# COLLINS GEM WEBSTER'S DICTIONARY

**EDITOR**
Eugene Ehrlich
Columbia University

HarperCollins*Publishers*

New York

London

First published in this edition 1990
**Latest reprint 1992**
© HarperCollins Publishers 1990
ISBN 0-06-276504-3

Printed and Published by
HarperCollins Publishers

# PREFACE

The Collins Gem Webster's Dictionary, edited by an American for users of American English, is the newest member of the large family of Collins Gem dictionaries.

It contains short, clear explanations of all the words in everyday use that an ordinary reader is likely to look up, along with many specialized and technical terms (see, for example, *oviparous, oxide, oxymoron,* and *ozone*), sports terms (eg *strike, huddle,* and *crease*), and slang (eg *buttinsky, poop out,* and *rail* (of cocaine)).

The guide to the pronunciation, using a simple respelling scheme, will enable users to see at once how to pronounce words properly. Seldom will it be necessary to go back to the essay on pronunciation on page vii, but this gives fuller guidance should it ever be required. In addition, each entry word is divided into syllables, giving guidance both on pronunciation and on end-of-line hyphenation.

At the back of the dictionary the user will find guidance on punctuation and useful tables of presidents, states, and cities, foreign countries and their currencies, signs of the zodiac, roman numerals, chemical elements, and the planets of the solar system.

The aim, in short, has been to compile a durable reference work that is both comprehensive and yet small enough to be tucked away in a desk drawer, purse, schoolbag, or coat pocket. The user will find the *Collins Gem Webster's Dictionary* not only authoritative and clear, but also helpful and easy to use.

E.E.
January 1990

# CONTENTS

# ARRANGEMENT OF ENTRIES

All main entries are arranged in a single alphabetical listing, including abbreviations, foreign words, and combining forms or prefixes. Each such entry consists of a paragraph, with a headword, that is, a main or core word, at the head of it in large bold type. Derived or related words, in smaller bold type, appear later in the paragraph in alphabetical order, with phrases included at the end. Thus, "**laborer**" and "**laborious**" will be found under "**labor**", just as "**lends itself to**" will be found under "**lend**" and so on.

Alternative spellings are shown by enclosing optional letters in parentheses, for example, "**ab·sinth(e)**" or by placing the variants side by side (**mol·lusk, mol·lusc**), but if the divergence in spelling is very great there is a separate entry.

Center dots, as in "**ab·sinthe**" and "**mol·lusk**" above, are used to indicate divisions between syllables.

The part of speech is shown by an abbreviation placed after the pronunciation of the entry word (or after the entry word if it does not require pronouncing), for example, "**dog** (dawg) *n.*" for noun. Words used as more than one part of speech are written out only once, the change being indicated by a new part of speech label, for example, "**rav·age** (RAV-ij) *vt.* lay waste, plunder —*n.* destruction." In the case of very short, simple entries, parts of speech may be combined, for example, "**jest** *n./vi.* joke."

The past tense and participles of verbs are shown in parentheses after the verb label when such information is considered helpful. The comparative and superlative forms of adjectives are also shown in parentheses after the adjective label when helpful to the reader. When it is considered helpful to readers to show the plural form or forms of a noun entry, this is also done in parentheses after the noun label.

When a derived word is included within an entry, its meaning may be understood from the meaning of the headword or another derived word within the paragraph.

Field labels (such as *Radio*) and usage notes (such as *Inf.*) are added in italic type and abbreviated where there will be no confusion.

# PRONUNCIATION

The pronunciation of some words is adequately shown by placing a mark (') immediately after the syllable that carries the main stress, as in **'mon·soon'** *n.*

In most words, however, simple phonetic respelling is used to show pronunciation and stress. The respelled word appears in parentheses immediately after the headword, and the stressed syllable is given in capital letters.

Typical examples are: **cache** (kash); **ca·chet** (ka-SHAY); **cais·son** (KAY-son); **cap·puc·ci·no** (kap-ə-CHEE-noh); **cap·tious** (KAP-shəs).

Take note of the use of the schwa (ə), the neutral vowel sound typically occurring in unstressed syllables, as in the second syllable of **cap·puc·ci·no** and the second syllable of **cap·tious**.

The schwa and other special letters and letter combinations used in the phonetic respelling system are listed below. All letters that are not listed have their normal pronunciation.

| | | | | | |
|---|---|---|---|---|---|
| a | sat | oh | rope | u | but |
| ah | calm | oi | boil | uu | book |
| ai | air | oo | food | ch | church |
| aw | law | yoo | sin*uou*s | ng | ring |
| ay | mate | or | four | sh | shin |
| e | met | ow | how | th | thin |
| ee | freeze | ə | *ago* | *th* | this |
| i | bit | | emer*a*ld | y | yes |
| ī | tight | | penc*i*l | z | zebra |
| ī | del*igh*t | | ven*o*m | *zh* | vi*si*on |
| o | hot | | s*u*pport | | |

vii

# ABBREVIATIONS USED IN THE DICTIONARY

| | | | |
|---|---|---|---|
| *abbrev.* | abbreviation | m | meter(s) |
| *adv.* | adverb | *masc.* | masculine |
| *adj.* | adjective | mm | millimeter(s) |
| Afr. | Africa(n) | N | North |
| Amer. | America(n) | *n.* | noun |
| Aust. | Australia(n) | *n. pl.* | plural noun |
| Brit. | Britain, British | N.Z. | New Zealand |
| Canad. | Canada, Canadian | *obs.* | obsolete, obsolescent |
| cent. | century | *offens.* | offensive |
| cm | centimeter(s) | oft. | often |
| *comb.* | combining | *orig.* | originally |
| *comp.* | comparative | *pers.* | person |
| *conj.* | conjunction | pert. | pertaining |
| cu. | cubic | *pl.* | plural |
| *dial.* | dialect | *poss.* | possessive |
| *dim.* | diminutive | *pp.* | past participle |
| eg | for example | *prep.* | preposition |
| *esp.* | especially | *pres.t.* | present tense |
| *fem.* | feminine | *pron.* | pronoun |
| *fig.* | figuratively | *pr.p.* | present participle |
| Fr. | French | *pt.* | past tense |
| g | gram(s) | R.C. | Roman Catholic |
| Ger. | German | *refl.* | reflexive |
| Gr. | Greek | S | South |
| *ie* | that is | *sing.* | singular |
| *impers.* | impersonal | *sl.* | slang |
| *ind.* | indicative | Sp. | Spanish |
| *inf.* | informal | sq. | square |
| *interj.* | interjection | *sup.* | superlative |
| *intr.* | intransitive | *tr.* | transitive |
| It. | Italian | *usu.* | usually |
| k | kilogram(s) | *v.* | verb |
| km | kilometer(s) | *v.aux.* | auxiliary verb |
| l | liter(s) | *vi.* | intransitive verb |
| Lat. | Latin | *vt.* | transitive verb |
| *lit.* | literally | | |

| | | |
|---|---|---|
| R | | Trademark |
| A | | Australian |
| UK | | United Kingdom |
| US | | United States |
| C | | Canadian |
| SA | | South African |

# A

**a, an** *adj.* the indefinite article meaning one; *an* is used before words beginning with vowel sounds, and sometimes before unaccented syllables beginning with *h* aspirate

**aard·vark** (AHRD-vahrk) *n.* S African mammal feeding on ants and termites

**a·back** (ə-BAK) *adv.* —taken aback startled

**ab·a·cus** (AB-ə-kəs) *n.* counting device of beads on wire frame; flat tablet at top of architectural column

**ab·a·lone** (ab-ə-LOH-nee) *n.* edible shellfish, yielding mother-of-pearl

**a·ban·don** (ə-BAN-dən) *vt.* desert; give up altogether —*n.* freedom from inhibitions *etc.* —a·ban'doned *adj.* deserted, forsaken; uninhibited; wicked

**a·base** (ə-BAYS) *vt.* (-based, -basing) humiliate, degrade —a·base'ment *n.*

**a·bash** (ə-BASH) *vt.* (*usu. passive*) confuse, make ashamed

**a·bate** (ə-BAYT) *v.* (-bated, -bating) make or become less, diminish —a·bate'ment *n.*

**ab·at·toir** (AB-ə-twahr) *n.* slaughterhouse

**ab·bey** (AB-ee) *n.* (*pl.* -beys) dwelling place of community of monks or nuns; church of an abbey

**ab·bot** (AB-ət) *n.* head of abbey or monastery —ab'bess *fem.*)

**ab·bre·vi·ate** (ə-BREE-vee-ayt) *vt.* (-at·ed, -at·ing) shorten,

abridge —ab·bre·vi·a'tion *n.* shortened form of word or phrase

**ab·di·cate** (AB-di-kayt) *v.* (-cat·ed, -cat·ing) formally give up (throne *etc.*) —ab·di·ca'tion *n.*

**ab·do·men** (AB-də-mən) *n.* belly —ab·dom'i·nal *adj.*

**ab·duct** (ab-DUKT) *vt.* carry off, kidnap —ab·duc'tion *n.*

**ab·er·ra·tion** (ab-ə-RAY-shən) *n.* deviation from what is normal; flaw; lapse —ab·er·rant (ə-BER-ənt) *adj.*

**a·bet** (ə-BET) *vt.* (-bet·ted, -bet·ting) assist, encourage, *esp.* in doing wrong —a·bet'tor, -ter *n.*

**a·bey·ance** (ə-BAY-əns) *n.* condition of not being in use or action

**ab·hor'** *vt.* (-horred, -hor·ring) dislike strongly, loathe —ab·hor'rent *adj.* hateful

**a·bide** (ə-BID) *v.* (a·bode' or a·bid'ed, a·bid'ing) *vt.* endure, put up with —*vi. obs.* stay, reside —abide by obey

**a·bil·i·ty** (ə-BIL-i-tee) *n.* (*pl.* -ties) competence, power; talent

**ab·ject** (AB-jekt) *adj.* humiliated, wretched; despicable

**a·blaze** (ə-BLAYZ) *adj.* burning

**a·ble** (AY-bəl) *adj.* capable, competent —a'bly *adv.* —a'ble·bod'ied *adj.*

**ab·lu·tion** (ə-BLOO-shən) *n.* (*usu. pl.*) act of washing (oneself)

**ab·ne·gate** (AB-ni-gayt) *vt.* (-gat·ed, -gat·ing) give up, renounce —ab·ne·ga'tion *n.*

**ab·nor·mal** (ab-NOR-məl) *adj.* irregular; not usual or typical;

freakish, odd —**ab·nor·mal'i·ty** *n.* (*pl.* -ties) —**ab·nor'mal·ly** *adv.*

**a·board** (ə-BORD) *adv.* on board, on ship, train, or aircraft

**a·bode** (ə-BOHD) *n.* home; dwelling —*pt./pp. of* ABIDE

**a·bol·ish** (ə-BOL-ish) *vt.* do away with —**ab·o·li'tion** *n.* —**ab·o·li'tion·ist** *n.* one who wishes to do away with something, *esp.* slavery

**a·bom·i·nate** (ə-BOM-ə-nayt) *vt.* (-nat·ed, -nat·ing) detest —**a·bom'i·na·ble** *adj.* —**a·bom·i·na'tion** *n.* loathing; the object loathed —**abominable snowman** large legendary apelike creature said to inhabit the Himalayas

**ab·o·rig·i·nal** (ab-ə-RIJ-ə-nl) *adj.* (of people *etc.*) original or earliest known in an area; of, relating to aborigines —**ab·o·rig'i·ne** (-ə-nee) *n.* one of race of people inhabiting an area when European settlers arrived; original inhabitant of country *etc.*

**a·bort** (ə-BORT) *v.* (cause to) end prematurely (*esp.* pregnancy) —*vi.* give birth to dead fetus; fail —**a·bor'tion** *n.* operation to terminate pregnancy; something deformed —**a·bor'tion·ist** *n.* one who performs abortion, *esp.* illegally —**a·bor'tive** *adj.* unsuccessful

**a·bound** (ə-BOWND) *vi.* be plentiful; overflow —**a·bound'ing** *adj.*

**a·bout** (ə-BOWT) *adv.* on all sides; nearly; up and down; out, on the move —*prep.* around; near; concerning; ready to —**about turn** reversal, complete change

**a·bove** (ə-BUV) *adv.* higher up —*prep.* over; higher than, more than; beyond

**a·brade** (ə-BRAYD) *vt.* (-brad·ed, -brad·ing) rub off, scrape away

**a·bra·sion** (ə-BRAY-zhən) *n.* place scraped or worn by rubbing (*eg* on skin); scraping, rubbing —**a·bra'sive** (-siv) *n.* substance for grinding, polishing *etc.* —*adj.* causing abrasion; grating —**a·bra'sive·ness** *n.* tendency to annoy

**a·breast** (ə-BREST) *adv.* side by side; keeping up with

**a·bridge** (ə-BRIJ) *vt.* cut short, abbreviate —**a·bridg'ment** *n.*

**a·broad** (ə-BRAWD) *adv.* to or in a foreign country; at large

**ab·ro·gate** (AB-rə-gayt) *vt.* cancel, repeal —**ab·ro·ga'tion** *n.*

**ab·rupt** (ə-BRUPT) *adj.* sudden; blunt; hasty; steep

**ab·scess** (AB-ses) *n.* gathering of pus in any part of the body

**ab·scis·sa** (ab-SIS-ə) *n.* *Math.* (*pl.* -sae *pr.* -see) distance of point from the axis of coordinates

**ab·scond** (ab-SKOND) *vi.* leave secretly, *esp.* having stolen something

**ab·sent** (AB-sənt) *adj.* away; not attentive —*vt.* (ab-SENT) keep away —**ab'sence** *n.* —**ab·sen·tee'** *n.* one who stays away *esp.* habitually —**ab·sen·tee'ism** *n.* persistent absence from work *etc.*

**ab·sinthe** (AB-sinth) *n.* potent aniseed-flavored liqueur

**ab·so·lute** (AB-sə-loot) *adj.* complete; not limited, unconditional; pure (as absolute alcohol) —*n.* —**ab'so·lute·ly** *adv.* completely —*interj.* (-LOOT-lee) certainly

**ab·solve** (ab-ZOLV) *vt.* (-solved, -solv·ing) free from, pardon, acquit —**ab·so·lu'tion** (-sə-LOO-shən) *n.*

**ab·sorb'** *vt.* suck up, drink in; engage, occupy (attention *etc.*); receive impact —**absorb'ent** *adj.* —**ab·sorp'tion** *n.*

**ab·stain** (ab-STAYN) *vi.* keep from, refrain from drinking alcohol, voting *etc.* —**ab·sten'tion** *n.* —**ab'sti·nence** *n.*

**ab·ste·mi·ous** (ab-STEE-mee-əs) *adj.* sparing in food or *esp.* drink, temperate —**ab·ste'mi·ous·ness** *n.*

**ab·stract** (ab-STRAKT) *adj.* existing only in the mind; not concrete; (of art) not representational —*n.* (AB-strakt) summary, abridgment —*vt.* (ab-STRAKT) draw from, remove; steal —**ab·stract'ed** *adj.* preoccupied —**abstrac'tion** *n.*

**ab·struse** (ab-STROOS) *adj.* obscure, difficult to understand, profound

**ab·surd** (əb-SURD) *adj.* contrary to reason —**ab·surd'i·ty** *n.*

**a·bun·dance** (ə-BUN-dəns) *n.* great amount —**a·bun'dant** *adj.* plentiful

**a·buse** (ə-BYOOZ) *vt.* (-bused, -bus·ing) misuse; address rudely —*n.* (ə-BYOOS) —**a·bu'sive** (-siv) *adj.*—**a·bu'sive·ness** *n.*

**a·but** (ə-BUT) *vi.* (-but·ted, -but·ting) adjoin, border on —**a·but'ment** *n.* support, edge of bridge or arch

**a·bys·mal** (ə-BIZ-məl) *adj.* immeasurable, very great; *inf.* extremely bad —**a·bys'mal·ly** *adv.*

**a·byss** (ə-BIS) *n.* very deep gulf or pit

**Ac** *Chem* actinium

**a·cad·e·my** (ə-KAD-ə-mee) *n.* (pl. -mies) society to advance arts or sciences; institution for specialized training; secondary school —**a·ca·dem'ic** (ak-ə-DEM-ik) *adj.* of academy, university *etc.*; theoretical

**ac·cede** (ak-SEED) *vi.* (-ced·ed, -ced·ing) agree, consent; attain (office, right *etc.*)

**ac·cel·er·ate** (ak-SEL-ə-rayt) *v.* (-at·ed, -at·ing) (cause to) increase speed, hasten —**ac·cel·er·a'tion** *n.* —**ac·cel'er·a·tor** *n.*

mechanism to increase speed, *esp.* in automobile

**ac·cent** (AK-sent) *n.* stress or pitch in speaking; mark to show such stress; local or national style of pronunciation; particular attention or emphasis —*vt.* (ak-SENT)

**ac·cen·tu·ate** (ak-SEN-choo-ayt) *vt.* (-at·ed, -at·ing) stress, emphasize

**ac·cept** (ak-SEPT) *vt.* take, receive; admit, believe; agree to —**ac·cept'a·ble** *adj.* —**ac·cept'ance** *n.*

**ac·cess** (AK-ses) *n.* act, right or means of entry —**ac·ces'si·ble** *adj.* easy to approach

**ac·ces·sion** (ak-SESH-ən) *n.* attaining of office, right *etc.*; increase, addition

**ac·ces·so·ry** (ak-SES-ə-ree) *n.* (pl. -ries) additional or supplementary part of automobile, woman's dress *etc.*; person inciting or assisting in crime —*adj.* contributory, assisting

**ac·ci·dent** (AK-si-dənt) *n.* event happening by chance; misfortune or mishap, *esp.* causing injury; nonessential quality —**ac·ci·den'tal** *adj.*

**ac·claim** (ə-KLAYM) *vt.* applaud, praise —*n.* applause —**ac·clama'tion** *n.*

**ac·cli·mate** (AK-klə-mayt) *v.* (-mat·ed, -mat·ing) acclimatize

**ac·cli·ma·tize** (ə-KLĪ-mə-tīz) *v.* (-tized, -tiz·ing) accustom to new climate or environment —**ac·cli·ma·ti·za'tion** *n.*

**ac·co·lade** (AK-ə-layd) *n.* praise, public approval; award, honor; token of award of knighthood *etc.*

**ac·com·mo·date** (ə-KOM-ə-dayt) *vt.* (-dat·ed, -dat·ing) supply, *esp.* with board and lodging; oblige; harmonize, adapt —**ac·com'mo-**

**dat·ing** adj. obliging —**ac·com·mo·da·tions** n. pl. lodgings

**ac·com·pa·ny** (ɔ-KUM-pɔ-nee) vt. (-nied, -ny·ing) go with; supplement; occur with; provide a musical accompaniment —**ac·com'pa·ni·ment** n. that which accompanies, esp. in music, part that goes with solos etc. —**ac·com'pa·nist** n.

**ac·com·plice** (ɔ-KOM-plis) n. one assisting another in criminal deed

**ac·com·plish** (ɔ-KOM-plish) vt. carry out; finish —**ac·com'plished** adj. complete, perfect; proficient —**ac·com'plish·ment** n. completion; personal ability

**ac·cord** (ɔ-KORD) n. (esp. in accord with) agreement, harmony —v. (cause to) be in accord with —vt. grant —**ac·cord'ing·ly** adv. as the circumstances suggest; therefore

**ac·cor·di·on** (ɔ-KOR-dee-ɔn) n. portable musical instrument with keys, metal reeds and a bellows

**ac·cost** (ɔ-KAWST) vi. approach and speak to, ask question etc.

**ac·count** (ɔ-KOWNT) n. report, description; importance, value; statement of moneys received, paid, or owed; person's money held in bank; credit available to person at store etc. —v. reckon; judge —vi. give reason, answer (for) —**ac·count'a·ble** adj. responsible —**ac·count'an·cy** n. keeping, preparation of business accounts, financial records etc. —**ac·count'ant** n. one practicing accountancy —**ac·count'ing** n. skill or practice of keeping and preparing business accounts —adj.

**ac·cred·it·ed** (ɔ-KRED-i-tid) adj. authorized, officially recognized

**ac·cre·tion** (ɔ-KREE-shɔn) n. growth; something added on

**dat·ing** adj. obliging

**ac·crue** (ɔ-KROO) vi. (-crued, -cru·ing) be added; result

**ac·cu·mu·late** (ɔ-KYOO-myɔ-layt) v. (-lat·ed, -lat·ing) gather, become gathered in increasing quantity; collect —**ac·cu·mu·la·tion** n.

**ac·cu·rate** (AK-yɔr-it) adj. exact, correct, without errors —**ac'cu·ra·cy** n.

**ac·curs·ed** (ɔ-KUR-sid) adj. under a curse; hateful, detestable

**ac·cuse** (ɔ-KYOOZ) vt. (-cused, -cus·ing) charge with wrongdoing; blame —**ac·cu·sa·tion** (ak-yɔ-ZAY-shɔn) n. —**ac·cu'sa·tive** n. grammatical case indicating the direct object —**ac·cu'sa·to·ry** adj.

**ac·cus·tom** (ɔ-KUS-tɔm) vt. make used to, familiarize —**ac·cus'tomed** adj. usual; used (to); in the habit (of)

**ace** n. the one at dice, cards, dominoes; Tennis winning serve untouched by opponent; very successful fighter pilot —vt. (aced, ac·ing) score an ace; Golf make hole in one; inf. make grade of A —adj. excellent

**a·cer·bi·ty** (ɔ-SUR-bi-tee) n. severity, sharpness; sour tasting —**a·cerb'** adj.

**ac·e·tate** (AS-i-tayt n. salt or ester of acetic acid; synthetic textile fiber

**a·ce·tic** (ɔ-SEE-tik) adj. derived from or having the nature of vinegar

**ac·e·tone** (AS-i-tohn) n. colorless liquid used as a solvent

**a·cet·y·lene** (ɔ-SET-l-een) n. colorless, flammable gas used esp. in welding metals

**ache** (ayk) n. continuous pain —vi. (ached, ach·ing) to be in pain

**a·chieve** (ɔ-CHEEV) vt. (-chieved, -chiev·ing) accomplish, perform successfully; gain —a·chieve'·ment n. something accomplished

ac·id (AS-id) adj. sharp, sour —n. sour substance; Chem. one of a class of compounds that combine with bases (alkalis, oxides etc.) to form salts —a·cid'ic adj. —a·cid'i·fy vt. (-fied, -fy·ing) —a·cid'i·ty n. (-fied, -fy·ing) —a·cid'u·lous adj. caustic —acid rain rain acidified by atmospheric pollution —acid test conclusive test of value

ac·knowl·edge (ak-NOL-ij) vt. (-edged, -edg·ing) admit, own to knowing, recognize; say one has received —ac·knowl'edg·ment n.

ac·me (AK-mee) n. highest point

ac·ne (AK-nee) n. pimply skin disease

ac·o·lyte (AK-ə-lit) n. follower or attendant, esp. of priest

a·cous·tic (ə-KOO-stik) adj. pert. to sound and to hearing —a·cous'tics n. science of sounds (with sing. v.); (pl.) features of room or building as regards sounds heard within it

ac·quaint (ə-KWAYNT) vt. make familiar, inform —ac·quaint'ance n. person known; personal knowledge

ac·qui·esce (ak-wee-ES) vi. (-esced, -esc·ing) agree, consent without complaint —ac·qui·es'cence n.

ac·quire (ə-KWIR) vt. (-quired, -quir·ing) gain, get —ac·qui·si·tion (ak-wə-ZISH-ən) n. act of getting; material gain —ac·quis'i·tive adj. desirous of gaining

ac·quit (ə-KWIT) vt. (-quit·ted, -quit·ting) declare innocent; settle, discharge, as a debt; behave (oneself) —ac·quit'tal n. declaration of innocence in court

a·cre (AY-kər) n. measure of land, 43,560 square feet —pl. lands, estates; inf. large area or plenty of —a'cre·age n. the extent of land in acres

ac·rid (AK-rid) adj. pungent, sharp; irritating

ac·ri·mo·ny (AK-rə-moh-nee) n. bitterness of feeling or language —ac·ri·mo'ni·ous adj.

ac·ro·bat (AK-rə-bat) n. one skilled in gymnastic feats, esp. as entertainer in circus etc. —acro·bat'ic adj. —ac·ro·bat'ics n. pl. activities requiring agility

ac·ro·nym (AK-rə-nim) n. word formed from initial letters of other words eg radar, NATO

a·crop·o·lis (ə-KROP-ə-lis) n. citadel, esp. in ancient Greece

a·cross (ə-KRAWS) adv./prep. crosswise; from side to side; on or to the other side —get (or put) it across explain, make (something) understood

a·cros·tic (ə-KRAW-stik) n. word puzzle (or verse) in which the first, middle, or last letters of each line spell a word or words

a·cryl·ic (ə-KRIL-ik) n. variety of synthetic materials, esp. paint and textiles

act (akt) n. thing done, deed; doing; law or decree; section of a play —v. perform, as in a play —vi. exert force, work, as mechanism; behave —act'ing n. performance of a part —adj. temporarily performing the duties of —ac'tion n. operation; deed; gesture; expenditure of energy; battle; lawsuit —ac'tionable adj. subject to lawsuit —ac'ti·vate vt. (-vat·ed, -vat·ing) make active; make radioactive; make chemically active —ac·ti·va'tion n. —ac'tive adj. moving, working; brisk, energetic —ac'ti·vist n. one who takes (direct) action to achieve political or social ends —ac·tiv'i·ty n. —ac·tor

(AK-tər) *n*. one who acts in a play, film *etc.* (*fem.* -**tress**)

**ac·tin·i·um** (ak-TIN-ee-əm) *n*. radioactive element occurring as decay product of uranium

**ac·tu·al** (AK-choo-əl) *adj*. existing in the present; real —**ac·tu·al'i·ty** *n*. —**ac'tu·al·ly** *adv*. really, indeed

**ac·tu·ar·y** (AK-choo-er-ee) *n*. (*pl.* -**ar·ies**) statistician who calculates insurance risks, premiums *etc.* —**ac·tu·ar'i·al** *adj.*

**ac·tu·ate** (AK-choo-ayt) *vt*. (-at·ed, -at·ing) activate; motivate —**ac'tu·a·tor** *n*. mechanism for controlling or moving something indirectly

**a·cu·i·ty** (ə-KYOO-i-tee) *n*. keenness, *esp.* in vision or thought

**a·cu·men** (ə-KYOO-mən) *n*. sharpness of wit, perception, penetration

**ac·u·punc·ture** (AK-yə-pungk-chər) *n*. orig. Chinese medical treatment involving insertion of needles at various points on the body

**a·cute** (ə-KYOOT) *adj*. keen, shrewd; sharp; severe; of angle, less than 90° — **ac·cent** (´) over a letter to indicate the quality or length of its sound *eg* **abé** —**a·cute'ness** *n*.

**ad·age** (AD-ij) *n*. much used wise saying, proverb

**a·da·gio** (ə-DAH-joh) *adv./n. Mus.* (*pl.* -**gios**) leisurely, slow (passage)

**ad·a·mant** (AD-ə-mənt) *adj*. very hard, unyielding —**ad·a·man'tine** (-MAN-teen) *adj.*

**Adam's apple** (AD-əmz) projecting part at front of the throat, the thyroid cartilage

**a·dapt** (ə-DAPT) *vt*. alter for new use; fit, modify; change —**a·dapt'a·ble** *adj.* —**ad·ap·ta'tion** *n*. —**a·dapt'er, -tor** *n. esp.*

appliance for connecting two parts (*eg* electrical)

**add** *v*. join; increase by; say further —**ad·di'tion** (ə-DISH-ən) *n*. —**ad·di'tion·al** *adj.* —**ad'di·tive** *n*. something added, *esp.* to food

**ad·den·dum** (ə-DEN-dəm) *n*. (*pl.* -**da** *pr*. -də) thing to be added

**ad·der** (AD-ər) *n*. small poisonous snake

**ad·dict** (AD-ikt) *n*. one who has become dependent on something, *eg* drugs (a *drug addict*) —*vt*. (ə-DIKT) (*usu. passive*) —**ad·dict'ed** *adj.* —**ad·dic'tion** *n*. —**ad·dic'tive** *adj*. causing addiction

**ad·dle** (AD-l) *v*. (-dled, -dling) make or become rotten, muddled

**ad·dress** (ə-DRES) *n*. direction on letter; place where one lives; speech —*vt*. mark destination, as on envelope; speak to; direct; dispatch —**address ball** *Golf* adjust club before striking ball —**address·ee'** *n*. person addressed

**ad·duce** (ə-DOOS) *vt*. (-duced, -duc·ing) offer as proof; cite —**ad·duc'i·ble** *adj.*

**ad·e·noids** (AD-n-oidz) *pl. n*. tissue at back of nose and throat, sometimes causing breathing

**a·dept** (ə-DEPT) *adj*. skilled —*n*. (AD-ept) expert

**ad·e·quate** (AD-i-kwit) *adj*. sufficient, enough, suitable; not outstanding —**ad'e·qua·cy** *n.*

**ad·here** (ad-HEER) *vi*. (-hered, -her·ing) stick to; be firm in opinion *etc.* —**ad·her'ent** *n./adj.* —**ad·he'sion** (-HEE-zhən) *n*. —**ad·he'sive** (-siv) *adj./n.*

**ad hoc** (ad-HOK) *adj./adv*. for a particular occasion only; improvised

**a·dieu** (ə-DYOO) *interj*. farewell —*n*. (*pl.* **a·dieus, a·dieux,** *pr*. ə-DYOOZ) act of taking leave

**ad in·fi·ni·tum** (in-fə-NI-təm) *Lat.* endlessly

**ad·i·pose** (AD-ə-pohs) *adj.* of fat, fatty

**ad·ja·cent** (ə-JAY-sənt) *adj.* lying near, next (to)

**ad·jec·tive** (AJ-ik-tiv) *n.* word that modifies or limits a noun —**ad·jec·ti´val** (-TĪ-vəl) *adj.* of adjective

**ad·join** (ə-JOIN) *v.* be next to; join —**ad·join´ing** *adj.* next to, near

**ad·journ** (ə-JURN) *v.* postpone temporarily, as meeting; *inf.* move elsewhere

**ad·judge** (ə-JUJ) *v.* (-judged, -judg·ing) declare; decide; award

**ad·ju·di·cate** (ə-JOO-di-kayt) *v.* (-cat·ed, -cat·ing) try, judge; sit in judgment —**ad·ju·di·ca´tion** *n.*

**ad·junct** (AJ-ungkt) *adj.* joined, added —*n.* person or thing added or subordinate

**ad·jure** (ə-JOOR) *vt.* (-jured, -jur·ing) beg, earnestly entreat —**ad·ju·ra´tion** (aj-ə-RAY-shən) *n.*

**ad·just** (ə-JUST) *v.* make suitable, adapt; alter slightly, regulate —*vi.* adapt or conform to new conditions *etc.* —**ad·just´a·ble** *adj.*

**ad·ju·tant** (AJ-ə-tənt) *n.* military officer who assists superiors —**ad·ju·tan·cy** *n.* office, rank of adjutant

**ad·lib** *v.* (-libbed, -lib·bing) improvise and speak spontaneously —**ad lib** *n.* such speech *etc.*

**ad·min·is·ter** (ad-MIN-ə-stər) *vt.* manage, look after; dispense, as justice *etc.*; apply —**ad·min·is·tra´tion** *n.* —**ad·min´is·tra·tive** *adj.*

**ad·mi·ral** (AD-mər-əl) *n.* naval officer of highest rank —**ad´mi·ral·ty** *Law* court having jurisdiction over maritime matters

**ad·mire** (ad-MĪR) *vt.* (-mired, -mir·ing) look on with wonder and pleasure; respect highly —**ad´mi·ra·ble** *adj.* —**ad´mi·ra·bly** *adv.* —**ad·mi·ra´tion** *n.* —**ad·mir´er** *n.* —**ad·mir´ing·ly** *adv.*

**ad·mit** (ad-MIT) *vt.* (-mit·ted, -mit·ting) confess; accept as true; allow; let in —**ad·mis´si·ble** *adj.* —**ad·mis´sion** *n.* permission to enter; entrance fee; confession —**ad·mit´tance** *n.* permission to enter —**ad·mit´ted·ly** *adv.*

**ad·mix·ture** (ad-MIKS-chər) *n.* mixture; ingredient

**ad·mon·ish** (ad-MON-ish) *vt.* reprove; advise; warn; exhort —**ad·mo·ni´tion** (-mə-NISH-ən) *n.* —**ad·mon´i·to·ry** *adj.*

**ad nau·se·am** (NAW-zee-əm) *Lat.* to a boring or disgusting extent

**a·do** (ə-DOO) *n.* fuss

**a·do·be** (ə-DOH-bee) *n.* sun-dried brick

**ad·o·les·cence** (ad-l-ES-ens) *n.* period of life just before maturity —**ad·o·les´cent** *n.* a youth —*adj.*

**a·dopt** (ə-DOPT) *vt.* take into relationship, *esp.* as one's child; take up, as principle, resolution —**a·dop´tion** *n.* —**a·dop´tive** *adj.* that which adopts or is adopted

**a·dore** (ə-DOR) *v.* (-dored, -dor·ing) love intensely; worship —**a·dor´a·ble** *adj.* —**ad·o·ra´tion** *n.*

**a·dorn** (ə-DORN) *v.* beautify, embellish, deck —**a·dorn´ment** *n.* ornament, decoration

**ad·re·nal** (ə-DREEN-l) *adj.* near the kidney —**adrenal gland** —**a·dren´a·line** (-DREN-l-in) *n.* hormone secreted by adrenal glands; this substance used as drug

**a·drift** (ə-DRIFT) *adj./adv.* drifting free; *inf.* detached; *inf.* off course

**a·droit** (ə-DROIT) *adj.* skillful, expert; clever —**a·droit´ness** *n.* dexterity

**ad·sorb** (ad-SORB) v. (of gas, vapor) condense and form thin film on surface —**ad·sorb'ent** adj./n. —**ad·sorp'tion** n.

**ad·u·la·tion** (aj-ə-LAY-shən) n. flattery —**ad'u·late** vt. (-lat·ed, -lat·ing) flatter —**ad'u·la·to·ry** adj.

**a·dult** (ə-DULT) adj. grown-up, mature —n. grown-up person; full-grown animal or plant

**a·dul·ter·ate** (ə-DUL-tə-rayt) vt. (-at·ed, -at·ing) make impure by addition —**a·dul'ter·ant** n.

**a·dul·ter·y** (ə-DUL-tə-ree) n. sexual unfaithfulness of a husband or wife —**a·dul'ter·er** n. masc. (-ter·ess fem.) —**a·dul'ter·ous** adj.

**ad·vance** (ad-VANS) v. (-vanced, -vanc·ing) —vt. bring forward; suggest; encourage; pay beforehand; Auto. to time spark earlier in engine cycle —vi. go forward; improve in position or value —n. movement forward; improvement; a loan —pl. personal approach(es) to gain favor etc. —adj. ahead in time or position —**ad·vanced'** adj. at a late stage; not elementary; ahead of the times —**ad·vance'ment** n. promotion

**ad·van·tage** (ad-VAN-tij) n. superiority; more favorable position or state; benefit —**ad·vanta'geous** (-vən-TAY-jəs) adj.

**ad·vent** (AD-vent) n. a coming, arrival; (A-) the four weeks before Christmas —the Advent the coming of Christ —**Ad'vent·ist** n. one of number of Christian sects believing in imminent return of Christ

**ad·ven·ti·tious** (ad-vən-TISH-əs) adj. added; accidental, casual

**ad·ven·ture** (ad-VEN-chər) n. risk; bold exploit; remarkable happening; enterprise; commercial speculation —**ad·ven'tur·er** n. one who seeks adventures; one who lives on his wits —(-tur·ess fem.) —**ad·ven'tur·ous** adj.

**ad·verb** (AD-vurb) n. word used with verb, adjective, or other adverb to modify meaning —**ad·ver'bi·al** adj.

**ad·verse** (ad-VURS) adj. opposed to; hostile; unfavorable, bringing harm —**ad'ver·sar·y** n. (pl. -sar·ies) enemy —**ad·verse'ly** adv. —**ad·ver'si·ty** n. distress, misfortune

**ad·ver·tise** (AD-vər-tiz) v. (-tised, -tis·ing) —vt. publicize; make known; give notice of, esp. in newspapers etc. —vi. make public request (for) —**ad·ver·tise'ment** n. —**ad·ver'tis·ing** adj./n.

**ad·vice** (ad-VĪS) n. opinion given; counsel; information; (formal) notification

**ad·vise** (ad-VĪZ) vt. (-vised, -vis·ing) offer advice; recommend a line of conduct; give notice (of) —**ad·vis'a·ble** adj. expedient —**ad·vised'** adj. considered, deliberate, as in well-advised —**ad·vis'ed·ly** (-zid-lee) adv. —**ad·vis'er** n. —**ad·vi'so·ry** adj.

**ad·vo·cate** (AD-və-kit) n. one who pleads the cause of another, esp. in court of law; attorney —vt. (-kayt) uphold, recommend —**ad'vo·ca·cy** (-kə-see) n.

**ae·gis** (EE-jis) n. sponsorship, protection (orig. shield of Zeus)

**aer·ate** (AIR-ayt) vt. (-at·ed, -at·ing) charge liquid with gas, as effervescent drink; expose to air —**aer·a'tion** n. —**aer'a·tor** n. apparatus for charging liquid with gas

**aer·i·al** (AIR-ee-əl) adj. of the air; operating in the air; pertaining to aircraft —n. part of radio etc. receiving or sending radio waves

**aer·ie, aer·y** n. see EYRIE

**aero-** (comb. form) air or aircraft as in aerodynamics

**aer·o·bat·ics** (air-ə-BAT-iks) n. (with sing. or pl. v.) stunt flying

**aer·o·bics** n. (with sing. or pl. v.) exercise system designed to increase the amount of oxygen in the blood

**aer·o·dy·nam·ics** (air-oh-di-NAM-iks) n. (with sing. v.) study of air flow, esp. around moving solid bodies

**aer·o·naut** (AIR-ə-nawt) n. pilot or navigator of lighter-than-air craft —**aer·o·nau·tics** n. (with sing. v.) science of air navigation and flying in general —**aer·o·nau′ti·cal** adj.

**aer·o·sol** (AIR-ə-sawl) n. (substance dispensed as fine spray from) pressurized can

**aer·o·space** (AIR-oh-spays) n. Earth's atmosphere and space beyond —adj.

**aes·thet·ic** (es-THET-ik) adj. relating to principles of beauty, taste and art —**aes·thet′ics** n. (with sing. or pl. v.) study of art, taste etc. —**aes·thete** (ES-theet) n. one who affects extravagant love of art

**a·far** (ə-FAHR) adv. from, at, or to, a great distance

**af·a·ble** (AF-ə-bəl) adj. easy to speak to, polite and friendly —**af·fa·bil′i·ty** n.

**af·fair** (ə-FAIR) n. thing done or attended to; business; happening; sexual liaison —pl. personal or business interests; matters of public interest

**af·fect** (ə-FEKT) vt. act on, influence; move feelings; make show of, make pretense; assume; have liking for —**affect** (AF-ekt) n. Psych. emotion, feeling, desire —**af·fec·ta′tion** n. show, pretense —**af·fect′ed** adj. making a pretense; moved; acted upon —**af·fect′ing** adj. moving the feelings —**af·fec′tion** n. fondness, love —**af·fec′tion·ate** adj.

**af·fi·da·vit** (af-i-DAY-vit) n. written statement under oath

**af·fil·i·ate** (ə-FIL-ee-ayt) vt. (-at·ed, -at·ing) connect, attach, as society to federation etc.; adopt —n. (-ee-it) affiliated organization

**af·fin·i·ty** (ə-FIN-i-tee) n. (pl. -ties) natural liking; resemblance; relationship by marriage; chemical attraction

**af·firm** (ə-FURM) v. assert positively, declare; maintain statement; make solemn declaration —**af·fir·ma′tion** n. —**af·firm′a·tive** adj. asserting —n. word of assent

**af·fix** (ə-FIKS) vt. fasten (to); attach, append —n. (AF-fiks) addition, esp. to word, as suffix, prefix

**af·flict** (ə-FLIKT) vt. give pain or grief to, distress; trouble, vex —**af·flic′tion** n.

**af·flu·ent** (AF-loo-ənt) adj. wealthy; abundant —n. tributary stream —**af′flu·ence** n. wealth, abundance

**af·ford** (ə-FORD) vt. be able to buy; be able to spare the time etc.; produce, yield, furnish

**af·front** (ə-FRUNT) vt. insult openly —n. insult; offense

**a·field** (ə-FEELD) adv. away from home; in or on the field

**a·fire** (ə-FIR) adv. on fire

**a·flame** (ə-FLAYM) adv. burning

**a·float** (ə-FLOHT) adv. floating; at sea; in circulation

**a·foot** (ə-FUUT) adv. astir; on foot

**a·fore** (ə-FOR) prep./adv. before, usually in compounds as **a·fore′said**, **a·fore′thought**, **a·fore′time**

**a·foul** (ə-FOWL) adj./adv. into difficulty (with)

**a·fraid** (ə-FRAYD) *adj.* frightened; regretful

**a·fresh** (ə-FRESH) *adv.* again, anew

**Af·ri·can** (AF-ri-kən) *adj.* belonging to Africa —*n.* native of Africa

**Af·ri·kaans** (af-ri-KAHNS) *n.* language used in S. Africa, derived from 17th cent. Dutch —**Af·ri·ka'ner** *n.* white native of S. Afr. with Afrikaans as mother tongue

**aft** *adv.* toward stern of ship or tail of aircraft

**af·ter** (AF-tər) *adv.* later; behind —*prep.* behind; later than; on the model of; pursuing —*conj.* at a later time than —*adj.* behind; later; nearer stern or tail of aircraft

**af·ter·birth** (-burth) *n.* membrane expelled after a birth

**af·ter·care** (-kair) *n.* care, *esp.* medical, bestowed on person after period of treatment

**af·ter·ef·fect** (-ə-fekt) *n.* subsequent effect of deed, event *etc.*

**af·ter·glow** (-gloh) *n.* light after sunset; reflection of past emotion

**af·ter·math** *n.* result, consequence

**af·ter·noon'** *n.* time from noon to evening

**af·ter·taste** (-tayst) *n.* taste remaining or recurring after eating or drinking something

**af·ter·thought** (-thawt) *n.* idea occurring later

**af·ter·ward(s)** (-wərd, -wərdz) *adv.* later

**Ag** *Chem.* silver

**a·gain** (ə-GEN) *adv.* once more; in addition; back, in return; besides

**a·gainst** (ə-GENST) *prep.* in opposition to; in contact with; opposite; in readiness for

**a·gape** (ə-GAYP) *adj./adv.* openmouthed as in wonder *etc.*

**ag·ate** (AG-it) *n.* colored, semi-precious, decorative form of quartz

**age** (ayj) *n.* length of time person or thing has existed; time of life; period of history; maturity; long time —*v.* (aged, ag·ing) make or grow old —**aged** (AY-jid *or* ayjd) *adj.* old —*n. pl.* (AY-jid) old people —**aging** *n./adj.* —**age'less** *adj.* not growing old, not showing signs of age —**age-old** *adj.* ancient

**a·gen·da** (ə-JEN-də) *n.* (*with sing. v.*) things to be done; program of business meeting

**a·gent** (AY-jənt) *n.* one authorized to carry on business or affairs for another; person or thing producing effect; cause; natural force —**a·gen·cy** *n.* instrumentality; business, place of business, of agent

**agent pro·vo·ca·teur** (prə-vok-ə-TUR) (*pl.* agents provocateurs) *Fr.* police or secret service spy

**ag·glu·ti·nate** (ə-GLOOT-n-ayt) *vt.* (-nat·ed, -nat·ing) unite with glue *etc.*; form words into compounds —*adj.* (-n-it) united, as by glue —**ag·glu·ti·na'tion** *n.*

**ag·gran·dize** (ə-GRAN-dīz) *vt.* (-dized, -diz·ing) make greater in size, power, or rank —**ag·gran'dize·ment** (-diz-mənt) *n.*

**ag·gra·vate** (AG-rə-vayt) *vt.* (-vat·ed, -vat·ing) make worse or more severe; *inf.* annoy —**aggra·va'tion** *n.*

**ag·gre·gate** (AG-ri-gayt) *vt.* (-gat·ed, -gat·ing) gather into mass —*adj.* (-git) gathered thus —*n.* (-git) mass, sum total; rock consisting of mixture of minerals; mixture of gravel *etc.* for concrete —**ag·gre·ga'tion** *n.*

**ag·gres·sion** (ə-GRESH-ən) *n.* unprovoked attack; hostile activity —**ag·gres'sive** *adj.* —**ag·gres'sive·ness** *n.* —**ag·gres'sor** *n.*

**ag·grieve** (ɔ-GREEV) *vt.* (-grieved, -griev·ing) pain, injure

**a·ghast** (ɔ-GAST) *adj.* struck, stupefied with horror or terror

**ag·ile** (AJ-ɔl) *adj.* nimble; active; quick —**a·gil'i·ty** *n.*

**ag·i·tate** (AJ-i-tayt) *v.* (-tat·ed, -tat·ing) —*vt.* disturb, shake up; keep in motion, stir, shake up; trouble —*vi.* stir up public opinion (for or against) —**ag'i·ta·tor** *n.*

**a·glow** (ɔ-GLOH) *adj.* glowing

**ag·nos·tic** (ag-NOS-tik) *n.* one who knows nothing of things outside the material world —*adj.* of this theory —**ag·nos'ti·cism** *n.*

**a·go** (ɔ-goh) *adv.* in the past

**a·gog** (ɔ-GOG) *adj./adv.* eager, astir

**ag·o·ny** (AG-ɔ-nee) *n.* (*pl.* -nies) extreme suffering of mind or body, violent struggle —**ag'o·nize** *vi.* (-nized, -niz·ing) suffer agony; worry greatly —**agony column** newspaper or magazine feature column containing advertisements relating to personal problems, *esp.* to missing friends or relatives

**ag·o·ra·pho·bi·a** (ag-ɔr-ɔ-FOH-bee-ɔ) *n.* abnormal fear of open spaces

**a·grar·i·an** (ɔ-GRAIR-ee-ɔn) *adj.* of agriculture, land or its management

**a·gree** (ɔ-GREE) *v.* (-greed, -gree·ing) be of same opinion; consent; harmonize; settle suit —**a·gree'a·ble** *adj.* willing; pleasant —**a·gree'ment** *n.* concord; contract

**ag·ri·cul·ture** (AG·ri·kul·chɔr) *n.* art, practice of cultivating land —**ag·ri·cul'tur·al** *adj.*

**a·gron·o·my** (ɔ-GRON-ɔ-mee) *n.* the study of the management of the land and the scientific cultivation of crops —**a·gron'o·mist** *n.*

**a·ground** (ɔ-GROWND) *adv.* (of boat) touching bottom

**a·head** (ɔ-HED) *adv.* in front; forward; in advance

**a·hoy** (ɔ-HOI) *interj.* shout used at sea for hailing

**aid** (ayd) *vt.* to help —*n.* help, support, assistance

**aide** (ayd) *n.* person acting as an assistant

**aide-de-camp** (AYD-dɔ-KAMP) (*pl.* aides-) *n.* (*also* aide) military officer personally assisting superior

**AIDS** acquired immune deficiency syndrome

**ail** (ayl) *vt.* trouble, afflict, disturb —*vi.* be ill —**ail'ing** *adj.* sickly —**ail'ment** *n.* illness

**ai·ler·on** (AY-lɔ-ron) *n.* movable section of wing of aircraft that gives lateral control

**aim** (aym) *v.* give direction to weapon *etc.*; direct effort toward, try to —*n.* direction; object, purpose —**aim'less** *adj.* without purpose

**ain't** (aynt) *nonstandard* am not; is not; are not; has not; have not

**air** *n.* mixture of gases we breathe, the atmosphere; breeze; tune; manner —*pl.* affected manners —*vt.* expose to air to dry or ventilate —**air'i·ly** *adv.* —**air'i·ness** *n.* —**air'ing** *v.* time spent in the open air; exposure to public view; radio or TV broadcast —**air'less** *adj.* stuffy —**air'y** *adj.* (air·i·er, air·i·est) of air —**air'borne** *adj.* flying, in the air —**air brake** brake worked by compressed air; method of slowing down an aircraft —**air'brush** *n.* atomizer spraying paint by compressed air —**air'-con·di·tion** *vt.* maintain constant stream of clean fresh air in building at correct temperature —**air conditioner** —**air'craft** *n.* collective name for flying machines; airplane —air-craft carrier —air cushion pocket of air supporting hovercraft —air′field n. landing and takeoff area for aircraft —air force military organization of country for air warfare —air gun gun discharged by force of compressed air —air′lift n. transport of goods etc. by aircraft —air′line n. company operating aircraft —air′lock n. air bubble obstructing flow of liquid in pipe; airtight chamber —air pocket less dense air that causes airplane to drop suddenly —air′port n. station for civilian aircraft —air pump machine to extract or supply air —air raid attack by aircraft —air shaft passage for air into a mine etc. —air′ship n. lighter-than-air flying machine with means of propulsion and steering —air′sickness n. nausea caused by motion of aircraft in flight —air′speed n. speed of aircraft relative to air —air′strip n. small airfield with only one runway —air′tight adj. not allowing passage of air —air′way n. regular aircraft route —air′wor·thy adj. fit for service in air —air′wor·thi·ness n.

air′plane (-playn) n. heavier-than-air flying machine

aisle (īl) n. passageway separating seating areas in church, theater etc.

a·jar (ǝ-JAHR) adv. partly open

a·kim·bo (ǝ-KIM-boh) adv. with hands on hips and elbows outward

a·kin (ǝ-KIN) adj. related by blood; alike, having like qualities

Al Chem. aluminum

al·a·bas·ter (AL-ǝ-bas-tǝr) n. soft, white, semitransparent stone —al·a·bas′trine (-BAS-trin) adj. of, like this

à la carte (ah lǝ KAHRT) selected freely from the menu

a·lac·ri·ty (ǝ-LAK-ri-tee) n. quickness, briskness, readiness

à la mode (ah lǝ MOHD) in fashion; topped with ice cream

a·larm (ǝ-LAHRM) n. sudden fright; apprehension; notice of danger; bell, buzzer; call to arms —vt. frighten; warn of danger —a·larm′ist n. one given to prophesying danger or exciting alarm esp. needlessly

a·las (ǝ-LAS) interj. cry of grief, pity, or concern

al·ba·tross (AL-bǝ-traws) n. large oceanic bird, of petrel family; someone or something thought to make accomplishment difficult

al·be·it (awl-BEE-it) conj. although

al·bi·no (al-BĪ-noh) n. (pl. -nos) person or animal with white skin and hair, and pink eyes, due to lack of pigment —al·bi·nism (AL-bǝ-niz-ǝm) n.

al·bum (AL-bǝm) n. book of blank leaves, for photographs, stamps, autographs etc.; one or more long-playing phonograph records or tape recordings

al·bu·men (al-BYOO-mǝn) n. egg white

al·bu·min (al-BYOO-mǝn) n. constituent of animal and vegetable matter, found nearly pure in white of egg

al·che·my (AL-kǝ-mee) n. medieval chemistry, esp. attempts to turn base metals into gold and find elixir of life —al′che·mist n.

al·co·hol (AL-kǝ-hawl) n. intoxicating fermented liquor; class of organic chemical substances —al·co·hol′ic adj. —n. one addicted to alcoholic drink —al′co·hol·ism n. disease, alcohol poisoning

al·cove (AL-kohv) n. recessed section of a room

**ale** (ayl) *n.* fermented malt liquor, type of beer, *orig.* without hops

**a·lert** (ə-LURT) *adj.* watchful; brisk, active —*n.* warning of sudden attack or surprise —*vt.* warn, *esp.* of danger; draw attention to —a·lert'ness *n.* —on the alert watchful

**al·fal·fa** (al-FAL-fə) *n.* plant widely used as fodder

**al·fres·co** (al-FRES-koh) *adv./adj.* in the open air

**al·gae** (AL-jee) *n. pl.* (*sing.* -ga *pr.* -gə) various water plants, including seaweed

**al·ge·bra** (AL-jə-brə) *n.* method of calculating, using symbols to represent quantities and to show relations between them, making a kind of abstract arithmetic —al·ge·bra'ic (-BRAY-ik) *adj.*

**ALGOL, Algol** (AL-gol) *Computers* algorithmic oriented language

**al·go·rithm** (AL-gə-*rith*-əm) *n.* procedural model for complicated calculations

**a·li·as** (AY-lee-əs) *adv.* otherwise known as —*n.* (*pl.* -as·es) assumed name

**al·i·bi** (AL-ə-bī) *n.* plea of being somewhere else when crime was committed; *inf.* excuse

**a·li·en** (AY-lee-ən) *adj.* foreign; different in nature; repugnant (to) —*n.* foreigner —a'li·en·a·ble *adj.* able to be transferred to another owner —a'li·en·ate (-ə-nayt) *vt.* (-at·ed, -at·ing) estrange; transfer —a·li·en·a'tion *n.*

**a·light¹** (ə-LĪT) *vi.* get down; land, settle

**a·light²** *adj.* lit up

**a·lign** (ə-LĪN) *vt.* bring into line or agreement

**a·like** (ə-LĪK) *adj.* like, similar —*adv.* in the same way

**al·i·men·ta·ry** (al-ə-MEN-tə-ree) *adj.* of food —alimentary canal food passage in body

**al·i·mo·ny** (AL-ə-moh-nee) *n.* allowance paid under court order to separated or divorced spouse

**a·live** (ə-LĪV) *adj.* living; active; aware; swarming

**al·ka·li** (AL-kə-lī) *n.* (*pl.* -lis) substance that combines with acid and neutralizes it, forming a salt: potash, soda *etc.* —al'ka·line *adj.* —al·ka·lin'i·ty *n.*

**all** (awl) *adj.* the whole of, every one of —*adv.* wholly, entirely —*n.* the whole; everything, everyone —*pron.* everything, everyone —all fours hands and feet —all in exhausted —all'-a·round' *adj.* showing ability in many fields —all right satisfactory; well, safe; pleasing; very well; beyond doubt

**Al·lah** (AH-lə) *n.* Muslim name for the Supreme Being

**al·lay** (ə-LAY) *vt.* lighten, relieve, calm, soothe

**al·lege** (ə-LEJ) *vt.* (-leged, -leg·ing) state without or before proof; produce as argument —al·le·ga·tion (al-i-GAY-shən) *n.* —al·leged' *adj.* —al·leg·ed·ly *adv.*

**al·le·giance** (ə-LEE-jəns) *n.* duty of a subject or citizen to sovereign or government; loyalty (to person or cause)

**al·le·go·ry** (AL-i-gor-ee) *n.* (*pl.* -ries) story with a meaning other than literal one; description of one thing under image of another —al·le·gor'i·cal *adj.*

**al·le·gret·to** (a-li-GRET-oh) *adv./adj./n. Mus.* lively (passage) but not so quick as allegro

**al·le·gro** (ə-LEG-roh) *adv./adj./n. Mus.* fast (a lively passage)

**al·ler·gy** (AL-ər-jee) *n.* (*pl.* -gies) abnormal sensitivity to some food or substance harmless to most people —al'ler·gen *n.* substance capable of inducing an allergy —**al·ler·gic** (ə-LUR-jik) *adj.* having or caused by an allergy; *inf.* having an aversion (to)

**al·le·vi·ate** (ə-LEE-vee-ayt) *vt.* (-at·ed, -at·ing) ease, lessen, mitigate; make light —**al·le·vi·a'·tion** *n.*

**al·ley** (AL-ee) *n.* (*pl.* -leys) narrow street *esp.* through the middle of a block; walk, path; hardwood lane for bowling; building housing bowling lanes

**al·li·ance** (ə-LI-əns) *n.* state of being allied; union between families by marriage, and states by treaty; confederation

**al·li·ga·tor** (AL-i-gay-tər) *n.* animal of crocodile family; leather made from its hide

**al·lit·er·a·tion** (ə-lit-ə-RAY-shən) *n.* beginning of two or more words in close succession with same sound, *eg* Sing a Song of Sixpence —**al·lit'·er·a·tive** *adj.*

**al·lo·cate** (AL-ə-kayt) *vt.* (-cat·ed, -cat·ing) assign as a share; designate —**al·lo·ca'tion** *n.*

**al·lo·mor·phism** (al-ə-MOR-fiz-əm) *n.* variation of form without change in essential nature; variation of crystalline form of chemical compound —**al'lo·morph** *n.* —**al·lo·morph'ic** *adj.*

**al·lop·a·thy** (ə-LOP-ə-thee) *n.* orthodox practice of medicine; opposite of homeopathy

**al·lot** (ə-LOT) *vt.* (-lot·ted, -lot·ting) distribute as shares; give out —**al·lot'ment** *n.* distribution; portion of land rented for cultivation; portion of land, pay *etc.* allotted

**al·low** (ə-LOW) *vt.* let happen; permit; acknowledge; set aside —*vi.* (*usu. with* for) take into account —**al·low'a·ble** *adj.* —**al·low'ance** *n.* portion or amount allowed, *esp.* at regular times

**al·loy** (AL-oi) *n.* mixture of two or more metals —*vt.* (ə-LOI) mix metals, debase

**all right** *see* ALL

**all·spice** (AWL-spīs) *n.* berry of West Indian tree; the tree; aromatic spice prepared from its berries

**al·lude** (ə-LOOD) *vi.* (-lud·ed, -lud·ing) mention lightly, hint at, make indirect reference to; refer to —**al·lu'sion** (-LOO-zhən) *n.* —**al·lu'sive** (-siv) *adj.*

**al·lure** (ə-LOOR) *vt.* (-lured, -lur·ing) entice, win over, fascinate —*n.* attractiveness —**al·lur'ing** *adj.* charming, seductive

**al·lu·vi·al** (ə-LOO-vee-əl) *adj.* deposited by rivers —**al·lu'vi·on** (-vee-ən) *n.* land formed by washed-up deposit —**al·lu'vi·um** (-vee-əm) *n.* (*pl.* -vi·a *pr.* -vee-ə) water-borne matter deposited by rivers, floods *etc.*

**al·ly** (ə-LĪ) *vt.* (-lied, -ly·ing) join in relationship by treaty, marriage, or friendship *etc.* —**al·ly** (AL-ī) *n.* (*pl.* -lies) country or ruler bound to another by treaty; confederate

**al·ma ma·ter** (AL-mə MAH-tər) one's school, college, or university; its song or hymn

**al·ma·nac** (AWL-mə-nak) *n.* yearly publication with detailed information on tides, events *etc.*

**al·might·y** (awl-MĪ-tee) *adj.* having all power, omnipotent; *inf.* very great —**The Almighty** God

**al·mond** (AH-mənd) *n.* kernel of the fruit of a tree related to the peach; tree that bears it

**al·most** (AWL-mohst) *adv.* very nearly, all but

**alms** (ahmz) *n. pl.* gifts to the poor

**al·oe** (AL-oh) *n.* genus of plants of medicinal value —**aloes** *n.* with *sing. v.* bitter drug made from plant

**a·loft** (ɔ-LAWFT) *adv.* on high; overhead; in ship's rigging

**a·lone** (ɔ-LOHN) *adj.* single, solitary —*adv.* separately, only

**a·long** (ɔ-LAWNG) *adv.* lengthwise; together (with); forward —*prep.* over the length of —**a·long'side'** *adv./prep.* beside

**a·loof** (ɔ-LOOF) *adv.* withdrawn; at a distance; apart —*adj.* uninvolved —**a·loof'ness** *n.*

**al·o·pe·ci·a** (al-ɔ-PEE-shee-ɔ) *n.* baldness

**a·loud** (ɔ-LOWD) *adj.* in a voice loud enough to be heard —*adv.* loudly; audibly

**alp** *n.* high mountain —**Alps** *pl. esp.* mountains of Switzerland —**al·pine** (AL-pin) *adj.* of, growing on, high mountains; (A-) of the Alps —*n.* mountain plant —alpinist (AL-pɔ-nist) *n.* mountain climber —**al'pen·stock** (-pɔn-stok) *n.* iron-tipped staff used by climbers

**al·pac·a** (al-PAK-ɔ) *n.* Peruvian llama; its wool; cloth made from this

**al·pha·bet** (AL-fɔ-bet) *n.* the set of letters used in writing a language —**al·pha·bet'i·cal** *adj.* in the standard order of the letters

**al·read·y** (awl-RED-ee) *adv.* before, previously; sooner than expected

**al·so** (AWL-soh) *adv.* as well, too; besides, moreover

**al·tar** (AWL-tɔr) *n.* raised place, stone *etc.*, on which sacrifices are offered; in Christian church, table on which priest consecrates the eucharist elements, as **al'tar·cloth** *n.*, **al'tar·piece** *n.*, **al'tar rails**

**altar boy** acolyte

**al·ter** (AWL-tɔr) *v.* change, make or become different; castrate;

spay (animal) —**al'ter·a·ble** *adj.* —**al'ter·a·bly** *adv.* —**al·ter·a·tion** *n.*

**al·ter·ca·tion** (awl-tɔr-KAY-shɔn) *n.* dispute, wrangling, noisy controversy

**al·ter e·go** (AWL-tɔr EE-goh) second self; close friend

**al·ter·nate** (AWL-tɔr-nayt) *v.* (-nat·ed, -nat·ing) occur or cause to occur by turns —**al'ter·nate** (-nit) *adj./n.* (one) after the other, by turns —**al·ter·na·tive** (awl-TUR-nɔ-tiv) *n.* one of two choices —*adj.* offering or expressing a choice —**al'ter·na·tor** *n.* electric generator for producing alternating current

**al·though** (awl-THOH) *conj.* despite the fact that

**al·tim·e·ter** (al-TIM-i-tɔr) *n.* instrument for measuring height

**al·ti·tude** (AL-ti-tood) *n.* height, eminence, elevation, loftiness

**al·to** (AL-toh) *n. Mus.* (*pl.* -tos) male singing voice or instrument above tenor; contralto

**al·to·geth·er** (awl-tɔ-GETH-ɔr) *adv.* entirely; on the whole; in total —**in the altogether** nude

**al·tru·ism** (AL-troo-iz-ɔm) *n.* principle of living and acting for good of others —**al'tru·ist** *n.* —**al·tru·is'tic** *adj.*

**a·lu·mi·num** (ɔ-LOO-mɔ-nɔm) *n.* light nonrusting metal resembling silver —**a·lu'mi·na** *n.* oxide of aluminum

**a·lum·na** (ɔ-LUM-nɔ) *n.* (*pl.* -nae *pr.* -nee) girl or woman graduate of a particular school, college, or university

**a·lum·nus** (ɔ-LUM-nɔs) *n.* (*pl.* -ni *pr.* -nī) graduate of a particular school, college, or university

**al·ways** (AWL-wayz) *adv.* at all times; forever

**am** *first person sing. pres. ind. of* BE

**Am** *Chem.* americium

**A.M., a.m.** ante meridiem (before noon)

**a·mal·gam** (ɔ-MAL-gɔm) *n.* compound of mercury and another metal; soft, plastic mixture; combination of elements

**a·mal·ga·mate** (ɔ-MAL-gɔ-mayt) *v.* (-mat·ed, -mat·ing) mix, combine or cause to combine —**a·mal·ga·ma′tion** *n.*

**a·man·u·en·sis** (ɔ-man-yoo-EN-sis) *n.* (*pl.* -ses *pr.* -seez) one who writes from dictation; copyist, secretary

**a·mass** (ɔ-MAS) *v.* collect in quantity

**am·a·teur** (AM-ɔ-chuur) *n.* one who carries on an art, study, game *etc.* for the love of it, not for money; unskilled practitioner —**am·a·teur′ish** *adj.* imperfect, untrained

**am·a·to·ry** (AM-ɔ-tor-ee) *adj.* relating to love

**a·maze** (ɔ-MAYZ) *vt.* (-mazed, -maz·ing) surprise greatly, astound —**a·maze′ment** *n.* —**amazing** *adj.*

**Am·a·zon** (AM-ɔ-zon) *n.* female warrior of legend; tall, strong woman —**Am·a·zo′ni·an** (-ZOH-nee-ɔn) *adj.*

**am·bas·sa·dor** (am-BAS-ɔ-dɔr) *n.* senior diplomatic representative sent by one government to another —**am·bas·sa·do′ri·al** *adj.*

**am·ber** (AM-bɔr) *n.* yellowish, translucent fossil resin —*adj.* made of, colored like amber

**am·ber·gris** (AM-bɔr-gris) *n.* waxy substance secreted by the sperm whale, used in making perfumes

**am·bi·dex·trous** (am-bi-DEK-strɔs) *adj.* able to use both hands with equal ease —**am·bi·dex·ter′i·ty** *n.*

**am·bi·ence, -ance** (AM-bee-ɔns) *n.* atmosphere of a place

**am·bi·ent** (AM-bee-ɔnt) *adj.* surrounding

**am·big·u·ous** (am-BIG-yoo-ɔs) *adj.* having more than one meaning; obscure —**am·bi·gu′i·ty** *n.*

**am·bi·tion** (am-BISH-ɔn) *n.* desire for power, fame, honor; the object of that desire —**am·bi′tious** *adj.*

**am·biv·a·lence** (am-BIV-ɔ-lɔns) *n.* simultaneous existence of two conflicting desires, opinions *etc.* —**am·biv′a·lent** *adj.*

**am·ble** (AM-bɔl) *vi.* (-bled, -bling) move along easily and gently; move at an easy pace —*n.* this movement or pace

**am·bro·sia** (am-BROH-zhɔ) *n. Myth.* food of the gods; anything smelling, tasting particularly good

**am·bu·lance** (AM-byɔ-lɔns) *n.* conveyance for sick or injured

**am·bus·cade** (AM-bɔ-skayd) *n.* a hiding to attack by surprise; ambush

**am·bush** (AM-buush) *n.* a lying in wait (for) —*vt.* waylay, attack from hiding, lie in wait for

**a·mel·io·rate** (ɔ-MEEL-yɔ-rayt) *v.* (-rat·ed, -rat·ing) make better, improve —**a·mel·io·ra′tion** *n.*

**a·men** (AY-MEN) *interj.* surely; so let it be

**a·me·na·ble** (ɔ-MEE-nɔ-bɔl) *adj.* easy to be led or controlled; subject to, liable —**a·me′na·bly** *adv.*

**a·mend** (ɔ-MEND) *v.* grow better —*vt.* correct; improve; alter in detail, as bill in legislature *etc.* —**a·mend′ment** *n.* —**a·mends′** *n. pl.* reparation

**a·men·i·ty** (ɔ-MEN-i-tee) *n.* (*pl.* -ties) useful or pleasant facility or service

**A·mer·i·can** (ɔ-MER-i-kɔn) *adj.*

of, relating to, the North American continent or the United States of America

**am·e·thyst** (AM-ə-thist) *n.* bluish-violet precious stone; its color

**a·mi·a·ble** (AY-mee-ə-bəl) *adj.* friendly, kindly —**a·mi·a·bil'·i·ty** *n.*

**am·i·ca·ble** (AM-i-kə-bəl) *adj.* friendly —**am·i·ca·bil'i·ty** *n.*

**a·mid** (ə-MID), **a·midst** (ə-MIDST) *prep.* in the middle of, among; during

**a·mid·ships** (ə-MID-ships) *adv.* near, toward, middle of ship

**a·mi·no acid** (ə-MEE-noh) organic compound found in protein

**a·miss** (ə-MIS) *adj.* wrong —*adv.* faultily, badly —**take amiss** be offended by

**am·i·ty** (AM-i-tee) *n.* friendship

**am·me·ter** (AM-mee-tər) *n.* instrument for measuring electric current

**am·mo·ni·a** (ə-MOHN-yə) *n.* pungent alkaline gas containing hydrogen and nitrogen

**am·mo·nite** (AM-ə-nit) *n.* whorled fossil shell like ram's horn

**am·mu·ni·tion** (am-yə-NISH-ən) *n.* any projectiles (bullets, rockets *etc.*) that can be discharged from a weapon: also *fig.*

**am·ne·sia** (am-NEE-zhə) *n.* loss of memory

**am·nes·ty** (AM-nə-stee) *n.* (pl. -ties) general pardon —*vt.* (-tied, -ty·ing) grant this

**am·ni·ot·ic fluid** (am-nee-OT-ik) fluid surrounding fetus in womb

**a·moe·ba** (ə-MEE-bə) *n.* (pl. -bas) microscopic single-celled animal found in ponds *etc.* and able to change its shape

**a·mok**, **a·muck** (ə-MUK) *adv.* —**run amok** rush about in murderous frenzy

**a·mong** (ə-MUNG), **a·mongst** (ə-MUNGST) *prep.* mixed with, in the midst of, of the number of, between

**a·mor·al** (ay-MOR-əl) *adj.* nonmoral, having no moral qualities —**a·mo·ral·i·ty** (ay-mo-RAL-i-tee) *n.*

**am·o·rous** (AM-ər-əs) *adj.* inclined to love; in love —**am'o·rous·ness** *n.*

**a·mor·phous** (ə-MOR-fəs) *adj.* without distinct shape

**am·or·tize** (AM-ər-tiz) *vt.* pay off a debt by a sinking fund —**am'or·tiz·a·ble** *adj.*

**a·mount** (ə-MOWNT) *vi.* come, be equal (to) —*n.* quantity; sum total

**a·mour** (ə-MOOR) *n.* (illicit) love affair

**am·pere** (AM-peer) *n.* unit of electric current —**am·per·age** (AM-pə-rij) *n.* strength of current in amperes

**am·per·sand** (AM-pər-sand) *n.* the sign & (and)

**am·phet·a·mine** (am-FET-ə-meen) *n.* synthetic liquid used medicinally as stimulant, a dangerous drug if misused

**am·phib·i·ous** (am-FIB-ee-əs) *adj.* living or operating both on land and in water —**am·phib'i·an** *n.* animal that lives first in water then on land; vehicle able to travel on land or water; aircraft that can alight on land or water

**am·phi·the·a·ter** (AM-fə-thee-ə-tər) *n.* building with tiers of seats rising around an arena; room with gallery above from which one can observe surgical operations *etc.*

**am·pho·ra** (AM-fər-ə) *n.* (pl. -rae pr. -ree) two-handled vessel of ancient Greece and Rome

**am·ple** (AM-pəl) *adj.* big enough; large, spacious —**am'ply** *adv.*

**am·pli·fy** (AM-plə-fi) *vt.* (-fied, -fy·ing) increase; make bigger, louder *etc.* —am·pli·fi·ca'tion *n.* —am'pli·fi·er *n.*

am·pli·tude (AM-pli-tood) *n.* spaciousness, width; maximum departure from average of alternating current *etc.* —amplitude modulation modulation of amplitude of radio carrier wave; broadcasting system using this

am·pule (AM-pyool) *n.* container for hypodermic dose

am·pu·tate (AM-pyə-tayt) *vi.* (-tat·ed, -tat·ing) cut off (limb *etc.*) —am·pu·ta'tion *n.*

amuck *see* AMOK

am·u·let (AM-yə-lit) *n.* something carried or worn as a charm

a·muse (ə-MYOOZ) *vt.* (-mused, -mus·ing) divert; occupy pleasantly; cause to laugh or smile —a·muse'ment *n.* entertainment, pastime

an *see* A

an·a·bol·ic ster·oid (an-ə-BOL-ik STEER-oid) any of various hormones used by athletes to encourage muscle growth

a·nach·ro·nism (ə-NAK-rə-niz-əm) *n.* mistake of time, by which something is put in wrong historical period; something out-of-date

an·a·con·da (an-ə-KON-də) *n.* large semi-aquatic snake that kills by constriction

an·a·gram (AN-ə-gram) *n.* word or sentence made by reordering the letters of another word or sentence, *eg* ant from ran

anal *see* ANUS

an·al·ge·si·a (an-l-JEE-zee-ə) *n.* absence of pain —an·al·ge'sic *adj./n.* (drug) relieving pain

a·nal·o·gy (ə-NAL-ə-jee) *n.* (pl. -gies) agreement or likeness in certain respects; correspondence —a·nal'o·gize *v.* (-gized, -giz·ing) explain by analogy —a·nal'o·gous (-ə-gəs) *adj.* similar; parallel

a·nal·y·sis (ə-NAL-ə-sis) *n.* (pl. -ses *pr.* -seez) separation into elements or components —an·a·lyze (AN-l-īz) *vt.* (-lyzed, -lyz·ing) examine critically; determine the constituent parts —an·a·lyst (AN-l-ist) *n.* one skilled in analysis, *esp.* chemical analysis; psychoanalyst —an·a·lyt·ic (an-l-IT-ik) *adj.*

an·a·pest (AN-ə-pest) *n.* metrical foot of two short syllables followed by one long —an·a·pes'tic *adj.*

an·ar·chy (AN-ər-kee) *n.* lawlessness; lack of government in a country; confusion —an·ar·chic (an-AHR-kik) *adj.* —an'ar·chism *n.* —an'ar·chist *n.* one who opposes all government

a·nath·e·ma (ə-NATH-ə-mə) *n.* (pl. -mas) anything detested, hateful; ban of the church; curse —a·nath'e·ma·tize *vt.* (-tized, -tiz·ing)

a·nat·o·my (ə-NAT-ə-mee) *n.* science of structure of the body; detailed analysis; the body —an·a·tom'i·cal *adj.*

an·ces·tor (AN-ses-tər) *n.* person from whom another is descended; early type of later form or product —an·ces'tral *adj.* —an'·ces·try *n.*

an·chor (ANG-kər) *n.* heavy (*usu.* hooked) implement dropped on cable, chain *etc.* to bottom of sea *etc.* to secure vessel; *Radio and TV* principal announcer in program of news, sports *etc.* —*vt.* fasten by or as with anchor; perform as anchor —an'chor·age *n.* act of, place of anchoring

an·cho·rite (ANG-kə-rīt) *n.* hermit, recluse

an·cho·vy (AN-choh-vee) *n.* (pl. -vies) small fish of herring family

an·cient (AYN-shənt) *adj.* belonging to former age; old; timeworn

—*n.* one who lived in an earlier age (*esp. in pl.*) —**ancient history** history of ancient times; common knowledge

an·cil·lar·y (AN-sə-ler-ee) *adj.* subordinate, subservient, auxiliary —*n.* (*pl.* -ies )

**and** *conj.* joins words, phrases, clauses, and sentences to introduce a consequence *etc.*

an·dan·te (ahn-DAHN-tay) *adv./n. Mus.* moderately slow (passage)

and·i·ron (AND-ī-ərn) *n.* steel bar or bracket for supporting logs in a fireplace

an·drog·y·nous (an-DROJ-ə-nəs) *adj.* having characteristics of both male and female

an·ec·dote (AN-ik-doht) *n.* very short story dealing with single incident —**an·ec·do·tal** *adj.* —**an·ec·do·tal·ist** —*n.* one given to recounting anecdotes

a·ne·mi·a (ə-NEE-mee-ə) *n.* deficiency in number of red blood cells —**a·ne′mic** *adj.* suffering from anemia; pale, sickly

an·e·mom·e·ter (an-ə-MOM-i-tər) *n.* wind gauge

a·nem·o·ne (ə-NEM-ə-nee) *n.* flower related to buttercup —**sea anemone** plantlike sea animal

an·er·oid (AN-ə-roid) *adj.* denoting a barometer that measures atmospheric pressure without use of mercury or other liquid

an·es·the·si·ol·o·gy (an-is-thee-zi-OL-ə-jee) *n.* branch of medicine dealing with anesthetics

an·es·thet·ic (an-əs-THET-ik) *n./adj.* (drug) causing loss of sensation —**an·es·the·sia** (-THEE-zhə) *n.* loss of sensation —**an·es·the·tist** (ə-NES-thi-tist) *n.* expert in use of anesthetics —**an·es′the·tize** *vt.* (-tized, -tiz·ing)

an·eu·rism (AN-yə-riz-əm) *n.* swelling out of a part of an artery

a·new (ə-NOO) *adv.* afresh, again

an·gel (AYN-jəl) *n.* divine messenger; ministering or attendant spirit; person with the qualities of such a spirit, as gentleness, purity *etc.* —**an·gel′ic** *adj.*

An·ge·lus (AN-jə-ləs) *n.* devotional service in R.C. Church in memory of the Incarnation, said at morning, noon and sunset; bell announcing the time for this service

an·ger (ANG-gər) *n.* strong emotion excited by a real or supposed injury; wrath; rage —*vt.* excite to wrath; enrage —**an′gri·ly** *adv.* —**an′gry** *adj.* full of anger; inflamed

an·gi·na (pec·to·ris) (an-JĪ-nə PEK-tə-ris) *n.* severe pain accompanying some heart diseases

an·gle¹ (ANG-gəl) *vi.* (-gled, -gling) fish with hook and line —**an′gler** *n.*

angle² *n.* meeting of two lines or surfaces; corner; point of view; *inf.* devious motive —*vt.* bend at an angle

An·gli·can (ANG-gli-kən) *adj./n.* (member) of the Church of England —**An′gli·can·ism** *n.*

an·gli·cize (ANG-glə-sīz) *vt.* (-cized, -ciz·ing) express in English; turn into English form —**An′gli·cism** *n.* English idiom or peculiarity

Anglo- (*comb. form*) English, as Anglo-American

an·glo·phil·i·a (ang-glə-FIL-ee-ə)*n.* excessive admiration for English people (-fil) *n.*

An·glo·pho·bi·a (ang-glə-FOH-bee-ə) *n.* dislike of England *etc.* —**an′glo·phobe** *n.*

an·go·ra (ang-GOR-ə) *n.* goat with long white silky hair which is used in the making of mohair; cloth or wool made from this hair —**angora cat, rabbit** varieties of cat and rabbit with long, silky fur

**an·gos·tu·ra bark** (ang-gə-STOOR-ə) *n.* bitter bark of certain **SA** trees, used as flavoring in alcoholic drinks

**ang·strom** (ANG-strəm) *n.* unit of length for measuring wavelengths of electromagnetic radiation

**an·guish** (ANG-gwish) *n.* great mental or bodily pain — *v.* suffer this pain; cause to suffer it

**an·gu·lar** (ANG-gyə-lər) *adj.* (of people) bony, awkward; having angles; measured by an angle —**an·gu·lar'i·ty** *n.*

**an·hy·drous** (an-HĪ-drəs) *adj.* (of chemical substances) free from water

**an·i·line** (AN-l-in) *n.* product of coal tar or indigo that yields dyes

**an·i·mad·vert** (an-ə-mad-VURT) *vi.* (*with* (up)on) criticize, pass censure —**an·i·mad·ver·sion** (-VUR-zhən) *n.* criticism, censure; unfair criticism

**an·i·mal** (AN-ə-məl) *n.* living creature, having sensation and power of voluntary motion; beast —*adj.* of, pert. to animals; sensual —**an·i·mal·cule** (an-ə-MAL-kyool) *n.* very small animal, *esp.* one that cannot be seen by naked eye —**animal husbandry** branch of agriculture concerned with raising domestic animals

**an·i·mate** (AN-ə-mayt) *vt.* (-mat·ed, -mat·ing) give life to; enliven; inspire; actuate; make cartoon film of —**an'i·mat·ed** *adj.* lively; in form of cartoons —**an·i·ma'tion** *n.* life, vigor; cartoon film

**an·i·mism** (AN-ə-miz-əm) *n.* primitive religion, belief that natural effects are due to spirits, that inanimate things have spirits —**an'i·mist** *n.*

**an·i·mos·i·ty** (an-ə-MOS-i-tee) *n.* (*pl.* -ties) hostility, enmity

**an·i·mus** (AN-ə-məs) *n.* hatred; animosity

**an·i·on** (AN-ī-ən) *n.* ion with negative charge

**an·ise** (AN-is) *n.* plant with aromatic seeds, which are used for flavoring

**an·i·seed** (AN-ə-seed) *n.* the licorice-flavored seed of anise

**an·kle** (ANG-kəl) *n.* joint between foot and leg —**an·klet** (ANG-klit) *n.* ankle ornament; short sock reaching just above the ankle

**an·nals** (AN-lz) *n. pl.* historical records of events —**an'nal·ist** *n.*

**an·neal** (ə-NEEL) *vt.* toughen (metal or glass) by heating and slow cooling; temper

**an·ne·lid** (AN-l-id) *n.* one of class of invertebrate animals, including the earthworm *etc.*

**an·nex** (ə-NEKS) *vt.* add, append, attach; take possession of (*esp.* territory) —**an·nex·a·tion** (an-ik-SAY-shən) *n.* —**annex** *n.* (AN-eks) supplementary building; something added

**an·ni·hi·late** (ə-NĪ-ə-layt) *vt.* (-lat·ed, -lat·ing) reduce to nothing, destroy utterly —**an·ni·hi·la'tion** *n.*

**an·ni·ver·sa·ry** (an-ə-VUR-sə-ree) *n.* yearly return of a date; celebration of this

**an·no Dom·i·ni** (AN-oh DOM-ə-nee) *Lat.* in the year of our Lord

**an·no·tate** (AN-ə-tayt) *vt.* (-tat·ed, -tat·ing) make notes upon, comment —**an·no·ta'tion** *n.*

**an·nounce** (ə-NOWNS) *vt.* (-nounced, -nounc·ing) make known, proclaim —**an·nounce'ment** *n.* —**an·nounc'er** *n.* broadcaster who announces items in program, introduces speakers *etc.*

**an·noy** (ə-NOI) *vt.* vex; make slightly angry; tease —**an·noy'·ance** *n.*

**an·nu·al** (AN-yoo-əl) *adj.* yearly; of, for a year —*n.* plant that completes its life cycle in a year; book published each year —**an'·nu·al·ly** *adv.*

**an·nu·i·ty** (ə-NOO-i-tee) *n.* (*pl.* -ties) sum or grant paid every year —**an·nu'·i·tant** (-tnt) *n.* holder of annuity

**an·nul** (ə-NUL) *vt.* (-nulled, -nul·ling) make void, cancel, abolish

**an·nu·lar** (AN-yə-lər) *adj.* ring-shaped —**an'·nu·lat·ed** (-lay-tid) *adj.* formed in rings —**an'·nu·let** (-lit) *n.* small ring or molding in shape of ring

**An·nun·ci·a·tion** (ə-nun-see-AY-shən) *n.* angel's announcement of Incarnation to the Virgin Mary; (a-) announcing; announcement —**an·nun'·ci·ate** *vt.* (-at·ed, -at·ing) proclaim, announce

**an·ode** (AN-ohd) *n. Electricity* the positive electrode or terminal —**an·o·dize** (AN-ə-dīz) *vt.* cover (metal object) with protective film by using it as an anode in electrolysis

**an·o·dyne** (AN-ə-dīn) *adj.* relieving pain, soothing —*n.* pain-relieving drug; something that soothes

**a·noint** (ə-NOINT) *vt.* smear with oil or ointment; consecrate with oil —**a·noint'·ment** *n.* —**the Anointed** the Messiah

**a·nom·a·lous** (ə-NOM-ə-ləs) *adj.* irregular, abnormal —**a·nom'·a·ly** *n.* (*pl.* -lies) irregularity; deviation from rule

**a·non** (ə-NON) *obs. adv.* in a short time, soon; now and then

**a·non·y·mous** (ə-NON-ə-məs) *adj.* nameless, *esp.* without an author's name —**an·o·nym·i·ty** (an-ə-NIM-i-tee) *n.*

**an·o·rak** (AN-ə-rak) *n.* lightweight, warm, waterproof, *usu.* hooded jacket; parka

**an·o·rex·i·a** (an-ə-REK-see-ə) *n.* loss of appetite —**anorexia nervosa** (nur-VOH-sə) chronic psychological condition characterized by refusal to eat

**an·oth·er** (ə-NUTH-ər) *pron./adj.* one other; a different one; one more

**an·ser·ine** (AN-sə-rīn) *adj.* of or like a goose; silly

**an·swer** (AN-sər) *v.* reply (to); solve; reply correctly; pay; meet; be accountable (for, to); match; satisfy, suit —*n.* reply; solution —**an'·swer·a·ble** *adj.* accountable —**answering machine** apparatus for answering a telephone automatically and recording messages

**ant** *n.* small social insect, proverbial for industry —**ant'·eat·er** *n.* animal that feeds on ants by means of a long, sticky tongue —**ant'·hill** the mound raised by ants

**an·tag·o·nist** (an-TAG-ə-nist) *n.* opponent, adversary —**an·tag'o·nism** *n.* —**an·tag·o·nis'·tic** *adj.* —**an·tag'o·nize** *vt.* (-nized, -niz·ing) arouse hostility in

**Ant·arc·tic** (ant-AHRK-tik) *adj.* south polar —*n.* these regions

**an·te** (AN-tee) *n.* player's stake in poker —*vt.* (-ted, -te·ing) (*often with up*) stake

**ante-** (*prefix*) before, as in ante-chamber and antedate *in.* Such words are not given here when their meanings can easily be inferred from the simple word

**an·te·ced·ent** (an-tə-SEED-nt) *adj./n.* (thing) going before

**an·te·di·lu·vi·an** (an-tee-di-LOO-vee-ɔn) *adj.* before the Flood; ancient

**an·te·lope** (AN-tl-ohp) *n.* deer-like ruminant animal, remarkable for grace and speed

**ante me·rid·i·em** (AN-tee mɔ-RID-ee-ɔm) *Lat.* before noon

**an·te·na·tal** (an-tee-NAYT-l) *adj.* of care *etc.* during pregnancy

**an·ten·na** (an-TEN-ɔ) *n.* (*pl.* -nae *pr.* -nee) insect's feeler; aerial

**an·te·pe·nult** (an-tee-PEE-nult) *n.* last syllable but two in a word —an·te·pe·nul'ti·mate *adj./n.*

**an·te·ri·or** (an-TEER-ee-ɔr) *adj.* to the front; before

**an·them** (AN-thɔm) *n.* song of loyalty, *esp.* to a country; Scripture passage set to music; piece of sacred music, originally sung in alternate parts by two choirs

**an·ther** (AN-thɔr) *n.* in flower, part at top of stamen containing pollen

**an·thol·o·gy** (an-THOL-ɔ-jee) *n.* (*pl.* -gies) collection of poems, literary extracts *etc.* —an·thol'o·gist *n.* maker of such —anthol'o·gize *vt.* (-gized, -giz·ing) compile or publish in an anthology

**an·thra·cite** (AN-thrɔ-sīt) *n.* hard coal burning slowly almost without flame or smoke

**an·thrax** (AN-thraks) *n.* malignant disease in cattle, communicable to people; sore caused by this

**an·thro·poid** (AN-thrɔ-poid) *adj.* like man —*n.* ape resembling human being

**an·thro·pol·o·gy** (an-thrɔ-POL-ɔ-jee) *n.* scientific study of origins, development of human race —an·thro·po·log'i·cal (-pɔ-LOJ-i-kɔl) *adj.* —an·thro·pol'o·gist *n.*

**an·thro·po·mor·phize** (an-thrɔ-pɔ-MOR-fīz) *vt.* (-pized, -piz·ing) ascribe human attributes to God

or an animal —an·thro·po·mor'phic *adj.*

**anti-, ant-** (*prefix*) against, as in antiaircraft *adj.* —antispasmodic *adj./n. etc.* Such words are not given here when their meanings can easily be inferred from the simple word

**an·ti·bi·ot·ic** (an-ti-bī-OT-ik) *n.* any of various chemical, fungal or synthetic substances, *esp.* penicillin, used against bacterial infection —*adj.*

**an·ti·bod·y** (AN-ti-bod-ee) *n.* substance in, or introduced into, blood serum that counteracts the growth and harmful action of bacteria

**an·tic·i·pate** (an-TIS-ɔ-payt) *vt.* (-pat·ed, -pat·ing) expect; take or consider beforehand; foresee; enjoy in advance —an·tic·i·pa'tion *n.* —an·tic'i·pa·to·ry (-pɔ-tor-ee) *adj.*

**an·ti·cli·max** (an-ti-KLĪ-maks) *n.* sudden descent to the trivial or ludicrous —an·ti·cli·mac'tic *adj.*

**an·tics** (AN-tiks) *n. pl.* absurd or grotesque movements or acts

**an·ti·cy·clone** (an-tee-SĪ-klohn) *n.* system of winds moving around center of high barometric pressure

**an·ti·dote** (AN-ti-doht) *n.* counteracting remedy

**an·ti·freeze** (AN-ti-freez) *n.* liquid added to water to lower its freezing point, as in automobile radiators

**an·ti·gen** (AN-ti-jɔn) *n.* substance stimulating production of antibodies in the blood

**an·ti·his·ta·mine** (an-ti-HIS-tɔ-meen) *n.* drug used *esp.* to treat allergies

**an·ti·ma·cas·sar** (an-ti-mɔ-KAS-ɔr) *n.* cover to protect back or arms of chairs

**an·ti·mo·ny** (AN-tə-moh-nee) *n.* brittle, bluish-white metal

**an·tip·a·thy** (an-TIP-ə-thee) *n.* (*pl.* -thies) dislike, aversion

**an·ti·per·spi·rant** (an-ti-PUR-spər-ənt) *n.* substance used to reduce sweating

**an·ti·phon** (AN-tə-fon) *n.* composition in which verses, lines are sung alternately by two choirs; anthem —**an·tiph·o·nal** (an-TIF-ə-nl) *adj.*

**an·tip·o·des** (an-TIP-ə-deez) *n. pl.* countries, peoples on opposite side of the globe (often refers to Aust. and N Zealand) —**an·tip·o·de·an** *adj.*

**an·ti·pope** (n. ti-pohp) *n.* pope elected in opposition to the one regularly chosen

**an·tique** (an-TEEK) *n.* relic of former times, usu. a piece of furniture *etc.* that is collected —*adj.* ancient; old-fashioned —**an·ti·quar·i·an** *n.* student or collector of old things —**an·ti·quated** *adj.* out-of-date —**an·tiq·ui·ty** (an-TIK-wi-tee) *n.* great age; former times

**an·ti-Sem·it·ic** (an-tee-sə-MIT-ik) *adj.* hostile or discriminating against Jews —**an·ti-Sem'i·tism**, **an·ti-Sem'ite** *n.*

**an·ti·sep·tic** (an-tə-SEPT-tik) *n./adj.* (substance) preventing infection —*adj.* free from infection

**an·tith·e·sis** (an-TITH-ə-sis) *n.* (*pl.* -ses *pr.* -seez) direct opposite; contrast; opposition of ideas —**an·ti·thet'i·cal** *adj.*

**an·ti·tox·in** (an-ti-TOK-sin) *n.* serum used to neutralize disease poisons

**an·ti·tus·sive** (an-ti-TUS-iv) *n./adj.* (substance) controlling or preventing coughing

**an·ti·ven·in** (an-tee-VEN-in) *n.* antitoxin to counteract specific venom, *eg* of snake or spider

**ant·ler** (ANT-lər) *n.* branching horn of certain deer

**an·to·nym** (AN-tə-nim) *n.* word of opposite meaning to another *eg cold* is an antonym of *hot*

**a·nus** (AY-nəs) *n.* the lower opening of the bowels —**a'nal** *adj.*

**an·vil** *n.* heavy iron block with steel face on which a blacksmith hammers metal into shape

**anx·ious** (ANGK-shəs) *adj.* troubled, uneasy; concerned —**anx·i·e·ty** (ang-Zl-ə-tee) *n.*

**an·y** (EN-ee) *adj./pron.* one indefinitely; some; every —**an'y·bod·y** *n./pron* —**an'y·how** *adv.* —**an'y·one** *n./pron* —**an'y·thing** *n./pron* —**an'y·way** *adv.* —**an'y·where** *adv.*

**a·or·ta** (ay-OR-tə) *n.* great artery rising from left ventricle of heart —**a·or'tal** *adj.*

**a·pace** (ə-PAYS) *adv.* swiftly

**a·part** (ə-PAHRT) *adv.* separately, aside; in pieces

**a·part·heid** (ə-PAHRT-hayt) *n.* (*esp.* in S Africa) official government policy of racial segregation

**a·part·ment** (ə-PAHRT-mənt) *n.* room or suite of rooms in larger building used for dwelling

**ap·a·thy** (AP-ə-thee) *n.* (*pl.* -thies) indifference; lack of emotion —**ap·a·thet'ic** *adj.*

**ape** (ayp) *n.* tailless monkey (*eg* chimpanzee, gorilla); coarse, clumsy person; imitator —*vt.* (aped, ap·ing) imitate

**a·pe·ri·ent** (ə-PEER-ee-ənt) *adj.* mildly laxative —*n.* any such medicine

**a·pe·ri·od·ic** (ay-peer-ee-OD-ik) *adj. Electricity* having no natural period or frequency

**a·pe·ri·tif** (ə-per-i-TEEF) *n.* alcoholic appetizer

**ap·er·ture** (AP-ər-chər) *n.* opening, hole

**a·pex** (AY-peks) *n.* (*pl.* **a·pex·es**) top, peak; vertex

**a·pha·sia** (ə-FAY-zhə) *n.* dumbness, or loss of speech control, due to disease of the brain

**a·phe·li·on** (ə-FEE-lee-ən) *n.* point of planet's orbit farthest from the sun

**a·phid** (AY-fid) *n.* any of various sap-sucking insects

**a·phis** (AY-fis) *n.* (*pl.* **a·phi·des** *pr.* AY-fi-deez) an aphid

**aph·o·rism** (AF-ə-riz-əm) *n.* maxim, pithy saying —**aph·o·ris'tic** (-RIS-tik) *adj.*

**aph·ro·dis·i·ac** (af-rə-DEE-zee-ak) *adj.* exciting sexual desire —*n.* substance that so excites

**a·pi·ar·y** (AY-pee-er-ee) *n.* (*pl.* **-ar·ies**) place where bees are kept —**a'pi·a·rist** *n.* beekeeper —**a'pi·cul·ture** *n.*

**a·piece** (ə-PEES) *adv.* for each

**a·plomb** (ə-PLOM) *n.* self-possession, coolness, assurance

**a·poc·a·lypse** (ə-POK-ə-lips) *n.* prophetic revelation *esp.* of future of the world; (A-) in last book of the New Testament —**a·poc·a·lyp'tic** *adj.*

**a·poc·ry·pha** (ə-POK-rə-fə) *n. pl.* religious writing of doubtful authenticity; (A-) *n. pl.* collective name for 14 books originally in the Old Testament —**a·poc'ry·phal** *adj.* spurious

**ap·o·gee** (AP-ə-jee) *n.* point farthest from Earth in orbit of moon or satellite; climax; highest point

**a·pol·o·gy** (ə-POL-ə-jee) *n.* (*pl.* **-gies**) acknowledgment of offense and expression of regret; written or spoken defense; poor substitute (*with* for) —**a·pol·o·get'ic** *adj.* —**a·pol·o·get'ics** *n.* branch of theology charged with defense of Christianity —**a·pol'o·**

**gist** *n.* —**a·pol'o·gize** *vi.* (**-gized, -giz·ing**)

**ap·o·plex·y** (AP-ə-plek-see) *n.* loss of sense and often paralysis caused by broken or blocked blood vessel in the brain; a stroke —**ap·o·plec'tic** *adj.*

**a·pos·ta·sy** (ə-POS-tə-see) *n.* (*pl.* **-sies**) abandonment of one's religious or other faith —**a·pos'tate** (-tayt) *n./adj.*

**a pos·te·ri·o·ri** (ay po-steer-ee-OR-I) *adj.* denoting form of inductive reasoning that arrives at causes from effects; empirical

**a·pos·tle** (ə-POS-əl) *n.* ardent supporter; leader of reform —(A-) one sent to preach the Gospel, *esp.* one of the first disciples of Jesus; founder of Christian church in a country —**a·pos·tol'ic** *adj.*

**a·pos·tro·phe** (ə-POS-trə-fee) *n.* a mark (') showing the omission of a letter or letters in a word; digression to appeal to someone dead or absent

**ap·o·thegm** (AP-ə-them) *n.* terse saying, maxim

**a·poth·e·o·sis** (ə-poth-ee-OH-sis) *n.* (*pl.* **-ses** *pr.* -seez) deification, act of raising any person or thing into a god

**ap·pall** (ə-PAWL) *vt.* dismay, terrify —**ap·pall'ing** *adj. inf.* dreadful, terrible

**ap·pa·ra·tus** (ap-ə-RAT-əs) *n.* equipment, tools, instruments, for performing any experiment, operation *etc.*; means by which something operates

**ap·par·el** (ə-PAR-əl) *n.* clothing —*vt.* (**-eled, -el·ing**) clothe

**ap·par·ent** (ə-PAR-ənt) *adj.* seeming; obvious; acknowledged, as in *heir apparent*

**ap·pa·ri·tion** (ap-ə-RISH-ən) *n.* appearance, *esp.* of ghost

**ap·peal** (ə-PEEL) *vi.* (*with* to) call

upon, make earnest request; be attractive; refer to, have recourse to; refer to higher court —n. request, reference, supplication —ap·peal'ing adj. making appeal; pleasant, attractive —ap·pel'lant (-PEL-ənt) ·n. one who appeals to higher court —ap·pel'late (-it) adj. of appeals

ap·pear (ə-PEER) vi. become visible or present; seem, be plain; be seen in public —ap·pear'ance n. an appearing; aspect; pretense

ap·pease (ə-PEEZ) vt. (-peased, -peas·ing) pacify, quiet, allay, satisfy —ap·pease'ment n.

appellant see APPEAL

ap·pel·la·tion (ap-ə-LAY-shən) n. name

ap·pend (ə-PEND) vt. join on, add —ap·pend'age n.

ap·pen·di·ci·tis (ə-pen-də-SĪ-tis) n. inflammation of vermiform appendix

ap·pen·dix (ə-PEN-diks) n. (pl. -di·ces pr. -də-seez) subsidiary addition to book etc.; Anatomy projection, esp. the small worm-shaped (vermiform) part of the intestine

ap·per·cep·tion (ap-ər-SEP-shən) n. perception; apprehension; the mind's perception of itself as a conscious agent

ap·per·tain (ap-ər-TAYN) vi. belong, relate to; be appropriate

ap·pe·tite (AP-i-tīt) n. desire, inclination; desire for food —ap'pe·tiz·er n. something stimulating to appetite —ap'pe·tiz·ing adj.

ap·plaud (ə-PLAWD) vt. praise by handclapping; praise loudly —ap·plause' (-PLAWZ n.) loud approval

ap·ple (AP-əl) n. round, firm, fleshy fruit; tree bearing it

ap·pli·ance (ə-PLĪ-əns) n. piece of equipment esp. electrical

ap·pli·qué (ap-li-KAY) n. orna-

ments, embroidery etc., secured to surface of material —vt. (-quéd, -qué·ing) ornament thus

ap·ply (ə-PLĪ) vt. (-plied, -ply·ing) —vt. utilize, employ; lay or place on; administer, devote —vi. have reference (to); make request (to) —ap'pli·ca·ble adj. relevant —ap'pli·cant n. —ap·pli·ca'tion n. applying something for a particular use; relevance; request for a job etc.; concentration, diligence —applied' adj. (of skill, science etc.) put to practical use

ap·point (ə-POINT) vt. name, assign to a job or position; fix, settle; equip —ap·point'ment n. engagement to meet; (selection for a) position —pl. equipment, furnishings

ap·por·tion (ə-POR-shən) vt. divide out in shares —ap·por'tion·ment n.

ap·po·site (AP-ə-zit) adj. suitable, apt —ap'po·site·ness n. —ap·po·si'tion (-ZISH-ən) n. proximity; the placing of one word beside another that it describes

ap·praise (ə-PRAYZ) vt. (-praised, -prais·ing) set price on, estimate value of —ap·prais'al n. —ap·prais'er n.

ap·pre·ci·ate (ə-PREE-shee-ayt) v. (-at·ed, -at·ing) —vt. value at true worth; be grateful for; understand; enjoy —vi. rise in value —ap·pre'ci·a·ble (-shə-bəl) adj. estimable; substantial —ap·pre'ci·a·bly adv. —ap·pre·ci·a'tion n. —ap·pre'ci·a·tive (-shə-tiv) adj. capable of expressing pleasurable recognition

ap·pre·hend (ap-ri-HEND) vt. arrest, seize by authority; take hold of; recognize, understand; dread —ap·pre·hen·si·ble (-HEN-sə-bəl) adj. —ap·pre·hen'sion (-shən) n. dread, anxiety; arrest; conception; ability to understand —appre·hen'sive (-siv) *adj.* — ap·pre·hen'sive·ly *adv.*

ap·pren·tice (ə-PREN-tis) *n.* person learning a trade under specified conditions; novice —*vt.* (-ticed, -tic·ing) bind, set to work, as apprentice —ap·pren'tice·ship *n.*

ap·prise (ə-PRĪZ) *vt.* (-prised, -pris·ing) inform

ap·proach (ə-PROHCH) *v.* draw near (to); set about; address request to; approximate to; make advances to —*n.* a drawing near; means of reaching or doing; approximation; (*oft. pl.*) friendly or amatory overture(s) —ap·proach'a·ble *adj.*

ap·pro·ba·tion (ap-rə-BAY-shən) *n.* approval

ap·pro·pri·ate (ə-PROH-pree-ayt) *vt.* (-at·ed, -at·ing) take for oneself; put aside for particular purpose —*adj.* (-it) suitable, fitting —ap·pro'pri·ate·ness (-it-nis) *n.* —ap·pro·pri·a'tion *n.* act of setting apart for purpose; legislative vote of money

ap·prove (ə-PROOV) *vt.* (-proved, -prov·ing) think well of, commend; authorize, agree to —ap·prov'al *n.* —ap·prov'ing·ly *adv.*

ap·prox·i·mate (ə-PROK-sə-mit) *adj.* very near, nearly correct; inexact, imprecise —*v.* (-mayt) (-mat·ed, -mat·ing) —*vt.* bring close —*vi.* come near; be almost the same as —ap·prox'i·mate·ly *adv.*

ap·pur·te·nance (ə-PUR-te- əns) *n.* thing that appertains to; accessory

après-ski (ah-pray-SKEE) *n.* social activities after day's skiing

ap·ri·cot (AP-ri-kot) *n.* orange-colored fruit related to the plum —*adj.* of the color of the fruit

A·pril fool (AY-prəl) butt of a joke or trick played on April Fools' Day, April 1

a pri·o·ri (ay-prī-OR-ī) *adj.* denoting deductive reasoning from general principle to expected facts or effects; denoting knowledge gained independently of experience

a·pron (AY-prən) *n.* cloth, piece of leather *etc.*, worn in front to protect clothes, or as part of costume; in theater, strip of stage before curtain; on airfield, paved area where aircraft stand, are refueled *etc.*; *fig.* any of a variety of things resembling these

ap·ro·pos (ap-rə-POH) *adv.* to the purpose; with reference to —*adj.* apt, appropriate —apropos of concerning

apse (aps) *n.* arched recess, *esp.* in a church

apt (apt) *adj.* suitable; likely; prompt, quick-witted; dexterous —ap·ti·tude (AP-ti-tood) *n.* capacity, fitness —apt'ly *adv.* —apt'ness *n.*

aq·ua·ma·rine (ak-wə-mə-REEN) *n.* precious stone, a transparent beryl —*adj.* greenish-blue, sea-colored

aq·ua·plane (AK-wə-playn) *n.* plank or boat towed by fast motorboat and ridden by person standing on it —*vi.* (-planed, -plan·ing) ride on aquaplane; (of automobile) be in contact with water on road, not with road surface —aquaplaning *n.*

a·quar·i·um (ə-KWAIR-ee-əm) *n.* (*pl.* -i·ums) tank or pond for keeping water animals or plants

a·quat·ic (ə-KWAT-ik) *adj.* living, growing, done in or on water —a·quat'ics *n. sing.* water sport

aq·ua·vit (AH-kwə-veet) *n.* Scandinavian liquor *usu.* flavored with caraway seeds

aq·ue·duct (AK-wi-dukt) *n.* artificial channel for water, *esp.* one like a bridge; conduit

**a·que·ous** (AY-kwee-ɔs) *adj.* of, like, containing water

**aq·ui·fer** (AK-wɔ-fɔr) *n.* geological formation containing or conveying ground water

**aq·ui·line** (AK-wɔ-lin) *adj.* relating to eagle; hooked like an eagle's beak

**Ar** *Chem.* argon

**Ar·ab** (AR-ɔb) *n.* general term for inhabitants of Middle Eastern countries; Arabian horse —**Ar'a·bic** *n.* language of Arabs —*adj.* —**Ar'ab·ist** *n.* specialist in Arabic language or in Arabic culture

**ar·a·besque** (ar-ɔ-BESK) *n.* classical ballet position; fanciful painted or carved ornament of Arabian origin —*adj.*

**ar·a·ble** (AR-ɔ-bɔl) *adj.* suitable for plowing or planting crops

**a·rach·nid** (ɔ-RAK-nid) *n.* one of the Arachnida (spiders, scorpions, and mites) —**a·rach'noid** *adj.*

**ar·bi·ter** (AHR-bi-tɔr) *n.* judge, umpire —**ar·bi·trar'i·ly** (-TRER-ɔ-lee) *adv.* —**ar'bi·trar·y** *adj.* not bound by rules, despotic; random —**ar'bi·trate** (-trayt) *v.* decide dispute; submit to, settle by arbitration; act as an umpire —**ar·bi·tra'tion** *n.* hearing, settling of disputes, *esp.* industrial and legal, by impartial referee —**ar'bi·tra·tor** *n.*

**ar·bor** (AHR-bɔr) *n.* leafy glade *etc.*, sheltered by trees

**ar·bo·re·al** (ahr-BOR-ee-ɔl) *adj.* relating to trees —**ar·bo·re'tum** (-bɔ-REE-tɔm) *n.* (*pl.* -tums) place for cultivating specimens of trees —**ar·bor·i·cul·ture** (AHR-bɔr-i-kul-chɔr) *n.* forestry, cultivation of trees —**ar'bor·ist** *n.*

**ar·bor vi·tae** (ahr-bɔr VĪ-tee) *n.* a kind of evergreen conifer

**arc** (ahrk) *n.* part of circumfer-ence of circle or similar curve; luminous electric discharge between two conductors —**arc lamp, arc light**

**ar·cade** (ahr-KAYD) *n.* row of arches on pillars; covered walk or avenue, *esp.* lined by shops

**ar·cane** (ahr-KAYN) *adj.* mysterious; esoteric

**arch**[1] (ahrch) *n.* curved structure in building, supporting itself over open space by pressure of stones one against the other; any similar structure; a curved shape; curved part of sole of the foot —*v.* form, make into, an arch —**arched** *adj.* —**arch'way** *n.*

**arch**[2] *adj.* chief; experienced, expert; superior, knowing, coyly playful —**arch'ly** *adv.* —**arch'ness** *n.*

**arch-** (*comb. form*) chief, as in **archangel** *n.*, **archenemy** *n. etc.* Such words are not given here where the meaning can easily be inferred from the simple word

**ar·cha·ic** (ahr-KAY-ik) *adj.* old, primitive —**ar·cha·ism** (AHR-kee-iz-ɔm) *n.* obsolete word or phrase

**arch·bish·op** (ahrch-BISH-ɔp) *n.* chief bishop —**arch·bish'op·ric** *n.*

**ar·che·ol·o·gy** (ahr-kee-OL-ɔ-jee) *n.* study of ancient times from remains of art, implements *etc.* —**ar·che·o·log'i·cal** *adj.* —**ar·che·ol'o·gist** *n.*

**ar·cher·y** (AHR-chɔ-ree) *n.* skill, sport of shooting with bow and arrow —**arch'er** *n.*

**ar·che·type** (AHR-ki-tīp) *n.* prototype; perfect specimen —**ar·che·typ'i·cal** (-TIP-i-kɔl) *adj.*

**ar·chi·pel·a·go** (ahr-kɔ-PEL-ɔ-goh) *n.* (*pl.* -goes, -gos) group of islands; sea with many small islands, *esp.* Aegean

**ar·chi·tect** (AHR-ki-tekt) *n.* one qualified to design and supervise construction of buildings; contriver —ar·chi·tec'tur·al (-TEK-chər-əl) adj. —ar'chi·tec·ture n.

ar·chives (AHR-kīvz) n. pl. collection of records, documents etc. about an institution, family etc.; place where these are kept —archi'val adj. —ar'chi·vist (-kə-vist) n.

Arc·tic (AHRK-tik) adj. of northern polar regions; (a-) very cold —n. region around north pole

ar·dent (AHR-dnt) adj. fiery; passionate —ar'dent·ly adv. —ar'dor (-dər) n. enthusiasm; zeal

ar·du·ous (AHR-joo-əs) adj. laborious, hard to accomplish, difficult, strenuous

are¹ (ahr) pres. ind. pl. of BE

are² (air) n. unit of measure, 100 square meters

ar·e·a (AIR-ee-ə) n. extent, expanse of any surface; two-dimensional expanse enclosed by boundary (area of square, circle etc.); region; part, section; subject, field of activity

a·re·na (ə-REE-nə) n. enclosure for sports events etc.; space in middle of amphitheater or stadium; sphere, scene of conflict

ar·gon (AHR-gon) n. a gas, inert constituent of air

ar·go·sy (AHR-gə-see) n. Poet. (pl. -sies) large richly-laden merchant ship

ar·got (AHR-goh) n. slang

ar·gue (AHR-gyoo) v. (-gued, -gu·ing) —vi. quarrel, dispute; prove; offer reasons —vt. prove by reasoning; discuss —ar'gu·a·ble adj. —ar'gu·ment n. quarrel; reasoning; discussion; theme —ar·gu·men·ta'tion n. —ar·gu·men'ta·tive adj.

a·ri·a (AHR-ee-ə) n. air or rhythmical song in cantata, opera etc.

ar'id adj. parched with heat, dry; dull —a·rid·i·ty (ə-RID-i-tee) n.

a·right (ə-RĪT) adv. rightly

a·rise (ə-RĪZ) vi. (a·rose, a·ris·en pr. ə-RIZ-ən, a·ris·ing) come about; get up; rise (up), ascend

ar·is·toc·ra·cy (ar-ə-STOK-rə-see) n. (pl. -cies) government by the best in birth or fortune; nobility; upper classes —a·ris·to·crat (ə-RIS-tə-krat) n. —a·ris·to·crat'ic adj. noble; elegant

a·rith·me·tic (ə-RITH-mə-tik) n. science of numbers; art of reckoning by figures —ar·ith·met'ic adj. —ar·ith·met'i·cal·ly adv.

ark (ahrk) n. Noah's vessel; (A-) coffer containing scrolls of the Torah

arm¹ (ahrm) n. limb extending from shoulder to wrist; anything projecting from main body, as branch of sea, supporting rail of chair etc. —arm'chair n. —arm'ful n. (pl. -fuls) —arm'hole n. —arm'pit n. hollow under arm at shoulder —arm-twisting n. use of personal pressure to achieve a desired result

arm² (ahrm) vt. supply with weapons, furnish; prepare bomb etc. for use —vi. take up arms —n. weapon; branch of army —pl. weapons; war, military exploits; official heraldic symbols —ar'ma·ment n.

ar·ma·da (ahr-MAH-də) n. large number of ships or aircraft

ar·ma·dil·lo (ahr-mə-DIL-oh) n. (pl. -los) small Amer. animal protected by bands of bony plates

ar·ma·ture (AHR-mə-chər) n. revolving structure in electric motor, generator; framework used by a sculptor to support modeling clay etc.

ar·mi·stice (AHR-mə-stis) n. truce, suspension of fighting

ar·mor (AHR-mər) n. defensive covering or dress; plating of tanks, warships etc.; armored fighting vehicles, as tanks —**ar'·mor·y** n. (pl. **-mor·ies**)

**ar·my** (AHR-mee) n. (pl. **-mies**) large body of soldiers armed for warfare and under military command; host; great number

**a·ro·ma** (ə-ROH-mə) n. sweet smell; fragrance; peculiar charm —**ar·o·mat·ic** (ar-ə-MAT-ik) adj.

**a·rose** pt. of ARISE

**a·round** (ə-ROWND) prep. on all sides of; somewhere in or near; approximately (of time) —adv. on every side; in a circle; here and there, nowhere in particular; inf. present in or at some place

**a·rouse** (ə-ROWZ) vt. (**-roused, -rous·ing**) awaken, stimulate

**ar·peg·gi·o** (ahr-PEJ-ee-oh) n. Mus. (pl. **-gi·os**) notes sounded in quick succession, not together; chord so played

**ar·rack** (AR-ək) n. alcoholic beverage of Far East and Middle East distilled from rice etc.

**ar·raign** (ə-RAYN) vt. accuse, indict, put on trial —**ar·raign'·ment** n.

**ar·range** (ə-RAYNJ) v. (**-ranged, -rang·ing**) set in order; make agreement; adjust; plan; adapt, as music; settle, as dispute —**ar·range'ment** n.

**ar·rant** (AR-ənt) adj. downright, notorious

**ar·ras** (AR-əs) n. tapestry

**ar·ray** (ə-RAY) n. order, esp. military order; dress; imposing show, splendor —vt. set in order; dress, equip, adorn

**ar·rears** (ə-REERZ) n. pl. amount unpaid or undone

**ar·rest** (ə-REST) vt. detain by legal authority; stop; catch attention —n. seizure by warrant; making prisoner —**ar·rest'ing** adj. attracting attention, striking —**ar·rest'er** n. person who ar-rests; mechanism to stop or slow moving object

**ar·rive** (ə-RĪV) vi. (**-rived, -riving**) reach destination; (with at) reach, attain; inf. succeed —**arri'·val** n.

**ar·ro·gance** (AR-ə-gəns) n. aggressive conceit —**ar'ro·gant** adj. proud; overbearing

**ar·ro·gate** (AR-ə-gayt) vt. (**-gat·ed, -gat·ing**) seize or claim without right

**ar·row** (AR-oh) n. pointed shaft shot from bow —**ar'row·head** n. head of arrow; any triangular shape

**ar·row·root** (AR-oh-root) n. nutritious starch from W Indian plant, used as a food

**ar·se·nal** (AHR-sə-nl) n. place for manufacture, storage weapons and ammunition; fig. repertoire (of skills, skilled personnel etc.)

**ar·se·nic** (AHR-sə-nik) n. soft, gray, metallic element; its oxide, a powerful poison —**ar'se·nate** (-nayt) n. —**ar·sen'i·cal** adj.

**ar·son** (AHR-sən) n. crime of intentionally setting property on fire

**art** (ahrt) n. skill; human skill as opposed to nature; creative skill in painting, poetry, music etc.; any of the works produced thus; profession, craft, knack; contrivance, cunning, trick; system of rules —pl. certain branches of learning, languages, history etc., as distinct from natural science; wiles —art'ful adj. wily —art'fully adv. —art'ist n. one who practices fine art, esp. painting; one who makes a fine art of a craft —art·iste' (-TEEST) n. professional entertainer, singer, dancer etc. —ar·tis'tic adj. —art'ist·ry n. —art'less adj. natural, frank —art'less·ness n. —art'y adj.

(art·i·er, art·i·est) ostentatiously artistic

**ar·te·ri·o·scle·ro·sis** (ahr-teer-ee-oh-sklə-ROH-sis) *n.* hardening of the arteries —**ar·te·ri·o·scle·rot'ic** *adj.*

**ar·ter·y** (AHR-tə-ree) *n.* (*pl.* -ter·ies) one of the vessels carrying blood from heart; any main channel of communications —**ar·te'ri·al** (-TEER-ee-əl) *adj.* pert. to an artery; main, important as arterial highway

**ar·te·sian** (ahr-TEE-zhən) *adj.* describes deep well in which water rises by internal pressure

**ar·thri·tis** (ahr-THRĪ-tis) *n.* painful inflammation of joint(s) —**ar·thrit'ic** (-THRIT-ik) *adj./n.*

**ar·thro·pod** (AHR-thrə-pod) *n.* invertebrate with jointed limbs and segmented body *eg* insect, spider

**ar·ti·choke** (AHR-ti-chohk) *n.* thistle-like perennial, edible flower

**ar·ti·cle** (AHR-ti-kəl) *n.* item, object; short written piece; paragraph, section; *Grammar* words *the*, *a*, *an*; clause in a contract; rule, condition

**ar·tic·u·late** (ahr-TIK-yə-lit) *adj.* able to express oneself fluently; jointed; of speech, clear, distinct —*v.* (-layt) (-lat·ed, -lat·ing) —*vt.* joint; utter distinctly —*vi.* speak —**ar·tic'u·late·ly** *adv.* —**ar·tic·u·la'tion** *n.*

**ar·ti·fact** (AHR-tə-fakt) *n.* something made by a person, *esp.* by hand

**ar·ti·fice** (AHR-tə-fis) *n.* contrivance, trick, cunning, skill —**ar·tif'i·cer** (-TIF-ə-sər) *n.* craftsperson —**ar·ti·fi'cial** (-FISH-əl) *adj.* manufactured, synthetic; insincere —**ar·ti·fi'cial·ly** *adv.* —artificial intelligence ability of machines, *esp.* computers, to imitate intelligent human behav-

ior —artificial respiration method of restarting person's breathing after it has stopped

**ar·til·ler·y** (ahr-TIL-ə-ree) *n.* large guns on wheels; the troops that use them

**ar·ti·san** (AHR-tə-zən) *n.* craftsperson, skilled mechanic, manual worker

**ar·tiste** *see* ART

**Ar·y·an** (AIR-ee-ən) *adj.* relating to Indo-European family of nations and languages

**As** *Chem.* arsenic

**as** (az) *adv./conj.* denoting: comparison; similarity; equality; identity; concurrence; reason

**as·bes·tos** (as-BES-təs) *n.* fibrous mineral that does not burn —**as·bes·to·sis** (as-be-STOH-sis) *n.* lung disease caused by inhalation of asbestos fiber

**as·cend** (ə-SEND) *vi.* climb, rise —*vt.* walk up, climb, mount —**as·cend'an·cy** *n.* control, dominance —**as·cend'ant** *adj.* rising —**as·cen'sion** (-shən) *n.* —**as·cent'** *n.* rise

**as·cer·tain** (as-ər-TAYN) *v.* get to know, find out, determine —**as·cer·tain'a·ble** *adj.*

**as·cet·ic** (ə-SET-ik) *n.* one who practices severe self-denial —*adj.* rigidly abstinent, austere —**as·cet'i·cism** (-ə-siz-əm) *n.*

**a·scor·bic acid** (ə-SKOR-bik) vitamin C, present in green vegetables, citrus fruits *etc.*

**as·cribe** (ə-SKRĪB) *vt.* (-cribed, -crib·ing) attribute, impute, assign —**a·scrib'a·ble** *adj.*

**a·sep·tic** (ay-SEP-tik) *adj.* germ-free —**a·sep'sis** *n.*

**a·sex·u·al** (ay-SEK-shoo-əl) *adj.* without sex

**ash'** *n.* dust or remains of anything burned —*pl.* ruins; remains, *eg* of cremated body —**ash'en** *adj.* like ashes; pale

**ash**[2] *n.* deciduous timber tree; its wood —**ash'en** *adj.*

**a·shamed** (ɔSHAYMD) *adj.* affected with shame, abashed

**a·shore** (ɔSHOR) *adv.* on shore

**Ash Wednesday** first day of Lent

**A·sian** (AY-zhɔn) *adj.* pert. to continent of Asia —*n.* native of Asia or descendant of one —**A·si·at·ic** (-zhee-AT-ik) *adj.*

**a·side** (ɔSID) *adv.* to or on one side; privately —*n.* words spoken in an undertone not to be heard by some person present

**as·i·nine** (AS-ɔ-nin) *adj.* of or like an ass, silly —**as·i·nin'i·ty** (-NIN-i-tee) *n.*

**ask** *vt.* request, require, question, invite —*vi.* make inquiry or request

**a·skance** (ɔSKANS) *adv.* sideways, awry; with a side look or meaning —**look askance** view with suspicion

**a·skew** (ɔSKYOO) *adv.* aside, awry

**a·sleep** (ɔSLEEP) *adj./adv.* sleeping, at rest

**asp** *n.* small venomous snake

**as·par·a·gus** (ɔ-SPA-rɔ-gɔs) *n.* plant whose young shoots make a table delicacy

**as·pect** (AS-pekt) *n.* look, view, appearance, expression

**as·pen** (AS-pɔn) *n.* type of poplar tree

**as·per·i·ty** (ɔ-SPER-i-tee) *n.* (*pl.* -ties) roughness; harshness; coldness

**as·per·sion** (ɔ-SPUR-zhɔn) *n.* (*usu. in pl.*) malicious remarks; slanderous attack

**as·phalt** (AS-fawlt) *n.* black, hard bituminous substance used for road surfaces *etc.*

**as·phyx·i·a** (as-FIK-see-ɔ) *n.* suffocation —**as·phyx'i·ate** (-ayt) *v.*

(-at·ed, -at·ing) —**as·phyx·i·a'tion** *n.*

**as·pic** (AS-pik) *n.* jelly used to coat or make a mold of meat, eggs, fish *etc.*

**as·pire** (ɔSPIR) *vi.* (-pired, -pir·ing) desire eagerly; aim at high things; rise to great height —**as·pi·rant** (AS-pɔr-ɔnt) *n.* one who aspires; candidate —**as'pi·rate** (-pɔ-rayt) *vt.* pronounce with full breathing, as "h" —**aspir'ing** *adj.*

**as·pi·rin** (AS-pɔr-in) *n.* (a tablet of) drug used to allay pain and fever

**ass** *n.* quadruped of horse family; stupid person

**as·sail** (ɔSAYL) *vt.* attack, assault —**as·sail'a·ble** *adj.* —**as·sail'ant** *n.*

**as·sas·sin** (ɔ-SAS-in) *n.* one who kills, *esp.* prominent person, by treacherous violence; murderer —**as·sas'si·nate** *vt.* (-nat·ed, -nat·ing) —**as·sas·si·na'tion** *n.*

**as·sault** (ɔSAWLT) *n.* attack, *esp.* sudden —*vt.* attack

**as·say** (ɔSAY) *vt.* test, *esp.* proportions of metals in alloy or ore —*n.* (AS·ay) analysis, *esp.* of metals; trial, test

**as·sem·ble** (ɔ-SEM-bɔl) *v.* (-bled, -bling) meet, bring together; collect; put together (of machinery *etc.*) —**as·sem'bly** *n.* (*pl.* -blies) gathering, meeting; assembling —**assembly line** sequence of machines, workers in factory assembling product

**as·sent** (ɔSENT) *vi.* concur, agree —*n.* acquiescence, agreement, compliance

**as·sert** (ɔSURT) *vt.* declare strongly, insist upon —**as·ser'tion** *n.* —**as·sert'ive** *adj.* —**as·ser'tive·ly** *adv.*

**as·sess** (ɔSES) *vt.* fix value; evaluate, estimate, *esp.* for taxation; fix amount (of tax or fine); tax or fine —as·sess'ment n. —as·ses'sor n.

as·set (AS-et) n. valuable or useful person, thing —pl. property available to pay debts, esp. of insolvent debtor

as·sev·er·ate (ɔ-SEV-ɔ-rayt) v. (-at·ed, -at·ing) assert solemnly —as·sev·er·a'tion n.

as·sid·u·ous (ɔ-SIJ-oo-ɔs) adj. persevering, attentive, diligent —as·si·du·i·ty (as-i-DOO-i-tee) n.

as·sign (ɔ-SĪN) vt. appoint to job etc.; allot, apportion, fix; ascribe; transfer —as·sign'a·ble adj. —as·sig·na·tion (as-ig-NAY-shɔn) n. secret meeting (esp.) tryst; appointment to meet —as·sign'ment n. act of assigning; allotted duty

as·sim·i·late (ɔ-SIM-ɔ-layt) vt. (-lat·ed, -lat·ing) learn and understand; make similar; absorb into the system —as·sim·i·la'tion n.

as·sist (ɔ-SIST) v. give help; aid —as·sis'tance n. —as·sis'tant n. helper

as·so·ci·ate (ɔ-SOH-shee-ayt) v. (-at·ed, -at·ing) —vt. link, connect, esp. as ideas in mind; join —vi. formerly, keep company with; combine, unite —n. (-it) companion, partner; friend, ally; subordinate member of association —adj. affiliated —as·so·ci·a'tion n. society, club

as·sort (ɔ-SORT) vt. classify, arrange —vi. match, agree with, harmonize —as·sort'ed adj. mixed —as·sort'ment n.

as·suage (ɔ-SWAYJ) vt. (-suaged, -suag·ing) soften, pacify; soothe

as·sume (ɔ-SOOM) vt. (-sumed, -sum·ing) take for granted; pretend; take upon oneself; claim —as·sump'tion (-SUMP-shɔn) n.

as·sure (ɔ-SHOOR) vt. (-sured,

-sur·ing) tell positively; promise; make sure; insure against loss, esp. of life; affirm —as·sured' adj. sure —as·sur'ed·ly (-id-lee) adv.

as·ter·isk (AS-tɔ-risk) n. star (*) used in printing —vt. mark thus

a·stern (ɔ-STURN) adv. in, behind the stern; backward in direction

as·ter·oid (AS-tɔ-roid) n. small planet —adj. star-shaped

asth·ma (AZ-mɔ) n. illness in which one has difficulty in breathing —asth·mat'ic adj./n.

a·stig·ma·tism (ɔ-STIG-mɔ-tiz-ɔm) n. inability of lens (esp. of eye) to focus properly —as·tig·mat·ic (as-tig-MAT-ik) adj.

a·stir (ɔ-STUR) adv. on the move; out of bed; in excitement

as·ton·ish (ɔ-STON-ish) vt. amaze, surprise —as·ton'ish·ing adj. —as·ton'ish·ment n.

as·tound (ɔ-STOWND) vt. astonish greatly; stun with amazement —as·tound'ing adj. startling

as·tra·khan (AS-trɔ-kɔn) n. lambskin with curled wool

as·tral (AS-trɔl) adj. of the stars or spirit world —astral body

a·stray (ɔ-STRAY) adv. off the right path, wanderingly

a·stride (ɔ-STRID) adv. with the legs apart, straddling

as·trin·gent (ɔ-STRIN-jɔnt) adj. severe, harsh; sharp; constricting (body tissues, blood vessels etc.) —n. astringent substance

as·trol·o·gy (ɔ-STROL-ɔ-jee) n. foretelling of events by stars; medieval astronomy —as·trol'o·ger n. —as·tro·log'i·cal adj.

as·tro·naut (AS-trɔ-nawt) n. one trained for travel in space

as·tron·o·my (ɔ-STRON-ɔ-mee) n. scientific study of heavenly bodies —as·tron'o·mer n. —as·tro·nom'i·cal (-trɔ-NOM-i-kɔl) adj. very large; of astronomy —astronomical unit unit of distance used in astronomy equal to the mean distance between Earth and the sun

**as·tro·phys·ics** (as-troh-FIZ-iks) *n.* the science of the chemical and physical characteristics of heavenly bodies —**as·tro·phys′i·cist** *n.*

**as·tute** (ə-STOOT) *adj.* perceptive, shrewd —**as·tute′ly** *adv.* —**as·tute′ness** *n.*

**a·sun·der** (ə-SUN-dər) *adv.* apart; in pieces

**a·sy·lum** (ə-SI-ləm) *n.* refuge, sanctuary, place of safety; *old name for* home for care of the unfortunate, *esp.* of mentally ill

**a·sym·me·try** (ay-SIM-i-tree) *n.* lack of symmetry —**a·sym·met′-ric** (-sə-MET′-rik) *adj.*

**as·ymp·tote** (AS-im-toht) *n.* straight line that continually approaches a curve, but never meets it

**at** *prep./adv.* denoting: location in space or time; rate; condition or state; amount; direction; cause

**At** *Chem.* astatine

**at·a·vism** (AT-ə-viz-əm) *n.* appearance of ancestral, not parental, characteristics in human beings, animals or plants —**at·a·vis′-tic** *adj.*

**a·tax·i·a** (ə-TAK-see-ə) *n.* lack of muscular coordination

**ate** (ayt) *pt. of* EAT

**at·el·ier** (at-l-YAY) *n.* workshop, artist's studio

**a·the·ism** (AY-thee-iz-əm) *n.* belief that there is no God —**a′the·ist** *n.* —**a·the·is′tic** *adj.*

**ath·lete** (ATH-leet) *n.* one trained for physical exercises, feats or contests of strength; one good at sports —**ath·let′ic** *adj.* —**ath·let′-ics** *n. with sing. v.* sports such as running, jumping, throwing *etc.* —**ath·let′i·cal·ly** *adv.*

**a·thwart** (ə-THWORT) *prep.* across —*adv.* across, *esp.* obliquely

**at·las** (AT-ləs) *n.* volume of maps

**at·mos·phere** (AT-məs-feer) *n.* mass of gas surrounding heavenly body, *esp.* Earth; prevailing tone or mood (of place *etc.*); unit of pressure in cgs system —**at·mos·pher′ic** (-FER-ik) *adj.* —**at·mos·pher′ics** *n. pl.* noises in radio reception due to electrical disturbance in the atmosphere; *Politics* mood or atmosphere

**at·oll** (AT-awl) *n.* ring-shaped coral island enclosing lagoon

**at·om** (AT-əm) *n.* smallest unit of matter that can enter into chemical combination; any very small particle —**a·tom·ic** (ə-TOM-ik) *adj.* of, arising from atoms —**at·o·mic·i·ty** (at-ə-MIS-i-tee) *n.* number of atoms in molecule of an element —**at′om·ize** *vt.* (-ized, -iz·ing) reduce to atoms or small particles —**at′om·iz·er** *n.* instrument for discharging liquids in a fine spray —**atom(ic) bomb** one whose immense power derives from nuclear fission or fusion, nuclear bomb —**atomic energy** nuclear energy —**atomic number** the number of protons in the nucleus of an atom —**atomic re·actor** *see* REACTOR —**atomic weight** the weight of an atom of an element relative to that of carbon 12

**a·tone** (ə-TOHN) *vi.* (-toned, -ton·ing) make reparation, amends (for); expiate; give satisfaction —**a·tone′ment** *n.*

**a·ton·ic** (ay-TON-ik) *adj.* unaccented

**a·top** (ə-TOP) *adv.* at or on the top; above

**a·tro·cious** (ə-TROH-shəs) *adj.* extremely cruel or wicked; horrifying; very bad —**a·troc′i·ty**

(-TROS-i-tee) *n.* (*pl.* -ties) wickedness

**at·ro·phy** (A-trə-fee) *n.* wasting away, emaciation —*vi.* (-phied, -phy·ing) waste away, become useless —atrophied *adj.*

**at·tach** (ə-TACH) *v.* (*mainly tr.*) join, fasten; unite; be connected with; attribute; appoint; seize by law —at·tached *adj.* (with to) fond of —at·tach'ment *n.*

**at·ta·ché** (a-ta-SHAY) *n.* (*pl.* -chés) specialist attached to diplomatic mission —attaché case small suitcase for papers

**at·tack** (ə-TAK) *vt.* take action against (in war *etc.*); criticize; set about with vigor; affect adversely —*n.* attacking action; bout of sickness

**at·tain** (ə-TAYN) *vt.* arrive at; reach, gain by effort, accomplish —at·tain'a·ble *adj.* —at·tain'ment *n.* *esp.* personal accomplishment

**at·tain·der** (ə-TAYN-dər) *n.* Hist. loss of civil rights *usu.* through conviction of treason

**at·tar** (AT-ər) *n.* a fragrant oil made *esp.* from rose petals

**at·tempt** (ə-TEMPT) *vt.* try, endeavor —*n.* trial, effort

**at·tend** (ə-TEND) *vt.* be present at; accompany —*vi.* (with to) take care of; give the mind to), pay attention to —at·tend'ance *n.* an attending; presence; persons attending —at·tend·ee (ə-ten-DEE) *n.* —at·tend'ant *n./adj.* —at·ten'tion *n.* notice; heed; act of attending; care; courtesy —at·ten'tive *adj.* —at·ten'tive·ness *n.*

**at·ten·u·ate** (ə-TEN-yoo-ayt) *v.* (-at·ed, -at·ing) weaken or become weak; make or become thin —atten'u·at·ed *adj.* —at·ten·u·a'tion *n.* reduction of intensity —at·ten'u·a·tor *n.* device for

attenuating, *esp.* for reducing the amplitude of an electrical signal

**at·test** (ə-TEST) *vt.* bear witness to, certify —at·tes·ta·tion (a-tes-TAY-shən) *n.* formal confirmation by oath *etc.*

**at·tic** (AT-ik) *n.* space within roof where ceiling follows line of roof —**Attic** *adj.* of Attica, Athens; (of literary or artistic style) pure, refined, elegant

**at·tire** (ə-TIR) *vt.* (-tired, -tir·ing) dress, array —*n.* dress, clothing

**at·ti·tude** (AT-i-tood) *n.* mental view, opinion; posture, pose; disposition, behavior —at·ti·tu'dinize *vi.* (-nized, -niz·ing) assume affected attitudes

**at·tor·ney** (ə-TUR-nee) *n.* (*pl.* -neys) one legally appointed to act for another, *esp.* a lawyer —attorney-at-law *n.* (*pl.* -neys-at-law) a lawyer

**at·tract** (ə-TRAKT) *v.* draw (attention *etc.*); arouse interest of; cause to come closer (as magnet *etc.*) —at·trac'tion *n.* power to attract; something offered so as to interest, please —at·trac'tive *adj.* —at·trac'tive·ness *n.*

**at·trib·ute** (ə-TRIB-yoot) *vt.* (-ut·ed, -ut·ing) regard as belonging to or produced by —*n.* (A-trə-byoot) quality, property or characteristic of anything —at·trib'ut·a·ble *adj.* —at·tri·bu'tion *n.*

**at·tri·tion** (ə-TRISH-ən) *n.* wearing away of strength *etc.*; rubbing away, friction

**at·tune** (ə-TOON) *vt.* (-tuned, -tun·ing) tune, harmonize; make accordant

**Au** Chem. gold

**au·burn** (AW-bərn) *adj.* reddish brown —*n.* this color

**au cou·rant** (oh koo-RAHN) up-to-date; acquainted with

**auc·tion** (AWK-shən) *n.* public

sale in which bidder offers increase of price over another and what is sold goes to one who bids highest —v. —**auc·tion·eer′** n. —auction bridge card game —Dutch auction one in which price starts high and is reduced until purchaser is found

**au·da·cious** (aw-DAY-shos) adj. bold; daring; impudent —**au·dac′·i·ty** (-DAS-i-tee) n.

**au·di·ble** (AW-do-bol) adj. able to be heard —**au′di·bly** adv.

**au·di·ence** (AW-dee-ons) n. assembly of spectators or listeners; act of hearing; judicial hearing; formal interview

**audio-** (comb. form) relating to sound or hearing

**au·di·o·phile** (AW-dee-o-fil) n. one who is enthusiastic about sound reproduction, esp. of music

**au·di·o·vis·u·al** (aw-dee-oh-VIZH-oo-ol) adj. (esp. of teaching aids) involving, directed at, both sight and hearing, as film etc.

**au·dit** (AW-dit) n. formal examination or settlement of financial accounts —vt. examine such accounts —**au′di·tor** n.

**au·di·tion** (aw-DISH-on) n. screen or other test of prospective performer; hearing —vt. conduct such a test —**au·di·to′ri·um** n. (pl. -ri·ums) hall; place where audience sits —**au′di·to·ry** adj. pert. to sense of hearing

**auf Wie·der·seh·en** (owf VEE-dor-zay-on) Ger. goodbye

**au·ger** (AW-gor) n. carpenter's tool for boring holes, large gimlet

**aught** (awt) n. obs. anything —adv. obs. to any extent

**aug·ment** (awg-MENT) v. increase, enlarge —**aug·men·ta′·tion** n. —**aug·ment′a·ble** adj. able to increase in force or size

**au gra·tin** (oh GRAHT-n) cooked or baked to form light crust

**au·gur** (AW-gor) n. among the Romans, soothsayer —v. be a sign of future events, foretell —**au′gu·ry** (-gyo-ree) n. divination from omens etc.; omen

**au·gust** (aw-GUST) adj. majestic, dignified —**au·gust′ly** adv.

**auk** (awk) n. northern web-footed seabird with short wings used only as paddles

**aunt** (ant) n. father's or mother's sister, uncle's wife

**au pair** (oh PAIR) n. young foreign person, usu. a girl, who receives free board and lodging and usu. an allowance in return for housework etc.

**au·ra** (OR-o) n. (pl. -ras) quality, air, atmosphere considered distinctive of person or thing; medical symptom warning of impending epileptic seizure etc.

**au·ral** (OR-ol) adj. of, by ear —**au′ral·ly** adv.

**au·re·ole** (AR-ee-ohl) n. gold disk around head in sacred pictures; halo

**au re·voir** (oh ro-VWAHR) Fr. goodbye

**au·ri·cle** (OR-i-kol) n. outside ear; an upper cavity of heart —**au·ric·u·lar** (aw-RIK-yo-lor) adj. of the auricle; aural

**au·rif·er·ous** (aw-RIF-or-os) adj. gold-bearing

**au·ro·ra** (aw-ROR-o) n. (pl. -ras) dawn; lights in the atmosphere seen radiating from regions of the poles —aurora bo·re·al·is (bor-ee-AL-is) the northern lights —aurora aus·tra·lis (aw-STRAY-lis) the southern lights

**aus·cul·ta·tion** (aw-skol-TAY-shon) n. listening to sounds of heart and lungs with stethoscope

**aus·pice** (AW-spis) n. omen, augury —pl. (-pi·ces pr. -siz) patronage —**aus·pi·cious** (aw-

SPISH-əs) *adj.* of good omen, favorable

**aus·tere** (aw-STEER) *adj.* harsh, strict, severe; without luxury —**aus·tere′ly** *adv.* —**aus·ter·i·ty** (aw-STER-i-tee) *n.*

**aus·tral** (AW-strəl) *adj.* southern —Austral *adj.* Australian

**Aus·tral·a·sian** (aw-strə-LAY-zhən) *adj./n.* (native or inhabitant) of Australasia (Australia, N Zealand and adjacent islands)

**Aus·tral·ian** (aw-STRAYL-yən) *n./adj.* (native or inhabitant) of Australia

**au·tar·chy** (AW-tahr-kee) *n.* (*pl.* -chies) despotism, absolute power, dictatorship

**au·then·tic** (aw-THEN-tik) *adj.* real, genuine, true; trustworthy —**au·then′ti·cal·ly** *adv.* —**au·then′ti·cate** (-ti-kayt) *vt.* make valid, confirm; establish truth, authorship *etc.* of —**au·then·tic′i·ty** *n.*

**au·thor** (AW-thər) *n.* writer of book; originator, constructor

**au·thor·i·ty** (ə-THOR-i-tee) *n.* (*pl.* -ties) legal power or right; delegated power; influence; permission; expert; body or board in control, *esp.* in *pl.* —**au·thor′i·ta·tive** (-tay-tiv) *adj.* —**au·thor′i·ta·tive·ly** *adv.* —**au·thor·i·za·tion** (aw-thor-) *n.* —**au′thor·ize** *vt.* (-ized, -iz·ing) empower; permit, sanction

**au·tis·tic** (aw-TIS-tik) *adj.* withdrawn and divorced from reality —**au′tism** *n.* this condition

**auto-** (*comb. form*) self, as in *autograph, autosuggestion etc.* Such words are not given here where the meaning can easily be inferred from the simple word

**au·to** (AW-toh) *n.* automobile

**au·to·bi·og·ra·phy** (aw-tə-bi-OG-rə-fee) *n.* (*pl.* -phies) life of person written by that person —**au·to·bi·o·graph′i·cal** *adj.*

**au·toch·thon** (aw-TOK-thən) *n.* primitive or original inhabitant; native plant or animal —**autoch′tho·nous** *adj.* indigenous, native

**au·to·crat** (AW-tə-krat) *n.* absolute ruler; despotic person —**au·toc′ra·cy** (-TOK-rə-see) *n.* (*pl.* -cies) —**au·to·crat′ic** *adj.*

**au·to·cross** (AW-toh-kraws) *n.* motor racing sport over rough course

**au·to·er·o·tism** (aw-toh-ER-ə-tiz-əm) *n.* self-produced sexual arousal

**au·tog·e·nous** (aw-TOJ-ə-nəs) *adj.* self-generated

**au·to·gi·ro** (aw-tə-JI-roh) *n.* (*pl.* -ros) aircraft like helicopter using horizontal airscrew for vertical ascent and descent

**au·to·graph** (AW-tə-graf) *n.* a signature; one's own handwriting —*vt.* sign

**au·to·in·tox·i·ca·tion** (aw-toh-in-tok-si-KAY-shən) *n.* poisoning of tissues of the body as a result of the absorption of bodily waste

**au·to·mate** (AW-tə-mayt) *vt.* (-mat·ed, -mat·ing) make manufacturing process *etc.* automatic —**au·to·ma′tion** *n.* use of automatic devices in industrial production

**au·to·mat·ic** (aw-tə-MAT-ik) *adj.* operated or controlled mechanically; done without conscious thought —*adj./n.* self-loading (weapon) —**au·to·mat′i·cal·ly** *adv.* —**au·tom′a·ton** *n.* (*pl.* -ta *pr.* -tə) self-acting machine, *esp.* simulating a human being

**au·to·mo·bile** (aw-tə-mə-BEEL) *n.* motor car

**au·ton·o·my** (aw-TON-ə-mee) *n.* (*pl.* -mies) self-government —**au·ton′o·mous** *adj.*

**au·top·sy** (AW-top-see) *n.* (*pl.*

**-sies)** postmortem examination to determine cause of death

**au·to·sug·ges·tion** (aw-toh-səg-JES-chən) *n.* process of influencing the mind (toward health *etc.*), conducted by oneself

**au·tumn** (AW-təm) *n./adj.* (typical of) the season after summer —**au·tum·nal** (aw-TUM-nl) *adj.* typical of the onset of winter

**aux·il·i·ary** (awg-ZIL-yə-ree) *adj.* helping, subsidiary —*n.* (*pl.* -ries) helper; something subsidiary, as troops; verb used to form tenses of others

**a·vail** (ə-VAYL) *v.* be of use, advantage, value (to) —*n.* benefit, as to be of little avail *etc.* —**a·vail·a·bil'i·ty** *n.* —**a·vail'a·ble** *adj.* obtainable; accessible —**avail oneself of** make use of

**av·a·lanche** (AV-ə-lanch) *n.* mass of snow, ice, sliding down mountain; a sudden overwhelming quantity of anything

**a·vant-garde** (ah-vahnt-GAHRD) *adj.* markedly experimental or in advance

**av·a·rice** (AV-ər-is) *n.* greed for wealth —**av·a·ri'cious** (-RISH-əs) *adj.*

**a·vast** (ə-VAST) *imperative v.* stop

**a·va·tar** (AV-ə-tahr) *n.* (Hinduism) descent of god to Earth in bodily form

**a·venge** (ə-VENJ) *vt.* (-venged, -veng·ing) take vengeance on behalf of (person) or on account of (thing) —**a·veng'er** *n.*

**av·e·nue** (AV-ə-nyoo) *n.* route; a way of approach, a channel

**a·ver** (ə-VUR) *vt.* (-verred, -ver·ring) affirm, assert

**av·er·age** (AV-rij) *n.* the mean value or quantity of a number of values or quantities —*adj.* calculated as an average; medium, ordinary —*v.* (-aged, -ag·ing)

—*vt.* fix or calculate a mean —*vi.* exist in or form a mean

**a·verse** (ə-VURS) *adj.* disinclined, unwilling —**a·ver'sion** (-zhən) *n.* dislike; person or thing disliked

**a·vert** (ə-VURT) *vt.* turn away; ward off

**a·vi·ar·y** (AY-vee-er-ee) *n.* (*pl.* -ar·ies) enclosure for birds —**a'vi·a·rist** *n.*

**a·vi·a·tion** (ay-vee-AY-shən) *n.* art of flying aircraft; transport by aircraft —**a'vi·a·tor** *n.*

**av·id** (AV-id) *adj.* keen, enthusiastic; greedy (for) —**a·vid'i·ty** *n.* —**av'id·ly** *adv.*

**av·o·ca·do** (a-və-KAH-doh) *n.* tropical tree; its green-skinned edible fruit, alligator pear

**a·vo·ca·tion** (av-ə-KAY-shən) *n.* vocation; employment, business

**a·void** (ə-VOID) *vt.* keep away from; refrain from; not allow to happen —**a·void'a·ble** *adj.* —**a·void'ance** *n.*

**av·oir·du·pois** (av-ər-də-POIZ) *n.* system of weights used in many English-speaking countries based on pounds and ounces

**a·vow** (ə-VOW) *vt.* declare; admit —**a·vow'a·ble** *adj.* —**a·vow'al** *n.* —**a·vowed** *adj.* —**a·vow'ed·ly** *adv.*

**a·vun·cu·lar** (ə-VUNG-kyə-lər) *adj.* like or of an uncle *esp.* in manner

**a·wait** (ə-WAYT) *vt.* wait or stay for; be in store for

**a·wake** (ə-WAYK) *v.* (**a·woke** *or* **a·waked, awoke** *or* **awaked** *or* **a·wo·ken, a·wak·ing**) emerge or rouse from sleep; become or cause to become alert (Also **a·wak'en** —*adj.* not sleeping; alert —**a·wak'en·ing** *n.*

**a·ward** (ə-WORD) *vt.* to give formally (*esp.* a prize or punishment) —*n.* prize; judicial decision, amount awarded

**a·ware** (ə-WAIR) *adj.* informed, conscious —**a·ware′ness** *n.*

**a·wash** (ə-WOSH) *adv.* level with the surface of water; filled or overflowing with water —**awash** in marked by an abundance of

**a·way** (ə-WAY) *adv.* absent, apart, at a distance, out of the way —*adj. Sports* played on opponent's grounds

**awe** (aw) *n.* dread mingled with reverence —**awe′some** (-səm) *adj.* **awe′some·ly** *adv.* —**awe′some·ness** *n.* —**awe′struck,** **awe′strick·en** *adj.* filled with awe

**aw·ful** (AW-fəl) *adj.* very bad, unpleasant; inspiring awe; *inf.* very great —**aw′ful·ly** *adv.* in an unpleasant way; *inf.* very much

**a·while** (ə-HWIL) *adv.* for a time

**awk·ward** (AWK-wərd) *adj.* clumsy, ungainly; difficult; inconvenient; embarrassed —**awk′ward·ly** *adv.* —**awk′ward·ness** *n.*

**awl** *n.* pointed tool for marking or boring wood, leather *etc.*

**awn′ing** *n.* (canvas *etc.*) roof or shelter, to protect from weather

**awoke** *pt./pp.* of AWAKE

**a·wry** (ə-RI) *adv.* crookedly; amiss; at a slant —*adj.* crooked, distorted; wrong

**ax, axe** (aks) *n.* tool with handle and heavy, sharp blade for chopping; *inf.* dismissal from employment *etc.* —*vt. inf.* (**axed, ax·ing**) dismiss, dispense with

**ax·iom** (AK-see-əm) *n.* received or accepted principle; self-evident truth —**ax·i·o·mat′ic** *adj.*

**ax·is** (AK-sis) *n.* (*pl.* **ax·es** *pr.* AK-seez) (imaginary) line around which a body spins; line or column about which parts are arranged —**ax′i·al** *adj.* —**ax′i·al·ly** *adv.*

**Ax·is** *n.* coalition of Germany, Italy and Japan, 1936-45

**ax·le** (AK-səl) *n.* shaft on which wheel turns

**a·ya·tol·lah** (ah-yə-TOH-lə) *adj.* one of a class of Islamic religious leaders

**aye** (i) *adv.* yes —*n.* affirmative answer or vote —*pl.* those voting for motion

**a·zal·ea** (ə-ZAYL-yə) *n.* any of group of shrubby plants of the rhododendron genus

**az·i·muth** (AZ-ə-məth) *n.* vertical arc from zenith to horizon; angular distance of this from meridian

**Az·tec** (AZ-tek) *adj./n.* (member) of people ruling Mexico before Spanish conquest

**az·ure** (AZH-ər) *n.* sky-blue color; clear sky —*adj.* sky-blue

# B

**B** *Chem.* boron

**Ba** *Chem.* barium

**bab·ble** (BAB-əl) *v.* (**-bled, -bling**) speak foolishly, incoherently, or childishly —*n.* foolish, confused talk —**bab′bler** *n.*

**babe** (bayb) *n.* baby; guileless person

**ba·bel** (BAY-bəl) *n.* confused noise or scene, uproar

**ba·boon** (ba-BOON) *n.* large monkey of Africa and Asia

**ba·by** (BAY-bee) *n.* (*pl.* **-bies**) very young child, infant —**ba′by·ish** *adj.* —**ba′by·sit** *v.* (**-sat,** **-sit·ting**)—**ba′by·sit·ter** *n.* one who cares for children when parents are out

**bac·ca·lau·re·ate** (bak-ə-LOR-ee-it) *n.* degree of bachelor; service held at college or university awarding degree; sermon delivered at this service

**bac·ca·rat** (BAH-kə-rah) *n.* gambling card game

**bach·e·lor** (BACH-lər) *n.* unmarried man; holder of lowest four-year college or university degree

**ba·cil·lus** (bə-SIL-əs) *n.* (*pl.* -cil·li *pr.* -SIL-ī) minute organism sometimes causing disease

**back** (bak) *n.* hinder part of anything, eg human body; part opposite front; part or side of something farther away or less used; (position of) player in football and other games behind other (forward) players —*adj.* situated behind; earlier —*adv.* at, to the back; in, into the past; in return —*vi.* move backward —*vt.* support; put wager on; provide with back or backing —**back'er** *n.* one supporting another, esp. in contest or election campaign; one betting on horse *etc.* in race —**back'ing** *n.* support; material to protect the back of something; —**back'ward(s)** *adv.* to the rear; to the past; to worse state —**back'ward** *adj.* directed toward the rear; (of a country, region or people) retarded in economic development; behind in education; reluctant, bashful —**back'ward·ness** *n.* —**back'bite** *vt.* (-bit, -bit·ten, -bit·ing) slander absent person —**back'bit·er** *n.* —**back'bit·ing** *n.* —**back'bone** *n.* spinal column —**back'date** *vt.* (-dat·ed, -dat·ing) make effective from earlier date —**back'drop** *n.* painted cloth at back of stage —**back'fire** *vi.* (-fired, -fir·ing) ignite at wrong time, as fuel in cylinder of internal-combustion engine; (of plan, scheme *etc.*) fail to work, esp. to the detriment of the instigator; ignite wrongly, as gas burner *etc.* —**back'gam·mon** (-gam·ən) *n.* game played with counters and dice —**back'ground**

*n.* space behind chief figures of picture *etc.*; past history of person —**back'hand** *n.* stroke with hand turned backward —**back'hand·ed** *adj.* (of compliment *etc.*) with second, uncomplimentary meaning —**back'lash** *n.* sudden and adverse reaction —**back'log** *n.* accumulation of work *etc.* to be dealt with —**back'pack** *n.* type of knapsack —*vi.* (-packed, -pack·ing) hike with this —**back'side** *n.* buttocks —**back'slide** *vi.* (-slid, -slid *or* -slid·den, -slid·ing) fall back in faith or morals —**back'stroke** *n.* swimming stroke performed on the back —**back'talk** *n.* impudent or insolent answer —**back'up** *n.* musical accompaniment, esp. for pop singer —**back'wash** *n.* water thrown back by ship's propellers *etc.*; a backward current; a reaction —**back'wa·ter** *n.* still water fed by back flow of stream; backward or isolated place or condition —**back'woods** *n. pl.* remote forest areas; remote or backward area

**ba·con** (BAY-kən) *n.* cured and smoked meat from side of pig

**bac·te·ri·a** (bak-TEER-ee-ə) *n. pl.* (*sing.* -ri·um) microscopic organisms, some causing disease —**bac·te'ri·al** *adj.* —**bac·te·ri·cide** (-TEER-ə-sīd) *n.* substance that destroys bacteria —**bac·te·ri·ol'o·gist** (-OL-ə-jist) *n.* —**bac·te·ri·ol'o·gy** *n.* study of bacteria

**bad** *adj.* (worse, worst) of poor quality; faulty; evil; immoral; offensive; severe; rotten, decayed —**bad'ly** *adv.* —**bad'ness** *n.*

**bade** (bad) *pt.* of BID

**badge** (baj) *n.* distinguishing emblem or sign

**badg·er** (BAJ-ər) *n.* burrowing night animal, about the size of fox; its pelt or fur —*vt.* pester, worry

**bad·i·nage** (bad-n-AHZH) *n.* playful talk, banter

**bad·min·ton** (BAD-min-tn) *n.* game like tennis, played with rackets and shuttlecocks over high net

**baf·fle** (BAF-əl) *vt.* (-fled, -fling) check, frustrate, bewilder —**baffling** *adj.* —**baffle** *n.* device to regulate or divert flow of liquid, gas, sound waves *etc.*

**bag** *n.* sack, pouch; measure of quantity; woman's handbag; *offens.* unattractive woman —*v.* (bagged, bag·ging) —*vi.* swell out; bulge; sag —*vt.* put in bag; kill as game, *etc.* —**bag'gy** *adj.* (-gi·er, -gi·est) loose, drooping —**bag lady** homeless woman who carries her possessions in shopping bags *etc.* —**bag'man** *n.* (*pl.* -men) person who collects and distributes illicitly obtained money for another

**ba·gasse** (bə-GAS) *n.* sugar cane refuse

**bag·a·telle** (bag-ə-TEL) *n.* trifle; pinball

**bag·gage** (BAG-ij) *n.* suitcases *etc.*, packed for journey; *offens.* woman

**bag·pipe** (BAG-pīp) *n.* oft. pl. musical wind instrument, of windbag and pipes —**bag'pip·er** *n.*

**bail**[1] (bayl) *n. Law* security given for person's reappearance in court; one giving such security —*vt.* release, or obtain release of, on security; *inf.* help a person, firm *etc.* out of trouble

**bail**[2] *vt.* empty out water from boat —**bail out** leave aircraft by parachute; give up on or abandon something

**bail·iff** (BAY-lif) *n.* minor court officer

**bail·i·wick** (BAY-li-wik) *n.* a per-

son's domain or special area of competence

**bait** (bayt) *n.* food to entice fish; any lure or enticement —*vt.* set a lure; annoy, persecute

**baize** (bayz) *n.* smooth woolen cloth

**bake** (bayk) *v.* (baked, bak·ing) —*vt.* cook or harden by dry heat —*vi.* make bread, cakes *etc.*; be scorched or tanned —**bak'er** *n.* —**bak'er·y** *n.* —**baking** *n.* —**baking powder** leavening agent containing sodium bicarbonate *etc.* used in making baked goods

**bal·a·cla·va** (bal-ə-KLAH-və) *n.* close-fitting woolen helmet, covering head and neck

**bal·a·lai·ka** (bal-ə-LI-kə) *n.* Russian musical instrument, like guitar

**bal·ance** (BAL-əns) *n.* pair of scales; equilibrium; surplus; sum due on an account; difference between two sums —*vt.* (-anced, -anc·ing) weigh; bring to equilibrium —**balance sheet** tabular statement of assets and liabilities —**balance wheel** regulating wheel of watch

**bal·co·ny** (BAL-kə-nee) *n.* (*pl.* -nies) railed platform outside window; upper seats in theater

**bald** (bawld) *adj.* hairless; plain; bare —**bald'ing** *a.* becoming bald —**bald'ness** *n.*

**bale** (bayl) *n.* bundle or package —*vt.* (baled, bal·ing) make into bundles or pack into cartons —**bal'er** *n.* machine that does this

**ba·leen** (bə-LEEN) *n.* whalebone

**bale·ful** (BAYL-fəl) *adj.* menacing —**bale'ful·ly** *adv.*

**balk** (bawk) *vi.* swerve, pull up; *Baseball* commit a balk —*vt.* thwart, hinder; shirk —*n.* hindrance; rafter, beam; *Baseball* illegal motion of pitcher before releasing ball to batter —**balk at** recoil; stop short

**ball**[1] (bawl) *n.* anything round; globe, sphere, *esp.* as used in games; a ball as pitched; bullet —*vi.* clog, gather into a mass —**ball bearings** hardened steel balls used to lessen friction on bearings —**ball'point (pen)** pen with tiny ball bearing as nib

**ball**[2] *n.* formal social gathering for dancing; (*inf.*) a very good time —**ball'room** *n.*

**bal·lad** (BAL-əd) *n.* narrative poem; simple song

**bal·lade** (bə-LAHD) *n.* short poem with refrain and envoi; piece of music

**bal·last** (BAL-əst) *n.* heavy material put in ship to give steadiness; that which renders anything steady —*vt.* load with ballast, steady

**bal·let** (ba-LAY) *n.* theatrical presentation of dancing and miming to musical accompaniment —**bal·le·ri·na** (bal-ə-REE-nə) *n.*

**bal·lis·tic** (bə-LIS-tik) *adj.* moving as, or pertaining to motion of, a projectile —**bal·lis'tics** *n.* (*with sing. v.*) scientific study of ballistic motion

**bal·loon** (bə-LOON) *n.* large bag filled with air or gas to make it rise in the air —*vi.* puff out; increase rapidly —**bal·loon'ing** *n.* —**bal·loon'ist** *n.*

**bal·lot** (BAL-ət) *n.* method of voting secretly, usually by marking ballot paper and putting it into box —*vi.* vote or decide by ballot —**ballot box**

**bal·ly·hoo** (BAL-ee-hoo) *n.* noisy confusion or uproar; flamboyant, exaggerated publicity or advertising

**balm** (bahm) *n.* aromatic substance, healing or soothing oint-

ment; anything soothing —**balm'y** *adj.* (**balm·i·er, balm·i·est**) soothing; (of climate) mild; (of a person) foolish —**balm'i·ness** *n.*

**bal·sa** (BAWL-sə) *n.* Amer. tree with light but strong wood

**bal·sam** (BAWL-səm) *n.* resinous aromatic substance obtained from various trees and shrubs; soothing ointment —**bal·sam'ic** *adj.*

**Baltimore oriole** oriole of eastern N Amer.

**bal·us·ter** (BAL-ə-stər) *n.* short pillar used as support to rail of staircase *etc.* —**bal'us·trade** (-strayd) *n.* row of short pillars topped by rail

**bam·boo** (bam-BOO) *n.* (*pl.* -**boos**) large tropical treelike reed

**bam·boo·zle** (bam-BOO-zəl) *vt.* (-**zled, -zling**) mystify, hoodwink

**ban** *vt.* (**banned, ban·ning**) prohibit, forbid, outlaw —*n.* prohibition; proclamation —**banns** *n. pl.* proclamation of marriage

**ba·nal** (bə-NAL) *adj.* commonplace, trivial, trite —**ba·nal'i·ty** *n.*

**ba·nan·a** (bə-NAN-ə) *n.* tropical treelike plant; its fruit

**band**[1] *n.* strip used to bind; range of values, frequencies *etc.*, between two limits —**band·age** (BAN-dij) *n.* strip of cloth for binding wound

**band**[2] *n.* company, group; company of musicians —*v.* bind together —**band'mas·ter** *n.* —**band'stand** *n.*

**ban·dan·na** (ban-DAN-ə) *n.* large decorated handkerchief

**band·box** (BAND-boks) *n.* light box of cardboard for hats *etc.*; theater or other public structure of small interior dimensions

**ban·deau** (ban-DOH) *n.* (*pl.* -**deaux** *pr.* -DOHZ) band, ribbon for the hair

**ban'dit** *n.* outlaw; robber; brigand

**ban·do·leer** (ban-də-LEER) n. shoulder belt for cartridges

**band·wag·on** (BAND-wag-ən) n. —climb, jump, get on the bandwagon join something that seems sure of success

**ban·dy** (BAN-dee) vt. (-died, -dying) beat to and fro, toss from one to another —ban'dy-leg·ged (-leg-id) adj. bowlegged, having legs curving outward

**bane** (bayn) n. poison; person or thing causing misery or distress —bane'ful adj.

**bang**[1] n. sudden loud noise, explosion; heavy blow —vt. make loud noise; beat; strike violently, slam

**bang**[2] n. fringe of hair cut straight across forehead

**ban·gle** (BANG-gəl) n. ring worn on arm or leg

**ban·ish** vt. condemn to exile; drive away; dismiss —ban'ish·ment n. exile

**ban·is·ters** (BAN-ə-stərz) n. pl. railing and supporting uprights on staircase

**ban·jo** (BAN-joh) n. (pl. -jos) musical instrument like guitar, with circular body —ban'jo·ist n.

**bank**[1] (bangk) n. mound or ridge of earth; edge of river, lake etc.; rising ground in sea —v. enclose with ridge; pile up; (of aircraft) tilt upward in turning

**bank**[2] n. establishment for keeping, lending, exchanging etc. money; any supply or store for future use, as a blood bank —vt. put in bank —vi. keep with bank —bank'er n. —bank'ing n. —bank teller bank cashier —bank'note n. written promise of payment acceptable as money —bank on rely on

**bank**[3] n. tier of objects eg telephones

**bank·rupt** (BANGK-rupt) n. one who fails in business, insolvent

debtor —adj. financially ruined; broken; destitute —vt. make, cause to be, bankrupt —bank'rupt·cy n.

**ban·ner** (BAN-ər) n. long strip with slogan etc.; placard; flag used as ensign

**banns** n. see BAN

**ban·quet** (BANG-kwit) n. feast —vi. feast —vt. treat with feast

**ban·quette** (bang-KET) n. upholstered bench usu. along a wall; raised firing step behind parapet

**ban'shee** n. (in Irish folklore) female spirit with a wail portending death

**ban·tam** (BAN-təm) n. dwarf variety of domestic fowl; person of diminutive stature —ban'tam·weight n. boxer weighing no more than 118 pounds

**ban·ter** (BAN-tər) vt. make fun of —n. light, teasing language

**Ban·tu** (BAN-too) n. collective name for large group of related tribes in Africa; family of languages spoken by Bantu peoples

**ban·yan** (BAN-yən) n. Indian fig tree with spreading branches that take root

**ba·o·bab** (BAY-oh-bab) n. Afr. tree with thick trunk and angular branches

**Bap'tist** n. member of Protestant Christian denomination believing in necessity of baptism by immersion, esp. of adults —baptist n. one who baptizes

**bap·tize** (BAP-tīz) vt. (-tized, -tiz·ing) immerse, sprinkle with water ceremonially; christen —bap'tism (-tiz-əm) n. —bap·tis'mal (-TIZ-məl) adj. —bap'tistry n. (pl. -ries) place where baptism is performed

**bar**[1] (bahr) n. rod or block of any substance; obstacle; bank of sand at mouth of river; rail in law court; body of lawyers; room or counter where drinks are served, *esp.* in hotel *etc.*; unit of music —*vt.* (barred, bar·ring) fasten; obstruct; exclude —*prep.* except —barring *prep.* excepting —bar code arrangement of numbers and parallel lines on package, electronically scanned at checkout to give price *etc.* —bar'maid *n.* —bar'ten·der *n.*

**bar**² *n.* unit of pressure

**barb** (bahrb) *n.* sharp point curving backward behind main point of spear, fishhook *etc.*; cutting remark —barbed *adj.* —barbed wire fencing wire with barbs at close intervals

**bar·ba·rous** (BAHR-bər-əs) *adj.* savage, brutal, uncivilized —bar·bar'ian (-BAIR-ee-ən) *n.* —barbar'ic *adj.* —bar'ba·rism *n.* —barbar'i·ty *n.*

**bar·be·cue** (BAHR-bi-kyoo) *n.* meal, *oft.* entire big event *etc.*, cooked outdoors over open fire; fireplace, grill used for this —*vt.* (-cued, cu·ing) cook meat *etc.* in this manner

**bar·ber** (BAHR-bər) *n.* one whose job is to cut hair and shave beards—*v.* (-bered, -ber·ing) perform this service

**bar·bi·tu·rate** (bahr-BICH-ər-it) *n.* derivative of barbituric acid used as sedative drug

**bar·ca·role** (BAHR-kə-rohl) *n.* gondolier's song; music imitative of this

**bard** (bahrd) *n.* Celtic poet; wandering minstrel; poet —the Bard of Avon Shakespeare

**bare** (bair) *adj.* (bar·er, bar·est) uncovered; naked; plain; scanty —*vt.* (bared, bar·ing) make bare —bare'ly *adv.* only just, scarcely —bare'back, -backed *adj.* on unsaddled horse —bare'faced *adj.* shameless

**bar·gain** (BAHR-gən) *n.* some-thing bought at price favorable to purchaser; contract, agreement —*vi.* haggle, negotiate; make bargain

**barge** (bahrj) *n.* flat-bottomed freight boat propelled by towing; roomy pleasure boat —*vi. inf.* (barged, barg·ing) interrupt; *inf.* bump (into), push

**bar·i·tone** (BAR-i-tohn) *n.* (singer with) second lowest adult male voice —*adj.* written for or possessing this vocal range

**bar·i·um** (BA-ree-əm) *n.* white metallic element

**bark**¹ (bahrk) *n.* sharp loud cry of dog *etc.* —*v.* make, utter with such sound —bark'er *n.* one who stands outside entrance to a circus *etc.* calling out its attractions —bark up the wrong tree misdirect one's efforts; pursue a wrong course

**bark**² *n.* outer layer of trunk, branches of tree —*vt.* strip bark from; rub off (skin), graze (shins *etc.*)

**bark**³ *n.* sailing ship, *esp.* large, three-masted one

**bar·ley** (BAHR-lee) *n.* grain used for food and making malt —bar'ley·corn *n.* a grain of barley —John Barleycorn personification of intoxicating liquor

**bar mitz·vah** (bahr MITS-və) *n.* Jewish boy at age 13 who participates in religious ceremony signifying entry into adulthood; the ceremony

**barn** (bahrn) *n.* building to store grain, hay *etc.* —barn dance (party with) country music and dancing —barn'yard *n.* area adjoining barn —barnyard humor earthy or smutty humor

**bar·na·cle** (BAHR-nə-kəl) *n.* shellfish that adheres to rocks, logs, ships' bottoms *etc.*

**ba·rom·e·ter** (bə-ROM-i-tər) *n.*

instrument to measure pressure of atmosphere —bar·o·met·ric (bar-ɔ-ME-trik) adj. —bar·o·graph (BA-rɔ-graf) n. recording barometer

bar·on (BA-rɔn) n. member of lowest rank of peerage in Great Britain; powerful businessman (fem. -ess) —bar'o·ny n. —ba·ro'ni·al (-ROH-nee-ɔl) adj.

bar·on·et (BA-rɔ-nit) n. lowest British hereditary title, below baron but above knight —bar'o·net·cy n.

ba·roque (bɔ-ROHK) adj. extravagantly ornamented, esp. in architecture and music —baroque pearl one irregularly shaped

bar·rack (BA-rɔk) n. (usu. in pl.) building for housing soldiers; bare, barnlike building —vt. house in barracks

bar·ra·cu·da (bar-ɔ-KOO-dɔ) n. type of large, elongated, predatory fish, mostly tropical

bar·rage (bɔ-RAHZH) n. heavy artillery fire; continuous and heavy delivery of questions etc.

bar·rel (BA-rɔl) n. round wooden vessel, made of curved staves bound with hoops; its capacity; great amount or number; anything long and hollow, as tube of gun etc. —over a barrel helpless —v. (-reled, -rel·ing) put in barrel; move at high speed —bar'rel·ful n. (pl. -fuls) as much, as many, as a barrel can hold; large amount or number

bar·ren (BA-rɔn) adj. unfruitful, sterile; unprofitable; dull —bar'ren·ness n.

bar·ri·cade (BA-ri-kayd) n. improvised fortification, barrier —vt. (-cad·ed, -cad·ing) to protect by building barrier; block

bar·ri·er (BAR-ee-ɔr) n. fence, obstruction, obstacle, boundary

—barrier reef coral reef lying parallel to shore

bar·row[1] (BA-roh) n. small wheeled handcart; wheelbarrow

barrow[2] n. castrated male swine

barrow[3] n. burial mound of earth or stones

bar·ter (BAHR-tɔr) v. trade by exchange of goods —n.

bar·y·on (BA-ree-on) n. Physics elementary particle of matter

ba·salt (bɔ-SAWLT) n. dark-colored, hard, compact, igneous rock —ba·sal'tic adj.

base[1] (bays) n. bottom, foundation; starting point; center of operations; fixed point; Chem. compound that combines with an acid to form a salt; medium into which other substances are mixed —vt. (based, bas·ing) found, establish —base'less adj. —base'ment n. lowest floor of building, partly or entirely below ground

base[2] adj. (-er, -est) low, mean; despicable —base'ly adv. —base'ness n.

base·ball (BAYS-bawl) n. game played with bat and ball between teams of 9 (sometimes 10) players; the ball they use

ba·sen·ji (bɔ-SEN-jee) n. small African hunting dog that seldom barks

bash v. inf. strike violently —n. blow; attempt; festive party

bash·ful (BASH-fɔl) adj. shy, modest —bash'ful·ly adv.

BASIC (BAY-sik) Computers Beginner's All-purpose Symbolic Instruction Code

ba·sic (BAY-sik) adj. ba·si·cal·ly adv. relating to, serving as base; fundamental; necessary

ba·sil·i·ca (bɔ-SIL-i-kɔ) n. type of church with long hall and pillars

bas·i·lisk (BAS-ɔ-lisk) n. legendary small fire-breathing dragon;

type of tropical lizard related to iguanas

**ba·sin** (BAY-son) n. deep circular dish; harbor; land drained by river

**basis** (BAY-sis) n. (pl. **-ses** pr. -seez) foundation; principal constituent

**bask** vi. lie in warmth and sunshine (often fig.)

**bas·ket** (BAS-kit) n. vessel made of woven cane, straw etc. —**bas'ket·ry** (-ki-tree) n. —**bas'ket·ball** n. ball game played by two teams of 5 players who score points by throwing ball through baskets suspended above ends of playing area; the ball they use

**Basque** (bask) n. one of a people from W Pyrenees; their language

**bas·re·lief** (bah-ri-LEEF) n. sculpture with figures standing out slightly from background

**bass¹** (bays) n. lowest part in music; bass singer or voice —adj.

**bass²** (bas) n. any of large variety of freshwater or seawater fishes

**bas·set hound** (BAS-it) n. type of smooth-haired short-legged dog

**bas·soon** (bo-SOON) n. woodwind instrument of low tone —**bas·soon'ist** n.

**bas·tard** (BAS-tord) n. child born of unmarried parents; sl. person, as in lucky, poor etc. bastard —adj. illegitimate; spurious

**baste¹** (bayst) vt. (**bast·ed, bast·ing**) moisten (meat) during cooking with hot fat; beat severely —**bast'er** n.

**baste²** (bast-ed, bast·ing) sew loosely; tack

**bas·ti·na·do** (bas-to-NAY-doh) n. (pl. **-does**) beating with stick etc. esp. on soles of feet —vt. (**-doed, -do·ing**)

**bas·tion** (BAS-chon) n. projecting part of fortification; tower; strong defense or bulwark

**bat¹** n. any of various types of clubs used to hit ball in certain sports, eg baseball —v. (**bat·ted, bat·ting**) strike with bat or use bat in sport —**batting** n. performance with bat

**bat²** n. nocturnal mouselike flying animal

**bat³** vt. (**bat·ted, bat·ting**) flutter (one's eyelids)

**batch** (bach) n. group or set of similar objects, esp. cakes etc. baked together

**bat·ed** (BAY-tid) adj. —with bated breath anxiously

**bath** n. vessel or place to bathe in; water for bathing; act of bathing —**bath'house** n. building with dressing and washing facilities for bathers —**bath'room** n. room with toilet and washing facilities —**take a bath** sl. esp. experience serious financial losses in a venture

**bathe** (bayth) v. (**bathed, bath'ing**) swim; apply liquid; wash; immerse in water —n. —**bath'er** n.

**ba·thos** (BAY-thos) n. ludicrous descent from the elevated to the ordinary in writing or speech

**ba·tik** (bo-TEEK) n. dyeing process using wax

**ba·ton** (bo-TON) n. stick, esp. of conductor, marshal, member of relay team

**ba·tra·chi·an** (bo-TRAY-kee-on) n./adj. (of) any amphibian, esp. frog or toad

**bat·tal·ion** (bo-TAL-yon) n. military unit consisting of three or more companies; fig. a large group

**bat·ten¹** (BAT-n) n. narrow piece of board, strip of wood etc. (esp. with down) fasten, make secure

**batten²** vi. (usu. with on) thrive, esp. at someone else's expense

**bat·ter** (BAT-or) vt. strike continuously —*n.* mixture of flour, eggs, liquid, used in cooking

**bat·ter·y** (BAT-ə-ree) *n.* (*pl.* -ter·ies) connected group of electrical cells; any electrical cell; number of similar things occurring together; *Law* assault by beating; number of guns; place where they are mounted; unit of artillery; *Baseball* pitcher and catcher as a unit

**bat·ting** (BAT-ing) *n.* cotton or wool fiber as stuffing or lining

**bat·tle** (BAT-l) *n.* fight between armies, combat —*vi.* (-tled, -tling) fight, struggle —**battle·ax** *n. sl.* sharp-tempered, domineering woman

**bat·tle·ment** (BAT-l-mənt) *n.* wall, parapet for fortification with openings for cannon

**bat·tle·ship** (BAT-l-ship) *n.* heavily armed and armored fighting ship of the largest and heaviest class

**bat·ty** (BAT-ee) *adj. inf.* (-ti·er, -ti·est) crazy, silly

**bau·ble** (BAW-bəl) *n.* showy trinket

**baud** (bawd) *n.* unit of data transmission speed

**baux·ite** (BAWK-sīt) *n.* mineral yielding aluminum

**bawd** *n.* prostitute; brothel keeper —**bawd′y** *adj.* (bawd·i·er, bawd·i·est) obscene, lewd

**bawl** *vi.* cry; shout —*n.* —**bawl out** *vt. inf.* reprimand severely

**bay¹** *n.* wide inlet of sea; space between two columns; recess —**bay window**

**bay²** *n.* bark; cry of hounds in pursuit —*v.* bark (at) —**at bay** cornered

**bay³** *n.* laurel tree —*pl.* honorary crown of victory

**bay⁴** *adj.* reddish-brown —*n.* horse with body of this color and black mane

**bay·o·net** (BAY-ə-nit) *n.* stabbing weapon fixed to rifle —*vt.* (-net·ed, -net·ing) stab with this

**bay·ou** (BĪ-oo) *n.* (*pl.* -ous) marshy inlet or outlet of lake, river *etc.*, *usu.* sluggish

**ba·zaar** (bə-ZAHR) *n.* market (*esp.* in Orient); sale of goods for charity

**ba·zoo·ka** (bə-ZOO-kə) *n.* antitank rocket launcher

**be** *vi.* (I am, he is; we, you, they are, *pr. ind.* —was, *pl.* were, *pt.* —been *pp.* —be′ing *pr. p.*) live; exist; have a state or quality

**beach** (beech) *n.* shore of sea —*vt.* run boat on shore —**beach′·comb·er** (-koh-mər) *n.* one who habitually searches shore debris for items of value; loafer spending days aimlessly on beach —**beach′head** *n.* area on beach captured from enemy; base for operations; foothold

**bea·con** (BEE-kən) *n.* signal fire; lighthouse, buoy; (radio) signal used for navigation

**bead** (beed) *n.* little ball pierced for threading on string of necklace, rosary *etc.*; drop of liquid; narrow molding —*vt.* string together or furnish with beads —**bead′ing** *n.* —**bead′y** *adj.* (bead·i·er, bead·i·est) small and bright

**bea·gle** (BEE-gəl) *n.* small hound

**beak** (beek) *n.* projecting horny jaws of bird; anything pointed or projecting; *sl.* nose

**beak·er** (BEE-kər) *n.* large drinking cup; glass vessel used by chemists

**beam** (beem) *n.* long squared piece of wood; ship's cross timber, side, or width; ray of light *etc.*; broad smile; bar of a balance —*vt.* aim light, radio waves *etc.* (to) —*vi.* shine; smile benignly

**bean** (been) *n.* any of various leguminous plants or their seeds; head —**full of beans** *inf.* lively —**bean sprout** edible sprout of newly germinated bean, *esp.* mung bean

**bear**[1] (bair) *vt.* (**bore, borne** *or* **born, bear·ing**) carry; support; produce; endure; press (upon) —**bear′er** *n.*

**bear**[2] *n.* heavy carnivorous quadruped; other bearlike animals, *eg* koala —**bear′skin** *n.* tall fur helmet

**beard** (beerd) *n.* hair on chin —*vt.* oppose boldly

**bear·ing** (BAIR-ing) *n.* support or guide for mechanical part, *esp.* one reducing friction; relevance; behavior; direction; relative position

**beast** (beest) *n.* animal; four-footed animal; brutal man —**beast′li·ness** *n.* —**beast′ly** *adj.*

**beat** (beet) *v.* (**beat, beat·en, beat·ing**) —*vt.* strike repeatedly; overcome; surpass; stir vigorously with striking action; flap (wings); make, wear (path) —*vi.* throb; sail against wind —*n.* stroke; pulsation; appointed course; basic rhythmic unit in piece of music —*adj. sl.* exhausted —**beat′er** *n.* instrument for beating; one who rouses game for shooters

**be·at·i·fy** (bee-AT-ə-fī) *vt.* (**-fied, -fy·ing**) make happy; *R.C. Church* pronounce in eternal happiness (first step in canonization) —**be·a·tif′ic** (bee-ə-TIF-ik) *adj.* —**be·at·i·fi·ca′tion** *n.* —**be·at′i·tude** *n.* blessedness

**beau** (boh) *n.* (*pl.* **beaux** *pr.* bohz) suitor

**Beau·fort scale** (BOH-fərt) system of indicating wind strength (from 0, calm, to 17, hurricane)

**beau·ty** (BYOO-tee) *n.* (*pl.* **-ties**) loveliness, grace; beautiful person or thing —**beau·ti·cian** (byoo-TISH-ən) *n.* one who gives treatment in beauty parlor —**beau′ti·ful** *adj.* —**beau·ti·fy** (-tə-fī) *vt.* (**-fied, -fy·ing**) —**beauty parlor** establishment offering hair-dressing, manicure *etc.*

**bea·ver** (BEE-vər) *n.* amphibious rodent; its fur; exceptionally hard-working person

**be·calmed** (bi-KAHMD) *adj.* (of ship) motionless through lack of wind

**became** *pt. of* BECOME

**be·cause** (bi-KAWZ) *adv./conj.* by reason of, since

**beck** (bek) *n.* —**at someone's beck and call** subject to someone's slightest whim

**beck·on** (BEK-ən) *v.* summon or lure by silent signal

**be·come** (bi-KUM) *v.* (**be·came, be·come, be·com·ing**) —*vi.* come to be —*vt.* suit —**becoming** *adj.* suitable to; proper

**bed** *n.* piece of furniture for sleeping on; garden plot; supporting structure; bottom of river; layer, stratum —*vt.* (**bed·ded, bed·ding**) lay in a bed; plant —**bedding** *n.* —**bed′bug** *n.* wingless bug infesting beds and sucking blood —**bed′pan** *n.* container used as toilet by bedridden person —**bed′rid·den** *adj.* confined to bed by age or sickness —**bed′room** *n.* —**bed′spread** (-spred) *n.* cover for bed when not in use —**bed′stead** (-sted) *n.* framework of a bed

**be·dev·il** (bi-DEV-əl) *vt.* (**-iled, -il·ing**) confuse; torment —**be·dev′il·ment** *n.*

**bed·lam** (BED-ləm) *n.* noisy confused scene

**Bed·ou·in** (BED-oo-in) *n.* nomadic Arab of the desert; nomad

**be·drag·gle** (bi-DRAG-əl) vt. (-gled, -gling) dirty by trailing in wet or mud

**bee** n. insect that makes honey —**bee'hive** n. —**bee'line** n. shortest route —**bees'wax** n. wax secreted by bees —**bee in one's bonnet** an obsession

**beech** n. tree with smooth grayish bark and small nuts; its wood

**beef** n. flesh of cattle raised and killed for eating; inf. complaint —vi. inf. complain —**beef'y** adj. (**beef·i·er, beef·i·est**) fleshy, stolid —**beef'burg·er** n. hamburger

**been** pp. of BE

**beep** n. short, loud sound of automobile horn etc. —v. make this sound —**beep'er** n. small portable electronic signaling device

**beer** n. fermented alcoholic drink made from hops and malt —**beer'y** adj. (**beer·i·er, beer·i·est**) affected by, smelling of, beer

**beet** n. any of various plants with root used for food or extraction of sugar

**bee·tle** (BEET-l) n. class of insect with hard upper-wing cases closed over the back for protection —**bee'tle-browed** (browd) adj. with prominent brows

**be·fall** (bi-FAWL) v. (**be·fell, be·fall·en, be·fall·ing**) happen (to)

**be·fit** (bi-FIT) vt. (**be·fit·ted, be·fit·ting**) be suitable to

**be·fog** (bi-FOG) vt. (**-fogged, -fog·ging**) perplex, confuse

**be·fore** (bi-FOR) prep. in front of; in presence of; in preference to; earlier than —adv. earlier; in front —conj. sooner than —**be·fore'hand** adv. previously

**be·foul** (bi-FOWL) vt. make filthy

**be·friend** (bi-FREND) vt. make friend of

**beg** v. (**begged, beg·ging**) —vt. ask earnestly, beseech —vi. ask for or live on charity —**beg·gar** (BEG-ər) n.

**began** pt. of BEGIN

**be·get** (bi-GET) vt. (**be·got** or obs. **be·gat, be·got·ten** or **be·got, be·get·ting**) produce, generate

**be·gin** (bi-GIN) v. (**be·gan, begun, be·gin·ning**) (cause to) start; initiate; originate —**be·gin'ner** n. novice

**be·go·nia** (bi-GOHN-yə) n. genus of tropical plant

**be·got** pt./pp. of BEGET

**be·grudge** (bi-GRUJ) vt. (**-grudged, -grudg·ing**) grudge, envy anyone the possession of

**be·guile** (bi-GIL) vt. (**-guiled, -guil·ing**) charm, fascinate; amuse; deceive —**beguiling** adj.

**be·gun** pp. of BEGIN

**be·half** (bi-HAF) n. favor, benefit, interest, esp. in on behalf of

**be·have** (bi-HAYV) vi. (**-haved, -hav·ing**) act, function in particular way —**be·hav·ior** (bi-HAYV-yər) n. conduct —**behave oneself** conduct oneself well

**be·head** (bi-HED) vt. cut off head

**be·held** pt./pp. of BEHOLD

**be·hest** (bi-HEST) n. charge, command

**be·hind** (bi-HIND) prep. farther back or earlier than; in support of —adv. in the rear —**behind-the-scenes** kept or made in secret

**be·hold** (bi-HOHLD) vt. (**be·held, be·hold·ing**) watch, see —**be·hold'er** n.

**be·hold·en** (bi-HOHL-dən) adj. bound in gratitude

**be·hoove** (bi-HOOV) vi. (**-hooved, -hoov·ing**) be fit, necessary (only impersonal)

**beige** (bayzh) n. color of undyed woolen cloth

**be·ing** (BEE-ing) n. existence; that which exists; creature —pr. p. of BE

**bel** *n.* unit for comparing two power levels

**be·la·bor** (bi-LAY-bər) *vt.* beat soundly; discuss (a subject) endlessly

**be·lat·ed** (bi-LAY-tid) *adj.* late; too late

**be·lay** (bi-LAY) *vt.* fasten rope to peg, pin *etc.*

**belch** *vi.* void gas by mouth —*vt.* eject violently; cast up —*n.* emission of gas *etc.*

**be·lea·guer** (bi-LEE-gər) *vt.* besiege

**bel·fry** (BEL-free) *n.* (*pl.* -fries) bell tower

**be·lie** (bi-LI) *vt.* (-lied, -ly·ing) contradict; misrepresent

**be·lieve** (bi-LEEV) *v.* (-lieved, -liev·ing) —*vt.* regard as true or real —*vi.* have faith —**be·lief'** *n.* —**be·liev'a·ble** *adj.* credible —**be·liev'er** *n. esp.* one of same religious faith

**be·lit·tle** (bi-LIT-l) *vt.* (-tled, -tling) regard, speak of, as having little worth or value —**be·lit'tler** *n.*

**bell** *n.* hollow metal instrument giving ringing sound when struck; electrical device emitting ring or buzz as signal —**bell'hop** *n.* hotel employee who carries luggage, conducts guests to rooms *etc.*

**bel·la·don·na** (bel-ə-DON-ə) *n.* deadly nightshade

**belle** (bel) *n.* beautiful woman, reigning beauty

**bel·li·cose** (BEL-i-kohs) *adj.* warlike

**bel·lig·er·ent** (bə-LIJ-ər-ənt) *adj.* hostile, aggressive; making war —*n.* warring person or nation

**bel·low** (BEL-oh) *vi.* roar like bull; shout —*n.* roar of bull; any deep cry or shout

**bel·lows** (BEL-ohz) *n. pl.* instrument for creating stream of air

**bel·ly** (BEL-ee) *n.* (*pl.* -lies) part of body that contains intestines; stomach —*v.* (-lied, -ly·ing) swell out —**belly laugh** *n.* hearty laugh

**be·long** (bi-LAWNG) *vi.* be the property or attribute of; be a member or inhabitant of; have an allotted place; pertain to —**be·long'ings** *n. pl.* personal possessions

**be·lov·ed** (bi-LUV-id *or* bi-LUVD) *adj.* much loved —*n.* dear one

**be·low** (bi-LOH) *adv.* beneath —*prep.* lower than

**belt** *n.* band; girdle; zone or district —*vt.* surround, fasten with belt; mark with band; *inf.* thrash

**be·moan** (bi-MOHN) *vt.* grieve over (loss *etc.*)

**be·muse** (bi-MYOOZ) *v.* (-mused, -mus·ing) confuse, bewilder

**bench** *n.* long seat; seat or body of judges *etc.* —*vt.* provide with benches —**bench'mark** *n.* fixed point, criterion

**bend** *v.* (bent, bend·ing) (cause to) form a curve —*n.* curve —the bends *n. pl.* decompression sickness —**bend over backward** exert oneself to the utmost

**be·neath** (bi-NEETH) *prep.* under, lower than —*adv.* below

**ben·e·dic·tion** (ben-i-DIK-shən) *n.* invocation of divine blessing

**ben·e·fit** (BEN-ə-fit) *n.* advantage, favor, profit, good; money paid by a government or business *etc.* to unemployed *etc.* —*v.* (-fit·ed, -fit·ing) do good to; receive good —**ben'e·fac·tor** *n.* one who helps or does good to others; patron —**ben'e·fice** (-ə-fis) *n.* an ecclesiastical livelihood —**be·nef'i·cence** *n.* —**be·nef'i·cent** *adj.* doing good; kind —**ben·e·fi'cial** (-FISH-əl) *adj.* advantageous, helpful —**ben·e·fi'ci·ar·y** *n.* (*pl.* -ar·ies)

**be·nev·o·lent** (bə-NEV-ə-lənt)

*adj.* kindly, charitable —benev'o-lence *n.*

be·night·ed (bi-NĪ-tid) *adj.* ignorant, uncultured

be·nign (bi-NĪN) *adj.* kindly, mild, favorable —be·nign'ly *adv.*

bent *pt./pp.* of BEND —*adj.* curved; resolved (on); determined —*n.* inclination, personal propensity

be·numb (bi-NUM) *vt.* make numb, deaden

ben·zene (BEN-zeen) *n.* one of group of related flammable liquids used in chemistry and as solvents, cleaning agents *etc.*

be·queath (bi-KWEETH) *vt.* leave property *etc.* by will —be·quest (bi-KWEST) *n.* bequeathing; legacy

be·rate (bi-RAYT) *vt.* (-rat·ed, -rat·ing) scold harshly

be·reave (bi-REEV) *vt.* (-reaved, -reft, -reav·ing) deprive of, *esp.* by death —be·reave'ment *n.* loss, *esp.* by death

be·ret (be-RAY) *n.* round, close-fitting hat

ber·i·ber·i (ber-ee-BER-ee) *n.* tropical disease caused by vitamin B deficiency

ber·ke·li·um (bər-KEE-lee-əm) *n.* artificial radioactive metallic element

ber·ry (BER-ee) *n.* (*pl.* -ries) small juicy stoneless fruit —*vi.* (-ried, -ry·ing) look for, pick, berries

ber·serk (bər-SURK) *adj.* frenzied

berth (burth) *n.* ship's mooring place; place to sleep on ship or train —*vt.* to moor

ber·yl (BER-əl) *n.* variety of crystalline mineral including aquamarine and emerald

be·ryl·li·um (bə-RIL-ee-əm) *n.* strong brittle metallic element

be·seech (bi-SEECH) *vt.* (-sought

or -seeched, -seech·ing) entreat, implore

be·set (bi-SET) *vt.* (-set, -setting) assail, surround with danger, problems

be·side (bi-SĪD) *adv./prep.* by the side of, near; distinct from —besides' *adv./prep.* in addition (to)

be·siege (bi-SEEJ) *vt.* (-sieged, -sieg·ing) surround with armed forces *etc.*)

be·sot·ted (bi-SOT-id) *adj.* drunk; foolish; infatuated

besought *pt./pp.* of BESEECH

be·speak (bi-SPEEK) *vt.* (-spoke, -spok·en, -speak·ing) engage beforehand

best *adj./adv. sup.* of GOOD or WELL —*vt.* defeat —best seller book or other product sold in great numbers; author of one or more of these books

bes·tial (BES-chəl) *adj.* like a beast, brutish —bes·ti·al'i·ty (-chee-AL-i-tee) *n.*

be·stir (bi-STUR) *vt.* (-stirred, -stir·ring) rouse (oneself) to activity

be·stow (bi-STOH) *vt.* give, confer —be·stow'al *n.*

be·stride (bi-STRĪD) *vt.* (-strode or -strid, -strid·den or -strid, -strid·ing) sit or stand over with legs apart, mount horse

bet *v.* (bet or bet·ted, bet·ting) agree to pay money *etc.* if wrong (or win if right) in guessing result of contest *etc.* —*n.* money risked in this way

be·tel (BEET-l) *n.* species of pepper —betel nut the nut of the betel palm

bête noire (bet NWAHR) *n.* (*pl.* bêtes noires) *Fr.* pet aversion

be·tide (bi-TĪD) *v.* (-tid·ed, -tid·ing) happen (to)

be·to·ken (bi-TOH-kən) *vt.* be a sign of

be·tray (bi-TRAY) *vt.* be disloyal

to, *esp.* by assisting an enemy; reveal, divulge; show signs of —be·tray'al *n.* —be·tray'er *n.*

be·troth (bi-TROHTH) *vt.* promise to marry —be·troth'al *n.* —be·trothed' *n./adj.*

bet·ter (BET-ər) *adj /adv comp* of GOOD and WELL —*v.* improve —bet'ter·ment *n.*

be·tween (bi-TWEEN) *prep./adv.* in the intermediate part in space or time; indicating reciprocal relation or comparison

be·twixt (bi-TWIKST) *prep./adv. obs.* between

bev·el (BEV-əl) *n.* surface not at right angle to another; slant —*v.* (-eled, -el·ing) slope, slant; cut on slant —bev'eled *adj.* slanted

bev·er·age (BEV-rij) *n.* drink

bev·y (BEV-ee) *n.* (*pl.* bev·ies) flock or group

be·wail (bi-WAYL) *vt.* lament

be·ware (bi-WAIR) *vi.* be on one's guard, take care

be·wil·der (bi-WIL-dər) *vt.* puzzle, confuse —be·wil'der·ing *adj.* —be·wil'der·ment *n.*

be·witch (bi-WICH) *vt.* cast spell over; charm, fascinate —be·witch'ing *adj.*

be·yond (bee-OND) *adv.* farther away; besides —*prep.* on the farther side of; later than; surpassing, out of reach of

Bi *Chem.* bismuth

bi·as (BI-əs) *n.* (*pl.* -as·es) personal slant; inclination or preference; onesided inclination —*vt.* (-ased, -as·ing) influence, affect —bi'ased *adj.* prejudiced

bib *n.* cloth put under child's chin to protect clothes when eating; part of apron or overalls above waist

Bi·ble (BI-bəl) *n.* the sacred writings of Christianity and Judaism —bible *n. fig.* book or journal considered unchallengeably

authoritative —Bib·li·cal (BIB-li-kəl) *adj.*

bib·li·og·ra·phy (bib-lee-OG-rə-fee) *n.* (*pl.* -phies) list of books on a subject; history and description of books —bib·li·og'ra·pher *n.*

bib·li·o·phile (BIB-lee-ə-fil) *n.* lover, collector of books

bib·u·lous (BIB-yə-ləs) *adj.* given to drinking

bi·cam·er·al (bī-KAM-ər-əl) *adj.* (of a legislature) having two chambers

bi·car·bo·nate (bī-KAHR-bə-nit) *n.* chemical compound releasing carbon dioxide when mixed with acid

bi·cen·ten·ni·al (bī-sen-TEN-ee-əl) *n.* two hundredth anniversary; its celebration —*adj.* relating to this

bi·ceps (BI-seps) *n.* two-headed muscle, *esp.* muscle of upper arm

bick·er (BIK-ər) *vi./n.* quarrel over petty things —bick'er·ing *n.*

bi·cy·cle (BI-si-kəl) *n.* vehicle with two wheels, one in front of other, pedaled by rider —bi'cy·clist *n.*

bid *vt.* (bade, bid or bid·den, bid·ding) offer; say; command; invite —*n.* offer, *esp.* of price; try —bid'der *n.*

bide (bid) *v.* (bid·ed, bid·ing) —*vi.* remain; dwell —*vt.* await —bid'ing *n.*

bi·det (bi-DAY) *n.* low basin for washing genital area

bi·en·ni·al (bī-EN-ee-əl) *adj.* happening every two years; lasting two years —*n.* plant living two years —bi·en'ni·um (-əm) *n.* period of two years

bier (beer) *n.* frame for bearing dead to grave; stand for holding dead; coffin and its stand

bi·fo·cal (bī-FOH-kəl) *adj.* having two different focal lengths —bi-

**fo·cals** *n. pl.* eyeglasses having bifocal lenses for near and distant vision

**big** *adj.* (**big·ger, big·gest**) of great or considerable size, height, number, power *etc.* —**big'head** *n. inf.* conceit —**big'head·ed** *adj.* —**big shot** *inf.* important or influential person

**big·a·my** (BIG-ə-mee) *n.* (*pl.* -**mies**) crime of marrying a person while one is still legally married to someone else —**big'a·mist** *n.*

**bight** (bīt) *n.* curve or loop in rope; long curved shoreline or water bounded by it

**big·ot** (BIG-ət) *n.* person intolerant or not receptive to ideas of others (*esp.* on religion, race *etc.*) —**big'ot·ed** *adj.* —**big'ot·ry** *n.*

**bike** (bīk) *n. short for* BICYCLE *or* MOTOR BIKE

**bi·ki·ni** (bi-KEE-nee) *n.* (*pl.* -**nis**) woman's brief two-piece swimming costume

**bi·lat·er·al** (bī-LAT-ər-əl) *adj.* two-sided

**bile** (bīl) *n.* fluid secreted by the liver; anger, ill temper —**bil·ious** (BIL-yəs) *adj.* nauseous, nauseating —**bil'ious·ness** *n.*

**bilge** (bilj) *n.* bottom of ship's hull; dirty water collecting there; *inf.* nonsense

**bi·lin·gual** (bī-LING-gwəl) *adj.* speaking, or written in, two languages —**bi·lin'gual·ism** *n.*

**bill**[1] *n.* written account of charges; draft of legislative act; poster; commercial document; paper money —*vt.* present account of charges; announce by advertisement —**bill'ing** *n.* degree of importance (*esp.* in theater *etc.*)—**bill'board** *n.* large panel for outdoor advertising

**bill**[2] *n.* bird's beak —*vi.* touch bills, as doves; caress affectionately

**bil·let** (BIL-it) *n.* civilian quarters for troops; resting place —*vt.* quarter, as troops

**bil·let-doux** (bil-ee-DOO) *n.* (*pl.* **billets-doux** *pr.* bil-ee-DOOZ) love letter

**bil·liards** (BIL-yərdz) *n.* game played on table with balls and cues

**bil·lion** (BIL-yən) *n.* thousand millions

**bil·low** (BIL-oh) *n.* great swelling wave —*vi.* surge; swell out

**bi·month·ly** (bī-MUNTH-lee) *adv./adj.* every two months; *oft.* twice a month

**bin** *n.* box *etc.* used for storage

**bi·na·ry** (BĪ-nə-ree) *adj.* composed of, characterized by, two; dual

**bind** (bīnd) *v.* (**bound, bind·ing**) —*vt.* tie fast; tie around, gird; tie together; oblige; seal; constrain; bandage; cohere; unite; put (book) into cover —**bind'er** *n.* one who, or that which binds —**bind'er·y** *n.* (*pl.* -**er·ies**) —**bind'ing** *n.* cover of book; tape for hem *etc.*

**binge** (binj) *n. inf.* excessive indulgence in eating or drinking; spree

**bin·go** (BING-goh) *n.* game of chance in which numbers drawn are matched with those on a card

**bin·na·cle** (BIN-ə-kəl) *n.* box holding ship's compass

**bin·oc·u·lar** (bə-NOK-yə-lər) *adj.* seeing with, made for, both eyes —**bin·oc'u·lars** *n. pl.* telescope made for both eyes

**bi·no·mi·al** (bī-NOH-mee-əl) *adj./n.* (denoting) algebraic expression consisting of two terms

**bio-** (*comb. form*) life, living, as in **biochemistry** *n.* Such words are not given here where the meaning can easily be inferred from the simple word

**bi·o·de·grad·a·ble** (bī-oh-di-GRAY-də-bəl) *adj.* capable of decomposition by natural means

**bi·og·ra·phy** (bī-OG-rə-fee) *n.* (*pl.* -phies) story of one person's life —bi·og'ra·pher *n.* —bi·o·graph'i·cal *adj.*

**bi·ol·o·gy** (bī-OL-ə-jee) *n.* study of living organisms —bi·o·log'i·cal *adj.* —bi·ol'o·gist *n.*

**bi·on·ics** (bī-ON-iks) *n.* (*with sing. v.*) study of relation of biological and electronic processes —**bionic** *adj.* having physical functions controlled, augmented by electronic equipment

**bi·op·sy** (BĪ-op-see) *n.* (*pl.* -sies) examination of tissue removed surgically from a living body

**bi·o·rhythm** (BĪ-oh-rith-əm) *n.* cyclically recurring pattern of physiological states

**bi·par·ti·san** (bī-PAHR-tə-zən) *adj.* consisting of or supported by two political parties

**bi·par·tite** (bī-PAHR-tīt) *adj.* consisting of two parts, parties

**bi·ped** (BĪ-ped) *n.* two-footed animal

**bi·plane** (BĪ-playn) *n.* airplane with two pairs of wings

**birch** (burch) *n.* tree with silvery bark; rod for punishment, made of birch twigs —*vt.* flog —birch'en *adj.*

**bird** (burd) *n.* feathered animal —*vi.* observe or identify wild birds as a hobby —bird'brain *n.* stupid person

**bird·ie** (BUR-dee) *n./v.* Golf (make) score of one under par for a hole

**bi·ret·ta** (bə-RET-ə) *n.* square cap with three or four ridges worn usu. by Catholic clergy

**birth** (burth) *n.* bearing, or the being born, of offspring; parentage, origin —**birth control** limitation of childbearing usu. by artificial means —**birth'mark** *n.* blemish, *usu.* dark, formed on skin before birth —birth'right *n.* right one has by birth

**bis·cuit** (BIS-kit) *n.* quick bread made from spoonful of rolled dough

**bi·sect** (bī-SEKT) *vt.* divide into two equal parts

**bi·sex·ual** (bī-SEK-shoo-əl) *adj.* sexually attracted to both men and women; of both sexes

**bish·op** (BISH-əp) *n.* clergyman typically governing diocese; chess piece —bish'op·ric *n.* diocese or office of a bishop

**bis·muth** (BIZ-məth) *n.* reddish-white metal used in medicine *etc.*

**bi·son** (BĪ-sən) *n.* large wild ox; N Amer. buffalo

**bis·tro** (BIS-troh) *n.* (*pl.* -tros) small restaurant

**bit**[1] *n.* fragment, piece; biting, cutting part of tool; mouthpiece of horse's bridle

**bit**[2] *pt./pp.* of BITE

**bit**[3] *n.* Computers smallest unit of information

**bitch** (bich) *n.* female dog, fox or wolf; *offens. sl.* spiteful woman; *inf.* complaint —*vi. inf.* complain —bitch'y *adj. sl.* (bitch·i·er, bitch·i·est) —bitch'i·ness *n. sl.*

**bite** (bīt) *vt.* (bit, bit·ten, bit·ing) cut into *esp.* with teeth; grip; rise to bait; etch with acid —*n.* act of biting; wound so made; mouthful —biting *adj.* having power to bite

**bit·ter** (BIT-ər) *adj.* (-er, -est) sharp, sour tasting; unpleasant; (of person) angry, resentful; sarcastic —bit'ter·ly *adv.* —bit'ter·ness *n.* —bit'ters *n. pl.* essence of bitter usu. aromatic herbs —**bitter end** final extremity

**bi·tu·men** (bi-TOO-mən) *n.* viscous substance occurring in asphalt, tar *etc.* —**bi·tu'mi·nous** coal coal yielding much bitumen on burning

**bi·valve** (BĪ-valv) *adj.* having a double shell —*n.* mollusk with such shell

**biv·ou·ac** (BIV-oo-ak) *n.* temporary encampment of soldiers, hikers *etc.* — *vi.* (-acked, -ack·ing) pass the night in temporary camp

**bi·zarre** (bi-ZAHR) *adj.* unusual, weird

**Bk** *Chem.* berkelium

**blab** *v.* (blabbed, blab·bing) reveal secrets; chatter idly —*n.* chatter —**blab·ber** *v.* (-bered, -ber·ing) blab

**black** (blak) *adj.* of the darkest color; without light; dark; evil; somber; dishonorable — *n.* darkest color; black dye, clothing *etc.*; (B-) person of dark-skinned race; African-American —**black'en** *v.* —**black'ing** *n.* substance used for blacking and cleaning leather *etc.* —**black'ball** *vt.* vote against, exclude —**black'bird** *n.* common American black bird —**black'board** *n.* dark-colored surface for writing on with chalk —**black box** *inf.* name for FLIGHT RE-CORDER —**black economy** illegally undeclared income —**black'head** *n.* dark, fatty plug blocking pore in skin —**black'list** *n.* list of people, organizations considered suspicious, untrustworthy *etc.* —*vt.* put on blacklist —**Black Ma·ri·a** (mə-RĪ-ə) police van for transporting prisoners —**black market** illegal buying and selling of goods —**black widow** highly poisonous N Amer. spider

**black·guard** (BLAG-ahrd) *n.* scoundrel

**black·mail** (BLAK-mayl) *vt.* extort money from (a person) by threats —*n.* act of blackmailing; money extorted thus —**black'mail·er** *n.*

**black·out** (BLAK-owt) *n.* complete failure of electricity supply; sudden turning off of all stagelights; state of temporary unconsciousness; obscuring of all lights as precaution against night air attack —**black out** *vi.* lose consciousness, memory, or vision temporarily

**black·smith** (BLAK-smith) *n.* smith who works in iron

**blad·der** (BLAD-ər) *n.* membranous bag to contain liquid, *esp.* urinary bladder

**blade** (blayd) *n.* edge, cutting part of knife or tool; leaf of grass *etc.*; sword; *obs.* dashing fellow; flat of oar

**blame** (blaym) *n.* censure; culpability —*vt.* (blamed, blam·ing) find fault with; censure —**blame'less** *adj.* —**blame'wor·thy** (-wur·thee) *adj.*

**blanch** *v.* whiten, bleach, take color out of; (of foodstuffs) briefly boil or fry; turn pale

**bland** *adj.* (-er, -est) devoid of distinctive characteristics; smooth in manner

**blan·dish** *vt.* coax; flatter —**blan'dish·ment** *n.*

**blank** *adj.* with no marks or writing; empty; vacant, confused; (of verse) without rhyme —*n.* empty space; void; cartridge containing no bullet

**blan·ket** (BLANG-kit) *n.* thick woven covering for bed, horse *etc.*; concealing cover —*vt.* cover with blanket; cover, stifle

**blare** (blair) *v.* (blared, blar·ing) sound loudly and harshly —*n.* such sound

**blar·ney** (BLAHR-nee) *n.* flattering talk

**blasé** (blah-ZAY) *adj.* indifferent through familiarity; bored

**blas·pheme** (blas-FEEM) *v.* show contempt for God or sacred things, *esp.* in speech —**blas·phem'er** *n.* —**blas·phe·mous** (-fə-məs) *adj.* —**blas'phe·my** *n.*

**blast** *n.* explosion; high-pressure wave of air coming from an explosion; current of air; gust of wind or air; loud sound; reprimand; *sl.* riotous party —*vt.* blow up; remove, open *etc.* by explosion; blight; ruin —**blast furnace** furnace for smelting ore, using blast of heated air

**bla·tant** (BLAYT-nt) *adj.* obvious —**bla'tan·cy** *n.*

**blaze**[1] (blayz) *n.* strong fire or flame; brightness; outburst —*vi.* (blazed, blaz·ing) burn strongly; be very angry

**blaze**[2] *v.* (blazed, blaz·ing) (mark trees to) establish trail —*n.* mark on tree; white mark on horse's face

**blaze**[3] *vt.* (blazed, blaz·ing) proclaim

**blaz·er** (BLAY-zər) *n.* type of sports jacket

**bla·zon** (BLAY-zən) *vt.* make public, proclaim

**bleach** (bleech) *v.* make or become white —*n.* bleaching substance

**bleak** (bleek) *adj.* (-er, -est) cold and cheerless; exposed —**bleak'ly** *adv.* **bleak'ness** *n.*

**blear·y** (BLEER-ee) *adj.* (blear·i·er, blear·i·est) (of the eyes) dimmed, as with tears, sleep

**bleat** (bleet) *v.* cry, as sheep; say, speak, plaintively —*n.* sheep's cry

**bleed** *v.* (bled, bleed·ing) lose blood; draw blood or liquid from; extort money from

**bleep** *n.* short high-pitched sound *eg* from electronic device —*vt.* obscure sound *eg* of TV program by making bleep

**blem'ish** *n.* defect; stain —*vt.* make (something) defective, dirty *etc.* —**blem'ished** *adj.*

**blend** *v.* mix —*n.* mixture —**blend'er** *n.* one who, that which blends, *esp.* electrical kitchen appliance for mixing food

**bless** *vt.* (blessed *or* blest, bless·ing) consecrate; give thanks to; ask God's favor for; (*usu.* passive) endow (with); glorify; make happy —**bless'ed** (-id) *adj.* —**blessing** *n.* (ceremony asking for) God's protection, aid; short prayer; approval; welcome event, benefit

**blew** *pt.* of BLOW

**blight** (blīt) *n.* plant disease; harmful influence —*vt.* injure as with blight

**blimp** *n.* small, nonrigid airship used for observing

**blind** (blīnd) *adj.* unable to see; heedless; random; dim; closed at one end; *sl.* very drunk —*vt.* deprive of sight —*n.* something cutting off light; window screen; pretext; place of concealment for hunters —**blind'ly** *adv.* —**blind'ness** *n.* —**blind flying** navigation of aircraft by use of instruments alone —**blind'fold** *vt.* cover the eyes of so as to prevent vision —*n./adj.* —**blind·man's buff** game in which one player is blindfolded

**blink** (blingk) *vi.* wink; twinkle; shine intermittently —*vi.* gleam —**blink'ers** *n. pl.* leather flaps to prevent horse from seeing to the side —**blink at** see, know about, but ignore —**on the blink** *inf.* not working (properly)

**blip** *n.* repetitive sound or visible pulse, *eg* on radar screen —*vt.* (blipped, blip·ping) bleep

**bliss** *n.* perfect happiness —**bliss'ful** *adj.* —**bliss'ful·ly** *adv.*

**blis·ter** (BLIS-tər) n. bubble on skin; surface swelling, eg on paint —v. form blisters (on) —**blis'ter·ing** adj. (of verbal attack) bitter —**blister pack** package for goods with hard, raised, transparent cover

**blithe** (blith) adj. happy, gay; heedless —**blithe'ly** adv. —**blithe'ness** n.

**blitz** (blits) n. sudden, concentrated attack —**blitz'krieg** (-kreeg) n. sudden concentrated military attack; war conducted in this way

**bliz·zard** (BLIZ-ərd) n. blinding storm of wind and snow

**bloat** (bloht) v. puff or swell out —n. distension of stomach of cow etc. by gas —**bloat'ed** adj. swollen

**blob** n. soft mass, esp. drop of liquid; shapeless form

**bloc** (blok) n. (political) grouping of people or countries

**block** (blok) n. solid (rectangular) piece of wood, stone etc., esp. Hist. that on which people were beheaded; obstacle; stoppage; pulley with frame; group of buildings; urban area enclosed by intersecting streets —vt. obstruct, stop up; shape on block; sketch (in) —**block'age** n. obstruction —**block'head** n. fool, simpleton —**block letters** written capital letters

**block·ade** (blo-KAYD) n. physical prevention of access, esp. to port etc. —vt. (-ad·ed, -ad·ing)

**blond** adj. (of hair) light-colored —n. (**blonde** fem. same pr.) someone with blond hair

**blood** (blud) n. red fluid in veins; race; kindred; good parentage; temperament; passion —vt. initiate (into hunting, war etc.) —**blood'less** adj. —**blood'y** adj. (-i·er, -i·est) covered in blood; slaughterous —adj./adv. sl. a common intensifier —v. make bloody —**blood bank** (institution managing) store of human blood preserved for transfusion —**blood'cur·dling** adj. horrifying —**blood'hound** n. breed of large hound noted for keen powers of scent —**blood'shed** n. slaughter, killing —**blood'shot** adj. inflamed (said of eyes) —**blood sport** sport in which animals are killed, eg fox hunting —**blood'suck·er** n. parasite (eg mosquito) living on host's blood; parasitic person —**blood test** examination of sample of blood —**blood'thirst·y** adj. murderous, cruel —**blood transfusion** transfer of blood from one person to another

**bloom** n. flower of plant; blossoming; prime, perfection; glow; powdery deposit on fruit —vi. be in flower; flourish

**bloom·er** (BLOO-mər) n. inf. blunder in bloom; person reaching full competence; ludicrous mistake

**bloo·mers** (BLOO-mərz) n. pl. girls' or women's wide, baggy underpants

**blos·som** (BLOS-əm) n. flower; flower bud —vi. flower; develop

**blot** n. spot, stain; disgrace —vt. (-ted, -ting) spot, stain; obliterate; detract from; soak up ink etc. from —**blot'ter** —**blotting paper**

**blotch** (bloch) n. dark spot on skin —vt. make spotted —**blotch'y** adj. (blotch·i·er, blotch·i·est)

**blouse** (blows) n. light, loose upper garment

**blow¹** (bloh) v. (**blew, blown, blow·ing**) vi. make a current of air; pant; emit sound —vt. drive air upon or into; drive by current of air; sound; spout (of whales); fan; sl. squander —n. blast; gale —**blow-dry** vt. (-dried, -dry·ing) style hair after washing using stream of hot air —**blow'pipe** *n.* dart tube —**blow'out** *n.* sudden puncture in tire; uncontrolled escape of oil, gas, from well; *sl.* festive party; uncontrolled eruption of oil or gas well —**blow up** explode; inflate; enlarge (photograph); *inf.* lose one's temper

**blow²** *n.* stroke, knock; sudden misfortune, loss

**blown** *pp. of* BLOW¹

**blows·y** (BLOW-zee) *adj.* (**blows·i·er, blows·i·est**) slovenly, sluttish; red-faced

**blub·ber** (BLUB-ǝr) *vi.* weep —*n.* fat of whales; weeping

**bludg·eon** (BLUJ-ǝn) *n.* short thick club —*vt.* strike with one; coerce (someone into)

**blue** (bloo) *adj.* (**blu·er, blu·est**) of the color of sky or shades of that color; livid; depressed; indecent —*n.* the color; dye or pigment —*vt.* (**blued, blu·ing**) make blue; dip in blue liquid —**blues** *n. pl. inf.* (*oft. with sing. v.*) depression; song in slow tempo originating with African-Americans; employed in jazz music —**blu'ish** *adj.* —**blue baby** baby born with bluish skin caused by heart defect —**blue blood** (person) of royal or aristocratic descent —**blue·col·lar** *adj.* denoting factory workers —**blue jeans** pants made usu. of blue denim —**blue-pen·cil** *vt.* (**-ciled, -cil·ing**) alter, delete parts of, *esp.* to censor —**blue'print** *n.* copy of drawing; original plan —**blue'stock·ing** *n.* scholarly, intellectual woman

**bluff¹** *n.* cliff, steep bank —*adj.* (**-er, -est**) hearty; blunt; steep; abrupt

**bluff²** *vt.* deceive by pretense of strength —*n.* pretense

**blu·ing** (BLOO-ing) *n.* indigo powder used in laundering

**blun·der** (BLUN-dǝr) *n.* clumsy mistake —*vi.* make stupid mistake; act clumsily

**blun·der·buss** (BLUN-dǝr-bus) *n.* obsolete short gun with wide bore

**blunt** *adj.* (**-er, -est**) not sharp; (of speech) abrupt —*vt.* make blunt —**blunt'ly** *adv.* —**blunt'ness** *n.*

**blur** *v.* (**blurred, blur·ring**) make, become less distinct —*n.* something vague, indistinct —**blur'ry** *adj.* (**-ri·er, -ri·est**)

**blurb** *n.* statement advertising, recommending book *etc.*

**blurt** *vt.* utter suddenly or unadvisedly (*usually with* out)

**blush** *vi.* become red in face; be ashamed; redden —*n.* this effect

**blus·ter** (BLUS-tǝr) *vi./n.* (indulge in) noisy, aggressive behavior —**blus'ter·ing, -ter·y** *adj.* (of wind *etc.*) noisy and gusty

**bo·a** (BOH-ǝ) *n.* (*pl.* **bo·as**) large, nonvenomous snake, *esp.* boa constrictor; long scarf of fur or feathers

**boar** (bor) *n.* male pig; wild pig

**board** (bord) *n.* broad, flat piece of wood; sheet of rigid material for specific purpose; table; meals; group of people who administer company; governing body; thick, stiff paper —*pl.* stage —*vt.* cover with planks; supply food daily; enter ship *etc.* —*vi.* take daily meals —**board'er** *n.* —**board'ing house** lodging house where meals may be had —**boarding school** school providing living accommodation for pupils —**board'room** *n.* room where board of company or governing body meets —**above board** beyond suspicion —**on board** aboard

**boast** (bohst) *vi.* speak too much

in praise of oneself, one's possessions —vt. brag of; have to show —n. something boasted (of) —boast'er n. —boast'ful adj.

**boat** (boht) n. small open vessel; ship —vi. sail about in boat —boat'ing n. —boat'swain (BOHsən) n. ship's petty officer in charge of maintenance

**bob** v. (bobbed, bob·bing) —vi. move up and down —vt. move jerkily; cut (women's) hair short —n. short, jerking motion; short hair style; weight on pendulum etc. —bobbed adj.

**bob·bin** (BOB-in) n. cylinder on which thread is wound

**bob·ble** (BOB-əl) v./n. Baseball (-bled, -bling) fumble —n. fumbled ball

**bob·cat** (BOB-kat) n. N Amer. lynx

**bob·o·link** (BOB-ə-lingk) n. N Amer. songbird

**bode** (bohd) vt. (bod·ed, bod·ing) be an omen of

**bod·ice** (BOD-is) n. upper part of woman's dress

**bod·y** (BOD-ee) n. (pl. bod·ies) entire frame of person or animal; main part of anything; corpse; main part of anything; substance; mass; person; number of persons united or organized; matter, opposed to spirit —bod'i·ly adj./adv. —bod'y·guard n. escort to protect important persons —body stocking undergarment covering body, oft. including arms and legs —bod'y·work n. body of motor vehicle; repair of this

**Boer** (bor) n. a S Afr. of Dutch or Huguenot descent

**bof·fo** (BOF-oh) adj. sl. excellent; highly successful

**bog** n. wet, soft ground —bog'gy adj. (-gi·er, -gi·est) marshy —bog down stick as in a bog

**bo·gey** (BOH-gee) n. evil or mischievous spirit; source of fear; Golf one stroke over par on a hole —bo'gey·man n.

**bog·gle** (BOG-əl) v. (-gled, -gling) —vi. be surprised; be baffled —vt. overwhelm with wonder; bewilder

**bo·gus** (BOH-gəs) adj. sham, false

**bo·he·mi·an** (boh-HEE-mee-ən) adj. unconventional —n. one who leads an unsettled life —bo·he'·mi·a n. district, social circles of bohemians

**boil¹** vi. change from liquid to gas, esp. by heating; become cooked by boiling; bubble; be agitated; seethe; inf. be hot; inf. be angry —vt. cause to boil; cook by boiling —n. boiling state —boil'er n. vessel for boiling —boil'ermak·er n. repairman, worker on boilers; whiskey with beer chaser —boiling point temperature at which boiling occurs; point at which anger becomes uncontrollable

**boil²** n. inflamed suppurating swelling on skin

**bois·ter·ous** (BOI-stər-əs) adj. wild; noisy; turbulent —bois'ter·ous·ness n.

**bold** (bohld) adj. (-er, -est) daring, fearless; presumptuous; striking, prominent —bold'ly adv. —bold'ness n. —bold'face n. Printing heavy-faced type

**bole** (bohl) n. trunk of a tree

**bo·le·ro** (bə-LAIR-oh) n. (pl. -ros) Spanish dance; short loose jacket

**boll** (bohl) n. seed capsule of cotton, flax etc. —boll weevil beetle infesting the cotton plant

**Bol·she·vik** (BOHL-shə-vik) n. violent revolutionary; esp. member of Russian group active in overthrow of czarist regime

**bol·ster** (BOHL-stər) vt. support, uphold —n. long pillow; pad, support

**bolt** (bohlt) n. bar or pin (esp.

with thread for nut); rush; discharge of lightning; roll of cloth —vt. fasten with bolt; swallow hastily —vi. rush away; break from control

**bomb** (bom) n. explosive projectile; any explosive device; a failure —**the bomb** nuclear bomb —vt. attack with bombs —**bombard'** —vt. shell; attack (verbally) —**bom·bar·dier'** (-bər-DEER) n. person in military aircraft who aims and releases bombs —**bombard'ment** n. —**bomb'er** n. aircraft capable of carrying bombs; person using bombs illegally —**bomb'shell** n. shell of bomb; surprise; inf. very attractive woman

**bom'bast** n. pompous language; pomposity —**bom·bas'tic** adj.

**bo·na fide** (BOH-nə fīd) Lat. genuine(ly); sincere(ly) —**bona fi·des** (FĪ-deez) good faith, sincerity

**bo·nan·za** (bə-NAN-zə) n. sudden good luck or wealth

**bond** n. that which binds; link, union; written promise to pay money or carry out contract —vt. bind; store goods until duty is paid on them —**bond'ed** adj. placed in bond; mortgaged —**bonds'man** (-mən) n. Law one whose work is to enter into bonds as surety

**bond·age** (BON-dij) n. slavery

**bone** (bohn) n. hard substance forming animal's skeleton; piece of this —v. (boned, bon·ing) —vt. take out bone —vi. inf. (with up) study hard —**bone'less** adj. —**bon'y** adj. (bon·i·er, bon·i·est) —**bone'head** n. inf. stupid person

**bon·fire** (BON-fir) n. large outdoor fire

**bon·go** (BONG-goh) n. (pl. -gos, -goes) small drum, usu. one of a pair, played with the fingers

**bon·net** (BON-it) n. hat (usu.) with strings

**bon·sai** (BON-sī) n. (art of growing) dwarf trees, shrubs

**bo·nus** (BOH-nəs) n. (pl. -nus·es) extra (oft. unexpected) payment or gift

**boob** n. fool; offens. sl. female breast

**boo·by** (BOO-bee) n. (pl. -bies) fool; tropical marine bird —**booby hatch** inf. insane asylum —**booby prize** mock prize for poor performance —**booby trap** harmless-looking object that explodes when disturbed; form of practical joke

**boo·dle** (BOOD-l) n. (bribe) money

**boog·ie-woog·ie** (BUUG-ee-WUUG-ee) n. kind of jazz piano playing, emphasizing a rolling bass in syncopated eighth notes

**book** (buuk) n. collection of sheets of paper bound together; literary work; main division of this —vt. reserve (table, ticket etc.); charge with legal offense; enter name in book; schedule engagements for —**book'ing** n. scheduled performance for entertainer etc.; reservation —**book'ish** adj. studious, fond of reading —**book'keep·ing** n. systematic recording of business transactions —**book'keep·er** n. —**book'let** n. —**book'mak·er** n. one whose work is taking bets (also inf. book'ie) —**book'worm** n. great reader

**boom**[1] n. sudden commercial activity; prosperity —vi. become active, prosperous

**boom**[2] vi./n. (make) loud, deep sound

**boom**[3] n. long spar, as for stretching the bottom of a sail; barrier across harbor, river etc.; pole carrying overhead microphone *etc.*

**boo·mer·ang** (BOO-mə-rang) *n.* curved wooden missile of Aust. Aborigines that returns to the thrower —*vi.* recoil; return unexpectedly; backfire

**boon** *n.* something helpful, favor

**boon·docks** (BOON-doks) *n. pl.* rural, backward area

**boon·dog·gle** (BOON-dog-əl) *n./vi.* (-gled, -gling) (do) work of no practical value performed merely to appear busy

**boor** *n.* rude person —**boor'ish** *adj.* —**boor'ish·ness** *n.*

**boost** *n.* encouragement; help; upward push; increase —*vt.* —**boost'er** *n.* person or thing that supports, increases power *etc.*

**boot** *n.* covering for the foot and ankle; *inf.* kick —*vt. inf.* kick —**boot'ed** *adj.*

**booth** *n.* stall; cubicle

**boot'leg** *v.* -legged, -leg·ging) make, carry, sell illicit goods, *esp.* alcohol —*adj.* —**boot'leg·ger** *n.*

**boo·ty** (BOO-tee) *n.* (*pl.* -ties) plunder, spoil

**booze** (booz) *n./vi. inf.* (boozed, booz·ing) (consume) alcoholic drink; drinking spree —**booz'er** *n. inf.* person fond of drinking

**bo·rax** (BOR-aks) *n.* white soluble substance, compound of boron —**bo·rac·ic** (bə-RAS-ik) *adj.*

**bor·der** (BOR-dər) *n.* margin; frontier; limit; strip of garden —*v.* provide with border; adjoin

**bore**[1] (bor) *vt.* (bored, bor·ing) pierce, making a hole; *n.* hole; caliber of gun —**bor'er** *n.* instrument for making holes; insect that bores holes

**bore**[2] *vt.* (bored, bor·ing) make weary by repetition *etc.* —*n.* tiresome person or thing —**bore'dom** (-dəm) *n.*

**bore**[3] *pt. of* BEAR

**borne, born** *pp. of* BEAR

**bo·ron** (BOR-on) *n.* chemical element used in hardening steel, *etc.*

**bor·ough** (BUR-oh) *n.* political subdivision in some states

**bor·row** (BO-roh) *vt.* obtain on loan or trust; appropriate

**bor·zoi** *n.* breed of tall hound with long, silky coat

**bos·om** (BUUZ-əm) *n.* human breast; seat of passions and feelings

**boss**[1] (baws) *n.* person in charge of or employing others —*vt.* be in charge of; be domineering over —**boss'y** *adj.* (boss·i·er, boss·i·est) overbearing

**boss**[2] *n.* knob or stud; raised ornament —*vt.* emboss

**bo·sun** (BOH-sən) *n.* boatswain

**bot·a·ny** (BOT-n-ee) *n.* study of plants —**bo·tan·i·cal** (bə-TAN-ik-əl) *adj.* —**bot'a·nist** *n.* —**botanical garden** garden for exhibition and study of plants

**botch** (boch) *vt.* spoil by clumsiness

**both** (bohth) *adj./pron.* the two —*adv./conj.* as well

**both·er** (BOTH-ər) *vt.* pester; perplex —*vi./n.* fuss, trouble

**bot·tle** (BOT-l) *n.* vessel for holding liquid; its contents —*vt.* (-tled, -tling) put into bottle; restrain —**bot'tler** *n.* —**bot'tle·neck** *n.* narrow outlet that impedes smooth flow of traffic of production of goods; person who hampers flow of work, information *etc.*

**bot·tom** (BOT-əm) *n.* lowest part of anything; bed of sea, river *etc.*; buttocks —*vt.* put bottom to; base (upon); get to bottom of —**bot'tom·less** *adj.* —**bottom line** last line of financial statement; crucial or deciding factor

**bot·u·lism** (BOCH-ə-liz-əm) *n.* kind of food poisoning

**bou·clé** (boo-KLAY) *n.* looped yarn giving knobby effect

**bou·doir** (BOO-dwahr) *n.* woman's bedroom, private sitting room

**bough** (bow, *rhymes with cow*) *n.* branch of tree

**bought** *pt./pp.* of BUY

**boul·der** (BOHL-dər) *n.* large weather-worn rounded stone

**boul·e·vard** (BUUL-ə-vahrd) *n.* broad street or promenade

**bounce** (bowns) *v.* (bounced, bounc·ing) (cause to) rebound (repeatedly) on impact, as a ball —*n.* rebounding; quality in object causing this; *inf.* vitality, vigor —**bounc'er** *n.* one employed to evict undesirables (forcibly) —**bounc'ing** *adj.* vigorous, robust —**bounc'y** *adj.* (bounc·i·er, bounc·i·est) lively

**bound**[1] bownd *n./vt.* limit —**bound'a·ry** *n.* (*pl.* -ries) —**bound'ed** *adj.* —**bound'less** *adj.*

**bound**[2] *vi./n.* spring, leap

**bound**[3] *adj.* on a specified course, as outward bound

**bound**[4] *pt./pp.* of BIND —*adj.* committed; certain; tied

**boun·ty** (BOWN-tee) *n.* (*pl.* -ties) liberality; gift; premium —**boun'te·ous** (-tee-əs), **boun'ti·ful** *adj.* liberal, generous

**bou·quet** (boo-KAY) *n.* bunch of flowers; perfume of wine; compliment

**bour·bon** (BUR-bən) *n.* whiskey made from corn, malt and rye

**bour·geois** (buur-ZHWAH) *n./adj.* (*oft. disparaging*) middle class; smugly conventional (person)

**bout** (bowt) *n.* contest, fight; period of time spent doing something

**bou·tique** (boo-TEEK) *n.* small shop, *esp.* one selling clothes

**bo·vine** (BOH-vīn) *adj.* of cattle; oxlike; stolid, dull

**bow**[1] (boh) *n.* weapon for shooting arrows; implement for playing violin *etc.*; ornamental knot of ribbon *etc.*; bend, bent line —*v.* bend —**bow'leg·ged** (-leg-id) *adj.* having legs curved outward —**bow window** one with outward curve

**bow**[2] (*rhymes with cow*) *vi.* bend body in respect, assent *etc.*; submit —*vt.* bend downward; cause to stoop; crush —*n.*

**bow**[3] (*rhymes with cow*) *n.* fore end of ship; prow; rower nearest bow

**bowd·ler·ize** (BOHD-lə-rīz) *vt.* (-ized, -iz·ing) expurgate, censor

**bow·el** (BOW-əl) *n.* (*oft. pl.*) part of intestine (*esp.* with reference to defecation); inside of anything

**bow·er** (BOW-ər) *n.* shady retreat, arbor

**bowl**[1] (bohl) *n.* round vessel, deep basin; drinking cup; hollow

**bowl**[2] *n.* wooden ball —*pl.* outdoor game played with such balls —**bowl'ing** *n.* similar game, played indoors usu. with large, heavy balls —*v.* roll or throw ball in various ways —**bowling green** place where bowls is played —**bowling alley** place where bowling is played

**box**[1] (boks) *n.* (wooden) container, usu. rectangular with lid; its contents; small enclosure; any boxlike cubicle, shelter or receptacle (*eg* mailbox) —*vt.* put in box; confine

**box**[2] *v.* fight with fists, *esp.* with padded gloves on —*vt.* strike —*n.* blow —**box'er** *n.* one who boxes; breed of pug-faced large dog

**boy** (boi) *n.* male child; young man —**boy'hood** (-huud) *n.*

**boy·cott** (BOI-kot) *v.* refuse to deal with or participate in —*n.*

**Br** *Chem.* bromine

**bra** (brah) *n.* brassiere

**brace** (brays) *n.* tool for boring; clasp, clamp; pair, couple; strut, support —*pl.* dental appliance worn to help straighten teeth —*vt.* (braced, brac·ing) steady (oneself) as before a blow; support, make firm —**bracing** *adj.* invigorating —**brace'let** *n.* ornament for the arm —*pl. sl.* handcuffs

**brack·et** (BRAK-it) *n.* support for shelf *etc.*; group —*pl.* marks (), used to enclose words *etc.* —*vt.* enclose in brackets; connect

**brack·ish** (BRAK-ish) *adj.* (of water) slightly salty

**bract** (brakt) *n.* small scalelike leaf

**brad** *n.* small nail

**brag** *vi.* (bragged, brag·ging) boast —*n.* boastful talk —**brag·gart** (-ərt) *n.*

**Brah·man** (BRAY-mən) *n.* breed of beef cattle

**Brah·min** (BRAH-min) *n.* member of priestly Hindu caste; socially or intellectually aloof person

**braid** (brayd) *vt.* interweave, *eg* hair; trim with braid —*n.* length of anything interwoven or plaited; ornamental tape

**Braille** (brayl) *n.* system of printing for blind, with raised dots instead of letters

**brain** (brayn) *n.* mass of nerve tissue in head; intellect —*vt.* kill by hitting on head —**brain'less** *adj.* —**brain'y** *adj.* (brain·i·er, brain·i·est) —**brain'child** *n.* invention —**brain'storm** *n.* sudden mental aberration; sudden clever idea —*v.* practice, subject to, brainstorming —**brain'storm·ing** *n.* technique for coming upon innovative ideas —**brain trust** group of experts without official status who advise government officials —**brain'wash** *vt.* change, distort a person's ideas or beliefs

—**brain wave** electrical impulse in brain

**braise** (brayz) *vt.* (braised, brais·ing) cook slowly in covered pan

**brake** (brayk) *n.* instrument for retarding motion of wheel or vehicle —*vt.* (braked, brak·ing) apply brake to

**bram·ble** (BRAM-bəl) *n.* prickly shrub —**bram'bly** *adj.* (-bli·er, -bli·est)

**bran** *n.* sifted husks of cereal grain

**branch** *n.* limb of tree; offshoot or subsidiary part of something larger or primary —*vi.* bear branches; diverge; spread —**branched** *adj.* —**branch'less** *adj.*

**brand** *n.* trademark; class of goods; particular kind, sort; mark made by hot iron; burning piece of wood; sword; mark of disgrace —*vt.* burn with iron; mark; stigmatize —**brand-new** *adj.* absolutely new

**bran'dish** *vt.* flourish, wave (weapon *etc.*)

**bran·dy** (BRAN-dee) *n.* (*pl.* -dies) alcoholic liquor distilled from wine or fruit juice —**brandy** (-died, -dy·ing) *vt.* flavor or preserve with brandy

**brash** *adj.* (-er, -est) bold, impudent

**brass** *n.* alloy of copper and zinc; group of brass wind instruments forming part of orchestra or band; *inf.* (military) officers —*adj.* —**brass'y** *adj.* (brass·i·er, brass·i·est) showy; harsh —**brass'i·ness** *n.*

**bras·siere** (brə-ZEER) *n.* woman's undergarment, supporting breasts, bra

**brat** *n.* contemptuous term for a child

**bra·va·do** (brə-VAH-doh) *n.* showy display of boldness

**brave** (brayv) *adj.* (**brav·er, brav·est**) bold, courageous; splendid, fine —*n.* N Amer. Indian warrior —*vt.* (**braved, brav·ing**) defy, meet boldly —**brav'er·y** *n.* (*pl.* **-er·ies**)

**bra·vo** (BRAH-voh) *interj.* well done!

**brawl** *vi.* fight noisily —*n.* —**brawl'er** *n.*

**brawn** *n.* muscle; strength —**brawn'y** *adj.* (**brawn·i·er, brawn·i·est**) muscular

**bray** *n.* donkey's cry —*vi.* utter this; give out harsh or loud sounds

**braze** (brayz) *vt.* (**brazed, braz·ing**) solder with alloy of brass or zinc

**bra·zen** (BRAY-zən) *adj.* of, like brass; impudent, shameless —*vt.* (*usu.* **with** out or through) face, carry through with impudence —**bra'zen·ness** *n.* effrontery —**bra'zier** (-zhər) *n.* brassworker

**bra·zier** (BRAY-zhər) *n.* pan for burning charcoal or coals

**breach** (breech) *n.* break, opening; breaking of rule, duty *etc.*; quarrel —*vt.* make a gap in; break (rule *etc.*)

**bread** (bred) *n.* food made of flour or meal baked; food; *sl.* money —**bread'fruit** *n.* breadlike fruit found in Pacific islands —**bread'win·ner** *n.* person who works to support family

**breadth** (bredth) *n.* extent across, width; largeness of view, mind

**break** (brayk) *v.* (**broke, bro·ken, break·ing**) —*vt.* part by force; shatter; burst, destroy; fail to observe; disclose; interrupt; surpass; make bankrupt; relax; mitigate; accustom (horse) to being ridden; decipher (code) —*vi.* become broken, shattered, divided; open, appear; come suddenly; crack, give way; part, fall out; (of voice) change in tone, pitch —*n.* fracture; gap; opening; separation; interruption; respite; interval; *inf.* opportunity; dawn; *Pool* opening shot in a game; *Boxing* separation after a clinch; —**break'a·ble** *adj.* —**break'age** *n.* —**break'er** *n.* person or device that breaks, *eg* electrical circuit; wave beating on rocks or shore —**break dance** acrobatic dance style of 1980s —**break'down** *n.* collapse, as nervous breakdown; failure to function effectively; analysis —**break'fast** (BREK-fəst) *n.* first meal of the day —**break'·in** *n.* illegal entering of building, *esp.* by thieves —**break'neck** *adj.* dangerous —**break'through** *n.* important advance —**break'·wa·ter** *n.* barrier to break force of waves

**breast** (brest) *n.* human chest; milk-secreting gland on chest of human female; seat of the affections; any protuberance —*vt.* face, oppose; reach summit of —**breast'stroke** *n.* stroke in swimming

**breath** (breth) *n.* air used by lungs; life; respiration; slight breeze —**breathe** (breeth) *v.* (**breathed, breath·ing**) —*vi.* inhale and exhale air from lungs; live; pause, rest —*vt.* inhale and exhale; utter softly, whisper —**breath'er** (-thər) *n.* short rest —**breath·less** (BRETH-lis) *adj.* —**breath'tak·ing** *adj.* causing awe or excitement

**Breath·a·lyz·er** (BRETH-ə-lī-zər) R device that estimates amount of alcohol in breath

**bred** *pt./pp.* of BREED

**breech** *n.* buttocks; hinder part of anything, *esp.* gun —**breech'·load·er** *n.*

**breed** *v.* (**bred, breed·ing**) —*vt.*

generate, bring forth, give rise to; rear —vi. be produced; be with young —n. offspring produced; race, kind —**breed**·**ing** n. producing; manners; ancestry —**breeder reactor** nuclear reactor producing more fissionable material than it consumes

**breeze** (breez) n. gentle wind —**breez**′i·**ly** adv. —**breez**′y adj. (breez·i·er, breez·i·est) windy; jovial, lively; casual —**in a breeze** easily

**breth·ren** (BRETH-rən) obs. pl. of BROTHER

**breve** (breev) n. long musical note

**bre·vi·a·ry** (BREE-vee-er-ee) n. (pl. -ar·ies) book of daily prayers, hymns etc.

**brev·i·ty** (BREV-i-tee) n. conciseness of expression; short duration

**brew** (broo) vt. prepare liquor, as beer from malt etc.; make drink, as tea, by infusion; plot, contrive —vi. be in preparation —n. beverage produced by brewing —**brew**′er n. —**brew**′er·y n.

**bri·ar**[1], **-er**[1] (BRI-ər) n. prickly shrub, esp. the wild rose

**briar**[2], **-er**[2] n. European shrub —briar pipe made from its root

**bribe** (brīb) n. anything offered or given to someone to gain favor, influence —vt. (bribed, brib·ing) ·influence by bribe —**brib**′er·y n. (pl. -er·ies)

**bric-a-brac** (BRIK-ə-brak) n. miscellaneous small objects, used for ornament

**brick** (brik) n. oblong mass of hardened clay used in building; good-hearted person —vt. build, block etc. with bricks

**bride** (brīd) n. woman about to be, or just, married —**brid**′al adj. of, relating to, a bride or wedding —**bride**′**groom** n. man about to

be, or just, married —**brides**′**maid** n.

**bridge**[1] (brij) n. structure for crossing river etc.; something joining or supporting other parts; raised narrow platform on ship; upper part of nose; part of violin supporting strings —vt. (bridged, bridg·ing) make bridge over, span

**bridge**[2] n. card game

**bri·dle** (BRID-l) n. headgear of horse harness; curb v. (-dled, -dling) —vt. put on bridle; restrain —vi. show resentment —**bridle path** path suitable for riding horses

**brief** (breef) adj. (-er, -est) short in duration; concise; scanty —n. summary of case for judge or lawyer's use; papal letter; instructions —pl. underpants; panties —vt. give instructions, information —**brief**′**ly** adv. —**brief**′**case** n. hand case for carrying papers —**brief**·**ing** book one prepared to provide (participant) information on meeting etc.

**brier** see BRIAR

**brig** n. two-masted, square-rigged ship; inf. ship's jail, guardhouse

**bri·gade** (bri-GAYD) n. subdivision of army; organized band —**brig**·**a·dier**′ (-ə-DEER) **gen·er·al** one-star general

**brig·an·tine** (BRIG-ən-teen) n. two-masted vessel, with square-rigged foremast and fore-and-aft mainmast

**bright** (brīt) adj. (-er, -est) shining; full of light; cheerful; clever —**bright**′**en** v.

**bril·liant** (BRIL-yənt) adj. shining; sparkling; splendid; very intelligent or clever; distinguished —**bril**′**liance** n.

**brim** n. margin, edge, esp. of river, cup, hat —**brim**·**ful** adj.

—brim'less adj. —brim'ming adj. —to the brim until it can hold no more

brim·stone (BRIM-stohn) n. sulfur

brin·dled (BRIN-dld) adj. brownish with streaks of other color —brin'dle n. this color; a brindled animal

brine (brin) n. salt water —brin'y adj. (brin·i·er, brin·i·est) very salty —n. inf. the sea

bring vt. (brought, bring·ing) fetch; carry with one; cause to come

brink (bringk) n. edge of steep place; verge, margin —brink'man·ship n. technique of attempting to gain advantage through maneuvering dangerous situation to limit of tolerance

bri·quette (bri-KET) n. block of compressed coal dust

brisk adj. (-er, -est) active, vigorous —brisk'ly adv. —brisk'ness n.

bris·ket (BRIS-kit) n. cut of meat from breast of animal

bris·tle (BRIS-ol) n. short stiff hair —vi. (-tled, -tling) stand erect; show temper —bris'tly adj. (-tli·er, -tli·est)

British thermal unit unit of heat equal to 1055 joules, abbrev. Btu

brit·tle (BRIT-l) adj. easily broken, fragile; curt, irritable —brit'tle·ness n.

broach (brohch) vt. pierce (cask); open, begin

broad (brawd) adj. (-er, -est) wide, spacious, open; plain, obvious; coarse; general; tolerant; (of pronunciation) dialectal —broad'en vt. —broad'ly adv. —broad'ness n. —broad'cast vt. (-cast or -cast·ed, -cast·ing) transmit by radio or television; make widely known; scatter, as seed —n. radio or TV program —broad'cast·er n. —broad'loom

n./adj. (carpet) woven on wide loom —broad·mind·ed (-MIN-did) adj. tolerant; generous —broad'side n. discharge of all guns on one side; strong (verbal) attack

bro·cade (broh-KAYD) n. rich woven fabric with raised design

broc·co·li (BROK-ə-lee) n. type of cabbage

bro·chette (broh-SHET) n. small spit; skewer

bro·chure (broh-SHUUR) n. pamphlet, booklet

brogue (brohg) n. stout shoe; dialect, esp. Irish accent

broil vt. cook over hot coals; grill —vi. be heated

broke see BREAK —adj. inf. penniless

bro·ker (BROH-kər) n. one employed to buy and sell for others; dealer —bro'ker·age n. business of broker; payment to broker

bro·mide (BROH-mid) n. chemical compound used in medicine and photography; hackneyed, commonplace statement —bro-mid'ic (-MID-ik) adj. lacking in originality

bro·mine (BROH-meen) n. liquid element used in production of chemicals

bron·chus (BRONG-kəs) n. (pl. -chi pr. -kee) branch of windpipe —bron'chi·al adj. —bron·chi'tis (-Kl-tis) n. inflammation of bronchi

bron·co (BRONG-koh) n. (pl. -cos) N Amer. half-tamed horse

bron·to·sau·rus (bron-tə-SOR-əs) n. very large herbivorous dinosaur

bronze (bronz) n. alloy of copper and tin —adj. made of, or colored like, bronze —vt. (bronzed, bronz·ing) give appearance of bronze to

brooch (brohch) n. ornamental pin or fastening

**brood** n. family of young, esp. of birds; tribe, race —v. sit, as hen on eggs; meditate, fret over —**brood′y** adj. (**brood·i·er, brood·i·est**) moody, sullen

**brook**[1] (bruuk) n. small stream

**brook**[2] vt. put up with, endure, tolerate

**broom** n. brush for sweeping; yellow-flowered shrub —**broom′stick** n. handle of broom

**broth** (brawth) n. thick soup; stock

**broth·el** (BROTH-əl) n. house of prostitution

**broth·er** (BRUTH-ər) n. son of same parents; one closely united with another —**broth′er·hood** (-huud) n. relationship; fraternity, company —**broth′er·ly** adj. —**broth′er-in-law** n. brother of husband or wife; husband of sister

**brought** pt./pp. of BRING

**brow** n. ridge over eyes; forehead; eyebrow; edge of hill —**brow′beat** vt. (**-beat, -beat·en, -beat·ing**) bully

**brown** adj. (**-er, -est**) of dark color inclining to red or yellow —n. the color —v. make, become brown —**browned off** sl. angry; fed up

**Brown·ie** (BROW-nee) n. Girl Scout 7 to 10 years old; (**b-**) small, nutted square of chocolate cake —**Brownie point** notional mark to one's credit for being seen to do the right thing

**browse** (browz) vi. (**browsed, brows·ing**) look through (book, articles for sale etc.) in a casual manner; feed on shoots and leaves

**bruise** (brooz) vt. (**bruised, bruis·ing**) injure without breaking skin —n. contusion, discoloration caused by blow —**bruis′er** n. inf. strong, tough person

**brunch** n. inf. breakfast and lunch combined

**bru·nette** (broo-NET) n. person of dark complexion and hair —adj. dark brown

**brunt** n. shock of attack, chief stress; first blow

**brush** n. device with bristles, hairs, wires etc. used for cleaning, painting etc.; act, instance of brushing; brief contact; skirmish, fight; bushy tail, bushy haircut; dense growth of bushes, shrubs etc. (carbon) device taking electric current from moving to stationary parts of generator etc. —v. apply, remove, clean, with brush; touch, discuss lightly —**brush′off** n. inf. dismissal; refusal; snub; rebuff —**brush′fire** n. fire in area of bushes, shrubs etc. —**brush′wood** n. broken-off branches; land covered with scrub

**brusque** (brusk) adj. rough in manner, curt, blunt

**brute** (broot) n. any animal except man; crude, vicious person —adj. animal; sensual, stupid; physical —**bru′tal** adj. —**bru·tal′i·ty** n. —**bru′tal·ize** vt. (**-ized, -iz·ing**) —**brut′ish** adj. bestial, gross

**Btu** British thermal unit

**bub·ble** (BUB-əl) n. hollow globe of liquid, blown out with air; something insubstantial, not serious; transparent dome —vi. (**-bled, -bling**) rise in bubbles; make gurgling sound

**bu·bon·ic plague** (byoo-BON-ik playg) n. acute infectious disease characterized by swellings and fever

**buc·ca·neer** (buk-ə-NEER) n. pirate; unscrupulous adventurer —**buc·ca·neer′ing** n.

**buck** (buk) n. male deer, or other male animal; act of bucking; sl.

dollar —*v.* of horse, attempt to throw rider by jumping upward *etc.*; resist, oppose (something) —**buck'shot** *n.* lead shot in shotgun shell —**buck-teeth** *n. pl.* projecting upper teeth —**pass the buck** shift blame or responsibility to another person

**buck·et** (BUK-it) *n.* vessel, round with arched handle, for water *etc.*; anything resembling this —**buck'et·ful** *n.* (*pl.* **-fuls**) —**bucket seat** seat with back shaped to occupier's figure

**buck·le** (BUK-əl) *n.* metal clasp for fastening belt, strap *etc.* —*v.* (**-led, -ling**) —*vt.* fasten with buckle —*vi.* warp, bend —**buckle down** start work

**buck·ram** (BUK-rəm) *n.* coarse cloth stiffened with size

**bu·col·ic** (byoo-KOL-ik) *adj.* rustic

**bud** *n.* shoot or sprout on plant containing unopened leaf, flower *etc.* —*v.* (**bud·ded, bud·ding**) —*vi.* begin to grow —*vt.* to graft

**Bud·dhism** (BOO-diz-əm) *n.* religion founded in India by Buddha —**Bud'dhist** *adj./n.*

**bud·dy** (BUD-ee) *n. inf.* (*pl.* **-dies**) pal, chum

**budge** (buj) *vi.* (**budged, budging**) move, stir

**budg·et** (BUJ-it) *n.* annual financial statement; plan of systematic spending —*vi.* prepare financial statement; plan financially

**buff**[1] *n.* light yellow color; bare skin; polishing pad —*vt.* polish

**buff**[2] *n. inf.* expert on some subject

**buf·fa·lo** (BUF-ə-loh) *n.* (*pl.* **-los, -loes**) any of several species of large oxen

**buff·er** (BUF-ər) *n.* contrivance to lessen shock of concussion; person, country that shields another against annoyance *etc.*

**buf·fet**[1] (BUF-it) *n.* blow, slap;

misfortune —*vt.* strike with blows; contend against —**buf'fet·ing** *n.*

**buf·fet**[2] (bə-FAY) *n.* refreshment bar; meal at which guests serve themselves; sideboard

**buf·foon** (bə-FOON) *n.* clown; fool —**buf·foon'er·y** *n.* clowning

**bug** *n.* any small insect; *inf.* disease, infection; concealed listening device —*vt.* (**bugged, bugging**) install secret microphone in

**bug·a·boo** (BUG-ə-boo) *n.* (*pl.* **-boos**) something that causes fear or worry

**bug·bear** (BUG-bair) *n.* object of needless terror; nuisance

**bug·ger** (BUG-ər) *n. vulgar* sodomite; *inf.* worthless person; *inf.* lad

**bu·gle** (BYOO-gəl) *n.* instrument like trumpet —**bu'gler** *n.*

**build** (bild) *v.* (**built, build·ing**) make, construct, by putting together parts or materials —*n.* make, form; physique —**build'ing** *n.*

**bulb** *n.* modified leaf bud emitting roots from base, *eg* onion; anything resembling this; globe surrounding filament of electric light —*vi.* form bulbs —**bul'bous** *adj.*

**bulge** (bulj) *n.* swelling, protuberance; temporary increase —*vi.* (**bulged, bulg·ing**) swell out —**bulg'i·ness** *n.*

**bulk** *n.* size; volume; greater part; cargo —*vi.* be of weight or importance —**bulk'i·ness** *n.* —**bulk'y** *adj.* (**bulk·i·er, bulk·i·est**)

**bulk·head** (BULK-hed) *n.* partition in interior of ship

**bull**[1] (buul) *n.* male of cattle; male of various other animals —**bull'-dog** *n.* thickset breed of dog —**bull'doze** (-dohz) *v.* (**-dozed, -doz·ing**) —**bull'doz·er** *n.* powerful tractor with blade for excavating *etc.* —**bul′lock** (-lɔk) *n.* castrated bull —**bull′s′-eye** *n.* (*pl.* -**eyes**) middle part of target

**bull**[2] *n.* papal edict

**bull**[3] *n. sl.* nonsense —*v.* talk nonsense (to)

**bul·let** (BUUL-it) *n.* projectile discharged from rifle, pistol *etc.*

**bul·le·tin** (BUUL-i-tn) *n.* official report

**bul·lion** (BUUL-yɔn) *n.* gold or silver in mass

**bul·ly** (BUUL-ee) *n.* (*pl.* -**lies**) one who hurts, persecutes, or intimidates weaker people —*vt.* (-**lied,** -**ly·ing**) intimidate, overawe; illtreat —*adj./interj.* first-rate

**bul·rush** (BUUL-rush) *n.* tall reedlike marsh plant with brown velvety spike

**bul·wark** (BUUL-wɔrk) *n.* rampart; any defense or means of security; raised side of ship; breakwater

**bum** *n.* loafer, scrounger —*vt. inf.* (**bummed, bum·ming**) get by scrounging —*adj. sl.* worthless; inferior; disabled

**bum·ble** (BUM-bɔl) *v.* (-**bled,** -**bling**) perform clumsily —**bum′bler** *n.*

**bum·ble·bee** (BUM-bɔl-bee) *n.* large bee

**bump** *n.* heavy blow, dull in sound; swelling caused by blow; protuberance; sudden movement —*vt.* strike or push against —**bump′er** *n.* horizontal bar at front and rear of automobile to protect against damage; full glass —*adj.* full, abundant —**bump off** *sl.* murder

**bump·kin** (BUMP-kin) *n.* rustic

**bump·tious** (BUMP-shɔs) *adj.* offensively self-assertive

**bun** *n.* small, round bread or cake; round knot of hair; *sl.* enough liquor to make one drunk

**bunch** *n.* number of things tied or growing together; cluster; tuft, knot; group, party —*vt.* put together in bunch —*vi.* gather together

**bun·dle** (BUN-dl) *n.* package; number of things tied together; *sl.* lot of money —*vt.* (-**dled,** -**dling**) tie in bundle; send (off) without ceremony

**bung** *n.* stopper for cask; large cork —*vt.* stop up, seal, close —**bung′hole** *n.*

**bun·ga·low** (BUNG-gɔ-loh) *n.* onestoried house

**bun·gle** (BUNG-gɔl) *v.* (-**gled,** -**gling**) *vt.* do badly from lack of skill, botch —*vi.* act clumsily, awkwardly —*n.* blunder, muddle —**bun′gler** *n.*

**bun·ion** (BUN-yɔn) *n.* inflamed swelling on foot or toe

**bunk**[1] (bungk) *n.* narrow, shelflike bed —*vi.* stay the night (with) —**bunk bed** one of pair of beds constructed one above the other

**bunk**[2] *n.* bunkum

**bun·ker** (BUNG-kɔr) *n.* large storage container for oil, coal *etc.*; sandy hollow on golf course; (military) underground defensive position

**bun·ko** (BUNG-koh) *n.* (*pl.* -**kos**) swindling scheme or game

**bun·kum** (BUNG-kɔm) *n.* nonsense

**bun·ny** (BUN-ee) *n. inf.* (*pl.* -**nies**) rabbit

**Bun·sen burner** (BUN-sɔn) gas burner, producing great heat, used for chemical experiments

**bun′ting**[1] *n.* material for flags

**bun·ting**[2] *n.* bird with short, stout bill

**bu·oy** (BOO-ee) *n.* floating marker anchored in sea; lifebuoy —*vt.* mark with buoy; keep from sink-

ing; support —**buoy·an·cy** (BOI-
ən-see) *n.* —**buoy'ant** *adj.*

**bur·ble** (BUR-bəl) *vi.* (**-bled,
-bling**) gurgle, as stream or baby;
talk idly

**bur·den** (BUR-dn) *n.* load; weight,
cargo; anything difficult to bear
—*vt.* load, encumber —**bur'den·
some** (-səm) *adj.*

**bu·reau** (BYUUR-oh) *n.* (*pl.*
**-reaus, -reaux** *both pr.* -rohz)
office; government department
—**bu·reauc·ra·cy** (byuu-ROK-rə-
see) *n.* (*pl.* -cies) government by
officials; body of officials —**bu·
reau·crat** (BYUUR-ə-krat) *n.*

**bur·geon** (BUR-jən) *vi.* bud; develop rapidly

**burg·er** (BUR-gər) *n.* hamburger

**bur·gess** (BUR-jis) *n.* member of
colonial Maryland or Virginia
legislature

**bur·glar** (BUR-glər) *n.* one who
enters building to commit theft
—**bur'gla·ry** (-glə-ree) *n.* —**bur'·
gle** (-gəl) *vt.* (**-gled, -gling**)

**bur·gun·dy** (BUR-gən-dee) *n.* (*pl.*
**-dies**) name of various wines,
white and red

**bur'lap** *n.* coarse canvas

**bur·lesque** (bər-LESK) *n.* (artistic) caricature; ludicrous imitation; provocative and humorous
stage show —*vt.* (**-lesqued,
-lesqu·ing**) caricature

**bur·ly** (BUR-lee) *adj.* (**-li·er, -liest**)
sturdy, stout, robust

**burn** *v.* (**burned** *or* **burnt, burning**) —*vt.* destroy or injure by
fire —*vi.* be on fire, *lit.* or *fig.*; be
consumed by fire —*n.* injury,
mark caused by fire

**bur'nish** *vt.* make bright by rubbing; polish —*n.* gloss, luster

**burp** *v. inf.* belch (*esp.* of
baby)

**burr¹** *n.* soft trilling sound given to
letter *r* in some dialects

**burr²** *n.* rough edge left after
cutting, drilling *etc.*

**burr³** *n.* head of plant with prick-
les or hooks

**bur·ro** (BUR-oh) *n.* (*pl.* -ros) small
donkey

**bur·row** (BUR-oh) *n.* hole dug by
rabbit *etc.* —*vt.* make holes in
ground; bore; conceal oneself

**bur·sar** (BUR-sər) *n.* official managing finances of college, monastery *etc.*

**burst** *v.* (**burst, burst·ing**) —*vi.*
fly asunder; break into pieces;
rend; break suddenly into some
expression of feeling —*vt.* shatter, break violently —*n.* bursting;
explosion; outbreak; spurt

**bur·y** (BER-ee) *vt.* (**bur·ied, bur·y·
ing**) put underground; inter; conceal —**bur'i·al** *n./adj.*

**bus** *n.* (*orig.* omnibus) large motor vehicle for passengers —*v.*
travel or transport by bus; work
as busboy —**bus'man's holiday**
vacation spent in an activity
closely resembling one's work

**bus·boy** (BUS-boi) *n.* waiter's
helper in public dining room

**bush** (buush) *n.* shrub; woodland,
thicket; uncleared country, back-
woods, interior —**bushed** *adj. inf.*
tired out —**bush'y** *adj.* (**bush·i·er,
bush·i·est**) shaggy —**bush jacket**
shirtlike jacket with patch pock-
ets

**bush·el** (BUUSH-əl) *n.* dry measure of eight gallons

**busi·ness** (BIZ-nis) *n.* profession,
occupation; commercial or industrial establishment; commerce, trade; responsibility, affair, matter; work

**bust¹** *n.* sculpture of head and
shoulders of human body; woman's breasts

**bust²** *v. inf.* burst; make, become
bankrupt —*vt. sl.* raid; arrest
—*adj. inf.* broken; bankrupt —*n.*

*sl.* police raid or arrest; *inf.* punch

**bus·tle**[1] (BUS-əl) *vi.* (-tled, -tling) be noisily busy, active —*n.* fuss, commotion

**bustle**[2] *n. Hist.* pad worn by ladies to support back of the skirt

**bus·y** (BIZ-ee) *adj.* (bus·i·er, bus·i·est) actively employed; full of activity —*vt.* (bus·ied, bus·y·ing) occupy —**bus'y·bod·y** *n.* (*pl.* -bod·ies) meddler

**but** *prep./conj.* without; except; only; yet; still; besides

**bu·tane** (BYOO-tayn) *n.* gas used for fuel

**butch** (buuch) *adj./n. sl.* markedly or aggressively masculine (person)

**butch·er** (BUUCH-ər) *n.* one who kills, dresses animals for food, or sells meat; bloody, savage man —*vt.* slaughter, murder; spoil work —**butch'er·y** *n.*

**but·ler** (BUT-lər) *n.* chief male servant

**butt**[1] *n.* the thick end; target; object of ridicule; bottom or unused end of anything —*v.* lie, be placed end on to

**butt**[2] *v.* strike with head; push —*n.* blow with head, as of sheep —**butt in** interfere; meddle —**butt·in'sky** *n. sl.* (*pl.* -skies) meddler

**but·ter** (BUT-ər) *n.* fatty substance got from cream by churning —*vt.* spread with or as if with butter; flatter

**but·ter·fly** (BUT-ər-flī) *n.* (*pl.* -flies) insect with large wings; inconstant person; stroke in swimming —*vt.* (-flied, -fly·ing) split (foodstuff) into shape resembling butterfly

**but·ter·milk** (BUT-ər-milk) *n.* milk that remains after churning

**but·tock** (BUT-ək) *n.* (*usu. pl.*) rump, protruding hinder part

**but·ton** (BUT-ən) *n.* knob, stud for fastening dress; knob that operates doorbell, machine *etc.* —*vt.* fasten with buttons —**but'tonhole** *n.* slit in garment to pass button through as fastening —*vt.* (-holed, -hol·ing) detain (unwilling) person in conversation

**but·tress** (BU-tris) *n.* structure to support wall; prop —*vt.*

**bux·om** (BUK-səm) *adj.* full of health, plump, gay; large-breasted

**buy** (bī) *vt.* (bought, buy·ing) get by payment, purchase; bribe —**buy'er** *n.*

**buzz** *vi.* make humming sound —*n.* humming sound of bees; *inf.* telephone call —**buzz'er** *n.* any apparatus that makes buzzing sound —**buzz word** *inf.* word, *oft.* orig. jargon, that becomes fashionable

**buz·zard** (BUZ-ərd) *n.* bird of prey of hawk family

**by** (bī) *prep.* near; along; across; past; during; not later than; through use or agency of; in units of —*adv.* near; away, aside; past —**by and by** soon, in the future —**by and large** on the whole; speaking generally —**come by** obtain

**by-** (*comb. form*) subsidiary, incidental, out-of-the-way, near, as in *bypath, byproduct, bystander*

**bye** (bī) *n. Sports* in early round of a tournament, a situation in which player, team not paired with opponent advances to next round without playing

**by-law** (BĪ-law) *n.* law, regulation made by an organization

**by-line** (BĪ-līn) *n.* printed line identifying author of news story, article *etc.*

**by·gone** (BĪ-gawn) *adj.* past, former —*n.* (*oft. pl.*) past occurrence

**by·pass** (BĪ-pas) n. road for diversion of traffic from crowded centers; secondary channel carrying fluid around a part and back to the main stream —vt.

**by·play** (BĪ-play) n. diversion, action apart from main action of play

**byte** (bīt) n. Computers sequence of bits processed as single unit of information

**by·word** (BĪ-wurd) n. a well-known name, saying

# C

**C** Chem. Celsius

**Ca** Chem. calcium

**cab** n. taxi; driver's enclosed compartment on locomotive, truck etc. —**cab'driv·er** n. —**cab'stand** n. place where taxis may wait to be hired

**ca·bal** (kɔ-BAL) n. small group of intriguers; secret plot

**cab·a·ret** (kab-ɔ-RAY) n. night club

**cab·bage** (KAB-ij) n. green vegetable with usu. round head of leaves

**ca·ber** (KAY-bɔr) n. pole tossed as trial of strength at Scottish games

**cab·in** (KAB-in) n. hut, shed; small room esp. in ship —**cabin cruiser** power boat with cabin, bunks etc.

**cab·i·net** (KAB-ɔ-nit) n. piece of furniture with drawers or shelves; outer case of television, radio etc.; body of advisers to head of state —**cab'i·net·mak·er** n. artisan who makes fine furniture

**ca·ble** (KAY-bɔl) n. strong rope; wire or bundle of wires conveying electric power, telegraph signals etc.; message sent by this; nautical unit of measurement (100-120 fathoms) —v. (-**bled**, -**bling**) telegraph by cable —**ca'ble·gram** n. cabled message —**ca·ble** (TV) TV service conveyed by cable to subscribers

**ca·boo·dle** (kɔ-BOOD-l) n. inf. —**the whole caboodle** the whole lot

**ca·boose** (kɔ-BOOS) n. (usu. last) car of freight train, for use by train crew

**ca·ca·o** (kɔ-KAH-oh) n. tropical tree from the seeds of which chocolate and cocoa are made

**cache** (kash) n. secret hiding place; store of food, arms etc.

**ca·chet** (ka-SHAY) n. mark, stamp; mark of authenticity; prestige, distinction

**cack·le** (KAK-ɔl) vi. (-**led**, -**ling**) make chattering noise, as hen —n. cackling noise or laughter; empty chatter

**ca·coph·o·ny** (kɔ-KOF-ɔ-nee) n. (pl. -**nies**) disagreeable sound; discord of sounds —**ca·coph'o·nous** adj.

**cac·tus** (KAK-tɔs) n. (pl. -**ti** pr. -**tī**) spiny succulent plant

**cad** n. dishonorable, ungentlemanly person

**ca·dav·er** (kɔ-DAV-ɔr) n. corpse —**ca·dav'er·ous** adj. corpselike; sickly-looking; gaunt

**cad·die** (KAD-ee) n. person hired to carry golfer's clubs, find the ball etc.

**ca·dence** (KAYD-ns) n. fall or modulation of voice in music, speech, or verse

**ca·den·za** (kɔ-DEN-zɔ) n. Mus. elaborate passage for solo instrument or singer

**ca·det** (kɔ-DET) n. youth in training, esp. for officer status in armed forces

**cadge** (kaj) v. (**cadged, cadg·ing**)

get (food, money *etc.*) by begging —**cadg'er** *n.* sponger

**cad·mi·um** (KAD-mee-əm) *n.* metallic element

**ca·dre** (KAD-ree) *n.* nucleus or framework, *esp.* skeleton of military unit

**Cae·sar·e·an section** (si-ZAIR-ee-ən) surgical incision through abdominal wall to deliver a baby

**café** (ka-FAY) *n.* small or inexpensive restaurant serving light refreshments; bar —**caf·e·te·ri·a** (kaf-ə-TEE-ree-ə) *n.* restaurant designed for self-service

**caf·feine** (ka-FEEN) *n.* stimulating alkaloid found in tea and coffee plants

**caf·tan** (KAF-tan) *n.* long coatlike Eastern garment; imitation of it, *esp.* as woman's long, loose dress with sleeves

**cage** (kayj) *n.* enclosure, box with bars or wires, *esp.* for keeping animals or birds; place of confinement; enclosed platform of elevator, *esp.* in mine —*vt.* (caged, cag·ing) put in cage, confine —**cag'ey** *adj.* (cag·i·er, cag·i·est) wary, shrewd

**ca·hoots** (kə-HOOTS) *n. pl. sl.* partnership, as in cahoots with

**cairn** (kairn) *n.* heap of stones, *esp.* as monument or landmark

**cais·son** (KAY-son) *n.* chamber for working under water; apparatus for lifting vessel out of the water; ammunition wagon —**caisson disease** the bends

**ca·jole** (kə-JOHL) *vt.* (-joled, -jol·ing) persuade by flattery, wheedle —**ca·jol'er** *n.*

**cake** (kayk) *n.* baked, sweetened, bread-like food; compact mass —*v.* (caked, cak·ing) make into a cake; harden (as of mud)

**cal·a·boose** (KAL-ə-boos) *n. inf.* jail

**cal·a·mine** (KAL-ə-mīn) *n.* pink powder used medicinally in soothing ointment

**ca·lam·i·ty** (kə-LAM-i-tee) *n.* (*pl.* -ties) great misfortune; deep distress, disaster —**ca·lam'i·tous** *adj.*

**cal·ci·um** (KAL-see-əm) *n.* metallic element, the basis of lime —**cal·car'e·ous** (-KAIR-ee-əs) *adj.* containing lime —**cal'ci·fy** *v.* (-fied, -fy·ing) convert, be converted, to lime

**cal·cu·late** (KAL-kyə-layt) *v.* (-lat·ed, -lat·ing) *vt.* estimate; compute —*vi.* make reckonings —**cal'cu·lat·ing** *adj.* able to perform calculations; shrewd, designing, scheming —**cal'cu·la·tor** *n.* electronic or mechanical device for making calculations —**cal'cu·lus** *n.* (*pl.* -li *pr.* -lī) branch of mathematics; stone in body

**cal·en·dar** (KAL-ən-dər) *n.* table of months and days in the year; list of events, documents; register

**calf¹** (kaf) *n.* (*pl.* calves *pr.* kavz) young of cow and of other animals; leather made of calf's skin —**calve** (kav) *vi.* (-calved, calv·ing) give birth to calf

**calf²** *n.* (*pl.* calves) fleshy back part of leg below knee

**cal·i·ber** (KAL-ə-bər) *n.* size of bore of gun; capacity, character —**cal'i·brate** (-brayt) *vt.* (-brat·ed, -brat·ing) mark scale of measuring instrument *etc.* —**cal·i·bra'tion** *n.*

**cal·i·co** (KAL-i-koh) *n.* (*pl.* -coes, -cos) printed cotton fabric

**cal·i·per** (KAL-ə-pər) *n.* instrument for measuring diameters; thickness, *esp.* of tree, paper

**cal·is·then·ics** (kal-əs-THEN-iks) *n. pl.* light gymnastic exercises

**call** (kawl) *vt.* speak loudly to attract attention; summon; (*oft.*

**with** up) telephone; name —*vi.* shout; (pay visit —*vi.* shout; animal's cry; visit; inner urge, summons, as to be minister *etc.*; need, demand —**call'ing** *n.* vocation, profession —**call box** outdoor telephone for calling police or fire department —**call girl** prostitute who accepts appointments by telephone —**call up** summon to serve in army; imagine

**cal·lig·ra·phy** (kə-LIG-rə-fee) *n.* handwriting, penmanship —**calli·graph'ic** *adj.*

**cal·lous** (KAL-əs) *adj.* hardened, unfeeling —**cal'lous·ness** *n.*

**cal·low** (KAL-oh) *adj.* inexperienced; immature

**cal·lus** (KAL-əs) *n.* (*pl.* -lus·es) area of thick, hardened skin

**calm** (kahm) *adj.* (-er, -est) still, quiet, tranquil —*n.* stillness; tranquility; absence of wind —*v.* become, make, still or quiet —**calm'ly** *adv.*

**cal·o·rie** (KAL-ə-ree) *n.* unit of heat; unit of energy obtained from foods —**cal·o·rif'ic** *adj.* heat-making —**cal·o·rim'e·ter** *n.*

**cal·u·met** (KAL-yə-met) *n.* tobacco pipe of N Amer. Indians; peace pipe

**cal·um·ny** (KAL-əm-nee) *n.* (*pl.* -nies) slander, false accusation —**ca·lum'ni·ate** *vt.* (-at·ed, -at·ing) —**ca·lum·ni·a'tion** *n.*

**ca·lyp·so** (kə-LIP-soh) *n.* (*pl.* -sos) (West Indies) improvised song on topical subject

**ca·lyx** (KAY-liks) *n.* (*pl.* -lyx·es) covering of bud

**cam** (kam) *n.* device to change rotary to reciprocating motion —**cam'shaft** *n.* in motor vehicles, rotating shaft to which cams are fixed to lift valves

**ca·ma·ra·de·rie** (kah-mə-RAH-

də-ree) *n.* spirit of comradeship, trust

**cam·ber** (KAM-bər) *n.* convexity on upper surface of road, bridge *etc.*; curvature of aircraft wing; setting of motor vehicle wheels closer together at bottom than at top

**cam·bric** (KAYM-brik) *n.* fine white linen or cotton cloth

**cam·cord·er** (KAM-kor-dər) *n.* combined portable video camera and recorder

**came** *pt.* of COME

**cam·el** (KAM-əl) *n.* animal of Asia and Africa, with humped back, used as beast of burden

**cam·e·o** (KAM-ee-oh) *n.* (*pl.* -e·os) medallion, brooch *etc.* with profile head or design carved in relief; single brief scene or appearance in film *etc.* by well-known performer

**cam·er·a** (KAM-ər-ə) *n.* apparatus used to make photographs —**cam'er·a·man** *n.* photographer, *esp.* for TV or film —**camera ob·scu·ra** (ob-SKYUUR-ə) darkened chamber in which views of external objects are shown on sheet by means of lenses —**in camera** (of legal proceedings *etc.*) conducted in private

**cam·i·sole** (KAM-ə-sohl) *n.* woman's short sleeveless undergarment

**cam·ou·flage** (KAM-ə-flahzh) *n.* disguise, means of deceiving enemy observation, *eg* by paint, screen —*vt.* (-flaged, -flag·ing) disguise

**camp** (kamp) *n.* (place for) tents of hikers, army *etc.*; cabins *etc.* for temporary accommodation; group supporting political party *etc.* —*adj. inf.* consciously artificial —*vi.* form or lodge in a camp

**cam·paign** (kam-PAYN) *n.* series of coordinated activities for some purpose, *eg* political or military campaign —*vi.* serve in campaign —**cam·paign'er** *n.*

**cam·pa·nol·o·gy** (kam-pə-NOL-ə-jee) *n.* art of ringing bells musically

**cam·phor** (KAM-fər) *n.* solid essential oil with aromatic taste and smell —**cam'phor·at·ed** *adj.*

**cam·pus** (KAM-pəs) *n.* (*pl.* -pus·es) grounds of college or university

**can**¹ (kan) *vi.* (could *pt.*) be able; have the power; be allowed

**can**² *n.* container, usu. metal, for liquids, foods —*v.* (canned, canning) put in can; prepare (food) for canning —**canned** *adj.* preserved in jar or can; (of music, TV or radio programs *etc.*) previously recorded —**can'ner·y** *n.* (*pl.* -ner·ies) factory where food is canned

**Can·a·da Day** (KAN-ə-də) July 1st, anniversary of establishment of Confederation in 1867

**Canada goose** large grayish-brown N Amer. goose

**Ca·na·di·an** (kə-NAY-dee-ən) *n./adj.* (native) of Canada

**ca·nal** (kə-NAL) *n.* artificial watercourse; duct in body —**can·al·ize** (KAN-l-īz) *vt.* (-ized, -iz·ing) convert into canal; direct (thoughts, energies *etc.*) into one channel

**can·a·pé** (KAN-ə-pay) *n.* small piece of toast *etc.* with cheese *etc.* topping

**ca·nar·y** (kə-NAIR-ee) *n.* (*pl.* -nar·ies) yellow singing bird

**ca·nas·ta** (kə-NAS-tə) *n.* card game played with two packs

**can·can** (KAN-kan) *n.* high-kicking (orig. French music-hall) dance

**can·cel** (KAN-səl) *vt.* (-celed, -cel·ing) cross out; annul; invalidate; call off —**can·cel·la'tion** *n.*

**can·cer** (KAN-sər) *n.* malignant growth or tumor —**can'cer·ous** *adj.*

**can·de·la** (kan-DEE-lə) *n.* basic unit of luminous intensity

**can·did** (KAN-did) *adj.* frank, open, impartial —**can'did·ly** *adv.* —**can'dor** (-dər) *n.* frankness

**can·di·date** (KAN-di-dayt) *n.* one who seeks office, employment *etc.*; person taking examination or test —**can'di·da·cy** (-də-see) *n.* (*pl.* -cies)

**can·dle** (KAN-dl) *n.* stick of wax with wick; light —**can·de·la'brum** (-AH-brəm) (*pl.* -bra *pr.* -brə) *n.* large, branched candle holder —**can'dle·pow·er** *n.* unit for measuring light —**can't hold a candle to** compare unfavorably with

**can·dy** (KAN-dee) *n.* (*pl.* -dies) crystallized sugar; confectionery in general —*v.* (-died, -dy·ing) preserve with sugar; become encrusted with sugar

**cane** (kayn) *n.* stem of small palm or large grass; walking stick —*vt.* (caned, can·ing) beat with cane

**ca·nine** (KAY-nīn) *adj.* like, pert. to, dog —**canine tooth** one of four sharp, pointed teeth, two in each jaw

**can·is·ter** (KAN-ə-stər) *n.* container, *oft.* of metal, for storing dry food

**can·ker** (KANG-kər) *n.* spreading sore; thing that eats away, destroys, corrupts —**canker sore** painful ulcer *esp.* in mouth

**can·na·bis** (KAN-ə-bis) *n.* hemp plant; drug derived from this; marijuana; hashish

**can·nel·lo·ni** (kan-l-OH-nee) *n.* tubular pieces of pasta filled with meat *etc.*

**can·ni·bal** (KAN-ə-bəl) *n.* one who eats human flesh —*adj.* relating

to this practice —**can·ni·bal·ism**
*n.* —**can·ni·bal·ize** *vt.* (-ized,
-iz·ing) use parts from one machine *etc.* to repair another

**can·non** (KAN-ən) *n.* (*pl.* -nons *or*
-non) large gun —**can·non·ball** *n.*

**can·not** (KAN-ot) *negative form*
*of* CAN[1]

**can·ny** (KAN-ee) *adj.* (-ni·er,
-ni·est) shrewd; cautious; crafty
—**can'ni·ly** *adv.*

**ca·noe** (kə-NOO) *n.* (*pl.* -noes)
very light boat propelled with
paddle or paddles —**ca·noe'ist** *n.*

**can·on**[1] (KAN-ən) *n.* law or rule,
*esp.* of church; standard; body of
books accepted as genuine; list of
saints —**can·on·i·za'tion** *n.*
—**can'on·ize** *vt.* (-ized, -iz·ing)
enroll in list of saints

**canon**[2] *n.* church dignitary, member of cathedral or collegiate
chapter or staff —**ca·non'i·cal**
*adj.* —**ca·non'i·cals** *n. pl.* canonical vestments

**can·o·py** (KAN-ə-pee) *n.* (*pl.*
-pies) covering over throne, bed
*etc.*; any overhanging shelter
—*vt.* (-pied, -py·ing) cover with
canopy

**cant**[1] (kant) *n.* hypocritical
speech; whining; language of a
sect; technical jargon; slang, *esp.*
of thieves

**cant**[2] *v.* (cant·ed, cant·ing) tilt,
slope; bevel

**can·ta·loupe** (KAN-tl-ohp) *n.* variety of muskmelon

**can·tan·ker·ous** (kan-TANG-kər-əs) *adj.* ill-natured, quarrelsome

**can·ta·ta** (kən-TAH-tə) *n.* choral
work like, but shorter than, oratorio

**can·teen** (kan-TEEN) *n.* flask for
carrying water; place in factory,
school *etc.* where light meals are
provided; post exchange

**can·ter** (KAN-tər) *n.* easy gallop
—*v.* move at, make to canter

**can·ti·le·ver** (KAN-tl-ee-vər) *n.* beam, girder *etc.*
fixed at one end only —*vi.* project like a cantilever —*vt.* build to
project in this manner

**can·to** (KAN-toh) *n.* (*pl.* -tos) division of a poem

**can·ton** (KAN-tn) *n.* division of
country, *esp.* Swiss federal state

**can·ton·ment** (kan-TON-mənt) *n.*
quarters for troops

**can·tor** (KAN-tər) *n.* chief singer
of liturgy in synagogue

**can·vas** (KAN-vəs) *n.* coarse cloth
used for sails, painting on *etc.*;
sails of ship; picture

**can·vass** (KAN-vəs) *vt.* solicit
votes, contributions *etc.*; discuss,
examine —*n.* solicitation

**can·yon** (KAN-yən) *n.* deep gorge

**cap** (kap) *n.* covering for head;
lid, top, or other covering —*vt.*
(capped, cap·ping) put a limit on;
outdo; seal (a well)

**ca·pa·ble** (KAY-pə-bəl) *adj.* able,
gifted; competent; having the capacity, power —**ca·pa·bil'i·ty** *n.*

**ca·pac·i·ty** (kə-PAS-i-tee) *n.* (*pl.*
-ties) power of holding or grasping; room; volume; character;
ability, power of mind —**ca·pa'cious** (-PAY-shəs) *adj.* roomy
—**ca·pac'i·tance** *n.* (measure of)
ability of system to store electric
charge —**ca·pac'i·tor** *n.*

**cape**[1] (kayp) *n.* covering for
shoulders

**cape**[2] *n.* point of land running into
sea, headland —**Cape Cod** common type of cottage in Mass. and
elsewhere in Northeast

**ca·per**[1] (KAY-pər) *n.* skip; frolic;
escapade —*vi.* skip, dance

**caper**[2] *n.* pickled flower bud of
Sicilian shrub

**cap·il·lar·y** (KAP-ə-ler-ee) *adj.*
hairlike —*n.* (*pl.* -lar·ies) tube
with very small bore, *esp.* small
blood vessel

**cap·i·tal** (KAP-i-tl) *n.* chief town;

money, stock, funds; large-sized letter; headpiece of column —*adj.* involving or punishable by death; serious; chief; leading; excellent —**cap'i·tal·ism** *n.* economic system based on private ownership of industry —**cap'i·tal·ist** *n.* owner of capital; supporter of capitalism —*adj.* run by, possessing, capital, as capitalist state —**cap'i·tal·ize** *v.* (-ized, -iz·ing) convert into capital; (*with* on) turn to advantage

**Cap·i·tol** (KAP-i-tl) *n.* building in which US Congress meets; (c-) a state legislature building

**ca·pit·u·late** (kə-PICH-ə-layt) *vi.* (-lat·ed, -lat·ing) surrender on terms, give in —**ca·pit·u·la'tion** *n.*

**ca·pon** (KAY-pon) *n.* castrated male fowl fattened for eating —**ca'pon·ize** *vt.* (-ized, -iz·ing)

**cap·puc·ci·no** (kap-ə-CHEE-noh) *n.* espresso coffee with steamed milk

**ca·price** (kə-PREES) *n.* whim, freak —**ca·pri'cious** (-PRISH-əs) *adj.* —**ca·pri'cious·ness** *n.*

**cap·size** (KAP-siz) *v.* (-sized, -siz·ing) —*vt.* (of boat) upset —*vi.* be overturned

**cap·stan** (KAP-stən) *n.* machine to wind cable, *esp.* to hoist anchor

**cap·sule** (KAP-səl) *n.* gelatin case for dose of medicine or drug; any small enclosed area or container; seed vessel of plant —**cap'sul·ize** *vt.* (-ized, -iz·ing) enclose in a capsule; put (news or information) in concise form

**cap·tain** (KAP-tən) *n.* commander of ship or company of soldiers; leader, chief —*vt.* be captain of

**cap·tion** (KAP-shən) *n.* heading, title of article, picture *etc.*

**cap·tious** (KAP-shəs) *adj.* ready to find fault; critical; peevish —**cap'tious·ness** *n.*

**cap·tive** (KAP-tiv) *n.* prisoner —*adj.* taken, imprisoned —**cap'ti·vate** *vt.* (-vat·ed, -vat·ing) fascinate —**cap'ti·vat·ing** *adj.* delightful —**cap·tiv'i·ty** *n.*

**cap·ture** (KAP-chər) *vt.* (-tured, -tur·ing) seize, make prisoner —*n.* seizure, taking —**cap'tor** *n.*

**car** (kahr) *n.* automobile; passenger compartment, as in cable car; vehicle running on rails —**car park** area, building where vehicles may be left for a time

**ca·rafe** (kə-RAF) *n.* glass water bottle for the table, decanter

**car·a·mel** (KAR-ə-məl) *n.* burned sugar or syrup for sweetening; type of confectionery —**car'a·mel·ize** *v.* (-ized, -iz·ing) change (sugar *etc.*) into caramel; become caramel

**car·at** (KAR-ət) *n.* small weight used for gold, diamonds *etc.*; proportional measure of twenty-fourths used to state fineness of gold

**car·a·van** (KAR-ə-van) *n.* company of merchants traveling together for safety in the East

**car·a·way** (KAR-ə-way) *n.* plant whose seeds are used as a spice in bread *etc.*

**car·bide** (KAHR-bid) *n.* compound of carbon with an element, *esp.* calcium carbide

**car·bine** (KAHR-been) *n.* light rifle

**car·bo·hy·drate** (kahr-boh-HĪ-drayt) *n.* any of large group of compounds containing carbon, hydrogen and oxygen, *esp.* sugars and starches as components of food

**car·bol·ic ac·id** (kahr-BOL-ik) disinfectant derived from coal tar

**car·bon** (KAHR-bən) *n.* nonmetallic element, substance of pure charcoal, found in all organic matter —**car'bon·ate** n. salt of carbonic acid —**car·bon'ic** adj. —**car'bon·ize** vt. (-ized, -iz·ing) —**carbonic acid carbon dioxide;** compound formed by carbon dioxide and water —**carbon dioxide** colorless gas exhaled in respiration of animals —**carbon paper** paper coated with a dark, waxy pigment, used for duplicating written or typed matter, producing **carbon copy**

**car·bo·run·dum** (kahr-bə-RUN-dəm) n. artificial silicate of carbon

**car·bun·cle** (KAHR-bung-kəl) n. inflamed ulcer, boil or tumor

**car·bu·re·tor** (KAHR-bə-ray-tər) n. device for vaporizing and mixing gasoline with air in internal combustion engine

**car·cass** (KAHR-kəs) n. dead animal body; orig. skeleton

**car·cin·o·gen** (kahr-SIN-ə-jən) n. substance producing cancer

**car·ci·no·ma** (kahr-sə-NOH-mə) n. (pl. -mas) a cancer

**card** (kahrd) n. thick, stiff paper; piece of this giving identification etc.; greeting card; one of the 48 or 52 playing cards making up a pack; inf. a character, eccentric —pl. any card game —**card'-board** n. thin, stiff board made of paper pulp

**card** [2] n. instrument for combing wool etc. —vt. comb —**card'er** n.

**car·di·ac** (KAHR·dee·ak) adj. pert. to the heart —n. person with heart disease —**car'di·o·graph** (-ə-graf) n. instrument that records movements of the heart —**car'di·o·gram** n. graph of such

**car·di·gan** (KAHR·di·gən) n. knitted sweater opening in front

**car·di·nal** (KAHR·dn·l) adj. chief, principal —n. highest rank; next

to the Pope in Cath. church; N Amer. finch, male of which is bright red in summer —**cardinal numbers** 1, 2, 3, etc. —**cardinal points** N, S, E, W

**care** (kair) vi. (cared, car·ing) be anxious; have regard or liking (for); look after; be disposed to —n. attention; pains; heed; charge, protection; anxiety; caution —**care'free** adj. —**care'ful** adj. —**care'less** adj. —**care'tak·er** n. person in charge of premises —adj. temporary, interim

**ca·reen** (kə-REEN) vt. cause ship to list; lay ship over on its side for cleaning and repair —vi. keel over; sway dangerously

**ca·reer** (kə-REER) n. course through life; profession; rapid motion —vi. run or move at full speed

**ca·ress** (kə-RES) vt. fondle, embrace, treat with affection —n. act or expression of affection

**car·et** (KAR·it) n. mark (∧) showing where to insert something omitted

**car·go** (KAHR·goh) n. (pl. -goes) load, freight, carried by ship, plane etc.

**car·i·bou** (KAR·ə·boo) n. N Amer. reindeer

**car·i·ca·ture** (KAR·i·kə·chər) n. likeness exaggerated or distorted to appear ridiculous —vt. (-tured, -tur·ing) portray in this way —**car'i·ca·tur·ist** n.

**car·ies** (KAIR·eez) n. (pl. same form) decay of tooth or bone

**car·il·lon** (KAR·ə·lon) n. set of bells usu. hung in tower and played by set of keys, pedals etc.; tune so played

**car·min·a·tive** (kahr·MIN·ə·tiv) n. medicine to remedy flatulence —adj. acting as this

**car·mine** (KAHR·min) n. brilliant

red color (prepared from cochineal) —*adj.* of this color

**car·nage** (KAHR-nij) *n.* slaughter

**car·nal** (KAHR-nl) *adj.* fleshly, sensual; worldly

**car·na·tion** (kahr-NAY-shən) *n.* cultivated flower; flesh color

**car·ni·val** (KAHR-nə-vəl) *n.* festive occasion; traveling fair; show or display for amusement

**car·niv·o·rous** (kahr-NIV-ər-əs) *adj.* flesh-eating —**car'ni·vore** (-nə-vor) *n.*

**car·ob** (KAR-əb) *n.* Mediterranean tree with edible pods

**car·ol** (KAR-əl) *n.* song or hymn of joy or praise (*esp.* Christmas carol) —*vi.* (-oled, -ol·ing) sing (carols)

**car·om** (KAR-əm) *n.* billiard stroke, hitting both object balls with one's own —*vi.* make this stroke; rebound, collide

**ca·rouse** (kə-ROWZ) *vi.* (-roused, -rous·ing) have merry drinking spree —*n.* —**ca·rous'er** *n.*

**car·ou·sel** (kar-ə-SEL) *n.* merry-go-round

**carp**[1] (kahrp) *n.* freshwater fish

**carp**[2] *vi.* complain about small faults or errors; nag —**carp'er** *n.* —**carp'ing** *adj.*

**car·pen·ter** (KAHR-pən-tər) *n.* worker in timber as in building *etc.* —**car'pen·try** (*pr.* -tree) *n.* this art

**car·pet** (KAHR-pit) *n.* heavy fabric for covering floor —*vt.* cover floor —**car'pet·bag** *n.* traveling bag —**car'pet·bag·ger** *n.* political adventurer —**on the carpet** called up for censure

**car·riage** (KA-rij) *n.* bearing, conduct; horse-drawn vehicle; act, cost, of carrying

**car·ri·on** (KA-ree-ən) *n.* rotting dead flesh

**car·rot** (KA-rət) *n.* plant with orange-red edible root; inducement —**car'rot-top** *n.* person with red hair

**car·ry** (KA-ree) *v.* (-ried, -ry·ing) —*vt.* convey, transport; capture, win; effect; behave —*vi.* (of projectile, sound) reach —*n.* range —**car'ri·er** *n.* one that carries goods; immune person who communicates a disease to others; aircraft carrier; kind of pigeon —**carry on** continue; *inf.* fuss unnecessarily

**cart** (kahrt) *n.* open (two-wheeled) vehicle, *esp.* pulled by horse —*vt.* convey in cart; carry with effort —**cart'er** *n.* —**cart'-horse** *n.* —**cart'wheel** *n.* large, spoked wheel; sideways somersault —**cart'wright** *n.* maker of carts

**carte blanche** (kahrt blanch) *n.* (*pl.* **cartes blanches** *pr.* kahrts blanch) complete discretion or authority

**car·tel** (kahr-TEL) *n.* commercial combination for the purpose of fixing output, prices *etc.*; alliance of political parties *etc.* to further common aims

**Car·te·sian** (kahr-TEE-zhən) *adj.* pert. to the French philosopher René Descartes (1596-1650) or his system of coordinates —*n.* an adherent of his philosophy

**car·ti·lage** (KAHR-tl-ij) *n.* firm elastic tissue in the body; gristle —**car·ti·lag'i·nous** *adj.*

**car·tog·ra·phy** (kahr-TOG-rə-fee) *n.* map making —**car·tog'ra·pher** *n.*

**car·ton** (KAHR-tn) *n.* cardboard or plastic container

**car·toon** (kahr-TOON) *n.* drawing, *esp.* humorous or satirical; sequence of drawings telling story; animated cartoon

**car·tridge** (KAHR-trij) *n.* case containing charge for gun; container for film, magnetic tape *etc.*; unit in head of phonograph pickup

**carve** (kahrv) *vt.* (**carved, carving**) cut; hew; sculpture; engrave; cut in pieces or slices (meat) —**carv'er** *n.*

**car·y·at·id** (kar-ee-AT-id) *n.* supporting column in shape of female figure

**cas·cade** (kas-KAYD) *n.* waterfall; anything resembling this —*vi.* (**-cad·ed, -cad·ing**) fall in cascades

**case**[1] (kays) *n.* instance; event, circumstance; question at issue; state of affairs, condition; arguments supporting particular action *etc.*; *Med.* patient under treatment; law suit; grounds for suit; grammatical relation of words in sentence

**case**[2] *n.* box, sheath, covering; receptacle; box and contents —*vt.* (**cased, cas·ing**) put in a case —**case'hard·en** *vt.* harden by carbonizing the surface of (*esp.* iron) by converting into steel; make hard, callous

**ca·se·in** (KAY-seen) *n.* protein in milk and its products —**ca'se·ous** (-see-əs) *adj.* like cheese

**case·ment** (KAYS-mənt) *n.* window opening on hinges

**cash** (kash) *n.* money, bills and coin —*vt.* turn into or exchange for money —**cash·ier** (ka-SHEER) *n.* one in charge of receiving and paying of money —**cash dispenser** computerized device outside a bank for supplying cash —**cash register** till that records amount of money put in

**cash·ier** (ka-SHEER) *vt.* dismiss from office or service

**cash·mere** (KAZH-meer) *n.* fine soft fabric; yarn made from goat's wool

**ca·si·no** (kə-SEE-noh) *n.* (*pl.* **-nos**) building, institution for gambling; type of card game

**cask** (kask) *n.* barrel; container for wine

**cas·ket** (KAS-kit) *n.* small case for jewels *etc.*; coffin

**Cas·san·dra** (kə-SAN-drə) *n.* prophet of misfortune or disaster

**cas·se·role** (KAS-ə-rohl) *n.* fireproof cooking and serving dish; food cooked in this

**cas·sette** (kə-SET) *n.* plastic container for film, magnetic tape *etc.*

**cas·sock** (KAS-ək) *n.* long tunic worn by clergymen

**cast** (kast) *v.* throw or fling; shed; throw down; deposit (a vote); allot, as parts in play; mold, as metal —*n.* throw; distance thrown; squint; mold; that which is shed or ejected; set of actors; type or quality —**cast'ing** *n.* —**cast'a·way** *n.* shipwrecked person

**cas·ta·nets** (kas-tə-NETS) *n. pl.* (in Spanish dancing) two small curved pieces of wood *etc.* clicked together in hand

**caste** (kast) *n.* section of society in India; social rank

**cast·er** (KAS-tər) *n.* container for salt *etc.* with perforated top; small swiveled wheel on table leg *etc.*

**cas·ti·gate** (KAS-ti-gayt) *vt.* (**-gat·ed, -gat·ing**) punish, rebuke severely, correct; chastise —**cas'ti·ga·tor** *n.*

**cas·tle** (KAS-əl) *n.* fortress; mansion; chess piece —**castle in the air** pipe dream

**cas·tor oil** (KAS-tər) vegetable medicinal oil

**cas·trate** (KAS-trayt) *vt.* (**-trat·ed, -trat·ing**) remove testicles, deprive of power of generation; deprive of vigor —**cas·tra'tion** *n.*

**cas·tra·to** (ka-STRAH-toh) n. (pl. -ti pr. -tee) singer castrated in boyhood to preserve soprano or alto voice

**cas·u·al** (KAZH-oo-ɔl) adj. accidental; unforeseen; occasional; unconcerned; informal —**cas'ual·ty** n. (pl. -ties) person killed or injured in accident, war etc.; thing lost, destroyed, in accident etc.

**cas·u·ist** (KAZH-oo-ist) n. one who studies and solves moral problems; quibbler —**cas'u·ist·ry** n.

**cat** (kat) n. any of various feline animals, including, eg small domesticated furred animal, and lions, tigers etc. —**cat'ty** (-ti·er, -ti·est) adj. spiteful —**cat'call** n. derisive cry —**cat'fish** n. mainly freshwater fish with catlike whiskers —**cat'kin** n. drooping flower spike —**cat'nap** vi./n. doze —**cat's'·eye** n. (pl. -eyes) glass reflector set in road to reflect beams from automobile headlights —**cat'walk** n. narrow, raised path or plank

**ca·tab·o·lism** (kɔ-TAB-ɔ-liz-ɔm) n. breaking down of complex molecules, destructive metabolism

**cat·a·clysm** (KAT-ɔ-kliz-ɔm) n. (disastrous) upheaval; deluge —**cat·a·clys'mic** adj.

**cat·a·comb** (KAT-ɔ-kohm) n. underground gallery for burial —pl. series of underground tunnels and caves

**cat·a·lep·sy** (KAT-l-ep-see) n. condition of unconsciousness with rigidity of muscles —**cat·a·lep'tic** adj.

**cat·a·log** (KAT-l-awg) n. descriptive list —vt. make such list of; enter in catalog

**cat·a·lyst** (KAT-l-ist) n. substance causing or assisting a chemical reaction without taking part in it; person or thing that precipitates event or change —**cat'a·lyze** vt. (-lyzed, -lyz·ing) —**ca·tal'y·sis** n. —**cat·a·lyt'ic** adj. —catalytic converter type of antipollution device for automotive exhaust system

**cat·a·ma·ran** (kat-ɔ-mɔ-RAN) n. type of sailing boat with twin hulls; raft of logs

**cat·a·pult** (KAT-ɔ-pult) n. small forked stick with elastic sling used for throwing stones; Hist. engine of war for hurling arrows, stones etc.; launching device —vt.

**cat·a·ract** (KAT-ɔ-rakt) n. waterfall; downpour; disease of eye

**ca·tas·tro·phe** (kɔ-TAS-trɔ-fee) n. great disaster, calamity; culmination of a tragedy —**cat·a·stroph'ic** adj.

**catch** (kach) v. (caught, catching) —vt. take hold of, seize, understand; hear; contract (disease); be in time for; surprise, detect —vi. be contagious; get entangled; begin to burn —n. seizure; thing that holds, stops etc.; what is caught; inf. snag, disadvantage; form of musical composition; thing, person worth catching, esp. as spouse —**catch'er** n. —**catching** adj. —**catch'y** adj. (catch·i·er, catch·i·est) pleasant, memorable; tricky —**catch'word** n. popular phrase or idea —**catch 22** inescapable dilemma —**catch·ment** area drainage basin, area in which rainfall collects to form the supply of river etc.; area from which people are allocated to a particular social service agency, hospital etc. —**catch-as-catch-can** adj. using any method that can be applied

**cat·e·chize** (KAT-i-kīz) vt.

(-chized, -chiz·ing) instruct by question and answer; question —**cat'e·chism** n. such instruction —**cat'e·chist** n. —**cat·e·chu'men** (-KYOO-mən) n. one under instruction in Christianity

**cat·e·go·ry** (KAT-i-gohr-ee) n. (pl. -ries) class, order, division —**cat·e·gor'i·cal** adj. positive; of category —**cat·e·gor'i·cal·ly** adv. —**cat'e·go·rize** vt. (-ized, -iz·ing)

**ca·ter** (KAY-tər) vi. provide what is required or desired, esp. food etc. —**ca'ter·er** n.

**cat·er·pil·lar** (KAT-ə-pil-ər) n. hairy grub of moth or butterfly

**cat·er·waul** (KAT-ər-wawl) vi. wail, howl; argue noisily

**ca·the·dral** (kə-THEE-drəl) n. principal church of diocese —adj. pert. to, containing cathedral

**cath·ode** (KATH-ohd) n. negative electrode —**cathode rays** stream of electrons

**cath·o·lic** (KATH-lik) adj. universal; including whole body of Christians; (C-) relating to Catholic Church —n. (C-) adherent of Catholic Church —**Ca·thol·i·cism** (kə-THOL-ə-siz-əm) n. —**cath·o·lic·i·ty** (kath-ə-LIS-i-tee) n.

**CAT scan** (kat skan) computerized axial tomography (also CT scan)

**cat·tle** (KAT-l) n. pl. beasts of pasture, esp. steers, cows —**cat'tle·man** n. —**cattle guard** heavy grid over ditch in road to prevent passage of livestock

**Cau·ca·sian** (kaw-KAY-zhən) adj./n. (of, pert. to) light-complexioned racial group of mankind —**Cau'ca·soid** (-kə-soid) adj./n.

**cau·cus** (KAW-kəs) n. group, meeting, esp. of members of political party, with power to decide policy etc.

**caught** pt./pp. of CATCH

**caul·dron** (KAWL-drən) large pot used for boiling

**cau·li·flow·er** (KAW-li-flow-ər) n. variety of cabbage with edible white flowering head

**caulk** (kawk) vt. stop up cracks (orig. of ship) with waterproof filler —**caulk'er** n. —**caulk'ing** n. —**caulking compound** filler used in caulking

**cause** (kawz) n. that which produces an effect; reason, origin; motive, purpose; charity, movement; lawsuit —vt. (caused, caus·ing) bring about, make happen —**caus'al** adj. —**cau·sal'i·ty** n. —**cau·sa'tion** n. —**cause'less** adj. groundless

**cause cé·lè·bre** (kawz sə-LEB-rə) n. (pl. **causes cé·lè·bres** pr. kawz sə-LEB-rəz) great controversy eg famous legal case

**cause·way** (KAWZ-way) n. raised way over marsh etc.; highway

**caus·tic** (KAW-stik) adj. burning; bitter, severe —n. corrosive substance —**caus'ti·cal·ly** adv.

**cau·ter·ize** (KAW-tə-rīz) vt. (-ized, -iz·ing) burn with caustic or hot iron —**cau·ter·i·za'tion** n.

**cau·tion** (KAW-shən) n. heedfulness, care; warning —vt. warn —**cau'tion·ar·y** adj. containing warning or precept —**cau'tious** adj.

**cav·al·cade** (KAV-əl-kayd) n. column or procession of riders; series

**cav·a·lier** (kav-ə-LEER) adj. careless, disdainful —n. courtly gentleman; obs. horseman

**cav·al·ry** (KAV-əl-ree) n. (pl. -ries) mounted troops

**cave** (kayv) n. hollow place in the earth; den —**cav·ern** (KAV-ərn) n. deep cave —**cav'ern·ous** adj. —**cav'i·ty** n. (pl. -ties) hollow —**cave'man** n. prehistoric cave dweller —**cave in** fall inward; submit; give in

**cav·i·ar** (KAV-ee-ahr) *n.* salted sturgeon roe

**cav·il** (KAV-əl) *vi.* (-iled, -il·ing) find fault without sufficient reason, make trifling objections —**cav'il·ing** *n.* —**cav'il·er** *n.*

**cav·i·ta·tion** (kav-i-TAY-shən) *n.* rapid formation of cavities or bubbles —**cav'i·tate** *vi.* (-tat·ed, -tat·ing) undergo cavitation

**ca·vort** (kə-VORT) *vi.* prance, frisk

**caw** (kaw) *n.* crow's cry —*vi.* cry so

**cay·enne pepper** (kī-EN) *n.* pungent red pepper

**Cd** *Chem.* cadmium

**CD** certificate of deposit; compact disk —**CD-ROM** compact disk storing digitized read-only data

**cease** (sees) *v.* (ceased, ceas·ing) bring or come to an end —**cease'less** *adj.*

**ce·dar** (SEE-dər) *n.* large evergreen tree; its wood

**cede** (seed) *vt.* (ced·ed, ced·ing) yield, give up, transfer, *esp.* of territory

**ce·dil·la** (si-DIL-ə) *n.* hooklike mark placed under a letter *c* to show the sound of *s*

**ceil·ing** (SEE-ling) *n.* inner, upper surface of a room; maximum price, wage *etc.*; *Aviation* lower level of clouds; limit of height to which aircraft can climb

**cel·e·brate** (SEL-ə-brayt) *v.* (-brat·ed, -brat·ing) rejoice or have festivities to mark (happy day, event *etc.*) —*vt.* observe (birthday *etc.*); perform (religious ceremony *etc.*); praise publicly —**cel'e·brant** *n.* —**celebrat·ed** *adj.* famous —**cel·e·bra'tion** *n.* —**ce·leb'ri·ty** *n.* (*pl.* -ties) famous person; fame

**ce·ler·i·ty** (sə-LER-i-tee) *n.* swiftness

**cel·er·y** (SEL-ə-ree) *n.* vegetable with long juicy edible stalks

**ce·les·tial** (sə-LES-chəl) *adj.* heavenly, divine; of the sky

**cel·i·ba·cy** (SEL-ə-bə-see) *n.* single life, unmarried state —**cel'i·bate** (-bit) *n./adj.*

**cell** (sel) *n.* small room, *esp.* in prison; small cavity; minute, basic unit of living matter; device converting chemical energy into electrical energy; small local group operating as nucleus of larger political or religious organization —**cel·lu·lar** (SEL-yə-lər) *adj.*

**cel·lar** (SEL-ər) *n.* underground room or story; stock of wine; wine cellar

**cel·lo** (CHEL-oh) *n.* (*pl.* -los) stringed instrument of violin family

**cel·lo·phane** (SEL-ə-fayn) *n.* transparent wrapping

**cel·lu·loid** (SEL-yə-loid) *n.* synthetic plastic substance with wide range of uses; motionpicture film

**cel·lu·lose** (SEL-yə-lohs) *n.* substance of vegetable cell wall; group of carbohydrates

**Cel·si·us** (SEL-see-əs) *adj./n.* (of) scale of temperature from 0° (melting point of ice) to 100° (boiling point of water)

**Celt·ic** (KEL-tik *or* SEL-) *n.* branch of language including Gaelic and Welsh —*adj.* of, or relating to the Celtic peoples or languages

**ce·ment** (si-MENT) *n.* fine mortar; adhesive, glue —*vt.* unite with cement; join firmly

**cem·e·ter·y** (SEM-i-ter-ee) *n.* (*pl.* -ter·ies) burial ground

**cen·o·taph** (SEN-ə-taf) *n.* monument to one buried elsewhere

**cen·ser** (SEN-sər) *n.* pan in which incense is burned

**cen·sor** (SEN-sər) *n.* one authorized to examine films, books *etc.* and suppress all or part if considered morally or otherwise unacceptable —*vt.* —**cen·so·ri·al** (sen-SOHR-ee-əl) *adj.* of censor —**cen·so'ri·ous** *adj.* faultfinding —**cen'sor·ship** *n.*

**cen·sure** (SEN-shər) *n.* blame; harsh criticism —*vt.* (-sured, -sur·ing) blame; criticize harshly

**cen·sus** (SEN-səs) *n.* (*pl.* -sus·es) official counting of people, things *etc.*

**cent** (sent) *n.* hundredth part of dollar *etc.*

**cen·taur** (SEN-tor) *n.* mythical creature, half man, half horse

**cen·te·nar·y** (sen-TEN-ə-ree) *n./adj.* centennial —**cen·te·nar·i·an** (sen-tn-AIR-ee-ən) *n.* person a hundred years old

**cen·ten·ni·al** (sen-TEN-ee-əl) *adj.* lasting, happening every hundred years —*n.* 100 years; celebration of hundredth anniversary

**cen·ter** (SEN-tər) *n.* midpoint; pivot, axis; point to or from which things move or are drawn; place for specific organization or activity —**cen'tral** (-trəl) *adj.* —**central·i·ty** *n.* —**cen'tral·ize** *vt.* (-ized, -iz·ing) bring to a center; concentrate under one control —**cen'tral·ly** *adv.* —**cen·trif'u·gal** (-TRIF-yə-gəl) *adj.* tending away from center —**cen·trip'e·tal** (-TRIP-i-tl) *adj.* tending toward center —**central heating** method of heating building from one central source —**central processing unit** Computers part of a computer that performs logical and arithmetical operations

**cen·ti·grade** (SEN-ti-grayd) *adj.*

another name for Celsius; having one hundred degrees

**cen·ti·me·ter** (SEN-tə-mee-tər) *n.* hundredth part of meter

**cen·ti·pede** (SEN-tə-peed) *n.* small segmented animal with many legs

**cen·tu·ry** (SEN-chə-ree) *n.* (*pl.* -ries) 100 years; any set of 100

**ce·ram·ic** (sə-RAM-ik) *n.* hard brittle material of baked clay; object made of this —*adj.* —**ce·ram'ics** (*with sing. v.*) art, techniques of making ceramic objects; such objects

**ce·re·al** (SEER-ee-əl) *n.* any edible grain, *eg* wheat, rice *etc.*; (breakfast) food made from grain —*adj.*

**ce·re·bral** (sə-REE-brəl) *adj.* pert. to brain or intellect

**cer·e·mo·ny** (SER-ə-moh-nee) *n.* (*pl.* -nies) formal observance; sacred rite; courteous act —**cer·e·mo'ni·al** *adj./n.* —**cer·e·mo'ni·ous** *adj.*

**ce·rise** (sə-REES) *n./adj.* clear, pinkish red

**cer·tain** (SUR-tn) *adj.* sure; settled, inevitable; some, one; of moderate (quantity, degree *etc.*) —**cer'tain·ly** *adv.* —**cer'tain·ty** *n.* (*pl.* -ties) —**cer'ti·tude** *n.* confidence

**cer·ti·fy** (SUR-tə-fī) *vt.* (-fied, -fy·ing) declare formally; endorse, guarantee; declare legally insane —**cer·tif'i·cate** (-kit) *n.* written declaration —*vt.* (-kayt) (-cat·ed, -cat·ing) give written declaration —**cer·ti·fi·ca'tion** *n.*

**ce·ru·le·an** (sə-ROO-lee-ən) *adj.* sky blue; deep blue

**cer·vix** (SUR-viks) *n.* (*pl.* -vix·es) neck, *esp.* of womb —**cer'vi·cal** *adj.*

**ces·sa·tion** (se-SAY-shən) *n.* ceasing or stopping, pause

**ces·sion** (SESH-ən) *n.* yielding up

**cess·pit** (SES-pit) *n.* pit for receiving sewage or other refuse

**cess·pool** (SES-pool) *n.* catch basin in which sewage collects; filthy place; place of moral filth

**Cf** *Chem.* californium

**cf.** *confer* (Lat.) compare

**cgs units** metric system of units based on *centimeter, gram, second*

**chafe** (chayf) *vt.* (**chafed, chafing**) make sore or worn by rubbing; make warm by rubbing; vex, irritate

**chaff** *n.* husks of corn; worthless matter; banter —*v.* tease good-naturedly

**cha·grin** (shə-GRIN) *n.* vexation, disappointment —*vt.* embarrass; annoy; disappoint

**chain** (chayn) *n.* series of connected links or rings; thing that binds; connected series of things or events; surveyor's measure Makes compound nouns as chain gang, chain reaction, chain smoker, chain stitch, chain store *etc.* —*vt.* fasten with a chain; confine; restrain

**chair** *n.* movable seat, with back, for one person; seat of authority; professorship —*vt.* preside over; carry in triumph —**chair'lift** *n.* series of chairs fixed to cable for conveying people (*esp.* skiers) up mountain —**chair'per·son, -wom·an, -man** *n.* one who presides over meeting —**chair'man·ship** *n.*

**chaise** (shayz) *n.* light horse-drawn carriage —**chaise longue** (lawng) sofa

**chal·ced·o·ny** (kal-SED-n-ee) *n.* whitish, bluish-white variety of quartz

**cha·let** (sha-LAY) *n.* Swiss wooden house; house in this style

**chal·ice** (CHAL-is) *n. Poet.* cup or bowl; communion cup

**chalk** (chawk) *n.* white substance, carbonate of lime; crayon —*v.* rub, draw, mark with chalk —**chalk'y** *adj.* (**chalk·i·er, chalk·i·est**)

**chal·lenge** (CHAL-inj) *vt.* (**-lenged, -leng·ing**) call to fight or account; dispute; stimulate; object to; claim —*n.* —**chal'leng·er** *n.* —**chal'leng·ing** *adj.* difficult but stimulating

**cham·ber** (CHAYM-bər) *n.* room for assembly; assembly, body of legislators; compartment; cavity; *obs.* room —*pl.* office of lawyer or judge; lodgings —**cham'ber·lain** (-lin) *n.* official at court of a monarch having charge of domestic and ceremonial affairs —**cham'ber·maid** *n.* female servant with care of bedrooms —**chamber music** music for performance by a few instruments —**chamber (pot)** vessel for urine

**cha·me·le·on** (kə-MEEL-yən) *n.* small lizard famous for its power of changing color

**cham·fer** (CHAM-fər) *vt.* groove; bevel; flute —*n.* groove

**cham·ois** (SHAM-ee) *n.* goatlike mountain antelope; a soft pliable leather

**champ**[1] *v.* munch forcibly, noisily, as horse; be nervous, impatient

**champ**[2] *n. short for* CHAMPION

**cham·pagne** (sham-PAYN) *n.* light, sparkling white wine of several varieties

**cham·pi·on** (CHAM-pee-ən) *n.* one that excels all others; defender of a cause; one who fights for another; hero —*vt.* fight for, maintain —**cham'pi·on·ship** *n.*

**chance** (chans) *n.* unpredictable course of events; fortune, luck; opportunity; possibility; risk; probability —*v.* (**chanced, chancing**) —*vt.* risk —*vi.* happen —*adj.* casual, unexpected —**chanc'y**

*adj.* (**chanc·i·er, chanc·i·est**) risky

**chan·cel** (CHAN-səl) *n.* part of a church where altar is

**chan·cel·lor** (CHAN-sə-lər) *n.* high officer of state; head of university, state educational system

**chan·cer·y** (CHAN-sə-ree) *n.* (*pl.* -ies) court of equity

**chan·de·lier** (shan-dl-EER) *n.* hanging frame with branches for holding lights

**change** (chaynj) *v.* (**changed, chang·ing**) alter, make or become different; put on (different clothes, fresh coverings) —*v.t.* put or give for another; exchange, interchange —*n.* alteration, variation; variety; conversion of money; small money, coins; balance received on payment —**change'a·ble** *adj.* —**change'less** *adj.* —**change'ling** *n.* child exchanged for another

**chan·nel** (CHAN-l) *n.* bed of stream; strait; deeper part of strait, bay, harbor; groove; means of passing or conveying; band of radio frequencies; TV broadcasting station —*v.t.* groove, furrow; guide, convey

**chant** *n.* simple song or melody; rhythmic or repetitious slogan —*v.* sing or utter chant; speak monotonously or repetitiously

**chan·tey** (SHAN-tee) *n.* sailor's song with chorus

**chan·ti·cleer** (CHAN-tə-kleer) *n.* rooster

**cha·os** (KAY-os) *n.* disorder, confusion; state of universe before Creation —**chaot'ic** *adj.* —**cha·ot'i·cal·ly** *adv.*

**chap**[1] *v.* (**chapped, chap·ping**) of skin, become dry, raw and cracked, *esp.* by exposure to cold and wind —**chapped** *adj.*

**chap**[2] *n. inf.* fellow, man

**chap·el** (CHAP-əl) *n.* private church; subordinate place of worship; division of church with its own altar; place of worship used by a nonconforming Christian group; print shop

**chap·er·on(e)** (SHAP-ə-rohn) *n.* one who attends young unmarried woman in public as protector —*v.t.* (-**oned, -on·ing**) attend in this way

**chap·lain** (CHAP-lin) *n.* clergyman attached to chapel, regiment, warship, institution *etc.* —**chap'lain·cy** *n.* office or term of chaplain

**chaps** *n. pl.* cowboy's leggings of thick leather

**chap·ter** (CHAP-tər) *n.* division of book; section, heading; assembly of clergy, bishop's council *etc.*; organized branch of society, fraternity

**char** (chahr) *v.t.* (**charred, char·ring**) scorch, burn to charcoal —**charred** *adj.*

**char·ac·ter** (KAR-ik-tər) *n.* nature; total of qualities making up individuality; moral qualities; reputation of possessing them; statement of qualities of person; an eccentric; personality in play or novel; letter, sign, or any distinctive mark; essential feature —**char·ac·ter·is'tic** *adj./n.* —**char·ac·ter·is'ti·cal·ly** *adv.* —**char'ac·ter·ize** *vt.* (-**ized, -iz·ing**) mark out, distinguish; describe by peculiar qualities

**char·ade** (shə-RAYD) *n.* absurd act; travesty —*pl.* word-guessing parlor game with syllables of word acted

**char·coal** (CHAHR-kohl) *n.* black residue of wood, bones *etc.*, produced by smothered burning; charred wood

**charge** (chahrj) *v.* (**charged, charg·ing**) —*v.t.* ask as price;

bring accusation against; lay task on; command; attack; deliver injunction; fill with electricity; fill, load —vi. make onrush, attack —n. cost, price; accusation; attack, onrush; command; exhortation; accumulation of electricity —pl. expenses —**charge'a·ble** adj. —**charg'er** n. strong, fast battle horse; that which charges, esp. electrically

**char·i·ot** (CHAR-ee-ət) n. two-wheeled vehicle used in ancient fighting —**char·i·ot·eer'** n.

**cha·ris·ma** (kə·RIZ-mə) n. special power of person to inspire fascination, loyalty etc. —**char·is·mat·ic** (kar-iz-MAT-ik) adj.

**char·i·ty** (CHAR-i-tee) n. (pl. -ties) the giving of help, money etc. to those in need; organization for doing this; the money etc. given; love, kindness; disposition to think kindly of others —**char'i·ta·ble** adj.

**char·la·tan** (SHAHR-lə-tn) n. quack, impostor

**charm** (chahrm) n. attractiveness; anything that fascinates; amulet; magic spell —vt. bewitch; delight, attract —**charmed** adj. —**charm'ing** adj.

**char·nel house** (CHAHR-nl) n. vault for bones of the dead

**chart** (chahrt) n. map of sea; diagram or tabulated statement —vt. map; represent on chart

**char·ter** (CHAHR-tər) n. document granting privileges etc.; —vt. let or hire; establish by charter

**char·wom·an** (CHAHR-wuum-ən) n. woman paid to clean office, house etc.

**char·y** (CHAIR-ee) adj. (char·i·er, char·i·est) cautious, sparing —**char'i·ly** adv. —**char'i·ness** n. caution

**chase**[1] (chays) vt. (chased, chas-ing) hunt, pursue; drive from, away, into etc. —n. pursuit, hunting; the hunted; hunting ground —**chas'er** n. drink of beer, soda etc., taken after straight whiskey

**chase**[2] vt. (chased, chas·ing) ornament, engrave (metal) —**chas'er** n. —**chas'ing** n.

**chasm** (KAZ-əm) n. deep cleft, fissure; abyss

**chas·sis** (CHAS-ee) n. (pl. same form pr. -eez) frame, wheels and machinery of motor vehicle on which body is supported

**chaste** (chayst) adj. virginal; pure; modest; virtuous —**chas·ti·ty** (CHAS-ti-tee) n.

**chas·ten** (CHAY-sən) vt. correct by punishment; restrain, subdue —**chas'tened** adj. —**chas·tise** (chas-TIZ) vt. (-tised, -tis·ing) inflict punishment on

**chas·u·ble** (CHAZ-yə-bəl) n. priest's long sleeveless outer vestment

**chat** vi. (chat·ted, chat·ting) talk idly, or familiarly —n. familiar idle talk

**châ·teau** (shat-TOH) n. (pl. -teaus or -teaux both pr. -TOHZ) (esp. in France) castle, country house

**chat·tel** (CHAT-l) n. any movable property

**chat·ter** (CHAT-ər) vi. talk idly or rapidly; rattle teeth —n. idle talk —**chat'ter·er** n. —**chat'ter·box** n. one who chatters incessantly

**chauf·feur** (SHOH-fər) n. paid driver of automobile —vt. perform this work

**chau·vin·ism** (SHOH-və-niz-əm) n. aggressive patriotism —**male chauvinism** smug sense of male superiority over women —**chau'vin·ist** n.

**cheap** (cheep) adj. (-er, -est) low in price; inexpensive; easily obtained; of little value or estimation; mean, inferior —**cheap'en** vt.

**cheat** (cheet) vt. deceive, defraud, swindle, impose upon —vi. practice deceit to gain advantage; (oft. followed by on) be sexually unfaithful —**cheat**, **cheat'er** n. one who cheats —**cheat'ers** n. sl. eyeglasses

**check** (chek) vt. stop; restrain; hinder; repress; control; examine for accuracy, quality etc. —n. repulse; stoppage; restraint; brief examination for correctness or accuracy; pattern of squares on fabric; threat to king at chess; written order to banker to pay money from one's account; printed slip of paper used for this —**check'book** n. book of checks —**check'mate** n. Chess final winning move; any overthrow, defeat —vt. Chess (-**mat·ed**, **-mat·ing**) make game-ending move; defeat —**check'out** n. counter in supermarket where customers pay —**check'up** n. examination (esp. medical) to see if all is in order

**checked** (chekt) adj. having pattern of small squares

**check·er** (CHEK-ər) n. marking as on checkerboard; playing piece in game of checkers —vt. mark in squares; variegate —**check'ered** adj. marked in squares; uneven, varied —**check'ers** n. game played on checkered board of 64 squares with flat round playing pieces —**check'er·board** n.

**ched·dar** (CHED-ər) n. (also C-) smooth hard cheese

**cheek** n. side of face below eye; impudence; buttock —vt. inf. address impudently —**cheek by jowl** in close intimacy

**cheep** vi./n. (utter) high-pitched cry, as of young bird

**cheer** vt. comfort; gladden; encourage by shouts —vi. shout applause —n. shout of approval; happiness, good spirits; mood —**cheer'ful** adj. —**cheer'i·ly** adv. —**cheer'less** adj.

**cheese** (cheez) n. curd of milk coagulated, separated from the whey and pressed —**chees'y** adj. (**chees·i·er**, **chees·i·est**) suggesting cheese in aroma etc.; (sl.) cheap, shabby —**cheese'cake** n. cake made with cottage or cream cheese and oft. with fruit mixture; inf. photograph of shapely, scantily clad woman —**cheese'cloth** n. loosely woven cotton cloth

**chee·tah** (CHEE-tə) n. large, swift, spotted feline animal

**chef** (shef) n. head cook, esp. in restaurant

**chef-d'oeu·vre** (shay-DUR-vr) Fr. masterpiece

**chem·is·try** (KEM-ə-stree) n. science concerned with properties of substances and their combinations and reactions; interaction of one personality with another —**chem'i·cal** n./adj. —**chem'ist** n. one trained in chemistry

**che·mo·ther·a·py** (kee-moh-THER-ə-pee) n. treatment of disease by chemical means

**che·nille** (shə-NEEL) n. soft yarn, fabric of silk, wool etc.

**cheong·sam** (chawng-sahm) n. (Chinese) straight dress with slit in one side of skirt

**cher'ish** vt. treat with affection; protect; foster

**che·root** (shə-ROOT) n. cigar with both ends open

**cher·ry** (CHER-ee) n. small red fruit with stone; tree bearing it —adj. ruddy, bright red

**cher·ub** (CHER-əb) n. (pl. **cher·u·bim**, **-ubs**) winged creature with human face; angel —che·ru·bic (chə-ROO-bik) adj.

cher·vil (CHUR-vil) n. an herb

chess n. game of skill played by two with 32 pieces on checkered board of 64 squares —chess'·board n. —chess'men n. pl. pieces used in chess

chest n. upper part of trunk of body; large, strong box —chest of drawers piece of furniture containing drawers

chest·nut (CHES-nut) n. large reddish-brown nut growing in prickly husk; tree bearing it; horse of chestnut color; old joke —adj. reddish-brown

chev·ron (SHEV-rən) n. Mil. V-shaped band of braid worn on sleeve to designate rank

chew (choo) v. grind with teeth —n. —chew'y adj. (chew·i·er, chew·i·est) firm, sticky when chewed

chi·an·ti (kee-AHN-tee) n. Italian wine

chic (sheek) adj. (-er, -est) stylish, elegant —n.

chi·can·er·y (shi-KAY-nə-ree) n. (pl. -er·ies) quibbling; trick, artifice

chick (chik), chick·en (CHIK-ən) n. young of birds, esp. of hen; sl. oft. offens. girl, young woman —chicken feed trifling amount of money —chick'en-heart·ed adj. cowardly —chick'en-pox n. infectious disease, esp. of children —chick'pea n. legume bearing pods containing pealike seeds; seed of this plant

chic·o·ry (CHIK-ə-ree) n. salad plant; ground root of the plant used with, or instead of, coffee

chide (chid) vt. (chid·ed or chid, chid·ed or chid or chid·den, chid·ing) scold, reprove, censure

chief (cheef) n. head or principal person —adj. principal, foremost, leading —chief'ly adv. —chief'·tain (-tən) n. leader, chief of clan or tribe

chif·fon (shi-FON) n. thin gauzy material

chi·gnon (SHEEN-yon) n. roll, knot, of hair worn at back of head

chi·hua·hua (chi-WAH-wah) n. breed of tiny dog, orig. from Mexico

chil·blain (CHIL-blayn) n. inflamed sore on hands, legs etc., due to cold

child (chield) n. (pl. chil·dren pr. CHIL-drən) young human being; offspring —child'ish adj. of or like a child; silly; trifling —child'·ish·ly adv. —child'less adj. —child'like adj. of or like a child; innocent; frank; docile —child'·birth n. —child'hood n. period between birth and puberty —child's play very easy task

chil·i (CHIL-ee) n. (pl. chil·ies) small red hot-tasting seed pod; plant producing it; chili con car·ne —chili con carne (kon KAHR-nee) Mexican-style dish of chilies or chili powder, ground beef, onions etc.

chill n. coldness; cold with shivering; anything that damps, discourages —v. make, become cold (esp. food, drink) —chill'i·ness n. —chill'y adj. (chill·i·er, chill·i·est)

chime (chim) n. sound of bell; harmonious, ringing sound —v. (chimed, chim·ing) —vi. ring harmoniously; agree —vt. strike (bells) —chime in break into a conversation to express an opinion

chi·me·ra (ki-MEER-ə) n. fabled monster, made up of parts of various animals; wild fancy —chi·mer'i·cal (-MER-i-kəl) adj. fanciful

chim·ney (CHIM-nee) n. (pl.

-neys) a passage for smoke; narrow vertical cleft in rock

**chim·pan·zee** (chim-pan-ZEE) *n.* gregarious, intelligent ape of Africa

**chin** *n.* part of face below mouth

**chi·na** (CHI-nə) *n.* fine earthenware, porcelain; cups, saucers *etc.* collectively

**chin·chil·la** (chin-CHIL-ə) *n.* S Amer. rodent with soft, gray fur; its fur

**chine** (chīn) *n.* backbone; cut of meat including backbone; ridge or crest of land; intersection of bottom and side of boat

**chink**[1] (chingk) *n.* cleft, crack

**chink**[2] *n.* light metallic sound — *v.* (cause to) make this sound

**chintz** (chints) *n.* cotton cloth printed in colored designs

**chip** *n.* splinter; place where piece has been broken off; tiny wafer of silicon forming integrated circuit in computer *etc.* — *v.* (chipped, chip·ping) — *vt.* chop into small pieces; break small pieces from; shape by cutting off pieces — *vi.* break off — **chip** in contribute; butt in

**chip·munk** (CHIP-mungk) *n.* small, striped N Amer. squirrel

**chi·rop·o·dist** (ki-ROP-ə-dist) *n.* one who treats disorders of feet — **chi·rop′o·dy** *n.*

**chi·ro·prac·tor** (KI-rə-prak-tər) *n.* one skilled in treating bodily disorders by manipulation, massage *etc.* — **chi·ro·prac′tic** *n.*

**chirp** (churp) *n.* short, sharp cry of bird — *vi.* make this sound — **chirp′y** *adj. inf.* **chirp·i·er, chirp·i·est**) happy

**chis·el** (CHIZ-əl) *n.* cutting tool, usu. bar of steel with edge across main axis — *vt.* (**-eled, -el·ing**) cut, carve with chisel; *sl.* cheat

**chit**[1] *n.* signed note for money owed; informal receipt

**chit**[2] *n.* child, *esp.* young girl

**chiv·al·ry** (SHIV-əl-ree) *n.* bravery and courtesy; medieval system of knighthood — **chiv′al·rous** *adj.*

**chive** (chīv) *n.* herb with mild onion flavor

**chlo·rine** (KLOR-een) *n.* nonmetallic element, yellowish-green poison gas, used as disinfectant — **chlo′rate** (-ayt) *n.* salt of chloric acid — **chlo′ric** *adj.* — **chlo′ride** *n.* compound of chlorine; bleaching agent — **chlo·ri·nate** (KLOR-ə-nayt) *vt.* (**-nat·ed, -nat·ing**) disinfect; purify with chlorine

**chlo·ro·form** (KLOR-ə-form) *n.* volatile liquid formerly used as anesthetic — *vt.* render insensible with it

**chlo·ro·phyll** (KLOR-ə-fil) *n.* green coloring matter in plants

**chock** (chok) *n.* block or wedge to prevent heavy object from rolling or sliding — **chock′-full** *adj.* packed full

**choc·o·late** (CHAWK-lit) *n.* paste from ground cacao seeds; candy, drink made from this — *adj.* dark brown

**choice** (chois) *n.* act or power of choosing; alternative; thing or person chosen — *adj.* select, fine, worthy of being chosen

**choir** (kwir) *n.* company of singers, *esp.* in church; part of church set aside for them

**choke** (chohk) *v.* (**choked, chok·ing**) — *v.* hinder, stop the breathing of; smother, stifle; obstruct — *vi.* suffer choking — *n.* act, noise of choking; device in carburetor to increase richness of fuel-air mixture

**chol·er** (KOL-ər) *n.* bile, anger — **chol′er·ic** *adj.* irritable

**chol·er·a** (KOL-ər-ə) *n.* deadly infectious disease marked by vomiting and diarrhea

**cho·les·ter·ol** (kə-LES-tə-rawl) n. substance found in animal tissue and fat

**chomp** v. chew noisily

**choose** (chooz) v. (**chose**, **chosen**, **choos·ing**) —vt. pick out, select; take by preference —vi. decide, think fit —**choos'y** adj. (**choos·i·er**, **choos·i·est**) fussy

**chop** vt. (**chopped**, **chop·ping**) cut with blow; hack —n. hewing blow; slice of meat containing rib or other bone —**chop'per** n. short axe; inf. helicopter; sl. helicopter —**chop'py** adj. (**-pi·er**, **-pi·est**) (of sea) having short, broken waves

**chops** n. pl. jaw, mouth

**chop·sticks** (CHOP-stiks) n. pl. implements used by Chinese and others for eating food

**cho·ral** (KOR-əl) adj. of, for, sung by, a choir

**cho·rale** (kə-RAL) n. slow, stately hymn tune

**chord** (kord) n. emotional response, esp. of sympathy; simultaneous sounding of musical notes; straight line joining ends of arc

**chore** (chor) n. (unpleasant) task; odd job

**cho·re·og·ra·phy** (kor-ee-OG-rə-fee) n. art of arranging dances, esp. ballet; art, notation of ballet dancing —**cho·re·og'ra·pher** n. —**cho·re·o·graph'ic** adj.

**chor·tle** (CHOR-tl) vi. (**-tled**, **-tling**) chuckle happily —n.

**cho·rus** (KOR-əs) n. group of singers; combination of voices singing together; refrain —vt. (**-rused**, **-rus·ing**) sing or say together —**chor'is·ter** n.

**chose** pt. —**cho'sen** pp. of CHOOSE

**chow'** n. inf. food —**chow'hound** n. sl. glutton

**chow'** n. thick-coated dog with curled tail, orig. from China

**chow·der** (CHOW-dər) n. thick soup of seafood, vegetables etc.; soup resembling it eg corn chowder

**Christ** (krist) n. Jesus of Nazareth, regarded by Christians as the Messiah

**Chris·tian** (KRIS-chən) n. follower of Christ —adj. following Christ; relating to Christ or his religion —**chris'ten** (-ən) vt. baptize, give name to —**Chris'ten·dom** (-ən-dəm) n. all the Christian world —**Chris·ti·an'i·ty** (-chee-AN-i-tee) n. religion of Christ —**Christian name** name given at baptism —**Christian Science** religious system founded by Mary Baker Eddy

**Christ·mas** (KRIS-məs) n. festival of birth of Christ

**chro·mat·ic** (kroh-MAT-ik) adj. of color; Mus. of scale proceeding by semitones

**chro·ma·tin** (KROH-mə-tin) n. part of protoplasmic substance in nucleus of cells that takes color in staining tests

**chrome** (krohm), **chro'mi·um** (-mee-əm) n. metal used in alloys and for plating

**chro·mo·some** (KROH-mə-sohm) n. microscopic gene-carrying body in the tissue of a cell

**Chron.** Chronicles

**chron·ic** (KRON-ik) adj. lasting a long time; habitual

**chron·i·cle** (KRON-i-kəl) n. record of events in order of time; account —vt. (**-cled**, **-cling**) record —**chron'i·cler** n.

**chro·nol·o·gy** (krə-NOL-ə-jee) n. (pl. **-gies**) determination of sequence of past events; arrangement in order of occurrence; account of events, reference work arranged in order of time —**chron·o·log·i·cal** (kron-l-OJ-i-kəl) adj. arranged in order of time

**chro·nom·e·ter** (krə-NOM-i-tər) n. instrument for measuring time exactly; watch

**chrys·a·lis** (KRIS-ə-lis) n. (pl. **chry·sal·i·des** pr. kri-SAL-i-deez) resting state of insect between grub and butterfly etc.; case enclosing it

**chry·san·the·mum** (kri-SAN-thə-məm) n. garden flower of various colors

**chub·by** (CHUB-ee) adj. (-bi·er, -bi·est) plump

**chuck**[1] (chuk) vt. inf. throw; pat affectionately (under chin); give up, reject

**chuck**[2] n. cut of beef; device for gripping, adjusting bit in power drill etc.

**chuck·le** (CHUK-əl) vi. (-led, -ling) laugh softly —n. such laugh

**chuk·ker** (CHUK-ər) n. period of play in game of polo

**chum** n. inf. close friend —**chum'my** adj. (-mi·er, -mi·est)

**chunk** (chungk) n. thick, solid piece —**chunk'y** adj. (chunk·i·er, chunk·i·est)

**church** n. building for Christian worship; (C-) whole body or sect of Christians; clergy —**church'ward·en** n. officer who represents interests of Anglican parish; long clay pipe —**church'yard** n.

**churl** n. rustic, rude, boorish person —**churl'ish** adj. —**churl'ish·ness** n.

**churn** n. vessel for making butter —v. shake up, stir (liquid) violently; make (butter) in churn; (of a stockbroker) trade (stocks) excessively to increase commissions

**chute** (shoot) n. slide for sending down parcels, coal etc.; channel; narrow passageway, eg for spraying, counting cattle, sheep etc.; inf. short for PARACHUTE

**chut·ney** (CHUT-nee) n. condiment of fruit, spices etc.

**chutz·pah** (HUUT-spə) n. shameless audacity; gall

**ci·ca·da** (si-KAY-də) n. cricketlike insect

**cic·a·trix** (SIK-ə-triks) n. scar of healed wound

**cic·e·ro·ne** (sis-ə-ROH-nee) n. guide for sightseers

**ci·der** (SĪ-dər) n. drink made from apples —**hard cider**, after fermentation —**soft cider**, before fermentation

**ci·gar** (si-GAHR) n. roll of tobacco leaves for smoking —**cig·a·rette** (sig-ə-RET) n. finely cut tobacco rolled in paper for smoking

**cinch** (sinch) n. inf. easy task, certainty; strong girth used on saddle

**cin·der** (SIN-dər) n. remains of burned coal

**cin·e·ma** (SIN-ə-mə) n. building used for showing of motion pictures; these generally or collectively

**cin·na·mon** (SIN-ə-mən) n. spice got from bark of Asian tree; the tree —adj. light-brown color

**ci·pher** (SĪ-fər) n. secret writing; arithmetical symbol; person of no importance; monogram —vt. write in cipher

**cir·ca** (SUR-kə) Lat. about, approximately

**cir·cle** (SUR-kəl) n. perfectly round figure; ring; Theater balcony or tier of seats above main level of auditorium; group, society with common interest; class of society etc. —v. (-cled, -cling) —vt. surround —vi. move in circle —**cir'cu·lar** (-kyə-lər) adj. round; in a circle —n. letter etc. intended for wide distribution —**cir'cu·late** (-kyə-layt) v. (-lat·ed,

**-lat·ing)** —*vi.* move around; pass from hand to hand or place to place —*vt.* send around —**cir·cu·la'tion** *n.* flow of blood from, and back to; act of moving around; extent of sale of newspaper *etc.* —**cir'cu·la·to·ry** *adj.*

**cir·cuit** (SUR-kit) *n.* complete round or course; area; path of electric current; round of visitation, *esp.* of judges; series of sporting events; district —**circu·i·tous** (sər-KYOO-i-təs) *adj.* roundabout, indirect —**cir'cuit·ry** *n.* electrical circuit(s)

**cir·cum·cise** (SUR-kəm-sīz) *vt.* (-cised, -cis·ing) cut off foreskin of (penis) —**cir·cum·ci'sion** (-SIZH-ən) *n.*

**cir·cum·fer·ence** (sər-KUM-fər-əns) *n.* boundary line, *esp.* of circle

**cir·cum·flex** (SUR-kəm-fleks) *n.* accent (ˆ) over vowel to indicate length of its sound

**cir·cum·lo·cu·tion** (sur-kəm-loh-KYOO-shən) *n.* roundabout speech

**cir·cum·nav·i·gate** (sur-kəm-NAV-i-gayt) *vt.* (-gat·ed, -gat·ing) sail or fly right around

**cir·cum·scribe** (SUR-kəm-skrīb) *vt.* (-scribed, -scrib·ing) confine, bound, limit, hamper

**cir·cum·spect** (SUR-kəm-spekt) *adj.* watchful, cautious, prudent —**cir·cum·spec'tion** *n.*

**cir·cum·stance** (SUR-kəm-stans) *n.* detail; event; matter of fact —*pl.* state of affairs; condition in life, *esp.* financial; surroundings or things accompanying an action —**cir·cum·stan'tial** *adj.* depending on detail or circumstances; detailed, minute; incidental

**cir·cum·vent** (sur-kəm-VENT) *vt.* outwit, evade, get round —**cir·cum·ven'tion** *n.*

**cir·cus** (SUR-kəs) *n.* (*pl.* -cus·es) (performance of) traveling group of acrobats, clowns, performing animals *etc.*; circular structure for public shows

**cir·rho·sis** (si-ROH-sis) *n.* any of various chronic progressive diseases of liver —**cir·rhot'ic** (-ROT-ik) *adj.*

**cir·rus** (SIR-əs) *n.* (*pl. same form*) high wispy cloud

**cis·tern** (SIS-tərn) *n.* water tank, *esp.* for rain water

**cit·a·del** (SIT-ə-dl) *n.* fortress in, near, or commanding a city

**cite** (sīt) *vt.* (cit·ed, cit·ing) quote; bring forward as proof —**ci·ta·tion** (si-TAY-shən) *n.* quoting; commendation for bravery *etc.*

**cit·i·zen** (SIT-ə-zən) *n.* native, naturalized member of state, nation *etc.*; inhabitant of city —**cit'i·zen·ship** *n.*

**cit·ron** (SI-trən) *n.* fruit like a lemon, the tree —**cit'ric** *adj.* of the acid of lemon or citron —**cit·rus** fruit citrons, lemons, limes, oranges *etc.*

**cit·y** (SIT-ee) *n.* (*pl.* cit·ies) a large town

**civ·et** (SIV-it) *n.* strong, musky perfume —**civet cat** catlike animal producing it

**civ·ic** (SIV-ik) *adj.* pert. to city or citizen —**civ'ics** *n.* (*with sing. v.*) study of the responsibilities and rights of citizenship

**civ·il** (SIV-əl) *adj.* relating to citizens of state; not military; refined, polite; *Law* not criminal —**ci·vil·ian** (si-VIL-yən) *n.* nonmilitary person —**ci·vil'i·ty** *n.* (*pl.* -ties) —**civ'il·ly** *adv.* —**civil service** service responsible for the public administration of the government of a city, state, or country

**civ·i·lize** (SIV-ə-līz) *vt.* (-lized,

-liz·ing) bring out of barbarism; refine —**civ·i·li·za′tion** n.

**Cl** *Chem.* chlorine

**clack** (klak) n. sound, as of two pieces of wood striking together —v.

**clad** pt./pp. of CLOTHE

**clad·ding** (KLAD-ing) n. metal bonded to inner core of another metal, as protection against corrosion

**claim** (klaym) vt. demand as right; assert; call for —n. demand for thing supposed due; right; thing claimed; plot of mining land marked out by stakes as required by law —**claim′ant** (-mənt) n.

**clair·voy·ance** (klair-VOI-əns) n. power of seeing things not present to senses, second sight —**clair·voy′ant** n./adj.

**clam** (klam) n. edible mollusk

**clam·ber** (KLAM-bər) vi. to climb with difficulty or awkwardly

**clam·my** (KLAM-ee) adj. (-mi·er, -mi·est) moist and sticky —**clam′mi·ness** n.

**clam·or** (KLAM-ər) n. loud shouting, outcry, noise —vi. shout, call noisily (for) —**clam′or·ous** adj.

**clamp** (klamp) n. tool for holding or compressing —vt. fasten, strengthen with or as with clamp

**clan** (klan) n. tribe or collection of families under chief and of common ancestry; faction, group —**clan′nish** adj.

**clan·des·tine** (klan-DES-tin) adj. secret; sly

**clang** (klang) v. (cause to) make loud ringing sound —n. loud ringing sound

**clank** (klangk) n. short sound as of pieces of metal struck together —v. cause, move with, such sound

**clap**¹ (klap) v. (clapped, clapping) (cause to) strike with noise;

strike (hands) together; applaud —vt. pat; place or put quickly —n. hard, explosive sound; slap —**clap′per** n. —**clap′trap** n. empty words

**clap**² n. sl. gonorrhea

**clar·et** (KLAR-it) n. a dry dark red wine of Bordeaux; similar wine made elsewhere

**clar·i·fy** (KLAR-ə-fi) v. (-fied, -fy·ing) make or become clear, pure, or more easily understood —**clar·i·fi·ca′tion** n. —**clar′i·ty** n. clearness

**clar·i·net** (klar-ə-NET) n. woodwind musical instrument

**clar·i·on** (KLAR-ee-ən) n. clear-sounding trumpet; rousing sound

**clash** (klash) n. loud noise, as of weapons striking; conflict, collision —vi. make clash; come into conflict; (of events) coincide; (of colors) look ugly together —vt. strike together to make clash

**clasp** (klasp) n. hook or other means of fastening; embrace —vt. fasten; embrace, grasp

**class** (klas) n. any division, order, kind, sort; rank; group of school pupils etc. taught together; division by merit; quality; inf. excellence or elegance —vt. assign to proper division —**clas′si·fy** (-ə-fi) vt. (-fied, -fy·ing) arrange methodically in classes —**clas·si·fi·ca′tion** n. —**clas·si·fied** adj. arranged in classes; secret; (of advertisements) arranged under headings in newspapers etc. —**class′y** adj. inf. (**class·i·er**, **class·i·est**) stylish, elegant

**clas·sic** (KLAS-ik) adj. of first rank; of highest rank generally, but esp. of art; refined; typical; famous —n. (literary) work of recognized excellence —n. pl. ancient Latin and Greek literature —**clas′si·cal** adj. of Greek and Roman literature, art, culture; of classic quality; *Mus.* of established standards of form, complexity *etc.* —**clas′si·cism** *n.* —**clas′si·cist** *n.*

**clat·ter** (KLAT-ər) *n.* rattling noise; noisy conversation —*v.* (cause to) make clatter

**clause** (klawz) *n.* part of sentence, containing verb; article in formal document as treaty, contract *etc.*

**claus·tro·pho·bia** (klaw-strə-FOH-bee-ə) *n.* abnormal fear of confined spaces

**clav·i·chord** (KLAV-i-kord) *n.* musical instrument with keyboard, forerunner of piano

**clav·i·cle** (KLAV-i-kəl) *n.* collarbone

**claw** (klaw) *n.* sharp hooked nail of bird or beast; foot of bird or prey; clawlike article —*vt.* tear with claws; grip

**clay** (klay) *n.* fine-grained earth, plastic when wet, hardening when baked; earth

**clean** (kleen) *adj.* (-er, -est) free from dirt, stain, or defilement; pure; guiltless; trim, shapely —*adv.* (-er, -est) so as to leave no dirt; entirely —*vt.* free from dirt —**clean·li·ness** (KLEN-lee-nis) *n.* —**clean·ly** (KLEEN-lee) *adv.* —*adj.* (KLEN-lee) clean (-li-er, -li·est) —**cleanse** (klenz) *vt.* (cleansed, cleans·ing) make clean —**come clean** *inf.* confess

**clear** (kleer) *adj.* (-er, -est) pure, undimmed, bright; free from cloud; transparent; plain, distinct; without defect or drawback; unimpeded —*adv.* (-er, -est) brightly; wholly, quite —*vt.* make clear; acquit; pass over or through; make as profit; free from obstruction, debt, difficulty —*vi.* become clear, bright, free, transparent —**clear′ance** *n.* making clear; removal of obstructions,

surplus stock *etc.*; certificate that ship has been cleared at custom house; space for moving part, vehicle, to pass within, through or past something —**clear′ing** *n.* land cleared of trees —**clear′ly** *adv.* —**clear′head·ed** (-hed-id) *adj.* discerning

**cleat** (kleet) *n.* wedge; piece of wood or iron with two projecting ends round which ropes are made fast; (on shoes) projecting piece to furnish a grip —*n. pl.* shoes equipped with cleats

**cleave**[1] (kleev) *v.* (cleft *or* cleaved *or* clove, cleft *or* cleaved *or* clo·ven, cleav·ing) —*vt.* split asunder —*vi.* crack, part asunder —**cleav′age** *n.* (*esp.*) area between a woman's breasts —**cleav′er** *n.* butcher's heavy knife

**cleave**[2] *vi.* (cleaved, cleav·ing) stick, adhere; be loyal

**clef** *n. Mus.* mark showing pitch of music on staff

**cleft** *n.* crack, fissure, chasm; opening made by cleaving —*pt./pp. of* CLEAVE[1]

**clem·ent** (KLEM-ənt) *adj.* merciful; gentle; mild —**clem′en·cy** *n.*

**clench** *vt.* set firmly together; grasp, close (fist)

**cler·gy** (KLUR-jee) *n.* body of ordained ministers in a religion —**cler′gy·man** *n.*

**cler·ic** (KLER-ik) *n.* member of clergy

**cler·i·cal** (KLER-i-kəl) *adj.* of clergy; of, connected with, office work

**clerk** (klurk) *n.* employee who keeps files *etc.* in an office; officer in charge of records, correspondence *etc.* of court, government department *etc.*; sales or service employee

**clev·er** (KLEV-ər) *adj.* quick to

understand; able, skillful, adroit —**clev'er·ly** adv. —**clev'er·ness** n.

**clew** n. see CLUE

**cli·ché** (klee-SHAY) n. (pl. -**chés**) stereotyped hackneyed phrase

**click**[1] (klik) n. short, sharp sound, as of latch in door; catch —vi. make this sound

**click**[2] vi. sl. be a success; inf. become clear; inf. strike up friendship

**cli·ent** (KLI-ɔnt) n. customer; one who employs professional person —**cli·en·tele'** (-ɔn-TEL) n. body of clients

**cliff** (klif) n. steep rock face —**cliff'hang·er** n. tense situation

**cli·mate** (KLI-mit) n. condition of region with regard to weather; prevailing feeling, atmosphere —**cli·mat'ic** adj. of climate

**cli·max** (KLI-maks) n. highest point, culmination; point of greatest excitement, tension in story etc. —**cli·mac'tic** adj.

**climb** (klim) v. go up or ascend; progress with difficulty; creep up, mount; slope upwards

**clinch** (klinch) vt. clench; settle, conclude (an agreement) —vi. (in boxing) hold opponent close with arm or arms; sl. embrace, esp. passionately —n. clinching; sl. embrace —**clinch'er** n. inf. something decisive

**cling** vi. (**clung, cling·ing**) adhere; be firmly attached to; be dependent

**clin·ic** (KLIN-ik) n. hospital facility for examination, treatment of outpatients; medical training session with hospital patients as subjects —**clin'i·cal** adj. relating to clinic, care of sick etc.; objective, unemotional; bare, plain —**clinical thermometer** used for taking body temperature

**clink**[1] (klingk) n. sharp metallic

sound —v. (cause to) make this sound

**clink**[2] n. sl. prison

**clink·er** (KLING-kɔr) n. fused coal residues from fire or furnace; hard brick

**clip**[1] vt. (**clipped, clip·ping**) cut with scissors; cut short; sl. cheat —n. inf. sharp blow —**clip'per** n.

**clip**[2] n. device for gripping or holding together, esp. hair, clothing etc.

**clip·per** (KLIP-ɔr) n. fast sailing ship

**clique** (kleek) n. small exclusive set; faction, group of people —**cli'quish** adj. —**cli'quish·ness** n.

**clit·o·ris** (KLIT-ɔr-is) n. small erectile part of female genitals

**cloak** (klohk) n. loose outer garment; disguise, pretext —vt. cover with cloak; disguise, conceal

**clob·ber** (KLOB-ɔr) vt. inf. beat, batter; defeat utterly

**clock** (klok) n. instrument for measuring time; device with dial for recording or measuring —**clock'wise** adv./adj. in the direction that the hands of a clock rotate —**clock'work** n. mechanism similar to that of a clock, as in a windup toy —**clock in** or **on, out** or **off** record arrival or departure on automatic time recorder

**clod** (klod) n. lump of earth; blockhead —**clod'dish** adj.

**clog** (klog) vt. (**clogged, clog·ging**) hamper, impede, choke up —n. obstruction, impediment; wooden-soled shoe

**cloi·son·né** (kloi-zɔ-NAY) n. enamel decoration in compartments formed by small strips of metal —adj.

**clois·ter** (KLOI-stɔr) n. covered pillared arcade; monastery or convent —**clois'tered** adj. confined, secluded, sheltered

**clone** (klohn) *n.* group of organisms, cells of same genetic constitution as another, derived by asexual reproduction, as graft of plant *etc.*; person closely resembling another in appearance, behavior *etc.* —*v.* (cloned, clon·ing)

**clop** (klop) *vi.* move, sound, as horse's hooves

**close**[1] (klohs) *adj.* (clos·er, clos·est) adjacent, near; compact; crowded; affectionate, intimate; almost equal; careful, searching; confined; secret; unventilated; stifling; reticent; niggardly; strict, restricted —*adv.* nearly; tightly —**close·ly** *adv.* —**close·fist'ed** *adj.* mean; avaricious —**close·up** *n.* close view, *esp.* portion of motion picture

**close**[2] (klohz) *v.* (closed, clos·ing) —*vt.* shut; stop up; prevent access to; finish —*vi.* come together; grapple —*n.* end —**closed season** when it is illegal to kill certain kinds of game and fish —**closed shop** place of work in which all workers must belong to a union

**clos·et** (KLOZ-it) *n.* small room *etc.* for storing clothing; small private room —*vt.* shut up in private room, *esp.* for conference —**clos'et·ful** *n.* (*pl.* -fuls)

**clo·sure** (KLOH-zhər) *n.* act of closing; cloture

**clot** (klot) *n.* mass or lump; *Med.* coagulated mass of blood —*v.* (clot·ted, clot·ting) form into lumps; coagulate

**cloth** (klawth) *n.* woven fabric —**clothes** (klohthz) *n. pl.* dress; bed coverings —**clothe** (klohth) *vt.* (clothed *or* clad, cloth·ing) put clothes on —**cloth·ier** (KLOHTH-yər) *n.* —**cloth·ing** (KLOH-thing) *n.*

**clo·ture** (KLOH-chər) *n.* ending of debate by majority vote or other authority

**cloud** (klowd) *n.* condensed water vapor floating in air; state of gloom; multitude —*vt.* overshadow, dim, darken —*vi.* become cloudy —**cloud'less** *adj.* —**cloud'y** *adj.* (cloud·i·er, cloud·i·est)

**clout** (klowt) *n. inf.* blow; influence, power —*vt.* strike

**clove**[1] (klohv) *n.* dried flower bud of tropical tree, used as spice; one of small bulbs making up compound bulb

**clove**[2] *pt.* —**clo'ven** *pp.* of CLEAVE[1]

**clo·ver** (KLOH-vər) *n.* low-growing forage plant —**be in clover** live in luxury

**clown** (klown) *n.* comic entertainer in circus; jester, fool

**cloy** (kloi) *vt.* weary by sweetness, sameness *etc.*

**club** (klub) *n.* thick stick; bat, stick used in some games; association for pursuance of common interest; building used by such association; one of the suits at cards —*v.* (clubbed, club·bing) strike with club; combine for a common object —**club foot** deformed foot

**cluck** (kluk) *vi./n.* (make) noise of hen

**clue** (kloo) *n.* indication, *esp.* of solution of mystery or puzzle —**not have a clue** be ignorant or incompetent

**clump**[1] (klump) *n.* cluster of trees or plants; compact mass

**clump**[2] *vi.* walk, tread heavily —*n.*

**clum·sy** (KLUM-zee) *adj.* (-si·er, -si·est) awkward, unwieldy, ungainly; badly made or arranged —**clum'si·ly** *adv.* —**clum'si·ness** *n.*

**clung** *pt./pp.* of CLING

**clunk** (klungk) n. (sound of) blow or something falling

**clus·ter** (KLUS-tər) n. group, bunch —v. gather, grow in cluster

**clutch¹** (kluch) v. grasp eagerly; snatch (at) —n. grasp, tight grip; device enabling two rotating shafts to be connected and disconnected at will

**clutch²** n. set of eggs hatched at one time; brood of chickens

**clut·ter** (KLUT-ər) v. strew; crowd together in disorder —n. disordered, obstructive mass of objects

**Cm** Chem. curium

**Co** Chem. cobalt

**coach** (kohch) n. large four-wheeled carriage; railway carriage; class of airline travel; tutor, instructor —vt. instruct

**co·ag·u·late** (koh-AG-yə-layt) v. (-lat·ed, -lat·ing) curdle, clot, form into a mass; congeal, solidify —co·ag·u·la'tion n.

**coal** (kohl) n. mineral consisting of carbonized vegetable matter, used as fuel; glowing ember —v. supply with or take in coal —coal'field n. area in which coal is found

**co·a·lesce** (koh-ə-LES) vi. (-lesced, -lesc·ing) unite, merge —co·a·les'cence n.

**co·a·li·tion** (koh-ə-LISH-ən) n. alliance, esp. of political parties

**coarse** (kors) adj. (coars·er, coars·est) rough, harsh; unrefined; indecent —coarse'ness n.

**coast** (kohst) n. seashore —v. move under momentum; proceed without making much effort; sail by the coast —coast'er n. small ship; that which, one who, coasts; small table mat for glasses etc.

**coat** (koht) n. sleeved outer garment; animal's fur or feathers; covering layer —vt. cover with layer; clothe —coat of arms armorial bearings

**coax** (kohks) vt. wheedle, cajole, persuade, force gently

**co·ax·i·al** (koh-AK-see-əl) adj. having the same axis —co·ax'i-al·ly adv.

**co·balt** (KOH-bawlt) n. metallic element; blue pigment from it

**cob·ble** (KOB-əl) n. (vt. (-bled, -bling) patch roughly; mend shoes —n. round stone —cob'bler n. shoe mender

**co·bra** (KOH-brə) n. venomous, hooded snake of Asia and Africa

**cob'web** n. spider's web

**co·caine** (koh-KAYN) n. addictive narcotic drug used medicinally as anesthetic

**coch·i·neal** (koch-ə-NEEL) n. scarlet dye from Mexican insect

**cock** (kok) n. male bird, esp. of domestic fowl; tap for liquids; hammer of gun; its position drawn back —vt. draw back (gun hammer) to firing position; raise, turn in alert or jaunty manner —cock'eyed (-īd) adj. crosseyed; with a squint; askew —cock'fight n. staged fight between roosters

**cock·a·trice** (KOK-ə-tris) n. fabulous animal similar to basilisk

**cock·chaf·er** (KOK-chay-fər) n. large, flying beetle

**cock·le** (KOK-əl) n. shellfish

**Cock·ney** (KOK-nee) n. (pl. -neys) native of London

**cock·pit** (KOK-pit) n. pilot's seat, compartment in small aircraft; driver's seat in racing car; orig. enclosure for cockfighting

**cock·roach** (KOK-rohch) n. kind of insect, household pest

**cock·tail** (KOK-tayl) n. short drink of whiskey, gin etc. with flavorings etc.

**cock·y** (KOK-ee) adj. (cock·i·er, cock·i·est) conceited, pert —cock'i·ness n.

**co·coa** (KOH-koh) *n.* powder made from seed of cacao (tropical) tree; drink made from the powder

**co·co·nut** (KOH-kə-nut) *n.* tropical palm; very large, hard nut from this palm

**co·coon** (kə-KOON) *n.* sheath of insect in chrysalis stage; any protective covering

**co·da** (KOH-də) *n. Mus.* final part of musical composition

**cod·dle** (KOD-l) *vt.* (-dled, -dling) overprotect, pamper; cook (eggs) lightly

**code** (kohd) *n.* system of letters, symbols and rules for their association to transmit messages secretly or briefly; scheme of conduct; collection of laws —**cod′i·fy** (KOD-) *vt.* (-fied, -fy·ing) —**cod·i·fi·ca′tion** *n.*

**co·deine** (KOH-deen) *n.* alkaline sedative, analgesic drug

**co·dex** (KOH-deks) *n.* (pl. -di·ces pr. -də-seez) ancient manuscript volume, *esp.* of Bible *etc.*

**codg·er** (KOJ-ər) *n. inf.* man, *esp.* old

**cod·i·cil** (KOD-ə-səl) *n.* addition to will

**co·ed·u·ca·tion·al** (koh-ej-ə-KAY-shə-nl) *adj.* of education of boys and girls together in mixed classes —**co·ed** (koh-ed) *n.* (female student at) coeducational school —*adj.*

**co·ef·fi·cient** (koh-ə-FISH-ənt) *n. Math.* numerical or constant factor

**co·erce** (koh-URS) *vt.* (-erced, -erc·ing) compel, force —**co·er′cion** (-UR-shən) *n.* forcible compulsion or restraint

**co·ex·ist** (koh-ig-ZIST) *vi.* exist together —**co·ex·ist′ence** *n.*

**cof·fee** (KAW-fee) *n.* seeds of tropical shrub; drink made from roasting and grinding these

**cof·fer** (KAW-fər) *n.* chest for valuables; treasury, funds

**cof·fer·dam** (KAW-fər-dam) *n.* watertight structure enabling construction work to be done underwater

**cof·fin** (KAW-fin) *n.* box for corpse

**cog** (kog) *n.* one of series of teeth on rim of wheel; person, thing forming small part of big process, organization *etc.*

**co·gent** (KOH-jənt) *adj.* convincing, compelling, persuasive —**co′gen·cy** *n.*

**cog·i·tate** (KOJ-i-tayt) *vi.* (-tat·ed, -tat·ing) think, reflect, ponder

**co·gnac** (KOHN-yak) *n.* French brandy

**cog·nate** (KOG-nayt) *adj.* of same stock, related, kindred

**cog·ni·tion** (kog-NISH-ən) *n.* act or faculty of knowing —**cog′ni·tive** *adj.*

**cog·ni·zance** (KOG-nə-zəns) *n.* knowledge, perception —**cog′ni·zant** *adj.*

**co·gno·scen·ti** (kon-yə-SHEN-tee) *n. pl.* people with knowledge in particular field, *esp.* arts

**co·hab·it** (koh-HAB-it) *vi.* live together as husband and wife

**co·here** (koh-HEER) *vi.* (-hered, -her·ing) stick together, be consistent —**co·her′ence** *n.* —**coher′ent** *adj.* capable of logical speech, thought; connected, making sense; sticking together —**co·he′sion** (-HEE-zhən) *n.* cohering —**co·he′sive** *adj.*

**co·hort** (KOH-hort) *n.* troop; associate

**coif·feur** (kwah-FUUR) *n.* hairdresser

**coif·fure** (kwah-FYUUR) *n.* hairstyle

**coil** (koil) *vt.* lay in rings; twist into winding shape —*vi.* twist, take up a winding shape or spiral —n. series of rings; device in vehicle etc. to transform low-voltage direct current to higher voltage for ignition purposes; contraceptive device inserted in womb

**coin** (koin) n. piece of money; money —vt. make into money, stamp; invent —**coin'age** n. coining; coins collectively —**coin money** inf. make money rapidly

**co·in·cide** (koh-in-SID) vi. (-cid·ed, -cid·ing) happen together; agree exactly —**co·in'ci·dence** (-si-dəns) n. —**co·in'ci·dent** adj. coinciding —**co·in·ci·den'tal** adj.

**co·i·tion** (koh-ISH-ən) n. sexual intercourse (also **co·i·tus** (KOH-i-təs))

**coke**[1] (kohk) n. residue left from distillation of coal, used as fuel

**coke**[2] n. sl. cocaine

**Col.** Colossians

**co·la** (KOH-lə) n. tropical tree; its nut, used to flavor drink

**col·an·der** (KUL-ən-dər) n. culinary strainer perforated with small holes

**cold** (kohld) adj. (-er, -est) lacking heat; indifferent, unmoved, apathetic; dispiriting; reserved or unfriendly; (of colors) giving an impression of coldness —n. lack of heat; illness, marked by runny nose etc. —**cold'ly** adv. —**cold'-blood·ed** adj. lacking pity, mercy; having body temperature that varies with that of the surroundings —**cold chisel** toughened steel chisel —**cold feet** fear —**cold storage** method of preserving perishable foods etc. by keeping them at artificially reduced temperature —**cold turkey** sl. abrupt halt in use of addictive drug etc. —**cold war** economic, diplomatic but nonmilitary hostility

**cole·slaw** (KOHL-slaw) n. salad dish based on shredded cabbage

**col·ic** (KOL-ik) n. severe pains in the intestines —**co·li·tis** (kə-LI-tis) n. inflammation of the colon

**col·lab·o·rate** (kə-LAB-ə-rayt) vi. (-rat·ed, -rat·ing) work with another on a project —**col·lab'o·ra·tor** n. one who works with another, esp. one who aids an enemy in occupation of his own country

**col·lage** (kə-LAHZH) n. (artistic) composition of bits and pieces stuck together on background

**col·lapse** (kə-LAPS) vi. (-lapsed, -laps·ing) fall; give way; lose strength, fail —n. act of collapsing; breakdown —**col·laps'i·ble** adj.

**col·lar** (KOL-ər) n. band, part of garment, worn round neck; inf. police arrest —vt. seize by collar; inf. capture, seize —**col'lar·bone** n. bone from shoulder to breastbone

**col·late** (kə-LAYT) vt. (-lat·ed, -lat·ing) compare carefully; place in order (as printed sheets for binding) —**col·la'tion** n. collating; light meal

**col·lat·er·al** (kə-LAT-ər-əl) n. security pledged for repayment of loan —adj. accompanying; side by side; of same stock but different line; subordinate

**col·league** (KOL-eeg) n. associate, companion in office or employment, fellow worker

**col·lect** (kə-LEKT) vt. gather, bring together —vi. come together; inf. receive money —**col·lect'ed** adj. calm; gathered —**col·lec'tion** n. —**col·lec'tive** n. factory, farm etc., run on principles of collectivism —adj. —**col·lec'tiv·ism** n. theory that a government should own all means of production

**col·lege** (KOL-ij) n. place of higher education; society of scholars; association —**col·le·giate** (kə-LEE-jit) *adj.* —**col·le·gian** *n.* student

**col·lide** (kə-LID) *vi.* (-**lid·ed**, -**lid·ing**) strike or dash together; come into conflict —**col·li·sion** (-LIZH-ən) *n.* colliding

**col·lo·di·on** (kə-LOH-dee-ən) *n.* chemical solution used in photography and medicine

**col·loid** (KOL-oid) *n.* suspension of particles in a solution

**col·lo·qui·al** (kə-LOH-kwee-əl) *adj.* pert. to or used in informal conversation —**col·lo·qui·al·ism** *n.* —**col·lo·quy** (KOL-ə-kwee) *n.* (*pl.* -**quies**) conversation; dialogue

**col·lu·sion** (kə-LOO-zhən) *n.* secret agreement for a fraudulent purpose, *esp.* in legal proceedings —**col·lu·sive** (-siv) *adj.*

**co·logne** (kə-LOHN) *n.* perfumed liquid

**co·lon**[1] (KOH-lən) *n.* mark (:) indicating break in a sentence

**co·lon**[2] *n.* part of large intestine from cecum to rectum

**colo·nel** (KUR-nl) *n.* commander of regiment or battalion

**col·on·nade** (kol-ə-NAYD) *n.* row of columns

**col·o·ny** (KOL-ə-nee) *n.* (*pl.* -**nies**) body of people who settle in new country but remain subject to parent country; country so settled; distinctive group living together —**co·lo·ni·al** (kə-LOH-nee-əl) *adj.* of colony —**col'o·nist** *n.* —**col·o·ni·za'tion** *n.* —**col'o·nize** *vt.* (-**nized**, -**niz·ing**)

**col·or** (KUL-ər) *n.* hue, tint; complexion; paint; pigment; *fig.* semblance, pretext; timbre, quality; mood —*pl.* flag; distinguishing symbol —*vt.* stain, dye, paint, give color to; disguise; influence or distort —*vi.* become colored;

blush —**col·or·a'tion** *n.* —**col'or·ful** *adj.* with bright or varied colors; distinctive

**co·los·sus** (kə-LOS-əs) *n.* (*pl.* -**los·si** *pr.* -LOS-i) huge statue; something, somebody very large —**co·los'sal** *adj.* huge, gigantic

**colt** (kohlt) *n.* young male horse

**col·umn** (KOL-əm) *n.* long vertical cylinder, pillar; support; division of page; body of troops —**co·lum·nar** (kə-LUM-nər) *adj.* —**col'um·nist** *n.* journalist writing regular feature for newspaper

**co·ma** (KOH-mə) *n.* state of unconsciousness —**co'ma·tose** (-tohs) *adj.*

**comb** (kohm) *n.* toothed instrument for tidying, arranging, or ornamenting hair; rooster's crest; mass of honey cells —*vt.* use comb on; search with great care

**com·bat** (KOM-bat *n.*, kəm-BAT *vt.*) fight, contest —**com·bat·ant** (kəm-BAT-nt) *n.* —**com'bat'ive** *adj.*

**com·bine** (kəm-BIN) *v.* join together; ally —*n.* (KOM-bin) trust, syndicate, *esp.* of businesses, trade organizations *etc.* —**com·bi·na·tion** (kom-bə-NAY-shən) *n.* —**com'bine** *n.* machine to harvest and thresh grain in one operation

**com·bus·tion** (kəm-BUS-chən) *n.* process of burning —**com·bus'ti·ble** *adj.*

**come** (kum) *vi.* (**came**, **come**, **com·ing**) approach, arrive, move toward; reach; happen to; occur; be available; originate (from); become; turn out to be —**come'back** *n. inf.* return to active life after retirement; *inf.* retort —**come'down** *n.* setback; descent in social status

**com·e·dy** (KOM-i-dee) *n.* (*pl.* -**dies**) dramatic or other work of light, amusing character; humor

**come·ly** (KUM-lee) *adj.* fair, pretty, good-looking —**come'li·ness** *n.*

**co·mes·ti·bles** (ka-MES-ta-balz) *n.* food

**com·et** (KOM-it) *n.* luminous heavenly body consisting of diffuse head, nucleus and long tail

**com·fort** (KUM-fart) *n.* well-being; ease; consolation; means of consolation or satisfaction —*vt.* soothe; cheer, gladden, console —**com·fort·a·ble** (KUMF-ta-bal) *adj.* free from pain *etc.*; *inf.* financially secure —**com'fort·a·bly** *adv.* —**com'fort·er** *n.* one who comforts; woolen scarf; quilt

**com·ic** (KOM-ik) *adj.* relating to comedy; funny, laughable —*n.* comedian; magazine consisting of strip cartoons —**com'i·cal** *adj.*

**com·ma** (KOM-a) *n.* punctuation mark (,) separating parts of sentence

**com·mand** (ka-MAND) *vt.* order; rule; compel; have in one's power; overlook, dominate —*vi.* exercise rule —*n.* order; power of controlling, ruling, dominating, overlooking; knowledge, mastery; post of one commanding; district commanded, jurisdiction —**com'man·dant** (KOM-an-dant) *n.* —**com·man·deer'** *vt.* seize for military use, appropriate —**com·mand'er** *n.* —**com·mand'ing** *adj.* in command; with air of authority —**com·mand'ment** *n.*

**com·man·do** (ka-MAN-doh) *n.* (*pl.* -dos) (member of) special military unit trained for airborne, amphibious attack

**com·mem·o·rate** (ka-MEM-a-rayt) *vt.* (-rat·ed, -rat·ing) celebrate, keep in memory by ceremony; be a memorial of —**com·mem·o·ra'tion** *n.* —**com·mem'o·ra·tive** *adj.*

**com·mence** (ka-MENS) *v.* (-menced, -menc·ing) begin —**com·mence'ment** *n.* beginning; graduation of students

**com·mend** (ka-MEND) *vt.* praise; commit, entrust —**com·mend'a·ble** *adj.* —**com·men·da'tion** *n.*

**com·men·su·rate** (ka-MEN-sar-it) *adj.* equal in size or length of time; in proportion, adequate

**com·ment** (KOM-ent) *n.* remark, criticism; gossip; note, explanation —*vi.* remark, note; annotate, criticize —**com'men·tar·y** *n.* (*pl.* -tar·ies) explanatory notes or comments; spoken accompaniment to film *etc.* —**com'men·ta·tor** *n.* author, speaker of commentary

**com·merce** (KOM-ars) *n.* buying and selling; dealings; trade —**com·mer·cial** (ka-MUR-shal) *adj.* of, concerning, business, trade, profit *etc.* —*n.* advertisement on radio or TV

**com·mis·er·ate** (ka-MIZ-a-rayt) *vt.* (-at·ed, -at·ing) pity, condole, sympathize with

**com·mis·sion** (ka-MISH-an) *n.* something entrusted to be done; delegated authority; body entrusted with some special duty; payment by percentage for doing something; warrant, *esp.* presidential warrant, giving authority; document appointing person to officer's rank; doing, committing —*vt.* charge with duty or task; *Mil.* confer a rank; give order for —**com·mis'sion·er** *n.* one empowered to act by commission or warrant; member of commission or government board; administrative head of professional department

**com·mit** (ka-MIT) *vt.* (-mit·ted, -mit·ting) entrust, give in charge; perpetrate, be guilty of; pledge;

promise; compromise, entangle; place in prison or mental institution —com·mit′ment *n.*

**com·mit·tee** (kə-MIT-ee) *n.* body appointed, elected for special business usu. from larger body

**com·mode** (kə-MOHD) *n.* chest of drawers; toilet

**com·mo·di·ous** (kə-MOH-dee-əs) *adj.* roomy

**com·mod·i·ty** (kə-MOD-i-tee) *n.* (*pl.* -ties) article of trade; anything useful

**com·mon** (KOM-ən) *adj.* shared by or belonging to all, or to several; public, general; ordinary, usual, frequent; inferior; vulgar —*n.* land belonging to community —*pl.* ordinary people; (C-) lower house of British parliament —com′mon·ly *adv.* —**Common Market** *see* EUROPEAN ECONOMIC COMMUNITY —com′mon·place *adj.* ordinary, everyday —*n.* trite remark; anything occurring frequently —**common sense** sound, practical understanding —com′mon·wealth *n.* republic; state of the US; federation of self-governing countries

**com·mo·tion** (kə-MOH-shən) *n.* stir, disturbance, tumult

**com·mune**[1] (kə-MYOON) *vi.* (-muned, -mun·ing) converse together intimately —com·mun′ion *n.* sharing of thoughts, feelings *etc.;* fellowship; body with common faith; (C-) participation in sacrament of the Lord's Supper; (C-) that sacrament, Eucharist

**com·mune**[2] (KOM-yoon) *n.* group of families, individuals living together and sharing property, responsibility *etc.* —com·mu·nal (kə-MYOON-l) *adj.* for common use

**com·mu·ni·cate** (kə-MYOO-ni-kayt) *v.* (-cat·ed, -cat·ing) —*vt.* impart, convey; reveal —*vi.* give or exchange information; have connecting passage, door; receive Communion —com·mu′ni·ca·ble *adj.* —com·mu′ni·cant *n.* one who receives Communion —com·mu·ni·ca′tion *n.* act of giving, *esp.* information; information, message; (*usu. pl.*) passage (road, railway *etc.*), or means of exchanging messages (radio, mail *etc.*) between places —*pl.* connections between military base and front —com·mu′ni·ca·tive *adj.* free with information

**com·mu·ni·qué** (kə-myoo-ni-KAY) *n.* official announcement

**com·mu·nism** (KOM-yə-niz-əm) *n.* doctrine that all goods, means of production *etc.*, should be property of community —com′mu·nist *n./adj.*

**com·mu·ni·ty** (kə-MYOO-ni-tee) *n.* (*pl.* -ties) body of people with something in common, *eg* neighborhood, religion *etc.;* society, the public; joint ownership; similarity, agreement

**com·mute** (kə-MYOOT) *v.* (-mut·ed, -mut·ing) —*vi.* travel daily some distance to work —*vt.* exchange; change (punishment *etc.*) into something less severe; change (payment *etc.*) into another form —com·mu·ta·tion (kom-yə-TAY-shən) *n.* —com′mu·ta·tor *n.* device to change alternating electric current into direct current —com·mut′er *n.* one who daily travels some distance to work

**com·pact**[1] (kəm-PAKT) *adj.* neatly arranged or packed; solid, concentrated; terse —*v.* make, become compact; compress —com·pact′ness *n.* —**com·pact disk** (KOM-pakt) small disk on which sound is recorded as series of metallic pits enclosed in polyvinyl chloride and played back by optical scanning by laser

**com·pact²** (KOM-pakt) *n.* small case to hold face powder, powder puff and mirror

**com·pact³** (KOM-pakt) *n.* agreement, covenant, treaty, contract

**com·pan·ion¹** (kəm-PAN-yən) *n.* chum, fellow, comrade, associate; person employed to live with another —com·pan'ion·a·ble *adj.*

**companion²** *n.* raised cover over staircase from deck to cabin of ship; deck skylight —compan'ionway *n.* staircase from deck to cabin

**com·pa·ny** (KUM-pə-nee) *n.* (*pl.* -nies) gathering of persons; companionship, fellowship; guests; business firm; division of regiment under captain; crew of ship; actors in play

**com·pare** (kəm-PAIR) *vt.* (-pared, -par·ing) notice or point out likenesses and differences of things; liken; make comparative and superlative of adjective or adverb —*vi.* be like; compete with —com·pa·ra·bil·i·ty (kom-pər-ə-BIL-i-tee) *n.* —com·pa·ra·ble *adj.* —com·par'a·tive *adj.* that may be compared; not absolute; relative, partial; *Grammar* denoting form of adjective, adverb, indicating "more" —*n.* —com·par'a·tive·ly *adv.* —com·par'i·son *n.* act of comparing

**com·part·ment** (kəm-PAHRT-mənt) *n.* division or part divided off, *eg* in airplane; section

**com·pass** (KUM-pəs) *n.* instrument for showing the north; instrument for drawing circles; circumference, measurement around; space, area; scope, reach —*vt.* surround; comprehend; attain, accomplish

**com·pas·sion** (kəm-PASH-ən) *n.*

pity, sympathy —com·pas'sion·ate (-it) *adj.*

**com·pat·i·ble** (kəm-PAT-ə-bəl) *adj.* capable of harmonious existence; consistent, agreeing with —com·pat·i·bil'i·ty *adv.*

**com·pa·tri·ot** (kəm-PAY-tree-ət) *n.* fellow countryman —*adj.*

**com·pel** (kəm-PEL) *vt.* (-pelled, -pel·ling ) force, oblige; bring about by force

**com·pen·di·um** (kəm-PEN-dee-əm) *n.* (*pl.* -diums) abridgment, summary —com·pen'di·ous *adj.* brief but inclusive

**com·pen·sate** (KOM-pən-sayt) *vt.* (-sat·ed, -sat·ing) make up for; recompense suitably; reward —com·pen·sa'tion *n.*

**com·pete** (kəm-PEET) *vi.* (-pet·ed, -pet·ing) (*oft.* with with) strive in rivalry, contend for, vie with —com·pe·ti·tion (kom-pi-TISH-ən) *n.* —com·pet'i·tive (kəm-) *adj.* —com·pet'i·tor *n.*

**com·pe·tent** (KOM-pi-tənt) *adj.* able, skillful; properly qualified; proper, due, legitimate; suitable, sufficient —com'pe·tence *n.* efficiency

**com·pile** (kəm-PIL) *vt.* (-piled, -pil·ing) make up (*eg* book) from various sources or materials; gather, put together —com·pi·la·tion (kom-pə-LAY-shən) *n.* —com·pil'er *n.*

**com·pla·cent** (kəm-PLAY-sənt) *adj.* self-satisfied; pleased or gratified —com·pla'cen·cy *n.*

**com·plain** (kəm-PLAYN) *vi.* grumble; bring charge, make known a grievance; (*with of*) make known that one is suffering from —com·plaint' *n.* statement of a wrong, grievance; ailment, illness —com·plain'ant *n.*

**com·ple·ment** (KOM-plə-mənt) *n.* something making up a whole;

full allowance, equipment *etc.* —*vt.* add to, make complete —**com·ple·men·ta·ry** *adj.*

**com·plete** (kəm-PLEET) *adj.* full, perfect; finished, ended; entire; thorough —*vt.* (-**plet·ed**, -**plet·ing**) make whole, perfect; finish —**com·plete·ly** *adv.* —**com·ple′tion** *n.*

**com·plex** (kəm-PLEKS) *adj.* intricate, compound, involved —*n.* (KOM-pleks) complicated whole; group of related buildings; psychological abnormality, obsession —**com·plex′i·ty** *n.*

**com·plex·ion** (kəm-PLEK-shən) *n.* look, color, of skin, *esp.* of face, appearance; aspect, character; disposition

**compliant** *see* COMPLY

**com·pli·cate** (KOM-pli-kayt) *vt.* (-**cat·ed**, -**cat·ing**) make intricate, involved, difficult; mix up —**com·pli·ca′tion** *n.*

**com·plic·i·ty** (kəm-PLIS-i-tee) *n.* (*pl.* -**ties**) partnership in wrongdoing

**com·pli·ment** (KOM-plə-mənt) *n.* expression of regard, praise; flattering speech —*pl.* expression of courtesy, formal greetings —*vt.* praise, congratulate —**com·pli·men′ta·ry** *adj.* expressing praise; free of charge

**com·ply** (kəm-PLĪ) *vi.* (-**plied**, -**ply·ing**) consent, yield, do as asked —**com·pli′ance** *n.* —**com·pli′ant** *adj.*

**com·po·nent** (kəm-POH-nənt) *n.* part, element, constituent of whole —*adj.* composing, making up

**com·port** (kəm-PORT) *v.* agree; behave

**com·pose** (kəm-POHZ) *vt.* (-**posed**, -**pos·ing**) arrange, put in order; write, invent; make up; calm; settle, adjust —**com·posed′** *adj.* calm —**com·pos′er** *n.* one who composes, *esp.* music —**com·po·site** (kəm-POZ-it) *adj.* made up of distinct parts —**com·po·si·tion** (kom-pə-ZISH-ən) *n.* —**com·pos·i·tor** (kəm-POZ-i-tər) *n.* typesetter, one who arranges type for printing —**com·po·sure** (kəm-POH-zhər) *n.* calmness

**com·pos men·tis** (KOM-pəs MEN-tis) *Lat.* of sound mind

**com·post** (KOM-pohst) *n.* fertilizing mixture of decayed vegetable matter for soil

**com·pote** (KOM-poht) *n.* fruit stewed or preserved in syrup

**com·pound**[1] (KOM-pownd) *n.* mixture, joining; substance, word, made up of parts —*adj.* not simple; composite, mixed —*vt.* (kəm-POWND) mix, make up, put together; intensify, make worse; compromise, settle debt by partial payment

**com·pound**[2] (KOM-pownd) *n.* (fenced or walled) enclosure containing houses *etc.*

**com·pre·hend** (kom-pri-HEND) *vt.* understand, take in; include, comprise —**com·pre·hen′si·ble** *adj.* —**com·pre·hen′sion** *n.* —**com·pre·hen′sive** *adj.* wide, full; taking in much

**com·press** (kəm-PRES) *vt.* squeeze together; make smaller in size, bulk —*n.* (KOM-pres) pad of cloth applied to wound, inflamed part *etc.* —**com·press′i·ble** *adj.* —**com·pres·sion** (kəm-PRESH-ən) *n.* internal combustion engine, squeezing of explosive charge before ignition, to give additional force —**com·pres′sor** *n.* *esp.* machine to compress air, gas

**com·prise** (kəm-PRĪZ) *vt.* (-**prised**, -**pris·ing**) include, contain

**com·pro·mise** (KOM-prə-mīz) *n.* meeting halfway, coming to terms by giving up part of claim; middle course —v. (-mised, -mis·ing) settle (dispute) by making concessions —vt. expose to risk or suspicion

**comp·trol·ler** (kən-TROH-lər) n. controller (in some titles)

**com·pul·sion** (kəm-PUL-shən) n. act of compelling; irresistible impulse —**compul'sive** adj. —**com·pul'so·ri·ly** (-sə-rə-lee) adv. —**com·pul'so·ry** adj. not optional

**com·punc·tion** (kəm-PUNGK-shən) n. regret for wrongdoing

**com·pute** (kəm-PYOOT) vt. (-put·ed, -put·ing) reckon, calculate, esp. using computer —**com·pu·ta·tion** (kom-pyə-TAY-shən) n. reckoning, estimate —**comput'er** n. electronic device for storing, retrieving information and performing calculations —**com·put'er·ize** v. (-ized, -iz·ing) equip with, perform by computer

**com·rade** (KOM-rad) n. chum, companion, friend —**com'rade·ship** n. —**com'rade·ly** adj.

**con**[1] (kon) v. inf. (conned, con·ning) swindle, defraud; cajole —**con game**

**con**[2] n. abbrev. of contra, against —**pros and cons** (arguments) for and against

**con**[3] vt. (conned, con·ning) direct steering (of ship)

**con·cat·e·nate** (kon-KAT-n-ayt) vt. (-nat·ed, -nat·ing) link together —**con·cat·e·na'tion** n. connected chain (as of circumstances)

**con·cave** (kon-KAYV) adj. hollow, rounded inward —**con·cav'i·ty** n.

**con·ceal** (kən-SEEL) vt. hide, keep secret

**con·cede** (kən-SEED) vt. (-ced·ed, -ced·ing) admit, admit truth of; grant, allow, yield

**con·ceit** (kən-SEET) n. vanity, overweening opinion of oneself;

far-fetched comparison —**con·ceit'ed** adj.

**con·ceive** (kən-SEEV) v. (-ceived, -ceiv·ing) think of, imagine; believe; form in the mind; become pregnant —**con·ceiv'a·ble** adj.

**con·cen·trate** (KON-sən-trayt) v. (-trat·ed, -trat·ing) —vt. focus (one's efforts etc.); increase in strength; reduce to small space —vi. devote all attention; come together —n. concentrated material or solution —**con·cen·tra'tion** n. —**concentration camp** prison camp, esp. one in Nazi Germany

**con·cen·tric** (kən-SEN-trik) adj. having the same center

**con·cept** (KON-sept) n. abstract idea; mental expression —**con·cep·tu·al** (kən-SEP-choo-əl) adj.

**con·cep·tion** (kən-SEP-shən) n. idea, notion; act of conceiving

**con·cern** (kən-SURN) vt. relate, apply to; interest, affect, trouble; (with in or with) involve (oneself) —n. affair; regard, worry; importance; business, enterprise —**con·cerned'** adj. connected with; interested; worried; involved —**con·cern'ing** prep. respecting, about

**con·cert** (KON-surt) n. musical entertainment; harmony, agreement —vt. (kən-SURT) arrange, plan together —**con·cert'ed** adj. mutually arranged, planned; determined —**con·cer·ti·na** (kon-sər-TEE-nə) n. musical instrument with bellows and keys —**con·cer·to** (kən-CHER-toh) n. (pl. -tos) musical composition for solo instrument and orchestra

**con·ces·sion** (kən-SESH-ən) n. act of conceding; thing conceded; grant; special privilege

**conch** (kongk) n. seashell —**con·chol·o·gy** (kong-KOL-ə-jee) n.

study, collection of shells and shellfish

**con·cierge** (kon-see-AIRZH) n. in France esp., caretaker, door-keeper

**con·cil·i·ate** (kən-SIL-e-ayt) vt. (-at·ed, -at·ing) pacify, win over from hostility —**con·cil'i·a·tor** n. —**con·cil'i·a·to·ry** adj.

**con·cise** (kən-SIS) adj. brief, terse —**con·cise'ly** adv. —**con·cise'-ness** n.

**con·clave** (KON-klayv) n. private meeting; assembly for election of a pope

**con·clude** (kən-KLOOD) v. (-clud·ed, -clud·ing) —vt. end, finish; deduce; settle —vi. come to end; decide —**con·clu'sion** (-KLOO-zhən) n. —**con·clu'sive** adj. decisive, convincing

**con·coct** (kən-KOKT) vt. make mixture, prepare with various ingredients; make up; contrive, plan —**con·coc'tion** n.

**con·com·i·tant** (kən-KOM-i-tənt) adj. accompanying

**con·cord** (KON-kord) n. agreement; harmony —vi. (kən-KORD) agree —**con·cord'ance** (-əns) n. agreement; index to words of book (esp.Bible)

**con·course** (KON-kors) n. crowd; large, open place in public area; boulevard

**con·crete** (KON-kreet) n. mixture of sand, cement etc., used in building —adj. made of concrete; particular, specific; perceptible, actual; solid —**con·crete'ly** adv.

**con·cu·bine** (KONG-kyə-bin) n. woman living with man as his wife, but not married to him; mistress —**con·cu·bi·nage** (kon-KYOO-bə-nij) n.

**con·cu·pis·cence** (kon-KYOO-pi-səns) n. lust

**con·cur** (kən-KUR) vi. (-curred, -cur·ring) agree, express agree-ment; happen together; coincide —**con·cur'rence** n. —**con·cur'-rent** adj. —**con·cur'rent·ly** adv. at the same time

**con·cus·sion** (kən-KUSH-ən) n. brain injury; physical shock

**con·demn** (kən-DEM) vt. blame; find guilty; doom; find, declare unfit for use —**con·dem·na·tion** (kon-dem-NAY-shən) n. —**con·dem'na·to·ry** adj.

**con·dense** (kən-DENS) v. (-densed, -dens·ing) vt. concen-trate, make more solid; turn from gas into liquid; pack into few words —vi. turn from gas to liquid —**con·den·sa·tion** (kon-den-SAY-shən) n. —**con·dens'er** n. Electricity apparatus for storing electrical energy, a capacitor; apparatus for reducing gas to liquid form; a lens or mirror for focusing light

**con·de·scend** (kon-də-SEND) vi. treat graciously one regarded as inferior; do something below one's dignity —**con·de·scend'ing** adj. —**con·de·scen'sion** n.

**con·di·ment** (KON-də-mənt) n. sauce, seasoning for food

**con·di·tion** (kən-DISH-ən) n. state or circumstances of anything; thing on which statement or hap-pening or existing depends; stipu-lation, prerequisite; health, physical fitness; rank —vt. accus-tom; regulate; make fit, healthy; be essential to happening or ex-istence of; stipulate —**con·di'tion·al** adj. dependent on circum-stances or events —n. Grammar form of verbs

**con·dole** (kən-DOHL) vi. (-doled, -dol·ing) grieve with, offer sym-pathy; commiserate with —**con·do'lence** n.

**con·dom** (KON-dəm) n. sheath-like usu. rubber contraceptive device worn by man

**con·do·min·i·um** (kon-də-MIN-ee-əm) *n.* joint rule by two or more countries; building with apartments, offices *etc.* individually owned

**con·done** (kən-DOHN) *vt.* (-doned, -don·ing) overlook, forgive, treat as not existing

**con·duce** (kən-DOOS) *vi.* (-duced, -duc·ing) help, promote; tend toward —**con·du'cive** *adj.*

**con·duct** (KON-dukt) *n.* behavior; management —*vt.* (kən-DUKT) escort, guide; lead, direct; manage; transmit (heat, electricity) —**con·duc'tion** *n.* —**con·duc'tive** *adj.* —**con·duc·tiv'i·ty** *n.* —**con·duc'tor** *n.* employee on bus, train *etc.* who collects fares; director of orchestra; one who leads, guides; substance capable of transmitting heat, electricity *etc.*

**con·du·it** (KON-doo-it) *n.* channel or pipe for conveying water, electric cables *etc.*

**cone** (kohn) *n.* solid figure with circular base, tapering to a point; fruit of pine, fir *etc.* —**con·ic** (KON-ik), —**con'i·cal** *adj.*

**con·fab·u·late** (kən-FAB-yə-layt) *vi.* (-lat·ed, -lat·ing) chat —**con·fab** (KON-fab) *n. inf.* shortened form of **con·fab·u·la'tion** *n.* confidential conversation

**con·fec·tion** (kən-FEK-shən) *n.* prepared delicacy, *esp.* something sweet; candy —**con·fec'tion·er** *n.* dealer in candies, fancy cakes *etc.* —**con·fec'tion·er·y** *n.* confectioner's shop; things confectioner sells

**con·fed·er·ate** (kən-FED-ər-it) *n.* ally; accomplice —*v.* (-ə-rayt) (-at·ed, -at·ing) unite —**con·fed'er·a·cy** *n.* —**con·fed·er·a'tion** *n.* alliance of political unions

**con·fer** (kən-FUR) *v.* (-ferred, -fer·ring) *vt.* grant, give; bestow; award *vi.* talk with, take advice

—**con·fer·ence** (KON-fər-əns) *n.* meeting for consultation or deliberation

**con·fess** (kən-FES) *vt.* admit, own; (of priest) hear sins of —*vi.* acknowledge; declare one's sins orally to priest —**con·fes'sion** (-FESH-ən) *n.* —**con·fes'sion·al** *n.* confessor's stall —**con·fes'sor** *n.* priest who hears confessions

**con·fet·ti** (kən-FET-ee) *n. pl.* small bits of colored paper for throwing at weddings

**con·fide** (kən-FID) *v.* (-fid·ed, -fid·ing) —*vi.* (with in) tell secrets, trust —*vt.* entrust —**con·fi·dant** (KON-fi-dant) *n.* one entrusted with secrets —**con'fi·dence** *n.* trust; boldness, assurance; intimacy; something confided, secret —**con'fi·dent** *adj.* —**con·fi·den'tial** (-shəl) *adj.* private; secret; entrusted with another's confidences —**con'fi·dent·ly** *adv.* —**confidence game** con game, swindle in which victim entrusts money *etc.* to thief, believed honest

**con·fig·u·ra·tion** (kən-fig-yə-RAY-shən) *n.* shape, aspect, conformation, arrangement

**con·fine** (kən-FIN) *vt.* (-fined, -fin·ing) keep within bounds; keep in house, bed *etc.*; shut up, imprison —**con·fines** (KON-finz) *n. pl.* boundaries, limits —**confine'ment** *n. esp.* childbirth; imprisonment

**con·firm** (kən-FURM) *vt.* make sure, verify; strengthen; settle; make valid, ratify; administer confirmation to —**con·fir·ma·tion** (kon-fər-MAY-shən) *n.* making strong, certain; Christian rite administered to confirm vows made at baptism; Jewish ceremony to admit boys, girls to adult status —**con·firm'a·to·ry** *adj.* tending to confirm or establish; corroborative —**con·firmed'** *adj.* (of habit *etc.*) long-established

**con·fis·cate** (KON-fə-skayt) *vt.* (-cat·ed, -cat·ing) seize by authority —**con·fis·ca'tion** *n.* —**con·fis·ca·to·ry** (kən-FIS-kə-tor-ee) *adj.*

**con·fla·gra·tion** (kon-flə-GRAY-shən) *n.* great destructive fire

**con·flict** (KON-flikt) *n.* struggle, trial of strength; disagreement —*vi.* (kən-FLIKT) be at odds with, be inconsistent with; clash

**con·flu·ence** (KON-floo- əns) *n.* union of streams; meeting place —**con'flu·ent** *adj.*

**con·form** (kən-FORM) *v.* comply with accepted standards, conventions *etc.*; adapt to rule, pattern, custom *etc.* —**con·for·ma·tion** (kon-for-MAY-shən) *n.* structure, adaptation —**con·form'ist** *n.* one who conforms, agrees —**con·form'i·ty** *n.* compliance

**con·found** (kon-FOWND) *vt.* baffle, perplex; confuse; defeat —**con·found'ed** *adj. esp. inf.* damned

**con·front** (kən-FRUNT) *vt.* face; bring face to face with —**con·fron·ta·tion** (kon-frən-TAY-shən) *n.*

**con·fuse** (kən-FYOOZ) *vt.* (-fused, -fus·ing) bewilder; jumble; make unclear; mistake (one thing) for another; disconcert —**con·fu'sion** *n.*

**con·geal** (kən-JEEL) *v.* solidify by cooling or freezing

**con·gen·ial** (kən-JEEN-yəl) *adj.* pleasant, to one's liking; of similar disposition, tastes *etc.* —**con·ge·ni·al'i·ty** *n.*

**con·gen·i·tal** (kən-JEN-i-tl) *adj.* existing at birth; dating from birth

**con·ge·ries** (KON-jə-reez) *n. sing.*

*and pl.* collection or mass of small bodies, conglomeration

**con·gest** (kən-JEST) *v.* overcrowd or clog —**con·ges'tion** *n.* abnormal accumulation, overcrowding —**con·gest'ed** *adj.*

**con·glom·er·ate** (kən-GLOM-ər-it) *n.* thing, substance (*esp.* rock) composed of mixture of other, smaller elements or pieces; business organization comprising many companies —*v.* (-ə-rayt) (-at·ed, -at·ing) gather together —*adj.* —**con·glom·er·a'tion** *n.*

**con·grat·u·late** (kən-GRACH-ə-layt) *vt.* (-lat·ed, -lat·ing) express pleasure at good fortune, success *etc.* —**con·grat·u·la'tion** *n.* —**con·grat'u·la·to·ry** *adj.*

**con·gre·gate** (KONG-gri-gayt) *v.* (-gat·ed, -gat·ing) assemble; collect, flock together —**con·grega'tion** *n.* assembly, *esp.* for worship —**con·gre·ga'tion·al** *adj.* —**con·gre·ga'tion·al·ism** *n.* form of Protestant church organization in which local churches are self-governing

**con·gress** (KONG-gris) *n.* meeting; sexual intercourse; formal assembly for discussion; legislative body —**con·gres·sion·al** (kən-GRESH-ə-nl) *adj.* —**con'gress·man** *n.* member of US House of Representatives

**con·gru·ent** (KONG-groo-ənt) *adj.* suitable, accordant; fitting together, *esp.* triangles —**con'gru·ence** *n.* —**con·gru'i·ty** *n.* —**con'gru·ous** *adj.*

**conic** *see* CONE

**con·i·fer** (KON-ə-fər) *n.* cone-bearing tree, as fir, pine *etc.* —**co·nif·er·ous** (koh-NIF-ər-əs) *adj.*

**con·jec·ture** (kən-JEK-chər) *n.* guess, guesswork —*v.* (-tured, -tur·ing) guess, surmise —**con·jec'tur·al** *adj.*

**con·ju·gal** (KON-jə-gəl) *adj.* relating to marriage; between married persons —**con·ju·gal'i·ty** *n.*

**con·ju·gate** (KON-jə-gayt) *v.* (-gat·ed, -gat·ing) inflect verb in its various forms (past, present *etc.*) —**con·ju·ga'tion** *n.*

**con·junc·tion** (kən-JUNGK-shən) *n.* union; simultaneous happening; part of speech joining words, phrases *etc.* —**con·junc'tive** *adj.*

**con·junc·ti·va** (kon-jungk-TI-və) *n.* mucous membrane lining eyelid —**con·junc·ti·vi·tis** (kon-jungk-tə-VI-tis) *n.* inflammation of this

**con·jure** (KON-jər) *v.* (-jured, -jur·ing) produce magic effects; perform tricks by sleight of hand *etc.*; invoke devils; (kən-JUUR) implore earnestly —**con·jur·a·tion** (kon-jə-RAY-shən) *n.* —**con'·jur·er** *n.*

**conk** (kongk) *vt. inf.* strike (*esp.* on head) —*vi. inf.* (*oft. with* out) break down, stall; faint; fall asleep

**con·nect** (kə-NEKT) *v.* join together, unite; associate in the mind —**con·nec'tion** *n.* association; train, *etc.* timed to enable passengers to transfer from another; family relation; social, commercial *etc.* relationship —**con·nec'tive** *adj.* —**connecting rod** part of engine that transfers motion from piston to crankshaft

**con·ning tower** (KON-ing) armored control position in submarine, battleship *etc.*; *see* CON[?]

**con·nive** (kə-NIV) *vi.* (-nived, -niv·ing) plot, conspire; assent, refrain from preventing or forbidding —**con·niv'ance** *n.*

**con·nois·seur** (kon-ə-SUR) *n.* critical expert in matters of taste, *esp.* fine arts; competent judge

**con·note** (kə-NOHT) *vt.* (-not·ed,

-not·ing) imply, mean in addition to primary meaning —**con·no·ta·tion** (kon-ə-TAY-shən) *n.*

**con·nu·bi·al** (kə-NOO-bee-əl) *adj.* of marriage

**con·quer** (KONG-kər) *vt.* win by force of arms, overcome; defeat —*vi.* be victorious —**con'quer·or** *n.* —**con·quest** (KON-kwest) *n.*

**con·san·guin·i·ty** (kon-sang-GWIN-i-tee) *n.* kinship —**con·san·guin'e·ous** *adj.*

**con·science** (KON-shəns) *n.* sense of right or wrong governing person's words and actions —**con·sci·en'tious** (-shee-EN-shəs) *adj.* scrupulous; obedient to the dictates of conscience —**con·sci·en'tious·ly** *adv.* —**conscientious objector** one who refuses military service on moral or religious grounds

**con·scious** (KON-shəs) *adj.* aware; awake to one's surroundings and identity; deliberate, intentional —**con'scious·ly** *adv.* —**con'scious·ness** *n.* being conscious

**con·script** (KON-skript)*n.* one compulsorily enlisted for military service —*vt.* (kən-SKRIPT) —**con·scrip'tion** *n.*

**con·se·crate** (KON-si-krayt) *vt.* (-crat·ed, -crat·ing) make sacred —**con·se·cra'tion** *n.*

**con·sec·u·tive** (kən-SEK-yə-tiv) *adj.* in unbroken succession

**con·sen·sus** (kən-SEN-səs) *n.* widespread agreement, unanimity

**con·sent** (kən-SENT) *vi.* agree to, comply —*n.* acquiescence; permission; agreement

**con·se·quence** (KON-si-kwens) *n.* result, effect, outcome; that which naturally follows; significance, importance —**con'se·quent** *adj.* —**con·se·quen'tial** *adj.*

important —con'se·quent·ly adv. therefore, as a result

con·serv·a·to·ry (kon-SUR-və-tor-ee) n. (pl. -ries) school for teaching music or painting etc.; greenhouse

con·serve (kon-SURV) vt. (-served, -serv·ing) keep from change or decay; preserve; maintain —n. (KON-surv) jam, preserved fruit etc. —con·ser·va·tion (kon-sor-VAY-shon) n. protection, careful management of natural resources and environment —con·ser·va'tion·ist n./adj. —con·serv'a·tive adj. tending to or wishing to conserve; moderate —n. Politics one who desires to preserve institutions of country against change and innovation; one opposed to hasty changes or innovations —con·serv'a·tism n.

con·sid·er (kon-SID-or) vt. think over; examine; make allowance for; be of opinion that; discuss —con·sid'er·a·ble adj. important; somewhat large —con·sid'er·ate (-it) adj. thoughtful for others' feelings, careful —con·sid'er·ate·ly adv. —con·sid·er·a'tion n. deliberation; point of importance; thoughtfulness; bribe, recompense

con·sign (kon-SIN) vt. commit, hand over; entrust to carrier —con·sign·ee (kon-si-NEE), —con·sign'or n. —con·sign'ment n. goods consigned

con·sist (kon-SIST) vi. be composed of; (with in) have as basis; agree with, be compatible —con·sist'en·cy n. agreement; harmony; degree of firmness —con·sist'ent adj. unchanging, constant; agreeing (with)

con·sis·to·ry (kon-SIS-tə-ree) n. (pl. -ries) ecclesiastical court or council, esp. of pope and cardinals

con·sole¹ (kon-SOHL) vt. (-soled, -sol·ing) comfort, cheer in distress —con·so·la·tion (kon-sə-LAY-shon) n.

con·sole² (KON-sohl) n. bracket supporting shelf; keyboard, stops etc., of organ; cabinet for TV, radio etc.

con·sol·i·date (kon-SOL-i-dayt) vt. (-dat·ed, -dat·ing) combine into connected whole; make firm, secure —con·sol·i·da'tion n.

con·som·mé (kon-sə-MAY) n. clear meat soup

con·so·nant (KON-sə-nənt) n. sound making a syllable only with vowel; non-vowel —adj. agreeing with, in accord —con'so·nance n.

con·sort (kon-SORT) vi. associate, keep company with —n. (KON-sort) husband, wife, esp. of ruler; ship sailing with another —con·sor'ti·um (-SOR-shee-əm) (pl. -ti·a pr. -shee-ə) n. association of banks, companies etc.

con·spic·u·ous (kon-SPIK-yoo-əs) adj. striking, noticeable, outstanding; prominent; eminent

con·spire (kon-SPIR) vi. (-spired, -spir·ing) combine for evil purpose; plot, devise —con·spir'a·cy (-SPIR-ə-see) n. (pl. -cies) —con·spir'a·tor n. —con·spir·a·to'ri·al adj.

con·stant (KON-stənt) adj. fixed, unchanging, steadfast; always duly happening or continuing —n. quantity that does not vary —con'stan·cy n. steadfastness; loyalty

con·stel·la·tion (kon-stə-LAY-shən) n. group of stars

con·ster·na·tion (kon-stər-NAY-shən) n. alarm, dismay, panic —con'ster·nate v. (-nat·ed, -nat·ing)

con·sti·pa·tion (kon-stə-PAY-shən) n. difficulty in emptying bowels —con'sti·pate vt. (-pat·ed, -pat·ing) affect with this disorder

con·stit·u·ent (kən-STICH-oo-ənt) adj. going toward making up whole; having power to make, alter constitution of a government —n. component part; element; voter —con·stit'u·en·cy n. body of constituents, supporters

con·sti·tute (KON-sti-toot) vt. (-tut·ed, -tut·ing) compose, set up, establish, form; make into, found, give form to —con·sti·tu'tion n. structure, composition; health; character, disposition; principles on which country, state is governed —con·sti·tu'tion·al adj. pert. to constitution; in harmony with political constitution —n. walk taken for health's sake

con·strain (kən-STRAYN) vt. force, compel —con·straint' n. compulsion; restraint; embarrassment, tension

con·stric·tion (kən-STRIK-shən) n. compression, squeezing together —con·strict' vt. —con·stric'tive adj. —con·stric'tor n. that which constricts; see also BOA

con·struct (kən-STRUKT) vt. make, build, form; put together; compose —con·struct (KON-strukt) n. —con·struc'tion n. —con·struc'tive adj. serving to improve; positive

con·strue (kən-STROO) vt. (-strued, -stru·ing) interpret; deduce; analyze grammatically

con·sul (KON-səl) n. official appointed by a government to represent it in a foreign country; in ancient Rome, one of the chief magistrates —con'su·lar adj. —con'su·late (-lit) n.

con·sult (kən-SULT) v. seek counsel, advice, information from —con·sult'ant n. specialist, expert —con·sul·ta·tion (kon-səl-TAY-shən) n. consulting; appointment to seek professional advice, esp. of doctor, lawyer —con·sul·ta·tive (kən-SUL-tə-tiv) adj. having privilege of consulting, but not of voting; advisory

con·sume (kən-SOOM) vt. (-sumed, -sum·ing) eat or drink; engross, possess; use up; destroy —con·sum'er n. buyer or user of commodity; one who consumes —con·sump'tion (-SUMP-shən) n. using up; destruction; wasting disease, esp. obs. pulmonary tuberculosis —con·sump'tive adj./n.

con·sum·mate (KON-sə-mayt) vt. (-mat·ed, -mat·ing) perfect; fulfill; complete (esp. marriage by sexual intercourse) —adj. (kən-SUM-it) of greatest perfection or completeness —con·sum'mate·ly adv. —con·sum·ma'tion n.

con·tact (KON-takt) n. touching; being in touch; junction of two or more electrical conductors; useful acquaintance —vt. —contact lens lens fitting over eyeball to correct defect of vision

con·ta·gion (kən-TAY-jən) n. passing on of disease by touch, contact; contagious disease; harmful physical or moral influence —con·ta'gious adj. communicable by contact, catching

con·tain (kən-TAYN) vt. hold; have room for; include, comprise; restrain (oneself) —con·tain'er n. box etc. for holding; large cargo-carrying standardsized receptacle for various modes of transport

con·tam·i·nate (kən-TAM-ə-nayt) vt. (-nat·ed, -nat·ing) stain, pollute, infect; make radioactive —con·tam·i·na'tion n. pollution

con·tem·plate (KON-təm-playt) vt. (-plat·ed, -plat·ing) reflect, meditate on; gaze upon; intend —con·tem·pla'tion n. thoughtful consideration; spiritual meditation —con·tem·pla·tive (kən-TEM-plə-tiv) adj./n. (one) given to contemplation

con·tem·po·rar·y (kən-TEM-pə-rer-ee) adj. existing or lasting at same time; of same age; modern —n. (pl. -rar·ies) one existing at same time as another —con·tem·po·ra'ne·ous (-RAY-nee-əs) adj.

con·tempt (kən-TEMPT) n. feeling that something is worthless, despicable etc.; expression of this feeling; state of being despised, disregarded; willful disrespect of authority

con·tend (kən-TEND) vi. strive, fight; dispute —vt. maintain (that) —con·ten'tion n. strife; debate; subject matter of dispute —con·ten'tious adj. quarrelsome; causing dispute

con·tent¹ (KON-tent) n. that contained; holding capacity —pl. that contained; index of topics in book

con·tent² (kən-TENT) adj. satisfied; willing (to) —vt. satisfy —n. satisfaction —con·tent'ed adj.

con·ter·mi·nous (kən-TUR-mə-nəs) adj. of the same extent (in time etc.); meeting along a common boundary; meeting end to end —con·ter'mi·nous adj.

con·test (KON-test) n. competition; conflict —vt. (kən-TEST) dispute, debate; fight or compete for —con·test'a·ble adj. —con·test'ant n.

con·text (KON-tekst) n. words coming before, after a word or passage; conditions and circumstances of event, fact etc. —con·tex·tu·al (kən-TEKS-choo-əl) adj.

con·tig·u·ous (kən-TIG-yoo-əs) adj. touching, near —con·ti·gu'i·ty n.

con·ti·nent¹ (KON-tə-nənt) n. large continuous mass of land —con·ti·nen'tal adj.

continent² adj. able to control one's urination and defecation; sexually chaste —con'ti·nence n.

con·tin·gent (kən-TIN-jənt) adj. depending (on); possible; accidental —n. group (of troops, supporters etc.) part of or representative of a larger group —con·tin'gen·cy n.

con·tin·ue (kən-TIN-yoo) v. (-ued, -u·ing) remain, keep in existence; carry on, last, go on; resume; prolong —con·tin'u·al adj. —con·tin·u·a'tion n. extension, extra part; resumption; constant succession, prolongation —con·tin·u'i·ty n. logical sequence; state of being continuous —con·tin'u·ous adj.

con·tort (kən-TORT) vt. twist out of normal shape —con·tor'tion n. —con·tor'tion·ist n. one who contorts own body to entertain

con·tour (KON-tuur) n. outline, shape, esp. of mountains, coast etc. —contour line line on map drawn through places of same height —contour map

contra- (prefix) against, as in contradistinction, contraposition etc. Such words are omitted where the meaning can easily be inferred from the simple word

con·tra·band (KON-trə-band) n. smuggled goods; illegal traffic in such goods —adj. prohibited by law

con·tra·cep·tion (kon-trə-SEP-shən) n. prevention of conception usu. by artificial means, birth control —con·tra·cep'tive adj./n.

**con·tract** (kɔn-TRAKT) v. make or become smaller, shorter; enter into agreement; agree upon —vt. incur, become affected by —n. (KON-trakt) bargain, agreement; formal document recording agreement; agreement enforceable by law —**con·tract'ed** adj. drawn together —**con·trac·tile** (kɔn-TRAK-tl) adj. tending to contract —**con·trac'tion** n. —**con'trac·tor** n. one making contract, esp. builder —**con·trac'tu·al** (-choo-əl) adj.

**con·tra·dict** (kon-trə-DIKT) vt. deny; be at variance or inconsistent with —**con·tra·dic'tion** n. —**con·tra·dic'to·ry** adj.

**con·tral·to** (kɔn-TRAL-toh) n. (pl. -tos) lowest of female voices

**con·trap·tion** (kɔn-TRAP-shən) n. gadget; device; construction, device often overelaborate or eccentric

**con·tra·pun·tal** (kon-trə-PUN-tl) adj. Mus. pert. to counterpoint

**con·trar·y** (KON-trer-ee) adj. opposed; opposite, other; (kɔn-TRAIR-ee) perverse, obstinate —n. (KON-trer-ee) something the exact opposite of another —adv. in opposition —**con'trar·i·ness** n.

**con·trast** (kɔn-TRAST) vt. bring out differences; set in opposition for comparison —vi. show great difference —n. (KON-trast) striking difference; TV sharpness of image

**con·tra·vene** (kon-trə-VEEN) vt. (-vened, -ven·ing) transgress, infringe; conflict with; contradict —**con·tra·ven'tion** n.

**con·tre·temps** (KON-trə-tahn) n. unexpected and embarrassing event or mishap

**con·trib·ute** (kɔn-TRIB-yoot) v. (-ut·ed, -ut·ing) give, pay to common fund; help to occur; write for the press —**con·tri·bu-**

**tion** (kon-trə-BYOO-shən) n. —**con·trib'u·tive** adj. —**con·trib'u·tor** n. one who writes articles for newspapers etc.; one who donates —**con·trib'u·to·ry** adj. partly responsible; giving to pension fund etc.

**con·trite** (kɔn-TRIT) adj. remorseful for wrongdoing, penitent —**con·trite'ly** adv. —**con·tri'tion** (-TRISH-ən) n.

**con·trive** (kɔn-TRIV) vt. (-trived, -triv·ing) manage; devise, invent, design —**con·triv'ance** n. artifice or device —**con·trived'** adj. obviously planned, artificial

**con·trol** (kɔn-TROHL) vt. (-trolled, -trol·ling) command, dominate; regulate; direct, check, test —n. power to direct or determine; curb, check; standard of comparison in experiment —n. pl. system of instruments to control automobile, aircraft etc. —**con·trol'la·ble** adj. —**con·trol'ler** n. one who controls; official controlling expenditure —**control tower** tower in airport from which takeoffs and landings are directed

**con·tro·ver·sy** (KON-trə-vur-see) n. (pl. -sies) dispute, debate, esp. over public issues —**con·tro·ver'sial** adj. —**con'tro·vert** vt. deny; argue —**con·tro·vert'i·ble** adj.

**con·tu·ma·cy** (KON-tuu-mə-see) n. (pl. -cies) stubborn disobedience —**con·tu·ma'cious** (-MAY-shəs) adj.

**con·tu·me·ly** (kon-TUU-mə-lee) n. (pl. -lies) insulting language or treatment —**con·tu·me'li·ous** (-MEE-lee-əs) adj. abusive, insolent

**con·tu·sion** (kɔn-TOO-zhən) n. bruise

**co·nun·drum** (kə-NUN-drəm) n. riddle, esp. with punning answer

**con·ur·ba·tion** (kon-ər-BAY-**

shon) *n.* densely populated urban sprawl formed by spreading of towns

**con·va·lesce** (kon-vo-LES) *vi.* (-lesced, -lesc·ing) recover health after illness, operation *etc.* —con·va·les'cence *n.* —con·va·les'cent *adj./n.*

**con·vec·tion** (kon-VEK-shon) *n.* transmission, *esp.* of heat, by currents in liquids or gases —con·vec'tor *n.* —con·vec'tive *adj.*

**con·vene** (kon-VEEN) *vt.* (-vened, -ven·ing) call together, assemble, convoke —con·ven'tion *n.* assembly; treaty, agreement; rule; practice based on agreement; accepted usage —con·ven'tion·al *adj.* (slavishly) observing customs of society; customary; (of weapons, war *etc.*) not nuclear

**con·ven·ient** (kon-VEEN-yont) *adj.* handy; favorable to needs, comfort; well adapted to one's purpose —con·ven'ience *n.* ease, comfort, suitability —*adj.* (of food) quick to prepare

**con·vent** (KON-vent) *n.* religious community, *esp.* of nuns; their building

**con·verge** (kon-VURJ) *vi.* (-verged, -verg·ing) approach, tend to meet —con·ver'gence, -gen·cy *n.* —con·ver'gent *adj.*

**con·ver·sant** (kon-VUR-sont) *adj.* acquainted, familiar (with), versed in

**conversation** *see* CONVERSE[1]

**con·verse**[1] (kon-VURS) *vi.* (-versed, -vers·ing) talk (with) —con·ver·sa'tion *n.* —con·ver·sa'tion·al *adj.*

**con·verse**[2] (KON-vurs) *adj.* opposite, turned around, reversed —*n.* the opposite, contrary

**con·vert** (kon-VURT) *vt.* apply to another purpose; change; trans-

form; cause to adopt (another) religion, opinion; *Football* make a conversion —*n.* (KON-vurt) converted person —con·ver'sion (-zhon) *n.* change of state; unauthorized appropriation; change of opinion, religion, or party; *Football* extra point scored after a touchdown —con·vert'er *n.* one who, that which converts; electrical device for changing alternating current into direct current; vessel in which molten metal is refined —con·vert'i·ble *n.* car with folding roof —*adj.*

**con·vex** (kon-VEKS) *adj.* curved outward; of a rounded form —con·vex'i·ty *n.*

**con·vey** (kon-VAY) *vt.* carry, transport; impart, communicate; *Law* make over, transfer —con·vey'ance *n.* carrying; vehicle; act by which title to property is transferred —con·vey'or belt continuous moving belt for transporting things, *esp.* in factory

**con·vict** (kon-VIKT) *vt.* prove or declare guilty —*n.* (KON-vikt) person found guilty of crime; criminal serving prison sentence —con·vic'tion *n.* verdict of guilty; being convinced, firm belief, state of being sure

**con·vince** (kon-VINS) *vt.* (-vinced, -vinc·ing) firmly persuade, satisfy by evidence or argument —con·vinc'ing *adj.* capable of compelling belief, effective

**con·viv·i·al** (kon-VIV-ee-ol) *adj.* sociable, festive, jovial —con·viv·i·al'i·ty *n.*

**con·voke** (kon-VOHK) *vt.* (-voked, -vok·ing) call together —con·vo·ca·tion (kon-vo-KAY-shon) *n.* calling together, assembly, *esp.* of clergy, college faculty *etc.*

**con·vo·lute** (KON-vo-loot) *vt.*

(-lut·ed, -lut·ing) twist, coil, tangle —con'vo·lut·ed adj. —con·vo·lu'tion n.

**con·voy** (KON-voi) n. party (of ships, troops, trucks etc.) traveling together for protection —vt. escort for protection

**con·vulse** (kən-VULS) vt. (-vulsed, -vuls·ing) shake violently; affect with violent involuntary contractions of muscles —con·vul'sion n. violent upheaval —pl. spasms; fits of laughter or hysteria —con·vul'sive adj.

**coo** (koo) n. cry of doves —vi. (cooed, coo·ing) make such cry

**cook** (kuuk) vt. prepare (food) for table, esp. by heat; inf. falsify (accounts etc.) —vi. undergo cooking; act as cook —n. one who prepares food for table —cook'er n. cooking apparatus —cook'ie n. small cake made from sweet dough —cook'out n. (party featuring) meal cooked and served outdoors —cook up inf. invent, plan; prepare (meal)

**cool** (kool) adj. moderately cold; unexcited, calm; lacking friendliness or interest; inf. calmly insolent; inf. sophisticated, elegant —v. make, become cool —n. cool time, place etc.; inf. calmness, composure —cool'ant n. fluid used for cooling tool, machinery etc. —cool'er n. vessel in which liquids are cooled; iced drink usu. with wine or whiskey base; sl. jail —cool one's heels be kept waiting, esp. because of deliberate discourtesy

**coon** (koon) n. raccoon

**coop** (koop) n. cage or pen for pigeons etc. —vt. shut up in a coop; confine

**co-op** (KOH-op) n. cooperative enterprise; apartment or business run by one

**coop·er** (KOO-pər) n. one who makes casks

**co·op·er·ate** (koh-OP-ə-rayt) vi. (-at·ed, -at·ing) work together —co·op·er·a'tion n. —co·op'er·a·tive adj. willing to cooperate; (of an enterprise) owned collectively and managed for joint economic benefit (also n.)

**co-opt** (koh-OPT) vt. preempt, appropriate as one's own; elect by votes of existing members

**co·or·di·nate** (koh-OR-dn-ayt) vt. (-nat·ed, -nat·ing) bring into order as parts of whole; place in same rank; put into harmony —n. (-it) Math. any of set of numbers defining location of point —adj. equal in degree, status etc. —co·or·di·na'tion n.

**coot** (koot) n. small black water fowl; inf. silly (old) person

**cop** (kop) vt. sl. (copped, cop·ping) catch —n. inf. policeman —cop a plea sl. plead guilty in return for light sentence

**cope** (kohp) vi. (coped, cop·ing) deal successfully (with)

**Co·per·ni·can** (koh-PUR-ni-kən) adj. pert. to Copernicus, Polish astronomer (1473-1543), or to his system

**cop·ing** (KOH-ping) n. top course of wall, usu. sloping to throw off rain

**co·pi·ous** (KOH-pee-əs) adj. abundant; plentiful; full, ample

**cop·per**[1] (KOP-ər) n. reddish-brown malleable ductile metal; bronze money, coin —vt. cover with copper —copper beech tree with reddish leaves —cop'per·plate (-playt) n. plate of copper for engraving, etching; print from this; copybook writing; first-class handwriting

**cop·per**[2] n. sl. policeman

**copse** (kops) n. a wood of small trees

**co·pra** (KOH-prə) *n.* dried coconut kernels

**cop·u·la** (KOP-yə-lə) *n.* (*pl.* -las) word, *esp.* verb acting as connecting link in sentence; connection, tie

**cop·u·late** (KOP-yə-layt) *vi.* (-lat·ed, -lat·ing) unite sexually —**cop·u·la′tion** *n.*

**cop·y** (KOP-ee) *n.* (*pl.* cop·ies) imitation; single specimen of book; matter for printing —*vt.* (cop·ied, cop·y·ing) make copy of, imitate; transcribe; follow an example —**cop′y·right** *n.* legal exclusive right to print and publish book, article, work of art *etc.* —*vt.* protect by copyright —**cop′y·writ·er** *n.* one who writes advertisements

**co·quette** (koh-KET) *n.* woman who flirts —**co·quet·ry** (KOH-ki-tree) *n.* —**co·quet′tish** *adj.*

**Cor.** Corinthians

**cor·al** (KOR-əl) *n.* hard substance made by sea polyps and forming growths, islands, reefs; ornament of coral —*adj.* made of coral; of deep pink color

**cord** (kord) *n.* thin rope or thick string; rib on cloth; ribbed fabric —*vt.* fasten with cord —**cord′age** *n.*

**cor·date** (KOR-dayt) *adj.* heart-shaped

**cor·dial** (KOR-jəl) *adj.* hearty, sincere, warm —*n.* sweet, fruit-flavored alcoholic drink; liqueur —**cor·di·al·i·ty** (kor-jee-AL-i-tee) *n.* warmth

**cord·ite** (KOR-dīt) *n.* explosive compound

**cor·don** (KOR-dn) *n.* chain of troops or police; fruit tree grown as single stem —*vt.* form cordon around

**cor·don bleu** (kor-DAWN BLUU) *adj.* (*esp.* of food preparation) of highest standard

**cor·du·roy** (KOR-də-roi) *n.* cotton fabric with velvety, ribbed surface

**core** (kor) *n.* horny seed case of apple and other fruits; central or innermost part of thing —*vt.* (cored, cor·ing) take out the core

**co·re·spond·ent** (koh-ri-SPON-dənt) *n.* one cited in divorce case, alleged to have committed adultery with the respondent

**cor·gi** (KOR-gee) *n.* a small Welsh dog

**co·ri·an·der** (KOR-ee-an-dər) *n.* an herb

**Co·rin·thi·an** (kə-RIN-thee-ən) *adj.* of Corinth; Corinthian order of architecture, ornate Greek; (*pl.*) books in New Testament

**cork** (kork) *n.* bark of an evergreen Mediterranean oak tree; piece of it or other material, *esp.* used as stopper for bottle *etc.* —*vt.* stop up with cork —**cork′age** *n.* charge for opening wine bottles in restaurant —**cork′er** *n.* *sl.* something, someone outstanding —**cork′screw** *n.* tool for pulling out corks

**corn**[1] (korn) *n.* (kernels of) sweet corn, corn on the cob; *inf.* oversentimental, trite quality in play, film *etc.* —*vt.* preserve (meat) with salt or brine —**corn′y** *adj.* *inf.* (corn·i·er, corn·i·est) trite, oversentimental, hackneyed —**corn·cob** *n.* ear of sweet corn —**corn′flour** *n.* finely ground corn —**corn′flow·er** *n.* blue flower, *oft.* growing in grainfields

**corn**[2] *n.* painful horny growth on foot or toe

**cor·ne·a** (KOR-nee-ə) *n.* transparent membrane covering front of eye

**cor·ner** (KOR-nər) *n.* part of room where two sides meet; remote or humble place; point where two walls, streets *etc.* meet; angle, projection; *Business* buying up of whole existing stock of commodity, shares —*vt.* drive into position of difficulty, or leaving no escape; establish monopoly —*vi.* turn around corner —**cor'ner-stone** *n.* indispensable part, basis —**corner kick** *Soccer* free kick from corner of field

**cor-net** (kor-NET) *n.* trumpet with valves

**cor-nice** (KOR-nis) *n.* projection near top of wall; ornamental, carved molding below ceiling

**cor-nu-co-pi-a** (kor-nə-KOH-pee-ə) *n.* symbol of plenty, consisting of goat's horn, overflowing with fruit and flowers

**co-rol-la** (kə-ROL-ə) *n.* flower's inner envelope of petals

**cor-ol-lar-y** (KOR-ə-lee-ee) *n.* (*pl.* -lar-ies) inference from a preceding statement; deduction; result

**co-ro-na** (kə-ROH-nə) *n.* (*pl.* -nas) halo around heavenly body; flat projecting part of cornice; top or crown

**cor-o-nar-y** (KOR-ə-ner-ee) *adj.* of blood vessels surrounding heart —*n.* (*pl.* -nar-ies) short for coronary thrombosis, disease of the heart

**cor-o-na-tion** (kor-ə-NAY-shən) *n.* ceremony of crowning a sovereign

**cor-o-ner** (KOR-ə-nər) *n.* officer who holds inquests on bodies of persons supposed killed by violence, accident *etc.*

**cor-o-net** (KOR-ə-net) *n.* small crown

**cor-po-ral**[1] (KOR-pər-əl) *adj.* of the body; material, not spiritual —**corporal punishment** (flogging *etc.*) of physical nature

**corporal**[2] *n.* noncommissioned officer below sergeant

**cor-po-ra-tion** (kor-pə-RAY-shən) *n.* association, body of persons legally authorized to act as an individual; authorities of town or city —**cor'po-rate** (-rit) *adj.*

**cor-po-re-al** (kor-POR-ee-əl) *adj.* of the body, material; tangible

**corps** (kor) *n.* (*pl.* **corps** *pr.* korz) military force, body of troops; any organized body of persons

**corpse** (korps) *n.* dead body

**cor-pu-lent** (KOR-pyə-lənt) *adj.* fat —**cor'pu-lence** *n.*

**cor-pus** (KOR-pəs) *n.* collection or body of works, *esp.* by single author; main part or body of something

**cor-pus-cle** (KOR-pə-səl) *n.* minute organism or particle, *esp.* red and white corpuscles of blood

**cor-ral** (kə-RAL) *n.* enclosure for cattle, or for defense —*vt.* (-ralled, -ral-ling)

**cor-rect** (kə-REKT) *vt.* set right; indicate errors in; rebuke, punish; counteract, rectify —*adj.* right, exact, accurate; in accordance with facts or standards —**cor-rec'tion** *n.* —**cor-rec'tive** *n./adj.*

**cor-re-late** (KOR-ə-layt) *vt.* (-lat-ed, -lat-ing) bring into reciprocal relation —*n.* (-lit) either of two things or words necessarily implying the other —**cor-re-la'tion** *n.* —**cor-re-la-tive** (kə-REL-ə-tiv) *adj./n.*

**cor-re-spond** (kor-ə-SPOND) *vi.* be in agreement, be consistent with; be similar (to); exchange letters —**cor-re-spond'ence** *n.* agreement, corresponding; similarity; exchange of letters; letters received —**cor-re-spond'ent** *n.* writer of letters; one employed by newspaper *etc.* to report on particular topic, country *etc.*

**cor-ri-dor** (KOR-i-dər) *n.* passage in building *etc.*; strip of territory (or air route) not under control of country through which it passes; densely populated area incl. two or more major cities

**cor·ri·gen·dum** (kor-i-JEN-dəm) *n.* (*pl.* -da *pr.* -də) thing to be corrected

**cor·rob·o·rate** (kə-ROB-ə-rayt) *vt.* (-rat·ed, -rat·ing) confirm, support (statement *etc.*) —**cor·rob·o·ra'tion** *n.* —**cor·rob'o·ra·tive** *adj.*

**cor·rode** (kə-ROHD) *vt.* (-rod·ed, -rod·ing) eat, wear away, eat into (by chemical action, disease *etc.*) —**cor·ro'sion** (-ROH-zhən) *n.* —**cor·ro'sive** *adj.*

**cor·ru·gate** (KOR-ə-gayt) *v.* (-gat·ed, -gat·ing) wrinkle, bend into wavy ridges

**cor·rupt** (kə-RUPT) *adj.* lacking integrity; open to, or involving, bribery; wicked; spoiled by mistakes, altered for the worse (of words, literary passages *etc.*) —*vt.* make evil, pervert; bribe; make rotten —**cor·rupt'i·ble** *adj.* —**cor·rup'tion** *n.*

**cor·sage** (kor-SAHZH) *n.* (flower, spray, worn on) bodice of woman's dress

**cor·sair** (KOR-sair) *n.* pirate (ship)

**cor·set** (KOR-sit) *n.* close-fitting undergarment stiffened to give support or shape to the body

**cor·tege** (kor-TEZH) *n.* formal (funeral) procession

**cor·tex** (KOR-teks) *n. Anat.* (*pl.* -ti·ces *pr.* -tə-seez) outer layer; bark; sheath —**cor'ti·cal** *adj.*

**cor·ti·sone** (KOR-tə-zohn) *n.* synthetic hormone used in the treatment of a variety of diseases

**cor·vette** (kor-VET) *n.* lightly armed warship for escort and antisubmarine duties

**co·sine** (KOH-sīn) *n.* in a right triangle, the ratio of a side adjacent to a given angle and the hypotenuse

**cos·met·ic** (koz-MET-ik) *n.* preparation to beautify or improve skin, hair *etc.* —*adj.* designed to improve appearance only

**cos·mic** (KOZ-mik) *adj.* relating to the universe; of the vastness of the universe —**cos·mog'ra·pher** *n.* —**cos·mog'ra·phy** *n.* description or mapping of the universe —**cos·mo·log·i·cal** (koz-mə-LOJ-i-kəl) *adj.* —**cos·mol'o·gy** *n.* the science or study of the universe

**cosmic rays** high-energy electromagnetic rays from space

**cos·mo·naut** (KOZ-mə-nawt) *n.* Soviet astronaut

**cos·mo·pol·i·tan** (koz-mə-POL-i-tn) *n.* person who has lived and traveled in many countries —*adj.* familiar with many countries; sophisticated; free from national prejudice

**cos·mos**[1] (KOZ-məs) *n.* the world or universe considered as an ordered system

**cos·mos**[2] *n.* (*pl.* -mos) plant cultivated for brightly colored flowers

**cos·sack** (KOS-ak) *n.* member of tribe in SE Russia

**cost** (kawst) *n.* price; expenditure of time, labor *etc.* —*pl.* expenses of lawsuit —*vt.* (cost, cost·ing) have as price; entail payment, or loss, or sacrifice of —**cost'ing** *n.* system of calculating cost of production, sale —**cost'li·ness** *n.* —**cost'ly** *adj.* (-li·er, -li·est) valuable; expensive —**cost** (price) price at which article is bought by one intending to resell it

**cos·tal** (KOS-tl) *adj.* pert. to side of body or ribs

**cos·tume** (KOS-toom) *n.* style of dress of particular place or time, or for particular activity; theatrical clothes —cos'tum·er *n.* dealer in costumes —costume jewelry inexpensive jewelry

cot (kot) *n.* narrow, usu. collapsible bed

cote (koht) *n.* shelter, shed for animals or birds, *eg* dovecote

co·te·rie (KOH-tə-ree) *n.* exclusive group of people with common interests; social clique

coterminous *see* CONTERMINOUS

cot·tage (KOT-ij) *n.* small house —cottage cheese mild, soft cheese —cottage industry industry in which workers work in their own homes

cot·ter (KOT-ər) *n.* pin, wedge *etc.* to prevent relative motion of two parts of machine *etc.*

cot·ton (KOT-n) *n.* plant; white downy fibrous covering of its seeds; thread or cloth made of this —cotton (on) to begin to like, understand (idea, person *etc.*)

cot·y·le·don (kot-l-EED-n) *n.* primary leaf of plant embryos

couch (kowch) *n.* piece of furniture for sitting or reclining on by day, sofa —*vt.* put into (words), phrase; cause to lie down —on the couch under psychiatric treatment

cou·gar (KOO-gər) *n.* mountain lion

cough (kawf) *vi.* expel air from lungs with sudden effort and noise, often to remove obstruction —*n.* act of coughing

could *pt.* of CAN[1]

cou·lomb (KOO-lom) *n.* unit of quantity of electricity

coun·cil (KOWN-səl) *n.* deliberative or administrative body; one of its meetings; local governing authority of town *etc.* —coun'cilor *n.* member of council

coun·sel (KOWN-səl) *n.* advice, deliberation or debate; lawyer or lawyers; plan, policy —*vt.* advise, recommend —coun'se·lor *n.* adviser; lawyer —keep one's counsel keep a secret

count[1] (kownt) *vt.* reckon, calculate, number; include; consider to be —*vi.* be reckoned in; depend (on); be of importance —*n.* reckoning; total number reached by counting; item in list of charges or indictment; act of counting —count'less *adj.* too many to be counted

count[2] *n.* European nobleman of rank corresponding to that of British earl —count'ess *n. fem.* wife or widow of count or earl

coun·te·nance (KOWN-tn-əns) *n.* face, its expression; support, approval —*vt.* (-nanced, -nanc·ing) give support, approve

count·er[1] (KOWN-tər) *n.* horizontal surface in bank, store *etc.*, on which business is transacted; work surface in kitchen; disk, token used for counting or scoring, *esp.* in board games

coun·ter[2] *adv.* in opposite direction; contrary —*vi.* oppose, contradict; Fencing parry —*n.* parry

counter- (*comb. form*) reversed, opposite, rival, retaliatory, as in counterclaim *n.* —counterirritant *n.* —countermarch *vi.* —counterpunch *vi.* —counterrevolution *n. etc.* Such words are not given here where the meaning can be inferred from the simple word

coun·ter·act (kown-tər-AKT) *vt.* neutralize or hinder

coun·ter·at·tack (KOWN-tər-ə-tak) *v./n.* attack after enemy's advance

coun·ter·bal·ance (KOWN-tər-bal-əns) *n.* weight balancing or neutralizing another —*vt.* (-anced, anc·ing)

coun·ter·feit (KOWN-tər-fit) *adj.*

sham, forged —n. imitation, forgery —vt. imitate with intent to deceive; forge

coun·ter·mand (kown-tər-MAND) vt. cancel (previous order)

coun·ter·part (KOWN-tər-pahrt) n. thing so like another as to be mistaken for it; something complementary to or correlative of another

coun·ter·point (KOWN-tər-point) n. melody added as accompaniment to given melody; art of so adding melodies

coun·ter·sign (KOWN-tər-sīn) vt. sign document already signed by another; ratify —n. Military secret sign

coun·ter·sink (KOWN-tər-singk) v. (-sunk, -sink·ing) enlarge upper part of hole (drilled in wood etc.) to take head of screw, bolt etc. below surface

countess n. see COUNT[2]

coun·try (KUN-tree) n. (pl. -tries) region, district; territory of nation; land of birth, residence etc.; rural districts as opposed to city; nation —coun'tri·fied (fid) adj. rural in manner or appearance —coun'try·man n. rustic; compatriot —country music popular music based on Amer. folk music —coun'try·side n. rural district; its inhabitants

coun·ty (KOWN-tee) n. (pl. -ties) division of a state

coup (koo) n. (pl. coups pr. kooz) successful stroke, move or gamble; (short for coup d'é·tat pr. koo-day-TAH) sudden, violent seizure of government

cou·ple (KUP-əl) n. two, pair; husband and wife; any two persons —v. (-pled, -pling) vt. connect, fasten together; associate, connect in the mind —vi. join, associate —cou'plet n. two lines of verse, esp. rhyming and of equal length —cou'pling n. connection

cou·pon (KOO-pon) n. ticket or voucher entitling holder to discount, gift etc.; detachable slip used as order form

cour·age (KUR-ij) n. bravery, boldness —cou·ra·geous (kə-RAY-jəs) adj.

cour·i·er (KUUR-ee-ər) n. express messenger

course (kors) n. movement in space or time; direction of movement; successive development, sequence; line of conduct or action; series of lessons, exercises etc.; any of successive parts of meal; continuous line of masonry at particular level in building; area where golf is played; track or ground on which a race is run —v. (coursed, cours·ing) vt. hunt —vi. run swiftly, gallop about; (of blood) circulate

court (kort) n. space enclosed by buildings, yard; area marked off or enclosed for playing various games; retinue and establishment of sovereign; body with judicial powers, place where it meets, one of its sittings; attention, homage, flattery —vt. woo, try to win or attract; seek, invite —cour·ti·er (KOR-tee-ər) n. one who frequents royal court —court'li·ness n. —court'ly adj. (-li·er, -li·est) ceremoniously polite; characteristic of a court —court martial (pl. court martials) court of naval or military officers for trying naval or military offenses —court'yard n. paved space enclosed by buildings or walls

cour·te·san (KOR-tə-zən) n. court mistress; high-class prostitute

cour·te·sy (KUR-tə-see) n. (pl. -sies) politeness, good manners;

act of civility —**cour'te·ous** adj. polite

**court·ship** (KORT-ship) n. wooing

**cous·in** (KUZ-ən) n. son or daughter of uncle or aunt

**cove** (kohv) n. small inlet of coast, sheltered bay

**cov·en** (KUV-ən) n. gathering of witches

**cov·e·nant** (KUV-ə-nənt) n. contract, mutual agreement; compact —v. agree to a covenant

**cov·er** (KUV-ər) vt. place or spread over; extend, spread; bring upon (oneself); screen, protect; travel over; include; be sufficient; Journalism etc. report; point a gun at —n. lid, wrapper, envelope, binding, screen, anything that covers —**cov'er·age** n. amount, extent covered —**cov'er·let** n. bedspread —**cover girl** attractive model whose picture appears on magazine cover

**co·vert** (KOH-vərt) adj. secret, veiled, concealed, sly —n. (KUV-ərt) thicket, place sheltering game

**cov·et** (KUV-it) vt. long to possess, esp. what belongs to another —**cov'et·ous** adj. greedy

**cov·ey** (KUV-ee) n. (pl. -eys) brood of partridges or quail

**cow**[1] (kow) n. the female of the bovine and of certain other animals (eg elephant, whale) —**cow'boy** n. ranch hand in charge of cattle on western plains of US; inf. reckless driver etc.

**cow**[2] vt. frighten into submission, overawe, subdue

**cow·ard** (KOW-ərd) n. one who lacks courage, shrinks from danger —**cow'ard·ice** (-dis) n. —**cow'ard·ly** adj.

**cow·er** (KOW-ər) vi. crouch, shrink in fear

**cowl** (kowl) n. monk's hooded cloak; its hood; cowling

**cowl·ing** (KOW-ling) n. covering for aircraft engine

**cow·rie** (KOW-ree) n. brightly colored sea shell

**cox·swain** (KOK-sən) n. steersman of boat —**cox** v. inf. act as coxswain

**coy** (koi) adj. (-er, -est) (pretending to be) shy, modest —**coy'ness** n.

**coy·o·te** (kī-OH-tee) n. N Amer. prairie wolf

**co·zy** (KOH-zee) adj. (-zi·er, -zi·est) snug, comfortable, sheltered; suggesting conspiratorial intimacy —**co'zi·ly** adv. —**co'ziness** n.

**Cr** Chem. chromium

**crab** (krab) n. edible crustacean with ten legs, noted for sidelong and backward walk; type of louse —vi. (crabbed, crab·bing) catch crabs; move sideways —**crab·bed** (KRAB-id) adj. of handwriting, hard to read —**crab'by** adj. (-bi·er, -bi·est) irritable

**crack** (krak) vt. break, split partially; break with sharp noise; cause to make sharp noise, as of whip, rifle etc.; break down, yield; inf. tell (joke); solve, decipher —vi. make sharp noise; split, fissure; of the voice, lose clearness when changing from boy's to man's —n. sharp explosive noise; split, fissure; flaw; inf. joke, esp. sarcastic; chat; sl. pure, highly addictive form of cocaine —adj. inf. special, smart, of great reputation for skill or fashion —**crack'er** n. thin dry biscuit; (C-) n. sl. offens. native or inhabitant of Georgia —**crack'le** (-əl) n. sound of repeated small cracks —vi. (-led, -ling) make this sound —**crack'ling** n. crackle; crisp skin of roast pork etc.

**cra·dle** (KRAYD-l) n. infant's bed

(on rockers); *fig.* earliest resting place or home; supporting framework —*vt.* (-dled, -dling) hold or rock as in a cradle; cherish

**craft**[1] (kraft) *n.* skill, ability, *esp.* manual ability; cunning; skilled trade; members of a trade —**craft'i·ly** *adv.* —**craft'y** *adj.* (-craft·i·er, craft·i·est) cunning, shrewd —**crafts'man** *n.* —**crafts'man·ship** *n.*

**craft**[2] *n.* vessel; ship

**crag** (krag) *n.* steep rugged rock —**crag'gy** *adj.* (-gi·er, -gi·est) rugged

**cram** (kram) *vt.* (crammed, cram·ming) fill quite full; stuff, force; pack tightly —*vi.* feed to excess; prepare quickly for examination

**cramp** (kramp) *n.* painful muscular contraction; clamp for holding masonry, wood *etc.* together —*vt.* restrict or hamper; hem in, keep within too narrow limits

**cram·pon** (KRAM-pon) *n.* spike in shoe for mountain climbing *esp.* on ice

**crane** (krayn) *n.* wading bird with long legs, neck, and bill; machine for moving heavy weights —*vi.* (craned, cran·ing) stretch neck to see

**cra·ni·um** (KRAY-nee-əm) *n.* skull —**cra'ni·al** *adj.*

**crank** (krangk) *n.* arm at right angles to axis, for turning main shaft, changing reciprocal into rotary motion *etc.*; *inf.* eccentric person, faddist —*v.* start (engine) by turning crank —**crank'y** *adj.* (crank·i·er, crank·i·est) bad-tempered; eccentric —**crank'shaft** *n.* principal shaft of engine

**cran·ny** (KRAN-ee) *n.* (*pl.* -nies) small opening, chink —**cran'nied** *adj.*

**crap** (krap) *n.* gambling game played with two dice (*also* **craps**)

**crape** (krayp) *n.* crepe, *esp.* when used for mourning clothes

**crash** (krash) *v.* (cause to) make loud noise; (cause to) fall with crash —*vi.* break, smash; collapse, fail, *esp.* financially; cause (aircraft) to hit land or water; collide with (another car *etc.*); move noisily or violently —*n.* loud, violent fall or impact; collision, *esp.* between vehicles; sudden, uncontrolled descent of aircraft to land; sudden collapse or downfall, *esp.* of economy; bankruptcy —*adj.* requiring, using, great effort to achieve results quickly —**crash helmet** helmet worn by motorcyclists *etc.* to protect head

**crass** (kras) *adj.* (-er, -est) grossly stupid; insensitive —**crass'ness** *n.*

**crate** (krayt) *n.* large (*usu.* wooden) container for packing goods

**cra·ter** (KRAY-tər) *n.* mouth of volcano; bowl-shaped cavity, *esp.* one made by explosion of large shell, bomb, mine *etc.*

**cra·vat** (krə-VAT) *n.* man's neckband or scarf

**crave** (krayv) *v.* (craved, craving) have very strong desire for, long for —*vt.* ask humbly; beg —**craving** *n.*

**cra·ven** (KRAY-vən) *adj.* cowardly, abject, spineless —*n.* coward —**cra'ven·ness** *n.*

**craw** (kraw) *n.* bird's or animal's stomach; bird's crop

**crawl** (krawl) *vi.* move on belly or on hands and knees; move very slowly; ingratiate oneself, cringe; swim with crawl stroke; be overrun (with) —*n.* crawling motion; very slow walk; racing stroke at swimming

**cray·fish** (KRAY-fish) *n.* edible

freshwater crustacean like lobster (also **craw'fish**)

**cray·on** (KRAY-ǝn) *n.* stick or pencil of colored chalk, wax *etc.*

**craze** (krayz) *n.* short-lived current fashion; strong desire or passion, mania; madness —**crazed** *adj.* demented; (of porcelain) having fine cracks —**cra'zy** *adj.* (**-zi·er, -zi·est**) insane; very foolish; madly eager (for) —**crazy quilt** patchwork quilt of irregular patches; jumble

**creak** (kreek) *n.* harsh grating noise —*vi.* make creaking sound

**cream** (kreem) *n.* fatty part of milk; various foods, dishes, resembling cream; cosmetic *etc.* with creamlike consistency; yellowish-white color; best part of anything —*vt.* take cream from; take best part from; beat to creamy consistency —**cream'y** *adj.* (**cream·i·er, cream·i·est**)

**crease** (krees) *n.* line made by folding; wrinkle; *Ice Hockey* marked rectangular area in front of goal cage; superficial bullet wound —*v.* (**creased, creas·ing**) make, develop creases

**cre·ate** (kree-AYT) *v.* (**-at·ed, -at·ing**) —*vt.* bring into being; give rise to; make —*vi. inf.* make a fuss —**cre·a'tion** *n.* —**cre·a'tive** *adj.* —**cre·a'tor** *n.*

**crea·ture** (KREE-chǝr) *n.* living being; thing created; dependent, too (of another) —**creature comforts** bodily comforts

**crèche** (kresh) *n.* representation of the Nativity scene

**cre·dence** (KREED-ns) *n.* belief, credit; small table for bread and wine of the Eucharist

**cre·den·tials** (kri-DEN-shǝlz) *n. pl.* testimonials; letters of introduction, *esp.* those given to ambassador

**cred·i·ble** (KRED-ǝ-bǝl) *adj.* worthy of belief; trustworthy —**cred·i·bil'i·ty** *n.*

**cred·it** (KRED-it) *n.* commendation, approval; source, cause, of honor; belief, trust; good name; influence, honor or power based on trust of others; system of allowing customers to take goods for later payment; money at one's disposal in bank *etc.*; side of ledger on which such sums are entered; reputation for financial reliability —*pl.* list of those responsible for production of film *etc.* —*vt.* attribute, believe that person has; believe; put on credit side of account —**cred'it·a·ble** *adj.* bringing honor —**cred'i·tor** *n.* one to whom debt is due

**cred·u·lous** (KREJ-ǝ-lǝs) *adj.* too easy of belief, easily deceived or imposed on, gullible —**cre·du·li·ty** (krǝ-DOO-li-tee) *n.*

**creed** (kreed) *n.* formal statement of religious beliefs; statement, system of beliefs or principles

**creek** (kreek) *n.* narrow inlet on seacoast

**creel** (kreel) *n.* angler's fishing basket

**creep** (kreep) *vi.* (**crept, creep·ing**) make way along ground, as snake; move with stealthy, slow movements; crawl; act in servile way; of skin or flesh, feel shrinking, shivering sensation, due to fear or repugnance —*n.* creeping; *sl.* repulsive person —*pl.* feeling of fear or repugnance —**creep'er** *n.* creeping or climbing plant, *eg* ivy —**creep'y** *inf. adj.* (**creep·i·er, creep·i·est**) uncanny, unpleasant; causing flesh to creep

**cre·ma·tion** (kri-MAY-shǝn) *n.* burning as means of disposing of corpses —**cre·mate** (KREE-mayt) *vt.* (**-mat·ed, -mat·ing**) —**cre·ma·**

**to·ri·um** (kree-mə-TOR-ee-əm) n. place for cremation

**cre·ole** (KREE-ohl) n. hybrid language; (C-) native born W Indian, Latin American, of European descent

**cre·o·sote** (KREE-ə-soht) n. oily antiseptic liquid distilled from coal or wood tar, used for preserving wood —vt. (-sot·ed, -sot·ing) coat or impregnate with creosote

**crepe** (krayp) n. fabric with crimped surface; crape; thin, light pancake —**crepe rubber** rough-surfaced rubber used for soles of shoes

**crept** pt./pp. of CREEP

**cre·scen·do** (kri-SHEN-doh) n. gradual increase of loudness, esp. in music —adj./adv.

**cres·cent** (KRES-ənt) n. (shape of) moon as seen in first or last quarter; any figure of this shape; curved portion of a street

**crest** (krest) n. comb or tuft on bird's or animal's head; plume on top of helmet; top of mountain, ridge, wave etc.; feather above shield of coat of arms, also used separately on seal, plate etc. —vi. crown —vt. reach top of —**crest'fall·en** adj. cast down by failure, dejected

**cre·ta·ceous** (kri-TAY-shəs) adj. chalky

**cre·tin** (KREET-n) n. person afflicted with cretinism; inf. stupid or mentally defective person —**cre'tin·ism** n. deficiency in thyroid gland causing physical and mental retardation

**cre·vasse** (kri-VAS) n. deep open chasm, esp. in glacier

**crev·ice** (KREV-is) n. cleft, fissure, chink

**crew** (kroo) n. ship's, boat's or aircraft's company, excluding passengers; inf. gang or set —v.

serve as crew —**crew cut** man's closely cropped haircut

**crew·el** (KROO-əl) n. fine worsted yarn, used in needlework and embroidery

**crib** (krib) n. child's cot; barred rack used for fodder; plagiarism; translation used by students, sometimes illicitly —vt. (cribbed, crib·bing) confine in small space; copy unfairly

**crib·bage** (KRIB-ij) n. card game for two, three, or four players

**crick** (krik) n. spasm or cramp in muscles, esp. in neck

**crick·et¹** (KRIK-it) n. chirping insect

**crick·et²** n. outdoor game played esp. in England with bats, ball and wickets by teams of eleven a side —**crick'et·er** n.

**crime** (krīm) n. violation of law (usu. a serious offense); wicked or forbidden act; inf. something to be regretted —**crim·i·nal** (KRIM-ə-nl) adj./n. —**crim·i·nal'i·ty** n. —**crim·i·nol'o·gy** n. study of crime and criminals

**crimp** (krimp) vt. pinch into tiny parallel pleats; wrinkle

**crim·son** (KRIM-zən) adj./n. (of) rich deep red

**cringe** (krinj) vi. (cringed, cring·ing) shrink, cower; behave obsequiously

**crin·kle** (KRING-kəl) v./n. (-kled, -kling) wrinkle

**crin·o·line** (KRIN-l-in) n. hooped petticoat or skirt of stiff material

**crip·ple** (KRIP-əl) n. one not having normal use of limbs, disabled or deformed person —vt. (-pled, -pling) maim, disable, impair; weaken, lessen efficiency of

**cri·sis** (KRĪ-sis) n. (pl. -ses pr. -seez) turning point or decisive moment, esp. in illness; time of acute danger or difficulty

**crisp** (krisp) adj. (-er, -est) brittle

but firm; brisk, decided; clear-cut; fresh, invigorating; crackling; of hair, curly —*n.* dessert of fruit baked with a crunchy mixture —**crisp'er** *n.* refrigerator compartment for storing salads *etc.*

**cri·te·ri·on** (krī-TEER-ee-ən) *n.* (*pl.* -ri·a *pr.* -ree-ə) standard of judgment

**crit·i·cal** (KRIT-i-kəl) *adj.* faultfinding; discerning; skilled in or given to judging; of great importance, crucial, decisive —**crit'ic** *n.* one who passes judgment; writer expert in judging works of literature, art *etc.* —**crit'i·cism** *n.* —**crit'i·cize** *vt.* (-cized, ciz·ing) —**cri·tique** (kri-TEEK) *n.* critical essay, carefully written criticism

**croak** (krohk) *v.* utter deep hoarse cry, as raven, frog; talk dismally —*vi. sl.* die —*n.* deep hoarse cry

**cro·chet** (kroh-SHAY) *n.* kind of handicraft like knitting, done with small hooked needle —*v.* do, make such work

**crock** (krok) *n.* earthenware jar or pot; broken piece of earthenware —**crock'er·y** *n.* earthenware dishes, utensils *etc.*

**croc·o·dile** (KROK-ə-dīl) *n.* large amphibious reptile —**crocodile tears** insincere grief

**crois·sant** (krwah-SAHN) *n.* buttery, crescent-shaped roll of leavened dough or puff paste

**crone** (krohn) *n.* witchlike old woman

**cro·ny** (KROH-nee) *n.* (*pl.* -nies) intimate friend

**crook** (kruuk) *n.* hooked staff; any hook, bend, sharp turn; *inf.* swindler, criminal —**crook'ed** *adj.* bent; twisted; deformed; dishonest

**croon** (kroon) *v.* hum, sing in soft, low tone —**croon'er** *n.*

**crop** (krop) *n.* produce of cultivation of any plant or plants; harvest, *lit.* or *fig.*; pouch in bird's gullet; stock of whip; hunting whip; short haircut —*v.* (cropped, crop·ping) cut short; raise, produce or occupy land with crop; (of animals) bite, eat down; poll or clip —**crop'·dust·ing** *n.* spreading fungicide *etc.* on crops from aircraft —**crop up** *inf.* happen unexpectedly

**cro·quet** (kroh-KAY) *n.* lawn game played with balls, wooden mallets and hoops

**cro·quette** (kroh-KET) *n.* breaded, fried ball of minced meat, fish *etc.*

**cro·sier** (KROH-zhər) *n.* bishop's or abbot's staff

**cross** (kraws) *n.* structure or symbol of two intersecting lines or pieces (at right angles); such a structure of wood as means of execution by tying or nailing victim to it; symbol of Christian faith; any thing or mark in the shape of cross; misfortune, annoyance, affliction; intermixture of breeds, hybrid —*v.* move or go across (something); intersect; meet and pass —*vt.* mark with lines across; (*with* out) delete; place or put in form of cross; make sign of cross on or over; modify breed of animals or plants by intermixture; thwart; oppose —*adj.* out of temper, angry; peevish, perverse; transverse; intersecting; contrary; adverse —**cross'ing** *n.* intersection of roads, rails *etc.*; part of street where pedestrians are expected to cross —**cross'ly** *adv.* —**cross'·wise** *adv./adj.* —**cross'bow** (-boh) *n.* bow fixed across wooden shoulder stock —cross'breed n. breed produced from parents of different breeds —cross-country adj./n. (long race) held over open ground —cross'-ex·am'ine vt. examine witness already examined by other side —cross'-eyed adj. having eye(s) turning inward —cross'-fer·ti·li·za'tion n. fertilization of one plant by pollen of another —cross'-grained' adj. having fibers running diagonally etc.; perverse —cross'-ref'er·ence n. reference within text to another part of text —cross section transverse section; group of people fully representative of a nation, community etc. —cross'word puzzle puzzle built up of intersecting words, of which some letters are common, the words being indicated by clues

crotch (kroch) n. angle between legs, genital area; fork

crotch·et (KROCH-it) n. musical note, equal to half the length of a minim

crotch·et·y (KROCH-i-tee) adj. peevish; irritable

crouch (krowch) vi. bend low; huddle down close to ground; stoop servilely, cringe —n.

croup (kroop) n. throat disease of children, with cough

crou·pi·er (KROO-pee-ər) n. person dealing cards, collecting money etc. at gambling table

crow¹ (kroh) n. large black scavenging bird —crow's'-foot n. wrinkle at corner of eye —crow's'-nest n. lookout platform high on ship's mast

crow² vi. utter rooster's cry; boast one's happiness or superiority —n. rooster's cry

crow·bar (KROH-bahr) n. iron or steel bar, usu. wedge-shaped, for levering

crowd (krowd) n. throng, mass —vi. flock together —vt. cram, force, thrust, pack; fill with people —crowd out exclude by excess already in

crown (krown) n. monarch's headdress; wreath for head; monarch; monarchy; royal power; various foreign coins; top of head; summit, top; completion or perfection of thing —vt. put crown on; confer title; occur as culmination of series of events; inf. hit on head —crown prince heir to throne

cru·cial (KROO-shəl) adj. decisive, critical; inf. very important

cru·ci·ble (KROO-sə-bəl) n. small melting pot

cru·ci·fy (KROO-sə-fī) vt. (-fied, -fy·ing) put to death on cross; treat cruelly; inf. ridicule —cru'ci·fix (-fiks) n. cross; image of (Christ on the) Cross —cru·ci·fix'ion n.

crude (krood) adj. (crud·er, crud·est) lacking taste, vulgar; in natural or raw state, unrefined; rough, unfinished —cru'di·ty n. (pl. -ties)

cru·el (KROO-əl) adj. (-er, -est) delighting in others' pain; causing pain or suffering —cru'el·ly adv. —cru'el·ty n. (pl. -ties)

cru·et (KROO-it) n. small container for salt, pepper, vinegar, oil etc.; stand holding such containers

cruise (krooz) vi. (cruised, cruis·ing) travel about in a ship for pleasure etc.; (of vehicle, aircraft) travel at safe, average speed —n. cruising voyage —cruis'er n. ship that cruises; warship lighter and faster than battleship —cruise missile subsonic missile guided throughout its flight

crumb (krum) n. small particle,

fragment, *esp.* of bread; *sl.* contemptible person —*vt.* reduce to, break into, cover with crumbs

**crum·ble** (KRUM-bəl) *v.* (-bled, -bling) break into small fragments, disintegrate, crush; perish, decay —*vi.* fall apart or away —**crum'bly** *adj.* (-bli·er, -bli·est)

**crum·my** (KRUM-ee) *adj. sl.* (-mi·er, -mi·est) inferior, contemptible

**crum·ple** (KRUM-pəl) *v.* (-pled, -pling) (cause to) collapse; make or become crushed, wrinkled, creased

**crunch** (krunch) *n.* sound made by chewing crisp food, treading on gravel, hard snow *etc.*; *inf.* critical moment or situation —*v.* make crunching sound

**cru·sade** (kroo-SAYD) *n.* medieval Christian war to recover Holy Land; campaign against something believed to be evil; concerted action to further a cause —*vi.* (-sad·ed, -sad·ing) —**cru·sad'er** *n.*

**crush**[1] (krush) *vt.* compress so as to break, bruise, crumple; break to small pieces; defeat utterly; overthrow —*n.* act of crushing; crowd of people *etc.*

**crush**[2] *n. inf.* infatuation

**crust** (krust) *n.* hard outer part of bread; similar hard outer casing on anything —*v.* cover with, form, crust —**crust'i·ly** *adv.* —**crust'y** *adj.* (crust·i·er, crust·i·est) having, or like, crust; harsh, surly; rude

**crus·ta·cean** (kru-STAY-shən) *n.* hard-shelled animal, *eg* crab, lobster —*adj.*

**crutch** (kruch) *n.* staff with crosspiece to go under armpit of lame person, device resembling this; support; groin, crotch

**crux** (kruks) *n.* (*pl.* -es) that on

which a decision turns; anything that puzzles very much

**cry** (krī) *v.* (**cried, cry·ing**) —*vi.* weep; wail; utter call; shout; clamor or beg (for) —*vt.* utter loudly, proclaim —*n.* loud utterance; scream, wail, shout; call of animal; fit of weeping; watchword

**cry·o·gen·ics** (krī-ə-JEN-iks) *n.* branch of physics concerned with phenomena at very low temperatures —**cry·o·gen'ic** *adj.*

**crypt** (kript) *n.* vault, *esp.* under church —**cryp'tic** *adj.* secret, mysterious —**cryp'ti·cal·ly** *adv.* —**cryp'to·gram** *n.* piece of writing in code —**cryp·tog'ra·phy** *n.* art of writing, decoding ciphers

**crys·tal** (KRIS-tl) *n.* clear transparent mineral; very clear glass; cut-glass ware; characteristic form assumed by many substances, with definite internal structure and external shape of symmetrically arranged plane surfaces —**crys'tal·line** (-tl-in) —**crys·tal·li·za'tion** *n.* **crys'tal·lize** *v.* (-lized, -liz·ing) form into crystals; become definite

**Cs** *Chem.* cesium

**Cu** *Chem.* copper

**cub** (kub) *n.* young of fox and other animals; cub scout —*v.* (**cubbed, cub·bing**) bring forth cubs —**cub scout** member of junior division of the Boy Scouts

**cub·by·hole** (KUB-ee-hohl) *n.* small, enclosed space or room; pigeonhole

**cube** (kyoob) *n.* regular solid figure contained by six equal square sides; cube-shaped block; product obtained by multiplying number by itself twice —*vt.* (**cubed, cub·ing**) multiply thus —**cu'bic** *adj.* —**cub'ism** *n.* style of art in which objects are present-

ed as assemblage of geometrical
shapes —**cub′ist** n./adj.

**cu·bi·cle** (KYOO-bi-kəl) n. partially or totally enclosed section of
room, as in study hall

**cu·bit** (KYOO-bit) n. old measure
of length, about 18 inches

**cuck·old** (KUK-əld) n. man whose
wife has committed adultery
—vt.

**cuck·oo** (KOO-koo) n. (pl. -oos)
migratory bird that deposits its
eggs in the nests of other birds;
its call —adj. sl. crazy —vi.
(-ooed, -oo·ing)

**cu·cum·ber** (KYOO-kum-bər) n.
plant with long fleshy green fruit;
the fruit, used in salad

**cud** (kud) n. food that ruminant
animal brings back into mouth to
chew again —**chew the cud** reflect, meditate

**cud·dle** (KUD-l) v. (-dled, -dling)
vt. hug —vi. lie close and snug,
nestle —n.

**cudg·el** (KUJ-əl) n. short thick
stick —vt. (-eled, -el·ing) beat
with cudgel

**cue**[1] (kyoo) n. last words of actor's speech etc. as signal to
another to act or speak; signal,
hint, example for action

**cue**[2] n. long tapering rod used in
billiards

**cuff**[1] (kuf) n. ending of sleeve;
wristband —**off the cuff** inf. without preparation

**cuff**[2] vt. strike with open hand
—n. blow with hand

**cui·sine** (kwi-ZEEN) n. style of
cooking; menu, food offered by
restaurant etc.

**cul-de-sac** (KUL-də-SAK) n. (pl.
culs- pr. kulz-) street, lane open
only at one end; blind alley

**cu·li·nar·y** (KYOO-lə-ner-ee) adj.
of, for, suitable for, cooking or
kitchen

**cull** (kul) vt. gather, select; take

out selected animals from herd
—n. something culled

**cul·mi·nate** (KUL-mə-nayt) vi.
(-nat·ed, -nat·ing) reach highest
point; come to climax, to a head
—**cul·mi·na′tion** n.

**cul·pa·ble** (KUL-pə-bəl) adj.
blameworthy —**cul·pa·bil′i·ty** n.

**cul·prit** (KUL-prit) n. one guilty of
usu. minor offense

**cult** (kult) n. system of religious
worship; pursuit of, devotion to,
some person, thing, or activity
—**cult′ism** n. practices of a religious cult —**cult′ist** n.

**cul·ti·vate** (KUL-tə-vayt) vt.
(-vat·ed, -vat·ing) till and prepare (soil) to raise crops; develop, improve, refine; devote attention to, cherish; practice; foster
—**cul·ti·va′tion** n.

**cul·ture** (KUL-chər) n. state of
manners, taste, and intellectual
development at a time or place;
cultivating; artificial rearing; set
of bacteria so reared —**cul′tur·al**
adj. —**cul′tured** adj. refined,
showing culture —**cultured pearl**
pearl artificially induced to grow
in oyster shell

**cul·vert** (KUL-vərt) n. tunneled
drain for passage of water under
road, railroad etc.

**cum·ber·some** (KUM-bər-səm)
adj. awkward, unwieldy

**cu·mu·la·tive** (KYOO-myə-lə-tiv)
adj. becoming greater by successive additions; representing the
sum of many items

**cu·mu·lus** (KYOO-myə-ləs) n. (pl.
-li pr. -lī) cloud shaped in rounded
white woolly masses

**cu·ne·i·form** (kyoo-NEE-ə-form)
adj. wedge-shaped, esp. of ancient Babylonian writing

**cun·ning** (KUN-ing) adj. crafty,
sly; ingenious; cute —n. skill in
deceit or evasion; skill, ingenuity

**cup** (kup) n. small drinking vessel

with handle at one side; any small drinking vessel; contents of cup; various cup-shaped formations, cavities, sockets etc.; cup-shaped trophy as prize; portion or lot; iced drink of wine and other ingredients —vt. (cupped, cup-ping) shape as cup (hands etc.) —cup-ful n. (pl. -fuls) —cup-board (KUB-ərd) n. piece of furniture, recess in room, with door, for storage

**Cu-pid** (KYOO-pid) n. god of love

**cu-pid-i-ty** (kyoo-PID-i-tee) n. greed for possessions; covetousness

**cu-po-la** (KYOO-pə-lə) n. dome

**cu-pre-ous** (KYOO-pree-əs) adj. of, containing, copper

**cur** (kur) n. dog of mixed breed; surly, contemptible, or mean person

**cu-ra-re** (kyuu-RAHR-ee) n. poisonous resin of S Amer. tree, now used as muscle relaxant in medicine

**cu-rate** (KYUUR-it) n. parish priest —cu'ra-cy n. office or term of office of curate

**cur-a-tive** (KYUUR-ə-tiv) adj. tending to cure disease —n.

**cu-ra-tor** (kyuur-AY-tər) n. person in charge, esp. of museum, library etc.

**curb** (kurb) n. check, restraint; chain or strap passing under horse's lower jaw and giving powerful control with reins; edging, esp. of stone or concrete, along street, path etc. —vt. restrain; apply curb to

**curd** (kurd) n. coagulated milk —cur-dle (KUR-dl) v. (-dled, -dling) turn into curd, coagulate —blood'cur-dling adj. terrifying, making blood appear to curdle

**cure** (kyuur) vt. (cured, cur-ing) heal, restore to health; remedy; preserve (fish, skins etc.) —n.

remedy; course of medical treatment; successful treatment, restoration to health —cur'a-ble adj.

**cu-rette** (kyuu-RET) n. surgical instrument for removing dead tissue etc. from some body cavities —cu-ret-tage (kyuur-i-TAHZH) n.

**cur-few** (KUR-fyoo) n. official regulation restricting or prohibiting movement of people, esp. at night; time set as deadline by such regulation

**cu-rie** (KYUUR-ee) n. standard unit of radium emanation

**cu-ri-o** (KYUUR-ee-oh) n. (pl. -ri-os) rare or curious thing of the kind sought for collections

**cu-ri-ous** (KYUUR-ee-əs) adj. eager to know, inquisitive; prying; puzzling, strange, odd —curi-os'i-ty n. (pl. -ties) eagerness to know; inquisitiveness; strange or rare thing

**cu-ri-um** (KYUUR-ee-əm) n. element produced from plutonium

**curl** (kurl) vi. take spiral or curved shape or path —vt. bend into spiral or curved shape —n. spiral lock of hair; spiral, curved state, form or motion —curl'ing n. game like bowls, played with large rounded stones on ice —curl'y adj. (curl-i-er, curl-i-est)

**cur-mudg-eon** (kər-MUJ-ən) n. surly or miserly person

**cur-rent** (KUR-ənt) adj. of immediate present, going on; up-to-date, not yet superseded; in circulation or general use —n. body of water or air in motion; tendency, drift; transmission of electricity through conductor —cur'ren-cy n. money in use; state of being in use; time during which thing is current

**cur-ric-u-lum** (kə-RIK-yə-ləm) n. (pl. -la pr. -lə) specified course of study

**cur·ry**[1] (KUR-ee) n. (pl. -ries) highly-flavored, pungent condiment; meat etc. dish flavored with curry —vt. (-ried, -ry·ing) prepare, flavor dish with curry

**curry**[2] vt. (-ried, -ry·ing) groom (horse) with comb; dress (leather) —curry favor try to win favor unworthily, ingratiate oneself

**curse** (kurs) n. profane or obscene expression of anger etc.; utterance expressing extreme ill will toward some person or thing; affliction, misfortune, scourge —v. (cursed, curs·ing) utter curse, swear (at); afflict —curs·ed (KUR-sid) adj. hateful; wicked; deserving of, or under, a curse

**cur·sive** (KUR-siv) adj./n. (written in) running script, with letters joined

**cur·so·ry** (KUR-sə-ree) adj. rapid, hasty, not detailed, superficial —cur'so·ri·ly adv.

**curt** (kurt) adj. (-er, -est) short, rudely brief, abrupt —curt'ness n.

**cur·tail** (kər-TAYL) vt. cut short, diminish

**cur·tain** (KUR-tn) n. hanging drapery at window etc.; cloth hung as screen; screen separating audience and stage in theater; end to act or scene etc.; (pl. sl.) death —vt. provide, cover with curtain —curtain call return to stage by performers to acknowledge applause

**curt·sy** (KURT-see) n. (pl. -sies) woman's bow or respectful gesture made by bending knees and lowering body —vi. (-sied, -sy·ing)

**curve** (kurv) n. line of which no part is straight; bent line or part —v. bend into curve —cur·va'ceous (-VAY-shəs) adj. shapely

—cur'va·ture (-və-chər) n. a bending; bent shape

**cush·ion** (KUUSH-ən) n. bag filled with soft stuffing or air, to support or ease body; any soft pad or support; resilient rim of pool table —vt. provide, protect with cushion; lessen effects of

**cusp** (kusp) n. pointed end, esp. of tooth; Astrology point marking the beginning of a house or sign —cus'pid n. pointed tooth

**cus·pi·dor** (KUS-pi-dor) n. spittoon

**cus·tard** (KUS-tərd) n. dessert made of eggs, sugar and milk

**cus·to·dy** (KUS-tə-dee) n. (pl. -dies) safekeeping, guardianship, imprisonment —cus·to'di·an n. keeper, caretaker

**cus·tom** (KUS-təm) n. habit; practice; fashion, usage; business patronage; tax —pl. duties levied on imports; government department that collects these; area in airport etc. where customs officials examine baggage for dutiable goods —cus·tom·ar'i·ly adv. —cus'tom·ar·y adj. usual, habitual —cus'tom·er n. one who enters store to buy, esp. regularly; purchaser

**cut** (kut) vt. (cut, cut·ting) sever, penetrate, wound, divide, or separate with pressure of sharp or edged instrument; pare, detach, trim, or shape by cutting; divide; intersect; reduce, decrease; abridge; inf. ignore (person); strike (with whip etc.); inf. deliberately stay away from —n. act of cutting; stroke; blow, wound (of knife, whip etc.); reduction, decrease; fashion, shape; incision; engraving; piece cut off; division; excavation for road, canal etc.) through high ground; inf. share, esp. of profits —cut'ter n. one who, that which, cuts;

ship's boat for carrying stores *etc.*; small armed government boat —cut'ting *n.* act of cutting, thing cut off or out; shoot, twig of plant —*adj.* sarcastic, unkind —cut'throat *adj.* merciless —*n.* murderer —cut dead refuse to recognize an acquaintance

cu·ta·ne·ous (kyoo-TAY-nee-əs) *adj.* of skin

cute (kyoot) *adj.* (cut·er, cut·est) appealing, attractive, pretty

cu·ti·cle (KYOO-ti-kəl) *n.* dead skin, *esp.* at base of fingernail

cut·lass (KUT-ləs) *n.* short broad-bladed sword

cut·ler·y (KUT-lə-ree) *n.* knives, forks, spoons *etc.*

cut·let (KUT-lit) *n.* small piece of meat broiled or fried

cy·a·nide (SĪ-ə-nīd) *n.* extremely poisonous chemical compound

cy·a·no·sis (sī-ə-NOH-sis) *n.* blueness of the skin —cy·a·not'ic *adj.*

cy·ber·net·ics (sī-bər-NET-iks) *n.* (with sing. v.) comparative study of control mechanisms of electronic and biological systems

cy·cle (SĪ-kəl) *n.* recurrent series or period; rotation of events; complete series or period; development following course of stages; series of poems *etc.*; bicycle —*vi.* (-cled, -cling) move in cycles; ride bicycle —cy'clist *n.* bicycle rider

cy·clone (SĪ-klohn) *n.* system of winds moving around center of low pressure; circular storm —cy·clon'ic (-KLON-ik) *adj.*

cy·clo·tron (SĪ-klə-tron) *n.* powerful apparatus that accelerates the circular movement of subatomic particles in a magnetic field, used for work in nuclear disintegration *etc.*

cyg·net (SIG-nit) *n.* young swan

cyl·in·der (SIL-in-dər) *n.* roller-shaped solid or hollow body, of uniform diameter; piston chamber of engine —cy·lin'dri·cal *adj.*

cym·bal (SIM-bəl) *n.* one of pair of two brass plates struck together to produce ringing or clashing sound in music

cyn·ic (SIN-ik) *n.* one who expects, believes, the worst about people, their motives, or outcome of events —cyn'i·cal *adj.* —cyn'i·cism *n.* being cynical

cy·no·sure (SĪN-ə-shuur) *n.* center of attraction

cyst (sist) *n.* sac containing liquid secretion or pus —cys'tic *adj.* of cysts; of the bladder —cys·ti'tis *n.* inflammation of bladder

Czar (zahr) *n.* emperor, king, *esp.* of Russia 1547-1917 —Cza·ri·na (zah-REE-nə) *n.* wife of Czar

# D

D *Chem.* deuterium

dab *vt.* (dabbed, dab·bing) apply with momentary pressure, *esp.* anything wet and soft; strike feebly —*n.* smear; slight blow or tap; small mass

dab·ble (DAB-əl) *vi.* (-bled, -bling) splash about; be desultory student or amateur (in) —dab'bler *n.*

dac·tyl (DAK-til) *n.* metrical foot of one long followed by two short syllables

dad·dy (DAD-ee) *n.* inf. (pl. -dies) father

da·do (DAY-doh) *n.* (pl. -dos) lower part of room wall when lined and painted separately

dag·ger (DAG-ər) *n.* short, edged stabbing weapon

da·guerre·o·type (də-GAIR-ə-tīp) *n.* early photographic process; photograph by it

**dahl·ia** (DAL-yɔ) n. garden plant of various colors

**dai·ly** (DAY-lee) adj. done, occurring, published every day —adv. every day —n. (pl. -lies) daily newspaper

**dain·ty** (DAYN-tee) adj. (-ti-er, -ti-est) delicate; elegant, choice; pretty and neat; fastidious —n. (pl. -ties) delicacy —dain'ti·ly adv. —dain'ti·ness n.

**dair·y** (DAIR-ee) n.(pl. -ries) place for processing milk and its products —dair'y·ing n.

**da·is** (DAY-is) n. raised platform, usually at end of hall

**dai·sy** (DAY-zee) n. (pl. -sies) flower with yellow center and white petals

**Da·lai La·ma** (DAH-lī LAH-mɔ) n. head of Buddhist hierarchy in Tibet

**dale** (dayl) n. valley

**dal·ly** (DAL-ee) vi. (-lied, -ly·ing) trifle, spend time in idleness or amusement; loiter —dal'li·ance n.

**Dal·ma·tian** (dal-MAY-shɔn) n. large dog, white with black spots

**dam**[1] n. barrier to hold back flow of waters; water so collected —vt. (dammed, dam'ming) hold with or as with dam

**dam**[2] n. female parent (used of animals)

**dam·age** (DAM-ij) n. injury, harm, loss —pl. sum claimed or adjudged in compensation for injury —vt. (-maged, -mag·ing) harm

**dam·ask** (DAM-ɔsk) n. figured woven material of silk or linen, esp. white table linen with design shown up by light; color of damask rose, velvety red

**dame** (daym) n. obs. lady; sl. woman

**damn** (dam) v. (damned, damn·ing) —vt. condemn to hell; be the ruin of; give hostile reception to

—vi. curse —interj. expression of annoyance, impatience etc. —dam'na·ble adj. deserving damnation; hateful, annoying —damna'tion n.

**damp** adj. moist; slightly moist —n. diffused moisture; in coal mines, dangerous gas —vt. make damp; (often with down) deaden, discourage —damp'en v. make, become damp —vt. stifle, deaden —damp'er n. anything that discourages or depresses; plate in a flue to control draft

**Dan.** Daniel

**dance** (dans) v. (danced, danc·ing) —vi. move with measured rhythmic steps, usu. to music; be in lively movement; bob up and down —vt. perform (dance); cause to dance —n. lively, rhythmical movement; arrangement of such movements; tune for them; social gathering for the purpose of dancing —danc'er n. —dan·seuse (dan-SUUZ) n. female battle dancer

**dan·de·li·on** (DAN-dl-ī-ɔn) n. yellow-flowered wild plant

**dan·der** (DAN-dɔr) n. inf. temper, fighting spirit

**dan·druff** (DAN-drɔf) n. dead skin in small scales on the scalp, in hair

**dan·dy** (DAN-dee) n. (pl. -dies) man excessively concerned with smartness of dress —adj. inf. excellent

**dan·ger** (DAYN-jɔr) n. liability or exposure to harm; risk, peril —dan'ger·ous adj.

**dan·gle** (DANG-gɔl) v. (-gled, -gling) hang loosely and swaying; hold suspended; tempt with

**dank** (dangk) adj. (-er, -est) unpleasantly damp and chilly —dank'ness n.

**dap·per** (DAP-ɔr) adj. neat and precise, esp. in dress, spruce

**dap·ple** (DAP-əl) v. (-pled, -pling) mark with spots —**dappled** adj. spotted; mottled; variegated —**dapple-gray** adj. (of horse) gray marked with darker spots

**dare** (dair) vt. (dared, dar·ing) venture, have courage (to); challenge —n. challenge —**daring** adj. bold —n. adventurous courage —**dare'dev·il** adj./n. reckless (person)

**dark** (dahrk) adj. (-er, -est) without light; gloomy; deep in tint; dim, secret; unenlightened; wicked —n. absence of light or color or knowledge —**dark'en** v. —**dark'ness** n. —**dark horse** somebody, something, esp. competitor in race, about whom little is known —**dark'room** n. darkened room for processing film

**dar·ling** (DAHR-ling) adj./n. much loved or very lovable (person)

**darn¹** (dahrn) vt. mend by filling (hole) with yarn —n. place so mended —**darn'ing** n.

**darn²** interj. mild expletive

**dart** (dahrt) n. small light pointed missile; darting motion; small seam or intake in garment —pl. indoor game played with numbered target and miniature darts —vt. cast, throw rapidly (dart glance etc.) —vi. go rapidly or abruptly

**dash** vt. smash, throw, thrust, send with violence; cast down; tinge, flavor, mix —vi. move, go with great speed or violence —n. rush; vigor; smartness; small quantity, tinge; stroke (—) between words —**dash'ing** adj. spirited, showy —**dash'board** n. in car etc., instrument panel in front of driver

**da·shi·ki** (də-SHEE-kee) n. (pl. -kis) loose pullover garment, orig. African

**das·tard** (DAS-tərd) n. obs. contemptible, sneaking coward —**das'tard·ly** adj.

**da·ta** (DAY-tə) n. pl. of DATUM (oft. with sing. v.) series of observations, measurements, or facts; information —**data base** systematized collection of data that can be manipulated by data-processing system for specific purpose —**data processing** handling of data by computer

**date¹** (dayt) n. day of the month; statement on document of its time of writing; time of occurrence; period of work of art etc.; engagement, appointment —v. (dat·ed, dat·ing) —vt. mark with date; refer to date; reveal age of; inf. accompany on social outing —vi. exist (from); betray time or period of origin, become old-fashioned —**date'less** adj. without date; immemorial

**date²** n. sweet, single-stone fruit of palm; the palm

**da·tive** (DAY-tiv) n. case indicating indirect object etc.

**da·tum** n. (see DATA) thing given, known, or assumed as basis for reckoning, reasoning etc.

**daub** (dawb) vt. coat, plaster, paint coarsely or roughly —n. crude picture; smear —**daub'er** n.

**daugh·ter** (DAW-tər) n. one's female child —**daugh'ter-in-law** n. (pl. daugh'ters-) son's wife

**daunt** (dawnt) vt. frighten, esp. into giving up purpose —**daunt'less** adj. intrepid, fearless

**dav·en·port** (DAV-ən-port) n. small writing table with drawers; large couch or settee

**Da·vy Jones's locker** (DAY-vee JOHN-ziz) bottom of sea, considered as sailors' grave

**daw·dle** (DAWD-l) vi. (-dled, -dling) idle, waste time, loiter —**daw'dler** n.

**dawn** *n.* first light, daybreak; first gleam or beginning of anything —*vi.* begin to grow light; appear, begin; (begin to) be understood

**day** *n.* period of 24 hours; time when sun is above horizon; point or unit of time; daylight; part of day occupied by certain activity, time period; special or designated day —**day′break** *n.* dawn —**day′-care center** place providing daytime care, meals *etc.* for preschool children *etc.* —**day′dream** *n.* idle fancy —*vi.* —**day′light** *n.* natural light; dawn —*pl.* consciousness, wits —**daylight saving** in summer, time set one hour ahead of local standard time, giving extra daylight in evenings —**day′time** *n.* time between sunrise and sunset

**daze** (dayz) *vt.* (**dazed**, **daz·ing**) stupefy, stun, bewilder —*n.* stupefied or bewildered state

**daz·zle** (DAZ-əl) *vt.* (**-zled**, **-zling**) blind, confuse or overpower with brightness, light, brilliant display or prospects —*n.* brightness that dazzles the vision

**D-day** (DEE-day) day selected for start of something, *esp.* Allied invasion of Europe in 1944

**de-** (*prefix*) removal of, from, reversal of, as in **delouse**, **desegregate** Such words are omitted where their meaning can easily be inferred from the simple word

**dea·con** (DEE-kən) *n.* in hierarchical churches, member of the clergy next below priest; in other churches, one who superintends secular affairs (**dea′con·ess** *fem.*)

**dead** (ded) *adj.* (**-er**, **-est**) no longer alive; obsolete; numb, without sensation; no longer functioning, extinguished; lacking luster or movement or vigor; sure, complete —*n.* dead person or persons (*oft. in pl.*, **the dead**) —*adv.* utterly, completely —**dead′en** *vt.* —**dead′ly** *adj.* (**-li·er**, **-li·est**) fatal; deathlike —*adv.* as if dead —**dead′beat** *n. inf.* one who avoids payment of debts; lazy, useless person —**dead′head** *n.* log sticking out of water as hindrance to navigation; boring person; train, aircraft *etc.* operating empty, as when returning to terminal —**dead heat** race in which competitors finish exactly even —**dead letter** rule no longer observed; letter that post office cannot deliver —**dead′line** *n.* limit of time allowed —**dead′lock** *n.* standstill —**dead′pan** *adj.* expressionless —**dead reckoning** calculation of ship's position from log and compass, when observations cannot be taken —**dead set** absolutely, resolute attack —**dead of night** time of greatest stillness and darkness

**deaf** (def) *adj.* (**-er**, **-est**) wholly or partly without hearing; unwilling to listen —**deaf′en** *vt.* make deaf

**deal** (deel) *v.* (**dealt**, **deal′ing**) —*vt.* distribute, give out; inflict —*vi.* act; treat; do business (**with**, **in**) —*n.* agreement; treatment; share; business transaction —**deal′er** *n.* one who deals (*esp.* cards); trader —**deal′ings** *n. pl.* transactions or relations with others —**deal with** handle, act toward (someone)

**dean** (deen) *n.* university or college official; head of cathedral chapter

**dear** (deer) *adj.* beloved; precious; costly, expensive —*n.* beloved one —*adv.* at a high price —**dear′ly** *adv.*

**dearth** (durth) *n.* scarcity

**death** (deth) *n.* dying; end of life; end, extinction; annihilation; (D-)

personification of death, as skeleton —**death′less** adj. immortal —**death′ly** adj./adv. like death —**death mask** cast of person's face taken after death —**death′watch** n. vigil at dying person's bedside

**de·ba·cle** (day-BAH-kəl) n. utter collapse, rout, disaster

**de·bar** (di-BAHR) vt. (**-barred**, **-bar′ring**) shut out from; stop; prohibit; preclude

**de·bark** (di-BAHRK) v. disembark

**de·base** (di-BASE) vt. (**-based**, **-bas·ing**) lower in value, quality or character; adulterate coinage —**de·base′ment** n.

**de·bate** (di-BAYT) v. (**-bat·ed**, **-bat·ing**) argue, discuss, esp. in a formal assembly; consider —n. discussion; controversy —**debat′a·ble** adj.

**de·bauch** (di-BAWCH) vt. lead into a life of depraved self-indulgence —n. bout of sensual indulgence —**de·bauch·ee** (deb-aw-CHEE) n. dissipated person —**de·bauch′er·y** n.

**de·ben·ture** (di-BEN-chər) n. bond of company or corporation

**de·bil·i·ty** (di-BIL-i-tee) n. (pl. **-ties**) feebleness, esp. of health; languor —**de·bil′i·tate** vt. weaken, enervate

**deb′it** n. Accounting entry in account of sum owed; side of ledger in which such sums are entered —vt. charge, enter as due

**deb·o·nair** (deb-ə-NAIR) adj. suave, genial, affable

**de·brief** (dee-BREEF) v. of soldier etc., report to superior on result of mission

**de·bris** (də-BREE) n. fragments, rubbish

**debt** (det) n. what is owed; state of owing —**debt′or** n.

**de·bunk** (di-BUNGK) vt. expose

falseness, pretentiousness of, esp. by ridicule

**de·but** (day-BYOO) n. first appearance in public —**deb·u·tante** (DEB-yuu-tahnt) n. young woman making official debut into society

**deca-** (comb. form) ten, as in decagon

**dec·ade** (DEK-ayd) n. period of ten years; set of ten

**dec·a·dent** (DEK-ə-dənt) adj. declining, deteriorating; morally corrupt —**dec′a·dence** n.

**de·caf·fein·at·ed** (dee-KAF-ə-nay-tid) adj. (of coffee) with the caffeine removed

**dec·a·gon** (DEK-ə-gon) n. figure of 10 angles

**dec·a·he·dron** (dek-ə-HEE-drən) n. solid of 10 faces

**de·cal·ci·fy** (dee-KAL-si-fī) vt. (**-fied**, **-fy·ing**) deprive of lime, as bones or teeth

**dec·a·logue** (also D-) (DEK-ə-lawg) n. the Ten Commandments

**de·camp** (di-KAMP) vi. make off, break camp, abscond

**de·cant** (di-KANT) vt. pour off (liquid, as wine) to leave sediment —**de·cant′er** n. stoppered bottle for wine or whiskey

**de·cap·i·tate** (di-KAP-i-tayt) vt. behead —**de·cap·i·ta′tion** n.

**de·cath·lon** (di-KATH-lon) n. athletic contest with ten events

**de·cay** (di-KAY) v. rot, decompose; fall off, decline —n. rotting; a falling away, break up

**de·cease** (di-SEES) n. death —vi. (**-ceased**, **-ceas·ing**) die —**deceased** adj. dead —n. person lately dead

**de·ceive** (di-SEEV) vt. (**-ceived**, **-ceiv·ing**) mislead, delude, cheat —**de·ceit′** n. fraud; duplicity —**de·ceit′ful** adj.

**de·cel·er·ate** (dee-SEL-ə-rayt) vi. (**-at·ed**, **-at·ing**) slow down

**de·cen·ni·al** (di-SEN-ee-əl) *adj.* of period of ten years

**de·cent** (DEE-sənt) *adj.* respectable; fitting, seemly; not obscene; adequate; *inf.* kind —**de·cen·cy** *n.*

**de·cen·tral·ize** (dee-SEN-trə-līz) *vt.* (-ized, -iz·ing) divide (government, organization) among local centers

**de·cep·tion** (di-SEP-shən) *n.* deceiving; illusion; fraud; trick —**de·cep·tive** *adj.* misleading; apt to mislead

**dec·i·bel** (DES-ə-bəl) *n.* unit for measuring intensity of a sound

**de·cide** (di-SĪD) *v.* (-cid·ed, -cid·ing) *vt.* settle, determine, bring to resolution; give judgment —*vi.* come to a decision, conclusion —**de·cid·ed** *adj.* unmistakable; settled; resolute —**de·cid·ed·ly** *adv.* certainly, undoubtedly —**de·ci·sion** (-SIZH-ən) *n.* —**de·ci·sive** *adj.* —**de·ci·sive·ness** *n.*

**de·cid·u·ous** (di-SIJ-oo-əs) *adj.* of trees, losing leaves annually; of antlers, teeth *etc.* being shed at the end of a period of growth

**dec·i·mal** (DES-ə-məl) *adj.* relating to tenths; proceeding by tens —*n.* decimal fraction —**decimal system** system of weights and measures, or coinage, in which value of each denomination is ten times the one below it —**dec'i·gram** *n.* tenth of gram —**dec'i·li·ter** *n.* tenth of liter —**dec'i·me·ter** *n.* tenth of meter

**dec·i·mate** (DES-ə-mayt) *vt.* (-mat·ed, -mat·ing) destroy or kill a tenth of, large proportion of —**dec·i·ma'tion** *n.*

**de·ci·pher** (di-SĪ-fər) *vt.* make out meaning of; decode —**de·ci'pher·a·ble** *adj.*

**deck** (dek) *n.* platform or floor, *esp.* one covering whole or part of ship's hull; cassette deck; pack of playing cards; *sl.* small packet of a narcotic —*vt.* array, decorate —**deck chair** folding chair made of canvas suspended in wooden frame

**de·claim** (di-KLAYM) *v.* speak dramatically, rhetorically or passionately; protest loudly —**dec·la·ma·tion** (dek-lə-MAY-shən) *n.* —**de·clam'a·to·ry** *adj.*

**de·clare** (di-KLAIR) *v.* (-clared, -clar·ing) —*vt.* announce formally; state emphatically; show; name (as liable to customs duty) —*vi.* take sides (for); *Bridge* bid (a suit or no trump) —**dec·la·ra·tion** (dek-lə-RAY-shən) *n.* —**de·clar'a·tive** *adj.* —**de·clar'er** *n.* *Bridge* person who plays the contract

**de·cline** (di-KLĪN) *v.* (-clined, -clin·ing) refuse; slope, bend or sink downward; deteriorate gradually; grow smaller, diminish; list the case endings of nouns, pronouns, adjectives —*n.* gradual deterioration; movement downward; diminution; downward slope —**de·clen'sion** *n.* in grammar, set of nouns, pronouns *etc.*; falling off; declining —**de·clin'a·ble** *adj.* —**dec·li·na'tion** *n.* sloping away, deviation; angle

**de·cliv·i·ty** (di-KLIV-i-tee) *n.* downward slope

**de·code** (dee-KOHD) *vt.* (-cod·ed, -cod·ing) put in intelligible terms a message in code or secret alphabet

**dé·col·le·té** (day-kol-TAY) *adj.* (of women's garment) having a low-cut neckline —**de·colle·tage'** (-TAHZH) *n.* low-cut neckline

**de·com·mis·sion** (dee-kə-MISH-ən) *vt.* dismantle (nuclear reactor, industrial plant) sufficiently to abandon safely; remove (ship) from service

**de·com·pose** (dee-kəm-POHZ) *v.*

(-posed, -pos·ing) separate into elements; rot —de·com·po·si·tion (dee-kom-pə-ZISH-ən) n. decay

**de·com·press** (dee-kəm-PRES) vt. free from pressure; return to condition of normal atmospheric pressure —de·com·pres'sion n.

**de·con·ges·tant** (dee-kən-JES-tənt) adj./n. (drug) relieving (esp. nasal) congestion

**de·con·tam·i·nate** (dee-kən-TAM-ə-nayt) vt. (-nat·ed, -nat·ing) free from contamination eg from poisons, radioactive substances

**de·con·trol** (dee-kən-TROHL) vt. (-trolled, -trol·ling) release from government control

**de·cor** (day-KOR) n. decorative scheme of a room etc.; stage decoration, scenery

**dec·o·rate** (DEK-ə-rayt) vt. (-rat·ed, -rat·ing) beautify by additions; select paint, furniture etc. for room, apartment etc.; award (medal etc.) —dec·o·ra'tion n. —dec'o·ra·tive (-rə-tiv) adj.

**de·co·rum** (di-KOR-əm) n. seemly behavior, propriety, decency —dec·o·rous (DEK-ə-rəs) adj.

**de·coy** (DEE-koi) n. something used to entrap others or to distract their attention; bait, lure —v. (di-KOI) lure, be lured as with decoy

**de·crease** (di-KREES) v. (-creased, -creas·ing) diminish, lessen —n. (DEE-krees) lessening

**de·cree** (di-KREE) n. order having the force of law; edict —v. (-creed, -cree·ing) determine judicially; order

**dec·re·ment** (DEK-rə-mənt) n. act or state of decreasing; quantity lost by decrease

**de·crep·it** (di-KREP-it) adj. old and feeble; broken down, worn out —de·crep'i·tude n.

**de·cry** (di-KRĪ) vt. (-cried, -cry·ing) disparage

**ded·i·cate** (DED-i-kayt) vt. (-cat·ed, -cat·ing) commit wholly to special purpose or cause; inscribe or address (book etc.); devote to God's service —ded·i·ca'tion n. —ded'i·ca·to·ry (-kə-tor-ee) adj.

**de·duce** (di-DOOS) vt. (-duced, -duc·ing) draw as conclusion from facts —de·duct (di-DUKT) vt. take away, subtract —de·duct'i·ble adj. —de·duc'tion n. deducting; amount subtracted; conclusion deduced; inference from general to particular —de·duc'tive adj.

**deed** n. action or fact; exploit; legal document

**deem** vt. judge, consider, regard

**deep** adj. (-er, -est) extending far down, in or back; at, of given depth; profound; heartfelt; hard to fathom; cunning; engrossed, immersed; of color, dark and rich; of sound, low and full —n. deep place; the sea —adv. far down etc. —deep'en vt. —deep'ly adv. —deep freeze condition or period of suspended activity

**deer** n. (pl. deer) family of ruminant animals typically with antlers in male —deer'stalk·er n. one who stalks deer; kind of cloth hat with visor in front and behind

**de·face** (di-FAYS) vt. (-faced, -fac·ing) spoil or mar surface; disfigure —de·face'ment n.

**de fac·to** (day FAK-toh) Lat. existing in fact, whether legally recognized or not

**de·fal·ca·tion** (dee-fal-KAY-shən) n. misappropriation of money held by trustee etc.; the money taken —de·fal·cate (di-FAL-kayt) vi. (-cat·ed, -cat·ing)

**de·fame** (di-FAYM) vt. (-famed, -fam·ing) speak ill of, dishonor by slander or rumor —**de·fa·ma·tion** (def-ə-MAY-shən) n. —**de·fam′a·to·ry** adj.

**de·fault** (di-FAWLT) n. failure, neglect to act, appear or pay —v. fail (to pay) —**de·fault′er** n. one who defaults

**de·feat** (di-FEET) vt. overcome, vanquish; thwart —n. overthrow; lost battle or encounter; frustration —**de·feat′ism** n. attitude tending to accept defeat —**de·feat′ist** n./adj.

**def·e·cate** (DEF-i-kayt) vt. (-cat·ed, -cat·ing) empty the bowels; clear of impurities —**def·e·ca′tion** n.

**de·fect** (DEE-fekt) n. lack, blemish, failing —vi. (di-FEKT) desert one's country, cause etc., esp. to join opponents —**de·fec′tion** n. abandonment of duty or allegiance —**de·fec′tive** adj. incomplete; faulty

**de·fend** (di-FEND) vt. protect, ward off attack; support by argument, evidence; (try to) maintain (title etc.) against challenger —**de·fense′** n. —**de·fend′ant** n. person accused in court —**de·fend′er** n. —**de·fen′si·ble** adj. —**de·fen′sive** adj. serving for defense —n. position or attitude of defense

**de·fer**[1] (di-FUR) vt. (-ferred, -fer·ring) put off, postpone —**de·fer′ment**, **de·fer′ral** n.

**de·fer**[2] vi. (-ferred, -fer·ring) submit to opinion or judgment of another —**def′er·ence** n. respectful submission to views etc. of another —**def·er·en′tial** (-shəl) adj.

**defiance, defiant** see DEFY

**de·fi·cient** (di-FISH-ənt) adj. lacking or falling short in something, insufficient —**de·fi′cien·cy** n. —**def·i·cit** (DEF-ə-sit) n. amount

by which sum of money is too small; lack, shortage

**de·file**[1] (di-FIL) vt. (-filed, -fil·ing) make dirty, pollute, soil; sully; desecrate

**de·file**[2] n. narrow pass or valley —vi. (-filed, fil·ing) march in file

**de·fine** (di-FIN) vt. (-fined, -fin·ing) state contents or meaning of; show clearly the form; lay down clearly, fix; mark out —**de·fin′a·ble** adj. —**def·i·ni′tion** (-NISH-ən) n. —**def′i·nite** (-nit) adj. exact, defined; clear, specific; certain, sure —**de·fin′i·tive** adj. conclusive, to be looked on as final

**de·flate** (di-FLAYT) v. (-flat·ed, -flat·ing) (cause to) collapse by release of gas from; take away (person's) self-esteem; Economics cause deflation —**de·fla′tion** n. deflating; Economics reduction of economic and industrial activity —**de·fla′tion·ar·y** adj.

**de·flect** (di-FLEKT) v. (cause to) turn from straight course —**de·flec′tion** n.

**de·flow·er** (di-FLOW-ər) vt. deprive of virginity, innocence etc. —**def·lo·ra′tion** n.

**de·fo·li·ate** (dee-FOH-lee-ayt) v. (-at·ed, -at·ing) (cause to) lose leaves, esp. by action of chemicals —**defo′li·ant** n. —**de·fo·li·a′tion** n.

**de·form** (di-FORM) vt. spoil shape of; make ugly; disfigure —**de·formed′** adj. —**de·form′i·ty** n. (pl. -ties)

**de·fraud** (di-FRAWD) vt. cheat, swindle

**de·fray** (di-FRAY) vt. provide money for (expenses etc.)

**de·frock** (dee-FROK) vt. deprive (priest, minister) of ecclesiastical status

**de·frost** (di-FRAWST) v. make, become free of frost, ice; thaw

**deft** adj. (-er, -est) skillful, adroit —**deft**·ly adv. —**deft**'ness n.

**de·funct** (di-FUNGKT) adj. dead, obsolete

**de·fuse** (dee-FYOOZ) vt. (-fused, -fus·ing) remove fuse of bomb, etc.; remove tension (from situation etc.)

**de·fy** (di-FĪ) vt. (-fied, -fy·ing) challenge, resist successfully; disregard —**de·fi**'ance n. resistance —**de·fi**'ant adj. openly and aggressively hostile; insolent

**de·gauss** (dee-GOWS) vt. neutralize magnetic field (of ship's hull, electronic apparatus, etc.)

**de·gen·er·ate** (di-JEN-ə-rayt) vi. (-rat·ed, -rat·ing) deteriorate to lower mental, moral, or physical level —adj. (-rit) fallen away in quality —n. (-rit) degenerate person —**de·gen**'er·a·cy n.

**de·grade** (di-GRAYD) v. (-grad·ed, -grad·ing) —vt. dishonor; debase; reduce to lower rank —vi. decompose chemically —**de·gra**'da·ble adj. capable of chemical, biological decomposition —**de·grad**'ed adj. shamed, humiliated —**deg·ra·da**'tion n.

**de·gree** (di-GREE) n. step, stage in process, scale, relative rank, order, condition, manner, way; academic title conferred by university or college; unit of measurement of temperature or angle —**third degree** severe, lengthy examination, esp. of accused person by police, to extract information, confession

**de·hu·mid·i·fy** (dee-hyoo-MID-ə-fī) vt. (-fied, -fy·ing) extract moisture from

**de·hy·drate** (dee-HĪ-drayt) vt. (-drat·ed, -drat·ing) remove moisture from —**de·hy·dra**'tion n.

**de·ice** (dee-ĪS) vt. (-iced, -ic·ing)

to dislodge ice from (eg windshield) or prevent its forming

**de·i·fy** (DEE-ə-fī) vt. (-fied, -fy·ing) make god of; treat, worship as god —**de·i·fi·ca**'tion n.

**deign** (dayn) vt. condescend, stoop; think fit

**de·ism** (DEE-iz-əm) n. belief in god but not in revelation —**de**'ist n. —**de·i·ty** (DEE-i-tee) n. (pl. -ties) divine status or attributes; a god

**dé·jà vu** (DAY-zhah VOO) Fr. experience of perceiving new situation as if it had occurred before

**de·ject** (di-JEKT) vt. dishearten, cast down, depress —**de·ject**'ed adj. —**de·jec**'tion n.

**de ju·re** (di JUUR-ee) Lat. in law, by right

**de·lay** (di-LAY) vt. postpone, hold back —vi. be tardy, linger —n. act or instance of delaying; interval of time between events

**de·lec·ta·ble** (di-LEK-tə-bəl) adj. delightful delicious —**de·lec·ta**'tion (dee-lek-TAY-shən) n. pleasure

**del·e·gate** (DEL-i-git) n. person chosen to represent another —v. (-gayt) (-gat·ed, -gat·ing) send as deputy; commit (authority, business etc.) to a deputy —**del·e·ga**'tion n.

**de·lete** (di-LEET) vt. (-let·ed, -let·ing) remove, cancel, erase —**de·le**'tion n.

**del·e·te·ri·ous** (del-i-TEER-ee-əs) adj. harmful, harmful

**de·lib·er·ate** (di-LIB-ər-it) adj. intentional; well considered; without haste, slow —v. (-rayt) (-rat·ed, -rat·ing) consider, debate —**de·lib·er·a**'tion n.

**del·i·cate** (DEL-i-kit) adj. exquisite; not robust, fragile; sensitive; requiring tact; deft —**del**'i·ca·cy n.

**del·i·ca·tes·sen** (del-i-kə-TES-ən)

*n.* store selling ready-to-eat foods; the food sold

**de·li·cious** (di-LISH-əs) *adj.* delightful, pleasing to senses, *esp.* taste

**de·light** (di-LĪT) *vt.* please greatly —*vi.* take great pleasure (in) —*n.* great pleasure —**de·light'ful** *adj.* charming

**de·lin·e·ate** (di-LIN-ee-ayt) *vt.* (-at·ed, -at·ing) portray by drawing or description; represent accurately —**de·lin·e·a'tion** *n.*

**de·lin·quent** (di-LING-kwənt) *n.* someone, *esp.* young person, guilty of delinquency —*adj.* —**de·lin'quen·cy** *n.* (*pl.* -cies) (minor) offense or misdeed

**del·i·quesce** (del-i-KWES) *vi.* (-quesced, -quesc·ing) become liquid —**del·i·ques'cence** *n.* —**del·i·ques'cent** *adj.*

**de·lir·i·um** (di-LEER-ee-əm) *n.* disorder of the mind, *esp.* in feverish illness; violent excitement —**de·lir'i·ous** *adj.* raving; light-headed, wildly excited

**de·liv·er** (di-LIV-ər) *vt.* carry (goods *etc.*) to destination; hand over; release; give birth or assist in birth (of); utter or present (speech *etc.*) —**de·liv'er·ance** *n.* rescue —**de·liv'er·y** *n.*

**Del·phic** (DEL-fik) *adj.* pert. to Delphi or to the oracle of Apollo

**del·ta** (DEL-tə) *n.* alluvial tract where river at mouth breaks into several streams; Greek letter (Δ); shape of this letter

**de·lude** (di-LOOD) *vt.* (-lud·ed, -lud·ing) deceive; mislead —**de·lu'sion** (-zhən) *n.*

**del·uge** (DEL-yooj) *n.* flood, great flow, rush, downpour, cloudburst —*vt.* (-uged, -ug·ing) flood, overwhelm

**de luxe** (də LUKS) *adj.* rich, sumptuous; superior in quality

**delve** (delv) *v.* (delved, delv·ing)

(*with* into) search intensively; dig

**de·mag·net·ize** (dee-MAG-ni-tīz) *vt.* (-tized, -tiz·ing) deprive of magnetic polarity

**dem·a·gogue** (DEM-ə-gog) *n.* mob leader or agitator —**dem·a·gog'ic** (-GOJ-ik) *adj.* —**dem'a·go·gy** (-goh-jee) *n.*

**de·mand** (di-MAND) *vt.* ask as giving an order; ask as by right; call for as due, right or necessary —*n.* urgent request, claim, requirement; call for (specific commodity) —**de·mand'ing** *adj.* requiring great skill, patience *etc.*

**de·mar·cate** (di-MAHR-kayt) *vt.* (-cat·ed, -cat·ing) mark boundaries or limits of —**de·mar·ca'tion** *n.*

**de·mean** (di-MEEN) *vt.* degrade, lower, humiliate

**de·mean·or** (di-MEEN-ər) *n.* conduct, bearing, behavior

**de·ment·ed** (di-MEN-tid) *adj.* mad, crazy; beside oneself —**de·men'tia** (-shə) *n.* form of insanity

**de·mer·it** (di-MER-it) *n.* bad mark; undesirable quality

**demi-** (*comb. form*) half, as in demigod Such words are not given here where meaning can be inferred from the simple word

**de·mil·i·ta·rize** (dee-MIL-i-tə-rīz) *vt.* (-rized, -riz·ing) prohibit military presence or function in (an area)

**dem·i·monde** (DEM-ee-mond) *n.* class of women of doubtful reputation; group behaving with doubtful legality *etc.*

**de·mise** (di-MĪZ) *n.* death; conveyance by will or bequest; transfer of sovereignty on death or abdication

**dem·i·urge** (DEM-ee-urj) *n.* name given in some philosophies (*esp.*

Platonic) to the creator of the world and man

**dem·o** (DEM-oh) *n. inf.* short for DEMONSTRATION

**de·mo·bi·lize** (dee-MOH-bə-līz) *vt.* (-lized, -liz·ing) disband (troops); discharge (soldier)

**de·moc·ra·cy** (di-MOK-rə-see) *n.* (*pl.* -cies) government by the people or their elected representatives; country so governed —**dem·o·crat** (DEM-ə-krat) *n.* advocate of democracy —**dem·o·crat'ic** *adj.* connected with democracy; favoring popular rights —**de·moc'ra·tize** *vt.* (-tized, -tiz·ing)

**de·mog·ra·phy** (di-MOG-rə-fee) *n.* study of population statistics, as births, deaths, diseases —**dem·o·graph·ic** (dem-ə-GRAF-ik) *adj.*

**de·mol·ish** (di-MOL-ish) *vt.* knock to pieces; destroy utterly, raze —**dem·o·li·tion** (dem-ə-LISH-ən) *n.*

**de·mon** (DEE-mən) *n.* devil, evil spirit; very cruel or malignant person; person very good at or devoted to a given activity —**de·mo·ni·ac** (di-MOH-nee-ak) *n.* one possessed by a devil —**de·mo·ni·a·cal** (dee-mə-NĪ-ə-kəl) *adj.* —**de·mon·ic** (di-MON-ik) *adj.* of the nature of a demon —**de·mon·ol'o·gy** (dee-) *n.* study of demons

**dem·on·strate** (DEM-ən-strayt) *v.* (-strat·ed, -strat·ing) *vt.* show by reasoning, prove; describe, explain by specimens or experiments —*vi.* make exhibition of support, protest *etc.* by public parade, demonstration; make show of armed force —**dem·on·stra·ble** (di-MON-strə-bəl) *adj.* —**dem·on·stra'tion** *n.* making clear, proving by evidence; exhibition and description; organized public expression of opinion; display of armed force —**dem·on'stra·tive** *adj.* expressing feelings, emotions easily and unreservedly; pointing out; conclusive —**de'mon·stra·tor** *n.* one who demonstrates equipment, products *etc.*; one who takes part in a public demonstration

**de·mor·al·ize** (di-MOR-ə-līz) *vt.* (-ized, -iz·ing) deprive of courage and discipline; undermine morally —**de·mor·al·i·za'tion** *n.*

**de·mote** (di-MOHT) *vt.* (-mot·ed, -mot·ing) reduce in status or rank —**de·mo'tion** *n.*

**de·mur** (di-MUR) *vi.* (-murred, -mur·ring) make difficulties, object —**de·mur'ral** *n.* raising of objection; objection raised —**de·mur'rer** *n.*

**de·mure** (di-MYUUR) *adj.* (-mur·er, -mur·est) reserved, quiet —**de·mure'ly** *adv.*

**den** *n.* cave or hole of wild beast; lair; small room, *esp.* study; site, haunt

**de·na·tion·a·lize** (dee-NASH-ə-nl-īz) *vt.* (-lized, -liz·ing) return (an industry) from public to private ownership

**de·na·ture** (dee-NAY-chər) *vt.* (-tured, -tur·ing) deprive of essential qualities, adulterate —**de·natured** alcohol alcohol made undrinkable

**den·gue** (DENG-gee) *n.* an infectious tropical fever

**denial** *see* DENY

**de·nier** (DEN-yər) *n.* unit of weight of silk and synthetic yarn

**den·i·grate** (DEN-i-grayt) *vt.* (-grat·ed, -grat·ing) belittle or disparage character of

**den·im** (DEN-əm) *n.* strong twilled cotton fabric for trousers, overalls *etc.*; *pl.* garment made of this

**den·i·zen** (DEN-ə-zən) *n.* inhabitant

**de·nom·i·nate** (di-NOM-ə-nayt) vt. (-nat·ed, -nat·ing) give name to —de·nom·i·na'tion n. distinctly named church or sect; name, esp. of class or group —de·nom·i·na'tion·al adj. —de·nom'i·na·tor n. Arithmetic divisor in fraction

**de·note** (di-NOHT) vt. (-not·ed, -not·ing) stand for, be the name of; mark, indicate, show —de·no·ta·tion (dee-noh-TAY-shən) n. esp. explicit meaning of word or phrase

**de·noue·ment** (day-noo-MAHN) n. unraveling of dramatic plot; final solution of mystery

**de·nounce** (di-NOWNS) vt. (-nounced, -nounc·ing) speak violently against; accuse; terminate (treaty) —de·nun·ci·a'tion n. denouncing

**dense** (dens) adj. (dens·er, dens·est) thick, compact; stupid —den'si·ty n. (pl. -ties) mass per unit of volume

**dent** n. hollow or mark left by blow or pressure —vt. make dent in; mark with dent

**den·tal** (DEN-tl) adj. of, pert. to teeth or dentistry; pronounced by applying tongue to teeth —den'ti·frice (-fris) n. powder, paste, or wash for cleaning teeth —den'tist n. one skilled in care, repair of teeth —den'tis·try n. art of dentist —den·ti'tion n. teething; arrangement of teeth —den'ture (-chər) n. (usu. pl.) set of false teeth —dental floss soft thread, oft. waxed, for cleaning between teeth

**den·tine** (DEN-teen) n. the hard bonelike part of a tooth

**de·nude** (di-NOOD) vt. (-nud·ed, -nud·ing) strip, make bare; expose (rock) by erosion of plants, soil etc.

**denunciation** see DENOUNCE

**de·ny** (di-NĪ) vt. (-nied, -ny·ing) declare untrue; contradict; reject, disown; refuse to give; refuse; (reflex.) abstain from —de·ni'a·ble adj. —de·ni'al n.

**de·o·dor·ize** (dee-OH-də-rīz) vt. (-ized, -iz·ing) rid of smell or mask smell of —de·o'dor·ant n. —de·o'dor·iz·er n.

**de·ox·i·dize** (dee-OK-si-dīz) vt. (-dized, -diz·ing) deprive of oxygen

**de·part** (di-PAHRT) vi. go away; start out, set forth; deviate, vary; die —de·par'ture (-chər) n.

**de·part·ment** (di-PAHRT-mənt) n. division; branch; province —de·part·men'tal adj.

**de·pend** (di-PEND) vi. (usu. with on) rely entirely; live; be contingent, await settlement or decision —de·pend·a·ble adj. reliable —de·pend'ent n. one for whose maintenance another is responsible —adj. depending on —de·pend'ence n. —de·pend'en·cy n. dependence; subject territory

**de·pict** (di-PIKT) vt. give picture of; describe in words —de·pic'tion n.

**de·pil·a·to·ry** (di-PIL-ə-tor-ee) n. (pl. -ries) substance that removes unwanted hair —adj.

**de·plete** (di-PLEET) vt. (-plet·ed, -plet·ing) empty; reduce; exhaust —de·ple'tion n.

**de·plore** (di-PLOR) vt. (-plored, -plor·ing) lament, regret; deprecate, complain of —de·plor'a·ble adj. lamentable; disgraceful

**de·ploy** (di-PLOI) v. of troops, ships, aircraft (cause to) adopt battle formation; arrange —de·ploy'ment n.

**de·po·nent** (di-POH-nənt) adj. of verb, having passive form but active meaning —n. deponent verb; one who makes statement under oath

**de·pop·u·late** (di-POP-yə-layt) v.

(-lat·ed, -lat·ing) (cause to) be reduced in population —de·pop·u·la'tion n.

**de·port** (di-PORT) vt. expel from foreign country, banish —de·por·ta'tion (dee-) n.

**de·port·ment** (di-PORT-mənt) n. behavior, conduct, bearing —de·port' v. behave, carry (oneself)

**de·pose** (di-POHZ) v. (-posed, -pos·ing) —vt. remove from office, esp. of ruler —vi. make statement under oath, give evidence —de·pos'al n. removal from office

**de·pos·it** (di-POZ-it) vt. set down, esp. carefully; give into safekeeping, esp. in bank; let fall (as sediment) —n. thing deposited; money given in part payment or as security; sediment (dep·o·sish (dep-ə-ZISH-ən) n. statement written and attested; act of deposing or depositing —de·pos'i·tor n. —de·pos'i·to·ry n. (pl. -ries) place for safekeeping

**dep·ot** (DEE-poh) n. storehouse; building for storage and servicing of buses, trains etc.; railroad, bus station

**de·prave** (di-PRAYV) vt. (-praved, -prav·ing) make bad, corrupt, pervert —de·prav'i·ty n. (pl. -ties) wickedness, viciousness

**dep·re·cate** (DEP-ri-kayt) vt. (-cat·ed, -cat·ing) express disapproval of; advise against —dep·re·ca'tion n. —dep're·ca·to·ry adj.

**de·pre·ci·ate** (di-PREE-shee-ayt) v. (-at·ed, -at·ing) —vt. lower price, value or purchasing power of; belittle —vi. fall in value —de·pre·ci·a'tion n.

**dep·re·da·tion** (dep-ri-DAY-shən) n. plundering, pillage —dep're·date vt. (-dat·ed, -dat·ing) plunder, despoil

**de·press** (di-PRES) vt. affect with low spirits; lower, in level or activity —de·pres'sion (-PRESH-ən) n. hollow; low spirits, dejection, despondency; poor condition of business, slump —de·pres'sant adj./n.

**de·prive** (di-PRIV) vt. (-prived, -priv·ing) strip, dispossess —dep·ri·va·tion (dep-rə-VAY-shən) n. —deprived adj. lacking adequate food, care, amenities etc.

**depth** n. (degree of) deepness; deep place, abyss; intensity (of color, feeling); profundity (of mind) —depth charge bomb for use against submarines

**de·pute** (di-PYOOT) vt. (-put·ed, -put·ing) vt. allot; appoint as an agent or substitute —dep·u·ta·tion (dep-yə-TAY-shən) n. persons sent to speak for others —dep'u·tize vi. (-tized, -tiz·ing) act for another —vt. depute —dep'u·ty n. (pl. -ties) assistant; substitute, delegate

**de·rail** (dee-RAYL) v. (cause to) go off the rails, as train etc. —de·rail'ment n.

**de·rail·leur** (di-RAY-lər) n. gear-changing mechanism for bicycles

**de·range** (di-RAYNJ) vt. (-ranged, -rang·ing) put out of place, out of order; upset; make insane —de·range'ment n.

**der·by** (DUR-bee) n. horserace, esp. Kentucky Derby, held at Churchill Downs, Kentucky; contest between teams of skaters etc.; man's low-crowned stiff felt hat

**de·reg·u·late** (dee-REG-yə-layt) vt. (-lat·ed, -lat·ing) remove regulations or controls from

**der·e·lict** (DER-ə-likt) adj. abandoned, forsaken; falling into ruins, dilapidated —n. social outcast, vagrant; abandoned property, ship *etc.* —**der·e·lic'tion** *n.* neglect (of duty); abandoning

**de·ride** (di-RĪD) *vt.* (-rid·ed, -rid·ing) speak of or treat with contempt, ridicule —**de·ri'sion** (-RIZH-ən) *n.* ridicule —**de·ri'sive** (-RĪ-siv) *adj.*

**de ri·gueur** (də ri-GUR) *Fr.* required by etiquette, fashion or custom

**de·rive** (di-RĪV) *vt.* (-rived, -riv·ing) deduce, get from; show origin of —*vi.* issue, be descended (from) —**der·i·va'tion** (-də-VAY-shən) *n.* —**de·riv·a·tive** (di-RIV-ə-tiv) *adj./n.*

**der·ma·ti·tis** (dur-mə-TĪ-tis) *n.* inflammation of the skin

**der·ma·tol·o·gy** (dur-mə-TOL-ə-jee) *n.* science of skin —**der·ma·tol'o·gist** *n.* physician specializing in skin diseases

**de·rog·a·to·ry** (di-ROG-ə-tor-ee) *adj.* disparaging, belittling, intentionally offensive —**der·o·gate** (DER-ə-gayt) *v.* (-gat·ed, -gat·ing) *vt.* disparage —*vi.* detract

**der·rick** (DER-ik) *n.* hoisting machine; framework over oil well *etc.*

**der·ring-do** (DER·ing DOO) *n.* (act of) spirited bravery, boldness

**der·rin·ger** (DER-in-jər) *n.* short-barreled pocket pistol

**der·vish** (DUR-vish) *n.* member of Muslim ascetic order, noted for frenzied, whirling dance

**des·cant** (DES-kant) *n. Mus.* decorative variation sung as accompaniment to basic melody —*vi.* (des-KANT) sing or play a descant; talk about in detail; dwell (on) at length

**de·scend** (di-SEND) *vi.* come or go down; slope down; stoop, condescend; spring from (ancestor *etc.*); pass to heir, be transmitted; swoop down or attack —*vt.* go or

come down —**de·scend'ant** *n.* person descended from an ancestor —**de·scent'** *n.*

**de·scribe** (di-SKRĪB) *vt.* (-scribed, -scrib·ing) give detailed account of; pronounce or label; trace out (geometric figure *etc.*) —**de·scrip'tion** (-SKRIP-shən) *n.* detailed account; marking out; kind, sort, species —**de·scrip'tive** *adj.*

**de·scry** (di-SKRĪ) *vt.* (-scried, -scry·ing) make out, catch sight of, *esp.* at a distance espy

**des·e·crate** (DES-i-krayt) *vt.* (-crat·ed, -crat·ing) violate sanctity of; profane; convert to evil use —**des·e·cra'tion** *n.*

**des·ert¹** (DEZ-ərt) *n.* uninhabited and barren region —*adj.* barren, uninhabited, desolate

**de·sert²** (di-ZURT) *vt.* abandon, forsake, leave —*vi.* run away from service, *esp.* of soldiers, sailors *etc.* —**de·sert'er** *n.* —**de·ser'tion** *n.*

**de·sert³** (di-ZURT) *n.* (*usu. pl.*) what is due as reward or punishment; merit, virtue

**de·serve** (di-ZURV) *vt.* (-served, -serv·ing) show oneself worthy of; have by conduct a claim to —**de·serv'ed·ly** *adv.* —**de·serv'ing** *adj.* worthy (of reward *etc.*)

**deshabille** *n. see* DISHABILLE

**des·ic·cate** (DES-i-kayt) *v.* (-cat·ed, -cat·ing) dry; dry up

**de·sid·er·a·tum** (di-sid-ə-RAH-təm) *n.* (*pl.* -ta *pr.* -tə) something lacked and wanted

**de·sign** (di-ZĪN) *vt.* make working drawings for; sketch; plan out; intend, select for —*vi.* outline sketch; working plan; art of making decorative patterns *etc.*; project, purpose, mental plan —**de·sign'ed·ly** *adv.* on purpose —**de·sign'er** *n. esp.* one who draws designs for manufacturers or selects typefaces *etc.* for books *etc.*

—de·sign'ing adj. crafty, scheming

des·ig·nate (DEZ-ig-nayt) vt. (-nat·ed, -nat·ing) name, pick out, appoint to office —adj. (-nit) appointed but not yet installed —des·ig·na'tion n. name, appellation

de·sire (di-ZIR) vt. (-sired, -siring) wish, long for; ask for, entreat —n. longing, craving; expressed wish, request; sexual appetite; something wished for or requested —de·sir'a·ble adj. worth desiring —de·sir'ous adj. filled with desire

de·sist (di-ZIST) vi. cease, stop

desk n. table or other piece of furniture designed for reading or writing; counter; editorial section of newspaper etc. covering specific subject; section of State Department having responsibility for particular operations

des·o·late (DES-ə-lit) adj. uninhabited; neglected, barren, ruinous; solitary; dreary, dismal, forlorn —vt. (-layt) (-lat·ed, -lat·ing) depopulate, lay waste; overwhelm with grief —des·o·la'tion n.

de·spair (di-SPAIR) vi. lose hope —n. loss of all hope; cause of this; despondency

despatch see DISPATCH

des·pe·rate (DES-pər-it) adj. reckless from despair; difficult or dangerous; frantic; hopelessly bad; leaving no room for hope —des·per·a'do (-pə-RAH-doh) n. (pl. -dos) reckless, lawless person —des'per·ate·ly adv. —des·per·a'tion n.

de·spise (di-SPIZ) vt. (-spised, -spis·ing) look down on as contemptible, inferior —des·pi·ca·ble (DES-pi-kə-bəl) adj. base, contemptible, vile

de·spite (di-SPIT) prep. in spite of

de·spoil (di-SPOIL) vt. plunder, rob, strip of —de·spo·li·a·tion (dispoh-lee-AY-shən) n.

de·spond·ent (di-SPON-dənt) adj. dejected, depressed —de·spond'en·cy n.

des·pot (DES-pot) n. tyrant, oppressor —des·pot·ic (de-SPOT-ik) adj. —des'pot·ism n. autocratic government, tyranny

des·sert (di-ZURT) n. course of pastry, fruit etc. served at end of meal

des·ti·na·tion (des-tə-NAY-shən) n. place a person or thing is bound for; goal; purpose

des·tine (DES-tin) vt. (-tined, -tin·ing) ordain or fix beforehand; set apart, devote

des·ti·ny (DES-tə-nee) n. (pl. -nies) course of events or person's fate; the power that foreordains

des·ti·tute (DES-ti-toot) adj. in absolute want; in great need, devoid (of); penniless —des·ti·tu'tion n.

de·stroy (di-STROI) vt. ruin; pull to pieces; undo; put an end to; demolish; annihilate —de·stroy'er n. one who destroys; small, swift, heavily armed warship —de·struct (di-STRUKT) v. destroy (one's own missile etc.) for safety; be destroyed —de·struct'i·ble adj. —de·struc'tion n. ruin, overthrow; death —de·struc'tive adj. destroying; negative, not constructive

des·ue·tude (DES-wi-tood) n. disuse, discontinuance

des·ul·to·ry (DES-əl-tor-ee) adj. passing, changing fitfully from one thing to another; aimless; unmethodical

de·tach (di-TACH) vt. unfasten, disconnect, separate —de·tach'a·ble adj. —de·tached' adj. standing apart, isolated; impersonal, disinterested —de·tach'ment n. aloofness; detaching; a body of troops detached for special duty

de·tail (di-TAYL) n. particular; small or unimportant part; treatment of anything item by item; party or personnel assigned for duty in military unit —vt. relate in full; appoint for duty

de·tain (di-TAYN) vt. keep under restraint; hinder; keep waiting —de·ten'tion n. confinement; arrest; detaining

de·tect (di-TEKT) vt. find out or discover existence, presence, nature or identity of —de·tec'tion n. —de·tec'tive n. police officer or private agent employed in detecting crime —adj. employed in detection —de·tec'tor n. esp. mechanical sensing device or device for detecting radio signals etc.

dé·tente (day-TAHNT) n. lessening of tension in political or international affairs

detention n. see DETAIN

de·ter (di-TUR) vt. (-terred, -ter·ring) discourage, frighten; hinder, prevent —de·ter'rent adj./n.

de·ter·gent (di-TUR-jənt) n. cleansing, purifying substance —adj. having cleansing power

de·te·ri·o·rate (di-TEER-ee-ə-rayt) v. (-rat·ed, -rat·ing) become or make worse —de·te·ri·o·ra'tion n.

de·ter·mine (di-TUR-min) v. (-mined, -min·ing) vt. make up one's mind, decide; fix as known; bring to a decision; be deciding factor in; Law end —vi. come to an end; come to a decision —de·ter'mi·nant adj./n. —de·ter'mi·nate (-nit) adj. fixed in scope or nature —de·ter·mi·na'tion n. determining; firm or resolute conduct or purpose; resolve —deter-

mined adj. resolute —de·ter'min·ism n. theory that human action is settled by forces independent of human will

de·test (di-TEST) vt. hate, loathe —de·test'a·ble adj. —de·tes·ta'tion (dee·te-STAY-shən) n.

de·throne (dee-THROHN) vt. (-throned, -thron·ing) remove from throne, depose

det·o·nate (DET-n-ayt) v. of bomb, mine, explosives etc., (cause to) explode —det·o·na'tion n. —det'o·na·tor n. mechanical, electrical device, or small amount of explosive, used to set off main explosive charge

de·tour (DEE-tuur) n. course that leaves main route to rejoin it later; roundabout way —vi.

de·tract (di-TRAKT) v. take away (a part) from, diminish —de·trac'tor n.

det·ri·ment (DE-trə-mənt) n. harm done, loss, damage —det·ri·men'tal adj. damaging, injurious

de·tri·tus (di-TRI-təs) n. worn-down matter such as gravel, or rock debris; debris

de trop (də TROH) Fr. not wanted, superfluous

deuce (doos) n. two; playing card with two spots; Tennis forty all; in exclamatory phrases, the devil

Deut. Deuteronomy

deu·te·ri·um (doo-TEER-ee-əm) n. isotope of hydrogen twice as heavy as the normal gas

de·val·ue (dee-VAL-yoo) (-ued, -u·ing), de·val·u·ate (-at·ed, -at·ing) v. (of currency) reduce or be reduced in value; reduce the value or worth of —de·val·u·a'tion n.

dev·as·tate (DEV-ə-stayt) vt. (-tat·ed, -tat·ing) lay waste; ravage; inf. overwhelm —dev·as·ta'tion n.

**de·vel·op** (di-VEL-əp) *vt.* bring to maturity; elaborate; bring forth, bring out; evolve; treat photographic plate or film to bring out image; improve value or change use (of land) by building *etc.* —*vi.* grow to maturer state —**de·vel′op·er** *n.* one who develops land; chemical for developing film —**de·vel′op·ment** *n.*

**de·vi·ate** (DEE-vee-ayt) *vi.* (-at·ed, -at·ing) leave the way, turn aside, diverge —**de′vi·ant** *n./adj.* (person) deviating from normal *esp.* in sexual practices —**de·vi·a′tion** *n.* —**de′vi·ous** *adj.* deceitful, underhanded; roundabout, rambling; erring

**de·vice** (di-VĪS) *n.* contrivance, invention; apparatus; stratagem; scheme, plot; heraldic or emblematic figure or design

**dev·il** (DEV-əl) *n.* personified spirit of evil; superhuman evil being; person of great wickedness, cruelty *etc.*; *inf.* fellow; *inf.* something difficult or annoying; energy, dash, unconquerable spirit; *inf.* rogue, rascal —*vt.* (-iled, -il·ing) prepare (eggs *etc.*) with spicy seasoning —**dev′il·ish** *adj.* like, of the devil; evil —*adv. inf.* very, extremely —**dev′il·try** *n.* (*pl.* -tries) wickedness; wild and reckless mischief, revelry, high spirits —**dev′il·may·care′** *adj.* happy-go-lucky —**devil's advocate** one who advocates opposing, unpopular view, *usu.* for sake of argument; *Catholic Church* one appointed to state disqualifications of person who has been proposed for sainthood

**devious** *adj. see* DEVIATE

**de·vise** (di-VĪZ) *vt.* (-vised, -vis·ing) plan, contrive; invent; plot; leave by will

**de·void** (di-VOID) *adj.* (*usu.* with of) empty, lacking, free from

**de·volve** (di-VOLV) *vi.* (-volved, -volv·ing) pass or fall (to, upon) —*vt.* throw (duty *etc.*) on to another —**dev·o·lu·tion** (dev-ə-LOO-shən) *n.* transfer of authority from central to regional government

**de·vote** (di-VOHT) *vt.* (-vot·ed, -vot·ing) set apart, give up exclusively (to person, purpose *etc.*) —**de·vot′ed** *adj.* loving, attached —**dev·o·tee** (dev-ə-TEE) *n.* ardent enthusiast; zealous worshiper —**de·vo′tion** *n.* deep affection, loyalty; dedication; religious earnestness —*pl.* prayers, religious exercises —**de·vo′tion·al** *adj.*

**de·vour** (di-VOWR) *vt.* eat greedily; consume, destroy; read, gaze at eagerly

**de·vout** (di-VOWT) *adj.* earnestly religious, pious; sincere, heartfelt

**dew** (doo) *n.* moisture from air deposited as small drops on cool surface between nightfall and morning; any beaded moisture —*vt.* wet with or as with dew —**dew′y** *adj.* (dew·i·er, dew·i·est) —**dew′claw** *n.* partly developed inner toe of dogs —**dew′lap** *n.* fold of loose skin hanging from neck

**dex·ter·i·ty** (dek-STER-i-tee) *n.* manual skill, neatness, deftness, adroitness —**dex′ter·ous** *adj.* showing dexterity, skillful

**dex·trose** (DEK-strohs) *n.* white, soluble, sweet-tasting crystalline solid, occurring naturally in fruit, honey, animal tissue

**dia–** (*prefix*) through

**di·a·be·tes** (dī-ə-BEE-tis) *n.* various disorders characterized by excretion of abnormal amount of urine, *esp.* diabetes mel·li·tus (MEL-i-təs), in which body fails to store and utilize glucose —**di·a·bet′ic** *n./adj.*

**di·a·bol·ic** (dī-ə-BOL-ik), **di·a-**

**bol′i·cal** adj. devilish; inf. very bad —di·a·bol′i·cal·ly adv.

**di·a·crit·ic** (dī-ə-KRIT-ik) n. sign above letter or character indicating special phonetic value etc. —di·a·crit′i·cal adj. of a diacritic; showing a distinction

**di·a·dem** (DĪ-ə-dem) n. a crown

**di·ag·no·sis** (dī-əg-NOH-sis) n. (pl. -ses pr. -seez) identification of disease from symptoms —di′ag·nose (-nohz) vt. (-nosed, -nosing) —di·ag·nos′tic (-NOS-tik) adj.

**di·ag·o·nal** (dī-AG-ə-nl) adj. from corner to corner; oblique —n. line from corner to corner —di·ag′o·nal·ly adv.

**di·a·gram** (DĪ-ə-gram) n. drawing, figure in lines, to illustrate something being expounded —di·a·gram·mat′i·cal·ly adv.

**di·al** (DĪ-əl) n. face of clock etc.; plate marked with graduations on which a pointer moves (as on a meter, radio, scale etc.); numbered disk on front of telephone —vt. operate telephone; indicate on dial

**di·a·lect** (DĪ-ə-lekt) n. characteristic speech of region; local variety of a language —di·a·lec′tal adj.

**di·a·lec·tic** (dī-ə-LEK-tik) n. art of arguing —di·a·lec′ti·cal adj. —di·a·lec·ti′cian (-TISH-ən) n. logician; reasoner

**di·a·logue** (DĪ-ə-lawg) n. conversation between two or more (persons); representation of such conversation in drama, novel etc.; discussion between representatives of two governments etc.

**di·al·y·sis** (dī-AL-ə-sis) n. Med. (pl. -ses pr. -seez) filtering of blood through membrane to remove waste products

**di·am·e·ter** (dī-AM-i-tər) n. (length of) straight line from side to side of figure or body (esp. circle) through center ; thickness —di·a·met′ri·cal adj. opposite —di·a·met′ri·cal·ly adv.

**di·a·mond** (DĪ-mənd) n. very hard and brilliant precious stone, also used in industry; rhomboid figure; suit at cards; playing field in baseball —diamond jubilee, wedding 60th or 75th anniversary

**di·a·pa·son** (dī-ə-PAY-zən) n. fundamental organ stop; compass of voice or instrument

**di·a·per** (DĪ-pər) n. garment of absorbent material to absorb an infant's excrement —vt. put a diaper on

**di·aph·a·nous** (dī-AF-ə-nəs) adj. transparent

**di·a·pho·ret·ic** (dī-ə-fə-RET-ik) n. drug promoting perspiration —adj.

**di·a·phragm** (DĪ-ə-fram) n. muscular partition dividing two cavities of body, midriff; plate or disk wholly or partly closing tube or opening; any thin dividing or covering membrane

**di·ar·rhe·a** (dī-ə-REE-ə) n. excessive looseness of the bowels

**di·a·ry** (DĪ-ə-ree) n. (pl. -ries) daily record of events or thoughts; book for this; book for noting appointments, memoranda etc. —di′a·rist n. writer of diary

**di·as·to·le** (dī-AS-tl-ee) n. dilatation of the chambers of the heart

**di·a·ther·my** (DĪ-ə-thur-mee) n. heating of body tissues with electric current for medical or surgical purposes

**di·a·tom** (DĪ-ə-tom) n. one of order of microscopic algae —di·a·tom′ic adj. of two atoms

**di·a·ton·ic** (dī-ə-TON-ik) adj. Mus. pert. to regular major and minor scales; (of melody) composed in such a scale

**di·a·tribe** (DĪ-ə-trīb) n. violently

bitter verbal attack, invective, denunciation

**dice** (dīs) *n. pl.* (*sing.* **die** *pr.* dī) cubes each with six sides marked one to six for games of chance —*v.* (**diced, dic·ing**) —*vi.* gamble with dice —*vt. Cookery* cut vegetables into small cubes —**dic'er** *n.* —**dic'ey** *adj. inf.* (**dic·i·er, dic·i·est**) dangerous, risky

**di·chot·o·my** (dī-KOT-ə-mee) *n.* (*pl.* -**mies**) division into two parts

**dictate** (DIK-tayt) *v.* (-**tat·ed,** -**tat·ing**) say or read for another to transcribe; prescribe, lay down; impose (as terms) —*n.* bidding —**dic·ta'tion** *n.* —**dictator** *n.* absolute ruler —**dic·ta·to'ri·al** *adj.* despotic; overbearing —**dic·ta'tor·ship** *n.*

**dic·tion** (DIK-shən) *n.* choice and use of words; enunciation

**dic·tion·ar·y** (DIK-shə-ner-ee) *n.* (*pl.* -**ar·ies**) book setting forth, alphabetically, words of language with meanings *etc.*; reference book with items in alphabetical order

**dic·tum** (DIK-təm) *n.* (*pl.* -**ta** *pr.* -tə) pronouncement, saying, maxim

**did** *pt. of* DO

**di·dac·tic** (dī-DAK-tik) *adj.* designed to instruct; (of people) opinionated, dictatorial

**die**[1] (dī) *vi.* (**died, dy·ing**) cease to live; come to an end; stop functioning; *inf.* be nearly overcome (with laughter *etc.*); *inf.* look forward (to) —**die'hard** *n.* one who resists (reform *etc.*) to the end

**die**[2] *see* DICE

**die**[3] *n.* shaped block of hard material to form metal in forge, press *etc.*; tool for cutting thread on pipe *etc.*

**di·e·lec·tric** (dī-i-LEK-trik) *n.* substance through or across which electric induction takes place; nonconductor; insulator

**di·er·e·sis** (dī-ER-ə-sis) *n.* (*pl.* -**ses** *pr.* -seez) mark (¨) placed over vowel to show that it is sounded separately from preceding one

**die·sel** (DEE-zəl) *adj.* pert. to internal-combustion engine using oil as fuel —*n.* this engine; vehicle powered by it

**di·et**[1] (DĪ-it) *n.* restricted or regulated course of feeding; kind of food lived on; food —*vi.* follow a dietary regimen, as to lose weight —**di'e·ta·ry** *adj.* relating to a regulated diet —**di·e·tet'ic** *adj.* —**di·e·tet'ics** *n.* science of diet —**di·e·ti'tian** (-TISH-ən) *n.* one skilled in dietetics —**dietary fiber** fibrous substances in fruit and vegetables, consumption of which aids digestion (*also* **roughage**)

**diet**[2] *n.* parliament of some countries; formal assembly

**dif·fer** (DIF-ər) *vi.* be unlike; disagree —**dif'fer·ence** *n.* unlikeness; degree or point of unlikeness; disagreement; remainder left after subtraction —**dif'fer·ent** *adj.* unlike

**dif·fer·en·tial** (dif-ə-REN-shəl) *adj.* varying with circumstances; special; *Math.* pert. to an infinitesimal change in variable quantity; *Physics etc.* relating to difference between sets of motions acting in the same direction or between pressures *etc.* —*n. Math.* infinitesimal difference between two consecutive states of variable quantity; mechanism in automobile *etc.* permitting back wheels to revolve at different speeds when rounding corner; difference between rates of pay for different types of labor —**dif·fer·en'ti·ate** (-shee-ayt) *v.*

(-at·ed, -at·ing) —*vt.* serve to distinguish between, make different —*vi.* discriminate —**dif·fer·en·ti·a'tion** *n.* —**differential calculus** method of calculating relative rate of change for continuously varying quantities

**dif·fi·cult** (DIF-i-kult) *adj.* requiring effort, skill *etc.* to do or understand, not easy; obscure —**dif'fi·cul·ty** *n.* (*pl.* -ties) being difficult; difficult task, problem; embarrassment; hindrance; obscurity; trouble

**dif·fi·dent** (DIF-i-dənt) *adj.* lacking confidence, timid, shy —**dif'fi·dence** *n.* shyness

**dif·fract** (di-FRAKT) *vt.* break up, *esp.* of rays of light, sound waves —**dif·frac'tion** (-FRAK-shən) *n.* deflection of ray of light, electromagnetic wave caused by an obstacle

**dif·fuse** (di-FYOOZ) *vt.* (-fused, -fus·ing) spread abroad —*adj.* (-FYOOS) widely spread; loose, verbose, wordy —**dif·fuse'ly** *adv.* loosely; wordily —**dif·fu'sion** (-zhən) *n.* —**dif·fu'sive** *adj.*

**dig** *v.* (dug, dig·ging) —*vi.* work with spade; search, investigate —*vt.* turn up with spade; hollow out, make hole in; excavate; thrust into; discover by searching; *sl.* understand —*n.* archaeological excavation; thrust; gibe, taunt —**dig'ger** *n.*

**di·gest** (di-JEST) *vt.* prepare (food) in stomach *etc.* for assimilation; bring into handy form by sorting, tabulating, summarizing; reflect on; absorb —*vi.* of food, undergo digestion —*n.* (Di-jest) methodical summary, of laws, research *etc.*; magazine containing condensed version of articles *etc.* already published elsewhere —**di·gest'i·ble** *adj.* —**di·ges'tion** *n.* digesting

**dig·it** (DIJ-it) *n.* finger or toe; any of the numbers 0 to 9 —**dig'it·al** *adj.* of, resembling digits; performed with fingers; displaying information (time *etc.*) by numbers rather than by pointer on dial —**digital recording** sound recording process that converts audio signals into pulses corresponding to voltage level

**dig·i·tal·is** (dij-i-TAL-is) *n.* drug made from foxglove

**dig·ni·ty** (DIG-ni-tee) *n.* (*pl.* -ties) stateliness, gravity; worthiness, excellence, repute; honorable office or title —**dig'ni·fy** *vt.* (-fied, -fy·ing) give dignity to —**dignified** *adj.* stately, majestic —**dig'ni·tar·y** (-ter-ee) *n.* (*pl.* -tar·ies) holder of high office

**di·gress** (di-GRES) *vi.* turn from main course, *esp.* to deviate from subject in speaking or writing —**di·gres'sion** *n.*

**di·he·dral** (dī-HEE-drəl) *adj.* having two plane faces or sides

**dike** (dīk) *n.* embankment to prevent flooding; ditch

**di·lap·i·dat·ed** (di-LAP-i-day-tid) *adj.* in ruins; decayed

**dil·a·ta·tion** (dil-ə-TAY-shən) *n.* widening of body aperture for medical treatment (*eg* for curettage)

**di·late** (dī-LAYT) *v.* (-lat·ed, -lat·ing) —*vt.* widen, expand —*vi.* expand; talk or write at length (on) —**di·la'tion** *n.*

**dil·a·to·ry** (DIL-ə-tor-ee) *adj.* tardy, slow, belated —**dil'a·to·ri·ness** *n.* delay

**di·lem·ma** (di-LEM-ə) *n.* position in fact or argument offering choice only between unwelcome alternatives; predicament

**dil·et·tante** (DIL-i-tahnt) *n.* person with taste and knowledge of fine arts as pastime; dabbler

—*adj.* amateur, desultory —**dil'et·tant·ism** *n.*

**dil·i·gent** (DIL-i-jənt) *adj.* unremitting in effort, industrious, hardworking —**dil'i·gence** *n.*

**di·lute** (di-LOOT) *vt.* (-lut·ed, -lut·ing) reduce (liquid) in strength, *esp.* by adding water; thin; reduce in force, effect *etc.* —*adj.* weakened thus —**di·lu'tion** *n.*

**dim** *adj.* (dim·mer, dim·mest) indistinct, faint, not bright; mentally dull; unfavorable —*v.* (dimmed, dim·ming) make, grow dim —**dim'ly** *adv.* —**dim'mer** *n.* device for dimming electric lights —**dim'ness** *n.*

**dime** (dīm) *n.* 10-cent piece, coin of US and Canada

**di·men·sion** (di-MEN-shən) *n.* measurement, size; aspect —**fourth dimension** *Physics* time; supernatural, fictional dimension additional to those of length, breadth, thickness

**di·min·ish** *v.* lessen —**dim·i·nu·tion** (dim-ə-NOO-shən) *n.* —**di·min·u·tive** (di-MIN-yə-tiv) *adj.* very small —*n.* derivative word, affix implying smallness

**di·min·u·en·do** (di-min-yoo-EN-doh) *adj./adv. Mus.* of sound, dying away

**dim·ple** (DIM-pəl) *n.* small hollow in surface of skin, *esp.* of cheek; any small hollow —*v.* (-pled, -pling) mark with, show dimples

**din** *n.* continuous roar of confused noises —*vt.* (dinned, din·ning) repeat to weariness, ram (fact, opinion *etc.*) into

**dine** (dīn) *v.* (dined, din·ing) —*vi.* eat *esp.* dinner —*vt.* give dinner to —**din'er** *n.* one who dines; *informal usu.* cheap restaurant —**dining room**

**din·ghy** (DING-gee) *n.* (*pl.* -ghies) small open boat; inflatable life raft

**din·go** (DING-goh) *n.* (*pl.* -goes) Aust. wild dog

**din·gy** (DIN-jee) *adj.* (-gi·er, -gi·est) dirty-looking, shabby —**din'gi·ness** *n.*

**din·ner** (DIN-ər) *n.* chief meal of the day; official banquet

**di·no·saur** (DĪ-nə-sor) *n.* extinct reptile, often of gigantic size

**dint** *n.* force, power —**by dint of** by means of

**di·o·cese** (DĪ-ə-sis) *n.* ecclesiastical district under jurisdiction of bishop —**di·oc·e·san** (dī-OS-ə-sən) *adj.* —*n.* bishop having jurisdiction over diocese

**di·ode** (DĪ-ohd) *n. Electronics* device for converting alternating current to direct current

**di·op·ter** (dī-OP-tər) *n.* unit for measuring refractive power of lens

**di·o·ram·a** (dī-ə-RAM-ə) *n.* miniature three-dimensional scene, *esp.* as museum exhibit

**di·ox·ide** (dī-OK-sīd) *n.* oxide with two parts of oxygen to one of the other constituents

**di·ox·in** (dī-OK-sin) *n.* extremely toxic byproduct of the manufacture of certain herbicides and bactericides

**dip** *v.* (dipped, dip·ping) *vt.* put partly or for a moment into liquid; immerse, involve; lower and raise again; take up in ladle, bucket *etc.* —*vi.* plunge partially or temporarily; go down, sink; slope downward —*n.* act of dipping; brief swim; liquid chemical in which livestock are immersed to treat insect pests *etc.*; downward slope; hollow; creamy mixture in which cracker *etc.* is dipped before being eaten —**dip into** glance at (book *etc.*)

**diph·the·ri·a** (dif-THEER-ee-ə) *n.* infectious disease of throat with membranous growth

**diph·thong** (DIF-thawng) *n.* union of two vowel sounds in single compound sound

**di·plo·ma** (di-PLOH-mə) *n.* (*pl.* -mas) document vouching for person's proficiency; title to degree, honor *etc.*

**di·plo·ma·cy** (di-PLOH-mə-see) *n.* management of international relations; skill in negotiation; tactful, adroit dealing —**dip·lo·mat** (DIP-lə-mat) *n.* one engaged in official diplomacy —**dip·lo·mat'ic** *adj.* —**di·plo'ma·tist** *n.* tactful person

**di·plo·pi·a** (di-PLOH-pee-ə) *n.* double vision

**di·po·lar** (di-POH-lər) *adj.* having two poles

**di·pole** (Dl-pohl) *n.* type of radio and television antenna

**dip·per** (DIP-ər) *n.* ladle, bucket, scoop

**dip·so·ma·ni·a** (dip-sə-MAY-nee-ə) *n.* uncontrollable craving for alcohol —**dip·so·ma'ni·ac** *n.* victim of this

**dip·tych** (DIP-tik) *n.* ancient tablet hinged in the middle, folding together like a book; painting, carving on two hinged panels

**dire** (dir) *adj.* (**dir·er, dir·est**) terrible; urgent

**di·rect** (di-REKT) *vt.* control, manage, order; point out the way; aim, point, turn; address (letter *etc.*); supervise actors *etc.* in play or film —*adj.* frank, straightforward; straight; going straight to the point; immediate; lineal —**di·rec'tion** *n.* directing; aim, course of movement; address, instruction —**di·rec'tive** *adj./n.* —**di·rec'tor** *n.* one who directs, *esp.* a film; member of board of directors of company —**di·rec'to·rate** (-tər-it) *n.* body of directors; office of director —**di·rec'to·ry** *n.* (*pl.* -ries) book of names, addresses, streets *etc.* —**direction finder** radio receiver that determines the direction of incoming waves

**dirge** (durj) *n.* song of mourning

**dir·i·gi·ble** (DIR-i-jə-bəl) *adj.* steerable —*n.* airship

**dirt** (durt) *n.* filth; soil; earth; obscene material; contamination —**dirt'i·ness** *n.* —**dirt'y** *adj.* (-i·er, -i·est) unclean, filthy; obscene; unfair; dishonest

**dis-** (*prefix*) negation, opposition, deprivation; in many verbs indicates undoing of the action of simple verb In the list below, the meaning can be inferred from the word to which *dis-* is prefixed

| | | |
|---|---|---|
| dis·ap·pro·ba'tion | dis·cour'te·sy | dis·in'ter' |
| dis·ap·prov'al | dis·em·bark' | dis·loy'al |
| dis·ap·prove' | dis·en·gage' | dis·mount' |
| dis·ar·range' | dis·en·gage'ment | dis·or·gan·i·za'tion |
| dis·as·so'ci·ate | dis·en·tan'gle | dis·or'gan·ize |
| dis·band' | dis·es·tab'lish | dis·pro·por'tion |
| dis·be·lief' | dis·es·tab'lish·ment | dis·prove' |
| dis·com·pose' | dis·fa'vor | dis·rep'u·ta·ble |
| dis·com·po'sure | dis·fran'chise | dis·re·pute' |
| dis·con·nect' | dis·har'mo·ny | dis·re·spect'(ful) |
| dis·con·tent' | dis·heart'en | dis·sat·is·fac'tion |
| dis·con·tent'ment | dis·hon'est | dis·sat'is·fy |
| dis·con·tin'ue | dis·hon'es·ty | dis·sim'i·lar |
| dis·cour'te·ous | dis·hon'or·a·ble | dis·sim·i·lar'i·ty |

**dis·a·ble** (dis-AY-bəl) *vt.* (-bled, -bling) make unable; cripple; maim —dis·a·bil'i·ty *n.* (*pl.* -ties) incapacity; drawback

**dis·a·buse** (dis-ə-BYOOZ) *vt.* (-bused, -bus·ing) undeceive, disillusion; free from error

**dis·ad·van·tage** (dis-əd-VAN-tij) *n.* drawback; hindrance; detriment —*vt.* (-taged, -tag·ing) handicap —**disadvantaged** *adj.* deprived, discriminated against, underprivileged —dis·ad·van·ta·geous (-TAY-jəs) *adj.*

**dis·af·fect·ed** (dis-ə-FEK-tid) *adj.* ill-disposed, alienated, estranged —dis·af·fec'tion *n.*

**dis·a·gree** (dis-ə-GREE) *vt.* (-greed, -gree·ing) be at variance; conflict; (of food *etc.*) have bad effect on —dis·a·gree'ment *n.* difference of opinion; discord; discrepancy —dis·a·gree'a·ble *adj.* unpleasant

**dis·al·low** (dis-ə-LOW) *vt.* reject as untrue or invalid

**dis·ap·pear** (dis-ə-PEER) *vi.* vanish; cease to exist; be lost —dis·ap·pear'ance *n.*

**dis·ap·point** (dis-ə-POINT) *vt.* fail to fulfill (hope), frustrate —dis·ap·point'ment *n.*

**dis·arm** (dis-AHRM) *v.* deprive of arms or weapons; reduce country's war weapons; win over —dis·ar'ma·ment *n.* —dis·arm'ing *adj.* removing hostility, suspicion

**dis·ar·ray** (dis-ə-RAY) *vt.* throw into disorder, derange —*n.* disorderliness, *esp.* of clothing

**dis·as·ter** (di-ZAS-tər) *n.* calamity, sudden or great misfortune —dis·as'trous *adj.* calamitous

**dis·bar** (dis-BAHR) *vt.* (-barred, -bar·ring) *Law* expel from the bar

**dis·bud'** *vt.* (-bud·ded, -bud·ding) remove superfluous buds, shoots from

**dis·burse** (dis-BURS) *vt.* (-bursed, -burs·ing) pay out (money) —dis·burse'ment *n.*

**disc** *see* DISK

**dis·card** (di-SKAHRD) *v.* reject; give up; cast off, dismiss

**dis·cern** (di-SURN) *vt.* make out; distinguish —dis·cern'i·ble *adj.* —dis·cern'ing *adj.* discriminating; penetrating —dis·cern'ment *n.* insight

**dis·charge** (dis-CHAHRJ) *vt.* (-charged, -charg·ing) release; dismiss; emit; perform (duties); fulfill (obligations); let go; fire off; unload; pay —*n.* (DIS-chahrj) discharging; being discharged; release; matter emitted; document certifying release, payment *etc.*

**dis·ci·ple** (di-SĪ-pəl) *n.* follower, one who takes another as teacher and model

**dis·ci·pline** (DIS-ə-plin) *n.* training that produces orderliness, obedience, self-control; result of such training in order, conduct *etc.*; system of rules, *etc.* —*vt.* (-plined, -plin·ing) train; punish —dis·ci·pli·nar'i·an *n.* one who enforces rigid discipline —dis'ci·pli·nar·y *adj.*

**dis·claim** (dis-KLAYM) *vt.* deny, renounce —dis·claim'er *n.* repudiation, denial

**dis·close** (dis-SKLOHZ) *vt.* (-closed, -clos·ing) allow to be seen; make known —dis·clo'sure (-zhər) *n.* revelation

**dis·col·or** (dis-KUL-ər) *vt.* alter color of, stain —dis·col·or·a'tion *n.*

**dis·com·fit** (dis-KUM-fit) *vt.* embarrass, disconcert, baffle —dis·com'fi·ture (-fi-chər) *n.*

---

dis·sym'me·try         dis·trust'

**dis·com·mode** (dis-kə-MOHD) vt. (-mod·ed, -mod·ing) put to inconvenience; disturb

**dis·con·cert** (dis-kən-SURT) vt. ruffle, confuse, upset, embarrass

**dis·con·so·late** (dis-KON-sə-lit) adj. unhappy, downcast, forlorn

**dis·cord** (DIS-kord) n. strife; difference, dissension; disagreement of sounds —dis·cord'ant adj.

**dis·co·theque** (DIS-kə-tek) n. club etc. for dancing to recorded music

**dis·count** (dis-KOWNT) vt. consider as possibility but reject as unsuitable, inappropriate etc.; deduct (amount, percentage) from usual price; sell at reduced price —n. (DIS-kownt) amount deducted as cash amount or percentage

**dis·coun·te·nance** (dis-KOWN-tn-əns) vt. (-nanced, -nanc·ing) abash; discourage; frown upon

**dis·cour·age** (di-SKUR-ij) vt. (-aged, -ag·ing) reduce confidence of; deter; show disapproval of

**dis·course** (DIS-kors) n. conversation; speech, treatise, sermon —vi. (dis-KORS) (-coursed, -cours·ing) speak, converse, lecture

**dis·cov·er** (di-SKUV-ər) vt. (be the first to) find out, light upon; make known —dis·cov'er·a·ble adj. —dis·cov'er·er n. —dis·cov'er·y n. (pl. -er·ies)

**dis·cred·it** (dis-KRED-it) vt. damage reputation of; cast doubt on; reject as untrue —n. disgrace; doubt —dis·cred'it·a·ble adj.

**dis·creet** (di-SKREET) adj. prudent, circumspect —dis·creet'ness n.

**dis·crep·an·cy** (di-SKREP-ən-see) n. (pl. -cies) conflict, variation, as between figures —dis·crep'ant adj.

**dis·crete** (di-SKREET) adj. separate, disunited, discontinuous

**dis·cre·tion** (di-SKRESH-ən) n. quality of being discreet; prudence; freedom to act as one chooses —dis·cre'tion·ar·y adj.

**dis·crim·i·nate** (di-SKRIM-ə-nayt) vi. (-nat·ed, -nat·ing) single out for special favor or disfavor; distinguish between; be discerning —dis·crim·i·na'tion n.

**dis·cur·sive** (di-SKUR-siv) adj. passing from subject to subject, rambling

**dis·cus** (DIS-kəs) n. disk-shaped object thrown in athletic competition

**dis·cuss** (di-SKUS) vt. exchange opinions about; debate —dis·cus'sion n.

**dis·dain** (dis-DAYN) n. scorn, contempt —vt. scorn —dis·dain'ful adj.

**dis·ease** (di-ZEEZ) n. illness; disorder of health

**dis·em·bod·ied** (dis-em-BOD-eed) adj. (of spirit) released from bodily form

**dis·em·bow·el** (dis-em-BOW-əl) vt. take out entrails of

**dis·en·chant·ed** (dis-en-CHAN-tid) adj. disillusioned

**dis·fig·ure** (dis-FIG-yər) vt. (-ured, -ur·ing) mar appearance of —dis·fig·ur·a'tion n. —dis·fig'ure·ment n. blemish, defect

**dis·gorge** (dis-GORJ) vt. (-gorged, -gorg·ing) vomit; give up

**dis·grace** (dis-GRAYS) n. shame, loss of reputation, dishonor —vt. (-graced, -grac·ing) bring shame or discredit upon —dis·grace'ful adj. shameful

**dis·grun·tled** (dis-GRUN-tld) adj. vexed; put out

**dis·guise** (dis-GĪZ) vt. (-guised, -guis·ing) change appearance of, make unrecognizable; conceal, cloak; misrepresent —n. false appearance; device to conceal identity

**dis·gust'** n. violent distaste, loathing, repugnance —vt. affect with loathing

**dish** n. shallow vessel for food; portion or variety of food; contents of dish; sl. attractive woman —**dish out** inf. put in dish; serve up; dispense (money, abuse etc.)

**dis·ha·bille** (dis-ə-BEEL) n. state of being partly or carelessly dressed

**di·shev·eled** (di-SHEV-əld) adj. with disordered hair; ruffled, untidy, unkempt

**dis·il·lu·sion** (dis-i-LOO-zhən) vt. destroy ideals, illusions, or false ideas of —n.

**dis·in·fect·ant** (dis-in-FEK-tənt) n. substance that prevents or removes infection —**dis·in·fect'** vt.

**dis·in·for·ma·tion** (dis-in-fər-MAY-shən) n. false information intended to deceive or mislead

**dis·in·gen·u·ous** (dis-in-JEN-yoo-əs) adj. not sincere or frank

**dis·in·her·it** (dis-in-HE-rit) vt. to deprive of inheritance

**dis·in·te·grate** (dis-IN-tə-grayt) v. (-grat·ed, -grat·ing) break up, fall to pieces

**dis·in·ter·est** (dis-IN-trist) n. freedom from bias or involvement —**dis·in'ter·est·ed** adj.

**dis·joint'** vt. put out of joint; break the natural order or logical arrangement of —**dis·joint'ed** adj. (of discourse) incoherent; disconnected

**disk** thin, flat, circular object like a coin; phonograph record —**disk harrow** harrow that cuts the soil with inclined disks

**dis·lo·cate** (DIS-loh-kayt) vt.

(-cat·ed, -cat·ing) put out of joint (eg dislocate shoulder); disrupt, displace —**dis·lo·ca'tion** n.

**dis·lodge** (dis-LOJ) vt. (-lodged, -lodg·ing) drive out or remove from hiding place or previous position

**dis·mal** (DIZ-məl) adj. depressing; depressed; cheerless, dreary, gloomy —**dis'mal·ly** adv.

**dis·man·tle** (dis-MAN-tl) vt. (-tled, -tling) take apart —**dis·man'tle·ment** n.

**dis·may'** vt. dishearten, daunt —n. consternation, horrified amazement; apprehension

**dis·mem·ber** (dis-MEM-bər) vt. tear or cut limb from limb; divide, partition —**dis·mem'ber·ment** n.

**dis·miss'** vt. remove, discharge from employment; send away; reject —**dis·miss'al** n.

**dis·o·bey** (dis-ə-BAY) v. refuse or fail to obey —**dis·o·be'di·ence** (-BEE-dee-əns) n.

**dis·o·blige** (dis-ə-BLIJ) vt. (-bliged, -blig·ing) disregard the wishes, preferences of

**dis·or·der** (dis-OR-dər) n. disarray, confusion, disturbance; upset of health, ailment —vt. upset order of; disturb health of —**dis·or'der·ly** adj. untidy; unruly

**dis·o·ri·ent** (dis-OR-ee-ənt) vt. cause to lose one's bearings, confuse

**dis·own** (dis-OHN) vt. refuse to acknowledge

**dis·par·age** (di-SPAR-ij) vt. (-aged, -ag·ing) speak slightingly of; belittle —**dis·par'age·ment** n.

**dis·pa·rate** (DIS-pər-it) adj. essentially different, unrelated —**dis·par'i·ty** n. (pl. -ties) inequality; difference

**dis·pas·sion·ate** (dis-PASH-ə-nit) adj. unswayed by passion; calm, impartial

**dis·patch** (di-SPACH) *vt.* send off to destination or on an errand; send off; finish off, get done with speed; *inf.* eat up; kill —*n.* sending off; efficient speed; official message, report

**dis·pel** (di-SPEL) *vt.* (-pelled, -pel·ling) clear, drive away, scatter

**dis·pense** (di-SPENS) *vt.* (-pensed, -pens·ing) deal out; make up (medicine); administer (justice); grant exemption from —**dis·pen'sa·ble** *adj.* —**dis·pen'sa·ry** *n.* (*pl.* -ries) place where medical aid is given —**dis·pen·sa'tion** *n.* act of dispensing; license or exemption; provision of nature or providence —**dis·pens'er** *n.* —dispense with do away with; manage without

**dis·perse** (di-SPURS) *vt.* (-persed, -pers·ing) scatter —dispersed *adj.* scattered; placed here and there —**dis·per'sal, dis·per'sion** (-zhən) *n.*

**dis·pir·it·ed** (di-SPIR-i-tid) *adj.* dejected, disheartened —**dis·pir'it·ing** *adj.*

**dis·place** (dis-PLAYS) *vt.* (-placed, -plac·ing) move from its place; remove from office; take place of —**dis·place'ment** *n.* displacing; weight of liquid displaced by a solid in it

**dis·play** (di-SPLAY) *vt.* spread out for show; show, expose to view —*n.* displaying; parade; show, exhibition; ostentation

**dis·please** (dis-PLEEZ) *v.* (-pleased, pleas·ing) offend; annoy —**dis·pleas·ure** (-PLEZH-ər) *n.* anger, vexation

**dis·port** (di-SPORT) *v. refl.* gambol, amuse oneself, frolic

**dis·pose** (di-SPOHZ) *v.* (-posed, -pos·ing) —*vt.* arrange; distribute; incline; adjust —*vi.* determine —**dis·pos'a·ble** *adj.* de-

signed to be thrown away after use —**dis·pos'al** *n.* —**dis·po·si·tion** (dis-pə-ZISH-ən) *n.* inclination; temperament; arrangement; plan —dispose of sell, get rid of; have authority over, deal with

**dis·pos·sess** (dis-pə-ZES) *vt.* cause to give up possession (of)

**dis·pute** (di-SPYOOT) *v.* (-put·ed, -put·ing) —*vi.* debate, discuss —*vt.* call in question; debate, argue; oppose, contest —**dis·put'a·ble** *adj.* —**dis·pu'tant** *n.* —**dis·pu·ta'tious** *adj.* argumentative; quarrelsome

**dis·qual·i·fy** (dis-KWOL-ə-fī) *vt.* (-fied, -fy·ing) make ineligible, unfit for some special purpose

**dis·qui·et** (dis-KWĪ-it) *n.* anxiety, uneasiness —*vt.* cause (someone) to feel this

**dis·qui·si·tion** (dis-kwə-ZISH-ən) *n.* learned or elaborate treatise, discourse or essay

**dis·rupt'** *vt.* interrupt; throw into turmoil or disorder —**dis·rup'tion** *n.* —**dis·rup'tive** *adj.*

**dis·sect** (di-SEKT) *vt.* cut up (body, organism) for detailed examination; examine or criticize in detail —**dis·sec'tion** *n.*

**dis·sem·ble** (di-SEM-bəl) *v.* (-bled, -bling) conceal, disguise (feelings *etc.*); act the hypocrite —**dis·sem'bler** *n.*

**dis·sem·i·nate** (di-SEM-ə-nayt) *vt.* (-nat·ed, -nat·ing) spread abroad, scatter —**dis·sem·i·na'tion** *n.*

**dis·sent** (di-SENT) *vi.* differ in opinion; express such difference; disagree with doctrine *etc.* of established church *etc.* —*n.* such disagreement —**dis·sent'er** *n.*

**dis·ser·ta·tion** (dis-ər-TAY-shən) *n.* written thesis; formal discourse

**dis·serv·ice** (dis-SUR-vis) n. ill turn, wrong, injury

**dis·si·dent** (DIS-i-dənt) n./adj. (one) not in agreement, esp. with government —**dis'si·dence** n. dissent; disagreement

**dis·sim·u·late** (di-SIM-yə-layt) v. (-lat·ed, -lat·ing) pretend not to have; practice deceit —**dis·sim·u·la'tion** n.

**dis·si·pate** (DIS-ə-payt) vt. (-pat·ed, -pat·ing) waste, squander —**dis'si·pat·ed** adj. indulging in pleasure without restraint, dissolute; scattered, wasted —**dis·si·pa'tion** n. scattering; frivolous, dissolute way of life

**dis·so·ci·ate** (di-SOH-shee-ayt) v. (-at·ed, -at·ing) separate, sever; disconnect

**dis·so·lute** (DIS-ə-loot) adj. lacking restraint, esp. lax in morals

**dis·so·lu·tion** (dis-ə-LOO-shon) n. breakup; termination of legislature, meeting or legal relationship; destruction; death

**dis·solve** (di-ZOLV) v. (-solved, -solv·ing) —vt. absorb or melt in fluid; break up, put an end to, annul —vi. melt in fluid; disappear, vanish; break up, scatter —**dis·sol·u·ble** (di-SOL-yə-bəl) adj. capable of being dissolved

**dis·so·nant** (DIS-ə-nənt) adj. jarring, discordant —**dis'so·nance** n.

**dis·suade** (di-SWAYD) vt. (-suad·ed, -suad·ing) advise to refrain, persuade not to —**dis·sua'sion** (-zhən) n. —**dis·sua'sive** adj.

**dis·taff** (DIS-taf) n. cleft stick to hold wool etc., for spinning —**distaff side** maternal side; female line

**dis·tance** (DIS-təns) n. amount of space between two things; remoteness; aloofness, reserve —vt. (-tanced, -tanc·ing) hold or

place at distance —**dis'tant** adj. far off, remote; haughty, cold

**dis·taste** (dis-TAYST) n. dislike of food or drink; aversion, disgust —**dis·taste'ful** adj. unpleasant, displeasing to feelings —**dis·taste'ful·ness** n.

**dis·tem·per** (dis-TEM-pər) n. disease of dogs; method of painting on plaster without oil; paint used for this —vt. paint with distemper

**dis·tend** (di-STEND) v. swell out by pressure from within, inflate —**dis·ten'sion** n.

**dis·tich** (DIS-tik) n. couplet

**dis·till** (di-STIL) vt. vaporize and recondense a liquid; purify, separate, concentrate liquids by this method; fig. extract quality of —vi. trickle down —**dis·til·late** (DIS-tə-lit) n. distilled liquid, esp. as fuel for some engines —**dis·till'er** n. one who distills, esp. manufacturer of whiskey

**dis·tinct** (di-STINGKT) adj. clear, easily seen; definite; separate, different —**dis·tinc'tion** n. point of difference; act of distinguishing; eminence, repute, high honor, high quality —**dis·tinc'tive** adj. characteristic —**dis·tinct'ly** adv.

**dis·tin·guish** (di-STING-gwish) vt. make difference in; recognize, make out; honor; make prominent or honored (usu. refl.); classify —vi. (usu. with between or among) draw distinction, grasp difference —**dis·tin'guish·a·ble** adj. —**dis·tin'guished** adj. dignified; famous, eminent

**dis·tort** (di-STORT) vt. put out of shape, deform; misrepresent; garble, falsify —**dis·tor'tion** n.

**dis·tract** (di-STRAKT) vt. draw attention of (someone) away from work etc.; divert; perplex, bewilder, drive mad —**dis·trac'·tion** n.

**dis·traught** (di-STRAWT) adj. bewildered, crazed with grief; frantic, distracted

**dis·tress** (dis-STRES) n. severe trouble, mental pain; severe pressure of hunger, fatigue or want; —vt. afflict, give mental pain —**dis·tress'ful** adj.

**dis·trib·ute** (di-STRIB-yoot) vt. (-ut·ed, -ut·ing) deal out, dispense; spread, dispose at intervals; classify —**dis·tri·bu'tion** n. —**dis·trib'u·tive** adj. —**dis·trib'u·tor** n. rotary switch distributing electricity in automotive engine

**dis·trict** (DIS-trikt) n. region, locality; portion of territory

**dis·turb'** vt. trouble, agitate, unsettle, derange —**dis·turb'ance** n.

**dis·use** (dis-YOOS) n. state of being no longer used —**dis·used'** (-YOOZD) adj.

**ditch** (dich) n. long narrow hollow dug in ground for drainage etc. —v. make, repair ditches; run car etc. into ditch —vt. sl. abandon, discard

**dith·er** (DITH-ər) vi. be uncertain or indecisive —n. this state

**dith·y·ramb** (DITH-ə-ram) n. ancient Greek hymn sung in honor of Dionysus

**dit·to** (DIT-oh) n. (pl. -tos) same, aforesaid (used to avoid repetition in lists etc.)

**dit·ty** (DIT-ee) n. (pl. -ties) simple song

**di·u·ret·ic** (di-ə-RET-ik) adj. increasing the discharge of urine —n. substance with this property

**di·ur·nal** (di-UR-nəl) adj. daily; in or of daytime; taking a day

**di·va·lent** (di-VAY-lənt) adj. capable of combining with two atoms of hydrogen or their equivalent

**di·van'** n. bed, couch without back or head

**dive** (div) vi. (**dived** or **dove**, **div·ing**) plunge under surface of water; descend deeply; disappear; go deep down into; reach quickly —n. act of diving; sl. disreputable bar, club etc. —**div'·er** n. one who descends into deep water —**dive bomber** aircraft that attacks after diving steeply

**di·verge** (di-VURJ) vi. (-verged, -verg·ing) get farther apart; separate —**di·ver'gence** n. —**di·ver'gent** adj.

**di·vers** (DI-vərz) adj. obs. some, various

**di·verse** (di-VURS) adj. different, varied —**di·ver'si·fy** vt. (-fied, -fy·ing) make diverse or varied; give variety to —**di·ver·si·fi·ca'tion** n.

**di·vert** (di-VURT) vt. turn aside, ward off; amuse, entertain —**di·ver'sion** (-zhən) n. a diverting; official detour for traffic when main route is closed; amusement

**di·vest'** vt. unclothe, strip; dispossess, deprive; sell off

**di·vide** (di-VID) vt. (-vid·ed, -vid·ing) vt. make into two or more parts, split up, separate; distribute, share; diverge in opinion; classify —vi. become separated; part into two groups for voting etc. —n. division esp. between adjacent drainage areas —**div'i·dend** n. share of profits, of money divided among shareholders etc.; number to be divided by another —**di·vid'ers** n. pl. pair of compasses

**di·vine** (di-VIN) adj. (-vin·er, -vin·est) of, pert. to, proceeding from, God; sacred; heavenly —n. theologian; clergyman —v. (-vined, -vin·ing) guess; predict, foresee, tell by inspiration or magic —**div·i·na·tion** (div-ə-NAY-

shən) *n.* divining —di·vine·ly *adv.*
—di·vin′er *n.* —di·vin′i·ty *n.* quality of being divine; god; theology —divining rod (forked) stick *etc.* said to move when held over ground where water is present

di·vi·sion (di-VIZH-ən) *n.* act of dividing; part of whole; barrier; section; difference in opinion *etc.*; Math. method of finding how many times one number is contained in another; army unit; separation, disunion —di·vis′i·ble *adj.* capable of division —di·vi′sive (-VI-siv) *adj.* causing disagreement —di·vi′sor (-VI-zər) *n.* Math. number that divides dividend

di·vorce (di-VORS) *n.* legal dissolution of marriage; complete separation, disunion —vt. (-vorced, -vorc·ing) dissolve marriage; separate; sunder —di·vor·cee′ (-SAY) *n.*

div·ot (DIV-ət) *n.* piece of turf

di·vulge (di-VULJ) *vt.* (-vulged, -vulg·ing) reveal, let out (secret)

Dix·ie (DIK-see) *n.* southern states of the US

diz·zy (DIZ-ee) *adj.* (-zi·er, -zi·est) feeling dazed, unsteady, as if about to fall; causing or fit to cause dizziness, as speed *etc.*; inf. silly —vt. (-zied, -zy·ing) make dizzy —diz′zi·ly *adv.* —diz′zi·ness *n.*

DNA *n. abbrev.* for deoxyribonucleic acid, main constituent of the chromosomes of all organisms

do¹ (doo) *v.* (did, done, do·ing) —vt. perform, effect, transact, bring about, finish; work at; work out, solve; suit; cover (distance); provide, prepare; *inf.* cheat, trick; frustrate; look after —vi. act; manage; work; fare; serve; suffice; happen —v. aux. makes negative and interrogative sentences and expresses emphasis —n. *inf.* celebration, festivity —do away with destroy —do up fasten; renovate —do with need; make use of —do without deny oneself

do² (doh) *n.* first sol-fa note

doc·ile (DOS-əl) *adj.* willing to obey, submissive

dock¹ (dok) *n.* artificial enclosure near harbor for loading or repairing ships; platform for loading and unloading trucks —v. of vessel, put or go into dock; (of spacecraft) link or be linked together in space —dock′er *n.* longshoreman —dock′yard *n.* enclosure with docks, for building or repairing ships

dock² *n.* solid part of animal's tail; cut end, stump —vt. cut short, *esp.* tail; curtail, deduct (an amount) from

dock³ *n.* enclosure in criminal court for prisoner

dock·et (DOK-it) *n.* agenda; list of court cases to be heard —vt. place on docket

doc·tor (DOK-tər) *n.* medical practitioner; one holding university's highest degree in any faculty —vt. treat medically; repair, mend; falsify (accounts *etc.*) —doc′tor·al (-əl) *adj.* —doc′tor·ate (-it) *n.*

doc·trine (DOK-trin) *n.* what is taught; teaching of church, school, or person; belief, opinion, dogma —doc·tri·naire′ (-trə-NAIR) *adj.* stubbornly insistent on applying theory without regard for circumstances —n. —doc′tri·nal (-nəl) *adj.*

doc·u·ment (DOK-yə-mənt) *n.* piece of paper *etc.* providing information or evidence —vt. furnish with proofs, illustrations, certificates —doc·u·men′ta·ry *adj./n.* (*pl.* -ries) (of) type of film, TV program dealing with real life, not fiction —**doc·u·men·ta′tion** n.

**dod·der** (DOD-ər) vi. totter or tremble, as with age

**dodge** (doj) v. avoid or attempt to avoid (blow, discovery etc.) as by moving quickly; evade questions by cleverness —n. trick, artifice; ingenious method; act of dodging —**dodg′er** n. shifty person; evader

**do·do** (DOH-doh) n. (pl. -dos) large extinct bird; person with old-fashioned ideas

**doe** (doh) n. female of deer, hare, rabbit

**does** (duz) third pers. sing., pres. ind. active of DO

**doff** (dof) vt. take off (hat, clothing); discard, lay aside

**dog** (dawg) n. domesticated carnivorous four-legged mammal; person (in contempt, abuse or playfully); name given to various mechanical contrivances for gripping, holding; device with tooth that penetrates or grips object and detains it; andiron or firedog; sl. ugly person; sl. thing of extremely poor quality; inf. a fellow —vt. (dogged, dog·ging) follow steadily or closely —**dog′ged** (-gid) adj. persistent, resolute, tenacious —**dog′gy** adj. (-gi·er, -gi·est) —dog days hot season of the rising of Dog Star; period of inactivity —**dog′·ear** n. turned-down corner of page in book —vt. turn down corners of pages —**dog′-eat-dog′** n. action based on complete cynicism, ruthless competition —**dog′fight** n. skirmish between fighter planes; savage contest characterized by disregard of rules —doggy bag bag in which diner may take leftovers (ostensibly) for dog) —**dog′house** n. kennel; inf. disfavor, as in the doghouse

—**dog′leg** n. sharp bend or angle —**dog's age** quite a long time —Dog Star star Sirius —go to the dogs degenerate

**doge** (dohj) n. formerly, chief magistrate in Venice

**dog·ger·el** (DAW-gər-əl) n. slipshod, unpoetic or trivial verse

**do·gie** (DOH-gee) n. motherless calf

**dog·ma** (DAWG-mə) n. (pl. -mas) article of belief, esp. one laid down authoritatively by church; body of beliefs —**dog·mat′ic** adj. asserting opinions with arrogance; relating to dogma —**dog·mat′i·cal·ly** adv. —**dog′ma·tism** n. arrogant assertion of opinion

**doi·ly** (DOI-lee) n. (pl. -lies) small cloth, paper, piece of lace to place under cake, dish etc.

**Dol·by** (DOHL-bee) R system used in tape recording to reduce unwanted noise

**dol·ce** (DOHL-chay) adj. Mus. sweet

**dol·drums** (DOHL-drəmz) n. pl. state of depression, dumps; region of light winds and calms near the equator

**dole** (dohl) n. charitable allotment, gift —vt. (doled, dol·ing) (usu. with out) deal out sparingly

**dole·ful** (DOHL-fəl) adj. dreary, mournful —**dole′ful·ly** adv.

**doll** (dol) n. child's toy image of human being; sl. attractive person —v. dress (up) in latest fashion or smartly

**dol·lar** (DOL-ər) n. standard monetary unit of many countries, esp. US and Canada

**dol·lop** (DOL-əp) n. inf. semisolid lump; unmeasured amount, a dash

**dol·ly** (DOL-ee) n. (pl. -lies) doll; wheeled support for film, TV camera; platform on wheels for moving heavy objects; various metal devices used as aids in hammering, riveting

**dol·men** (DOHL-mən) *n.* prehistoric monument; stone table

**do·lo·mite** (DOH-lə-mīt) *n.* a type of limestone

**do·lor** (DOH-lər) *n.* grief, sadness, distress —**dol'or·ous** (DOL-) *adj.*

**dol·phin** (DOL-fin) *n.* sea mammal, smaller than whale, with beaklike snout

**dolt** (dohlt) *n.* stupid fellow —**dolt'ish** *adj.*

**do·main** (doh-MAYN) *n.* lands held or ruled over; sphere, field of influence; province

**dome** (dohm) *n.* a rounded vault forming a roof; something of this shape

**Domes·day Book** (DOOMZ-day) record of survey of England in 1086

**do·mes·tic** (də-MES-tik) *adj.* of, in the home; homeloving; (of animals) tamed, kept by man; of, in one's own country, not foreign —*n.* household servant —**domes'ti·cate** (-kayt) *vt.* (-cat·ed, -cat·ing) tame (animals); accustom to home life; adapt to an environment —**domes·tic·i·ty** (doh-me-STIS-i-tee) *n.*

**dom·i·cile** (DOM-ə-sil) *n.* person's regular place of abode —**dom'iciled** *adj.* living

**dom·i·nate** (DOM-ə-nayt) *vt.* (-nat·ed, -nat·ing) rule, control, sway; of heights, overlook —*vi.* control, be the most powerful or influential member or part of something —**dom'i·nant** *adj.* —**dom·i·na'tion** *n.* —**dom'i·neer'** *v.* act imperiously, tyrannize

**Do·min·i·can** (də-MIN-i-kən) *n.* priest or nun of the order of St. Dominic —*adj.* pert. to this order

**do·min·ion** (də-MIN-yən) *n.* sovereignty, rule; territory of government

**dom·i·noes** (DOM-ə-nohz) *n. with sing. v.* game played with 28 oblong flat pieces marked on one side with 0 to 6 spots on each half of the face —**dom·i·no** *n.* one of these pieces; cloak with eye mask for masquerading

**don¹** *vt.* (donned, don·ning) put on (clothes)

**don²** *n.* in English universities, fellow or tutor of college; Spanish title, Sir; in Mafia, head of a family or syndicate

**do·nate** (DOH-nayt) *vt.* (-nat·ed, -nat·ing) give —**do·na'tion** *n.* gift to fund —**do·nor** (DOH-nər) *n.* —**donor card** card specifying organs that may be used for transplant after cardholder's death

**done** *pp.* of DO

**don·key** (DONG-kee) *n. (pl. -keys)* ass; stupid or obstinate person —**donkey engine** auxiliary engine —**don'key·work** *n.* drudgery

**donned** *pt./pp.* of DON

**doo·dle** (DOOD-l) *vi.* (-dled, -dling) scribble absentmindedly —*n.*

**doom** *n.* fate, destiny; ruin; judicial sentence, condemnation; the Last Judgment —*vt.* sentence, condemn; destine to destruction or suffering —**dooms'day** *n.* the day of the Last Judgment

**door** (dor) *n.* hinged or sliding barrier to close any entrance —**door'way** *n.* entrance with or without door

**dope** (dohp) *n.* kind of varnish; *sl.* drug, *esp.* illegal, narcotic drug; *inf.* information; *inf.* stupid person —*vt.* (doped, dop·ing) drug (*esp.* of racehorses) —**dop·ey** (DOH-pee) *adj. inf.* (dop·i·er, dop·i·est) foolish; drugged; half-asleep

**Dop·pler effect** (DOP-lər) *n.* shift in frequency of sound, light, other waves when emitting source moves closer or farther from the observer

**Dor·ic** (DOR-ik) n. dialect of Dorians; style of Greek architecture; rustic dialect —adj. —Do·ri·an (DOR-ee-ən) adj./n. (member) of early Greek race

**dor·mant** (DOR-mənt) adj. not active, in state of suspension; sleeping —dor'man·cy n.

**dor·mer** (DOR-mər) n. upright window set in sloping roof; such a projecting structure

**dor·mi·to·ry** (DOR-mi-tor-ee) n. (pl. -ries) sleeping room with many beds —dormitory suburb suburb whose inhabitants commute to work

**dor·mouse** (DOR-mows) n. small hibernating mouselike rodent

**dor·sal** (DOR-səl) adj. of, on back

**do·ry** (DOR-ee) n. (pl. -ries) flat-bottomed boat with high bow and flaring sides

**dose** (dohs) n. amount (of drug etc.) administered at one time; inf. instance or period of something unpleasant, esp. disease —vt. (dosed, dos·ing) give doses to —dos'age n.

**dos·si·er** (DOS-ee-ay) n. set of papers on some particular subject or event

**dot** n. small spot, mark —vt. (dot·ted, dot·ting) mark with dot(s); sprinkle —dot'ty adj. inf. (-ti·er, -ti·est) eccentric; crazy; inf. (with over or about) extremely fond of

**dote** (doht) vi. (dot·ed, dot·ing) (with on or upon) be passionately fond of; be silly or weak-minded —dot'age (-ij) n. senility —do'tard (-tərd) n. —dot'ing adj. blindly affectionate

**dotty** see DOT

**dou·ble** (DUB-əl) adj. of two parts, layers etc., folded; twice as much or many; of two kinds; designed for two users; ambiguous; deceitful —adv. twice; to twice the amount or extent; in a pair —n. person or thing exactly like, or mistaken for, another; quantity twice as much as another; sharp turn; running pace —v. (-bled, -bling) make, become double; increase twofold; fold in two; turn sharply; get around, sail around —dou'bly adv. —double agent spy employed simultaneously by two opposing sides —double bass largest and lowest-toned instrument in violin form —dou'ble-cross' v. betray, swindle a colleague —dou'ble-cross'er n. —dou'ble-deal'ing n. artifice, duplicity —double Dutch sl. incomprehensible talk, gibberish; (d-) form of the game of jump rope —double glazing two panes of glass in a window to insulate against cold, sound etc. —dou'ble-head'er n. Sports two games played consecutively on same day in same stadium —dou'ble-quick' adj./adv. very fast —double take delayed reaction to a remark, situation etc. —dou'ble-talk n./vt. (engage in) intentionally garbled speech

**dou·ble en·ten·dre** (DUB-əl ahn-TAHN-drə) n. (pl. -dres pr. -drəz) word or phrase with two meanings, one usu. indelicate

**dou·blet** (DUB-lit) n. close-fitting body garment formerly worn by men; one of two words from same root but differing in form and usu. in meaning, as warden and guardian; counterfeit gem of thin layer of gemstone fused onto base of glass etc.

**dou·bloon** (də-BLOON) n. ancient Spanish gold coin

**doubt** (dowt) vt. hesitate to believe; call in question; suspect —vi. be wavering or uncertain in belief or opinion —*n.* uncertainty, wavering in belief; state of affairs giving cause for uncertainty —*doubt'ful adj.* —*doubt'less adv.*

**douche** (doosh) *n.* jet or spray of water applied to (part of) body; device for douching —*vt.* (douched, douch·ing) give douche to

**dough** (doh) *n.* flour or meal kneaded with water; *sl.* money —*dough'nut n.* sweetened and fried, usu. ring-shaped, piece of dough

**dough·ty** (DOW-tee) *adj.* (-ti·er, -ti·est) valiant —*dough'ti·ness n.* boldness

**dour** (duur) *adj.* grim, stubborn, severe

**douse** (dows) *vt.* (doused, dous·ing) thrust into water; extinguish (light)

**dove** (duv) *n.* bird of pigeon family; person opposed to war —*dove'cote* (-koht) *n.* house for doves —*dove'tail n.* joint made with fan-shaped tenon —*v.* fit closely, neatly, firmly together

**dow·a·ger** (DOW-ə-jər) *n.* widow with title or property derived from deceased husband; dignified elderly woman, *esp.* with wealth or social prominence

**dow·dy** (DOW-dee) *adj.* (-di·er, -di·est) unattractively or shabbily dressed —*n.* woman so dressed

**dow·el** (DOW-əl) *n.* wooden, metal peg, *esp.* joining two adjacent parts

**dow·er** (DOW-ər) *n.* widow's share for life of husband's estate —*vt.* endow —*dow'ry n.* property wife brings to husband at marriage; any endowment

**down¹** *adv.* to, in, or toward, lower position; below the horizon; (of payment) on the spot, immediate —*prep.* from higher to lower part of; at lower part of; along —*adj.* depressed, miserable —*vt.* knock, pull, push down; *inf.* drink, eat quickly —*down'ward adj./adv.* —*down'wards adv.* —*down'cast adj.* dejected; looking down —*down'pour n.* heavy rainfall —*down'right adj.* plain, straightforward —*adv.* quite, thoroughly —*down·stage adj./adv.* at, to front of stage —*down'-and-out'* finished, defeated —*down in the mouth* dejected, discouraged —*down East* New England, *esp.* the state of Maine —*down under* Australia and New Zealand

**down²** *n.* soft underfeathers, hair or fiber; fluff —*down'y adj.* (down·i·er, down·i·est)

**Down syndrome** genetic disorder characterized by degree of mental and physical retardation

**dowry** *see* DOWER

**dowse** (dowz) *v.* (dowsed, dows·ing) use divining rod —*dows'er n.* water diviner

**dox·ol·o·gy** (dok-SOL-ə-jee) *n.* short hymn of praise to God

**doy·en** (doi-EN) *n.* senior member of a body or profession (-enne *fem.*)

**doze** (dohz) *vi.* (dozed, doz·ing) sleep drowsily, be half-asleep —*n.* nap

**doz·en** (DUZ-ən) *n.* (set of) twelve

**drab** *adj.* dull, monotonous; of a dingy brown color —*n.* mud color; slut, prostitute

**drach·ma** (DRAK-mə) *n.* (pl. -mas) monetary unit of Greece

**Dra·co·ni·an** (dray-KOH-nee-ən) *adj.* like the laws of Draco; (*oft.* d-) very harsh, cruel

**draft¹** *n.* design, sketch; preliminary plan or layout for work to be executed; rough copy of document; order for money; current of air between apertures in room *etc.*; act or action of drawing; act or action of drinking; amount drunk at once; inhaling; depth of ship in water —*vt.* make sketch, plan, or rough design of; make rough copy (of writing *etc.*) —*adj.* of beer *etc.*, for drawing; drawn —*draft'y adj.* (draft·i·er, draft·i·est) full of air currents —**draft horse** horse for vehicles carrying heavy loads —**drafts'·man** *n.* (*pl.* -men), -per·son one who makes drawings, plans *etc.* —**drafts'man·ship** *n.*

**draft²** *vt.* select for compulsory military service; select (professional athlete) by draft; compel (person) to serve

**drag** *v.* (dragged, drag·ging) —*vt.* pull along with difficulty or friction; trail, go heavily; sweep with net or grapnels; protract —*vi.* lag, trail; be tediously protracted —*n.* check on progress; checked motion; sledge, net, grapnel, rake; *sl.* influence; *sl.* tedious person or thing; *sl.* women's clothes worn by (transvestite) man —**drag'ster** *n.* automobile designed, modified for drag racing; driver of such car —**drag'net** *n.* fishing net to be dragged along sea floor; comprehensive search, *esp.* by police for criminal *etc.* —**drag race** automobile race where cars are timed over measured distance

**drag·on** (DRAG-ən) *n.* mythical fire-breathing monster, like winged crocodile; type of large lizard —**drag'on·fly** *n.* (*pl.* -flies) long-bodied insect with gauzy wings

**dra·goon** (drə-GOON) *n.* formerly, cavalryman of certain regiments —*vt.* oppress; coerce

**drain** (drayn) *vt.* draw off (liquid) by pipes, ditches *etc.*; dry; drink to dregs; empty, exhaust —*vi.*

flow off or away; become rid of liquid —*n.* channel for removing liquid; sewer; depletion, strain —**drain'age** (-ij) *n.*

**drake** (drayk) *n.* male duck

**dram** *n.* small draft of strong drink; unit of weight, 1/8 of fluid ounce, 1/16 of avoirdupois ounce

**dra·ma** (DRAH-mə) *n.* stage play; art or literature of plays; playlike series of events —**dra·mat·ic** (drə-MAT-ik) *adj.* pert. to drama; suitable for stage representation; with force and vividness of drama; striking; tense; exciting —**dram'a·tist** *n.* writer of plays —**dram·a·ti·za'tion** *n.* —**dram'a·tize** *vt.* (-tized, -tiz·ing) adapt story, novel for acting

**dram·a·tur·gy** (DRAM-ə-tur-jee) *n.* the technique of writing and producing plays —**dram'a·tur·gist** *n.* playwright

**drape** (drayp) *vt.* (draped, drap·ing) cover, adorn with cloth; arrange in graceful folds —**dra·per·y** (DRAY-pə-ree) *n.* (*pl.* -per·ies) covering, curtain *etc.* of cloth

**dras·tic** (DRAS-tik) *adj.* extreme, forceful; severe

**draw** *v.* (drew, drawn, draw·ing) —*vt.* pull, pull along, haul; inhale; entice; delineate, portray with pencil *etc.*; frame, compose, draft, write; attract; bring (upon, out *etc.*); get by lot; of ship, require (depth of water); take from (well, barrel *etc.*); receive (money); bend (bow) —*vi.* pull, shrink; attract; make, admit current of air; make pictures with pencil *etc.*; finish game in tie; write orders for money; come, approach (near) —*n.* act of drawing; casting of lots; unfinished game, tie —**draw'er** *n.* one who or that which draws; sliding box in table or chest —*pl.* undergarment for the lower body —**draw'ing** *n.* art of depicting in line; sketch so done; action of verb —**draw'back** *n.* anything that takes away from satisfaction; snag —**draw'bridge** *n.* hinged bridge to pull up —**drawing room** living room, sitting room —**draw near** approach —**draw out** lengthen —**draw up** arrange; come to a halt

**drawl** *v.* speak slowly —*n.* such speech

**drawn** *pp.* of DRAW

**dread** (dred) *vt.* fear greatly —*n.* awe, terror —*adj.* feared, awful —**dread'ful** *adj.* disagreeable, shocking or bad —**dread'locks** *n. pl.* Rastafarian hair style of long matted or tightly curled strands —**dread'nought** *n.* large battleship mounting heavy guns

**dream** (dreem) *n.* vision during sleep; fancy, reverie, aspiration; very pleasant idea, person, thing —*v.* (**dreamed** *or* **dreamt, dreaming**) —*vi.* have dreams —*vt.* see, imagine in dreams; think of as possible —**dream'y** *adj.* (**dream-i-er, dream-i-est**) given to daydreams, impractical, vague; *inf.* wonderful

**drear-y** (DREER-ee) *adj.* (**drear-i-er, drear-i-est**) dismal, dull —**drear'i-ly** *adv.* —**drear'i-ness** *n.* gloom

**dredge**[1] (drej) *v.* (**dredged, dredg-ing**) bring up mud *etc.*, from sea bottom; deepen channel by dredge; search for, produce obscure, remote, unlikely material —*n.* form of scoop or grab —**dredg'er** *n.* ship for dredging

**dredge**[2] *vt.* sprinkle with flour *etc.* —**dredg'er** *n.*

**dregs** (dregz) *n. pl.* sediment, grounds; worthless part

**drench** *vt.* wet thoroughly, soak; make (an animal) take dose of medicine —*n.* soaking; dose for animal

**dress** *vt.* clothe; array for show; trim, smooth, prepare surface of; prepare (food) for market or table; put dressing on (wound); align (troops) —*vi.* put on one's clothes; form in proper line —*n.* one-piece garment for woman; clothing; clothing for ceremonial evening wear —**dress'er** *n.* one who dresses, *esp.* actors or actresses; chest of drawers, oft. with mirror —**dress'ing** *n.* something applied to something else, as sauce to food, ointment to wound, manure to land, *etc.*; *inf.* scolding, as in **dressing down** —**dress'y** *adj.* (**dress-i-er, dress-i-est**) stylish; fond of dress —**dress circle** (*usu.*) first gallery in theater —**dressing gown** —**dressing table** —**dress'-mak-er** *n.*

**dres-sage** (drə-SAHZH) *n.* method of training horse in special maneuvers to show obedience

**drew** *pt.* of DRAW

**drib-ble** (DRIB-əl) *v.* (**-bled, -bling**) flow in drops, trickle; run at the mouth; *Basketball* work ball forward with short bounces; *Soccer* work ball forward with short kicks —*n.* trickle, drop —**drib'let** *n.* small portion or installment

**drift** *vi.* be carried as by current of air, water; move aimlessly or passively —*n.* process of being driven by current; slow current or course; deviation from course; tendency; speaker's, writer's meaning; wind-heaped mass of snow, sand *etc.*; material driven or carried by water —**drift'er** *n.* one who, that which drifts; *inf.* aimless person with no fixed job *etc.* —**drift'wood** (-wuud) *n.* wood washed ashore by sea

**drill**[1] *n.* boring tool or machine; exercise of soldiers or others in handling of arms and maneuvers; repeated routine in teaching —*vt.* bore, pierce hole; exercise in military and other routine —*vi.* practice routine

**drill**[2] *n.* machine for sowing seed; small furrow for seed; row of plants —*vt.* sow seed in drills or furrows

**drill**[3] *n.* coarsely woven twilled fabric

**drink** (dringk) *v.* (**drank, drunk, drink·ing**) swallow liquid; absorb; take intoxicating liquor, *esp.* to excess —*n.* liquid for drinking; portion of this; act of drinking; intoxicating liquor; excessive use of it —**drink'a·ble** *adj.* —**drink to,** drink the health of express good wishes *etc.* by drinking a toast to

**drip** *v.* (**dripped, drip·ping**) fall or let fall in drops —*n.* act of dripping; drop; *Med.* intravenous administration of solution; *sl.* dull, insipid person —**drippings** *n.* melted fat that drips from roasting meat —*adj.* very wet —**drip-dry** (-drī) *adj.* (of fabric) drying free of creases if hung up while wet

**drive** (drīv) *v.* (**drove, driv·en, driv·ing**) —*vt.* urge in some direction; make move and steer (vehicle, animal *etc.*); urge, impel; fix by blows, as nail; chase; convey in vehicle; hit a ball with force as in golf, baseball —*vi.* keep machine, animal, going; steer it; be conveyed in vehicle; rush, dash, drift fast —*n.* act, action of driving; journey in vehicle; private road leading to house; capacity for getting things done; united effort, campaign; energy; forceful stroke in golf, baseball —**driv'er** *n.* one that drives; golf club

**driv·el** (DRIV-əl) *vi.* run at the mouth or nose; talk nonsense —*n.* silly nonsense

**driz·zle** (DRIZ-əl) *vi.* (**-zled, -zling**) rain in fine drops —*n.* fine, light rain

**drogue** (drohg) *n.* any funnel-like device, *esp.* of canvas, used as sea anchor; small parachute; wind indicator; windsock towed behind target aircraft; funnel-shaped device on end of refueling hose of tanker aircraft to receive probe of aircraft being refueled

**droll** (drohl) *adj.* (**-er, -est**) funny, odd, comical —**droll'ness** *n.* —**drol'ly** *adv.*

**drone** (drohn) *n.* male of honey bee; lazy idler; deep humming; bass pipe of bagpipe; its note —*v.* (**droned, dron·ing**) hum; talk in monotonous tone

**drool** *vi.* to slaver, drivel

**droop** *vi.* hang down; wilt, flag —*vt.* let hang down —*n.* drooping condition —**droop'y** *adj.* (**droop·i·er, droop·i·est**)

**drop** *n.* globule of liquid; very small quantity; fall, descent; distance through which thing falls; thing that falls, as gallows platform —*v.* (**dropped, drop·ping**) —*vt.* let fall; let fall in drops; utter casually; set down, unload; discontinue —*vi.* fall; fall in drops; lapse; come or go casually —**drop'let** *n.* —**drop'pings** *n. pl.* dung of birds, rabbits *etc.* —**drop'out** *n.* person who fails to complete course of study or one who rejects conventional society

**dross** (draws) *n.* scum of molten metal; impurity, refuse; anything of little or no value

**drought** (drowt) *n.* long spell of dry weather

**drove**[1] (drohv) *pt. of* DRIVE

**drove**[2] *n.* herd, flock, crowd, *esp.*

in motion —**drov'er** n. driver of cattle

**drown** v. die or be killed by immersion in liquid; get rid of as by submerging in liquid; make sound inaudible by louder sound

**drow·sy** (DROW-zee) adj. (-si·er, -si·est) half-asleep; lulling; dull —**drowse** vi. —**drow'si·ly** adv. —**drow'si·ness** n.

**drub** vt. (drubbed, drub·bing) thrash, beat —**drubbing** n. beating

**drudge** (druj) vi. work at menial or distasteful tasks, slave —n. one who drudges, hack —**drudg'er·y** n. (pl. -er·ies)

**drug** n. medical substance; narcotic; merchandise that is unsalable because of overproduction —vt. (drugged, drug·ging) mix drugs with; administer drug to, esp. one inducing unconsciousness —**drug'store** n. pharmacy where wide variety of goods is available —**drug·gist** n.

**dru·id** (DROO-id) n. (also **D-**) member of ancient order of Celtic priests

**drum** n. percussion instrument of skin stretched over round hollow frame, played by beating with sticks; various things shaped like drum; part of ear — v. (drummed, drum·ming) play drum; tap, thump continuously —**drum'mer** n. one who plays drum; traveling salesman —**drum'head** n. part of drum that is struck —**drumhead court-martial** summary one held at war front —**drum major** leader of military band —**drum'stick** n. stick for beating drum; lower joint of cooked fowl's leg —**drum out** expel from military service etc.

**drunk** (drungk) adj. (-er, -est) overcome by strong drink; fig. under influence of strong emotion —**drunk'ard** (-ərd) n. one given to excessive drinking —**drunk'en** adj. drunk; caused by, showing intoxication —**drunk'en·ness** n.

**dry** (drī) adj. (dri·er, dri·est) without moisture; rainless; not yielding milk, or other liquid; cold, unfriendly; caustically witty; having prohibition of alcoholic drink; uninteresting; needing effort to study; lacking sweetness (as wines) —v. (dried, dry·ing) remove water, moisture; become dry; evaporate —**dri'ly** adv. —**dry'ness** n. —**dry'er** n. person or thing that dries; apparatus for removing moisture —**dry battery** electric battery without liquid —**dry'-clean** v. clean clothes with solvent other than water —**dry'-clean·er** n. —**dry ice** solid carbon dioxide —**dry'point** needle for engraving without acid; engraving so made —**dry rot** fungoid decay in wood —**dry run** practice, rehearsal in simulated conditions

**dry·ad** (DRĪ-əd) n. wood nymph

**du·al** (DOO-əl) adj. twofold; of two, double, forming pair —**du'al·ism** n. recognition of two independent powers or principles, eg good and evil, mind and matter —**du·al'i·ty** n.

**dub** vt. (dubbed, dub·bing) give title to; confer knighthood on; provide film with soundtrack not in original language; smear with grease, dubbin —**dub'bin, dub'bing** n. grease for making leather supple

**du·bi·ous** (DOO-bee-əs) adj. causing doubt, not clear or decided; of suspect character —**du·bi'e·ty** (-BĪ-i·tee) n. (-ties) uncertainty, doubt

**du·cal** (DOO-kəl) adj. of, like a duke

**duch·ess** (DUCH-is) *n.* duke's wife or widow

**duch·y** (DUCH-ee) *n.* (*pl.* duch·ies) territory of duke, dukedom

**duck**[1] (duk) *n.* common swimming bird (drake *masc.*) —*v.* plunge (someone) under water; bob down —**duck'ling** *n.* —duck'billed platypus *see* PLATYPUS

**duck**[2] *n.* strong linen or cotton fabric —*pl.* trousers of it

**duct** (dukt) *n.* channel, tube —**duc·tile** (DUK-tl) *adj.* capable of being drawn into wire; flexible and tough; easily led —**duc·til'i·ty** *n.* —**duct'less** *adj.* (of glands) secreting directly certain substances essential to health

**dud** *n.* futile, worthless person or thing; shell that fails to explode —*adj.* worthless

**dude** (dood) *n.* city man, *esp.* Easterner in the West; *sl.* fellow —dude ranch ranch operating as vacation resort

**dudg·eon** (DUJ-ən) *n.* anger, indignation, resentment

**duds** (dudz) *n. pl. inf.* clothes

**due** (doo) *adj.* owing; proper to be given, inflicted etc.; adequate, fitting; under engagement to arrive, be present; timed for —*adv.* (with points of compass) exactly —*n.* person's right; (*usu. pl.*) charge, fee etc. —**du'ly** *adv.* properly; fitly; rightly; punctually —due to attributable to; caused by

**du·el** (DOO-əl) *n.* arranged fight with deadly weapons, between two persons; keen two-sided contest —*vi.* (-eled, -el·ing) fight in duel —**du'el·ist** *n.*

**du·en·na** (doo-EN-ə) *n.* in Spain or Portugal, elderly governess, guardian, chaperone

**du·et** (doo-ET) *n.* piece of music for two performers

**duff** *n. sl.* buttocks

**duf·fel** (DUF-əl) *n.* coarse woolen cloth; coat of this

**duff·er** (DUF-ər) *n. inf.* stupid inefficient person; (in golf) inept player

**dug**[1] *pt./pp. of* DIG

**dug**[2] *n.* udder, teat of animal

**dug·out** (DUG-owt) *n.* covered excavation to provide shelter for troops etc.; canoe of hollowed-out tree; *Baseball* roofed structure with bench for players when not on the field

**duke** (dook) *n.* in Great Britain, peer of rank next below prince; ruler of duchy (duch'ess *fem.*) —**duke'dom** (-dəm) *n.*

**dukes** (dooks) *n. pl. sl.* fists

**dul·cet** (DUL-sit) *adj.* (of sounds) sweet, melodious

**dul·ci·mer** (DUL-sə-mər) *n.* stringed instrument played with light hammers, ancestor of piano

**dull** *adj.* (-er, -est) stupid; insensible; sluggish; tedious; lacking liveliness or variety; gloomy, overcast —*v.* make or become dull —**dull'ard** (-ərd) *n.*

**duly** *see* DUE

**dumb** (dum) *adj.* (-er, -est) incapable of speech; silent; *inf.* stupid —**dumb'ly** *adv.* —**dumb'ness** *n.* —**dumb'bell** *n.* weight for exercises; dolt —**dumb·found'** *vt.* confound into silence —**dumb show** gestures without speech

**dum'dum** *n.* soft-nosed expanding bullet

**dum·my** (DUM-ee) *n.* (*pl.* -mies) tailor's, dressmaker's model; imitation object; *Cards* hand exposed on table and played by partner —*adj.* sham, bogus —dummy up *inf.* to keep silent

**dump** *vt.* throw down in mass; deposit; unload; send (low-priced goods) for sale abroad —*n.* place where garbage is dumped; *inf.* dirty, unpleasant place; temporary depot of stores or munitions —*pl.* low spirits, dejection —**dump'ling** *n.* small round mass of boiled or steamed dough; dessert of fruit wrapped in dough and baked —**dump truck** truck for hauling and dumping sand, stone *etc.* —**dump'y** *adj.* (**dump·i·er, dump·i·est**) short, stout

**dun**[1] *vt.* (**dunned, dun·ning**) persistently demand payment of debts —*n.* one who duns; urgent request for payment

**dun**[2] *adj.* of dull grayish brown —*n.* this color; dun horse

**dunce** (duns) *n.* slow learner, stupid pupil

**dune** (doon) *n.* sandhill on coast or desert

**dung** *n.* excrement of animals; manure —*vt.* fertilize or spread with manure

**dun·ga·ree** (dung-gɔ-REE) *n.* blue denim —*pl.* work clothes *etc.* of this material

**dun·geon** (DUN-jɔn) *n.* underground cell or vault for prisoners; formerly, tower or keep of castle

**dunk** (dungk) *vt.* dip bread *etc.* in liquid before eating it; submerge —**dunk shot** *Basketball* shot made by jumping high to thrust ball through basket

**dun·nage** (DUN-ij) *n.* padding, loose material for packing cargo

**du·o** (DOO-oh) *n.* (*pl.* **du·os**) pair of performers *etc.*

**du·o·dec·i·mal** (doo-ɔ-DES-ɔ-mɔl) *adj.* computed by twelves; twelfth

**du·o·dec·i·mo** (doo-ɔ-DES-ɔ-moh) *n.* (*pl.* **-mos**) size of book in which each sheet is folded into 12 leaves before cutting; book of this size —*adj.* of this size

**du·o·de·num** (doo-ɔ-DEE-nɔm) *n.*

upper part of small intestine —**du·o·de'nal** *adj.*

**dupe** (doop) *n.* victim of delusion or sharp practice —*vt.* (**duped, dup·ing**) deceive for advantage, impose upon

**du·plex** (DOO-pleks) *adj.* twofold —*n.* apartment with rooms on two floors; two-family house

**du·pli·cate** (DOO-pli-kayt) *vt.* (**-cat·ed, -cat·ing**) make exact copy of; double —*adj.* (-kit) double; exactly the same as something else —*n.* exact copy —**du'pli·ca·tor** *n.* machine for making copies of typewritten matter *etc.*) —**du·plic'i·ty** (-PLIS-i-tee) *n.* (*pl.* **-ties**) deceitfulness, double-dealing, bad faith

**du·ra·ble** (DUUR-ɔ-bɔl) *adj.* lasting, resisting wear —**du·ra·bil'i·ty** *n.*

**du·ra·tion** (duu-RAY-shɔn) *n.* time thing lasts

**du·ress** (duu-RES) *n.* compulsion by use of force or threats

**dur·ing** (DUUR-ing) *prep.* throughout, in the time of, in the course of

**dusk** *n.* darker stage of twilight; partial darkness —**dusk'y** *adj.* (**dusk·i·er, dusk·i·est**) dark; dark-colored

**dust** *n.* fine particles, powder of earth or other matter, lying on surface or blown along by wind; ashes of the dead —*vt.* sprinkle with powder, fertilizer *etc.*; rid of dust —**dust'er** *n.* cloth for removing dust; housecoat —**dust'y** *adj.* (**dust·i·er, dust·i·est**) covered with dust —**dust'bowl** (-bohl) *n.* area in which dust storms have carried away the top soil

**Dutch** (duch) *adj.* pert. to the Netherlands, its inhabitants, its language —**Dutch courage** drunken bravado —**Dutch treat**

one where each person pays own share

**du·ty** (DOO-tee) *n.* (*pl.* -ties) moral or legal obligation; that which is due; tax on goods; military service; one's proper employment —du'te·ous *adj.* —du'ti·a·ble *adj.* liable to customs duty —du'ti·ful *adj.*

**du·vet** (doo-VAY) *n.* quilt filled with down or artificial fiber

**dwarf** (dworf) *n.* (*pl.* dwarfs, dwarves *pr.* dworvz) very undersized person; mythological, small, manlike creature —*adj.* unusually small, stunted —*vt.* make seem small by contrast; make stunted

**dwell** *vi.* (dwelt *or* dwelled, dwell·ing) live, make one's abode (in); fix one's attention, write or speak at length (on) —dwell'er *n.* —dwell'ing *n.* house

**dwin·dle** (DWIN-dl) *vi.* (-dled, -dling) grow less, waste away, decline

**dye** (dī) *vt.* (dyed, dye·ing) impregnate (cloth *etc.*) with coloring matter; color thus —*n.* coloring matter in solution or that can be dissolved for dyeing; tinge, color —dy'er *n.*

**dy·nam·ics** (dī-NAM-iks) *n. pl.* (*with sing. v.*) branch of physics dealing with force as producing or affecting motion; physical forces —dy·nam'ic *adj.* of, relating to motive force, force in operation; energetic and forceful —dy·nam'i·cal·ly *adv.*

**dy·na·mite** (DĪ-nə-mīt) *n.* high explosive mixture —*vt.* (-mit·ed, -mit·ing) blow up with this —*adj. inf.* topnotch

**dy·na·mo** (DĪ-nə-moh) *n.* (*pl.* -mos) machine to convert mechanical into electrical energy, generator of electricity —dy·na-

**mom'e·ter** *n.* instrument to measure energy expended

**dy·nas·ty** (DĪ-nəs-stee) *n.* (*pl.* -ties) line, family, succession of hereditary rulers —dy'nast *n.* ruler —dy·nas'tic *adj.* of dynasty

**dyne** (dīn) *n.* cgs unit of force

**dys·en·ter·y** (DIS-ən-ter-ee) *n.* infection of intestine causing severe diarrhea

**dys·func·tion** (dis-FUNGK-shən) *n.* abnormal, impaired functioning, *esp.* of bodily organ

**dys·lex·ia** (dis-LEK-see-ə) *n.* impaired ability to read, caused by condition of the brain —dys·lex'ic *adj./n.*

**dys·pep·sia** (dis-PEP-see-ə) *n.* indigestion —dys·pep'tic *adj./n.*

**dys·tro·phy** (DIS-trə-fee) *n.* wasting of body tissues, *esp.* muscles

# E

**each** (eech) *adj./pron.* every one taken separately

**ea·ger** (EE-gər) *adj.* having a strong wish (for something); keen, impatient —ea'ger·ness *n.*

**ea·gle** (EE-gəl) *n.* large bird with keen sight that preys on small birds and animals; Golf score of two strokes under par for a hole —ea'glet (EE-glit) *n.* young eagle

**ear**[1] (eer) *n.* organ of hearing, *esp.* external part of it; sense of hearing; sensitiveness to sounds; attention —ear'ache *n.* acute pain in ear —ear'mark *vt.* assign, reserve for definite purpose —ear'phone *n.* receiver for radio *etc.* held to or put in ear —ear'ring *n.* ornament for lobe of the ear —ear'shot *n.* hearing distance

**ear**[2] *n.* spike, head of corn

**earl** (url) *n.* British nobleman ranking next below marquis

**ear·ly** (UR-lee) *adj./adv.* -li·er, -li·est) before expected or usual time; in first part, near or nearer beginning of some portion of time

**earn** (urn) *vt.* obtain by work or merit; gain —**earn'ings** *n. pl.*

**ear·nest**[1] (UR-nist) *adj.* serious, ardent, sincere —**in earnest** serious, determined

**earnest**[2] *n.* money paid over in token to bind bargain; pledge; token, foretaste

**earth** (urth) *n.* (E-) planet or world we live on; ground, dry land; mold, soil, mineral —**earth'en** *adj.* made of clay or earth —**earth'ly** *adj.* possible, feasible —**earth'y** *adj.* (**earth·i·er, earth·i·est**) of earth; uninhibited; vulgar —**earth'en·ware** *n.* (vessels of) baked clay —**earth'quake** *n.* convulsion of Earth's surface

**ease** (eez) *n.* comfort; freedom from constraint, annoyance, awkwardness, pain or trouble; idleness —*v.* (**eased, eas·ing**) reduce burden; give bodily or mental ease to; slacken; (cause to) move carefully or gradually; relieve of pain —**ease'ment** *n.* Law right of way etc., over another's land —**eas'i·ly** *adv.* —**eas'y** *adj.* (**eas·i·er, eas·i·est**) not difficult; free from pain, care, constraint or anxiety; compliant; characterized by low demand; fitting loosely; *inf.* having no preference for any particular course of action —**easy-going** *adj.* not fussy; indolent

**ea·sel** (EE-zəl) *n.* frame to support picture etc.

**east** (eest) *n.* part of horizon where sun rises; (E-) eastern lands, Orient —*adj.* on, in, or near, east; coming from east —*adv.* from, or to, east —**east'er·ly** *adj./adv.* from, or to, east —**east'ern** *adj.* of, dwelling in, east —**east'ern·er** (*also* E-) *n.* —**east'ward** *adj./adv./n.* —**east'ward(s)** *adv.*

**Eas·ter** (EE-stər) *n.* annual festival of the resurrection of Christ

**easy** *see* EASE

**eat** (eet) *v.* (**ate, eat·en, eat·ing**) chew and swallow; consume, destroy; gnaw; wear away

**eaves** (eevz) *n. pl.* overhanging edges of roof —**eaves'drop** *v.* (-**dropped, -drop·ping**) listen secretly —**eaves'drop·per** *n.*

**ebb** *vi.* flow back; decay —*n.* flowing back of tide; decline, decay —**ebb tide**

**eb·on·y** (EB-ə-nee) *n.* (**-on·ies**) hard black wood —*adj.* made of, black as ebony

**e·bul·lient** (i-BUUL-yənt) *adj.* exuberant; boiling —**e·bul'lience** *n.* —**eb·ul·li·tion** (eb-ə-LISH-ən) *n.* boiling; effervescence; outburst

**ec·cen·tric** (ik-SEN-trik) *adj.* odd, unconventional; irregular; not placed, or not having axis placed, centrally; not circular (in orbit) —*n.* odd, unconventional person; mechanical device to change circular into to-and-fro movement —**ec·cen·tric'i·ty** *n.*

**Eccles.** Ecclesiastes

**ec·cle·si·as·tic** (i-klee-zee-AS-tik) *n.* clergyman —*adj.* of, relating to the Christian Church —**ec·cle·si·as'ti·cal** *adj.*

**ech·e·lon** (ESH-ə-lon) *n.* level, grade, of responsibility or command; formation of troops, planes etc. in parallel divisions each slightly to left or right of the one in front

**ech·o** (EK-oh) *n.* (*pl.* **ech·oes**) repetition of sounds by reflection; close imitation —*v.* (**ech·oed, ech·o·ing**) —*vt.* repeat as echo, send back the sound of; imitate closely —vi. resound; be repeated —**echo sounder** —**echo sounding** system of ascertaining depth of water by measuring time required to receive an echo from sea bottom or submerged object

**éclair** (ay-KLAIR) n. finger-shaped, chocolate-frosted cake filled with whipped cream or custard

**éclat** (ay-KLAH) n. splendor, renown, acclamation

**e·clec·tic** (i-KLEK-tik) adj. selecting; borrowing one's philosophy from various sources; catholic in views or taste —n. —**e·clec'ti·cism** n.

**e·clipse** (i-KLIPS) n. blotting out of sun, moon etc. by another heavenly body; obscurity —vt. (-clipsed, -clips·ing) obscure, hide; surpass —**e·clip'tic** adj. of eclipse —n. apparent path of sun

**e·col·o·gy** (i-KOL-ə-jee) n. science of plants and animals in relation to their environment —**ec·o·log'i·cal** adj. —**e·col'o·gist** n. specialist in or advocate of ecological studies

**e·con·o·my** (i-KON-ə-mee) n. (pl. -mies) careful management of resources to avoid unnecessary expenditure or waste; sparing, restrained or efficient use; system of interrelationship of money, industry and employment in a country —**ec·o·nom'ic** adj. of economics; profitable; economical —**ec·o·nom'i·cal** adj. not wasteful of money, time, effort etc.; frugal —**ec·o·nom'ics** n. (with pl. v.) study of economies of nations; (with pl. v.) financial aspects —**e·con'o·mist** n. specialist in economics —**e·con'o·mize** v. (-mized, -miz·ing) limit or reduce expense, waste etc.

**ec·ru** (EK-roo) n./adj. (of) color of unbleached linen

**ec·sta·sy** (EK-stə-see) n. (pl. -sies) exalted state of feeling, mystic trance; frenzy —**ec·stat'ic** (ik-STAT-ik) adj. —**ec·stat'i·cal·ly** adv.

**ec·u·men·i·cal** (ek-yuu-MEN-i-kəl) adj. of the Christian Church throughout the world, esp. with regard to its unity; interdenominational; universal —**ec·u·men'i·cism** n.

**ec·ze·ma** (EK-sə-mə) n. skin disease

**ed·dy** (ED-ee) n. (pl. -dies) small whirl in water, smoke etc. —vi. (-died, -dy·ing) move in whirls

**e·del·weiss** (AY-dəl-vīs) n. white-flowered alpine plant

**e·de·ma** (i-DEE-mə) n. an abnormal excess of fluid in tissues, organs; swelling due to this

**E·den** (EE-dən) n. garden in which Adam and Eve were placed at the Creation; any delightful, happy place or condition

**edge** (ej) n. border, boundary; cutting side of blade; sharpness; advantage; acrimony, bitterness v. (edged, edg·ing) —vt. sharpen, give edge or border to; move gradually —vi. advance sideways or gradually —**edge'ways, -wise** adv. —**edg'ing** n. —**edg'y** adj. (edg·i·er, edg·i·est) irritable, sharp or keen in temper —**on edge** nervous, irritable; excited

**ed·i·ble** (ED-ə-bəl) adj. eatable, fit for eating

**e·dict** (EE-dikt) n. order proclaimed by authority, decree

**ed·i·fice** (ED-ə-fis) n. building, esp. big one

**ed·i·fy** (ED-ə-fī) vt. (-fied, -fy·ing) improve morally, instruct —**ed·i·fi·ca'tion** n. improvement of the mind or morals

**ed'it** vt. prepare book, film, tape

*etc.* for publication or broadcast —**e·di·tion** (i-DISH-ən) *n.* form in which something is published; number of copies of new publication printed at one time —**ed·i·to'ri·al** *adj.* of editor —*n.* article stating opinion of newspaper *etc.*

**ed·u·cate** (EJ-uu-kayt) *vt.* (-cat·ed, -cat·ing) provide schooling for; teach; train mentally and morally; train; improve, develop —**ed·u·ca'tion** *n.* —**ed·u·ca'tion·al** *adj.* —**ed'u·ca·tive** *adj.* —**ed'u·ca·tor** *n.*

**e·duce** (i-DOOS) *vt.* (-duced, -duc·ing) bring out, elicit, develop; infer, deduce

**ee·rie** (EER-ee) *adj.* (-ri·er, -ri·est) weird, uncanny; causing superstitious fear

**ef·face** (i-FAYS) *vt.* (-faced, -fac·ing) wipe or rub out —**ef·face'a·ble** *adj.*

**ef·fect** (i-FEKT) *n.* result, consequence; efficacy; impression; condition of being operative —*pl.* movable property; lighting, sounds *etc.* to accompany film, broadcast *etc.* —*vt.* bring about, accomplish —**ef·fec'tive** *adj.* having power to produce effects; in effect, operative; serviceable; powerful; striking —**ef·fec'tive·ly** *adv.* —**ef·fec'tu·al** (-choo-əl) *adj.* successful in producing desired effect; satisfactory; efficacious —**ef·fec'tu·ate** (-choo-ayt) *vt.* (-at·ed, -at·ing) bring about, effect

**ef·fem·i·nate** (i-FEM-ə-nit) *adj.* womanish, unmanly —**ef·fem'i·na·cy** *n.*

**ef·fer·ent** (EF-ər-ənt) *adj.* conveying outward or away

**ef·fer·vesce** (ef-ər-VES) *vi.* (-vesced, -vesc·ing) give off bubbles; be in high spirits —**ef·fer·ves'cent** *adj.*

**ef·fete** (i-FEET) *adj.* worn out, feeble

**ef·fi·ca·cious** (ef-i-KAY-shəs) *adj.* producing or sure to produce desired effect; effective; powerful; adequate —**ef'fi·ca·cy** (-kə-see) *n.* (-cies) potency; force; efficiency

**ef·fi·cient** (i-FISH-ənt) *adj.* capable, competent, producing effect —**ef·fi'cien·cy** *n. esp.* compact apartment (*pl.* -cies)

**ef·fi·gy** (EF-i-jee) *n.* (*pl.* -gies) image, likeness

**ef·flo·resce** (ef-lə-RES) *vi.* (-resced, -resc·ing) burst into flower —**ef·flo·res'cence** *n.*

**ef·flu·ent** (EF-loo-ənt) *n.* liquid discharged as waste; stream flowing from larger stream, lake *etc.* —*adj.* flowing out —**ef·flu·vi·um** (i-FLOO-vee-əm) *n.* (*pl.* -vi·a) something flowing out invisibly, *esp.* affecting lungs or sense of smell

**ef·fort** (EF-ərt) *n.* exertion, endeavor, attempt or something achieved —**ef'fort·less** *adj.*

**ef·fron·ter·y** (i-FRUN-tə-ree) *n.* (*pl.* -ter·ies) brazen impudence

**ef·ful·gent** (i-FUL-jənt) *adj.* radiant, shining brightly —**ef·ful'gence** *n.*

**ef·fu·sion** (i-FYOO-zhən) *n.* (unrestrained) outpouring —**ef·fuse** (i-FYOOZ) *v.* (-fused, -fus·ing) pour out, shed; radiate —**ef·fu'sive** (-siv) *adj.* gushing, demonstrative

**e.g.** exempli gratia (Lat.) for example

**e·gal·i·tar·i·an** (i-gal-i-TAIR-ee-ən) *adj.* believing that all people should be equal; promoting this ideal —*n.*

**egg[1]** *n.* oval or round object produced by female of bird *etc.*, from which young emerge, *esp.* egg of domestic hen, used as food

—**egg′plant** n. egg-shaped dark purple fruit; plant bearing it

**egg²** vt. —**egg on** encourage, urge; incite

**e·go** (EE-goh) n. (pl. **e·gos**) the self; the conscious thinking subject; one's image of oneself; morale —**e′go·ism** n. systematic selfishness; theory that bases morality on self-interest —**eg′o·ist** n. —**e·go·is′tic** adj. —**e′go·tism** n. selfishness; self-conceit —**e′go·tist** n. —**e·go·tis′tic** adj. —**e·go·cen′tric** adj. self-centered; egoistic; centered in the ego

**e·gre·gious** (i-GREE-jəs) adj. outstandingly bad, blatant; absurdly obvious, esp. of mistake etc.

**e·gress** (EE-gres) n. way out; departure

**e·gret** (EE-grit) n. one of several white herons

**ei·der** (Ī-dər) n. any of several northern sea ducks; eiderdown —**ei′der·down** n. its breast feathers; quilt (stuffed with feathers)

**eight** (ayt) n. cardinal number one above seven; crew of eight-oared shell —adj. —**eight·een′** adj./n. eight more than ten —**eight-eenth′** adj./n. —**eighth** (ayth) adj./n. ordinal number —**eight′i·eth** adj./n. —**eight′y** adj./n. (pl. **eight·ies**) ten times eight —**figure** eight a skating figure; any figure shaped as 8

**ei·ther** (EE-thər) adj./pron. one or the other; one of two; each —adv./conj. bringing in first of alternatives or strengthening an added negation

**e·jac·u·late** (i-JAK-yə-layt) v. (-lat·ed, -lat·ing) eject (semen); exclaim, utter suddenly —**e·jac·u·la′tion** n.

**e·ject** (i-JEKT) vt. throw out; expel, drive out —**e·jec′tion** n.

**eke out** (eek) make (supply) last, esp. by frugal use; supply deficiencies of; make with difficulty (a living etc.)

**e·lab·o·rate** (i-LAB-ər-it) adj. carefully worked out, detailed; complicated —v. (-ayt) (-rat·ed, -rat·ing) —vi. expand (upon) —vt. work out in detail; take pains with

**élan** (ay-LAHN) n. dash; ardor; impetuosity —**élan vi·tal** (vee-TAL) in Bergsonian philosophy, the creative force within an organism that is responsible for growth, change etc.

**e·lapse** (i-LAPS) vi. (-lapsed, -laps·ing) of time, pass

**e·las·tic** (i-LAS-tik) adj. resuming normal shape after distortion, springy; flexible —n. tape, fabric, containing interwoven strands of flexible rubber etc. —**e·las′ti·cized** (-sīzd) adj. —**e·las·tic′i·ty** n.

**e·la·tion** (i-LAY-shən) n. high spirits; pride —**e·late** (i-LAYT) vt. (-lat·ed, -lat·ing) (usu. passive be elated etc.) raise the spirits of; make happy; exhilarate

**el·bow** (EL-boh) n. joint between fore and upper parts of arm (esp. outer part of it); part of sleeve covering this; something resembling this, esp. angular pipe fitting —vt. shove, strike with elbow —**elbow grease** hard work —**el′bow-room** n. sufficient room

**eld·er¹** (EL-dər) adj. older, senior —comp. of OLD —n. person of greater age; old person; official of certain churches —**eld′er·ly** adj. growing old —**eld′est** adj. oldest —sup. of OLD

**el·der²** n. white-flowered tree or shrub

**El Do·ra·do** (el də-RAH-doh) n. fictitious country rich in gold

**e·lect** (i-LEKT) vt. choose by vote; choose —adj. appointed but not yet in office; chosen, select, choice —**e·lec′tion** n. choosing, *esp.* by voting —e·lec·tion·eer' *vi.* work in political campaign —e·lec'tive *adj.* appointed, filled, or chosen by election —e·lec'tor *n.* one who elects —e·lec'tor·al *adj.* —electoral college body of electors chosen by voters to elect President and Vice President —e·lec'tor·ate *n.* body of persons entitled to vote

e·lec·tric·i·ty (i-lek-TRIS-i-tee) *n.* form of energy associated with stationary or moving electrons or other charged particles; electric current or charge; science dealing with electricity —e·lec'tric *adj.* derived from, produced by, producing, transmitting or powered by electricity; excited, emotionally charged —e·lec'tri·cal *adj.* —e·lec·tri'cian *n.* one trained in installation *etc.* of electrical wiring and devices —e·lec·tri·fi·ca'tion *n.* —e·lec'tri·fy *vt.* (-fied, -fy·ing) —electric chair chair in which criminals sentenced to death are electrocuted —electric organ *Mus.* organ in which sound is produced by electric devices instead of wind

electro- (*comb. form*) by, caused by electricity, as in electrotherapy *n.* Such words are not given here where the meaning can easily be inferred from the simple word

e·lec·tro·car·di·o·graph (i-lek-troh-KAHR-dee-ə-graf) *n.* instrument for recording electrical activity of heart —e·lec·tro·car'di·o·gram *n.* tracing produced by this

e·lec·tro·cute (i-LEK-trə-kyoot) *vt.* (-cut·ed, -cut·ing) execute, kill by electricity —e·lec·tro·cu'tion *n.*

e·lec·trode (i-LEK-trohd) *n.* conductor by which electric current

enters or leaves battery, vacuum tube *etc.*

e·lec·tro·en·ceph·a·lo·graph (i-lek-troh-en-SEF-ə-lə-graf) *n.* instrument for recording electrical activity of brain —e·lec·tro·en·ceph'a·lo·gram *n.* tracing produced by this

e·lec·tro·lyte (i-LEK-trə-lit) *n.* solution, molten substance that conducts electricity —e·lec·tro·lyt'ic (-LIT-ik) *adj.*

e·lec·tro·lyze (i-LEK-trə-līz) *vt.* (-lyzed, -lyz·ing) decompose by electricity —e·lec·trol'y·sis (-TROL-ə-sis) *n.*

e·lec·tro·mag·net (i-lek-troh-MAG-nit) *n.* magnet containing coil of wire through which electric current is passed —e·lec·tro·mag·net'ic *adj.*

e·lec·tron (i-LEK-tron) *n.* one of fundamental particles of matter identified with unit of charge of negative electricity and essential component of the atom —e·lec·tron'ic *adj.* of electrons or electronics; using devices, such as semiconductors, transistors or vacuum tubes, dependent on action of electrons -e·lec·tron'ics *n.* (*with sing. v.*) technology concerned with development of electronic devices and circuits; science of behavior and control of electrons —electron volt unit of energy used in nuclear physics

e·lec·tro·plate (i-LEK-trə-playt) *vt.* (-plat·ed, -plat·ing) coat with silver *etc.* by electrolysis —*n.* articles electroplated

el·ee·mos·y·nar·y (el-ə-MOS-ner-ee) *adj.* charitable; dependent on charity

el·e·gant (EL-ə-gənt) *adj.* graceful, tasteful; refined —el'e·gance *n.*

el·e·gy (EL-ə-jee) *n.* (*pl.* -gies) lament for the dead in poem or song —el·e·gi·ac (el-ɔ-Jī-ɔk) adj. suited to elegies; plaintive

el·e·ment (EL-ɔ-mɔnt) n. substance that cannot be separated into other substances by ordinary chemical techniques; component part; small amount, trace; heating wire in electric kettle, stove etc.; proper abode or sphere —pl. powers of atmosphere; rudiments, first principles —el·e·men·tal adj. fundamental; of powers of nature —el·e·men·ta·ry adj. rudimentary, simple

el·e·phant (EL-ɔ-fɔnt) n. huge four-footed, thick-skinned animal with ivory tusks and long trunk —el·e·phan·ti·a·sis n. disease with hardening of skin and enlargement of legs etc. —el·e·phan·tine (-FAN-teen) adj. unwieldy, clumsy, heavily big

el·e·vate (EL-ɔ-vayt) vt. (-vat·ed, -vat·ing) raise, lift up, exalt —el·e·va·tion n. raising; height, esp. above sea level; angle above horizon, of gun; drawing of one side of building etc. —el·e·va·tor n. cage raised and lowered in vertical shaft to transport people etc.

el·ev·en (i-LEV-ɔn) n. number next above 10; team of 11 persons —adj. —el·ev·en·fold adj./adv. —el·ev·enth adj. the ordinal number —eleventh hour latest possible time

elf n. (pl. elves) fairy; woodland sprite —elf·in, elf·ish, elv·ish adj. roguish, mischievous

e·lic·it (i-LIS-it) vt. draw out, evoke; bring to light

e·lide (i-LĪD) vt. (e·lid·ed, e·lid·ing) omit in pronunciation a vowel or syllable —e·li·sion (i-LIZH-ɔn) n.

el·i·gi·ble (EL-ɔ-jɔ-bɔl) adj. fit or qualified to be chosen; suitable, desirable —el·i·gi·bil'i·ty n.

e·lim·i·nate (i-LIM-ɔ-nayt) vt. (-nat·ed, -nat·ing) remove, get rid of, set aside —e·lim·i·na'tion n.

elision see ELIDE

e·lite (i-LEET) n. choice or select body; the pick or best part of society; typewriter type size (12 letters to inch) —adj. —e·lit'ism n. —e·lit'ist n.

e·lix·ir (i-LIK-sɔr) n. preparation sought by alchemists to change base metals into gold, or to prolong life; panacea

elk n. large deer

e·clipse (i-LIPS) n. oval —el·lip'ti·cal adj.

el·lip·sis (i-LIP-sis) n. (pl. -ses pr. -seez) Grammar omission of parts of word or sentence; mark (as ... or ∗∗∗) indicating this

el·o·cu·tion (el-ɔ-KYOO-shɔn) n. art of public speaking, voice management —el·o·cu'tion·ist n. teacher of this

e·lon·gate (i-LAWNG-gayt) vt. (-gat·ed, -gat·ing) lengthen, extend, prolong —e·lon·ga'tion n.

e·lope (i-LOHP) vi. (-loped, -lop·ing) run away from home with lover; do this with intention of marrying —e·lope'ment n.

el·o·quence (EL-ɔ-kwɔns) n. fluent, powerful use of language —el'o·quent adj.

else (els) adv. besides; instead; otherwise —else·where adv. in or to some other place

e·lu·ci·date (i-LOO-si-dayt) vt. (-dat·ed, -dat·ing) throw light upon, explain —e·lu·ci·da'tion n.

e·lude (i-LOOD) vt. (-lud·ed, -lud·ing) escape, slip away from, dodge; baffle —e·lu'sion n. act of eluding; evasion —e·lu'sive adj. difficult to catch hold of, deceptive —e·lu'sive·ness n.

elves, elvish see ELF

**em** n. Printing the square of any size of type

**em-** prefix see EN-

**e·ma·ci·ate** (i-MAY-shee-ayt) v. (-at·ed, -at·ing) make or become abnormally thin —**e·ma·ci·a'tion** n.

**em·a·nate** (EM-ə-nayt) vi. (-nat·ed, -nat·ing) issue, proceed from, originate —**em·a·na'tion** n.

**e·man·ci·pate** (i-MAN-sə-payt) vt. (-pat·ed, -pat·ing) set free —**e·man·ci·pa'tion** n. act of setting free, esp. from social, legal restraint; state of being set free —**e·man'ci·pa·tor** n.

**e·mas·cu·late** (i-MAS-kyə-layt) vt. (-lat·ed, -lat·ing) castrate; enfeeble, weaken —**e·mas·cu·la'tion** n.

**em·balm** (em-BAHM) vt. preserve corpse from decay by use of chemicals, herbs etc. —**em·balm'er** n.

**em·bank·ment** (em-BANGK-mənt) n. artificial mound carrying road, railway, or serving to dam water

**em·bar·go** (em-BAHR-goh) n. (pl. -goes) order stopping movement of ships; suspension of commerce; ban —vt. (-goed, -go·ing) put under embargo

**em·bark** (em-BAHRK) v. put, go, on board ship, aircraft etc.; (with on or upon) commence new project, venture etc. —**em·bar·ka'tion** n.

**em·bar·rass** (em-BAR-əs) vt. perplex, disconcert; abash; confuse; encumber —**em·bar'rass·ment** n.

**em·bas·sy** (EM-bə-see) n. (pl. -sies) office, work or official residence of ambassador; deputation

**em·bed'** vt. (-bed·ded, -bed·ding) fix fast in something solid

**em·bel'lish** vt. adorn, enrich —**em·bel'lish·ment** n.

**em·ber** (EM-bər) n. glowing cinder —pl. red-hot ashes

**em·bez·zle** (em-BEZ-əl) vt. (-zled, -zling) divert fraudulently, misappropriate (money in trust etc.) —**em·bez'zle·ment** n. —**em·bez'zler** n.

**em·bit·ter** (em-BIT-ər) vt. make bitter —**em·bit'ter·ment** n.

**em·bla·zon** (em-BLAY-zən) vt. adorn richly, esp. heraldically

**em·blem** (EM-bləm) n. symbol; badge, device —**em·ble·mat'ic** adj.

**em·bod·y** (em-BOD-ee) vt. (-bod·ied, -bod·y·ing) give body, concrete expression to; represent, include, be expression of —**em·bod'i·ment** n.

**em·bo·lism** (EM-bə-liz-əm) n. Med. obstruction of artery by blood clot or air bubble

**em·boss** (em-BAWS) vt. mold, stamp or carve in relief

**em·brace** (em-BRAYS) vt. (-braced, -brac·ing) clasp in arms, hug; seize, avail oneself of, accept; comprise —n.

**em·bra·sure** (em-BRAY-zhər) n. opening in wall for cannon; beveling of wall at sides of window

**em·bro·ca·tion** (em-brə-KAY-shən) n. lotion for rubbing limbs etc. to relieve pain —**em'bro·cate** vt. (-cat·ed, -cat·ing) apply lotion etc.

**em·broi·der** (em-BROI-dər) vt. ornament with needlework; embellish, exaggerate (story) —**em·broi'der·y** n.

**em·broil'** vt. bring into confusion; involve in hostility —**em·broil'ment** n.

**em·bry·o** (EM-bree-oh) n. (pl. -os) unborn or undeveloped offspring, germ; undeveloped thing —**em·bry·ol'o·gist** n. —**em·bry·ol'o·gy** n. —**em·bry·on'ic** adj.

**e·mend** (i-MEND) vt. remove errors from, correct —e·men·da'·tion n.

em·er·ald (EM-ər-əld) n. bright green precious stone —adj. of the color of emerald

e·merge (i-MURJ) vi. (-merged, -merg·ing) come up, out; rise to notice; come into view; come out on inquiry —e·mer'gence n. —e·mer'gent adj.

e·mer·gen·cy (i-MUR-jən-see) n. (pl. -cies) sudden unforeseen thing or event needing prompt action; difficult situation; exigency, crisis

e·mer·i·tus (i-MER-i-təs) adj. retired, honorably discharged but retaining one's title (eg professor) on honorary basis

em·er·y (EM-ər-ee) n. hard mineral used for polishing —emery board cardboard coated with powdered emery

e·met·ic (i-MET-ik) n./adj. (medicine or agent) causing vomiting

em·i·grate (EM-i-grayt) vt. (-grat·ed, -grat·ing) go and settle in another country —em'i·grant (-grənt) n. —em·i·gra'tion n.

é·mi·gré (EM-i-gray) n. (pl. -grés) emigrant, esp. one forced to leave native land for political reasons

em·i·nent (EM-ə-nənt) adj. distinguished, notable —em'i·nence n. distinction; height; rank; fame; rising ground; (E-) title of cardinal —em'i·nent·ly adv. —é·mi·nence grise (ay-mee-nahns GREEZ) Fr. person wielding unofficial power, oft. surreptitiously

em·is·sar·y (EM-ə-ser-ee) n. (pl. -sar·ies) agent, representative (esp. of government) sent on mission

e·mit (i-MIT) vt. (-mit·ted, -mit·ting) give out, put forth —e·mis'sion n. —e·mit'ter n.

e·mol·lient (i-MOL-yənt) adj. softening, soothing —n. ointment or other softening application

e·mol·u·ment (i-MOL-yə-mənt) n. salary, pay, profit from work

e·mo·tion (i-MOH-shən) n. mental agitation, excited state of feeling, as joy, fear etc. —e·mo'tion·al adj. given to emotion; appealing to the emotions —e·mo'tive adj. tending to arouse emotion

em·pa·thy (EM-pə-thee) n. power of understanding, imaginatively entering into, another's feelings

em·per·or (EM-pər-ər, -prər) n. ruler of an empire —em'press (-pris) fem.

em·pha·sis (EM-fə-sis) n. (pl. -ses pr. -seez) importance attached; stress on words; vigor of speech, expression —em·pha·size vt. (-sized, -siz·ing) —em·phat'ic (-FAT-ik) adj. forceful, decided; stressed

em·pire (EM-pīr) n. large territory or peoples under supreme ruler, supreme control

em·pir·i·cal (em-PIR-i-kəl) adj. relying on experiment or experience, not on theory —em·pir'i·cal·ly adv. —em·pir'i·cist (-ə-sist) n. one who relies solely on experience and observation —em·pir'i·cism n.

em·place·ment (em-PLAYS-mənt) n. putting in position; gun platform

em·ploy (em-PLOI) vt. provide work for (a person) in return for money, hire; keep busy; use —em·ploy·ee' n. —em·ploy'er n. —em·ploy'ment n. an employing, being employed; work, trade; occupation

em·po·ri·um (em-POHR-ee-əm) n. (pl. -ri·ums) large store, esp. one carrying general merchandise; center of commerce

em·pow·er (em-POW-ər) vt. enable, authorize —**em·pow·er·ment** n.

**empress** see EMPEROR

**emp·ty** (EM-tee) adj. (-ti·er, -ti·est) containing nothing; unoccupied; senseless; vain, foolish —v. (-tied, -ty·ing) make, become devoid of content; discharge (contents) into —**emp'·ties** n. pl. empty boxes, bottles etc. —**emp'ti·ness** n.

**e·mu** (EE-myoo) n. large Aust. flightless bird like ostrich

**em·u·late** (EM-yə·layt) vt. (-lat·ed, -lat·ing) strive to equal or excel; imitate —**em·u·la'tion** n. rivalry; competition —**em'u·la·tive** adj. —**em'u·la·tor** n.

**e·mul·sion** (i-MUL-shən) n. light-sensitive coating of film; milky liquid with oily or resinous particles in suspension; paint etc. in this form —**e·mul'si·fi·er** n. —**e·mul'si·fy** vt. (-fied, -fy·ing)

**en** n. Printing unit of measurement, half an em

**en-** (also **em-** before labials) (prefix) put in, into, on, as **enrage** vt. Such words are not given here where the meaning can easily be inferred from the simple word

**en·a·ble** (en-AY-bəl) vt. (-bled, -bling) make able, authorize, empower, supply with means (to do something)

**en·act** (en-AKT) vi. make law; act part —**en·act'ment** n.

**e·nam·el** (i-NAM-əl) n. glasslike coating applied to metal etc. to preserve surface; coating of teeth; any hard outer coating —vt. (-eled, -el·ing)

**e·nam·or** (i-NAM-ər) vt. inspire with love; charm; bewitch

**en·camp** (en-KAMP) v. set up (in) camp —**en·camp'ment** n. camp

**en·cap·su·late** (en-KAP-sə-layt) vt. (-lat·ed, -lat·ing) enclose in capsule; put in concise or

abridged form —**en·cap·su·la'tion** n.

**en·ceph·a·lo·gram** (en-SEF-ə-lə-gram) n. X-ray photograph of brain

**en·chant'** vt. bewitch, delight —**en·chant'er** n. (-**chan·tress** fem.) —**en·chant'ment** n.

**en·chi·la·da** (en-chə-LAH-də) n. Mexican rolled tortilla filled with sauce of meat etc.

**en·cir·cle** (en-SUR-kəl) vt. (-cled, -cling) surround; enfold; go around so as to surround

**en·clave** (EN-klayv) n. portion of territory entirely surrounded by foreign land; distinct area or group isolated within larger one

**en·close** (en-KLOHZ) vt. (-closed, -clos·ing) shut in; surround; envelop; place in with something else (in letter etc.) —**en·clo'sure** (-zhər) n.

**en·co·mi·um** (en-KOH-mee-əm) n. (-mi·ums) formal praise; eulogy —**en·co'mi·ast** n. one who composes encomiums

**en·com·pass** (en-KUM-pəs) vt. surround, encircle, contain

**en·core** (ONG-kor) interj. again, once more —n. call for repetition of song etc.; the repetition

**en·coun·ter** (en-KOWN-tər) vt. meet unexpectedly; meet in conflict; be faced with (difficulty etc.) —n.

**en·cour·age** (en-KUR-ij) vt. (-aged, -ag·ing) hearten, animate, inspire with hope; embolden —**en·cour'age·ment** n.

**en·croach** (en-KROHCH) vi. intrude (on) as usurper; trespass —**en·croach'ment** n.

**en·crust** (en-KRUST) v. incrust —**en·crus·ta'tion** n.

**en·cum·ber** (en-KUM-bər) vt. hamper; burden —**en·cum'brance** n. impediment, burden

**en·cyc·li·cal** (en-SIK-li-kəl) adj.

sent to many persons or places —*n.* circular letter, *esp.* papal letter to all Catholic bishops

**en·cy·clo·pe·di·a** (en-sī-klə-PEE-dee-ə) *n.* book, set of books of information on all subjects, or on every branch of subject, usu. arranged alphabetically —**en·cy·clo·pe′dic** *adj.*

**end** *n.* limit; extremity; conclusion, finishing; fragment; latter part; death; event, issue; purpose, aim; Football one of two linemen stationed farthest from the center —*v.* put an end to; come to an end, finish —**end′ing** *n.* —**end′less** *adj.* —**end′pa·pers** *n. pl.* blank pages at beginning and end of book

**en·dear** (en-DEER) *vt* to make dear or beloved —**en·dear′ing** *adj.* —**en·dear′ment** *n.* loving word; tender affection

**en·deav·or** (en-DEV-ər) *vi.* try, strive after —*n.* attempt, effort

**en·dem·ic** (en-DEM-ik) *adj.* found only among a particular people or in a particular place —*n.* endemic disease

**en·dive** (EN-dīv) *n.* curly-leaved chicory used as salad; developing crown of chicory blanched for use as salad, Belgian endive

**endo-** (*comb. form*) within, as in *endocrine etc.* Such words are not given here where the meaning can easily be inferred from the simple word

**en·do·car·di·um** (en-doh-KAHR-dee-əm) *n.* lining membrane of the heart —**en·do·car·di′tis** (-DĪ-tis) *n.* inflammation of this

**en·do·crine** (EN-ə-krin) *adj.* of those glands (thyroid, pituitary *etc.*) that secrete hormones directly into bloodstream —**en·do·cri·nol′o·gy** *n.* science dealing with endocrine glands

**en·dorse** (en-DORS) *vt.* (-dorsed,

-dors·ing) sanction; confirm; write (*esp.* sign name) on back of —**en·dorse′ment** *n.*

**en·dow′** *vt.* provide permanent income for; furnish (with) —**en·dow′ment** *n.*

**en·dure** (en-DUUR) *v.* (-dured, -dur·ing) undergo; tolerate; bear; last —**en·dur′a·ble** *adj.* —**en·dur′ance** *n.* act or power of enduring

**en·e·ma** (EN-ə-mə) *n.* medicine, liquid injected into rectum

**en·e·my** (EN-ə-mee) *n.* (*pl.* -mies) *n.* hostile person; opponent; armed foe; hostile force

**en·er·gy** (EN-ər-jee) *n.* (*pl.* -gies) vigor, force, activity; source(s) of power, as oil, coal *etc.*; capacity of machine, battery *etc.* for work or output of power —**en·er·get′ic** *adj.* —**en′er·gize** (-gized, -giz·ing) *vt.* give vigor to

**en·er·vate** (EN-ər-vayt) *vt.* (-vat·ed, -vat·ing) weaken, deprive of vigor —**en·er·va′tion** *n.* lassitude, weakness

**en·fee·ble** (en-FEE-bəl) *vt.* (-bled, -bling) weaken, debilitate

**en·fi·lade** (EN-fi-layd) *n.* fire from artillery, sweeping line from end to end

**en·force** (en-FORS) *vt.* compel obedience to; impose (action) upon; drive home —**en·force′a·ble** *adj.*

**en·fran·chise** (en-FRAN-chīz) *vt.* (-chised, -chis·ing) give right of voting to; give legislative representation to; set free —**en·fran′chise·ment** (-chiz-mənt) *n.*

**en·gage** (en-GAYJ) *v.* (-gaged, -gag·ing) —*vt.* employ; reserve, hire; bind by contract or promise; order; pledge oneself; betroth; undertake; attract; occupy; bring into conflict; interlock —*vi.* employ oneself (in); promise; begin to fight —**en·gaged′** *adj.* betrothed; in use; occupied, busy

—en·gage'ment *n.* —engaging *adj.* charming

en·gen·der (en-JEN-dər) *vt.* give rise to; beget; rouse

en·gine (EN-jin) *n.* any machine to convert energy into mechanical work, as steam or gasoline engine; railroad locomotive; fire engine —en·gi·neer' *n.* one who is in charge of engines, machinery *etc.* or construction work (*eg* roads, bridges); one who originates, organizes something; one trained and skilled in engineering —*vt.* construct as engineer; contrive —en·gi·neer'ing *n.*

Eng·lish (ING-glish) *n.* the language of the US, Britain, most parts of the British Commonwealth and certain other countries; the people of England —*adj.* relating to England

engrain *vt. see* INGRAIN

en·grave (en-GRAYV) *vt.* (-graved, -grav·ing) cut in lines on metal for printing; carve, incise; impress deeply —en·grav'er *n.* —en·grav'ing *n.* copy of picture printed from engraved plate

en·gross (en-GROHS) *vt.* absorb (attention); occupy wholly; write out in large letters or in legal form; monopolize

en·gulf' *vt.* swallow up

en·hance (en-HANS) *vt.* (-hanced, -hanc·ing) heighten, intensify, increase value or attractiveness —en·hance'ment *n.*

e·nig·ma (ə-NIG-mə) *n.* (*pl.* -mas) *n.* puzzling thing or person; riddle —en·ig·mat'ic *adj.*

en·join *vt.* command; impose, prescribe

en·joy (en-JOI) *vt.* delight in; take pleasure in; have use or benefit of —*v. refl.* be happy —en·joy'·a·ble *adj.*

en·large (en-LAHRJ) *v.* (-larged, -larg·ing) —*vt.* make bigger; reproduce on larger scale, as photograph —*vi.* grow bigger; talk, write about, in greater detail —en·large'a·ble *adj.* —en·large'ment *n.* —en·larg'er *n.* optical instrument for enlarging photographs

en·light·en (en-LI-tən) *vt.* give information to; instruct, inform, shed light on —en·light'en·ment *n.*

en·list' *v.* engage as soldier or helper —en·list'ment *n.*

en·liv·en (en-LI-vən) *vt.* brighten, make more lively, animate

en masse (ahn MAS) *adv.* in a group, body; all together

en·mesh' *vt.* entangle

en·mi·ty (EN-mi-tee) *n.* (*pl.* -ties) ill will, hostility

en·no·ble (en-NOH-bəl) *vt.* (-bled, -bling) make noble, elevate —en·no'ble·ment *n.*

en·nui (ahn-WEE) *n.* boredom

e·nor·mous (i-NOR-məs) *adj.* very big, vast —e·nor'mi·ty *n.* a gross offense; great wickedness; *inf.* great size

e·nough (i-NUF) *adj.* as much or as many as need be; sufficient —*n.* sufficient quantity —*adv.* (just) sufficiently

enquire *see* INQUIRE

en·rap·ture (en-RAP-chər) *vt.* (-tured, -tur·ing) delight excessively; charm

en·rich' *vt.* make rich; add to —en·rich'ment *n.*

en·roll (en-ROHL) *vt.* write name of on roll or list; engage, enlist, take in as member; enter, record —*vi.* become member —en·roll'ment *n.*

en route (ahn ROOT) *Fr.* on the way

en·sconce (en-SKONS) *vt.* (-sconced, -sconc·ing) place snugly; establish in safety

en·sem·ble (ahn-SAHM-bəl) *n.*

whole; all parts taken together; woman's complete outfit; company of actors, dancers etc.; *Mus.* group of soloists performing together; *Mus.* concerted passage; general effect

**en·shrine** (en-SHRĪN) *vt.* (-shrined, -shrin·ing) set in shrine, preserve with great care and sacred affection

**en·sign** (EN-sin) *n.* naval or military flag; badge; *Navy, Coast Guard* lowest commissioned officer

**ensilage** *see* SILAGE

**en·slave** (en-SLAYV) *vt.* (-slaved, -slav·ing) make into slave —**en·slave'ment** *n.* bondage

**en·snare** (en-SNAIR) *vt.* (-snared, -snar·ing) capture in snare or trap; trick into false position; entangle

**en·sue** (en-SOO) *vi.* (-sued, -su·ing) follow, happen after

**en·sure** (en-SHUUR) *vt.* (-sured, -sur·ing) make safe or sure; make certain to happen; secure

**en·tail** (en-TAYL) *vt.* involve as result, necessitate; *Law* restrict ownership of property to designated line of heirs —**en·tail'ment** *n.*

**en·tan·gle** (en-TANG-gəl) *vt.* (-gled, -gling) ensnare; perplex —**en·tan'gle·ment** *n.*

**en·tente** (ahn-TAHNT) *n.* friendly understanding between nations

**en·ter** (EN-tər) *vt.* go, come into; penetrate; join; write in, register —*vi.* go, come in, join, begin —**en'trance** (-trəns) *n.* going, coming in; door, passage to enter; right to enter; fee paid for this —**en'trant** *n.* one who enters, *esp.* contest —**en'try** *n.* (*pl.* -tries) entrance; entering; item entered, *eg* in account, list

**en·ter·ic** (en-TER-ik) *adj.* of or relating to the intestines —**en·ter·i'tis** *n.* inflammation of intestines

**en·ter·prise** (EN-tər-prīz) *n.* bold or difficult undertaking; bold spirit; force of character in launching out; business, company —**en'ter·pris·ing** *adj.*

**en·ter·tain** (en-tər-TAYN) *vt.* amuse, divert; receive as guest; maintain; consider favorable, take into consideration —**en·ter·tain'er** *n.*

**en·thrall** (en-THRAWL) *vt.* captivate, thrill, hold spellbound

**en·thu·si·asm** (en-THOO-zee-az-əm) *n.* ardent eagerness, zeal —**en·thuse'** *v.* (cause to) show enthusiasm —**en·thu'si·ast** *n.* ardent supporter of —**en·thu·si·as'tic** *adj.*

**en·tice** (en-TĪS) *vt.* (-ticed, -tic·ing) allure, attract, inveigle, tempt —**en·tic'ing** *adj.* alluring

**en·tire** (en-TĪR) *adj.* whole, complete, unbroken —**en·tire'ly** *adv.* —**en·tire'ty** *n.* (*pl.* -ties)

**en·ti·tle** (en-TĪ-təl) *vi.* (-tled, -tling) lay claim to; qualify; give title to

**en·ti·ty** (EN-ti-tee) *n.* (*pl.* -ties) thing's being or existence; reality; thing having real existence

**en·to·mol·o·gy** (en-tə-MOL-ə-jee) *n.* study of insects —**en·to·mol'o·gist** *n.*

**en·tou·rage** (ahn-tuu-RAHZH) *n.* associates, retinue; surroundings

**en·trails** (EN-traylz) *n. pl.* bowels, intestines; inner parts

**en·trance**[1] *n. see* ENTER

**en·trance**[2] (en-TRANS) *vt.* (-tranced, -tranc·ing) delight; throw into a trance

**en·treat** (en-TREET) *vt.* ask earnestly; beg, implore —**en·treat'y** *n.* (*pl.* -treat·ies) earnest request

**en·trée** (AHN-tray) *n.* main course of meal; right of access, admission

**en·trench′** vt. establish in fortified position with trenches; establish firmly

**en·tre·pre·neur** (ahn-trə-prə-NUR) n. person who attempts to profit by risk and initiative

**en·tro·py** (EN-trə-pee) n. unavailability of the heat energy of a system for mechanical work; measurement of this

**en·trust′** vt. commit, charge with; put into care or protection of

**en·twine** (en-TWIN) vt. (-twined, -twin·ing) interweave; wreathe with; embrace

**e·nu·mer·ate** (i-NOO-mə-rayt) vt. (-at·ed, -at·ing) mention one by one; count —**e·nu·mer·a′tion** n. —**e·nu′mer·a·tor** n.

**e·nun·ci·ate** (i-NUN-see-ayt) vt. (-at·ed, -at·ing) state clearly; proclaim; pronounce —**e·nun·ci·a′tion** n.

**en·vel·op** (en-VEL-əp) vt. wrap up, enclose, surround; encircle —**en·vel′op·ment** n.

**en·vel·ope** (EN-və-lohp) n. folded, gummed cover of letter; covering, wrapper

**en·ven·om** (en-VEN-əm) vt. put poison, venom in; embitter

**en·vi·ron** (en-VI-rən) vt. surround —**en·vi′ron·ment** n. surroundings; conditions of life or growth —**en·vi·ron·men′tal** adj. —**en·vi·ron·men′tal·ist** n. ecologist —**en·vi′rons** n. pl. districts around (town etc.), outskirts

**en·vis·age** (en-VIZ-ij) vt. (-aged, -ag·ing) conceive of as possibility; visualize

**en·voy** (EN-voi) n. messenger, representative; diplomatic agent of rank below ambassador

**en·vy** (EN-vee) n. pl. (-vies) bitter contemplation of another's good fortune; object of this feeling —vt. (-vied, -vy·ing) grudge another's good fortune, success or qualities; feel envy of —**en′vi·a·ble** adj. arousing envy —**en′vi·ous** adj. full of envy

**en·zyme** (EN-zim) n. any of group of complex proteins produced by living cells and acting as catalysts in biochemical reactions

**e·on** (EE-ən) n. age, very long period of time

**ep-, eph-, epi-** (prefix) upon, during, as in ephemeral, epitaph, epoch etc. Such words are not given here where the meaning can easily be inferred from the simple word

**ep·au·lette** (EP-ə-let) n. shoulder ornament on uniform

**Eph.** Ephesians

**e·phem·er·al** (i-FEM-ər-əl) adj. short-lived, transient —**e·phem′er·on** n. (pl. -er·ons, -er·a pr. -ər-ə) ephemeral thing Also **e·phem′er·a** (pl. -er·as, -er·ae pr. -ər-ee)

**ep·ic** (EP-ik) n. long poem or story telling of achievements of hero or heroes; film etc. about heroic deeds —adj. of, like, an epic; impressive, grand

**ep·i·cene** (EP-i-seen) adj. common to both sexes; effeminate; weak —n. epicene person or thing

**ep·i·cen·ter** (EP-i-sen-tər) n. focus of earthquake

**ep·i·cure** (EP-i-kyuur) n. one delighting in eating and drinking —**ep·i·cu·re′an** adj. of Epicurus, who taught that pleasure, in the shape of practice of virtue, was highest good; given to refined sensuous enjoyment —n. such person or philosopher —**ep·i·cu·re′an·ism** n.

**ep·i·dem·ic** (ep·i-DEM-ik) adj. (esp. of disease) prevalent and spreading rapidly; widespread —n.

**ep·i·der·mis** (ep-i-DUR-mis) *n.* outer skin

**ep·i·du·ral** (ep-i-DUUR-əl) *n./adj.* (of) spinal anesthetic used esp. for relief of pain during childbirth

**ep·i·glot'tis** *n.* (*pl.* **-tis·es**) cartilage that covers opening of larynx in swallowing **—ep·i·glot'tal** (-GLOT-əl) *adj.*

**ep·i·gone** (EP-i-gohn) *n.* imitative follower

**ep'i·gram** *n.* concise, witty poem or saying **—ep·i·gram·mat'ic** (-grə-MAT-ik) *adj.* **—ep·i·gram'ma·tist** (-GRAM-ə-tist) *n.*

**ep·i·graph** (EP-i-graf) *n.* inscription

**ep·i·lep·sy** (EP-ə-lep-see) *n.* disorder of nervous system causing convulsions **—ep·i·lep'tic** *n.* sufferer from this **—***adj.* of, subject to, this

**ep·i·logue** (EP-ə-lawg) *n.* short speech or poem at end, *esp.* of play

**E·piph·a·ny** (i-PIF-ə-nee) *n.* (*pl.* **-nies**) festival of the announcement of Christ to the Magi, celebrated January 6; (e-) sudden intuitive perception or insight

**e·pis·co·pal** (i-PIS-kə-pəl) *adj.* of bishop; ruled by bishops **—e·pis'co·pa·cy** (-pə-see) *n.* government by body of bishops **—E·pis·co·pa'li·an** (-PAYL-yən) *adj./n.* (member, adherent) of Episcopalian church **—e·pis'co·pate** (-kə-pit) *n.* bishop's office, see, or duration of office; body of bishops

**ep·i·sode** (EP-ə-sohd) *n.* incident; section of (serialized) book, TV program *etc.* **—ep·i·sod'ic** (-SOD-ik) *adj.*

**e·pis·te·mol·o·gy** (i-pis-tə-MOL-ə-jee) *n.* study of source, nature and limitations of knowledge **—e·pis·te·mo·log'i·cal** *adj.*

**e·pis·tle** (i-PIS-əl) *n.* letter, *esp.* of apostle; poem in letter form **—e·pis'to·lar·y** (-tə-ler-ee) *adj.*

**ep·i·taph** (EP-i-taf) *n.* memorial inscription on tomb

**ep·i·thet** (EP-ə-thet) *n.* additional, descriptive word or name

**e·pit·o·me** (i-PIT-ə-mee) *n.* embodiment, typical example; summary **—e·pit'o·mize** (-ə-miz) *vt.* (-mized, -miz·ing) typify

**ep·och** (EP-ək) *n.* beginning of period; period, era, *esp.* one of notable events **—ep'och·al** (-kəl) *adj.*

**e·qua·ble** (EK-wə-bəl) *adj.* even-tempered, placid; uniform, not easily disturbed **—e·qua·bly** *adv.* **—e·qua·bil'i·ty** *n.*

**e·qual** (EE-kwəl) *adj.* the same in number, size, merit *etc.*; identical; fit or qualified; evenly balanced **—***n.* one equal to another **—***vt.* be equal to **—e·qual·i·ty** (i-KWOL-i-tee) *n.* (*pl.* **-ties**) state of being equal; uniformity **—e'qual·ize** *v.* (-ized, -iz·ing) make, become, equal **—e·qual·ly** *adv.* **—equal opportunity** nondiscrimination as to sex, race *etc.* in employment, pay *etc.*

**e·qua·nim·i·ty** (ee-kwə-NIM-i-tee) *n.* calmness, composure, steadiness

**e·quate** (i-KWAYT) *vt.* (-quat·ed, -quat·ing) make equal; bring to a common standard **—e·qua'tion** (-zhən) *n.* equating of two mathematical expressions; balancing

**e·qua·tor** (i-KWAY-tər) *n.* imaginary circle around Earth equidistant from the poles **—e·qua·to·ri·al** (ee-kwə-TOR-ee-əl) *adj.*

**e·ques·tri·an** (i-KWES-tree-ən) *adj.* of, skilled in, horseback riding; mounted on horse **—***n.* rider

**equi-** (*comb. form*) equal, at equal, as in **equidistant** *adj.* Such words are not given here where

the meaning can easily be inferred from the simple word

**e·qui·an·gu·lar** (ee-kwee-ANG-
gyə-lər) *adj.* having equal angles

**e·qui·lat·er·al** (ee-kwə-LAT-ər-əl)
*adj.* having equal sides

**e·qui·lib·ri·um** (ee-kwə-LIB-ree-
əm) *n.* state of steadiness, equi-
poise or stability

**e·quine** (EE-kwin) *adj.* of, like a
horse

**e·qui·nox** (EE-kwə-noks) *n.* time
when sun crosses equator and
day and night are equal; either
point at which sun crosses equator

**e·quip** (i-KWIP) *vt.* (-quipped,
-quip·ping) supply, fit out, array
—**e·quip′ment** *n.*

**e·qui·poise** (EK-wə-poiz) *n.* perfect balance; counterpoise; equa-
nimity

**eq·ui·ty** (EK-wə-tee) *n.* (*pl.* -ties)
fairness; use of principles of justice to supplement law; system of
law so made —**eq′ui·ta·ble** *adj.*
fair, reasonable, just

**e·quiv·a·lent** (i-KWIV-ə-lənt) *adj.*
equal in value; having the same
meaning or result; tantamount;
corresponding —**e·quiv′a·lence**
*n.* —**e·quiv′a·len·cy** *n.*

**e·quiv·o·cal** (i-KWIV-ə-kəl) *adj.* of
double or doubtful meaning;
questionable; liable to suspicion
—**e·quiv′o·cate** *vi.* (-cat·ed,
-cat·ing) use equivocal words to
mislead —**e·quiv·o·ca′tion** *n.*

**Er** *Chem.* erbium

**e·ra** (EER-ə) *n.* system of time in
which years are numbered from
particular event; time of the
event; memorable date, period

**e·rad·i·cate** (i-RAD-i-kayt) *vt.*
(-cat·ed, -cat·ing) wipe out, ex-
terminate; root out —**e·rad′i·
ca·ble** *adj.* —**e·rad·i·ca′tion** *n.*

**e·rase** (i-RAYS) *vt.* (-rased,
-ras·ing) rub out; remove, *eg* re-

cording from magnetic tape
—**e·ra′ser** *n.* —**e·ra′sure**
(-shər) *n.*

**ere** (air) *prep./conj. Poet.* before;
sooner than

**e·rect** (i-REKT) *adj.* upright —*vt.*
set up; build —**e·rec′tile** (-tl) *adj.*
—**e·rec′tion** *n. esp.* an erect penis

**erg** (urg) *n.* cgs unit of work or
energy

**er·go·nom·ics** (ur-gə-NOM-iks) *n.*
(*with sing. v.*) study of relationship between workers and their
environment

**er·got** (UR-gət) *n.* disease of
grain; diseased seed used as drug
—**er′got·ism** *n.* disease caused by
eating ergot-infested grain

**er·mine** (UR-min) *n.* weasel in
northern regions, *esp.* in winter;
its white winter fur

**e·rode** (i-ROHD) *vt.* (-rod·ed,
-rod·ing) wear away; eat into
—**e·ro′sion** (-zhən) *n.*

**e·rog·e·nous** (i-ROJ-ə-nəs) *adj.*
sensitive to sexual stimulation

**e·rot·ic** (i-ROT-ik) *adj.* relating to,
or treating of, sexual pleasure
—**e·rot′i·ca** (-i-kə) *n. used with
sing. or pl. v.* sexual literature or
art —**e·rot′i·cism** (-ə-sizm) *n.*

**err** (er) *vi.* make mistakes; be
wrong; sin —**er·rat·ic** (i-RAT-ik)
*adj.* irregular in movement, conduct *etc.* —**er·rat′i·cal·ly** *adv.*
—**er·ra·tum** (i-RAH-təm) *n.* (*pl.*
-ta *pr.* -tə) printing mistake noted
for correction —**er·ro·ne·ous** (i-
ROH-nee-əs) *adj.* mistaken, wrong
—**er′ror** *n.* mistake; wrong opinion; sin

**er·rand** (ER-ənd) *n.* short journey
for simple business; the business,
mission of messenger; purpose

**er·rant** (ER-ənt) *adj.* wandering
in search of adventure; erring
—**er′ran·cy** *n.* (*pl.* -cies) erring
state or conduct —**er′rant·ry** *n.*

(*pl.* -ries) state or conduct of knight errant

**erst·while** (URST-hwīl) *adj.* of times past, former

**er·u·dite** (ER-ya-dīt) *adj.* learned —**er·u·di'tion** (-DISH-ən) *n.* learning

**e·rupt** (i-RUPT) *vi.* burst out —**e·rup'tion** *n.* bursting out, *esp.* volcanic outbreak; rash on the skin

**er·y·sip·e·las** (er-ə-SIP-ə-ləs) *n.* acute skin infection

**Es** *Chem.* einsteinium

**es·ca·late** (ES-kə-layt) *v.* (-lat·ed, -lat·ing) increase, be increased, in extent, intensity *etc.*

**es·ca·la·tor** (ES-kə-lay-tər) *n.* moving staircase

**es·cape** (i-SKAYP) *v.* (-caped, -cap·ing) —*vi.* get free; get off safely; go unpunished; find way out —*vt.* elude; be forgotten by —*n.* escaping —**es'ca·pade** *n.* wild (mischievous) adventure —**es·cap'ism** (-KAYP-izm) *n.* taking refuge in fantasy to avoid facing disagreeable facts

**es·carp·ment** (i-SKAHRP-mənt) *n.* steep hillside

**es·cha·tol·o·gy** (es-kə-TOL-ə-jee) *n.* study of death, judgment and last things —**es·cha·to·log'i·cal** *adj.*

**es·chew** (es-CHOO) *vt.* avoid, abstain from, shun

**es·cort** (ES-kort) *n.* armed guard for traveler *etc.*; person or persons accompanying another —**es·cort'** *vt.*

**es·cri·toire** (es-kri-TWAHR) *n.* type of writing desk

**es·cut·cheon** (i-SKUCH-ən) *n.* shield with coat of arms; ornamental plate around keyhole *etc.*

**Es·ki·mo** (ES-kə-moh) *n.* (*pl.* -mos) one of aboriginal people inhabiting N Amer., Greenland *etc.*; their language

**e·soph·a·gus** (i-SOF-ə-gəs) *n.* (*pl.* -gi *pr.* -jī) canal from mouth to stomach; gullet —**e·soph·a·ge'al** (-JEE-əl) *adj.*

**es·o·ter·ic** (es-ə-TER-ik) *adj.* abstruse, obscure; secret; restricted to initiates

**ESP** extrasensory perception

**es·pal·ier** (i-SPAL-yər) *n.* shrub, (fruit) tree trained to grow flat, as against wall *etc.*; trellis for this

**es·pe·cial** (i-SPESH-əl) *adj.* preeminent, more than ordinary; particular —**es·pe'cial·ly** *adv.*

**Es·pe·ran·to** (es-pə-RAHN-toh) *n.* artificial language designed for universal use

**es·pi·o·nage** (ES-pee-ə-nahzh) *n.* spying; use of secret agents

**es·pla·nade** (ES-plə-nahd) *n.* level space, *esp.* one used as public promenade

**es·pouse** (i-SPOWZ) *vt.* (-poused, -pous·ing) support, embrace (cause *etc.*); marry —**es·pous'al** *n.*

**es·pres·so** (e-SPRES-oh) *n.* strong coffee made by forcing steam through ground coffee beans; cup of espresso

**es·prit** (e-SPREE) *n.* spirit; animation —**esprit de corps** (də kor) attachment, loyalty to the society *etc.*, one belongs to

**es·py** (i-SPĪ) *vt.* (-pied, -py·ing) catch sight of

**es·quire** (ES-kwīr) *n.* gentleman's courtesy title used on letters; formerly, a squire

**es·say** *n.* prose composition; short treatise; attempt —**es·say'** *vt.* (-sayed, -say·ing) try, attempt; test —**es'say·ist** *n.*

**es·sence** (ES-əns) *n.* all that makes thing what it is; existence, being; entity, reality; extract got by distillation —**es·sen'tial** (ə-SEN-shəl) *adj.* necessary, indispensable; inherent; of, constituting essence of thing —n. indispensable element; chief point

**es·tab·lish** (i-STAB-lish) vt. make secure; set up; settle; prove —es·tab'lish·ment n. establishing; permanent organized body; place of business together with its employees, equipment etc.; household; public institution —**established church** church officially recognized as national institution —**the Establishment** n. group, class of people holding authority within a profession, society etc.

**es·tate** (i-STAYT) n. landed property; person's property; deceased person's property; class as part of nation; rank, state, condition of life

**es·teem** (i-STEEM) vt. think highly of; consider —n. favorable opinion, regard, respect

**es·ter** (ES-tər) n. Chem. organic compound produced by reaction between acid and alcohol

**es·ti·mate** (ES-tə-mayt) vt. (-mat·ed, -mat·ing) form approximate idea of (amounts, measurements etc.); form opinion of; quote probable price for —n. (-mit) approximate judgment of amounts etc.; amount etc., arrived at; opinion; price quoted by contractor —es·ti·ma·ble adj. worthy of regard —es·ti·ma'tion n. opinion, judgment, esteem

**es·ti·vate** (ES-tə-vayt) vi. (-vat·ed, -vat·ing) spend the summer

**es·trange** (i-STRAYNJ) vt. (-tranged, -trang·ing) lose affection of; alienate —es·trange'ment n.

**es·tro·gen** (ES-trə-jən) n. hormone in females esp. controlling changes, cycles, in reproductive organs —es·tro·gen'ic adj.

**es·tu·ar·y** (ES-choo-er-ee) n. (pl. -ar·ies) tidal mouth of river, inlet etc. et cetera

**et cet·er·a** (et SET-ər-ə) Lat. and the rest, and others, and so on (abbrev. etc.)

**etch** (ech) vt. make engraving by eating away surface of metal plate with acids etc.; imprint vividly —etch'er n. —etch'ing n.

**e·ter·nal** (i-TUR-nəl) adj. without beginning or end; everlasting; changeless —e·ter'ni·ty n. (pl. -ties)

**e·ther** (EE-thər) n. colorless volatile liquid used as anesthetic; intangible fluid formerly supposed to fill all space; the clear sky, region above clouds —e·the·re·al (i-THEER-ee-əl) adj. light, airy; heavenly, spirit-like

**eth·i·cal** (ETH-i-kəl) adj. relating to morals —eth'i·cal·ly adv. —eth'ics n. (with sing. or pl. v.) science of morals; moral principles, rules of conduct

**eth·nic** (ETH-nik) adj. of race or relating to classification of humans into social, cultural etc., groups —eth·nog'ra·phy (-NOG-rə-fee) n. description of races of men —eth·nol'o·gy n. study of human races

**e·thos** (EE-thos) n. distinctive character, spirit etc. of people, culture etc.

**eth·yl** (ETH-əl) n. ($C_2H_5$) radical of ordinary alcohol and ether —eth'y·lene (-leen) n. poisonous gas used as anesthetic and fuel

**e·ti·ol·o·gy** (ee-tee-OL-ə-jee) n. (pl. -gies) study of causes, esp. inquiry into origin of disease —e·ti·o·log'i·cal adj.

**et·i·quette** (ET-i-kit) n. conventional code of conduct or behavior

**é·tude** (AY-tood) n. short musical

composition, study, intended often as technical exercise

**et·y·mol·o·gy** (et-ə-MOL-ə-jee) n. tracing, account of, formation of word's origin, development; study of this —**et·y·mo·log·i·cal** adj. —**et·y·mol'o·gist** n.

**eu-, ev-** (comb. form) well, as in eugenic, euphony, evangelist etc.

**eu·ca·lyp·tus** (yoo-kə-LIP-təs) n. mostly Aust. genus of tree, the gum tree, yielding timber and oil, used medicinally from leaves

**Eu·cha·rist** (YOO-kə-rist) n. Christian sacrament of the Lord's Supper; the consecrated elements; (e-) thanksgiving

**eu·gen·ic** (yoo-JEN-ik) adj. relating to, or tending toward, production of fine offspring —**eu·gen'ics** n. (with sing. v.) this science

**eu·lo·gy** (YOO-lə-jee) n. (pl. -gies) speech or writing in praise of person esp. dead person; praise —**eu'lo·gist** n. —**eu'lo·gize** (-jīz) vt. (-gized, -giz·ing)

**eu·nuch** (YOO-nək) n. castrated man, esp. formerly one employed in harem

**eu·phe·mism** (YOO-fə-miz-əm) n. substitution of mild term for offensive or hurtful one; instance of this —**eu·phe·mis'tic** adj. —**eu·phe·mis'ti·cal·ly** adv.

**eu·pho·ny** (YOO-fə-nee) n. (pl. -nies) pleasantness of sound —**eu·phon'ic** (-FON-ik) adj. —**eu·pho'ni·ous** (-FOH-nee-əs) adj. pleasing to ear

**eu·pho·ri·a** (yoo-FOR-ee-ə) n. sense of well-being or elation —**eu·phor'ic** adj.

**eu·phu·ism** (YOO-fyoo-iz-əm) n. affected high-flown manner of writing, esp. in imitation of Lyly's Euphues (1580) —**eu·phu·is'tic** adj.

**Eu·ra·sian** (yuu-RAY-zhən) adj. of mixed European and Asiatic descent; of Europe and Asia —n. one of this descent

**eu·re·ka** (yuu-REE-kə) interj. exclamation of triumph at finding something

**Eu·ro·pe·an** (yuur-ə-PEE-ən) n./adj. (native) of Europe —European Economic Community association of a number of European nations for trade

**Eu·sta·chian tube** (yoo-STAY-shən) passage leading from pharynx to middle ear

**eu·tha·na·sia** (yoo-thə-NAY-zhə) n. gentle, painless death; putting to death in this way, esp. to relieve suffering

**e·vac·u·ate** (i-VAK-yoo-ayt) vt. (-at·ed, -at·ing) empty; withdraw from; discharge —**e·vac·u·a'tion** n. —**e·vac·u·ee'** n. person moved from dangerous area esp. in time of war

**e·vade** (i-VAYD) vt. (-vad·ed, -vad·ing) avoid, escape from; elude —**e·va'sion** (-zhən) n. subterfuge; excuse; equivocation —**e·va'sive** adj. elusive, not straightforward

**e·val·u·ate** (i-VAL-yoo-ayt) vt. (-at·ed, -at·ing) find or judge value of —**e·val·u·a'tion** n.

**ev·a·nesce** (ev-ə-NES) vi. (-nesced, -nesc·ing) fade away —**ev·a·nes'cence** n. —**ev·a·nes'cent** adj. fleeting, transient

**e·van·gel·i·cal** (ee-van-JEL-i-kəl) adj. of, or according to, gospel teaching; of Protestant sect that stresses salvation by faith —n. member of evangelical sect —**e·van'gel·ism** n. —**e·van'ge·list** n. writer of one of the four gospels; ardent, zealous preacher of the gospel; revivalist —**e·van'ge·lize** vt. (-lized, -liz·ing) preach gospel to; convert

**e·vap·o·rate** (i-VAP-ə-rayt) v. (-rat·ed, -rat·ing) —vi. turn into, pass off in, vapor —*vt.* turn into vapor —**e·vap·o·ra'tion** *n.*

**evasion** *see* EVADE

**eve** (eev) *n.* evening before (holiday *etc.*); time just before (event *etc.*)

**e·ven** (EE·vən) *adj.* flat, smooth; uniform in quality, equal in amount, balanced; divisible by two; impartial —*vt.* make even; smooth; equalize —*adv.* equally; simply; notwithstanding; (used to express emphasis)

**eve·ning** (EEV·ning) *n.* the close of day or early part of night; decline, end

**e·vent** (i-VENT) *n.* happening; notable occurrence; issue, result; any one contest in series in sports program —**e·vent'ful** *adj.* full of exciting events —**e·ven·tu·al** (-choo-əl) *adj.* resulting in the end; ultimate; final —**e·ven·tu·al'i·ty** (-AL·i-tee) *n.* possible event —**e·ven'tu·ate** *vi.* (-at·ed, -at·ing) turn out; happen; end

**ev·er** (EV·ər) *adv.* always; constantly; at any time —**ev'er·green** *n./adj.* (tree or shrub) bearing foliage throughout year —**ev·er·more** *adv.*

**eve·ry** (EV·ree) *adj.* each of all; all possible —**eve'ry·body** *pron.* —**eve'ry·day** *adj.* usual, ordinary —**eve'ry·one** *pron.* —**eve'ry·thing** *pron./n.* —**eve'ry·where** *adv.* in all places

**e·vict** (i-VIKT) *vt.* expel by legal process, turn out —**e·vic'tion** (-shən) *n.*

**ev·i·dent** (EV·i-dənt) *adj.* plain, obvious —**ev'i·dence** *n.* ground of belief; sign, indication; testimony —*vt.* (-denced, -denc·ing) indicate, prove —**ev·i·den'tial** *adj.* —**ev'i·dent·ly** *adv.* —**in evidence** conspicuous

**e·vil** (EE·vəl) *adj.* bad, harmful —*n.* what is bad or harmful; sin

—**e'vil·ly** *adv.* —**e'vil·do·er** *n.* sinner

**e·vince** (i-VINS) *vt.* (-vinced, -vinc·ing) show, indicate

**e·voke** (i-VOHK) *vt.* (-voked, -vok·ing) draw forth; call to mind —**ev·o·ca·tion** (ev-ə-KAY-shən) *n.* —**e·voc·a·tive** (i-VOK-ə-tiv) *adj.*

**e·volve** (i-VOLV) *v.* (-volved, -volv·ing) develop or cause to develop gradually —*vi.* undergo slow changes in process of growth —**ev·o·lu·tion** (ev-ə-LOO-shən) *n.* evolving; development of species from earlier forms —**ev·o·lu'tion·ar·y** *adj.* —**ev·o·lu'tion·ist** *n.* one who supports theory of evolution

**ewe** (yoo) *n.* female sheep

**ew·er** (YOO·ər) *n.* pitcher with wide spout

**Ex.** Exodus

**ex-, e-, ef-** (*prefix*) out from, from, out of, formerly, as in *ex·claim, evade, effusive, exodus* Such words are not given here where the meaning can easily be inferred from the simple word

**ex·ac·er·bate** (ig-ZAS·ər-bayt) *vt.* (-bat·ed, -bat·ing) aggravate, embitter, make worse —**ex·ac·er·ba'tion** *n.*

**ex·act** (ig-ZAKT) *adj.* precise, accurate, strictly correct —*vt.* demand, extort; insist upon; enforce —**ex·act'ing** *adj.* making rigorous or excessive demands —**ex·ac'tion** *n.* act of exacting; that which is exacted, as excessive work *etc.*; oppressive demand —**ex·act'ly** *adv.* —**ex·act'ness** *n.* accuracy; precision

**ex·ag·ger·ate** (ig-ZAJ·ə-rayt) *vt.* (-at·ed, -at·ing) magnify beyond truth, overstate; overestimate —**ex·ag·ger·a'tion** *n.*

**ex·alt** (ig-ZAWLT) *vt.* raise up; praise; make noble, dignify —**ex·al·ta·tion** (eg-zawl-TAY-shən) *n.*

an exalting; elevation in rank, dignity or position; rapture

**ex·am·ine** (ig-ZAM-in) *vt.* (-ined, -in·ing) investigate; look at closely; ask questions of; test knowledge or proficiency of; inquire into —**ex·am·i·na'tion** *n.* —**exam'in·er** *n.*

**ex·am·ple** (ig-ZAM-pəl) *n.* thing illustrating general rule; specimen; model; warning, precedent, instance

**ex·as·per·ate** (ig-ZAS-pə-rayt) *vt.* (-at·ed, -at·ing) irritate, enrage; intensify, make worse —**ex·as·per·a'tion** *n.*

**ex·ca·vate** (EKS-kə-vayt) *vt.* (-vat·ed, -vat·ing) hollow out; make hole by digging; unearth —**ex·ca·va'tion** *n.*

**ex·ceed** (ik-SEED) *vt.* be greater than; do more than authorized; go beyond; surpass —**ex·ceed'ing·ly** *adv.* very; greatly

**ex·cel** (ik-SEL) *v.* (-celled, -cel·ling) —*vt.* surpass, be better than —*vi.* be very good, preeminent —**ex'cel·lence** *n.* —**ex'cel·len·cy** *n.* title borne by certain high officials —**ex'cel·lent** *adj.* very good

**ex·cept** (ik-SEPT) *prep.* not including; but —*vt.* leave or take out; exclude —**ex·cept'ing** *prep.* not including —**ex·cep'tion** *n.* thing excepted, not included in a rule; objection —**ex·cep'tion·a·ble** *adj.* open to objection —**ex·cep'tion·al** *adj.* not ordinary, esp. much above average

**ex·cerpt** (EK·surpt) *n.* quoted or extracted passage from book *etc.* —**ex·cerpt'** *vt.* extract, quote (passage from book *etc.*)

**ex·cess** (EK-ses) *n.* an exceeding; amount by which thing exceeds; too great amount; intemperance or immoderate conduct —**ex·ces'sive** (-siv) *adj.*

**ex·change** (iks-CHAYNJ) *vt.* (-changed, -chang·ing) give (something) in return for something else; barter —*n.* giving one thing and receiving another; giving or receiving currency of one country for that of another; thing given for another; building where merchants, dealers meet for business; central telephone office —**ex·change'a·ble** *adj.*

**ex·cheq·uer** (eks-CHEK-ər) *n.* treasury, *eg* of a government; *inf.* personal funds

**ex·cise**[1] (EK-sīz) *n.* tax levied on domestic goods during manufacture or before sale

**ex·cise**[2] (ik-SĪZ) *vt.* (-cised, -cis·ing) cut out, cut away —**ex·ci·sion** (-SIZH-ən) *n.*

**ex·cite** (ik-SĪT) *vt.* (-cit·ed, -cit·ing) arouse to strong emotion, stimulate; rouse up, set in motion; *Electricity* energize to produce electric activity or a magnetic field —**ex·cit'a·ble** *adj.* —**ex·ci·ta·tion** (ek-si-TAY-shən) *n.* —**ex·cite'ment** *n.* —**ex·cit'ing** *adj.* thrilling; rousing to action

**ex·claim** (ik-SKLAYM) *v.* speak suddenly, cry out —**ex·cla·ma·tion** (ek-sklə-MAY-shən) *n.* —**ex·clam·a·to·ry** (ik-SKLAM-ə-tor-ee) *adj.*

**ex·clude** (ik-SKLOOD) *vt.* (-clud·ed, -clud·ing) shut out; debar from; reject, not consider —**ex·clu'sion** (-zhən) *n.* —**ex·clu'sive** *adj.* excluding; inclined to keep out (from society *etc.*); sole, only; select —*n.* something exclusive, *esp.* story appearing only in one newspaper —**ex·clu·sive·ly** *adv.*

**ex·com·mu·ni·cate** (eks-kə-MYOO-ni-kayt) *vt.* (-cat·ed, -cat·ing) cut off from the sacraments of the Church —**ex·com·mu·ni·ca'tion** *n.*

**ex·cre·ment** (EKS-kra-mənt) n. waste matter from body, esp. from bowels; dung —**ex·cre·ta** (ik-SKREE-tə) n. (usu. with pl. v.) excrement —**ex·crete** vi. (-cret·ed, -cret·ing) discharge from the system —**ex·cre'tion** n. —**ex'cre·to·ry** adj.

**ex·cres·cent** (ik-SKRES-ənt) adj. growing out of; redundant —**ex·cres'cence** n. unnatural outgrowth

**ex·cru·ci·ate** (ik-SKROO-shee-ayt) vt. (-at·ed, -at·ing) torment acutely, torture in body or mind

**ex·cul·pate** (EK-skul-payt) vt. (-pat·ed, -pat·ing) free from blame, acquit —**ex·cul·pa·tion** n. —**ex·cul'pa·to·ry** adj.

**ex·cur·sion** (ik-SKUR-zhən) n. journey, ramble, trip for pleasure; digression

**ex·cuse** (ik-SKYOOZ) vt. (-cused, -cus·ing) forgive, overlook; try to clear from blame; gain exemption; set free, remit —n. (-SKYOOS) that which serves to excuse; apology —**ex·cus·a·ble** (ik-SKYOO-zə-bəl) adj.

**ex·e·cra·ble** (EK-si-krə-bəl) adj. abominable, hatefully bad

**ex·e·cute** (EK-si-kyoot) vt. (-cut·ed, -cut·ing) inflict capital punishment on, kill; carry out, perform; make, produce; sign (document) —**ex·e·cu'tion** n. —**ex·e·cu'tion·er** n. one employed to execute criminals —**ex·ec'u·tive** n. person in administrative position; executive body; executive branch of government —adj. carrying into effect, esp. of branch of government executing laws —**ex·ec·u·tor** (ig-ZEK-yə-tər) n. person appointed to carry out provisions of a will —**ex·ec'u·trix** fem.)

**ex·e·ge·sis** (ek-si-JEE-sis) n. (pl. -ses pr. -seez) explanation, esp. of Scripture —**ex'e·gete** (-jeet) one skilled in exegesis

**ex·em·plar** (ig-ZEM-plər) n. model type —**ex·em'pla·ry** (-plə-ree) adj. fit to be imitated, serving as example; commendable; typical

**ex·em·pli·fy** (ig-ZEM-plə-fi) vt. (-fied, -fy·ing) serve as example of; illustrate; exhibit; make attested copy of —**ex·em·pli·fi·ca'tion** n.

**ex·empt** (ig-ZEMPT) vt. free from; excuse —adj. freed from, not liable for; not affected by —**ex·emp'tion** n.

**ex·e·quies** (EK-si-kweez) n. pl. funeral rites or procession

**ex·er·cise** (EK-sər-sīz) v. (-cised, -cis·ing) —vt. use, employ; give exercise to; carry out, discharge; trouble, harass —vi. take exercise —n. use of limbs for health; practice for training; task for training; lesson; employment; use (of limbs, mind etc.)

**ex·ert** (ig-ZURT) vt. apply (oneself) diligently, make effort; bring to bear —**ex·er'tion** n. effort, physical activity

**ex·hale** (eks-HAYL) v. (-haled, -hal·ing) breathe out; give, pass off as vapor

**ex·haust** (ig-ZAWST) vt. tire out; use up; empty; draw off; treat, discuss thoroughly —n. used steam or fluid from engine; waste gases from internal combustion engine; passage for, or coming out of this —**ex·haust'i·ble** adj. —**ex·haus'tion** (-chən) n. state of extreme fatigue; limit of endurance —**ex·haus'tive** adj. thorough; comprehensive

**ex·hib·it** (ig-ZIB-it) vt. show, display; manifest; show publicly (often in competition) —n. thing shown, esp. in competition or as evidence in court —**ex·hi·bi·tion** (ek-sə-BISH-ən) n. display, act of displaying; public show (of works of art *etc.*) —**ex·hi·bi'tion·ist** *n.* one with compulsive desire to draw attention to self or to expose genitals publicly —**ex·hib'i·tor** *n.* one who exhibits, *esp.* in show

**ex·hil·a·rate** (ig-ZIL-ǝ-rayt) *vt.* (-rat·ed, -rat·ing) enliven, gladden —**ex·hil·a·ra'tion** *n.* high spirits, enlivenment

**ex·hort** (ig-ZORT) *vt.* urge, admonish earnestly —**ex·hor·ta·tion** (eg-zor-TAY-shǝn) *n.* —**ex·hort'er** *n.*

**ex·hume** (ig-ZOOM) *vt.* (-humed, -hum·ing) unearth what has been buried, disinter —**ex·hu·ma·tion** (eks-hyuu-MAY-shǝn) *n.*

**ex·i·gent** (EK-si-jǝnt) *adj.* exacting; urgent, pressing —**ex'i·gen·cy** *n.* (*pl.* -cies) pressing need; emergency

**ex·ig·u·ous** (ig-ZIG-yoo-ǝs) *adj.* scanty, meager

**ex·ile** (EG-zīl) *n.* banishment, expulsion from one's own country; long absence abroad; one banished or permanently living away from home or country —*vt.* (-iled, -il·ing) banish, expel

**ex·ist** (ig-ZIST) *vi.* be, have being, live —**ex·ist'ence** *n.* —**ex·ist'ent** *adj.*

**ex·is·ten·tial·ism** (eg-zi-STEN-shǝ-liz-ǝm) *n.* philosophy stressing importance of personal responsibility and the free agency of the individual in a seemingly meaningless universe

**ex·it** (EG-zit) *n.* way out; going out; death; actor's departure from stage —*vi.* go out

**ex li·bris** (eks LEE-bris) *Lat.* from the library of

**ex·o·crine** (EK-sǝ-krin) *adj.* of gland (*e.g.* salivary, sweat) secreting its products through ducts

**ex·o·dus** (EK-sǝ-dǝs) *n.* depar-

ture, *esp.* of crowd; (E-) second book of Old Testament —**the Exodus** departure of Israelites from Egypt

**ex of·fi·ci·o** (eks ǝ-FISH-ee-oh) *Lat.* by right of position or office

**ex·on·er·ate** (ig-ZON-ǝ-rayt) *vt.* (-at·ed, -at·ing) free, declare free, from blame; exculpate; acquit —**ex·on·er·a'tion** *n.*

**ex·or·bi·tant** (ig-ZOR-bi-tǝnt) *adj.* very excessive, inordinate, immoderate —**ex·or'bi·tance** *n.*

**ex·or·cise** (EK-sor-sīz) *vt.* (-cised, -cis·ing) cast out (evil spirits) by invocation; free person of evil spirits —**ex'or·cism** *n.* —**ex'or·cist** *n.*

**ex·ot·ic** (ig-ZOT-ik) *adj.* brought in from abroad, foreign; rare, unusual, having strange or bizarre allure —*n.* exotic plant *etc.* —**ex·ot'i·ca** (-i-kǝ) *n. pl.* (collection of) exotic objects —**ex·ot'i·cism** *n.* —**exotic dancer** stripper

**ex·pand** (ik-SPAND) *v.* increase, spread out, dilate, develop —**ex·pand'a·ble, -i·ble** *adj.* —**ex·panse'** *n.* wide space; open stretch of land —**ex·pan'si·ble** *adj.* —**ex·pan'sion** *n.* —**ex·pan'sive** *adj.* wide; extensive; friendly, talkative

**ex·pa·ti·ate** (ik-SPAY-shee-ayt) *vi.* (-at·ed, -at·ing) speak or write at great length (on); enlarge (upon) —**ex·pa·ti·a'tion** *n.*

**ex·pa·tri·ate** (eks-PAY-tree-ayt) *vt.* (-at·ed, -at·ing) banish; exile; withdraw (oneself) from one's native land —*adj./n.* (-tree-it) —**ex·pa·tri·a'tion** *n.*

**ex·pect** (ik-SPEKT) *vt.* regard as probable; look forward to; await, hope —**ex·pect'an·cy** *n.* state or act of expecting; that which is expected; hope —**ex·pect'ant** *adj.* looking or waiting for, *esp.* for birth of child —**ex·pect'ant·ly**

*adv.* —ex·pec·ta·tion (ek-spek-TAY-shən) *n.* act or state of expecting; prospect of future good; what is expected; promise; value of something expected —*pl.* prospect of fortune or profit *esp.* by inheritance

ex·pec·to·rate (ik-SPEK-tə-rayt) *v.* (-rat·ed, -rat·ing) spit out (phlegm *etc.*) —ex·pec·to·ra'·tion *n.*

ex·pe·di·ent (ik-SPEE-dee-ont) *adj.* fitting, advisable; politic; suitable; convenient —*n.* something suitable, useful, *esp.* in emergency —ex·pe'di·en·cy *n.*

ex·pe·dite (EK-spi-dīt) *vt.* help on, hasten; dispatch —ex·pe·di·tion (-DISH-ən) *n.* journey for definite (often scientific or military) purpose; people, equipment engaged in expedition; excursion; promptness —ex·pe·di'tion·ar·y *adj.* —ex·pe·di'tious *adj.* prompt, speedy

ex·pel (ik-SPEL) *vt.* (-pelled, -pel·ling) drive, cast out; exclude; discharge —ex·pul'sion *n.*

ex·pend (ik-SPEND) *vt.* spend, pay out; use up —ex·pend'a·ble *adj.* likely, or meant, to be used up or destroyed —ex·pend'i·ture (-i-chər) *n.* —ex·pense' *n.* cost; (cause of) spending —*pl.* charges, outlay incurred —ex·pen'sive *adj.*

ex·pe·ri·ence (ik-SPEER-ee-əns) *n.* observation of facts as source of knowledge; being affected consciously by event; the event; knowledge, skill, gained from life, by contact with facts and events —*vt.* (-enced, -enc·ing) undergo, suffer, meet with —ex·pe'ri·enced *adj.* skilled, expert, capable —ex·pe·ri·en·tial (ik-speer-ee-EN-shəl) *adj.*

ex·per·i·ment (ik-SPER-ə-mənt) *n.* test, trial, something done in the hope that it may succeed, or to test hypothesis, principle *etc.* —*vi.* conduct experiment —ex·per·i·men'tal *adj.*

ex·pert (EK-spurt) *n.* one skillful, knowledgeable, in something; authority —*adj.* practiced, skillful —ex·per·tise (ek-spər-TEEZ) *n.* expertness; know-how

ex·pi·ate (EK-spee-ayt) *vt.* (-at·ed, -at·ing) pay penalty for; make amends for —ex·pi·a'tion *n.* —ex'pi·a·to·ry (-ə-tor-ee) *adj.*

ex·pire (ik-SPĪR) *vi.* (-pired, -pir·ing) come to an end; give out breath; die —*vt.* breathe out —ex·pi·ra·tion *n.*

ex·plain (ik-SPLAYN) *vt.* make clear, intelligible; interpret; elucidate; give details of; account for —ex·pla·na·tion (ek-splə-NAY-shən) *n.* —ex·plan'a·to·ry *adj.*

ex·ple·tive (EK-spli-tiv) *n.* exclamation; exclamatory oath —*adj.* serving only to fill out sentence *etc.*

ex·pli·ca·ble (EK-splik-ə-bəl) *adj.* explainable —ex'pli·cate (-cat·ed, -cat·ing) develop, explain —ex'pli·ca·to·ry *adj.*

ex·plic·it (ik-SPLIS-it) *adj.* stated in detail; stated, not merely implied; outspoken; clear, plain; unequivocal

ex·plode (ik-SPLOHD) *v.* (-plod·ed, -plod·ing) —*vi.* go off with bang; burst violently; (of population) increase rapidly —*vt.* make explode; discredit, expose (a theory *etc.*) —ex·plo'sion (-zhən) *n.* —ex·plo'sive *adj./n.*

ex·ploit (EK-sploit) *n.* brilliant feat, deed —*vt.* (ik-SPLOIT) turn to advantage; make use of for one's own ends —ex·ploi·ta'tion (ek-) *n.*

ex·plore (ik-SPLOHR) *vt.* (-plored, -plor·ing) investigate; examine; scrutinize; examine (country etc.) by going through it —**ex·plo·ra·tion** (ek-splə-RAY-shən) n. —**ex·plor·a·to·ry** (ek-SPLOR-ə-tor·ee) adj. —**ex·plor'er** n.

**explosion** see EXPLODE

**exponent** see EXPOUND

**ex·port** (ik-SPORT) vt. send (goods) out of the country —**ex·port** (EK-sport) n./adj. —**ex·por·ta'tion** (-TAY-shən) n. —**ex·port'er** n.

**ex·pose** (ik-SPOHZ) vt. (-posed, -pos·ing) exhibit; disclose, reveal; lay open (to); leave unprotected; expose photographic plate or film to light —**ex·po·sure** (-zhər) n.

**ex·po·sé** (ek-spoh-ZAY) n. newspaper article etc., disclosing scandal, crime etc.

**exposition** see EXPOUND

**ex·pos·tu·late** (ik-SPOS-chə-layt) vi. (-lat·ed, -lat·ing) remonstrate; reason with (in a kindly manner) —**ex·pos·tu·la'tion** n.

**ex·pound** (ik-SPOWND) vt. explain, interpret —**ex·po·nent** (ik-SPOH-nənt) n. one who expounds or promotes (idea, cause etc.); performer, executant; Math. small, raised number showing the power of a factor —**ex·po·nen·tial** (ek-spə-NEN-shəl) adj. —**ex·po·si'tion** (-ZISH-ən) n. explanation, description; exhibition of goods etc. —**ex·pos·i·tor** (ik-SPOZ-i-tər) n. one who explains, interpreter —**ex·pos'i·to·ry** adj. explanatory

**ex·press** (ik-SPRES) vt. put into words; make known or understood by words, behavior etc.; squeeze out —adj. definitely stated; specially designed; clear; positive; speedy; of train, fast and making few stops —adv. by express; with speed —n. express train; rapid parcel delivery service —**ex·press'i·ble** adj. —**ex·**

**pres'sion** (-shən) n. expressing; word, phrase; look, aspect; feeling; utterance —**ex·pres·sion·ism** n. theory that art depends on expression of artist's creative self, not on mere reproduction —**ex·pres'sive** adj. —**ex·press'ly** adv. —**ex·pres'sive·ness** n.

**ex·pro·pri·ate** (eks-PROH-pree-ayt) vt. (-at·ed, -at·ing) dispossess; take out of owner's hands —**ex·pro·pri·a'tion** n.

**expulsion** see EXPEL

**ex·punge** (ik-SPUNJ) vt. (-punged, -pung·ing) strike out, erase

**ex·pur·gate** (EK-spər-gayt) vt. (-gat·ed, -gat·ing) remove objectionable parts (from book etc.), purge —**ex·pur·ga'tion** n.

**ex·quis·ite** (EK-skwiz-it) adj. of extreme beauty or delicacy; keen, acute; keenly sensitive —**ex·quis'ite·ly** adv.

**ex·tant** (EK-stənt) adj. still existing

**ex·tem·po·re** (ik-STEM-pə-ree) adj./adv. without previous thought or preparation —**ex·tem·po·ra·ne·ous** adj. —**ex·tem·po·rize** vt. (-rized, -riz·ing) speak without preparation; devise for the occasion

**ex·tend** (ik-STEND) vt. stretch out, lengthen; prolong in duration; widen in area, scope; accord, grant —vi. reach; cover area; have range or scope; become larger or wider —**ex·tend'i·ble, -a·ble, ex·ten'si·ble** adj. —**ex·ten·sile** (ik-STEN-səl) adj. that can be extended —**ex·ten'sion** n. stretching out, prolongation or enlargement; expansion; continuation, additional part, as of telephone etc. —**ex·ten'sive** adj. wide, large, comprehensive —**ex·ten'sor** n. straightening muscle —**ex·tent'** n. space or degree to which thing is extended; size; compass; volume

**ex·ten·u·ate** (ik-STEN-yoo-ayt) *vt.* (-at·ed, -at·ing) make less blameworthy, lessen; mitigate —**ex·ten·u·a′tion** *n.*

**ex·te·ri·or** (ik-STEER-ee-ər) *n.* the outside; outward appearance —*adj.* outer, outward, external

**ex·ter·mi·nate** (ik-STUR-mə-nayt) *vt.* (-nat·ed, -nat·ing) destroy utterly, annihilate, root out, eliminate —**ex·ter·mi·na′tion** *n.* —**ex·ter′mi·na·tor** *n.* destroyer

**ex·ter·nal** (ik-STUR-nəl) *adj.* outside, outward —**ex·ter′nal·ly** *adv.*

**ex·tinct** (ik-STINGKT) *adj.* having died out or come to an end; no longer existing; quenched, no longer burning —**ex·tinc′tion** *n.*

**ex·tin·guish** (ik-STING-gwish) *vt.* put out, quench; wipe out —**ex·tin′guish·er** *n.* device, *esp.* spraying liquid or foam, used to put out fires

**ex·tir·pate** (EK-stər-payt) *vt.* (-pat·ed, -pat·ing) root out, destroy utterly —**ex·tir·pa′tion** *n.* —**ex′tir·pa·tor** *n.*

**ex·tol** (ik-STOHL) *vt.* (-tolled, -tol·ling) praise highly

**ex·tort** (ik-STORT) *vt.* get by force or threats; wring out; exact —**ex·tor′tion** *n.*

**ex·tra** (EK-strə) *adj.* additional; larger, better, than usual —*adv.* additionally; more than usually —*n.* extra thing; something charged as additional; *Films* actor hired for crowd scenes

**extra-** (prefix) beyond, as in *extradition, extramural, extraterritorial etc.* Such words are not given here where the meaning can easily be inferred from the simple word

**ex·tract** (ik-STRAKT) *vt.* take out, *esp.* by force; obtain against person's will; get by pressure, distil-

lation *etc.*; deduce, derive; copy out, quote —*n.* (EK-strakt) passage from book, film *etc.*; matter got by distillation; concentrated solution —**ex·trac′tion** *n.* extracting, *esp.* of tooth; ancestry

**ex·tra·di·tion** (ek-strə-DISH-ən) *n.* delivery, under treaty, of foreign fugitive from justice to authorities concerned —**ex′tra·dite** (-dīt) *vt.* (-dit·ed, -dit·ing) give or obtain such delivery

**ex·tra·mu·ral** (ek-strə-MYUUR-əl) *adj.* connected with but outside normal courses *etc.* of college or school; situated outside walls or boundaries of a place

**ex·tra·ne·ous** (ik-STRAY-nee-əs) *adj.* not essential; irrelevant; added from without, not belonging

**ex·tra·or·di·na·ry** (ik-STROR-dn-er-ee) *adj.* out of the usual course; additional; unusual, surprising, exceptional

**ex·trap·o·late** (ik-STRAP-ə-layt) *vt.* (-lat·ed, -lat·ing) infer something not known from something not known from known facts; *Math.* estimate a value beyond known values

**ex·tra·sen·so·ry** (ek-strə-SEN-sə-ree) *adj.* of perception apparently gained without use of known senses

**ex·tra·ter·res·tri·al** (ek-strə-RES-tree-əl) *adj.* of, or from outside Earth's atmosphere

**ex·trav·a·gant** (ik-STRAV-ə-gənt) *adj.* wasteful; exorbitant; wild, absurd —**ex·trav′a·gance** (- gəns) *n.* —**ex·trav′a·gant·ly** *adv.* —**ex·trav·a·gan′za** (-GAN-zə) *n.* elaborate, lavish, entertainment, display *etc.*

**extravert** *see* EXTROVERT

**ex·treme** (ik-STREEM) *adj.* (-trem·er, -trem·est) of high or highest degree; severe; going beyond moderation; at the end; outermost —*n.* utmost degree;

thing at one end or the other, first and last of series —**ex·trem'ist** n. advocate of extreme measures —**ex·trem'i·ty** (-TREM-i-tee) n. end (pl. -ties) hands and feet; utmost distress; extreme measures

**ex·tri·cate** (EK-stri-kayt) vt. (-cat·ed, -cat·ing) disentangle, unravel, set free —**ex·tri·ca'tion** n.

**ex·trin·sic** (ik-STRIN-sik) adj. accessory, not belonging, not intrinsic —**ex·trin'si·cal·ly** adv.

**ex·tro·vert** (EK-strə-vurt) n. one who is interested in other people and things rather than own feelings —**ex·tro·ver'sion** (-VUR-zhən) n.

**ex·trude** (ik-STROOD) vt. (-trud·ed, -trud·ing) squeeze, force out; (esp. of molten metal or plastic etc.) shape by squeezing through suitable nozzle or die

**ex·u·ber·ant** (ig-ZOO-bər-ənt) adj. high-spirited, vivacious; prolific, abundant, luxurious —**ex·u'ber·ance** n.

**ex·ude** (ig-ZOOD) v. (-ud·ed, -ud·ing) —vi. ooze out —vt. give off (moisture)

**ex·ult** (ig-ZULT) vi. rejoice, triumph —**exult'an·cy** n. —**ex·ul'tant** adj. triumphant —**ex·ul·ta'tion** (eg-zul-TAY-shən) n.

**eye** (i) n. organ of sight; look, glance; attention; aperture; view; judgment; watch, vigilance; thing, mark resembling eye; slit in needle for thread —vt. (eyed, ey·ing) look at; observe —**eye'less** adj. —**eye'ball** n. ball of eye —**eye'brow** n. fringe of hair above eye —**eye'glass** n. glass to assist sight; monocle —**eye'lash** n. hair fringing eyelid —**eye'let** n. small hole for rope etc. to pass through —**eye'lid** n. lid or cover of eye —**eye'o·pen·er** n. surprising news; revealing statement —**eye shadow** colored cosmetic put on around the eyes —**eye'sore** n. ugly object; thing that annoys one to see —**eye'tooth** n. canine tooth —**eye'wash** inf. n. deceptive talk etc., nonsense —**eye'wit·ness** n. one who actually sees something and can give firsthand account of it

**ey·rie** (AIR-ee) n. nest of bird of prey, esp. eagle; high dwelling place

# F

**fa** (fah) n. fourth sol-fa note

**fa·ble** (FAY-bəl) n. short story with moral, esp. one with animals as characters; tale; legend; fiction or lie —vt. invent, tell fables about —**fab'u·list** n. writer of fables —**fab'u·lous** (-yə-ləs) adj. amazing; inf. extremely good; told of in fables; unhistorical

**fab·ric** (FAB-rik) n. cloth; texture; frame, structure —**fab'ri·cate** vt. (-cat·ed, -cat·ing) build; frame; construct; invent (lie etc.); forge (document) —**fab·ri·ca'tion** n.

**fa·cade** (fə-SAHD) n. front of building; fig. outward appearance

**face** (fays) n. front of head; distorted expression; outward appearance; front, upper surface, or chief side of anything; dial of a clock etc.; dignity —v. (faced, fac·ing) vt. look or front toward; meet (boldly); give a covering surface —vi. turn —**fac·et** (FAS-it) n. one side of many-sided body, esp. cut gem; one aspect —**fa·cial** (FAY-shəl) adj. pert. to face —n. cosmetic treatment for face —**fac′ings** n. pl. lining for decoration or reinforcement, sewn on collar, cuff etc. —**face′less** adj. without a face; anonymous —**face′lift·ing** n. operation to tighten skin of face to remove wrinkles

fa·ce·tious (fə-SEE-shəs) adj. (sarcastically) witty; humorous, given to jesting, esp. at inappropriate time

facia n. see FASCIA

fac·ile (FAS-il) adj. easy; working easily; easygoing; superficial, silly —**fa·cil′i·tate** vt. make easy, help —**fa·cil′i·ta·tor** n. —**fa·cil′i·ty** n. easiness, dexterity —pl. (-ties) good conditions; means, equipment for doing something

fac·sim·i·le (fak-SIM-ə-lee) n. an exact copy

fact (fakt) n. thing known to be true; deed; reality —**fac′tu·al** (-choo-əl) adj.

fac·tion (FAK-shən) n. (dissenting) minority group within larger body; dissension —**fac′tious** adj. of or producing factions

fac·ti·tious (fak-TISH-əs) adj. artificial; specially made up; unreal

fac·tor (FAK-tər) n. something contributing to a result; one of numbers that multiplied together give a given number; agent, dealer; business that provides money to finance commerce —**fac·to′tum** (-TOH-təm) n. one performing all types of work

fac·to·ry (FAK-tə-ree) n. building in which things are manufactured

fac·ul·ty (FAK-əl-tee) n. (pl. -ties) inherent power; power of the mind; ability, aptitude; staff of school, college or university; department of university

fad (fad) n. short-lived fashion; whim —**fad′dish** adj. —**fad′dism** n. —**fad′dist** n.

fade (fayd) n. (fad·ed, fad·ing) —vi. lose color, strength; wither; grow dim; disappear gradually —vt. cause to fade —**fade′-in,** **-out** n. Radio variation in strength of signals; TV, Film gradual appearance and disappearance of picture

fag·got (FAG-ət) n. bundle of sticks for fuel etc.; sl. offens. male homosexual

Fahr·en·heit (FAR-ən-hīt) adj. measured by thermometric scale with freezing point of water 32°, boiling point 212°

fa·ience (FAY-ahns) n. glazed earthenware or china

fail (fayl) vi. be unsuccessful; stop operating or working; be below the required standard; be insufficient; run short; be wanting when in need; lose power; die away; become bankrupt —vt. disappoint, give no help to; neglect, forget to do; judge (student) to be below required standard —**fail′-ing** n. deficiency; fault —prep. in default of —**fail′ure** n. —**fail′-safe** adj. of device ensuring safety or remedy of malfunction in machine, weapon etc. —**without fail** in spite of every difficulty; certainly

faint (faynt) adj. (-er, -est) feeble, dim, pale; weak; dizzy, about to lose consciousness —vi. lose consciousness temporarily

fair[1] adj. (-er, -est) just, impartial; according to rules, legitimate; blond; beautiful; ample; of moderate quality or amount; unblemished; plausible; middling; (of weather) favorable —adv. honestly —**fair′ing** n. Aviation streamlined structure, or any part so shaped that it provides streamlined form —**fair′ly** adv. —**fair′ness** n. —**fair′way** n. Golf trimmed turf between rough; navigable channel

**fair**[2] *n.* traveling entertainment with sideshows, amusements *etc.*; large exhibition of farm, commercial or industrial products; periodical market often with amusements —**fair′ground** *n.*

**fair·y** (FAIR-ee) *n.* (*pl.* fair·ies) imaginary small creature with powers of magic; *sl. offens.* male homosexual —*adj.* of fairies; like fairy, beautiful and delicate, imaginary —**fair′y·land** *n.* —**fair′y·tale** *adj.* of or like fairy tale —**fairy tale** story of imaginary beings and happenings, *esp.* as told to children

**fait ac·com·pli** (fay ta-kawn-PLEE) *Fr.* (*pl.* faits accomplis *pr.* (fe za-kawn-PLEE) something already done that cannot be altered

**faith** (fayth) *n.* trust; belief; belief without proof; religion; promise; loyalty, constancy —faith′ful *adj.* constant, true —**faith′ful·ly** *adv.* —**faith′less** *adj.*

**fake** (fayk) *vt.* (faked, fak·ing) conceal defects of by artifice; touch up; counterfeit —*n.* fraudulent object, person, act —*adj.* —**fak′er** *n.* one who deals in fakes; swindler

**fa·kir** (fɔ-KEER) *n.* member of Islamic religious order; Hindu ascetic

**fa·la·fel** (fɔ-LAH-fɔl) *n.* seasoned croquette of flour or ground chick peas

**fal·con** (FAL-kɔn) *n.* small bird of prey, *esp.* trained in hawking for sport —**fal′con·er** *n.* one who keeps, trains, or hunts with falcons —**fal′con·ry** *n.* hawking

**fall** (fawl) *vi.* (fell, fall·en) drop, come down freely; become lower; decrease; hang down; come to the ground, cease to stand; per-ish; collapse; be captured; revert; lapse; be uttered; become; happen —*n.* falling; amount that falls; amount of descent; decrease; collapse, ruin; drop; (*oft. pl.*) cascade; cadence; yielding to temptation; autumn —fall′out *n.* radioactive particles spread as result of nuclear explosion; incidental effect or outcome —fall for *inf.* fall in love with; *inf.* be taken in by

**fal·la·cy** (FAL-ɔ-see) *n.* (*pl.* -cies) incorrect, misleading opinion or argument; flaw in logic; illusion —fal·la·cious (fɔ-LAY-shɔs) *adj.* —**fal·li·bil′i·ty** *n.* —**fal′li·ble** *adj.* liable to error

**fallen** *pp.* of FALL

**Fal·lo·pi·an tube** (fɔ-LOH-pee-ɔn) either of a pair of tubes through which egg cells pass from ovary to womb

**fal·low**[1] (FAL-oh) *adj.* plowed and harrowed but left without crop; uncultivated; neglected

**fallow**[2] *adj.* brown or reddish yellow —fallow deer deer of this color

**false** (fawls) *adj.* (fals·er, fals·est) wrong, erroneous; deceptive; faithless; sham, artificial —false′ly *adv.* —false′ness *n.* faithlessness —fal·si·fi·ca′tion *n.* —fal′si·fy *vt.* (-fied, -fy·ing) alter fraudulently; misrepresent —fal′si·ty *n.* (*pl.* -ties) —false′hood *n.* lie

**fal·set·to** (fawl-SET-oh) *n.* (*pl.* -tos) forced voice above natural range

**Fal·staff·i·an** (fawl-STAF-ee-ɔn) *adj.* like Shakespeare's Falstaff; fat; convivial; boasting

**fal·ter** (FAWL-tɔr) *vi.* hesitate; waver; stumble —fal′ter·ing·ly *adv.*

**fame** (faym) *n.* reputation; renown —**famed** adj. —**fa'mous** adj. widely known; excellent

**fa·mil·i·ar** (fə-MIL-yər) adj. well-known; frequent, customary; intimate; closely acquainted; unceremonious; impertinent, too friendly —n. familiar friend; familiar demon —**fa·mil·i·ar'·i·ty** (pl. -ties) n. —**fa·mil'iar·ize** vt. (-ized, -iz·ing)

**fam·i·ly** (FAM-ə-lee) n. (pl. -lies) group of parents and children, or near relatives; person's children; all descendants of common ancestor; household; group of allied objects —**fa·mil·ial** (fə-MIL-yəl) adj.

**fam·ine** (FAM-in) n. extreme scarcity of food; starvation —**fam'ished** adj. very hungry

**famous** see FAME

**fan¹** n. instrument for producing current of air, esp. for ventilating or cooling; folding object of paper etc., used, esp. formerly, for cooling the face; outspread feathers of a bird's tail —v. (fanned, fan·ning) spread out like fan —vt. blow or cool with fan —**fan'light** n. (fan-shaped) window over door

**fan²** n. inf. devoted admirer, an enthusiast, particularly of a sport etc.

**fa·nat·ic** (fə-NAT-ik) adj. filled with abnormal enthusiasm, esp. in religion —n. fanatic person —**fa·nat'i·cal** adj. —**fa·nat'i·cism** n.

**fan·cy** (FAN-see) adj. (-ci·er, -ci·est) ornamental, not plain; of whimsical or arbitrary kind —n. (pl. -cies) whim, caprice; liking, inclination; imagination; mental image —vt. (-cied, -cy·ing) imagine; be inclined to believe; inf. have a liking for —**fan'ci·er** n. one with liking and expert knowledge (respecting some specific thing) —**fan'ci·ful** adj. —**fan'ci·ful·ly** adv.

**fan·dan·go** (fan-DANG-goh) n. (pl. -goes) lively Spanish dance with castanets; music for this dance

**fan·fare** (FAN-fair) n. a flourish of trumpets or bugles; ostentatious display

**fang** n. snake's poison tooth; long, pointed tooth

**fan·tail** (FAN-tayl) n. (kind of bird with) fan-shaped tail; projecting part of ship's stern

**fan·ta·sy** (FAN-tə-see) n. (pl. -sies) power of imagination, esp. extravagant; mental image; fanciful invention or design —**fan·ta'sia** (-TAY-zhə) n. fanciful musical composition —**fan'ta·size** v. (-sized, -siz·ing) —**fan·tas'tic** adj. quaint, grotesque, extremely fanciful, wild; inf. very good; inf. very large —**fan·tas'ti·cal·ly** adv.

**far** adv. (far·ther or further, far·thest or fur·thest) at or to a great distance, or advanced point; at or to a remote time; by very much —adj. distant; more distant —**far'·fetched'** adj. incredible

**far·ad** (FA-rəd) n. unit of electrical capacitance

**farce** (fahrs) n. comedy of boisterous humor; absurd and futile proceeding —**far'ci·cal** adj. ludicrous

**fare** (fair) n. charge for passenger's transport; passenger; food —vi. (fared, far·ing) get on; happen; travel, progress —**fare·well'** interj. goodbye —n. leave-taking

**far·i·na·ceous** (far-ə-NAY-shəs) adj. mealy, starchy; made of flour or meal

**farm** (fahrm) n. tract of land for cultivation or rearing livestock; unit of land, water, for growing or rearing a particular crop, animal etc. —v. cultivate (land);

rear livestock (on farm) —**farm′er** n. —**farm′house** n. —**farm′yard** n. —**farm out** send (work) to be done by others; put into care of others

**far·o** (FAIR-oh) n. card game

**far·ra·go** (fə-RAH-goh) n. (pl. -gos) medley, hodgepodge

**far·row** (FA-roh) n. litter of pigs —vi. produce this

**fart** (fahrt) n. vulg. (audible) emission of gas from anus —vi.

**far·ther** (FAHR-thər) adv./adj. further; comp. of FAR —far′thest adv./adj. furthest; sup. of FAR

**fas·ces** (FAS-eez) n. pl. bundle of rods bound together around ax, forming Roman badge of authority, emblem of Italian fascists

**fas·cia** (FAY-shə) n. (pl. -cias) Architecture long flat surface between moldings under eaves; face of wood or stone in a building

**fas·ci·nate** (FAS-ə-nayt) vt. (-nat·ed, -nat·ing) attract and delight by arousing interest and curiosity; render motionless, as with a fixed stare —**fas·ci·na′tion** n.

**fas·cism** (FASH-iz-əm) n. authoritarian political system opposed to democracy and liberalism; behavior (esp. by those in authority) supposedly typical of this system —**fas′cist** adj./n. —**fa·scis·tic** (fə-SHIS-tik) adj.

**fash·ion** (FASH-ən) n. (latest) style, esp. of dress etc.; manner, mode; form, type etc.; —vt. shape, make —**fash′ion·a·ble** adj. —**fash′ion·a·bly** adv.

**fast**[1] adj. (-er, -est) (capable of) moving quickly; permitting, providing, rapid progress; ahead of true time; firm, steady; permanent —adv. rapidly; tightly —**fast′ness** n. fast state; fortress, stronghold —**fast′back** n. car

with back forming continuous slope from roof to rear —**fast food** food, esp. hamburgers etc., prepared and served very quickly

**fast**[2] vi. (fast·ed, fast·ing) go without food, or some kinds of food —n. —**fast′ing** n.

**fas·ten** (FAS-ən) vt. attach, fix, secure —vi. become joined; seize (upon)

**fas·tid·i·ous** (fa-STID-ee-əs) adj. hard to please; discriminating; particular

**fat** n. oily animal substance; fat part —adj. (fat·ter, fat·test) having too much fat; containing fat, greasy; profitable; fertile —**fat′ten** vt. feed (animals) for slaughter —vi. become fat —**fat′ness** n. —**fat′ty** adj. (-ti·er, -i·est) —n. (pl. -ties) —**fat′head** n. sl. dolt, fool —**fat farm** resort for helping people lose weight

**fate** (fayt) n. power supposed to predetermine events; goddess of destiny; destiny; person's appointed lot or condition; death or destruction —vt. (fat·ed, fat·ing) preordain —**fa′tal** adj. deadly, ending in death; destructive; disastrous; inevitable —**fa′tal·ism** n. belief that everything is predetermined; submission to fate —**fa′tal·ist** n. —**fa·tal·is′tic** adj. —**fa·tal′i·ty** n. (pl. -ties) accident resulting in death; person killed in war, accident —**fa′tal·ly** adv. —**fate′ful** adj. fraught with destiny, prophetic

**fa·ther** (FAH-thər) n. male parent; forefather, ancestor; (F-) God; originator, early leader; priest, confessor; oldest member of a society —vt. beget; originate; pass as father or author of; act as father to —**fa′ther·hood** n. —**fa′ther·less** adj. —**fa′ther·ly** adj.

—**fa·ther-in-law** *n.* husband's or wife's father

**fath·om** (FATH-əm) *n.* measure of six feet of water —*vt.* sound (water); get to bottom of; understand —**fath'om·a·ble** *adj.* —**fath'om·less** *adj.* too deep to fathom

**fa·tigue** (fə-TEEG) *n.* weariness; toil; weakness of metals *etc.*, subjected to stress; soldier's nonmilitary duty; *pl.* clothing worn for such duty —*vt.* (-tigued, -tigu·ing) weary

**fat·u·ous** (FACH-oo-əs) *adj.* very silly, idiotic —**fat'u·ous·ness** *n.*

**fau·cet** (FAW-sit) *n.* device for controlling flow of liquid; tap

**fault** (fawlt) *n.* defect; flaw; misdeed; blame, culpability; blunder; mistake; *Tennis* ball wrongly served; *Geology* break in strata —*v.* find fault in; (cause to) undergo or commit fault —**fault'i·ly** *adv.* —**fault'less** *adj.* —**fault'y** *adj.* (fault·i·er, fault·i·est)

**faun** (fawn) *n.* mythological woodland being with tail and horns

**fau·na** (FAW-nə) *n.* (*pl.* -nas, -nae *pr.* -nee) animals of region or period collectively

**faux pas** (foh-PAH) *n.* (*pl.* same form *pr.* -PAHZ) social blunder or indiscretion

**fa·vor** (FAY-vər) *n.* goodwill; approval; special kindness; partiality; *pl.* sexual intimacy granted by woman; small party gift for a guest —*vt.* regard or treat with favor; oblige; treat with partiality; aid; support; resemble —**fa'vor·a·ble** *adj.* —**fa'vor·ite** (-it) *n.* favored person or thing; horse, team *etc.* expected to win race (or game) —*adj.* chosen, preferred —**fa'vor·it·ism** *n.* practice of showing undue preference

**fawn¹** *n.* young deer —*adj.* light yellowish brown

**fawn²** *vi.* of person, cringe, court favor servilely; *esp.* of dog, show affection by wagging tail and groveling

**fax** (faks) *n.* facsimile —*vt.* transmit facsimile of (printed matter *etc.*) electronically

**faze** (fayz) *vt.* (fazed, faz·ing) fluster; daunt

**Fe** *Chem.* iron

**fear** (feer) *n.* dread, alarm, anxiety, unpleasant emotion caused by coming evil or danger —*vi.* have this feeling, be afraid —*vt.* regard with fear; hesitate, shrink from; revere —**fear'ful** *adj.* —**fear'ful·ly** *adv.* —**fear'less** *adj.* intrepid

**fea·si·ble** (FEE-zə-bəl) *adj.* able to be done; likely —**fea·si·bil'i·ty** *n.*

**feast** (feest) *n.* banquet, lavish meal; religious anniversary; something very pleasant, sumptuous —*vi.* partake of banquet, fare sumptuously —*vt.* regale with feast; provide delight for

**feat** (feet) *n.* notable deed; surprising or striking trick

**feath·er** (FETH-ər) *n.* one of the barbed shafts that form covering of birds; anything resembling this —*vt.* provide, line with feathers —*vi.* grow feathers —*v.* turn (oar, propeller) edgewise —**feath'er·y** *adj.* —**feath'erweight** *n.* very light person (*esp.* boxer) or thing; *inf.* person of small consequence or ability —**feather one's nest** enrich oneself —**in fine feather** in good form

**fea·ture** (FEE-chər) *n.* (*usu. pl.*) part of face; characteristic or notable part of anything; main or special item —*v.* (-tured, -tur·ing) —*vt.* portray; *Film* present in leading role in a film; give prominence to —*vi.* be prominent (in) —**fea'ture·less** *adj.* without striking features

**fe·brile** (FEE-brəl) *adj.* of fever; feverish

**fe·ces** (FEE-seez) *n. pl.* excrement, waste matter —**fe'cal** (-kəl) *adj.*

**feck·less** (FEK-lis) *adj.* spiritless, weak, irresponsible —**feck'less·ness** *n.*

**fec·u·lent** (FEK-yə-lənt) *adj.* full of sediment, turbid, foul —**fec'u·lence** *n.*

**fe·cund** (FEE-kund) *adj.* fertile, fruitful, fertilizing —**fe·cun·date** *vt.* (-dat·ed, -dat·ing) fertilize, impregnate —**fe·cun·di·ty** (fi-KUN-di-tee) *n.*

**fed** *pt./pp.* of FEED —**fed up** bored, dissatisfied

**fed·er·al** (FED-ər-əl) *adj.* of, or like, the government of countries that are united but retain internal independence of the separate states —**fed'er·al·ism** *n.* —**fed'er·ate** (-ə-rayt) *v.* (-at·ed, -at·ing) form into, become, a federation —**fed·er·a'tion** *n.* league; federal union

**fee** *n.* payment for professional and other services

**fee·ble** (FEE-bəl) *adj.* (-bler, -blest) weak; lacking strength or effectiveness, insipid —**fee'bly** *adv.*

**feed** *v.* (fed, feed·ing) give food to; supply, support; take food —*n.* feeding; fodder, pasturage; allowance of fodder; material supplied to machine; part of machine taking in material —**feed'er** *n.* one who or that which feeds —**feed'back** *n.* return of part of output of electrical circuit or loudspeakers; information received in response to inquiry *etc.*

—**feed'lot** *n.* area, building where cattle are fattened for market

**feel** *v.* (felt, feel·ing) perceive, examine by touch; experience; proceed, find (one's way) cautiously; be sensitive to; show emotion (for); believe, consider —*n.* act or instance of feeling; quality or impression of something perceived by feeling; sense of touch —**feel'er** *n.* special organ of touch in some animals; proposal put forward to test others' opinions; that which feels —**feel'ing** *n.* sense of touch; ability to feel; physical sensation; emotion; sympathy, tenderness; conviction or opinion not solely based on reason —*pl.* susceptibilities —*adj.* sensitive, sympathetic, heartfelt —**feel like** have an inclination for

**feet** *see* FOOT; **feet of clay** hidden flaw in person's character

**feign** (fayn) *v.* pretend, sham

**feint** (faynt) *n.* sham attack or blow meant to deceive opponent; semblance, pretense —*vi.* make feint

**feist·y** (FI-stee) *adj.* (feist·i·er, feist·i·est) spirited, spunky, plucky; ill-tempered —**feist'i·ness** *n.*

**feld·spar** (FELD-spahr) *n.* crystalline mineral found in granite *etc.*

**fe·lic·i·ty** (fi-LIS-i-tee) *n.* (*pl.* -ties) great happiness, bliss; appropriateness of wording —**fe·lic'i·tate** *vt.* (-tat·ed, -tat·ing) congratulate —**fe·lic·i·ta'tion** *n.* (*usu.* in *pl.*) —**fe·lic'i·tous** *adj.* apt, well-chosen; happy

**fe·line** (FEE-lin) *adj.* of cats; cat-like

**fell**[1] *pt.* of FALL

**fell**[2] *vt.* knock down; cut down (tree)

**fell**[3] *adj.* fierce, terrible

**fell**[4] *n.* skin or hide with hair

**fel·low** (FEL-oh) *n. inf.* man, boy; person; comrade, associate; counterpart; like thing; member (of society); student granted university fellowship —*adj.* of the same class, associated —**fel'low·ship** *n.* fraternity; friendship; (in university *etc.*) research post or special scholarship

**fel·on** (FEL-ən) *n.* one guilty of felony —**fe·lo·ni·ous** (fə-LOH-nee-əs) *adj.* —**fel'o·ny** *n.* (*pl.* -nies) serious crime

**felt**[1] *pt./pp.* of FEEL

**felt**[2] *n.* soft, matted fabric made by bonding fibers chemically and by pressure; thing made of this —*vt.* make into, or cover with, felt —*vi.* become matted like felt —**felt'-tip pen** pen with writing point made of pressed fibers

**fe·male** (FEE-mayl) *adj.* of sex that bears offspring; relating to this sex —*n.* one of this sex

**fem·i·nine** (FEM-ə-nin) *adj.* of women; womanly; class or type of grammatical inflection in some languages —**fem'i·nism** *n.* advocacy of equal rights for women —**fem'i·nist** *n./adj.* —**fem·i·nin'i·ty** *n.*

**fem·o·ral** (FEM-ər-əl) *adj.* of the thigh

**fe·mur** (FEE-mər) *n.* thigh bone

**fen** *n.* tract of marshy land, swamp

**fence** (fens) *n.* structure of wire, wood *etc.* enclosing an area; (machinery) guard, guide; *sl.* dealer in stolen property —*v.* (fenced, fenc·ing) erect fence; enclose; fight (as sport) with swords; avoid question *etc.*; *sl.* deal in stolen property —**fencing** *n.* art of swordplay

**fend** *vt.* ward off, repel —*vi.* provide (for oneself *etc.*) —**fend'er** *n.* low metal frame in front of fireplace; name for various protective devices; frame; edge; buffer; mudguard of car —**fender bender** *inf.* collision between automobiles causing minor damage

**fen·es·tra·tion** (fen-ə-STRAY-shən) *n.* arrangement of windows in a building; (in medicine) perforation in a structure; operation to create this

**fe·ral**[1] (FER-əl) *adj.* wild, uncultivated

**feral**[2] *adj.* funereal, gloomy; causing death

**fer·ment** (FUR-ment) *n.* leaven, substance causing thing to ferment; excitement, tumult —*v.* (fər-MENT) (cause to) undergo chemical change with effervescence, liberation of heat and alteration of properties, *eg* process set up in dough by yeast; (cause to) become excited —**fer·men·ta'tion** (fur-) *n.*

**fern** (furn) *n.* plant with feathery fronds

**fe·ro·cious** (fə-ROH-shəs) *adj.* fierce, savage, cruel —**fe·roc'i·ty** (-ROS-i-tee) *n.*

**fer·ret** (FER-it) *n.* tamed animal like weasel, used to catch rabbits, rats *etc.* —*vt.* drive out with ferrets; search out —*vi.* search about, rummage

**fer·ric** (FER-ik), **fer·rous** (FER-əs) *adj.* pert. to, containing, iron —**fer·ru·gi·nous** (fə-ROO-jə-nəs) *adj.* containing iron; reddish-brown —**fer·ro·con'crete** *n.* reinforced concrete (strengthened by framework of metal)

**Fer·ris wheel** (FER-is) in amusement park, large, vertical wheel with seats for riding

**fer·rule** (FER-əl) *n.* metal cap to strengthen end of stick *etc.*

**fer·ry** (FER-ee) *n.* (*pl.* -ries) boat *etc.* for transporting people, vehicles, across body of water, *esp.* as repeated or regular service —*v.* (-ried, -ry·ing) carry, travel, by ferry; deliver (airplanes *etc.*) by air

**fer·tile** (FUR-tl) *adj.* (capable of) producing offspring, bearing crops *etc.*; fruitful, producing abundantly; inventive —**fer·til·i·ty** (fər-TIL-ĭ-tee) *n.* —**fer·ti·li·za'tion** *n.* —**fer'ti·lize** *vt.* (-lized, -liz·ing) make fertile —**fer'ti·liz·er** *n.*

**fer·vent** (FUR-vənt), **fer·vid** (-vid) *adj.* ardent, vehement, intense —**fer'ven·cy** *n.* —**fer'vent·ly** *adv.* —**fer'vor** (-vər) *n.*

**fes·cue** (FES-kyoo) *n.* grass for pasture or lawns, with stiff narrow leaves

**fes·tal** (FES-tl) *adj.* of feast or holiday; merry, gay

**fes·ter** (FES-tər) *v.* (cause to) form pus —*vi.* rankle; become embittered

**fes·ti·val** (FES-tə-vəl) *n.* day, period set aside for celebration, *esp.* of religious feast; organized series of events, performances *etc.* *usu.* in one place —**fes·tive** (-tiv) *adj.* joyous, merry; of feast —**fes·tiv'i·ty** *n.* gaiety, mirth; rejoicing —*pl.* (-ties) festive proceedings

**fe·stoon'** *n.* chain of flowers, ribbons *etc.* hung in curve between two points —*vt.* form, adorn with festoons

**fetch** (fech) *vt.* go and bring; draw forth; be sold for; attract —*n.* act of fetching —**fetch'ing** *adj.* attractive

**fete** (fayt) *n.* (*pl.* fetes) gala, bazaar *etc.*, *esp.* one held out of doors; festival, holiday, celebration —*vt.* (fet·ed, fet·ing) feast; honor with festive entertainment

**fet'id** *adj.* stinking

**fet'ish** *n.* (inanimate) object believed to have magical powers;

excessive attention to something; object, activity, to which excessive devotion is paid —**fet'ish·ism**, **fet'ish·ist** *n.*

**fet·lock** (FET-lok) *n.* projection behind and above horse's hoof, or tuft of hair on this

**fet·ter** (FET-ər) *n.* chain or shackle for feet; check, restraint —*pl.* captivity —*vt.* chain up; restrain, hamper

**fet·tle** (FET-l) *n.* condition, state of health

**fe·tus** (FEE-təs) *n.* (*pl.* -tus·es) fully developed young in womb or egg —**fe·tal** (FEET-l) *adj.*

**feud** (fyood) *n.* bitter, lasting, mutual hostility, *esp.* between two families or tribes; vendetta —*vi.* carry on feud

**feu·dal** (FYOOD-l) *adj.* of, like, medieval social and economic system based on holding land from superior in return for service —**feu'dal·ism** *n.*

**fe·ver** (FEE-vər) *n.* condition of illness with high body temperature; intense nervous excitement —**fe'vered**, **fe'ver·ish** *adj.* having fever; accompanied by, caused by, fever; in a state of restless excitement —**fe'ver·ish·ly** *adv.* —fever pitch very fast pace; intense excitement

**few** (fyoo) *adj.* (-er, -est) not many —*n.* small number —quite a few several

**fey** (fay) *adj.* supernatural, unreal; enchanted

**fez** *n.* (*pl.* fez·zes) red, brimless, orig. Turkish tasseled cap

**fi·an·cé** (fee-ahn-SAY) *n.* man engaged to be married (-cée *fem.*)

**fi·as·co** (fee-AS-koh) *n.* (*pl.* -cos) breakdown, total failure

**fi·at** (FEE-aht) *n.* decree; official permission

**fib** *n.* trivial lie, falsehood —*vt.*

(fibbed, fib·bing) tell fib —fib'·ber n.

**fi·ber** (FI-bər) n. filament forming part of animal or plant tissue; substance that can be spun (eg wool, cotton) —fi'brous adj. made of fiber —fi'ber·board n. building material of compressed plant fibers —fi'ber·glass n. material made of fine glass fibers —fiber optics (with sing. v.) use of bundles of long transparent glass fibers in transmitting light

**fib·u·la** (FIB-yə-lə) n. slender outer bone of lower leg —fib'u·lar adj.

**fick·le** (FIK-əl) adj. changeable, inconstant —fick'le·ness n.

**fic·tion** (FIK-shən) n. prose, literary works of the imagination; invented statement or story —fic'tion·al adj. —fic·ti'tious (-TISH-əs) adj. not genuine; false; imaginary; assumed

**fid·dle** (FID-l) n. violin —v. (-dled, -dling) vi. play fiddle; make idle movements, fidget, trifle —fid'dle·sticks interj. nonsense

**Fi·de·i De·fen·sor** (FEE-dee-ee de-FEN-sor) Lat. defender of the faith

**fi·del·i·ty** (fi-DEL-i-tee) n. (pl. -ties) (conjugal) faithfulness; quality of sound reproduction

**fidg·et** (FIJ-it) vi. move restlessly; be uneasy —n. (oft. pl.) nervous restlessness, restless mood; one who fidgets —fidg'et·y adj.

**fi·du·ci·ar·y** (fi-DOO-shee-er-ee) adj. held, given in trust; relating to trustee —n. trustee

**fief** (feef) n. Hist. land held of a superior in return for service —fief'dom (-dəm) n. estate of a feudal lord; inf. organization etc. owned by controlled by one person

**field** (feeld) n. area of (farming) land; enclosed piece of land; tract of land rich in specified product (eg gold field); players in a game or sport collectively; all competitors but the favorite; battlefield; area over which electric, gravitational, magnetic force can be exerted; sphere of knowledge; range, area of operation —v. Baseball stop and return ball; send player, team, on to field —field'er n. —field day day of outdoor activities; important occasion —field events throwing and jumping events in athletics —field glasses binoculars —field hockey hockey played on field, as distinct from ice hockey —field marshal (in some countries) army officer of highest rank —field'work n. research, practical work, conducted away from the classroom, laboratory etc. —field of view area covered in telescope, camera etc.

**fiend** (feend) n. demon, devil; wicked person; person very fond of or addicted to something eg fresh-air fiend, drug fiend —fiend'ish adj. wicked, difficult, unpleasant

**fierce** (feers) adj. fierc·er, fierc·est) savage, wild, violent; rough; severe; intense —fierce'ly adv. —fierce'ness n.

**fier·y** (FI-ə-ree) adj. (fier·i·er, fier·i·est) consisting of fire; blazing, glowing, flashing; irritable; spirited —fier'i·ness n.

**fi·es·ta** (fee-ES-tə) n. (religious) celebration, carnival

**fife** (fif) n. high-pitched flute —v. play on fife —fif'er n.

**fifteen, fifth, fifty** see FIVE

**fig** n. soft, pear-shaped fruit; tree bearing it

**fight** (fit) v. (fought, fight·ing) contend with in battle or in single combat; maintain against opponent; settle by combat —n.

—**fight'er** *n.* one who fights; prizefighter; *Mil.* aircraft designed for destroying other aircraft —*adj.*

**fig·ment** (FIG-mənt) *n.* invention, purely imaginary thing

**fig·ure** (FIG-yər) *n.* numerical symbol; amount, number; form, shape; bodily shape; appearance, *esp.* conspicuous appearance; space enclosed by lines, or surfaces; diagram, illustration; likeness; image; pattern, movement in dancing, skating, *etc.*; abnormal form of expression for effect in speech, *eg* metaphor —*v.* (-ured, -ur·ing) —*vt.* calculate, estimate; represent by picture or diagram; ornament —*vi.* (*oft.* with in) show, appear, be conspicuous, be included —**fig'ur·a·tive** *adj.* metaphorical; full of figures of speech —**fig'ur·a·tive·ly** *adv.* —**fig·ur·ine'** (-REEN) *n.* statuette —**fig'ure·head** *n.* nominal leader; ornamental figure under bowsprit of ship

**fil·a·ment** (FIL-ə-mənt) *n.* fine wire in electric light bulb and vacuum tube that is heated by electric current; threadlike body

**filch** *vt.* steal, pilfer

**file**[1] (fil) *n.* box, folder, clip *etc.* holding papers for reference; papers so kept; information about specific person, subject; orderly line, as of soldiers, one behind the other —*v.* (**filed, fil·ing**) —*vt.* arrange (papers *etc.*) and put them away for reference; transmit (*eg* tax return); *Law* place on records of a court; bring suit in law court —*vi.* march in file —**filing** *n.* —**single** (*or* **Indian**) **file** single line of people one behind the other

**file**[2] *n.* roughened tool for smoothing or shaping —*vt.* (**filed, fil·ing**) apply file to, smooth, polish —**fil·**

**ing** *n.* action of using file; scrap of metal removed by file

**filet** *see* FILLET

**fil·i·al** (FIL-ee-əl) *adj.* of, befitting, son or daughter

**fil·i·bus·ter** (FIL-ə-bus-tər) *n.* process of obstructing legislation by using delaying tactics —*vi.*

**fil·i·gree** (FIL-i-gree) *n.* fine tracery or openwork of metal, usu. gold or silver wire

**fill** *vt.* make full; occupy completely; hold, discharge duties of; stop up; satisfy; fulfill —*vi.* become full —*n.* full supply; as much as desired; soil *etc.*, to bring area of ground up to required level —**fill'ing** *n.* —**filling station** business selling oil, gasoline *etc.* —**fill the bill** *inf.* supply all that is wanted

**fil·let** (fi-LAY) *n.* boneless slice of meat, fish; narrow strip —*vt.* cut into fillets, bone

**fil·lip** (FIL-əp) *n.* stimulus; sudden release of finger bent against thumb; snap so produced

**fil·ly** (FIL-ee) *n.* (*pl.* **-lies**) young female horse; *inf.* girl, young woman

**film** *n.* sequence of images projected on screen, creating illusion of movement; story *etc.* presented thus, and shown in movie theater or on TV; sensitized celluloid roll used in photography, cinematography; thin skin or layer; dimness on eyes; slight haze —*adj.* connected with movies —*vt.* photograph with movie camera; make movie of (scene, story *etc.*) —*v.* cover, become covered, with film —**film'y** *adj.* (**film·i·er, film·i·est**) membranous; gauzy —**film star** popular movie actor or actress

**fil·ter** (FIL-tər) *n.* cloth or other material, or a device, permitting fluid to pass but retaining solid particles; anything performing similar function —vt. act as filter, or as if passing through filter —vi. pass slowly (through) —**fil·trate** (FIL-trayt) n. filtered gas or liquid —**fil·tra·tion** n.

**filth** n. disgusting dirt; pollution; obscenity —**filth'i·ly** adv. —**filth'i·ness** n. —**filth'y** adj. (**filth·i·er**, **filth·i·est**) unclean; foul

**fin** n. propelling or steering organ of fish; anything like this, eg stabilizing surface of airplane; sl. five-dollar bill

**fi·nal** (FIN-l) adj. at the end; conclusive —n. game, heat, examination etc., coming at end of series or school term —**fi·na·le** (fi-NAL-ee) n. closing part of musical composition, opera etc.; termination —**fi·nal·i·ty** (fi-NAL-i-tee) n. —**fi'na·lize** v. (-**lized**, -**liz·ing**) —**fi'nal·ly** adv.

**fi·nance** (fi-NANS) n. management of money; pl. money resources —vt. (-**nanced**, -**nanc·ing**) find capital for —**fi·nan'cial** (-shəl) adj. of finance —**fin·an·ci·er'** (-SEER) n.

**finch** n. one of family of small songbirds

**find** (find) vt. (**found**, **find·ing**) come across; light upon; obtain; recognize; experience; discover; find by searching; ascertain; supply (as funds); Law give a verdict —n. finding; (valuable) thing found —**find'er** n. —**find·ing** n. judicial verdict

**fine**[1] (fin) adj. (**fin·er**, **fin·est**) choice, of high quality; delicate; subtle; pure; in small particles; slender; excellent; handsome; showy; inf. healthy, at ease, comfortable; free of rain —vt. (**fined**, **fin·ing**) make clear or pure; refine; thin —**fine'ly** adv. —**fine'ness** n. —**fin'er·y** n. (pl. -**er·ies**) showy dress —**fi·nesse** (fi-NES) n.

elegant, skillful management —**fine art** art produced for its aesthetic value —**fine-tune** v.t. make fine adjustments to for optimum performance

**fine**[2] n. sum fixed as penalty —vt. (**fined**, **fin·ing**) punish by fine —**in fine** in conclusion; in brief

**fin·ger** (FING-gər) n. one of the jointed branches of the hand; various things like this —vt. touch or handle with fingers; sl. inform against (a criminal) —**fin'ger·ing** n. manner or act of touching; choice of fingers, as in playing musical instrument; indication of this —**fin'ger·board** n. part of violin etc. against which fingers are placed —**fin'ger·print** n. impression of tip of finger, esp. as used for identifying criminals

**fin·i·al** (FIN-ee-əl) n. ornament at apex of gable, spire, furniture etc.

**fin·ick·y** (FIN-i-kee) adj. (-**ick·i·er**, -**ick·i·est**) fastidious, fussy; too fine

**fin'is** Lat. end, esp. of book

**fin'ish** v. (mainly tr.) bring, come to an end, conclude; complete; perfect; kill —n. end; way in which thing is finished, as oak finish, of furniture; final appearance

**fi·nite** (FĪ-nīt) adj. bounded, limited

**fiord** see FJORD

**fir** (fur) n. kind of coniferous resinous tree; its wood

**fire** (fir) n. state of burning, combustion, flame, glow; mass of burning fuel; destructive burning, conflagration; burning fuel for heating a room etc.; ardor, keenness, spirit; shooting of firearms —v. (**fired**, **fir·ing**) —vt. discharge (firearm); propel from firearm; inf. dismiss from employment; bake; make burn; supply with fuel; inspire; explode —*vi.* discharge firearm; begin to burn; become excited —**fire´arm** *n.* gun, rifle, pistol *etc.* —**fire´-brand** *n.* burning piece of wood; energetic (troublesome) person —**fire´break** (-brayk) *n.* strip of cleared land to arrest progress of forest or grass fire —**fire´bug** *n. inf.* person who practices arson —**fire department** organized body of personnel and equipment to put out fires and rescue those in danger —**fire drill** rehearsal of procedures for escape from fire —**fire engine** vehicle with apparatus for extinguishing fires —**fire escape** means, *esp.* metal stairs, for escaping from burning buildings —**fire´fight·er** *n.* member of fire department; person employed to fight forest fires —**fire´fly** *n.* (*pl.* -flies) insect giving off phosphorescent glow —**fire´guard, fire screen** protective grating in front of fire —**fire irons** tongs, poker and shovel —**fire´man** firefighter; stoker; assistant to locomotive driver —**fire´place** *n.* recess in room for fire —**fire house** building housing fire department equipment and personnel —**fire´work** *n.* (*oft. pl.*) device to give spectacular effects by explosions and colored sparks —*pl.* outburst of temper, anger —**firing squad** detachment sent to fire volleys at military funeral, or to execute criminal

**fir·kin** (FUR-kin) *n.* small cask

**firm** (furm) *adj.* (-er, -est) solid, fixed, stable; steadfast; resolute; settled —*v.* make, become firm —*n.* commercial enterprise; partnership

**fir·ma·ment** (FUR-mə-mənt) *n.* expanse of sky, heavens

**first** (furst) *adj.* earliest in time or order; foremost in rank or posi-

tion; most excellent; highest, chief —*n.* beginning; first occurrence of something; *Baseball* first base —*adv.* before others in time, order *etc.* —**first´ly** *adv.* —**first aid** help given to injured person before arrival of doctor —**first-hand** *adj.* obtained directly from the first source —**first mate, first officer** officer of merchant vessel immediately below captain —**first-rate** *adj.* of highest class or quality —**first-strike** *adj.* (of a nuclear missile) for use in an opening attack to destroy enemy nuclear weapons

**fis·cal** (FIS-kəl) *adj.* of (government) finances

**fish** *n.* (*pl.* **fish, fish·es**) vertebrate cold-blooded animal with gills, living in water; its flesh as food —*v.* (attempt to) catch fish; search (for); try to get information indirectly —**fish´er** *n.* —**fish´er·y** *n.* (*pl.* -er·ies) business of fishing; fishing ground —**fish´y** *adj.* (fish·i·er, fish·i·est) of, like, or full of fish; dubious, open to suspicion; unsafe —**fish´er·man** *n.* one who catches fish for a living or for pleasure —**fish´plate** *n.* piece of metal holding wooden beams *etc.* together —**fish stick** small piece of fish covered in breadcrumbs

**fis·sure** (FISH-ər) *n.* cleft, split, cleavage —**fis´sile** (-əl) *adj.* capable of splitting; tending to split —**fis·sion** (FISH-ən) *n.* splitting; reproduction by division of living cells with two parts, each of which becomes complete organism; splitting of atomic nucleus with release of large amount of energy —**fis´sion·a·ble** *adj.* capable of undergoing nuclear fission —**fis·sip·a·rous** (fi-SIP-ər-əs) *adj.* reproducing by fission

**fist** n. clenched hand —**fist′i·cuffs** n. pl. fighting

**fis·tu·la** (FIS-chuu-lə) n. (pl. -las) pipelike ulcer

**fit**[1] v. (fit·ted or fit, fit·ting) —vt. be suited to; be properly adjusted to; arrange, adjust, apply, insert; supply, furnish —vi. be correctly adjusted or adapted; be of right size —adj. (fit·ter, fit·test) well-suited, worthy; qualified; proper, becoming; ready; in good condition or health —n. way anything fits, its style; adjustment —fit′ly adv. —fit′ment n. piece of equipment —fit′ness n. —fit·ter n. one who, that which, makes fit; one who supervises making and fitting of garments; mechanic skilled in fitting up metal work —fitting adj. appropriate, suitable; proper —n. fixture; apparatus; action of fitting

**fit**[2] n. seizure with convulsions, spasms, loss of consciousness etc., as of epilepsy, hysteria etc.; sudden passing attack of illness; passing state, mood —fit′ful adj. spasmodic, capricious —fit′ful·ly adv.

**five** (fiv) adj./n. cardinal number after four —fifth adj./n. ordinal number —fif′th·ly adv. —fif′teen adj./n. ten plus five —fif′teenth adj./n. —fif·ti·eth adj./n. —fif′ty adj./n. (pl. -ties) five tens —fifth column organization spying for enemy within country at war

**fix** (fiks) vt. fasten, make firm or stable; set, establish; appoint, assign, determine; make fast; repair; inf. influence the outcome of unfairly or by deception; bribe; sl. treat someone vengefully —vi. become firm or solidified; determine —n. difficult situation; position of ship, aircraft ascertained by radar, observation etc.; sl. dose of narcotic drug —fix·a′tion n. act of fixing; preoccupation, obsession; situation of being set in some way of acting or thinking —fix′a·tive adj. capable of, or tending to fix —n. —fix′ed·ly (-sid-lee) adv. intently —fix′ture (-chər) n. thing fixed in position; thing attached to house; sporting event that takes place regularly; person long-established in a place —fix up arrange —fix (someone) up attend to person's needs; esp. arrange date

**fizz** vi. hiss, splutter —n. hissing noise; effervescent liquid as soda water, champagne —fiz′zle (-əl) vi. (-zled, -zling) splutter weakly —n. fizzling noise; fiasco —fizzle out inf. come to nothing, fail

**fjord** (fyord) n. (esp. in Norway) long, narrow inlet of sea

**flab·ber·gast** (FLAB-ər-gast) vt. overwhelm with astonishment

**flab·by** (FLAB-ee) adj. (-bi·er, -bi·est) hanging loose, limp; out of condition, too fat; feeble; yielding —flab n. inf. unsightly fat on the body —flab′bi·ness n.

**flac·cid** (FLAK-sid) adj. flabby, lacking firmness —flac·cid′i·ty n.

**flag**[1] n. banner, piece of bunting attached to staff or halyard as standard or signal —vt. (flagged, flag·ging) inform by flag signals —Flag Day June 14 —flag′ship n. admiral's flag; most important ship of fleet —flag′staff n. pole for flag

**flag**[2] n. flat slab of stone —pl. pavement of flags —vt. (flagged, flag·ging) pave with flags —flag′stone n.

**flag**[3] vi. (flagged, flag·ging) droop, fade; lose vigor

**flag·el·late** (FLAJ-ə-layt) vt. (-lat·ed, -lat·ing) scourge, flog —flag′el·lant (-lənt) n. one who scourges self, esp. in religious

penance —**flag·el·la'tion** n.
—**flag'el·la·tor** n.

**flag·eo·let** (flaj-ɔ-LET) n. small
flutelike instrument

**fla·gi·tious** (flɔ-JISH-ɔs) adj.
shamefully wicked; infamous

**flag·on** (FLAG-ɔn) n. large bottle
of wine etc.

**fla·grant** (FLAY-grɔnt) adj. glar-
ing, scandalous, blatant —**fla'-
gran·cy** n.

**flail** (flayl) n. instrument for
threshing grain by hand —v. beat
with, move as, flail

**flair** n. natural ability; elegance

**flak** n. antiaircraft fire; inf. adverse criticism

**flake** (flayk) n. small, thin piece,
esp. particle of snow; piece
chipped off —v. (flaked, flak·ing)
(cause to) peel off in flakes
—**flak'y** adj. (flak·i·er, flak·i·est)
of or like flakes; sl. eccentric
—**flake out** inf. collapse, sleep
from exhaustion

**flam·boy·ant** (flam-BOI-ɔnt) adj.
florid, gorgeous, showy; exuberant, ostentatious

**flame** (flaym) n. burning gas, esp.
above fire; visible burning; passion, esp. love; inf. sweetheart
—vi. (flamed, flam·ing) give out
flames, blaze; shine; burst out

**fla·men·co** (flɔ-MENG-koh) n.
Spanish dance to guitar; music
for this

**fla·min·go** (flɔ-MING-goh) n. (pl.
-gos, -goes) large pink to scarlet
bird with long neck and legs

**flam·ma·ble** (FLAM-ɔ-bɔl) adj.
liable to catch fire, inflammable

**flan** n. open sweet dessert with
caramel topping; tartlike pastry

**flange** (flanj) n. projecting flat
rim, collar, or rib —v. (flanged,
flang·ing) provide with or take
form of flange

**flank** (flangk) n. part of side between hips and ribs; side of any-

thing, eg body of troops —vt.
guard or strengthen on flank;
attack or take in flank; be at,
move along either side of

**flan·nel** (FLAN-l) n. soft woolen
fabric for clothing, esp. trousers
—**flan'nel·mouth** n. person of
slow, thick speech or deceptively
smooth speech

**flap** v. (flapped, flap·ping) move
(wings, arms etc.) as bird flying;
(cause to) sway; strike with flat
object; sl. be agitated, flustered
—n. act of flapping; broad piece
of anything hanging from hinge
or loosely from one side; movable part of aircraft wing; inf.
state of excitement or panic
—**flap'pa·ble** adj. inf. easily confused, esp. under stress

**flare** (flair) vi. (flared, flar·ing)
blaze with unsteady flame; inf.
(with up) burst suddenly into anger; spread outward, as bottom of
skirt —n. instance of flaring; signal light

**flash** n. sudden burst of light or
flame; sudden short blaze; very
short time; brief news item; display —vi. break into sudden
flame; gleam; burst into view;
move very fast; appear suddenly;
sl. expose oneself indecently
—vt. cause to gleam; emit (light
etc.) suddenly —**flash'er** n. thing
that flashes; sl. one who indecently exposes self —**flash'back**
n. break in continuity of book,
play or film, to introduce what
has taken place previously
—**flash'i·er** (flash·i·er, flash·i·
est) showy, sham —**flash point**
temperature at which a vapor
ignites; point at which violence
or anger breaks out

**flask** n. long-necked bottle for
scientific use; metal or glass
pocket bottle

**flat¹** adj. (flat·ter, flat·test) level;

spread out; at full length; smooth; downright; dull, lifeless; *Mus.* below true pitch; (of vehicle tire) deflated, punctured *n.* what is flat; *Mus.* note half tone below natural pitch —**flat′ly** *adv.* —**flat′ness** *n.* —**flat′ten** *vt.* —**flat feet** feet with abnormally flattened arches —**flat′foot** *n. sl.* (*pl.* -foots) police officer —**flat race** horse race over level ground with no jumps —**flat rate** the same price in all cases —**flat out** at, with maximum speed or effort

**flat²** *n.* apartment

**flat·ter** (FLAT-*ə*r) *vt.* fawn on; praise insincerely; inspire unfounded belief; gratify (senses); represent too favorably —**flat′ter·er** *n.* —**flat′ter·y** *n.* (*pl.* -ter·ies)

**flat·u·lent** (FLACH-*ə*-l*ə*nt) *adj.* suffering from, generating (excess) gases in intestines; pretentious —**flat′u·lence** *n.* flatulent condition; verbosity, emptiness

**flaunt** (flawnt) *v.* show off; wave proudly

**flautist** *n.* see FLUTE

**fla·vor** (FLAY-v*ə*r) *n.* mixed sensation of smell and taste; distinctive taste, savor; undefinable characteristic, quality of anything —*vt.* give flavor to; season —**fla′vor·ing** *n.* —**fla′vor·ful** *adj.*

**flaw** *n.* crack; defect, blemish —*vt.* make flaw in —**flaw′less** *adj.* perfect

**flax** (flaks) *n.* plant grown for its textile fiber and seeds; its fibers, spun into linen thread —**flax′en** *adj.* of flax; light yellow or strawcolored

**flay** *vt.* strip skin off; criticize severely

**flea** (flee) *n.* small, wingless, jumping, blood-sucking insect —**flea′bag** *n. sl.* worthless race-

horse, unkempt dog *etc.*; shabby hotel *etc.* —**flea′bite** *n.* insect's bite; trifling injury; trifle —**flea′-bit·ten** *adj.* bitten by flea; mean, worthless; scruffy —**flea market** market, *usu.* held outdoors, for used articles, cheap goods

**fleck** (flek) *n.* small mark, streak, or particle —*vt.* mark with flecks

**fled** *pt./pp.* of FLEE

**fledged** (flejd) *adj.* (of birds) able to fly; experienced, trained —**fledg′ling** *n.* young bird; inexperienced person

**flee** *v.* (fled, flee·ing) run away from

**fleece** (flees) *n.* sheep's wool —*vt.* (fleeced, fleec·ing) rob —**fleec′y** *adj.* (fleec·i·er, fleec·i·est) resembling wool

**fleet¹** *n.* number of warships organized as unit; number of ships, automobiles *etc.* operating together

**fleet²** *adj.* (-er, -est) swift, nimble —**fleet′ing** *adj.* passing, transient —**fleet′ing·ly** *adv.*

**flense** (flens) *vt.* (flensed, flens·ing) strip (*esp.* whale) of flesh

**flesh** *n.* soft part, muscular substance, between skin and bone; in plants, pulp; fat; person's family —**flesh′ly** *adj.* (-li·er, -li·est) carnal, material —**flesh′y** *adj.* (flesh·i·er, flesh·i·est) plump, pulpy —**flesh′pots** *n. pl.* (places catering to) self-indulgent living —in the flesh in person, actually present

**fleur-de-lis** (flur-dl-EE) (*pl.* fleurs-de-lis *pr.* -dl-EEZ) *n.* heraldic lily with three petals

**flew** *pt.* of FLY

**flex** (fleks) *n.* act of flexing —*v.* bend, be bent —**flex·i·bil′i·ty** *n.* —**flex′i·ble** *adj.* easily bent; manageable; adaptable —**flex′time** *n.* system permitting variation in starting and finishing times of work, providing agreed total time is worked over a specified period

**flib·ber·ti·gib·bet** (FLIB-ər-tee-jib-it) n. flighty, chattering person

**flick** (flik) vt. strike lightly, jerk —n. light blow; jerk; sl. motion picture

**flick·er** (FLIK-ər) vi. burn, shine, unsteadily; waver, quiver —n. unsteady light or movement

**flight** (flit) n. act or manner of flying through air; number flying together, as birds; journey in aircraft; air force unit of command; power of flying; swift movement or passage; sally; distance flown; stairs between two landings; running away —**flight recorder** electronic device in aircraft storing information about its flight

**flight·y** (FLI-tee) adj. (flight·i·er, flight·i·est) frivolous, erratic

**flim·sy** (FLIM-zee) adj. (-si·er, -si·est) frail, weak, thin; easily destroyed —**flim'si·ness** n.

**flinch** vi. shrink, draw back, wince

**fling** v. (mainly tr.) (flung, fling·ing) throw, send, move, with force —n. throw; hasty attempt; spell of indulgence; vigorous dance

**flint** n. hard steel-gray stone; piece of this; hard substance used (as flint) for striking fire —**flint'y** adj. (flint·i·er, flint·i·est) like or consisting of flint; hard, cruel

**flip** v. (flipped, flip·ping) throw or flick lightly; turn over; sl. react with astonishment, become irrational —n. instance, act, of flipping; drink with beaten egg —**flip'pan·cy** n. (pl. -cies) —**flip'pant** adj. treating serious things lightly —**flip'per** n. limb, fin for swimming —pl. fin-shaped rubber devices worn on feet to help in swimming

**flirt** (flurt) vi. toy, play with another's affections; trifle, toy (with) —n. person who flirts —**flir·ta'tion** (-TAY-shən) n. —**flir·ta'tious** adj.

**flit** vi. (flit·ted, flit·ting) pass lightly and rapidly; dart; inf. go away hastily, secretly

**flitch** (flich) n. side of bacon

**float** (floht) vi. rest, drift on surface of liquid; be suspended freely; move aimlessly —vt. of liquid, support, bear alone; in commerce, get (company) started; obtain loan —n. anything small that floats (esp. to support something else, eg fishing net); motor vehicle carrying tableau etc., in parade; uncollected checks etc. in process of transfer between banks etc. —**flo·ta'tion** n. act of floating, esp. floating of business venture

**floc·cu·late** (FLOK-yə-layt) vt. (-lat·ed, -lat·ing) form into masses of particles —**floc'cu·lant** (-lənt) n. chemical for accomplishing this

**floc·cu·lent** (FLOK-yə-lənt) adj. like tufts of wool

**flock**[1] (flok) n. number of animals of one kind together; fig. body of people; religious congregation —vi. gather in a crowd

**flock**[2] n. lock, tuft of wool etc.; wool refuse for stuffing cushions etc.

**floe** (floh) n. sheet of floating ice

**flog** vt. (flogged, flog·ging) beat with whip, stick etc.; sl. sell, esp. vigorously

**flood** (flud) n. inundation, overflow of water; rising of tide; outpouring; flowing water —vt. inundate; cover, fill with water; arrive, move etc. in great numbers —**flood'gate** n. gate, sluice for letting water in or out —**flood'light** n. broad, intense beam of artificial light —**flood'lit** adj. —**flood tide** the rising tide

**floor** (flor) n. lower surface of room; set of rooms on one level, story; flat space; (right to speak in) meeting or legislative chamber; lower limit —vt. supply with floor; knock down; confound —**floor'ing** n. material for floors —**floor show** entertainment in nightclub etc.

**flop** vi. (flopped, flop·ping) bend, fall, collapse loosely, carelessly; fall flat on floor, on water etc.; inf. go to sleep; inf. fail —n. flopping movement or sound; inf. failure —**flop'pi·ness** n. —**flop'py** adj. (-pi·er, -pi·est) limp, unsteady —**flop'house** n. run-down rooming house —**floppy disk** Computers flexible magnetic disk that stores information

**flo·ra** (FLOR-ɔ) n. plants of a region; list of them —**flor'al** adj. of flowers —**flo·res'cence** (-ɔns) n. state or time of flowering —**flo·ret** (FLOR-it) n. small flower forming part of composite flower —**flo'ri·cul·ture** n. cultivation of flowers —**flo·ri·cul'tur·ist** n. —**flo'rist** n. dealer in flowers

**flor'id** adj. with red, flushed complexion; ornate

**floss** (flaws) n. mass of fine, silky fibers, eg of cotton, silk; fluff —**floss'y** adj. (floss·i·er, floss·i·est) light and downy; excessively fancy

**flotation** see FLOAT

**flo·til·la** (floh-TIL-ɔ) n. fleet of small vessels, esp. naval vessels

**flot·sam** (FLOT-sɔm) n. floating wreckage; discarded waste objects; penniless population of city etc.

**flounce**[1] (flowns) vi. (flounced, flounc·ing) go, move abruptly and impatiently —n. fling, jerk of body or limb

**flounce**[2] n. ornamental gathered strip on woman's garment

**floun·der**[1] (FLOWN-dɔr) vi. plunge and struggle, esp. in water or mud; proceed in bungling, hesitating manner —n. act of floundering

**flounder**[2] n. type of flatfish

**flour** (FLOW-ɔr) n. powder prepared by sifting and grinding wheat etc.; fine soft powder —vt. sprinkle with flour

**flour·ish** (FLUR-ish) vi. thrive; be in the prime —vt. brandish, display; wave about —n. ornamental curve; showy gesture in speech etc.; waving of hand, weapon etc.; fanfare (of trumpets)

**flout** (flowt) vt. show contempt for, mock; defy

**flow** (floh) vi. glide along as stream; circulate, as the blood; move easily; move in waves; hang loose; be present in abundance —n. act, instance of flowing; quantity that flows; rise of tide; ample supply —**flow chart** diagram showing sequence of operations in industrial etc. process

**flow·er** (FLOW-ɔr) n. colored (not green) part of plant from which fruit is developed; bloom, blossom; ornamentation; choicest part, pick —vi. produce flowers; bloom; come to prime condition —vt. ornament with flowers —**flow'er·et** n. small flower —**flow'er·y** adj. (-er·i·er, -er·i·est) abounding in flowers; full of fine words, ornamented with figures of speech —**flower girl** girl selling flowers; young girl designated to attend bride at wedding ceremony

**flown** pp. of FLY

**flu** n. short for INFLUENZA

**fluc·tu·ate** (FLUK-choo-ayt) v. (-at·ed, -at·ing) vary, rise and fall, undulate —**fluc·tu·a'tion** n.

**flue** (floo) n. passage or pipe for smoke or hot air, chimney

**flu·ent** (FLOO-ənt) adj. speaking, writing a given language easily and well; easy, graceful

**fluff** n. soft, feathery stuff; down; inf. mistake; inf. anything insubstantial —v. make or become soft, light; inf. make mistake —**fluff'y** adj. (fluff·i·er, fluff·i·est)

**flu·id** (FLOO-id) adj. flowing easily, not solid —n. gas or liquid —**flu·id'i·ty** n. —**fluid ounce** unit of capacity 1/16 of pint

**fluke¹** (flook) n. flat triangular point of anchor —pl. whale's tail

**fluke²** n. stroke of luck, accident —**fluk'y** adj. (fluk·i·er, fluk·i·est) uncertain; got by luck

**fluke³** n. type of flatfish; parasitic worm

**flume** (floom) n. narrow (artificial) channel for water

**flum·mer·y** (FLUM-ə-ree) n. (pl. -mer·ies) nonsense, idle talk, humbug; dish of milk, flour, eggs etc.

**flum·mox** (FLUM-əks) vt. inf. bewilder, perplex

**flung** prf./pp. of FLING

**flun·ky** (FLUNG-kee) n. (pl. -kies) servant, esp. liveried man-servant; assistant doing menial work; servile person

**fluo·res·cence** (fluu-RES-əns) n. emission of light or other radiation from substance when bombarded by particles (electrons etc.) or other radiation, as in fluorescent lamp —**fluo·res'cent** adj.

**flur·ry** (FLUR-ee) n. (pl. -ries) squall, gust; bustle, commotion; fluttering (as of snowflakes) —vt. (-ried, -ry·ing) agitate, bewilder, fluster

**flush¹** vi. blush; of skin, redden; flow suddenly or violently; be excited —vt. cleanse (eg toilet) by rush of water; excite —n. reddening, blush; rush of water; excitement; elation; glow of color; freshness, vigor —adj. full, in flood; well supplied; level with surrounding surface

**flush²** v. (cause to) leave cover and take flight

**flush³** n. set of cards all of one suit

**flus·ter** (FLUS-tər) v. make or become nervous, agitated —n.

**flute** (floot) n. wind instrument of tube with holes stopped by fingers or keys and blowhole in side; groove, channel —v. (flut·ed, flut·ing) —vi. play on flute —vt. make grooves in —**flut'ist, flaut'ist** (FLOWT-) n. flute player

**flut·ter** (FLUT-ər) v. flap (as wings) rapidly without flight or in short flights; quiver; be or make excited, agitated —n. flapping movement; nervous agitation

**flu·vi·al** (FLOO-vee-əl) adj. of rivers

**flux** (fluks) n. discharge; constant succession of changes; substance mixed with metal to clean, aid adhesion in soldering etc.; measure of strength in magnetic field

**fly¹** (flī) v. (flew, flown, fly·ing) move through air on wings or in aircraft; pass quickly (through air); float loosely; spring, rush; flee, run away —vt. operate aircraft; cause to fly; set flying —vi. run from —n. (zipper or buttons fastening) opening in trousers; flap in garment or tent; flying —flying adj. hurried, brief —fly'fish v. fish with artificial fly as lure —flying boat airplane fitted with floats instead of landing wheels —flying buttress

*Architecture* arched or slanting structure attached at only one point to a mass of masonry —**fly•ing colors** conspicuous success —**flying fish** fish with winglike fins used for gliding above the sea —**flying saucer** unidentified (disk-shaped) flying object, supposedly from outer space —**flying squad** special detachment of police *etc.*, ready to act quickly —**fly′leaf** *n.* (*pl.* -**leaves**) blank leaf at beginning or end of book —**fly′o•ver** *n.* formation of aircraft in flight for observation from ground —**fly′wheel** *n.* heavy wheel regulating speed of machine

**fly²** *n.* (*pl.* **flies**) two-winged insect, *esp.* common housefly —**fly′-catch•er** *n.* small insect-eating songbird

**Fm** *Chem.* fermium

**foal** (fohl) *n.* young of horse, ass *etc.* —*v.* bear (foal)

**foam** (fohm) *n.* collection of small bubbles on liquid; froth of saliva or sweat; light cellular solid used for insulation, packing *etc.* —*v.* (cause to) produce foam; be very angry —**foam′y** *adj.* (**foam•i•er, foam•i•est**)

**fob¹** *n.* short watch chain; small pocket in waistband of trousers or vest

**fob off** (**fobbed, fob′bing**) ignore, dismiss someone or something in offhand (insulting) manner; dispose of

**foci** *pl. of* FOCUS

**fo•cus** (FOH-kəs) *n.* (*pl.* -**cus•es,** -**ci** *pr.* -**sī**) point at which rays meet after being reflected or refracted; state of optical image when it is clearly defined; state of instrument producing such image; point of convergence; point on which interest, activity is centered —*v.* (-**cused,** -**cus•ing**) —*vt.*

bring to focus, adjust; concentrate —*vi.* come to focus; converge —**fo′cal** (-kəl) *adj.* of, at focus

**fod•der** (FOD-ər) *n.* bulk food for livestock

**foe** (foh) *n.* enemy

**fog** *n.* thick mist; dense watery vapor in lower atmosphere; cloud of anything reducing visibility; stupor —*vt.* (**fogged, fog′ging**) cover in fog; puzzle —**fog′gy** *adj.* (-**gi•er, -gi•est**) —**fog′horn** *n.* instrument to warn ships in fog

**fo•gy** (FOH-gee) *n.* (*pl.* -**gies**) old-fashioned person

**foi•ble** (FOI-bəl) *n.* minor weakness, idiosyncrasy

**foil¹** *vt.* baffle, defeat, frustrate —*n.* blunt sword, with button on point for fencing

**foil²** *n.* metal in thin sheet; anything or person that sets off another to advantage

**foist** *vt.* (*usu. with* on *or* upon) sell, pass off inferior or unwanted thing as valuable

**fold¹** (fohld) *vt.* double up, bend part of; interlace (arms); wrap up; clasp (in arms); *Cooking* mix gently —*vi.* become folded; admit of being folded; *inf.* fail —*n.* folding; coil; winding; line made by folding; crease; foldlike geological formation —**fold′er** *n.* binder, file for loose papers

**fold²** *n.* enclosure for sheep; body of believers; church

**fo•li•age** (FOH-lee-ij) *n.* leaves collectively, leafage —**fo•li•a′ceous** (-AY-shəs) *adj.* of or like leaf —**fo′li•ate** (-it) *adj.* leaflike, having leaves

**fo•li•o** (FOH-lee-oh) *n.* (*pl.* -**li•os**) sheet of paper folded in half to make two leaves of book; book of largest common size made up of such sheets; page numbered on one side only; page number

**folk** (fohk) *n.* people in general; family, relatives; race of people —**folk dance** —**folk′lore** *n.* tradition, customs, beliefs popularly held —**folk song** music originating among a people

**fol·li·cle** (FOL-i-kəl) *n.* small cavity, sac; seed vessel

**fol·low** (FOL-oh) *v.* go or come after —*vt.* accompany, attend on; keep to (path *etc.*); take as guide, conform to; engage in; have a keen interest in; be consequent on; grasp meaning of —*vi.* come next; result —**fol′low·er** *n.* disciple, supporter —**fol′low·ing** *adj.* about to be mentioned —*n.* body of supporters —**fol′low-through** *n.* in ball games, continuation of stroke after impact with ball —**fol′low-up** *n.* something done to reinforce initial action

**fol·ly** (FOL-ee) *n.* (*pl.* **-lies**) foolishness; foolish action, idea *etc.*; useless, extravagant structure

**fo·ment** (foh-MENT) *vt.* foster, stir up; bathe with warm lotions

**fond** *adj.* (**-er**, **-est**) tender, loving —**fond′ly** *adv.* —**fond′ness** *n.* —**fond** of having liking for

**fon·dant** (FON-dənt) *n.* soft sugar mixture for candies; candy made of this

**fon·dle** (FON-dl) *vt.* (**-dled**, **-dling**) caress

**fon·due** (fon-DOO) *n.* Swiss dish of cheese and seasonings into which pieces of bread *etc.* are dipped

**font** *n.* bowl for baptismal water usu. on pedestal; productive source; assortment of printing type of one size

**fon·ta·nel** (fon-tn-EL) *n.* soft, membraneous gap between bones of baby's skull

**food** *n.* solid nourishment; what

one eats; mental or spiritual nourishment —**food additive** natural or synthetic substance added to commercially processed food as preservative or to add color, flavor *etc.* —**food processor** electric kitchen appliance for automatic chopping, blending *etc.* of foodstuffs —**food′stuff** *n.* food

**fool** *n.* silly, empty-headed person; dupe; simpleton; *Hist.* jester, clown —*vt.* delude; dupe —*vi.* act as fool —**fool′er·y** *n.* (*pl.* **-er·ies**) habitual folly; act of playing the fool; absurdity —**fool′har·di·ness** *n.* —**fool′har·dy** *adj.* (**-di·er**, **-di·est**) foolishly adventurous —**fool′ish** *adj.* ill-considered, silly, stupid —**fool′proof** *adj.* proof against failure —**fool's cap** jester's or dunce's cap —**fools′cap** *n.* inexpensive paper *esp.* legal-size (formerly with fool's cap as watermark)

**foot** (fuut) *n.* (*pl.* **feet**) lowest part of leg, from ankle down; lowest part of anything, base, stand; end of bed *etc.*; measure of twelve inches; division of line of verse —*v.* (*usu.* **foot·**) dance; walk (*esp.* **foot it**); pay cost of (*esp.* in **foot the bill**) —**foot′age** *n.* length in feet; length, extent, of film used —**foot′ing** *n.* basis, foundation; firm standing, relations, conditions —*pl.* (*concrete*) foundations for walls of buildings —**foot′-and-mouth′ disease** infectious viral disease in sheep, cattle *etc.* —**foot′ball** *n.* game played with inflated oval ball; the ball —**foot′ball pool** form of gambling on results of football games —**foot brake** brake operated by pressure on foot pedal —**foot fault** *Tennis* fault of overstepping baseline while serving —**foot′hold** *n.* place affording secure grip for the foot; secure position from which progress may be made —**foot′lights** n. pl. lights across front of stage —**foot′loose** adj. free of any ties —**foot′note** n. note of reference or explanation printed at foot of page —**foot′pound** n. unit of measurement of work in fps system —**foot′print** n. mark left by foot —playing foot′sie flirting or sharing a surreptitious intimacy —**foot′slog** vt. (-slogged, slogging) walk, go on foot —**foot′slog·ger** n.

**fop** n. man excessively concerned with fashion —**fop′per·y** n. (pl. -per·ies) —**fop′pish** adj.

**for** prep. intended to reach, directed or belonging to; because of; instead of; toward; on account of; in favor of; respecting; during; in search of; in payment of; in the character of; in spite of —conj. because —**in for it** inf. liable for punishment or blame

**for-** (prefix) from, away, against, as in forswear, forbid Such words are not given here where the meaning can easily be inferred from the simple word

**for·age** (FOR-ij) n. food for cattle and horses —vi. (-aged, -ag·ing) collect forage; make roving search

**for′ay** n. raid, inroad —vi. make one

**for·bear** (for-BAIR) v. (-bore, -borne, -bear·ing) (esp. with from) cease; refrain (from); be patient pp.) —**for·bear′ance** n. self-control, patience

**for·bid** (for-BID) vt. (-bade or -bad or -bid, -bid·den or -bid, -bid·ding) prohibit; refuse to allow —**forbidding** adj. uninviting, threatening

**force** (fors) n. strength, power; compulsion; that which tends to produce a change in a physical system; mental or moral strength; body of troops, police etc.; group of people organized for particular task or duty; effectiveness, operative state; violence —vt. (forced, forc·ing) constrain, compel; produce by effort, strength; break open; urge, strain; drive; hasten maturity of —**forced** adj. accomplished by great effort, compulsory; unnatural; strained; excessive —**force′ful** adj. powerful, persuasive —**for′ci·ble** adj. done by force; efficacious, compelling, impressive; strong —**for′ci·bly** adv.

**for·ceps** (FOR-səps) n. pl. surgical pincers

**ford** n. shallow place where river may be crossed —vt. —**ford′a·ble** adj.

**fore**[1] (for) adj. in front —n. front part

**fore**[2] interj. golfer's warning

**fore-** (prefix) previous, before, front

**fore-and-aft** (FOR-ənd-AFT) adj. placed in line from bow to stern of ship

**fore·arm** (FOR-ahrm) n. arm between wrist and elbow —vt. (for-AHRM) arm beforehand

**fore·bear** (FOR-bair) n. ancestor

**fore·bode** (for-BOHD) vt. (-bod·ed, -bod·ing) indicate in advance —**foreboding** n. anticipation of evil

**fore·cast** (FOR-kast) vt. estimate beforehand (esp. weather); prophesy —**prediction**

**fore·castle** (FOHK-səl) n. forward raised part of ship; sailors' quarters

**fore·close** (for-KLOHZ) vt. (-closed, -clos·ing) take away power of redeeming (mortgage); prevent, shut out, bar —**fore·clo′sure** (-zhər) n.

**fore·court** (FOR-kort) n. courtyard, open space, in front of building; *Tennis* part of court between service line and net

**fore·fa·ther** (FOR-fah-*th*ər) *n.* ancestor

**fore·fin·ger** (FOR-fing-gər) *n.* finger next to thumb, index finger

**foregather** *see* FORGATHER

**fore·go** (for-GOH) *vt.* (-went, -gone, -go·ing) precede in time, place —**foregoing** *adj.* going before, preceding —**foregone** *adj.* determined beforehand; preceding —**foregone** conclusion result that might have been foreseen

**fore·ground** (FOR-grownd) *n.* part of view, *esp.* in picture, nearest observer

**fore·hand** (FOR-hand) *adj.* of stroke in racquet games made with inner side of wrist leading

**fore·head** (FOR-id) *n.* part of face above eyebrows and between temples

**for·eign** (FOR-in) *adj.* not of, or in, one's own country; relating to, or connected with other countries; irrelevant; coming from outside; unfamiliar, strange —**for'eign·er** *n.*

**fore·man** (FOR-mən) *n.* (*pl.* -men) one in charge of work; leader of jury

**fore·mast** (FOR-mast) *n.* mast nearest bow

**fore·most** (FOR-mohst) *adj./adv.* first in time, place, importance *etc.*

**fore·noon** (FOR-noon) *n.* morning

**fo·ren·sic** (fə-REN-sik) *adj.* of courts of law —**forensic** medicine application of medical knowledge in legal matters

**fore·play** (FOR-play) *n.* sexual stimulation before intercourse

**fore·run·ner** (FOR-run-ər) *n.* one that goes before, precursor

**fore·see** (for-SEE) *vt.* (-saw, -seen, -see·ing) see beforehand

**fore·shad·ow** (for-SHAD-oh) *vt.* show, suggest beforehand, be a type of

**fore·short·en** (for-SHOR-tn) *vt.* draw (object) so that it appears shortened; make shorter

**fore·sight** (FOR-sīt) *n.* foreseeing; care for future

**fore·skin** (FOR-skin) *n.* skin that covers end of penis

**for·est** (FOR-ist) *n.* area with heavy growth of trees and plants; these trees; *fig.* something resembling forest —*vt.* plant, create forest (in an area) —**for'est·er** *n.* one skilled in forestry —**for'est·ry** *n.* study, management of forest planting and maintenance

**fore·stall** (for-STAWL) *vt.* anticipate; prevent, guard against in advance

**fore·taste** (FOR-tayst) *n.* anticipation; taste beforehand

**fore·tell** (for-TEL) *vt.* (-told, -tel·ling) prophesy

**fore·thought** (FOR-thawt) *n.* thoughtful consideration of future events

**for·ev·er** (for-EV-ər) *adv.* always; eternally; *inf.* for a long time

**fore·warn** (for-WORN) *vt.* warn, caution in advance

**forewent** *see* FOREGO

**fore·word** (FOR-wurd) *n.* preface

**for·feit** (FOR-fit) *n.* thing lost by crime or fault; penalty, fine —*adj.* lost by crime or fault —*vt.* lose by penalty —**for'fei·ture** (-fi-chər) *n.*

**for·gath·er** (for-GA*TH*-ər) *vt.* meet together, assemble, associate

**forge**[1] (forj) *n.* place where metal is worked, smithy; furnace, workshop for melting or refining metal —*vt.* (forged, forg·ing) shape (metal) by heating in fire and hammering; make, shape, invent; make a fraudulent imitation of thing; counterfeit —**forg′er** *n.* —**for′ger•y** *n.* (*pl.* -ger•ies) forged artwork, document, currency *etc.*; the making of it

**forge²** *vi.* (forged, forg•ing) advance steadily

**for•get** (fɔr-GET) *vt.* (-got, -got•ten *or* -got, -get•ting) lose memory of, neglect, overlook —**for•get′ful** *adj.* liable to forget

**for•give** (fɔr-GIV) *v.* (-gave, -giv•en, -giv•ing) cease to blame or hold resentment against; pardon —**for•give′ness** *n.*

**for•go** (for-GOH) *vt.* (-went, -gone, -go•ing) go without; give up

**forgot, forgotten** *see* FORGET

**fork** *n.* pronged instrument for eating food; pronged tool for digging or lifting; division into branches; point of this division; one of the branches —*vi.* branch —*vt.* dig, lift, throw, work with fork; make fork-shaped —**fork out** *or* **over** *inf.* pay (reluctantly)

**for•lorn′** *adj.* forsaken; desperate —**forlorn hope** anything undertaken with little hope of success

**form** *n.* shape, visible appearance; visible person or animal; structure; nature; species, kind; regularly drawn up document, *esp.* printed one with blanks for particulars; condition, good condition; customary way of doing things; set order of words; *Printing* frame for type —*vt.* shape, mold, arrange, organize; train, shape in the mind, conceive; go to make up, make part of —*vi.* come into existence or shape —**for•ma′tion** *n.* forming; thing formed; structure, shape, arrangement; military order —**form′a•tive** *adj.* of, relating to,

development; serving or tending to form; used in forming —**form′-less** *adj.*

**for•mal** (FOR-mɔl) *adj.* ceremonial, according to rule; of outward form or routine; of, for, formal occasions; according to rule that does not matter; precise; stiff —*n.* formal dance —**for′mal•ism** *n.* quality of being formal; exclusive concern for form, structure, technique in an activity, *eg* art —**for•mal′i•ty** *n.* (*pl.* -ties) observance required by custom or etiquette; condition or quality of being formal; conformity to custom; conventionality, mere form; in art, precision, stiffness, as opposed to originality

**for•mal•de•hyde** (for-MAL-dɔ-hid) *n.* colorless, poisonous, pungent gas, used in making antiseptics and in chemistry —**for′ma•lin** (-mɔ-lin) *n.* solution of formaldehyde in water, used as disinfectant, preservative *etc.*

**for′mat** *n.* size and shape of book; organization of TV show *etc.*

**for•mer** (FOR-mɔr) *adj.* earlier in time; of past times; first named —*pron.* first named thing or person or fact —**for′mer•ly** *adv.* previously

**for•mi•da•ble** (FOR-mi-dɔ-bɔl) *adj.* to be feared; overwhelming, terrible, redoubtable; likely to be difficult, serious —**for′mi•da•bly** *adv.*

**for•mu•la** (FOR-myɔ-lɔ) *n.* (*pl.* -las, -lae *pr.* -lee) set form of words setting forth principle, method or rule for doing, producing something; substance so prepared; specific category of racing car; recipe; *Science, Math.* rule, fact expressed in symbols and figures —**for′mu•late** (-layt) *vt.* (-lat•ed, -lat•ing) reduce to, express in formula, or in definite form; devise —**for·mu·la'tion** n.

**for·ni·ca·tion** (for-ni-KAY-shən) n. sexual intercourse outside marriage —**for'ni·cate** vi. (-cat·ed, -cat·ing)

**for·sake** (for-SAYK) vt. (-sook, -sak·en, -sak·ing) abandon, desert; give up

**for·sooth'** adv. obs. in truth

**for·swear** (for-SWAIR) vt. (-swore, -sworn, -swear·ing) renounce, deny —refl. perjure

**for·syth·i·a** (for-SITH-ee-ə) n. widely cultivated shrub with yellow flowers

**fort** n. fortified place, stronghold

**forte[1]** (fort) n. one's strong point, that in which one excels

**for·te[2]** (FOR-tay) adv. Mus. loudly —**for·tis'si·mo** sup.

**forth** adv. onward, into view —**forth·com'ing** adj. about to come; ready when wanted; willing to talk, communicative —**forth·with'** adv. at once, immediately

**forth·right** (FORTH-rīt) adj. direct; outspoken

**for·ti·eth** see FOUR

**for·ti·fy** (FOR-tə-fī) vt. (-fied, -fy·ing) strengthen; provide with defensive works —**for·ti·fi·ca'·tion** n.

**for·ti·tude** (FOR-ti-tood) n. courage in adversity or pain, endurance

**fort·night** (FORT-nīt) n. two weeks —**fort'night·ly** adv.

**FORTRAN** (FOR-tran) Computers a programming language for mathematical and scientific purposes

**for·tress** (FOR-tris) n. fortified place, eg castle, stronghold

**for·tu·i·tous** (for-TOO-i-təs) adj. accidental, by chance —**for·tu'i·tous·ly** adv.

**for·tune** (FOR-chən) n. good luck, prosperity; wealth; stock of wealth; chance, luck —**for'tu·nate** (-nit) adj. —**for'tu·nate·ly** adv. —**fortune hunter** person seeking fortune, esp. by marriage —**fortuneteller** n. one who predicts a person's future

**forty** see FOUR

**fo·rum** (FOR-əm) n. (place or medium for) meeting, assembly for open discussion or debate

**for·ward** (FOR-wərd) adj. lying in front of; onward; presumptuous, impudent; advanced, progressive; relating to the future —n. player placed in forward position in various team games, eg basketball —adv. toward the future; toward the front, to the front, into view; as, in fore part of ship; onward, so as to make progress —vt. help forward; send, dispatch —**for'ward·ly** adv. —**for'ward·ness** n. —**for'wards** (-wərdz) adv.

**forwent** see FORGO

**fos·sil** (FOS-əl) n. remnant or impression of animal or plant, esp. prehistoric one, preserved in earth; inf. person, idea etc. that is outdated and incapable of change —adj. —**fos'sil·ize** v. (-ized, -iz·ing) turn into fossil; petrify

**fos·ter** (FAW-stər) vt. promote growth or development of; bring up child, esp. not one's own —**foster brother** one related by upbringing not blood; thus, —**foster father, mother, parent, child** etc.

**fought** pt./pp. of FIGHT

**foul** (fowl) adj. (-er, -est) loathsome, offensive; stinking; dirty; unfair; wet, rough; obscene, disgustingly abusive; charged with harmful matter, clogged, choked —n. act of unfair play; the breaking of a rule —adv. unfairly —v.

*(mainly tr.)* make, become foul; jam; collide with —**foul'ly** *adv.*

**found**[1] (fownd) *pt./pp. of* FIND

**found**[2] *vt.* establish, institute; lay base of; base, ground —**foun·da'tion** *n.* basis; base, lowest part of building; founding; endowed institution *etc.* —**found'er** *n.* —**foundation stone** one of stones forming foundation of building, *esp.* stone laid with public ceremony

**found**[3] *vt.* melt and run into mold; cast —**found'er** *n.* —**found'ry** *n.* (*pl.* -ries) place for casting; art of this

**found·er** (FOWN-dər) *vi.* collapse; sink; become stuck as in mud *etc.*

**found·ling** (FOWND-ling) *n.* deserted infant

**fount** (fownt) *n.* fountain

**foun·tain** (FOWN-tn) *n.* jet of water, *esp.* ornamental one; spring; source —**foun'tain·head** (-hed) *n.* source —**fountain pen** pen with ink reservoir

**four** (for) *n./adj.* cardinal number next after three —**fourth** *adj.* the ordinal number —**fourth'ly** *adv.* —**for'ti·eth** *adj.* —**for'ty** *n./adj.* (*pl.* -ties) four tens —**four'teen** *n./adj.* four plus ten —**fourteenth'** *adj.* —**four-cycle, four-stroke** *adj.* describing an internal-combustion engine firing once every four strokes of piston —**four'post·er** *n.* bed with four posts for curtains *etc.* —**four'some** *n.* group of four people; game or dance for four people —*adj.* —**four'square** *adj.* firm, steady —**on all fours** on hands and knees

**fowl** *n.* domestic rooster or hen; bird, its flesh —*vi.* hunt wild birds —**fowling piece** shotgun for fowling

**fox** (foks) *n.* red bushy-tailed animal; its fur; cunning person —*vt.* perplex; discolor (paper) with brown spots; mislead —*vi.* act craftily; sham —**fox'y** *adj.* (**fox·i·er, fox·i·est**) foxlike; *sl.* sexually appealing; attractive —**fox'hole** *n.* in war, small trench giving protection —**fox'hound** *n.* dog bred for hunting foxes —**fox terrier** small dog now mainly kept as a pet —**fox'trot** *n.* (music for) ballroom dance —*v.*

**foy·er** (FOI-ər) *n.* entrance hall in theaters, hotels *etc.*; vestibule

**Fr** *Chem.* francium

**fra·cas** (FRAY-kəs) *n.* noisy quarrel; uproar, brawl

**frac·tion** (FRAK-shən) *n.* numerical quantity not an integer; fragment, piece —**frac'tion·al** *adj.* constituting a fraction; forming but a small part; insignificant

**frac·tious** (FRAK-shəs) *adj.* unruly, irritable

**frac·ture** (FRAK-chər) *n.* breakage, part broken; breaking of bone; breach, rupture —*v.* (-tured, -tur·ing) break

**frag·ile** (FRAJ-əl) *adj.* breakable; frail; delicate —**fra·gil'i·ty** *n.*

**frag·ment** (FRAG-mənt) *n.* piece broken off; small portion, incomplete part —*v.* (-ment) —**frag'men·tar·y** (-te-ree) *adj.*

**fra·grant** (FRAY-grənt) *adj.* sweet-smelling —**fra'grance** *n.* scent

**frail** (frayl) *adj.* (-er, -est) fragile, delicate; infirm; in weak health; morally weak —**frail'ly** *adv.* —**frail'ty** *n.* (*pl.* -ties)

**frame** (fraym) *n.* that in which thing is set, as square of wood around picture *etc.*; structure; build of body; constitution; mood; individual exposure on strip of film —*vt.* put together, make; adapt; put into words; put into frame; bring false charge against —**frame-up** *n. inf.* plot, manufactured evidence —**frame'work** *n.*

structure into which completing parts can be fitted; supporting work

**franc** (frangk) *n.* monetary unit of France, Switzerland and other countries

**fran·chise** (FRAN-chīz) *n.* right of voting; citizenship; privilege or right, *esp.* right to sell certain goods —*v.* (-chised, -chis·ing)

**fran·gi·pane** (FRAN-jə-payn) *n.* type of pastry cake; its filling

**fran·gi·pan·i** (fran-jə-PAN-ee) *n.* tropical American shrub; perfume made of its flower

**frank** (frangk) *adj.* (-er, -est) candid, outspoken; sincere —*n.* official mark on letter either canceling stamp or ensuring delivery without stamp —*vt.* mark letter thus —**frank'ly** *adv.* candidly —**frank'ness** *n.*

**frank·furt·er** (FRANGK-fər-tər) *n.* smoked sausage, hot dog

**frank·in·cense** (FRANG-kin-sens) *n.* aromatic gum resin burned as incense

**fran·tic** (FRAN-tik) *adj.* distracted with rage, grief, joy *etc.*; frenzied —**fran'ti·cal·ly** *adv.*

**fra·ter·nal** (frə-TUR-nl) *adj.* of brother, brotherly —**fra·ter'nal·ly** *adv.* —**fra·ter'ni·ty** *n.* (pl. -ties) brotherliness; brotherhood; college society —**frat·er·ni·za'tion** *n.* —**frat'er·nize** *vi.* (-nized, -niz·ing) to associate, make friends —**frat·ri·cid'al** *adj.* —**frat'ri·cide** *n.* killing, killer of brother or sister

**fraud** (frawd) *n.* criminal deception; swindle, imposture —**fraud·u·lence** (FRAW-jə-ləns) *n.* —**fraud'u·lent** *adj.*

**fraught** (frawt) *adj.* filled (with), involving

**fray**[1] *n.* fight; noisy quarrel

**fray**[2] *v.* wear through by rubbing; make, become ragged at edge

**fraz·zle** (FRAZ-əl) *inf. v.* (-zled, -zling) make or become exhausted; make or become irritated —*n.* exhausted state

**freak** (freek) *n.* abnormal person, animal, thing —*adj.* —**freak'ish.** **freak'y** *adj.* (freak·i·er, freak·i·est) —**freak out** *sl.* (cause to) hallucinate, be wildly excited *etc.*

**freck·le** (FREK-əl) *n.* light brown spot on skin, *esp.* caused by sun; any small spot —*v.* (-led, -ling) bring, come out in freckles

**free** (free) *adj.* (fre·er, fre·est) able to act at will, not under compulsion or restraint; not restricted or affected by; not subject to cost or tax; independent; not exact or literal; generous; not in use; (of person) not occupied, having no appointment; loose, not fixed —*vt.* (freed, free·ing) set at liberty; remove (obstacles, pain *etc.*); rid (of) —**free'dom** *n.* —**free'ly** *adv.* —**free-for-all** *n.* brawl —**free'hand** *adj.* drawn without guiding instruments —**free'lance** (-lans) *adj./n.* (of) self-employed, unattached person —**Free·ma·son** (-may-sən) *n.* member of secret fraternity for mutual help —**freemasonry** *n.* principles of Freemasons; fellowship, secret brotherhood —**free'-range** *adj.* (of livestock and poultry) kept, produced in natural, nonintensive conditions —**free space** region that has no gravitational and electromagnetic fields —**free speech** right to express opinions publicly —**free-swinging** *adj.* recklessly daring —**free-think'er** *n.* skeptic who forms own opinions, *esp.* in religion —**free trade** international trade free of protective tariffs —**free'way** *n.* express highway

**freeze** (freez) *v.* (froze, fro·zen, freez·ing) change (by reduction of temperature) from liquid to solid, as water to ice —*vt.* preserve (food *etc.*) by extreme cold, in freezer; fix (prices *etc.*) —*vi.* feel very cold; become rigid as with fear; stop —**freez′er** *n.* insulated cabinet for long-term storage of perishable foodstuffs —**frozen** *adj.* of assets *etc.*, unrealizable —**freezing point** temperature at which liquid becomes solid

**freight** (frayt) *n.* commercial transport (*esp.* by rail, ship); cost of this; goods so carried —*vt.* send as or by freight —**freight′er** *n.*

**French** *n.* language spoken by people of France —*adj.* of, or pertaining to France —**French dressing** salad dressing —**French fries** deep-fried strips of potato —**French horn** musical wind instrument —**French leave** unauthorized leave —**French window** window extended to floor level and used as door

**fre·net·ic** (frə-NET-ik) *adj.* frenzied

**fren·zy** (FREN-zee) *n.* (*pl.* -zies) violent mental derangement; wild excitement —**fren′zied** *adj.*

**fre·quent** (FREE-kwənt) *adj.* happening often; common; numerous —*vt.* (fri-KWENT) go often to —**fre′quen·cy** *n.* (*pl.* -cies) rate of occurrence; in radio *etc.* cycles per second of alternating current —**fre·quen·ta·tive** (fri-KWEN-tə-tiv) *adj.* expressing repetition

**fres·co** (FRES-koh) *n.* (*pl.* -coes) method of painting in water color on plaster of wall before it dries; painting done thus

**fresh** *adj.* (-er, -est) not stale; new; additional; different; recent; inexperienced; pure; not pickled, frozen *etc.*; not faded or dimmed; not tired; of wind, strong; *inf.*

impudent; forward —**fresh′en** *v.* —**fresh′et** *n.* rush of water at river mouth; flood of river water —**fresh′ly** *adv.* —**fresh′man** *n.* first-year high school or college student

**fret**[1] *v.* (fret·ted, fret·ting) be irritated, worry —*n.* irritation —**fret′ful** *adj.* irritable, (easily) upset

**fret**[2] *n.* repetitive geometrical pattern; small bar on fingerboard of guitar *etc.* —*vt.* (fret·ted, fret·ting) ornament with carved pattern —**fret saw** saw with narrow blade and fine teeth, used for fretwork —**fret′work** *n.* carved or open woodwork in ornamental patterns and devices

**Freud·i·an** (FROI-dee-ən) *adj.* pert. to Austrian psychologist Sigmund Freud, or his theories

**fri·a·ble** (FRI-ə-bəl) *adj.* easily crumbled —**fri·a·bil′i·ty,** *n.*

**fri·ar** (FRI-ər) *n.* member of mendicant religious order —**fri′ar·y** *n.* house of friars

**fric·as·see** (frik-ə-SEE) *n.* dish of pieces of chicken or meat, fried or stewed and served with rich sauce —*vt.* (-seed, -see·ing) cook thus

**fric·tion** (FRIK-shən) *n.* rubbing; resistance met with by body moving over another; clash of wills *etc.*, disagreement —**fric′tion·al** *adj.*

**fried** *pt./pp.* of FRY

**friend** (frend) *n.* one well known to another and regarded with affection and loyalty; intimate associate; supporter; (F-) Quaker —**friend′less** *adj.* —**friend′li·ness** *n.* —**friend′ly** *adj.* (-li·er, -li·est) having disposition of, being kind; favorable —**friend′ship** *n.*

**frieze** (freez) *n.* ornamental band, strip (on wall)

**frig·ate** (FRIG-it) *n.* old (sailing)

warship corresponding to modern cruiser; fast warship equipped for escort and antisubmarine duties

**fright** (frīt) *n.* sudden fear; shock; alarm; grotesque or ludicrous person or thing —**fright'en** *vt.* cause fear, fright in —**fright'ful** *adj.* terrible, calamitous; shocking; *inf.* very great, very large —**fright'ful·ly** *adv. inf.* terribly; very

**frig·id** (FRIJ-id) *adj.* formal, dull; (sexually) unfeeling; cold —**frigid'i·ty** *n.* —**frig'id·ly** *adv.*

**frill** *n.* fluted strip of fabric gathered at one edge; ruff of hair, feathers around neck of dog, bird *etc.*; fringe; unnecessary words, politeness; superfluous thing; adornment —*vt.* make into, decorate with frill

**fringe** (frinj) *n.* ornamental edge of hanging threads, tassels *etc.*; anything like this; edge, limit —*vt.* (**fringed, fring·ing**) adorn with, serve as, fringe —**fringe benefit** benefit provided in addition to regular pay

**frip·per·y** (FRIP-ə-ree) *n.* (*pl.* **-er·ies**) finery; trivia

**frisk** *vi.* move, leap, playfully —*vt.* wave briskly; search (person) for concealed weapons *etc.* —*n.* —**frisk'y** *adj.* (**frisk·i·er, frisk·i·est**)

**frit·ter¹** (FRIT-ər) *vt.* waste —**fritter away** throw away, waste

**fritter²** *n.* small deep-fried cake of batter oft. containing corn

**friv·o·lous** (FRIV-ə-ləs) *adj.* not serious, unimportant; flippant —**fri·vol'i·ty** *n.*

**frizz** *vt.* curl into small crisp curls —*n.* frizzed hair —**friz'zy** *adj.* (**-zi·er, -zi·est**)

**fro** (froh) *adv.* away, from (*only* in **to and fro**)

**frock** (frok) *n.* woman's dress;

various similar garments —*vt.* dress with frock; invest with office of priest

**frog¹** *n.* tailless amphibious animal developed from tadpole —**frog'man** *n.* swimmer equipped for swimming, working, underwater

**frog²** *n.* ornamental coat fastening of button and loop; (military) attachment to belt to carry sword

**frol·ic** (FROL-ik) *n.* merrymaking —*vi.* (**-icked, -ick·ing**) behave playfully —**frol'ic·some** *adj.*

**from** (frum) *prep.* expressing point of departure, source, distance, cause, change of state *etc.*

**frond** *n.* plant organ consisting of stem and foliage, usually with fruit forms, *esp.* in ferns

**front** (frunt) *n.* fore part; position directly before or ahead; battle line or area; *Meteorology* dividing line between two air masses of different characteristics; outward aspect, bearing; *inf.* something serving as a respectable cover for another, *usu.* criminal, activity; field of activity; group with common goal —*v.* look, face; *inf.* be a cover for —*adj.* of, at, the front —**front'age** (-ij) *n.* front of building; property line along street, lake *etc.* —**fron'tal** (-əl) *adj.* —**fron'tier** (-TEER) *n.* part of country that borders on another —**fron'tis·piece** *n.* illustration facing title page of book

**frost** (frawst) *n.* frozen dew or mist; act or state of freezing; weather in which temperature falls below point at which water turns to ice —*v.* cover, be covered with frost or something similar in appearance; give slightly roughened surface —**frost'i·ly** *adv.* —**frost'y** *adj.* (**frost·i·er, frost·i·est**) accompanied by frost; chilly; cold; unfriendly —**frost′bite** n. destruction by cold of tissue, esp. of fingers, ears etc.

**froth** (frawth) n. collection of small bubbles, foam; scum; idle talk —v. (cause to) foam —**froth′i·ly** adv. —**froth′y** adj. (froth·i·er, froth·i·est)

**frown** vi. wrinkle brows —n.

**frowz·y** (FROW-zee) adj. (frowz·i·er, frowz·i·est) dirty, unkempt

**froze** pt. —**frozen** pp. of FREEZE

**fruc·ti·fy** (FRUK-tə-fī) v. (-fied, -fy·ing) (cause to) bear fruit

**fru·gal** (FROO-gəl) adj. sparing; thrifty; economical; meager —**fru·gal′i·ty** n.

**fruit** (froot) n. seed and its envelope, esp. edible one; vegetable product; (usu. in pl.) result, benefit —vi. bear fruit —**fruit′ful** (-fəl) adj. —**fru·i·tion** (froo-ISH-ən) n. enjoyment; realization of hopes —**fruit′less** adj. —**fruit′y** adj. (fruit·i·er, fruit·i·est)

**frump** n. dowdy woman —**frump′ish**, **frump′y** adj. (frump·i·er, frump·i·est)

**frus·trate** (FRUS-trayt) v. (-trat·ed, -trat·ing) thwart, balk; baffle, disappoint —**frus·tra′tion** n.

**fry**[1] (frī) v. (fried, fry·ing) cook with fat; be cooked thus; sl. be executed by electrocution

**fry**[2] n. (pl. same form) young of fish —**small fry** young or insignificant beings

**fuch·sia** (FYOO-shə) n. ornamental shrub with purple-red flowers

**fud·dle** (FUD-l) v. (-dled, -dling) (cause to) be intoxicated, confused —n. this state

**fudge**[1] (fuj) n. soft, variously flavored candy

**fudge**[2] v. (fudged, fudg·ing) make, do carelessly or dishonestly; fake

**fuel** (FYOO-əl) n. material for burning as source of heat or power; something that nourishes —vt. provide with fuel

**fu·gi·tive** (FYOO-ji-tiv) n. one who flees, esp. from arrest or pursuit —adj. fleeing, elusive

**fugue** (fyoog) n. musical composition in which themes are repeated in different parts

**Füh·rer** (FYUUR-ər) n. leader, title of German dictator, esp. Hitler

**ful·crum** (FUUL-krəm) n. (pl. -crums) point on which a lever is placed for support

**ful·fill** (fuul-FIL) vt. satisfy; carry out; obey; satisfy (desire etc.) —**ful·fill′ment** n.

**full** (fuul) adj. (-er, -est) containing as much as possible; abundant; complete; ample; plump; (of garment) of ample cut —adv. very; quite; exactly —**ful′ly** adv. —**full′ness** n. —**ful·some** (FUUL-səm) adj. excessive —**full-blown′** (-BLOHN) adj. fully developed

**ful·mi·nate** (FUL-mə-nayt) vi. (-nat·ed, -nat·ing) esp. with against) criticize harshly —n. chemical compound exploding readily —**ful·mi·na′tion** n.

**fulsome** see FULL

**fum·ble** (FUM-bəl) v. (-bled, -bling) grope about; handle awkwardly; in football etc., drop (ball) —n. awkward attempt

**fume** (fyoom) vi. be angry; emit smoke or vapor —n. smoke; vapor —**fu′mi·gate** vt. (-gat·ed, -gat·ing) apply fumes or smoke to, esp. for disinfection —**fu′mi·ga·tor** n.

**fun** n. anything enjoyable, amusing etc. —**fun′ni·ly** adv. —**fun′ny** adj. (-ni·er, -ni·est) comical; odd; difficult to explain

**func·tion** (FUNGK-shən) n. work a thing is designed to do; (large) social event; duty; profession; *Math.* quantity whose value depends on varying value of another —*vi.* operate, work —**func′tion·al** *adj.* having a special purpose; practical, necessary; capable of operating —**func′tion·ar·y** *n.* (*pl.* **-ar·ies**) official

**fund** *n.* stock or sum of money; supply, store —*pl.* money resources —*vt.* (in financial, business dealings) provide or obtain funds in various ways

**fun·da·men·tal** (fun-də-MEN-tl) *adj.* of, affecting, or serving as, the base; essential, primary —*n.* basic rule or fact —**fun′da·ment** (-mənt) *n.* buttocks; foundation —**fun·da·men′tal·ism** *n.* —**fun·da·men′tal·ist** *n.* one laying stress on belief in literal and verbal inspiration of Bible and other traditional creeds

**fu·ner·al** (FYOO-nər-əl) *n.* (ceremony associated with) burial or cremation of dead —**fu·ne′re·al** (-NEE-ree-əl) *adj.* like a funeral; dark; gloomy

**fun·gi·ble** (FUN-jə-bəl) *adj.* (of assets) freely exchangeable

**fun·gus** (FUNG-gəs) *n.* (*pl.* **-gi** *pr.* -jī, **-gus·es**) plant without leaves, flowers, or roots, as mushroom, mold —**fun′gal**, **fun′gous** *adj.* —**fun′gi·cide** (-jə-sid) *n.* fungus destroyer

**fu·nic·u·lar** (fyoo-NIK-yə-lər) *n.* cable railway on mountainside with two counterbalanced cars

**funk** (fungk) *n.* panic (*esp.* **blue funk**)

**fun·nel** (FUN-l) *n.* cone-shaped vessel or tube; chimney of locomotive or ship; ventilating shaft —*v.* (**-neled, -nel·ing**) (cause to) move as through funnel; concentrate, focus

**funny** *see* FUN

**fur** *n.* soft hair of animal; garment *etc.* of dressed skins with such hair; furlike coating —*vt.* (**furred, fur·ring**) cover with fur —**fur′ri·er** *n.* dealer in furs; repairer, dresser of furs —**fur′ry** *adj.* (**-ri·er, -ri·est**) of, like fur

**fur′bish** *vt.* clean up

**fu·ri·ous** (FYUUR-ee-əs) *adj.* extremely angry; violent —**fu′ri·ous·ly** *adv.*

**furl** *vt.* roll up and bind (sail, umbrella *etc.*)

**fur·long** (FUR-lawng) *n.* eighth of mile

**fur·lough** (FUR-loh) *n.* leave of absence, *esp.* to soldier

**fur·nace** (FUR-nis) *n.* apparatus for applying great heat to metals; closed fireplace for heating boiler *etc.*; hot place

**fur′nish** *vt.* fit up house with furniture; equip; supply, yield —**fur′ni·ture** (-chər) *n.* movable contents of a house or room

**fu·ror** (FYUUR-or) *n.* public outburst, *esp.* of protest; sudden enthusiasm

**fur·row** (FUR-oh) *n.* trench as made by plow; groove —*vt.* make furrows in

**fur·ther** (FUR-thər) *adv.* more; in addition; at or to a greater distance or extent —*adj.* additional; more distant —*comp. of* FAR —*vt.* help forward; promote —**fur′ther·ance** *n.* —**fur′ther·more** *adv.* besides —**fur′thest** *adj. sup. of* FAR —*adv.* —**fur′ther·most** *adj.*

**fur·tive** (FUR-tiv) *adj.* stealthy, sly, secret —**fur′tive·ly** *adv.*

**fu·ry** (FYUUR-ee) *n.* (*pl.* **-ries**) wild rage, violent anger; violence of storm *etc.*; (*usu. pl.*) snake-haired avenging deity

**fus·cous** (FUS-kəs) *adj.* dark-colored

**fuse** (fyooz) *v.* (**fused, fus·ing**) blend by melting; melt with heat;

amalgamate; —*n.* (*also* **fuze**) soft wire, with low melting point, used as safety device in electrical systems; (*also* **fuze**) device (*orig.* combustible cord) for igniting bomb *etc.* —**fu′si·ble** (-zǝ-bǝl) *adj.* —**fu·sion** (FYOO-zhǝn) *n.* melting; state of being melted; union of things, as atomic nuclei, as if melted together

**fu·se·lage** (FYOO-sǝ-lahzh) *n.* body of aircraft

**fu·sil·lade** (FYOO-sǝ-layd) *n.* continuous discharge of firearms

**fuss** *n.* needless bustle or concern; complaint; objection —*v.* make fuss —**fuss′i·ly** *adv.* —**fuss′i·ness** *n.* —**fuss′y** *adj.* (**fuss·i·er, fuss·i·est**) particular; hard to please; overmeticulous; overelaborate

**fus·tian** (FUS-chǝn) *n.* thick cotton cloth; inflated language

**fus·ty** (FUS-tee) *adj.* (**-ti·er, -ti·est**) moldy; smelling of damp; old-fashioned —**fus′ti·ness** *n.*

**fu·tile** (FYOOT-l) *adj.* useless, ineffectual, trifling —**fu·til′i·ty** *n.* (*pl.* **-ties**)

**fu·ton** (FOO-ton) *n.* Japanese padded quilt, laid on floor as bed

**fu·ture** (FYOO-chǝr) *n.* time to come; what will happen; tense of verb indicating this; likelihood of development —*adj.* that will be; of, relating to, time to come —**fu′tur·ism** *n.* movement in art marked by revolt against tradition —**fu′tur·ist** *n./adj.* —**fu·tur·is′tic** *adj.* ultramodern —**fu·tu′r·i·ty** (-TUUR-i·tee) *n.* (*pl.* **-ties**) future time

**fuze** *see* FUSE

**fuzz** *n.* fluff; fluffy or frizzed hair; blur; *sl.* police (officer) —**fuzz′y** *adj.* (**fuzz·i·er, fuzz·i·est**) fluffy, frizzy; blurred, indistinct

# G

**Ga** *Chem.* gallium

**gab·ar·dine** (GAB-ǝr-deen) *n.* fine twill cloth like serge; *Hist.* (**gab·erdine**) loose outer garment worn by Orthodox Jews

**gab·ble** (GAB-ǝl) *v.* (**-bled, -bling**) talk, utter inarticulately or too fast —*n.* such talk —**gab** *inf. n./v.* (**gabbed, gab·bing**) talk, chatter —**gab′by** *adj. inf.* (**-bi·er, -bi·est**) talkative —**gift of gab** eloquence, loquacity

**ga·ble** (GAY-bǝl) *n.* triangular upper part of wall at end of ridged roof —**gable end**

**gad** *vi.* (**gad·ded, gad·ding**) (*esp. with* about) go around in search of pleasure —**gad′a·bout** *n.* pleasure seeker

**gad·fly** (GAD-flī) *n.* (*pl.* **-flies**) cattle-biting fly; worrying person

**gadg·et** (GAJ-it) *n.* small mechanical device; object valued for its novelty or ingenuity —**gadg′et·ry** *n.*

**Gael** (gayl) *n.* one who speaks Gaelic —**Gael′ic** *n.* language of Ireland and Scottish Highlands —*adj.* of Gaels, their language or customs

**gaff** *n.* stick with iron hook for landing fish; spar for top of foreand-aft sail —*vt.* seize (fish) with gaff

**gaffe** (gaf) *n.* blunder; tactless remark

**gaf·fer** (GAF-ǝr) *n.* old man; *Film, TV* chief electrician

**gag**[1] *v.* (**gagged, gag·ging**) stop up (person's mouth) with cloth *etc.*; retch, choke —*n.* cloth *etc.* put into, tied across mouth

**gag**[2] *n.* joke, funny story

**ga·ga** (GAH-gah) *inf.* foolishly enthusiastic; infatuated

**gage**[1] (gayj) *n.* pledge, thing given as security; challenge, or something symbolizing one

**gage**[2] *see* GAUGE

**gag·gle** (GAG-əl) *n.* flock of geese; *inf.* disorderly crowd

**gaiety** *see* GAY

**gain** (gayn) *vt.* obtain, secure; obtain as profit; win; earn; reach —*vi.* increase, improve; get nearer; (of watch, clock) operate too fast —*n.* profit; increase, improvement —**gain'ful·ly** *adv.* profitably; for a wage, salary

**gain·say** (GAYN-say) *vt.* (-said, -say·ing) deny, contradict

**gait** (gayt) *n.* manner of walking; pace

**Gal.** Galatians

**ga·la** (GAY-lə) *n.* festive occasion; celebration; special entertainment —*adj.* festive; showy

**gal·ax·y** (GAL-ək-see) *n.* (pl. -ax·ies) system of stars bound by gravitational forces; splendid gathering, *esp.* of famous people —**ga·lac·tic** (gə-LAK-tik) *adj.*

**gale** (gayl) *n.* strong wind; *inf.* loud outburst, *esp.* of laughter

**gall**[1] (gawl) *n. inf.* impudence; bitterness —**gall'blad·der** *n.* sac attached to liver, reservoir for bile —**gall'stone** *n.* hard secretion in gallbladder or ducts leading from it

**gall**[2] *n.* painful swelling, *esp.* on horse; sore caused by chafing —*vt.* make sore by rubbing; vex, irritate

**gall**[3] *n.* abnormal growth or excrescence on trees *etc.*

**gal·lant** (GAL-ənt) *adj.* fine, stately, brave; chivalrous, very attentive to women —*n.* (gə-LANT) lover, suitor; dashing, fashionable young man —**gal'-**

lant·ly *adv.* —**gal'lant·ry** *n.* (pl. -ries)

**gal·le·on** (GAL-ee-ən) *n.* large, high-built sailing ship of war

**gal·ler·y** (GAL-ə-ree) *n.* (pl. -ler·ies) covered walk with side openings, colonnade; platform or projecting upper floor in theater *etc.*; group of spectators; long, narrow platform on outside of building; room or rooms for special purposes, *eg* showing works of art; passage in wall, open to interior of building

**gal·ley** (GAL-ee) *n.* (pl. -leys) one-decked vessel with sails and oars, usu. rowed by slaves or criminals; kitchen of ship or aircraft; printer's tray for composed type —**galley proof** printer's proof before being made up into pages —**galley slave** one condemned to row in galley; drudge

**Gal·lic** (GAL-ik) *adj.* of ancient Gaul; French —**Gal'li·cism** *n.* French word or idiom

**gal·li·um** (GAL-ee-əm) *n.* soft, gray metal of great fusibility

**gal·li·vant** (GAL-ə-vant) *vi.* gad about

**gal·lon** (GAL-ən) *n.* liquid measure of four quarts (3.7853 liters)

**gal·lop** (GAL-əp) *v.* go, ride at gallop; move fast —*n.* horse's fastest pace with all four feet off ground together in each stride; ride at this pace —**gal'lop·ing** *adj.* at a gallop; speedy, swift

**gal·lows** (GAL-ohz) *n.* structure, usu. of two upright beams and crossbar, *esp.* for hanging criminals

**Gal·lup poll** (GAL-əp) *n.* method of finding out public opinion by questioning a cross section of the population

**ga·loot** (gə-LOOT) *n. inf.* silly, clumsy person

**ga·lore** (gə-LOR) *adv.* in plenty

**ga·losh·es** (gə-LOSH-əz) *n. pl.* waterproof overshoes

**gal·van·ic** (gal-VAN-ik) *adj.* of, producing, concerning electric current, *esp.* when produced chemically; *inf.* resembling effect of electric shock, startling —**gal′va·nize** (-və-nīz) *vt.* (-nized, -niz·ing) stimulate to action; excite, startle; cover (iron *etc.*) with protective zinc coating

**gam′bit** *n. Chess* opening involving sacrifice of a piece; any opening maneuver, comment *etc.* intended to secure an advantage

**gam·ble** (GAM-bəl) *vi.* (-bled, -bling) play games of chance to win money; act on expectation of something —*n.* risky undertaking; bet, wager —**gam′bler** *n.*

**gam·bol** (GAM-bəl) *vi.* (-boled, -bol·ing) skip, jump playfully —*n.*

**game**[1] (gaym) *n.* diversion, pastime; jest; contest for amusement; scheme, strategy; animals or birds hunted; their flesh —*adj.* (gam·er, gam·est) brave; willing —**game′ster** *n.* gambler —**game′cock** *n.* rooster bred for fighting —**game′keep·er** *n.* person employed to breed game, prevent poaching

**game**[2] *adj.* lame, crippled (leg)

**gam·ete** (GAM-eet) *n. Biology* a sexual cell that unites with another for reproduction or the formation of a new individual

**gam·ma** (GAM-ə) *n.* third letter of the Greek alphabet —**gamma ray** a very penetrative electromagnetic ray

**gam·mon** (GAM-ən) *n.* cured or smoked ham; lower end of side of bacon

**gam·ut** (GAM-ət) *n.* whole range or scale (*orig.* of musical notes)

**gan·der** (GAN-dər) *n.* male goose; *sl.* a quick look

**gang** *n.* (criminal) group; organized group of persons working together —*vi.* (*esp.* with together) form gang —**gang up (on)** *inf.* combine against

**gang′ling** *adj.* lanky, awkward in movement

**gan·gli·on** (GANG-glee-ən) *n.* (*pl.* -gli·a *pr.* -glee-ə) nerve nucleus

**gang′plank** (GANG-plangk) *n.* portable bridge for boarding or leaving vessel

**gan·grene** (GANG-green) *n.* death or decay of body tissue as a result of disease or injury —**gan′gre·nous** (-grə-nəs) *adj.*

**gang′ster** (GANG-stər) *n.* member of criminal gang; notorious or hardened criminal

**gang′way** *n.* bridge from ship to shore; anything similar —*interj.* make way!

**gan·try** (GAN-tree) *n.* (*pl.* -tries) structure to support crane, railway signals *etc.*; framework beside rocket on launching pad

**gap** *n.* breach, opening, interval; cleft; empty space

**gape** (gayp) *vi.* (gaped, gap·ing) stare in wonder; open mouth wide, as in yawning; be, become wide open —*n.*

**ga·rage** (gə-RAHZH) *n.* (part of) building to house automobiles; refueling and repair center for them —*vt.* (-raged, -rag·ing) leave automobile in garage

**garb** (gahrb) *n.* dress; fashion of dress —*vt.* dress, clothe

**gar·bage** (GAHR-bij) *n.* rubbish; refuse —**garbage can** large, *usu.* cylindrical container for household rubbish

**gar·ble** (GAHR-bəl) *vt.* (-bled, -bling) jumble or distort (story, account *etc.*)

**gar·den** (GAHR-dn) *n.* ground for growing flowers, fruit, or vegetables —*vi.* cultivate garden —**gar-**

**den·er** (GAHRD-nər) n. —**gar·den·ing** (GAHRD-ning) n.

**gar·de·nia** (gahr-DEE-nyə) n. (sub)tropical shrub, with fragrant white or yellow flowers

**gar·gan·tu·an** (gahr-GAN-choo-ən) adj. immense, enormous, huge

**gar·gle** (GAHR-gəl) v. (-gled, -gling) —vi. wash throat with liquid kept moving by the breath —vt. wash (throat) thus —n. gargling; preparation for this purpose

**gar·goyle** (GAHR-goil) n. carved (grotesque) face on waterspout, esp. on Gothic church

**gar·ish** (GAIR-ish) adj. showy; gaudy

**gar·land** (GAHR-lənd) n. wreath of flowers worn or hung as decoration —vt. decorate with garlands

**gar·lic** (GAHR-lik) n. (bulb of) plant with strong smell and taste, used in cooking and seasoning

**gar·ment** (GAHR-mənt) n. article of clothing —pl. clothes

**gar·ner** (GAHR-nər) vt. store up, collect, as if in granary

**gar·net** (GAHR-nit) n. red semiprecious stone

**gar·nish** (GAHR-nish) vt. adorn, decorate (esp. food) —n. material for this

**gar·ret** (GAR-it) n. small (usu. wretched) room on top floor, attic

**gar·ri·son** (GAR-ə-sən) n. troops stationed in town, fort etc.; fortified place —vt. furnish or occupy with garrison

**gar·rote** (gə-ROHT) n. Hist. capital punishment by strangling; apparatus for this —v. (-rot·ed, -rot·ing) execute, kill thus —**gar·rot'er** n.

**gar·ru·lous** (GAR-ə-ləs) adj. (frivolously) talkative —**gar·ru·li·ty** (gə-ROO-li-tee) n. loquacity

**gar·ter** (GAHR-tər) n. band worn around leg to hold up sock or stocking —**garter snake** type of harmless snake

**gas** n. (pl. -es) airlike substance, esp. one that does not liquefy or solidify at ordinary temperatures; fossil fuel in form of gas, used for heating or lighting; gaseous anesthetic; poisonous or irritant substance dispersed through atmosphere in warfare etc.; gasoline; automobile accelerator; sl. idle, boastful talk —v. (gassed, gas·sing) project gas over; poison with gas; fill with gas; sl. talk idly, boastfully —**gas'e·ous** (-ee-əs) adj. of, like gas —**gas'y** adj. (-sl·er, -si·est) —**gas'bag** n. sl. person who talks idly —**gas mask** mask with chemical filter to guard against poisoning by gas

**gash** n. gaping wound, slash —vt. cut deeply

**gas·ket** (GAS-kit) n. rubber, neoprene etc. used as seal between metal faces, esp. in engines

**gas·o·hol** (GAS-ə-hawl) n. mixture of gasoline and ethyl alcohol used as fuel for automobiles

**gas·o·line** (gas-ə-LEEN) n. refined petroleum used in automobiles etc.

**gasp** vi. catch breath with open mouth, as in exhaustion or surprise —n. convulsive catching of breath

**gas·tric** (GAS-trik) adj. of stomach —**gas·tro·nom'i·cal** (-trə-NOM-ə-kəl) adj. —**gas·tron·o·my** (ga-STRON-ə-mee) n. art of good eating

**gas·tro·en·ter·i·tis** (gas-troh-en-tə-RĪ-tis) n. inflammation of stomach and intestines

**gas·tro·pod** (GAS-trə-pod) n. mollusk, *eg* snail, with disklike organ of locomotion on ventral surface

**gate** (gayt) *n.* opening in wall, fence *etc.*; barrier for closing it; sluice; any entrance or way out; (entrance money paid by) those attending sports event —**gate′-crash-er** *n. inf.* person who enters sports event, social function *etc.* uninvited

**gath-er** (GATH-ər) *v.* (cause to) assemble; increase gradually; draw together —*vt.* collect; learn, understand; draw material into small tucks or folds —**gath′er-ing** *n.* assembly

**gauche** (gohsh) *adj.* tactless, blundering —**gau′che-rie** *n.* awkwardness, clumsiness

**gau-cho** (GOW-choh) *n.* (*pl.* -chos) cowboy of S Amer. pampas

**gaud** (gawd) *n.* showy ornament —**gaud′i-ly** *adv.* —**gaud′iness** *n.* —**gaud′y** *adj.* (gaud-i-er, gaud-i-est) showy in tasteless way

**gauge, gage** (gayj) *n.* standard measure, as of diameter of wire, thickness of sheet metal *etc.*; distance between rails of railway; capacity, extent; instrument for measuring such things as wire, rainfall, height of water in boiler *etc.* —*vt.* (gauged, gaug-ing) measure; estimate

**gaunt** (gawnt) *adj.* (-er, -est) extremely lean, haggard

**gaunt-let** (GAWNT-lit) *n.* armored glove; glove covering part of arm —**run the gauntlet** formerly, run as punishment between two lines of men striking at runner with sticks *etc.*; be exposed to criticism or unpleasant treatment; undergo ordeal —**throw down the gauntlet** offer challenge

**gauss** (gows) *n.* unit of density of magnetic field

**gauze** (gawz) *n.* thin transparent fabric of silk, wire *etc.*; this as surgical dressing

**gave** *pt.* of GIVE

**gav-el** (GAV-əl) *n.* mallet of presiding officer or auctioneer

**ga-votte** (gə-VOT) *n.* lively dance; music for it

**gawk** *vi.* stare stupidly —**gawk′y** *adj.* (gawk-i-er, gawk-i-est) clumsy, awkward

**gay** *adj.* (-er, -est) merry; lively; cheerful; bright; lighthearted; showy; given to pleasure; homosexual —**gai′e-ty** *n.* (*pl.* -ties) —**gai′ly** *adv.*

**gaze** (gayz) *vi.* (gazed, gaz-ing) look fixedly —*n.* fixed look

**ga-ze-bo** (gə-ZAY-boh) *n.* summerhouse, small roofed structure, with extensive view

**ga-zelle** (gə-ZEL) *n.* small graceful antelope

**ga-zette** (gə-ZET) *n.* name for newspaper —**gaz-et-teer′** *n.* geographical dictionary

**Gd** *Chem.* gadolinium

**gear** (geer) *n.* set of wheels working together, *esp.* by engaging cogs; connection by which driving wheel of cycle, automobile *etc.* performs more or fewer revolutions relative to pedals, pistons *etc.*; equipment; clothing; goods, utensils; apparatus, tackle, tools; rigging; harness —*vt.* adapt (one thing) so as to conform with another; provide with gear; put in gear —**gear′box** *n.* case protecting gearing of bicycle, automobile *etc.* —**in gear** connected up and ready for work —**out of gear** disconnected

**geese** (gees) *pl.* of GOOSE

**gee-zer** (GEE-zər) *n. sl.* (old, eccentric) man

**ge-fil-te fish** (gə-FIL-tə) in Jewish cookery, a dish of various freshwater fish chopped and blended with eggs, matzo meal *etc.*

**Gei·ger count·er** (GI-gər) *n.* instrument for detecting radioactivity, cosmic radiation and charged atomic particles

**gei·sha** (GAY-shə) *n.* in Japan, professional female entertainer and companion for men

**gel** (jel) *n.* jelly-like substance —*vi.* gelled, gel·ling) form a gel; jell

**gel·a·tin** (JEL-ə-tn) *n.* substance prepared from animal bones *etc.*, producing edible jelly; anything resembling this —**ge·lat·i·nous** (jə-LAT-n-əs) *adj.* like gelatin or jelly

**geld** *vt.* castrate —**geld'ing** *n.* castrated horse

**gel·id** (JEL-id) *adj.* very cold

**gem** (jem) *n.* precious stone, *esp.* when cut and polished; treasure —*vt.* (gemmed, gem·ming) adorn with gems

**Gen.** Genesis

**gen·darme** (ZHAHN-dahrm) *n.* policeman in France

**gen·der** (JEN-dər) *n.* sex, male or female; grammatical classification of nouns, according to sex (actual or attributed)

**gene** (jeen) *n.* biological factor determining inherited characteristics

**ge·ne·al·o·gy** (jee-nee-AL-ə-jee) *n.* (*pl.* -gies) account of descent from ancestors; pedigree; study of pedigrees —**ge·ne·a·log'i·cal** (-LOJ-ə-kəl) *adj.*

**genera** *pl. of* GENUS

**gen·er·al** (JEN-ər-əl) *adj.* common, widespread; not particular or specific; applicable to all or most; usual, prevalent; miscellaneous; dealing with main element only; vague, indefinite —*n.* army officer of rank above colo-

nel —**gen·er·al'i·ty** *n.* (*pl.* -ties) general principle; vague statement; indefiniteness —**gen·er·al·i·za'tion** *n.* general conclusion from particular instance; inference —**gen'er·al·ize** *v.* (-ized, -iz·ing) —*vt.* reduce to general laws —*vi.* draw general conclusions —**general practitioner** physician with practice not restricted to particular branch of medicine

**gen·er·ate** (JEN-ə-rayt) *vt.* (-at·ed, -at·ing) bring into being; produce —**gen·er·a'tion** *n.* bringing into being; all persons born about same time; average time between two such generations (about 30 years) —**gen'er·a·tor** *n.* apparatus for producing (steam, electricity *etc.*); begetter

**ge·ner·ic** (ji-NER-ik) *adj.* belonging to, characteristic of class or genus —**ge·ner'i·cal·ly** *adv.* —**generic drug** one sold without brand name

**gen·er·ous** (JEN-ər-əs) *adj.* liberal, free in giving; abundant —**gen·er·os'i·ty** *n.* (*pl.* -ties)

**gen·e·sis** (JEN-ə-sis) *n.* (*pl.* -ses *pr.* -seez) origin; mode of formation; (G-) first book of Bible

**ge·net·ics** (jə-NET-iks) *n.* (*with sing. v.*) scientific study of heredity and variation in organisms —**ge·net'ic** *adj.* —**ge·net'i·cist** *n.* —**genetic engineering** deliberate modification of heredity characteristics by treatment of DNA to transfer selected genes

**gen·ial** (JEEN-yəl) *adj.* cheerful, warm in behavior; mild, conducive to growth —**ge·ni·al'i·ty** *n.*

**ge·nie** (JEE-nee) *n.* in fairy tales, servant appearing by, and working, magic

**gen·i·tal** (JEN-i-tl) *adj.* relating to sexual organs or reproduction

—**gen'i·tals** *n. pl.* the sexual organs

**gen·i·tive** (JEN-i-tiv) *adj./n.* possessive (case)

**gen·ius** (JEEN-yɔs) *n.* (person with) exceptional power or ability, *esp.* of mind; distinctive spirit or nature (of nation *etc.*)

**gen·o·cide** (JEN-ɔ-sīd) *n.* murder of a nationality or ethnic group

**gen·re** (ZHAHN-rɔ) *n.* kind; sort; style; painting of homely scene

**gen·teel** (jen-TEEL) *adj.* well-bred; stylish; affectedly proper

**gen·tile** (JEN-tīl) *adj.* of people other than Jewish; heathen —*n.*

**gen·tle** (JEN-tl) *adj.* (-**tler**, -**tlest**) mild, quiet, not rough or severe; soft and soothing; courteous; moderate; gradual; wellborn —**gen·til'i·ty** *n.* respectability, (pretentious) politeness —**gen'tle·ness** *n.* quality of being gentle; tenderness —**gent'ly** *adv.* —**gen·tri·fi·ca'tion** *n.* buying of properties in run-down urban neighborhoods by affluent people, thus increasing property values but displacing less affluent residents and owners of small businesses —**gent'ry** *n.* wellborn people —**gen'tle·man** *n.* well-bred man; man of good social position; man (used as a mark of politeness) —**gen'tle·man·ly** *adj.* —gentlemen's agreement agreement binding by honor but not valid in law; unwritten law in private club *etc.* to discriminate against members of certain groups —**gen'tri·fy** *v.* (-**fied**, -**fy-ing**) change by gentrification, undergo this change

**gen·u·flect** (JEN-yɔ-flekt) *vi.* bend knee, *esp.* in worship —**gen·u·flec'tion** *n.*

**gen·u·ine** (JEN-yoo-in) *adj.* real, true, not sham, authentic; sincere; pure

**ge·nus** (JEE-nɔs) *n.* (*pl.* **gen·e·ra** *pr.* JEN-ɔr-ɔ) class, order, group (*esp.* of insects, animals *etc.*) with common characteristics usu. comprising several species

**ge·o·cen·tric** (jee-oh-SEN-trik) *adj. Astronomy* measured, seen from Earth; having Earth as center

**ge·ode** (JEE-ohd) *n.* cavity lined with crystals; stone containing this

**ge·o·des·ic** (jee-ɔ-DES-ik) *adj.* of geometry of curved surfaces —geodesic dome light but strong hemispherical construction formed from set of polygons

**ge·og·ra·phy** (jee-OG-rɔ-fee) *n.* (*pl.* -**phies**) science of Earth's form, physical features, climate, population *etc.* —**ge·og'ra·pher** *n.*

**ge·ol·o·gy** (jee-OL-ɔ-jee) *n.* science of Earth's crust, rocks, strata *etc.* —**ge·o·log'ic·al** *adj.*

**ge·om·e·try** (jee-OM-i-tree) *n.* science of properties and relations of lines, surfaces *etc.* —**ge·o·met'ric** *adj.*

**ge·o·phys·ics** (jee-oh-FIZ-iks) *n.* science dealing with physics of Earth —**ge·o·phys'i·cal** *adj.*

**ge·o·sta·tion·ar·y** (jee-oh-STAY-shɔ-ner-ee) *adj.* (of satellite) in orbit around Earth so satellite remains over same point on surface

**ger·bil** (JUR-bɔl) *n.* burrowing, desert rodent of Asia and Africa

**ger·i·at·rics** (jer-ee-A-triks) *n.* branch of medicine dealing with old age and its diseases —**ger·i·at'ric** *adj.* old —*n. sl.* old person

**germ** (jurm) *n.* microbe, *esp.* causing disease; elementary thing; rudiment of new organism, of animal or plant —**ger'mi·cide** (-mɔ-sīd) *n.* substance for destroying disease germs

**Ger·man** (JUR-mən) *n./adj.* (language or native) of Germany —**German measles** rubella, mild disease with symptoms like measles

**german** *adj.* of the same parents; closely akin (*only in* brother-, sister-, cousin-german)

**ger·mane** (jər-MAYN) *adj.* relevant, pertinent

**ger·mi·nate** (JUR-mə-nayt) *v.* (-nat·ed, -nat·ing) (cause to) sprout or begin to grow

**ger·ry·man·der** (JER-i-man-dər) *vt.* manipulate election districts so as to favor one side

**ger·und** (JER-ənd) *n.* noun formed from verb, *eg* living

**ges·ta·tion** (je-STAY-shən) *n.* carrying of young in womb between conception and birth; this period

**ges·tic·u·late** (je-STIK-yə-layt) *vi.* use expressive movements of hands and arms when speaking

**ges·ture** (JES-chər) *n.* movement to convey meaning; indication of state of mind —*vi.* (-tured, -tur·ing) make such a movement

**get** *v.* (got, got *or* got·ten, get·ting) —*vt.* obtain, procure; contract; catch; earn; cause to go or come; bring into position or state; induce; engender; be in possession of, have (to do); *inf.* understand —*vi.* succeed in coming or going; reach, attain; become —**get·a·way** *n.* escape —**get across** be understood —**get at** gain access to; annoy; criticize; influence —**get (one's) goat** *sl.* make (one) angry, annoyed

**gey·ser** (GI-zər) *n.* hot spring throwing up spout of water from time to time

**ghast·ly** (GAST-lee) *adj. inf.* (-li·er, -li·est) unpleasant; death-like, pallid; horrible —*adv.* horribly

**gher·kin** (GUR-kin) *n.* small cucumber used in pickling

**ghet·to** (GET-oh) *n.* (*pl.* -tos) densely populated (*esp.* by one racial or ethnic group) slum area

**ghost** (gohst) *n.* spirit, dead person appearing again; specter; semblance; faint trace; one who writes work to appear under another's name, ghostwriter —*v.* (*also* **ghostwrite**) write another's work, speeches *etc.* —**ghost'ly** *adj.*

**ghoul** (gool) *n.* malevolent spirit; person with morbid interests; fiend —**ghoul'ish** *adj.* of or like ghoul; horrible

**gi·ant** (JI-ənt) *n.* mythical being of superhuman size; very tall person, plant *etc.* —*adj.* huge —**gi·gan'tic** *adj.* enormous, huge

**gib·ber** (JIB-ər) *vi.* make meaningless sounds with mouth, jabber, chatter —**gib'ber·ish** *n.* meaningless speech or words

**gib·bet** (JIB-it) *n.* gallows; post with arm on which executed criminal was hung; death by hanging —*vt.* hang on gibbet; hold up to scorn

**gib·bon** (GIB-ən) *n.* type of ape

**gibe** (jīb) *v.* (gibed, gib·ing) utter taunts; mock; jeer —*n.*

**gib·lets** (JIB-lits) *n. pl.* internal edible parts of fowl, as liver, gizzard *etc.*

**gid·dy** (GID-ee) *adj.* (-di·er, -di·est) dizzy, feeling as if about to fall; liable to cause this feeling; flighty, frivolous —**gid'di·ness** *n.*

**gift** *n.* thing given, present; faculty, power —*vt.* present (with); endow, bestow —**gift'ed** *adj.* talented

**gig** *n.* light, two-wheeled carriage; *inf.* single booking of musicians to play at club *etc.*

**giga-** (*comb. form*) billion *eg*

**gigacycle** one billion cycles, **gigahertz** one billion hertz

**gigantic** *see* GIANT

**gig·gle** (GIG-əl) *vi.* (**-gled, -gling**) laugh nervously, foolishly —*n.* such a laugh

**gig·o·lo** (JIG-ə-loh) *n.* (*pl.* **-los**) man kept, paid, by (older) woman to be her escort, lover

**gild**[1] *vt.* (**gilded** *or* **gilt, gild·ing**) put thin layer of gold on; make falsely attractive —**gilt** *adj.* gilded —*n.* thin layer of gold put on

**gill**[1] *n.* breathing organ in fish (*usu. pl.*)

**gill**[2] (jil) *n.* liquid measure, quarter of pint

**gim·bals** (JIM-bəlz) *n. pl.* pivoted rings, for keeping things, *eg* compass, horizontal at sea or in space

**gim·let** (GIM-lit) *n.* boring tool, usu. with screw point; drink of vodka or gin with lime juice

**gim·mick** (GIM-ik) *n.* clever device, stratagem *etc.*, *esp.* one designed to attract attention or publicity

**gimp** *n.* narrow fabric or braid used as edging or trimming; *sl.* a limp; person who limps

**gin**[1] (jin) *n.* alcoholic liquor flavored with juniper berries

**gin**[2] *n.* primitive engine in which vertical shaft is turned to drive horizontal beam in a circle; machine for separating cotton from seeds

**gin·ger** (JIN-jər) *n.* plant with pungent spicy root used in cooking *etc.*; the root; *inf.* spirit, mettle; light reddish-yellow color —*vt. inf.* stimulate —**gin'ger·y** *adj.* of, like ginger; spicy; highspirited; reddish —**ginger ale, beer** ginger-flavored soft drink —**gin'ger·bread** *n.* cake, cookie flavored with ginger

**gin·ger·ly** (JIN-jər-lee) *adv.* cautiously, warily, reluctantly

**ging·ham** (GING-əm) *n.* cotton cloth, usu. checked, woven from dyed yarn

**gink·go** (GING-koh) *n.* (*pl.* **-goes**) large Chinese shade tree

**gin·seng** (JIN-seng) *n.* (root of) plant believed to have tonic and energy-giving properties

**gi·raffe** (jə-RAF) *n.* Afr. ruminant animal, with spotted coat and very long neck and legs

**gird** (gurd) *vt.* (**gird·ed** *or* **girt, gird·ing**) put belt around; fasten clothes thus; equip with, or belt on, a sword; prepare (oneself); encircle —**gird'er** *n.* large beam, *esp.* of steel

**gir·dle** (GURD-l) *n.* corset; waistband; anything that surrounds, encircles —*vt.* (**-dled, -dling**) surround, encircle; remove bark (of tree) from a band around it

**girl** (gurl) *n.* female child; young (formerly, an unmarried) woman —**girl'hood** (-huud) *n.*

**girt** *pt./pp. of* GIRD

**girth** (gurth) *n.* measurement around thing; leather or cloth band put around horse to hold saddle *etc.* —*vt.* surround, secure with girth; girdle

**gist** (jist) *n.* substance, main point (of remarks *etc.*)

**give** (giv) *v.* (**gave, giv·en, giv·ing**) *vt.* bestow, confer ownership of, make present of; deliver; impart; assign; yield; supply; utter; emit; be host of (party *etc.*); make over; cause to have —*vi.* yield, give way, move —*n.* yielding, elasticity —**give'a·way** *n.* act of giving something away; what is given away; telltale sign —**give up** acknowledge defeat; abandon

**giz·zard** (GIZ-ərd) *n.* part of bird's stomach

**gla·brous** (GLAY-brəs) *adj.*

smooth; without hairs or any un-evenness

**gla·cier** (GLAY-shər) *n.* river of ice, slow-moving mass of ice formed by accumulated snow in mountain valleys —**gla'cial** *adj.* of ice, or of glaciers; very cold —**gla·ci·a'tion** *n.*

**glad** *adj.* (-der, -dest) pleased; happy, joyous; giving joy —**glad'-den** *vt.* make glad —**glad'ly** *adv.* —**glad rags** *inf.* dressy clothes for party *etc.*

**glade** (glayd) *n.* clear, grassy space in wood or forest

**glad·i·a·tor** (GLAD-ee-ay-tər) *n.* trained fighter in ancient Roman arena

**glam·our** (GLAM-ər) *n.* alluring charm, fascination —**glam'or·ize** *vt.* (-ized, -iz·ing) make appear glamorous —**glam'or·ous** *adj.*

**glance** (glans) *vi.* (glanced, glanc·ing) look rapidly or briefly; allude, touch; glide off something struck; pass quickly —*n.* brief look; flash; gleam; sudden (deflected) blow

**gland** *n.* one of various small organs controlling different bodily functions by chemical means —**glan·du·lar** (GLAN-jə-lər) *adj.*

**glare** (glair) *vi.* (glared, glar·ing) look fiercely; shine brightly, intensely; be conspicuous —*n.*

**glass** *n.* hard transparent substance made by fusing sand, soda, potash *etc.*; things made of it; tumbler; its contents; lens; mirror; spyglass —*pl.* eyeglasses —**glass'i·ness** *n.* —**glass'y** *adj.* (glass·i·er, glass·i·est) like glass; expressionless —**glass wool** insulating fabric of spun glass

**glau·co·ma** (glow-KOH-mə) *n.* eye disease

**glaze** (glayz) *v.* (glazed, glaz·ing) —*vt.* furnish with glass; cover with glassy substance —*vi.* become glassy —*n.* transparent coating; substance used for this; glossy surface —**gla·zier** (GLAY-zhər) *n.* one who glazes windows

**gleam** (gleem) *n.* slight or passing beam of light; faint or momentary show —*vi.* give out gleams

**glean** (gleen) *v.* pick up (facts *etc.*); gather, pick up (*orig.*) after reapers in grainfields —**glean'-er** *n.*

**glee** *n.* mirth, merriment; musical composition for three or more voices —**glee'ful** *adj.* —**glee club** chorus organized for singing choral music

**glen** *n.* narrow valley, usu. wooded and with a stream

**glib** *adj.* (-ber, -best) fluent but insincere or superficial; plausible —**glib'ness** *n.*

**glide** (glīd) *vi.* (glid·ed, glid·ing) pass smoothly and continuously; of airplane, move without use of engines —*n.* smooth, silent movement; *Mus.* sounds made in passing from tone to tone —**glid'-er** *n.* aircraft without engine that moves through the action of gravity and air currents; porch swing —**glid'ing** *n.* sport of flying gliders

**glim·mer** (GLIM-ər) *vi.* shine faintly, flicker —*n.* —**glim'mer-ing** *n.* faint gleam of light; faint idea, notion

**glimpse** (glimps) *n.* brief or incomplete view —*vt.* (glimpsed, glimps·ing) catch glimpse of

**glint** (glint) *v.* flash, glance, glitter; reflect —*n.*

**glis·ten** (GLIS-ən) *vi.* gleam by reflecting light

**glit·ter** (GLIT-ər) *vi.* shine with bright quivering light, sparkle; be showy —*n.* luster; sparkle

**gloam·ing** (GLOH-ming) *n.* evening twilight

**gloat** (gloht) *vi.* regard, dwell on with smugness or malicious satisfaction

**glob** *n.* soft lump or mass

**globe** (glohb) *n.* sphere with map of Earth or stars; heavenly sphere, *esp.* Earth; ball, sphere —**glob′al** *adj.* of globe; relating to whole world —**glob′u·lar** (-yə lər) *adj.* globe-shaped —**glob′ule** (-yool) *n.* small round particle; drop —**glob′u·lin** *n.* kind of simple protein —**globe′trot·ter** *n.* (habitual) world traveler

**glock·en·spiel** (GLOK-ən-speel) *n.* percussion instrument of metal bars struck with hammers

**gloom** *n.* darkness; melancholy, depression —**gloom′y** *adj,* (gloom·i·er, gloom·i·est)

**glo·ry** (GLOR-ee) *n.* renown, honorable fame; splendor; exalted or prosperous state; heavenly bliss —*vi.* (-ried, -ry·ing) take pride (in) —**glor′i·fy** *vt.* (-fied, -fy·ing) make glorious; invest with glory —**glo′ri·ous** *adj.* illustrious; splendid; excellent; delightful

**gloss**[1] *n.* surface shine, luster —*vt.* put gloss on; (*esp.* with over) (try to) cover up, pass over (fault, error) —**gloss′i·ness** *n.* —**gloss′y** (gloss·i·er, gloss·i·est) *adj.* smooth, shiny —*n.* photograph printed on shiny paper

**gloss**[2] *n.* marginal interpretation of word; comment, explanation —*vt.* interpret; comment; explain away —**glos′sa·ry** *n.* (*pl.* -ries) dictionary, vocabulary of special words

**glot′tis** *n.* human vocal apparatus, larynx —**glot′tal** (GLOT-l) *adj.*

**glove** (gluv) *n.* covering for the hand —*vt.* (gloved, glov·ing) cover with, or as with glove —**glove compartment** storage area in dashboard of automobile —**the gloves** boxing gloves

**glow** (gloh) *vi.* give out light and heat without flames; shine; experience well-being or satisfaction; be or look hot; burn with emotion —*n.* shining heat; warmth of color; feeling of well-being; ardor —**glow·worm** (GLOH-wurm) *n.* female insect giving out green light

**glow·er** (GLOW-ər) *vi.* scowl

**glu·cose** (GLOO-kohs) *n.* type of sugar found in fruit *etc.*

**glue** (gloo) *n.* any natural or synthetic adhesive; any sticky substance —*vt.* (glued, glu·ing) fasten (as if) with glue —**glue sniffing** practice of inhaling fumes of glue for intoxicating or hallucinatory effects

**glum** *adj.* (glum·mer, glum·mest) sullen, moody, gloomy

**glut** *n.* surfeit, excessive amount —*vt.* (glut·ted, glut·ting) feed, gratify to the full or to excess; overstock

**glu·ten** (GLOOT-n) *n.* protein present in cereal grain —**glu′ti·nous** *adj.* sticky, gluey

**glut·ton** (GLUT-n) *n.* greedy person; one with great liking or capacity for something, *esp.* food and drink —**glut′ton·ous** *adj.* like glutton, greedy —**glut′ton·y** *n.*

**glyc·er·in** (GLIS-ər-in) *n.* colorless sweet liquid with wide application in chemistry and industry

**gnarled** (nahrld) *adj.* knobby, rugged, twisted

**gnash** (nash) *v.* grind (teeth) together as in anger or pain

**gnat** (nat) *n.* small, biting, two-winged fly

**gnaw** (naw) *v.* bite or chew steadily; (*esp. with* at) cause distress to

**gneiss** (nīs) *n.* coarse-grained metamorphic rock

**gnome** (nohm) *n.* legendary creature like small old man;

international financier —gnom'-ish adj.

gno·mic (NOH-mik) adj. of or like an aphorism

gnos·tic (NOS-tik) adj. of, relating to knowledge, esp. spiritual knowledge

gnu (noo) n. S Afr. antelope somewhat like ox

go (goh) vi. (went, gone, go·ing) move along, make way; be moving; depart; function; make specified sound; fail, give way, break down; elapse; be kept, put; be able to put; result; contribute to result; tend to; be accepted, have force; become —n. going; energy, vigor; attempt; turn —go-go dancer dancer, usu. scantily dressed, who performs rhythmic and oft. erotic modern dance routines, esp. in nightclub

goad (gohd) n. spiked stick for driving cattle; anything that urges to action; incentive —vt. urge on; torment

goal (gohl) n. end of race; object of effort; posts through which ball is to be driven in various games; the score so made

goat (goht) n. four-footed animal with long hair, horns and beard —goat·ee' n. beard like goat's —get (someone's) goat inf. annoy (someone)

gob n. lump; sl. sailor —gob·ble (GOB-əl) vt. (-bled, -bling) eat hastily, noisily or greedily

gob·ble n. throaty, gurgling cry of male turkey —vi. (-bled, -bling) make such a noise

gob·ble·de·gook, -dy·gook (GOB-əl-dee-guuk) n. pretentious, usu. incomprehensible language, esp. as used by officials

gob·let (GOB-lit) n. drinking cup

gob·lin n. Folklore small, usu. malevolent being

god n. superhuman being wor-

shipped as having supernatural power; object of worship, idol; (G-) in monotheistic religions, the Supreme Being, creator and ruler of universe (god'dess fem.) —god'like adj. —god'li·ness n. —god'ly adj. (-li·er, -li·est) devout, pious —god'child n. one considered in relation to godparent n. —god'father, -mother n. sponsor at baptism —God-fearing adj. religious, good —god'for·sak·en (-for·say·ken) adj. hopeless, dismal —God'head n. divine nature or deity —god'send n. something unexpected but welcome

gog·gle (GOG-əl) vi. (-gled, -gling) (of eyes) bulge; stare —n. pl. protective eyeglasses

goi·ter (GOI-tər) n. neck swelling due to enlargement of thyroid gland

go-kart, go-cart see KART

gold (gohld) n. yellow precious metal; coins of this; wealth; beautiful or precious thing; color of gold —adj. of, like gold —gold'en adj. —gold digger inf. woman skillful in extracting money from men —golden mean middle way between extremes —gold'en·rod n. tall plant with golden flower spikes —golden rule important principle —golden wedding fiftieth wedding anniversary —gold'field n. place where gold deposits are known to exist —gold'finch n. bird with yellow feathers —gold'fish n. any of various ornamental pond or aquarium fish —gold standard financial arrangement whereby currencies of countries accepting it are expressed in fixed terms of gold

golf n. outdoor game in which small hard ball is struck with clubs into a succession of holes —vi. play this game

**go·nad** (GOH-nad) n. gland producing gametes

**gon·do·la** (GON-dl-ɔ) n. Venetian canal boat —**gon·do·lier'** n. rower of gondola

**gone** (gawn) pp. of GO

**gong** n. metal plate with turned rim that resounds as bell when struck with soft mallet; anything used thus

**gon·or·rhea** (gon-ɔ-REE-ɔ) n. a venereal disease

**good** (guud) adj. (**bet·ter, best**) commendable; right; proper; excellent; beneficial; well-behaved; virtuous; kind; safe; adequate; sound; valid —n. benefit; well-being; profit —pl. property; wares —**good'ly** adj. large, considerable —**good'ness** n. —**good will** kindly feeling, heartiness; value of a business in reputation etc. over and above its tangible assets

**good-bye** (guud-BI) interj./n. form of address on parting

**goof** n. inf. mistake; stupid person —vi. make mistake —**goof'y** adj. (**goof·i·er, -i·est**) silly

**goon** n. sl. stupid, awkward fellow; inf. hired thug, hoodlum

**goose** (goos) n. (pl. **geese**) webfooted bird; its flesh; simpleton —**goose flesh** bristling of skin due to cold, fright —**goose step** formal parade step

**go·pher** (GOH-fɔr) n. various species of Amer. burrowing rodents —**gopher ball** Baseball sl. pitched ball hit for home run

**gore**[1] (gor) n. (dried) blood from wound —**gor'y** adj. (**gor·i·er, -i·est**)

**gore**[2] vt. (**gored, gor·ing**) pierce with horns

**gore**[3] n. triangular piece inserted

to shape garment —vt. (**gored, gor·ing**) shape thus

**gorge** (gorj) n. ravine; disgust, resentment —vi. (**gorged, gorg·ing**) feed greedily

**gor·geous** (GOR-jɔs) adj. splendid, showy, dazzling; inf. extremely pleasing

**gor·gon** (GOR-gɔn) n. terrifying or repulsive woman; (G-) in Greek mythology, any of three sisters whose appearance turned any viewer to stone

**go·ril·la** (gɔ-RIL-ɔ) n. largest anthropoid ape, found in Afr.

**gor·mand·ize** (GOR-mɔn-dīz) vt. (**-ized, -iz·ing**) eat hurriedly or like a glutton

**gory** see GORE[1]

**gos'hawk** n. large hawk

**gos·ling** (GOZ-ling) n. young goose

**gos·pel** (GOS-pɔl) n. unquestionable truth; (G-) any of first four books of New Testament

**gos·sa·mer** (GOS-ɔ-mɔr) n. filmy substance like spider's web; thin gauze or silk fabric

**gos·sip** (GOS-ɔp) n. idle (malicious) talk about other persons, esp. regardless of fact; one who talks thus —vi. (**-siped, -sip·ing**) engage in gossip; chatter

**got** see GET

**Goth·ic** (GOTH-ik) adj. Architecture of the pointed arch style common in Europe from twelfth to sixteenth century; of Goths; barbarous; gloomy; grotesque; (of type) German black letter

**gouge** (gowj) vt. (**gouged, gouging**) scoop out; force out; extort from; overcharge —n. chisel with curved cutting edge

**gou·lash** (GOO-lahsh) n. stew of meat and vegetables seasoned with paprika etc.

**gourd** (gord) n. trailing or climbing plant; its large fleshy fruit; its rind as vessel

**gour·mand** (guur-MAHND) n. glutton

**gour·met** (guur-MAY) n. connoisseur of wine, food; epicure

**gout** (gowt) n. disease with inflammation, esp. of joints

**gov·ern** (GUV-ərn) vt. rule, direct, guide, control; decide or determine; be followed by (grammatical case etc.) —gov·ern·a·ble adj. —gov'ern·ess n. woman teacher in private household —gov'ern·ment n. exercise of political authority in directing a people, country etc.; system by which community is ruled; body of people in charge of government of country; executive power; control; direction; exercise of authority —gov'ern·or n. one who governs, esp. one invested with supreme authority in a state etc.; chief administrator of an institution; member of committee responsible for an organization or institution; regulator for speed of engine

**gown** n. loose flowing outer garment; woman's (long) dress; official robe, as in university etc.

**grab** vt. (grabbed, grab·bing) grasp suddenly; snatch —n. sudden clutch; quick attempt to seize; device or implement for clutching

**grace** (grays) n. charm, elegance, accomplishment; goodwill, favor; sense of propriety; postponement granted; short thanksgiving before or after meal —vt. (graced, grac·ing) add grace to, honor —grace'ful adj. —grace'less adj. shameless, depraved —gra'cious (-shəs) adj. favorable; kind; pleasing; indulgent, beneficent, condescending —grace note Mus. melodic ornament

**grade** (grayd) n. step, stage; degree of rank etc.; class; mark, rating; slope —vt. (grad·ed, grad·ing) arrange in classes; assign grade to; level ground, move earth with grader —gra·da'tion n. series of degrees or steps; each of them; arrangement in steps; in painting, gradual passing from one shade etc. to another —grad'er n. esp. machine with wide blade used in road making —make the grade succeed

**gra·di·ent** (GRAY-dee-ənt) n. (degree of) slope

**grad·u·al** (GRAJ-oo-əl) adj. taking place by degrees; slow and steady; not steep —grad'u·al·ly adv.

**grad·u·ate** (GRAJ-oo-ayt) v. (-at·ed, -at·ing) —vi. receive diploma or degree on completing course of study —vt. divide into degrees; mark, arrange according to scale —n. (-it) holder of diploma or degree —grad·u·a'tion n.

**graf·fi·ti** (grə-FEE-tee) n. pl. (sing. -fi·to) (oft. obscene) writing, drawing on walls

**graft**[1] n. shoot of plant set in stalk of another; the process; surgical transplant of skin, tissue —vt. insert (shoot) in another stalk; transplant (living tissue in surgery)

**graft**[2] n. inf. self-advancement, profit by unfair means, esp. through official or political privilege; bribe; swindle

**grail** (grayl) n. (usu. Holy Grail) cup or dish used by Christ at the Last Supper

**grain** (grayn) n. seed, fruit of cereal plant; wheat and allied plants; small hard particle; unit of weight, 0.0648 gram; texture; arrangement of fibers; any very small amount; natural temperament or disposition

**gram** n. unit of weight (equivalent to 0.035 ounce) in metric system, one thousandth of a kilogram

**gram·mar** (GRAM-ər) n. science of structure and usage of language; book on this; correct use of words —**gram·mar·i·an** (gra-MAIR-ee-ən) n. —**gram·mat·i·cal** adj. according to grammar —**grammar school** elementary school

**gra·na·ry** (GRAY-nə-ree) n. (pl. -ries) storehouse for grain; rich grain-growing region

**grand** adj. (-er, -est) imposing; magnificent; majestic; noble; splendid; eminent; lofty; chief, of chief importance; final (total) —**gran·deur** (GRAN-jər) n. nobility; magnificence; dignity —**gran·dil·o·quence** n. —**gran·dil·o·quent** adj. pompous in speech —**gran·di·ose** (-dee-ohs) adj. imposing; affectedly grand; striking —**grand'child** n. child of one's child (**grand'son** or **grand'daugh·ter**) —**grand'par·ent** n. parent of parent —**grand'fa·ther**, **-moth·er** —**grand'pi·an·o** large harp-shaped piano with horizontal strings —**grand'stand** n. structure with tiered seats for spectators

**grange** (graynj) n. farm with its farmhouse and farm buildings

**gran·ite** (GRAN-it) n. hard crystalline igneous rock —**gran'ite·like** adj.

**gran·ny** (GRAN-ee) n. inf. (pl. -nies) grandmother

**grant** vt. consent to fulfill (request); permit; bestow; admit —n. sum of money provided by government or other source for specific purpose, as education; gift; allowance, concession

**gran·ule** (GRAN-yool) n. small grain; small particle —**gran'u·lar** (-yə-lər) adj. of or like grains

**grape** (grayp) n. fruit of vine —**grape'shot** n. bullets scattering when fired —**grape'vine** (-vīn) n. grape-bearing vine; inf. unofficial means of conveying information

**grape·fruit** (GRAYP-froot) n. subtropical citrus fruit

**graph** (graf) n. drawing depicting relation of different numbers, quantities etc. —vt. represent by graph

**graph·ic** (GRAF-ik) adj. vividly descriptive; of, in, relating to, writing, drawing, painting etc. —**graph'i·cal·ly** adv. —**graph'ite** (-īt) n. form of carbon (used in pencils) —**graph·ol'o·gy** n. study of handwriting

**grap·nel** (GRAP-nl) n. hooked iron instrument for seizing anything; small anchor with several flukes

**grap·ple** (GRAP-əl) v. (-pled, -pling) come to grips with, wrestle; cope or contend —n. grappling; grapnel

**grasp** v. (try, struggle to) seize hold; understand —n. act of grasping; grip; comprehension —**grasp'ing** adj. greedy, avaricious

**grass** n. common type of plant with jointed stems and long narrow leaves (including cereals, bamboo etc.); such plants grown as lawn; pasture; sl. marijuana —vt. cover with grass —**grass'hop·per** n. jumping, chirping insect —**grass roots** ordinary people; fundamentals —**grass-roots** adj. coming from ordinary people, the rank and file

**grate**[1] (grayt) n. framework of metal bars for holding fuel in fireplace —**grat'ing** n. frame-

work of parallel or latticed bars
covering opening

**grate**[2] v. (**grat·ed, grat·ing**) —vt.
rub into small bits on rough surface —vi. rub with harsh noise;
have irritating effect —**grat'er** n.
utensil with rough surface for
reducing substance to small particles —**grating** adj. harsh; irritating

**grate·ful** (GRAYT-fəl) adj. thankful; appreciative; pleasing
—**grat·i·tude** (GRAT-ə-tood) n.
sense of being thankful for favor

**grat·i·fy** (GRAT-ə-fi) vt. (**-fied, -fy-
ing**) satisfy; please; indulge
—**grat·i·fi·ca'tion** n.

**gratin** see AU GRATIN

**grat'is** adv./adj. free, for nothing

**gra·tu·i·tous** (grə-TOO-i-təs) adj.
given free; uncalled for —**gra·
tu'i·tous·ly** adv. —**gra·tu'i·ty** n.
(pl. **-ties**) a tip

**grave**[1] (grayv) n. hole dug to bury
corpse; death —**grave'stone** n.
monument on grave —**grave'-
yard** n.

**grave**[2] adj. (**grav·er, grav·est**) serious, weighty; dignified, solemn;
plain, dark in color; deep in note
—**grave'ly** adv.

**grave**[3] n. accent (`) over vowel to
indicate special sound quality

**grav·el** (GRAV-əl) n. small stones;
coarse sand —vt. (**-eled, -el·ing**)
cover with gravel —**grav'el·ly**
adj.

**grav·en** (GRAY-vən) adj. carved,
engraved

**grav·i·tate** (GRAV-i-tayt) vi.
(**-tat·ed, -tat·ing**) move by gravity; tend (toward) center of attraction; sink, settle down
—**grav·i·ta'tion** n.

**grav·i·ty** (GRAV-i-tee) n. (pl.
**-ties**) force of attraction of one
body for another, esp. of objects
to Earth; heaviness; importance;
seriousness; staidness

**gra·vy** (GRAY-vee) n. (pl. **-vies**)
juices from meat in cooking;
sauce for food made from these;
thing of value obtained unexpectedly

**gray** adj. between black and
white, as ashes or lead; clouded;
dismal; turning white; aged;
intermediate, indeterminate —n.
gray color; gray or white horse

**graze**[1] (grayz) v. (**grazed, grazing**) feed on grass, pasture

**graze**[2] vt. (**grazed, graz·ing**) touch
lightly in passing, scratch, scrape
—n. grazing; abrasion

**grease** (grees) n. soft melted fat
of animals; thick oil as lubricant
—vt. (**greased, greas·ing**) apply
grease to —**greas'i·ness** n.
—**greas'y** adj. (**greas·i·er,
greas·i·est**) —**grease gun** appliance for injecting grease into
machinery —**grease monkey** inf.
mechanic —**grease'paint** n. theatrical makeup

**great** (grayt) adj. (**-er, -est**)
large, big; important; preeminent, distinguished; inf. excellent —prefix indicates a degree
further removed in relationship,
eg **great-grand'fa·ther** n.
—**great'ly** adv. —**great'ness** n.
—**Great Dane** breed of very large
dog

**Gre·cian** (GREE-shən) adj. of (ancient) Greece

**greed** n. excessive consumption
of, desire for, food, wealth
—**greed'y** adj. (**greed·i·er,
greed·i·est**) gluttonous; eagerly
desirous; voracious; covetous
—**greed'i·ly** adv.

**Greek** n. native language of
Greece —adj. of Greece or
Greek

**green** adj. (**-er, -est**) of color
between blue and yellow; grass-
colored; emerald; unripe; inexperienced; gullible; envious —n.

color; area of grass, *esp.* in golf, for putting; —*pl.* green vegetables —**green′er·y** *n.* (*pl.* -er·ies) vegetation —**green belt** area of farms, open country around a community —**green′horn** *n.* inexperienced person; *sl.* recent immigrant, newcomer —**green′house** *n.* (*pl.* -hous·es, *pr.* -howziz) (usu.) glass house for rearing plants —**green′room** *n.* room for actors, TV performers, when offstage —**green thumb** talent for gardening

**greet** *vt.* meet with expressions of welcome; accost, salute; receive —**greet′ing** *n.*

**gre·gar·i·ous** (gri-GAIR-ee-əs) *adj.* fond of company, sociable; living in flocks —**gre·gar′i·ous·ness** *n.*

**grem′lin** *n.* imaginary being blamed for mechanical and other troubles

**gre·nade** (gri-NAYD) *n.* explosive shell or bomb, thrown by hand or shot from rifle

**gren·a·dine** (gren-ə-DEEN) *n.* syrup made from pomegranate juice, for sweetening and coloring drinks

**grew** *pt. of* GROW

**grey′hound** (GRAY-hownd) *n.* swift slender dog used in racing

**grid** *n.* network of horizontal and vertical lines, bars *etc.*; any interconnecting system of links; regional network of electricity supply

**grid·dle** (GRID-l) *n.* frying pan, flat iron plate for cooking —**grid′dle·cake** *n.* pancake

**grid·i·ron** (GRID-i-ərn) *n.* frame of metal bars for grilling; (field of play for) football

**grief** (greef) *n.* deep sorrow —**griev·ance** (GREE-vəns) *n.* real or imaginary ground of complaint —**grieve** *v.* (grieved, griev-ing) —*vi.* feel grief —*vt.* cause grief to —**griev′ous** *adj.* painful, oppressive; very serious

**grif·fin, grif·fon, gryph·on** (all GRIF-in) *n.* fabulous monster with eagle's head and wings and lion's body

**grill** *n.* grated utensil for broiling meat *etc.*; food cooked on grill; grillroom —*v.* cook (food) on grill; subject to severe questioning —**grill′ing** *n.* severe cross-examination —**grill′room** *n.* restaurant specializing in grilled food

**grille** (gril) *n.* grating, crosswork of bars over opening

**grim** *adj.* (grim·mer, grim·mest) stern; of stern or forbidding aspect, relentless; joyless

**grim·ace** (GRIM-əs) *n.* wry face —*vi.* (-aced, -ac·ing) make wry face

**grime** (grīm) *n.* ingrained dirt, soot —*vt.* (grimed, grim·ing) soil; dirty; blacken —**grim′y** *adj.* (grim·i·er, grim·i·est)

**grin** *vi.* (grinned, grin·ning) show teeth, as in laughter —*n.* grinning smile

**grind** (grīnd) *v.* (ground, grind·ing) —*vt.* crush to powder; oppress; make sharp, smooth; grate —*vi.* perform action of grinding; *inf.* (with away) work (*esp.* study) hard; grate —*n. inf.* hard work, excessively diligent student; action of grinding

**grin·go** (GRING-goh) *n.* (*pl.* -gos) in Mexico, contemptuous name for foreigner, esp. American or Englishman

**grip** *n.* firm hold, grasp; grasping power; mastery; handle; suitcase or traveling bag —*vt.* (gripped, grip·ping) grasp or hold tightly; hold interest or attention of

**gripe** (grīp) *vi. inf.* (griped, grip·ing) complain (persistently) —*n.*

*inf.* complaint —*pl.* intestinal pain

**gris·ly** (GRIZ-lee) *adj.* (-li·er, -li·est) grim, causing terror, ghastly

**grist** *n.* grain to be ground —**grist for one's mill** something that can be turned to advantage

**gris·tle** (GRIS-əl) *n.* cartilage, tough flexible tissue

**grit** *n.* rough particles of sand; coarse sandstone; courage —*pl.* hominy *etc.* coarsely ground and cooked as breakfast food —*vt.* (grit·ted, grit·ting) clench, grind (teeth) —**grit'ty** *adj.* (-ti·er, -ti·est)

**griz·zle** (GRIZ-əl) *v.* (-zled, -zling) make, become gray —**griz'zly** (bear) large Amer. bear

**groan** (grohn) *vi.* make low, deep sound of grief or pain; be in pain or overburdened —*n.*

**groats** (grohts) *n.* hulled grain or kernels of oats, wheat *etc.* broken into fragments

**gro·cer** (GROH-sər) *n.* dealer in foodstuffs —**gro'cer·ies** *n. pl.* commodities sold by a grocer —**gro'cer·y** *n.* (*pl.* -cer·ies) trade, premises of grocer

**grog·gy** (GROG-ee) *adj. inf.* (-gier, -gi·est) unsteady, shaky, weak

**groin** *n.* fold where legs meet abdomen; euphemism for genitals

**groom** *n.* person caring for horses; bridegroom —*vt.* tend or look after; brush or clean (*esp.* horse); train (someone for something) —**well-groomed** *adj.* neat, smart

**groove** (groov) *n.* narrow channel, hollow, *esp.* cut by tool; rut, routine —*vt.* (grooved, groov·ing) cut groove in —*v. inf. sl.* (groov·i·er, groov·i·est) attractive, exciting

**grope** (grohp) *vi.* (groped, grop·ing) feel about, search blindly

**gros·beak** (GROHS-beek) *n.* finch with large powerful bill

**gross** (grohs) *adj.* (-er, -est) very fat; total, not net; coarse; indecent; flagrant; thick, rank —*n.* twelve dozen

**gro·tesque** (groh-TESK) *adj.* (horribly) distorted; absurd —*n.* grotesque person, thing

**grot·to** (GROT-oh) *n.* (*pl.* -toes) cave

**grouch** (growch) *n. inf.* persistent grumbler; discontented mood —*vi.* grumble, be peevish

**ground**[1] (grownd) *n.* surface of Earth; soil, earth; reason, motive; coating to work on with paint; background, main surface worked on in painting, embroidery *etc.*; special area; bottom of sea —*pl.* dregs; land around house and belonging to it —*vt.* establish; instruct (in elements); place on ground —*vi.* run ashore; strike ground —**ground'ed** *adj.* of aircraft or pilot, unable or not permitted to fly; *inf.* of child, punished by restriction of activities —**ground'ing** *n.* basic general knowledge of a subject —**ground'less** *adj.* without reason —**ground'speed** *n.* aircraft's speed in relation to ground

**ground**[2] *pt./pp.* of GRIND

**group** (groop) *n.* number of persons or things near together, or placed or classified together; small musical band of players or singers; class; two or more figures forming one artistic design —*v.* place, fall into group

**grouse**[1] (grows) *n.* (*pl. same form*) game bird; its flesh

**grouse**[2] *vi.* (groused, grous·ing) grumble, complain —*n.* complaint —**grous'er** *n.* grumbler

**grout** (growt) *n.* thin fluid mortar —*vt.* fill up with grout

**grove** (grohv) n. small group of trees

**grov·el** (GRUV-əl) vi. (-eled, -el·ing) abase oneself; lie or crawl facedown

**grow** (groh) v. (grew, grown, grow·ing) —vi. develop naturally; increase in size, height etc.; be produced; become by degrees —vt. produce by cultivation —**growth** n. growing; increase; what has grown or is growing —**grown-up** adj. —**grownup** n. adult

**growl** vi. make low guttural sound of anger; rumble; murmur, complain —n.

**grub** v. (grubbed, grub·bing) dig superficially; root up; dig, rummage; plod; drudge —n. larva of insect; sl. food —**grub'by** adj. (-bi·er, -bi·est) dirty

**grudge** (gruj) vt. (grudged, grudg·ing) be unwilling to give, allow —n. ill will

**gru·el** (GROO-əl) n. food of cereal boiled in milk or water —**gru'el·ing** adj./n. exhausting, severe (experience)

**grue·some** (GROO-səm) adj. fearful, horrible, grisly —**grue'some·ness** n.

**gruff** adj. (-er, -est) rough in manner or voice, surly —**gruff'ness** n.

**grum·ble** (GRUM-bəl) vi. (-bled, -bling) complain; rumble, murmur; make growling sounds —n. complaint; low growl

**grump·y** (GRUM-pee) adj. (grump·i·er, grump·i·est) ill-tempered, surly —**grump'i·ness** n.

**grunt** vi. make sound characteristic of pig —n. pig's sound; gruff noise

**gryphon** n. see GRIFFIN

**G-string** (JEE-string) n. very small covering for genitals; Mus. string tuned to G

**gua·no** (GWAH-noh) n. manure of seabird

**guar·an·tee** (gar-ən-TEE) n. formal assurance (esp. in writing) that product etc. will meet certain standards, last for given time etc. —vt. (-teed, -tee'ing) give guarantee of, for something; secure (against risk etc.) —**guar'an·tor** n. one who guarantees —**guar'an·ty** n. (pl. -ties)

**guard** (gahrd) vt. protect, defend —vi. be careful, take precautions (against) —n. person, group that protects, supervises, keeps watch; sentry; soldiers protecting anything; official in charge of train; protection; screen for enclosing anything dangerous; protector; posture of defense —**guard'i·an** (-ee·ən) n. keeper, protector; person having custody of infant etc. —**guard'i·an·ship** n. care —**guard'house** n. place for stationing those on guard or for prisoners

**gua·va** (GWAH-və) n. tropical tree with fruit used to make jelly

**guer·ril·la** (gə-RIL-ə) n. member of irregular armed force, esp. fighting established force, government etc.

**Guern·sey** (GURN-zee) n. (pl. -seys) breed of cattle

**guess** (ges) vt. estimate without calculation; conjecture, suppose; consider, think —vi. form conjectures —n.

**guest** (gest) n. one entertained at another's house; one living in hotel —**guest'house** n. small house for guests, separate from main house

**guff** n. inf. silly talk; insolent talk

**guf·faw** (gə-FAW) n. burst of boisterous laughter —vi.

**guide** (gīd) n. one who shows the

way; adviser; book of instruction or information; contrivance for directing motion —vt. (guid·ed, guid·ing) lead, act as guide to; arrange —guid'ance (-əns) n. —guided missile n. whose flight path is controlled by radio signals or programmed homing mechanism

**guild** (gild) n. organization; club; society for mutual help, or with common object; Hist. society of merchants or tradesmen

**guile** (gīl) n. cunning, deceit —guile'ful adj. —guile'less adj. sincere, straightforward

**guil·lo·tine** (GIL-ə-teen) n. machine for beheading —vt. (-tined, -tin·ing) behead

**guilt** (gilt) n. fact, state of having done wrong; responsibility for criminal or moral offense —guilt'less adj. innocent —guilt'y adj. (guilt·i·er, guilt·i·est) having committed an offense

**guin·ea** (GIN-ee) n. pig rodent originating in S Amer.; inf. person used in experiments

**guise** (gīz) n. external appearance, esp. one assumed

**gui·tar** (gi-TAHR) n. usu. six-stringed instrument played by plucking or strumming —gui-tar'ist n.

**gulch** n. ravine; gully

**gulf** n. large inlet of the sea; chasm; large gap

**gull[1]** n. long-winged web-footed seabird

**gull[2]** n. dupe, fool —vt. dupe, cheat —gul·li·bil'i·ty n. —gul'li·ble adj. easily imposed on, credulous

**gul·let** (GUL-it) n. food passage from mouth to stomach

**gul·ly** (GUL-ee) n. (pl. -lies) channel or ravine worn by water

**gulp** vt. swallow eagerly —vi. gasp, choke —n.

**gum[1]** n. firm flesh in which teeth are set —vt. (gummed, gum·ming) chew with the gums

**gum[2]** n. sticky substance issuing from certain trees; an adhesive; chewing gum; gum tree, eucalyptus —vt. (gummed, gum·ming) stick with gum —gum'my adj. (-mi·er, -mi·est) —gum'shoe n. shoe of rubber; sl. detective —gum tree any species of eucalyptus —gum up the works sl. impede progress

**gump·tion** (GUM-shən) n. resourcefulness; shrewdness; common sense

**gun** n. weapon with metal tube from which missiles are discharged by explosion; cannon, pistol etc. —v. (gunned, gun·ning) shoot; pursue as with gun; race engine (of car) —gun'ner n. —gun'ner·y n. use or science of large guns —gun'boat n. small warship —gun dog (breed of) dog used to retrieve etc. game —gun'man n. armed criminal —gun'met·al n. alloy of copper and tin or zinc, formerly used for guns —gun'pow·der n. explosive mixture of saltpeter, sulfur, charcoal —gun'shot n. shot or range of gun —adj. caused by missile from gun —gun'wale, gun'nel (both GUN-l) n. upper edge of ship's side

**gunk** (gungk) n. inf. any sticky, oily matter

**gun·ny** (GUN-ee) n. (pl. -nies) strong, coarse sacking made from jute

**gup·py** (GUP-ee) n. (pl. -pies) small colorful aquarium fish

**gur·gle** (GUR-gəl) n. bubbling noise —vi. (-gled, -gling) utter, flow with gurgle

**gu·ru** (GUUR-oo) n. a spiritual teacher, guide in India

**gush** vi. flow out suddenly and copiously; spurt —n. sudden and copious flow; effusiveness —**gush'er** *n.* gushing person; oil well

**gus·set** (GUS-it) *n.* triangle or diamond-shaped piece of material let into garment —**gus'set·ed** *adj.*

**gust** *n.* sudden blast of wind; burst of rain, anger, passion *etc.* —**gust'y** *adj.* (gust·i·er, gust·i·est)

**gus·to** (GUS-toh) *n.* enjoyment, zest

**gut** *n.* (*oft. pl.*) entrails, intestines; material made from guts of animals, *eg* for violin strings *etc.* —*pl. inf.* essential, fundamental part; courage —*vt.* (gut·ted, gut·ting) remove guts from (fish *etc.*); remove, destroy contents of (house) —**guts'y** *adj. inf.* (guts·i·er, guts·i·est) courageous; vigorous

**gut·ter** (GUT-ər) *n.* shallow trough for carrying off water from roof or side of street —*vt.* make channels in —*vi.* flow in streams; of candle, melt away by wax forming channels and running down —**gutter press** journalism that relies on sensationalism —**gut'ter·snipe** (-snip) *n.* neglected slum child

**gut·tur·al** (GUT-ər-əl) *adj.* of, relating to, or produced in, the throat —*n.* guttural sound or letter

**guy**[1] (gī) *n.* inf. person (*usu.* male) —*vt.* (guyed, guy·ing) make fun of; ridicule —**wise guy** *inf., usu.* disparaging clever person

**guy**[2] *n.* rope, chain *etc.* to steady, secure something, *eg* tent —*vt.* (guyed, guy·ing) keep in position by guy

**guz·zle** (GUZ-əl) *v.* (-zled, -zling) eat or drink greedily —

**gym** (jim) *n.* short for GYMNASIUM *or* GYMNASTICS

**gym·kha·na** (jim-KAH-nə) *n.* competition or display of horse riding or gymnastics; place for this

**gym·na·si·um** (jim-NAY-zee-əm) *n.* place equipped for muscular exercises, athletic training —**gym'nast** *n.* expert in gymnastics —**gym·nas'tics** *n. pl.* muscular exercises, with or without apparatus, *eg* parallel bars

**gy·ne·col·o·gy** (gī-ni-KOL-ə-jee) *n.* branch of medicine dealing with functions and diseases of women —**gy·ne·col'o·gist** *n.*

**gyp·sum** (JIP-səm) *n.* crystalline sulfate of lime, a source of plaster

**Gyp·sy** (JIP-see) *n.* (*pl.* -sies) one of a wandering people originally from NW India, Romany

**gy·rate** (JĪ-rayt) *vi.* (-rat·ed, -rat·ing) move in circle, spirally, revolve —**gy·ra'tion** *n.*

**gy·ro·com·pass** (JĪ-roh-kum-pəs) *n.* compass using gyroscope

**gy·ro·scope** (JĪ-rə-skohp) *n.* disk or wheel so mounted as to be able to rotate about any axis, *esp.* to keep disk (with compass *etc.*) level despite movement of ship *etc.* —**gy·ro·scop'ic** (-SKOP-ik) *adj.*

**gy·ro·sta·bi·liz·er** (jī-rə-STAY-bə-lī-zər) *n.* gyroscopic device to prevent rolling of ship or airplane

# H

**H** *Chem.* hydrogen

**ha·be·as cor·pus** (HAY-bee-əs KOR-pəs) *n.* writ issued to produce prisoner in court

**hab·er·dash·er** (HAB-ər-dash-ər) *n.* dealer in articles of dress, ribbons, pins, needles etc. —hab'er·dash·er·y n. (-er·ies)

hab'it n. settled tendency or practice; constitution; customary apparel esp. of nun or monk; woman's riding dress —ha·bit·u·al (hə-BICH-oo-əl) adj. formed or acquired by habit; usual, customary —ha·bit'u·ate (-ayt) vt. (-at·ed, -at·ing) accustom —ha·bit·u·a'tion n. —ha·bit'u·é (-oo-ay) n. constant visitor

hab·it·a·ble (HAB-i-tə-bəl) adj. fit to live in —hab'i·tat n. natural home (of animal etc.) —hab·i·ta'tion (-TAY-shon) n. dwelling place

ha·ci·en·da (hah-see-EN-də) n. (pl. -das) ranch or large estate in Sp. Amer.

hack¹ (hak) vt. cut, chop (at) violently; inf. utter harsh, dry cough; sl. deal or cope with —n. —hack'er n. sl. computer fanatic, esp. one who through personal computer breaks into computer system of company or government —hack around sl. pass time idly

hack² n. drudge; writer of inferior literary works; cabdriver —hack'work n. dull, repetitive work

hack·le (HAK-əl) n. neck feathers of rooster etc. —pl. hairs on back of neck of dog and other animals that are raised in anger

hack·ney (HAK-nee) n. (pl. -neys) harness horse, carriage, coach kept for hire

hack·neyed (HAK-need) adj. (of words etc.) stale, trite because of overuse

hack·saw (HAK-saw) n. handsaw for cutting metal

had pt./pp. of HAVE

Ha·des (HAY-deez) n. abode of the dead; underworld; (oft. h-) hell

haft n. handle (of knife etc.) —vt. fit with one

hag n. ugly old woman; witch

hag·gard (HAG-ərd) adj. wild-looking; anxious, careworn

hag'gis n. Scottish dish made from sheep's heart, lungs, liver, chopped with oatmeal, suet, onion etc., and boiled in the stomach

hag·gle (HAG-əl) vi. (-gled, -gling) bargain, wrangle over price —n.

hag·i·ol·o·gy (hag-ee-OL-ə-jee) n. (pl. -gies) literature of the lives of saints —hag·i·og'ra·pher (-rə-fər) n. —hag·i·og'ra·phy n. (pl. -phies) writing of this

hail¹ (hayl) n. (shower of) pellets of ice; intense shower, barrage —v. pour down as shower of hail —hail'stone n.

hail² vt. greet (esp. enthusiastically); acclaim, acknowledge; call —vi. come (from)

hair n. filament growing from skin of animal, as covering of person's head; such filaments collectively —hair'i·ness n. —hair'y adj. (hair·i·er, hair·i·est) —hair'do (-doo) n. (pl. -dos) way of styling hair —hair'dress·er n. one who attends to and cuts hair, esp. women's hair —hair'line adj./n. very fine (line); lower edge of human hair eg on forehead —hair'pin n. pin for keeping hair in place —hairpin bend U-shaped turn in road —hair'split·ting n. making of overly fine distinctions —hair'spring n. very fine, delicate spring in timepiece —hair trigger trigger operated by light touch —hair-trigger adj. easily set off, eg temper

hal·cy·on (HAL-see-ən) n. bird fabled to calm the sea and to breed on floating nest —halcyon days time of peace and happiness

hale (hayl) adj. (hal·er, hal·est)

robust, healthy, *esp. in* hale and hearty

**half** (haf) *n.* (*pl.* halves *pr.* havz) either of two equal parts of thing —*adj.* forming half —*adv.* to the extent of half —**half′back** *n.* Football one of two players lining up on each side of fullback —**half-baked** *adj.* underdone; *inf.* immature, silly —**half′-breed** (*offens.*), **half′-caste** *n.* person with parents of different races —**half′-broth·er, -sis·ter** *n.* brother (sister) by one parent only —**half-cocked** *adj.* ill-prepared —**half′-heart·ed** *adj.* unenthusiastic —**half′-life** *n.* (*pl. -lives*) time taken for half the atoms in radioactive material to decay —**half nel′son** hold in wrestling —**half′time** *n.* Sports rest period between two halves of a game —**half′tone** *n.* illustration printed by photoengraving from plate, showing lights and shadows by means of minute dots —**half vol′ley** Tennis etc. striking of a ball the moment it bounces —**half′wit** *n.* feebleminded person; stupid person

**hal·i·but** (HAL-ə-bət) *n.* large edible flatfish

**hal·i·to·sis** (hal-i-TOH-sis) *n.* bad-smelling breath

**hall** (hawl) *n.* (entrance) passage; large room or building belonging to particular group or used for particular purpose *esp.* public assembly

**hal·le·lu·jah** (hal-ə-LOO-yə) *n./interj.* exclamation of praise to God

**hall′mark** (HAWL-mahrk) *n.* mark used to indicate standard of tested gold and silver; mark of excellence; distinguishing feature

**hal·low** (HAL-oh) *vt.* make, or honor as holy —**Hal·low·een** (hal-ə-WEEN) *n.* the evening of Oct.

31st, the day before All Saints' Day

**hal·lu·ci·nate** (hə-LOO-sə-nayt) *vi.* (*-nat·ed, -nat·ing*) suffer illusions —**hal·lu·ci·na′tion** *n.* illusion —**hal·lu′ci·na·to·ry** *adj.* —**hal·lu′ci·no·gen** (*-jən*) *n.* drug inducing hallucinations

**ha·lo** (HAY-loh) *n.* (*pl. -los, -loes*) circle of light around moon, sun *etc.*; disk of light around saint's head in picture; ideal glory attaching to person —*vt.* (*-loed, -lo·ing*) surround with halo

**halt**[1] *n.* interruption or end to progress *etc.* (*esp.* as command to stop marching) —*v.* (cause to) stop

**halt**[2] *vi.* falter, fail —**halt′ing** *adj.* hesitant, lame

**hal·ter** (HAWL-tər) *n.* rope or strap with headgear to fasten horses or cattle; low-cut dress style with strap passing behind neck —*vt.* put halter on, fasten with one

**halve** (hav) *vt.* (halved, halv·ing) cut in half; reduce to half; share

**hal·yard** (HAL-yərd) *n.* rope for raising sail, signal flags *etc.*

**ham** *n.* meat (*esp.* salted or smoked) from thigh of pig; actor adopting exaggerated, unconvincing style (*also adj. and v.*); amateur radio enthusiast —**ham′string** *n.* tendon at back of knee —*vt.* (*-strung, -string·ing*) cripple by cutting this; render useless; thwart

**ham·burg·er** (HAM-burg-gər) *n.* broiled, fried patty of ground beef, *esp.* served in bread roll

**ham·let** (HAM-lit) *n.* small village

**ham·mer** (HAM-ər) *n.* tool usu. with heavy head at end of handle, for beating, driving nails *etc.*; machine for same purposes; contrivance for exploding charge of gun; auctioneer's mallet; heavy metal ball on wire thrown in sports —v. strike with, or as with, hammer —ham'mer·head (-hed) n. shark with wide, flattened head —ham'mer·toe n. deformed toe —hammer out solve problem by painstaking work

ham·mock (HAM-ək) n. bed of canvas etc., hung on cords

ham·per[1] (HAM-pər) n. large covered basket; large parcel, box etc. of food, wines etc., esp. one sent as gift

hamper[2] vt. impede, obstruct movements of

ham·ster (HAM-stər) n. type of rodent, sometimes kept as pet

ham'strung adj. crippled, thwarted; see HAM

hand n. extremity of arm beyond wrist; side, quarter, direction; style of writing; cards dealt to player; measure of four inches; manual worker; sailor; help, aid; pointer on dial; applause —vt. pass; deliver; hold out —hand'ful n. (pl. -fuls) small amount or number; inf. person, thing causing problems —hand'i·ly adv. —hand'i·ness n. dexterity; state of being near, available —hand'y adj. (hand·i·er, hand·i·est) convenient; clever with the hands —hand'bag n. woman's bag for personal articles; bag for carrying in hand —hand'bill n. small printed notice —hand'book n. small reference or instruction book —hand'cuff n. fetter for wrist, usu. joined in pair —vt. secure thus —hand'i·craft n. manual occupation or skill —hand'i·work n. thing done by particular person —hand·ker·chief (HANG-kər-chif) n. small square of fabric carried in pocket for wiping nose etc. —hand'out n. inf. money, food etc. given free; pamphlet giving news, in-

formation etc. —hands-on adj. involving practical experience of equipment —hand'stand n. act of supporting body in upside-down position by hands alone —hand'writ·ing n. way person writes —hand'y·man n. one employed to do various tasks; one skilled in odd jobs —hand in glove very intimate

hand·i·cap (HAN-dee-kap) n. something that hampers or hinders; race, contest in which chances are equalized by weights carried, golf strokes etc.; condition so imposed; any physical disability —vt. (-capped, -capping) hamper; impose handicap on; attempt to predict winner of race, game

han·dle (HAN-dl) n. part of thing to hold it by —vi. (-dled, -dling) touch, feel with hands; manage; deal with; trade —han'dle·bars n. pl. curved metal bars used to steer bicycle, motorbike etc. —handlebar mustache one resembling handlebar

hand·some (HAN-səm) adj. of fine appearance; generous; ample

hang v. (hung or hanged, hanging) —vt. suspend; kill by suspension by neck; attach, set up (wallpaper, doors etc.) —vi. be suspended, cling —hang'er n. frame on which clothes etc. can be hung —hang'dog adj. sullen, dejected —hang glider glider like large kite, with pilot hanging in frame below —hang gliding —hang'man n. executioner —hang'o·ver n. aftereffects of too much drinking —hang out inf. reside, frequent —hang-up n. sl. persistent emotional problem; preoccupation

hang·ar (HANG-ər) n. large shed for aircraft

**hank** (hangk) *n.* coil, skein, length, *esp.* as measure of yarn

**hank·er** (HANG-kər) *vi.* oft. with *after* or *for*, crave

**han·ky-pan·ky** (HANG-kee-PANG-kee) *n. inf.* trickery; illicit sexual relations

**han·som** (HAN-səm) *n.* two-wheeled horse-drawn cab for two to ride inside with driver mounted up behind

**hap·haz·ard** (hap-HAZ-ərd) *adj.* random, careless

**hap·less** (HAP-lis) *adj.* unlucky

**hap·pen** (HAP-ən) *vi.* come about, occur; chance to do —**hap'pen·ing** *n.* occurrence, event

**hap·py** *adj.* (-pi·er, -pi·est) glad, content; lucky, fortunate; apt —**hap'pi·ly** *adv.* —**hap'pi·ness** *n.* —**hap'py·go·luck'y** *adj.* casual, lighthearted

**ha·ra·ki·ri** (HAHR-ə-KEER-ee) *n.* in Japan, ritual suicide by disemboweling

**ha·rangue** (hə-RANG) *n.* vehement speech; tirade —*v.* (-rangued, -rangu·ing)

**ha·rass** (hə-RAS) *vt.* worry, trouble, torment —**ha·rass'ment** *n.*

**har·bin·ger** (HAHR-bin-jər) *n.* one who announces another's approach; forerunner, herald

**har·bor** (HAHR-bər) *n.* shelter for ships; shelter —*v.* give shelter, protection to; maintain (secretly) *esp.* grudge *etc.*

**hard** (hahrd) *adj.* (-er, -est) firm, resisting pressure; solid; difficult to understand; harsh, unfeeling; difficult to bear; practical, shrewd; heavy; strenuous; of water, not making lather well with soap; of drugs, highly addictive —*adv.* vigorously; with difficulty; close —**hard'en** *v.* —**hard'ly** *adv.* unkindly, harshly; scarcely, not quite; only just —**hard'ship** *n.* bad luck; severe toil, suffering; in-

stance of this —**hard-boiled** *adj.* boiled so long as to be hard; *inf.* of person, unemotional, unsentimental —**hard-hat** *n. inf.* construction worker —**hard'head'ed** *adj.* shrewd —**hard-pressed** *adj.* heavily burdened —**hard'ware** *n.* tools, implements; necessary (parts of) machinery; Computers mechanical and electronic parts —**hard'wood** *n.* wood from deciduous trees —**hard of hearing** rather deaf —**hard up** very short of money

**har·dy** (HAHR-dee) *adj.* (-di·er, -di·est) robust, vigorous; bold; of plants, able to grow in the open all the year round —**har'di·hood** (-huud) *n.* extreme boldness, audacity —**hard'i·ly** *adv.* —**har'di·ness** *n.*

**hare** (hair) *n.* animal like large rabbit, with longer legs and ears, noted for speed —**hare'brained** *adj.* rash, wild —**hare'lip** *n.* fissure of upper lip

**har·em** (HAIR-əm) *n.* women's part of Muslim dwelling; one man's wives and concubines

**hark** (hahrk) *vi.* listen —**hark back** return to previous subject of discussion

**har·le·quin** (HAHR-lə-kwin) *n.* stock comic character, *esp.* masked clown in diamond-patterned costume —**har·le·quin·ade'** (-NAYD) *n.* scene in pantomime; buffoonery

**har·lot** (HAHR-lət) *n.* whore, prostitute —**har'lot·ry** *n.*

**harm** (hahrm) *n.* damage, injury —*vt.* cause harm to —**harm'ful** *adj.* —**harm'less** *adj.* unable or unlikely to hurt

**har·mo·ny** (HAHR-mə-nee) *n.* (*pl.* -nies) agreement; concord; peace; combination of notes to make chords; melodious sound —**har·mon'ic** *adj.* of harmony

—n. tone or note whose frequency is a multiple of its pitch —**har·mon·ics** n. with sing. v. science of musical sounds; (with pl. v.) harmonious sounds —**har·mo·ni·ca** n. various musical instruments, but esp. mouth organ —**har·mo'ni·ous** adj. —**har'mo·nize** (-mə·niz) v. (-nized, -niz·ing) —vt. bring into harmony; cause to agree; reconcile —vi. be in harmony

**har·ness** (HAHR-nis) n. equipment for attaching horse to cart, plow etc.; any such equipment —vt. put on, in harness; utilize energy or power of (waterfall etc.)

**harp** (hahrp) n. musical instrument of strings played by hand —vi. play on harp; dwell (on) persistently —**harp'ist** n. —**harp'si·chord** (-si-kord) n. stringed instrument like piano

**har·poon** (hahr-POON) n. barbed spear with rope attached for catching whales —vt. catch, kill with this —**har·poon'er** n. —**harpoon gun** gun for firing harpoon in whaling

**Har·py** (HAHR-pee) n. (pl. -pies) monster with body of woman and wings and claws of bird; (h-) cruel, grasping person

**har·ri·dan** (HAHR-i-dn) n. shrewish old woman, hag

**har·row** (HAR-oh) n. implement for smoothing, leveling or stirring up soil —vt. draw harrow over; distress greatly —**har'row·ing** adj. heartrending; distressful

**har·ry** (HAR-ee) vt. (-ried, -ry·ing) harass; ravage

**harsh** (hahrsh) adj. (-er, -est) rough, discordant; severe; unfeeling —**harsh·ness** n.

**har·um-scar·um** (HAIR-əm-SKAIR-əm) adj. reckless, wild; disorganized

**har·vest** (HAHR-vist) n. (season for) gathering in grain; gathering; crop; product of action —vt. reap and gather in

**has** (haz) third person sing. pres. indicative of HAVE

**hash** n. dish of hashed meat etc.; inf. short for HASHISH; mess, jumble —vt. cut up small, chop; mix up

**hash·ish** (hash-EESH) n. resinous extract of Indian hemp, esp. used as hallucinogen

**hasp** n. clasp passing over a staple for fastening door etc. —vt. fasten, secure with hasp

**has·sle** (HAS-əl) n. inf. quarrel; a lot of bother, trouble —v. (-sled, -sling)

**has·sock** (HAS-ək) n. cushion used as footstool, ottoman; tuft of grass

**haste** (hayst) n. speed, quickness, hurry —v. (hast·ed, hast·ing) vi. hasten —**has·ten** (HAY-sən) v. (cause to) hurry, increase speed —**hast'i·ly** adv. —**hast'y** adj. (hast·i·er, hast·i·est)

**hat** n. head covering, usu. with brim —**hat'ter** n. dealer in, maker of hats —**hat trick** any three successive achievements, esp. in sports

**hatch¹** (hach) v. of young, esp. of birds, (cause to) emerge from egg; contrive, devise —**hatch'er·y** n. (pl. -er·ies)

**hatch²** n. hatchway; trapdoor over it; lower half of divided door —**hatch'back** n. automobile with single lifting door in rear —**hatch'way** n. opening in deck of ship etc.

**hatch³** vt. engrave or draw lines on for shading; shade with parallel lines

**hatch·et** (HACH-it) n. small ax —**hatchet job** malicious verbal attack —**hatchet man** person carrying out unpleasant assignments for another; professional assassin —**bury the hatchet** make peace

**hate** (hayt) *vt.* (**hat·ed, hat·ing**) dislike strongly; bear malice toward —*n.* this feeling; that which is hated —**hate'ful** *adj.* detestable —**ha·tred** (HAY-trid) *n.* extreme dislike, active ill will

**haugh·ty** (HAW-tee) *adj.* (**-ti·er, -ti·est**) proud, arrogant —**haugh'ti·ness** *n.*

**haul** (hawl) *vt.* pull, drag with effort —*vi.* of wind, shift in direction —*n.* hauling; what is hauled; catch of fish; acquisition; distance (to be) covered —**haul·age** (HAW-lij) *n.* carrying of loads; charge for this —**haul'er** *n.* firm, person that transports goods by road

**haunch** (hawnch) *n.* human hip or fleshy hindquarter of animal; leg and loin of animal as food

**haunt** (hawnt) *vt.* visit regularly; visit in form of ghost; recur to —*n. esp.* place frequently visited —**haunt'ed** *adj.* frequented by ghosts; worried

**hau·teur** (hoh-TUR) *n.* haughty spirit; arrogance

**have** (hav) *vt.* (**had, hav·ing**) hold, possess; be possessed, affected with; be obliged (to do); cheat, outwit; engage in, obtain; contain; allow; cause to be done; give birth to; (as auxiliary, forms perfect and other tenses) (*pres. tense:* I *have,* you *have,* he *has,* we, you, they *have*)

**ha·ven** (HAY-vən) *n.* place of safety

**hav·er·sack** (HAV-ər-sak) *n.* canvas bag for provisions *etc.* carried on back or shoulder when hiking *etc.*

**hav·oc** (HAV-ək) *n.* devastation, ruin; *inf.* confusion, chaos

**hawk**[1] *n.* bird of prey smaller than eagle; supporter, advocate, of warlike policies —*vi.* hunt with hawks; attack like hawk

**hawk**[2] *vt.* offer (goods) for sale, as in street —**hawk'er** *n.*

**hawk**[3] *vi.* clear throat noisily

**haw·ser** (HAW-zər) *n.* large rope or cable

**hay** *n.* grass mown and dried —**hay'cock** *n.* conical pile of hay for drying —**hay fever** allergic reaction to pollen, dust *etc.* —**hay'stack** *n.* large pile of hay —**hay'wire** *adj.* crazy; disorganized

**haz·ard** (HAZ-ərd) *n.* chance; risk, danger —*vt.* expose to risk; run risk of —**haz'ard·ous** *adj.* risky

**haze** (hayz) *n.* mist, often due to heat; obscurity —**ha'zy** *adj.* (**-zi·er, -zi·est**) misty; obscured; vague

**ha·zel** (HAY-zəl) *n.* bush or small tree bearing nuts; yellowish-brown color of the nuts —*adj.* light brown

**He** *Chem.* helium

**he** (hee) *pron.* (*third person masculine pronoun*) person, animal already referred to; (*comb. form*) male, as **he-goat**

**head** (hed) *n.* upper part of person's or animal's body, containing mouth, sense organs and brain; upper part of anything; chief of organization, school *etc.;* chief part; aptitude, capacity; crisis; leader; title; headland; person, animal considered as unit; white froth on beer *etc.; inf.* headache; *sl.* addict, habitual user of drug —*adj.* chief, principal; of wind, contrary —*vt.* be at the top, head of; lead, direct; provide with head; hit (ball) with head —*vi.* make for; form a head —**head'er** *n.* headfirst plunge; brick laid with end in face of wall; action of striking ball with head —**head'ing** n. title —**heads** adv. inf. with obverse side (of coin) uppermost —**head'y** adj. (**head·i·er, head·i·est**) apt to intoxicate or excite —**head'ache** (-ayk) n. continuous pain in head; worrying circumstance —**head'board** n. vertical board at head of bed —**head'land** (-lənd) n. promontory —**head'light** n. powerful lamp carried on front of locomotive, motor vehicle etc. —**head'line** n. news summary, in large type in newspaper —**head'long** adv. head foremost, in rush —**head'quar·ters** n. pl. residence of commander-in-chief; center of operations —**head'stone** n. gravestone —**head'strong** adj. self-willed —**head'way** n. advance, progress

**heal** (heel) v. make or become well —**health** (pr. helth) n. soundness of body; condition of body; toast drunk in person's honor —**health'i·ly** adv. —**health'y** adj. (**health·i·er, health·i·est**) of strong constitution; of or producing good health, well-being etc.; vigorous —**health food** vegetarian food, organically grown, eaten for dietary value

**heap** (heep) n. pile of things lying one on another; great quantity —vt. pile, load with

**hear** (heer) v. (**heard**, pr. hurd, **hear·ing**) perceive by ear; listen to; Law try (case); heed; perceive sound; learn —**hear'ing** n. ability to hear; earshot; judicial examination —**hear'say** n. rumor —adj.

**hark·en** (HAHR-kən) vi. listen

**hearse** (hurs) n. funeral carriage for coffin

**heart** (hahrt) n. organ that makes blood circulate; seat of emotions and affections; mind, soul, courage; central part; play-

ing card marked with figure of heart; one of these marks —**heart'en** v. make, become cheerful —**heart'i·ly** adv. —**heart'less** (-lis) adj. unfeeling —**heart'y** adj. (**heart·i·er, heart·i·est**) friendly; vigorous; in good health; satisfying the appetite —**heart attack** sudden severe malfunction of heart —**heart'burn** n. pain in upper intestine —**heart'rend·ing** adj. overwhelming with grief; agonizing —**heart'throb** n. object of infatuation —**heart'-to-heart'** adj. frank, sincere —**by heart** by memory

**hearth** (hahrth) n. floor of fireplace; part of room where fire is made; home

**heat** (heet) n. hotness; sensation of this; hot weather or climate; warmth of feeling, anger etc.; sexual excitement caused by readiness to mate in female animals; one of many races etc. to decide persons to compete in finals —v. make, become hot —**heat'ed** adj. esp. angry

**heath** (heeth) n. tract of wasteland; low-growing evergreen shrub

**hea·then** (HEE-thən) adj. not adhering to a religious system; pagan; barbarous; unenlightened —n. heathen person —**hea'then·ish** adj. of or like heathen; rough; barbarous

**heath·er** (HETH-ər) n. shrub growing on heaths and mountains

**heave** (heev) v. (**heaved, heav·ing**) —vt. lift with effort; throw (something heavy); utter (sigh) —vi. swell, rise; vomit —n.

**heav·en** (HEV-ən) n. abode of God; place of bliss; sky (also pl.) —**heav'en·ly** adj. lovely, delightful, divine; beautiful; of or like heaven

**heav·y** (HEV-ee) *adj.* (heav·i·er, heav·i·est) weighty, striking, falling with force; dense; sluggish; difficult, severe; sorrowful; serious; dull; *sl.* serious, excellent —heav'i·ly *adv.* —heav'i·ness *n.* —heavy industry basic, large-scale industry producing metal, machinery *etc.* —heavy metal rock music with strong beat and amplified instrumental effects —heavy water deuterium oxide, water in which normal hydrogen content has been replaced by deuterium

**Heb.** Hebrews

**He·brew** (HEE-broo) *n.* member of an ancient Semitic people; their language; its modern form, used in Israel —*pl.* book of New Testament —*adj.*

**heck·le** (HEK-əl) *v.* (-led, -ling) interrupt or try to annoy (speaker) by questions, taunts *etc.*

**hect-, hecto-** (*comb. form*) one hundred, *esp.* in metric system, as in **hectoliter, hectometer**

**hec·tare** (HEK-tahr) *n.* one hundred ares (10,000 square meters, 2.471 acres)

**hec·tic** (HEK-tik) *adj.* rushed, busy

**hec·tor** (HEK-tər) *v.* bully, bluster —*n.* bully

**hedge** (hej) *n.* fence of bushes —*v.* (hedged, hedg·ing) —*vt.* surround with hedge; obstruct; hem in; bet on both sides —*vi.* make hedge; be evasive; secure against loss —hedge'hog *n.* small animal covered with spines

**he·don·ism** (HEED-n-iz-əm) *n.* doctrine that pleasure is the chief good —he'don·ist *n.*

**heed** *vt.* take notice of, care for —heed'ful *adj.* —heed'less *adj.* careless

**heel¹** *n.* hinder part of foot; part of shoe supporting this; undesirable person —*vt.* supply with heel; touch ground with heel —*vi.* of dog, follow at one's heels

**heel²** *v.* of ship, (cause to) lean to one side —*n.* heeling, list

**heft·y** (HEF-tee) *adj.* (heft·i·er, heft·i·est) bulky; weighty; strong

**he·gem·o·ny** (hi-JEM-ə-nee) *n.* (*pl.* -nies) leadership, political domination

**heif·er** (HEF-ər) *n.* young cow

**height** (hit) *n.* measure from base to top; quality of being high; elevation; highest degree; (*oft. pl.*) hilltop —height'en *vt.* make higher; intensify

**hei·nous** (HAY-nəs) *adj.* atrocious, extremely wicked, detestable

**heir** (air) *n.* person entitled to inherit property or rank (heir'ess *fem.*) —heir'loom *n.* thing that has been in family for generations

**held** *pt./pp.* of HOLD

**hel·i·cal** (HEL-i-kəl) *adj.* spiral

**hel·i·cop·ter** (HEL-i-kop-tər) *n.* aircraft made to rise vertically by pull of rotating blades turning horizontally —hel'i·port *n.* airport for helicopters

**helio-** (*comb. form*) sun

**he·li·o·graph** (HEE-lee-ə-graf) *n.* signaling apparatus employing a mirror to reflect sun's rays

**he·li·o·ther·a·py** (hee-lee-oh-THER-ə-pee) *n.* therapeutic use of sunlight

**he·li·o·trope** (HEE-lee-ə-trohp) *n.* plant with purple flowers; color of the flowers —he·li·o·trop'ic (-TROP-ik) *adj.* growing, turning toward source of light

**he·li·um** (HEE-lee-əm) *n.* very light, nonflammable gaseous element

**he·lix** (HEE-liks) *n.* spiral

**hell** *n.* abode of the damned; abode of the dead generally;

place or state of wickedness, or misery, or torture —**hell'ish** adj.

**Hel·len·ic** (he-LEN-ik) adj. pert. to inhabitants of Greece

**hel·lo** (he-LOH) interj. expression of greeting or surprise

**helm** n. tiller, wheel for turning ship's rudder

**hel·met** (HEL-mit) n. defensive or protective covering for head

**help** vt. aid, assist; support; succor; remedy, prevent —n. —**help'ful** adj. —**help'ing** n. single portion of food taken at a meal —**help'less** (-lis) adj. useless, incompetent; unaided; unable to help —**help'mate, -meet** n. helpful companion; husband or wife

**hel·ter-skel·ter** (HEL-tər-SKEL-tər) adv./adj./n. (in) hurry and confusion

**hem** n. border of cloth, esp. one made by turning over edge and sewing it down —vt. (hemmed, hem·ming) sew thus; confine, shut in —**hem'stitch** n. ornamental stitch —vt.

**hemi-** (comb. form) half

**hem·i·ple·gi·a** (hem-i-PLEE-jə) n. paralysis of one side of body —**hem·i·ple'gic** adj./n.

**hem·i·sphere** (HEM-i-sfeer) n. half sphere; half of celestial sphere; half of Earth —**hem·i·spher'i·cal** (-sfe-rə-kəl) adj.

**hem·lock** (HEM-lok) n. poisonous plant; poison extracted from it; evergreen of pine family

**hemo-, hema-** (comb. form) blood

**he·mo·glo·bin** (HEE-mə-gloh-bin) n. coloring and oxygen-bearing matter of red blood corpuscles

**he·mo·phil·i·a** (hee-mə-FIL-ee-ə) n. hereditary tendency to intensive bleeding as blood fails to clot —**he·mo·phil'i·ac** n.

**hem·or·rhage** (HEM-ər-ij) n. pro-fuse bleeding —vi. (-rhaged, -rhag·ing) bleed profusely; lose assets, esp. in large amounts

**hem·or·rhoids** (HEM-ə-roidz) n. pl. swollen veins in rectum (also called **piles**)

**hemp** n. Indian plant; its fiber used for rope etc.; any of several narcotic drugs made from varieties of hemp —**hemp'en** (-pən) adj. made of hemp or rope

**hen** n. female of domestic fowl and others —**hen'peck** vt. (of a woman) harass (a man, esp. husband) by nagging

**hence** (hens) adv. from this point; for this reason —**hence·for'ward, hence'forth** adv. from now onward

**hench·man** (HENCH-mən) n. trusty follower; unscrupulous supporter

**hen·na** (HEN-ə) n. flowering shrub; reddish dye made from it

**hen·o·the·ism** (HEN-ə-thee-iz-əm) n. belief in one god (of several) as special god of one's family, tribe etc.

**hen·ry** (HEN-ree) n. (pl. -ries) SI unit of electrical inductance

**he·pat·ic** (hi-PAT-ik) adj. pert. to the liver —**hep·a·ti·tis** (hep-ə-TI-tis) n. inflammation of the liver

**hepta-** (comb. form) seven

**hep·ta·gon** (HEP-tə-gon) n. figure with seven angles —**hep·tag'o·nal** adj.

**her** (hur) adj. objective and possessive case of SHE —**hers** pron. of her —**her·self'** pron. emphatic form of SHE

**her·ald** (HER-əld) n. messenger, envoy; officer who makes royal proclamations, arranges ceremonies etc. —vt. announce; proclaim approach of —**he·ral·dic** (hi-RAL-dik) adj. —**her'ald·ry** n. study of (right to have) heraldic bearings

**herb** (urb) n. plant with soft stem that dies down after flowering; plant of which parts are used in cookery or medicine —her·ba·ceous (hur-BAY-shəs) adj. of, like herbs; perennially flowering —herb·al (HUR-bəl) adj. of herbs —n. book on herbs —herb'al·ist n. writer on herbs; collector, dealer in medicinal herbs —herb'i·cide (-sīd) n. chemical that destroys plants —her·biv'o·rous (-ə-rəs) adj. feeding on plants

**Her·cu·les** (HUR-kyə-leez) n. mythical hero noted for strength —her·cu·le'an (-kyə-LEE-ən) adj. requiring great strength, courage; hard to perform

**herd** (hurd) n. company of animals, usu. of same species, feeding or traveling together —v. crowd together —vt. tend (herd) —herds·man (HURDZ-mən) n.

**here** (heer) adv. in this place; at or to this point —here·af'ter adv. in time to come —n. future existence after death —here·to·fore' (-tə-FOR) adv. before

**he·red·i·ty** (hə-RED-i-tee) n. tendency of organism to transmit its nature to its descendants —he·red'i·tar·y (-ter-ee) adj. descending by inheritance; holding office by inheritance; that can be transmitted from one generation to another

**her·e·sy** (HER-ə-see) n. (pl. -sies pr. -seez) opinion contrary to orthodox opinion or belief —her'e·tic n. one holding opinions contrary to orthodox faith —he·ret'i·cal (-kəl) adj.

**her·it·age** (HER-i-tij) n. what may be or is inherited; anything from past, esp. owned or handed down by tradition —her'it·a·ble adj. that can be inherited

**her·maph·ro·dite** (hur-MAF-rə-dīt) n. person, animal with characteristics or reproductive organs of both sexes

**her·met·ic** (hur-MET-ik) adj. sealed so as to be airtight —her·met'i·cal·ly adv.

**her·mit** (HUR-mit) n. one living in solitude, esp. from religious motives —her'mit·age (-tij) n. this person's abode

**her·ni·a** (HUR-nee-ə) n. projection of (part of) organ through lining encasing it

**he·ro** (HEER-oh) n. (pl. -roes) —her·o·ine fem. pr. HER-oh-in) one greatly regarded for achievements or qualities; principal character in poem, play, story; illustrious warrior; demigod —he·ro'ic (hi-ROH-ik) adj. of, like hero; courageous, daring —he·ro'i·cal·ly adv. —he·ro'ics n. pl. extravagant behavior —her'o·ism n. qualities of hero; courage, boldness —hero sandwich large sandwich of meats etc. on loaf of Italian bread —hero worship admiration of heroes or of great men; excessive admiration of others

**her·o·in** (HER-oh-in) n. white crystalline derivative of morphine, a highly addictive narcotic

**her·on** (HER-ən) n. long-legged wading bird

**her·pes** (HUR-peez) n. any of several diseases, including shingles and cold sores

**her'ring** n. important food fish of northern hemisphere

**hertz** (hurts) n. (pl. same form) SI unit of frequency

**hes·i·tate** (HEZ-i-tayt) vi. (-tat·ed, -tat·ing) hold back; feel, or show indecision; be reluctant —hes'i·tan·cy (-tən-see), hes·i·ta'tion n. wavering; doubt; stammering —hes'i·tant adj. undecided, pausing

**hetero-** (*comb. form*) other or different

**het·er·o·dox** (HET-ɔr-ɔ-doks) *adj.* not orthodox —**het'er·o·dox·y** *n.* (*pl.* -**dox·ies**)

**het·er·o·ge·ne·ous** (het-ɔr-ɔ-JEE-nee-ɔs) *adj.* composed of diverse elements —**het·er·o·ge·ne'i·ty** (-jɔ-NEE-i-tee) *n.*

**het·er·o·sex·u·al** (het-ɔr-ɔ-SEK-shoo-ɔl) *n.* person sexually attracted to members of the opposite sex

**heu·ris·tic** (hyuu-RIS-tik) *adj.* serving to find out or to stimulate investigation

**hew** (hyoo) *v.* (**hewed**, **hewed** or **hewn**, **hew·ing**) chop, cut with axe —**hew'er** *n.*

**hex** (heks) *n.* magic spell —*v.* bewitch

**hex-, hexa-** (*comb. form*) six

**hex·a·gon** (HEK-sɔ-gon) *n.* figure with six angles —**hex·ag'o·nal** *adj.*

**hex·am·e·ter** (hek-SAM-i-tɔr) *n.* line of verse six feet

**hey·day** (HAY-day) *n.* bloom, prime

**Hf** *Chem.* hafnium

**Hg** *Chem.* mercury

**hi·a·tus** (hī-AY-tɔs) *n.* (*pl.* -**tus·es**) break or gap where something is missing

**hi·ber·nate** (HĪ-bɔr-nayt) *vi.* (-**nat·ed**, -**nat·ing**) pass the winter, *esp.* in a torpid state —**hi·ber·na'tion** *n.*

**hi·bis·cus** (hī-BIS-kɔs) *n.* flowering (sub)tropical shrub

**hic·cup** (HIK-up) *n.* spasm of the breathing organs with an abrupt cough-like sound —*vi.* (-**cupped**, -**cup·ping**) have this

**hick** (hik) *adj. inf.* rustic; unsophisticated —*n.* person, place like this

**hick·o·ry** (HIK-ɔ-ree) *n.* (*pl.* -**o·ries**) N Amer. nut-bearing tree; its tough wood

**hide**[1] (hīd) *v.* (**hid**, **hid·den** or **hid**, **hid·ing**) —*vt.* put, keep out of sight; conceal, keep secret —*vi.* conceal oneself —**hide'out** *n.* hiding place

**hide**[2] *n.* skin of animal —**hid'ing** *n. sl.* thrashing —**hide'bound** *adj.* restricted, *esp.* by petty rules *etc.*; narrow-minded

**hid·e·ous** (HID-ee-ɔs) *adj.* repulsive, revolting

**hi·er·ar·chy** (HĪ-ɔ-rahr-kee) *n.* (*pl.* -**chies**) system of persons or things arranged in graded order —**hi·er·ar'chi·cal** *adj.*

**hi·er·o·glyph·ic** (hī-ɔr-ɔ-GLIF-ik) *adj.* of a system of picture writing, as used in ancient Egypt *n.* symbol representing object, concept or sound; symbol, picture, difficult to decipher —**hi'er·o·glyph** *n.*

**hi-fi** (HĪ-FĪ) *adj. short for* HIGH-FIDELITY —*n.* high-fidelity equipment

**high** (hī) *adj.* (-**er**, -**est**) tall, lofty; far up; of roads, main; of meat, tainted; of sound, acute in pitch; expensive; of great importance, quality, or rank; *inf.* in state of euphoria, *esp.* induced by alcohol or drugs —*adv.* far up; strongly, to a great extent; at, to a high pitch; at a high rate —**high'ly** *adv.* —**high'ness** *n.* quality of being high; (H-) title of prince and princess —**high'brow** *n.* intellectual, *esp.* intellectual snob —*adj.* intellectual; difficult; serious —**high'-fi·del'i·ty** *adj.* of high-quality sound-reproducing equipment —**high-flown** *adj.* extravagant, bombastic —**high'-hand'ed** *adj.* domineering, dogmatic —**high'land** (-lɔnd) *n.* relatively high ground —**High'land** *adj.* of, from the highlands of Scotland

—**high′light** n. lightest or brightest area in painting, photograph etc.; outstanding feature —vt. bring into prominence —**high′-rise** adj./n. (of) building that has many stories and elevators —**high′-sound′ing** adj. pompous, imposing —**high-strung** adj. excitable, nervous —**high-tech** n. technology requiring sophisticated scientific equipment and engineering techniques; interior design using features of industrial equipment —adj. —**high time** latest possible time —**high′way** n. main road —**highway robbery** inf. exorbitant fee or charge —**high′way·man** (-mən) n. (formerly) robber on road, esp. mounted

**hi·jack** (HĪ-jak) vt. divert or wrongfully take command of a vehicle (esp. aircraft) or its contents or passengers; rob —**hi′jack·er** n.

**hike** (hīk) v. (hiked, hik·ing) —vi. walk a long way (for pleasure) in country —vt. pull (up), hitch —n. —**hik′er** n.

**hi·lar·i·ty** (hi-LAR-i-tee) n. cheerfulness, gaiety —**hi·lar′i·ous** adj.

**hill** n. natural elevation, small mountain; mound —**hill′ock** (-ɔk) n. little hill —**hill′y** adj. (hill·i·er, hill·i·est) —**hill′bil·ly** n. offens. (pl. -lies) unsophisticated country person

**hilt** n. handle of sword etc. —(up) to the hilt completely

**him** pron. objective case of pronoun HE —**him·self′** pron. emphatic form of HE

**hind**¹ (hīnd) n. female of deer

**hind**² adj. at the back, posterior (also hind·er pr. (HĪN-dər)

**hin·der** (HIN-dər) vt. obstruct, impede, delay —**hin′drance** (-drəns) n.

**Hin·di** (HIN-dee) n. language of N central India —**Hin′du** (-doo) n. person who adheres to Hin′du·ism, the dominant religion of India

**hinge** (hinj) n. movable joint, as that on which door hangs —v. (hinged, hing·ing) —vt. attach with, or as with, hinge —vi. turn, depend on

**hint** n. slight indication or suggestion —v. give hint of

**hin·ter·land** (HIN-tər-land) n. district lying behind coast, or near city, port etc.

**hip** n. either side of body below waist and above thigh; angle formed where sloping sides of roof meet; fruit of rose, esp. wild

**hip·pie** (HIP-ee) n. (formerly) (young) person whose behavior, dress etc. implies rejection of conventional values

**hip·po·pot·a·mus** (hip-ɔ-POT-ɔ-mɔs) n. (pl. -mus·es, -mi pr. -mī) large Afr. animal living in and near rivers

**hire** (hīr) vt. (hired, hir·ing) obtain temporary use of by payment; engage for wage —n. hiring or being hired; payment for use of thing —**hire′ling** n. one who works for wages

**hir·sute** (HUR-soot) adj. hairy

**his** (hiz) pron./adj. belonging to him

**his′pid** adj. rough with bristles or minute spines; bristly, shaggy

**hiss** vi. make sharp sound of letter S, esp. in disapproval —vt. express disapproval, deride thus —n.

**his·ta·mine** (HIS-tɔ-meen) n. substance released by body tissues, sometimes creating allergic reactions

**his·tol·o·gy** (hi-STOL-ɔ-jee) n. science that treats of minute structure of organic tissues

**his·to·ry** (HIS-tɔ-ree) n. (pl. -ries)

record of past events; study of these; past events; train of events, public or private; course of life or existence; systematic account of phenomena —his·to'ri·an n. writer of history —his·tor'ic adj. noted in history —his·tor'i·cal adj. of, based on, history; belonging to past —his·tor·ic'i·ty (-tə·RIS·it·tee) n. historical authenticity —his·to·ri·og'ra·pher n. official historian; one who studies historical method —his·to·ri·og'ra·phy n. methods of historical research

his·tri·on·ic (his·tree·ON·ik) adj. excessively theatrical, insincere, artificial in manner —his·tri·on'ics n. (with sing. or pl. v.) behavior like this

hit v. (hit, hit·ting) —vt. strike with blow or missile; affect injuriously; find —vi. strike; light (upon) —n. blow; success —hit'ter n. —hit man sl. hired assassin —hit it off inf. get along with (person) —hit or miss haphazard(ly) —hit the hay inf. go to bed —hit the road inf. proceed on journey; depart

hitch (hich) vt. fasten with loop etc.; raise, move with jerk —vi. be caught or fastened —n. difficulty; knot, fastening; jerk —hitch'hike vi. (-hiked, -hik·ing) travel by begging free rides

hith·er (HITH·ər) adv. to or toward this place —hith'er·to adv. up to now or to this time

hive (hīv) n. structure in which bees live or are housed; fig. place swarming with busy occupants —v. (hived, hiv·ing) gather, place bees, in hive

hives (hīvz) n. pl. eruptive skin disease

hoard (hord) n. stock, store, esp. hidden away —vt. amass and hide away; store

hoarse (hors) adj. (hoars·er, hoars·est) rough, harsh sounding, husky

hoar·y (HOR·ee) adj. (hoar·i·er, hoar·i·est) gray with age; grayish-white; of great antiquity; venerable —hoar'frost n. frozen dew

hoax (hohks) n. practical joke; deceptive trick —vt. play trick on; deceive —hoax'er n.

hob (hob) n. projection or shelf at side or back of fireplace, used for keeping food warm; tool for cutting gear teeth etc. —hob'nail (-nayl) n. large-headed nail for boot soles

hob·ble (HOB·əl) v. (-bled, -bling) —vi. walk lamely —vt. tie legs together (of horse etc.); impede, hamper —n. straps or ropes put on an animal's legs to prevent it from straying; limping gait

hob·by (HOB·ee) n. (pl. -bies) favorite occupation as pastime —hob'by·horse n. toy horse; favorite topic, preoccupation

hob'gob·lin n. mischievous fairy

hob'nob vi. (-nobbed, -nob·bing) associate, be familiar (with)

ho·bo (HOH·boh) n. (pl. -boes) shiftless, wandering person

hock (hok) n. backward-pointing joint on leg of horse etc., corresponding to human ankle —vt. disable by cutting tendons of hock, hamstring

hock·ey (HOK·ee) n. team game played on a field with ball and curved sticks; ice hockey

ho·cus-po·cus (HOH·kəs·POH·kəs) n. trickery; mystifying jargon

hod n. small trough on a pole for carrying mortar, bricks etc.

hoe (hoh) n. tool for weeding, breaking ground etc. —vt. (hoed, hoe·ing)

hog (hawg) n. pig, esp. castrated

male for fattening; greedy, dirty person —vt. inf. (hogged, hog·ging) eat, use (something) selfishly —hogs·head (HAWGZ-hed) n. large cask; liquid measure of 63 to 140 gallons (238 to 530 liters) —hog'tie vt. (-tied, -ty·ing) hobble; hamper —hog'wash n. nonsense; pig food

ho·gan (HOH-gon) n. Navajo Indian dwelling of earth, branches etc.

hoi pol·loi (HOI po-LOI) n. the common mass of people; the masses

hoist vt. raise aloft, raise with tackle etc.

hold[1] (hohld) v. (held, hold·ing) —vt. keep fast, grasp; support in or with hands etc.; maintain in position; have capacity for; own, occupy; contain; detain; celebrate; keep back; believe —vi. cling; not to give away; abide (by); keep (to); last, proceed, be in force; occur —n. grasp; influence —hold'ing n. (oft. pl.) property, as land or stocks and bonds —hold'up n. armed robbery; delay

hold[2] n. space in ship or aircraft for cargo

hole (hohl) n. hollow place, cavity; perforation; opening; inf. unattractive place; inf. difficult situation —v. (holed, hol·ing) make holes in; go into a hole; drive into a hole

hol'i·day n. day or other period of rest from work etc., esp. spent away from home

hol·low (HOL-oh) adj. (-er, -est) having a cavity, not solid; empty; false; insincere; not full-toned —n. cavity, hole, valley —v. make hollow, make hole in; excavate

hol·ly (HOL-ee) n. (pl. -lies pr.

-leez) evergreen shrub usu. with prickly leaves and red berries

hol·o·caust (HOL-ə-kawst) n. great destruction of life, esp. by fire; (H-) mass slaughter of Jews in Nazi concentration camps during World War II

hol·o·graph (HOL-ə-graf) n. document wholly written by the signer

ho·log·ra·phy (hə-LOG-rə-fee) n. science of using lasers to produce a photographic record (hol'o·gram) that can reproduce a three-dimensional image

hol·ster (HOHL-stər) n. case for pistol, hung from belt etc.

ho·ly (HOH-lee) adj. (-li·er, -li·est) belonging, devoted to God; free from sin; divine; consecrated —ho'li·ness n. sanctity; (H-) Pope's title —holy day day of religious festival —Holy Communion service of the Eucharist —Holy Week that before Easter Sunday

hom·age (HOM-ij) n. tribute, respect, reverence; formal acknowledgment of allegiance

home (hohm) n. dwelling place; residence; native place; institution for the elderly, infirm etc. —adj. of, connected with, home; native —adv. to, at one's home; to the point —v. (homed, hom·ing) direct or be directed onto a point or target —home fries boiled potatoes, sliced and fried in butter etc. —home'less adj. —home'ly adj. (-li·er, -li·est) unpretentious; warm and domesticated; plain —home'ward (-wərd) adj./adv. —home'wards adv. —home-brew n. alcoholic drink made at home, esp. beer —home'sick adj. depressed by absence from home —home'spun adj. domestic; simple —n. cloth made of homespun yarn

—home′stead (-sted) n. house with outbuildings, esp. on farm —home′stead·er n. —home′work n. school work done usu. at home —bring home to impress deeply upon —home free sure of success

ho·me·op·a·thy (hoh-mee-OP-ə-thee) n. treatment of disease by small doses of what would produce symptoms in healthy person —ho·me·o·path′ic adj.

hom·i·cide (HOM-ə-sīd) n. killing of human being; killer —hom·i·ci′dal adj.

hom·i·ly (HOM-ə-lee) n. (pl. -lies pr. -leez) sermon; religious discourse —hom·i·let′ic adj. of sermons —hom·i·let′ics n. with sing. v. art of preaching

Ho·mo (HOH-moh) n. genus to which modern man belongs

homo- (comb. form) same, as in homophone, homosexual etc. Such words are not given here where the meaning can easily be inferred from the simple word

ho·mo·ge·ne·ous (hoh-mə-JEE-nee-əs) adj. formed of uniform parts; similar, uniform; of the same nature —ho·mo·ge·ne′i·ty n. —ho·mog·e·nize (hə-MOJ-ə-nīz) vt. (-nized, -niz·ing) break up fat globules in milk and cream to distribute them evenly; make uniform or similar

ho·mol·o·gous (hə-MOL-ə-gəs) adj. having the same relation, relative position etc. —ho·mo·logue (HOH-mə-lawg) n. homologous thing

hom·o·nym (HOM-ə-nim) n. word of same form as another, but of different sense

ho·mo·sex·u·al (hoh-mə-SEK-shoo-əl) n. person sexually attracted to members of the same sex —adj. —ho·mo·sex·u·al′i·ty n. —ho·mo·pho′bi·a (-PHOH-bee-

ə) n. hate or fear of homosexuals and homosexuality

hone (hohn) n. whetstone for sharpening razors etc. —vt. (honed, hon·ing) sharpen on one

hon·est (ON-ist) adj. not cheating, lying, stealing etc.; genuine; without pretension —hon′es·ty n. quality of being honest

hon·ey (HUN-ee) n. (pl. -eys) sweet fluid made by bees —hon′ey·comb (-kohm) n. wax structure in hexagonal cells in which bees place honey, eggs etc. —vt. fill with cells or perforations —hon′ey·dew (-doo) n. sweet sticky substance found on plants; type of sweet melon —hon′ey·moon n. holiday taken by newly wedded couple; any new relationship with initial period of harmony —vi. spend one's honeymoon

honk (hongk) n. call of goose; any sound like this, esp. sound of automobile horn —vi. make this sound —vt. cause (automobile horn) to sound

hon·or (ON-ər) n. personal integrity; renown; reputation; sense of what is right or due; chastity; high rank or position; source, cause of honor; pleasure, privilege —pl. mark of respect; distinction in examination —vt. respect highly; confer honor on; accept or pay (bill etc.) when due —hon′or·a·ble adj. —hon·o·rar′i·um n. a fee (pl. -rar·i·a) —hon′or·ar·y adj. conferred for the sake of honor only; holding position without pay or usual requirements; giving services without pay —hon·or·if′ic adj. conferring, indicating honor —n. in certain languages, form used to show respect, esp. in direct address

hood[1] (huud) n. covering for head

and neck, often part of cloak or gown; hoodlike thing, as covering of engine compartment of automobile etc. —**hood′ed** adj. covered with or shaped like a hood —**hood′wink** vt. deceive

**hood²** n. sl. hoodlum

**hood·lum** (HUUD-ləm) n. gangster; street ruffian

**hoo′doo** n. cause of bad luck

**hoof** (huuf) n. (pl. **hoofs** or **hooves**) horny casing of foot of horse etc. —**on the hoof** (of livestock) alive

**hoo-ha** (HOO-hah) n. uproar —interj. exclamation expressing excitement or surprise

**hook** (huuk) n. bent piece of metal etc., for catching hold, hanging up etc.; something resembling hook in shape or function; curved cutting tool; enticement; Boxing blow delivered with elbow bent —vt. grasp, catch, hold, as with hook; fasten with hook; Golf drive (ball) widely to the left (of right-handed golfer, and vice versa) —**hooked** adj. shaped like hook; caught; inf. addicted to; sl. married —**hook′er** n. sl. prostitute —**hook′up** n. linking of radio, television stations —**hook′worm** (-wurm) n. parasitic worm infesting humans and animals

**hook·ah** (HUUK-ə) n. oriental pipe in which smoke is drawn through cooling water and long tube

**hoo·li·gan** (HOO-li-gən) n. violent, irresponsible (young) person; ruffian —**hoo′li·gan·ism** n.

**hoop** n. rigid circular band of metal, wood etc.; such a band used for binding barrel etc., for use as a toy, or for jumping through as in circus acts —vt. bind with hoops; encircle —**put through the hoops** inf. subject to ordeal or test

**hoop·la** (HOOP-lah) n. inf. excitement; hullabaloo

**hoot** n. owl's cry or similar sound; cry of disapproval or derision; sl. funny person or thing —vi. utter hoot (esp. in derision) —vt. assail (someone) with derisive cries; drive (someone) away by hooting

**hop¹** vi. (**hopped, hop·ping**) spring on one foot; inf. move quickly —n. leap, skip; one stage of journey —**hop′scotch** (-skoch) n. children's game of hopping in pattern drawn on ground

**hop²** n. climbing plant with bitter cones used to flavor beer etc. —pl. the cones

**hope** (hohp) n. expectation of something desired; thing that gives, or object of, this feeling —v. (**hoped, hop·ing**) feel hope (for) —**hope′ful** adj. —**hope′less** adj. —**young hopeful** promising boy or girl

**hop·per** (HOP-ər) n. one who hops; device for feeding material into mill or machine or grain into truck etc. —**hopper car** railroad freight car, usu. open at top and containing one or more hoppers, for transport and discharge of grain etc.

**horde** (hord) n. large crowd (esp. moving together)

**ho·ri·zon** (hə-RĪ-zən) n. boundary of part of Earth seen from any given point; lines where Earth and sky seem to meet; boundary of mental outlook —**hor·i·zon·tal** (hor-ə-ZON-tl) adj. parallel with horizon, level

**hor·mone** (HOR-mohn) n. substance secreted by certain glands that stimulates organs of the body; synthetic substance with same effect

**horn** n. hard projection on heads

of certain animals, *eg* cattle; substance of it; various things made of, or resembling it; *Music* wind instrument *orig.* made of a horn; device (*esp.* in car) emitting sound as alarm, warning *etc.* —**horned** *adj.* having horns —**horn'y** *adj.* (horn·i·er, horn·i·est) hornlike; *sl. vulgar* lustful —**horn'pipe** *n.* lively dance, *esp.* associated with sailors

**hor·net** (HOR-nit) *n.* large insect of wasp family —**hornet's nest** much opposition, animosity

**hor·o·scope** (HOR-ə-skohp) *n.* observation of, or scheme showing disposition of planets *etc.* at given moment, *esp.* birth, by which character and abilities of individual are predicted; telling of person's fortune by this method

**hor·ren·dous** (haw-REN-dəs) *adj.* horrific

**hor·ror** (HOR-ər) *n.* terror; loathing, fear of; its cause —**hor'ri·ble** *adj.* exciting horror, hideous, shocking —**hor'ri·bly** *adv.* —**hor'rid** *adj.* unpleasant, repulsive; *inf.* unkind —**hor'ri·fy** *vt.* (-fied, -fy·ing) move to horror —**hor·rif'ic** *adj.* particularly horrible

**hors d'oeu·vre** (or-DURV) *n.* (*pl.* -vres *pr.* -DURVZ) small appetizer served before main meal

**horse** (hors) *n.* four-legged animal used for riding and work; cavalry; vaulting horse; frame for support; *sl.* heroin —*vt.* (horsed, hors·ing) provide with horse or horses —**hors'y** *adj.* (hors·i·er, hors·i·est) having to do with horses; devoted to horses or horse racing —**horse'fly** *n.* (*pl.* -flies) large, bloodsucking fly —**horse laugh** harsh boisterous laugh usu. expressing derision —**horse'man** (-mən) *n.* (-wom·an *fem.*) rider on horse —**horse'play** *n.* rough, boisterous play

—**horse'pow·er** *n.* unit of power of engine *etc.* 550 foot-pounds per second —**horse'shoe** (-shoo) *n.* protective U-shaped piece of iron nailed to horse's hoof; thing so shaped —**horse around** *sl.* play roughly, boisterously

**hor·ti·cul·ture** (HOR-ti-kul-chər) *n.* art or science of gardening —**hor·ti·cul'tur·al** *adj.*

**Hos.** Hosea

**ho·san·na** (hoh-ZAN-ə) *n.* (*pl.* -nas) cry of praise, adoration

**hose** (hohz) *n.* flexible tube for conveying liquid or gas; stockings —*vt.* (hosed, hos·ing) water with hose —**ho'sier·y** *n.* stockings or socks

**hos·pice** (HOS-pis) *n.* traveler's house of rest kept by religious order; residence for care of terminally ill

**hos·pi·tal** (HOS-pi-tl) *n.* institution for care of sick —**hos·pi·tal·i·za'tion** *n.* —**hos'pi·tal·ize** *vt.* (-ized, -iz·ing) to place for care in a hospital

**hos·pi·tal·i·ty** (hos-pi-TAL-i-tee) *n.* (*pl.* -ties) friendly and liberal reception of strangers or guests —**hos'pi·ta·ble** *adj.* welcoming, kindly

**host**[1] (hohst) *n.* one who entertains another (-ess *fem.*); master of ceremonies of show; animal, plant on which parasite lives —*vt.* act as a host

**host**[2] *n.* large number

**Host** *n.* consecrated bread of the Eucharist

**hos·tage** (HOS-tij) *n.* person taken or given as pledge or security

**hos·tel** (HOS-tl) *n.* building providing accommodation at low cost for particular category of people, as students, or the homeless

**hos·tile** (HOS-tl) *adj.* opposed, antagonistic; warlike; of an enemy;

unfriendly —hos·til'i·ty n. enmity —pl. -ties) acts of warfare

hot adj. (hot·ter, hot·test) of high temperature, very warm, giving or feeling heat; angry; severe; recent, new; much favored; spicy; sl. good, quick, smart, lucky, successful; sl. stolen —hot'ly adv. —hot'ness n. —hot air inf. boastful, empty talk —hot'bed n. bed of earth heated by manure and grass for young plants; any place encouraging growth; center of activity —hot'-blood·ed (-blud-id) adj. passionate, excitable —hot dog frankfurter (in split bread roll) —hot'foot (-fuut) v./adv. (go) quickly —hot'head (-hed) n. hasty, intemperate person —hot'house n. forcing house for plants; heated building for cultivating tropical plants in cold or temperate climates —hot line direct communication link between heads of governments etc. —hot pants extremely brief and close-fitting pants for women; sl. strong sexual desire —hot'plate n. heated plate on electric cooker; portable device for keeping food warm

ho·tel (hoh-TEL) n. commercial establishment providing lodging

hound (hownd) n. hunting dog —vt. chase, urge, pursue

hour (owr) n. twenty-fourth part of day; sixty minutes; time of day; appointed time —pl. fixed periods for work, prayers etc.; book of prayers —hour'ly adv. every hour; frequently —adj. frequent; happening every hour —hour'glass n. instrument using dropping sand or mercury to indicate passage of an hour

hou·ri (HUUR-ee) (pl. -ris) n. beautiful virgin provided in the Muslim paradise

house (hows) n. (pl. hous·es pr. HOW-ziz) building for human habitation; building for other specified purpose; legislative or other assembly; family; business firm; theater audience, performance —vt. (howz) (housed, hous·ing) give or receive shelter, lodging or storage; cover or contain —housing n. (providing of) houses; part or structure designed to cover, protect, contain —house'boat n. boat for living in on river etc. —house'break·er (-brayk-ər) n. burglar —house'coat n. woman's long loose garment for casual wear at home —house'hold n. inmates of house collectively —house'hold·er n. occupier of house as own dwelling; head of household —house'keep·er n. person managing affairs of household —house'keep·ing n. running household —house'warm·ing n. party to celebrate entry into new house —house'wife, -hus·band n. woman (man) who runs a household

hov·el (HUV-əl) n. mean dwelling

hov·er (HUV-ər) vi. hang in the air (of bird etc.); loiter; be in state of indecision —hov'er·craft n. type of craft that can travel over land and sea on a cushion of air

how adv. in what way; by what means; in what condition; to what degree; (in direct or dependent question) —how·ev'er conj. nevertheless —adv. in whatever way, degree; all the same

how·dah (HOW-də) n. (canopied) seat on elephant's back

how·itz·er (HOW-it-sər) n. short gun firing shells at high elevation

howl vi. utter long loud cry —n. such cry —howl'er n. one that howls; embarrassing mistake

**hoy·den** (HOID-n) n. wild, boisterous girl, tomboy

**hub** n. middle part of wheel, from which spokes radiate; central point of activity

**hub'bub** n. confused noise of many voices; uproar

**huck·ster** (HUK-stər) n. retailer, peddler; person using aggressive or questionable methods of selling —vt. sell goods thus

**hud·dle** (HUD-l) n. crowded mass; inf. impromptu conference, esp. of offensive football team during game —v. (-dled, -dling) heap, crowd together; hunch; confer

**hue** (hyoo) n. color, complexion

**hue and cry** public uproar, outcry; loud outcry usually in pursuit of wrongdoer

**huff** n. passing mood of anger —v. make or become angry, resentful —vi. blow, puff heavily —huff'i·ly adv. —huff'y adj. (huff·i·er, huff·i·est)

**hug** vt. (hugged, hug·ging) clasp tightly in the arms; cling; keep close to —n. fond embrace

**huge** (hyooj) adj. very big —huge'ly adv. very much

**hu·la** (HOO-lə) n. native dance of Hawaii

**hulk** n. body of abandoned vessel; large, unwieldy person or thing —hulk'ing adj. unwieldy, bulky

**hull** n. frame, body of ship; calyx of strawberry, raspberry, or similar fruit; shell, husk —vt. remove shell, hull

**hul·la·ba·loo** (HUL-ə-bə-loo) n. (pl. -loos) uproar, clamor, row

**hum** v. (hummed, hum·ming) —vi. make low continuous sound as bee; be very active —vt. sing with closed lips —n. humming sound; smell; great activity; in radio, disturbance affecting reception —hum'ming·bird n. very

small bird whose wings make humming noise

**hu·man** (HYOO-mən) adj. of people; relating to, characteristic of, people's nature —hu·mane' (-MAYN) adj. benevolent; kind; merciful —hu'man·ism n. belief in human effort rather than religion; interest in human welfare and affairs; classical literary culture —hu'man·ist n. —hu·man·i·tar'i·an n. philanthropist —adj. —hu·man'i·ty n. human nature; human race; kindliness —hu·man'i·ties (-teez) n. pl. study of literature, philosophy, the arts —hu'man·ize vt. (-ized, -iz·ing) make human; civilize —hu'man·ly adv. —hu'man·kind (-kīnd) n. human race as a whole

**hum·ble** (HUM-bəl) adj. (-bler, -blest) lowly, modest —vt. (-bled, -bling) bring low, abase, humiliate —hum'bly adv.

**hum'bug** n. impostor; sham, nonsense, deception —vt. (-bugged, -bug·ging) deceive; defraud

**hum·ding·er** (HUM-DING-ər) n. inf. excellent person or thing

**hum'drum** adj. commonplace, dull, monotonous

**hu·mer·us** (HYOO-mər-əs) n. (pl. -mer·i pr. -mə-rī) long bone of upper arm

**hu·mid** (HYOO-mid) adj. moist, damp —hu·mid'i·fi·er n. device for increasing amount of water vapor in air in room etc. —hu·mid'i·fy vt. (-fied, -fy·ing) —hu·mid'i·ty n.

**hu·mil·i·ate** (hyoo-MIL-ee-ayt) vt. (-at·ed, -at·ing) lower dignity of, abase, mortify

**hu·mil·i·ty** (hyoo-MIL-i-tee) n. state of being humble; meekness

**hum·mock** (HUM-ək) n. low knoll, hillock; ridge of ice

**hu·mor** (HYOO-mər) n. faculty of saying or perceiving what excites amusement; state of mind, mood; temperament; *obs.* one of four chief fluids of body —*vt.* gratify, indulge —**hu'mor·ist** *n.* person who acts, speaks, writes humorously —**hu'mor·ous** *adj.* funny; amusing

**hump** *n.* normal or deforming lump, *esp.* on back; hillock —*vt.* make hump-shaped; *inf.* exert (oneself), hurry; *sl.* carry or heave —**hump'back** *n.* person with hump —**hump'backed** *adj.* having a hump

**hu·mus** (HYOO-məs) *n.* decayed vegetable and animal mold

**hunch** *n. inf.* intuition or premonition; hump —*vt.* thrust, bend into hump —**hunch'back** *n.* humpback

**hun·dred** (HUN-drid) *n./adj.* cardinal number, ten times ten —**hun'dredth** (-dridth) *adj.* the ordinal number —**hun'dred·fold** *adj./adv.* —**hun'dred·weight** *n.* weight of 100 lbs. (45.359 kg)

**hung** *pt./pp.* of HANG —*adj.* (of jury *etc.*) unable to decide; not having majority —**hung'o'ver** *inf.* experiencing a hangover —**hung up** *inf.* delayed; stymied; baffled —**hung up on** *sl.* obsessed by

**hun·ger** (HUNG-gər) *n.* discomfort, exhaustion from lack of food; strong desire —*vi.* —**hun'gri·ly** *adv.* —**hun'gry** *adj.* (-gri·er, -gri·est) having keen appetite —**hunger strike** refusal of all food, as a protest

**hunk** (hungk) *n.* thick piece; *sl.* attractive man with excellent physique

**hunt** *vt.* seek out to kill or capture for sport or food; search (for) —*n.* chase, search; track of country hunted over; (party organized for) hunting; pack of hounds; hunting club —**hunt'er** *n.* one

who hunts (**-ress** *fem.*); horse, dog bred for hunting

**hur·dle** (HUR-dl) *n.* portable frame of bars for temporary fences or for jumping over; obstacle —*vi.* (-dled, -dling) race over hurdles —**hurdles** *n.* with *sing.* v. a race over hurdles —**hur'dler** *n.*

**hurl** *vt.* throw violently —**hurl·y-burl·y** (HUR-lee-BUR-lee) *n.* (*pl.* -burl·ies) loud confusion

**hur·rah** (hə-RAH), **hur·ray** (-RAY) *interj.* exclamation of joy or applause —**last hurrah** final occasion of achievement

**hur·ri·cane** (HUR-i-kayn) *n.* very strong, potentially destructive wind or storm —**hurricane lamp** lamp with glass chimney around flame

**hur·ry** (HUR-ee) *v.* (-ried, -ry·ing) (cause to) move or act in great haste —*n.* (*pl.* -ries) undue haste; eagerness —**hur'ried·ly** *adv.*

**hurt** *v.* (hurt, hurt·ing) —*vt.* injure, damage, give pain to; wound feelings of; distress —*vi. inf.* feel pain —*n.* wound, injury, harm —**hurt'ful** *adj.*

**hur·tle** (HUR-tl) *vi.* (-tled, -tling) move rapidly; rush violently; whirl

**hus·band** (HUZ-bənd) *n.* married man —*vt.* economize; use to best advantage —**hus'band·ry** (-dree) *n.* farming; economy

**hush** *v.* make or be silent —*n.* stillness; quietness —**hush** *adj. inf.* secret —**hush up** suppress rumors, information; make secret

**husk** *n.* dry covering of certain seeds and fruits; worthless outside part —*vt.* remove husk from eg ear of corn —**husk'y** *adj.* (husk·i·er, husk·i·est) rough in tone; hoarse; dry as husk, dry in the throat; of, full of, husks; big and strong

**husk·y** (HUS-kee) *n.* (*pl.* husk·ies) Eskimo dog

**hus·sy** (HUS-ee) *n.* (*pl.* -sies) brazen or immoral woman; impudent girl or young woman

**hus·tings** (HUS-tingz) *n. pl.* any place from which political campaign speeches are made; political campaigning

**hus·tle** (HUS-əl) *v.* (-tled, -tling) push about, jostle, hurry —*vi. sl.* solicit clients *esp.* for prostitution —*n.* —**hus·tler** (HUS-lər) industrious person; *sl.* prostitute

**hut** *n.* any small house or shelter, usu. of wood or metal

**hutch** (huch) *n.* boxlike pen for rabbits *etc.*

**hy·brid** (HI-brid) *n.* offspring of two plants or animals of different species; mongrel —*adj.* crossbred —**hy'brid·ism** *n.* —**hy'brid·ize** *v.* (-ized, -iz·ing) make hybrid; crossbreed

**hy·dra** (HI-drə) *n.* (*pl.* -dras *pr.* —drəz) fabulous many-headed water serpent; any persistent problem; freshwater polyp —**hy'dra-head·ed** *adj.* hard to understand, root out

**hy·dran·gea** (hi-DRAYN-jə) *n.* ornamental shrub with pink, blue, or white flowers

**hy·drant** (HI-drənt) *n.* water pipe with nozzle for hose

**hy·drau·lic** (hi-DRAW-lik) *adj.* concerned with, operated by, pressure transmitted through liquid in pipe —**hy·drau'lics** *n. with sing. v.* science of mechanical properties of liquid in motion

**hydro-** (*comb. form*) water, as *hydroelectric*; presence of hydrogen, as *hydrocarbon*

**hy·dro·car·bon** (hi-drə-KAHR-bən) *n.* compound of hydrogen and carbon

**hy·dro·chlor·ic ac·id** (hi-drə-KLOR-ik) strong colorless acid used in many industrial and laboratory processes

**hy·dro·dy·nam·ics** (hi-droh-di-NAM-iks) *n. with sing. v.* science of the motions of system wholly or partly fluid

**hy·dro·e·lec·tric** (hi-droh-i-LEK-trik) *adj.* pert. to generation of electricity by use of water

**hy·dro·foil** (HI-drə-foil) *n.* fast, light vessel with hull raised out of water at speed by action of vanes in water

**hy·dro·gen** (HI-drə-jən) *n.* colorless gas that combines with oxygen to form water —**hydrogen bomb** atom bomb of enormous power in which hydrogen nuclei are converted into helium nuclei —**hydrogen peroxide** colorless liquid used as antiseptic and bleach

**hy·drog·ra·phy** (hi-DROG-rə-fee) *n.* description of waters of the earth —**hy·dro·graph'ic** *adj.*

**hy·drol·y·sis** (hi-DROL-ə-sis) *n.* decomposition of chemical compound reacting with water

**hy·drom·e·ter** (hi-DROM-i-tər) *n.* device for measuring relative density of liquid

**hy·dro·pho·bi·a** (hi-drə-FOH-bee-ə) *n.* aversion to water, esp. as symptom of rabies; rabies

**hy·dro·plane** (HI-drə-playn) *n.* light skimming motorboat; seaplane; vane controlling motion of submarine *etc.*

**hy·dro·pon·ics** (hi-drə-PON-iks) *n. with sing. v.* science of cultivating plants in water without using soil

**hy·dro·ther·a·py** (hi-drə-THER-ə-pee) *n. Med.* treatment of disease by external application of water

**hy·drous** (HI-drəs) *adj.* containing water

**hy·e·na** (hī-EE-nə) *n.* wild animal related to dog

**hy·giene** (HĪ-jeen) *n.* principles and practice of health and cleanliness; study of these principles —**hy·gi·en·ic** (hī-jee-EN-ik) *adj.* —**hy·gien′ist** (-JEE-nist) *n.*

**hy·grom·e·ter** (hī-GROM-i-tər) *n.* instrument for measuring humidity of air

**hy·gro·scop·ic** (hī-grə-SKOP-ik) *adj.* readily absorbing moisture from the atmosphere

**hy·men** (HĪ-mən) *n.* membrane partly covering vagina of virgin; (H-) Greek god of marriage

**hymn** (him) *n.* song of praise, *esp.* to God —*vt.* praise in song —**hym·nal** (HIM-nl) *adj.* of hymns —*n.* book of hymns *Also* **hymn book**

**hype**[1] (hīp) *n.* *sl.* hypodermic syringe; drug addict

**hype**[2] *n.* *inf.* deception, racket; intensive publicity —*v.* *inf.* (hyped, hyp·ing) promote (a product) using intensive publicity

**hyper-** (*comb. form*) over, above, excessively, as in **hyperactive** *etc.* Such words are not given here where the meaning can easily be inferred from the simple word

**hy·per·bo·la** (hī-PUR-bə-lə) *n.* curve produced when cone is cut by plane making larger angle with the base than the side makes

**hy·per·bo·le** (hī-PUR-bə-lee) *n.* rhetorical exaggeration —**hy·per·bol′ic** *adj.*

**hy·per·bo·re·an** (hī-pər-BOR-ee-ən) *adj./n.* (inhabitant) of extreme north

**hy·per·crit·i·cal** (hī-pər-KRIT-i-kəl) *adj.* too critical

**hy·per·sen·si·tive** (hī-pər-SEN-si-tiv) *adj.* unduly vulnerable emotionally or physically

**hy·per·ten·sion** (hī-pər-TEN-shən) *n.* abnormally high blood pressure

**hy·phen** (HĪ-fən) *n.* short line (-) indicating that two words or syllables are to be connected —**hy·phen·ate** (-nayt) *vt.* (-at·ed, -at·ing) join by a hyphen

**hyp·no·sis** (HIP-noh-sis) *n.* (*pl.* -ses *pr.* -seez) induced state like deep sleep in which subject acts on external suggestion —**hyp·not′ic** *adj.* of hypnosis or of the person or thing producing it; like something that induces hypnosis —**hyp·no·tism** (HIP-nə-tiz-əm) *n.* —**hyp′no·tist** *n.* —**hyp·no·tize** *vt.* (-tized, -tiz·ing) affect with hypnosis; affect in way resembling hypnotic state

**hy·po** (HĪ-poh) *n.* short for **hyposulfite** (sodium thiosulfate), used as fixer in developing photographs

**hypo-, hyph-, hyp-** (*comb. forms*) under, below, less, as in *hypocrite, hyphen etc.* Such words are not given here where meaning can easily be inferred from simple word

**hy·po·al·ler·gen·ic** (hī-poh-al-ər-JEN-ik) *adj.* (of cosmetics *etc.*) not likely to cause allergic reaction

**hy·po·chon·dri·a** (hī-pə-KON-dree-ə) *n.* morbid depression, without cause, about one's own health —**hy·po·chon′dri·ac** *adj./n.*

**hy·poc·ri·sy** (hi-POK-rə-see) *n.* (*pl.* -sies *pr.* -seez) assuming of false appearance of virtue; insincerity —**hyp·o·crite** (HIP-ə-krit) *n.* —**hyp·o·crit′i·cal** *adj.*

**hy·po·der·mic** (hī-pə-DUR-mik) *adj.* introduced, injected beneath the skin —*n.* hypodermic syringe or needle

**hy·po·gas·tric** (hī-pə-GAS-trik)

*adj.* relating to, situated in, lower part of abdomen

**hy·pot·e·nuse** (hī-POT-ə-noos) *n.* side of a right triangle opposite the right angle

**hy·po·ther·mi·a** (hī-pə-THUR-mee-ə) *n.* condition of having body temperature reduced to dangerously low level

**hy·poth·e·sis** (hī-POTH-ə-sis) *n.* (*pl.* -ses *pr.* -seez) suggested explanation of something; assumption as basis of reasoning —**hy·po·thet′i·cal** *adj.* —**hy·poth′e·size** (-POTH-ə-sīz) *v.* (-sized, -siz·ing)

**hypso-** (*comb. form*) height, as in *hypsometry*

**hyp·sog·ra·phy** (hip-SOG-rə-fee) *n.* branch of geography dealing with altitudes

**hyp·som·e·ter** (hip-SOM-i-tər) *n.* instrument for measuring altitudes —**hyp·som′e·try** (-tree) *n.* science of measuring altitudes

**hys·ter·ec·to·my** (his-tə-REK-tə-mee) *n.* (*pl.* -mies) surgical operation for removing the uterus

**hys·ter·e·sis** (his-tə-REE-sis) *n.* *Physics* lag or delay in changes in variable property of a system

**hys·ter·i·a** (hi-STER-ee-ə) *n.* mental disorder with emotional outbursts; any frenzied emotional state; fit of crying or laughing —**hys·ter′i·cal** *adj.* —**hys·ter′ics** *n. pl.* fits of hysteria

**Hz** hertz

# I

**I** *Chem.* iodine
**I** *pron.* the pronoun of the first person singular
**i·amb** (Ī-amb) *n.* metrical foot of

short and long syllable —**i·am′bic** *adj.*

**i·bex** (Ī-beks) *n.* (*pl.* -bex·es) wild goat with large horns

**ibid.** (IB-id) *short for* ibidem (Lat. in the same place)

**i·bis** (Ī-bis) *n.* storklike bird

**ice** (īs) *n.* frozen water; frozen dessert made of sweetened water and fruit flavoring —*v.* (iced, ic·ing) cover, become covered with ice; cool with ice; cover with icing —**i′ci·cle** (-sə-kəl) *n.* tapering spike of ice hanging where water has dripped —**i′ci·ly** *adv.* in icy manner —**i′ci·ness** *n.* —**i′cing** *n.* mixture of sugar and water *etc.* used to decorate cakes —**i′cy** *adj.* (**i·ci·er, i·ci·est**) covered with ice; cold; chilling —**ice′berg** (-burg) *n.* large floating mass of ice —**ice cream** sweetened frozen dessert made from cream, eggs *etc.* —**ice floe** (-floh) sheet of floating ice —**ice hockey** team game played on ice with puck

**ich·thy·ol·o·gy** (ik-thee-OL-ə-jee) *n.* scientific study of fish

**icicle** *see* ICE

**i·con** (Ī-kon) *n.* image, representation, *esp.* of religious figure —**i·con′o·clast** *n.* one who attacks established principles *etc.*; breaker of icons —**i·con·o·clas′tic** *adj.* —**i·co·nog′ra·phy** *n.* icons collectively; study of icons

**id** *n.* *Psychoanalysis* the mind's instinctive energies

**i·de·a** (ī-DEE-ə) *n.* notion in the mind; conception; vague belief; plan, aim —**i·de′al** *n.* conception of something that is perfect; perfect person or thing —*adj.* perfect; visionary; existing only in idea —**i·de′al·ism** *n.* tendency to seek perfection in everything; philosophy that mind is the only reality —**i·de′al·ist** *n.* one who holds doctrine of idealism; one who strives after the ideal; impractical person —i·de·al·is'tic adj. —i·de'al·ize vt. (-ized, -iz·ing) portray as ideal

i·dem (I-dem) Lat. the same

i·den·ti·ty (ī-DEN-ti-tee) n. (pl. -ties) individuality; being the same, exactly alike —i·den'ti·cal adj. very same —i·den'ti·fi·able adj. —i·den'ti·fy v. (-fied, -fy·ing) establish identity of; associate (oneself) with; treat as identical

id·e·o·graph (ID-ee-ə-graf) n. picture, symbol, figure etc., suggesting an object without naming it Also id'e·o·gram

i·de·ol·o·gy (ī-dee-OL-ə-jee) n. (pl. -gies) body of ideas, beliefs of group, nation etc. —i·de·o·log'i·cal adj. —i'de·o·logue (-lawg) n. zealous advocate of an ideology

ides (īdz) n. pl. or sing. the 15th of March, May, July and Oct. and the 13th of other months of the ancient Roman calendar

idiocy see IDIOT

id·i·om (ID-ee-əm) n. way of expression natural to or peculiar to a language or group; characteristic style of expression —id·i·o·mat'ic adj. using idioms; colloquial

id·i·o·syn·cra·sy (id-ee-ə-SING-krə-see) n. peculiarity of mind, temper or disposition in a person —id·i·o·syn·crat'ic (-oh-sing-KRAT-ik) adj.

id·i·ot (ID-ee-ət) n. mentally deficient person; foolish, senseless person —id'i·o·cy (-ə-see) n. —id·i·ot'ic adj. utterly senseless or stupid

i·dle (ID-l) adj. (-dler, -dlest) unemployed; lazy; useless, vain, groundless —vi. (-dled, -dling) be idle; (of engine) run slowly with gears disengaged —vt. (esp. with away) waste —i'dle·ness n. —i'dler n. —i'dly adv.

i·dol (ID-l) n. image of deity as object of worship; object of excessive devotion —i·dol'a·ter n. worshiper of idols —i·dol'a·trous (-trəs) adj. —i·dol'a·try n. —i'dol·ize vt. (-ized, -iz·ing) love or venerate to excess; make an idol of

i·dyll (ID-l) n. short descriptive poem of picturesque or charming scene or episode, esp. of rustic life —i·dyl·lic (ī-DIL-ik) adj. of, like, idyll; delightful

if conj. on condition or supposition that; whether; although —n. uncertainty or doubt (esp. in ifs and buts) —if'fy (-ee) adj. inf. (-fi·er, -fi·est) dubious

ig'loo n. dome-shaped Eskimo house of snow and ice

ig·ne·ous (IG-nee-əs) adj. esp. of rocks, formed as molten rock cools and hardens

ig·nite (ig-NIT) v. (-nit·ed, -nit·ing) (cause to) burn —ig·ni'tion (-NISH-ən) n. act of kindling or setting on fire; in internal combustion engine, means of firing explosive mixture, usu. electric spark

ig·no·ble (ig-NOH-bəl) adj. mean, base; of low birth —ig·no'bly adv.

ig·no·min·y (IG-nə-min-ee) n. (pl. -min·ies) dishonor, disgrace; shameful act —ig·no·min'i·ous (-ee-əs) adj.

ig·nore (ig-NOR) vt. (-nored, -nor·ing) disregard, leave out of account —ig·no·ra'mus (-RA-məs) n. (pl. -mus·es) ignorant person —ig'no·rance (-rəns) n. lack of knowledge —ig'no·rant adj. lacking knowledge; uneducated; unaware

i·gua·na (i-GWAH-nə) n. large tropical American lizard

il Chem. illinium

il- (prefix) for in- before l: see IN- and listed words

**il·e·um** (IL-ee-əm) *n.* lower part of small intestine —**il′e·ac** *adj.*

**ilk** *adj.* same —of that ilk of the same type or class

**ill** *adj.* not in good health; bad, evil; faulty; unfavorable —*n.* evil, harm; mild disease —*adv.* badly; hardly, with difficulty —**ill′ness** *n.* —**ill′-ad·vised′** *adj.* imprudent; injudicious —**ill′-fat′ed** (-FAY-tid) *adj.* unfortunate —**ill′-fa′vored** (-FAY-vərd) *adj.* ugly, deformed; offensive —**ill′-got·ten** *adj.* obtained dishonestly —**ill′-man′nered** *adj.* boorish, uncivil —**ill-timed** *adj.* inopportune —**ill-treat** *vt.* treat cruelly —**ill will** unkind feeling, hostility

**il·le·git·i·mate** (il-i-JIT-ə-mit) *adj.* born out of wedlock; unlawful; not regular —*n.* bastard

**il·lic·it** (i-LIS-it) *adj.* illegal; prohibited, forbidden

**il·lit·er·ate** (i-LIT-ər-it) *adj.* not literate; unable to read or write —*n.* illiterate person —**il·lit′er·a·cy** *n.*

**il·lu·mi·nate** (i-LOO-mə-nayt) *vt.* (-nat·ed, -nat·ing) light up; clarify; decorate with lights; decorate with gold and colors —**il·lu·mi·na′tion** *n.* —**il·lu′mine** *vt.* (-mined, -min·ing) illuminate

**il·lu·sion** (i-LOO-zhən) *n.* deceptive appearance or belief —**il·lu′sion·ist** *n.* conjurer —**il·lu′so·ry** (-LOO-sə-ree) *adj.* deceptive

**il·lus·trate** (IL-ə-strayt) *vt.* (-trat·ed, -trat·ing) provide with pictures or examples; exemplify —**il·lus′tra·tion** *n.* picture, diagram; example; act of illustrating —**il·lus′tra·tive** *adj.* providing explanation

**il·lus·tri·ous** (i-LUS-tree-əs) *adj.* famous; distinguished; exalted

**im-** (prefix) for *in-* before *m, b,* and *p: see* IN- and listed words

**im·age** (IM-ij) *n.* representation

or likeness of person or thing; optical counterpart, as in mirror; double, copy; general impression; mental picture created by words, *esp.* in literature —*vt.* (-aged, -mag·ing) make image of; reflect —**im′age·ry** *n.* images collectively, *esp.* in literature

**im·ag·ine** (i-MAJ-in) *vt.* picture to oneself; think; conjecture —**im·ag′i·na·ble** *adj.* —**im·ag′i·nar·y** *adj.* existing only in fancy —**im·ag·i·na′tion** *n.* faculty of making mental images of things not present; fancy; resourcefulness —**im·ag′i·na·tive** *adj.*

**i·mam** (i-MAHM) *n.* Islamic minister or priest

**im·bal·ance** (im-BAL-əns) *n.* lack of balance, proportion

**im·be·cile** (IM-bə-sil) *n.* idiot —*adj.* idiotic —**im·be·cil′i·ty** *n.*

**im·bibe** (im-BIB) *v.* (-bibed, -bib·ing) —*vt.* drink in; absorb —*vi.* drink

**im·bri·cate** (IM-brə-kit) *adj.* lying over each other in regular order, like tiles or shingles on roof —**im·bri·ca′tion** *n.*

**im·bro·glio** (im-BROHL-yoh) *n.* (*pl.* -glios) disagreemnet; complicated situation, plot

**im·bue** (im-BYOO) *vt.* (-bued, -bu·ing) inspire; saturate

**im·i·tate** (IM-i-tayt) *vt.* (-tat·ed, -tat·ing) take as model; mimic, copy —**im′i·ta·ble** *adj.* —**im·i·ta′tion** *n.* act of imitating; copy of original; likeness; counterfeit —**im′i·ta·tive** *adj.* —**im′i·ta·tor** *n.*

**im·mac·u·late** (im-AK-yə-lit) *adj.* spotless; pure; immaculate

**im·ma·nent** (IM-mə-nənt) *adj.* abiding in, inherent —**im′ma·nence** *n.*

**im·ma·te·ri·al** (im-ə-TEER-ee-əl) *adj.* unimportant, trifling; not consisting of matter; spiritual

**im·me·di·ate** (i-MEE-dee-it) *adj.*

occurring at once; direct, not separated by others —im·me′di·a·cy n.

im·me·mo·ri·al (im-ɔ-MOR-ee-ɔl) adj. beyond memory

im·mense (i-MENS) adj. huge, vast —im·men′si·ty n. vastness

im·merse (i-MURS) vt. (-mersed, -mers·ing) dip, plunge, into liquid; involve; engross —im·mer′sion (-zhɔn) n. immersing —immersion heater n. electric appliance for heating liquid in which it is immersed

im·mi·grate (IM-i-grayt) vi. (-grat·ed, -grat·ing) come into country as settler —im′mi·grant (-grɔnt) n./adj. —im·mi·gra′tion n.

im·mi·nent (IM-ɔ-nɔnt) adj. liable to happen soon; close at hand —im′mi·nence n.

im·mo·late (IM-ɔ-layt) vt. (-lat·ed, -lat·ing) kill, sacrifice —im·mo·la′tion n.

im·mor·al (i-MOR-ɔl) adj. corrupt; promiscuous; indecent; unethical —im·mo·ral′i·ty n. (pl. -ties)

im·mor·tal (i-MOR-tl) adj. deathless; famed for all time —n. immortal being; god; one whose fame will last —im·mor·tal′i·ty n. —im·mor′tal·ize vt. (-ized, -iz·ing)

im·mune (i-MYOON) adj. proof (against a disease etc.); secure, exempt —im·mu′ni·ty n. state of being immune; freedom from prosecution etc. —im·mu·ni·za′tion n. process of making immune to disease —im′mu·nize vt. (-nized, -niz·ing) make immune —im·mu·nol′o·gy n. branch of biology concerned with study of immunity

im·mu·ta·ble (i-MYOO-tɔ-bɔl) adj. unchangeable

imp n. little devil; mischievous child

im·pact (IM-pakt) n. collision; profound effect —impact (im-PAKT) vt. drive, press

im·pair′ vt. weaken, damage —im·pair′ment n.

im·pa·la (im-PAL-ɔ) n. (pl. -pal·as) antelope of Africa

im·pale (im-PAYL) vt. (-paled, -pal·ing) pierce with sharp instrument; make helpless as if pierced through

im·part (im-PAHRT) vt. communicate (information etc.); give

im·par·tial (im-PAHR-shɔl) adj. not biased or prejudiced; fair —im·par·ti·al′i·ty n.

im·passe (IM-pas) n. deadlock; place, situation, from which there is no outlet

im·pas·sioned (im-PASH-ɔnd) adj. deeply moved, ardent

im·pas·sive (im-PAS-iv) adj. showing no emotion; calm —im·pas·siv′i·ty n.

im·peach (im-PEECH) vt. charge with crime; call to account; Law challenge credibility of (a witness) —im·peach′a·ble adj.

im·pec·ca·ble (im-PEK-ɔ-bɔl) adj. without flaw or error

im·pe·cu·ni·ous (im-pi-KYOO-nee-ɔs) adj. poor —im·pe·cu′ni·ous·ness, im·pe·cu·ni·os′i·ty n.

im·pede (im-PEED) vt. (-ped·ed, -ped·ing) hinder —im·ped′ance n. Electricity measure of opposition offered to flow of alternating current —im·ped′i·ment (-PED-ɔ-mɔnt) n. obstruction; defect

im·pel′ vt. (-pelled, -pel·ling) induce, incite; drive, force —im·pel′ler n.

im·pend′ vi. threaten; be imminent; hang over —im·pend′ing adj.

im·per·a·tive (im-PER-ɔ-tiv) adj. necessary; peremptory; expressing command —n. imperative mood

**im·pe·ri·al** (im-PEER-ee-əl) *adj.* of empire, or emperor; majestic —**im·pe′ri·al·ism** *n.* extension of empire; belief in colonial empire —**im·pe′ri·al·ist** *n.*

**im·per·il** (im-PER-əl) *vt.* (-iled, -il·ing) bring into peril, endanger

**im·pe·ri·ous** (im-PEER-ee-əs) *adj.* domineering; haughty; dictatorial —**im·pe′ri·ous·ness** *n.*

**im·per·son·al** (im-PUR-sə-nl) *adj.* objective, having no personal significance; devoid of human warmth, personality *etc.*; (of verb) without personal subject —**im·per·son·al′i·ty** *n.*

**im·per·son·ate** (im-PUR-sə-nayt) *vt.* (-at·ed, -at·ing) pretend to be (another person); play the part of —**im·per·son·a′tion** *n.*

**im·per·ti·nent** (im-PUR-tn-ənt) *adj.* insolent, rude —**im·per′ti·nence** *n.*

**im·per·turb·a·ble** (im-pər-TUR-bə-bəl) *adj.* calm, not excitable —**im·per·turb′a·bly** *adv.*

**im·per·vi·ous** (im-PUR-vee-əs) *adj.* not affording passage; impenetrable (to feeling, argument *etc.*)

**im·pe·ti·go** (im-pi-TĪ-goh) *n.* contagious skin disease

**im·pet·u·ous** (im-PECH-oo-əs) *adj.* likely to act without consideration, rash —**im·pet·u·os′i·ty** *n.*

**im·pe·tus** (IM-pi-təs) *n.* force with which body moves; impulse

**im·pinge** (im-PINJ) *vi.* (-pinged, -ping·ing) encroach (upon); collide (with) —**im·pinge′ment** *n.*

**im·pi·ous** (IM-pee-əs) *adj.* irreverent, profane, wicked —**im·pi′e·ty** (-PĪ-i-tee) *n.*

**im·plac·a·ble** (im-PLAK-ə-bəl) *adj.* not to be appeased; unyielding —**im·plac·a·bil′i·ty** *n.*

**im·plant′** *vt.* insert, fix —**im′plant** *n.* Dentistry artificial tooth implanted permanently in jaw

**im·ple·ment** (IM-plə-mənt) *n.* tool, instrument, utensil —*vt.* (-ment) carry out (instructions *etc.*); put into effect

**im·pli·cate** (IM-pli-kayt) *vt.* (-cat·ed, -cat·ing) involve, include; entangle; imply —**im·pli·ca′tion** *n.* something implied —**im·plic′it** (-PLIS-it) *adj.* implied but not expressed; absolute and unreserved

**im·plore** (im-PLOR) *vt.* (-plored, -plor·ing) entreat earnestly —**im·plor′ing·ly** *adv.*

**im·ply** (im-PLĪ) *vt.* (-plied, -ply·ing) indicate by hint, suggest; mean

**im·port′** *vt.* bring in, introduce (*esp.* goods from foreign country); imply —**im′port** *n.* thing imported; meaning; importance —**im·port′er** *n.*

**im·por·tant** (im-POR-tnt) *adj.* of great consequence; momentous; pompous —**im·por′tance** *n.*

**im·por·tune** (im-por-TOON) *vt.* (-tuned, -tun·ing) request, demand persistently —**im·por′tu·nate** (-POR-chə-nit) *adj.* persistent, demanding —**im·por·tu′ni·ty** *n.*

**im·pose** (im-POHZ) *vt.* (-posed, -pos·ing) levy (tax, duty *etc.*, upon) —*vi.* take advantage (of), practice deceit on —**im·pos′ing** *adj.* impressive —**im·po·si′tion** *n.* that which is imposed; tax; burden; deception —**im′post** *n.* duty, tax on imports

**im·pos·si·ble** (im-POS-ə-bəl) *adj.* incapable of being done or experienced; absurd; unreasonable —**im·pos·si·bil′i·ty** *n.* (*pl.* -ties)

**im·pos·tor** (im-POS-tər) *n.* deceiver, one who assumes false identity —**im·pos′ture** (-POS-chər) *n.*

**im·po·tent** (IM-pə-tənt) *adj.* powerless; (of males) incapable of sexual intercourse —im'po·tence n.

**im·pound** (im-POWND) vt. take legal possession of and, often, place in a pound (automobile, animal etc.); confiscate

**im·pov·er·ish** (im-POV-ər-ish) vt. make poor or weak —im·pov'er·ish·ment n.

**im·pre·ca·tion** (im-pri-KAY-shən) n. invoking of evil; curse —im'pre·cate vt. (-cat·ed, -cat·ing)

**im·preg·na·ble** (im-PREG-nə-bəl) adj. proof against attack; unassailable; unable to be broken into —im·preg·na·bil'i·ty n.

**im·preg·nate** (im-PREG-nayt) vt. (-nat·ed, -nat·ing) saturate, infuse; make pregnant —im·preg·na'tion n.

**im·pre·sa·ri·o** (im-prə-SAHR-ee-oh) n. (pl. -ri·os) organizer of public entertainment; manager of opera, ballet etc.

**im·press'**[1] vt. affect deeply, usu. favorably; imprint, stamp; fix —n. (IM-pres) act of impressing; mark impressed —im·pres'sion n. effect produced, esp. on mind; notion, belief; imprint; a printing; total of copies printed at once; printed copy —im·pres'sion·a·ble adj. susceptible to external influences —im·pres'sion·ism n. art style that renders general effect without detail —im·pres'sion·ist n. —im·pres'sive adj. making deep impression

**im·press'**[2] vt. press into service —im·press'ment n.

**im·pri·ma·tur** (im-pri-MAH-tər) n. license to print book etc.; sanction, approval

**im'print** n. mark made by pressure; characteristic mark —vt. (im-PRINT) produce mark; stamp; fix in mind

**im·promp·tu** (im-PROMP-too) adv./adj. on the spur of the moment; unrehearsed

**im·prove** (im-PROOV) v. (-proved, -prov·ing) make or become better in quality, standard, value etc. —im·prov'a·ble adj.

**im·prov·i·dent** (im-PROV-i-dənt) adj. thriftless; negligent; imprudent —im·prov'i·dence n.

**im·pro·vise** (IM-prə-vīz) v. (-vised, -vis·ing) make use of materials at hand; compose, utter without preparation —im·prov·i·sa'tion (-ZAY-shən) n.

**im·pu·dent** (IM-pyə-dənt) adj. disrespectful, impertinent —im'·pu·dence n.

**im·pugn** (im-PYOON) vt. (-pugned, -pugn·ing) call in question, challenge as false

**im·pulse** (IM-puls) n. sudden inclination to act; sudden application of force; motion caused by it; stimulation of nerve moving muscle —im·pul'sion n. impulse, usu. in its first sense —im·pul'sive adj. given to acting without reflection, rash

**im·pu·ni·ty** (im-PYOO-ni-tee) n. freedom, exemption from injurious consequences or punishment

**im·pute** (im-PYOOT) vt. (-put·ed, -put·ing) ascribe, attribute to —im·pu·ta'tion n. that which is imputed as a charge or fault; reproach, censure

**in** prep. expresses inclusion within limits of space, time, circumstance, sphere etc. —adv. in or into some state, place etc.; inf. in vogue etc. —adj. inf. fashionable

**In** Chem. indium

**in-** (prefix) with its forms il-, im-, ir- negatives the idea of the simple word: also forms compounds with the meaning of in, into, upon, as inter, impend, irrigate. The list below contains some compounds that will be understood if *not* or *lack of* is used with the meaning of the simple word

**in·ad·vert·ent** (in-əd-VUR-tnt) *adj.* not attentive; negligent; unintentional —**in·ad·vert'ence**, in·ad·vert'en·cy *n.*

**in·ane** (i-NAYN) *adj.* foolish, silly, vacant —**in·a·ni'tion** (-NISH-ən) *n.* exhaustion; silliness —**in·an'i·ty** *n.*

**in·an·i·mate** (in-AN-ə-mit) *adj.* lacking qualities of living beings; appearing dead; lacking vitality

**in·as·much** (in-əz-MUCH) *adv.* seeing that (only in inasmuch as)

**in·au·gu·rate** (in-AW-gyə-rayt) *vt.* (-rat·ed, -rat·ing) begin, initiate the use of, *esp.* with ceremony; admit to office —**in·au'gu·ral** *adj.* —**in·au·gu·ra'tion** *n.* act of inaugurating; ceremony to celebrate the initiation or admittance of

**in·aus·pi·cious** (in-aw-SPISH-əs) *adj.* not auspicious; unlucky; un-

favorable —**in·aus·pi'cious·ly** *adv.*

**in·board** (IN-bord) *adj.* inside hull or bulwarks

**in'born** *adj.* existing from birth; inherent

**in'bred** *vt.* (-bred, -breed·ing) breed from union of closely related individuals —**in'bred** *adj.* produced as result of inbreeding; inborn, ingrained

**in·cal·cu·la·ble** (in-KAL-kyə-lə-bəl) *adj.* beyond calculation; very great

**in cam·er·a** (KAM-ə-rə) in secret or private session

**in·can·des·cent** (in-kən-DES-ənt) *adj.* glowing with heat, shining; of artificial light, produced by glowing filament —**in·can·des'cence** *n.*

**in·can·ta·tion** (in-kan-TAY-shən) *n.* magic spell or formula, charm

**in·ca·pac·i·tate** (in-kə-PAS-i-tayt) *vt.* (-tat·ed, -tat·ing) disable;

il·le'gal
il·leg'i·ble
il·log'i·cal
im·ma·ture'
im·mo'bile
im·mod'er·ate
im·mod'est
im·mov'a·ble
im·pa'tient
im·per·cep'ti·ble
im·per'fect
im·po·lite'
im·prac'ti·ca·ble
im·prac'ti·cal
im·prob'a·ble
im·pro·pri'e·ty
im·pure'
in·a·bil'i·ty
in·ac'cu·rate
in·ad'e·quate
in·ap·pro'pri·ate
in·ca'pa·ble

in·com'pa·ra·ble
in·com·pat'i·ble
in·com'pe·tent
in·com·plete'
in·con·sid'er·ate
in·con·sist'ent
in·con·ven'ience
in·cor·rect'
in·cur'a·ble
in·de'cent
in·de·ci'sive
in·def'i·nite
in·di·rect'
in·dis·creet'
in·ef·fi'cient
in·ex·pen'sive
in·ex·pe'ri·enced
in·fer'tile
in·for'mal
in·fre'quent
in·grat'i·tude
in·hos·pi'ta·ble

in·of·fen'sive
in·san'i·tar·y
in·sen'si·tive
in·sig·nif'i·cant
in·sin·cere'
in·sol'vent
in·suf·fi'cient
in·tan'gi·ble
in·tol'er·a·ble
in·val'id
in·var'i·a·ble
in·vis'i·ble
in·vul'ner·a·ble
ir·ra'tion·al
ir·reg'u·lar
ir·rel'e·vant
ir·re·place'a·ble
ir·re·sist'i·ble
ir·res'o·lute
ir·re·spon'si·ble

make unfit; disqualify —**in·ca·pac'i·ty** n.

**in·car·cer·ate** (in-KAHR-sə-rayt) vt. (-at·ed, -at·ing) imprison —**in·car·cer·a'tion** n.

**in·car·nate** (in-KAR-nayt) vt. (-nat·ed, -nat·ing) embody in flesh, esp. in human form —adj. (-nit) embodied in flesh, in human form; typified —**in·car·na'tion** n.

**in·cen·di·ar·y** (in-SEN-dee-er-ee) adj. of malicious setting on fire of property; creating strife, violence etc.; designed to cause fires —n. arsonist; agitator; bomb etc. filled with inflammatory substance

**in·cense¹** (in-SENS) vt. (-censed, -cens·ing) enrage

**in·cense²** (IN-sens) n. gum, spice giving perfume when burned; its smoke —vt. (-censed, -cens·ing) burn incense to; perfume with it

**in·cen·tive** (in-SEN-tiv) n. something that arouses to effort or action; stimulus

**in·cep·tion** (in-SEP-shən) n. beginning —**in·cep'tive** (-tiv) adj.

**in·ces·sant** (in-SES-ənt) adj. unceasing

**in·cest** (IN-sest) n. sexual intercourse between two people too closely related to marry —**in·ces'tu·ous** (-SES-choo-əs) adj.

**inch** n. one twelfth of foot, or 2.54 centimeters —v. move very slowly

**in·cho·ate** (in-KOH-it) adj. just begun; undeveloped

**in·ci·dent** (IN-si-dənt) n. event, occurrence —adj. naturally attaching to; striking, falling (upon) —**in'ci·dence** n. degree, extent or frequency of occurrence; a falling on, or affecting —**in·ci·den'tal** adj. occurring as a minor part or an inevitable accompaniment or by chance —**in·ci·den'tal·ly**

adv. by chance; by the way —**in·ci·den'tals** n. pl. accompanying items

**in·cin·er·ate** (in-SIN-ə-rayt) vt. (-at·ed, -at·ing) burn up completely; reduce to ashes —**in·cin'er·a·tor** n.

**in·cip·i·ent** (in-SIP-ee-ənt) adj. beginning

**in·cise** (in-SĪZ) vt. (-cised, -cis·ing) cut into; engrave —**in·ci'sion** (-SIZH-ən) n. —**in·ci'sive** adj. keen or biting (of remark etc.); sharp —**in·ci'sor** n. cutting tooth

**in·cite** (in-SĪT) vt. (-cit·ed, -cit·ing) urge, stir up —**in·cite'ment** n.

**in·clem·ent** (in-KLEM-ənt) adj. of weather, stormy, severe, cold —**in·clem'en·cy** n.

**in·cline** (in-KLĪN) v. (-clined, -clin·ing) lean, slope; (cause to) be disposed; bend or lower (the head etc.) —n. (in-klīn) slope —**in·cli·na'tion** n. liking, tendency or preference; sloping surface; degree of deviation

**in·clude** (in-KLOOD) vt. (-clud·ed, -clud·ing) have as (part of) contents; comprise; add in; take in —**in·clu'sion** (-zhən) n. —**in·clu'sive** adj. including (everything)

**in·cog·ni·to** (in-kog-NEE-toh) adv./adj. under assumed identity —n. (pl. -tos) assumed identity

**in·co·her·ent** (in-koh-HEER-ənt) adj. lacking clarity, disorganized; inarticulate —**in·co·her'ence** n.

**in·come** (IN-kum) n. amount of money, esp. annual, from salary, investments etc.; receipts —income tax personal, corporate tax levied on annual income

**in·com·ing** (IN-kum-ing) adj. coming in; about to come into office; next

**in·com·mode** (in-kə-MOHD) vt. (-mod·ed, -mod·ing) trouble, inconvenience; disturb —in·com·mo′di·ous *adj.* cramped; inconvenient

in·com·mu·ni·ca·do (in-kə-MYOO-ni-kah-doh) *adj./adv.* deprived (by force or choice) of communication with others

in·con·gru·ous (in-KONG-groo-əs) *adj.* not appropriate; inconsistent, inconsistent, absurd —in·con·gru′i·ty *n.*

in·con·se·quen·tial (in-kon-si-KWEN-shəl) *adj.* illogical; irrelevant, trivial

in·con·tro·vert·i·ble (in-kon-trə-VUR-tə-bəl) *adj.* undeniable; indisputable

in·cor·po·rate (in-KOR-pə-rayt) *vt.* (-rat·ed, -rat·ing) include; unite into one body; form into corporation

in·cor·ri·gi·ble (in-KOR-i-jə-bəl) *adj.* beyond correction or reform; firmly rooted

in·crease (in-KREES) *v.* (-creased, -creas·ing) make or become greater in size, number *etc.* —*n.* (IN-krees) growth, enlargement, profit —in·creas′ing·ly *adv.* more and more

in·cred·i·ble (in-KRED-ə-bəl) *adj.* unbelievable; *inf.* marvelous, amazing

in·cred·u·lous (in-KREJ-ə-ləs) *adj.* unbelieving —in·cre·du′li·ty (-krə-DOO-lə-tee) *n.*

in·cre·ment (IN-krə-mənt) *n.* increase, *esp.* one of a series —in·cre·men′tal *adj.*

in·crim·i·nate (in-KRIM-ə-nayt) *vt.* (-nat·ed, -nat·ing) imply guilt of; accuse of crime —in·crim′i·na·to·ry *adj.*

in·crust (in-KRUST) *v.* cover with or form a crust or hard covering

in·cu·bate (in-kyə-bayt) *vt.* (-bat·ed, -bat·ing) provide (eggs, embryos, bacteria *etc.*) with heat or other favorable condition for development —*vi.* develop in this way —in·cu·ba′tion *n.* —in′cu·ba·tor *n.* apparatus for artificially hatching eggs, for rearing premature babies

in·cu·bus (IN-kyə-bəs) *n.* (*pl.* -bi *pr.* -bī) nightmare or obsession; (*orig.*) demon believed to afflict sleeping person

in·cul·cate (in-KUL-kayt) *vt.* (-cat·ed, -cat·ing) impress on the mind —in·cul·ca′tion *n.*

in·cum·bent (in-KUM-bənt) *adj.* lying, resting (on) —*n.* holder of office, *esp.* elective office in government —in·cum′ben·cy *n.* obligation; office or tenure of incumbent —it is incumbent on it is the duty of

in·cur (in-KUR) *vt.* (-curred, -cur·ring) fall into, bring upon oneself —in·cur′sion (-zhən) *n.* invasion, penetration

in·debt·ed (in-DET-id) *adj.* owing gratitude for help, favors *etc.*; owing money —in·debt′ed·ness *n.*

in·deed′ *adv.* in truth; really; in fact; certainly —*interj.* denoting surprise, doubt *etc.*

in·de·fat·i·ga·ble (in-di-FAT-i-gə-bəl) *adj.* untiring —in·de·fat′i·ga·bly *adv.*

in·de·fen·si·ble (in-di-FEN-sə-bəl) *adj.* not justifiable or defensible

in·del·i·ble (in-DEL-ə-bəl) *adj.* that cannot be blotted out, effaced or erased; producing such a mark —in·del′i·bly *adv.*

in·del·i·cate (in-DEL-i-kit) *adj.* coarse, embarrassing, tasteless

in·dem·ni·ty (in-DEM-ni-tee) *n.* (*pl.* -ties) compensation; security against loss —in·dem·ni·fi·ca′tion *n.* —in·dem′ni·fy (-fī) *vt.* (-fied, -fy·ing) give indemnity to; compensate

in·dent′ *v.* set in (from margin

*etc.*); make notches in —*n.* (IN-dent) indentation; notch —**in·den·ta'tion** *n.* —**in·den'ture** *n.* contract, *esp.* one binding apprentice to master; indentation —*vt.* (-tured, -tur·ing) bind by indenture

**in·de·pend·ent** (in-di-PEN-dont) *adj.* not subject to others; self-reliant; free; valid in itself; politically of no party —**in·de·pend'ence** *n.* being independent; self-reliance; self-support

**in·de·scrib·a·ble** (in-di-SKRI-bol) *adj.* beyond description; too intense *etc.* for words —**in·de·scrib'a·bly** *adv.*

**in·de·ter·mi·nate** (in-di-TUR-mo-nit) *adj.* uncertain; inconclusive; incalculable

**in·dex** (IN-deks) *n.* (*pl.* -dex·es, -di·ces *pr.* -do-seez) alphabetical list of references, usu. at end of book; pointer, indicator; *Math.* exponent; *Econ.* quantity relating relative level of wages, prices *etc.* compared with date established as standard —*vt.* provide book with index; insert in index; adjust wages, prices *etc.* to reflect change in some economic indicator

**In·di·an** (IN-dee-on) *n.* native of India; aboriginal American —*adj.*

**in·di·cate** (IN-di-kayt) *vt.* (-cat·ed, -cat·ing) point out; state briefly; signify —**in·di·ca'tion** *n.* sign; token; explanation —**in·dic'a·tive** *adj.* pointing to; *Grammar* stating fact —**in'di·ca·tor** *n.* one who, that which, indicates; on vehicle, flashing light showing driver's intention to turn

**in·dict** (in-DIT) *vt.* accuse, *esp.* by legal process —**in·dict'ment** (-mont) *n.*

**in·dif·fer·ent** (in-DIF-or-ont) *adj.* uninterested; unimportant; neither good nor bad; inferior; neutral —**in·dif'fer·ence** *n.*

**in·dig·e·nous** (in-DIJ-o-nos) *adj.* born in or natural to a country

**in·di·gent** (IN-di-jont) *adj.* poor, needy —**in'di·gence** *n.* poverty

**in·di·ges·tion** (in-di-JES-chon) *n.* (discomfort, pain caused by) difficulty in digesting food —**in·di·gest'i·ble** *adj.*

**in·dig·nant** (in-DIG-nont) *adj.* moved by anger and scorn; angered by sense of injury or injustice —**in·dig·na'tion** *n.* —**in·dig'ni·ty** *n.* humiliation, insult, slight

**in·di·go** (IN-do-goh) *n.* (*pl.* -gos) blue dye from plant; the plant —*adj.* deep blue

**in·dis·crim·i·nate** (in-di-SKRIM-o-nit) *adj.* lacking discrimination; jumbled

**in·dis·pen·sa·ble** (in-di-SPEN-so-bol) *adj.* necessary; essential

**in·dis·po·si·tion** (in-dis-po-ZISH-on) *n.* sickness; disinclination —**in·dis·posed'** (-POHZD) *adj.* unwell, not fit; disinclined

**in·dis·sol·u·ble** (in-di-SOL-yo-bol) *adj.* permanent

**in·di·um** (IN-dee-om) *n.* soft silver-white metallic element

**in·di·vid·u·al** (in-do-VIJ-oo-ol) *adj.* single; characteristic of single person or thing; distinctive —*n.* single person or thing —**in·di·vid'u·al·ism** *n.* principle of asserting one's independence —**in·di·vid'u·al·ist** *n.* —**in·di·vid·u·al'i·ty** *n.* distinctive character; personality —**in·di·vid'u·al·ize** *vt.* (-ized, -iz·ing) make (or treat as) individual —**in·di·vid'u·al·ly** *adv.* singly

**in·doc·tri·nate** (in-DOK-tro-nayt) *vt.* (-nat·ed, -nat·ing) implant beliefs in the mind of

**in·do·lent** (IN-dl-ont) *adj.* lazy —**in'do·lence** *n.*

**in·dom·i·ta·ble** (in-DOM-i-tə-bəl) *adj.* unyielding

**in·door** (IN-dor) *adj.* within doors; under cover —**in·doors** (in-DORZ) *adv.*

**in·du·bi·ta·ble** (in-DOO-bi-tə-bəl) *adj.* beyond doubt; certain —**in·du·bi·ta·bly** *adv.*

**in·duce** (in-DOOS) *vt.* (-duced, -duc·ing) persuade; bring on; cause; produce by induction —**in·duce'ment** *n.* incentive, attraction

**in·duct** (in-DUKT) *vt.* install in office —**in·duc'tion** *n.* an inducting; general inference from particular instances; production of electric or magnetic state in body by its being near (not touching) electrified or magnetized body —**in·duc'tance** (-təns) *n.* —**in·duc'tive** *adj.*

**in·dulge** (in-DULJ) *vt.* (-dulged, -dulg·ing) gratify; give free course to; pamper; spoil —**in·dul'gence** (-jəns) *n.* an indulging; extravagance; something granted as a favor or privilege; *RC Ch.* remission of temporal punishment due after absolution —**in·dul'gent** (-jənt) *adj.*

**in·dus·try** (IN-də-stree) *n.* manufacture, processing *etc.* of goods; branch of this; diligence; habitual hard work —**in·dus'tri·al** *adj.* of industries, trades —**in·dus'tri·al·ize** *vt.* (-ized, -iz·ing) —**in·dus'tri·ous** (-tree-əs) *adj.* diligent

**in·e·bri·ate** (in-EE-bree-ayt) *vt.* (-at·ed, -at·ing) make drunk; intoxicate —*adj.* (-bree-it) drunken —*n.* habitual drunkard —**in·e·bri·a'tion** *n.* drunkenness

**in·ed·i·ble** (in-ED-ə-bəl) *adj.* not eatable; unfit for food

**in·ed·u·ca·ble** (in-EJ-uu-kə-bəl) *adj.* incapable of being educated, *eg* through mental retardation

**in·ef·fa·ble** (in-EF-ə-bəl) *adj.* too great or sacred for words; unutterable —**in·ef·fa·bil'i·ty** *n.*

**in·el·i·gi·ble** (in-EL-i-jə-bəl) *adj.* not fit or qualified (for something) —**in·el·i·gi·bil'i·ty** *n.*

**in·ept'** *adj.* absurd; out of place; clumsy —**in·ept'i·tude** *n.*

**in·ert** (in-URT) *adj.* without power of action or resistance; slow, sluggish; chemically unreactive —**in·er'tia** (-UR-shə) *n.* inactivity; property by which matter continues in its existing state of rest or motion in straight line, unless that state is changed by external force

**in·es·ti·ma·ble** (in-ES-tə-mə-bəl) *adj.* too good, too great, to be estimated

**in·ev·i·ta·ble** (in-EV-i-tə-bəl) *adj.* unavoidable; sure to happen —**in·ev·i·ta·bil'i·ty** *n.*

**in·ex·o·ra·ble** (in-EK-sər-ə-bəl) *adj.* relentless —**in·ex'o·ra·bly** *adv.*

**in·ex·pli·ca·ble** (in-EK-spli-kə-bəl) *adj.* impossible to explain

**in ex·tre·mis** (eks-TREE-mis) *Lat.* at the point of death

**in·fal·li·ble** (in-FAL-ə-bəl) *adj.* unerring; not liable to fail; certain, sure —**in·fal·li·bil'i·ty** *n.*

**in·fa·mous** (IN-fə-məs) *adj.* notorious; shocking —**in'fa·my** (-mee) *n.* (*pl.* -mies)

**in·fant** (IN-fənt) *n.* very young child —**in'fan·cy** *n.* —**in·fan'ti·cide** (-FAN-tə-sid) *n.* murder of newborn child; person guilty of this —**in'fan·tile** (-fən-til) *adj.* childish

**in·fan·try** (IN-fən-tree) *n.* (*pl.* -tries) foot soldiers

**in·fat·u·ate** (in-FACH-oo-ayt) *vt.* (-at·ed, -at·ing) inspire with folly or foolish passion —**in·fat'u·at·ed** *adj.* foolishly enamored —**in·fat·u·a'tion** *n.*

**in·fect** (in-FEKT) *vt.* affect (with

disease); contaminate —in·fec'·tion (-shən) n. —in·fec'·tious (-shəs) adj. catching, spreading, pestilential

in·fer (in-FUR) vt. (-ferred, -fer·ring) deduce, conclude —in'·fer·ence (-fər-əns) n. —in·fer·en'·tial (-fər-EN-shəl) adj. deduced

in·fe·ri·or (in-FEER-ee-ər) adj. of poor quality; lower —n. one lower (in rank etc.) —in·fe·ri·or'i·ty n. —inferiority complex Psychoanalysis intense sense of inferiority

in·fer·nal (in-FUR-nl) adj. devilish; hellish; inf. irritating, confounded

in·fer·no (in-FUR-noh) n. region of hell; great destructive fire

in·fest' vt. inhabit or overrun in dangerously or unpleasantly large numbers —in·fes·ta'tion n.

in·fi·del·i·ty (in-fi-DEL-i-tee) n. unfaithfulness; religious disbelief; disloyalty; treachery —in'fi·del (-dl) n. unbeliever —adj.

in·fil·trate (in-FIL-trayt) v. (-trat·ed, -trat·ing) trickle through; cause to pass through pores; gain access surreptitiously —in·fil·tra'tion n.

in·fi·nite (in-fə-nit) adj. boundless —in'fi·nite·ly adv. exceedingly —in·fin·i·tes'i·mal (-TES-ə-məl) adj. extremely, infinitely small —in·fin'i·ty n. unlimited and endless extent

in·fin·i·tive (in-FIN-i-tiv) adj. Grammar in form expressing notion of verb without limitation of tense, person, or number —n. verb in this form

in·firm (in-FURM) adj. physically weak; mentally weak; irresolute —in·fir'ma·ry (-mə-ree) n. hospital; dispensary —in·fir'mi·ty n. (pl. -ties)

in·flame (in-FLAYM) v. (-flamed, -flam·ing) rouse to anger, excite-

ment; cause inflammation in; become inflamed —in·flam·ma·bil'·i·ty n. —in·flam'ma·ble adj. easily set on fire; excitable —in·flam·ma'tion n. infection of part of the body, with pain, heat, swelling, and redness

in·flate (in-FLAYT) v. (-flat·ed, -flat·ing) blow up with air, gas; swell; cause economic inflation; raise price, esp. artificially —in·fla'tion n. increase in prices and fall in value of money —in·fla'tion·ar·y adj.

in·flect (in-FLEKT) vt. modify (words) to show grammatical relationships; bend inward —in·flec'tion n. modification of word; modulation of voice

in·flex·i·ble (in-FLEK-sə-bəl) adj. incapable of being bent; stern —in·flex·i·bil'i·ty n.

in·flict (in-FLIKT) vt. impose, deliver forcibly —in·flic'tion n. inflicting; punishment

in·flu·ence (IN-floo-əns) n. effect of one person or thing on another; power of person or thing having an effect; thing, person exercising this —vt. (-enced, -enc·ing) sway; induce; affect —in·flu·en'tial adj.

in·flu·en·za (in-floo-EN-zə) n. contagious feverish respiratory virus disease

in·flux (IN-fluks) n. a flowing in; inflow

in·form' vt. tell; animate —vi. give information (about) —in·form'ant (-ənt) n. one who tells —in·for·ma'tion n. what is told, knowledge —in·form'a·tive adj.

infraction n. see INFRINGE

in·fra·red (in-frə-RED) adj. denoting rays below red end of visible spectrum

in·fra·struc·ture (IN-frə-struk-chər) n. basic structure or fixed capital items of an organization or economic system

**in·fringe** (in-FRINJ) *vt.* (-fringed, -fring·ing) transgress, break —**in·fringe′ment** *n.* —**in·frac′tion** *n.* breach; violation

**in·fu·ri·ate** (in-FYUUR-ee-ayt) *vt.* (-at·ed, -at·ing) enrage

**in·fuse** (in-FYOOZ) *v.* (-fused, -fus·ing) soak to extract flavor *etc.*; instill, charge —**in·fu′sion** (-FYOO-zhon) *n.* an infusing; liquid extract obtained

**in·gen·ious** (in-JEEN-yos) *adj.* clever at contriving; cleverly contrived —**in·ge·nu′i·ty** (-jo-NOO-o-tee) *n.*

**in·gé·nue** (AN-zho-noo) *n.* artless girl or young woman; actress playing such a part

**in·gen·u·ous** (in-JEN-yoo-os) *adj.* frank; naive, innocent —**in·gen′u·ous·ness** *n.*

**in·ges·tion** (in-JES-chon) *n.* act of introducing food into the body

**in·got** (ING-got) *n.* brick of cast metal, *esp.* gold

**in·grain** (in-GRAYN) *vt.* implant deeply —**in·grained′** *adj.* deep-rooted; inveterate

**in·gra·ti·ate** (in-GRAY-shee-ayt) *v. refl.* get (oneself) into favor —**in·gra′ti·at·ing·ly** *adv.*

**in·gre·di·ent** (in-GREE-dee-ont) *n.* component part of a mixture

**in′gress** *n.* entry, means, right of entrance

**in·hab′it** *vt.* dwell in —**in·hab′it·a·ble** *adj.* —**in·hab′it·ant** (-tont) *n.*

**in·hale** (in-HAYL) *v.* (-haled, -hal·ing) breathe in (air *etc.*) —**in·ha·la′tion** *n. esp.* medical preparation for inhaling —**in·ha′ler** *n.* person who inhales; *Also* **in′ha·la·tor** device producing, and assisting inhalation of therapeutic vapors

**in·here** (in-HEER) *vi.* (-hered,

-her·ing) of qualities, exist (in); of rights, be vested (in person) —**in·her′ent** (-HEER-ont) *adj.* existing as an inseparable part

**in·her′it** *vt.* receive as heir; derive from parents —*vi.* succeed as heir —**in·her′it·ance** (-ons) *n.*

**in·hib′it** *vt.* restrain (impulse, desire *etc.*); hinder (action); forbid —**in·hi·bi′tion** *n.* repression of emotion, instinct; a stopping or retarding —**in·hib′i·to·ry** *adj.*

**in·hu·man** (in-HYOO-mon) *adj.* cruel, brutal; not human —**in·hu·man′i·ty** *n.*

**in·im·i·cal** (i-NIM-i-kol) *adj.* unfavorable (to); unfriendly; hostile

**in·im·i·ta·ble** (i-NIM-i-to-bol) *adj.* defying imitation —**in·im′i·ta·bly** *adv.*

**in·iq·ui·ty** (i-NIK-wi-tee) *n.* (*pl.* -ties) gross injustice; wickedness, sin —**in·iq′ui·tous** *adj.* unfair, sinful, unjust

**in·i·tial** (i-NISH-ol) *adj.* of, occurring at the beginning —*n.* initial letter, *esp.* of person's name —*vt.* (-tialed, -tial·ing) mark, sign with one's initials

**in·i·ti·ate** (i-NISH-ee-ayt) *vt.* (-at·ed, -at·ing) originate; begin; admit into closed society; instruct in elements (of) —*n.* (-ee-it) initiated person —**in·i·ti·a′tion** *n.* —**in·i′ti·a·tive** *n.* first step, lead; ability to act independently —*adj.* originating

**in·ject** (in-JEKT) *vt.* introduce (*esp.* fluid, medicine *etc.* with syringe) —**in·jec′tion** *n.*

**in·junc·tion** (in-JUNGK-shon) *n.* judicial order to restrain; authoritative order

**in·ju·ry** (IN-jo-ree) *n.* (*pl.* -ries) physical damage or harm; wrong —**in·jure** (IN-jor) *vt.* (-jured, -jur·ing) do harm or damage to —**in·ju′ri·ous** (-JUU-ree-os) *adj.*

**in·jus·tice** (in-JUS-tis) *n.* want of justice; wrong; injury; unjust act

**ink** *n.* fluid used for writing or printing —*vt.* mark with ink; cover, smear with it

**ink·ling** (INGK-ling) *n.* hint, slight knowledge or suspicion

**inlaid** *see* INLAY

**in'land** *n.* interior of country —*adj.* (IN-land) in this; away from the sea; within a country —*adv.* (IN-land) in or toward the inland

**in'-law** *n.* relative by marriage *esp.* mother-in-law and father-in-law

**in'lay** *vt.* (-laid, -lay·ing) embed; decorate with inset pattern —*n.* inlaid piece or pattern

**in'let** *n.* entrance; small arm of sea, lake *etc.*; piece inserted

**in lo·co pa·ren·tis** (LOH-koh pə-REN-tis) *Lat.* in place of a parent

**in·mate** (IN-mayt) *n.* occupant, *esp.* of prison, hospital *etc.*

**in·most** (IN-mohst) *adj.* most inward, deepest; most secret

**inn** *n.* restaurant or tavern; country hotel —**inn'keep·er** *n.*

**in·nards** (IN-ərdz) *n. pl.* internal organs or working parts

**in·nate** (i-NAYT) *adj.* inborn; inherent

**in·ner** (IN-ər) *adj.* lying within —**in'ner·most** *adj.* —inner tube rubber air tube of pneumatic tire

**in'ning** *n. Sports* side's turn at bat; spell, turn

**in·no·cent** (IN-ə-sənt) *adj.* pure; guiltless; harmless *n.* innocent person, *esp.* young child —**in'no·cence** *n.*

**in·noc·u·ous** (i-NOK-yoo-əs) *adj.* harmless

**in·no·vate** (IN-ə-vayt) *vt.* (-vat·ed, -vat·ing) introduce changes, new things —**in·no·va'·tion** *n.*

**in·nu·en·do** (in-yoo-EN-doh) *n.* (*pl.* -dos) allusive remark, hint; indirect accusation

**in·nu·mer·a·ble** (i-NOO-mər-ə-bəl) *adj.* countless; very numerous

**in·oc·u·late** (i-NOK-yə-layt) *vt.* (-lat·ed, -lat·ing) immunize by injecting vaccine —**in·oc·u·la'·tion** *n.*

**in·op·er·a·ble** (in-OP-ər-ə-bəl) *adj.* unworkable; *Med.* that cannot be operated on —**in·op'er·a·tive** *adj.* not operative; ineffective

**in·op·por·tune** (in-op-ər-TOON) *adj.* badly timed

**in·or·di·nate** (in-OR-dn-it) *adj.* excessive

**in·or·gan·ic** (in-or-GAN-ik) *adj.* not having structure or characteristics of living organisms; of substances without carbon

**in·pa·tient** (IN-pay-shənt) *n.* patient who stays in hospital

**in·put** (IN-puut) *n.* act of putting in; that which is put in, as resource needed for industrial production *etc.*; data *etc.* fed into a computer

**in·quest** (IN-kwest) *n.* legal or judicial inquiry presided over by a coroner; detailed inquiry or discussion

**in·quire** (in-KWIR) *vi.* (-quired, -quir·ing) seek information —**in·quir'er** *n.* —**in·quir'y** *n.* (*pl.* -quir·ies) question; investigation

**in·qui·si·tion** (in-kwə-ZISH-ən) *n.* searching investigation, official inquiry; *Hist.* (I-) tribunal for suppression of heresy —**in·quis'i·tor** (-KWIZ-ə-tər) *n.*

**in·quis·i·tive** (in-KWIZ-i-tiv) *adj.* curious; prying

**in·road** (IN-rohd) *n.* incursion; encroachment

**in·sane** (in-SAYN) *adj.* mentally deranged; crazy, senseless —**in-**

**sane·ly** adv. like a lunatic, madly; excessively —in·san'i·ty n.

**in·sa·tia·ble** (in-SAY-sho-bol) adj. incapable of being satisfied

**in·scribe** (in-SKRĪB) vt. (-scribed, -scrib·ing) write, engrave (in or on something); mark; dedicate; trace (figure) within another —in·scrip'tion n. inscribing; words inscribed on monument etc.

**in·scru·ta·ble** (in-SKROO-to-bol) adj. mysterious, impenetrable; affording no explanation —in·scru·ta·bil'i·ty n.

**in·sect** (IN-sekt) n. small invertebrate animal with six legs, usu. segmented body and two or four wings —in·sec'ti·cide (-sīd) n. preparation for killing insects —in·sec·tiv'o·rous (-tiv') adj. insect-eating

**in·se·cure** (in-si-KYUUR) adj. not safe or firm; anxious, not confident

**in·sem·i·nate** (in-SEM-o-nayt) vt. (-nat·ed, -nat·ing) implant semen into —artificial insemination impregnation of the female by artificial means

**in·sen·sate** (in-SEN-sayt) adj. without sensation, unconscious; unfeeling

**in·sen·si·ble** (in-SEN-so-bol) adj. unconscious; without feeling; not aware; not perceptible —in·sen'si·bly adv. imperceptibly

**in·sert** (in-SURT) vt. introduce; place or put (in, into, between) —n. (IN-surt) something inserted —in·ser'tion (-shon) n.

**in·set** n. something extra inserted esp. as decoration —in·set' vt. (-set, -set·ting)

**in·shore** (IN-shor) adj. near shore —adv. toward shore

**in·side** (IN-sīd) n. inner side, surface, or part; inner circle of influence; sl. confidential infor-

mation; pl. inf. internal parts of body —adj. of, in, or on, inside —adv. (in-SĪD) in or into the inside; sl. in prison —prep. within, on inner side

**in·sid·i·ous** (in-SID-ee-os) adj. stealthy, treacherous; unseen but deadly

**in·sight** (IN-sīt) n. mental penetration, discernment

**in·sig·ni·a** (in-SIG-nee-o) n. pl. badges, emblems of honor or office (sing. in·sig'ne pr. -nee)

**in·sin·u·ate** (in-SIN-yoo-ayt) vt. (-at·ed, -at·ing) hint; work oneself into favor; introduce gradually or subtly —in·sin·u·a'tion n.

**in·sip·id** adj. dull, tasteless, spiritless

**in·sist'** vi. demand persistently; maintain; emphasize —in·sist'ence n. —in·sist'ent adj.

**in si·tu** (SĪ-too) Lat. in its original place or position

**in·so·lent** (IN-so-lont) adj. arrogantly impudent —in'so·lence n.

**in·som·ni·a** (in-SOM-nee-o) n. sleeplessness —in·som'ni·ac (-nee-ak) adj. or n.

**in·so·much** (in-so-MUCH) adv. to such an extent

**in·sou·ci·ant** (in-SOO-see-ont) adj. indifferent, careless, unconcerned —in·sou'ci·ance n.

**in·spect** (in-SPEKT) vt. examine closely or officially —in·spec'tion n. —in·spec'tor n. one who inspects; high-ranking police or fire officer

**in·spire** (in-SPĪR) vt. (-spired, -spir·ing) animate, invigorate; arouse, create feeling, thought; give rise to; breathe in, inhale —in·spi·ra'tion n. good idea; creative influence or stimulus

**in·stall** (in-STAWL) vt. have (apparatus) put in; establish; place (person in office etc.) with ceremony —in·stal·la'tion n. act of installing; that which is installed

in·stall·ment (IN-STAWL-mənt) n. payment of part of debt; any of parts of a whole delivered in succession

in·stance (IN-stəns) n. example; particular case; request —vt. (-stanced, -stanc·ing) cite

in·stant (IN-stənt) n. moment, point of time —adj. immediate; urgent; (of foods) requiring little preparation —in·stan·ta'ne·ous adj. happening in an instant —in·stan'ter adv. at once —in'stant·ly adv. at once

in·stead (IN-STED) adv. in place (of); as a substitute

in'step n. top of foot between toes and ankle

in·sti·gate (IN-sti·gayt) vt. (-gat·ed, -gat·ing) rouse, urge; bring about —in·sti·ga'tion n.

in·still' vt. implant; inculcate —in·still'ment n.

in·stinct (IN-stingkt) n. inborn impulse or propensity; unconscious skill; intuition —in·stinc'tive adj.

in·sti·tute (IN-sti·toot) vt. (-tut·ed, -tut·ing) establish, found; appoint; set in motion —n. society for promoting some public goal, esp. scientific; its building —in·sti·tu'tion n. a instituting; establishment for care or education, hospital, college etc.; an established custom or law or (inf.) person —in·sti·tu'tion·al adj. of institutions; routine —in·sti·tu'tion·al·ize vt. (-ized, -iz·ing) place in an institution esp. for care of mentally ill; make or become an institution

in·struct (IN-STRUKT) vt. teach; inform; order; brief (jury, lawyer) —in·struc'tion n. teaching; order —pl. directions —in·struc'tive adj. informative; useful

in·stru·ment (IN-strə-mənt) n. tool, implement, means, person, thing used to make, do, measure etc.; mechanism for producing musical sound; legal document —in·stru·men'tal adj. acting as instrument or means; helpful; belonging to, produced by musical instruments —in·stru·men'tal·ist n. player of musical instrument —in·stru·men·tal'i·ty n. (pl. -ties) agency, means —in·stru·men·ta'tion n. arrangement of music for instruments

in·sub·or·di·nate (in-sə-BOR-dn-it) adj. not submissive; mutinous, rebellious —in·sub·or·di·na'tion n.

in·su·lar (IN-sə-lər) adj. of an island; remote, detached; narrow-minded or prejudiced —in·su·lar'i·ty n.

in·su·late (IN-sə-layt) vt. (-lat·ed, -lat·ing) prevent or reduce transfer of electricity, heat, sound etc.; isolate, detach —in·su·la'tion n.

in·su·lin (IN-sə-lin) n. pancreatic hormone, used in treating diabetes

in·sult' vt. behave rudely to; offend —n. (IN·sult) offensive remark; affront —in·sult'ing adj.

in·su·per·a·ble (in-SOO-pər-ə-bəl) adj. that cannot be overcome or surmounted; unconquerable

in·sure (in-SHUUR) v. (-sured, -sur·ing) contract for payment in event of loss, death etc., by payment of premiums; make such contract about; make safe (against) —in·sur'a·ble adj. —in·sur'ance n. —in·sur'er n. —insurance policy contract of insurance

in·sur·gent (in-SUR-jənt) adj. in revolt —n. rebel —in·sur'gence, in·sur·rec'tion n. revolt

in·tact (in-TAKT) adj. untouched; uninjured

in·tagl·io (in-TAL-yoh) n. (pl.

-tagl·ios) engraved design; gem so cut

**in·take** (IN-tayk) *n.* what is taken in; quantity taken in; opening for taking in, in car, air passage into carburetor

**in·te·ger** (IN-ti-jər) *n.* whole number; whole of anything

**in·te·gral** (IN-ti-grəl) *adj.* constituting an essential part of a whole —**in'te·grate** *vt.* (-grat·ed, -grat·ing) combine into one whole; unify diverse elements (of community *etc.*) —**in·te·gra'tion** *n.* —**integral calculus** branch of mathematics of changing quantities that calculates total effects of the change —**integrated circuit** tiny electronic circuit, usu. on silicon chip

**in·teg·ri·ty** (in-TEG-ri-tee) *n.* honesty; original perfect state

**in·teg·u·ment** (in-TEG-yə-mənt) *n.* natural covering, skin, rind, husk

**in·tel·lect** (IN-tl-ekt) *n.* power of thinking and reasoning —**in·tel·lec'tu·al** *adj.* of, appealing to intellect; having good intellect —*n.* one endowed with intellect and attracted to intellectual things

**in·tel·li·gent** (in-TEL-i-jənt) *adj.* having, showing good intellect; quick at understanding; informed —**in·tel'li·gence** *n.* quickness of understanding; mental power or ability; intellect; information, news, *esp.* military information —**in·tel·li·gent'si·a** (-JENT-see-ə) *n.* intellectual or cultured classes —**in·tel'li·gi·ble** (-jə-bəl) *adj.* understandable

**in·tem·per·ate** (in-TEM-pər-it) *adj.* drinking alcohol to excess; immoderate; unrestrained —**in·tem'per·ance** (-əns) *n.*

**in·tend'** *vt.* propose, mean (to do, say *etc.*) —**in·tend'ed** *adj.*

planned, future —*n. inf.* proposed spouse

**in·tense** (in-TENS) *adj.* very strong or acute; emotional —**in·ten·si·fi·ca'tion** *n.* —**in·ten'si·fy** *v.* (-fied, -fy·ing) make or become stronger; increase —**in·ten'si·ty** *n.* intense quality; strength —**in·ten'sive** *adj.* characterized by intensity or emphasis on specified factor

**in·tent'** *n.* purpose —*adj.* concentrating (on); resolved, bent; preoccupied, absorbed —**in·ten'tion** *n.* purpose, aim —**in·ten'tion·al** *adj.*

**in·ter** (in-TUR) *vt.* (-terred, -ter·ring) bury —**in·ter'ment** *n.*

**inter-** (*prefix*) between, among, mutually *eg* interglacial, interrelation Such words are not given here where the meaning can easily be inferred from the simple word

**in·ter·act** (in-tər-AKT) *vi.* act on each other —**in·ter·ac'tion** *n.*

**in·ter·cede** (in-tər-SEED) *vi.* (-ced·ed, -ced·ing) plead in favor of; mediate —**in·ter·ces'sion** *n.*

**in·ter·cept** (in-tər-SEPT) *vt.* cut off; seize, stop in transit —**in·ter·cep'tion** *n.* —**in·ter·cep'tor, -er** *n.* one who, that which intercepts; fast fighter plane, missile *etc.*

**in·ter·change** (in-tər-CHAYNJ) *v.* (-changed, -chang·ing) (cause to) exchange places —*n.* (IN-tər-chaynj) interchanging; highway intersection —**in·ter·change'a·ble** *adj.* able to be exchanged in position or use

**in·ter·con·ti·nen·tal** (in-tər-kon-tn-EN-təl) *adj.* connecting continents; (of missile) able to reach one continent from another

**in·ter·course** (IN-tər-kors) *n.* mutual dealings; communication; sexual joining of two people; copulation

**in·ter·dict** (IN-tər-dikt) *n.* in Catholic church, decree restraining faithful from receiving certain sacraments; formal prohibition —**in·ter·dict'** *vt.* prohibit, forbid; restrain —**in·ter·dic'tion** *n.*

**in·ter·est** (IN-tər-ist) *n.* concern, curiosity; thing exciting this; sum paid for use of borrowed money (*also fig.*); legal concern; right, advantage, share —*vt.* excite, cause to feel interest —**in'ter·est·ing** *adj.*

**in·ter·face** (IN-tər-fays) *n.* area, surface, boundary linking two systems

**in·ter·fere** (in-tər-FEER) *vi.* (-fered, -fer·ing) meddle, intervene; clash —**in·ter·fer'ence** *n.* act of interfering; *Radio* interruption of reception by atmospherics or by unwanted signals

**in·ter·fer·on** (in-tər-FEER-on) *n.* a cellular protein that stops development of an invading virus

**in·ter·im** (IN-tər-əm) *n.* meantime —*adj.* temporary, intervening

**in·te·ri·or** (in-TEER-ee-ər) *adj.* inner; inland; indoors —*n.* inside; inland region

**in·ter·ject** (in-tər-JEKT) *vt.* interpose (remark *etc.*) —**in·ter·jec'tion** *n.* exclamation; interjected remark

**in·ter·lard** (in-tər-LAHRD) *v.* intersperse

**in·ter·loc·u·tor** (in-tər-LOK-yə-tər) *n.* one who takes part in conversation; middle man in line of minstrel performers —**in·ter·loc'u·to·ry** *adj.* of a court decree, issued before the final decision in an action

**in·ter·lop·er** (IN-tər-lohp-ər) *n.* one intruding upon another's affairs; intruder

**in·ter·lude** (IN-tər-lood) *n.* interval (in play *etc.*); something filling an interval

**in·ter·mar·ry** (in-tər-MAR-ee) *vi.* (-ried, -ry·ing) (of families, races, religions) become linked by marriage; marry within one's family —**in·ter·mar'riage** *n.*

**in·ter·me·di·ate** (in-tər-MEE-dee-it) *adj.* coming between; interposed —**in·ter·me'di·ar·y** *n.*

**in·ter·mez·zo** (in-tər-MET-soh) *n.* (*pl.* -zos) short performance between acts of play or opera

**in·ter·mi·na·ble** (in-TUR-mə-nə-bəl) *adj.* endless —**in·ter'mi·na·bly** *adv.*

**in·ter·mis·sion** (in-tər-MISH-ən) *n.* short interval between parts of a concert, play *etc.* —**in·ter·mit'tent** *adj.* occurring at intervals

**in·tern¹** (in-TURN) *vt.* confine to special area or camp —**in·tern'ment** *n.* —**in·tern·ee'** *n.*

**in·tern², in·terne** (IN-turn) *n.* recent medical school graduate residing in hospital and working under supervision as member of staff; trainee in occupation or profession —**in'tern·ship** *n.*

**in·ter·nal** (in-TUR-nl) *adj.* inward; interior; within (a country, organization) —**internal combustion** process of exploding mixture of air and fuel within engine cylinder

**in·ter·na·tion·al** (in-tər-NASH-ə-nl) *adj.* of relations between nations —*n.* labor union *etc.* with units, members, in more than one country

**in·ter·ne·cine** (in-tər-NEE-seen) *adj.* mutually destructive; deadly

**in·ter·po·late** (in-TUR-pə-layt) *vt.* (-lat·ed, -lat·ing) insert new (*esp.* misleading) matter (in book *etc.*); interject (remark); *Math.* estimate a value between known values —**in·ter·po·la'tion** *n.*

**in·ter·pose** (in-tər-POHZ) *v.*

(-posed, -pos·ing) —vt. insert; say as interruption; put in the way —vi. intervene; obstruct —in·ter·po·si'tion (-pə-ZISH-ən) n.

in·ter·pret (in-TUR-prit) v. explain; translate, esp. orally; Art render, represent —in·ter·pre·ta'tion n.

in·ter·reg·num (in-tər-REG-nəm) n. (pl. -nums) interval between reigns; gap in continuity

in·ter·ro·gate (in-TER-ə-gayt) vt. (-gat·ed, -gat·ing) question, esp. closely or officially —in·ter·ro·ga'tion n. —in·ter·rog'a·tive adj. questioning —n. word used in asking question —in·ter·rog'a·to·ry adj. of inquiry —n. question, set of questions

in·ter·rupt (in-tə-RUPT) v. break in (upon); stop the course of; block —in·ter·rup'tion n.

in·ter·sect (in-tər-SEKT) vt. divide by passing across or through —vi. meet and cross —in·ter·sec'tion n. point where lines, roads cross

in·ter·sperse (in-tər-SPURS) vt. (-spersed, -spers·ing) sprinkle (something with or something among or in)

in·ter·stel·lar (in-tər-STEL-ər) adj. (of the space) between stars

in·ter·stice (in-TUR-stis) n. (pl. -stic·es pr. -stə-seez) chink, gap, crevice —in·ter·sti'tial (-STISH-əl) adj.

in·ter·val (IN-tər-vəl) n. intervening time or space; pause, break; short period between parts of play, concert etc.; difference (of pitch)

in·ter·vene (in-tər-VEEN) vi. (-vened, -ven·ing) come into a situation in order to change it; be, come between or among; occur in meantime; interpose —in·ter·ven'tion n.

in·tes·tate (in-TES-tayt) adj. not

having made a will —n. person dying intestate —in·tes'ta·cy (-tə-see) n.

in·tes·tine (in-TES-tin) n. (usu. pl.) lower part of alimentary canal between stomach and anus —in·tes'ti·nal adj. of bowels

in·ti·mate[1] (IN-tə-mit) adj. closely acquainted, familiar; private; extensive; having sexual relations (with) —n. intimate friend —in'ti·ma·cy (-mə-see) n.

in·ti·mate[2] (IN-tə-mayt) vt. (-mat·ed, -mat·ing) imply; announce —in·ti·ma'tion n. notice

in·tim·i·date (in-TIM-i-dayt) vt. (-dat·ed, -dat·ing) frighten into submission; deter by threats —in·tim·i·da'tion n.

in·to (IN-too) prep. expresses motion to a point within; indicates change of state; indicates coming up against, encountering; indicates arithmetical division

in·tone (in-TOHN) vt. (-toned, -ton·ing) chant; recite in monotone —in·to·na'tion n. modulation of voice; intoning; accent

in·tox·i·cate (in-TOK-si-kayt) vt. (-cat·ed, -cat·ing) make drunk; excite to excess —in·tox'i·cant (-kənt) adj./n. intoxicating (liquor)

intr. intransitive

intra- (prefix) within

in·trac·ta·ble (in-TRAK-tə-bəl) adj. difficult to influence; hard to control

in·tran·si·gent (in-TRAN-si-jənt) adj. uncompromising, obstinate

in·tra·u·ter·ine (in-trə-YOO-tər-in) adj. within the womb

in·tra·ve·nous (in-trə-VEE-nəs) adj. into a vein

in·trep·id adj. fearless, undaunted —in·tre·pid'i·ty n.

in·tri·cate (in-TRI-kit) adj. involved, puzzlingly entangled —in'tri·ca·cy n. (pl. -cies)

**in·trigue** (in-TREEG) n. under-handed plot; secret love affair v. (-trigued, -tri·guing) —vi. carry on intrigue —vt. interest, puzzle

**in·trin·sic** (in-TRIN-sik) adj. inherent, essential —in·trin'si·cal·ly adv.

**intro-** (prefix) into, within, as in introduce, introvert, etc.

**in·tro·duce** (in-trə-DOOS) vt. (-duced, -duc·ing) make acquainted; present; bring in; bring forward; bring into practice; insert —in·tro·duc'tion n. an introducing; presentation of one person to another; preliminary section or treatment —in·tro·duc'to·ry adj. preliminary

**in·tro·spec·tion** (in-trə-SPEK-shən) n. examination of one's own thoughts —in·tro·spec'tive adj.

**in·tro·vert** (IN-trə-vurt) n. Psychoanalysis one who looks inward rather than at the external world —in·tro·ver'sion (-zhən) n. —in·tro·vert·ed adj.

**in·trude** (in-TROOD) v. (-trud·ed, -trud·ing) thrust (oneself) in uninvited —in·tru'sion (-zhən) n. —in·tru'sive adj.

**In·u·it** (IN-oo-it) n. Eskimo of N Amer. or Greenland

**in·un·date** (IN-ən-dayt) vt. (-dat·ed, -dat·ing) flood; overwhelm —in·un·da'tion n.

**in·ure** (in-YUUR) vt. (-ured, -ur·ing) accustom, esp. to hardship, danger etc.

**in·vade** (in-VAYD) vt. (-vad·ed, -vad·ing) enter by force with hostile intent; overrun; pervade —in·va'sion (-zhən) n.

**in·va·lid¹** (IN-və-lid) n. one suffering from chronic ill health —adj.

ill, suffering from sickness or injury —v. become an invalid; retire from active service because of illness etc.

**in·val·id²** (in-VAL-id) adj. not valid

**in·val·u·a·ble** (in-VAL-yoo-ə-bəl) adj. priceless

**invasion** see INVADE

**in·veigh** (in-VAY) vi. speak violently (against) —in·vec'tive n. abusive speech or writing, vituperation

**in·vei·gle** (in-VAY-gəl) vt. (-gled, -gling) entice, seduce, wheedle

**in·vent'** vt. devise, originate; fabricate (falsehoods etc.) —in·ven'tion n. that which is invented; ability to invent; contrivance; deceit; lie —in·ven'tive adj. resourceful; creative —in·ven'tor n.

**in·ven·to·ry** (IN-vən-tor·ee) n. (pl. -ries) detailed list of goods etc. —vt. (-ried, -ry·ing) make list of

**in·vert** (in-VURT) vt. turn upside down; reverse position, relations of —in·verse' adj. inverted; opposite —n. —in·verse'ly adv. —in·ver'sion (-zhən) n.

**in·ver·te·brate** (in-VUR-tə-brit) n. animal having no vertebral column —adj. spineless

**in·vest'** vt. lay out (money, time, effort etc.) for profit or advantage; install; endow; Poet. cover as with garment —in·ves'ti·ture (-chər) n. formal installation of person in office or rank —in·vest'ment n. investing; money invested; stocks, bonds etc. bought

**in·ves·ti·gate** (in-VES-ti-gayt) v. inquire into; examine —in·ves·ti·ga'tion n.

**in·vet·er·ate** (in-VET-ər-it) adj. deep-rooted; long established, confirmed

**in·vid·i·ous** (in-VID-ee-əs) *adj.* likely to cause ill will or envy

**in·vig·or·ate** (in-VIG-ə-rayt) *vt.* (-at·ed, -at·ing) give vigor to, strengthen

**in·vin·ci·ble** (in-VIN-sə-bəl) *adj.* unconquerable —**in·vin·ci·bil·i·ty** *n.*

**in·vi·o·la·ble** (in-VĪ-ə-lə-bəl) *adj.* not to be profaned; sacred; unalterable —**in·vi'o·late** (-ə-lit) *adj.* unhurt; unprofaned; unbroken

**in·vite** (in-VĪT) *vt.* (-vit·ed, -vit·ing) request the company of; ask courteously; ask for; attract, call forth —*n. inf.* (IN-vīt) an invitation —**in·vi·ta'tion** *n.*

**in·voice** (IN-vois) *n.* itemized bill for goods or services sold —*vt.* (-voiced, -voic·ing) make or present an invoice

**in·voke** (in-VOHK) *vt.* (-voked, -vok·ing) call on; appeal to; ask earnestly for; summon —**in·vo·ca'tion** *n.*

**in·vol·un·tar·y** (in-VOL-ən-ter-ee) *adj.* not done willingly; unintentional; instinctive

**in·vo·lute** (IN-və-loot) *adj.* complex; coiled spirally; rolled inward (*also* **in·vo·lut'ed**)

**in·volve** (in-VOLV) *vt.* (-volved, -volv·ing) include; entail; implicate (person); concern; entangle —**involved** *adj.* complicated; concerned (in)

**in·ward** (IN-wərd) *adj.* internal; situated within; spiritual, mental —*adv.* (*also* **in'wards**) toward the inside; into the mind —**in'ward·ly** *adv.* in the mind; internally

**i·o·dine** (Ī-ə-dīn) *n.* nonmetallic element found in seaweed and used in antiseptic solution, photography *etc.* —**i'o·dize** *vt.* (-dized, -diz·ing) treat or react with iodine

**i·on** (Ī-ən) *n.* electrically charged atom or group of atoms —**i·on'ic** *adj.* —**i·on·i·za'tion** *n.* —**i'on·ize** *vt.* (-ized, -iz·ing) change into ions —**i·on'o·sphere** *n.* region of atmosphere about 50 to 250 miles (80 to 400 km) above Earth

**I·on·ic** (Ī-ON-ik) *adj. Architecture* distinguished by scroll-like decoration on columns

**i·o·ta** (Ī-OH-tə) *n.* the Greek letter *ι*, (*usu.* with not) very small amount

**ip·so fac·to** (IP-soh FAK-toh) *Lat.* by that very fact

**Ir** *Chem.* iridium

**ir-** (*prefix*) for *in-* before *r:* see IN- and listed words

**ire** (ir) *n.* anger, wrath —**i·ras·ci·ble** (i-RAS-ə-bəl) *adj.* hottempered —**i·ras'ci·bly** *adv.* —**i·rate** (ī-RAYT) *adj.* angry

**ir·i·des·cent** (ir-i-DES-ənt) *adj.* exhibiting changing colors like those of the rainbow —**ir·i·des'cence** *n.*

**i·rid·i·um** (i-RID-ee-əm) *n.* very hard, corrosion-resistant metallic element

**i·ris** (Ī-ris) *n.* circular membrane of eye containing pupil; plant with sword-shaped leaves and showy flowers

**irk** (irk) *vt.* irritate, vex —**irk'some** (-sum) *adj.* tiresome

**i·ron** (Ī-ərn) *n.* metallic element, much used for tools *etc.*, and the raw material of steel; tool *etc.*, of this metal; appliance used, when heated, to smooth cloth; metalheaded golf club —*pl.* fetters —*adj.* of, like, iron; inflexible, unyielding; robust —*v.* smooth, cover, fetter *etc.*, with iron or an iron —**i'ron·clad** *adj.* protected with or as with iron —**iron** curtain any barrier that separates communities or ideologies —**iron** lung apparatus for administering artificial respiration

**i·ro·ny** (Ī-rə-nee) *n.* (*pl.* -nies)

(*usu.* humorous or mildly sarcastic) use of words to mean the opposite of what is said; event, situation opposite of that expected —i·ron'ic *adj.* of, using, irony

ir·ra·di·ate (i-RAY-dee-ayt) *vt.* (-at·ed, -at·ing) treat by radiation; shine upon, throw light upon, light up —ir·ra·di·a'tion *n.* impregnation by X-rays, light rays

ir·re·fran·gi·ble (ir-i-FRAN-jə-bəl) *adj.* inviolable; in optics, not susceptible to refraction

ir·ref·u·ta·ble (i-REF-yə-tə-bəl) *adj.* that cannot be refuted, disproved

ir·rep·a·ra·ble (i-REP-ər-ə-bəl) *adj.* not able to be repaired or remedied

ir·re·spec·tive (ir-i-SPEK-tiv) *adj.* without taking account (of)

ir·rev·o·ca·ble (i-REV-ə-kə-bəl) *adj.* not able to be changed, undone, altered

ir·ri·gate (IR-i-gayt) *vt.* (-gat·ed, -gat·ing) water by artificial channels, pipes *etc.* —ir·ri·ga'tion *n.*

ir·ri·tate (IR-i-tayt) *vt.* (-tat·ed, -tat·ing) annoy; inflame; stimulate —ir'ri·ta·ble *adj.* easily annoyed —ir'ri·tant *adj./n.* (person or thing) causing irritation —ir·ri·ta'tion *n.*

Is. Isaiah

is (iz) third person singular, *present indicative of* BE

Is·lam (iz-LAHM) *n.* Muslim faith or world —Is·lam'ic *adj.*

is·land (Ī-lənd) *n.* piece of land surrounded by water; anything like this *eg* safety island, raised area for pedestrians in middle of road

isle (īl) *n.* island —is·let (Ī-lit) *n.* little island

i·so·bar (Ī-sə-bahr) *n.* line on map connecting places of equal mean barometric pressure

i·so·late (Ī-sə-layt) *vt.* (-lat·ed, -lat·ing) place apart or alone —i·so·la'tion *n.* —i·so·la'tion·ism *n.* policy of not participating in international affairs

i·so·mer (Ī-sə-mər) *n.* substance with same molecules as another but different atomic arrangement —i·so·mer'ic *adj.*

i·so·met·ric (Ī-sə-ME-trik) *adj.* having equal dimensions; relating to muscular contraction without movement —i·so·met'rics *n. pl.* system of isometric exercises

i·sos·ce·les (Ī-SOS-ə-leez) *adj.* of triangle, having two sides equal

i·so·therm (Ī-sə-thurm) *n.* line on map connecting points of equal mean temperature

i·so·tope (Ī-sə-tohp) *n.* atom of element having a different nuclear mass and atomic weight from other atoms in same element —i·so·top'ic *adj.*

is·sue (ISH-oo) *n.* sending or giving out officially or publicly; number or amount so given out; discharge; offspring, children; topic of discussion; question, dispute; outcome, result —*v.* (-sued, -su·ing) —*vi.* go out; result in; arise (from) —*vt.* emit, give out, send out; distribute, publish

isth·mus (IS-məs) *n.* neck of land between two seas

it *pron.* neuter pronoun of the third person —its *adj.* belonging to it —it's *contraction* of it is —it·self' *pron.* emphatic form of it

i·tal·ic (i-TAL-ik) *adj.* of type, sloping —i·tal'ics *n. pl.* this type, now used for emphasis *etc.* —i·tal'i·cize (-sīz) *vt.* put in italics

itch (ich) *vi./n.* (feel) irritation in the skin —itch'y *adj.* (itch·i·er, itch·i·est)

**i·tem** (I-təm) *n.* single thing in list, collection *etc.*; piece of information; entry in account *etc.* —**i'tem·ize** *vt.* (-ized, -iz·ing)

**it·er·ate** (IT-ə-rayt) *vt.* (-at·ed, -at·ing) repeat —**it·er·a'tion** *n.* —**it'er·a·tive** *adj.*

**i·tin·er·ant** (ī-TIN-ər-ənt) *adj.* traveling from place to place; working for a short time in various places; traveling on circuit —**i·tin'er·ar·y** *n.* (*pl.* -ar·ies) record, line of travel; route; guidebook

**i·vo·ry** (I-və-ree) *n.* (*pl.* -ries) hard white substance of the tusks of elephants *etc.* —**ivory tower** seclusion, remoteness

**i·vy** (I-vee) *n.* (*pl.* -vies) climbing evergreen plant —**i'vied** *adj.* covered with ivy

# J

**jab** *vt.* (jabbed, jab·bing) poke roughly; thrust, stab abruptly —*n.* poke; punch

**jab·ber** (JAB-ər) *v.* chatter; utter, talk rapidly, incoherently —**Jab'ber·wock·y** *n.* nonsense, *esp.* in verse

**jack** (jak) *n.* fellow, man; *inf.* sailor; male of some animals; device for lifting heavy weight, *esp.* automobile; playing card with picture of soldier or servant; socket and plug connection for electrical equipment; small flag, *esp.* national, at sea —*vt.* (*usu.* with *up*) lift (an object) with a jack —**jack-of-all-trades** (*pl.* jacks-) person adept at many kinds of work

**jack·al** (JAK-əl) *n.* wild, gregarious animal of Asia and Africa closely allied to dog

**jack·ass** (JAK-as) *n.* male donkey; blockhead

**jack·et** (JAK-it) *n.* outer garment, short coat; outer casing, cover

**jack·knife** (JAK-nīf) *n.* (*pl.* -knives) clasp knife; dive with sharp bend at waist in midair —*v.* (-knifed, -knif·ing) bend sharply, *eg* an articulated truck forming a sharp angle with its trailer

**jack·pot** (JAK-pot) *n.* large prize; accumulated stakes, as in poker

**jac·quard** (JAK-ahrd) *n.* fabric in which design is incorporated into the weave

**Ja·cuz·zi** (jə-KOO-zee) R device that swirls water in a bath; bath with this device

**jade¹** (jayd) *n.* ornamental semi-precious stone, usu. dark green; this color

**jade²** *n.* sorry or worn-out horse; disreputable woman —**jad'ed** *adj.* tired; off-color

**jag** *n.* sharp or ragged projection; spree —**jag'ged** (-id) *adj.*

**jag·uar** (JAG-wahr) *n.* large S Amer. spotted cat

**jail** (jayl) *n.* building for confinement of criminals or suspects —*vt.* send to, confine in prison —**jail'bait** (-bayt) *n. sl.* underage girl with whom sexual intercourse is considered a crime —**jail'er** *n.* —**jail'bird** *n.* hardened criminal

**ja·lop·y** (jə-LOP-ee) *n. inf.* (*pl.* -lop·ies) old car

**jam** *vt.* (jammed, jam·ming) pack together; (cause to) stick together and become unworkable; apply fiercely; squeeze; *Radio* block (another station) with impulses of equal wavelength —*n.* fruit preserved by boiling with sugar; crush; delay of traffic; awkward situation —**jam-packed** *adj.* filled to capacity —**jam session** (improvised) jazz session

**jamb** (jam) n. side post of arch, door etc.

**jam·bo·ree** (jam-bə-REE) n. large gathering or rally of scouts; spree, celebration

**jan·gle** (JANG-gəl) v. (-gled, -gling) (cause to) sound harshly, as bell; (of nerves) irritate —n. harsh sound

**Jan·i·tor** (JAN-i-tər) n. custodian, cleaner

**jar**[1] (jahr) n. round vessel of glass, earthenware etc.; inf. drink of beer, whiskey etc.

**jar**[2] v. (jarred, jar·ring) (cause to) vibrate suddenly, violently; have disturbing, painful effect on —n. jarring sound; shock etc.

**jar·di·niere** (jahr-dn-EER) n. ornamental pot for growing plants

**jar·gon** (JAHR-gən) n. specialized language concerned with particular subject; pretentious or nonsensical language

**jas·per** (JAS-pər) n. red, yellow, dark green or brown quartz

**jaun·dice** (JAWN-dis) n. disease marked by yellowness of skin; bitterness, ill humor; prejudice —v. (-diced, -dic·ing) make, become prejudiced, bitter etc.

**jaunt** (jawnt) n. short pleasure trip —vi. make one

**jaun·ty** (JAWN-tee) adj. (-ti·er, -ti·est) sprightly; brisk; smart, trim —jaun′ti·ly adv.

**jave·lin** (JAV-lin) n. spear, esp. for throwing in sporting events

**jaw** n. one of bones in which teeth are set —pl. mouth; fig. narrow opening of a gorge or valley; gripping part of vise etc. —vi. sl. talk lengthily

**jay** n. noisy bird of brilliant plumage —**jay′walk·er** n. careless pedestrian —**jay′walk** vi.

**jazz** n. syncopated music and dance —**jazz′y** adj. (jazz·i·er, jazz·i·est) flashy, showy —**jazz up** inf. play as jazz; make more lively, appealing

**jeal·ous** (JEL-əs) adj. distrustful of the faithfulness (of); envious; suspiciously watchful

**jeans** (jeenz) n. pl. casual trousers, esp. of denim

**jeer** v. scoff, deride —n. scoff, taunt, gibe

**Je·ho·vah** (ji-HO-və) n. God

**je·june** (ji-JOON) adj. simple, naive; meager

**jell** v. congeal; assume definite form

**jel·ly** (JEL-ee) n. (pl. -lies) semitransparent food made with gelatin, becoming softly stiff as it cools; anything of the consistency of this —**jel′ly·fish** n. jellylike small sea animal

**jeop·ard·y** (JEP-ər-dee) n. danger —**jeop′ard·ize** vt. (-ized, -iz·ing) endanger

**Jer.** Jeremiah

**jerk** (jurk) n. sharp, abruptly stopped movement; twitch; sharp pull; sl. stupid person, inconsequential person —v. move or throw with a jerk —**jerk′i·ly** adv. —**jerk′y** adj. (jerk·i·er, jerk·i·est) uneven, spasmodic

**jer·sey** (JUR-zee) n. (pl. -seys) knitted sweater; machine-knitted fabric; (J-) breed of cow

**jest** n./vi. joke —**jest′er** n. joker, esp. Hist. court fool

**Jes·u·it** (JEZH-oo-it) n. member of Society of Jesus, order founded by Ignatius Loyola in 1534 —**Jes·u·it′i·cal** adj. of Jesuits; (j-) crafty, using overly subtle reasoning

**jet**[1] n. stream of liquid, gas etc., esp. shot from small hole; the small hole; spout, nozzle; aircraft driven by jet propulsion —v. (jet-ted, jet·ting) throw out; shoot forth —**jet-black** adj. deep black —**jet lag** fatigue caused by crossing time zones in jet aircraft —**jet propulsion** propulsion by thrust provided by jet of gas or liquid

**jet** n. hard black mineral capable of brilliant polish

**jet-sam** (JET-səm) n. goods thrown out to lighten ship and later washed ashore —**jet'ti-son** (-tə-sən) vt. abandon; throw overboard

**jet-ty** (JET-ee) n. (-ties) small pier, wharf

**Jew** (joo) n. one of Hebrew ancestry; one who practices Judaism —**Jew'ish** adj. —**Jew'ry** n. the Jews —**jew's harp** n. small musical instrument held between teeth and played by finger

**jew-el** (JOO-əl) n. precious stone; ornament containing one; precious thing —**jew'el-er** n. dealer in jewels —**jew'el-ry** n.

**jib** n. triangular sail set forward of mast; projecting arm of crane or derrick

**jibe** see GIBE

**jif-fy** (JIF-ee) n. inf. (pl. -fies) very short period of time

**jig** n. lively dance; music for it; small mechanical device; guide for cutting etc.; Angling any of various lures —vi. (jigged, jigging) dance jig; make jerky up-and-down movements —**jig'saw** n. machine-mounted saw for cutting curves etc. —**jigsaw puzzle** picture stuck on board and cut into interlocking pieces with jigsaw

**jig-ger** (JIG-ər) n. small glass holding and pouring measure of whiskey etc.

**jig-gle** (JIG-əl) v. (-gled, -gling) move (up and down etc.) with short jerky movements

**jilt** vt. cast off (lover)

**jim-my** (JIM-ee) n. (pl. -mies) short steel crowbar —vt. (-mied, -my-ing) force open with a jimmy etc.

**jin-gle** (JING-gəl) n. mixed metallic noise, as of shaken chain; catchy, rhythmic verse, song etc. —v. (-gled, -gling) (cause to) make jingling sound

**jin-go-ism** (JING-goh-iz-əm) n. chauvinism —**jin-go-is'tic** adj.

**jinks** (jingks) n. pl. —high jinks boisterous merrymaking

**jinx** (jingks) n. force, person, thing bringing bad luck —v.

**jit-ters** (JIT-ərz) n. pl. worried nervousness, anxiety —**jit'ter-y** adj. (-ter-i-er, -ter-i-est) nervous

**jiujitsu** n. see JUJITSU

**jive** (jiv) n. (dance performed to) swing music, esp. of 1950's —v. (jived, jiv-ing) play, dance to, swing music; sl. tease; fool

**job** n. piece of work, task; position, office; inf. difficult task; sl. a crime, eg robbery —**job'ber** n. wholesale merchant —**job'less** (-lis) adj./n. pl. unemployed (people)

**jock-ey** (JOK-ee) n.(pl. -eys) professional rider in horse races —v. (-eyed, -ey-ing) (esp. with for) maneuver

**jo-cose** (joh-KOHS) adj. waggish, humorous —**jo-cos'i-ty** (-KOS-i-tee) n. —**joc'u-lar** (-yə-lər) adj. joking; given to joking —**joc-u-lar'i-ty** n.

**joc-und** (JOK-ənd) adj. merry, cheerful —**jo-cun-di-ty** (joh-KUN-di-tee) n. (pl. -ties)

**jodh-purs** (JOD-pərz) n. pl. tight-legged riding breeches

**jog** v. (jogged, jog-ging) —vi. run slowly or move at trot, esp. for physical exercise —vt. jar, nudge; remind, stimulate —n. jogging —**jog'ger** n. —**jogging** n.

**jog-gle** (JOG-əl) v. (-gled, -gling)

move to and fro in jerks; shake —n.

**John** (jon) n. name; (j-) (sl.) toilet; (sl.) prostitute's customer

**joie de vi·vre** (zhwad VEE-vrə) Fr. enjoyment of life, ebullience

**join** vt. put together, fasten, unite; become a member (of) —vi. become united, connected; (with up) enlist; take part (in) —n. joining; place of joining, seam —join'er n. maker of finished woodwork; one who joins

**joint** n. arrangement by which two things fit together, rigidly or loosely; place of this sl. house, place etc.; sl. disreputable bar or nightclub; sl. marijuana cigarette —adj. common; shared by two or more —vt. connect by joints; divide at the joints —joint'ly adv. —out of joint dislocated; disorganized

**joist** n. one of the parallel beams stretched from wall to wall on which to fix floor or ceiling

**joke** (johk) n. thing said or done to cause laughter; something not in earnest, or ridiculous —vi. (joked, jok·ing) make jokes —jok'er n. one who jokes; inf. fellow; extra card in pack, counting as highest card in some games

**jol·ly** (JOL-ee) adj. (-li·er, -li·est) jovial; festive, merry —vt. (-lied, -ly·ing) (esp. with along) (try to) make person, occasion etc. happier

**jolt** (johlt) n. sudden jerk; bump; shock; inf. a strong drink —v. move, shake with jolts

**joss** (jos) n. Chinese idol —joss house Chinese temple —joss stick stick of Chinese incense

**jos·tle** (JOS-əl) v. (-tled, -tling) knock or push against

**jot** n. small amount, whit —vt. (jot·ted, jot·ting) write briefly; make note of —jot'ting n. quick note; memorandum

**joule** (jool) n. Electricity unit of work or energy

**jour·nal** (JUR-nl) n. daily newspaper or other periodical; daily record; logbook; part of axle or shaft resting on the bearings —jour·nal·ese' (-EEZ) n. journalist's jargon; style full of clichés —jour'nal·ism n. editing, writing in periodicals

**jour·ney** (JUR-nee) n. (pl. -neys) going to a place, excursion; distance traveled —vi. (-neyed, -ney·ing) travel

**joust** (jowst) n. Hist. encounter with lances between two mounted knights —vi. engage in joust

**jo·vi·al** (JOH-vee-əl) adj. convivial, merry, gay —jo·vi·al'i·ty n.

**jowl** n. cheek, jaw; outside of throat when prominent

**joy** (joi) n. gladness, pleasure, delight; cause of this —joy'ful (-fuul) adj. —joy'less (-lis) adj. —joy'ride n. (high-speed) automobile trip —joy'stick n. inf. control stick of aircraft or computer device

**ju'bi·lant** (JOO-bə-lənt) adj. exultant —ju·bi·la'tion n.

**ju·bi·lee** (JOO-bə-lee) n. time of rejoicing, esp. 25th (silver) or 50th (golden) anniversary

**Jud.** Judges

**Ju·da·ic** (joo-DAY-ik) adj. Jewish —Ju'da·ism n.

**judge** (juj) n. officer appointed to try cases in law courts; one who decides in a dispute, contest etc.; one able to form a reliable opinion, arbiter; umpire; in Jewish history, ruler —v. (judged, judg·ing) —vi. act as judge —vt. act as judge of; try, estimate; decide —judg'ment n. faculty of judging; sentence of court; opinion; misfortune regarded as sign of divine displeasure

**ju·di·ca·ture** (JOO-di-kə-chər) *n.* administration of justice; body of judges —**ju·di·cial** (-DISH-əl) *adj.* of or by a court or judge; proper to a judge; discriminating —**ju·di·ci·ar·y** (-shee-er-ee) *n.* (*pl.* -ar·ies) system of courts and judges —**ju·di·cious** (-shəs) *adj.* well-judged, sensible, prudent

**ju·do** (JOO-doh) *n.* modern sport derived from jujitsu

**jug** *n.* vessel for liquids, with handle and small spout; its contents; *sl.* prison —*vt.* (jugged, jug·ging) stew (*esp.* hare) in jug

**jug·ger·naut** (JUG-ər-nawt) *n.* large overpowering, destructive force

**jug·gle** (JUG-əl) *v.* (-gled, -gling) throw and catch (several objects) so most are in the air simultaneously; manage, manipulate (accounts *etc.*) to deceive —*n.* —**jug'gler** *n.*

**jug·u·lar vein** (JUG-yə-lər) one of three large veins of the neck returning blood from the head

**juice** (joos) *n.* liquid part of vegetable, fruit, or meat; *sl.* electric current; *sl.* fuel used to run engine; vigor, vitality —**juic'y** *adj.* (juic·i·er, juic·i·est) succulent; scandalous, improper

**ju·jit·su** (joo-JIT-soo) *n.* the Japanese art of wrestling and self-defense

**ju·jube** (JOO-joob) *n.* lozenge of gelatin, sugar *etc.*; a fruit

**ju·lep** (JOO-lip) *n.* sweet drink; medicated drink

**Jul·ian** (JOOL-yən) *adj.* of Julius Caesar —**Julian calendar** calendar as adjusted by Julius Caesar in 46 B.C., in which the year was made to consist of 365 days, 6 hours, instead of 365 days

**ju·li·enne** (joo-lee-EN) *n.* kind of

clear soup —*adj.* of food, cut into thin strips or small pieces

**jum·ble** (JUM-bəl) *vt.* (-bled, -bling) mingle, mix in confusion —*n.* confused heap, muddle

**jum·bo** (JUM-boh) *n. inf.* elephant; anything very large

**jump** *v.* (cause to) spring, leap (over); move hastily; pass or skip (over) —*vi.* move hastily; rise steeply; parachute from aircraft; start, jerk (with astonishment *etc.*); of faulty film *etc.*, make abrupt movements —*vt.* come off (tracks, rails *etc.*); attack without warning —*n.* act of jumping; obstacle to be jumped; distance, height jumped; sudden nervous jerk or start; sudden rise in prices —**jump'er** *n.* one who, that which jumps; sleeveless dress; electric cable to connect discharged car battery to external battery to aid starting of engine —**jump'y** *adj.* (jump·i·er, jump·i·est) nervous —**jump'suit** *n.* one-piece garment of trousers and top

**junc·tion** (JUNGK-shən) *n.* railroad station *etc.* where lines, routes join; place of joining; joining

**junc·ture** (JUNGK-chər) *n.* state of affairs

**jun·gle** (JUNG-gəl) *n.* tangled vegetation of equatorial forest; land covered with it; tangled mass; condition of intense competition, struggle for survival

**jun·ior** (JOON-yər) *adj.* younger; of lower standing —*n.* junior person

**ju·ni·per** (JOON-ə-pər) *n.* evergreen shrub with berries yielding oil of juniper, used for medicine and gin making

**junk** (jungk) *n.* discarded, useless objects; *inf.* nonsense; *sl.* narcotic drug *esp.* heroin —**junk'ie** *n. inf.*

(*pl.* **junk·ies**) drug addict —**junk food** food, oft. of low nutritional value, eaten in addition to or instead of regular meals

**junk²** *n.* Chinese sailing vessel

**jun·ket** (JUNG-kit) *n.* curdled milk flavored and sweetened; pleasure trip *esp.* one paid for by others —*vi.* go on a junket

**jun·ta** (HUUN-tə) *n.* group of military officers holding power in a country

**Ju·pi·ter** (JOO-pi-tər) *n.* Roman chief of gods; largest of the planets

**ju·ris·dic·tion** (juur-is-DIK-shən) *n.* administration of justice; authority; territory covered by it —**ju·ris·pru'dence** (-PROO-dəns) *n.* science of skill in law —**jur'ist** *n.* one skilled in law

**ju·ry** (JUUR-ee) *n.* (*pl.* **-ries**) body of persons sworn to render verdict in court of law; body of judges of competition —**ju'ror** *n.* one of jury —**jury box**

**just** *adj.* fair; upright; honest; proper, right, equitable —*adv.* exactly; barely; at this instant; merely, only; really —**jus'tice** *n.* quality of being just; fairness; judicial proceedings; judge, magistrate —**jus'ti·fy** *vt.* (**-fied, -fy·ing**) prove right, true or innocent; vindicate; excuse —**jus'ti·fi·a·ble** *adj.*

**jut** *vi.* (**jut·ted, jut·ting**) project, stick out —*n.* projection

**jute** (joot) *n.* fiber of certain plants, used for rope, canvas *etc.*

**ju·ve·nile** (JOO-və-nil) *adj.* young; of, for young children; immature —*n.* young person, child, male actor —**ju·ve·nil'i·a** *n. pl.* works produced in author's youth —**juvenile court** court dealing with young offenders or children in need of care —**juvenile delinquent** young person guilty of

some offense, antisocial behavior *etc.*

**jux·ta·pose** (juk-stə-POHZ) *vt.* (**-posed, -pos·ing**) put side by side —**jux·ta·po·si'tion** *n.* contiguity, being side by side

# K

**K** Kelvin; *Chem.* potassium

**ka·bob** (kə-BOB) *n.* dish of small pieces of meat, tomatoes *etc.* grilled on skewers (*also* **shish kebab**)

**kale** (kayl) *n.* type of cabbage

**ka·lei·do·scope** (kə-LI-də-skohp) *n.* optical toy for producing changing symmetrical patterns by multiple reflections of colored glass chips *etc.*, in inclined mirrors enclosed in tube; any complex, frequently changing pattern —**ka·lei·do·scop'ic** (-SKOP-ik) *adj.* swiftly changing

**ka·mi·ka·ze** (kah-mi-KAH-zə) *n.* suicidal attack, *esp.* as in World War II, by Japanese pilots

**kan·ga·roo** (kang-gə-ROO) *n.* (*pl.* **-roos**) Aust. marsupial with very strongly developed hind legs for jumping —**kangaroo court** irregular, illegal court

**ka·pok** (KAY-pok) *n.* tropical tree; fiber from its seed pods used to stuff cushions *etc.*

**ka·put** (kah-PUUT) *adj. sl.* ruined, out of order, no good

**ka·ra·te** (kə-RAH-tee) *n.* Japanese system of unarmed combat using feet, hands, elbows *etc.* as weapons in a variety of ways

**kar·ma** (KAHR-mə) *n. Buddhism, Hinduism* one's actions seen as affecting fate for next reincarnation

**kart** (kahrt) *n.* miniature low-powered racing car (*also* go-cart, go-kart)

**kay·ak** (KĪ-ak) *n.* Eskimo canoe made of sealskins stretched over frame; any canoe of this design

**ka·zoo** (kə-ZOO) *n.* (*pl.* -zoos) cigar-shaped musical instrument producing nasal sound; *sl.* the buttocks

**kebab, kebob** *see* KABOB

**ked·ger·ee** (KEJ-ə-ree) *n.* East Indian dish of fish cooked with rice, eggs *etc.*

**keel** *n.* lowest longitudinal support on which ship is built —**keel·haul** *vt.* formerly, punish by hauling under keel of ship; rebuke severely —**keel over** turn upside down; collapse suddenly

**keen**[1] *adj.* (-er, -est) sharp; acute; eager; shrewd, strong —**keen·ly** *adv.* —**keen·ness** *n.*

**keen**[2] *n.* funeral lament —*vi.* wail over the dead

**keep** *v.* (**kept**, **keep·ing**) retain possession of, not lose; store; cause to continue; take charge of; maintain, detain; provide upkeep; reserve; remain good; remain, continue —*n.* living or support; charge or care; central tower of castle, stronghold —**keep'er** *n.* —**keep·ing** *n.* harmony, agreement; care, charge, possession —**keep'sake** *n.* thing treasured for sake of giver

**keg** *n.* small barrel *usu.* holding 5 to 10 gallons (19 to 38 liters)

**kelp** *n.* large seaweed; its ashes, yielding iodine

**Kel'vin** *adj.* of thermometric scale starting at absolute zero (-273.15° Celsius) —*n.* SI unit of temperature

**ken** *n.* range of knowledge —*vt.* (**kenned, ken·ning**) (in Scotland) know

**ken·do** (KEN-doh) *n.* Japanese sport of fencing, using bamboo staves

**ken·nel** (KEN-l) *n.* house, shelter for dog; *oft. pl.*, place for breeding, boarding dogs —*vt.* (-neled, -nel·ing) put into kennel

**kept** *pt./pp. of* KEEP

**ker·chief** (KUR-chif) *n.* square scarf used as head covering; handkerchief

**ker·nel** (KUR-nl) *n.* inner seed of nut or fruit stone; central, essential part

**ker·o·sene** (KER-ə-seen) *n.* fuel distilled from petroleum or coal and shale

**ketch** (kech) *n.* two-masted sailing vessel

**ketch·up** (KECH-əp) *n.* condiment of vinegar, tomatoes *etc.*

**ket·tle** (KET-l) *n.* metal vessel with spout and handle, for boiling water —**ket'tle·drum** *n.* musical instrument made of membrane stretched over copper, brass *etc.* hemisphere —**a fine kettle of fish** awkward situation, mess

**key** (kee) *n.* instrument for operating lock, winding clock *etc.*; something providing control, explanation, means of achieving an end *etc.*; *Mus.* set of related notes; operating lever of typewriter, piano, organ *etc.*; mode of thought —*vt.* provide symbols on map *etc.* to assist identification of positions on it —*adj.* vital; most important —**key'board** (-bord) *n.* set of keys on piano *etc.* **key'hole** *n.* hole for inserting key into lock; any shape resembling this —**key'note** (-noht) *n.* dominant idea; basic note of musical key —**key'pad** *n.* small keyboard with push buttons —**key'stone** *n.* central stone of arch that locks all in position

**khak·i** (KAK-ee) *adj.* dull

yellowish-brown —n. (pl. **khakis**) khaki cloth; (usu. pl.) military uniform

**Khmer** (kmair) n. member of a people of Kampuchea

**Ki.** Kings

**kib·ble** (KIB-əl) vt. (-bled, -bling) grind into small pieces —n. dry dog food prepared in this way

**kib·butz** (ki-BUUTS) n. in Israel, Jewish communal agricultural settlement —**kib·butz′nik** n. member of kibbutz

**ki·bosh** (KĪ-bosh) n. inf. nonsense —to put the kibosh on silence; check; defeat

**kick** (kik) v. strike out with foot; score with a kick; be recalcitrant; recoil —vt. strike or hit with foot; sl. free oneself of (drug habit etc.) —n. foot blow; recoil; excitement, thrill —**kick′back** n. strong reaction; money paid illegally for favors done etc. —**kick off** v. start game of football; begin (discussion etc.) —**kick·start** v. start motorcycle engine etc. by pedal that is kicked downward

**kid** n. young goat; leather of its skin; inf. child —v. (**kid·ded, kid·ding**) of goat, give birth; inf. tease, deceive; inf. behave, speak in fun

**kid′nap** vt. (-**napped, -nap·ping**) seize and hold for ransom —**kid′nap·per** n.

**kid′ney** (KID-nee) n. (pl. -**neys**) either of the pair of organs that secrete urine; animal kidney used as food; nature, kind —**kid·ney bean** common bean, kidney-shaped at maturity

**kill** vt. deprive of life; destroy; neutralize; pass (time); weaken or dilute; inf. tire, exhaust; inf. cause to suffer pain; inf. squash, defeat, veto —n. act of killing; animals etc. killed in hunt; enemy troops, aircraft etc. killed or destroyed in combat —**kill′er** n. one who, that which, kills —**kill′ing** adj. inf. very tiring; very funny —n. sudden success, esp. on stock market

**kiln** n. furnace, oven

**kil·o** (KEE-loh) n. short for KILOGRAM

**kilo-** (comb. form) one thousand, as in **kiloliter** n., **kilometer** n.

**kil·o·gram** (KIL-ə-gram) n. weight of 1000 grams

**kil·o·hertz** (KIL-ə-hurts) n. one thousand cycles per second

**kil·o·watt** (KIL-ə-wot) n. Electricity one thousand watts

**kilt** n. short, usu. tartan, skirt, deeply pleated, worn orig. by Scottish Highlanders —**kilt′ed** adj.

**ki·mo·no** (kə-MOH-nə) n. (pl. -**nos**) loose, wide-sleeved Japanese robe, fastened with sash; woman's garment like this

**kin** n. family, relatives —adj. related by blood —**kin′dred** (-drid) n. relationship; relatives —adj. similar; related —**kin′folk** (-fohk) n. —**kin′ship** n.

**kind** (kīnd) n. genus, sort, class —adj. (-**er, -est**) sympathetic, considerate; good, benevolent; gentle —**kind′li·ness** n. —**kind′ly** adj. (-**li·er, -li·est**) kind, genial —adv. —**kind′ness** n. —**kind′heart·ed** adj. —**in kind** (of payment) in goods rather than money; with something similar

**kin·der·gar·ten** (KIN-dər-gahr-tn) n. class, school for children of about four to six years old

**kin·dle** (KIN-dl) n. (-**dled, -dling**) —vt. set on fire; inspire, excite —vi. catch fire —**kind′ling** n. small wood to kindle fires

**ki·net·ic** (ki-NET-ik) adj. of motion in relation to force —**ki·net′ics** n. with sing. v. science of this

**king** *n.* male sovereign ruler of independent country; monarch; piece in game of chess; playing card with picture of a king; *Checkers* two pieces on top of one another, allowed freedom of movement —**king'ly** *adj.* (**-li·er, -li·est**) royal; appropriate to a king —**king'dom** (**-dəm**) *n.* country ruled by king; realm; sphere —**king'fish** *n.* any of several types of fish; *inf.* person in position of authority —**king'pin** *n.* swivel pin; central or front pin in bowling; *inf.* chief thing or person —**king-size(d)** *adj. inf.* large; larger than standard size

**kink** (kingk) *n.* tight twist in rope, wire, hair *etc.*; crick, as of neck; *inf.* eccentricity —*v.* make, become kinked; put, make kink in; twist —**kink'y** *adj.* (**kink·i·er, kink·i·est**) full of kinks; *inf.* eccentric, *esp.* given to deviant (sexual) practices

**ki·osk** (KEE-osk) *n.* small, sometimes movable booth selling soft drinks, cigarettes, newspapers *etc.*

**kip·per** (KIP-ər) *vt.* cure (fish) by splitting open, rubbing with salt, and drying or smoking —*n.* kippered fish

**kirsch** (keersh) *n.* brandy made from cherries

**kis·met** (KIZ-mit) *n.* fate, destiny

**kiss** *n.* touch or caress with lips; light touch —*v.* kiss —**kiss'er** *n.* one who kisses; *sl.* mouth or face —**kissing kin** relative(s) familiar enough to greet with polite kiss —**kiss of death** apparently friendly ruinous act

**kit** *n.* outfit, equipment; personal effects, *esp.* of traveler; set of pieces of equipment sold ready to be assembled —**kit bag** small bag for holding soldier's or traveler's kit

**kitch·en** (KICH-ən) *n.* room used for cooking —**kitch·en·ette'** *n.* small compact kitchen —**kitchen garden** garden for raising vegetables, herbs *etc.* —**kitchen sink** sink in kitchen; final item imaginable

**kite** (kīt) *n.* light papered frame flown in wind; large hawk; check drawn against nonexistent funds —*vt.* (kit·ed, kit·ing) use check in this way; cash or pass such a check

**kith** *n.* acquaintance, kindred (*only in* kith and kin)

**kitsch** (kich) *n.* vulgarized, pretentious art, literature *etc.*, usu. with popular, sentimental appeal

**kit·ten** (KIT-n) *n.* young cat

**kit·ty** (KIT-ee) *n.* (*pl.* **-ties**) *short for* KITTEN; in some card games, pool of money; communal fund

**ki·wi** (KEE-wee) *n.* (*pl.* **-wis**) any N.Z. flightless bird of the genus *Apteryx*; *inf.* New Zealander —*n.* fuzzy fruit of Asian climbing plant, the Chinese gooseberry

**klax·on** (KLAK-sən) *n.* powerful electric horn, used as warning signal

**klep·to·ma·ni·a** (klep-tə-MAY-nee-ə) *n.* compulsive tendency to steal for the sake of theft —**klep·to·ma'ni·ac** *n.*

**knack** (nak) *n.* acquired facility or dexterity; trick; habit

**knap·sack** (NAP-sak) *n.* soldier's or traveler's bag to strap to the back, rucksack

**knave** (nayv) *n.* jack at cards; *obs.* rogue —**knav'er·y** *n.* villainy —**knav'ish** *adj.*

**knead** (need) *vt.* work (flour) into dough; work, massage

**knee** (nee) *n.* joint between thigh and lower leg; part of garment covering knee —*vt.* (**kneed, knee·ing**) strike, push with knee

—**knee′cap** n. bone in front of knee

**kneel** (neel) vi. (**knelt** or **kneeled**, **kneel·ing**) fall, rest on knees

**knell** (nel) n. sound of a bell, esp. at funeral or death; portent of doom

**knew** pt. of KNOW

**knick·ers** (NIK-ərz) n. pl. loose-fitting short trousers gathered in at knee

**knick-knack** (NIK-nak) n. trifle, trinket

**knife** (nīf) n. (pl. **knives**) cutting blade, esp. one in handle, used as implement or weapon —vt. (**knifed, knif·ing**) cut or stab with knife —**knife edge** critical, possibly dangerous situation

**knight** (nit) n. Brit. man of rank below baronet, having right to prefix Sir to his name; member of medieval order of chivalry; champion; piece in chess —vt. confer knighthood on —**knight′·hood** (-huud) n.

**knish** n. turnover filled with potato, meat etc. and fried or baked

**knit** (nit) v. (**knit′ted** or **knit, knit·ting**) form (garment etc.) by putting together series of loops in wool or other yarn; draw together; unite —**knit′ting** n. knitted work; act of knitting

**knob** (nob) n. rounded lump, esp. at end or on surface of anything —**knob·by** adj. (-**bi·er, -bi·est**)

**knock** (nok) vt. strike, hit; inf. disparage; rap audibly; (of engine) make metallic noise, ping —n. blow, rap —**knock′er** n. metal appliance for knocking on door; who or what knocks —**knock-kneed** adj. having incurved legs —**knocked out** exhausted, tired, worn out —**knock off** inf. cease work; inf. copy, plagiarize sl. kill; sl. steal —**knock out** inf. render (oppo-

nent) unconscious; overwhelm, amaze; make (something) hurriedly —**knock′out** n. blow etc. that renders unconscious; inf. person or thing overwhelmingly attractive —**knock up** sl. make pregnant

**knoll** (nohl) n. small rounded hill, mound

**knot** (not) n. fastening of strands by looping and pulling tight; cluster; small closely knit group; tie, bond; hard lump, esp. of wood where branch joins or has joined in; measure of ship's speed, eg ten knots means ten nautical miles per hour; difficulty —vt. (**knot′ted, knot·ting**) tie with knot, in knots —**knot′ty** adj. (**-ti·er, -ti·est**) full of knots; puzzling, difficult —**knot′hole** (-hohl) n. hole in wood where knot has been

**know** (noh) v. (**knew, known, know·ing**) —vt. be aware of, have information about, be acquainted with, recognize, have experience, understand —vi. have information or understanding —**know′ing** adj. cunning, shrewd —**know′ing·ly** adv. shrewdly; deliberately —**knowl′edge** (NOL-ij) n. knowing; what one knows; learning —**knowl′edge·a·ble** adj. intelligent, well-informed —**know-how** n. practical knowledge, experience, aptitude —**in the know** informed

**knuck·le** (NUK-əl) n. bone at finger joint; knee joint of calf or pig —vt. (**-led, -ling**) strike with knuckles —**knuckle ball** Baseball pitch delivered by holding ball by thumb and first joints or tips of first two or three fingers —**knuckle-dust·er** n. metal appliances worn on knuckles to add force to blow, brass knuckles —**knuckle down** get down (to work) —**knuckle under** yield, submit

**knurled** (nurld) adj. serrated; gnarled

**ko·a·la** (koh-AH-lə) n. marsupial Aust. animal, native bear

**kohl** n. powdered antimony used orig. in Eastern countries for darkening the eyelids

**kohl·ra·bi** (kohl-RAH-bee) n. (pl. -bies) type of cabbage with edible stem

**ko·peck** (KOH-pek) n. Soviet monetary unit, one hundredth of ruble

**Ko·ran** (kə-RAN) n. sacred book of Muslims

**ko·sher** (KOH-shər) adj. permitted, clean, good, as of food etc., conforming to the Jewish dietary law; inf. legitimate, authentic —n. inf. kosher food —vt. make (food etc.) kosher

**kow·tow** (kow-TOW) n. former Chinese custom of touching ground with head in respect; submission —vi. (esp. with to) prostrate oneself; be obsequious, fawn on

**Kr** Chem. krypton

**Krem·lin** n. central government of Soviet Union; citadel of Moscow

**krill** (kril) n. (pl. same form) small shrimplike marine animal

**kryp·ton** (KRIP-ton) n. rare gaseous element, present in atmosphere

**ku·dos** (KOO-dohz) n. honor; acclaim

**ku·du** (KOO-doo) n. Afr. antelope with spiral horns

**ku·lak** (kuu-LAHK) n. independent well-to-do Russian peasant of Czarist times

**kum·quat** (KUM-kwot) n. small Chinese tree; its round orange fruit

**kung fu** (kung foo) Chinese mar-

tial art combining techniques of judo and karate

# L

**la** see LAH

**La** Chem. lanthanum

**la·bel** (LAY-bəl) n. slip of paper, metal etc., fixed to object to give information about it; brief, descriptive phrase or term —vt. (-beled, -bel·ing)

**la·bi·al** (LAY-bee-əl) adj. of the lips; pronounced with the lips —n. labial consonant

**la·bor** (LAY-bər) n. exertion of body or mind; task; workers collectively; effort, pain, of childbirth or time taken for this —vi. work hard; strive; maintain normal motion with difficulty; (esp. of ship) to be tossed heavily —vt. elaborate; stress to excess —la'bored adj. uttered, done, with difficulty —la'bor·er n. one who labors, esp. person doing manual work for wages —la·bo·ri·ous (lə-BOR-ee-əs) adj. tedious

**lab·o·ra·to·ry** (LAB-rə-tor-ee) n. place for scientific investigations or for manufacture of chemicals

**lab·ra·dor** (LAB-rə-dor) n. breed of large, smooth-coated retriever dog

**lab·y·rinth** (LAB-ə-rinth) n. network of tortuous passages; maze; inexplicable difficulty; perplexity —lab·y·rin'thine (-RIN-thin) adj.

**lace** (lays) n. fine patterned openwork fabric; cord, usu. one of pair, to draw edges together, eg to tighten shoes etc.; ornamental braid —vt. (laced, lac·ing) fasten with laces; flavor with whiskey etc. —lac'y adj. (lac·i·er, lac·i·est) fine, like lace

**lac·er·ate** (LAS-ə-rayt) *vt.* (-at·ed, -at·ing) tear, mangle; distress —**lac·er·a'tion** *n.*

**lach·ry·mal** (LAK-rə-məl) *adj.* of tears —**lach'ry·ma·to·ry** (-mə-tor-ee) *adj.* causing tears or inflammation of eyes —**lach'ry·mose** (-mohs) *adj.* tearful

**lack** (lak) *n.* deficiency, need —*vt.* need, be short of —**lack'lus·ter** *adj.* lacking brilliance or vitality

**lack·a·dai·si·cal** (lak-ə-DAY-zi-kəl) *adj.* languid, listless; lazy, careless

**lack·ey** (LAK-ee) *n.* (*pl.* -eys) servile follower; footman —*v.* (-eyed, -ey·ing) be, or play, the lackey; wait upon

**la·con·ic** (lə-KON-ik) *adj.* using, expressed in few words; brief, terse; offhand, not caring —**la·con'i·cal·ly** *adv.*

**lac·quer** (LAK-ər) *n.* hard varnish —*vt.* coat with this

**la·crosse** (lə-KRAWS) *n.* ball game played with long-handled racket, or crosse

**lac·tic** (LAK-tik) *adj.* of milk —**lac'tate** *vi.* (-tat·ed, -tat·ing) secrete milk —**lac·ta'tion** *n.* —**lac'tose** (-tohs) *n.* white crystalline substance occurring in milk

**la·cu·na** (lə-KYOO-nə) *n.* (*pl.* -nae *pr.* -nee) gap, missing part, *esp.* in document or series

**lad** *n.* boy, young fellow

**lad·der** (LAD-ər) *n.* frame of two poles connected by crossbars called rungs, used for climbing; flaw in stockings, caused by running of torn stitch

**lade** (layd) *vt.* (lad·ed, lad·ed *or* lad·en, lad·ing) load; ship; burden, weigh down —**lad'ing** *n.* cargo, freight

**la·dle** (LAYD-l) *n.* spoon with long handle for large bowl —*vt.* (-dled, -dling) serve out liquid with a ladle

**la·dy** (LAY-dee) *n.* (*pl.* -dies) female counterpart of gentleman; *polite term for* a woman; title of some women of rank —**la'dy-like** *adj.* gracious; well-mannered —**Our Lady** the Virgin Mary —**la'dy·fin·ger** *n.* small sponge cake in shape of finger —**lady-of-the-night** *n.* (*pl.* ladies-) prostitute

**lag**[1] *vi.* (lagged, lag·ging) go too slowly, fall behind —*n.* lagging, interval of time between events —**lag'gard** (-ərd) *n.* one who lags —**lag'ging** *adj.* loitering, slow

**lag**[2] *vt.* (lagged, lag·ging) wrap boiler, pipes *etc.* with insulating material —**lag'ging** *n.* this material

**la·ger** (LAH-gər) *n.* a light-bodied type of beer —*vt.* age (beer) by storing in tanks

**la·goon** (lə-GOON) *n.* saltwater lake, enclosed by atoll, or separated by sandbank from sea

**lah, la** *n.* sixth sol-fa note

**la·ic** (LAY-ik) *adj.* secular, lay —**la'i·cize** (-sīz) *vt.* (-cized, -ciz·ing) render secular or lay

**laid** (layd) *pt./pp. of* LAY —**laid-back** *adj. inf.* relaxed

**lain** (layn) *pp. of* LIE

**lair** *n.* resting place, den of animal

**lais·sez faire** (les-ay FAIR) *n.* principle of nonintervention, *esp.* by government in commercial affairs; indifference

**la·i·ty** (LAY-i-tee) *n.* lay worshipers, the people as opposed to clergy

**lake** (layk) *n.* expanse of inland water

**lam** *n. sl.* hasty escape -*vi. sl.* (lammed, lam·ming) run away fast; escape —on the lam *sl.* escaping; hiding *esp.* from police

**Lam.** Lamentations

**la·ma** (LAH-mə) *n.* Buddhist priest in Tibet or Mongolia —**la'ma·ser·y** *n.* monastery of lamas

**lamb** (lam) *n.* young of the sheep; its meat; innocent or helpless creature —*vi.* (of sheep) give birth to lamb —**lamb'like** *adj.* meek, gentle

**lam·baste** (lam-BAYST) *vt.* (-bast·ed, -bast·ing) beat, reprimand

**lam·bent** (LAM-bənt) *adj.* (of flame) flickering softly; glowing

**lame** (laym) *adj.* (**lam·er, lam·est**) crippled in a limb, *esp.* leg; limping; (of excuse *etc.*) unconvincing —*vt.* (**lamed, lam·ing**) cripple —**lame duck** official serving out term of office while waiting for elected successor to assume office; disabled, weak person or thing

**la·mé** (la-MAY) *n./adj.* (fabric) interwoven with gold or silver thread

**la·ment** (lə-MENT) *v.* feel, express sorrow (for) —*n.* passionate expression of grief; song of grief —**lam'en·ta·ble** (LAM-) *adj.* deplorable —**lam·en·ta'tion** *n.*

**lam·i·na** (LAM-ə-nə) *n.* (*pl.* -nas) thin plate, scale, flake —**lam'i·nate** (-nayt) *v.* (-nat·ed, -nat·ing) make (sheet of material) by bonding together two or more thin sheets; split, beat, form into thin sheets; cover with thin sheet of material —*n.* (-nit) laminated sheet —**lam·i·na'tion** *n.*

**lamp** *n.* any of various appliances (*esp.* electrical) that produce light, heat, radiation *etc.*; formerly, vessel holding oil burned by wick for lighting —**lamp'black** *n.* pigment made from soot —**lamp'light** *n.* —**lamp'post** *n.* post supporting lamp in street

**lam·poon'** *n.* satire ridiculing person, literary work *etc.* —*vt.* satirize, ridicule —**lam·poon'ist** *n.*

**lam·prey** (LAM-pree) *n.* (*pl.* -preys) fish like an eel with a sucker mouth

**lance** (lans) *n.* horseman's spear —*vt.* (**lanced, lanc·ing**) pierce with lance or lancet —**lan'ce·o·late** (-see-ə-layt) *adj.* lance-shaped, tapering —**lanc'er** *n.* formerly, cavalry soldier armed with lance —**lan'cet** (-sit) *n.* pointed two-edged surgical knife

**land** *n.* solid part of Earth's surface; ground, soil; country; property consisting of land —*pl.* estates —*vi.* come to land, disembark; bring an aircraft from air to land or water; alight, step down; arrive on ground —*vt.* bring to land; come or bring to some point or condition; *inf.* obtain; catch —**land'ed** *adj.* possessing, consisting of lands —**land'ing** *n.* act of landing; platform between flights of stairs —**land'fall** *n.* ship's approach to land at end of voyage —**land'locked** *adj.* enclosed by land —**land'lord** *n.*, **-la·dy** *n.* person who lets land or houses *etc.*; owner of apartment house *etc.* —**land'lub·ber** *n.* person ignorant of the sea and ships —**land'mark** *n.* boundary mark, conspicuous object, as guide for direction *etc.*; event, decision *etc.* considered as important stage in development of something —**land'scape** *n.* piece of inland scenery; picture of it; prospect —*v.* (-scaped, -scap·ing) create, arrange, garden, park *etc.* —**landscape gardening** —**land·scape painter** —**land'slide** *n.* falling of soil, rock *etc.* down mountainside; overwhelming electoral victory

**lane** (layn) *n.* narrow road or street; specified route followed by shipping or aircraft; area of road for one stream of traffic

**lan·guage** (LANG-gwij) *n.* system of sounds, symbols *etc.* for communicating thought; specialized vocabulary used by a particular group; style of speech or expression

**lan·guish** (LANG-gwish) *vi.* be or become weak or faint; be in depressing or painful conditions; droop, pine —**lan'guid** *adj.* lacking energy, interest; spiritless, dull —**lan'guor** (-gor) *n.* want of energy or interest; faintness; tender mood; softness of atmosphere —**lan'guor·ous** *adj.*

**lank** (langk) *adj.* lean and tall; straight and limp —**lank'y** *adj.* (**lank·i·er, lank·i·est**)

**lan·o·lin** (LAN-l-in) *n.* grease from wool used in ointments *etc.*

**lan·tern** (LAN-torn) *n.* transparent case for lamp or candle; erection on dome or roof to let out smoke, admit light

**lan·tha·num** (LAN-tho-nom) *n.* silvery-white ductile metallic element

**lan·yard** (LAN-yord) *n.* short cord for securing knife or whistle; short nautical rope; cord for firing cannon

**lap**[1] *n.* the part between waist and knees of a person when sitting; *fig.* place where anything lies securely; single circuit of racetrack; track; stage or part of journey; single turn of wound thread *etc.* —*vt.* (**lapped, lap·ping**) enfold, wrap around; overtake opponent to be one or more circuits ahead —**lap dog** *n.* small pet dog

**lap**[2] *vt.* (**lapped, lap·ping**) drink by scooping up with tongue; (of waves *etc.*) beat softly

**la·pel** (lo-PEL) *n.* part of front of a jacket or coat folded back toward shoulders

**lap·i·dar·y** (LAP-i-der-ee) *adj.* of stones; engraved on stone; exhibiting extreme refinement; concise and dignified —*n.* (*pl.* **-dar·ies**) cutter, engraver of stones

**lap·is laz·u·li** (LAP-is LAZ-uu-lee) bright blue stone or pigment

**lapse** (laps) *n.* fall in (standard, condition, virtue *etc.*); slip; mistake; passing (of time *etc.*) —*vi.* (**lapsed, laps·ing**) fall away; end, *esp.* through disuse

**lar·board** (LAHR-bord) *n./adj.* old term for port (side of ship)

**lar·ce·ny** (LAHR-so-nee) *n.* (*pl.* **-nies**) theft

**lard** (lahrd) *n.* prepared pig fat —*vt.* insert strips of bacon in (meat); intersperse, decorate (speech with strange words *etc.*)

**lar·der** (LAHR-dor) *n.* storeroom for food

**large** (lahrj) *adj.* (**larg·er, larg·est**) broad in range or area; great in size, number *etc.*; liberal; generous —*adv.* in a big way —**large'ly** *adv.* —**lar·gess(e)** *n.* bounty; gift; donation —**at large** free, not confined; in general; fully

**lar·go** (LAHR-goh) *adv. Mus.* slow and dignified

**lar·i·at** (LAR-ee-ot) *n.* lasso

**lark**[1] (lahrk) *n.* small brown songbird, skylark

**lark**[2] *n.* frolic, spree —*vi.* indulge in lark

**lar·va** (LAHR-vo) *n.* (*pl.* **-vae** *pr.* **-vee**) insect in immature but active stage —**lar'val** *adj.*

**lar·ynx** (LAR-ingks) *n.* (*pl.* **-es**) part of throat containing vocal cords —**lar·yn·gi'tis** (-ji-tis) *n.* inflammation of this

**la·sa·gne** (lo-ZAHN-yo) *n.* pasta formed in wide, flat sheets;

baked dish of this with meat, cheese, tomato sauce *etc.*

**las·civ·i·ous** (lɔ-SIV-ee-ɔs) *adj.* lustful

**la·ser** (LAY-zɔr) *n.* device for concentrating electromagnetic radiation or light of mixed frequencies into an intense, narrow, concentrated beam

**lash**[1] *n.* stroke with whip; flexible part of whip; eyelash —*vt.* strike with whip, thong *etc.*; dash against (as waves); attack verbally, ridicule; flick, wave sharply to and fro —*vi.* (*with* out) hit, kick

**lash**[2] *vt.* fasten or bind tightly with cord *etc.*

**las·si·tude** (LAS-i-tood) *n.* weariness

**las·so** (LAS-oh) *n.* (*pl.* -sos, -soes) rope with noose for catching cattle *etc.* —*vt.* (-soed, -so·ing)

**last**[1] *adj./adv.* after all others, coming at the end; most recently —*adj.* only remaining —*sup.* of LATE —*n.* last person or thing —**last**'ly *adv.* finally

**last**[2] *vi.* continue, hold out, remain alive or unexhausted, endure

**last**[3] *n.* model of foot on which shoes are made, repaired

**latch** (lach) *n.* fastening for door, consisting of bar, catch for it, and lever to lift it; small lock with spring action —*vt.* fasten with latch —**latch**'key (-kee) *n.*

**late** (layt) *adj.* (lat·er or lat·ter, lat·est or last) coming after the appointed time; delayed; that was recently but now is not; recently dead; recent in date; of late stage of development —*adv.* (lat·er, lat·est) after proper time; recently; at, till late hour —**late**'ly *adv.* not long since

**la·tent** (LAYT-nt) *adj.* existing but not developed; hidden

**lat·er·al** (LAT-ɔr-ɔl) *adj.* of, at, from the side —**lat**'er·al·ly *adv.*

**la·tex** (LAY-teks) *n.* sap or fluid of plants, *esp.* of rubber tree

**lath** (*n.* laths *pr.* lathz) thin strip of wood, or wire mesh —**lath**'ing *n.*

**lathe** (layth) *n.* machine for turning object while it is being shaped

**lath·er** (LATH-ɔr) *n.* froth of soap and water; frothy sweat —*v.* make frothy; *inf.* beat

**Lat·in** (LAT-n) *n.* language of ancient Romans —*adj.* of ancient Romans, of, in their language; denoting people speaking a language descended from Latin *esp.* Spanish —**La·ti·no** (lɔ-TEE-noh) *n.* (*pl.* -nos) person of Central or S Amer. descent

**lat·i·tude** (LAT-i-tood) *n.* angular distance on meridian reckoned N or S from equator; deviation from a standard; freedom from restriction; scope —*pl.* regions

**la·trine** (lɔ-TREEN) *n.* in army *etc.*, toilet

**lat·ter** (LAT-ɔr) *adj.* second of two; later; more recent —**lat**'ter·ly *adv.*

**lat·tice** (LAT-is) *n.* structure of strips of wood, metal *etc.* crossing with spaces between; window, gate, so made —**lat**'ticed *adj.*

**laud** (lawd) *n.* hymn, song, of praise —*vt.* —**laud**'a·ble *adj.* praiseworthy —**laud**'a·bly *adv.* —**laud**'a·to·ry (-tor-ee) *adj.* expressing, containing, praise

**lau·da·num** (LAWD-n-ɔm) *n.* tincture of opium

**laugh** (laf) *vi.* make sounds instinctively expressing amusement, merriment, or scorn —**laugh**'a·ble *adj.* ludicrous —**laugh**'a·bly *adv.* —**laugh**'ter *n.* —**laughing gas** nitrous oxide as anesthetic —**laughing stock** object of general derision

**launch**[1] (lawnch) vt. set afloat; set in motion; start; propel (missile, spacecraft) into space; hurl, send —vi. enter on course —**launch'er** n. installation, vehicle, device for launching rockets, missiles etc.

**launch**[2] n. large engine-driven boat

**laun·dry** (LAWN-dree) n. (pl. -dries) place for washing clothes, esp. as a business; clothes etc. for washing —**laun'der** vt. wash and iron —**laun·der·ette'** n. self-service laundry with coin-operated washing, drying machines

**lau·re·ate** (LOR-ee-ət) adj. crowned with laurels —n. person honored for achievements —**poet laureate** poet honored as most eminent of country or region

**lau·rel** (LOR-əl) n. glossy-leaved shrub, bay tree —pl. its leaves, emblem of victory or merit

**la·va** (LAH-və) n. molten matter thrown out by volcanoes, solidifying as it cools

**lav·a·to·ry** (LAV-ə-tor-ee) n. (-ries) washroom; toilet

**lave** (layv) vt. (laved, lav·ing) wash, bathe

**lav·en·der** (LAV-ən-dər) n. shrub with fragrant flowers; color of the flowers, pale lilac

**lav·ish** adj. giving or spending profusely; very, too abundant —vt. spend, bestow, profusely

**law** n. rule binding on community; system of such rules; legal science; knowledge, administration of it; inf. (member of) police force; general principle deduced from facts; invariable sequence of events in nature —**law'ful** (-fəl) adj. allowed by law —**law'ful·ly**

adv. —**law'less** (-lis) adj. ignoring laws; violent —**law'yer** n. professional expert in law —**law'a·bid·ing** (-bīd-ing) adj. obedient to laws; well-behaved —**law'giv·er** n. one who makes laws —**law'suit** (-soot) n. prosecution of claim in court

**lawn**[1] n. stretch of carefully tended turf in garden etc. —**lawn tennis** tennis played on grass court

**lawn**[2] n. fine linen

**lawyer** see LAW

**lax** (laks) adj. not strict; lacking precision; loose, slack —**lax'a·tive** adj. having loosening effect on bowels —n. —**lax'i·ty, lax'ness** n. slackness; looseness of (moral) standards

**lay**[1] pt. of LIE[1]

**lay**[2] vt. (laid, lay·ing) deposit, set, cause to lie —**lay'er** n. single thickness of some substance, as stratum or coating on surface; laying hen; shoot of plant pegged down or partly covered with soil or plastic to encourage root growth —vt. propagate plants by making layers —**lay'down** n. in bridge, unbeatable hand held by declarer who plays with all cards exposed to view —**lay'out** n. arrangement, esp. of matter for printing —**lay off** dismiss employees during slack period (**lay'off** n.) —**lay on** provide, supply; apply; strike —**lay on hands** of healer, place hands on person to be cured —**lay out** display; expend; prepare for burial; plan copy for printing etc.; sl. knock out; sl. criticize severely —**lay waste** devastate

**lay**[3] n. minstrel's song

**lay**[4] adj. not clerical or professional; of, or done, by persons not clergymen —**lay'man, lay'per·son** n. ordinary person

**lay·ette** (lay-ET) *n.* clothes *etc.* for newborn child

**laz·ar** (LAZ-or) *n.* leper

**la·zy** (LAY-zee) *adj.* (-zi·er, -zi·est) averse to work, indolent —**laze** *vi.* (lazed, laz·ing) indulge in laziness —**la'zi·ly** *adv.* —**la'zi·ness** *n.*

**lead¹** (leed) *v.* (led, lead·ing) —*vt.* guide, conduct; persuade; direct; conduct people —*vi.* be, go, play first; result; give access to —*n.* leading; that which leads or is used to lead; example; front or principal place, role *etc.*; cable bringing current to electric instrument —**lead'er** *n.* one who leads; most important or prominent article in newspaper (*also* **leading article**) —**lead'er·ship** *n.* —**leading question** question worded to prompt answer desired —**lead time** time between design of product and its production

**lead²** (led) *n.* soft heavy gray metal; plummet, used for sounding depths of water; graphite —*vt.* (-ed, -ing) cover, weight or space with lead —**lead'en** *adj.* of, like lead; heavy; dull —**go over like a lead balloon** *sl.* fail to arouse interest or support

**leaf** (leef) *n.* (*pl.* **leaves**) organ of photosynthesis in plants, consisting of a flat, usu. green blade on stem; two pages of book *etc.*; thin sheet; flap, movable part of table *etc.* —*vt.* turn through (pages *etc.*) cursorily —**leaf'less** (-lis) *adj.* —**leaf'let** (-lit) *n.* small leaf; single sheet, often folded, of printed matter for distribution as *eg* notice or advertisement —**leaf'y** *adj.* (**leaf·i·er, leaf·i·est**)

**league¹** (leeg) *n.* agreement for mutual help; parties to it; federation of teams *etc.*; *inf.* class, level —*vi.* (**leagued, lea·guing**) unite in a league; combine in an association —**lea'guer** *n.* member of league

**league²** *n. obs.* measure of distance, about three miles

**leak** (leek) *n.* hole, defect, that allows escape or entrance of liquid, gas, radiation *etc.*; disclosure —*vi.* let fluid *etc.* in or out; (of fluid *etc.*) find its way through leak —*vt.* let escape —*v.* (allow to) become known little by little —**leak'age** (-ij) *n.* leaking; gradual escape or loss —**leak'y** *adj.* (**leak·i·er, leak·i·est**)

**lean¹** (leen) *adj.* (-er, -est) lacking fat; thin; meager; (of mixture of fuel and air) with too little fuel —*n.* lean part of meat, mainly muscular tissue

**lean²** *v.* (**leaned, lean·ing**) rest against; bend, incline; tend (toward); depend, rely (on) —**lean·ing** *n.* tendency —**lean-to** *n.* (*pl.* **-tos**) shed built against tree or post

**leap** (leep) *v.* (**leaped** or **leapt, leap·ing**) spring, jump; spring over —*n.* jump —**leap'frog** *n.* game in which player vaults over another bending down —**leap year** year with February 29th as extra day, occurring every fourth year

**learn** (lurn) *v.* (**learned** or **learnt, learn·ing**) gain skill, knowledge by study, practice or teaching; gain knowledge; be taught; find out —**learn'ed** (LUR-nid) *adj.* erudite, deeply read; showing much learning —**learn'er** *n.* —**learn'ing** *n.* knowledge acquired by study

**lease** (lees) *n.* contract by which land or property is rented for stated time by owner to tenant —*vt.* (**leased, leas·ing**) let, rent by, take on lease

**leash** (leesh) *n.* thong for holding

a dog; curb —*vt.* hold on leash; restrain

**least** (leest) *adj.* smallest —*sup. of* LITTLE —*n.* smallest one —*adv.* in smallest degree

**leath·er** (LETH-ər) *n.* prepared skin of animal —**leath·er·y** *adj.* like leather, tough

**leave**[1] (leev) *v.* (**left, leav·ing**) go away from; deposit; allow to remain; depart from; entrust; bequeath; go away, set out

**leave**[2] *n.* permission; permission to be absent from work, duty; period of such absence; formal parting

**leav·en** (LEV-ən) *n.* yeast; *fig.* transforming influence —*vt.* raise with leaven; influence; modify

**lech·er** (LECH-ər) *n.* man given to lewdness —**lech·er·ous** *adj.* lewd; provoking lust; lascivious —**lech'·er·ous·ly** *adv.* —**lech·er·ous·ness** *n.* —**lech'er·y** *n.* (*pl.* **-er·ies**)

**lec·tern** (LEK-tərn) *n.* reading desk, *esp.* in church; stand with slanted top to hold book, notes *etc.*

**lec·ture** (LEK-chər) *n.* instructive discourse; speech of reproof —*v.* (**-tured, -tur·ing**) —*vi.* deliver discourse —*vt.* reprove —**lec'tur·er** *n.*

**ledge** (lej) *n.* narrow shelf sticking out from wall, cliff *etc.*; ridge, rock below surface of sea

**ledg·er** (LEJ-ər) *n.* book of debit and credit accounts, chief account book of firm; flat stone —**ledger line** *Mus.* short line, above or below stave

**lee** *n.* shelter; side of anything, *esp.* ship, away from wind —**lee'·ward** (-wərd) *adj./n.* (on) lee side —*adv.* toward this side —**lee'way** *n.* leeward drift of ship; room for free movement within limits

**leech** *n.* species of bloodsucking worm

**leek** *n.* plant like onion with long bulb and thick stem

**leer** *vi.* glance with malign, sly, or lascivious expression —*n.* such glance

**lees** (leez) *n. pl.* sediment of wine *etc.*; dregs

**left**[1] *adj.* denotes the side that faces west when the front faces north; opposite to the right —*n.* the left hand or part; *Politics* reforming or radical party (*also* **left wing**) —*adv.* on or toward the left —**left'ist** *n./adj.* (person) of the political left

**left**[2] *pt./pp. of* LEAVE

**leg** *n.* one of limbs on which person or animal walks, runs, stands; part of garment covering leg; anything that supports, as leg of table; stage of journey —**leg'·gings** *n. pl.* covering of leather or other material for legs —**leg'gy** *adj.* (**-gi·er, -gi·est**) long-legged; (of plants) straggling —**leg'·warm·er** *n.* one of pair of long knitted footless socks worn over tights when exercising

**leg·a·cy** (LEG-ə-see) *n.* (*pl.* **-cies**) anything left by will, bequest; thing handed down to successor

**le·gal** (LEE-gəl) *adj.* of, appointed or permitted by, or based on, law —**le·gal'i·ty** *n.* —**le'gal·ize** *vt.* (**-ized, -iz·ing**) make legal

**leg·ate** (LEG-it) *n.* ambassador, *esp.* papal —**le·ga'tion** *n.* diplomatic minister and staff; headquarters for these

**leg·a·tee** (leg-ə-TEE) *n.* recipient of legacy

**le·ga·to** (lə-GAH-toh) *adv. Mus.* smoothly

**leg·end** (LEJ-ənd) *n.* traditional story or myth; traditional literature; famous, renowned, person or event; inscription —leg′end-ar-y adj.

leg·er·de·main (lej-or-do-MAYN) n. juggling, conjuring, sleight of hand, trickery

leg·i·ble (LEJ-o-bol) adj. easily read —leg·i·bil′i·ty n.

le·gion (LEE-jon) n. body of infantry in Roman army; various modern military bodies; association of veterans; large number —le′gion-ar-y adj./n. —le·gion-naires′ (-NAIRZ) disease serious bacterial disease similar to pneumonia

leg·is·la·tor (LEJ-is-lay-tor) n. maker of laws —leg′is-late vi. (-lat-ed, -lat-ing) make laws —leg-is-la′tion n. act of legislating; law or laws that are made —leg′is-la-tive adj. —leg′is-la-ture (-chor) n. body that makes laws of a country or state

le·git·i·mate (lo-JIT-o-mit) adj. born in wedlock; lawful, regular; fairly deduced —le·git′i-ma-cy (-mo-see) n. —le·git′i-mize (-mized, -miz-ing) vt. make legitimate

le·gu·mi·nous (li-GYOO-mo-nos) adj. (of plants) pod-bearing —leg-ume (LEG-yoom) n. leguminous plant

lei (lay) n. garland of flowers

lei·sure (LEE-zhor) n. freedom from occupation; spare time —lei′sure-ly adj. deliberate, unhurried —adv. slowly —lei′sured adj. with plenty of spare time

leit·mo·tif (LIT-moh-teef) n. Mus. recurring theme associated with some person, situation, thought

lem·ming (LEM-ing) n. rodent of northern regions

lem·on (LEM-on) n. pale yellow acid fruit; tree bearing it; its color; inf. useless or defective person or thing —lem-on-ade′ (-AYD) n. drink made from lemon juice

le·mur (LEE-mor) n. nocturnal animal like monkey

lend vt. (lent, lend-ing) give temporary use of; let out for hire or interest; give, bestow —lends it-self to is suitable for

length (lengkth) n. quality of being long; measurement from end to end; duration; extent; piece of a certain length —length′en v. make, become, longer; draw out —length′i·ly adv. —length′wise adj./adv. —length′y adj. (length-i-er, length-i-est) (over) long —at length in detail; at last

le·ni·ent (LEE-nee-ont) adj. mild, tolerant, not strict —le′ni-en-cy n.

len·i·ty (LEN-i-tee) n. (pl. -ties) mercy; clemency

lens (lenz) n. (pl. -es) piece of glass or similar material with one or both sides curved, used to converge or diverge light rays in cameras, eyeglasses, telescopes etc.

lent pt./pp. of LEND

Lent n. period of fasting from Ash Wednesday to Easter —Lent′en adj. of, in, or suitable to Lent

len′til n. edible seed of leguminous plant —len·tic′u·lar adj. like lentil

len·to (LEN-toh) adv. Mus. slowly

le·o·nine (LEE-o-nīn) adj. like a lion

leop·ard (LEP-ord) n. large, spotted, carnivorous animal of cat family, like panther

le·o·tard (LEE-o-tahrd) n. tight-fitting garment covering most of body, worn by acrobats, dancers etc.

lep·er (LEP-or) n. one suffering from leprosy; person ignored or despised —lep′ro·sy (-o-see) n. disease attacking nerves and skin resulting in loss of feeling in affected parts —**lep′rous** (-rəs) adj.

**lep·re·chaun** (LEP-rə-kawn) n. mischievous elf of Irish folklore

**les·bi·an** (LEZ-bee-ən) n. a homosexual woman —**les′bi·an·ism** n.

**lese maj·es·ty** (LEEZ) n. treason; taking of liberties

**le·sion** (LEE-zhən) n. injury, malignant change in texture or action of an organ of the body

**less** adj. comp. of LITTLE; not so much —n. smaller part, quantity; a lesser amount —adv. to a smaller extent or degree —prep. after deducting, minus —**less′en** vt. diminish; reduce —**less′er** adj. less; smaller; minor

**les·see** (le-SEE) n. one to whom lease is granted

**les·son** (LES-ən) n. installment of course of instruction; content of this; experience that teaches; portion of Scripture read in church

**les·sor** (LES-or) n. grantor of a lease

**lest** conj. in order that not; for fear that

**let**[1] v. (let, let·ting) —vt. allow, enable, cause; allow to escape; grant use of for rent, lease —vi. be leased —v. aux. used to express a proposal, command, threat, assumption

**let**[2] n. in law, obstacle or hindrance; in tennis etc., minor infringement, esp. obstruction of ball by net on service, requiring replaying of point

**le·thal** (LEE-thəl) adj. deadly

**leth·ar·gy** (LETH-ər-jee) n. (pl. -gies) apathy, want of energy or interest; unnatural drowsiness —**le·thar′gic** (-thar′jic) adj. —**le·thar′gi·cal·ly** adv.

**let·ter** (LET-ər) n. alphabetical symbol; written message; strict meaning, interpretation —pl. literature, knowledge of books —vt. mark with, in, letters —**let′tered** adj. learned —**let′ter·press** n. process of printing from raised type; matter printed in this way

**let·tuce** (LET-is) n. plant grown for use in salad

**leu·co·cyte** (LOO-kə-sit) n. one of white blood corpuscles

**leu·ke·mi·a** (loo-KEE-mee-ə) n. a progressive blood disease

**Lev.** Leviticus

**lev·ee**[1] n. Hist. reception held by sovereign on rising; reception in someone's honor

**levee**[2] n. river embankment, natural or artificial

**lev·el** (LEV-əl) adj. horizontal; even in surface; consistent in style, quality etc. —n. horizontal line or surface; instrument for showing, testing horizontal plane; position on scale; standard, grade; horizontal passage in mine —v. (-eled, -el·ing) make level; bring to same level; knock down; aim (gun, or, fig., accusation etc.) inf. (esp. with with) be honest, frank —**le′vel·head′ed** (-HED-id) adj. not apt to be carried away by emotion

**lev·er** (LEV-ər) n. rigid bar pivoted about a fulcrum to transfer a force with mechanical advantage; handle pressed, pulled etc. to operate something —vt. pry, move, with lever —**lev′er·age** (-ij) n. action, power of lever; influence; power to accomplish something; advantage

**le·vi·a·than** (lə-VI-ə-thən) n. sea monster; anything huge or formidable

**lev·i·ta·tion** (lev-i-TAY-shən) n. the power of raising a solid body into the air supernaturally —**lev′i·tate** v. (-tat·ed, -tat·ing) (cause to) do this

**lev·i·ty** (LEV-i-tee) n. (pl. -ties)

inclination to make a joke of serious matters, frivolity; facetiousness

**lev·y** (LEV-ee) vt. (lev·ied, lev·y·ing) impose (tax); raise (troops) —n. (pl. lev·ies) imposition or collection of taxes; enrolling of troops; amount, number levied

**lewd** (lood) adj. (-er, -est) lustful; indecent —lewd′ly adv. —lewd′ness n.

**lex·i·con** (LEK-si-kon) n. dictionary —lex·i·cog′ra·pher (-rə-fər) n. writer of dictionaries —lex·i·cog′ra·phy n.

**Li** Chem. lithium

**li·a·ble** (LI-ə-bəl) adj. answerable; exposed (to); subject (to); likely (to) —li·a·bil′i·ty n. state of being liable, obligation; hindrance, disadvantage —pl. (-ties) debts

**li·ai·son** (LEE-ə-zon) n. union; connection; intimacy, esp. secret; person who keeps others in touch with one another

**li·ar** (LI-ər) n. one who tells lies

**li·ba·tion** (li-BAY-shən) n. drink poured as offering to the gods; facetious drink of whiskey

**li·bel** (LI-bəl) n. published statement falsely damaging person's reputation —vt. (-beled, -bel·ing) defame falsely —li′bel·ous adj. defamatory

**lib·er·al** (LIB-ər-əl) adj. of political party favoring democratic reforms or favoring individual freedom; generous; tolerant; abundant; (of education) designed to develop general cultural interests —n. one who has liberal ideas or opinions —lib′er·al·ism n. —lib·er·al′i·ty n. (pl. -ties) munificence —lib′er·al·ize vt. (-ized, -iz·ing)

**lib·er·ate** (LIB-ə-rayt) vt. (-at·ed, -at·ing) set free —lib·er·a′tion n.

**lib·er·tar·i·an** (lib-ər-TAIR-ee-ən)

n. believer in freedom of thought etc., or in free will —adj.

**lib·er·tine** (LIB-ər-teen) n. morally dissolute person —adj. dissolute

**lib·er·ty** (LIB-ər-tee) n. freedom —pl. (-ties) rights, privileges —at liberty free; having the right; out of work —take liberties (with) be presumptuous

**li·bi·do** (li-BEE-doh) n. (pl. -dos) life force; emotional craving, esp. of sexual origin —li·bid′i·nous (-BID-n-əs) adj. lustful

**li·brar·y** (LI-brer-ee) n. (pl. -brar·ies) room, building where books are kept; collection of books, phonograph records etc.; reading, writing room in house —li·brar′i·an n. keeper of library

**li·bret·to** (li-BRET-oh) n. (pl. -tos, -ti pr. -tee) words of an opera —li·bret′tist n.

**lice** n. pl. see LOUSE

**li·cense** (LI-səns) n. (document, certificate, giving) leave, permission; excessive liberty; dissoluteness; writer's, artist's intentional transgression of rules of art (often poetic license) —li′cense vt. (-censed, -cens·ing) grant license to —li·cen·see′ n. holder of license

**li·cen·tious** (li-SEN-shəs) adj. dissolute; sexually immoral

**li·chen** (LI-kən) n. small flowerless plants forming crust on rocks, trees etc.

**lick** (lik) vt. pass the tongue over; touch lightly; inf. defeat; inf. flog, beat —n. act of licking; small amount (esp. of work etc.); block or natural deposit of salt or other chemical licked by cattle etc. —lick′ing n. beating; defeat

**lic·o·rice** (LIK-ər-ish) n. black substance used in medicine and as a candy; plant, its root from which it is obtained

**lid** n. movable cover; cover of the eye; sl. hat

**lie**¹ (lī) vi. (lay, lain, ly·ing) be horizontal, at rest; be situated; remain, be in certain state or position; exist, be found; recline —n. manner, direction, position in which thing lies; of a golf ball, its position relative to difficulty of hitting it

**lie**² vi. (lied, ly·ing) make false statement knowingly —n. deliberate falsehood —li'ar (-ər) n. —white lie untruth said without evil intent —give the lie to disprove

**lien** (leen) n. right to hold another's property until claim is met

**lieu** (loo) n. place —in lieu of instead of

**lieu·ten·ant** (loo-TEN-ənt) n. deputy; Army, Marines rank below captain; Navy rank below lieutenant commander; police, fire department officer

**life** (līf) n. (pl. lives) active principle of existence of animals and plants, animate existence; time of its lasting; history of such existence; way of living; vigor, vivacity —life'less (-lis) adj. dead; inert; dull —life'long adj. lasting a lifetime —life belt, jacket buoyant device to keep afloat person in danger of drowning —life style particular attitudes, habits etc. of person or group —life-support adj. of equipment or treatment necessary to keep a person alive —life'time n. length of time person, animal, or object lives or functions

**lift** vt. raise in position, status, mood, volume etc.; take up and remove; exalt spiritually; inf. steal —vi. rise —n. raising apparatus; ride in car etc., as passenger; force of air acting at right angles on aircraft wing, so lifting

it; inf. feeling of cheerfulness, uplift

**lig·a·ment** (LIG-ə-mənt) n. band of tissue joining bones —lig'a·ture (-chər) n. anything that binds; thread for tying up blood vessels or for removing tumors

**light**¹ (līt) adj. (-er, -est) of, or bearing, little weight; not severe; gentle; easy, requiring little effort; trivial; (of industry) producing small, usu. consumer goods, using light machinery —adv. in light manner —v. (light·ed or lit, light·ing) —vi. alight (from vehicle etc.); come by chance (upon) —light'en vt. reduce, remove (load etc.) —lights n. pl. lungs of animals as food —light'head'ed adj. dizzy, inclined to faint; delirious —light'heart'ed adj. carefree —light'weight n./adj. (person) of little weight or importance; boxer weighing between 126 and 135 pounds (56.7 to 61 kg)

**light**² n. electromagnetic radiation by which things are visible; source of this, lamp; window; light part of anything; means or act of setting fire to; understanding —pl. traffic lights —adj. (-er, -est) bright; pale, not dark —v. (light·ed or lit, light·ing) set burning; give light to; take fire; brighten —light'en vt. make light —light'ing n. apparatus for supplying artificial light —light'ning n. visible discharge of electricity in atmosphere —light'house n. tower with a light to guide ships —light-year n. Astronomy distance light travels in one year, about six trillion miles

**light·er** (Lī-tər) n. device for lighting cigarettes etc.; flat-bottomed boat for unloading ships

**like**¹ (līk) adj. resembling; similar; characteristic of —adv. in the manner of —*pron.* similar thing —**like'li·hood** (-huud) *n.* probability —**like'ly** *adj.* (-li·er, -li·est) probable; hopeful, promising —*adv.* probably —*vt.* compare —**like'ness** *n.* resemblance; portrait —**like'wise** *adv.* in like manner

**like²** *vt.* (liked, lik·ing) find agreeable, enjoy, love —**lik'a·ble** *adj.* —**liking** *n.* fondness; inclination, taste

**li·lac** (LI-lɔk) *n.* shrub bearing purple or white flowers; pale reddish purple —*adj.* of this color

**Lil·li·pu·tian** (lil-i-PYOO-shɔn) *adj.* diminutive —*n.* very small person

**lilt** *v.* sing merrily; move lightly —*n.* rhythmical effect in music, swing —**lilt'ing** *adj.*

**lil·y** (LIL-ee) *n.* (*pl.* lil·ies) bulbous flowering plant —**lil·y-white** *adj.* white; pure, above reproach; of an organization or community, forbidding admission to blacks

**limb¹** (lim) *n.* arm or leg; wing; branch of tree

**limb²** *n.* edge of sun or moon; edge of sextant

**lim·ber¹** (LIM-bɔr) *n.* detachable front of gun carriage

**lim·ber²** *adj.* pliant, lithe —**limber up** loosen stiff muscles by exercises

**lim·bo¹** (LIM-boh) *n.* (*pl.* -bos) supposed region intermediate between heaven and hell for the unbaptized; intermediate, indeterminate place or state

**lim·bo²** *n.* (*pl.* -bos) West Indian dance in which dancers pass under a bar

**lime¹** (lim) *n.* any of certain calcium compounds used in making fertilizer, cement —*vt.* (limed, lim·ing) treat (land) with lime —**lime'light** *n.* formerly, intense white light obtained by heating

lime; glare of publicity —**lime'stone** *n.* sedimentary rock used in building

**lime²** *n.* small acid fruit like lemon

**lim·er·ick** (LIM-ɔr-ik) *n.* self-contained, nonsensical, humorous verse of five lines

**lim'it** *n.* utmost extent or duration; boundary —*vt.* restrict, restrain, bound —**lim·i·ta'tion** *n.* —**lim'it·less** *adj.*

**lim·ou·sine** (LIM-ɔ-zeen) *n.* large, luxurious car

**limp¹** *adj.* (-er, -est) without firmness or stiffness —**limp'ly** *adv.*

**limp²** *vi.* walk lamely —*n.* limping gait

**lim'pid** *adj.* clear; translucent —**lim·pid'i·ty** *n.*

**linch'pin** *n.* pin to hold wheel on its axle; essential person or thing

**line** (lin) *n.* long narrow mark; stroke made with pen *etc.*; continuous length without breadth; row; series, course; telephone connection; progeny; province of activity; shipping company; railroad track; any class of goods; cord; string; wire; advice, guidance —*vt.* (lined, lin·ing) cover inside; mark with lines; bring into line; be, form border, edge —**lin'e·age** (-ee-ij) *n.* descent from, descendants of an ancestor —**lin'e·al** *adj.* of lines; in direct line of descent —**lin'e·a·ment** *n.* feature of face —**lin'e·ar** *adj.* of, in lines —**lin·er** (LIN-ɔr) *n.* large ship or aircraft of passenger line —**lines'man** (-mɔn) *n. Sports* official who helps referee, umpire —**get a line on** obtain all relevant information about

**lin·en** (LIN-ɔn) *adj.* made of flax —*n.* cloth made of flax; linen articles collectively; sheets, tablecloths *etc.*, or shirts (orig. made of linen)

**lin·ger** (LING-gər) vi. delay, loiter; remain long

**lin·ge·rie** (LAHN-zhə-ree) n. women's underwear or nightwear

**lin·go** (LING-goh) n. inf. language, speech esp. applied to jargon and slang

**lin·gua fran·ca** (LING-gwə FRANG-kə) (pl. -fran·cas) language used for communication between people of different mother tongues

**lin·gual** (LING-gwəl) adj. of the tongue or language —n. sound made by the tongue, as d, l, t —**lin'guist** n. one skilled in languages or language study —**lin·guis'tic** adj. of languages or their study —**lin·guis'tics** n. (with sing. v.) study, science of language

**lin·i·ment** (LIN-ə-mənt) n. lotion for rubbing on limbs etc. for relieving pain

**lin·ing** (LI-ning) n. covering for the inside of garment etc.

**link** (lingk) n. ring of a chain; connection; measure, 1-100th part of surveyor's chain —vt. join with, as with, link; intertwine —vi. be so joined —**link'age** (-ij) n.

**links** (lingks) n. pl. golf course

**li·no·le·um** (li-NOH-lee-əm) n. floor covering of burlap or canvas with smooth, hard, decorative coating of powdered cork etc.

**lin'seed** n. seed of flax plant

**lint** n. tiny shreds of yarn; bits of thread; soft material for dressing wounds

**lin·tel** (LIN-tl) n. top piece of door or window

**li·on** (LI-ən) n. large animal of cat family (li'on·ess fem.) —**li'on·ize** vt. (-ized, -iz·ing) treat as celebrity —**li'on·heart·ed** adj. exceptionally brave

**lip** n. upper or lower edge of mouth; edge or margin; sl. impudence —**lip gloss** cosmetic to give lips sheen —**lip'read·ing** n. method of understanding spoken words by interpreting movements of speaker's lips —**lip service** insincere tribute or respect —**lip'stick** n. cosmetic preparation, usu. in stick form, for coloring lips

**li·queur** (li-KUR) n. alcoholic liquor flavored and sweetened

**liq·uid** (LIK-wid) adj. fluid, not solid or gaseous; flowing smoothly; (of assets) in form of money or easily converted into money —n. substance in liquid form —**liq'ue·fy** (-wə-fi) v. (-fied, -fy·ing) make or become liquid —**liquid'i·ty** n. state of being able to meet financial obligations —**liquid air, liquefied** gas air, gas reduced to liquid state on application of increased pressure at low temperature

**liq·ui·date** (LIK-wi-dayt) vt. (-dat·ed, -dat·ing) pay (debt); arrange affairs of, and dissolve (company); wipe out, kill —**liq·ui·da'tion** n. process of clearing up financial affairs; state of being bankrupt —**liq'ui·da·tor** n. official appointed to liquidate business

**liq·uor** (LIK-ər) n. liquid, esp. an alcoholic one

**li·ra** (LEER-ə) n. (pl. -ras) monetary unit of Italy and Turkey

**lisle** (lil) n. fine hard-twisted cotton thread

**lisp** v. speak with faulty pronunciation of "s" and "z"; speak falteringly —n.

**lis·some** (LIS-əm) adj. supple, agile

**list¹** n. inventory, register; catalog; edge of cloth, selvage —pl. field for combat —vt. place on list

**list²** *vi.* (of ship) lean to one side —*n.* inclination of ship

**lis·ten** (LIS-ən) *vi.* try to hear, attend to —**lis'ten·er** *n.*

**list·less** (LIST-lis) *adj.* indifferent, languid

**lit** *pt./pp.* of LIGHT

**lit·a·ny** (LIT-nee) *n.* (*pl.* -nies) prayer with responses from congregation; tedious account

**li·ter** (LEE-tər) *n.* measure of volume of fluid, one cubic decimeter, about 1.05 quarts

**lit·er·al** (LIT-ər-əl) *adj.* according to sense of actual words, not figurative; exact in wording; of letters

**lit·er·ate** (LIT-ər-it) *adj.* able to read and write; educated —*n.* literate person —**lit'er·a·cy** *n.* —**lit·e·ra'ti** (-RAH-tee) *n. pl.* scholarly, literary people

**lit·er·a·ture** (LIT-ər-ə-chər) *n.* books and writings of a country, period or subject —**lit'er·ar·y** *adj.* of or learned in literature

**lithe** (līth) *adj.* (lith·er, lith·est) supple, pliant —**lithe'some** (-səm) *adj.* lissome, supple

**lith·i·um** (LITH-ee-əm) *n.* one of the lightest alkaline metallic elements; this substance used in treatment of depression *etc.*

**li·thog·ra·phy** (li-THOG-rə-fee) *n.* method of printing from metal or stone block using the antipathy of grease and water —**lith'o·graph** *n.* print so produced —*vt.* print thus —**li·thog'ra·pher** *n.*

**lit·i·gant** (LIT-i-gənt) *n./adj.* (person) conducting a lawsuit —**lit·i·ga'tion** *n.* lawsuit

**lit·i·gate** (LIT-i-gayt) *v.* (-gat·ed, -gat·ing) —*vt.* contest in law —*vi.* carry on a lawsuit —**li·ti'gious** (-jəs) *adj.* given to engaging in lawsuits; disputatious —**li·ti'gious·ness** *n.*

**lit·mus** (LIT-məs) *n.* blue · dye turned red by acids and restored to blue by alkali —**litmus paper** —**litmus test** *Chem.* use of litmus paper to test acidity or alkalinity of a solution; *inf.* any crucial test based on only one factor

**lit·ter** (LIT-ər) *n.* untidy refuse; odds and ends; young of animal produced at one birth; straw *etc.* as bedding for animals; portable couch; kind of stretcher for wounded —*vt.* strew with litter; bring forth

**lit·tle** (LIT-l) *adj.* small, not much —*n.* small quantity —*adv.* slightly

**lit·to·ral** (LIT-ər-əl) *adj.* pert. to the shore of sea, lake, ocean —*n.* littoral region

**lit·ur·gy** (LIT-ər-jee) *n.* (*pl.* -gies) prescribed form of public worship —**li·tur'gi·cal** *adj.*

**live** (liv) *v.* (lived, liv·ing) have life; pass one's life; continue in life; continue, last; dwell; feed —**liv'a·ble** *adj.* suitable for living in; tolerable —**living** *n.* action of being in life; people now alive; way of life; means of living; church benefice

**live²** (līv) *adj.* (liv·er, liv·est) living, alive, active, vital; flaming; (of transmission line *etc.*) carrying electric current; (of broadcast) transmitted during the actual performance —**live'ly** *adj.* (-li·er, -li·est) brisk, active, vivid —**live'li·ness** *n.* —**liv'en** *vt.* (*with* up) make (more) lively —**live'stock** *n.* domestic animals —**live wire** wire carrying electric current; able, very energetic person

**live·li·hood** (LĪV-lee-huud) *n.* means of living; subsistence, support

**live·long** (LIV-lawng) *adj.* of a period of time, lasting throughout, *esp.* as though forever

**liv·er** (LIV-ər) n. organ secreting bile; animal liver as food —**liv'er·ish** adj. unwell, as from liver upset; cross, touchy, irritable

**liv·er·y** (LIV-ə-ree) n. (pl. -er·ies) distinctive dress of person or group, esp. servant's; care, feeding of horses; a livery stable —**livery stable** where horses are kept at a charge or hired out

**liv'id** adj. of a bluish pale color; discolored, as by bruising; of reddish color; inf. angry, furious

**liz·ard** (LIZ-ərd) n. four-footed reptile

**Lk.** Luke

**lla·ma** (LAH-mə) n. woolly-haired animal used as beast of burden in S Amer.

**load** (lohd) n. burden; amount usu. carried at once; actual load carried by vehicle; resistance against which engine has to work; amount of electrical energy drawn from a source —vt. put load on or into; charge (gun); weigh down —**load'ed** adj. carrying a load; (of dice) dishonestly weighted; biased; (of question) containing hidden trap or implication; sl. wealthy; sl. drunk

**loadstar, -stone** n. see LODE

**loaf**[1] (lohf) n. (pl. loaves) mass of bread as baked; shaped mass of food

**loaf**[2] vi. idle, loiter —**loaf'er** n. idler

**loam** (lohm) n. fertile soil

**loan** (lohn) n. act of lending; thing lent; money borrowed at interest; permission to use —vt. grant loan of

**loath, loth** (lohth) adj. unwilling, reluctant (to) —**loathe** (lohth) vt. (loathed, loath·ing) hate, abhor —**loathing** (LOH·TH·ing) n. disgust; repulsion —**loath·some** (LOH·TH·səm) adj. disgusting

**lob** n. (lobbed, lob·bing) in tennis, artillery etc., ball, shell, sent high in air —v. hit, fire, thus

**lob·by** (LOB-ee) n. (pl. -bies) corridor into which rooms open; passage or room adjacent to legislative chamber; group of people who try to influence members of legislature —**lob'by·ing** n. activity of this group —**lob'by·ist** n.

**lobe** (lohb) n. any rounded projection; subdivision of body organ; soft, hanging part of ear —**lobed** adj. —**lo·bot·o·my** (lə-BOT-ə-mee) n. (pl. -mies) surgical incision into lobe of organ, esp. brain

**lob·ster** (LOB-stər) n. shellfish with long tail and claws, turning red when boiled

**lo·cal** (LOH-kəl) adj. of, existing in particular place; confined to a definite spot, district or part of the body; of place; (of train) making many stops —n. person belonging to a district; local branch of labor union; local train —**lo·cale** (loh-KAL) n. scene of event —**lo·cal'i·ty** n. place, situation; district —**lo'cal·ize** vt. (-ized, -iz·ing) assign, restrict to definite place —**local anesthetic** one that produces insensibility in part of body

**lo·cate** (loh-KAYT) vt. (-cat·ed, -cat·ing) attribute to a place; find the place of; situate —**lo·ca'tion** n. placing; situation; site of film production away from studio

**lock**[1] (lok) n. appliance for fastening door, lid etc.; mechanism for firing gun; enclosure in river or canal for moving boats from one level to another; air lock; appliance to check the motion of a mechanism; interlocking; block, jam —vt. fasten, make secure with lock; place in locked container; join firmly; cause to become immovable; embrace closely —*vi.* become fixed or united; become immovable —**lock′er** *n.* small closet with lock —**lock′jaw** *n.* tetanus —**lock′out** *n.* exclusion of workmen by employers as means of coercion —**lock′smith** *n.* one who makes and mends locks —**lock′up** *n.* prison

**lock**² *n.* tress of hair

**lock·et** (LOK-it) *n.* small hinged pendant for portrait *etc.*

**lo·co·mo·tive** (loh-kə-MOH-tiv) *n.* engine for pulling train on railway tracks —*adj.* having power of moving from place to place —**lo·co·mo′tion** *n.* action, power of moving

**lo·cus** (LOH-kəs) *n.* (*pl.* -ci *pr.* -sī) exact place or locality; curve made by all points satisfying certain mathematical condition, or by point, line or surface moving under such condition

**lo·cust** (LOH-kəst) *n.* destructive winged insect; N Amer. tree; wood of this tree

**lo·cu·tion** (loh-KYOO-shən) *n.* a phrase; speech; mode or style of speaking

**lode** (lohd) *n.* vein of ore —**lode′star** *n.* star that shows the way; any guide on which attention is fixed; Polaris —**lode′stone** *n.* magnetic iron ore

**lodge** (loj) *n.* house, cabin used seasonally or occasionally, *eg* for hunting, skiing; gatekeeper's house; meeting place of branch of certain fraternal organizations; the branch —*v.* (**lodged, lodg·ing**) —*vt.* house; deposit; bring (a charge *etc.*) against someone —*vi.* live in another's house at fixed rent; come to rest (in, on) —**lodg′er** *n.* —**lodgings** *n. pl.* rented room(s) in another person's house

**loft** (lawft) *n.* space between top

story and roof; upper story of warehouse, factory *etc.* typically with large unpartitioned space; gallery in church *etc.* —**loft building** building in which all stories have large unobstructed space once used for manufacturing but now usu. are converted to residences —*vt.* send (golf ball *etc.*) high —**loft′i·ly** *adv.* haughtily —**loft′i·ness** *n.* —**loft′y** *adj.* (**loft·i·er, loft·i·est**) of great height; elevated; haughty

**log**¹ (lawg) *n.* portion of felled tree stripped of branches; detailed record of voyages, time traveled *etc.* of ship, aircraft *etc.*; apparatus used formerly for measuring ship's speed —*vt.* (**logged, log·ging**) keep a record of; travel (specified distance, time) —**log′ging** *n.* cutting and transporting logs to river

**log**² *n.* logarithm

**log·a·rithm** (LAW-gə-rith-əm) *n.* one of series of arithmetical functions tabulated for use in calculation

**log·ger·head** (LAW-gər-hed) *n.* —**at loggerheads** quarreling, disputing

**log·ic** (LOJ-ik) *n.* art or philosophy of reasoning; reasoned thought or argument; coherence of various facts, events *etc.* —**log′i·cal** *adj.* of logic; according to reason; reasonable; apt to reason correctly —**lo·gi·cian** (loh-JISH-ən) *n.*

**lo·gis·tics** (loh-JIS-tiks) *n.* (with *sing.* or *pl. v.*) the transport, housing and feeding of troops; organization of any project, operation —**lo·gis′ti·cal** *adj.*

**lo·go** (LOH-goh) *n.* (*pl.* -gos) company emblem or similar device

**loin** *n.* part of body between ribs and hip; cut of meat from this —*pl.* hips and lower abdomen

—**loin′cloth** n. garment covering loins only

**loi·ter** (LOI-tər) vi. dawdle, hang about; idle —**loi′ter·er** n.

**loll** (lol) vi. sit, lie lazily; hang out —vt. allow to hang out

**lone** (lohn) adj. solitary —**lone′ly** adj. (-li·er, -li·est) sad because alone; unfrequented; solitary, alone —**lone′li·ness** n. —**lon′er** n. one who prefers to be alone —**lone′some** (-səm) adj.

**long**[1] (lawng) adj. (-er, -est) having length, esp. great length, in space or time; extensive; protracted —adv. for a long time —**long′hand** n. writing in which words are written out in full by hand rather than on typewriter etc. —**long′-play′ing** adj. (of record) lasting for 10 to 30 minutes because of its fine grooves —**long-range** adj. of the future; able to travel long distances without refueling; (of weapons) designed to hit distant target —**long shot** competitor, undertaking, bet etc. with small chance of success —**long ton** 2240 lbs. —**long′-wind′ed** adj. tediously loquacious

**long**[2] vi. have keen desire, yearn (for) —**long′ing** n. yearning

**lon·gev·i·ty** (lon-JEV-i-tee) n. long existence or life; length of existence or life; tenure

**lon·gi·tude** (LON-ji-tood) n. distance east or west from prime meridian —**lon·gi·tu′di·nal** adj. of length or longitude; lengthwise

**long·shore·man** (LAWNG-SHOR-mən) n. dock laborer

**look** (luuk) vi. direct, use eyes; face; seem; search (for); hope (for); (with after) take care of —n. looking; view; search; (pl.) appearance —**good looks** beauty —**look′a·like** n. person who is double of another —**look′out** n.

guard; place for watching; watchman; object of worry, concern —**look after** tend —**look down on** despise

**loom**[1] n. machine for weaving; middle part of oar

**loom**[2] vi. appear dimly; seem ominously close; assume great importance

**loon**[1] n. Amer. fish-eating diving bird

**loon**[2] n. stupid, foolish person —**loon′y** adj./n. (loon·i·er, loon·i·est) (loon·y bin inf. mental hospital or ward

**loop** n. figure made by curved line crossing itself; similar rounded shape in cord or rope etc. crossed on itself; contraceptive coil; aerial maneuver in which aircraft describes complete circle —v. form loop

**loop·hole** (LOOP-hohl) n. means of evading rule without infringing it; vertical slit in building wall, esp. for defense

**loose** (loos) adj. (loos·er, loos·est) not tight, fastened, fixed, or tense; slack; vague; dissolute —v. (loosed, loos·ing) —vt. free; unfasten; slacken —vi. (with off) shoot, let fly —**loose′ly** adv. —**loos′en** vt. make loose —**loose′ness** n. —**on the loose** free; on a spree

**loot** n./vt. plunder

**lop**[1] vt. (lopped, lop·ping) cut away twigs and branches; chop off

**lop**[2] vi. (lopped, lop·ping) hang limply —**lop′-eared** adj. having drooping ears —**lop′sid·ed** adj. with one side lower than the other; badly balanced

**lope** (lohp) vi. (loped, lop·ing) run with long, easy strides

**lo·qua·cious** (loh-KWAY-shəs) adj. talkative —**lo·quac′i·ty** (-KWAS-ə-tee) n.

**lord** *n*. British nobleman, peer of the realm; feudal superior; one ruling others; owner; (L-) God —*vi*. domineer —**lord'li·ness** *n*. —**lord'ly** *adj*. (**-li·er, -li·est**) imperious, proud; fit for a lord —**lord'ship** *n*. rule, ownership; domain; title of some noblemen

**lor·do·sis** (lor-DOH-sis) *n*. abnormal forward curvature of spine

**lore** (lor) *n*. learning; body of facts and traditions

**lor·gnette** (lorn-YET) *n*. pair of eyeglasses mounted on long handle

**lorn** *adj. poet.* abandoned; desolate

**lose** (looz) *v*. (**lost, los·ing**) —*vt*. be deprived of, fail to retain or use; let slip; fail to get; (of clock *etc.*) run slow (by specified amount); be defeated in —*vi*. suffer loss —**los·es** (laws) *n*. a losing; what is lost; harm or damage resulting from losing —**lost** *adj*. unable to be found; unable to find one's way; bewildered; not won; not utilized

**lot** *n*. great number; collection; large quantity; share; fate; destiny; item at auction; one of a set of objects used to decide something by chance, as in to cast lots; area of land —*pl*. great numbers or quantity —*adv*. a great deal

**loth** *see* LOATH

**lo·tion** (LOH-shon) *n*. liquid for washing to reduce itching *etc.*, improving skin *etc.*

**lot·ter·y** (LOT-ə-ree) *n*. (*pl.* **-ter·ies**) method of raising funds by selling tickets and prizes by chance; any gamble

**lot·to** (LOT-oh) *n*. game of chance like bingo

**lo·tus** (LOH-təs) *n*. (*pl.* **-tus·es**) legendary plant whose fruits induce forgetfulness when eaten;

Egyptian water lily —**lotus position** seated cross-legged position used in yoga *etc.*

**loud** (lowd) *adj*. (**-er, -est**) strongly audible; noisy; obtrusive —**loud'ly** *adv*. —**loud'speak·er** *n*. instrument for converting electrical signals into sound audible at a distance

**lounge** (lownj) *vi*. (**lounged, loung·ing**) sit, lie, walk, or stand in a relaxed manner —*n*. general waiting, relaxing area in airport, hotel *etc.*; bar —**loung'er** *n*. loafer

**louse** (lows) *n*. (*pl.* **lice**) a parasitic insect —**lous'y** *adj. inf.* (**lous·i·er, lous·i·est**) nasty, unpleasant; *sl.* (too) generously provided, thickly populated (with); bad, poor; having lice

**lout** (lowt) *n*. crude, oafish person —**lout'ish** *adj*.

**lou·ver** (LOO-vər) *n*. one of a set of boards or slats set parallel and slanted to admit air but not rain or sunlight; ventilating structure of these

**love** (luv) *n*. warm affection; benevolence; charity; sexual passion; sweetheart; *Tennis etc.* score of zero —*v*. (**loved, lov·ing**) —*vt*. admire passionately; delight in —*vi*. be in love —**lov'a·ble** *adj*. —**love'less** (-lis) *adj*. —**love'lorn** *adj*. forsaken by, pining for a lover —**love'li·ness** *n*. —**love'ly** *adj*. (**-li·er, -li·est**) beautiful, delightful —**loving** *adj*. affectionate; tender —**lov'ing·ly** *adv*. —**loving cup** bowl formerly passed around at banquet; large cup given as prize —**make love (to)** have sexual intercourse (with)

**low**[1] (loh) *adj*. (**-er, -est**) not tall, high or elevated; humble; commonplace; coarse; vulgar; dejected; ill; not loud; moderate; cheap —**low'er** *vt*. cause, allow to descend; move down; diminish, degrade —*adj.* below in position or rank; at an early stage, period of development —low'li·ness *n.* —low'ly *adj.* (-li·er, -li·est) modest, humble —low'brow *n.* person with no intellectual or cultural interests —*adj.* —**Low Church** section of Anglican Church stressing evangelical beliefs and practices —low'down *n. inf.* inside information —*adj.* mean, shabby, dishonorable —**low frequency** in electricity any frequency of alternating current from about 30 to 300 kilohertz; frequency within audible range —low-key (-kee) *adj.* subdued, restrained, not intense —low'land *n.* low-lying land —low-ten·sion *adj.* carrying, operating at low voltage

low[2] *vi.* of cattle, utter their cry, bellow —*n.* cry of cattle, bellow

low·er (LOW-ər) *vi.* look gloomy or threatening, as sky; scowl —*n.* scowl, frown

loy·al (LOI-əl) *adj.* faithful, true to allegiance —loy'al·ly *adv.* —loy'al·ty *n.*

loz·enge (LOZ-inj) *n.* small candy or tablet of medicine; rhombus, diamond figure

**LSD** lysergic acid diethylamide (hallucinogenic drug)

lub·ber (LUB-ər) *n.* clumsy fellow; unskilled seaman

lu·bri·cate (LOO-bri-kayt) *v.* (-cat·ed, -cat·ing) oil, grease; make slippery —lu'bri·cant (-kənt) *n.* substance used for this —lu·bri·ca'tion (-KAY-shən) *n.* —lu·bric'i·ty (-BRIS-i-tee) *n.* (pl. -ties) slipperiness, smoothness; lewdness

lu·cid (LOO-sid) *adj.* clear; easily understood; sane —lu·cid'i·ty *n.*

Lu·ci·fer (LOO-sə-fər) *n.* Satan

luck (luk) *n.* fortune, good or bad; good fortune; chance —luck'i·ly *adv.* fortunately —luck'less *adj.* having bad luck —luck'y *adj.* (luck·i·er, luck·i·est) having good luck

lu·cre (LOO-kər) *n.* money, wealth —lu'cra·tive (-krə-tiv) *adj.* very profitable —**filthy lucre** *inf.* money

lu·di·crous (LOO-di-krəs) *adj.* absurd, laughable, ridiculous

lug[1] *v.* (lugged, lug·ging) —*v.* drag with effort —*vi.* pull hard

lug[2] *n.* projection, tag serving as handle or support; *sl.* fellow, blockhead

lug·gage (LUG-ij) *n.* traveler's suitcases and other baggage

lu·gu·bri·ous (luu-GOO-bree-əs) *adj.* mournful, doleful, gloomy —lu·gu'bri·ous·ly *adv.*

luke·warm (look-worm) *adj.* moderately warm, tepid; indifferent

lull *vt.* soothe, sing to sleep; make quiet —*vi.* become quiet, subside —*n.* brief time of quiet in storm *etc.* —lull'a·by *n.* (pl. -bies) lulling song, *esp.* for children

lum·bar (LUM-bahr) *adj.* relating to body between lower ribs and hips —lum·ba'go (-BAY-goh) *n.* rheumatism in lower part of the back

lum·ber (LUM-bər) *n.* sawn timber; disused articles, useless rubbish —*vi.* move heavily —*vt.* convert (a number of trees) into lumber; burden with something unpleasant —lum'ber·jack *n.* logger

lu·men (LOO-mən) *n.* (pl. -mi·na pr. -mə·nə) SI unit of luminous flux

lu·mi·nous (LOO-mə-nəs) *adj.* bright; shedding light; glowing; lucid —lu'mi·nar·y (-ner·ee) *n.* learned person; prominent person; heavenly body giving light

—**lu·mi·nes′cence** (-NES-əns) n. emission of light at low temperatures by process (eg chemical) not involving burning —**lu·mi·nos′i·ty** n.

**lump** n. shapeless piece or mass; swelling; large sum —vt. throw together in one mass or sum —vi. move heavily —**lump′ish** adj. clumsy; stupid —**lump′y** adj. (**lump·i·er, lump·i·est**) full of lumps; uneven —**lump it** inf. put up with; accept and endure

**lu·nar** (LOO-nər) adj. relating to the moon

**lu·na·tic** (LOO-nə-tik) adj. insane —n. insane person —**lu′na·cy** n. (pl. -cies) —**lunatic fringe** extreme, radical section of group etc.

**lunch** n. meal taken in the middle of the day —v. eat, entertain at lunch —**lunch′eon** (-ən) n. a lunch

**lung** n. one of the two organs of respiration in vertebrates —**lung′fish** n. type of fish with air-breathing lung

**lunge** (lunj) vi. (**lunged, lung·ing**) thrust with sword etc. —n. such thrust; sudden movement of body, plunge

**lu·pine¹** (LOO-pin) n. leguminous plant with tall spikes of flowers

**lu·pine²** (LOO-pin) adj. like a wolf

**lu·pus** (LOO-pəs) n. skin disease

**lurch** n. sudden roll to one side —vi. stagger —**leave in the lurch** leave in difficulties

**lure** (luur) n. something that entices; bait; power to attract —vt. (**lured, lur·ing**) entice; attract

**lu·rid** (LUUR-id) adj. vivid in shocking detail, sensational; pale, wan; lit with unnatural glare

**lurk** vi. lie hidden —**lurk′ing** adj. (of suspicion) not definite

**lus·cious** (LUSH-əs) adj. sweet, juicy; extremely pleasurable or attractive

**lush¹** adj. (-er, -est) (of grass etc.) luxuriant and juicy, fresh

**lush²** n. sl. heavy drinker; alcoholic

**lust** n. strong desire for sexual gratification; any strong desire —vi. have passionate desire —**lust′ful** (-fəl) adj. —**lust′i·ly** adv. —**lust′y** adj. (**lust·i·er, lust·i·est**) vigorous, healthy

**lus·ter** (LUST-ər) n. gloss, sheen; splendor; renown; glory; glossy material; metallic pottery glaze —**lus′trous** (-trəs) adj. shining, luminous

**lute** (loot) n. old stringed musical instrument played with the fingers —**lu′te·nist** n.

**lux** (luks) n. (pl. **lu·ces** pr. LOO-seez) SI unit of illumination

**lux·u·ry** (LUK-shə-ree) n. (pl. -ries) possession and use of costly, choice things for enjoyment; enjoyable but not necessary thing; comfortable surroundings —**lux·u·ri·ance** (lug-ZHUUR-ee-əns) n. abundance, proliferation —**lux·u·ri·ant** adj. growing thickly; abundant —**lux·u′ri·ate** (-ayt) vi. (**-at·ed, -at·ing**) indulge in luxury; flourish profusely; take delight (in) —**lux·u′ri·ous** adj. fond of luxury; self-indulgent; sumptuous

**ly·ce·um** (lī-SEE-əm) n. institution for popular education eg concerts, lectures; public building for this purpose

**lye** (lī) n. water made alkaline with wood ashes etc. for washing

**lying** pr. p. of LIE

**lymph** (limf) n. colorless bodily fluid, mainly of white blood cells —**lym·phat′ic** adj. of lymph; flabby, sluggish —n. vessel in the body conveying lymph

**lynch** (linch) vt. put to death without trial —**lynch law** procedure of self-appointed court trying and punishing *esp.* executing accused

**lynx** (lingks) *n.* animal of cat family

**lyre** (līr) *n* instrument like harp —**lyr·ic** (LIR-ik) (also **lyr'i·cal**) *adj.* of short personal poems expressing emotion; of lyre; meant to be sung —**lyric** *n.* lyric poem —*pl.* words of popular song —**lyr'i·cist** (-sist) *n.* writer of lyrics; lyric poet —**wax lyrical** express great enthusiasm

# M

**ma·ca·bre** (mə-KAH-brə) *adj.* gruesome, ghastly

**mac·ad·am** (mə-KAD-əm) *n.* road surface made of pressed layers of small broken stones; this stone

**mac·a·roon** (mak-ə-ROON) *n.* small cookie made of egg whites, almond paste *etc.*

**ma·caw** (mə-KAW) *n.* kind of parrot

**mace** (mays) *n.* spice made of the husk of the nutmeg

**mac·er·ate** (MAS-ə-rayt) *vt.* (-at·ed, -at·ing) soften by soaking; cause to waste away

**mach** (**number**) (mahk) *n.* the ratio of the air speed of an aircraft to the velocity of sound under given conditions

**Mach·i·a·vel·li·an** (mak-ee-ə-VEL-ee-ən) *adj.* politically unprincipled, crafty, perfidious, subtle

**mach·i·na·tion** (mak-ə-NAY-shən) *n.* (*usu. pl.*) plotting, intrigue

**ma·chine** (mə-SHEEN) *n.* apparatus combining action of several parts to apply mechanical force; controlling organization; mechanical appliance; vehicle —*vt.* (-chined, -chin·ing) sew, print, shape *etc.* with machine —**ma·chin'er·y** *n.* (*pl.* -er·ies) parts of machine collectively; machines —**ma·chin'ist** *n.* one who makes or operates machines

**ma·chis·mo** (mah-CHEEZ-moh) *n.* strong or exaggerated masculine pride or masculinity —**ma'cho** (-choh) *adj.* denoting or exhibiting such pride in masculinity —*n.* (*pl.* -chos) person exhibiting this

**mack·er·el** (MAK-ər-əl) *n.* edible sea fish with blue and silver stripes

**mac·ra·mé** (MAK-rə-may) *n.* ornamental webbing of knotted cord

**mac·ro·bi·ot·ics** (mak-roh-bī-OT-iks) *n.* (*with sing. v.*) dietary system advocating grain and vegetables grown without chemical additives —**mac·ro·bi·ot'ic** *adj./n.* (relating to the diet of) person practicing macrobiotics

**mac·ro·cosm** (MAK-rə-koz-əm) *n.* the universe; any large, complete system

**mad** *adj.* (-der, -dest) suffering from mental disease, insane; wildly foolish; very enthusiastic (about); excited; furious, angry —**mad'den** *vt.* make mad —**mad'ly** *adv.* —**mad'man** *n.* —**mad'ness** *n.* insanity; folly

**mad·am** (MAD-əm) *n.* polite form of address to a woman; woman in charge of house; woman in charge of prostitution

**made** *pt./pp.* of MAKE

**Ma·don·na** (mə-DON-ə) *n.* the Virgin Mary; picture or statue of her

**mad·ri·gal** (MAD-ri-gəl) *n.* unaccompanied part song; short love poem or song

**mael·strom** (MAYL-strom) n. great whirlpool; turmoil

**ma·es·to·so** (mī-STOH-soh) adv. Mus. grandly, in majestic manner

**maes·tro** (MĪ-stroh) n. outstanding musician, conductor; man regarded as master of any art

**Ma·fi·a** (MAH-fee-ə) n. international secret organization allegedly engaging in crime, orig. Italian

**mag·a·zine** (mag-ə-ZEEN) n. periodical publication with stories and articles by different writers; appliance for supplying cartridges automatically to gun; storehouse for explosives or arms

**ma·gen·ta** (mə-JEN-tə) adj./n. (of) purplish-red color

**mag·got** (MAG-ət) n. grub, larva of certain flies —**mag'got·y** adj. infested with maggots

**Ma·gi** (MAY-jī) n. pl. priests of ancient Persia; the wise men from the East at the Nativity

**mag·ic** (MAJ-ik) n. art of supposedly invoking supernatural powers to influence events etc.; any mysterious agency or power; witchcraft, conjuring —adj. —**mag'i·cal** n. —**ma·gi'cian** n. one skilled in magic, wizard, conjurer, enchanter

**mag·is·trate** (MAJ-ə-strayt) n. civil officer administering law; justice of the peace —**mag·is·te'ri·al** (-STEER-ee-əl) adj. of, referring to magistrate; authoritative; weighty —**mag'is·tra·cy** (-stray-see) n. (pl. -cies) office of magistrate; magistrates collectively

**mag·ma** (MAG-mə) n. paste, suspension; molten rock inside Earth's crust

**mag·nan·i·mous** (mag-NAN-ə-məs) adj. noble, generous, not petty —**mag·na·nim'i·ty** n.

**mag·nate** (MAG-nayt) n. influential or wealthy person

**mag·ne·si·um** (mag-NEE-zee-əm) n. metallic element —**mag·ne'sia** (-zhə) n. white powder compound of this used in medicine

**mag·net** (MAG-nit) n. piece of iron, steel having properties of attracting iron, steel and pointing north and south when suspended; lodestone —**mag·net'ic** adj. with properties of magnet; exerting powerful attraction —**mag·net'i·cal·ly** adv. —**mag'net·ism** (-ni-tiz-əm) n. magnetic phenomena; science of this; personal charm or power of attracting others —**mag'net·ize** vt. (-ized, -iz·ing) make into a magnet; attract as if by magnet; fascinate —**mag·ne'to** (-NEE-toh) n. (pl. -tos) apparatus for ignition in internal combustion engine

**mag·nif·i·cent** (mag-NIF-ə-sənt) adj. splendid; stately, imposing; excellent —**mag·nif'i·cence** n.

**mag·ni·fy** (MAG-nə-fī) v. (-fied, -fy·ing) increase apparent size of, as with lens; exaggerate; make greater —**mag·ni·fi·ca'tion** (-KAY-shən) n.

**mag·nil·o·quent** (mag-NIL-ə-kwənt) adj. speaking pompously; grandiose —**mag·nil'o·quence** n.

**mag·ni·tude** (MAG-ni-tood) n. importance; greatness; size

**mag·num** (MAG-nəm) n. large wine bottle (approx. 1.6 quarts, 1.5 liters)

**mag·pie** (MAG-pī) n. black-and-white bird; incessantly talkative person

**ma·ha·ra·jah** (mah-hə-RAH-jə) n. former title of some Indian princes

**ma·ha·ri·shi** (mah-hə-REE-shee)

*n.* Hindu religious teacher or mystic

**ma·hat·ma** (mə-HAHT-mə) *n. Hinduism* man of saintly life with supernatural powers; one endowed with great wisdom and power

**mahl·stick** (MAHL-stik) *n.* light stick with ball at one end, held in other hand to support working hand while painting

**maid·en** (MAYD-n) *n. Literary* young unmarried woman —*adj.* unmarried; of, suited to maiden; first; having blank record —**maid** *n.* woman servant; *Literary* young unmarried woman —**maid′en·ly** *adj.* modest —**maid′en·hair** *n.* fern with delicate stalks and fronds —**maid′en·head** *n.* virginity —**maiden name** woman's surname before marriage

**mail**[1] (mayl) *n.* letters *etc.* transported and delivered by the post office; letters *etc.* conveyed at one time; the postal system; train, ship *etc.* carrying mail —*pl.* the postal system —*vt.* send by mail —**electronic mail** messages sent via telecommunication links between display terminals

**mail**[2] *n.* armor of interlaced rings or overlapping plates —**mailed** *adj.* covered with mail

**maim** (maym) *vt.* cripple, mutilate

**main** (mayn) *adj.* chief, principal, leading —*n.* principal pipe, line carrying water, gas *etc.;* chief part; strength, power; *obs.* open sea —**main′ly** *adv.* for the most part, chiefly —**main′frame** *Computers adj.* denoting a high-speed general-purpose computer —*n.* such a computer; the central processing unit of a computer —**main′land** *n.* stretch of land

that forms main part of a country —**main′mast** *n.* chief mast in ship —**main′sail** *n.* lowest sail of mainmast —**main′spring** *n.* chief spring of watch or clock; chief cause or motive —**main′stay** *n.* rope from mainmast; chief support

**main·tain** (mayn-TAYN) *vt.* carry on; preserve; support; sustain; keep up; keep supplied; affirm; support by argument; defend —**main′te·nance** (-tə-nəns) *n.* maintaining; means of support; upkeep of buildings *etc.;* provision of money for separated or divorced spouse

**mai·tre d'hô·tel** (may-tər doh-TEL) (*pl.* **mai·tres** *pr.* -torz) headwaiter, owner, or manager of hotel

**maize** (mayz) *n.* primitive corn with kernels of various colors, Indian corn

**maj·es·ty** (MAJ-ə-stee) *n.* stateliness; sovereignty; grandeur —**ma·jes′tic** (mə-) *adj.* splendid; regal —**ma·jes′ti·cal·ly** *adv.*

**ma·jor** (MAY-jər) *n.* military officer ranking next above captain; scale in music; principal field of study at college; person engaged in this —*adj.* greater in number, quality, extent; significant, serious —**ma·jor′i·ty** *n.* greater number; larger party voting together; more than half of votes cast in election; coming of age; rank of major —**major-do·mo** (-DOH-moh) *n.* (*pl.* -mos) male servant in charge of large household

**make** (mayk) *v.* (**made, mak·ing**) construct; produce; create; establish; appoint; amount to; cause to do something; accomplish; reach; earn; tend; contribute —*n.* brand, type, or style —**making** *n.* creation —*pl.* necessary requirements or qualities —**make allow-**

**ance** for take mitigating circumstance into consideration —**make′shift** n. temporary expedient —**make′up** n. cosmetics; characteristics; layout —**make up** compose; compile; complete; compensate; apply cosmetics; invent —**on the make** inf. intent on gain; sl. seeking sexual relations

**mal-, male-** (comb. form) ill, badly, as in malformation n. —**malevolent** adj.

**ma·lac·ca** (mə-LAK-ə) n. brown cane used for walking stick

**mal·a·droit** (mal-ə-DROIT) adj. clumsy, awkward

**mal·a·dy** (MAL-ə-dee) n. (pl. -dies) disease

**ma·laise** (ma-LAYZ′) n. vague, unlocated feeling of bodily discomfort

**mal·a·prop·ism** (MAL-ə-prop-iz-əm) n. ludicrous misuse of word

**ma·lar·i·a** (mə-LAIR-ee-ə) n. infectious disease caused by parasite transmitted by bite of some mosquitoes —**ma·lar′i·al** adj.

**mal·con·tent** (mal-kən-TENT) adj. actively discontented —n. malcontent person

**male** (mayl) adj. of sex producing gametes that fertilize female gametes; of men or male animals; of machine part, made to fit inside corresponding recessed female part —n. male person or animal

**mal·e·dic·tion** (mal-i-DIK-shən) n. curse

**mal·e·fac·tor** (MAL-ə-fak-tər) n. criminal

**ma·lev·o·lent** (mə-LEV-ə-lənt) adj. full of ill will —**ma·lev′o·lence** n.

**mal·fea·sance** (mal-FEE-zəns) n. illegal action; official misconduct

**mal·ice** (MAL-is) n. ill will; spite —**ma·li·cious** (mə-LISH-əs) adj. in-

tending evil or unkindness; spiteful; moved by hatred

**ma·lign** (mə-LIn) adj. evil in influence or effect —vt. slander, misrepresent —**ma·lig·nan·cy** (-LIG-nən-see) n. —**ma·lig′nant** adj. feeling extreme ill will; (of disease) resistant to therapy; tending to produce death —**ma·lig′ni·ty** n. malignant disposition

**ma·lin·ger** (mə-LING-gər) vi. feign illness to escape duty —**ma·lin′ger·er** n.

**mall** (mawl) n. level, shaded walk; street, shopping area closed to vehicles

**mal·le·a·ble** (MAL-ee-ə-bəl) adj. capable of being hammered into shape; adaptable

**mal·let** (MAL-it) n. (wooden etc.) hammer; croquet or pole stick

**mal·nu·tri·tion** (mal-noo-TRISH-ən) n. inadequate nutrition

**mal·o·dor·ous** (mal-OH-dər-əs) adj. evil-smelling

**mal·prac·tice** (mal-PRAK-tis) n. immoral, careless illegal or unethical conduct

**malt** (mawlt) n. grain used for brewing or distilling —vt. make into malt

**mam·bo** (MAHM-boh) n. (pl. -bos) Latin Amer. dance like rumba

**mam·mal** (MAM-əl) n. animal of type that suckles its young —**mam·ma′li·an** (-MAY-lee-ən) adj.

**mam·ma·ry** (MAM-ər-ee) adj. of, relating to breast or milk-producing gland

**mam·mon** (MAM-ən) n. wealth regarded as source of evil; (M-) false god of covetousness

**mam·moth** (MAM-əth) n. extinct animal like an elephant —adj. colossal

**man** n. (pl. men) human being; person; human race; adult male; manservant; piece used in chess *etc.* —*vt.* (**manned, man·ning**) supply (ship, artillery *etc.*) with necessary crew; fortify —**man′ful** *adj.* brave, vigorous —**man′li·ness** *n.* —**man′ly** (-li·er, -li·est) *adj.* —**man′nish** *adj.* like a man —**man·han·dle** *vt.* (**-dled, -dling**) treat roughly —**man′hole** *n.* opening through which person can pass to a drain, sewer *etc.* —**man′hood** (-huud) *n.* —**man′kind** (-KIND) *n.* human beings in general —**man′pow·er** *n.* power of human effort; available number of workers —**man′slaugh·ter** (-slaw·tor) *n.* culpable homicide without malice aforethought

**man·a·cle** (MAN-ə-kəl) *n.* fetter, handcuff —*vt.* (**-cled, -cling**) shackle

**man·age** (MAN-ij) *vt.* (**-aged, -ag·ing**) be in charge of, administer; succeed in doing; control; handle, cope with; conduct, carry on; persuade —**man′age·a·ble** *adj.* —**man′age·ment** *n.* those who manage, as board of directors *etc.*; administration; skillful use of means; conduct —**man′ag·er** *n.* one in charge of business, institution, actor *etc.*; one who manages efficiently —**man·a·ge′ri·al** *adj.*

**man·a·tee** (MAN-ə-tee) *n.* large, plant-eating aquatic mammal

**man·da·rin** (MAN-də-rin) *n. Hist.* Chinese high-ranking bureaucrat; *fig.* any high government official; Chinese variety of orange

**man·date** (MAN-dayt) *n.* command of, or commission to act for, another; commission from United Nations to govern a territory; instruction from electorate to representative or government —**man′dat·ed** *adj.* committed to a mandate —**man′da·to·ry** (-də·tor·ee) *n.* holder of a mandate —**man′da·to·ry** *adj.* compulsory

**man·di·ble** (MAN-də·bəl) *n.* lower jawbone; either part of bird's beak —**man·dib′u·lar** *adj.* of, like mandible

**man·do·lin** (MAN-dl-in) *n.* stringed musical instrument

**man·drel** (MAN-drəl) *n.* axis on which material is supported in a lathe; spindle around which metal is forged

**man′drill** *n.* large blue-faced baboon

**mane** (mayn) *n.* long hair on neck of horse, lion *etc.*

**ma·neu·ver** (mə-NOO-vər) *n.* contrived, complicated, perhaps deceptive plan or action; skillful management —*v.* employ stratagems, work adroitly; (cause to) perform maneuvers

**man·ga·nese** (MANG-gə-neez) *n.* metallic element; black oxide of this

**mange** (maynj) *n.* skin disease of dogs *etc.* —**man′gy** *adj.* (-gi·er, -gi·est) scruffy, shabby

**man·ger** (MAYN-jər) *n.* eating trough in stable

**man·gle¹** (MANG-gəl) *n.* machine for pressing clothes *etc.* to remove water —*vt.* (**-gled, -gling**) press in mangle

**man·gle²** *vt.* (**-gled, -gling**) mutilate, spoil, hack

**man·go** (MANG-goh) *n.* (*pl.* **-goes**) tropical fruit; tree bearing it

**man·grove** (MANG-grohv) *n.* tropical tree that grows on muddy banks of estuaries

**ma·ni·a** (MAY-nee-ə) *n.* madness; prevailing craze —**ma′ni·ac, ma·ni′a·cal, man′ic** *adj.* affected by mania —**maniac** *n. inf.* mad person; wild enthusiast

**man·i·cure** (MAN-i-kyuur) *n.* treatment and care of fingernails and hands —*vt.* (**-cured, -cur·ing**) apply such treatment —**man′i·cur·ist** *n.* one who does this professionally

**man·i·fest** (MAN-ə-fest) *adj.* clearly revealed, visible, undoubted —*vt.* make manifest —*n.* list of cargo for customs —**man·i·fes·ta'tion** *n.* —**man'i·fest·ly** *adv.* clearly —**man·i·fes'to** *n.* (pl. -toes) declaration of policy by political party, government, or movement

**man·i·fold** (MAN-ə-fohld) *adj.* numerous and varied —*n.* in internal combustion engine, pipe with several outlets

**ma·nip·u·late** (mə-NIP-yə-layt) *vt.* (-lat·ed, -lat·ing) handle; deal with skillfully; manage; falsify —**ma·nip·u·la'tion** *n.* act of manipulating, working by hand; skilled use of hands —**ma·nip'u·la·tive** *adj.*

**man·na** (MAN-ə) *n.* food of Israelites in the wilderness; unexpected benefit

**man·ne·quin** (MAN-i-kin) *n.* person who models clothes, *esp.* at fashion shows; clothing dummy

**man·ner** (MAN-ər) *n.* way thing happens or is done; sort, kind; custom; style —*pl.* social behavior —**man'ner·ism** *n.* person's distinctive habit, trait —**man'ner·ly** *adj.* polite

**man·or** (MAN-ər) *n.* main house of estate or plantation —**ma·no'ri·al** *adj.*

**man·sard** (MAN-sahrd) *n.* roof with break in its slope, lower part being steeper than upper

**man·sion** (MAN-shən) *n.* large house

**man·tel** (MAN-tl) *n.* structure around fireplace; mantelpiece —**man'tel·piece, -shelf** *n.* shelf at top of mantel

**man·til·la** (man-TIL-ə) *n.* in Spain, (lace) scarf worn as headdress

**man'tis** *n.* (pl. -tis·es) genus of insects including the stick insects and leaf insects

**man·tle** (MAN-tl) *n.* loose cloak; covering; incandescent fireproof network hood around gas jet —*vt.* (-tled, -tling) cover; conceal —**man·tle·piece** *n.* mantel

**man·u·al** (MAN-yoo-əl) *adj.* of, or done with, the hands; by human labor, not automatic —*n.* handbook; textbook; organ keyboard

**man·u·fac·ture** (man-yə-FAK-chər) *vt.* (-tured, -tur·ing) process, make (materials) into finished articles; produce (articles); invent, concoct —*n.* making of articles, materials, *esp.* in large quantities; anything produced from raw materials —**man·u·fac'tur·er** *n.*

**ma·nure** (mə-NUUR) *vt.* (-nured, -nur·ing) enrich land —*n.* dung, chemical fertilizer (used to enrich land)

**man·u·script** (MAN-yə-skript) *n.* book, document, written by hand; copy for printing —*adj.* handwritten or typed

**man·y** (MEN-ee) *adj.* (more, most) numerous —*n./pron.* large number

**Ma·o·ri** (MAH-aw-ree) *n.* member of New Zealand aboriginal population; their language

**map** *n.* flat representation of Earth or some part of it, or of the heavens —*vt.* (mapped, map·ping) make a map of; (with out) plan

**ma·ple** (MAY-pəl) *n.* tree of the *acer* genus, a variety of which yields sap that is made into syrup and sugar

**ma·quis** (mah-KEE) *n.* scrubby undergrowth of Mediterranean countries; name adopted by French resistance movement in WWII

**mar** (mahr) *vt.* (marred, mar·ring) spoil, impair

**mar·a·bou** (MAR-ə-boo) *n.* kind of

stork; its soft white lower tail feathers, formerly used to trim hats *etc.*; kind of silk

**ma·rac·a** (mə-RAH-kə) *n.* percussion instrument of gourd containing dried seeds *etc.*

**mar·a·schi·no** (mar-ə-SKEE-noh) *n.* liqueur made from cherries

**mar·a·thon** (MAR-ə-thon) *n.* long-distance race; endurance contest

**ma·raud** (mə-RAWD) *v.* make raid for plunder; pillage —**maraud'er** *n.*

**mar·ble** (MAHR-bəl) *n.* kind of limestone capable of taking polish; slab of, sculpture in this; small ball used in children's game —**mar'bled** *adj.* having mottled appearance, like marble; (of beef) streaked with fat

**march** (mahrch) *vi.* walk with military step; go, progress —*vt.* cause to march —*n.* action of marching; distance marched in day; tune to accompany marching

**mar·chion·ess** (MAHR-shə-nis) *n.* wife, widow of marquis

**Mar·di Gras** (MAHR-dee grah) *n.* festival of Shrove Tuesday; revelry celebrating this

**mare** (mair) *n.* female horse —**mare's-nest** *n.* supposed discovery that proves worthless

**mar·ga·rine** (MAHR-jər-in) *n.* butter substitute made from vegetable fats

**mar·gin** (MAHR-jin) *n.* border, edge; space around printed page; amount allowed beyond what is necessary —**mar'gin·al** *adj.*

**mar·i·gold** (MAR-i-gohld) *n.* plant with yellow flowers

**ma·ri·jua·na** (mar-ə-WAH-nə) *n.* dried flowers and leaves of hemp plant, used as narcotic

**ma·ri·na** (mə-REE-nə) *n.* mooring facility for yachts and pleasure boats

**mar·i·nade** (mar-ə-NAYD) *n.* seasoned, flavored liquid used to soak fish, meat *etc.* before cooking —**mar'i·nate** *vt.* (-nat·ed, -nat·ing)

**ma·rine** (mə-REEN) *adj.* of the sea or shipping; used at, found in sea —*n.* shipping, fleet; soldier trained for land or sea combat —**mar'i·ner** *n.* sailor

**mar·i·on·ette** (mar-ee-ə-NET) *n.* puppet worked with strings

**mar·i·tal** (MAR-i-tl) *adj.* relating to marriage

**mar·i·time** (MAR-i-tīm) *adj.* connected with seafaring; naval; bordering on the sea

**mar·jo·ram** (MAHR-jər-əm) *n.* aromatic herb

**mark**[1] (mahrk) *n.* line, dot, scar *etc.*; sign, token; inscription; letter, number showing evaluation of schoolwork *etc.*; indication; target —*vt.* make a mark on; be distinguishing mark of; indicate; notice; watch; assess, *eg* examination paper —*vi.* take notice —**mark'er** *n.* one who, that which marks; counter used at card playing *etc.*; *sl.* an IOU —**marks'man** *n.* skilled shot

**mark**[2] *n.* German monetary unit

**mar·ket** (MAHR-kit) *n.* assembly, place for buying and selling; demand for goods; center for trade —*vt.* offer or produce for sale —**mar'ket·a·ble** *adj.*

**mar·ma·lade** (MAHR-mə-layd) *n.* preserve usually made of oranges, lemons *etc.*

**mar·mo·re·al** (mahr-MOR-ee-əl) *adj.* of or like marble

**ma·roon**[1] (mə-ROON) *n.* brownish-red; firework —*adj.* of the color

**ma·roon**[2] *vt.* leave (person) on deserted island or coast; isolate, cut off by any means

**mar·quee** (mahr-KEE) *n.* rooflike

shelter with open sides; rooflike projection above theater *etc.* displaying name of play *etc.* being performed

**mar·quis** (MAHR-kwis) *n.* nobleman of rank below duke

**mar·row** (MAR-oh) *n.* fatty substance inside bones; vital part

**mar·ry** (MAR-ee) *v.* (-ried, -ry·ing) join as husband and wife; unite closely —**mar·riage** (MAR-ij) *n.* state of being married; wedding —**mar'riage·a·ble** *adj.*

**Mars** (mahrz) *n.* Roman god of war; planet nearest but one to Earth —**Mar·tian** (MAHR-shon) *n.* supposed inhabitant of Mars —*adj.* of Mars

**marsh** (mahrsh) *n.* low-lying wet land —**marsh'y** *adj.* (marsh·i·er, marsh·i·est) —**marsh'mal·low** *n.* spongy candy orig. made from root of marsh mallow, shrubby plant growing near marshes

**mar·shal** (MAHR-shol) *n.* high officer of state; law enforcement officer —*vt.* (-shaled, -shal·ing) arrange in due order; conduct with ceremony —**field marshal** in some nations, military officer of the highest rank

**mar·su·pi·al** (mahr-SOO-pee-ol) *n.* animal that carries its young in pouch, *eg* kangaroo —*adj.*

**mar·ten** (MAHR-tn) *n.* weasel-like animal; its fur

**mar·tial** (MAHR-shol) *adj.* relating to war; warlike, brave —**court martial** *see* COURT —**martial law** law enforced by military authorities in times of danger or emergency

**mar'tin** *n.* species of swallow

**mar·ti·net** (mahr-tn-ET) *n.* strict disciplinarian

**mar·ti·ni** (mahr-TEE-nee) *n.* (*pl.* -nis) cocktail containing gin and vermouth

**mar·tyr** (MAHR-tor) *n.* one put to death for not renouncing beliefs; one who suffers in some cause; one in constant suffering —*vt.* make martyr of —**mar'tyr·dom** (-dom) *n.*

**mar·vel** (MAHR-vol) *vi.* (-veled, -vel·ing) wonder —*n.* wonderful thing —**mar'vel·ous** *adj.* amazing; wonderful

**mar·zi·pan** (MAHR-zo-pan) *n.* paste of almonds, sugar *etc.* used in candies, cakes *etc.*

**mas·car·a** (ma-SKAR-o) *n.* cosmetic for darkening eyelashes and eyebrows

**mas·cot** (MAS-kot) *n.* animal, person or thing supposed to bring luck

**mas·cu·line** (MAS-kyo-lin) *adj.* relating to males; manly; of the grammatical gender to which names of males belong

**mash** *n.* grain, meal mixed with warm water; warm food for horses *etc.* —*vt.* make into a mash; crush into soft mass or pulp

**mask** *n.* covering for face; *Surgery* covering for nose and mouth; disguise, pretense —*vt.* cover with mask; hide, disguise

**mas·och·ism** (MAS-o-kiz-om) *n.* abnormal condition in which pleasure (*esp.* sexual) is derived from pain, humiliation *etc.* —**mas'och·ist** *n.* —**mas·och·is'tic** *adj.*

**ma·son** (MAY-son) *n.* worker in stone; (M-) Freemason —**Ma·son'ic** *adj.* of Freemasonry —**ma'son·ry** *n.* stonework; (M-) Freemasonry

**masque** (mask) *n. Hist.* form of theatrical performance —**mas·quer·ade'** *n.* masked ball —*vi.* (-ad·ed, -ad·ing) appear in disguise

**Mass** *n.* service of the Eucharist

**mass** *n.* quantity of matter; dense

collection of this; large quantity or number —v. form into a mass —mas'sive adj. large and heavy —mass-pro-duce' vt. (-duced, -duc-ing) produce standardized articles in large quantities —mass production —the masses the common people

mas-sa-cre (MAS-ə-kər) n. indiscriminate, large-scale killing, esp. of unresisting people —vt. (-cred, -cring) kill indiscriminately

mas-sage (mə-SAHZH) n. rubbing and kneading of muscles etc. as curative treatment —vt. (-saged, -sag-ing) apply this treatment to —mas'seur (-SUR) n. one who practices massage (-seuse fem. pr. -SOOS)

mast n. pole for supporting ship's sails; tall upright support for aerial etc.

mas-tec-to-my (ma-STEK-tə-mee) n. (pl. -mies) surgical removal of a breast

mas-ter (MAS-tər) n. one in control; employer; head of household; owner; document etc. from which copies are made; captain of merchant ship; expert; great artist; teacher —vt. overcome; acquire knowledge of or skill in —mas'ter-ful adj. imperious, domineering —mas'ter-ly adj. showing great competence —mas'ter-y n. full understanding (of); expertise; authority; victory —master key one that opens many different locks —mas'ter-mind vt. plan, direct —n. —mas'ter-piece n. outstanding work

mas-tic (MAS-tik) n. gum obtained from certain trees; pasty substance

mas-ti-cate (MAS-ti-kayt) vt. (-cat-ed, -cat-ing) chew —mas-ti-ca'tion n.

mas'tiff n. large dog

mas'toid adj. nipple-shaped —n. prominence on bone behind human ear —mas-toid-i'tis n. inflammation of this area

mas-tur-bate (MAS-tər-bayt) v. (-bat-ed, -bat-ing) stimulate (one's own) genital organs —mas-tur-ba'tion n.

mat[1] n. small rug; piece of fabric to protect another surface or to wipe feet on etc.; thick tangled mass —v. (mat-ted, mat-ting) form into such mass —go to the mat struggle unyieldingly

mat[2] see MATTE

mat-a-dor (MAT-ə-dor) n. bullfighter who slays bull in bullfights

match[1] (mach) n. contest, game; equal; person, thing exactly corresponding to another; marriage; person regarded as eligible for marriage —vt. get something corresponding to (color, pattern etc.); oppose, put in competition (with); arrange marriage for; join (in marriage) —vi. correspond —match'less adj. unequaled —match'mak-er n. one who schemes to bring about a marriage

match[2] n. small stick with head that ignites when rubbed; fuse —match'box n.

mate[1] (mayt) n. husband, wife; one of pair; officer in merchant ship —v. (mat-ed, mat-ing) marry; pair

mate[2] n./vt. Chess (mat-ed, mat-ing) checkmate

ma-te-ri-al (mə-TEER-ee-əl) n. substance from which thing is made; cloth, fabric —adj. of matter or body; affecting physical well-being; unspiritual; important, essential —ma-te'ri-al-ism n. excessive interest in, desire for money and possessions; doctrine that nothing but matter exists, denying independent existence of spirit —ma·te·ri·al·is'·tic adj. —ma·te'ri·al·ize v. (-ized, -iz·ing) —vi. come into existence or view —vt. make material —ma·te'ri·al·ly adv. appreciably

ma·ter·nal (mə·TUR-nl) adj. motherly; of a mother; related through mother —ma·ter'ni·ty n. motherhood

math·e·mat·ics (math-ə-MAT-iks) n. (with sing. v.) science of numbers, quantities and shapes —math·e·mat'i·cal adj. —math·e·ma·ti'cian (-TI-shən) n.

mat·i·née (mat-n-AY) n. afternoon performance in theater

ma·tri·arch (MAY-tree-ahrk) n. mother as head and ruler of family —ma'tri·ar·chy n. (pl. -chies) society with government by women and descent reckoned in female line

mat·ri·cide (MA-tri-sïd) n. the crime of killing one's mother; one who does this

ma·tric·u·late (mə·TRIK-yə-layt) v. (-lat·ed, -lat·ing) enroll, be enrolled as degree candidate in a college or university —ma·tric·u·la'tion n.

mat·ri·mo·ny (MA-trə-moh-nee) n. marriage —mat·ri·mo'ni·al adj.

ma·trix (MAY-triks) n. (pl. -tri·ces pr. -tri·seez) substance, situation in which something originates, takes form, or is enclosed; mold for casting; Math. rectangular array of elements set out in rows and columns

ma·tron (MAY-trən) n. married woman esp. of established social position; woman who superintends domestic arrangements of public institution, boarding school etc.; woman guard in prison etc. —ma'tron·ly adj. sedate

**Matt.** Matthew

matte (mat) adj. of photographic print, dull, lusterless, not shiny

mat·ter (MAT-ər) n. substance of which thing is made; physical or bodily substance; affair, business; cause of trouble; substance of book etc. —vi. be of importance, signify

mat·tock (MAT-ək) n. tool like pick with ends of blades flattened for cutting, hoeing

mat·tress (MA-tris) n. stuffed flat case, often with springs, or foam rubber pad, used as part of bed —air mattress inflatable mattress usu. of rubbery material

ma·ture (mə·CHUUR) adj. (-tur·er, -tur·est) ripe, completely developed; grown-up —v. (-tured, -tur·ing) bring, come to maturity —vi. (of bond etc.) come due —mat·u·ra'tion n. process of maturing —ma·tu'ri·ty n. full development

maud·lin (MAWD-lin) adj. weakly or tearfully sentimental

maul (mawl) vt. handle roughly; beat or bruise —n. heavy wooden hammer

maulstick n. see MAHLSTICK

maun·der (MAWN-dər) vi. talk, act aimlessly, dreamily

mau·so·le·um (maw-sə-LEE-əm) n. stately building as a tomb

mauve (mohv) adj./n. (of) pale purple color

mav·er·ick (MAV-ər-ik) n. unbranded steer, strayed cow; independent, unorthodox person

maw n. stomach, crop

mawk·ish (MAW-kish) adj. weakly sentimental, maudlin; sickening

max·im (MAK-sim) n. general truth, proverb; rule of conduct, principle

max·i·mum (MAK-sə-məm) n. greatest size or number; highest

point —*adj.* greatest —**max′i·m·ize** *vt.* (-mized, ·miz·ing)

**may** *v. aux.* (might *pt.*) expresses possibility, permission, opportunity *etc.* —**may′be** *adv.* perhaps; possibly

**May′day** *n.* international radio-telephone distress signal

**may·fly** (MAY-flī) *n.* short-lived flying insect, found near water —**may′pole** *n.* pole set up for dancing around on May Day, first day of May

**may′hem** *n.* in law, depriving person by violence of limb, member or organ, or causing mutilation of body; any violent destruction; confusion

**may·on·naise** (may-ɔ-NAYZ) *n.* creamy sauce of egg yolks *etc.*, *esp.* for salads

**may·or** (MAY-ɔr) *n.* head of municipality —**may′or·al** *adj.* —**may′or·al·ty** (-ɔl-tee) *n.* (time of) office of mayor

**maze** (mayz) *n.* labyrinth; network of paths, lines; state of confusion

**ma·zur·ka** (mɔ-ZUR-kɔ) *n.* lively Polish dance like polka; music for it

**me** (mee) *pron.* objective case singular of first personal pronoun I

**me·a cul·pa** (ME-ah KUUL-pah) *Lat.* my fault

**mead·ow** (MED-oh) *n.* tract of grassland

**mea·ger** (MEE-gɔr) *adj.* lean, thin, scanty, insufficient

**meal¹** (meel) *n.* occasion when food is served and eaten; the food

**meal²** *n.* grain ground to powder —**meal′y** *adj.* (meal·i·er, meal·i·est) —**meal′y-mouthed** (-mow*th*d) *adj.* euphemistic, insincere in what one says

**mean¹** (meen) *v.* (meant *pr. ment, mean·ing*) intend; signify;

have a meaning; have the intention of behaving —**mean′ing** *n.* sense, significance —*adj.* expressive —**mean′ing·ful** (-fɔl) *adj.* of great meaning or significance —**mean′ing·less** *adj.*

**mean²** *adj.* (-er, -est) ungenerous, petty; miserly, niggardly; unpleasant; callous; shabby; ashamed —**mean′ness** *n.*

**mean³** *n.* thing that is intermediate; middle point —*pl.* that by which thing is done; money; resources —*adj.* intermediate in time, quality *etc.*; average —**means** test inquiry into person's means to decide eligibility for pension, grant *etc.* —**mean′time, -while** *adv./n.* (during) time between one happening and another —**by all means** certainly —**by no means** not at all

**me·an·der** (mee-AN-dɔr) *vi.* flow windingly; wander aimlessly

**mea·sles** (MEE-zɔlz) *n.* infectious disease producing rash of red spots —**mea′sly** *adj. inf.* (-sli·er, -sli·est) poor, wretched, stingy; of measles

**meas·ure** (MEZH-ɔr) *n.* size, quantity; vessel, rod, line *etc.* for ascertaining size or quantity; unit of size or quantity; course, plan of action; law; poetical rhythm; musical time; *Poet.* tune; *obs.* dance —*vt.* (-ured, ur·ing) ascertain size, quantity of; be (so much) in size or quantity; indicate measurement of; estimate; bring into competition (against) —**meas′ur·a·ble** *adj.* —**meas′ured** *adj.* determined by measure; steady; rhythmical; carefully considered —**meas′ure·ment** *n.* measuring; size —*pl.* dimensions

**meat** (meet) *n.* animal flesh as food; food —**meat′y** *adj.* (meat·i·er, meat·i·est) (tasting) of, like meat; brawny; full of import or interest

**Mec·ca** (MEK-ə) *n.* holy city of Islam; (also **mecca**) place that attracts visitors

**me·chan·ic** (mə-KAN-ik) *n.* one employed in working with machinery; skilled worker —*pl.* scientific theory of motion —**me·chan'i·cal** *adj.* concerned with machines or operation of them; worked, produced (as though) by machine; acting without thought —**me·chan'i·cal·ly** *adv.*

**mech·an·ism** (MEK-ə-niz-əm) *n.* structure of machine; piece of machinery —**mech'a·nize** *vt.* (-nized, -niz·ing) equip with machinery; make mechanical, automatic; *Mil.* equip with armored vehicles

**med·al** (MED-l) *n.* piece of metal with inscription *etc.* used as reward or memento —**me·dal'lion** (mə-DAL-yən) *n.* large medal; various things like this in decorative work —**med'al·ist** *n.* winner of a medal; maker of medals

**med·dle** (MED-l) *vi.* (-dled, -dling) interfere, busy oneself with unnecessarily —**med'dle·some** (-səm) *adj.*

**me·di·a** (MEE-dee-ə) *n., pl.* of ME-DIUM, used *esp.* of the mass media, radio, TV *etc.* —**media event** event staged for or exploited by mass media

**mediaeval** *see* MEDIEVAL

**me·di·al** (MEE-dee-əl) *adj.* in the middle; pert. to a mean or average —**me'di·an** *adj./n.* middle (point or line)

**me·di·ate** (MEE-dee-ayt) *v.* (-at·ed, -at·ing) —*vi.* intervene to reconcile —*vt.* bring about by mediation —*adj.* depending on mediation —**me·di·a'tion** *n.* intervention on behalf of another; act of going between

**med·i·cine** (MED-i-sin) *n.* drug or remedy for treating disease; science of preventing, diagnosing, alleviating, or curing disease —**med'i·cal** (-kəl) *adj.* —**me·dic'a·ment** *n.* remedy —**med'i·cate** (-kayt) *vt.* (-cat·ed, -cat·ing) treat, impregnate with medicinal substances —**med·i·ca'tion** *n.* —**me·dic'i·nal** (-DIS-ə-nəl) *adj.* curative

**me·di·e·val** (mee-dee-EE-vəl) *adj.* of Middle Ages —**me·di·e'val·ist** *n.* student of the Middle Ages

**me·di·o·cre** (mee-dee-OH-kər) *adj.* neither bad nor good, ordinary, middling; second-rate —**me·di·oc'ri·ty** (-OK-rə-tee) *n.*

**med·i·tate** (MED-i-tayt) *v.* (-tat·ed, -tat·ing) —*vi.* be occupied in thought; reflect deeply on spiritual matters; engage in transcendental meditation —*vt.* think about; plan —**med·i·ta'tion** (-TAY-shən) *n.* thought; absorption in thought; religious contemplation —**med'i·ta·tive** *adj.* thoughtful; reflective

**me·di·um** (MEE-dee-əm) *adj.* between two qualities, degrees *etc.*, average —*n.* (*pl.* -di·a, -di·ums) middle quality, degree; intermediate substance conveying force; means, agency of communicating news *etc.* to public, as radio, newspapers *etc.*; person through whom communication can supposedly be held with spirit world; surroundings; environment

**med·ley** (MED-lee) *n.* (*pl.* -leys) miscellaneous mixture

**Me·du·sa** (mə-DOO-sə) *n. Myth.* (*pl.* -sas) Gorgon whose head turned beholders into stone

**meek** *adj.* (-er, -est) submissive, humble —**meek'ly** *adv.* —**meek'ness** *n.*

**meer·schaum** (MEER-shəm) *n.*

white substance like clay; tobacco pipe bowl of this

**meet** vt. (met, meet·ing) come face to face with, encounter; satisfy; pay; converge at specified point; assemble; come into contact —n. meeting, esp. for sports —**meeting** n. assembly; encounter

**meg·a·bit** (MEG-ə-bit) n. Computers approximately one million bits; $2^{20}$ bits

**meg·a·lith** (MEG-ə-lith) n. great stone —**meg·a·lith'ic** adj.

**meg·a·lo·ma'ni·a** (meg-ə-loh-MAY-nee-ə) n. desire for, delusions of grandeur, power etc.

**meg·a·ton** (MEG-ə-tun) n. one million tons; explosive power equal to that of million tons of TNT

**meg'ohm** n. Electricity one million ohms

**mel·an·chol·y** (MEL-ən-kol-ee) n. sadness, dejection, gloom —adj. gloomy, dejected —**mel·an·cho'li·a** (-KOH-lee-ə) n. mental disease accompanied by depression

**mé·lange** (may-LAHNZH) n. mixture

**mel·a·nin** (MEL-ə-nin) n. dark pigment found in hair, skin etc. of man

**me·lee** (MAY-lay) n. confused fight among several people; confusion; turmoil

**mel·io·rate** (MEEL-yə-rayt) v. (-rat·ed, -rat·ing) improve —**mel·io·ra'tion** n. —**mel'io·rism** n. doctrine that the world can be improved by human effort

**mel·lif·lu·ous** (mə-LIF-loo-əs) adj. (of sound, voice) smooth, sweet

**mel·low** (MEL-oh) adj. (-er, -est) ripe; softened by age, experience; soft, not harsh; genial, gay —v. make, become mellow

**mel·o·dra·ma** (MEL-ə-dram-ə) n.

play full of sensational and startling situations, often highly emotional; overly dramatic behavior, emotion —**mel·o·dra·mat'ic** (-drə-MAT-ik) adj.

**mel·o·dy** (MEL-ə-dee) n. (pl. -dies) series of musical notes that make tune; sweet sound —**me·lo·di·ous** (mə-LOH-dee-əs) adj. pleasing to the ear; tuneful

**mel·on** (MEL-ən) n. large, fleshy, juicy fruit

**melt** v. (melt·ed, melt·ed or molten, melt·ing) (cause to) become liquid by heat; dissolve; soften; waste away; blend (into); disappear —**melting** adj. softening; languishing; tender —**melt'down** n. in nuclear reactor, melting of fuel rods, with possible release of radiation

**mem·ber** (MEM-bər) n. any of individuals making up body or society; limb; any part of complex whole

**mem·brane** (MEM-brayn) n. thin flexible tissue in plant or animal body

**me·men·to** (mə-MEN-toh) n. (pl. -tos, -toes) thing serving to remind, souvenir

**mem·oir** (MEM-wahr) n. autobiography, personal history, biography; record of events

**mem·o·ry** (MEM-ə-ree) n. (pl. -ries) faculty of recollecting, recalling to mind; recollection; thing remembered; length of time one can remember; commemoration; part or faculty of computer that stores information —**me·mo'ri·al** adj. of, preserving memory —n. thing, esp. a monument, that serves to keep in memory —**mem'or·a·ble** adj. worthy of remembrance, noteworthy —**mem·o·ran'dum** n. (pl. -dums, -da) note to help the memory etc.; informal letter;

note of contract —me·mo'ri·al·ize vt. (-ized, -iz·ing) commemorate —mem'o·rize vt. (-ized, -iz·ing) commit to memory

men·ace (MEN-is) n. threat —vt. (-aced, -ac·ing) threaten, endanger

mé·nage (may-NAHZH) n. persons of a household —ménage à trois (ah TWAH) arrangement in which three persons, eg two men and one woman, share sexual relations while occupying same household

me·nag·er·ie (mə-NAJ-ə-ree) n. exhibition, collection of wild animals

mend vt. repair, patch; reform, correct, put right —vi. improve, esp. in health —n. repaired breakage, hole —on the mend regaining health

men·da·cious (men-DAY-shəs) adj. untruthful —men·dac'i·ty (-DAS'i-tee) n. (tendency to) untruthfulness

men·di·cant (MEN-di-kənt) adj. begging —n. beggar —men'di·can·cy n. begging

me·ni·al (MEE-nee-əl) adj. of work requiring little skill; of household duties or servants; servile —n. servant; servile person

men·in·gi·tis (men-in-JI-tis) n. inflammation of the membranes of the brain

me·nis·cus (mə-NIS-kəs) n. curved surface of liquid; curved lens

men·o·pause (MEN-ə-pawz) n. final cessation of menstruation

men·stru·a·tion (men-stroo-AY-shən) n. approximately monthly discharge of blood and cellular debris from womb of nonpregnant woman —men'stru·al adj. —men'stru·ate vi. (-at·ed, -at·ing)

men·su·ra·tion (men-shə-RAY-shən) n. measuring, esp. of areas

men·tal (MEN-təl) adj. of, done by the mind; inf. slightly mad —men·tal'i·ty n. state or quality of mind

men·thol (MEN-thawl) n. organic compound found in peppermint, used medicinally

men·tion (MEN-shən) vt. refer to briefly, speak of —n. acknowledgment; reference to or remark about (person or thing) —men'tion·a·ble adj. fit or suitable to be mentioned

men'tor n. wise, trusted adviser, guide, teacher

men·u (MEN-yoo) n. list of dishes to be served, or from which to order; Computers list of options available to user

mer·can·tile (MUR-kən-teel) adj. of, engaged in trade, commerce

mer·ce·nar·y (MUR-sə-ner-ee) adj. influenced by greed; working merely for reward —n. (-nar·ies) hired soldier

mer·chant (MUR-chənt) n. one engaged in trade; storekeeper —mer'chan·dise n. merchant's wares —mer'chant·man (-mən) n. trading ship —merchant navy ships engaged in a nation's commerce

mer·cu·ry (MUR-kyə-ree) n. silvery metal, liquid at ordinary temperature, quicksilver; (M-) Roman god of eloquence, messenger of the gods etc.; planet nearest to sun —mer·cu'ri·al (-KYOO-ree-əl) adj. relating to, containing mercury; lively, changeable

mer·cy (MUR-see) n. (pl. -cies) refraining from infliction of suffering by one who has right, power to inflict it, compassion —mer'ci·ful (-fəl) adj. —mer'ci·less (-lis) adj.

**mere** (meer) *adj.* (**mer·est** *sup.*) only; no more than; nothing but —**mere'ly** *adv.*

**mer·e·tri·cious** (mer-i-TRISH-əs) *adj.* superficially or garishly attractive; insincere

**merge** (murj) *v.* (**merged, merg·ing**) (cause to) lose identity or be absorbed —**mer'ger** *n.* combination of business firms into one; absorption into something greater

**me·rid·i·an** (mə-RID-ee-ən) *n.* circle of Earth passing through poles; imaginary circle in sky passing through celestial poles; highest point reached by star *etc.*; period of greatest splendor —*adj.* of meridian; at peak of something

**me·ringue** (mə-RANG) *n.* baked mixture of white of eggs and sugar; cake of this

**mer·it** *n.* excellence, worth; quality of deserving reward —*pl.* excellence —*vt.* deserve —**mer·i·to'ri·ous** *adj.* deserving praise

**mer·maid** (MUR-mayd) *n.* imaginary sea creature with upper part of woman and lower part of fish

**mer·ry** (MER-ee) *adj.* (**-ri·er, -ri·est**) joyous, cheerful —**mer'ri·ly** *adv.* —**mer'ri·ment** *n.*

**mesh** *n.* (one of the open spaces of, or wires *etc.* forming) network, net —*v.* entangle, become entangled; (of gears) engage —*vi.* coordinate (with)

**mes·mer·ism** (MEZ-mə-riz-əm) *n.* former term for HYPNOTISM —**mes'mer·ize** (-ized, -iz·ing) *vt.* hypnotize; fascinate; hold spellbound

**me·son** (MEE-zon) *n.* elementary atomic particle

**mess** *n.* untidy confusion; trouble, difficulty; place where military personnel group regularly eat together —*vi.* make mess; putter (about); *Mil.* eat in a mess —**mess up** make dirty; botch; spoil —**mess'y** *adj.* (**mess·i·er, mess·i·est**)

**mes·sage** (MES-ij) *n.* communication sent; meaning, moral —**mes'sen·ger** *n.* bearer of message

**Mes·si·ah** (mi-SI-ə) *n.* Jews' promised deliverer; Christ —**mes·si·an'ic** (mes-ee-AN-ik) *adj.*

**Messrs.** (MES-ərz) *pl. of* Mr.

**met** *pt./pp. of* MEET

**meta-** (*comb. form*) change, as in *metamorphose, metathesis etc.*

**me·tab·o·lism** (mə-TAB-ə-liz-əm) *n.* chemical process of living body —**met·a·bol'ic** *adj.* —**me·tab'o·lize** *vt.* (**-lized, -liz·ing**)

**met·al** (MET-l) *n.* mineral substance, opaque, fusible and malleable, capable of conducting heat and electricity; object made of metal —**me·tal'lic** *adj.* —**met'al·lur·gist** *n.* —**met'al·lur·gy** *n.* scientific study of extracting, refining metals, and their structure and properties

**met·a·mor·pho·sis** (met-ə-MOR-fə-sis) *n.* (*pl.* **-ses**) change of shape, character *etc.*; —**met·a·mor'phic** *adj.* (*esp.* of rocks) changed in texture, structure by heat, pressure *etc.* —**met·a·mor'phose** (-fohz) *vt.* (**-phosed, -phos·ing**) transform

**met·a·phor** (MET-ə-for) *n.* figure of speech in which term is transferred to something it does not literally apply to; instance of this —**met·a·phor'i·cal** *adj.* figurative

**met·a·phys·ics** (met-ə-FIZ-iks) *n.* (*with sing. v.*) branch of philosophy concerned with being and knowing

**me·tath·e·sis** (mə-TATH-ə-sis) *n.* (*pl.* **-ses** *pr.* **-seez**) transposition, *esp.* of letters in word, *eg* Old English *bridd* gives modern *bird*

**mete** (meet) *vt.* (-**met**-ed, **met**-ing) measure —**mete** out distribute; allot as punishment

**me·te·or** (MEE-tee-ər) *n.* small, fast-moving celestial body, visible as streak of incandescence if it enters Earth's atmosphere —**me·te·or'ic** *adj.* of, like meteor; brilliant but short-lived —**me'·te·or·ite** *n.* fallen meteor

**me·te·o·rol·o·gy** (mee-tee-ə-ROL-ə-jee) *n.* study of Earth's atmosphere, esp. for weather forecasting

**me·ter**[1] (MEE-tər) *n.* unit of length in decimal system; SI unit of length; rhythm of poem —**met'ric** *adj.* of system of weights and measures in which meter is a unit —**met'ri·cal** *adj.* of measurement of poetic meter

**meter**[2] *n.* that which measures; instrument for recording consumption of gas, electricity *etc.*

**meth·ane** (METH-ayn) *n.* inflammable gas, compound of carbon and hydrogen

**meth·od** (METH-əd) *n.* way, manner; technique; orderliness, system —**me·thod'i·cal** *adj.* orderly —**meth·od·ol'o·gy** *n.* (*pl.* -**gies**) particular method or procedure

**Meth·od·ist** (METH-ə-dist) *n.* member of any of the churches originated by Wesley and his followers —*adj.* —**Meth'od·ism** *n.*

**me·tic·u·lous** (mə-TIK-yə-ləs) *adj.* (over)particular about details

**mé·tier** (MAY-tyay) *n.* profession, vocation; one's forte

**me·ton·y·my** (mi-TON-ə-mee) *n.* figure of speech in which thing is replaced by another associated with it, *eg* "the Oval Office" for "the president"

**met·ro·nome** (ME-trə-nohm) *n.* instrument that marks musical time by means of ticking pendulum

**me·trop·o·lis** (mi-TROP-ə-lis) *n.* (*pl.* -**lis·es**) chief city of a country, region —**met·ro·pol'i·tan** *adj.* of metropolis —*n.* bishop with authority over other bishops of an ecclesiastical province

**met·tle** (MET-l) *n.* courage, spirit —**met'tle·some** (-səm) *adj.* high-spirited

**mew** (myoo) *n.* cry of cat, gull —*vi.* utter this cry

**mez·za·nine** (MEZ-ə-neen) *n.* in a theater, lowest balcony or forward part of balcony; in a building, low story between two other stories, *esp.* between first and second stories

**mez·zo·so·pran·o** (MET-soh-sə-PRAN-oh) *n.* (*pl.* -**pran·os**) voice, singer between soprano and contralto

**Mg** *Chem.* magnesium

**mi** (mee) *n.* third sol-fa note

**mi·as·ma** (mi-AZ-mə) *n.* (*pl.* -**mas**) unwholesome or foreboding atmosphere

**mi·ca** (MĪ-kə) *n.* mineral found as glittering scales, plates

**mi·crobe** (MĪ-krohb) *n.* minute organism; disease germ —**mi·cro'bi·al** *adj.*

**mi·cro·chip** (MĪ-kroh-chip) *n.* small wafer of silicon *etc.* containing electronic circuits, chip

**mi·cro·com·put·er** (MĪ-kroh-kəm-pyoo-tər) *n.* computer having a central processing unit contained in one or more silicon chips

**mi·cro·cosm** (MĪ-krə-koz-əm) *n.* miniature representation, model *etc.* of some larger system; human beings, society as epitome of universe

**mi·cro·fiche** (MĪ-krə-feesh) *n.* microfilm in sheet form

**mi·cro·film** (MĪ-krə-film) *n.* miniaturized recording of manuscript, book on roll of film

**mi·cro·groove** (MĪ-kroh-groov) *n.* narrow groove of long-playing phonograph record —*adj.*

**mi·crom·e·ter** (mī-KROM-i-tər) *n.* instrument for measuring very small distances or angles

**mi·cron** (MĪ-kron) *n.* unit of length, one millionth of a meter

**mi·cro·or·gan·ism** (mī-kroh-OR-gə·niz·əm) *n.* organism of microscopic size

**mi·cro·phone** (MĪ-krə-fohn) *n.* instrument for amplifying, transmitting sounds

**mi·cro·proc·es·sor** (MĪ-kroh-pros-es-ər) *n.* integrated circuit acting as central processing unit in small computer

**mi·cro·scope** (MĪ-krə-skohp) *n.* instrument by which very small body is magnified and made visible —**mi·cro·scop·ic** (-SKOP-ik) *adj.* of microscope; very small —**mi·cros·co·py** (-KROS-kə-pee) *n.* use of microscope

**mi·cro·wave** (MĪ-kroh-wayv) *n.* electromagnetic wave with wavelength of a few centimeters, used in radar, cooking *etc.*; microwave oven

**mid** *adj.* intermediate, in the middle of —**mid′day** *n.* noon —**mid′night** *n.* twelve o'clock at night —**mid′ship·man** (-mən) *n.* student, *eg* at US Naval Academy, training for commission as naval officer —**mid′sum′mer** *n.* middle of summer; summer solstice —**mid′way** *adj./adv.* halfway —**mid′win′ter** *n.*

**mid·dle** (MID-l) *adj.* equidistant from two extremes; medium, intermediate —*n.* middle point or part —**mid′dling** *adj.* mediocre; moderate —*adv.* —**Middle Ages** period from end of Roman Em-

pire to Renaissance, roughly A.D. 500-1350 —**middle class** social class of business, professional people *etc.*; middle economic class —**mid′dle-class** *adj.* —**mid′dle·man** *n.* business person between producer and consumer

**midge** (mij) *n.* gnat or similar insect

**midg·et** (MIJ-it) *n.* very small person or thing

**mid′riff** *n.* middle part of body

**midst** *prep.* in the middle of —*n.* middle —**in the midst of** surrounded by, among

**mid·wife** (MID-wīf) *n.* trained person who assists at childbirth —**mid·wife′ry** (-WĪF-ə-ree) *n.* art, practice of this

**mien** (meen) *n.* person's bearing, demeanor or appearance

**might**[1] (mīt) *see* MAY

**might**[2] *n.* power, strength —**might′i·ly** *adv.* strongly; powerfully —**might′y** *adj.* (might·i·er, might·i·est) of great power; strong; valiant; important —*adv. inf.* very

**mi·graine** (MĪ-grayn) *n.* severe headache, oft. with nausea and other symptoms

**mi·grate** (MĪ-grayt) *vi.* (-grat·ed, -grat·ing) move from one place to another —**mi′grant** (-grənt) *n./adj.* —**mi·gra′tion** *n.* act of passing from one place, condition to another; number migrating together —**mi′gra·to·ry** (-grə-TOR-ee) *adj.* of, capable of migration; (of animals) changing from one place to another according to season

**mild** (mīld) *adj.* (-er, -est) not strongly flavored; gentle, merciful; calm or temperate —**mild′ly** *adv.* —**mild′ness** *n.*

**mil·dew** (MIL-doo) *n.* destructive fungus on plants or things ex-

posed to damp —v. become tainted, affect with mildew

**mile** (mīl) n. measure of length,
1760 yards (1.609 km) —**mile′age**
n. distance in miles; travelling
expenses per mile; miles traveled (per gallon of gasoline)
—**mile′stone** n. stone marker
showing distance; significant
event, achievement

**mi·lieu** (mil-YUU) n. environment, condition in life

**mil·i·tar·y** (MIL-i-ter-ee) adj. of,
for, soldiers, armies or war —n.
armed services —**mil′i·tan·cy**
(-tən-see) n. —**mil′i·tant** adj. aggressive, vigorous in support of
cause; prepared, willing to fight
—**mil′i·ta·rism** (-tə-riz-əm) n. enthusiasm for military force and
methods —**mil′i·ta·rize** vt.
(-rized, -riz·ing) convert to military use —**mi·li′tia** (-LISH-ə) n.
military force of citizens serving
full time only in emergencies

**mil·i·tate** (MIL-i-tayt) vi. (-tat·ed,
-tat·ing) (esp. with against) have
strong influence, effect on

**milk** n. white fluid with which
mammals feed their young; fluid
in some plants —vt. draw milk
from —**milk′y** adj. (milk·i·er,
milk·i·est) containing, like milk;
(of liquids) opaque, clouded
—**milk′sop** n. weak, effeminate
fellow; milquetoast —**milk teeth**
first set of teeth in young mammals —**Milky Way** luminous band
of stars etc. stretching across
sky, the galaxy

**mill** n. factory; machine for grinding, pulverizing grain, paper etc.
—vt. put through mill; cut fine
grooves across edges of (eg
coins) —vi. move in confused
manner, as cattle or crowds of
people —**mill′er** n. —**mill′stone** n.
flat circular stone for grinding;

heavy emotional or mental burden

**mil·len·ni·um** (mi-LEN-ee-əm) n.
(pl. -ni·a pr. -nee-ə) period of a
thousand years during which
some claim Christ is to reign on
earth; period of a thousand years;
period of peace, happiness

**mil·let** (MIL-it) n. a cereal grass

**milli-** (comb. form) thousandth, as
in milligram n. thousandth part of
a gram —**milliliter** n. —**milli-
meter** n.

**mil·li·bar** (MIL-ə-bahr) n. unit of
atmospheric pressure

**mil·li·ner** (MIL-ə-nər) n. maker of,
dealer in women's hats, ribbons
etc. —**mil′li·ner·y** n. milliner's
goods or work

**mil·lion** (MIL-yən) n. 1000 thousands —**mil·lion·aire′** n. owner of
a million dollars etc. or more;
very rich person —**mil′lionth**
adj./n.

**mil·li·pede** (MIL-ə-peed) n. small
arthropod, like centipede, with
jointed body and many pairs of
legs

**milque·toast** (MILK-tohst) n. ineffectual person esp. one easily
dominated

**milt** n. spawn of male fish

**mime** (mīm) n. acting without the
use of words; actor who does this
—v. (mimed, mim·ing) act in
mime

**mim·ic** (MIM-ik) vt. (-icked,
-ick·ing) imitate (person, manner
etc.) esp. for satirical effect —n.
one who, or animal that does
this, or is adept at it —adj.
—**mim′ic·ry** n. (pl. -ries) mimick-
ing

**min·a·ret** (min-ə-RET) n. tall
slender tower of mosque

**mince** (mins) v. (minced, minc-
ing) —vt. cut, chop very small;
soften or moderate (words etc.)
—vi. walk, speak in affected

manner —n. something minced; mincemeat —**minc'ing** adj. affected in manner —**mince'meat** n. mixture of minced apples, currants, spices, sometimes meat etc. —**mince pie** pie containing mincemeat or mince

**mind** (mīnd) n. thinking faculties as distinguished from the body, intellectual faculties; memory, attention; intention; taste; sanity —vt. take offense at; care for; attend to; be cautious, careful about (something); be concerned, troubled about —vi. be careful; heed —**mind'ful** (fəl) adj. heedful; keeping in memory —**mind'less** (-lis) adj. stupid, careless

**mine**[1] (mīn) pron. belonging to me

**mine**[2] n. deep hole for digging out coal, metals etc.; in war, hidden deposit of explosive to blow up ship etc.; land mine; profitable source —v. (mined, min·ing) —vt. dig from mine; make mine in or under; place explosive mines in, on —vi. make, work in mine —**mi'ner** n. one who works in a mine —**mine'field** n. area of land or sea containing mines —**mine'lay·er** n. ship for laying mines —**mine'sweep·er** n. ship, helicopter for clearing away mines

**min·er·al** (MIN-ər-əl) n. naturally occurring inorganic substance, esp. as obtained by mining —adj. —**min·er·al'o·gy** n. science of minerals —**mineral water** water containing some mineral, esp. natural or artificial kinds for drinking

**min·e·stro·ne** (min-ə-STROH-nee) n. type of vegetable soup containing pasta

**min·gle** (MING-gəl) v. (-gled, -gling) mix, blend, unite, merge

**min·i** (MIN-ee) n. something small

or miniature; short skirt; small computer —adj.

**min·i·a·ture** (MIN-ee-ə-chər) n. small painted portrait; anything on small scale —adj. small-scale, minute

**min·i·bus** (MIN-ee-bus) n. small bus for about fifteen passengers

**min·im** (MIN-əm) n. unit of fluid measure, one-sixtieth of a dram; Mus. note half the length of semibreve

**min·i·mize** (MIN-ə-mīz) vt. (-mized, -miz·ing) bring to, estimate at smallest possible amount —**min'i·mal** (-məl) adj. —**min'i·mum** n. (pl. -mums) lowest size or quantity —adj. least possible

**min·ion** (MIN-yən) n. favorite; servile follower

**min·is·ter** (MIN-ə-stər) n. person in charge of government department; diplomatic representative; clergyman —vi. attend to needs of, take care of —**min·is·te'ri·al** (-STEER-ee-əl) adj. —**min·is·tra'tion** n. rendering help, esp. to sick —**min'is·try** n. (pl. -tries) office of clergyman; body of ministers forming government; act of ministering —**minister without portfolio** minister of state not in charge of specific department

**mink** (mingk) n. variety of weasel; its (brown) fur

**min·now** (MIN-oh) n. small freshwater fish

**mi·nor** (MĪ-nər) adj. lesser; under age —n. person below age of legal majority; scale in music —**mi·nor·i·ty** (mi-NOR-i-tee) n. lesser number; smaller party voting together; ethical or religious group in a minority in any country; state of being a minor

**Min·o·taur** (MIN-ə-tor) n. fabled monster, half bull, half man

**min·strel** (MIN-strəl) n. medieval singer, musician, poet —pl. performers in minstrel show —**minstrel show** formerly, an entertainment of songs and jokes provided by white performers with blackened faces

**mint¹** n. place where money is coined —vt. coin, invent

**mint²** n. aromatic plant

**min·u·et** (min-yoo-ET) n. stately dance; music for it

**mi·nus** (MĪ-nəs) prep./adj. less, with the deduction of, deprived of; lacking; negative —n. the sign of subtraction (-)

**mi·nute¹** (mī-NOOT) adj. (-nut·er, -nut·est) very small; precise —**mi·nute'ly** adv. —**mi·nu·ti·ae** (mi-NOO-shee-ee) n. pl. trifles, precise details

**min·ute²** (MIN-it) n. 60th part of hour or degree; moment; memorandum —pl. record of proceedings of meeting etc.

**minx** (mingks) n. bold, flirtatious girl

**mir·a·cle** (MIR-ə-kəl) n. supernatural event; marvel —**mi·rac'u·lous** adj. —**miracle play** drama (esp. medieval) based on sacred subject

**mi·rage** (mi-RAHZH) n. deceptive image in atmosphere, eg of lake in desert

**mire** (mīr) n. swampy ground, mud —vt. (mired, mir·ing) stick in, dirty with mud; entangle, involve

**mir·ror** (MIR-ər) n. glass or polished surface reflecting images —vt. reflect

**mirth** (murth) n. merriment, gaiety —**mirth'ful** adj.

**mis-** (prefix) wrong(ly), bad(ly), as in the list below

**mis·an·thrope** (MIS-ən-throhp) n. hater of mankind —**mis·an·throp'ic** adj.

**mis·ap·pro·pri·ate** (mis-ə-PROH-pree-ayt) vt. (-at·ed, -at·ing) put to dishonest use; embezzle

**mis·car·ry** (mis-KA-ree) vi. (-ried, -ry·ing) bring forth young prematurely; go wrong, fail —**mis·car'riage** (-KA-rij) n.

**mis·cast** v. (-cast, -cast·ing) distribute acting parts wrongly; assign to unsuitable role —adj.

**mis·cel·la·ne·ous** (mis-ə-LAY-nee-əs) adj. mixed, assorted —**mis'cel·la·ny** n. (pl. -nies) collection of assorted writings in one book; medley

**mis·chief** (MIS-chif) n. annoying behavior; inclination to tease, disturb; harm; source of harm or annoyance —**mis'chie·vous** (-chi-vəs) adj. of a child, full of pranks; disposed to mischief; having harmful effect

**mis·ci·ble** (MIS-ə-bəl) adj. capable of mixing

**mis·con·cep·tion** (mis-kən-SEP-shən) n. wrong idea, belief

**mis·cre·ant** (MIS-kree-ənt) n. wicked person, evildoer, villain

**mis·de·mean·or** (mis-di-MEE-nər) n. in law, offense less grave than a felony; minor offense

**mi·ser** (MĪ-zər) n. hoarder of

mis·behave'
mis·cal'cu·late
mis·con'duct
mis·deed'
mis·for'tune
mis·in·form'

mis·judge'
mis·man'age·ment
mis·place'
mis·print'
mis·pro·nounce'
mis·shap'en

mis·spell'
mis·spent'
mis·un·der·stand'
mis·use'

money; stingy person —**mi'ser·ly** *adj.* avaricious; niggardly

**mis·er·a·ble** (MIZ-ər-ə-bəl) *adj.* very unhappy, wretched; causing misery; worthless; squalid —**mis·er·y** *n.* (*pl.* **-er·ies**) great unhappiness; distress; poverty

**mis·fit** *n. esp.* person not suited to surroundings or work

**mis·giv·ing** *n.* (*oft. pl.*) feeling of fear, doubt *etc.*

**mis·guid·ed** (mis-GI-did) *adj.* foolish, unreasonable

**mis'hap** *n.* minor accident

**mis·lay'** *vt.* (**-laid, -lay·ing**) put in place that cannot later be remembered; place wrongly

**mis·lead** (mis-LEED) *vt.* (**-led, -lead·ing**) give false information to; lead astray —**misleading** *adj.* deceptive

**mis·no·mer** (mis-NOH-mər) *n.* wrong name or term; use of this

**mi·sog·y·ny** (mi-SOJ-ə-nee) *n.* hatred of women —**mi·sog'y·nist** *n.*

**miss** *vt.* fail to hit, reach, find, catch, or notice; be late for; omit; notice or regret absence of; avoid —*vi.* (of engine) misfire —*n.* fact, instance of missing —**mis'sing** *adj.* lost; absent

**mis·sal** (MIS-əl) *n.* book containing prayers *etc.* of the Mass

**mis·sile** (MIS-əl) *n.* that which may be thrown, shot, homed to damage, destroy —**guided missile** *see* GUIDE

**mis·sion** (MISH-ən) *n.* specific task or duty; calling in life; delegation; sending or being sent on some service; those sent —**mis'sion·ar·y** *n.* (*pl.* **-ar·ies**) one sent to a place, society to spread religion —*adj.*

**mis·sive** (MIS-iv) *n.* letter

**mist** *n.* water vapor in fine drops —**mist'y** *adj.* (**mist·i·er, mist·i·est**) full of mist; dim; obscure

**mis·take** (mi-STAYK) *n.* error,

blunder —*v.* (**-took** *pr.* **-TUUK, -tak·en, -tak·ing**) —*vt.* fail to understand; form wrong notion about; take (person or thing) for another —*vi.* be in error

**mis·ter** (MIS-tər) *n.* (*abbrev.* Mr.) title of courtesy to man

**mis·tle·toe** (MIS-əl-toh) *n.* evergreen parasitic plant with white berries that grows on trees

**mis·tress** (MIS-tris) *n.* object of man's illicit love; woman with mastery or control; woman owner; woman teacher; *obs.* title (*abbrev.* Mrs.) given to married woman

**mite** (mit) *n.* very small insect; anything very small; small contribution but all one can afford

**mi·ter** (MI-tər) *n.* bishop's headdress; joint between two pieces of wood *etc.* meeting at right angles —*vt.* join with, shape for a miter joint; put miter on

**mit·i·gate** (MIT-i-gayt) *vt.* (**-gat·ed, -gat·ing**) make less severe —**mit·i·ga'tion** *n.*

**mitt** *n.* baseball player's glove *esp.* for catcher, first baseman; *sl.* hand

**mit·ten** (MIT-n) *n.* glove with two compartments, one for thumb and one for fingers

**mix** (miks) *vt.* put together, combine, blend, mingle —*vi.* be mixed; associate —**mixed** *adj.* composed of different elements, races, sexes *etc.* —**mix'er** *n.* one who, that which mixes; informal party intended to help guests meet one another —**mix'ture** (-chər) *n.* —**mixed-up** *adj.* confused; emotionally unstable —**mix-up** *n.* confused situation; a fight

**mks units** metric system of units based on the meter, kilogram and second

**Mn** *Chem.* manganese

**mne·mon·ic** (ni-MON-ik) *adj.* helping the memory —*n.* something intended to help the memory

**Mo** *Chem.* molybdenum

**moan** (mohn) *n.* low murmur, usually of pain —*v.* utter with moan, lament

**moat** (moht) *n.* deep wide ditch *esp.* around castle —*vt.* surround with moat

**mob** *n.* disorderly crowd of people; mixed assembly —*vt.* (**mobbed, mob·bing**) attack in mob; crowd around boisterously

**mo·bile** (MOH-bəl) *adj.* capable of movement; easily moved or changed —*n.* (moh-BEEL) hanging structure of card, plastic *etc.* designed to move in air currents —**mo·bil´i·ty** *n.*

**mo·bi·lize** (MOH-bə-līz) *v.* (**-lized, -liz·ing**) (of armed services) prepare for military service —*v.t.* organize for a purpose —**mo·bi·li·za´tion** (-ZAY-shən) *n.* in war time, calling up of men and women for active service

**moc·ca·sin** (MOK-ə-sin) *n.* Amer. Indian soft shoe, usu. of deerskin

**mo·cha** (MOH-kə) *n.* type of strong, dark coffee; this flavor

**mock** (mok) *vt.* make fun of, ridicule; mimic —*vi.* scoff —*n.* act of mocking; laughingstock —*adj.* sham, imitation —**mock´er·y** *n.* (*pl.* **-er·ies**) derision; travesty —**mocking bird** N Amer. bird that imitates songs of others —**mock-up** *n.* scale model

**mode** (mohd) *n.* method, manner; prevailing fashion

**mod·el** (MOD-l) *n.* miniature representation; pattern; person or thing worthy of imitation; person employed by artist to pose, or by dress designer to display clothing —*vt.* (**-eled, -el·ing**) make model

of; mold; display (clothing) for dress designer

**mod·er·ate** (MOD-ər-it) *adj.* not going to extremes, temperate, medium —*n.* person of moderate views —*v.* (-ayt) make, become less violent or excessive; preside over meeting *etc.* —**mod´er·a·tor** *n.* mediator; president of Presbyterian body; arbitrator; person presiding over panel discussion

**mod·ern** (MOD-ərn) *adj.* of present or recent times; in, of current fashion —*n.* person living in modern times —**mod´ern·ism** *n.* (support of) modern tendencies, thoughts *etc.* —**mod·ern·i·za´tion** (-ZAY-shən) *n.* —**mod´ern·ize** (-īz) *vt.* (**-ized, -iz·ing**) bring up to date

**mod·est** (MOD-ist) *adj.* not overrating one's qualities or achievements; shy; moderate, not excessive; decorous, decent —**mod´es·ty** *n.*

**mod·i·cum** (MOD-i-kəm) *n.* small quantity

**mod·i·fy** (MOD-ə-fī) *v.* (mainly *tr.*) (**-fied, -fy·ing**) change slightly; tone down —**mod·i·fi·ca´tion** *n.* —**mod´i·fi·er** (-fī-ər) *n. esp.* word qualifying another

**mod·u·late** (MOD-jə-layt) (**-lat·ed, -lat·ing**) —*vt.* regulate; vary in tone —*vi.* change key of music —**mod·u·la´tion** *n.* modulating; *Electronics* superimposing signals onto high-frequency carrier

**mod·ule** (MOJ-ool) *n.* (detachable) unit, section, component with specific function

**mo·dus op·e·ran·di** (MOH-dəs op-ə-RAN-dee) *Lat.* method of operating, tackling task

**mo·gul** (MOH-gəl) *n.* important or powerful person; bump in ski slope

**mo·hair** (MOH-hair) *n.* fine cloth of goat hair; hair of Angora goat

**mo·hel** (MOH-əl) *n.* in Jewish tradition, person who performs rite of circumcision

**moi·e·ty** (MOI-i-tee) n. (pl. -ties) a half

**moist** adj. (-er, -est) damp, slightly wet —**moist'en** (MOI-sən) v. —**mois'ture** (-chər) n. liquid, esp. diffused in drops

**mo·lar** (MOH-lər) adj. (of teeth) for grinding —n. molar tooth

**mo·las·ses** (mə-LAS-iz) n. thick brown syrup, byproduct of process of sugar refining

**mold**[1] (mohld) n. hollow object in which metal etc. is cast; pattern for shaping; character; shape, form —vt. shape or pattern —**mold'ing** n. molded object; ornamental edging; decoration

**mold**[2] n. fungoid growth caused by dampness —**mold'y** adj. (**mold·i·er, mold·i·est**) stale, musty

**mold**[3] n. loose soil rich in organic matter —**mold'er** vi. decay into dust

**mole**[1] (mohl) n. small dark protuberant spot on the skin

**mole**[2] n. small burrowing animal; spy, informer

**mole**[3] n. SI unit of amount of substance

**mol·e·cule** (MOL-ə-kyool) n. simplest freely existing chemical unit, composed of two or more atoms; very small particle —**mo·lec'u·lar** adj. of, inherent in molecules

**mo·lest** (mə-LEST) vt. pester, interfere with so as to annoy or injure; make indecent sexual advances esp. to a child

**mol·li·fy** (MOL-ə-fi) vt. (**-fied, -fying**) calm down, placate, soften —**mol·li·fi·ca'tion** n.

**mol·lusk** (MOL-əsk) n. soft-bodied, usu. hard-shelled animal, eg snail, oyster

**molt** (mohlt) v. cast or shed fur, feathers etc. —n. molting

**molten** see MELT

**mo·lyb·de·num** (mə-LIB-də-nəm) n. silver-white metallic element

**mo·ment** (MOH-mənt) n. very short space of time; (present) point in time —**mo·men·tar'i·ly** adv. —**mo'men·tar·y** adj. lasting only a moment

**mo·men·tous** (moh-MEN-təs) adj. of great importance

**mo·men·tum** (moh-MEN-təm) n. force of a moving body; impetus gained from motion

**mon·arch** (MON-ərk) n. sovereign ruler of a country —**mo·nar'chi·cal** adj. —**mon'ar·chist** n. supporter of monarchy —**mon'arch·y** n. (pl. -chies) nation ruled by sovereign; monarch's rule

**mon·as·ter·y** (MON-ə-ster-ee) n. (pl. -ter·ies) house occupied by members of religious order —**mo·nas·tic** (mə-NAS-tik) adj. relating to monks, nuns, or monasteries —n. monk, recluse

**mon·ey** (MUN-ee) n. (pl. -eys, -ies) banknotes, coin etc., used as medium of exchange —**mon·e·ta·rism** (MON-ə-tə-riz-əm) n. theory that inflation is caused by increase in money supply —**mon'e·ta·rist** n./adj. —**mon'e·tar·y** adj. —**mon·eyed, -ied** (MUN-eed) adj. rich

**mon·gol·ism** (MONG-gə-liz-əm) n. old name for Down syndrome

**mon·goose** (MON-goos) n. (pl. -goos·es) small animal of Asia and Africa noted for killing snakes

**mon·grel** (MONG-grəl) n. animal, esp. dog, of mixed breed; hybrid —adj.

**mon·i·tor** (MON-i-tər) n. person or device that checks, controls, warns or keeps record of something; pupil assisting teacher with conduct of class; television set used in a studio for checking program being transmitted; *Computers* cathode ray tube with screen for viewing data; type of large lizard —*vt.* watch, check on —**mon'i·to·ry** (-tor-ee) *adj.* giving warning

**monk** (munk) *n.* one of a religious community of men living apart under vows —**monk'ish** *adj.*

**mon·key** (MUN-kee) *n.* (*pl.* -keys) long-tailed primate; mischievous child —*vi.* (-keyed, -key·ing) meddle, fool (with) —**monkey wrench** wrench with adjustable jaw

**mono-** (*comb. form*) single, as in monosyllabic *adj.*

**mon·o·chrome** (MON-ə-krohm) *n.* representation in one color —*adj.* of one color —**mon·o·chro·mat'ic** *adj.*

**mon·o·cle** (MON-ə-kəl) *n.* single eyeglass

**mo·noc·u·lar** (mə-NOK-yə-lər) *adj.* one-eyed

**mo·nog·a·my** (mə-NOG-ə-mee) *n.* custom of being married to one person at a time —**mo·nog'a·mous** *adj.*

**mon·o·gram** (MON-ə-gram) *n.* design of letters interwoven

**mon·o·graph** (MON-ə-graf) *n.* short scholarly book on single subject

**mon·o·lith** (MON-ə-lith) *n.* monument consisting of single standing stone —**mon·o·lith'ic** *adj.* of or like a monolith; massive, inflexible

**mon·o·logue** (MON-ə-lawg) *n.* dramatic composition with only one speaker; long speech by one person

**mon·o·ma·ni·a** (mon-ə-MAY-nee-ə) *n.* excessive preoccupation with one thing

**mo·nop·o·ly** (mə-NOP-ə-lee) *n.*

(*pl.* -lies) exclusive control of commerce, privilege *etc.* —**mo·nop'o·lize** *vt.* (-lized, -liz·ing) claim, take exclusive possession of

**mon·o·rail** (MON-ə-rayl) *n.* railway with cars running on or suspended from single rail

**mon·o·the·ism** (MON-ə-thee-iz-əm) *n.* belief in only one God

**mon·o·tone** (MON-ə-tohn) *n.* continuing on one note —**mo·not·o·nous** (mə-NOT-n-əs) *adj.* lacking in variety, dull, wearisome —**mo·not'o·ny** *n.*

**mon·soon'** *n.* seasonal wind of SE Asia; very heavy rainfall season

**mon·ster** (MON-stər) *n.* fantastic imaginary beast; misshapen animal or plant; very wicked person; huge person, animal or thing —*adj.* huge —**mon·stros'i·ty** *n.* monstrous being; deformity; distortion —**mon'strous** (-strəs) *adj.* of, like monster; unnatural; enormous; horrible

**mon·tage** (mon-TAHZH) *n.* elements of two or more pictures imposed upon a single background to give a unified effect; method of editing a film

**month** (munth) *n.* one of twelve periods into which the year is divided; period of moon's revolution around Earth —**month'ly** *adj.* happening or payable once a month —*adv.* once a month —*n.* magazine published every month

**mon·u·ment** (MON-yə-mənt) *n.* anything that commemorates, *esp.* a building or statue —**mon·u·men'tal** (-MEN-tl) *adj.* vast, lasting; of or serving as monument

**mooch** *vi. sl.* borrow without intending to repay; beg

**mood**[1] *n.* state of mind and feelings —**mood'y** *adj.* (mood·i·er, mood·i·est) gloomy, pensive; changeable in mood

mood² n. Grammar form indicating function of verb

moon n. satellite that takes lunar month to revolve around Earth; any secondary planet —vi. go about dreamily —moon'light n. —moon'shine n. inf. whiskey, esp. corn liquor, illicitly distilled; nonsense; moonlight —moon'stone n. transparent semiprecious stone

moor¹ n. tract of open uncultivated land, often hilly and overgrown with heath

moor² v. secure (ship) with chains or ropes —moor'ings n. pl. ropes etc. for mooring; something providing stability, security

moose (moos) n. N Amer. deer with large antlers

moot adj. that is open to argument, debatable; purely academic

mop n. bundle of yarn, cloth etc. on end of stick, used for cleaning; tangle (of hair etc.) —vt. (mopped, mop·ping) clean, wipe with mop or other absorbent material

mope vi. (moped, mop·ing) be gloomy, apathetic

mo·ped (MOH-ped) n. light motorized bicycle

mo·raine (mǝ-RAYN) n. accumulated mass of debris, earth, stones etc., deposited by glacier

mor·al (MOR-ǝl) adj. pert. to right and wrong conduct; of good conduct —n. practical lesson, eg of fable —pl. habits with respect to right and wrong, esp. in matters of sex —mor'al·ist n. teacher of morality —mor·al·i·ty (mǝ-RAL-ǝ-tee) n. good moral conduct; moral goodness or badness; kind of medieval drama, containing moral lesson —mor'al·ize v.

(-ized, -iz·ing) —vi. write, think about moral aspect of things —vt. interpret morally —moral victory triumph that is psychological rather than practical

mo·rale (mǝ-RAL) n. degree of confidence, hope of person or group

mo·rass (mǝ-RAS) n. marsh; mess

mor·a·to·ri·um (mor-ǝ-TOR-ee-ǝm) n. (pl. -ri·ums) act authorizing postponement of payments etc.; delay

mor'bid adj. unduly interested in death; gruesome; diseased

mor'dant (MOR-dnt) adj. biting; corrosive; scathing —n. substance that fixes dyes

more (mor) adj. greater in quantity or number —comp. of MANY and MUCH —adv. to a greater extent; in addition —pron. greater or additional amount or number —more·o'ver adv. besides, further

mor·ga·nat·ic marriage (mor-gǝ-NAT-ik) marriage of king or prince in which wife does not share husband's rank or possessions and children do not inherit from father

morgue (morg) n. mortuary; newspaper reference file or file room

mor·i·bund (MOR-ǝ-bund) adj. dying; stagnant

Mor·mon (MOR-mǝn) n. member of religious sect founded in US

morn'ing n. early part of day until noon —morning-after pill woman's contraceptive pill for use within hours after sexual intercourse —morning glory plant with trumpet-shaped flowers that close in late afternoon

mo·roc·co (mǝ-ROK-oh) n. (orig.) goatskin leather

mo·ron (MOR-on) n. mentally deficient person; fool —**mo·ron'ic** adj.

**mo·rose** (mɔ-ROHS) adj. sullen, moody

**mor·phine** (MOR-feen) n. narcotic extract of opium used to induce sleep and relieve pain

**mor·phol·o·gy** (mor-FOL-ɔ-jee) n. science of structure of organisms; form and structure of words of a language

**Morse** (mors) n. system of telegraphic signaling in which letters of alphabet are represented by combinations of dots and dashes, or short and long flashes

**mor·sel** (MOR-sɔl) n. fragment, small piece

**mor·tal** (MOR-tl) adj. subject to death; causing death —n. mortal creature —**mor·tal'i·ty** n. state of being mortal; great loss of life; death rate —**mor·tal·ly** adv. fatally; deeply, intensely

**mor·tar** (MOR-tɔr) n. mixture of lime, sand and water for holding bricks and stones together; small cannon firing over short range; vessel in which substances are pounded —**mor·tar·board** (-bord) n. square academic cap

**mort·gage** (MOR-gij) n. conveyance of property as security for debt with provision that property be reconveyed on payment within agreed time —vt. (-gaged, -gag·ing) convey by mortgage; pledge as security —**mort·ga·gee'** n. person to whom property is mortgaged —**mort'ga·gor, -ger** n. person who mortgages property

**mor·ti·fy** (MOR-tɔ-fi) v. (-fied, -fy·ing) humiliate; subdue by self-denial; (of flesh) be affected with gangrene —**mor·ti·fi·ca'tion** (-fi-KAY-shɔn) n.

**mor·tise** (MOR-tis) n. hole in piece of wood etc. to receive the tongue (tenon) and end of another piece —vt. (-tised, -tis·ing) make mortise in; fasten by mortise and tenon

**mor·tu·ar·y** (MOR-choo-er-ee) n. (pl. -ar·ies) funeral parlor —adj. of, for burial; pert. to death

**mo·sa·ic** (moh-ZAY-ik) n. picture or pattern of small bits of colored stone, glass etc.; this process of decoration

**Mo·sa·ic** (moh-ZAY-ik) adj. of Moses

**Moslem** n. see MUSLIM

**mosque** (mosk) n. Muslim temple

**mos·qui·to** (mɔ-SKEE-toh) n. (pl. -toes, -tos) any of various kinds of flying, biting insects

**moss** (maws) n. small plant growing in masses on moist surfaces —**moss'y** adj. (moss·i·er, moss·i·est) covered with moss

**most** (mohst) adj. greatest in size, number, or degree —sup. of MUCH and of MANY —n. greatest number, amount, or degree —adv. in the greatest degree; abbrev. of ALMOST —**most'ly** adv. for the most part, generally, on the whole

**mo·tel** (moh-TEL) n. roadside hotel with accommodation for motorists and their vehicles

**mo·tet** (moh-TET) n. short sacred vocal composition

**moth** (mawth) n. usu. nocturnal insect like butterfly; its grub —**moth'ball** n. small ball of camphor or naphthalene to repel moths from stored clothing etc. —vt. put in mothballs; store, postpone etc. —**moth'eat·en** adj. eaten, damaged by grub of moth; decayed, scruffy

**moth·er** (MUTH-ɔr) n. female parent; head of religious community of women —adj. natural, native, inborn —vt. act as moth-

er to —**moth'er·hood** (-huud) n.
—**moth'er·ly** adj. —**mother-in-
law** n. mother of one's wife or
husband —**mother of pearl** irides-
cent lining of certain shells

**mo·tif** (moh-TEEF) n. dominating
theme; recurring design

**mo·tion** (MOH-shən) n. process or
action or way of moving; proposal in meeting; application to
judge —vt. direct by sign —**mo'-
tion·less** (-lis) adj. still, immobile

**mo·tive** (MOH-tiv) n. that which
makes person act in particular
way; inner impulse —adj. causing
motion —**mo'ti·vate** vt. (-vat·ed,
-vat·ing) instigate; incite —**mo·ti·
va'tion** (-VAY-shən) n.

**mot·ley** (MOT-lee) adj. miscellaneous, varied; multicolored

**mo·to·cross** (MOH-toh-kraws) n.
motorcycle race over rough
course

**mo·tor** (MOH-tər) n. that which
imparts movement; machine to
supply motive power; automobile
—vi. travel by automobile —**mo'-
tor·ist** n. user of automobile
—**mo'tor·ize** vt. (-ized, -iz·ing)
equip with motor

**mot·tle** (MOT-l) vt. (-tled, -tling)
mark with blotches, variegate
—n. arrangement of blotches;
blotch on surface

**mot·to** (MOT-oh) n. (pl. -toes)
saying adopted as rule of conduct; short inscribed sentence;
word or sentence on badge or
banner

**mound** (mownd) n. heap of earth
or stones; small hill

**mount** (mownt) vi. rise; increase;
get on horseback —vt. get up on;
frame (picture); fix, set up; provide with horse —n. that on
which thing is supported or fitted; horse; hill

**moun·tain** (MOWN-tn) n. hill of
great size; surplus —**moun·tain·

eer'** n. one who lives among or
climbs mountains —**moun'tain·
ous** adj. very high, rugged

**moun·te·bank** (MOWN-tə-bangk)
n. charlatan, fake

**Moun·tie** (MOWN-tee) n. inf.
member of Royal Canadian
Mounted Police

**mourn** (morn) v. feel, show sorrow (for) —**mourn'er** n.
—**mourn'ful** (-fəl) adj. sad; dismal
—**mourn'ful·ly** adv. —**mourn'ing**
n. grieving; conventional signs of
grief for death; clothes of mourn-
er

**mouse** (mows) n. (pl. **mice** pr.
mis) small rodent —vi. catch,
hunt mice; prowl —**mous'er** n.
cat used for catching mice
—**mous'y** adj. (-mous·i·er,
mous·i·est) like mouse, esp. in
color; meek, shy

**mousse** (moos) n. sweet dessert
of flavored cream whipped and
frozen

**moustache** see MUSTACHE

**mouth** (mowth) n. opening in
head for eating, speaking etc.;
opening into anything hollow;
outfall of river; entrance to harbor etc. —vt. (mowth) declaim,
esp. in public; form (words) with
lips without speaking; take, move
in mouth —**mouth'piece** n. end of
anything placed between lips, eg
pipe; spokesman

**move** (moov) v. (moved, moving) —vt. change position of; stir
emotions of; incite; propose for
consideration —vi. change
places; change one's dwelling
etc.; take action —n. a moving;
motion toward some goal
—**mov'a·ble** adj./n. —**move'ment**
n. process, action of moving;
moving parts of machine; division of piece of music

**mow** (moh) v. (mowed, mowed
or mown, mow·ing) cut (grass

*etc.*) —**mow′er** *n.* person or machine that mows

**Mr.** mister

**Mrs.** title of married woman

**Ms.** title used instead of Miss or Mrs.

**much** *adj.* (**more, most**) existing in quantity —*n.* large amount; a great deal; important matter —*adv.* in a great degree; nearly

**mu·ci·lage** (MYOO-sə-lij) *n.* gum, glue

**muck** (muk) *n.* horse, cattle dung; unclean refuse; insulting remarks —*vt.* make dirty; (*with* out) remove muck from; *inf.* (*with* up) ruin, bungle, confuse —**muck′y** *adj.* (**muck·i·er, muck·i·est**) dirty; messy; unpleasant

**mu·cus** (MYOO-kəs) *n.* viscid fluid secreted by mucous membrane —**mu′cous** (-kəs) *adj.* resembling mucus; secreting mucus; slimy —**mucous membrane** lining of canals and cavities of the body

**mud** *n.* wet and soft earth; *inf.* slander —**mud′dy** *adj.* (**-di·er, -di·est**)

**mud·dle** (MUD-əl) *vt.* (**-dled, -dling**) (*esp. with* up) confuse; bewilder; mismanage —*n.* confusion; tangle

**mu·ez·zin** (myoo-EZ-in) *n.* crier who summons Muslims to prayer

**muff**[1] *n.* tube-shaped covering to keep the hands warm

**muff**[2] *vt.* miss, bungle, fail in

**muf·fin** *n.* cup-shaped quick bread

**muf·fle** (MUF-əl) *vt.* (**-fled, -fling**) wrap up, *esp.* to deaden sound —**muf′fler** (-lər) *n.* on motor vehicles, device for accomplishing this; scarf

**muf·ti** (MUF-tee) *n.* plain clothes as distinguished from uniform, *eg* of soldier

**mug**[1] *n.* drinking cup

**mug**[2] *n.* *sl.* face; *sl.* ruffian, criminal —*vt.* (**mugged, mug·ging**) rob violently —**mug′ger** (-ər) *n.*

**mug·gy** (MUG-ee) *adj.* (**-gi·er, -gi·est**) damp and stifling

**Mu·ham·mad, Mo·ham·med** (muu-HAM-əd) *n.* prophet and founder of Islam —**Mu·ham·mad·an** *adj./n.* Muslim

**mu·lat·to** (mə-LAT-oh) *n./adj.* (*pl.* -**oes**) (child) of one white and one black parent

**mul·ber·ry** (MUL-ber-ee) *n.* (*pl.* -**ries**) tree whose leaves are used to feed silkworms; its purplish fruit

**mulch** *n.* straw, leaves *etc.*, spread as protection for roots of plants —*vt.* protect thus

**mulct** (mulkt) *vt.* defraud; fine

**mule** (myool) *n.* animal that is cross between female horse and male donkey; hybrid; spinning machine; small locomotive; slipper —**mul′ish** *adj.* obstinate

**mull** *vt.* heat (wine) with sugar and spices; think (over), ponder

**mul·lah** (MUL-ə) *n.* Muslim theologian

**mul·lion** (MUL-yən) *n.* upright dividing bar in window

**multi-, mult-** (*comb. form*) many, as in multiracial *adj.*, multistory *adj.* Such words are omitted where the meaning can easily be found from the simple word

**mul·ti·far·i·ous** (mul-tə-FAIR-ee-əs) *adj.* of various kinds or parts

**mul·ti·ple** (MUL-tə-pəl) *adj.* having many parts —*n.* quantity that contains another an exact number of times —**mul·ti·pli·cand′** *n. Math.* number to be multiplied —**mul·ti·pli·ca′tion** (-PLI-kə) *n.* —**mul·ti·plic′i·ty** (-PLIS-ə-tee) *n.* variety, greatness in number —**mul′ti·ply** (-plī) *v.* (**-plied, -ply·ing**) (cause to) increase in number, quantity, or degree —*vt.* combine (two numbers or quantities) by multiplication; increase in number by reproduction

**mul·ti·plex** (MUL-tə-pleks) *adj.* Telecommunications capable of transmitting numerous messages over same wire or channel

**mul·ti·tude** (MUL-ti-tood) *n.* great number; great crowd; populace —**mul·ti·tu′di·nous** *adj.* very numerous

**mum** *adj.* silent —**mum's the word** keep silent

**mum·ble** (MUM-bəl) *v.* (-bled, -bling) speak indistinctly, mutter

**mum·my** (MUM-ee) *n.* (*pl.* -mies) embalmed body —**mum′mi·fy** *vt.* (-fied, -fy·ing)

**mumps** *n. pl.* infectious disease marked by swelling in the glands of the neck

**munch** *v.* chew noisily and vigorously; crunch

**mun·dane** (mun-DAYN) *adj.* ordinary, everyday; belonging to this world, earthly

**mu·nic·i·pal** (myuu-NIS-ə-pəl) *adj.* belonging to affairs of city or town —**mu·nic·i·pal′i·ty** *n.* (*pl.* -ties) city or town with local self-government; its governing body

**mu·nif·i·cent** (myoo-NIF-ə-sənt) *adj.* very generous —**mu·nif′i·cence** *n.* bounty

**mu·ni·tion** (myoo-NISH-ən) *n.* (*usu. pl.*) military stores

**mu·ral** (MYUUR-əl) *n.* painting on a wall —*adj.* of or on a wall

**mur·der** (MUR-dər) *n.* unlawful premeditated killing of human being —*vt.* kill thus —**mur′der·ous** *adj.*

**murk** *n.* thick darkness —**murk′y** *adj.* (murk·i·er, murk·i·est) gloomy

**mur·mur** (MUR-mər) *n.* low, indistinct sound —*vi.* make such a sound; complain —*vt.* utter in a low voice

**mus·cle** (MUS-əl) *n.* part of body that produces movement by contracting; system of muscles —**mus′cu·lar** (-kyə-lər) *adj.* with well-developed muscles; strong; of, like muscle —**mus′cle-bound** *adj.* with muscles stiff through overdevelopment —**muscular dystrophy** disease with wasting of muscles —**muscle in** *inf.* force one's way into

**muse** (myooz) *vi.* (mused, mus·ing) ponder; consider meditatively; be lost in thought

**Muse** (myooz) *n.* one of the nine goddesses inspiring learning and the arts

**museum** (myoo-ZEE-əm) *n.* place housing collection of natural, artistic, historical or scientific objects

**mush**[1] *n.* soft pulpy mass; cloying sentimentality —**mush′y** *adj.* (mush·i·er, mush·i·est)

**mush**[2] *vi.* travel over snow with dog team and sled —*vt.* spur on (sled) dogs —*interj.* go!

**mush′room** *n.* fungoid growth, typically with stem and cap structure, some species edible —*vi.* shoot up rapidly; expand —**mushroom cloud** large cloud resembling mushroom, *esp.* from nuclear explosion

**music** (MYOO-zik) *n.* art form using melodious and harmonious combination of notes; laws of this; composition in this art —**mu′si·cal** *adj.* of, like music; interested in, or with instinct for, music; pleasant to ear —*n.* play, motion picture in which music plays essential part —**mu·si′cian** *n.* —**mu·si·col′o·gist** (-jist) *n.* —**mu·si·col′o·gy** *n.* scientific study of music —**musical comedy** light dramatic entertainment of songs, dances *etc.*

**musk** *n.* scent obtained from

gland of **musk** deer; various plants with similar scent —**mus'ky** adj. (musk·i·er, musk·i·est) —musk ox ox of Arctic Amer. —**musk'rat** n. N Amer. rodent found near water; its fur

**mus·ket** (MUS-kit) n. Hist. infantryman's gun —**musket·eer'** n.

**Mus·lim** (MUZ-lim) n. follower of religion of Islam —adj. of religion, culture etc. of Islam

**mus·lin** (MUZ-lin) n. fine cotton fabric

**mus·sel** (MUS-əl) n. bivalve shellfish

**must**[1] v. aux. be obliged to, or certain to —n. something one must do

**must**[2] n. newly-pressed grape juice; unfermented wine

**mus·tache, mous·tache** (MUStash) n. hair on the upper lip

**mus'tang** n. wild horse

**mus·tard** (MUS-tərd) n. powder made from the seeds of a plant, used in paste as a condiment; the plant —**mustard gas** poisonous gas causing blistering, lung damage etc.

**mus·ter** (MUS-tər) v. assemble —n. assembly, esp. for exercise, inspection

**mus·ty** (MUS-tee) adj. (-ti·er, -ti·est) moldy, stale —**must, must'i·ness** n.

**mu·tate** (MYOO-tayt) v. (-tat·ed, -tat·ing) (cause to) undergo mutation —**mu'ta·ble** (-tə-bəl) adj. liable to change —**mu'tant** (-tənt) n. mutated animal, plant etc. —**mu·ta'tion** (-TAY-shən) n. change, esp. genetic change causing divergence from kind or racial type

**mute** (myoot) adj. (mut·er, mut·est) dumb; silent —n. person incapable of speech; Mus. contrivance to soften tone of instru-

ments —**mut'ed** adj. (of sound) muffled; calm; subdued

**mu·ti·late** (MYOOT-l-ayt) vt. (-lat·ed, -lat·ing) deprive of a limb or other part; damage; deface —**mu·ti·la'tion** n.

**mu·ti·ny** (MYOOT-n-ee) n. (pl. -nies) rebellion against authority, esp. against officers of disciplined body —vi. (-nied, -ny·ing) commit mutiny —**mu·ti·neer'** n. —**mu'ti·nous** adj. rebellious

**mutt** n. inf. (mongrel) dog

**mut·ter** (MUT-ər) vi. speak with mouth nearly closed, indistinctly; grumble —vt. utter in such tones —n. (act of) muttering

**mut·ton** (MUT-ən) n. flesh of sheep used as food —**mut·ton-chops** n. pl. side whiskers broad at jaw, narrow at temples —**mut'ton·head** (-hed) n. inf. slow-witted person

**mu·tu·al** (MYOO-choo-əl) adj. done, possessed etc., by each of two with respect to the other; reciprocal; common to both or all —**mu·tu·al'i·ty** n. —**mutual fund** investment company selling shares to public with repurchase on request

**muz·zle** (MUZ-əl) n. mouth and nose of animal; cover for these to prevent biting; open end of gun —vt. (-zled, -zling) put muzzle on; silence, gag

**my** (mi) adj. belonging to me —**my·self'** pron. emphatic or reflexive form of I or ME

**my·col·o·gy** (mī-KOL-ə-jee) n. science of fungi

**my·o·pi·a** (mī-OH-pee-ə) n. nearsightedness; obtuseness —**my·op'ic** adj.

**myr·i·ad** (MIR-ee-əd) adj. innumerable —n. large indefinite number

**myrrh** (mur) n. aromatic gum, formerly used as incense

**mys·ter·y** (MIS-tə-ree) n. (pl. -ter-ies) obscure or secret thing; anything strange or inexplicable; religious rite; in Middle Ages, biblical play —**mys·te'ri·ous** (-TEER-ree-əs) adj.

**mys·tic** (MIS-tik) n. one who seeks divine, spiritual knowledge, esp. by prayer, contemplation etc. —adj. of hidden meaning, esp. in religious sense —**mys'ti·cal** adj. —**mys'ti·cism** (-siz-əm) n.

**mys·ti·fy** (MIS-tə-fī) vt. (-fied, -fy-ing) bewilder, puzzle —**mys·ti·fi·ca'tion** (-KAY-shən) n.

**mys·tique** (mi-STEEK) n. aura of mystery, power etc.

**myth** (mith) n. tale with supernatural characters or events; invented story; imaginary person or object —**myth'i·cal** adj. —**myth·o·log'i·cal** (-LOJ-ə-kəl) adj. —**my·thol'o·gy** n. (pl. -gies) myths collectively; study of them

# N

**N** Chem. nitrogen; Physics newton

**Na** Chem. sodium

**na·bob** (NAY-bob) n. wealthy, powerful person

**na·cre** (NAY-kər) n. mother-of-pearl

**na·dir** (NAY-dər) n. point opposite the zenith; lowest point

**nag¹** v. (nagged, nag·ging) scold or annoy constantly; cause pain to constantly —n. nagging; one who nags

**nag²** n. old horse; sl. any horse; small horse for riding

**nai·ad** (NAY-ad) n. water nymph

**nail** (nayl) n. horny shield at ends of fingers, toes; claw; small metal spike for fastening wood etc. —vt. fasten with nails; inf. catch —**hit the nail on the head** do or say the right thing

**na·ive** (nah-EEV) adj. simple, unaffected, ingenuous —**na·ive·té** (-eev-TAY) n.

**nak·ed** (NAY-kid) adj. without clothes; exposed, bare; undisguised —**naked eye** the eye unassisted by any optical instrument

**name** (naym) n. word by which person, thing etc. is denoted; reputation; title; credit; family; famous person —vt. (named, nam·ing) give name to; call by name; entitle; appoint; mention; specify —**name'less** (-lis) adj. without a name; indescribable; too dreadful to be mentioned; obscure —**name'ly** adv. that is to say —**name'sake** n. person named after another; person with same name as another

**nap¹** vi. (napped, nap·ping) take short sleep, esp. in daytime —n. short sleep

**nap²** n. downy surface on cloth made by projecting fibers

**na·palm** (NAY-pahm) n. jellied gasoline, highly incendiary, used in bombs etc.

**nape** (nayp) n. back of neck

**naph·tha** (NAF-thə) n. inflammable oil distilled from coal etc. —**naph'tha·lene** (-leen) n. white crystalline product distilled from coal tar, used in disinfectants, mothballs etc.

**nap'kin** n. cloth, paper for wiping fingers or lips at table

**nar·cis·sus** (nahr-SIS-əs) n. (pl. same form) genus of bulbous plants including daffodil, jonquil, esp. one with white flowers —**nar'cis·sism** n. abnormal love and admiration of oneself —**nar'cis·sist** n.

**nar·cot·ic** (nahr-KOT-ik) n. any of a group of drugs, including morphine and opium, producing numbness and stupor, used medicinally but addictive —adj.

**nar·rate** (NAR-ayt) vt. (-rat·ed, -rat·ing) relate, recount, tell (story) —**nar·ra′tion** n. —**nar′ra·tive** (-rɔ-tiv) n. account, story —adj. relating —**nar′ra·tor** (-ray-tɔr) n.

**nar·row** (NAR-oh) adj. (-er, -est) of little breadth, or width esp. in comparison to length; limited; barely adequate or successful —v. make, become narrow —**nar′rows** n. pl. narrow part of straits —**nar′row·ness** n. —**narrow-minded** adj. illiberal; bigoted —**narrow-mindedness** n. prejudice, bigotry

**na·sal** (NAY-zɔl) adj. of nose —n. sound partly produced in nose —**na′sal·ly** adv.

**nas·cent** (NAYS-ɔnt) adj. just coming into existence; springing up

**nas·tur·ti·um** (na-STUR-shɔm) n. garden plant with red or orange flowers

**nas·ty** (NAS-tee) adj. (-ti·er, -ti·est) foul, disagreeable, unpleasant —**nas′ti·ly** adv. —**nas′ti·ness** n.

**na·tal** (NAYT-l) adj. of birth

**na·tion** (NAY-shɔn) n. people or race organized as a country —**na′tion·al** (NASH-ɔ-nl) adj. belonging or pert. to a nation; public, general —n. member of a nation —**na′tion·al·ism** n. loyalty, devotion to one's country; movement for independence of country, people, ruled by another —**na·tion·al′i·ty** n. (pl. -ties) national quality or feeling; fact of belonging to particular nation; member of this —**na′tion·al·ize** vt. (-ized, -iz·ing) convert (private industry, resources etc.) to government control

**na·tive** (NAY-tiv) adj. inborn; born in particular place; found in pure state; that was place of one's birth —n. one born in a place; member of indigenous people of a country; species of plant, animal etc. originating in a place

**na·tiv·i·ty** (nɔ-TIV-i-tee) n. (pl. -ties) birth; time, circumstances of birth; (N-) birth of Christ

**nat·ter** (NAT-ɔr) vi. talk idly

**nat·ty** (NAT-ee) adj. (-ti·er, -ti·est) neat and smart; spruce —**nat′ti·ly** adv.

**na·ture** (NAY-chɔr) n. innate or essential qualities of person or thing; class, sort; life force; (oft. N-) power underlying all phenomena in material world; material world as a whole; natural unspoiled scenery or countryside, and plants and animals in it; disposition; temperament —**nat′u·ral** (NACH-ɔr-ɔl) adj. of, according to, occurring in, provided by, nature; inborn; normal; unaffected; illegitimate —n. something, somebody well suited for something; Mus. character (♮) used to remove effect of sharp or flat preceding it —**nat′u·ral·ist** n. student of natural history —**nat′u·ral·is′tic** adj. of or imitating nature in effect or characteristics —**nat′u·ral·ize** vt. (-ized, -iz·ing) admit to citizenship; accustom to different climate or environment —**nat′u·ral·ly** adv. of or according to nature; by nature; of course —**natural history** study of animals and plants

**naught** (nawt) n. nothing; nought

**naugh·ty** (NAW-tee) adj. (-ti·er, -ti·est) disobedient, not behaving well; mildly indecent, tasteless —**naugh′ti·ly** adv.

**nau·se·a** (NAW-zee-ɔ) n. feeling that precedes vomiting —**nau**-

**se·ate** vt. (-at·ed, -at·ing) sicken —**nau'seous** pr. NAW-shəs, **nau'-se·at·ing** adj. disgusting; causing nausea

**nau·ti·cal** (NAW-ti-kəl) adj. of seamen or ships; marine —**nautical mile** 6080.20 feet (1853.25 meters)

**nau·ti·lus** (NAWT-l-əs) n. (pl. -lus·es) univalvular shellfish

**naval** see NAVY

**nave** (nayv) n. main part of church

**na·vel** (NAY-vəl) n. umbilicus, small scar, depression in middle of abdomen where umbilical cord was attached

**nav·i·gate** (NAV-i-gayt) v. (-gat·ed, -gat·ing) plan, direct, plot path or position of ship etc.; travel —**nav'i·ga·ble** adj. —**nav·i·ga'tion** n. science of directing course of seagoing vessel, or of aircraft in flight; shipping —**nav'i·ga·tor** n. one who navigates

**na·vy** (NAY-vee) n. (pl. -vies) fleet; warships of country with their crews and organization —adj. navy-blue —**na'val** adj. of the navy —**navy-blue** adj. very dark blue

**Na·zi** (NAHT-see) n. member of the National Socialist political party in Germany, 1919-45; one who thinks, acts, like a Nazi —adj.

**Nb** Chem. niobium

**Nd** Chem. neodymium

**Ne** Chem. neon

**Ne·an·der·thal** (nee-AN-dər-thawl) adj. of a type of primitive man; (n-) primitive

**neap** (neep) adj. low —**neap tide** the low tide at the first and third quarters of the moon

**near** (neer) prep. close to —adv. (-er, -est) at or to a short distance —adj. (-er, -est) close at hand; closely related; narrow, so

as barely to escape; stingy; (of vehicles, horses etc.) at driver's left —v. approach —**near'by** adj. adjacent —**near'ly** adv. closely; almost

**neat** (neet) adj. (-er, -est) tidy, orderly; efficient; precise, deft; cleverly worded; undiluted; simple and elegant —**neat'ly** adv.

**neb·u·la** (NEB-yə-lə) n. Astronomy (pl. -lae pr. -lee) diffuse cloud of particles, gases —**neb'u·lous** adj. cloudy; vague, indistinct

**nec·es·sary** (NES-ə-ser-ee) adj. needful, requisite, that must be done; unavoidable, inevitable —**nec'es·sar·i·ly** adv. —**ne·ces'si·tate** vt. (-tat·ed, -tat·ing) make necessary —**ne·ces'si·tous** adj. poor, needy, destitute —**ne·ces'si·ty** n. (pl. -ties) something needed, requisite; constraining power or force of affairs; compulsion; poverty

**neck** (nek) n. part of body joining head to shoulders; narrower part of a bottle etc.; narrow piece of anything between wider parts —vi. inf. embrace, cuddle —**neck'lace** (-lis) n. ornament around the neck

**nec·ro·man·cy** (NEK-rə-man-see) n. magic, esp. by communication with dead —**nec'ro·man·cer** n. wizard

**ne·crop·o·lis** (nə-KROP-ə-lis) n. (pl. -lis·es) cemetery

**nec·tar** (NEK-tər) n. honey of flowers; drink of the gods

**nec·tar·ine** (nek-tə-REEN) n. variety of peach

**nee** (nay) adj. indicating maiden name of married woman

**need** vt. want, require —n. (state, instance of) want; requirement; necessity; poverty —**need'ful** adj. necessary, requisite —**need'less** adj. unnecessary —**needs** adv. of necessity (esp. in needs must or

must needs) —**need′y** adj.
(**need·i·er, need·i·est**) poor, in
want

**nee·dle** (NEE-dl) n. (-**dled, -dling**)
pointed pin with an eye and no
head, for sewing; long, pointed
pin for knitting; pointer of gauge,
dial; magnetized bar of compass;
stylus for record player; leaf of
fir, pine etc.; obelisk; inf. hypodermic syringe —vt. inf. goad,
provoke —**nee′dle·craft, -work** n.
embroidery, sewing

**ne·far·i·ous** (ni-FAIR-ee-əs) adj.
wicked —**ne·far′i·ous·ness** n.

**ne·gate** (ni-GAYT) vt. (-**gat·ed,
-gat·ing**) deny, nullify —**ne·ga′-
tion** n. contradiction, denial

**neg·a·tive** (NEG-ə-tiv) adj. expressing denial or refusal; lacking enthusiasm, energy, interest;
not positive; of electrical charge
having the same polarity as the
charge of an electron —n. negative word or statement; Photography picture made by action of
light on chemicals in which
lights and shades are reversed

**ne·glect** (ni-GLEKT) vt. disregard, take no care of; fail to do;
omit through carelessness —n.
fact of neglecting or being neglected —**ne·glect′ful** adj.

**neg·li·gee** (NEG-li-zhay) n. woman's light, gauzy nightgown or
dressing gown

**neg·li·gence** (NEG-li-jəns) n. neglect; carelessness —**neg′li·gent**
adj. —**neg′li·gi·ble** adj. able to be
disregarded; very small or unimportant

**ne·go·ti·ate** (ni-GOH-shee-ayt) v.
(-**at·ed, -at·ing**) —vi. discuss with
view to mutual settlement —vt.
arrange by conference; transfer
(bill, check etc.); get over, past,
around (obstacle) —**ne·go′-
ti·a·ble** (-shə-bəl) adj. —**ne·go·
ti·a′tion** (-shee-AY-shən) n. deal-

ing with another on business;
discussion; transference (of bill,
check etc.)

**neigh** (nay) n. cry of horse —vi.
utter this cry

**neigh·bor** (NAY-bər) n. one who
lives near another —**neigh′bor-
hood** n. district; people of a district; region around about
—**neigh′bor·ing** adj. situated
nearby —**neigh′bor·ly** adj. as or
befitting a good or friendly
neighbor; friendly; helpful

**nei·ther** (NEE-thər) adj./pron.
not the one or the other —adv.
not on the one hand; not either
—conj. nor yet

**nem·e·sis** (NEM-ə-sis) n. (pl. -ses
pr. -seez) retribution; (N-) the
goddess of vengeance

**neo-** (comb. form) new, later,
revived in modified form, based
upon

**Ne·o·lith·ic** (nee-ə-LITH-ik) adj. of
the later Stone Age

**ne·ol·o·gism** (nee-OL-ə-jiz-əm) n.
newly coined word or phrase

**ne·on** (NEE-on) n. one of the inert
constituent gases of the atmosphere, used in illuminated signs
and lights

**ne·o·phyte** (NEE-ə-fit) n. new
convert; beginner, novice

**neph·ew** (NEF-yoo) n. brother's
or sister's son

**ne·phri·tis** (nə-FRI-tis) n. inflammation of kidneys —**ne·phro·sis**
(-FROH-sis) n. degenerative disease of kidneys

**nep·o·tism** (NEP-ə-tiz-əm) n. undue favoritism toward one's relations

**Nep·tune** (NEP-toon) n. god of
the sea; planet second farthest
from sun

**nep·tu·ni·um** (nep-TOO-nee-əm)
n. synthetic metallic element

**nerve** (nurv) n. sinew, tendon;
fiber or bundle of fibers convey-

ing feeling, impulses to motion *etc.* to and from brain and other parts of body; assurance; coolness in danger; audacity —*pl.* irritability, unusual sensitiveness to fear, annoyance *etc.* —**nerve'less** (-lis) *adj.* without nerves; useless; weak; paralyzed —**nerv'ous** (-əs) *adj.* excitable; timid, apprehensive, worried; of the nerves —**nerv'y** (-ee) *adj.* (**nerv.i.er, nerv.i.est**) nervous, jumpy, irritable; on edge —**nervous breakdown** condition of mental, emotional disturbance, disability

**nest** *n.* place in which bird lays and hatches its eggs; animal's breeding place; snug retreat —*vi.* make, have a nest —**nest egg** (fund of) money in reserve

**nes·tle** (NES-əl) *vi.* (-**tled, -tling**) settle comfortably, usu. pressing in or close to something

**nest'ling** *n.* bird too young to leave nest

**net**[1] *n.* openwork fabric of meshes of cord *etc.*; piece of it used to catch fish *etc.* —*vt.* (**net'ted, net·ting**) cover with, or catch in, net; catch, ensnare —**netting** *n.* string or wire net —**net'ball** *n.* Tennis return shot that hits top of net and remains in play

**net**[2] *adj.* left after all deductions; free from deduction —*vt.* (**net'ted, net·ting**) gain, yield as clear profit

**neth·er** (NETH-ər) *adj.* lower

**ne·tsu·ke** (NET-skee) *n.* carved wooden or ivory toggle or button worn in Japan

**net·tle** (NET-l) *n.* plant with stinging hairs on the leaves —*vt.* (-**tled, -tling**) irritate, provoke

**net·work** (NET-wurk) *n.* system of intersecting lines, roads *etc.*; interconnecting group of people or things; in broadcasting, group

of stations connected to transmit same programs simultaneously

**neu·ral** (NUUR-əl) *adj.* of the nerves

**neu·ral·gia** (nuu-RAL-jə) *n.* pain in, along nerves, *esp.* of face and head —**neu·ral'gic** (-jik) *adj.*

**neu·ri·tis** (nuu-RĪ-tis) *n.* inflammation of nerves

**neu·rol·o·gy** (nuu-ROL-ə-jee) *n.* science, study of nerves —**neu·rol'o·gist** *n.*

**neu·ro·sis** (nuu-ROH-sis) *n.* (*pl.* -**ses** *pr.* -seez) relatively mild mental disorder —**neu·rot'ic** *adj.* suffering from nervous disorder; abnormally sensitive —*n.* neurotic person

**neu·ter** (NOO-tər) *adj.* neither masculine nor feminine —*n.* neuter word; neuter gender —*vt.* castrate, spay (domestic animals)

**neu·tral** (NOO-trəl) *adj.* taking neither side in war, dispute *etc.*; without marked qualities; belonging to neither of two classes —*n.* neutral nation or a citizen of one; neutral gear —**neu·tral'i·ty** *n.* —**neu'tral·ize** *vt.* (-**ized, -iz·ing**) make ineffective; counterbalance —**neutral gear** in vehicle, position of gears that leaves transmission disengaged

**neu·tron** (NOO-tron) *n.* electrically neutral particle of the nucleus of an atom —**neutron bomb** nuclear bomb designed to destroy people but not buildings

**nev·er** (NEV-ər) *adv.* at no time —**nev'er·the·less'** *adv.* for all that, notwithstanding

**ne·vus** (NEE-vəs) *n.* congenital mark on skin; birthmark, mole

**new** (noo) *adj.* (-**er, -est**) not existing before, fresh; that has lately come into some state or existence; unfamiliar, strange —*adv.* (*usu.* new'ly) recently, fresh —**new′ness** *n.* —**new′-com·er** *n.* recent arrival —**new′-fan′gled** (-FANG-əld) *adj.* of new fashion

**new·el** (NOO-əl) *n.* central pillar of winding staircase; post at top or bottom of staircase rail —**newel post**

**news** (nooz) *n.* report of recent happenings, tidings; interesting fact not previously known —**news′cast** *n.* news broadcast —**news′deal·er** *n.* shopkeeper who sells newspapers and magazines —**news′flash** *n.* brief news item, *oft.* interrupting radio, TV program —**news′pa·per** *n.* periodical publication containing news, advertisements *etc.* —**news′print** *n.* paper of the kind used for newspapers *etc.* —**news′reel** *n.* motion picture giving news —**news′room** *n.* room where news is received and prepared for publication or broadcast —**news′wor·thy** (-wur-thee) *adj.* (-thi·er, -thi·est) sufficiently interesting and important to be reported as news

**newt** (noot) *n.* small, tailed amphibious creature

**new·ton** (NOOT-n) *n.* SI unit of force

**next** (nekst) *adj./adv.* nearest; immediately following —**next of kin** nearest relative(s)

**nex·us** (NEK-səs) *n.* (*pl. same form*) tie; connection, link

**Ni** *Chem.* nickel

**nib·ble** (NIB-əl) *v.* (-bled, -bling) take little bites of —*n.* little bite

**nice** (nis) *adj.* (nic·er, nic·est) pleasant; friendly, kind; attractive; subtle, fine; careful, exact; difficult to decide —**nice′ly** *adv.* —**ni′ce·ty** *n.* (*pl.* -ties) minute distinction or detail; subtlety; precision

**niche** (nich) *n.* recess in wall; suitable place in life, public estimation *etc.*

**nick** (nik) *vt.* make notch in, indent; *sl.* steal —*n.* notch; exact point of time —**in the nick of time** at the last possible moment

**nick·el** (NIK-əl) *n.* silver-white metal much used in alloys and plating; five-cent piece

**nick·name** (NIK-naym) *n.* familiar name added to or replacing an ordinary name

**nic·o·tine** (NIK-ə-teen) *n.* poisonous oily liquid in tobacco

**niece** (nees) *n.* brother's or sister's daughter

**nig·gard** (NIG-ərd) *n.* mean, stingy person —**nig′gard·ly** *adj./adv.* —**nig′gard·li·ness** *n.*

**nig·gle** (NIG-əl) *vi.* (-gled, -gling) find fault continually; annoy —**niggling** *adj.* petty; irritating and persistent

**nigh** (nī) *adj./adv./prep., obs. or Poet.* near

**night** (nīt) *n.* time of darkness between sunset and sunrise; end of daylight; dark —**night′ie** *n. inf.* nightgown —**night′ly** *adj.* happening, done every night; of the night —*adv.* every night; by night —**night′cap** *n.* cap worn in bed; *inf.* late-night (alcoholic) drink —**night′club** *n.* establishment for dancing, music *etc.* open until early morning —**night′gown** *n.* woman's or child's loose gown worn in bed —**night′in·gale** *n.* small Old World bird that sings *usu.* at night —**night′mare** (-mair) *n.* very bad dream; terrifying experience —**night′time** *n.*

**ni·hil·ism** (NĪ-ə-liz-əm) *n.* rejection of all religious and moral principles; opposition to all constituted authority, or government —**ni′hil·ist** *n.* —**ni·hil·ist′ic** *adj.*

**nim·ble** (NIM-bəl) *adj.* (-bler,

-blest) agile, active, quick, dexterous —nim'bly adv.

**nim·bus** (NIM-bəs) n. (pl. -bi pr. -bī, -bus·es) rain or storm cloud; cloud of glory, halo

**nine** (nīn) adj./n. cardinal number next above eight —ninth adj. —ninth'ly adv. —nine·teen' adj./n. nine more than ten —nine·teenth' adj. —nine'ty adj./n. nine tens —nine'ti·eth adj. —nine'pins n. (with sing. v.) game where wooden pins are set up to be knocked down by rolling ball, skittles

**nip** v. (nipped, nip·ping) pinch sharply; detach by pinching, bite; check growth (of plants) thus; inf. steal; inf. beat (opponent) by close margin; hurry —n. pinch; check to growth; sharp coldness of weather; small alcoholic drink —nip'per n. thing (eg crab's claw) that nips; inf. small boy —pl. pincers —nip'py adj. inf. (-pi·er, -pi·est) cold; quick

**nip·ple** (NIP-əl) n. point of a breast, teat; anything like this

**nir·va·na** (nir-VAH-nə) n. Buddhism absolute blessedness; Hinduism merging of individual in supreme spirit

**nit** n. egg of louse or other parasite —nit'pick·ing adj. inf. overconcerned with detail, esp. to find fault —nit'pick v. show such overconcern; criticize over petty faults —nit'wit n. inf. fool —nit·ty-grit·ty n. sl. basic facts, details

**ni·tro·gen** (NĪ-trə-jən) n. one of the gases making up the air —ni'trate n. compound of nitric acid and an alkali —ni'tric, ni'trous adj. —ni·trog'e·nous (-TROJ-ə-nəs) adj. of, containing nitrogen —ni·tro·glyc'er·in (-troh-GLIS-ə-rin) n. explosive liquid

**No** Chem. nobelium

**no** (noh) adj. not any, not a; not at all —adv. expresses negative reply to question or request —n. (pl. noes) refusal; denial; negative vote or voter —no one nobody —no-go adj. sl. not operating; canceled —no man's land waste or unclaimed land; contested land between two opposing forces —no way inf. absolutely not

**no·bel·i·um** (noh-BEL-ee-əm) n. synthetic element produced from curium

**no·ble** (NOH-bəl) adj. (-bler, -blest) of the nobility; showing, having high moral qualities; impressive, excellent —n. member of the nobility —no·bil'i·ty n. in some countries, class holding special rank, usu. hereditary; being noble —no'bly adv.

**no·bod·y** (NOH-bod-ee) pron. no person; no one —n. (pl. -bod·ies) person of no importance

**noc·tur·nal** (nok-TUR-nl) adj. of, in, by night; active by night

**noc·turne** (NOK-turn) n. dreamy piece of music

**nod** v. (nod·ded, nod·ding) bow head slightly and quickly in assent, command etc.; let head droop with sleep —n. act of nodding —nodding acquaintance slight knowledge of person or subject —give the nod to inf. express approval of —nod off fall asleep

**node** (nohd) n. knot or knob; point at which curve crosses itself —no'dal (-əl) adj.

**nod·ule** (NOJ-ool) n. little knot; rounded irregular mineral mass

**No·el** (noh-EL) n. Christmas; (n-) Christmas carol

**nog** n. drink made with beaten eggs; eggnog; peg, block

**nog·gin** (NOG-ən) n. small

amount of liquor; small mug; *inf.* head

**noise** (noyz) *n.* any sound, *esp.* disturbing one; clamor, din; loud outcry; talk or interest —*vt.* rumor —**noise'less** (-lis) *adj.* without noise, quiet, silent —**nois'i·ly** *adv.* —**nois'y** *adj.* (**nois·i·er, nois·i·est**) making much noise; clamorous

**noi·some** (NOI-səm) *adj.* disgusting; noxious

**no·mad** (NOH-mad) *n.* member of tribe with no fixed dwelling place; wanderer —**no·mad'ic** *adj.*

**nom de plume** (nom də PLOOM) *Fr.* writer's assumed name; pen name; pseudonym

**no·men·cla·ture** (NOH-mən-klay-chər) *n.* terminology of particular science *etc.*

**nom·i·nal** (NOM-ə-nəl) *adj.* in name only; (of fee *etc.*) small, insignificant; of a name or names —**nom'i·nal·ly** *adv.* in name only; not really

**nom·i·nate** (NOM-ə-nayt) *vt.* (**-nat·ed, -nat·ing**) propose as candidate; appoint to office —**nom·i·na'tion** *n.* —**nom'i·na·tive** (-nə·tiv) *adj./n.* (of) case of nouns, pronouns when subject of verb —**nom·i·nee'** *n.* candidate

**non-** (*prefix*) negates the idea of the simple word, as in list below

**non·a·ge·nar·i·an** (non-ə-jə-NAIR-ee-ən) *adj.* aged between ninety and ninety-nine —*n.* person of such age

**nonce** (nons) *n.* —**for the nonce** for the occasion only; for the present

**non·cha·lant** (non-shə-LAHNT) *adj.* casually unconcerned, indifferent, cool —**non'cha·lance** *n.*

**non·com·bat·ant** (non-kəm-BAT-nt) *n.* civilian during war; member of army who does not fight *eg* chaplain

**non·com·mit·tal** (non-kə-MIT-l) *adj.* avoiding definite preference or pledge

**non com·pos men·tis** (NON KOM-pohs MEN-tis) *Lat.* of unsound mind

**non·de·script** (non-di-SKRIPT) *adj.* lacking distinctive characteristics, indeterminate

**none** (nun) *pron.* no one, not any —*adj.* no —*adv.* in no way —**none·the·less'** *adv.* despite that, however

**non·en·ti·ty** (non-EN-ti-tee) *n.* (*pl.* **-ties**) insignificant person, thing; nonexistent thing

**non·pa·reil** (non-pə-REL) *adj.* unequaled, matchless —*n.* person or thing unequaled or unrivaled

**non·plus'** *vt.* (-plussed,

---

| | | |
|---|---|---|
| non·ag·gres'sion | non·e·vent' | non·se·lec'tive |
| non·al·co·hol'ic | non·ex·ist'ent | non·shrink'a·ble |
| non·be·liev'er | non·fic'tion | non·slip' |
| non·break'a·ble | non·in·ter·ven'tion | non·smok'er |
| non·com·bust'i·ble | mem·ber' | non·stand'ard |
| non·com·pet'i·tive | non·ne·go'ti·a·ble | non·start'er |
| non·con·duc'tive | non·par'ty | non·stick' |
| non·con·trib'u·to·ry | non·pay'ment | non·stop' |
| non·con·tro·ver'sial | non·prof·it | non·tax'a·ble |
| non·de·nom·i·  na'tion·al | non·read'er | non·tech'ni·cal |
| non·drink'er | non·res'i·dent | non·tox'ic |
| | non·re·turn'a·ble | non·vi'o·lent |

-plus·sing) disconcert, confound, or bewilder completely

**non·sense** (NON-sens) *n.* lack of sense; absurd language; absurdity; silly conduct —**non·sen'si·cal** *adj.* ridiculous; meaningless; without sense

**non se·qui·tur** (non SEK-wi-tər) *Lat.* statement with little or no relation to what preceded it

**noo·dle**[1] (NOOD-l) *n.* strip of pasta served in soup *etc.*

**noodle**[2] *n.* simpleton, fool; *sl.* the head

**nook** (nuuk) *n.* sheltered corner, retreat

**noon** *n.* midday, twelve o'clock —**noon'day** *n.* noon —**noon'tide** *n.* the time about noon

**noose** (noos) *n.* running loop; snare —*vt.* (noosed, noos·ing) catch, ensnare in noose, lasso

**nor** *conj.* and not

**Nor·dic** (NOR-dik) *adj.* pert. to peoples of Germanic stock *eg* Scandinavians

**norm** *n.* average level of achievement; rule or authoritative standard; model; standard type or pattern —**nor'mal** *adj.* ordinary; usual; conforming to type —*n.* *Geom.* perpendicular —**nor'mal·ly** *adv.*

**north** *n.* direction to the right of person facing the sunset; part of the world, of country *etc.* toward this point —*adv.* toward or in the north —*adj.* to, from, or in the north —**north·er·ly** (NOR-thər-lee) *adj.* —*n.* wind from the north —**north'ern** *adj.* —**north'ern·er** *n.* person from the north —**north'ward** (NORTH-wərd) *adj.* —**north'ward(s)** *adv.*

**nose** (nohz) *n.* organ of smell, used also in breathing; any projection resembling a nose, as prow of ship, aircraft *etc.* —*v.* (nosed, nos·ing) (cause to) move

forward slowly and carefully —*vt.* touch with nose; smell, sniff —*vi.* smell; pry —**nos·y** *adj.* (nos·i·er; nos·i·est) inquisitive —**nose'dive** *n.* downward sweep of aircraft; any sudden sharp fall —**nose'gay** *n.* bunch of flowers

**nos·tal·gia** (no-STAL-jə) *n.* longing for return of past events; homesickness —**nos·tal'gic** *adj.*

**nos·tril** (NOS-trəl) *n.* one of the two external openings of the nose

**nos·trum** (NOS-trəm) *n.* quack medicine; secret remedy

**not** *adv.* expressing negation, refusal, denial

**no·ta be·ne** (NOH-tah BE-ne) *Lat.* note well

**no·ta·ble** (NOH-tə-bəl) *adj.* worthy of note, remarkable —*n.* person of distinction —**no·ta·bil'i·ty** *n.* (*pl.* -ties) prominence; an eminent person —**no'ta·bly** *adv.*

**no·ta·tion** (noh-TAY-shən) *n.* representation of numbers, quantities, by symbols; set of such symbols

**notch** (noch) *n.* V-shaped cut or indentation; *inf.* step, grade —*vt.* make notches in

**note** (noht) *n.* brief comment or record; short letter; promissory note; symbol for musical sound; single tone; sign; indication, hint; fame; notice; regard —*pl.* brief jottings written down for future reference —*vt.* (not·ed, not·ing) observe, record; heed —**noted** *adj.* well-known; celebrated —**note'book** *n.* small book with blank pages for writing —**note'wor·thy** (-wur-*thee*) *adj.* worth noting, remarkable

**noth·ing** (NUTH-ing) *n.* no thing, not anything, nought —*adv.* not at all, in no way

**no·tice** (NOH-tis) *n.* observation; attention, consideration; warning, intimation, announcement; advance notification of intention to end a contract *etc.*, as of employment; review —*vt.* (-ticed, -tic·ing) observe, mention; give attention to —**no'tice·a·ble** *adj.* conspicuous; attracting attention; appreciable

**no·ti·fy** (NOH-tə-fī) *vt.* (-fied, -fy·ing) report; give notice of or to —**no·ti·fi·ca'tion** (-KAY-shən) *n.*

**no·tion** (NOH-shən) *n.* concept; opinion; whim; (*pl.*) small items *eg* buttons, thread for sale in store —**no'tion·al** *adj.* speculative, imaginary, abstract

**no·to·ri·ous** (noh-TOR-ee-əs) *adj.* known for something bad; well-known —**no·to·ri'e·ty** (-tə-RĪ-i-tee) *n.* discreditable publicity

**not·with·stand'ing** *prep.* in spite of —*adv.* all the same —*conj.* although

**nou·gat** (NOO-gət) *n.* chewy candy containing nuts, fruit *etc.*

**nought** (nawt) *n.* nothing; cipher 0

**noun** (nown) *n.* word used as name of person, idea, or thing, substantive

**nour·ish** (NUR-ish) *vt.* feed; nurture; tend; encourage

**nou·velle cui·sine** (noo-vel kwee-ZEEN) *Fr.* style of preparing and presenting food with light sauces and unusual combinations of flavors

**no·va** (NOH-və) *n.* (*pl.* -vas) star that suddenly becomes brighter then loses brightness through months or years

**nov·el**[1] (NOV-əl) *n.* fictitious tale in book form —**nov'el·ist** *n.* writer of novels

**nov·el**[2] *adj.* new, recent; strange —**nov'el·ty** *n.* (*pl.* -ties) newness; something new or unusual; small ornament, trinket

**no·ve·na** (noh-VEE-nə) *n.* R.C. *Church* prayers, services usu. extending over nine consecutive days

**nov·ice** (NOV-is) *n.* one new to anything; beginner; candidate for admission to religious order —**no·vi·ti·ate** (noh-VISH-ee-it) *n.* probationary period; part of religious house for novices; novice

**now** *adv.* at the present time; immediately; recently (*oft.* with just) —*conj.* seeing that, since —**now'a·days** *adv.* in these times, at present

**no·way** (NOH-way) *adv.* nowise

**no·where** (NOH-hwair) *adv.* not in any place or state

**no·wise** (NOH-wīz) *adv.* not in any manner or degree

**nox·ious** (NOK-shəs) *adj.* poisonous, harmful

**noz·zle** (NOZ-əl) *n.* pointed spout, *esp.* at end of hose

**Np** *Chem.* neptunium

**NT** New Testament

**nu·ance** (NOO-ahns) *n.* delicate shade of difference, in color, tone of voice *etc.*

**nub** *n.* small lump; main point (of story *etc.*)

**nu·bile** (NOO-bil) *adj.* marriageable —**nu·bil'i·ty** *n.*

**nu·cle·us** (NOO-klee-əs) *n.* (*pl.* -cle·i *pr.* -klee-ī) center, kernel; beginning meant to receive additions; core of the atom —**nu'cle·ar** (-klee-ər) *adj.* of, pert. to atomic nucleus —**nuclear energy** energy released by nuclear fission —**nuclear fission** disintegration of the atom —**nuclear reaction** change in structure and energy content of atomic nucleus by interaction with another nucleus, particle —**nuclear reactor** *see* REACTOR —**nuclear winter** period of extremely low temperatures and little light after nuclear war

**nude** (nood) *n.* state of being naked; (picture, statue *etc.* of) naked person —*adj.* naked —**nud'ism** *n.* practice of nudity —**nud'ist** *n.* —**nud'i·ty** *n.*

**nudge** (nuj) *vt.* (**nudged, nudg·ing**) touch slightly *esp.* with elbow to gain someone's attention, prod someone into action —*n.* such touch

**nu·ga·to·ry** (NOO-gə-tor-ee) *adj.* trifling; futile

**nug·get** (NUG-it) *n.* rough lump of native gold; anything of significance, value

**nui·sance** (NOO-səns) *n.* something or someone harmful, offensive, annoying or disagreeable

**null** *adj.* of no effect, void —**nul'li·fy** (-fī) *vt.* (**-fied, -fy·ing**) cancel; make useless or ineffective —**nul'li·ty** *n.* state of being null and void

**Num.** Numbers

**numb** (num) *adj.* (**-er, -est**) deprived of feeling, *esp.* by cold —*vt.* make numb; deaden

**num·ber** (NUM-bər) *n.* sum or aggregate; word or symbol saying how many; single issue of a journal *etc.*, issued in regular series; classification as to singular or plural; song, piece of music; performance; company, collection; identifying number, as of particular house, telephone *etc.*; *inf.* measure, correct estimation of —*vt.* count; class, reckon; give a number to; amount to —**num'ber·less** *adj.* countless —**number crunching** *inf.* large-scale processing of numerical data

**nu·mer·al** (NOO-mər-əl) *n.* sign or word denoting a number —**nu'mer·ate** *vt.* (**-at·ed, -at·ing**) count —**nu·mer·a'tion** *n.* —**nu·mer·a'tor** *n.* top part of fraction, figure showing how many of the fractional units are taken —**nu·mer'i·**cal *adj.* of, in respect of, number or numbers —**nu'mer·ous** (-əs) *adj.* many

**nu·mis·mat·ic** (noo-miz-MAT-ik) *adj.* of coins —**nu·mis·mat'ics** *n.* (*with sing. v.*) the study of coins —**nu·mis'ma·tist** (-mə-tist) *n.*

**nun** *n.* woman living (in convent) under religious vows —**nun'ner·y** *n.* (*pl.* **-ies**) convent of nuns

**nun·cu·pa·tive** (NUNG-kyə-pay-tiv) *adj.* of a will, oral; not written

**nup·tial** (NUP-shəl) *adj.* of, relating to marriage —**nup'tials** *n. pl.* marriage; wedding ceremony

**nurse** (nurs) *n.* person trained for care of sick or injured; woman tending another's child —*vt.* (**nursed, nurs·ing**) act as nurse to; suckle; pay special attention to; harbor (grudge *etc.*) —**nurs'er·y** *n.* (*pl.* **-er·ies**) room for children; rearing place for plants —**nurs'er·y·man** (-mən) *n.* one who raises plants for sale —**nurs·ing home** institution for housing and caring for the aged or chronically ill

**nur·ture** (NUR-chər) *n.* bringing up; education; rearing; nourishment —*vt.* (**-tured, -tur·ing**) bring up; educate

**nut** *n.* fruit consisting of hard shell and kernel; hollow metal collar into which a screw fits; *sl.* the head; *sl.* eccentric or crazy person —*vi.* (**nut·ted, nut·ting**) gather nuts —**nut'ty** *adj.* (**-ti·er, -ti·est**) of, like nut; pleasant to taste and bite; *sl.* insane, crazy; eccentric —**nuts** *adj. sl.* insane —**nut'hatch** *n.* small songbird —**nut'meg** *n.* aromatic seed of Indian tree

**nu·tri·ent** (NOO-tree-ənt) *adj.* nourishing —*n.* something nutritious

**nu·tri·ment** (NOO-trə-mənt) *n.* nourishing food —**nu·tri'tion**

(-TRISH-ən) *n.* food; act of nourishing; study of this process —**nu·tri'tion·ist** *n.* one trained in nutrition —**nu·tri'tious, nu'tri·tive** *adj.* nourishing; promoting growth

**nuz·zle** (NUZ-əl) *vi.* (**-zled, -zling**) burrow, press with nose; nestle

**ny·lon** (NI-lon) *n.* synthetic material used for fabrics, bristles, ropes *etc.* —*pl.* stockings made of this

**nymph** (nimf) *n.* legendary semidivine maiden of sea, woods, mountains *etc.*

**nym·pho·ma·ni·a** (nim-fə-MAY-nee-ə) *n.* abnormally intense sexual desire in women —**nym·pho·ma'ni·ac** *n.*

# O

**O** *Chem.* oxygen

**oaf** (ohf) *n.* lout; dolt

**oak** (ohk) *n.* common, deciduous forest tree —**oak'en** (-in) *adj.* of oak

**oa·kum** (OH-kəm) *n.* loose fiber, used for caulking, got by unraveling old rope

**oar** (or) *n.* wooden lever with broad blade worked by the hands to propel boat; oarsman —*v.* row —**oars·man** (ORZ-mən) *n.* (*pl.* **-men**) —**oars'man·ship** *n.* skill in rowing

**o·a·sis** (oh-AY-sis) *n.* (*pl.* **-ses** *pr.* -seez) fertile spot in desert; place serving as pleasant change from routine

**oat** (oht) *n.* (*usu. pl.*) grain of cereal grass; the plant —**oat'en** (-in) *adj.* —**oat'meal** (-meel) *n.*

**oath** (ohth) *n.* (*pl.* **oaths** *pr.* oh*thz*) confirmation of truth of statement by naming something sacred; curse

**ob·bli·ga·to** (ob-li-GAH-toh) *adj./n.* (*pl.* **-tos, -ti** *pr.* -tee) (in musical score) essential; essential part of a musical score

**ob·du·rate** (OB-duu-rit) *adj.* stubborn, unyielding —**ob'du·ra·cy** (-rə-see) *n.*

**o·be·di·ence** (oh-BEE-dee-əns) *n.* submission to authority —**o·be'di·ent** *adj.* willing to obey; compliant; dutiful

**o·bei·sance** (oh-BAY-səns) *n.* deference; a bow or curtsy

**ob·e·lisk** (OB-ə-lisk) *n.* tapering rectangular stone column, with pyramidal apex

**o·bese** (oh-BEES) *adj.* very fat, corpulent —**o·be'si·ty** *n.*

**o·bey** (oh-BAY) *vt.* do the bidding of; act in accordance with —*vi.* do as ordered; submit to authority

**ob·fus·cate** (OB-fə-skayt) *vt.* (**-cat·ed, -cat·ing**) perplex; darken; make obscure

**o·bit·u·ar·y** (oh-BICH-oo-er-ee) *n.* (*pl.* **-ar·ies**) notice, record of death; biographical sketch of deceased person, *esp.* in newspaper (*also inf.* **ob'it**)

**ob·ject**[1] (OB-jikt) *n.* material thing; that to which feeling or action is directed; end or aim; *Grammar* word dependent on verb or preposition —**object lesson** lesson with practical and concrete illustration —**no object** not an obstacle or hindrance

**ob·ject**[2] (əb-JEKT) *vt.* state in opposition —*vi.* feel dislike or reluctance to something —**ob·jec'tion** *n.* —**ob·jec'tion·a·ble** *adj.* disagreeable; justly liable to objection

**ob·jec·tive** (əb-JEK-tiv) *adj.* external to the mind; impartial —*n.* thing or place aimed at —**ob·jec·tiv'i·ty** (ob-jek-TIV-) *n.*

**ob·jur·gate** (OB-jər-gayt) *vt.*

(-gat·ed, -gat·ing) scold, reprove —**ob·jur·ga'tion** n.

**ob·late** (OB-layt) adj. of a sphere, flattened at the poles

**o·blige** (ɔ-BLIJ) vt. (o·bliged, o·blig·ing) bind morally or legally to do service to; compel —**ob'li·gate** vt. (-gat·ed, -gat·ing) bind esp. by legal contract; put under obligation —**ob·li·ga'tion** n. binding duty, promise; debt of gratitude —**o·blig·a·to·ry** adj. required; binding —**o·blig'ing** adj. ready to serve others, civil, helpful, courteous

**o·blique** (ɔ-BLEEK) adj. slanting; indirect —**o·blique'ly** adv. —**o·bliq'ui·ty** (ɔ-BLIK-wi-tee) n. (-ties) slant; dishonesty —**oblique angle** one not a right angle

**ob·lit·er·ate** (ɔ-BLIT-ɔ-rayt) vt. (-at·ed, -at·ing) blot out, efface, destroy completely

**o·bliv·i·on** (ɔ-BLIV-ee-ɔn) n. forgetting or being forgotten —**ob·liv'i·ous** adj. forgetful; unaware

**ob·long** (OB-lawng) adj. rectangular, with adjacent sides unequal —n. oblong figure

**ob·lo·quy** (OB-lɔ-kwee) n. (pl. -quies) reproach, abuse; disgrace; detraction

**ob·nox·ious** (ɔb-NOK-shɔs) adj. offensive, disliked, odious

**o·boe** (OH-boh) n. woodwind instrument —**o'bo·ist** n.

**ob·scene** (ɔb-SEEN) adj. indecent, lewd, repulsive —**ob·scen'i·ty** (-SEN-i-tee) n.

**ob·scure** (ɔb-SKYUUR) adj. (-scur·er, -scur·est) unclear, indistinct; unexplained; dark, dim; humble —vt. (-scured, -scur·ing) make unintelligible; dim; conceal —**ob·scu'rant** (-SKYUUR-ɔnt) n. one who opposes enlightenment or reform —**ob·scu'rant·ism** n. —**ob·scu'ri·ty** n. indistinctness;

lack of intelligibility; darkness; obscure, esp. unrecognized, place or position

**ob·se·quies** (OB-si-kweez) n. pl. funeral rites

**ob·se·qui·ous** (ɔb-SEE-kwee-ɔs) adj. servile, fawning

**ob·serve** (ɔb-ZURV) v. (-served, -serv·ing) notice, remark; watch; note systematically; keep, follow —vi. make a remark —**ob·serv'a·ble** adj. —**ob·serv'ance** (-ɔns) n. paying attention; keeping —**ob·serv'ant** adj. quick to notice; careful in observing —**ob·ser·va'tion** n. action, habit of observing; noticing; remark —**ob·serv·a·to·ry** (-ɔ-tor-ee) n. (pl. -ries) place for watching stars etc.

**ob·sess** (ɔb-SES) vt. haunt, fill the mind —**ob·ses'sion** (-SESH-ɔn) n. fixed idea; domination of the mind by one idea —**ob·ses'sive** adj.

**ob·sid·i·an** (ɔb-SID-ee-ɔn) n. fused volcanic rock, forming hard, dark, natural glass

**ob·so·lete** (OB-sɔ-LEET) adj. disused, out of date —**ob·so·les'cent** (-LES-ɔnt) adj. going out of use

**ob·sta·cle** (OB-stɔ-kɔl) n. hindrance; impediment, barrier, obstruction

**ob·stet·rics** (ɔb-STE-triks) n. (with sing. v.) branch of medicine concerned with childbirth and care of women before and after childbirth —**ob·stet'ric** adj. —**ob·ste·tri'cian** (-shɔn) n.

**ob·sti·nate** (OB-stɔ-nit) adj. stubborn; self-willed; unyielding; hard to overcome or cure —**ob'sti·na·cy** n.

**ob·strep·er·ous** (ɔb-STREP-ɔr-ɔs) adj. unruly, noisy, boisterous

**ob·struct** (ɔb-STRUKT) vt. block up; hinder; impede —**ob·struc'tion** n. —**ob·struc'tion·ist** n. one

who deliberately opposes transaction of business

**ob·tain** (əb-TAYN) *vt.* get; acquire; procure by effort —*vi.* be
customary —**ob·tain'a·ble** *adj.*
procurable

**ob·trude** (əb-TROOD) *vt.*
(-trud·ed, -trud·ing) thrust forward unduly —**ob·tru'sion**
(-TROO·zhən) *n.* —**ob·tru'sive** *adj.*
forward, pushing

**ob·tuse** (əb-TOOS) *adj.* dull of
perception; stupid; greater than
right angle; not pointed

**ob·verse** (OB-vurs) *n.* a fact, idea
*etc.* that is the complement of
another; side of coin, medal *etc.*
that has the principal design
—*adj.* (ob-VURS)

**ob·vi·ate** (OB-vee-ayt) *vt.* (-at·ed,
-at·ing) remove, make unnecessary

**ob·vi·ous** (OB-vee-əs) *adj.* clear,
evident; wanting in subtlety

**oc·ca·sion** (ə-KAY-zhən) *n.* time
when thing happens; reason,
need; opportunity; special event
—*vt.* cause —**oc·ca'sion·al** *adj.*
happening, found now and then;
produced for some special event,
as occasional music —**oc·ca'sion-
al·ly** *adv.* sometimes, now and
then

**Oc·ci·dent** (OK-si-dənt) *n.* the
West —**oc·ci·den'tal** *adj.*

**oc·ci·put** (OK-sə-put) *n.* back of
head —**oc·cip'i·tal** *adj.*

**oc·clude** (ə-KLOOD) *vt.* (-clud·ed,
-clud·ing) shut in or out —**oc·clu'-
sion** (-zhən) *n.* —**oc·clu'sive** *adj.*
serving to occlude

**oc·cult** (ə-KULT) *adj.* secret, mysterious; supernatural — esoteric knowledge —*vt.* hide from
view —**oc·cul·ta'tion** (ok-əl-TAY-
shən) *n.* eclipse —**oc'cult·ism** *n.*
study of supernatural

**oc·cu·py** (OK-yə-pī) *vt.* (-pied,
-py·ing) inhabit, fill; employ; take

possession of —**oc'cu·pan·cy** *n.*
fact of occupying; residing —**oc'-
cu·pant** *n.* tenant —**oc·cu·pa'tion**
*n.* employment; pursuit; fact of
occupying; seizure —**oc·cu·pa'-
tion·al** *adj.* pert. to occupation,
*esp.* of diseases arising from a
particular occupation; pert. to
use of occupations, *eg* craft, hob-
bies *etc.* as means of rehabilitation

**oc·cur** (ə-KUR) *vi.* (-curred,
-cur·ring) happen; come to mind
—**oc·cur'rence** *n.* happening

**o·cean** (OH-shən) *n.* great body of
water; large division of this; the
sea —**o·ce·an'ic** (-shee-AN-ik) *adj.*
—**o·cea·nol·o·gy** (oh-shə-NOL-ə-
jee) *n.* branch of science that
relates to ocean

**oc·e·lot** (OS-ə-lot) *n.* Amer.
leopardlike cat

**o·cher** (OH-kər) *n.* various earths
used as yellow or brown pig-
ments; this color, from yellow to
brown

**o'clock** (ə-KLOK) *adv.* by the
clock

**oct-, octa-, octo-** (*comb. form*)
eight

**oc·ta·gon** (OK-tə-gon) *n.* plane
figure with eight angles —**oc-
tag'o·nal** *adj.*

**oc·tane** (OK-tayn) *n.* ingredient of
gasoline —**octane number** measure of ability of gasoline to reduce engine knock

**oc·tave** (OK-tiv) *n. Mus.* eighth
note above or below given note;
this space; *Poetry* eight lines of
verse

**oc·ta·vo** (ok-TAY-voh) *n.* (*pl.*
-vos) book in which each sheet is
folded three times forming eight
leaves

**oc·tet** (ok-TET) *n.* group of eight;
music for eight instruments or
singers

**oc·to·ge·nar·i·an** (ok-tə-jə-NAIR-ee-ən) n. person aged between eighty and ninety —adj.

**oc·to·pus** (OK-tə-pəs) n. mollusk with eight arms covered with suckers —oc'to·poi n./adj. (mollusk) with eight feet

**oc·tu·ple** (ok-TUU-pol) adj. eight times as many or as much; eightfold

**oc·u·lar** (OK-yə-lər) adj. of eye or sight

**OD** (oh-dee) n. overdose esp. of dangerous drug; person who has taken overdose —vi. (-ed, -ing) take, die of, overdose

**odd** adj. (-er, -est) strange, queer; incidental, random; that is one in addition when the rest have been divided into equal groups; not even; not part of a set —odds n. pl. advantage conceded in betting; likelihood —odd'i·ty n. (pl. -ties) odd person or thing; quality of being odd —odd'ments (-mənts) n. pl. remnants, trifles —odds and ends odd fragments or scraps

**ode** (ohd) n. lyric poem on particular subject

**o·di·um** (OH-dee-əm) n. hatred, widespread dislike —o'di·ous adj. hateful, repulsive, obnoxious

**o·dor** (OH-dər) n. smell —o·dor·if·er·ous (oh-də-RIF-ər-əs) adj. spreading an odor —o'dor·ize vi. (-ized, -iz·ing) fill with scent —o'dor·ous adj. fragrant; scented —o'dor·less adj.

**Od·ys·sey** (OD-ə-see) n. Homer's epic describing Odysseus's return from Troy; (o-) (pl. -seys) any long adventurous journey

**of** (əv) prep. denotes removal, separation, ownership, attribute, material, quality

**off** (awf) adv. away —prep. away from —adj. not operative; canceled or postponed; bad, sour etc.; distant; of horses, vehicles

etc., to driver's right —off·color adj. slightly ill; risqué —off·hand' adj./adv. without previous thought; curt —off'set n. that which counterbalances, compensates; method of printing —off·set' vt. counterbalance —off'spring n. children, issue —in the offing likely to happen soon

**of·fal** (AW-fəl) n. edible entrails of animal; refuse

**of·fend** (ə-FEND) vt. hurt feelings of, displease —vi. do wrong —of·fense' n. wrong; crime; insult; Sports, Mil. attacking team, force —of·fen'sive adj. causing displeasure; aggressive —n. position or movement of attack

**of·fer** (AW-fər) vt. present for acceptance or refusal; tender; propose; attempt —vi. present itself —n. offering, bid —of'fer·er, -or n. —of'fer·to·ry n. (pl. -ies) offering of the bread and wine at the Eucharist; collection in church service

**of·fice** (AW-fis) n. room(s), building, in which business, clerical work etc. is done; commercial or professional organization; official position; service; duty; form of worship —n. task; service —of'fi·cer n. one in command in army, navy, etc.; official

**of·fi·cial** (ə-FISH-əl) adj. with, by, authority —n. one holding office, esp. in public body —of·fi'cial·dom (-dəm) n. officials collectively, or their attitudes, work, usu. in contemptuous sense

**of·fi·ci·ate** (ə-FISH-ee-ayt) vi. (-at·ed, -at·ing) perform duties of office; perform ceremony

**of·fi·cious** (ə-FISH-əs) adj. objectionably persistent in offering service; interfering

**of·ten** (AW-fən) adv. many times, frequently (Poet. oft)

**o·gle** (OH-gəl) v. (o·gled, o·gling)

stare, look (at) amorously —n. this look —o'gler n.

o·gre (OH-gər) n. Folklore man-eating giant; monster

ohm n. unit of electrical resistance —ohm'me·ter (-ee-tər) n.

oil n. any of a number of thick, viscous liquids with smooth, sticky feel and wide variety of uses; petroleum; any of variety of petroleum derivatives, esp. as fuel or lubricant —vt. lubricate with oil; apply oil to —oil'y adj. —oil·i·est —oil'skin n. cloth treated with oil to make it waterproof —oiled sl. drunk

oint·ment (OINT-mənt) n. greasy preparation for healing or beautifying the skin

OK, okay (oh-kay) inf. adj./adv. all right —n. (pl. OK'S) approval —vt. (OK'd, OK'ing) approve

o·ka·pi (oh-KAH-pee) n. (pl. -pis) Afr. animal like short-necked giraffe

old (ohld) adj. (old·er, old·est or eld·er, eld·est) aged, having lived or existed long; belonging to earlier period —old-fash'ioned (-FASH-ənd) adj. in style of earlier period, out of date; fond of old ways —old maid offens. elderly spinster; fussy person

o·le·ag·i·nous (oh-lee-AJ-ə-nəs) adj. oily, producing oil; unctuous, fawning

ol·fac·to·ry (ohl-FAK-tə-ree) adj. of smelling

ol·i·gar·chy (OL-i-gahr-kee) n. (pl. -chies) government by a few —ol·i·gar'chic adj.

ol·ive (OL-iv) n. evergreen tree; its oil-yielding fruit; its wood, color —adj. grayish-green

O·lym·pi·ad (ə-LIM-pee-ad) n. four-year period between Olympic games; celebration of modern Olympic games

om·buds·man (OM-bədz-mən) n. (pl. -men) official who investigates citizens' complaints against government; person appointed to perform analogous function in a business

o·me·ga (oh-MEE-gə) n. last letter of Greek alphabet; end

om·e·let (OM-lit) n. dish of eggs beaten up and cooked in melted butter with other ingredients and seasoning

o·men (OH-mən) n. prophetic object or happening —om·i·nous (OM-ə-nəs) adj. boding evil, threatening

o·mit (oh-MIT) vt. (o·mit·ted, o·mit·ting) leave out, neglect; leave undone —o·mis'sion (-MISH-ən) n.

omni- (comb. form) all

om·ni·bus (OM-nə-bəs) n. bus; book containing several works —adj. serving, containing several objects or subjects

om·ni·di·rec·tion·al adj. (om-nə-di-REK-shə-nl) in radio, denotes transmission, reception in all directions

om·nip·o·tent (om-NIP-ə-tənt) adj. all-powerful —om·nip'o·tence n.

om·ni·pres·ent (om-nə-PREZ-ənt) adj. present everywhere —om·ni·pres'ence n.

om·nis·cient (om-NISH-ənt) adj. knowing everything —om·nis'ci·ence n.

om·niv·o·rous (om-NIV-ər-əs) adj. devouring all foods; not selective eg in reading

on prep. above and touching, at, near, toward etc.; attached to; concerning; performed upon; during; taking regularly —adj. operating; taking place —adv. so as to be on; forward; continuously etc.; in progress

o·nan·ism (OH-nə-niz-əm) n. masturbation

**once** (wuns) *adv.* one time; formerly; ever —**once'-o·ver** *n. inf.* quick examination —**at once** immediately; simultaneously

**on·co·gene** (ONG-kɔ-jeen) *n.* any of several genes that when abnormally activated can cause cancer

**on·col·o·gy** (ong-KOL-ɔ-jee) *n.* branch of medicine dealing with tumors; study of cancer

**one** (wun) *adj.* lowest cardinal number; single; united; only, without others; identical —*n.* number or figure 1; unity; single specimen —*pron.* particular but not stated person; any person —**one'ness** *n.* unity; uniformity; singleness —**one·self** *pron.* —**one'-sid'ed** *adj.* partial; uneven —**one·way** *adj.* denotes system of traffic circulation in one direction only

**on·er·ous** (ON-ɔr-ɔs) *adj.* burdensome

**on·ion** (UN-yɔn) *n.* edible bulb of pungent flavor —**know one's onions** *sl.* know one's field *etc.* thoroughly

**on·ly** (OHN-lee) *adj.* being the one specimen —*adv.* solely, merely, exclusively —*conj.* but then, excepting that

**on·o·mas·tics** (on-ɔ-MAS-tiks) *n.* with *sing. v.* study of proper names

**on·o·mat·o·poe·ia** (on-ɔ-mat-ɔ-PEE-ɔ) *n.* formation of a word by using sounds that resemble or suggest the object or action to be named —**on·o·mat·o·poe'ic,** **on·o·mat·o·po·et'ic** *adj.*

**on·set** *n.* violent attack; assault; beginning

**on·slaught** (ON-slawt) *n.* attack

**on·to** (ON-too) *prep.* on top of; aware of

**on·tog·e·ny** (on-TOJ-ɔ-nee) *n.*

development of an individual organism

**on·tol·o·gy** (on-TOL-ɔ-jee) *n.* science of being or reality

**o·nus** (OH-nɔs) *n.* (*pl.* -nus·es) responsibility, burden

**on·ward** (ON-wɔrd) *adj.* advanced or advancing —*adv.* in advance, ahead, forward —**on'wards** *adv.*

**on·yx** (ON-iks) *n.* variety of chalcedony

**ooze** (ooz) *vi.* (**oozed, ooz·ing**) pass slowly out, exude (moisture) —*n.* sluggish flow; wet mud, slime

**o·pal** (OH-pɔl) *n.* glassy gemstone displaying variegated colors —**o·pal·es'cent** *adj.*

**o·paque** (oh-PAYK) *adj.* not allowing the passage of light, not transparent —**o·pac'i·ty** (-PAS-i-tee) *n.*

**op. cit.** (op sit) (*Lat.* opere citato) in the work cited

**o·pen** (OH-pɔn) *adj.* not shut or blocked up; without lid or door; bare; undisguised; not enclosed, covered or exclusive; spread out, accessible; frank, sincere —*vt.* set open, uncover, give access to; disclose, lay bare; begin; make a hole in —*vi.* become open; begin —*n.* clear space, unenclosed country; *Sports* competition in which all may enter —**o'pen·ing** *n.* hole, gap; beginning; opportunity —*adj.* first; initial —**o'pen·ly** *adv.* without concealment —**o'pen·hand'ed** *adj.* generous —**o'pen-heart'ed** *adj.* frank, magnanimous —**o'pen-mind'ed** *adj.* unprejudiced —**o'pen·work** *n.* pattern with interstices

**op·er·a** (OP-ɔr-ɔ) *n.* musical drama —**op·er·at'ic** *adj.* of opera —**op·er·et'ta** *n.* light, comic opera

**op·er·a·tion** (op-ɔ-RAY-shɔn)

working, way things work; scope; act of surgery; military action —**op'er·ate** v. (-at·ed, -at·ing) —vt. cause to function; effect —vi. work; produce an effect; perform act of surgery; exert power —**op·er·a'tion·al** adj. of operation(s); working —**op'er·a·tive** (-ɔ-tiv) adj. working —n. worker, esp. with a special skill; secret agent

**o·phid·i·an** (oh-FID-ee-ɔn) adj./n. (reptile) of the order including snakes

**oph·thal·mic** (of-THAL-mik) adj. of eyes —**oph·thal·mol'o·gist** (-jist) n. —**oph·thal·mol'o·gy** n. study of eye and its diseases —**oph·thal'mo·scope** (-skohp) n. instrument for examining interior of eye

**opiate** see OPIUM

**o·pin·ion** (ɔ-PIN-yɔn) n. what one thinks about something; belief, judgment —**o·pine** (oh-PIN) vt. (o·pined, o·pin·ing) think; utter opinion —**o·pin'ion·at·ed** adj. stubborn in one's opinions; dogmatic

**o·pi·um** (OH-pee-ɔm) n. sedative-narcotic drug made from poppy —**o'pi·ate** (-it) n. drug containing opium; narcotic —adj. inducing sleep; soothing

**o·pos·sum** (ɔ-POS-ɔm) n. small Amer. marsupial animal, possum

**op·po·nent** (ɔ-POH-nɔnt) n. adversary, antagonist

**op·por·tune** (op-ɔr-TOON) adj. seasonable, well-timed —**op·por·tun'ism** n. policy of doing what is expedient at the time regardless of principle —**op·por·tun'ist** n./adj. —**op·por·tu'ni·ty** n. (pl. -ties) favorable time or condition; good chance

**op·pose** (ɔ-POHZ) vt. (-posed, -pos·ing) resist, withstand; contrast; set against —**op·po·site**

(OP-ɔ-zit) adj. contrary; facing; diametrically different; adverse —n. the contrary —prep./adv. facing; on the other side —**op·po·si'tion** (-ZISH-ɔn) n. antithesis; resistance; obstruction; hostility; group opposing another; party opposing that in power

**op·press** (ɔ-PRES) vt. govern with tyranny; weigh down —**op·pres'sion** (-PRESH-ɔn) n. act of oppressing; severity; misery —**op·pres'sive** adj. tyrannical; hard to bear; heavy; hot and tiring (of weather) —**op·pres'sor** (-ɔr) n.

**op·pro·bri·um** (ɔ-PROH-bree-ɔm) n. disgrace —**op·pro'bri·ous** adj. reproachful; shameful; abusive

**opt** vi. make a choice —**op'ta·tive** (OP-tɔ-tiv) adj. expressing wish or desire

**op·tic** (OP-tik) adj. of eye or sight —n. eye —pl. (with sing. v.) science of sight and light —**op'ti·cal** adj. —optical character reader device for scanning magnetically coded data on labels, cans etc. —**op·ti'cian** (-TISH-ɔn) n. maker of, dealer in eyeglasses, contact lenses

**op·ti·mism** (OP-tɔ-miz-ɔm) n. disposition to look on the bright side; doctrine that good must prevail in the end; belief that the world is the best possible world —**op'ti·mist** n. —**op·ti·mis'tic** adj.

**op·ti·mum** (OP-tɔ-mɔm) adj./n. the best, the most favorable

**op·tion** (OP-shɔn) n. choice; preference; thing chosen; in business, purchased privilege of either buying or selling things at specified price within specified time —**op'tion·al** adj. leaving to choice

**op·tom·e·trist** (op-TOM-i-trist) n. person qualified in testing eyesight, prescribing corrective lenses etc. —**op·tom'e·try** n.

**op·u·lent** (OP-yə-lənt) *adj.* rich; copious —**op'u·lence** *n.* riches, wealth

**o·pus** (OH-pəs) *n.* (*pl.* **o·pus·es** or **op·er·a** *pr.* OHP-ə-rə) work; musical composition

**or** *conj.* introduces alternatives; if not

**or·a·cle** (OR-ə-kəl) *n.* divine utterance, prophecy, *oft.* ambiguous, given at shrine of god; the shrine; wise or mysterious adviser —**o·rac·u·lar** (aw-RAK-yə-lər) *adj.* of oracle; prophetic; authoritative; ambiguous

**o·ral** (OR-əl) *adj.* spoken; by mouth —*n.* spoken examination —**o'ral·ly** *adv.*

**or·ange** (OR-inj) *n.* bright reddish-yellow round fruit; tree bearing it; fruit's color

**o·rang·u·tan** (aw-RANG-uu-tan) *n.* large E. Indian ape

**or·a·tor** (OR-ə-tər) *n.* maker of speech; skillful speaker —**o·ra'tion** (aw-RAY-shən) *n.* formal speech —**or·a·tor'i·cal** *adj.* of orator or oration —**or'a·to·ry** *n.* speeches; eloquence; small private chapel

**or·a·to·ri·o** (or-ə-TOR-ee-oh) *n.* (*pl.* **-ri·os**) semidramatic composition of sacred music

**orb** *n.* globe, sphere; eye, eyeball

**or'bit** *n.* track of planet, satellite, comet *etc.*, around another heavenly body; field of influence, sphere; eye socket —*v.* move in, or put into, an orbit

**or·chard** (OR-chərd) *n.* area for cultivation of fruit trees; the trees

**or·ches·tra** (OR-kə-strə) *n.* band of musicians; place for such band in theater *etc.* —**or·ches'tral** *adj.* —**or'ches·trate** *vt.* (**-trat·ed, -trat·ing**) compose or arrange music for orchestra; organize, arrange

**or·chid** (OR-kid) *n.* genus of various flowering plants

**or·dain** (or-DAYN) *vt.* admit to religious ministry; confer holy orders upon; decree, enact; destine —**or·di·na'tion** *n.*

**or·deal** (or-DEEL) *n.* severe, trying experience; *Hist.* form of trial by which accused underwent severe physical test

**or·der** (OR-dər) *n.* regular or proper arrangement or condition; sequence; peaceful condition of society; rank, class; group; command; request for something to be supplied; mode of procedure; instruction; monastic society —*vt.* command; request (something) to be supplied or made; arrange —**or'der·li·ness** *n.* —**or'der·ly** *adj.* tidy; methodical; well-behaved —*n.* hospital attendant; soldier performing chores for officer —**or·di·nal** (OR-dn-əl) *adj.* showing position in a series —*n.* ordinal number

**or·di·nance** (OR-dn-əns) *n.* decree, rule; rite, ceremony

**or·di·nar·y** (OR-dn-er-ee) *adj.* usual, normal; common; plain; commonplace —*n.* average condition —**or'di·nar·i·ly** *adv.*

**ord·nance** (ORD-nəns) *n.* big guns, artillery; military stores

**or·dure** (OR-jər) *n.* dung; filth

**ore** *n.* naturally occurring mineral that yields metal

**o·reg·a·no** (ə-REG-ə-noh) *n.* herb, variety of marjoram

**or·gan** (OR-gən) *n.* musical wind instrument of pipes and stops, played by keys; member of animal or plant carrying out particular function; means of action; medium of information, *esp.* newspaper —**or·gan'ic** *adj.* of, derived from, living organisms; of bodily organs; affecting bodily organs; having vital organs;

*Chem.* of compounds formed from carbon; grown with fertilizers derived from animal or vegetable matter; organized, systematic —**or·gan'i·cal·ly** *adv.* —**or'gan·ist** *n.* organ player

**or·gan·ize** (OR-gə-nīz) *vt.* (**-nized, -niz'ing**) give definite structure; get up, arrange; put into working order; unite in a society —**or'gan·ism** *n.* organized body or system; plant, animal —**or·gan·i·za'tion** *n.* act of organizing; body of people; society

**or·gasm** (OR-gaz-əm) *n.* sexual climax

**or·gy** (OR-jee) *n.* (*pl.* **-gies**) drunken or licentious revel, debauch; act of immoderation, overindulgence

**o·ri·el** (OR-ee-ol) *n.* projecting part of an upper room with a window; the window

**o·ri·ent** (OR-ee-ənt) *n.* (**O-**) East; luster of best pearls —*adj.* rising; (**O-**) Eastern —*vt.* (OR-ee-ent) place so as to face east or other known direction; take bearings; determine one's position (*lit.* or *fig.*) —**or·i·en'tal** *adj./n.* —**o·ri·en'tal·ist** *n.* expert in Eastern languages and history —**o·ri·en·ta'tion** *n.*

**or·i·fice** (OR-ə-fis) *n.* opening, mouth of a cavity, *eg* pipe

**o·ri·ga·mi** (OR-ə-GAH-mee) *n.* Japanese art of paper folding

**or·i·gin** (OR-i-jin) *n.* beginning; source; parentage

**o·rig·i·nal** (ə-RIJ-ə-nl) *adj.* primitive, earliest; new, not copied or derived; thinking or acting for oneself; eccentric —*n.* pattern, thing from which another is copied; unconventional or strange person —**o·rig·i·nal'i·ty** *n.* power of producing something individual to oneself —**o·rig'i·nal·ly** *adv.* at first; in the beginning

**o·rig·i·nate** (ə-RIJ-ə-nayt) *v.* (**-nat·ed, -nat·ing**) come or bring into existence, begin —**o·rig'i·na·tor** (-tər) *n.*

**o·ri·ole** (OR-ee-ohl) *n.* any of several thrushlike birds

**O·ri·on** (ə-Rī-ən) *n.* bright constellation

**o·ri·son** (OR-ə-zən) *n.* prayer

**or·mo·lu** (OR-mə-loo) *n.* gilded bronze; gold-colored alloy; articles of these

**or·na·ment** (OR-nə-mənt) *n.* any object used to adorn or decorate; decoration —*vt.* (-ment) adorn —**or·na·men'tal** *adj.* —**or·na·men·ta'tion** *n.*

**or·nate** (or-NAYT) *adj.* highly decorated or elaborate

**or·ni·thol·o·gy** (OR-nə-THOL-ə-jee) *n.* science of birds —**or·ni·thol'o·gist** *n.*

**o·ro·tund** (OR-ə-tund) *adj.* full, clear, and musical; pompous

**or·phan** (OR-fən) *n.* child bereaved of one or both parents —**or'phan·age** (-fə-nij) *n.* institution for care of orphans

**ortho-** (*comb. form*) right, correct

**or·tho·dox** (OR-thə-doks) *adj.* holding accepted views; conventional —**or'tho·dox·y** *n.*

**or·thog·ra·phy** (or-THOG-rə-fee) *n.* correct spelling

**or·tho·pe·dic** (or-thə-PEE-dik) *adj.* for curing deformity, disorder of bones —**or·tho·pe'dics** *n.* with *sing.* v. medical specialty dealing with this —**or·tho·pe'dist** *n.*

**Os** *Chem.* osmium

**os·cil·late** (OS-ə-layt) *vi.* (**-lat·ed, -lat·ing**) swing to and fro; waver; fluctuate (regularly) —**os·cil·la'tion** *n.* —**os'cil·la·tor** *n.* —**os·cil'la·to·ry** *adj.* —**os·cil'lo·scope** *n.* electronic instrument producing visible representation of rapidly changing quantity

**os·mi·um** (OZ-mee-əm) *n.* heaviest of known metallic elements

**os·mo·sis** (oz-MOH-sis) *n.* percolation of fluids through porous partitions —**os·mot·ic** *adj.*

**os·se·ous** (OS-ee-əs) *adj.* of, like bone; bony —**os·si·fi·ca·tion** *n.* —**os·si·fy** (-fī) *v.* (-fied, -fy·ing) turn into bone; grow rigid

**os·ten·si·ble** (o-STEN-sə-bəl) *adj.* apparent; professed —**os·ten·si·bly** *adv.*

**os·ten·ta·tion** (os-ten-TAY-shən) *n.* show, pretentious display —**os·ten·ta·tious** *adj.* given to display; showing off

**os·te·op·a·thy** (os-tee-OP-ə-thee) *n.* art of treating disease by removing structural derangement by manipulation, *esp.* of spine —**os·te·o·path** *n.* one skilled in this art

**os·tra·cize** (OS-trə-sīz) *vt.* (-cized, -ciz·ing) exclude, banish from society, exile —**os·tra·cism** (-siz-əm) *n.* social boycotting

**os·trich** *n.* large swift-running flightless Afr. bird

**oth·er** (UTH-ər) *adj.* not this; not the same; alternative, different —*pron.* other person or thing —**oth·er·wise** *adv.* differently; in another way —*conj.* else, if not

**o·ti·tis** (oh-TI-tis) *n.* inflammation of the ear

**o·ti·ose** (OH-shee-ohs) *adj.* superfluous; useless

**ot·ter** (OT-ər) *n.* furry aquatic fish-eating animal

**Ot·to·man** (OT-ə-mən) *n.* Turkish —*n.* Turk; (o-) cushioned, backless seat; cushioned footstool

**ought** (awt) *v. aux.* expressing duty or obligation or advisability; be bound

**Oui·ja** (WEE-jə) R board with letters and symbols used to obtain messages at seances

**ounce** (owns) *n.* a weight, sixteenth of avoirdupois pound (28.349 grams), twelfth of troy pound (31.103 grams)

**our** (OW-ər) *adj.* belonging to us —**ours** *pron.* —**our·selves** *pron. pl.* emphatic or reflexive form of WE

**oust** (owst) *vt.* put out, expel

**out** (owt) *adv.* from within, away; wrong; on strike —*adj.* not worth considering; not allowed; unfashionable; unconscious; not in use, operation *etc.*; at an end; not burning; *Baseball* failed to get on base —**out'er** *adj.* away from the inside —**out'er·most** (-mohst) *adj.* on extreme outside —**out'ing** *n.* pleasure excursion —**out'ward** (-wurd) *adj./adv.* —**out'wards** (-wurdz) *adv.*

**out-** (*prefix*) beyond, in excess, as **outclass** *vt.*, **outdistance** *vt.*, **outsize** *adj.* Such compounds are not given here where the meaning can easily be inferred from the simple word

**out·bal·ance** (owt-BAL-əns) *vt.* (-anced, -anc·ing) outweigh; exceed in weight

**out·board** (OWT-bord) *adj.* of boat's engine, mounted on, outside stern

**out·break** (OWT-brayk) *n.* sudden occurrence, *esp.* of disease or strife

**out·burst** (OWT-burst) *n.* bursting out, *esp.* of violent emotion

**out·cast** (OWT-kast) *n.* someone rejected —*adj.*

**out·class** (owt-KLAS) *vt.* excel, surpass

**out·come** (OWT-kum) *n.* result

**out·crop** (OWT-krop) *n. Geology* rock coming out of stratum to the surface —*vi.* (owt-KROP)

(-cropped, -crop·ping) come out to the surface

**out·fit** (OWT-fit) *n.* equipment; clothes and accessories; *inf.* group or association regarded as a unit —**out'fit·ter** *n.* one who supplies clothing and accessories

**out·flank** (owt-FLANGK) *vt.* to get beyond the flank of (enemy army); circumvent; outmaneuver

**out·go·ing** (OWT-goh-ing) *adj.* departing; friendly, sociable

**out·grow** (owt-GROH) *vt.* (-grew, -grown, -grow·ing) become too large or too old for; surpass in growth

**out·house** (OWT-hows) *n.* outdoor toilet; shed *etc.* near main building

**out·land·ish** (owt-LAN-dish) *adj.* queer, extravagantly strange

**out·law** (OWT-law) *n.* one beyond protection of the law; exile, bandit —*vt.* make (someone) an outlaw; ban

**out·lay** (OWT-lay) *n.* expenditure

**out·let** (OWT-let) *n.* opening, vent; means of release or escape; market for product or service

**out·line** (OWT-līn) *n.* rough sketch; general plan; lines enclosing visible figure —*vt.* (-lined, lin·ing) sketch; summarize

**out·look** (OWT-luuk) *n.* point of view; probable outcome; view

**out·ly·ing** (OWT-lī-ing) *adj.* distant, remote

**out·mod·ed** (owt-MOH-did) *adj.* no longer fashionable or accepted

**out·pa·tient** (OWT-pay-shənt) *n.* patient treated but not kept at hospital

**out·put** (OWT-puut) *n.* quantity produced; *Computers* information produced

**out·rage** (OWT-rayj) *n.* violation of others' rights; gross or violent offense or indignity; anger arising from this —*vt.* (-raged, rag·ing) offend grossly; insult; injure, violate —**out·ra'geous** (-RAY-jəs) *adj.*

**ou·tré** (oo-TRAY) *adj.* extravagantly odd; bizarre

**out·rig·ger** (OWT-rig-ər) *n.* frame, *esp.* with float attached, outside boat's gunwale; frame on rowing boat's side with rowlock; boat with one

**out·right** (OWT-rīt) *adj.* undisputed; downright; positive —*adv.* (owt-rīt) completely; once for all; openly

**out·set** (OWT-set) *n.* beginning

**out·side** (OWT-sīd) *n.* exterior —*adv.* (owt-SĪD) not inside; in the open air —*adj.* (owt-SĪD) on exterior; remote, unlikely; greatest possible, probable —**out·sid'er** *n.* person outside specific group; contestant thought unlikely to win

**out·skirts** (OWT-skurts) *n. pl.* outer areas, districts, *esp.* of city

**out·spok·en** (OWT-SPOH-kən) *adj.* frank, candid

**out·stand·ing** (owt-STAN-ding) *adj.* excellent; remarkable; unsettled, unpaid

**out·strip** (owt-STRIP) *vt.* (-stripped, -strip·ping) outrun; surpass

**out·wit** (owt-WIT) *vt.* (-wit·ted, -wit·ting) get the better of by cunning

**o·val** (OH-vəl) *adj.* egg-shaped; elliptical —*n.* something of this shape

**o·va·ry** (OH-və-ree) *n.* (*pl.* -ries) female egg-producing organ —**o·var'i·an** (-VAIR-ee-ən) *adj.*

**o·va·tion** (oh-VAY-shən) *n.* enthusiastic burst of applause

**ov·en** (UV-ən) *n.* heated chamber for baking in

**o·ver** (OH-vər) *adv.* above, above and beyond, going beyond, in excess, too much, past, finished, in repetition, across, downward *etc.* —*prep.* above; on, upon; more than, in excess of, along *etc.* —*adj.* upper, outer

**over-** (*prefix*) too, too much, in excess, above, as in **o·ver·awe'**

**o·ver·all** (OH-vər-awl) *n.* loose garment worn as protection against dirt *etc.* (also *pl.*) —*adj.* total

**o·ver·bear·ing** (oh-vər-BAIR-ing) *adj.* domineering

**o·ver·blown** (OH-vər-BLOHN) *adj.* excessive, bombastic

**o·ver·board** (OH-vər-bord) *adv.* from a vessel into the water

**o·ver·cast** (OH-vər-KAST) *adj.* covered over, *esp.* by clouds

**o·ver·come** (oh-vər-KUM) *vt.* (-**came**, -**come**, -**com·ing**) conquer; surmount; make powerless

**o·ver·draft** (OH-vər-draft) *n.* withdrawal of money in excess of credit balance on bank account

**o·ver·haul** (oh-vər-HAWL) *vt.* examine and set in order, repair; overtake —*n.* (OH-vər-hawl) thorough examination, *esp.* for repairs

**o·ver·head** (OH-vər-hed) *adj.* over one's head, above —*n.* expense of running a business, over and above cost of manufacturing and of raw materials —*adv.* (OH-vər-HED) aloft, above

**o·ver·kill** (OH-vər-kil) *n.* capacity, advantage greater than required

**o·ver·look** (oh-vər-LUUK) *vt.* fail to notice; disregard; look over

**o·ver·ride** (oh-vər-RĪD) *vt.* (-**rode**, -**rid·den**, -**rid·ing**) set aside, disregard; cancel; trample down

**o·ver·seas** (OH-vər-SEEZ) *adj.* foreign —*adj./adv.* (*adv. pr.* oh-vər-SEEZ) to, from place over the sea

**o·ver·se·er** (OH-vər-see-ər) *n.* supervisor —**o·ver·see'** *vt.* (-**saw**, -**seen**, -**see·ing**) supervise

**o·ver·sight** (OH-vər-sīt) *n.* failure to notice; mistake; supervision

**o·vert** (oh-VURT) *adj.* open, unconcealed —**o·vert'ly** *adv.*

**o·ver·take** (oh-vər-TAYK) *vt.* (-**took**, -**tak·en**, -**tak·ing**) move past (vehicle, person) traveling in same direction; come up with in pursuit; catch up

**o·ver·tax** (oh-vər-TAKS) *vt.* tax too heavily; impose too great a strain on

**o·ver·throw** (oh-vər-THROH) *vt.* (-**threw**, -**thrown**, -**throw·ing**) upset, overturn; defeat —*n.* (OH-vər-throh) ruin; defeat; fall

**o·ver·tone** (oh-vər-tohn) *n.* additional meaning, nuance

**o·ver·ture** (OH-vər-chər) *n.* Mus. orchestral introduction; opening of negotiations; formal offer

**o·ver·ween·ing** (OH-vər-WEE-ning) *adj.* thinking too much of oneself

**o·ver·whelm** (oh-vər-HWELM) *vt.* crush; submerge, engulf —**o·ver·whelm'ing** *adj.* decisive; irresistible

| | | |
|---|---|---|
| o·ver·bal'ance | o·ver·due' | o·ver·re·act' |
| o'ver·coat | o·ver·flow' | o·ver·rule' |
| o·ver·crowd' | o·ver·lap' | o·ver·run' |
| o·ver·do' | o'ver·lord | o·ver·shoot' |
| o'ver·dose | o·ver·pow'er | o'ver·spill |

**o·ver·wrought** (OH-vər-RAWT) *adj.* overexcited; too elaborate

**o·vip·a·rous** (oh-VIP-ər-əs) *adj.* laying eggs

**ov·ule** (OV-yool) *n.* unfertilized seed —**ov·u·late** (-yə-layt) *vi.* (-lat·ed, -lat·ing) produce, discharge (egg) from ovary

**o·vum** (OH-vəm) *n.* (*pl.* **o·va** *pr.* OH-və) female egg cell, in which development of fetus takes place

**owe** (oh) *vt.* (**owed, ow·ing**) be bound to repay; be indebted for —**owing** *adj.* owed, due —**owing to** caused by, as result of

**owl** *n.* night bird of prey —**owl'ish** *adj.* resembling an owl

**own** (ohn) *adj.* emphasizes possession —*vt.* possess; acknowledge —*vi.* to confess —**own'er·ship** *n.* possession

**ox** (oks) *n.* (*pl.* **ox·en**) large cloven-footed and usu. horned farm animal; bull or cow —**ox'·bow** (-boh) *n.* U-shaped harness collar of ox; bow-shaped bend in river

**ox·ide** (OK-sīd) *n.* compound of oxygen and another element —**ox'i·dize** *v.* (-dized, -diz·ing) (cause to) combine with oxide, rust

**ox·y·gen** (OK-si-jən) *n.* gas in atmosphere essential to life, combustion *etc.* —**ox'y·gen·ate** *vt.* (-at·ed, -at·ing) combine or treat with oxygen

**ox·y·mo·ron** (ok-si-MOR-on) *n.* figure of speech in which two ideas of opposite meaning are combined to form an expressive phrase or epithet, *eg* "cruel kindness"

**oys·ter** (OI-stər) *n.* edible bivalve mollusk or shellfish

**o·zone** (OH-zohn) *n.* form of oxygen with pungent odor —**ozone layer** layer of upper atmosphere with concentration of ozone

# P

**P** *Chem.* phosphorus

**Pa** *Chem.* protactinium

**pace** (pays) *n.* step; its length; rate of movement; walk, gait *v.* (**paced, pac·ing**) —*vi.* step —*vt.* set speed for; cross, measure with steps —**pac'er** *n.* one who sets the pace for another; horse used for pacing in harness racing —**pace'mak·er** *n.* *esp.* electronic device surgically implanted in those with heart disease

**pa·chin·ko** (pə-CHING-koh) *n.* Japanese pinball machine

**pach·y·derm** (PAK-i-durm) *n.* thick-skinned animal, *eg* elephant —**pach·y·der'ma·tous** (-mə-təs) *adj.* thick-skinned, stolid

**pac·i·fy** (PAS-ə-fī) *vt.* (-fied, -fy·ing) calm; establish peace —**pa·cif'ic** *adj.* peaceable; calm, tranquil —**pac'i·fism** *n.* —**pac'i·fist** *n.* advocate of abolition of war; one who refuses to help in war

**pack** (pak) *n.* bundle; band of animals; large set of people or things; set of, container for, retail commodities; set of playing cards; mass of floating ice —*vt.* put together in suitcase *etc.*; make into a bundle; press tightly together, cram; fill with things; fill (meeting *etc.*) with one's own supporters; order off —**pack'age** (-ij) *n.* parcel; set of items offered together —*vt.* (-aged, -ag·ing) —**pack'et** (-it) *n.* small parcel; small container (and contents); *inf.* large sum of money; small mail, passenger, freight boat —**pack'horse** *n.* horse for carrying goods —**pack ice** loose floating ice that has been compacted together

**pact** (pakt) *n.* covenant, agreement, compact

**pad**[1] *n.* piece of soft material used as a cushion, protection *etc.*; block of sheets of paper; foot or sole of various animals; place for launching rockets; *sl.* residence —*vt.* (**pad·ded, pad·ding**) make soft, fill in, protect *etc.*, with pad or padding; add to dishonestly —**padding** *n.* material used for stuffing; literary matter put in simply to increase quantity

**pad**[2] *vi.* (**pad·ded, pad·ding**) walk with soft step; travel slowly —*n.* sound of soft footstep

**pad·dle**[1] (PAD-əl) *n.* short oar with broad blade at one or each end —*v.* (**-dled, -dling**) move by, as with, paddles; row gently —**paddle wheel** wheel with crosswise blades striking water successively to propel ship

**paddle**[2] *vt.* (**-dled, -dling**) walk with bare feet in shallow water —*n.* such a walk

**pad·dock** (PAD-ək) *n.* small grass field or enclosure

**pad·dy** (PAD-ee) *n.* (*pl.* **-dies**) rice growing or in the husk —**paddy field** field where rice is grown

**pad·lock** (PAD-lok) *n.* detachable lock with hinged hoop to go through staple or ring —*vt.* fasten thus

**pae·an** (PEE-ən) *n.* song of triumph or thanksgiving

**pa·gan** (PAY-gən) *adj./n.* heathen —**pa'gan·ism** *n.*

**page**[1] (payj) *n.* one side of leaf of book *etc.*

**page**[2] *n.* boy servant; attendant —*v.* (**paged, pag·ing**) summon by loudspeaker announcement —**page'boy** *n.* hair style with hair rolled under usu. at shoulder length

**pag·eant** (PAJ-ənt) *n.* show of persons in costume in procession, dramatic scenes *etc.*, usu. illustrating history; brilliant show —**pag'eant·ry** *n.* (*pl.* **-ies**)

**pag·i·nate** (PAJ-ə-nate) *vt.* (**-nat·ed, -nat·ing**) number pages of —**pag·i·na'tion** *n.*

**pa·go·da** (pə-GOH-də) *n.* pyramidal temple or tower of Chinese or Indian type

**paid** (payd) *pt.* of PAY —**paid-up** *adj.* paid in full

**pail** (payl) *n.* bucket —**pail'ful** (-fəl) *n.* (*pl.* **-fuls**)

**pain** (payn) *n.* bodily or mental suffering; penalty or punishment —*pl.* trouble, exertion —*vt.* inflict pain upon —**pain'ful** (-fəl) *adj.* —**pain'less** (-lis) *adj.* —**pain'kill·er** *n.* drug, as aspirin, that reduces pain —**pains'tak·ing** *adj.* diligent, careful

**paint** (paynt) *n.* coloring matter spread on a surface with brushes, roller, spray gun *etc.* —*vt.* portray, color, coat, or make picture of, with paint; apply makeup; describe —**paint'er** *n.* —**paint'ing** *n.* picture in paint

**paint·er** (PAYN-tər) *n.* line at bow of boat for tying it up

**pair** *n.* set of two, *esp.* existing or generally used together —*v.* arrange in twos; group or be grouped in twos

**pais·ley** (PAYZ-lee) *n.* (*pl.* **-leys**) pattern of small curving shapes

**pa·ja·mas** (pə-JAH-məz) *n. pl.* sleeping suit of loose-fitting trousers and jacket

**pal·ace** (PAL-is) *n.* residence of king, bishop *etc.*; stately mansion —**pa·la·tial** (pə-LAY-shəl) *adj.* like a palace; magnificent —**pal·a·tine** (PAL-ə-tin) *adj.* with royal privileges

**pal·ate** (PAL-it) *n.* roof of mouth; sense of taste —**pal'at·a·ble** *adj.*

agreeable to eat —**pal′a·tal** (-təl) adj. of the palate; made by placing tongue against palate

**palatial, palatine** see PALACE

**pa·lav·er** (pə-LAV-ər) n. fuss; conference, discussion

**pale¹** (payl) adj. (pal·er, pal·est) wan, dim, whitish —vi. (paled, pal·ing) whiten; lose superiority or importance

**pale²** n. stake, boundary —**pal′ing** n. upright stakes making up fence —**beyond the pale** beyond limits of propriety, safety etc.

**pa·le·o·lith·ic** (pay-lee-ə-LITH-ik) adj. of the old Stone Age

**pa·le·on·tol·o·gy** (pay-lee-ən-TOL-ə-jee) n. study of past geological periods and fossils

**pal·ette** (PAL-it) n. artist's flat board for mixing colors on

**pal·i·mo·ny** (PAL-ə-moh-nee) n. alimony awarded to partner in broken romantic relationship

**pal·in·drome** (PAL-in-drohm) n. word, verse or sentence that is the same when read backward or forward

**pal·i·sade** (pal-ə-SAYD) n. fence of stakes; —pl. line of cliffs —vt. (-sad·ed, -sad·ing) to enclose or protect with one

**pall¹** (pawl) n. cloth spread over a coffin; depressing; oppressive atmosphere —**pall′bear·er** n. one carrying, attending coffin at funeral

**pall²** vi. become tasteless or tiresome; cloy

**pal·let¹** (PAL-it) n. straw mattress; small bed

**pallet²** n. portable platform for storing and moving goods

**pal·li·ate** (PAL-ee-ayt) vt. (-at·ed, -at·ing) relieve without curing; excuse —**pal′li·a·tive** (-ə-tiv) adj. giving temporary or partial relief —n. that which excuses, mitigates or alleviates

**pal·lid** (PAL-id) adj. pale, wan, colorless —**pal′lor** (-ər) n. paleness

**palm** (pahm) n. inner surface of hand; tropical tree; leaf of the tree as symbol of victory —vt. conceal in palm of hand; pass off by trickery —**palm′is·try** n. fortune telling from lines on palm of hand —**palm′y** adj. (palm·i·er, palm·i·est) flourishing, successful —**Palm Sunday** Sunday before Easter

**pal·o·mi·no** (pal-ə-MEE-noh) n. (pl. -nos) golden horse with white mane and tail

**pal·pa·ble** (PAL-pə-bəl) adj. obvious; certain; that can be touched or felt —**pal′pa·bly** adv.

**pal·pate** (PAL-payt) vt. Med. (-pat·ed, -pat·ing) examine by touch

**pal·pi·tate** (PAL-pi-tayt) vi. (-tat·ed, -tat·ing) throb; pulsate violently —**pal·pi·ta′tion** n. throbbing; violent, irregular beating of heart

**pal·sy** (PAWL-zee) n. (pl. -sies) paralysis, esp. with tremors —**pal′sied** adj. affected with palsy

**pal·try** (PAWL-tree) adj. (-tri·er, -tri·est) worthless, contemptible, trifling

**pam·pas** (PAM-pəz) n. pl. vast grassy treeless plains in S Amer.

**pam·per** (PAM-pər) vt. overindulge, spoil by coddling

**pam·phlet** (PAM-flit) n. thin unbound book usu. on some topical subject —**pam·phlet·eer′** n. writer of these

**pan¹** n. broad, shallow vessel; depression in ground, esp. where salt forms —vt. (panned, pan·ning) wash gold ore in pan; inf. criticize harshly —**pan out** vi. inf. result, esp. successfully

**pan²** v. (panned, pan·ning) move motion picture or TV camera slowly while shooting to cover scene, follow moving object *etc.*

**pan-, pant-, panto-** (*comb. form*) all, as in *panacea, pantomime* Such words are not given here where the meaning can easily be inferred from simple word

**pan·a·ce·a** (pan-ə-SEE-ə) *n.* universal remedy, cure for all ills

**pa·nache** (pə-NASH) *n.* dashing style

**pan·cake** (PAN-kayk) *n.* thin cake of batter fried in pan; flat cake or stick of compressed makeup —*vi. Aviation* (-caked, -cak·ing) make flat landing by dropping in a level position

**pan·chro·mat·ic** (pan-kroh-MAT-ik) *adj. Photography* sensitive to light of all colors

**pan·cre·as** (PAN-kree-əs) *n.* digestive gland behind stomach —**pan·cre·at′ic** *adj.*

**pan·da** (PAN-də) *n.* large black and white bearlike mammal of China

**pan·dem·ic** (pan-DEM-ik) *adj.* (of disease) occurring over wide area

**pan·de·mo·ni·um** (pan-də-MOH-nee-əm) *n.* scene of din and uproar

**pan·der** (PAN-dər) *v.* (*esp. with* to) give gratification to (weakness or desires) —*n.* (*also* pan·der·er) pimp

**pane** (payn) *n.* single piece of glass in a window or door

**pan·e·gyr·ic** (pan-ə-JIR-ik) *n.* speech of praise —**pan·e·gyr′i·cal** *adj.* laudatory —**pan·e·gyr′ist** *n.*

**pan·el** (PAN-l) *n.* compartment of surface, usu. raised or sunk, *eg* in door; any distinct section of something, *eg* of automobile body; strip of material inserted in garment; group of persons as team in quiz game *etc.*; list of jurors, doctors *etc.*; thin board with picture on it —*vt.* (-eled, -el·ing) adorn with panels —**pan·el·ing** *n.* paneled work —**pan′el·ist** *n.* member of panel

**pang** *n.* sudden pain, sharp twinge; compunction

**pan·ic** (PAN-ik) *n.* sudden and infectious fear; extreme fright; unreasoning terror —*adj.* of fear *etc.* —*v.* (-icked, -ick·ing) feel or cause to feel panic —**pan′ick·y** *adj.* inclined to panic; nervous —**panic** button or switch that operates safety device, for use in emergency —**panic-stricken, -struck** *adj.* panicky

**pan·o·ply** (PAN-ə-plee) *n.* (*pl.* -plies) complete, magnificent array —**pan′o·plied** *adj.*

**pan·o·ram·a** (pan-ə-RAM-ə) *n.* wide or complete view; picture arranged around spectators or unrolled before them —**pan·o·ra′mic** *adj.*

**pan·sy** (PAN-zee) *n.* (*pl.* -sies) flower, species of violet; *sl. offens.* effeminate man

**pant** *vi.* gasp for breath; yearn; long; throb —*n.* gasp

**pan·ta·loon** (PAN-tl-oon) *n.* in pantomime, foolish old man who is the butt of clown —*pl.* baggy trousers

**pan·the·ism** (PAN-thee-iz-əm) *n.* identification of God with the universe —**pan·the·is′tic** *adj.* —**pan′the·on** (-thee-ən) *n.* temple of all gods

**pan·ther** (PAN-thər) *n.* cougar; puma; variety of leopard

**pant·ies** (PAN-teez) *n. pl.* women's undergarment

**pan·to·mime** (PAN-tə-mīm) *n.* dramatic entertainment without speech

**pan·try** (PAN-tree) *n.* (*pl.* -tries *pr.* -treez) room for storing food or utensils

**pants** *n. pl.* trousers; undergarment for lower trunk

**pant·y·hose** (PAN-tee-hohz) *n. pl.* women's one-piece garment combining stockings and panties

**pant·y·waist** (PAN-tee-wayst) *n. inf. offens.* effeminate man

**pap** *n.* soft food for infants, invalids *etc.*; pulp, mash; idea, book *etc.* lacking substance

**pa·pa·cy** (PAY-pə-see) *n.* (*pl.* -cies) office of Pope; papal system —**pa'pal** *adj.* of, relating to, the Pope —**pa'pist** *n.*

**pa·pa·raz·zo** (pah-pah-RAHT-soh) *n.* (*pl.* -raz·zi *pr.* -RAHT-see) freelance photographer specializing in candid shots of celebrities

**pa·pa·ya** (pə-PAH-yə) *n.* tree bearing melon-shaped fruit; its fruit

**pa·per** (PAY-pər) *n.* material made by pressing pulp of rags, straw, wood *etc.*, into thin, flat sheets; printed sheet of paper; newspaper; article, essay —*pl.* documents *etc.* —*vt.* cover, decorate with paper —**paper over** (try to) conceal (differences *etc.*) in order to preserve friendship *etc.*

**pa·pier-mâ·ché** (PAY-pər mə-SHAY) *n.* pulp from rags or paper mixed with size, shaped by molding and dried hard

**pa·poose** (pa-POOS) *n.* N Amer. Indian child

**pap·ri·ka** (pa-PREE-kə) *n.* (powdered seasoning prepared from) type of red pepper

**pa·py·rus** (pə-PI-rəs) *n.* (*pl.* -py·ri *pr.* -PI-ri) species of reed; (manuscript written on) kind of paper made from this plant

**par** (pahr) *n.* equality of value or standing; face value (of stocks and bonds); *Golf* estimated standard score —*vt. Golf* (parred, par·ring) make par on hole or round —**par'i·ty** *n.* equality; analogy

**para-, par-, pa-** (*comb. form*) beside, beyond, as in *paradigm, parallel, parody*

**par·a·ble** (PA-rə-bəl) *n.* allegory, story with a moral lesson

**pa·rab·o·la** (pə-RAB-ə-lə) *n.* section of cone cut by plane parallel to the cone's side

**par·a·chute** (PA-rə-shoot) *n.* apparatus extending like umbrella used to retard the descent of a falling body —*v.* (-chut·ed, -chut·ing) land or cause to land by parachute —**par'a·chut·ist** *n.* —**golden parachute** employment contract for key employee of company guaranteeing substantial severance pay *etc.* if company is sold

**pa·rade** (pə-RAYD) *n.* display; muster of troops; parade ground —*v.* (-rad·ed, -rad·ing) march; display

**par·a·digm** (PA-rə-dīm) *n.* example; model —**par·a·dig·mat·ic** (-dig-MAT-ik) *adj.*

**par·a·dise** (PA-rə-dīs) *n.* heaven; state of bliss; (P-) Garden of Eden

**par·a·dox** (PA-rə-doks) *n.* statement that seems absurd or self-contradictory but may be true —**par·a·dox'i·cal** *adj.*

**par·af·fin** (PA-rə-fin) *n.* waxlike or liquid hydrocarbon mixture used as fuel, solvent, in candles *etc.*

**par·a·gon** (PA-rə-gon) *n.* pattern or model of excellence

**par·a·graph** (PA-rə-graf) *n.* portion of chapter or book; short notice, as in newspaper —*vt.* arrange in paragraphs

**par·a·keet** (PA-rə-keet) *n.* small kind of parrot

**par·al·lax** (PA-rə-laks) *n.* apparent difference in object's position or direction as viewed from different points

**par·al·lel** (PA-rə-lel) *adj.* continuously at equal distances; precisely corresponding —*n.* line equidistant from another at all points; thing exactly like another; comparison; line of latitude —*vt.* (-leled, -lel·ing) represent as similar, compare —**par′al·lel·ism** *n.* —**par·al·lel′o·gram** (-ə-gram) *n.* four-sided plane figure with opposite sides parallel

**pa·ral·y·sis** (pə-RAL-ə-sis) *n.* (pl. -ses *pr.* -seez) incapacity to move or feel, due to damage to nervous system —**par·a·lyze** (PA-rə-līz) *vt.* (-lyzed, -lyz·ing) affect with paralysis; cripple; make useless or ineffectual —**par·a·lyt′ic** (-LIT-ik) *adj./n.* (person) affected with paralysis —**infantile paralysis poliomyelitis**

**par·a·med·i·cal** (pa-rə-MED-i-kəl) *adj.* of persons working in various capacities in support of medical profession —**par·a·med′ic** *n.*

**pa·ram·e·ter** (pə-RAM-i-tər) *n.* measurable characteristic; any constant limiting factor

**par·a·mil·i·tar·y** (pa-rə-MIL-i-teree) *adj.* of civilian group organized on military lines or in support of the military

**par·a·mount** (PA-rə-mownt) *adj.* supreme, eminent, preeminent, chief

**par·a·mour** (PA-rə-moor) *n. esp.* formerly, illicit lover, mistress

**par·a·noi·a** (pa-rə-NOI-ə) *n.* mental disease with delusions of fame, grandeur, persecution —**par·a·noi′ac** *adj./n.* —**par′a·noid** *adj.* of paranoia; *inf.* exhibiting fear of persecution *etc.* —*n.*

**par·a·pet** (PA-rə-pit) *n.* low wall, railing along edge of balcony, bridge *etc.*

**par·a·pher·na·lia** (pa-rə-fər-NAYL-yə) *n. pl.* (*sometimes with sing. v.*) personal belongings; odds and ends of equipment

**par·a·phrase** (PA-rə-frayz) *n.* expression of meaning of passage in other words; free translation —*vt.* (-phrased, -phras·ing) put into other words

**par·a·ple·gi·a** (pa-rə-PLEE-jee-ə) *n.* paralysis of lower half of body —**par·a·ple′gic** *n./adj.*

**par·a·psy·chol·o·gy** (pa-rə-sī-KOL-ə-jee) *n.* study of subjects pert. to extrasensory perception, *eg* telepathy

**par·a·site** (PA-rə-sīt) *n.* animal or plant living in or on another; self-interested hanger-on —**par·a·sit′ic** (-SIT-ik) *adj.* of the nature of, living as, parasite —**par′a·sit·ism** (-si-tiz-əm) *n.* —**par·a·si·tol′o·gy** *n.* study of animal and vegetable parasites, *esp.* as causes of disease

**par·a·sol** (PA-rə-sawl) *n.* lightweight umbrella used as sunshade

**par·a·troop·er** (PA-rə-troo-pər) *n.* soldier trained to descend from airplane by parachute

**par·a·ty·phoid** (pa-rə-TĪ-foid) *n.* an infectious disease similar to but distinct from typhoid fever

**par·boil** (PAHR-boil) *vt.* boil until partly cooked

**par·cel** (PAHR-səl) *n.* packet of goods, *esp.* one enclosed in paper; quantity dealt with at one time; tract of land —*vt.* (-celed, -cel·ing) wrap up; divide into, distribute in, parts

**parch** (pahrch) *v.* dry by heating; make, become hot and dry; scorch; toast slightly

**parch·ment** (PAHRCH-mənt) *n.* sheep, goat, calf skin prepared for writing; manuscript of this

**par·don** (PAHR-dn) *vt.* forgive,

excuse —*n.* forgiveness; release from punishment —**par·don·a·ble** *adj.*

**pare** (pair) *vt.* (pared, par·ing) trim, cut edge or surface of; decrease bit by bit —**par′ing** *n.* piece pared off, rind

**par·e·gor·ic** (pa-ri-GOR-ik) *n.* tincture of opium used to stop diarrhea

**par·ent** (PAIR-ənt) *n.* father or mother —**par′ent·age** *n.* descent, extraction —**pa·ren·tal** (pə-REN-tl) *adj.* —**par′ent·hood** (-huud) *n.*

**pa·ren·the·sis** (pə-REN-thə-sis) *n.* word, phrase *etc.* inserted in passage independently of grammatical sequence and usu. marked off by brackets, dashes, or commas —**pa·ren′the·ses** (-seez) *n. pl.* mark, ( ), used for this —**par·en·thet′i·cal** *adj.*

**pa·ri·ah** (pə-RĪ-ə) *n.* social outcast

**par·ish** (PA-rish) *n.* district under one clergyman; subdivision of county —**pa·rish′ion·er** *n.* member, inhabitant of parish

**parity** see PAR

**park** (pahrk) *n.* large area of land in natural state preserved for recreational use; field or stadium for sporting events; large enclosed piece of ground, usu. with grass or woodland, attached to country house or for public use; space in camp for military supplies —*vt.* leave for a short time; maneuver (automobile *etc.*) into a suitable space; *inf.* engage in caressing and kissing in parked automobile

**par·ka** (PAHR-kə) *n.* warm waterproof coat with hood

**par·lance** (PAHR-ləns) *n.* way of speaking, conversation; idiom

**par·ley** (PAHR-lee) *n.* (*pl.* -leys) meeting between leaders or representatives of opposing forces to discuss terms —*vi.* (-leyed, -ley·ing) hold discussion about terms

**par·lia·ment** (PAHR-lə-mənt) *n.* legislature of some countries —**par·lia·men·tar′i·an** (-TAIR-ee-ən) *n.* expert in rules and procedures of a legislature or other formal organization

**par·lor** (PAHR-lər) *n.* sitting room, room for receiving company in small house; place for milking cows; room or building as business premises, *esp.* undertaker, hairdresser *etc.*

**Par·me·san** (PAHR-mə-zahn) *n.* hard dry Italian cheese for grating

**pa·ro·chi·al** (pə-ROH-kee-əl) *adj.* narrow, provincial; of a parish —**pa·ro′chi·al·ism** *n.*

**par·o·dy** (PA-rə-dee) *n.* (*pl.* -dies) composition in which author's style is made fun of by imitation; travesty —*vt.* (-died, -dy·ing) write parody of —**par′o·dist** *n.*

**pa·role** (pə-ROHL) *n.* early freeing of prisoner on condition of good behavior; word of honor —*vt.* (-roled, rol·ing) place on parole

**par·ox·ysm** (PA-rək-siz-əm) *n.* sudden violent attack of pain, rage, laughter

**par·quet** (pahr-KAY) *n.* flooring of wooden blocks arranged in pattern —*vt.* (-queted *pr.* -KAYD, -quet·ing *pr.* -KAY-ing) lay a parquet

**par·ri·cide** (PA-rə-sīd) *n.* murder or murderer of a parent

**par·rot** (PA-rət) *n.* bird with short hooked beak, some varieties of which can imitate speaking; unintelligent imitator —*vt.* imitate or repeat without understanding

**par·ry** (PA-ree) *vt.* (-ried, -ry·ing) ward off, turn aside —*n.* (*pl.* -ries) act of parrying, *esp.* in fencing

**parse** (pahrs) *vt.* (parsed, parsing) describe (word), analyze (sentence) in terms of grammar

**par·si·mo·ny** (PAHR-sə-moh-nee) *n.* stinginess; undue economy —**par·si·mo'ni·ous** *adj.* sparing —**par·si·mo'ni·ous·ly** *adv.*

**pars·ley** (PAHR-slee) *n.* herb used for seasoning, garnish *etc.*

**pars·nip** (PAHR-snip) *n.* edible whitish root vegetable

**par·son** (PAHR-sən) *n.* member of clergy of parish or church —**par'son·age** *n.* parson's house

**part** (pahrt) *n.* portion, section, share; division; actor's role; duty; (*oft. pl.*) region; interest —*v.* divide; separate —**part'ing** *n.* division between sections of hair on head; separation; leave-taking —**part'ly** *adv.* in part —**part song** song for several voices singing in harmony

**par·take** (pahr-TAYK) *v.* (-took, -tak·en, -tak·ing) take or have share in; take food or drink

**par·tial** (PAHR-shəl) *adj.* not general or complete; prejudiced; fond of —**par'tial·ly** *adv.* partly —**par·ti·al·i·ty** (pahr-shee-AL-i-tee) *n.* favoritism; fondness for

**par·tic·i·pate** (pahr-TIS-ə-payt) *v.* (-pat·ed, -pat·ing) share in; take part in —**par·tic'i·pant** *n.* —**par·tic'i·pa·to·ry** *adj.*

**par·ti·ci·ple** (PAHR-tə-sip-əl) *n.* adjective made by inflection from verb and keeping verb's relation to dependent words —**par·ti·cip'i·al** *adj.*

**par·ti·cle** (PAHR-ti-kəl) *n.* minute portion of matter; least possible amount; minor part of speech in grammar, prefix, suffix

**par·ti·col·ored** (PAHR-tee-kul-ord) *adj.* differently colored in different parts, variegated

**par·tic·u·lar** (pahr-TIK-yə-lər) *adj.* relating to one, not general; distinct; minute; very exact; fastidious —*n.* detail, item —*pl.* detailed account; items of information —**par·tic'u·lar·ize** *vt.* (-ized, -iz·ing) mention in detail —**par·tic'u·lar·ly** *adv.*

**par·ti·san** (PAHR-tə-zən) *n.* adherent of a party; guerrilla, member of resistance movement —*adj.* adhering to faction; prejudiced

**par·ti·tion** (pahr-TISH-ən) *n.* division; interior dividing wall —*vt.* divide, cut into sections

**part·ner** (PAHRT-nər) *n.* ally or companion; member of a partnership; one who dances with another; a husband or wife; *Golf, Tennis etc.* one who plays with another against opponents —*vt.* be a partner of —**part'ner·ship** *n.* association of persons for business *etc.*

**par·tridge** (PAHR-trij) *n.* (*pl.* -tridg·es) game bird of the grouse family

**par·tu·ri·tion** (pahr-tyuu-RISH-ən) *n.* act of bringing forth young; childbirth

**par·ty** (PAHR-tee) *n.* (*pl.* -ties) social assembly; group of persons traveling or working together; group of persons united in opinion; side; person —*adj.* of, belonging to, a party or faction —**party line** telephone line serving two or more subscribers; policies of political party —**party wall** common wall separating adjoining premises

**par·ve·nu** (PAHR-və-noo) *n.* one newly risen into position of notice, power, wealth; upstart

**pas·chal** (PAS-kəl) *adj.* of Passover or Easter

**pass** *vt.* go by, beyond, through *etc.*; exceed; be accepted by; undergo successfully; spend; transfer; exchange; disregard; bring into force, sanction a legislative bill *etc.* —*vi.* go; be transferred from one state or person to another; elapse; undergo examination successfully; be taken as member of religious or racial group other than one's own —*n.* way, *esp.* a narrow and difficult way; permit, license, authorization; successful result from test; condition; *Sports* transfer of ball by kick or throw —**pass'a·ble** *adj.* (just) acceptable —**pass'ing** *adj.* transitory; cursory, casual —**pass off** present (something) under false pretenses —**pass up** ignore, neglect, reject

**pas·sage** (PAS-ij) *n.* channel, opening; way through, corridor; part of book *etc.*; journey, voyage, fare; enactment of rule, law by legislature *etc.*; conversation, dispute; incident

**pas·sé** (pa-SAY) *adj.* out-of-date; past the prime

**pas·sen·ger** (PAS-ən-jər) *n.* traveler, *esp.* by public conveyance

**pas·ser·ine** (PAS-ər-in) *adj.* of the order of perching birds

**pas'sim** *Lat.* everywhere, throughout

**pas·sion** (PASH-ən) *n.* ardent desire, *esp.* sexual; any strongly felt emotion; suffering (*esp.* that of Christ) —**pas'sion·ate** (-it) *adj.* (easily) moved by strong emotions

**pas·sive** (PAS-iv) *adj.* unresisting, submissive; inactive; denoting grammatical voice of verb in which the subject receives the action —**pas·siv'i·ty** *n.* —**passive smoking** involuntary inhalation of smoke from others' cigarettes by nonsmoker

**Pass·o·ver** (PAS-oh-vər) *n.* Jewish spring festival commemorating exodus of Jews from Egypt

**pass'port** *n.* official document

granting permission to pass, travel abroad *etc.*

**pass·word** (PAS-wurd) *n.* word, phrase, to distinguish friend from enemy; countersign

**past** *adj.* ended; gone by; elapsed —*n.* bygone times —*adv.* by; along —*prep.* beyond; after

**pas·ta** (PAH-stə) *n.* any of several variously shaped edible preparations of dough, *eg* spaghetti

**paste** (payst) *n.* soft composition, as toothpaste; soft plastic mixture or adhesive; fine glass to imitate gems —*vt.* (**past·ed, past·ing**) fasten with paste —**past·y** *adj.* (**past·i·er, past·i·est**) like paste; white; sickly

**pas·tel** (pa-STEL) *n.* colored crayon; art of drawing with crayons; pale, delicate color —*adj.* delicately tinted

**pas·teur·ize** (PAS-chə-rīz) *vt.* (**-ized, -iz·ing**) sterilize by heat —**pas·teur·i·za'tion** *n.*

**pas·tiche** (pa-STEESH) *n.* literary, musical, artistic work composed of parts borrowed from other works and loosely connected together; work imitating another's style

**pas·tille** (pa-STEEL) *n.* lozenge; aromatic substance burned as deodorant or fumigator

**pas·time** (PAS-tīm) *n.* that which makes time pass agreeably; recreation

**pas·tor** (PAS-tər) *n.* priest or minister in charge of a church —**pas'to·ral** *adj.* of, or like, shepherd's or rural life; of office of pastor —*n.* poem describing rural life

**pas·try** (PAY-stree) *n.* (*pl.* **-tries**) article of food made chiefly of flour, shortening and water

**pas·ture** (PAS-chər) *n.* grass for food of cattle; ground on which cattle graze —*v.* (**-tured,**

-tur·ing) (cause to) graze —**pas'·tur·age** n. (right to) pasture

**pat**[1] vt. (pat·ted, pat·ting) tap —n. light, quick blow; small mass, as of butter, beaten into shape

**pat**[2] adv. exactly; fluently; opportunely; glib; exactly right

**patch** (pach) n. piece of cloth sewn on garment; spot; plot of ground; protecting pad for the eye; small contrasting area; short period —vt. mend; repair clumsily —**patch'y** adj. (patch·i·er, patch·i·est) of uneven quality; full of patches —**patch'work** n. work composed of pieces sewn together; jumble

**patch·ou·li** (pə-CHOO-lee) n. Indian herb; perfume from it

**pate** (payt) n. head; top of head

**pâ·té** (pah-TAY) n. spread of finely chopped or puréed liver etc. —**pâté de foie gras** (də-fwah-GRAH) one made of goose liver

**pa·tel·la** (pə-TEL-ə) n. (pl. -las) kneecap —**pa·tel'lar** adj.

**pat·ent** (PAT-nt) n. document securing to person or organization exclusive right to invention —adj. open; evident; manifest; open to public perusal; as letters patent —vt. secure a patent —**pat·ent·ee'** n. one who has a patent —**pat'ent·ly** adv. obviously —**patent leather** (imitation) leather processed to give hard, glossy surface

**pa·ter·fa·mil·i·as** (pah-tər-fə-MIL-ee-əs n. (pl. -əs·es) father of a family

**pa·ter·nal** (pə-TUR-nl) adj. fatherly; of a father; related through a father —**pa·ter'nal·ism** n. authority exercised in a way that limits individual responsibility —**pa·ter·nal·is'tic** adj. —**pa·ter'ni·ty** n. relation of a father to his offspring; fatherhood

**pa·ter·nos·ter** (PAY-tər-NOS-tər) n. Lord's Prayer; beads of rosary

**path** n. (pl. paths pr. pathz) way or track; course of action

**pa·thet·ic** (pə-THET-ik) adj. affecting or moving tender emotions; distressingly inadequate —**pa·thet'i·cal·ly** adv.

**path·o·gen·ic** (path-ə-JEN-ik) adj. producing disease —**path'o·gen** n. disease-producing agent eg virus

**pa·thol·o·gy** (pə-THOL-ə-jee) n. science of diseases —**path·o·log'i·cal** (-LOJ-i-kəl) adj. of the science of disease; due to disease; compulsively motivated —**pa·thol'o·gist** n.

**pa·thos** (PAY-thos) n. power of exciting tender emotions

**pa·tient** (PAY-shənt) adj. bearing trials calmly —n. person under medical treatment —**pa'tience** n. quality of enduring; card game for one player

**pat·i·na** (pə-TEE-nə) n. fine layer on a surface; sheen of age on woodwork

**pat·i·o** (PAT-ee-oh) n. (pl. -i·os) (usu. paved) area adjoining house for lounging etc.

**pat·ois** (PA-twah) n. (pl. same form, pr. -twahz) regional dialect

**pa·tri·arch** (PAY-tree-ahrk) n. father and founder of family, esp. Biblical —**pa·tri·ar'chal** adj. venerable

**pa·tri·cian** (pə-TRISH-ən) n. noble of ancient Rome; one of noble birth —adj. of noble birth

**pat·ri·cide** (PA-trə-sīd) n. murder or murderer of father

**pat·ri·mo·ny** (PA-trə-moh-nee) n. (pl. -nies) property inherited from ancestors

**pa·tri·ot** (PAY-tree-ət) n. one who loves own country and maintains its interests —**pa'tri·ot·ism** n. (-ə-tiz-əm) love of, loyalty to one's country —**pa·tri·ot·ic** (-OT-ik) adj. inspired by love of one's country

**pa·trol** (pə-TROHL) n. regular circuit by guard; person, small group patrolling; unit of Boy Scouts or Girl Scouts —v. (-trolled, -trol·ling) go around on guard, or reconnoitering

**pa·tron** (PAY-trən) n. one who sponsors or aids artists, charities etc.; protector; regular customer; guardian saint; one who has disposition of benefice etc. —**pa'·tron·age** n. support given by, or position of, a patron —**pa'tron·ize** vt. (-ized, -iz·ing) assume air of superiority to, as customer; frequent as customer; encourage

**pat·ro·nym·ic** (pa-trə-NIM-ik) n. name derived from that of parent or an ancestor

**pat·ter** (PAT-ər) vi. make noise, as sound of quick, short steps; tap in quick succession; pray, talk rapidly —n. quick succession of taps; inf. glib, rapid speech

**pat·tern** (PAT-ərn) n. arrangement of repeated parts; design; shape to direct cutting of cloth etc.; specimen —vt. (with on, after) model; decorate with pattern

**pat·ty** (PAT-ee) n. (pl. -ties) a little pie; thin round piece of meat, candy etc.

**pau·ci·ty** (PAW-si-tee) n. scarcity; smallness of quantity; fewness

**paunch** (pawnch) n. belly; potbelly

**pau·per** (PAW-pər) n. poor person, esp. formerly, one supported by the public —**pau'per·ism** n. destitution; extreme poverty —**pau'per·ize** vt. (-ized, -iz·ing) reduce to pauperism

**pause** pawz) vi. (paused, paus·ing) cease for a time —n. stop or rest

**pave** (payv) vt. (paved, pav·ing) form surface with stone or brick —**pave'ment** (-mənt) n. paved floor, footpath; material for paving —**pave the way for** lead up to; facilitate entrance of

**pa·vil·ion** (pə-VIL-yən) n. clubhouse on playing field etc.; building for housing exhibition etc.; large ornate tent

**paw** n. foot of animal —v. scrape with forefoot; handle roughly; stroke with the hands

**pawn**[1] vt. deposit (article) as security for money borrowed —n. article deposited —**pawn'bro·ker** n. lender of money on goods pledged

**pawn**[2] n. piece in chess; fig. person used as mere tool

**pay** v. (paid, pay·ing) —vt. give money etc., for goods or services rendered; compensate; give or bestow; be profitable to; (with out) release bit by bit, as rope —vi. be remunerative; be profitable; (with out) spend —n. wages; paid employment —**pay'a·ble** adj. justly due; profitable —**pay·ee'** n. person to whom money is paid or due —**pay'ment** (-mənt) n. discharge of debt —**pay'load** n. part of cargo earning revenue; explosive power of missile etc. —**paying** guest boarder, lodger, esp. in private house —**pay television** programs provided for viewers who pay monthly or per-program fees

**Pb** Chem. lead

**Pd** Chem. palladium

**pea** (pee) n. fruit, growing in pods, of climbing plant; the plant —**pea-green** adj. of shade of green like color of green peas —**pea green** this color —**pea soup** thick soup made of green peas; inf. thick fog

**peace** (pees) n. freedom from war; harmony; quietness of mind;

calm; repose —**peace'a·ble** *adj.* disposed to peace —**peace'a·bly** *adv.* —**peace'ful** *adj.* free from war, tumult; mild; undisturbed

**peach** (peech) *n.* stone fruit of delicate flavor; *inf.* person or thing very pleasant; pinkish-yellow color —**peach'y** *adj.* (**peach·i·er, peach·i·est**) like peach; *inf.* fine, excellent

**pea·cock** (PEE-kok) *n.* male of bird (**pea'fowl**) with fanlike tail, brilliantly colored (**pea'hen** *fem.*) —*vt.* strut about or pose, like a peacock

**peak** (peek) *n.* pointed end of anything, *esp.* hill's sharp top; point of greatest development *etc.*; sharp increase; projecting piece on front of cap —*v.* (cause to) form, reach peaks —**peaked** *adj.* like, having a peak —**peak·ed** (PEE-kid) sickly, wan, drawn

**peal** (peel) *n.* loud sound or succession of loud sounds; changes rung on set of bells; chime —*vi.* sound loudly

**pea·nut** (PEE-nut) *n.* pea-shaped nut that ripens underground; the plant —*pl. inf.* trifling amount of money

**pear** (pair) *n.* tree yielding sweet, juicy fruit; the fruit —**pear-shaped** *adj.* shaped like a pear, heavier at the bottom than the top

**pearl** (purl) *n.* hard, lustrous structure found in several mollusks, *esp.* pearl oyster and used as jewel —**pearl'y** *adj.* (**pearl·i·er, pearl·i·est**) like pearls

**peas·ant** (PEZ-ənt) *n.* in certain countries, member of low social class, *esp.* in rural district; boorish person —**peas'ant·ry** *n.* peasants collectively

**peat** (peet) *n.* decomposed vegetable substance found in bogs; turf of it used for fuel —**peat moss** dried peat, used as mulch *etc.*

**peb·ble** (PEB-əl) *n.* small roundish stone; pale, transparent rock crystal; grainy, irregular surface —*vt.* (**-bled, -bling**) pave, cover with pebbles

**pe·can** (pi-KAHN) *n.* N Amer. tree, species of hickory, allied to walnut; its edible nut

**pec·ca·ble** (PEK-ə-bəl) *adj.* liable to sin —**pec'cant** (**-ənt**) *adj.* sinful; offensive

**pec·ca·dil·lo** (pek-ə-DIL-oh) *n.* (*pl.* **-loes**) slight offense; petty crime

**pec·ca·ry** (PEK-ə-ree) *n.* (*pl.* **-ries**) vicious Amer. animal allied to pig

**peck**[1] (pek) *n.* fourth part of bushel, equal to 8.81 liters; great deal

**peck**[2] *v.* pick, strike with or as with beak; nibble —*n.* quick kiss —*n.* —**peck'ish** *adj. inf.* irritable

**pec·tin** (PEK-tin) *n.* gelatinizing substance obtained from ripe fruits —**pec'tic** *adj.* congealing; denoting pectin

**pec·to·ral** (PEK-tər-əl) *adj.* of the breast —*n.* pectoral part of organ; breastplate

**pec·u·late** (PEK-yə-layt) *v.* (**-lated, -lating**) embezzle; steal —**pec·u·la'tion** *n.*

**pe·cu·liar** (pi-KYOOL-yər) *adj.* strange; particular; belonging to —**pe·cu·li·ar'i·ty** *n.* oddity; characteristic; distinguishing feature

**pe·cu·ni·ar·y** (pi-KYOO-nee-er-ee) *adj.* relating to, or consisting of, money

**ped·a·gogue** (PED-ə-gog) *n.* schoolmaster; pedant —**ped·a·gog'ic** (**-GOJ-ik**) *adj.*

**ped·al** (PED-l) *n.* something to transmit motion from foot; foot lever to modify tone or swell of musical instrument; *Mus.* note, usu. bass, held through successive harmonies —*adj.* of a foot —*v.* (-daled, -dal·ing) propel bicycle *etc.* by using its pedals; use pedal

**ped·ant** (PED-ənt) *n.* one who overvalues, or insists on, petty details of book learning, grammatical rules *etc.* —**pe·dan'tic** *adj.* —**ped'ant·ry** *n.* (*pl.* -tries)

**ped·dle** (PED-l) *vt.* (-dled, -dling) go around selling goods —**ped'dler, ped'lar** *n.*

**ped·er·ast** (PED-ə-rast) *n.* man who has homosexual relations with boy —**ped'er·as·ty** *n.*

**ped·es·tal** (PED-ə-stl) *n.* base of column, pillar —put on a pedestal idealize

**pe·des·tri·an** (pə-DES-tree-ən) *n.* one who goes on foot; walker —*adj.* going on foot; commonplace; dull, uninspiring

**pe·di·at·rics** (pee-dee-A-triks) *n.* (*with sing. v.*) branch of medicine dealing with diseases and disorders of children —**pe·di·a·tri'cian** (-ə-TRISH-ən) *n.*

**ped·i·cel** (PED-ə-səl) *n.* small, short stalk of leaf, flower or fruit

**ped·i·cure** (PED-i-kyoor) *n.* medical or cosmetic treatment of feet

**ped'i·gree** *n.* register of ancestors; genealogy

**ped·i·ment** (PED-ə-mənt) *n.* triangular part over Greek portico *etc.* —**ped·i·men'tal** (-MEN-tl) *adj.*

**pedlar** *see* PEDDLE

**pe·dom·e·ter** (pə-DOM-i-tər) *n.* instrument that measures the distance walked

**pe·dun·cle** (pi-DUNG-kəl) *n.* flower stalk; stalklike structure

**peek** *vi./n.* peep, glance

**peel** *vt.* strip off skin, rind or any form of covering —*vi.* come off, as skin, rind —*n.* skin, rind —**peeled** *adj. inf.* of eyes, watchful —**peel'ings** *n. pl.* parings

**peep**[1] *vi.* look slyly or quickly —*n.* such a look

**peep**[2] *vi.* cry, as chick; chirp —*n.* such a cry

**peer**[1] *n.* nobleman (**peer'ess** *fem.*); one of the same rank, ability *etc.* —**peer'age** (-ij) *n.* body of peers; rank of peer —**peer'less** (-lis) *adj.* without match or equal

**peer**[2] *vi.* look closely and intently

**peeved** (peevd) *adj.* sulky, irritated —**peeve** *vt.* (peeved, peev·ing) annoy; vex

**pee'vish** *adj.* fretful; irritable —**pee'vish·ly** *adv.* —**pee'vish·ness** (-nis) *n.* annoyance

**peg** *n.* nail or pin for joining, fastening, marking *etc.*; (mark of) level, standard *etc.* —*v.* (pegged, peg·ging) fasten with pegs; stabilize (prices); *inf.* throw; (*with* away) persevere —take down a peg humble (someone)

**peign·oir** (pain-WAHR) *n.* woman's dressing gown, jacket, wrapper

**pe·jo·ra·tive** (pi-JOR-ə-tiv) *adj.* (of words *etc.*) with unpleasant, disparaging connotation

**Pe·king·ese** (pee-kə-NEEZ) *n.* small Chinese dog

**pe·lag·ic** (pə-LAJ-ik) *adj.* of the deep sea

**pel·i·can** (PEL-i-kən) *n.* large, fish-eating waterfowl with large pouch beneath its bill

**pel·let** (PEL-it) *n.* little ball, pill

**pell-mell** *adv.* in utter confusion, headlong

**pel·lu·cid** (pə-LOO-sid) *adj.* translucent; clear

**pelt**[1] *vt.* strike with missiles —*vi.* throw missiles; rush; fall persistently, as rain

**pelt**[2] *n.* raw hide or skin

**pel'vis** *n.* (*pl.* -vis·es) bony cavity

at base of human trunk —**pel'vic** *adj.* pert. to pelvis

**pen**[1] *n.* instrument for writing —*vt.* (**penned, pen·ning**) compose; write —**pen name** author's pseudonym —**pen pal** person with whom one corresponds, usu. someone whom one has never met

**pen**[2] *n.* small enclosure, as for sheep —*vt.* (**penned, pen·ning**) put, keep in enclosure

**pen**[3] *n.* female swan

**pe·nal** (PEEN-l) *adj.* of, incurring, inflicting, punishment —**pe'nal·ize** *vt.* (**-ized, -iz·ing**) impose penalty on; handicap —**pen'al·ty** *n.* (*pl.* **-ties**) punishment for crime or offense; forfeit; *Sports* handicap or disadvantage imposed for infringement of rule *etc.*

**pen·ance** (PEN-ons) *n.* suffering submitted to as expression of penitence; repentance

**pen·chant** (PEN-chont) *n.* inclination, decided taste

**pen·cil** (PEN-sol) *n.* instrument as of graphite, for writing *etc.*; *Optics* narrow beam of light —*vt.* (**-ciled, -cil·ing**) paint or draw; mark with pencil

**pend·ant** (PEN-dont) *n.* hanging ornament —**pend'ent** *adj.* suspended; hanging; projecting

**pend'ing** *prep.* during, until —*adj.* awaiting settlement; undecided; imminent

**pen·du·lous** (PEN-jo-los) *adj.* hanging, swinging —**pen'du·lum** (-lom) *n.* suspended weight swinging to and fro, *esp.* as regulator for clock

**pen·e·trate** (PEN-i-trayt) *vt.* (**-trat·ed, trat·ing**) enter into; pierce; arrive at the meaning of —**pen·e·tra·bil'i·ty** *n.* quality of being penetrable —**pen'e·tra·ble** (-tra-bol) *adj.* capable of being entered or pierced —**penetrating**

*adj.* sharp; easily heard; subtle; quick to understand —**pen·e·tra'tion** *n.* insight, acuteness —**pen'e·tra·tive** (-tray-tiv) *adj.* piercing; discerning

**pen·guin** (PENG-gwin) *n.* flightless, short-legged swimming bird

**pen·i·cil·lin** (pen-o-SIL-in) *n.* antibiotic drug effective against a wide range of diseases, infections

**pen·in·su·la** (po-NINS-yo-lo) *n.* portion of land nearly surrounded by water —**pen·in'su·lar** *adj.*

**pe·nis** (PEE-nis) *n.* (*pl.* **-nis·es**) male organ of copulation (and of urination) in man and many mammals

**pen·i·tent** (PEN-i-tont) *adj.* affected by sense of guilt —*n.* one that repents of sin —**pen'i·tence** *n.* sorrow for sin; repentance —**pen·i·ten'tial** (-TEN·shol) *adj.* of, or expressing, penitence —**pen·i·ten'tia·ry** (-TEN-sho-ree) *adj.* relating to penance, or to the rules of penance —*n.* (*pl.* **-ries**) prison

**pen·nant** (PEN-ont) *n.* long narrow flag

**pen·non** (PEN-on) *n.* small pointed or swallow-tailed flag

**pen·ny** (PEN-ee) *n.* (*pl.* **-nies**) coin, 100th part of dollar; similar coin of other countries —**pen'ni·less** (-lis) *adj.* having no money; poor —**a pretty penny** *inf.* considerable amount of money

**pe·nol·o·gy** (pee-NOL-o-jee) *n.* study of punishment and prevention of crime

**pen·sion**[1] (PEN-shon) *n.* regular payment to old people, retired public officials, workers *etc.* —*vt.* grant pension to —**pen'sion·er** *n.*

**pen·sion**[2] (pahn-SYAWN) *n.* in France, boarding house; room and board

**pen·sive** (PEN-siv) *adj.* thoughtful with sadness; wistful

**pent** *adj.* shut up, kept in —**pent-up** *adj.* not released, repressed

**pen·ta·gon** (PEN-tə-gon) *n.* plane figure having five angles —**pen·tag·o·nal** (-TAG-ə-nl) *adj.*

**pen·tam·e·ter** (pen-TAM-i-tər) *n.* verse of five metrical feet

**Pen·ta·teuch** (PEN-tə-tyook) *n.* first five books of Old Testament

**pen·tath·lon** (pen-TATH-lən) *n.* athletic contest of five events

**Pen·te·cost** (PEN-ti-kawst) *n.* Christian festival of seventh Sunday after Easter

**pent·house** (PENT-hows) *n.* (*pl.* **-hous·es** *pr.* -howz-iz) apartment or other structure on top, or top floor, of building

**pen·tode** (PEN-tohd) *n. Electronics* five-electrode vacuum tube, having anode, cathode and three grids

**pe·nult** (PEE-nult) *n.* last syllable but one of word —**pen·ul·ti·mate** (pi-NUL-tə-mit) *adj.* next before the last

**pe·num·bra** (pi-NUM-brə) *n.* imperfect shadow; in an eclipse, the partially shadowed region that surrounds the full shadow

**pen·u·ry** (PEN-yə-ree) *n.* extreme poverty; extreme scarcity —**pe·nu·ri·ous** (pə-NUUR-ee-əs) *adj.* niggardly, stingy; poor, scanty

**peo·ple** (PEE-pəl) *n. pl.* persons generally; community, nation; race; family —*vt.* (**-pled, -pling**) stock with inhabitants; populate

**pep** *n. inf.* vigor; energy; enthusiasm —*vt.* (**pepped, pep·ping**) impart energy to; speed up

**pep·per** (PEP-ər) *n.* fruit of climbing plant that yields pungent aromatic spice; various slightly pungent vegetables *eg* capsicum —*vt.* season with pepper; sprinkle, dot; pelt with missiles —**pep′per·y** *adj.* having the qualities of pepper; irritable —**pep′per·corn** *n.* dried pepper berry; something trifling —**pep′per·mint** *n.* plant noted for aromatic pungent liquor distilled from it; a candy flavored with this

**pep·tic** (PEP-tik) *adj.* relating to digestion or digestive juices

**per** (pər) *prep.* for each; by; in manner of

**per-, pel-** (*prefix*) through, thoroughly, as in *perfect, pellucid*

**per·am·bu·late** (pər-AM-byə-layt) *v.* (**-lat·ed, -lat·ing**) —*vt.* walk through or over; traverse —*vi.* walk about —**per·am′bu·la·tor** *n.* baby carriage

**per an·num** (pər AN-əm) *Lat.* by the year

**per·cale** (pər-KAYL) *n.* woven cotton used *esp.* for sheets

**per cap·i·ta** (pər KAP-i-tə) *Lat.* for each person

**per·ceive** (pər-SEEV) *vt.* (**-ceived, -ceiv·ing**) obtain knowledge of through senses; observe; understand —**per·ceiv′a·ble** *adj.* —**per·cep′ti·ble** *adj.* discernible, recognizable —**per·cep′tion** *n.* faculty of perceiving; intuitive judgment —**per·cep′tive** *adj.*

**per·cent·age** (pər-SEN-tij) *n.* proportion or rate per hundred —**per cent** in each hundred

**perception** *n. see* PERCEIVE

**perch**[1] (purch) *n.* freshwater fish

**perch**[2] *n.* resting place, as for bird —*vt.* place, as on perch —*vi.* alight, settle on fixed body; roost; balance on

**per·cip·i·ent** (pər-SIP-ee-ənt) *adj.* having faculty of perception; perceiving —*n.* one who perceives

**per·co·late** (PUR-kə-layt) *v.* (**-lat·ed, -lat·ing**) pass through fine mesh as liquid; permeate; filter —**per′co·la·tor** *n.* coffeepot with filter

**per·cus·sion** (pər-KUSH-ən) *n.* collision; impact; vibratory shock —**percussion instrument** one played by being struck, *eg* drum

**per di·em** (pər DEE-əm) *Lat.* by the day; for each day

**per·di·tion** (pər-DISH-ən) *n.* spiritual ruin

**per·e·gri·nate** (per-i-grə-nayt) *vi.* (-nat·ed, -nat·ing) travel about; roam

**per·e·grine** (PER-i-grin) *n.* type of falcon

**per·emp·to·ry** (pə-REMP-tə-ree) *adj.* authoritative, imperious; forbidding debate; decisive

**per·en·ni·al** (pə-REN-ee-əl) *adj.* lasting through the years; perpetual, unfailing —*n.* plant lasting more than two years

**per·fect** (PUR-fikt) *adj.* complete; finished; whole; unspoiled; faultless; correct, precise; excellent; of highest quality —*n.* tense denoting a complete act —*vt.* (pər-FEKT) improve; finish; make skillful —**per·fect'·i·ble** *adj.* capable of becoming perfect —**per·fec'tion** (-FEK-shən) *n.* state of being perfect; faultlessness —**per'fect·ly** *adv.*

**per·fi·dy** (PUR-fi-dee) *n.* (-dies) treachery, disloyalty —**per·fid'i·ous** *adj.*

**per·fo·rate** (PUR-fə-rayt) *vt.* (-rat·ed, -rat·ing) make hole(s) in, penetrate —**per·fo·ra'tion** *n.* hole(s) made through ring

**per·force** (pər-FORS) *adv.* of necessity

**per·form** (pər-FORM) *vt.* bring to completion; accomplish; fulfill; represent on stage —*vi.* function; act part; play, as on musical instrument —**per·form'ance** (-məns) *n.*

**per·fume** (PUR-fyoom) *n.* agreeable scent; fragrance —*vt.* (pər-FYOOM) (-fumed, -fum·ing) imbue with an agreeable odor; scent —**per·fum'er** *n.*

**per·func·to·ry** (pər-FUNGK-tə-ree) *adj.* superficial; hasty; done indifferently

**per·go·la** (PUR-gə-lə) *n.* area covered by plants growing on trellis; the trellis

**per·haps** (pər-HAPS) *adv.* possibly

**peri-** (*prefix*) round, as in *perimeter, period, periphrasis*

**per·i·car·di·um** (per-i-KAHR-dee-əm) *n.* (*pl.* -di·a *pr.* -dee-ə) membrane enclosing the heart —**per·i·car·di'tis** (-Dl-tis) *n.* inflammation of this

**per·i·he·li·on** (per-ə-HEE-lee-ən) *n.* (*pl.* -li·a *pr.* -lee-ə) point in orbit of planet or comet nearest to sun

**per·il** (PER-əl) *n.* danger; exposure to injury —**per'il·ous** *adj.* full of peril, hazardous

**pe·rim·e·ter** (pə-RIM-i-tər) *n.* outer boundary of an area; length of this

**pe·ri·od** (PEER-ee-əd) *n.* particular portion of time; a series of years; single occurrence of menstruation; cycle; conclusion; full stop (.) at the end of a sentence; complete sentence —*adj.* of furniture, dress, play *etc.,* belonging to particular time in history —**pe·ri·od'ic** *adj.* recurring at regular intervals —**pe·ri·od'i·cal** *adj./n.* (of) publication issued at regular intervals —*adj.* of a period; periodic —**pe·ri·o·dic'i·ty** (-DIS-i-tee) *n.*

**per·i·pa·tet·ic** (per-ə-pə-TET-ik) *adj.* itinerant; walking, traveling about

**pe·riph·er·y** (pə-RIF-ə-ree) *n.* (*pl.* -er·ies) circumference; surface, outside —**pe·riph'er·al** (-ə-rəl) *adj.* minor, unimportant; of periphery

**pe·riph·ra·sis** (pə-RIF-rə-sis) n. (pl. -ses pr. -seez) roundabout speech or phrase; circumlocution —per·i·phras'tic adj.

**per·i·scope** (PER-ə-skohp) n. instrument used esp. in submarines, for giving view of objects on different level

**per·ish** vi. die, waste away; decay, rot —per·ish·a·ble adj. that will not last long —n. pl. perishable food

**per·i·to·ne·um** (per·i-tn-EE-əm) n. (pl. -ne·ums, -to·ne·a pr. -EE-ə) membrane lining internal surface of abdomen —per·i·to·ni'tis (-NI-tis) n. inflammation of it

**per·i·win·kle** (PER-i-wing-kəl) n. myrtle; small edible shellfish

**per·jure** (PUR-jər) vt. (-jured, -jur·ing) be guilty of perjury —per'ju·ry n. (pl. -ries) crime of false testimony under oath; false swearing

**perk·y** (PUR-kee) adj. (perk·i·er, perk·i·est) lively, cheerful, jaunty, gay —perk up make, become cheerful

**per·ma·frost** (PUR-mə-frawst) n. permanently frozen ground

**per·ma·nent** (PUR-mə-nənt) adj. continuing in same state; lasting —per'ma·nence, per'ma·nen·cy n. fixedness —permanent wave n. (treatment of hair producing) long-lasting style

**per·me·ate** (PUR-mee-ayt) vt. (-at·ed, -at·ing) pervade, saturate; pass through pores of —per'me·a·ble (-ə-bəl) adj. admitting of passage of fluids

**per·mit** (pər-MIT) vt. (-mit·ted, -mit·ting) allow; give leave to do something —n. (PUR-mit) license to do something; written permission —per·mis'si·ble adj. allowable —per·mis'sion n. authorization; leave, liberty —per·mis'sive adj.

(too) tolerant, lenient, esp. as parent

**per·mute** (pər-MYOOT) vt. (-mut·ed, -mut·ing) interchange —per·mu·ta·tion (pur-myuu-TAY-shən) n. mutual transference; Math. arrangement of a number of quantities in any possible order

**per·ni·cious** (pər-NISH-əs) adj. wicked or mischievous; extremely hurtful; having quality of destroying or injuring

**per·o·ra·tion** (per-ə-RAY-shən) n. concluding part of oration

**per·ox·ide** (pə-ROK-sid) n. oxide of a given base containing greatest quantity of oxygen; short for HYDROGEN PEROXIDE

**per·pen·dic·u·lar** (pur-pən-DIK-yə-lər) adj. at right angles to the plane of the horizon; at right angles to given line or surface; exactly upright —n. line falling at right angles on another line or plane

**per·pe·trate** (PUR-pi-trayt) vt. (-trat·ed, -trat·ing) perform or be responsible for (something bad)

**per·pet·u·al** (pər-PECH-oo-əl) adj. continuous; lasting for ever —per·pet'u·ate vt. (at·ed, -at·ing) make perpetual; not to allow to be forgotten —per·pet·u·a'tion n. —per·pe·tu'i·ty (pur-pi-TOO-i-tee) n.

**per·plex** (pər-PLEKS) vt. puzzle; bewilder; make difficult to understand —per·plex'i·ty n. (pl. -ties) puzzled or tangled state

**per·qui·site** (PUR-kwi-zit) n. any incidental benefit from a certain type of employment; casual payment in addition to salary; something due as a privilege

**per se** (pur SAY) Lat. by or in itself

**per·se·cute** (PUR-si-kyoot) vt. (-cut·ed, -cut·ing) oppress because of race, religion *etc.*; subject to persistent ill-treatment —per·se·cu'tion *n.*

per·se·vere (pur-sə-VEER) *vi.* (-vered, -ver·ing) persist, maintain effort —per·se·ver'ance (-əns) *n.* persistence

per·si·flage (PUR-sə-flahzh) *n.* idle talk; frivolous style of treating subject

per·sim·mon (pər-SIM-ən) *n.* Amer. tree; its hard wood; its fruit

per·sist (pər-SIST) *vi.* continue in spite of obstacles or objections —per·sist'ence (-əns), per·sis'ten·cy *n.* —per·sist'ent *adj.* persisting; steady; persevering; lasting

per·snick·et·y (pər-SNIK-i-tee) *adj. inf.* fussy; fastidious about trifles; snobbishly aloof; requiring great care

per·son (PUR-sən) *n.* individual (human) being; body of human being; *Grammar* classification, or one of the classes, of pronouns and verb forms according to the person speaking, spoken to, or spoken of —per·so·na (pər-SIM-nə) *n.* (*pl.* -nas) assumed character —per'son·a·ble *adj.* good-looking —per'son·age (-ij) *n.* notable person —per'son·al *adj.* individual, private, or one's own; of, relating to grammatical person —per·son·al'i·ty *n.* (*pl.* -ties) distinctive character; a celebrity —per'son·al·ly *adv.* in person —per'son·ate *vt.* (-at·ed, -at·ing) pass oneself off as —personal property *Law* all property except land and interests in land that pass to heir

per·son·i·fy (pər-SON-ə-fi) *vt.* (-fied, -fy·ing) represent as person; typify —per·son·i·fi·ca'tion *n.*

per·son·nel (pur-sə-NEL) *n.* staff

employed in a service or institution

per·spec·tive (pər-SPEK-tiv) *n.* mental view; art of drawing on flat surface to give effect of solidity and relative distances and sizes; drawing in perspective

per·spi·ca·cious (pur-spi-KAY-shəs) *adj.* having quick mental insight —per·spi·cac'i·ty (-KAS-i-tee) *n.*

per·spic·u·ous (pər-SPIK-yoo-əs) *adj.* clearly expressed; lucid; plain; obvious —per·spi·cu'i·ty *n.*

per·spire (pər-SPIR) *v.* (-spired, -spir·ing) sweat —per·spi·ra'tion (-spi-RAY-shən) *n.* sweating; sweat

per·suade (pər-SWAYD) *vt.* (-suad·ed, -suad·ing) bring (one to do something) by argument, charm *etc.*; convince —per·sua'sion (-SWAY-zhən) *n.* art, act of persuading; way of thinking or belief —per·sua'sive *adj.*

pert *adj.* (-er, -est) forward, saucy

per·tain (pər-TAYN) *vi.* belong, relate, have reference (to); concern

per·ti·na·cious (pur-tn-AY-shəs) *adj.* obstinate, persistent —per·ti·nac'i·ty (-AS-i-tee) *n.* doggedness, resolution

per·ti·nent (PUR-tn-ənt) *adj.* to the point —per'ti·nence *n.* relevance

per·turb (pər-TURB) *vt.* disturb greatly; alarm —per·tur·ba'tion (pur-tər-BAY-shən) *n.* disturbance; agitation of mind

pe·ruse (pə-ROOZ) *vt.* (-rused, -rus·ing) examine, read, *esp.* in slow and careful, or leisurely, manner —pe·rus'al *n.*

per·vade (pər-VAYD) *vt.* (-vad·ed, -vad·ing) spread through; be rife among —per·va'sive *adj.*

**per·vert** (pɔr-VURT) vt. turn to wrong use; lead astray —n. (PUR-vɔrt) one who shows unhealthy abnormality, esp. in sexual matters —**per·verse** (pɔr-VURS) adj. obstinately or unreasonably wrong; self-willed; headstrong; wayward —**per·ver'sion** (-VUR-zhɔn) n.

**per·vi·ous** (PUR-vee-ɔs) adj. permeable; penetrable; giving passage

**pes·sa·ry** (PES-ɔ-ree) n. (pl. -ries) instrument used to support mouth and neck of uterus; appliance to prevent conception; medicated suppository

**pes·si·mism** (PES-ɔ-miz-ɔm) n. tendency to see the worst side of things; theory that everything turns to evil —**pes'si·mist** n. —**pes·si·mis'tic** adj.

**pest** n. troublesome or harmful thing, person or insect; plague —**pest'i·cide** (-sid) n. chemical for killing pests, esp. insects —**pes·tif'er·ous** (-ɔr-ɔs) adj. troublesome; bringing plague

**pes·ter** (PES-tɔr) vt. trouble or vex persistently; harass

**pes·ti·lence** (PES-tl-ɔns) n. epidemic disease esp. bubonic plague —**pes'ti·lent** adj. troublesome; deadly —**pes·ti·len'tial** (-LEN-shɔl) adj.

**pes·tle** (PES-ɔl) n. instrument with which things are pounded in a mortar

**Pet.** Peter

**pet** n. animal or person kept or regarded with affection —vt. (pet·ted, pet·ting) make pet of; inf. hug, embrace, fondle

**pet·al** (PET-l) n. white or colored leaflike part of flower —**pet'aled** adj.

**pe·tard** (pi-TAHRD) n. formerly, an explosive device —hoist by one's own petard ruined, destroyed by plot one intended for another

**pe·ter** (PEE-tɔr) vi. —**peter out** inf. disappear, lose power gradually

**pe·tit** (PET-ee) adj. Law small, petty

**pe·tite** (pɔ-TEET) adj. small, dainty

**pe·ti·tion** (pɔ-TISH-ɔn) n. entreaty, request, esp. one presented to a governing body or person —vt. present petition to —**pe·ti'tion·er** n.

**pet·rel** (PE-trɔl) n. sea bird

**pet·ri·fy** (PE-trɔ-fi) vt. (-fied, -fy·ing) turn to stone; fig. make motionless with fear; make dumb with amazement —**pet·ri·fac'tion** n.

**pe·tro·le·um** (pɔ-TROH-lee-ɔm) n. unrefined oil

**pet·ti·coat** (PET-ee-koht) n. women's undergarment worn under skirts, dresses etc.

**pet·ti·fog·ger** (PET-ee-fog-ɔr) n. quibbler; unethical lawyer; one given to mean dealing in small matters

**pet·ty** (PET-ee) adj. (ti·er, -ti·est) unimportant, trivial; small-minded, mean; on a small scale —**petty cash** cash kept by firm to pay minor incidental expenses —**petty officer** noncommissioned officer in Navy

**pet·u·lant** (PECH-ɔ-lɔnt) adj. given to small fits of temper; peevish —**pet'u·lance** n. peevishness

**pe·tu·nia** (pi-TOON-yɔ) n. plant with funnel-shaped purple or white flowers

**pew** (pyoo) n. fixed seat in church; inf. chair, seat

**pew·ter** (PYOO-tɔr) n. alloy of tin and lead; utensil of this

**pha·lanx** (FAY-langks) n. (pl. -lanx·es) body of soldiers etc. formed in close array

**phal·lus** (FAL-əs) *n.* (*pl.* -lus·es) penis; symbol of it used in primitive rites —**phal′lic** *adj.*

**phan·tas·ma·go′ri·a** (fan-taz-mə-GOR-ee-ə) *n.* crowd of dim or unreal figures; exhibition of illusions

**phan·tom** (FAN-təm) *n.* apparition; specter, ghost; fancied vision

**Phar·aoh** (FAIR-oh) *n.* title of ancient Egyptian kings

**phar·i·see** (FA-rə-see) *n.* sanctimonious person; hypocrite —**phar·i·sa′ic** (-SAY-ik) *adj.*

**phar·ma·ceu·tic** (fahr-mə-SOO-tik) *adj.* of pharmacy —**phar·ma·ceu′ti·cal** *adj.* —**phar′ma·cist** *n.* person qualified to dispense drugs —**phar·ma·col′o·gy** (-KOL-ə-jee) *n.* study of drugs —**phar·ma·co·poe′ia** (-kə-PEE-ə) *n.* official book with list and directions for use of drugs —**phar′ma·cy** (-mə-see) *n.* preparation and dispensing of drugs; drugstore

**phar·ynx** (FA-ringks) *n.* (*pl.* pha·ryn·ges *pr.* fə-RIN-jeez) cavity forming back part of mouth and terminating in gullet —**pha·ryn′ge·al** *adj.*

**phase** (fayz) *n.* any distinct or characteristic period or stage in a development or chain of events —*vt.* (phased, phas·ing) arrange, execute in stages or to coincide with something else

**pheas·ant** (FEZ-ənt) *n.* game bird with bright plumage

**phe·no·bar·bi·tal** (fee-noh-BAHR-bi-tawl) *n.* drug inducing sleep

**phe·nom·e·non** (fi-NOM-ə-non) *n.* (*pl.* -na *pr.* -nə) anything appearing or observed; remarkable person or thing —**phe·nom′e·nal** *adj.* relating to phenomena; remarkable; recognizable or evidenced by senses

**Phil.** Philippians

**phil-** (*comb. form*) loving, as in *philanthropy, philosophy*

**phi·lan·der** (fi-LAN-dər) *vi.* (of man) flirt with, make love to, women, *esp.* with no intention of marrying them —**phi·lan′der·er** *n.*

**phi·lan·thro·py** (fi-LAN-thrə-pee) *n.* (*pl.* -pies) practice of doing good to people; love of mankind; a philanthropic organization —**phi·lan·throp′ic** *adj.* loving mankind; benevolent —**phi·lan′thro·pist** *n.*

**phi·lat·e·ly** (fi-LAT-l-ee) *n.* stamp collecting —**phi·lat′e·list** *n.*

**phi·lis·tine** (FIL-ə-steen) *n.* ignorant, smug person —*adj.*

**phi·lol·o·gy** (fi-LOL-ə-jee) *n.* science of structure and development of languages —**phi·lol′o·gist** *n.*

**phi·los·o·phy** (fi-LOS-ə-fee) *n.* pursuit of wisdom; study of realities and general principles; system of theories on nature of things or on conduct; calmness of mind —**phi·los′o·pher** *n.* one who studies, possesses, or originates philosophy —**phil·o·soph′i·cal** *adj.* of, like philosophy; wise, learned; calm, stoical —**phi·los′o·phize** (-fiz) *vi.* (-phized, -phiz·ing) reason like philosopher; theorize; moralize

**phle·bi·tis** (flə-BI-tis) *n.* inflammation of a vein

**phlegm** (flem) *n.* viscid substance formed by mucous membrane and ejected by coughing *etc.*; apathy, sluggishness —**phleg·mat·ic** (fleg-MAT-ik) *adj.* not easily agitated; composed

**pho·bi·a** (FOH-bee-ə) *n.* fear or aversion; unreasoning dislike

**phoe·nix** (FEE-niks) *n.* legendary bird; unique thing

**pho·net·ic** (fə-NET-ik) *adj.* of, or

relating to, vocal sounds —**phon·et'ics** n. (*used with sing. v.*) science of vocal sounds —**pho·ne·ti·cian** (foh-ni-TISH-ən) n.

**phono-** (*comb. form*) sound, as in *phonology*

**pho·no·graph** (FOH-nə-graf) n. instrument recording and reproducing sounds, record player

**phos·pho·rus** (FOS-fər-əs) n. toxic, flammable, nonmetallic element that appears luminous in the dark —**phos·phate** (FOS-fayt) n. compound of phosphorus —**phos·pho·res'cence** n. faint glow in the dark

**pho·to** (FOH-toh) n. inf. short for PHOTOGRAPH —**photo finish** photo taken at end of race to show placing of contestants

**photo-** (*comb. form*) light, as in *photometer, photosynthesis*

**pho·to·cop·y** (FOH-toh-kop-ee) n. (*pl.* -cop·ies) photographic reproduction —vt. (-cop·ied, -cop·y·ing)

**pho·to·e·lec·tron** (foh-toh-i-LEK-tron) n. electron liberated from metallic surface by action of beam of light

**pho·to·gen·ic** (foh-tə-JEN-ik) adj. capable of being photographed attractively

**pho·to·graph** (FOH-tə-graf) n. picture made by chemical action of light on sensitive film —vt. take photograph of —**pho·tog'ra·pher** (-rə-fər) n.

**pho·to·syn·the·sis** (foh-tə-SIN-thə-sis) n. process by which green plant uses sun's energy to build up carbohydrate reserves

**phrase** (frayz) n. group of words; pithy expression; mode of expression —vt. (phrased, phras·ing) express in words —**phrase·ol·o·gy** (fray-zee-OL-ə-jee) n. manner of expression, choice of words —**phras·al** (-əl) verb

phrase consisting of verb and preposition, often with meaning different to the parts (*eg* take in)

**phre·nol·o·gy** (frə-NOL-ə-jee) n. (formerly) study of skull's shape; theory that character and mental powers are indicated by shape of skull —**phre·nol'o·gist** n.

**phy·lac·ter·y** (fi-LAK-tə-ree) n. (*pl.* -ter·ies) leather case containing religious texts worn by Jewish men during weekday morning prayers

**phys·ic** (FIZ-ik) n. medicine, esp. cathartic —*pl.* science of properties of matter and energy —**phys'i·cal** adj. bodily, as opposed to mental or moral; material; of physics of body —**phy·si'cian** n. medical doctor —**phys'i·cist** n. one skilled in, or student of, physics

**phys·i·og·no·my** (fiz-ee-OG-nə-mee) n. (*pl.* -mies) judging character by face; face; outward appearance of something

**phys·i·ol·o·gy** (fiz-ee-OL-ə-jee) n. science of normal function of living things —**phys·i·ol'o·gist** n.

**phys·i·o·ther·a·py** (fiz-ee-oh-THER-ə-pee) n. therapeutic use of physical means, as massage etc. —**phys·i·o·ther'a·pist** n.

**phy·sique** (fi-ZEEK) n. bodily structure, constitution and development

**pi** (pī) n. Math. ratio of circumference of circle to its diameter, approx. 3.141592

**pi·an·o** (pee-AN-oh) n. (*pl.* -an·os) (*orig.* pianofor'te) musical instrument with strings that are struck by hammers worked by keyboard —adj./adv. Mus. softly —**pi·an·ist** (pee-AN-ist) n. performer on piano

**pi·az·za** (pee-AZ-ə) n. square, marketplace; veranda

**pi·ca** (PĪ-kə) n. printing type of 6

lines to the inch; size of type, 12 point; typewriter type size (10 letters to inch)

**pi·ca·dor** (PIK-ə-dor) *n.* mounted bullfighter with lance

**pic·a·resque** (pik-ə-RESK) *adj.* of fiction, *esp.* episodic and dealing with the adventures of rogues

**pic·co·lo** (PIK-ə-loh) *n.* (*pl.* -los) small flute

**pick**[1] (pik) *vt.* choose, select carefully; pluck, gather; peck at; pierce with something pointed; find occasion for —*n.* act of picking; choicest part —**pick'ings** *n. pl.* gleanings; odds and ends of profit —**pick–me–up** *n. inf.* tonic; stimulating drink —**pick'pock·et** *n.* one who steals from another's pocket —**pick'up** *n.* device for conversion of mechanical energy into electrical signals, as in record player *etc.*; pickup truck —**pick** to find fault with —**pick up** raise, lift; collect; improve, get better; accelerate

**pick**[2] *n.* tool with curved steel crossbar and wooden shaft, for breaking up hard ground or masonry —**pick'ax** *n.* pick

**pick·er·el** (PIK-ər-əl) *n.* small pike

**pick·et** (PIK-it) *n.* prong, pointed stake; person, *esp.* striker, posted outside building *etc.* to prevent use of facility, deter would-be workers during strike —*vt.* post as picket; beset with pickets; tether to peg —**picket fence** fence of pickets —**picket line** line of pickets

**pick·le** (PIK-əl) *n.* food, *esp.* cucumber, preserved in brine, vinegar *etc.*; liquid used for preserving; *inf.* awkward situation —*vt.* (-led, -ling) preserve in pickle —**pickled** *adj. sl.* drunk

**pic·nic** (PIK-nik) *n.* pleasure outing including meal out of doors —*vi.* (-nicked, -nick·ing) take part in picnic

**Pict** (pikt) *n.* member of ancient people of NE Scotland

**pic·ture** (PIK-chər) *n.* drawing or painting; mental image; beautiful or picturesque object —*pl. inf.* movies —*vt.* (-tured, -tur·ing) represent in, or as in, a picture —**pic·to'ri·al** *adj.* of, in, with painting or pictures; graphic —**pic·tur·esque** (pik-chə-RESK) *adj.* such as would be effective in picture; striking, vivid

**pidg·in** (PIJ-ən) *n.* language, not a mother tongue, made up of elements of two or more other languages

**pie** (pī) *n.* baked dish of fruit, meat *etc.*, usu. with pastry crust

**pie·bald** (PĪ-bawld) *adj.* irregularly marked with black and white; motley —*n.* piebald horse or other animal

**piece** (pees) *n.* bit, part, fragment; single object; literary or musical composition *etc.*; small object used in checkers, chess *etc.*; firearm —*vt.* (pieced, piec·ing) mend, put together —**piece'meal** *adv.* by, in, or into pieces, a bit at a time —**piece'work** *n.* work paid for according to quantity produced

**pièce de ré·sis·tance** (pyes də ray-zee-STAHNS) *Fr.* (*pl.* **pièces-**) principal item; most prized item

**pied** (pīd) *adj.* piebald; variegated

**pie–eyed** (PĪ-īd) *adj. sl.* drunk

**pier** (peer) *n.* structure running into sea as landing stage; piece of solid upright masonry as foundation for building *etc.*

**pierce** (peers) *vt.* (pierced, pierc·ing) make hole in; make a way through —**piercing** *adj.* keen; penetrating

**pi·e·ty** (PĪ-i-tee) *n.* (*pl.* -ties) godliness; devoutness; goodness; dutifulness

**pig** n. wild or domesticated mammal killed for pork, ham, bacon; inf. greedy, dirty person; offens. sl. policeman; oblong mass of smelted metal —vi. (pigged, pigging) of sow, produce litter —pig′gish adj. greedy; stubborn —pig′head·ed adj. obstinate —pig′tail n. braid of hair hanging from back of head

**pi·geon** (PIJ-ən) n. bird of many wild and domesticated varieties, often trained to carry messages; sl. dupe —pi′geon·hole (-hohl) n. compartment for papers in desk etc. —vt. (-holed, -hol·ing) defer; classify —pi′geon-toed (-tohd) adj. with feet, toes turned inward

**pig·ment** (PIG-mənt) n. coloring matter, paint or dye

**pigmy** see PYGMY

**pike**[1] (pīk) n. various types of large, predatory freshwater fish

**pike**[2] n. spear formerly used by infantry

**pi·laf** (PEE-lahf) n. Middle Eastern dish of steamed rice with spices, sometimes with meat or fowl etc.

**pi·las·ter** (pi-LAS-tər) n. square column, usu. set in wall

**pile**[1] (pīl) n. heap; great mass of building v. (piled, pil·ing) —vt. heap (up), stack load —vi. (with in, out, off etc.) move in a group —atomic pile nuclear reactor

**pile**[2] n. beam driven into the ground, esp. as foundation for building in water or wet ground —pile driver n. machine for driving down piles; person who operates this machine

**pile**[3] n. nap of cloth, esp. of velvet, carpet etc.; down

**piles** (pīlz) n. pl. tumors of veins of rectum, hemorrhoids

**pil·fer** (PIL-fər) v. steal in small

quantities —pil′fer·age (-ij) n. —pil′fer·er n.

**pil′grim** n. one who journeys to sacred place; wanderer, wayfarer —pil′grim·age (-ij) n.

**pill** n. small ball of medicine swallowed whole; anything disagreeable that has to be endured —the pill oral contraceptive —pill′box n. small box for pills; small concrete fort

**pil·lage** (PIL-ij) v. (-laged, -lag·ing) plunder, ravage, sack —n. seizure of goods, esp. in war; plunder

**pil·lar** (PIL-ər) n. slender, upright structure, column; prominent supporter

**pil·lo·ry** (PIL-ə-ree) n. (pl. -ries) frame with holes for head and hands in which offender was confined and exposed to public abuse and ridicule —vt. (-ried, -ry·ing) expose to ridicule and abuse; set in pillory

**pil·low** (PIL-oh) n. cushion for the head, esp. in bed —vt. lay on, or as on, pillow

**pi·lot** (PĪ-lət) n. person qualified to fly an aircraft or spacecraft; one qualified to take charge of ship entering or leaving harbor, or where knowledge of local water is needed; steersman; guide —adj. experimental and preliminary —vt. act as pilot to; steer —pilot light small auxiliary flame lighting main one in gas appliance etc.

**pi·mi·en·to** (pi-MYEN-toh) n. (pl. -tos) (fruit of the) sweet red pepper Also pi·men′to

**pimp** n. one who solicits for prostitute —vi. act as pimp

**pim·ple** (PIM-pəl) n. small pusfilled spot on the skin —pim′ply adj. (-pli·er, -li·est)

**pin** n. short thin piece of stiff wire with point and head, for fastening; wooden or metal peg or rivet —*vt.* (**pinned, pin·ning**) fasten with pin; seize and hold fast —**pin′ball** *n.* table game, where small ball is shot through various hazards —**pin money** trivial sum —**pin′point** *vt.* mark exactly

**pin·a·fore** (PIN-ə-for) *n.* child's apron; woman's dress with a bib top

**pince-nez** (PANS-nay) *n. sing.* (*pl. same form pr.* -nayz) eyeglasses kept on nose by spring

**pin·cers** (PIN-sərz) *n. pl.* tool for gripping, composed of two limbs crossed and pivoted; claws of lobster *etc.* —**pincers movement** military maneuver in which both flanks of a force are attacked simultaneously

**pinch** *vt.* nip, squeeze; stint; *sl.* steal; *sl.* arrest —*n.* nip; as much as can be taken up between finger and thumb; stress; emergency —**pinch′bar** *n.* crowbar

**pine**[1] (pīn) *n.* evergreen coniferous tree; its wood

**pine**[2] *vi.* (**pined, pin·ing**) yearn; waste away with grief *etc.*

**pin·e·al** (PIN-ee-əl) *adj.* shaped like pine cone —**pineal gland** small cone-shaped gland situated at base of brain

**pine·ap·ple** (PĪ-nap-əl) *n.* tropical plant with spiny leaves bearing large edible fruit; the fruit: *sl.* a bomb

**ping** *vi.* produce brief ringing sound; of engine, knock

**pin·guid** (PING-gwid) *adj.* oily; fat

**pin·ion**[1] (PIN-yən) *n.* bird's wing —*vt.* disable or confine by binding wings, arms *etc.*

**pinion**[2] *n.* small cogwheel

**pink** (pingk) *n.* pale red color; garden plant; best condition, fitness —*adj.* of color pink —*vt.* pierce; finish edge (of fabric) with perforations or scallops

**pin·na·cle** (PIN-ə-kəl) *n.* highest pitch or point; mountain peak; pointed turret on buttress or roof

**pint** (pīnt) *n.* liquid measure, half a quart, 1/8 gallon (.6 liter)

**pin·tle** (PIN-tl) *n.* pivot pin

**pin′up** *n.* picture of sexually attractive person, *esp.* (partly) naked

**pi·o·neer** (pī-ə-NEER) *n.* explorer; early settler; originator; one of advance party preparing road *etc.* for troops —*vi.* act as pioneer or leader

**pi·ous** (Pī-əs) *adj.* devout; righteous

**pip**[1] *n.* seed in fruit; *inf.* something or someone outstanding

**pip**[2] *n.* spot on playing cards, dice, or dominoes; *inf.* metal insigne on officer's shoulder showing rank

**pip**[3] *n.* disease of poultry

**pipe** (pīp) *n.* tube of metal or other material; tube with small bowl at end for smoking tobacco; musical instrument, whistle —*pl.* bagpipes —*v.* (**piped, pip·ing**) play on pipe; utter in shrill tone; convey by pipe; ornament with a piping or fancy edging —**pip′er** *n.* player on pipe or bagpipes —**pip·ing** *n.* system of pipes; fancy edging or trimming on clothes; act or art of playing on pipes, *esp.* bagpipes —**pipe down** *inf.* stop making noise; stop talking —**pipe dream** fanciful, impossible plan *etc.* —**pipe′line** *n.* long pipe for transporting oil, water *etc.*; means of communications —**pipe up** *inf.* assert oneself by speaking; speak louder —**in the pipeline** yet to come; in process of completion *etc.*

**pi·pette** (pī-PET) *n.* slender glass tube to transfer fluids from one vessel to another

**pip′pin** *n.* kind of apple

**pi·quant** (PEE-kənt) *adj.* pungent; stimulating —**pi′quan·cy** *n.*

**pique** (peek) *n.* feeling of injury, baffled curiosity or resentment —*vt.* (**piqued**, **piqu·ing**) hurt pride of; irritate; stimulate

**pi·qué** (pi-KAY) *n.* stiff ribbed cotton fabric

**pi·ra·nha** (pi-RAHN-yə) *n.* (*pl.* **-nhas**) small voracious freshwater fish of tropical Amer.

**pi·rate** (PI-rət) *n.* sea robber; publisher *etc.*, who infringes copyright —*n./adj.* (person) broadcasting illegally —*vt.* (**-rat·ed**, **-rat·ing**) use or reproduce (artistic work *etc.*) illicitly —**pi′ra·cy** (-see) *n.* (*pl.* **-cies**)

**pir·ou·ette** (pir-oo-ET) *n.* spinning around on the toe —*vi.* (**-et·ted**, **-et·ting**) do this

**pis·tach·i·o** (pi-STASH-ee-oh) *n.* (*pl.* **-i·os**) small hard-shelled, sweet-tasting nut; tree producing it

**pis·til** (PIS-tl) *n.* seed-bearing organ of flower

**pis·tol** (PIS-tl) *n.* small firearm for one hand —*vt.* (**-toled**, **-tol·ing**) shoot with pistol

**pis·ton** (PIS-tən) *n.* in internal combustion engine, steam engine *etc.*, cylindrical part propelled to and fro in hollow cylinder by pressure of gas *etc.* to convert reciprocating motion to rotation

**pit** *n.* deep hole in ground; mine or its shaft; depression; enclosure where cocks are set to fight; servicing, refueling area on automobile racetrack —*vt.* (**pit·ted**, **pit·ting**) set to fight, match; mark with small dents or scars —**pit′-fall** *n.* any hidden danger; covered pit for trapping animals or people

**pitch**[1] (pich) *vt.* cast or throw; set up; set the key of (a tune) —*vi.* fall headlong; of ship, plunge lengthwise —*n.* act of pitching; degree, height, intensity; slope; distance propeller advances during one revolution; distance between threads of screw, teeth of saw *etc.*; acuteness of tone; *Baseball* ball delivered by pitcher to batter *inf.* persuasive sales talk —**pitch′er** *n. Baseball* player who delivers ball to batter —**pitch′-fork** *n.* fork for lifting hay *etc.* —*vt.* throw with, as with, pitchfork —**pitch′out** *n. Baseball* pitch thrown intentionally beyond batter's reach to improve catcher's chance of putting out base runner attempting to steal

**pitch**[2] *n.* dark sticky substance obtained from tar or turpentine —*vt.* coat with this —**pitch′y** *adj.* (**pitch·i·er**, **pitch·i·est**) covered with pitch; black as pitch —**pitch-black**, **-dark** *adj.* very dark

**pitch·blende** (PICH-blend) *n.* mineral composed largely of uranium oxide, yielding radium

**pitch·er** (PICH-ər) *n.* large jug; *see also* PITCH

**pith** *n.* tissue in stems and branches of certain plants; essential substance, most important part —**pith′i·ly** *adv.* —**pith′y** *adj.* (**pith·i·er**, **pith·i·est**) terse, cogent, concise; consisting of pith

**pi·ton** (PEE-ton) *n.* metal spike used in mountain climbing

**pit·tance** (PIT-ns) *n.* small allowance; inadequate wages

**pi·tu·i·tar·y** (pi-TOO-i-ter·y) *adj.* of, pert. to, the endocrine gland at base of brain

**pit·y** (PIT-ee) *n.* (*pl.* **pit·ies**) sympathy, sorrow for others' suffering; regrettable fact —*vt.* (**pit·ied**, **pit·y·ing**) feel pity for —**pit′-e·ous** *adj.* deserving pity; sad, wretched —**pit′i·a·ble** *adj.* —**pit′i-ful** (-i-fəl) *adj.* woeful; contemptible —**pit'i·less** (-i-lis) adj. feeling no pity; hard, merciless

**piv·ot** (PIV-ət) n. shaft or pin on which thing turns —vt. furnish with pivot —vi. hinge on one —**piv'ot·al** (-ət-əl) adj. of, acting as, pivot; of crucial importance

**pix·ie** (PIK-see) n. fairy; mischievous person

**piz·za** (PEET-sə) n. dish (orig. It.) of baked disk of dough covered with cheese and tomato sauce and wide variety of garnishes —**piz·ze·ri'a** (-REE-ə) n. place selling pizzas

**pi·zazz** (pə-ZAZ) n. inf. sparkle, vitality, glamour

**piz·zi·ca·to** (pit-si-KAH-toh) adj./n. Mus. (pl. -ti pre -tee) (note, passage) played by plucking string of violin etc., with finger

**plac·ard** (PLAK-ahrd) n. paper or card with notice on one side for posting up or carrying, poster —vt. post placards on; advertise, display on placards

**pla·cate** (PLAY-klayt) vt. (-cat·ed, -cat·ing) conciliate, pacify, appease —**pla·ca·to'ry** (-kə-tor-ee) adj.

**place** (plays) n. locality; spot; position; stead; duty; town, village, residence, buildings; office, employment; seat, space —vt. (placed, plac·ing) put in particular place; set; identify; make (order, bet etc.)

**pla·ce·bo** (plə-SEE-boh n. (pl. -bos) sugar pill etc. given to unsuspecting patient as active drug

**pla·cen·ta** (plə-SEN-tə) n. (pl. -tas) organ formed in uterus during pregnancy, providing nutrients for fetus; afterbirth

**plac·id** (PLAS-id) adj. calm; equable —**pla·cid·i·ty** (plə-SID-i-tee) n. mildness, quiet

**pla·gia·rism** (PLAY-jə-riz-əm) n.

taking ideas, passages etc. from an author and presenting them, unacknowledged, as one's own —**pla'gia·rize** (-riz) v. (-rized, -riz·ing) —**pla'gia·rist** n.

**plague** (playg) n. highly contagious disease, esp. bubonic plague; nuisance; affliction —vt. (plagued, pla·guing) trouble, annoy

**plaid** (plad) n. checked or tartan pattern; fabric made of this

**plain** (playn) adj. (-er, -est) flat, level; unobstructed, not intricate; clear, obvious; easily understood; simple; ordinary; without decoration; not beautiful —n. tract of level country —adv. clearly —**plain'ly** (-lee) adv. —**plain'ness** (-nis) n. —**plain clothes** civilian dress, as opposed to uniform —**plain dealing** directness and honesty in transactions —**plain sailing** unobstructed course of action —**plain speaking** frankness, candor

**plain·tiff** (PLAYN-tif) n. Law one who sues in court

**plain·tive** (PLAYN-tiv) adj. sad, mournful, melancholy

**plait** (playt) n. braid of hair, straw etc. —vt. form or weave into braids

**plan** n. scheme; way of proceeding; project; design; drawing of horizontal section; diagram, map —vt. (planned, plan·ning) make plan of; arrange beforehand

**planch·et** (PLAN-chit) n. flat sheet of metal; disk of metal from which coin is stamped

**plan·chette** (plan-SHET) n. small board used in spiritualism

**plane¹** (playn) n. smooth surface; a level; carpenter's tool for smoothing wood —vt. (planed, plan·ing) make smooth with one —adj. perfectly flat or level —**plan'er** n. planing machine

**plane**[2] v. (**planed, plan·ing**) of airplane, glide; of boat, rise and partly skim over water —n. wing of airplane; airplane

**plan·et** (PLAN-it) n. heavenly body revolving around the sun —**plan'e·tar·y** (-i-ter-ee) adj. of, like, planets

**plan·e·tar·i·um** (plan-i-TAIR-ee-əm) n. an apparatus that shows the movement of sun, moon, stars and planets by projecting lights on the inside of a dome; building in which the apparatus is housed

**plan·gent** (PLAN-jənt) adj. resounding

**plank** (plangk) n. long flat piece of sawn timber —vt. cover with planks

**plank·ton** (PLANGK-tən) n. minute animal and vegetable organisms floating in ocean

**plant** n. living organism feeding on inorganic substances and without power of locomotion; such an organism that is smaller than tree or shrub; equipment or machinery needed for manufacture; building and equipment for manufacturing purposes; complete equipment used for heating, air conditioning etc. —vt. set in ground, to grow; support, establish; stock with plants; sl. hide, esp. to deceive or observe —**plant'er** n. one who plants; ornamental pot or stand for house plants

**plan·tain**[1] (PLAN-tin) n. low-growing weed with broad leaves

**plantain**[2] n. tropical plant like banana; its fruit

**plan·ta·tion** (plan-TAY-shən) n. estate or large farm for cultivation of tobacco, cotton etc.; wood of planted trees; formerly, colony

**plaque** (plak) n. ornamental plate, tablet; plate of clasp or brooch; filmy deposit on surfaces of teeth, conducive to decay

**plas·ma** (PLAZ-mə) n. clear, fluid portion of blood

**plas·ter** (PLAS-tər) n. mixture of lime, sand etc. for coating walls etc.; piece of fabric spread with medicinal or adhesive substance —vt. apply plaster to; apply like plaster; inf. defeat soundly —**plas'tered** adj. sl. drunk

**plas·tic** (PLAS-tik) n. any of a group of synthetic products derived from casein, cellulose etc. that can be readily molded into any form and are extremely durable —adj. made of plastic; easily molded, pliant; capable of being molded; produced by molding —**plas·tic·i·ty** (pla-STIS-i-tee) n. ability to be molded —**plastic surgery** repair or reconstruction of missing or malformed parts of the body for medical or cosmetic reasons

**plate** (playt) n. shallow round dish; flat thin sheet of metal, glass etc.; household utensils of gold or silver; device for printing; illustration in book; set of false teeth, part of this that adheres to roof of mouth —vt. (**plat·ed, plat·ing**) cover with thin coating of gold, silver, or other metal —**plate'ful** (-fəl) n. (pl. -fuls) —**plat'er** n. person who plates; inferior race horse —**plate glass** kind of thick glass used for mirrors, windows etc. —**plate tec·ton'ics** Geol. study of structure of Earth's crust, esp. movement of layers of rocks

**pla·teau** (pla-TOH) n. (pl. -teaus pr. -TOHZ) tract of level high land, tableland; period of stability

**plat·en** (PLAT-n) n. Printing plate by which paper is pressed against type; roller in typewriter

**plat·form** n. raised level surface

or floor, stage; raised area in station from which passengers board trains; political program

**plat·i·num** (PLAT-n-əm) n. white heavy malleable metal

**plat·i·tude** (PLAT-i-tood) n. commonplace remark —**plat·i·tu'di·nous** adj.

**Pla·ton·ic** (plə-TON-ik) adj. of Plato or his philosophy; (p-) (of love) purely spiritual, friendly

**pla·toon** (plə-TOON) n. two or more squads of soldiers employed as unit

**plat·ter** (PLAT-ər) n. flat dish

**plat·y·pus** (PLAT-i-pəs) n. (pl. -pus·es) small Aust. egg-laying amphibious mammal, with dense fur, webbed feet and ducklike bill; also **duckbilled platypus**

**plau·dit** (PLAW-dit) n. act of applause, handclapping

**plau·si·ble** (PLAW-zə-bəl) adj. apparently fair or reasonable; fair-spoken —**plau·si·bil'i·ty** n.

**play** vi. amuse oneself; take part in game; behave carelessly; act a part on the stage; perform on musical instrument; move with light or irregular motion, flicker etc. —vt. contend with in game; take part in (game); trifle; act the part of; perform (music); perform on (instrument); use, work (instrument) —n. dramatic piece or performance; sport; amusement; manner of action or conduct; activity; brisk or free movement; gambling —**play'ful** (-fəl) adj. lively —**play'group** (-groop) n. group of young children playing regularly under adult supervision —**play'house** n. theater; small house for children to play in —**playing card** one of set of usu. 52 cards used in card games —**playing field** extensive piece of ground for open-air games

—**play'thing** n. toy —**play'wright** (-rit) n. author of plays

**pla·za** (PLAH-zə) n. open space or square; complex of retail stores etc.

**plea** (plee) n. entreaty; statement of prisoner or defendant; excuse —**plead** v. (**plead·ed** or **pled**, **plead·ing**) make earnest appeal; address court of law; bring forward as excuse or plea —**plea bargaining** procedure in which defendant agrees to plead guilty in return for leniency in sentencing etc.

**please** (pleez) v. (**pleased, pleas·ing**) —vt. be agreeable to; gratify; delight —vi. like; be willing —adv. word of request —**pleas·ant** (PLEZ-ənt) adj. pleasing, agreeable —**pleas'ant·ry** (-ən-tree) n. (pl. -ries) joke, humor —**pleas·ur·a·ble** (PLEZH-ər-ə-bəl) adj. giving pleasure —**pleas'ure** n. enjoyment; satisfaction, will, choice

**pleat** (pleet) n. any of various types of fold made by doubling material back on itself —vi. make, gather into pleats

**plebe** (pleeb) n. at US military and naval academies, member of first-year class

**ple·be·ian** (pli-bee-ən) adj. belonging to the common people; low or rough —n. one of the common people

**pleb·i·scite** (PLEB-ə-sit) n. decision by direct voting of the electorate

**plec·trum** (PLEK-trəm) n. (pl. -trums) small implement for plucking strings of guitar etc.

**pledge** (plej) n. promise; thing given over as security; toast —vt. (**pledged, pledg·ing**) promise formally; bind or secure by pledge; give over as security

**Pleis·to·cene** (PLI-stə-seen)

adj./n. Geol. (of the) period of formation of the glaciers

**ple·na·ry** (PLEE-nə-ree) adj. complete, without limitations, absolute; of meeting etc., with all members present

**plen·i·po·ten·ti·ar·y** (plen-ə-po-TEN-shee-er-ee) adj./n. (envoy) having full powers

**plen·i·tude** (PLEN-i-tood) n. completeness, abundance, entirety

**plen·ty** n. (pl. -ties) abundance; quite enough —**plen'te·ous** (-tee-əs) adj. ample; rich; copious —**plen'ti·ful** (-ti-fəl) adj. abundant

**ple·num** (PLEE-nəm) n. (pl. -nums) space as considered to be full of matter (opposed to vacuum); condition of fullness; space above ceiling etc. for receiving, storing heated or cooled air

**ple·o·nasm** (PLEE-ə-naz-əm) n. use of more words than necessary —**ple·o·nas'tic** (-NAS-tik) adj. redundant

**pleth·o·ra** (PLETH-ər-ə) n. oversupply —**ple·thor·ic** (ple-THOR-ik) adj.

**pleu·ri·sy** (PLUUR-ə-see) n. inflammation of pleura, membrane lining the chest and covering the lungs

**plex·us** (PLEK-səs) n. (pl. -us·es) network of nerves, or fibers

**pli·a·ble** (PLI-ə-bəl) adj. easily bent or influenced —**pli·a·bil'i·ty** n. —**pli'an·cy** (-ən-see) n. —**pli'ant** adj. pliable

**pli·ers** (PLI-ərz) n. pl. tool with hinged arms and jaws for gripping

**plight**[1] (plīt) n. distressing state; predicament

**plight**[2] vt. promise, engage oneself to

**Plim·soll line** (PLIM-səl) mark on ships indicating maximum dis-

placement permitted when loaded

**Pli·o·cene** (PLI-ə-seen) n. Geol. the most recent tertiary deposits

**plod** vi. (plod·ded, plod·ding) walk or work doggedly

**plop** n. sound of object falling into water —vi. (plopped, plop·ping) fall with, as though with, such a sound; make the sound

**plot**[1] n. secret plan, conspiracy; essence of story, play etc. —v. (plot·ted, plot·ting) devise secretly; mark position of; make map of; conspire

**plot**[2] n. small piece of land

**plov·er** (PLUV-ər) n. one of various shore birds, typically with round head, straight bill and long pointed wings

**plow** n. implement for turning up soil; similar implement for clearing snow etc. —vt. turn up with plow, furrow etc.; work at slowly —**plow'share** (-shair) n. blade of plow —**plow under** bury beneath soil by plowing; overwhelm

**ploy** (ploi) n. stratagem; occupation; prank

**pluck** (pluk) vt. pull, pick off; strip from; sound strings of (guitar etc.) with fingers, plectrum —n. courage; sudden pull or tug —**pluck'y** adj. (pluck·i·er, pluck·i·est) courageous

**plug** n. thing fitting into and filling a hole; Electricity device connecting appliance to electricity supply; tobacco pressed hard; inf. recommendation, advertisement; sl. worn-out horse —vt. (plugged, plug·ging) stop with plug; inf. advertise anything by constant repetition; sl. punch; sl. shoot —**plug away** work hard —**plug in** connect (electrical appliance) with power source by means of plug

**plum** n. stone fruit; tree bearing

it; choicest part, piece, position *etc.*; dark reddish-purple color —*adj.* choice; plum-colored

**plumage** *see* PLUME

**plumb** (plum) *n.* ball of lead (plumb bob) attached to string used for sounding, finding the perpendicular *etc.* —*adj.* perpendicular —*adv.* perpendicularly; exactly; *inf.* downright; honestly —*vt.* set exactly upright; find depth of; reach, undergo; equip with, connect to plumbing system —**plumb'er** (PLUM-ər) *n.* worker who attends to water and sewage systems —**plumb'ing** *n.* trade of plumber; system of water and sewage pipes —**plumb'line** *n.* cord with plumb attached

**plume** (ploom) *n.* feather; ornament of feathers *etc.* —*vt.* (**plumed, plum·ing**) furnish with plumes; pride oneself —**plum·age** (PLOO-mij) *n.* bird's feathers collectively

**plum·met** (PLUM-it) *vi.* plunge headlong —*n.* plumbline

**plump**[1] *adj.* (**-er, -est**) of rounded form, moderately fat, chubby —*v.* make, become plump

**plump**[2] *vi.* sit, fall abruptly; (with *for*) support enthusiastically —*vt.* drop, throw abruptly —*adv.* suddenly; heavily; directly

**plun·der** (PLUN-dər) *vt.* take by force; rob systematically —*vi.* rob —*n.* pillage; booty, spoils

**plunge** (plunj) *v.* (**plunged, plung·ing**) —*vt.* put forcibly (into) —*vi.* throw oneself (into); enter, rush with violence; descend very suddenly —*n.* dive —**plung'er** *n.* rubber suction cap with handle to unblock drains —**take the plunge** *inf.* embark on risky enterprise; *inf.* get married

**plunk** *v.* pluck (string of banjo

*etc.*); drop, fall suddenly and heavily —*n.*

**plu·ral** (PLUUR-əl) *adj.* of, denoting more than one person or thing —*n.* word in its plural form —**plu'ral·ism** *n.* holding of more than one office at a time; coexistence of different social groups *etc.*, in one society —**plu·ral'i·ty** *n.* (*pl.* **-ties**) of three or more candidates *etc.* largest share of votes

**plus** *prep.* with addition of (*usu.* indicated by the sign +) —*adj.* to be added; positive

**plush** *n.* fabric with long nap, long-piled velvet —*adj.* (**-er, -est**) luxurious

**Plu·to** (PLOO-toh) *n.* Greek god of the underworld; farthest planet from the sun

**plu·toc·ra·cy** (ploo-TOK-rə-see) *n.* (*pl.* **-cies**) government by the rich; state ruled thus; wealthy class —**plu'to·crat** (**-tə-krat**) *n.* wealthy person

**plu·to·ni·um** (ploo-TOH-nee-əm) *n.* radioactive metallic element used *esp.* in nuclear reactors and weapons

**ply**[1] (plī) *v.* (**plied, ply·ing**) wield; work at; supply pressingly; urge; keep busy; go to and fro, run regularly

**ply**[2] *n.* fold or thickness; strand of yarn —**ply'wood** (**-wuud**) *n.* board of thin layers of wood glued together with grains at right angles

**pneu·mat·ic** (nuu-MAT-ik) *adj.* of, worked by, inflated with wind or air

**pneu·mo·nia** (nuu-MOHN-yə) *n.* inflammation of the lungs

**Po** *Chem.* polonium

**poach**[1] (pohch) *vt.* take (game) illegally; trample, make swampy or soft —*vi.* trespass for this purpose; encroach —**poach'er** *n.*

**poach²** *vt.* simmer (eggs, fish *etc.*) gently in water *etc.* —**poach'er** *n.*

**pock** (pok) *n.* pustule, as in smallpox *etc.* —**pock'marked** *adj.*

**pock·et** (POK-it) *n.* small bag inserted in garment; cavity filled with ore *etc.*; socket, cavity, pouch or hollow; mass of water or air differing from that surrounding it; isolated group or area —*vt.* put into one's pocket; appropriate, steal —*adj.* small —**pocket money** small, regular allowance given to children by parents; allowance for small, occasional expenses —**pocket veto** indirect veto of bill by president, governor, who retains bill unsigned until legislative adjournment

**pod** *n.* long seed vessel, as of peas, beans *etc.* —*v.* (**pod·ded, pod·ding**) —*vi.* form pods —*vt.* shell

**po·di·um** (POH-dee-əm) *n.* small raised platform

**po·em** (POH-əm) *n.* imaginative composition in rhythmic lines —**po'et** (-it) *n.* writer of poems —**po'et·ry** *n.* art or work of poet, verse —**po'e·sy** (-ə-see) *n.* poetry —**po·et'ic** (-ET-ik) *adj.* —**po·et'i·cal·ly** *adv.* —**po'et·as·ter** (-as-tər) *n.* would-be or inferior poet

**po·grom** (pə-GRUM) *n.* organized persecution and massacre, esp. of Jews

**poign·ant** (POIN-yənt) *adj.* moving; biting, stinging; vivid; pungent —**poign'an·cy** *n.* (*pl.* -**cies**)

**poin·set·ti·a** (poin-SET-ee-ə) *n.* orig. Amer. shrub, widely cultivated for its clusters of scarlet leaves, resembling petals

**point** *n.* dot, mark; punctuation mark; item, detail; unit of value; position, degree, stage; moment; gist of an argument; purpose; striking or effective part or quality; essential object or thing; sharp end; single unit in scoring; headland; one of direction marks of compass; fine kind of lace; act of pointing; printing unit, one-twelfth of a pica —*pl.* electrical contacts in distributor of engine —*vi.* show direction or position by extending finger; direct attention; (of dog) indicate position of game by standing facing it —*vt.* aim, direct; sharpen; fill up joints with mortar; give value to (words *etc.*) —**point'ed** *adj.* sharp; direct, telling —**point'er** *n.* index; indicating rod *etc.*, used for pointing; indication; dog trained to point —**point'less** (-lis) *adj.* blunt; futile, irrelevant —**point-blank** *adj.* aimed horizontally; plain, blunt —*adv.* with level aim (there being no necessity to elevate for distance); at short range

**poise** (poiz) *n.* composure; self-possession; balance, equilibrium, carriage (of body *etc.*) —*v.* (**poised, pois·ing**) (cause to be) balanced or suspended —*vt.* hold in readiness

**poi·son** (POI-zən) *n.* substance that kills or injures when introduced into living organism —*vt.* give poison to; infect; pervert, spoil —**poi'son·ous** *adj.* —**poison-pen letter** malicious anonymous letter

**poke¹** (pohk) *v.* (**poked, pok·ing**) —*vt.* push, thrust with finger, stick *etc.*; thrust forward —*vi.* make thrusts; pry —*n.* act of poking —**pok'er** *n.* metal rod for poking fire —**pok'y** *adj.* (**pok·i·er, pok·i·est**) small, confined, cramped

**poke²** —**pig in a poke** something bought *etc.* without previous inspection

**pok·er** (POHK-ər) *n.* card game

—**poker face** expressionless face; person with this

**polar.** adj. see POLE[2]

**Po·lar·oid** (POH-lə-roid) R type of plastic that polarizes light; camera that develops print very quickly inside itself

**pole**[1] (pohl) n. long rounded piece of wood etc. —vt. (poled, pol·ing) propel with pole

**pole**[2] n. each of the ends of axis of Earth or celestial sphere; each of opposite ends of magnet, electric battery etc. —**po·lar** (POH-lər) adj. pert. to the N and S pole, or to magnetic poles; directly opposite in tendency, character etc. —**po·lar'i·ty** n. —**po·lar·i·za'tion** (-ZAY-shən) n. —**po'lar·ize** vt. (-rized, -riz·ing) give polarity to; affect light in manner to restrict vibration of its waves to certain directions —**polar bear** white Arctic bear —**poles apart** having completely opposite interests etc.

**po·lem·ic** (pə-LEM-ik) adj. controversial —n. war of words, argument —**po·lem'i·cal** adj. —**po·lem'i·cize** (-siz) vt. (-cized, -ciz·ing)

**po·lice** (pə-LEES) n. the civil force that maintains public order —vt. (-liced, -lic·ing) keep in order —**police officer** n. member of police force

**pol·i·cy**[1] (POL-ə-see) n. (pl. -cies) course of action adopted, esp. in state affairs; prudence

**policy**[2] n. (pl. -cies) insurance contract

**po·li·o·my·e·li·tis** (poh-lee-oh-mī-ə-LĪ-tis) n. disease of spinal cord characterized by fever and possibly paralysis (abbrev. polio)

**pol'ish** vt. make smooth and glossy; refine —n. shine; polishing; substance for polishing; refinement

**po·lite** (pə-LĪT) adj. (-lit·er, -lit·est) showing regard for others in manners, speech etc. refined, cultured —**po·lite'ness** n. courtesy

**pol·i·tic** (POL-i-tik) adj. wise, shrewd, expedient, cunning —**pol'i·tics** n. (with sing. v.) art of government; political affairs or life —**po·lit'i·cal** adj. of the state or its affairs —**pol·i·ti'cian** (-TISH-ən) n. one engaged in politics —**pol'i·ty** n. (pl. -ties) form of government; organized state; civil government

**pol·ka** (POHL-kə) n. (pl. -kas) lively dance in 2/4 time; music for it —**polka dot** one of pattern of bold spots on fabric etc.

**poll** (pohl) n. voting; counting of votes; number of votes recorded; canvassing of sample of population to determine general opinion; (top of) head —pl. place where votes are cast —vt. receive (votes); take votes of; lop, shear; cut horns from animals —vi. vote —**polled** adj. hornless —**poll'ster** n. one who conducts polls —**poll tax** (esp. formerly) tax on each person

**pol·lard** (POL-ərd) n. hornless animal of normally horned variety; tree on which a close head of young branches has been made by polling —vt. make a pollard of

**pol·len** (POL-ən) n. fertilizing dust of flower —**pol'li·nate** vt. (-nat·ed, -nat·ing)

**pol·lute** (pə-LOOT) vt. (-lut·ed, -lut·ing) make foul; corrupt; desecrate —**pol·lu'tant** (-tənt) n. —**pol·lu'tion** n.

**po·lo** (POH-loh) n. game like hockey played by teams of 4 players on horseback —**water polo** game played similarly by swimmers seven to a side

**pol·o·naise** (pol-ə-NAYZ) *n.* Polish dance; music for it

**pol·ter·geist** (POHL-tər-gīst) *n.* noisy mischievous spirit

**poly-** (*comb. form*) many, as in **polysyllabic** *adj.*

**pol·y·an·dry** (POL-ee-an-dree) *n.* polygamy in which woman has more than one husband —**pol·y·an'drous** *adj.*

**pol·y·chrome** (POL-ee-krohm) *adj.* many colored —*n.* work of art in many colors —**pol·y·chro·mat'ic** *adj.*

**pol·y·es·ter** (POL-ee-es-tər) *n.* any of large class of synthetic materials used as plastics, textile fibers *etc.*

**pol·y·eth·yl·ene** (pol-ee-ETH-ə-leen) *n.* tough thermoplastic material

**po·lyg·a·my** (pə-LIG-ə-mee) *n.* custom of being married to several persons at a time —**po·lyg'a·mist** *n.*

**pol·y·glot** (POL-ee-glot) *adj.* speaking, writing in several languages —*n.* person who speaks, reads and writes in many languages

**pol·y·gon** (POL-ee-gon) *n.* figure with many angles or sides

**po·lyg·y·ny** (pə-LIJ-ə-nee) *n.* polygamy in which one man has more than one wife

**pol·y·he·dron** (pol-ee-HEE-drən) *n.* solid figure contained by many faces

**pol·y·math** (POL-ə-math) *n.* learned person

**pol·y·mer** (POL-ə-mər) *n.* compound, as polystyrene, that has large molecules formed from repeated units —**pol·y·mer·i·za·tion** (pə-lim-ər-ə-ZAY-shən) *n.* —**po·ly'mer·ize** (-LIM-ər-īz) *vt.* (-ized, -iz·ing)

**pol·y·yp** (POL-ip) *n.* sea anemone, or allied animal; tumor with branched roots

**pol·y·sty·rene** (pol-ee-STI-reen) *n.* synthetic material used *esp.* as white rigid foam for packing *etc.*

**pol·y·tech·nic** (pol-ee-TEK-nik) *n.* college dealing mainly with technical subjects —*adj.*

**pol·y·the·ism** (POL-ee-thee-iz-əm) *n.* belief in many gods —**pol·y·the·is'tic** *adj.*

**pol·y·un·sat·u·rat·ed** (pol-ee-un-SACH-ə-ray-tid) *adj.* of group of fats that do not form cholesterol in blood

**pol·y·u·re·thane** (pol-ee-YUUR-ə-thayn) *n.* class of synthetic materials, often in foam or flexible form

**po·made** (po-MAYD) *n.* scented ointment for hair

**po·me·gran·ate** (POM-ə-gran-it) *n.* tree; its fruit with thick rind containing many seeds in red pulp

**pom·mel** (PUM-əl) *n.* front of saddle; knob of sword hilt —*vt.* (-meled, -mel·ing) pummel

**pomp** *n.* splendid display or ceremony

**pom'pom** *n.* tuft of ribbon, wool, feathers *etc.*, decorating hat, shoe *etc.*

**pomp·ous** (POM-pəs) *adj.* self-important; ostentatious; of language, inflated, stilted —**pom·pos'i·ty** *n.* (*pl.* -ties)

**pon·cho** (PON-choh) *n.* (*pl.* -chos) loose circular cloak with hole for head

**pond** *n.* small body, pool or lake of still water

**pon·der** (PON-dər) *v.* muse, meditate, think over; consider, deliberate on

**pon·der·ous** (PON-dər-əs) *adj.* heavy, unwieldy; boring —**pon·der·a·ble** *adj.* able to be evaluated or weighed

**pon'tiff** *n.* Pope; high priest; bishop —**pon·tif'i·cal** *adj.* —**pon·tif'i·cate** (-kit) *n.* dignity or office of pontiff —**pon·tif'i·cate** (-kayt) *vi.* (-cat·ed, -cat·ing) speak bombastically; act as pontiff

**pon·toon'** *n.* flat-bottomed boat or metal drum for use in supporting temporary bridge

**po·ny** (POH-nee) *n.* (*pl.* -nies) horse of small breed; small horse; very small glass —**po'ny·tail** *n.* long hair tied in one bunch at back of head

**poo·dle** (POOD-l) *n.* pet dog with long curly hair often clipped delicately

**pool¹** *n.* small body of still water; deep place in river or stream; puddle; swimming pool

**pool²** *n.* common fund or resources; group of people, *eg* typists, any of whom can work for any of several employers; collective stakes in various games; cartel; variety of billiards —*vt.* put in common fund

**poop¹** *n.* ship's stern

**poop²** *vt. sl.* exhaust (someone) —**poop out** *sl.* fail in something; cease functioning

**poop³** *n. children's sl.* excrement —*vi.* defecate

**poop⁴** *n. sl.* pertinent information

**poor** (puur) *adj.* (-er, -est) having little money; unproductive; inadequate, insignificant; needy; miserable, pitiable; feeble; not fertile —**poor'ly** *adv./adj.* not in good health

**pop¹** *n.* (popped, pop·ping) —*vi.* make small explosive sound; *inf.* go or come unexpectedly or suddenly —*vt.* cause to make small explosive sound; put or place suddenly —*n.* small explosive sound; *inf.* nonalcoholic soda —**pop'corn** *n.* any kind of corn

with kernels that puff up when roasted; the roasted product

**pop²** *n. inf.* father; old man

**pop³** *n.* music of general appeal, *esp.* to young people —*adj.* short *for* popular

**Pope** (pohp) *n.* bishop of Rome and head of R.C. Church

**pop·lar** (POP-lər) *n.* tree noted for its slender tallness

**pop'lin** *n.* corded fabric *usu.* of cotton

**pop·pa·dom** (POP-ə-dəm) *n.* thin, round, crisp Indian bread

**pop·py** (POP-ee) *n.* (*pl.* -pies) bright-flowered plant yielding opium

**pop·u·lace** (POP-yə-ləs) *n.* the common people; the masses

**pop·u·lar** (POP-yə-lər) *adj.* finding general favor; of, by the people —**pop·u·lar'i·ty** *n.* state or quality of being generally liked —**pop'u·lar·ize** *vt.* (-ized, -iz·ing) make popular

**pop·u·late** (POP-yə-layt) *vt.* (-lat·ed, -lat·ing) fill with inhabitants —**pop·u·la'tion** (-LAY-shən) *n.* inhabitants; their number —**pop'u·lous** (-ləs) *adj.* thickly populated or inhabited

**pop·u·list** (POP-yə-list) *adj.* claiming to represent the whole of the people —*n.* —**pop'u·lism** (-liz·əm) *n.*

**por·ce·lain** (POR-sə-lin) *n.* fine earthenware, china

**porch** *n.* covered approach to entrance of building; veranda

**por·cine** (POR-sīn) *adj.* of, like a pig

**por·cu·pine** (POR-kyə-pīn) *n.* rodent covered with long, pointed quills

**pore¹** (por) *vi.* (pored, por·ing) fix eye or mind upon; study closely

**pore²** *n.* minute opening, *esp.* in skin —**po·ros·i·ty** (pə-ROS-i-tee) *n.* —**por·ous** (POR-əs) *adj.* allowing liquid to soak through; full of pores

**pork** n. pig's flesh as food —**pork'er** n. pig raised for food —**pork'y** adj. (**pork·i·er**, **pork·i·est**) fleshy, fat

**porn**, **por'no** n. inf. short for PORNOGRAPHY

**por·nog·ra·phy** (por-NOG-rə-fee) n. indecent literature, films etc. —**por·nog·ra·pher** n. —**por·no·graph'ic** adj.

**por·phy·ry** (POR-fə-ree) n. (pl. **-ries**) reddish stone with embedded crystals

**por·poise** (POR-pəs) n. blunt-nosed sea mammal like dolphin

**por·ridge** (POR-ij) n. soft food of oatmeal etc. boiled in water

**port**[1] n. harbor, haven; town with harbor

**port**[2] n. larboard or left side of ship —vt. turn to left side of a ship

**port**[3] n. strong red wine

**port**[4] n. opening in side of ship —**port'hole** n. small opening or window in side of ship

**port**[5] vt. Mil. carry rifle, etc. diagonally across body —n. this position

**port·a·ble** (POR-tə-bəl) n./adj. (something) easily carried

**por·tage** (POR-tij) n. (cost of) transport

**por·tal** (POR-tl) n. large doorway or imposing gate —**portal-to-portal pay** payment to worker that includes pay for all time spent on employer's premises

**port·cul·lis** (port-KUL-is) n. defense grating to raise or lower in front of castle gateway

**por·tend'** vt. foretell; be an omen of —**por'tent** n. omen, warning; marvel —**por·ten'tous** (-təs) adj. ominous; threatening; pompous

**por·ter** (POR-tər) n. person em-

ployed to carry burden, eg on railway; doorkeeper

**port·fo·li·o** (port-FOH-lee-oh) n. (pl. **-li·os**) flat portable case for loose papers; office of minister of state, member of cabinet

**por·ti·co** (POR-ti-koh) n. (pl. **-coes**, **-cos**) colonnade; covered walk

**por·tiere** (por-TYAIR) n. heavy door curtain

**por·tion** (POR-shən) n. part, share, helping; destiny, lot —vt. divide into shares

**port·ly** (PORT-lee) adj. (**-li·er**, **-li·est**) bulky, stout

**port·man·teau** (port-MAN-toh) n. (pl. **-teaus**) leather suitcase, esp. one opening into two compartments —**portmanteau word** word made by putting together parts of other words eg motel from motor and hotel

**por·tray'** vt. make pictures of, describe —**por'trait** (-trit) n. likeness (of face) of person —**por'trai·ture** (-tri·chər) n. —**por·tray'al** (-əl) n. act of portraying

**pose** (pohz) v. (**posed**, **pos·ing**) —vt. place in attitude; put forward —vi. assume attitude, affect or pretend to be a certain character —n. attitude, esp. one assumed for effect —**po·seur** (poh-ZUR) n. one who assumes affected attitude to create impression

**pos·er** (POH-zər) n. puzzling question

**posh** adj. inf. smart, elegant, stylish

**pos·it** (POZ-it) vt. lay down as principle

**po·si·tion** (pə-ZISH-ən) n. place; situation; location, attitude; status; state of affairs; employment; strategic point —vt. place in position

**pos·i·tive** (POZ-i·tiv) adj. certain; sure; definite, absolute, unquestionable; utter; downright; confident; not negative; greater than zero; *Electricity* having deficiency of electrons —*n.* something positive; *Photog.* print in which lights and shadows are not reversed —**pos′i·tiv·ism** *n.* philosophy recognizing only matters of fact and experience —**pos′i·tiv·ist** *n.* believer in this

**pos·i·tron** (POZ-i-tron) *n.* positive electron

**pos·se** (POS-ee) *n.* body of armed people, *esp.* for maintaining law and order

**pos·sess** (pə-ZES) *vt.* own; (of evil spirit *etc.*) have mastery of —**pos·ses′sion** *n.* act of possessing; thing possessed; ownership —**pos·ses′sive** *adj.* of, indicating possession; with excessive desire to possess, control —*n.* possessive case in grammar —**pos·ses′sor** *n.* owner

**pos·si·ble** (POS-ə-bəl) *adj.* that can, or may, be, exist, happen or be done; worthy of consideration —*n.* possible candidate —**pos·si·bil′i·ty** *n.* (*pl.* -ties) —**pos′si·bly** *adv.* perhaps

**pos·sum** (POS-əm) *n.* opossum —**play possum** pretend to be dead, asleep *etc.* to deceive opponent

**post**[1] (pohst) *n.* upright pole of timber or metal fixed firmly, usu. to support or mark something —*vt.* display; stick up (on notice board *etc.*) —**post′er** *n.* large advertising bill; one who posts bills —**poster paints**, colors flat paints suited for posters

**post**[2] *n.* mail; collection or delivery of this; office; situation; point, station, place of duty; place where soldier is stationed; place held by body of troops; fort —*vt.* put into mailbox; supply with latest information; station (soldiers *etc.*) in particular spot; transfer (entries) to ledger —*adv.* with haste —**post·age** (POH-stij) *n.* charge for carrying letter —**post′al** (-əl) *adj.* —**postal money order** written order, available at post office, for payment of sum of money —**post′card** *n.* stamped card sent by mail —**post′man** (-mən) *n.* (*pl.* -men) postal employee who collects or delivers mail —**post′mark** *n.* official mark with name of office *etc.* stamped on letters —**post′mas·ter**, (*fem.*) **-mis·tress** (-tris) *n.* official in charge of post office, place where postal business is conducted

**post-** (*prefix*) after, behind, later than, *eg* postwar *adj.* Such compounds are not given here when the meaning can easily be found from the simple word

**post·date** (pohst-DAYT) *vt.* (-dat·ed, -dat·ing) give date later than actual date

**poste res·tante** (pohst re-STAHNT) *Fr.* direction on mail to indicate that post office should keep traveler's letters till called for

**pos·te·ri·or** (po-STEER-ee-ər) *adj.* later, hinder —*n.* the buttocks

**pos·ter·i·ty** (po-STER-i-tee) *n.* later generations; descendants

**post·grad·u·ate** (pohst-GRAJ-oo-it) *adj.* carried on after graduation —*n.*

**post·hu·mous** (POS-chə-məs) *adj.* occurring after death; born after father's death; published after author's death —**post′hu·mous·ly** *adv.*

**post·mor·tem** (pohst-MOR-təm) *n.* medical examination of dead body; evaluation after event *etc.* ends —*adj.* taking place after death

**post·par·tum** (pohst-PAHR-təm) *adj.* occurring after childbirth

**post·pone** (pohs-POHN) *vt.* (-poned, -pon·ing) put off to later time, defer

**post·pran·di·al** (pohst-PRAN-dee-əl) *adj.* after a meal *esp.* dinner

**post·script** (POHST-skript) *n.* addition to letter, book *etc.*

**pos·tu·lant** (POS-chə-lənt) *n.* candidate for admission to religious order

**pos·tu·late** (POS-chə-layt) *vt.* (-lat·ed, -lat·ing) take for granted; lay down as self-evident; stipulate —*n.* (-lit) proposition assumed without proof; prerequisite

**pos·ture** (POS-chər) *n.* attitude, position of body —*v.* (-tured, -tur·ing) pose

**po·sy** (POH-zee) *n.* (*pl.* -sies) flower; bunch of flowers

**pot** *n.* round vessel; cooking vessel; trap, *esp.* for crabs, lobsters; *sl.* marijuana; *inf.* a lot —*vt.* (pot·ted, pot·ting) put into, preserve in pot —potted *adj.* cooked, preserved, in a pot; *sl.* drunk —**pot'·hole** *n.* pitlike cavity in rocks, usu. limestone, produced by faulting and water action; hole worn in road —**pot'·luck** *n.* whatever is to be had (to eat) —**pot'·sherd** (-shurd) *n.* broken fragment of pottery —**pot shot** easy or random shot

**po·ta·ble** (POH-tə-bəl) *adj.* drinkable —**po·ta'·tion** (-TAY-shən) *n.* drink; drinking

**pot'·ash** *n.* alkali used in soap *etc.*; crude potassium carbonate

**po·tas·si·um** (pə-TAS-ee-əm) *n.* white metallic element

**po·ta·to** (pə-TAY-toh) *n.* (*pl.* -toes) plant with tubers grown for food —**hot potato** topic *etc.* too threatening to bring up

—**sweet potato** trailing plant; its edible sweetish tubers

**po·tent** (POHT-nt) *adj.* powerful, influential; (of male) capable of sexual intercourse —**po'·ten·cy** *n.* physical or moral power; efficacy

**po·ten·tate** (POHT-n-tayt) *n.* ruler

**po·ten·tial** (pə-TEN-shəl) *adj.* latent, that may or might but does not now exist or act —*n.* possibility; amount of potential energy; *Electricity* level of electric pressure —**po·ten·ti·al'·i·ty** (-shee-AL-i-tee) *n.*

**po·tion** (POH-shən) *n.* dose of medicine or poison

**pot·pour·ri** (poh-puu-REE) *n.* mixture of rose petals, spices *etc.*; musical, literary medley

**pot·tage** (POT-ij) *n.* soup or stew

**pot·ter** (POT-ər) *n.* maker of earthenware vessels —**pot'·ter·y** *n.* (*pl.* -ter·ies) earthenware; where it is made; art of making it

**pouch** (powch) *n.* small bag; pocket —*vt.* put into one

**poul·tice** (POHL-tis) *n.* soft composition of cloth, bread *etc.*, applied hot to sore or inflamed parts of the body

**poul·try** (POHL-tree) *n.* domestic fowl collectively

**pounce**[1] (powns) *vi.* (pounced, pounc·ing) spring upon suddenly, swoop (upon) —*n.* swoop or sudden descent

**pounce**[2] *n.* fine powder used to prevent ink from spreading on unsized paper or in pattern making

**pound**[1] (pownd) *vt.* beat, thump; crush to pieces or powder; walk, run heavily

**pound**[2] *n.* unit of troy weight; unit of avoirdupois weight equal to 0.453 kg; monetary unit in United Kingdom

**pound**[3] n. enclosure for stray animals or officially removed vehicles; confined space

**pound·al** (POWN-dl) n. a unit of force in the foot-pound-second system

**pour** (por) vi. come out in a stream, crowd etc.; flow freely; rain heavily —vt. give out thus; cause to run out

**pout** (powt) v. thrust out (lips), look sulky —n. act of pouting —pout'er n. pigeon with power of inflating its crop

**pov·er·ty** (POV-ər-tee) n. state of being poor; poorness; lack of means; scarcity

**pow·der** (POW-dər) n. solid matter in fine dry particles; medicine in this form; gunpowder; face powder etc. —vt. apply powder to; reduce to powder —pow'der·y adj.

**pow·er** (POW-ər) n. ability to do or act; authority; control; person or thing having authority; mechanical energy; electricity supply; rate of doing work; product from continuous multiplication of number by itself —pow'ered adj. having or operated by mechanical or electrical power —pow'er·ful (-fəl) adj. —pow'er·less (-lis) adj. —pow'er·house, power station n. installation for generating and distributing electric power

**pow'wow** n. conference —vi. confer

**pox** (poks) n. one of several diseases marked by pustular eruptions of skin; inf. syphilis

**Pr** Chem. praseodymium

**prac·ti·cal** (PRAK-ti-kəl) adj. given to action rather than theory; relating to action or real existence; useful; in effect though not in name; virtual —prac'ti·cal·ly adv. —prac'ti·ca·ble (-kə-bəl) adj.

that can be done, used etc. —prac·ti'tion·er n. one engaged in a profession

**prac·tice** (PRAK-tis) v. (-ticed, -tic·ing) —vt. do repeatedly, work at to gain skill; do habitually; put into action —vi. exercise oneself; exercise profession —practice n. habit; mastery or skill; exercise of art or profession; action, not theory

**prag·mat·ic** (prag-MAT-ik) adj. concerned with practical consequence; of the affairs of state —prag'ma·tism (-mə-tiz-əm) n. —prag'ma·tist n.

**prai·rie** (PRAIR-ee) n. large mostly treeless tract of grassland —prairie dog small Amer. rodent allied to marmot —prairie oyster as remedy for hangover, a drink of raw egg usu. with seasonings; as food, testis of a calf

**praise** (prayz) n. commendation; fact, state of being praised —vt. (praised, prais·ing) express approval, admiration of; speak well of; glorify —praise'wor·thy (-wur-thee) adj.

**pra·line** (PRAH-leen) n. candy made of nuts with caramel covering

**prance** (prans) vi. (pranced, pranc·ing) swagger; caper; walk with bounds —n. prancing

**pran·di·al** (PRAN-dee-əl) adj. of a meal esp. dinner

**prank** (prangk) n. mischievous trick or escapade, frolic

**pra·se·o·dym·i·um** (pray-zee-oh-DIM-ee-əm) n. rare-earth chemical element

**prate** (prayt) vi. (prat·ed, prat·ing) talk idly, chatter —n. idle chatter

**prat·tle** (PRAT-l) vi. (-tled, -tling) talk like child —n. trifling, childish talk —prat'tler n. babbler

**prawn** n. edible sea crustacean like a shrimp

**pray** vt. ask earnestly; entreat —vi. offer prayers esp. to God —**prayer** (prair) n. action, practice of praying to God; earnest entreaty —**pray'er** n. one who prays

**pre-** (prefix) before, beforehand eg prenatal adj., prerecord vt., preshrunk adj. Such compounds are not given here where the meaning can easily be found from the simple word

**preach** (preech) vi. deliver sermon; give moral, religious advice —vt. set forth in religious discourse; advocate —**preach'er** n.

**pre·am·ble** (PREE-am-bəl) n. introductory part of document, story etc.

**pre·car·i·ous** (pri-KAIR-ee-əs) adj. insecure, unstable, perilous

**pre·cau·tion** (pri-KAW-shən) n. previous care to prevent evil or secure good; preventive measure —**pre·cau'tion·ar·y** adj.

**pre·cede** (pri-SEED) v. (-ced·ed, -ced·ing) go, come before in rank, order, time etc. —**prec·e·dence** (PRES-i-dəns) n. —n. priority in position, rank, time etc. —**prec'e·dent** n. previous case or occurrence taken as rule

**pre·cept** (PREE-sept) n. rule for conduct, maxim —**pre·cep'tor** n. instructor

**pre·ces·sion** (pree-SESH-ən) n. act of preceding; motion of spinning body (eg top, planet) wobbling so that axis of rotation marks out a cone

**pre·cinct** (PREE-singkt) n. enclosed, limited area; administrative area of city, esp. of police, board of elections —pl. environs —precinct house police station

**pre·cious** (PRESH-əs) adj. beloved, cherished; of great value,

highly valued; rare —**pre·cios·i·ty** (presh-ee-OS-i-tee) n. overrefinement in art or literature —**pre'cious·ly** adv.

**prec·i·pice** (PRES-ə-pis) n. very steep cliff or rockface —**pre·cip'i·tous** adj. sheer

**pre·cip·i·tant** (pra-SIP-i-tənt) adj. hasty, rash; abrupt —**pre·cip'i·tance**, **-tan·cy** n.

**pre·cip·i·tate** (pri-SIP-i-tayt) vt. (-tat·ed, -tat·ing) hasten happening of; throw headlong; Chem. cause to be deposited in solid form from solution —adj. (-i-tit) too sudden; rash, impetuous —n. (-i-tit) substance chemically precipitated —**pre·cip'i·tate·ly** (-tit-lee) adv. —**pre·cip·i·ta·tion** (-TAY-shən) n. esp. rain, snow etc.

**pré·cis** (PRAY-see) n. (pl. same form pr. PRAY-seez) abstract, summary

**pre·cise** (pri-SĪS) adj. definite; particular; exact, strictly worded; careful in observance; punctilious, formal —**pre·cise'ly** adv. —**pre·ci·sion** (-SIZH-ən) n. accuracy

**pre·clude** (pri-KLOOD) vt. (-clud·ed, -clud·ing) prevent from happening; shut out

**pre·co·cious** (pri-KOH-shəs) adj. developed, matured early or too soon —**pre·coc'i·ty** (-KOS-i-tee), **pre·co'cious·ness** (-KOH-shəs-nis) n.

**pre·con·ceive** (pree-kən-SEEV) vt. (-ceived, -ceiv·ing) form an idea beforehand —**pre·con·cep'tion** (-SEP-shən) n.

**pre·con·di·tion** (pree-kən-DISH-ən) n. necessary or required condition

**pre·cur·sor** (pri-KUR-sər) n. forerunner —**pre·cur'sive**, **pre·cur'so·ry** adj.

**pred·a·to·ry** (PRED-ə-tor-ee) adj. hunting, killing other animals *etc.* for food; plundering —**pred'a·tor** *n.* predatory animal

**pred·e·ces·sor** (PRED-ə-ses-ər) *n.* one who precedes another in an office or position; ancestor

**pre·des·tine** (pri-DES-tin) *vt.* (-tined, -tin·ing) decree beforehand, foreordain —**pre·des·ti·na'tion** *n.*

**pre·dic·a·ment** (pri-DIK-ə-mənt) *n.* perplexing, embarrassing, or difficult situation

**pred·i·cate** (PRED-i-kayt) *vt.* (-cat·ed, -cat·ing) affirm, assert; base (on or upon) —*n.* (-kit) that which is predicated; *Grammar* statement made about a subject

**pre·dict** (pri-DIKT) *vt.* foretell, prophesy —**pre·dict'a·ble** *adj.*

**pre·di·lec·tion** (pred-l-EK-shən) *n.* preference, liking, partiality

**pre·dis·pose** (pree-dis-POHZ) *vt.* (-posed, -pos·ing) incline, influence someone (toward); make susceptible (to)

**pre·dom·i·nate** (pri-DOM-ə-nayt) *vi.* (-nat·ed, -nat·ing) be main or controlling element —**pre·dom'i·nance** (-nəns) *n.* —**pre·dom'i·nant** *adj.* chief

**pre·em·i·nent** (pree-EM-ə-nənt) *adj.* excelling all others, outstanding —**pre·em'i·nence** *n.*

**pre·empt** (pree-EMPT) *vt.* acquire in advance or act in advance of or to exclusion of others —**pre·emp'tive** *adj.*

**preen** *vt.* trim (feathers) with beak, plume; smarten oneself

**pre·fab·ri·cate** (pree-FAB-ri-kayt) *vt.* (-cat·ed, -cat·ing) manufacture buildings *etc.* in shaped sections, for rapid assembly on the site —**pre'fab** *n.* building so made

**pref·ace** (PREF-is) *n.* introduction to book *etc.* —*vt.* (-faced, -fac·ing) introduce —**pref'a·to·ry** *adj.*

**pre·fect** (PREE-fekt) *n.* person put in authority —**pre·fec·ture** (PREE-fek-chər) *n.* office, residence, jurisdiction of a prefect

**pre·fer** (pri-FUR) *vt.* (-ferred, -fer·ring) like better; promote —**pref·er·a·ble** (PREF-ər-ə-bəl) *adj.* more desirable —**pref'er·a·bly** *adv.* —**pref'er·ence** (-əns) *n.* —**pref·er·en'tial** (-EN-shəl) *adj.* giving, receiving preference

**pre·fix** (PREE-fiks) *n.* preposition or particle put at beginning of word or title —*vt.* put as introduction; put before word to make compound

**preg·nant** (PREG-nənt) *adj.* carrying fetus in womb; full of meaning, significance; inventive —**preg'nan·cy** *n.*

**pre·hen·sile** (pri-HEN-sil) *adj.* capable of grasping

**pre·his·tor·ic** (pree-hi-STOR-ik) *adj.* before period in which written history begins —**pre·his'to·ry** *n.*

**prej·u·dice** (PREJ-ə-dis) *n.* preconceived opinion; bias, partiality; damage or injury likely to happen to person or person's rights as a result of others' action or judgment —*vt.* (-diced, -dic·ing) influence; bias; injure —**prej·u·di'cial** (-DISH-əl) *adj.* injurious; disadvantageous

**prel·ate** (PREL-it) *n.* bishop or other church dignitary of equal or higher rank —**prel'a·cy** (-ə-see) *n.* prelate's office

**pre·lim·i·nar·y** (pri-LIM-ə-ner-ee) *adj.* preparatory, introductory —*n.* (*pl.* -ies) introductory, preparatory statement, action

**prel·ude** (PREL-yood) *n. Mus.* introductory movement; performance, event *etc.* serving as introduction —*v.* (-ud·ed, -ud·ing) serve as prelude, introduce

**pre·mar·i·tal** (pree-MA-ri-tɔl) *adj.* occurring before marriage

**pre·ma·ture** (pree-mɔ-CHUUR) *adj.* happening, done before proper time

**pre·med·i·tate** (pri-MED-i-tayt) *vt.* (-tat·ed, -tat·ing) consider, plan beforehand —**pre·med·i·ta'·tion** *n.*

**pre·mier** (pri-MEER) *n.* prime minister —*adj.* chief, foremost; first —**pre·mier'ship** *n.* office of premier

**pre·miere** (pri-MEER) *n.* first performance of a play, film *etc.* —*vi.* (-miered, -mier·ing) have first performance

**prem·ise** (PREM-is) *n. Logic* proposition from which inference is drawn —*pl.* house, building with its belongings —**premise** *vt.* (-mised, -mis·ing) state by way of introduction

**pre·mi·um** (PREE-mee-ɔm) *n.* prize, bonus; sum paid for insurance; excess over nominal value; great value or regard

**pre·mo·ni·tion** (pree-mɔ-NISH-ɔn) *n.* presentiment, foreboding —**pre·mon·i·to·ry** (pri-MON-i-tor-ee) *adj.*

**pre·na·tal** (pree-NAYT-l) *adj.* occurring before birth

**pre·oc·cu·py** (pree-OK-yɔ-pī) *vt.* (-pied, -py·ing) occupy to the exclusion of other things —**pre·oc·cu·pa'tion** *n.* mental concentration or absorption

**pre·pare** (pri-PAIR) *v.* (-pared, -par·ing) —*vt.* make ready; make —*vi.* get ready —**prep·a·ra'tion** *n.* making ready beforehand; something that is prepared, as a medicine; at school, (time spent) preparing work for lesson —**pre·par·a·to·ry** (PA-rɔ-tor-ee) *adj.* serving to prepare; introductory —**pre·par'ed·ness** (-id-nis) *n.* state of being prepared

**pre·pon·der·ate** (pri-PON-dɔ-rayt) *vi.* (-at·ed, -at·ing) be of greater weight or power —**pre·pon'der·ance** (-ɔns) *n.* superiority of power, numbers *etc.*

**prep·o·si·tion** (prep-ɔ-ZISH-ɔn) *n.* word marking relation between noun or pronoun and other words —**prep·o·si'tion·al** *adj.*

**pre·pos·sess** (pree-pɔ-ZES) *vt.* impress, *esp.* favorably, beforehand; possess beforehand —**pre·pos·sess'ing** *adj.* inviting favorable opinion, attractive, winning

**pre·pos·ter·ous** (pri-POS-tɔr-ɔs) *adj.* utterly absurd, foolish

**pre·puce** (PRE-pyoos) *n.* retractable fold of skin covering tip of penis, foreskin

**pre·req·ui·site** (pri-REK-wɔ-zit) *n./adj.* (something) required as prior condition

**pre·rog·a·tive** (pri-ROG-ɔ-tiv) *n.* peculiar power or right, *esp.* as vested in ruler —*adj.* privileged

**pres·age** (PRES-ij) *n.* omen, indication of something to come —*vt.* (-aged, -ag·ing) foretell

**pres·by·o·pia** (prez-bee-OH-pee-ɔ) *n.* progressively diminishing ability of the eye to focus, *esp.* on near objects, farsightedness

**pres·by·ter** (PREZ-bi-tɔr) *n.* elder in early Christian church; priest; member of a presbytery —**Pres·by·te'ri·an** *adj./n.* (member) of Protestant church governed by lay elders —**pres'by·ter·y** *n.* church court composed of all ministers within a certain district and one or two ruling elders from each church; *R.C.Ch.* rectory

**pre·science** (PRESH-ɔns) *n.* foreknowledge —**pres'cient** *adj.*

**pre·scribe** (pri-SKRĪB) *v.* (-scribed, -scrib·ing) set out rules for; order; ordain; order use of (medicine) —**pre·scrip'tion** *n.*

prescribing; thing prescribed; written statement of it —pre·scrip′tive adj.

pres·ent¹ (PREZ-ənt) adj. that is here; now existing or happening —n. present time or tense —pres′ence n. being present; appearance, bearing —pres′ent·ly adv. soon; at present

present² (pri-ZENT) vt. introduce formally; bring; give; offer; point, aim —pres′ent n. gift —pre·sent′a·ble adj. fit to be seen —pres·en·ta′tion (-TAY-shən) n. —pre·sent′er n. person who presents, esp. an award

pre·sen·ti·ment (pri-ZEN-tə-mənt) n. sense of something (esp. evil) about to happen

pre·serve (pri-ZURV) vt. (-served, -serv·ing) keep from harm, injury or decay; maintain; pickle, can —n. special area; that which is preserved, as fruit etc.; place where game is kept for private fishing, shooting —pl. preserved vegetables, fruit etc. —pres·er·va′tion (-zur·VAY′tive n. chemical put into perishable foods, drinks etc. to keep them from going bad —adj. tending to preserve; having quality of preserving

pre·side (pri-ZID) vi. (-sid·ed, -sid·ing) be chairperson; superintend —pres′i·dent (-dənt) n. head of organization, company, republic etc. —pres′i·den·cy n. (pl. -cies) —pres·i·den′tial (-DEN-shəl) adj.

press¹ vt. subject to push or squeeze; smooth by pressure or heat; urge steadily, earnestly —vi. bring weight to bear; throng; hasten —n. a pressing; machine for pressing, esp. printing machine; printing house; its work or art; newspapers collectively; reporters, journalists;

crowd; stress —press′ing adj. urgent; persistent —press agent person employed to advertise and secure publicity for any person, enterprise etc. —press′man (-mən) n. printer who attends to the press

press² vt. force to serve esp. in navy or army —press gang formerly, body of men employed to press men into naval service

pres·sure (PRESH-ər) n. act of pressing; influence; authority; difficulties; Physics thrust per unit area —pres·sur·i·za′tion (-ZAY-shən) n. in aircraft, maintenance of normal atmospheric pressure at high altitudes —pres′sur·ize vt. (-ized, -iz·ing) —pressure cooker reinforced pot that cooks food rapidly by steam under pressure —pressure group organized group that exerts influence on policies, public opinion etc.

pres·ti·dig·i·ta·tion (pres-ti-dij-i-TAY-shən) n. sleight of hand —pres·ti·dig′i·ta·tor n.

pres·tige (pre-STEEZH) n. reputation; influence depending on it —pres·tig′i·ous (-STIJ-əs) adj.

pres·to (PRES-toh) adv. Mus. quickly

pre·stressed (PREE-strest) adj. (of concrete) containing stretched steel cables for strengthening

pre·sume (pri-ZOOM) v. (-sumed, -sum·ing) —vt. take for granted —vi. take liberties —pre·sum′a·bly adv. probably; doubtlessly —pre·sump′tion (-ZUM-shən) n. forward, arrogant opinion or conduct; strong probability —pre·sump′tive adj. that may be assumed as true or valid until contrary is proved —pre·sump′tu·ous (-shoo-əs) adj. forward, impudent, taking liberties

**pre·sup·pose** (pree-sə-POHZ) vt. (-posed, -pos·ing) assume or take for granted beforehand —**pre·sup·po·si'tion** (-ZI-shən) n. previous supposition

**pre·tend** (pri-TEND) vt. claim or allege (something untrue); make believe, as in play —vi. lay claim (to) —pretext —**pre·tense'** n. simulation; pretext —**pre·tend'er** n. claimant (to throne) —**pre·ten'sion** n. —**pre·ten'tious** (-shəs) adj. making claim to special merit or importance; given to outward show

**pre·ter·nat·u·ral** (pre-tər-NACH-ər-əl) adj. out of ordinary way of nature; abnormal, supernatural

**pre·text** (PREE tekst) n. excuse; pretense

**pret·ty** (PRIT-ee) adj. (-ti·er, -ti·est) having beauty that is attractive rather than imposing; charming etc. —adv. fairly, moderately —**pret'ti·ness** (-nis) n.

**pret·zel** (PRET-səl) n. crisp, dry biscuit usu. shaped as knot or stick

**pre·vail** (pri-VAYL) vi. gain mastery; triumph; be in fashion, generally established —**pre·vail'ing** adj. widespread; predominant —**prev'a·lence** (-ləns) n. —**prev'a·lent** (-lənt) adj. extensively existing, rife

**pre·var·i·cate** (pri-VA-ri-kayt) vi. (-cat·ed, -cat·ing) make evasive or misleading statements; lie —**pre·var'i·ca·tor** n.

**pre·vent** (pri-VENT) vt. stop, hinder —**pre·vent'a·ble** adj. —**pre·ven'tion** (-shən) n. —**pre·ven'tive** adj./n.

**pre·view** (PREE-vyoo) n. advance showing; a showing of scenes from a forthcoming film etc.

**pre·vi·ous** (PREE-vee-əs) adj. earlier; preceding; happening before —**pre'vi·ous·ly** adv. before

**prey** (pray) n. animal hunted and killed by carnivorous animals; victim —vi. seize for food; treat as prey; afflict, obsess (with upon)

**price** (pris) n. amount etc. for which thing is bought or sold; cost; value; reward; odds in betting —vt. (priced, pric·ing) fix, ask price for —**price'less** (-lis) adj. invaluable; very funny —**pric'ey** (-ee) (pric·i·er, pric·i·est) adj. expensive

**prick** (prik) vt. pierce slightly with sharp point; cause to feel mental pain; mark by prick; erect (ears) —n. slight hole made by pricking; pricking or being pricked; sting; remorse; that which pricks; sharp point —**prick'le** n. thorn, spike —vi. (-led, -ling) feel tingling or pricking sensation —**prick'ly** adj. (-li·er, -li·est) —prickly heat inflammation of skin with stinging pains

**pride** (prid) n. too high an opinion of oneself; worthy self-esteem; feeling of elation or great satisfaction; something causing this; group (of lions) —v. refl. (prid·ed, prid·ing) take pride

**priest** (preest) n. (-ess fem.) official minister of religion, member of clergy —**priest'hood** (-huud) n. —**priest'ly** adj. (-li·er, -li·est)

**prig** n. self-righteous person who professes superior culture, morality etc. —**prig'gish** adj.

**prim** adj. (prim·mer, prim·mest) very restrained, formally prudish

**pri·ma·cy** (PRI-mə-see) n. state of being first in rank, grade etc.; office of PRIMATE

**pri·ma don·na** (pree-mə DON-ə) (pl. donnas) principal female singer in opera; temperamental person

**pri·ma fa·ci·e** (PRI-mɔ FAY-shee) *Lat.* at first sight; obvious

**pri·mal** (PRI-mɔl) *adj.* of earliest age; first, original —**pri·ma′ri·ly** *adv.* —**pri′ma·ry** *adj.* chief; of the first stage, decision *etc.*; elementary

**pri·mate¹** (PRI-mit) *n.* archbishop

**primate²** (PRI-mayt) *n.* one of order of mammals including monkeys and man

**prime¹** (prim) *adj.* fundamental; original; chief; best —*n.* first, best part of anything; youth; full health and vigor —*vt.* (primed, prim·ing) prepare (gun, engine, pump *etc.*) for use; fill up, *eg* with information —**prime minister** leader of parliamentary government

**prime²** *vt.* (primed, prim·ing) prepare for paint with preliminary coating of oil *etc.* —**prim′er** (PRIM-ɔr) *n.* paint *etc.* for priming

**prim·er** (PRIM-ɔr) *n.* elementary schoolbook or manual

**pri·me·val** (pri-MEE-vɔl) *adj.* of the earliest age of the world

**prim·i·tive** (PRIM-i-tiv) *adj.* of an early undeveloped kind, ancient; crude, rough

**pri·mo·gen·i·ture** (pri-mɔ-JEN-i-chɔr) *n.* rule by which real estate passes to the first born son —**pri·mo·gen′i·tor** *n.* earliest ancestor; forefather

**pri·mor·di·al** (pri-MOR-dee-ɔl) *adj.* existing at or from the beginning

**prince** (prins) *n.* son or (in some countries) grandson of king or queen; ruler, chief; admirably fine person (**prin′cess** *fem.*) —**prince′ly** *adj.* (-li·er, -li·est) generous, lavish; stately; magnificent

**prin·ci·pal** (PRIN-sɔ-pɔl) *adj.* chief in importance —*n.* person for whom another is agent; head of institution, *esp.* school; sum of money lent and yielding interest; chief actor —**prin·ci·pal′i·ty** *n.* territory, dignity of prince

**prin·ci·ple** (PRIN-sɔ-pɔl) *n.* moral rule; settled reason of action; uprightness; fundamental truth or element

**print** *vt.* reproduce (words, pictures *etc.*), by pressing inked plates, type, blocks *etc.* to paper *etc.*; produce thus; write in imitation of this; impress; *Photog.* produce pictures from negatives; stamp (fabric) with colored design —*n.* printed matter; printed lettering; written imitation of printed type; photograph; impression, mark left on surface by thing that has pressed against it; printed cotton fabric —**print′er** *n.* person or device engaged in printing —**printed circuit** electronic circuit with wiring printed on an insulating base —**print′out** *n.* printed information from computer, teleprinter *etc.*

**pri·or** (PRI-ɔr) *adj.* earlier —*n.* chief of religious house (**pri′or·ess** *fem.*) or order —**pri·or′i·ty** *n.* (pl. -ties) precedence; something given special attention —**pri′o·ry** *n.* (pl. -ries) monastery, convent under prior, prioress —**prior to** before, earlier

**prise** (priz) *vt.* (prised, pris·ing) force open by levering; obtain (information *etc.*) with difficulty

**prism** (PRIZ-ɔm) *n.* transparent solid usu. with triangular ends and rectangular sides, used to disperse light into spectrum or refract it in optical instruments *etc.* —**pris·mat′ic** *adj.* of prism shape; (of color) such as is produced by refraction through prism, rainbowlike, brilliant

**pris·on** (PRIZ-ən) n. jail —**pris'on·er** n. one kept in prison; captive

**pris·sy** (PRIS-ee) adj. (-si·er, -si·est) fussy, prim

**pris·tine** (PRIS-teen) adj. original, primitive, unspoiled, good

**pri·vate** (PRĪ-vit) adj. secret, not public; reserved for, or belonging to, or concerning, an individual only; personal; secluded; denoting soldier or marine of lowest rank; not controlled by government —n. private soldier or marine —**pri'va·cy** (-vi-see) n. —**pri·va·tize** vt. (-tized, -tiz·ing) transfer from government or public ownership to private enterprise

**pri·va·tion** (prī-VAY-shən) n. want of comforts or necessities; hardship; act of depriving —**priv·a·tive** (PRIV-ə-tiv) adj. of privation or negation

**priv·et** (PRIV-it) n. bushy shrub used for hedges

**priv·i·lege** (PRIV-ə-lij) n. advantage or favor that only a few obtain; right, advantage belonging to person or class —**priv'i·leged** adj. enjoying special right or immunity

**priv·y** (PRIV-ee) adj. admitted to knowledge of secret —n. (pl. **priv·ies**) outhouse; Law person having interest in an action

**prize**[1] (priz) n. reward given for success in competition; thing striven for; thing won, eg in lottery —adj. winning or likely to win a prize —vt. (prized, priz·ing) value highly —**prize'fight** n. boxing match for money

**prize**[2] n. ship, property captured in (naval) warfare

**pro**[1] (proh) adj./adv. in favor of

**pro**[2] n. professional —adj. professional

**pro-** (prefix) for, instead of, be-

fore, in front, as in proconsul, pronoun, project Such compounds are not given here where the meaning can easily be found from the simple word

**prob·a·ble** (PROB-ə-bəl) adj. likely —**prob·a·bil'i·ty** n. likelihood; anything that has appearance of truth —**prob'a·bly** adv.

**pro·bate** (PROH-bayt) n. proving of authenticity of will; certificate of this —**probate court** court with power over administration of estates of dead persons

**pro·ba·tion** (proh-BAY-shən) n. system of releasing lawbreakers, but placing them under supervision for stated period; testing of candidate before admission to full membership

**probe** (prohb) vt. (probed, prob·ing) search into, examine, question closely —n. that which probes, or is used to probe; thorough inquiry

**pro·bi·ty** (PROH-bi-tee) n. honesty, uprightness, integrity

**prob·lem** (PROB-ləm) n. matter etc. difficult to deal with or solve; question set for solution; puzzle —**prob·le·mat'ic** adj. questionable; uncertain; doubtful

**pro·bos·cis** (proh-BOS-is) n. (pl. -cis·es) trunk or long snout, eg of elephant; inf. nose, esp. prominent one

**pro·ceed** (prə-SEED) vi. go forward, continue; be carried on; take legal action —**pro·ceeds** (PROH-seedz) n. pl. amount of money or profit received —**pro·ce'dur·al** (-SEE-jər-əl) adj. —**pro·ce'dure** n. act, manner of proceeding; conduct —**pro·ceed'ing** n. act or course of action; transaction —pl. minutes of meeting; methods of prosecuting charge, claim etc.

**proc·ess** (PROS-es) n. series of

actions or changes; method of operation; state of going on; action of law; outgrowth —*vt.* handle, treat, prepare by special method of manufacture *etc.* —**pro·ces·sion** (prə-SESH-ən) *n.* regular, orderly progress; line of persons in formal order —**pro·ces'sion·al** *adj.* —**proc'es·sor** *n.* person or device that processes

**pro·choice** (proh-CHOIS) *adj.* supporting legalized abortion

**pro·claim** (proh-KLAYM) *vt.* announce publicly, declare —**proc·la·ma'tion** (prok-lə-MAY-shən) *n.*

**pro·cliv·i·ty** (proh-KLIV-i-tee) *n.* (*pl.* -ties) inclination, tendency

**pro·cras·ti·nate** (proh-KRAS-tə-nayt) *vi.* (-nat·ed, -nat·ing) put off, delay —**pro·cras·ti·na'tion** *n.* —**pro·cras'ti·na·tor** *n.*

**pro·cre·ate** (PROH-kree-ayt) *vt.* (-at·ed, -at·ing) produce offspring, generate —**pro·cre·a'tion** *n.*

**Pro·crus·te·an** (proh-KRUS-tee-ən) *adj.* compelling uniformity by violence

**proc·tol·o·gy** (prok-TOL-ə-jee) *n.* medical specialty dealing with diseases of anus and rectum

**proc·tor** (PROK-tər) *n.* person appointed to supervise students during examinations; university official with administrative, *esp.* disciplinary, duties

**pro·cure** (prə-KYUUR) *v.* (-cured, -cur·ing) —*vt.* obtain, acquire; provide; bring about —*vi.* act as pimp —**pro·cure'ment** *n.* —**pro·cur'er** *n.* (-cur'ess *fem.*) one who procures; pimp

**prod** *vt.* (prod·ded, prod·ding) poke with something pointed; stimulate to action —*n.* prodding; goad; pointed instrument

**prod·i·gal** (PROD-i-gəl) *adj.* wasteful; extravagant —*n.* spendthrift —**prod·i·gal'i·ty** *n.* reckless extravagance

**prod·i·gy** (PROD-i-jee) *n.* (*pl.* -gies) person *esp.* precocious child with some marvelous gift; thing causing wonder —**pro·di·gious** (prə-DIJ-əs) *adj.* very great, immense; extraordinary —**pro·di'gious·ly** *adv.*

**pro·duce** (prə-DOOS) *vt.* (-duced, -duc·ing) bring into existence; yield; make; bring forward; manufacture; exhibit; present on stage, film, TV; *Geom.* extend in length —*n.* (PROD-oos) that which is yielded or made *esp.* vegetables —**pro·duc'er** *n.* person who produces, *esp.* play, film *etc.* —**prod'uct** (-əkt) *n.* result of process of manufacture; number resulting from multiplication —**pro·duc'tion** *n.* producing; things produced —**pro·duc'tive** *adj.* fertile; creative; efficient —**pro·duc·tiv'i·ty** *n.*

**pro·fam·i·ly** (proh-FAM-ə-lee) *adj.* antiabortion; pro-life

**pro·fane** (prə-FAYN) *adj.* irreverent, blasphemous; not sacred —*vt.* (-faned, -fan·ing) pollute, desecrate —**prof·a·na'tion** (prof-ə-NAY-shən) *n.* —**pro·fan·i·ty** (prə-FAN-i-tee) *n.* profane talk or behavior, blasphemy

**pro·fess** (prə-FES) —*vt.* affirm belief in; confess publicly; assert; claim, pretend —**pro·fess'ed·ly** *adv.* avowedly —**pro·fes'sion** *n.* calling or occupation, *esp.* learned, scientific or artistic; a professing; vow of religious faith on entering religious order —**pro·fes'sion·al** *adj.* engaged in a profession; engaged in a game or sport for money —*n.* member of profession; paid player —**pro·fes'sor** *n.* teacher of highest rank in college or university —**pro·fes·so'ri·al** *adj.*

**proffer** vt./n. offer

**pro·fi·cient** (prə-FISH-ənt) adj. skilled; expert —**pro·fi·cien·cy** n.

**pro·file** (PROH-fil) n. outline, esp. of face, as seen from side; brief biographical sketch

**prof·it** n. money gained; benefit obtained —v. benefit —**prof'it·a·ble** adj. yielding profit —**prof·it·eer'** n. one who makes excessive profits at the expense of the public —vi. to do this

**prof·li·gate** (PROF-li-git) adj. dissolute; reckless, wasteful —n. dissolute person —**prof'li·ga·cy** (-li-gi-see) n.

**pro for·ma** (proh FOR-mə) Lat. prescribing a set form; for the sake of form

**pro·found** (prə-FOWND) adj. (-er, -est) very learned; deep —**pro·fun'di·ty** n.

**pro·fuse** (prə-FYOOS) adj. abundant, prodigal —**pro·fu·sion** (-FYOO-zhən) n.

**prog·e·ny** (PROJ-ə-nee) n. children —**pro·gen·i·tor** (proh-JEN-i-tər) n. ancestor

**pro·ges·ter·one** (proh-JES-tə-rohn) n. hormone that prepares uterus for pregnancy and prevents further ovulation

**prog·na·thous** (prog-NAY-thəs) adj. with projecting lower jaw

**prog·no·sis** (prog-NOH-sis) n. (pl. -ses pr. -seez) art of foretelling course of disease by symptoms; forecast —**prog·nos'tic** adj. of, serving as prognosis —n. —**prog·nos'ti·cate** vt. (-cat·ed, -cat·ing) foretell

**pro·gram** (PROH-gram) n. plan, detailed notes of intended proceedings; broadcast on radio or television; detailed instructions for a computer —vt. (-grammed, -gram·ming) feed program into (computer); arrange detailed in-

structions for computer —**pro'gram·mer** n.

**prog'ress** n. onward movement; development —vi. (prə-GRES) go forward; improve —**pro·gres'sion** n. moving forward; advance, improvement; increase or decrease of numbers or magnitudes according to fixed law; Mus. regular succession of chords —**pro·gres'sive** adj. progressing by degrees; favoring political or social reform

**pro·hib·it** (proh-HIB-it) vt. forbid —**pro·hi·bi'tion** n. act of forbidding; interdict; interdiction of supply and consumption of alcoholic drinks —**pro·hib'i·tive** adj. tending to forbid or exclude; (of prices) very high

**pro·ject** (PROJ-ekt) n. plan, scheme; design —v. (prə-JEKT) —vt. plan; throw; cause to appear on distant background —vi. stick out, protrude —**pro·jec'tile** (-JEK-til) n. heavy missile, esp. shell or ball —adj. for throwing —**pro·jec'tion** n. —**pro·jec'tion·ist** n. operator of film projector —**pro·jec'tor** n. apparatus for projecting photographic images, films, slides on screen; one that forms scheme or design

**pro·lapse** (proh-LAPS) n. falling, slipping down of part of body from normal position —vi. fall or slip down in this way

**pro·le·tar·i·at** (proh-li-TAIR-ee-ət) n. lowest class of community, working class —**pro·le·tar'i·an** adj./n.

**pro·life** adj. see PROFAMILY

**pro·lif·er·ate** (prə-LIF-ə-rayt) v. (-at·ed, -at·ing) grow or reproduce rapidly —**pro·lif·er·a'tion** n.

**pro·li·fic** (prə-LIF-ik) adj. fruitful; producing much

**pro·lix** (proh-LIKS) adj. wordy, long-winded —**pro·lix'i·ty** n.

**pro·logue** (PROH-lawg) *n.* preface, *esp.* speech before a play

**pro·long** (prɔ-LAWNG) *vt.* lengthen; protract

**prom** *n.* school or college dance, *esp.* at end of school year

**prom·e·nade** (prom-ɔ-NAYD) *n.* leisurely walk; place made or used for this —*vi.* (-nad·ed, -nad·ing) take leisurely walk; go up and down

**prom·i·nent** (PROM-ɔ-nɔnt) *adj.* sticking out; conspicuous; distinguished —**prom'i·nence** *n.*

**pro·mis·cu·ous** (prɔ-MIS-kyoo-ɔs) *adj.* indiscriminate, *esp.* in sexual relations; mixed without distinction —**prom·is·cu'i·ty** (-KYOO-ɔ-tee) *n.*

**prom·ise** (PROM-is) *v.* (-mised, -mis·ing) —*vt.* give assurance —*vi.* be likely to —*n.* undertaking to do or not to do something; potential —**prom'is·ing** *adj.* showing good signs, hopeful —**prom'is·so·ry** *adj.* containing promise —**promissory note** written promise to pay sum to person named, at specified time

**prom·on·to·ry** (PROM-ɔn-tor-ee) *n.* (*pl.* -ries) point of high land jutting out into the sea, headland

**pro·mote** (prɔ-MOHT) *vt.* (-mot·ed, -mot·ing) help forward; move up to higher rank or position; work for; encourage sale of —**pro·mot'er** *n.* —**pro·mo'tion** *n.* advancement; preferment

**prompt** *adj.* (-er, -est) done at once; acting with alacrity; punctual; ready —*v.* urge, suggest; help out (actor or speaker) by reading or suggesting next words —**prompt'er** *n.* —**prompt'ness** (-nis) *n.* —**prompt'ly** *adv.*

**prom·ul·gate** (PROM-ɔl-gayt) *v.* (-gat·ed, -gat·ing) proclaim, publish —**prom·ul·ga'tion** *n.*

**prone** (prohn) *adj.* lying face or front downward; inclined (to) —**prone'ness** (-nis) *n.*

**prong** *n.* one tine of fork or similar instrument

**pro·noun** (PROH-nown) *n.* word used to replace noun —**pro·nom'i·nal** *adj.* pert. to, like pronoun

**pro·nounce** (prɔ-NOWNS) *v.* (-nounced, nounc·ing) —*vt.* utter formally; form with organs of speech; speak distinctly; declare —*vi.* give opinion or decision —**pro·nounce'able** *adj.* —**pro·nounced'** *adj.* strongly marked, decided —**pro·nounce'ment** *n.* declaration —**pro·nun·ci·a'tion** *n.* way word *etc.* is pronounced; articulation

**pron·to** (PRON-toh) *adv. inf.* at once, immediately, quickly

**proof** *n.* evidence; thing that proves; test, demonstration; trial impression from type or engraved plate; *Photog.* print from a negative; standard of strength of alcoholic drink —*adj.* giving impenetrable defense against; of proven strength —**proof'read** (-reed) *v.* (-read, -read·ing) read and correct proofs —**proof'read·er** *n.*

**prop**[1] *vt.* (propped, prop·ping) support, sustain, hold up —*n.* pole, beam *etc.* used as support

**prop**[2] *n.* short for PROPELLER

**prop**[3] *n.* short for (theatrical) PROPERTY

**prop·a·gan·da** (prop-ɔ-GAN-dɔ) *n.* organized dissemination of information to assist or damage political cause *etc.* —**prop·a·gan'dist** *n.* —**prop·a·gan'dize** (-dīz) *vt.* (-dized, -diz·ing)

**prop·a·gate** (pro-ɔ-gayt) *v.* (-gat·ed, -gat·ing) —*vt.* reproduce, breed, spread by sowing, breeding *etc.*; transmit —*vi.*

breed, multiply —**prop·a·ga'·tion** n.

**pro·pane** (PROH-payn) n. colorless, flammable gas from petroleum

**pro·pel** (prə-PEL) vt. (**-pelled, -pel·ling**) cause to move forward —**pro·pel'lant, -lent** n. something causing propulsion, eg rocket fuel —**pro·pel'er** n. revolving shaft with blades for driving ship or aircraft —**pro·pul'sion** n. act of, means of, driving forward —**pro·pul'sive, pro·pul'so·ry** adj. tending, having power to propel; urging on

**pro·pen·si·ty** (prə-PEN-si-tee) n. (pl. **-ties**) inclination or bent; tendency; disposition

**prop·er** (PROP-ər) adj. appropriate; correct; conforming to etiquette, decorous; strict; (of noun) denoting individual person or place

**prop·er·ty** (PROP-ər-tee) n. (pl. **-ties**) that which is owned; estate whether in lands, goods, or money; quality, attribute of something; article used on stage in play etc.

**proph·et** (PROF-it) n. inspired teacher or revealer of divine will; foreteller of future —**proph'e·cy** (-ə-see) n. (pl. **-cies**) prediction, prophetic utterance —**proph'e·sy** (-ə-sī) v. (**-sied, -sy·ing**) foretell, predict; make predictions —**pro·phet'ic** adj. —**pro·phet'i·cal·ly** adv.

**pro·phy·lac·tic** (prof-ə-LAK-tik) n./adj. (something) done or used to ward off disease; condom —**pro·phy·lax'is** n.

**pro·pin·qui·ty** (proh-PING-kwi-tee) n. nearness, proximity, close kinship

**pro·pi·ti·ate** (prə-PISH-ee-ayt) vt. (**-at·ed, -at·ing**) appease, gain favor of —**pro·pi'ti·a·to·ry** adj.

**pro·pi'tious** adj. favorable, auspicious

**pro·po·nent** (prə-POH-nənt) n. one who advocates something

**pro·por·tion** (prə-POR-shən) n. relative size or number; comparison; due relation between connected things or parts; share; relation —pl. dimensions —vt. arrange proportions of —**pro·por'tion·al, pro·por'tion·ate** adj. having a due proportion; corresponding in size, number etc. —**pro·por'tion·al·ly** adv.

**pro·pose** (prə-POHZ) v. (**-posed, -pos·ing**) —vt. put forward for consideration; nominate; intend —vi. offer marriage —**pro·pos'al** n. —**prop·o·si'tion** n. offer; statement, assertion; theorem; suggestion of terms; thing to be dealt with; proposal of illicit sexual relations

**pro·pound** (prə-POWND) vt. put forward for consideration or solution

**pro·pri·e·tor** (prə-PRĪ-i-tər) n. owner —**pro·pri·e·tar·y** (-ter-ee) adj. belonging to owner; made by firm with exclusive rights of manufacture

**pro·pri·e·ty** (prə-PRĪ-itee) n. (pl. **-ties**) properness, correct conduct, fitness

**propulsion** see PROPEL

**pro ra·ta** (proh RAY-tə) Lat. in proportion

**pro·sa·ic** (proh-ZAY-ik) adj. commonplace, unromantic

**pro·sce·ni·um** (proh-SEE-neeəm) n. (pl. **-ni·a** pr. -neeə) arch or opening framing stage

**pro·scribe** (proh-SKRĪB) vt. (**-scribed, -scrib·ing**) outlaw, condemn —**pro·scrip'tion** n.

**prose** (prohz) n. speech or writing not verse —**pros'y** adj. (**pros·i·er, pros·i·est**) tedious, dull

**pros·e·cute** (PROS-i-kyoot) *vt.* (-cut·ed, -cut·ing) carry on, bring legal proceedings against —**pros·e·cu'tion** *n.* —**pros'e·cu·tor** *n.*

**pros·e·lyte** (PROS-ə-līt) *n.* convert —**pros'e·lyt·ize** (li-tīz) *vt.* (-ized, -iz·ing)

**pros·o·dy** (PROS-ə-dee) *n.* system, study of versification —**pros'o·dist** *n.*

**pros·pect** (PROS-pekt) *n.* expectation, chance for success; view, outlook; likely customer or subscriber; mental view —*v.* explore, *esp.* for gold —**pros·pec'·tive** *adj.* anticipated; future —**pros·pec'tor** *n.* —**pro·spec'tus** (prə-SPEK-təs) *n.* (*pl.* -tus·es) document describing company, school *etc.*

**pros·per** (PROS-pər) *vi.* do well —**pros·per'i·ty** *n.* (*pl.* -ties) good fortune, well-being —**pros'per·ous** *adj.* doing well, successful; flourishing, rich, well-off

**pros·tate** (PROS-tayt) *n.* gland accessory to male generative organs

**pros·the·sis** (pros-THEE-sis) *n.* (*pl.* -ses *pr.* -seez) (replacement of part of body with) artificial substitute

**pros·ti·tute** (PROS-ti-toot) *n.* one who offers sexual intercourse in return for payment —*vt.* (-tut·ed, -tut·ing) make a prostitute of; put to unworthy use —**pros·ti·tu'tion** *n.*

**pros·trate** (PROS-trayt) *adj.* lying flat; crushed, submissive, overcome —*vt.* (-trat·ed, -trat·ing) throw flat on ground; reduce to exhaustion —**pros·tra'tion** *n.*

**pro·tag·o·nist** (proh-TAG-ə-nist) *n.* leading character; principal actor; champion of a cause

**pro·te·an** (PROH-tee-ən) *adj.* variable; versatile

**pro·tect** (prə-TEKT) *vt.* defend, guard, keep from harm —**pro·tec'tion** *n.* —**pro·tec'tion·ist** *n.* one who advocates protecting industries by taxing competing imports —**pro·tec'tive** *adj.* —**pro·tec'tor** *n.* one who protects; regent —**pro·tec'tor·ate** (-tor-it) *n.* relation of country to territory it protects and controls; such territory; office, period of protector of a country

**pro·té·gé** (PROH-tə-zhay) *n.* (-gée *fem.*) one under another's care, protection or patronage

**pro·tein** (PROH-teen) *n.* any of kinds of organic compounds that form most essential part of food of living creatures

**pro·test** (PROH-test) *n.* declaration or demonstration of objection —*vi.* (prə-TEST) object; make declaration against; assert formally —**prot·es·ta·tion** (prot-ə-STAY-shən) *n.* strong declaration

**Prot·es·tant** (PROT-ə-stənt) *adj.* belonging to any branch of the Western Christian Church outside the Roman Catholic Church —*n.* member of such church —**Prot'es·tant·ism** *n.*

**proto-, prot-** (*comb. form*) first, as in *prototype*

**pro·to·col** (PROH-tə-kawl) *n.* diplomatic etiquette; draft of terms signed by parties as basis of formal treaty

**pro·ton** (PROH-ton) *n.* positively charged particle in nucleus of atom

**pro·to·plasm** (PROH-tə-plaz-əm) *n.* substance that is living matter of all animal and plant cells

**pro·to·type** (PROH-tə-tīp) *n.* original, or model, after which thing is copied; pattern

**pro·to·zo·an** (proh-tə-ZOH-ən) *n.* minute animal of lowest and simplest class

**pro·tract** (proh-TRAKT) *vt.* lengthen; prolong; delay; draw to scale —**pro·tract'ed** *adj.* long drawn out; tedious —**pro·trac'tor** *n.* instrument for measuring angles on paper

**pro·trude** (proh-TROOD) *v.* (-trud·ed, -trud·ing) stick out, project —**pro·tru'sion** (-zhən) *n.* —**pro·tru'sive** (-siv) *adj.* thrusting forward

**pro·tu·ber·ant** (proh-TOO-bər-ənt) *adj.* bulging out —**pro·tu'ber·ance** (-əns) *n.* bulge, swelling

**proud** (prowd) *adj.* (-er, -est) feeling or displaying pride; arrogant; gratified; noble; self-respecting; stately —**proud'ly** *adv.* —**proud flesh** flesh growing around healing wound

**Prov.** Proverbs

**prove** (proov) *v.* (proved, proved or prov·en, prov·ing) —*vt.* establish validity of; demonstrate, test —*vi.* turn out (to be *etc.*); (of dough) rise in warm place before baking —**prov·en** *adj.* proved

**prov·e·nance** (PROV-ə-nəns) *n.* place of origin, source

**prov·en·der** (PROV-ən-dər) *n.* fodder

**prov·erb** (PROV-ərb) *n.* short, pithy, traditional saying in common use —**pro·ver'bi·al** (prə-VUR-bee-əl) *adj.*

**pro·vide** (prə-VID) *v.* (-vid·ed, -vid·ing) —*vi.* make preparation —*vt.* supply, equip, prepare, furnish, give —**pro·vid'er** *n.* —**provided that** on condition that

**prov·i·dent** (PROV-i-dənt) *adj.* thrifty; showing foresight —**prov'i·dence** *n.* kindly care of God or nature; foresight; economy —**prov·i·den'tial** (-DEN-shəl) *adj.* strikingly fortunate, lucky

**prov·ince** (PROV-əns) *n.* division of a country, district; sphere of action —*pl.* any part of country outside capital or largest cities —**pro·vin'cial** (prə-VIN-shəl) *adj.* of a province; unsophisticated; narrow in outlook —*n.* unsophisticated person; inhabitant of province —**pro·vin'cial·ism** *n.* narrowness of outlook; lack of refinement; idiom peculiar to district

**pro·vi·sion** (prə-VIZH-ən) *n.* a providing, *esp.* for the future; thing provided; *Law* article of instrument or statute —*pl.* food —*vt.* supply with food —**pro·vi'sion·al** *adj.* temporary; conditional

**pro·vi·so** (prə-VI-zoh) *n.* (*pl.* -sos, -soes) condition

**pro·vo·ca·teur** (prə-vok-ə-TUR) *n.* one who causes dissension, makes trouble; agitator; *see* AGENT PROVOCATEUR

**pro·voke** (prə-VOHK) *vt.* (-voked, -vok·ing) irritate; incense; arouse; excite; cause —**prov·o·ca'tion** (-ə-KAY-shən) *n.* —**pro·voc'a·tive** (-VOK-ə-tiv) *adj.*

**pro·vost** (PROH-vohst) *n.* one who superintends or presides; high administrative officer of university —**provost marshal** head of military police

**prow** (rhymes with cow) *n.* bow of vessel

**prow·ess** (PROW-is) *n.* skill; bravery, fighting capacity

**prowl** *vi.* roam stealthily, *esp.* in search of prey or booty —*n.* —**prowl'er** *n.* —**on the prowl** searching stealthily; seeking sexual partner

**prox·i·mate** (PROK-sə-mit) *adj.* nearest, next, immediate —**prox·im'i·ty** *n.*

**prox·y** (PROK-see) *n.* (*pl.* prox·ies) authorized agent or substitute; writing authorizing one to act as this

**prude** (prood) n. one who affects excessive modesty or propriety —prud'er·y n. (pl. -er·ies) —pru'dish adj.

**pru·dent** (PROOD-ǝnt) adj. careful, discreet; sensible —pru'dence n. habit of acting with careful deliberation; wisdom applied to practice —pru·den'tial adj.

**prune**[1] (proon) n. dried plum

**prune**[2] vt. (pruned, prun·ing) cut out dead parts, excessive branches etc.; shorten, reduce —pruning hook

**pru·ri·ent** (PRUUR-ee-ǝnt) adj. given to, springing from lewd thoughts; having unhealthy curiosity or desire —pru'ri·ence n.

**pry** (prī) vi. (pried, pry·ing) make furtive or impertinent inquiries; look curiously; force open

**Ps.** Psalm(s)

**psalm** (sahm) n. sacred song; (P-) any of the sacred songs making up the Book of Psalms in the Bible —psalm'ist n. writer of psalms —psal·mo·dy (SAHM-ǝ-dee) n. art, act of singing sacred music —psal·ter (SAWL-tǝr) n. book of psalms; (P-) copy of the Psalms as separate book —psal'ter·y (-tǝ-ree) n. (pl. -ter·ies) obsolete stringed instrument like lyre

**pseu·do** (SOO-doh) adj. sham, fake

**pseudo-** (comb. form) false, sham, as in pseudo-Gothic, pseudomodern etc. Such compounds are not given here where the meaning can easily be inferred from the simple word

**pseu·do·nym** (SOOD-n-im) n. false, fictitious name; pen name

**psit·ta·co·sis** (sit-ǝ-KOH-sis) n. dangerous infectious disease, germ of which is carried by parrots

**psych·e·del·ic** (sī-ki-DEL-ik) adj. of or causing hallucinations; like intense colors etc. experienced during hallucinations

**psy·chic** (SĪ-kik) adj. sensitive to phenomena lying outside range of normal experience; of soul or mind; that appears to be outside region of physical law —psy·chi·a·try (si-KĪ-ǝ-tree) n. medical treatment of mental diseases —psy·cho·a·nal'y·sis (sī-koh-) n. method of studying and treating mental disorders —psy·cho·an'a·lyst n. —psy·cho·log·i·cal (sī-kǝ-LOJ-i-kǝl) adj. of psychology; of the mind —psy·chol'o·gist n. —psy·chol'o·gy n. study of mind; person's mental makeup —psy·chom'e·try n. measurement, testing of psychological processes; supposed ability to divine unknown persons' qualities by handling object used or worn by them —psy'cho·path n. person afflicted with severe mental disorder causing him or her to commit antisocial, often violent acts —psy·cho·path'ic adj. —psy·cho'sis n. (pl. -ses pr. -seez) severe mental disorder in which person's contact with reality becomes distorted —psy·cho·so·mat'ic (-sǝ-MAT-ik) adj. of physical disorders thought to have psychological causes —psy·cho·ther'a·py n. treatment of disease by psychological, not physical, means

**psych up** (sīk) prepare (oneself or another) psychologically for action, performance etc.

**Pt** Chem. platinum

**ptar·mi·gan** (TAHR-mi-gǝn) n. bird of grouse family that turns white in winter

**PT boat** small, fast naval vessel used primarily for torpedoing enemy shipping

**pter·o·dac·tyl** (ter-ǝ-DAK-til) n.

extinct flying reptile with batlike wings

**pto·maine** (TOH-mayn) n. any of kinds of poisonous alkaloid found in decaying matter

**Pu** *Chem.* plutonium

**pu·ber·ty** (PYOO-bər-tee) n. sexual maturity

**pubic** (PYOO-bik) adj. of the lower abdomen

**pub·lic** (PUB-lik) adj. of or concerning the public as a whole; not private; open to general observation or knowledge; accessible to all; serving the people —n. the community or its members —**pub'lic·ly** adv. —**public re·lations** promotion of good relations of an organization or business with the general public —**public school** local elementary school —**public service** government employment —**public spirit** interest in and devotion to welfare of community

**pub·li·cist** (PUB-lə-sist) n. press agent; writer on public concerns —**pub·lic'i·ty** n. process of attracting public attention; attention thus gained —**pub'li·cize** vt. (-cized, -ciz·ing) give publicity to; bring to public notice

**pub'lish** vt. prepare and issue for sale (books, music *etc.*); make generally known; proclaim —**pub·li·ca'tion** (-KAY-shən) n. —**pub'lish·er** n.

**puce** (pyoos) adj./n. purplish-brown (color)

**puck¹** (puk) n. hard rubber disk used instead of ball in ice hockey

**puck²** n. mischievous sprite —**puck'ish** adj.

**puck·er** (PUK-ər) v. gather into wrinkles —n. crease, fold

**pud·ding** (PUUD-ing) n. thick, cooked dessert, often made from flour, milk, eggs, flavoring *etc.*

**pud·dle** (PUD-l) n. small pool of water; rough cement for lining walls of canals *etc.* —vt. (-dled, -dling) line with puddle; make muddy —**puddling** n. method of converting pig iron to wrought iron by oxidizing the carbon

**pu·den·dum** (PYOO-DEN-dəm) n. (*pl.* -da *pr.* -də) external genital organs, *esp.* of a woman; vulva

**pu·er·ile** (PYOO-ər-il) adj. childish; foolish; trivial

**puff** n. short blast of breath, wind *etc.*; its sound; type of pastry; laudatory review or advertisement —vi. blow abruptly; breathe hard —vt. send out in a puff; blow out, inflate; advertise; smoke hard —**puff'y** adj. (puff·i·er, puff·i·est) short-winded; swollen —**puff'ball** n. ball-shaped fungus

**puf'fin** n. sea bird with large brightly-colored beak

**pug** n. small snub-nosed dog; *sl.* boxer —**pug nose** snub nose

**pu·gi·list** (PYOO-jə-list) n. boxer —**pu'gi·lism** n. —**pu·gi·lis'tic** adj.

**pug·na·cious** (pug-NAY-shəs) adj. given to fighting —**pug·nac'i·ty** (-NAS-i-tee) n.

**puke** (pyook) vi. *sl.* (puked, puk·ing) vomit —n. *sl.* vomit

**pul·chri·tude** (PUL-kri-tood) n. beauty —**pul·chri·tu'di·nous** adj.

**pull** (puul) vt. exert force on object to move it toward source of force; strain or stretch; tear; propel by rowing —n. act of pulling; force exerted by it; drink of liquor; *inf.* power, influence —**pull in** (of train) arrive; attract; *sl.* arrest —**pull off** *inf.* carry through to successful issue —**pull out** withdraw; extract; (of train) depart; (of car *etc.*) move away from side of road or move out to overtake —**pull over** (of car *etc.*) drive to side of road and stop —**pull (someone's) leg** make fun of —**pull up** tear up; recover lost ground; improve; come to a stop; halt; reprimand

**pul·let** (PUUL-it) n. young hen

**pul·ley** (PUUL-ee) n. (pl. -leys) wheel with groove in rim for cord, used to raise weights by downward pull

**Pull·man** (PUUL-mən). n. R (pl. -mans) railroad sleeping car or parlor car

**pull·o·ver** (PUUL-oh-vər) n. sweater without fastening, to be pulled over head

**pul·mo·nar·y** (PUUL-mə-ner-ee) adj. of lungs

**pulp** n. soft, moist, vegetable or animal matter; flesh of fruit; any soft soggy mass —vt. reduce to pulp

**pul·pit** (PUUL-pit) n. (enclosed) platform for preacher, minister, rabbi etc.

**pul·sar** (PUL-sahr) n. small dense star emitting radio waves

**pulse** (puls) n. movement of blood in arteries corresponding to heartbeat, discernible to touch, eg in wrist; any regular beat or vibration —**pul·sate** (PUL-sayt) vi. (-sat·ed, -sat·ing) throb, quiver —**pul·sa'tion** (SAY-shən) n.

**pul·ver·ize** (PUL-və-rīz) vt. (-ized, -iz·ing) reduce to powder; smash or demolish

**pu·ma** (PYOO-mə) n. large Amer. feline carnivore, cougar

**pum·ice** (PUM-is) n. light porous variety of lava

**pum·mel** (PUM-əl) vt. (-meled, -mel·ing) strike repeatedly with fists

**pump¹** n. appliance in which piston and handle are used for raising water, or putting in or taking out air or liquid etc. —vt. raise, put in, take out etc. with pump; empty by means of a pump;

extract information from —vi. work pump; work like pump —**pump iron** lift weights as exercise

**pump²** n. light shoe

**pump·kin** n. any of varieties of gourd, eaten esp. as vegetable, in pie

**pun** n. play on words —vi. (punned, pun·ning) make one —**pun'ster** (-stər) n.

**punch¹** n. tool for perforating or stamping; blow with fist; vigor —vt. stamp, perforate with punch; strike with fist —**pull punches** punch lightly; inf. lessen, withhold, criticism —**punch-drunk** adj. inf. dazed, as by repeated blows

**punch²** n. drink of whiskey or wine with fruit juice, spice etc. —**fruit punch** punch made without alcohol

**punc·til·i·ous** (pungk-TIL-ee-əs) adj. making much of details of etiquette; very exact, particular —**punc·til'i·ous·ness** (-nis) n.

**punc·tu·al** (PUNGK-choo-əl) adj. in good time, not late, prompt —**punc·tu·al'i·ty** n.

**punc·tu·ate** (PUNGK-choo-ayt) vt. (-at·ed, -at·ing) put in punctuation marks; interrupt at intervals; emphasize —**punc·tu·a'tion** n. marks, eg commas, colons etc. put in writing to assist in making sense clear

**punc·ture** (PUNGK-chər) n. small hole made by sharp object, esp. in tire; act of puncturing —vt. (-tured, -tur·ing) prick hole in, perforate

**pun'dit** n. self-appointed expert

**pun·gent** (PUN-jənt) adj. biting; irritant; piercing; tart; caustic —**pun'gen·cy** n.

**pun·ish** n. cause to suffer for offense; inflict penalty on; use or treat roughly —**pun'ish·a·ble** adj.

—pun′ish·ment n. —pu′ni·tive (PYOO-ni-tiv) adj. inflicting or intending to inflict punishment

punk adj./n. inferior, rotten, worthless (person or thing); petty (hoodlum); (of) style of rock music

punt[1] n. flat-bottomed square-ended boat, propelled by pushing with pole —vt. propel thus

punt[2] vt. Football kick ball before it touches ground, when let fall from hands —n. such a kick

punt[3] vi. gamble, bet —punt′er n. one who punts; gambler

pu·ny (PYOO-nee) adj. (-ni·er, -ni·est) small and feeble

pup n. young of certain animals, eg dog, seal

pu·pa (PYOO-pə) n. (pl. -pas) stage between larva and adult in metamorphosis of insect, chrysalis —pu′pal adj.

pu·pil (PYOO-pəl) n. person being taught; opening in iris of eye

pup·pet (PUP-it) n. small doll or figure of person etc. controlled by operator's hand —pup·pet·eer′ n. —puppet show show with puppets worked by hidden performer

pup·py (PUP-ee) n. (pl. -pies) young dog

pur·chase (PUR-chəs) vt. (-chased, -chas·ing) buy —n. buying; what is bought; leverage, grip

pur·dah (PUR-də) n. Muslim, Hindu custom of keeping women in seclusion; screen, veil to achieve this

pure (pyuur) adj. (pur·er, pur·est) unmixed, untainted; simple; spotless; faultless; innocent; concerned with theory only —pure′ly adv. —pu·ri·fi·ca′tion n. —pu′ri·fy vt. (-fied, -fy·ing) make, become pure, clear or clean —pur′ism n. excessive insistence on correctness of language —pur′ist n. —pu′ri·ty n. state of being pure

pu·rée (pyuu-RAY) n. pulp, soup, of cooked fruit or vegetables put through sieve etc. —vt. (-réed, -ré·ing)

pur·ga·to·ry (PUR-gə-tor-ee) n. (-ries) place or state of torment, pain or distress, esp. temporary

purge (purj) vt. (purged, purg·ing) make clean, purify; remove, get rid of; clear out —n. act, process of purging; removal of undesirable members from political party, army etc. —pur′ga·tive (-gə-tiv) adj./n. cathartic

Pu·ri·tan (PYUUR-i-tn) n. Hist. member of extreme Protestant party; (p-) person of extreme strictness in morals or religion —pu·ri·tan′i·cal adj. strict in the observance of religious and moral duties; overscrupulous —pu′ri·tan·ism n.

purl n. stitch that forms ridge in knitting —vi. knit in purl

pur·loin (pər-LOIN) vt. steal; pilfer

pur·ple (PUR-pəl) n./adj. (-pler, -plest) (of) color between crimson and violet

pur·port (pər-PORT) vt. claim to be (true etc.); signify, imply —n. (PUR-port) meaning; apparent meaning; significance

pur·pose (PUR-pəs) n. reason, object; design; aim, intention —v. (-posed, -pos·ing) intend —pur′pose·ly adv. —on purpose intentionally

purr n. pleased noise that cat makes —vi. utter this

purse (purs) n. small bag for money; handbag; resources; money as prize —v. (pursed, purs·ing) —vt. pucker in wrinkles —vi. become wrinkled and drawn in —purs′er n. ship's officer who keeps accounts

**pur·sue** (pər-SOO) v. (-sued, -su·ing) —vt. run after; chase; aim at; engage in; continue; follow —vi. go in pursuit; continue —**pur·su'ance** (-əns) n. carrying out —**pur·su'ant** (-ənt) adv. accordingly —**pur·su'er** n. —**pur·suit'** (-SOOT) n. running after, attempt to catch; occupation

**purulent** adj. see PUS

**pur·vey** (pər-VAY) vt. supply (provisions) —**pur·vey'or** n.

**pur·view** (PUR-vyoo) n. scope, range

**pus** n. yellowish matter produced by suppuration —**pu·ru·lence** (PYUUR-ə-ləns) n. —**pu'ru·lent** adj. forming, discharging pus; septic

**push** (puush) vt. move, try to move away by pressure; drive or impel; sl. sell (esp. narcotic drugs) illegally —vi. make thrust; advance with steady effort —n. thrust; persevering self-assertion; big military advance —**push'y** adj. (push·i·er, push·i·est) given to pushing oneself

**pu·sil·lan·i·mous** (pyoo-sə-LAN-ə-məs) adj. cowardly —**pu·sil·la·nim'i·ty** (-lə-NIM-ə-tee) n.

**puss** (puus) n. cat: also **pus'sy** pl. **-sies**

**puss·y·foot** (PUUS-ee-fuut) vi. move stealthily; act indecisively, procrastinate

**pus·tule** (PUS-chuul) n. pimple containing pus

**put** (puut) vt. (put, put·ting) place; set; express; throw (esp. shot) —n. throw —**put across** express, carry out successfully —**put off** postpone; disconcert; repel —**put up** erect; accommodate; nominate

**pu·ta·tive** (PYOO-tə-tiv) adj. reputed, supposed

**pu·trid** (PYOO-trid) adj. decomposed; rotten —**pu'tre·fy** (-trə-fī)

v. (-fied, -fy·ing) make or become rotten —**pu·tre·fac'tion** n. —**pu·tres'cent** (-ənt) adj. becoming rotten

**putsch** (puuch) n. surprise attempt to overthrow the existing power, political revolt

**putt** (put) vt. strike (golf ball) along ground in direction of hole —**putt'er** n. golf club for putting; person who putts

**put·ter** (PUT-ər) vi. work, act in feeble, unsystematic way

**put·ty** (PUT-ee) n. pl. **-ties** paste of ground chalk and oil as used by glaziers —vt. (-tied, -ty·ing) fix, fill with putty

**puz·zle** (PUZ-əl) v. (-zled, -zling) perplex or be perplexed —n. bewildering, perplexing question, problem or toy —**puz'zle·ment** n.

**pyg·my, pig·my** (PIG-mee) n. (pl. **-mies**) abnormally undersized person; (P-) member of one of dwarf peoples of Equatorial Africa —adj. undersized

**py·lon** (PĪ-lon) n. post, tower, esp. for guiding aviators; steel tower for supporting power lines

**py·or·rhe·a** (pī-ə-REE-ə) n. inflammation of the gums with discharge of pus and loosening of teeth

**pyr·a·mid** (PIR-ə-mid) n. solid figure with sloping sides meeting at apex; structure of this shape, esp. ancient Egyptian; group of persons or things arranged, organized, like pyramid —**py·ram'i·dal** adj.

**pyre** (pīr) n. pile of wood for burning a dead body

**py·ri·tes** (pī-RĪ-teez) n. (pl. same form) sulfide of a metal, esp. iron pyrites

**py·ro·ma·ni·ac** (pī-rə-MAY-nee-ak) n. person with uncontrollable desire to set things on fire

**py·rom·e·ter** (pī-ROM-ə-tər) n. instrument for measuring very high temperature

**py·ro·tech·nics** (pī-rə-TEK-niks) *n.* manufacture, display of fireworks

**Pyr·rhic victory** (PIR-ik) one won at too high cost

**py·thon** (PĪ-thon) *n.* large nonpoisonous snake that crushes its prey

**pyx** (piks) *n.* vessel in which consecrated Host is preserved

# Q

**Q.E.D.** (Lat., *quod erat demonstrandum*) which was to be proved

**qua** (kway) *prep.* in the capacity of

**quack** (kwak) *n.* harsh cry of duck; pretender to medical or other skill —*vi.* (of duck) utter cry

**quadr-, quadri-** (*comb. form*) four

**quad·ran·gle** (KWOD-rang-gəl) *n.* four-sided figure; four-sided courtyard in a building —**quad·ran'gu·lar** (-gyə-lər) *adj.*

**quad·rant** (KWOD-rənt) *n.* quarter of circle; instrument for taking angular measurements —**quad·rat'ic** *adj.* of equation, involving square of unknown quantity

**quad·ra·phon·ic** (kwod-rə-FON-ik) *adj.* of a sound system using four independent speakers

**quad·ri·lat·er·al** (kwod-rə-LAT-ər-əl) *adj.* four-sided —*n.* four-sided figure

**quad·rille** (kwo-DRIL) *n.* square dance; music played for it

**quad·ril·lion** (kwo-DRIL-yən) *n.*

cardinal number of 1 followed by 15 zeros

**quad·ru·man·ous** (kwo-DROO-mə-nəs) *adj.* of apes *etc.* having four feet that can be used as hands

**quad·ru·ped** (KWOD-ruu-ped) *n.* four-footed animal

**quad·ru·ple** (kwo-DROO-pəl) *adj.* fourfold —*v.* (-pled, -pling) make, become four times as much —**quad·ru'pli·cate** (-kit) *adj.* fourfold

**quad·ru·plet** (kwo-DRUP-lit) *n.* one of four offspring born at one birth

**quaff** (kwof) *v.* drink heartily or in one swallow

**quag·mire** (KWAG-mīr) *n.* bog, swamp

**quail**[1] (kwayl) *n.* small bird of partridge family

**quail**[2] *vi.* flinch; cower

**quaint** (kwaynt) *adj.* (-er, -est) interestingly old-fashioned or odd; curious; whimsical —**quaint'ness** (-nis) *n.*

**quake** (kwayk) *vi.* (quaked, quaking) shake, tremble

**Quak·er** (KWAY-kər) *n.* member of Christian sect, the Society of Friends

**qual·i·fy** (KWOL-ə-fī) *v.* (-fied, -fying) make oneself competent; moderate; limit; make competent; ascribe quality to; describe —**qual·i·fi·ca'tion** *n.* thing that qualifies, attribute; restriction; qualifying

**qual·i·ty** (KWOL-i-tee) *n.* (*pl.* -ties) attribute, characteristic, property; degree of excellence; rank —**qual'i·ta·tive** *adj.* depending on quality

**qualm** (kwahm) *n.* misgiving; sudden feeling of sickness, nausea

**quan·da·ry** (KWON-də-ree) *n.* (*pl.*

-ries) state of perplexity, puzzling situation, dilemma

**quan·ti·ty** (KWON-ti-tee) n. (pl. -ties) size, number, amount; specified or considerable amount —**quan'ti·fy** (-fī) vt. (-fied, -fy-ing) discover, express quantity of —**quan'ti·ta·tive** adj. —**quan'tum** (-təm) n. (pl. -ta pr. -tə) desired or required amount —**quantum theory** theory that in radiation, energy of electrons is discharged not continuously but in discrete units, or **quanta**

**quar·an·tine** (KWOR-ən-teen) n. isolation to prevent spreading of infection —vt. (-tined, -tin·ing) put, keep in quarantine

**quark** (kwork) n. Physics any of several hypothetical particles thought to be fundamental units of matter

**quar·rel** (KWOR-əl) n. angry dispute; argument —vi. (-reled, -rel·ing) argue; find fault with —**quar'rel·some** (-səm) adj.

**quar·ry**[1] (KWOR-ee) n. (pl. -ries) object of hunt or pursuit; prey

**quarry**[2] n. (pl. -ries) excavation where stone etc. is obtained from ground for building etc. —v. (-ried, -ry·ing) get from quarry

**quart** (kwort) n. liquid measure, quarter of gallon or 2 pints (0.964 liter)

**quar·ter** (KWOR-tər) n. fourth part; 25 cents; region, district; mercy —pl. lodgings —vt. divide into quarters; lodge —**quar'ter·ly** adj. happening, due etc. each quarter of year —n. (pl. -lies) quarterly periodical —**quar·tet'** n. group of four musicians; music for four performers —**quar'to** n. (pl. -tos) size of book in which sheets are folded into four leaves —adj. of this size —**quar'ter·deck** n. after part of upper deck used esp. for official, ceremonial pur-

poses —**quarter horse** small, powerful breed of horse bred for short races —**quar'ter·mas·ter** n. officer responsible for quarters, clothing etc.

**quartz** (kworts) n. stone of pure crystalline silica —**quartz'ite** (-īt) n. quartz rock —**quartz timepiece** watch or clock operated by a vibrating quartz crystal

**qua·sar** (KWAY-zahr) n. extremely distant starlike object emitting powerful radio waves

**quash** (kwosh) vt. annul; reject; subdue forcibly

**qua·si-** (KWAY-zī) (comb. form) seemingly, resembling but not actually being, as in **quasi-scientific**

**quat·er·nar·y** (KWOT-ər-ner-ee) adj. of the number four; having four parts; Geology (Q-) of most recent period after Tertiary

**quat·rain** (KWO-trayn) n. four-line stanza, esp. rhymed alternately

**qua·ver** (KWAY-vər) vt. say or sing in quavering tones —vi. tremble, shake, vibrate —n. musical note half length of crotchet; quavering trill

**quay** (kee) n. solid, fixed landing stage; wharf

**quea·sy** (KWEE-zee) adj. (-si·er, -si·est) inclined to, or causing, sickness

**queen** (kween) n. king's wife; female ruler; piece in chess; fertile female bee, wasp etc.; playing card with picture of a queen, ranking between king and jack; sl. offens. male homosexual —**queen'ly** adj. (-li·er, -li·est) —adv.

**queer** (kweer) adj. (-er, -est) odd, strange; sl. offens. homosexual (also n.) —vt. spoil; interfere with

**quell** (kwel) *vt.* crush, put down; allay; pacify

**quench** (kwench) *vt.* slake; extinguish, put out, suppress

**quer·u·lous** (KWER-ə-ləs) *adj.* fretful, peevish, whining

**que·ry** (KWEER-ee) *n.* (*pl.* **-ries**) question; mark of interrogation —*vt.* (**-ried, -ry·ing**) question, ask

**quest** (kwest) *n./vi.* search

**ques·tion** (KWES-chən) *n.* sentence seeking for answer; that which is asked; interrogation; inquiry; problem; point for debate; debate, strife —*vt.* ask questions of, interrogate; dispute; doubt —**ques'tion·a·ble** *adj.* doubtful, *esp.* not really true or honest —**ques·tion·naire'** *n.* list of questions drawn up for formal answer

**queue** (kyoo) *n.* line of waiting persons, vehicles; sequence of computer tasks awaiting action —*vi.* (**queued, queu·ing**) wait in line (*with* up); arrange computer tasks in queue

**quib·ble** (KWIB-əl) *n.* trivial objection —*v.* (**-bled, -bling**) make this

**quiche** (keesh) *n.* open pielike dish of cheese *etc.* on light pastry shell

**quick** (kwik) *adj.* (**-er, -est**) rapid, swift; keen; brisk; hasty —*n.* part of body sensitive to pain; sensitive flesh; *obs.* (*with* the) living people —*adv.* rapidly —**quick'en** *v.* make, become faster or more lively —**quick'ie** *n. inf.* a quick drink *etc.* —**quick'ly** *adv.* —**quick'sand** *n.* loose wet sand easily yielding to pressure and engulfing persons, animals *etc.* —**quick'silver** *n.* mercury —**quick-tempered** *adj.* irascible

**quid pro quo** (KWID proh KWOH) *Lat.* something given in exchange

**qui·es·cent** (kwee-ES-ənt) *adj.* at

rest, inactive, inert; silent —**qui·es'cence** *n.*

**qui·et** (KWI-it) *adj.* (**-er, -est**) with little or no motion or noise; undisturbed; not showy or obtrusive —*n.* state of peacefulness, absence of noise or disturbance —*v.* make, become quiet —**qui'et·ly** *adv.* —**qui'e·tude** *n.*

**quill** (kwil) *n.* large feather; hollow stem of this; pen, plectrum made from feather; spine of porcupine

**quilt** (kwilt) *n.* padded coverlet —*vt.* stitch (two pieces of cloth) with pad between

**quince** (kwins) *n.* acid pear-shaped fruit; tree bearing it

**qui·nine** (KWI-nīn) *n.* bitter drug made from bark of tree, used to treat fever, and as mixer

**quin·quen·ni·al** (kwin-KWEN-ee-əl) *adj.* occurring once in, or lasting, five years

**quin·sy** (KWIN-zee) *n.* inflammation of throat or tonsils

**quint** (kwint) *n. short for* QUINTUPLET

**quin·tes·sence** (kwin-TES-əns) *n.* purest form, essential feature; embodiment —**quin·tes·sen'tial** (-tə-SEN-shəl) *adj.*

**quin·tet** (kwin-TET) *n.* set of five singers or players; composition for five voices or instruments

**quin·tu·plet** (kwin-TUP-lit) *n.* one of five offspring born at one birth

**quip** (kwip) *n./v.* (**quipped, quip·ping**) (utter) witty saying

**quire** (kwīr) *n.* 24 sheets of writing paper

**quirk** (kwurk) *n.* individual peculiarity of character; unexpected twist or turn

**quis·ling** (KWIZ-ling) *n.* traitor who aids occupying enemy force

**quit** (kwit) *v.* (**quit** *or* **quit·ted, quit·ting**) stop doing a thing; depart; leave, go away from; cease

from —*adj.* free, rid —**quits** *adj.*
on equal or even terms by repayment *etc.* —**quit'tance** (KWIT-ns)
*n.* discharge; receipt —**quit'ter** *n.*
one lacking perseverance

**quite** (kwit) *adv.* wholly, completely; very considerably; somewhat, rather —*interj.* exactly,
just so

**quiv·er**[1] (KWIV-ər) *vi.* shake or
tremble —*n.* quivering; vibration

**quiver**[2] *n.* carrying case for arrows

**quix·ot·ic** (kwik-SOT-ik) *adj.* unrealistically and impractically
optimistic, idealistic, chivalrous

**quiz** (kwiz) *n.* (*pl.* **quiz·zes**) entertainment in which general or
specific knowledge of players is
tested by questions; examination,
interrogation —*vt.* (**quizzed, quizzing**) question, interrogate
—**quiz'zi·cal** *adj.* questioning;
mocking

**quoit** (kwoit) *n.* ring for throwing
at peg as a game —*pl.* (*with sing.
v.*) the game

**quo·rum** (KWOR-əm) *n.* least
number that must be present in
meeting to make its transactions
valid

**quo·ta** (KWOH-tə) *n.* share to be
contributed or received; specified number, quantity, that may
be imported or admitted

**quote** (kwoht) *vt.* (**quot·ed, quoting**) copy or repeat passages
from; refer to, *esp.* to confirm
view; state price for —**quot'a·ble**
*adj.* —**quo·ta'tion** *n.*

**quoth** (kwohth) *obs.* said

**quo·tid·i·an** (kwoh-TID-ee-ən)
*adj.* daily; everyday, commonplace

**quo·tient** (KWOH-shənt) *n.* number resulting from dividing one
number by another

**q.v.** *quod vide* (*pr.* kwod VĪ-dee)
(Lat., which see)

# R

**Ra** *Chem.* radium

**rab·bet** (RAB-it) *n.* recess, groove
cut into piece of timber to join
with matching piece —*vt.*
(**-bet·ed, -bet·ing**) cut rabbet in

**rab·bi** (RAB-ī) *n.* (*pl.* **-bis**) Jewish
learned man, spiritual leader,
teacher —**rab·bin'i·cal** *adj.*

**rab'bit** *n.* small burrowing rodent
like hare —*vi.* hunt rabbits —**rabbit punch** sharp blow to back of
neck; *see* RAREBIT

**rab·ble** (RAB-əl) *n.* crowd of vulgar, noisy people; mob

**rab'id** *adj.* relating to or having
rabies; furious; mad; fanatical

**ra·bies** (RAY-beez) *n.* acute infectious viral disease transmitted by
dogs *etc.*

**rac·coon** (ra-KOON) *n.* small N
Amer. mammal

**race**[1] (rays) *n.* contest of speed,
as in running, swimming *etc.*;
contest, rivalry; strong current of
water, *esp.* leading to water
wheel —*pl.* meeting for horse
racing —*v.* (**raced, rac·ing**) —*vt.*
cause to run rapidly —*vi.* run
swiftly; of engine, pedal *etc.*, to
move rapidly and erratically,
*esp.* on removal of resistance
—**rac'er** *n.* person, vehicle, animal that races

**race**[2] *n.* group of people of common ancestry with distinguishing
physical features (skin color
*etc.*); species; type —**ra·cial** (RAY-
shəl) *adj.* —**rac'ism** *n.* belief in
innate superiority of particular
race; antagonism toward members of different race based on
this belief —**rac'ist** *adj./n.*

**rack**[1] (rak) *n.* framework for displaying or holding baggage, books, hats, bottles *etc.*; *Mechanics* straight bar with teeth on its edge, to work with pinion; instrument of torture by stretching —*vt.* stretch on rack or wheel; torture; stretch, strain —**rack′ing** *adj.* agonizing (pain)

**rack²** *n.* destruction *esp.* in rack and ruin

**rack³** *n.* neck or rib section of mutton, lamb, pork

**rack·et¹** (RAK-it) *n.* loud noise, uproar; occupation by which money is made illegally —**rack·et·eer** (rak-it-TEER) *n.* one making illegal profits —**rack′et·y** *adj.* noisy

**racket², rac·quet** (RAK-it) *n.* bat used in tennis *etc.* —*pl.* ball game played in paved, walled court

**rac·on·teur** (rak-ɔn-TUR) *n.* skilled storyteller

**racquet** *see* RACKET²

**rac·y** (RAY-see) *adj.* (rac·i·er, rac·i·est) spirited; lively; having strong flavor; spicy; piquant —**rac′i·ly** *adv.* —**rac′i·ness** *n.*

**ra·dar** (RAY-dahr) *n.* device for finding range and direction by ultrahigh frequency point-to-point radio waves, which reflect back to their source and reveal position and nature of objects sought

**radial** *see* RADIUS

**ra·di·ate** (RAY-dee-ayt) *v.* (-at·ed, -at·ing) emit, be emitted in rays; spread out from center —**ra′di·ance** (-ɔns) *n.* brightness; splendor —**ra′di·ant** (-ɔnt) *adj.* beaming; shining; emitting rays —**ra·di·a′tion** *n.* transmission of heat, light *etc.* from one body to another; particles, rays, emitted in nuclear decay; act of radiating —**ra′di·a·tor** *n.* that which radiates, *esp.* heating apparatus for rooms; cooling apparatus of automobile engine

**rad·i·cal** (RAD-i-kɔl) *adj.* fundamental, thorough; extreme; of root —*n.* person of extreme (political) views; number expressed as root of another; group of atoms of several elements that remain unchanged in a series of chemical compounds

**ra·di·o** (RAY-dee-oh) *n.* (*pl.* -di·os) use of electromagnetic waves for broadcasting, communication *etc.*; device for receiving, amplifying radio signals; broadcasting, content of radio program —*vt.* (-di·oed, -di·o·ing) transmit message by radio

**radio-** (*comb. form*) of rays, of radiation, of radium, as in *radiology*

**ra·di·o·ac·tive** (ray-dee-oh-AK-tiv) *adj.* emitting invisible rays that penetrate matter —**ra·di·o·ac·tiv′i·ty** *n.*

**ra·di·o·gra·phy** (ray-dee-OG-rɔ-fee) *n.* production of image on film or plate by radiation

**ra·di·ol·o·gy** (ray-dee-OL-ɔ-jee) *n.* science of use of rays in medicine —**ra·di·ol′o·gist** *n.*

**ra·di·o·ther·a·py** (ray-dee-oh-THER-ɔ-pee) *n.* diagnosis and treatment of disease by x-rays

**rad′ish** *n.* pungent root vegetable

**ra·di·um** (RAY-dee-ɔm) *n.* radioactive metallic element

**ra·di·us** (RAY-dee-ɔs) *n.* (*pl.* -di·i *pr.* -dee-i) straight line from center to circumference of circle; outer of two bones in forearm —**ra′di·al** (-ɔl) *adj.* arranged like radii of circle; of ray or rays; of radius

**ra·dome** (RAY-dohm) *n.* dome-shaped housing for radar

**ra·don** (RAY-don) *n.* radioactive gaseous element

**raf·fi·a** (RAF-fee-ə) *n.* prepared palm fiber for making mats *etc.*

**raff'ish** *adj.* disreputable

**raf·fle** (RAF-əl) *n.* lottery in which an article is assigned by lot to one of those buying tickets —*vt.* (-fled, -fling) dispose of by raffle

**raft** *n.* floating structure of logs, planks *etc.*

**raf·ter** (RAF-tər) *n.* one of the main beams of a roof

**raft·ing** (RAF-ting) *n.* sport of traveling on rivers by raft —**raft·er** *n.* participant in this

**rag**[1] *n.* fragment of cloth; torn piece; *inf.* newspaper *etc.*, *esp.* one considered worthless; piece of ragtime music —*pl.* tattered clothing —**rag·ged** (RAG-id) *adj.* shaggy; torn; clothed in torn clothes; lacking smoothness —**rag'bag** *n.* confused assortment —**rag'time** *n.* style of jazz piano music

**rag**[2] *vt.* (ragged, rag·ging) tease; torment; play practical jokes on

**rag·a·muf·fin** (RAG-ə-muf-in) *n.* ragged, dirty person or child

**rage** (rayj) *n.* violent anger or passion; fury —*vi.* (raged, rag·ing) speak, act with fury; proceed violently and without check (as storm, battle *etc.*); be widely and violently prevalent —**all the rage** very popular

**rag·lan** (RAG-lən) *adj.* of sleeves that continue to the neck so that there are no shoulder seams

**ra·gout** (ra-GOO) *n.* highly seasoned stew of meat and vegetables

**raid** (rayd) *n.* rush, attack; foray —*vt.* make raid on

**rail**[1] (rayl) *n.* horizontal bar, *esp.* as part of fence, track *etc.*; *sl.* line of cocaine for sniffing —**rail'ing** *n.* fence, barrier made of rails supported by posts —**rail'head** (-hed) *n.* farthest point to which

railway line extends —**rail'road**.

**rail'way** *n.* track of steel rails on which trains run; company operating railroad (*also pl.*)

**rail**[2] *vi.* utter abuse; scoff; scold; reproach —**rail'ler·y** (-ə-ree) *n.* (*pl.* **-ler·ies**) banter

**rail**[3] *n.* any of kinds of marsh birds

**rai·ment** (RAY-mənt) *n.* clothing

**rain** (rayn) *n.* moisture falling in drops from clouds; fall of such drops —*vi.* fall as rain —*vt.* pour down like rain —**rain'y** *adj.* (rain·i·er, rain·i·est) —**rain'bow** (-boh) *n.* arch of prismatic colors in sky —**rain'coat** *n.* light water-resistant overcoat

**raise** (rayz) *vt.* (raised, rais·ing) lift up; set up; build; increase; elevate; promote; heighten, as pitch of voice; breed into existence; levy, collect; end (siege) —**raise Cain** (KAYN) *be* riotous, angry *etc.*

**rai·sin** (RAY-zin) *n.* dried grape

**rai·son d'être** (RAY-zohn DE-trə) *Fr.* reason or justification for existence

**raj** (rahj) *n.* rule, sway, *esp.* in India —**ra'jah** *n.* Indian prince or ruler

**rake**[1] (rayk) *n.* tool with long handle and crosspiece with teeth for gathering hay, leaves *etc.* —*vt.* (raked, rak·ing) gather, smooth with rake; sweep, search over; sweep with shot —**rake-off** *n.* monetary commission, *esp.* illegal

**rake**[2] *n.* dissolute or dissipated man

**rake**[3] *n.* slope, *esp.* backward, of ship's funnel *etc.* —*v.* (raked, rak·ing) incline from perpendicular —**rak'ish** *adj.* appearing dashing or speedy

**ral·ly** (RAL-ee) *v.* (-lied, -ly·ing) bring together, *esp.* what has been scattered, as routed army or dispersed troops; come together; regain health or strength, revive —n. act of rallying; assembly, *esp.* outdoor, of any organization; *Tennis* lively exchange of strokes

**ram** n. male sheep; hydraulic machine; battering engine —vt. (**rammed, ram·ming**) force, drive; strike against with force; stuff; strike with ram

**ram·ble** (RAM-bəl) vi. (-**bled, -bling**) walk without definite route; wander; talk incoherently; spread in random fashion —n. rambling walk —**ram'bler** n. climbing rose; one who rambles

**ram·e·kin** (RAM-i-kin) n. small fireproof dish; food baked in it

**ram·i·fy** (RAM-ə-fī) v. (-**fied, -fy·ing**) spread in branches, subdivide; become complex —**ram·i·fi·ca'tion** n. branch, subdivision; process of branching out; consequence

**ra·mose** (RAY-mos) adj. branching

**ramp** n. gradual slope joining two level surfaces

**ram·page** (ram-PAYJ) vi. (-**paged, -pag·ing**) dash about violently —n. (RAM-payj) angry or destructive behavior —**ram·pa'geous** (-jəs) adj.

**ramp·ant** (RAM-pənt) adj. violent; rife; rearing

**ram·part** (RAM-pahrt) n. mound, wall for defense

**ram·shack·le** (RAM-shak-əl) adj. tumble-down, rickety, makeshift

**ran** pt. of RUN

**ranch** n. cattle farm —vi. manage one —**ranch'er** n.

**ran·cid** (RAN-sid) adj. smelling or tasting offensive, like stale fat

**ran·cor** (RANG-kər) n. bitter, inveterate hate —**ran'cor·ous** adj. malignant; virulent

**ran·dom** (RAN-dəm) adj. made or

done by chance, without plan —**at random** haphazard(ly)

**rand·y** (RAN-dee) adj. (**rand·i·er, rand·i·est**) sexually aroused

**rang** pt. of RING[2]

**range** (raynj) n. limits; row; scope, sphere; distance missile can travel; distance of mark shot at; place for shooting practice or rocket testing; rank; kitchen stove —v. (**ranged, rang·ing**) —vt. set in row; classify; roam —vi. extend; roam; pass from one point to another; fluctuate (as prices) —**rang'er** n. official in charge of or patrolling park *etc.* —**rang'y** (adj. (**rang·i·er, rang·i·est**) with long, slender limbs; spacious —**range'find·er** n. instrument for finding distance away of given object

**rank**[1] (rangk) n. row, line; order; social class; status; relative place or position —pl. common soldiers; great mass or majority of people (also *esp.* in labor unions **rank and file**) —vt. draw up in rank, classify —vi. have rank, place; have certain distinctions

**rank**[2] adj. (-**er, -est**) growing too thickly, coarse; offensively strong; rancid; vile; flagrant —**rank'ly** adv.

**ran·kle** (RANG-kəl) vi. (-**kled, -kling**) fester, continue to cause anger, resentment or bitterness

**ran·sack** (RAN-sak) vt. search thoroughly; pillage, plunder

**ran·som** (RAN-səm) n. release from captivity by payment; amount paid —vt. pay ransom for

**rant** vi. rave in violent, high-sounding language —n. noisy, boisterous speech; wild gaiety

**rap**[1] n. smart slight blow —v. (**rapped, rap·ping**) give rap to; utter abruptly; perform rhythmic monologue to music —**take the**

**rap** *sl.* take blame, suffer punishment (for) whether guilty or not

**rap²** *n.* —not care a rap not care at all

**ra·pa·cious** (rǝ-PAY-shǝs) *adj.* greedy; grasping —**ra·pac'i·ty** (-PAS-i-tee) *n.*

**rape** (rayp) *vt.* (**raped, rap·ing**) force (person) to submit unwillingly to sexual intercourse —*n.* act of raping; any violation or abuse —**rap'ist** *n.*

**rap'id** *adj.* quick, swift —*n.* (*esp. in pl.*) part of river with fast, turbulent current —**ra·pid'i·ty** *n.*

**ra·pi·er** (RAY-pee-ǝr) *n.* fine-bladed sword for thrusting only

**rap·ine** (RAP-in) *n.* plunder

**rap·port** (ra-POR) *n.* harmony, agreement

**rap·proche·ment** (rap-rohsh-MAHN) *n.* reestablishment of friendly relations, *esp.* between nations

**rapt** *adj.* engrossed, spellbound —**rap'ture** (-chǝr) *n.* ecstasy —**rap'tur·ous** *adj.*

**rare** (rair) *adj.* (**rar·er, rar·est**) uncommon; infrequent; of uncommon quality; of atmosphere, having low density, thin —**rare'ly** *adv.* seldom —**rar'i·ty** *n.* (*pl. -ties*) anything rare; rareness

**rare²** (rar·er, rar·est) *adj.* (of meat) lightly cooked

**rare·bit** (RAIR-bit) *n.* melted or toasted cheese dish *see* WELSH RABBIT

**rar·e·fy** (RAIR-ǝ-fī) *v.* (**-fied, -fy·ing**) make, become thin, rare, or less dense; refine

**rar·ing** (RAIR-ing) *adj. inf.* enthusiastically willing, ready

**ras·cal** (RAS-kǝl) *n.* rogue; naughty (young) person —**ras·cal'i·ty** (-KAL-i-tee) *n.* roguery, baseness —**ras'cal·ly** (-kǝl-ee) *adj.*

**rash¹** *adj.* (**-er, -est**) hasty, reckless, incautious

**rash²** *n.* skin eruption; outbreak, series of (unpleasant) occurrences

**rash·er** (RASH-ǝr) *n.* serving of bacon, usu. three or four slices; thin slice of bacon or ham

**rasp** *n.* harsh, grating noise; coarse file —*v.* scrape with rasp; make scraping noise; speak in grating voice; grate upon; irritate

**rasp·ber·ry** (RAZ-ber-ee) *n.* red, juicy edible berry; plant which bears it; *inf.* spluttering noise with tongue and lips to show contempt

**Ras·ta·far·i·an** (ras-tǝ-FAIR-ee-ǝn) *n.* member of Jamaican cult regarding Haile Selassie, late emperor of Ethiopia, as the messiah —*adj.*

**rat** *n.* small rodent; *sl.* contemptible person, *esp.* deserter, informer *etc.* —*vi.* (**rat·ted, rat·ting**) *sl.* inform (on), betray, desert, abandon; hunt rats —**rat'ty** *adj. sl.* (**-ti·er, -ti·est**) mean, ill-tempered, irritable —**rat race** continual hectic competitive activity —**rat'trap** *n.* device for catching rats; dilapidated dwelling

**ratch·et** (RACH-it) *n.* set of teeth on bar or wheel allowing motion in one direction only

**rate¹** (rayt) *n.* proportion between two things; charge; degree of speed *etc.* —*vt.* (**rat·ed, rat·ing**) value; estimate value of —**rat'a·ble** *adj.* that can be rated or appraised

**rate²** *vt.* (**rat·ed, rat·ing**) scold, chide

**rath·er** (RATH-ǝr) *adv.* to some extent; preferably; more willingly

**rat·i·fy** (RAT-ǝ-fī) *vt.* (**-fied, -fy·ing**) confirm —**rat·i·fi·ca'tion** (-fi-KAY-shǝn) *n.*

**rat·ing** (RAY-ting) *n.* credit standing; fixing a rate; classification, *esp.* of ship, enlisted member of armed forces; angry rebuke

**ra·tio** (RAY-shoh) *n.* (*pl.* -tios) proportion; quantitative relation

**ra·ti·oc·i·nate** (rash-ee-OS-ɔ-nayt) *vi.* (-nat·ed, -nat·ing) reason

**ra·tion** (RASH-ɔn) *n.* fixed allowance of food *etc.* —*vt.* supply with, limit to certain amount

**ra·tion·al** (RASH-ɔnl) *adj.* reasonable, sensible; capable of thinking, reasoning —**ra·tion·ale'** (-NAL) *n.* reasons given for actions *etc.* —**ra'tion·al·ism** *n.* philosophy that regards reason as only guide or authority —**ra·tion·al'i·ty** *n.* —**ra·tion·al·i·za'tion** *n.* —**ra'tion·al·ize** *vt.* (-ized, -iz·ing) justify by plausible reasoning; reorganize to improve efficiency

**rat·tan** (ra-TAN) *n.* climbing palm with jointed stems; cane of this *oft.* used for furniture

**rat·tle** (RAT-l) *v.* (-tled, -tling) —*vi.* give out succession of short sharp sounds; clatter —*vt.* shake briskly causing a sharp clatter of sounds; confuse, fluster —*n.* such sound; instrument for making it; set of horny rings in rattlesnake's tail —**rat'tle·snake** *n.* poisonous snake

**rau·cous** (RAW-kɔs) *adj.* hoarse; harsh

**raun·chy** (RAWN-chee) *adj.* *inf.* (-chi·er, -chi·est) earthy, vulgar, sexy; slovenly

**rav·age** (RAV-ij) *vt.* (-aged, -ag·ing) lay waste, plunder —*n.* destruction

**rave** (rayv) *vi.* (raved, rav·ing) talk wildly in delirium or enthusiastically —*n.*

**rav·el** (RAV-ɔl) *vt.* (-eled, -el·ing) entangle; fray out; disentangle

**ra·ven**[1] (RAY-vɔn) *n.* black bird like crow —*adj.* shiny black

**raven**[2] *v.* seek prey, plunder —**rav·en·ous** (RAV-ɔ-nɔs) *adj.* very hungry

**ra·vine** (rɔ-VEEN) *n.* narrow steep-sided valley worn by stream, gorge

**ra·vi·o·li** (rav-ee-OH-lee) *n. pl.* small, thin pieces of dough filled with highly seasoned, chopped meat and cooked

**rav·ish** *vt.* enrapture; commit rape upon —**rav'ish·ing** *adj.* lovely, entrancing

**raw** *adj.* (-er, -est) uncooked; not manufactured or refined; skinned; inexperienced, unpracticed, as recruits; sensitive; chilly —**raw deal** unfair or dishonest treatment —**raw'hide** *n.* untanned hide; whip of this

**ray**[1] *n.* single line or narrow beam of light, heat *etc.*; any of set of radiating lines —*vi.* come out in rays; radiate

**ray**[2] *n.* marine fish, often very large, with winglike pectoral fins and whiplike tail

**ray'on** *n.* (fabric of) synthetic fiber

**raze** (rayz) *vt.* (razed, raz·ing) destroy completely; wipe out, delete; level

**ra·zor** (RAY-zɔr) *n.* sharp instrument for shaving or for cutting hair

**Rb** *Chem.* rubidium

**re**[1] *n.* second sol-fa note

**re**[2] *prep.* with reference to, concerning

**Re** *Chem.* rhenium

**re-, red-, ren-** (*prefix*) again In the list below, the meaning can be inferred from the word to which *re-* is prefixed

re·ad·just'        re·ad·mis'sion

**reach** (reech) *vt.* arrive at; extend; succeed in touching; attain to —*vi.* stretch out hand; extend —*n.* act of reaching; power of touching; grasp, scope; range; straight stretch of river between two bends

**re·act** (ree-AKT) *vi.* act in return, opposition or toward former state —**re·ac'tance** (-əns) *n. Electricity* resistance in coil, apart from ohmic resistance, due to current reacting on itself —**re·ac'tion** (-AK-shən) *n.* any action resisting another; counter or backward tendency; response; chemical or nuclear change, combination or decomposition —**re·ac'tion·ar·y** *n./adj.* (pl. -ar·ies) (person) opposed to change, *esp.* in politics *etc.* —**re·ac'tive** *adj.* chemically active —**re·ac'tor** *n.* apparatus in which nuclear reaction is maintained and controlled to produce nuclear energy

**read** (reed) *v.* (**read** *pr.* red, **read·ing**) —*vt.* look at and understand written or printed matter; learn by reading; interpret mentally; read and utter; interpret; study; understand any indicating instrument; (of instrument) register —*vi.* be occupied in reading; find mentioned in reading —**read'·a·ble** *adj.* that can be read, or read with pleasure —**read'er** *n.* one who reads; university professor's assistant; school textbook; one who reads manuscripts submitted to publisher

**read·y** (RED-ee) *adj.* (**read·i·er, read·i·est**) prepared for use or action; willing, prompt —**read'i·ly** *adv.* promptly; willingly —**read'i·ness** (-nis) *n.*

**re·a·gent** (ree-AY-jənt) *n.* chemical substance that reacts with another and is used to detect presence of the other

**re·al** (REE-əl) *adj.* existing in fact; happening; actual; genuine; (of property) consisting of land and houses —**re'al·ism** *n.* regarding things as they are; artistic treatment with this outlook —**re·al·is'tic** *adj.* —**re·al'i·ty** *n.* real existence —**re'al·ly** *adv.* —**re'al·ty** *n.* real estate —**real estate** landed property

**re·al·ize** (REE-ə-līz) *vt.* (**-ized, -iz·ing**) apprehend, grasp significance of; make real; convert into money —**re·al·i·za'tion** *n.*

**realm** (relm) *n.* kingdom, province, domain, sphere

**ream**[1] (reem) *n.* twenty quires or 500 sheets of paper —*pl.* large quantity of written matter

**ream**[2] *vt.* enlarge, bevel out, as hole in metal —**ream'er** *n.* tool for this

**reap** (reep) *v.* cut and gather harvest; receive as fruit of previous activity —**reap'er** *n.*

| | | |
|---|---|---|
| re·ap·pear' | re·cov'er | re·heat' |
| re·arm' | re·cre·ate' | re·mar'ry |
| re·ar·range' | re·dec'o·rate | re·o'pen |
| re·born' | re·de·vel'op | re·print' |
| re·build' | re·dis·cov'er | re·route' |
| re·cap'ture | re·ech'o | re·set' |
| re·con·nect' | re·e·lect' | re·shuf'fle |
| re·con·sid'er | re·em'pha·size | re·sur'face |
| re·con·struct' | re·fill' | re·u·nite' |
| re·con·vene' | re·form' | re·wind' |

**rear**[1] (reer) *n.* back part; part of army, procession *etc.* behind others —*a.* rear admiral lowest flag rank in certain navies —**rear'guard** *n.* troops protecting rear of army —**rear'most** (-mohst) *adj.*

**rear**[2] *vt.* care for and educate (children); breed; erect —*vi.* rise, *esp.* on hind feet

**rea·son** (REE-zən) *n.* ground, motive; faculty of thinking; sanity; sensible or logical thought or view —*vi.* think logically in forming conclusions —*vt.* (*usu.* with with) persuade by logical argument into doing *etc.* —**rea'son·a·ble** *adj.* sensible, not excessive; suitable; logical

**re·as·sure** (ree-ə-SHUUR) *vt.* (-sured, -sur·ing) restore confidence to

**re·bate** (REE-bayt) *n.* discount, refund —*vt.* (-bat·ed, -bat·ing) deduct

**re·bel** (ri-BEL) *vi.* (-belled, -bel·ling) revolt, resist lawful authority, take arms against ruling power —*n.* (REB-əl) one who rebels; insurgent —*adj.* (REB-əl) in rebellion —**re·bel·lion** (ri-BEL-yən) *n.* organized open resistance to authority, revolt —**re·bel'lious** *adj.*

**re·bound** (ri-BOWND) *vi.* spring back; misfire, *esp.* so as to hurt perpetrator (of plan, deed *etc.*) —*n.* (REE-bownd) act of springing back or recoiling; return

**re·buff** (ri-BUF) *n.* blunt refusal; check —*vt.* repulse, snub

**re·buke** (ri-BYOOK) *vt.* (-buked, -buk·ing) reprove, reprimand, find fault with —*n.*

**re·bus** (REE-bəs) *n.* (*pl.* -bus·es) riddle in which names of things *etc.* are represented by pictures standing for syllables *etc.*

**re·but** (ri-BUT) *vt.* (-but·ted,

-but·ting) refute, disprove —**re·but'tal** *n.*

**re·cal·ci·trant** (ri-KAL-si-trənt) *adj./n.* willfully disobedient (person)

**re·call** (ri-KAWL) *vt.* recollect, remember; call, summon, order back; annul, cancel; revive, restore —*n.* (REE-kawl) summons to return; ability to remember

**re·cant** (ri-KANT) *vt.* withdraw statement, opinion *etc.* —**re·can·ta'tion** *n.*

**re·ca·pit·u·late** (ree-kə-PICH-ə-layt) *vt.* (-lat·ed, -lat·ing) state again briefly; repeat

**re·cede** (ri-SEED) *vi.* (-ced·ed, -ced·ing) go back; become distant; slope backward; begin balding

**re·ceipt** (ri-SEET) *n.* written acknowledgment of money received; receiving or being received —*vt.* acknowledge payment of in writing

**re·ceive** (ri-SEEV) *vt.* (-ceived, -ceiv·ing) take, accept, get; experience; greet (guests) —**re·ceiv'a·ble** *adj.* —**re·ceiv'er** *n.* official appointed to receive money; fence, one who takes stolen goods knowing them to have been stolen; equipment in telephone, radio or TV that converts electrical signals into sound, light

**re·cent** (REE-sənt) *adj.* that has lately happened; new —**re'cent·ly** *adv.*

**re·cep·ta·cle** (ri-SEP-tə-kəl) *n.* vessel, place or space, to contain anything

**re·cep·tion** (ri-SEP-shən) *n.* receiving; manner of receiving; welcome; formal party; in broadcasting, quality of signals received —**re·cep'tion·ist** *n.* person who receives guests, clients *etc.*

**re·cep·tive** (ri-SEP-tiv) *adj.* able, quick, willing to receive new ideas, suggestions *etc.* —re·cep·tiv'i·ty *n.*

re·cess (ri-SES) *n.* niche, alcove; hollow; secret, hidden place; remission or suspension of business; vacation, holiday

re·ces·sion (ri-SESH-ən) *n.* period of reduction in economic activity; act of receding —re·ces'sive *adj.* receding

re·ces·sion·al (ri-SESH-ə-nl) *n.* hymn sung while clergy retire

re·cher·ché (rə-SHAIR-shay) *adj.* of studied elegance; exquisite; choice

re·cid·i·vist (ri-SID-ə-vist) *n.* one who relapses into crime

rec·i·pe (RES-ə-pee) *n.* directions for cooking a dish; prescription; expedient

re·cip·i·ent (ri-SIP-ee-ənt) *adj.* that can or does receive —*n.* one who, that which receives

re·cip·ro·cal (ri-SIP-rə-kəl) *adj.* complementary; mutual; moving backward and forward; alternating —re·cip'ro·cate (-rə-kayt) *v.* (-cat·ed, -cat·ing) —*vt.* give and receive mutually; return —*vi.* move backward and forward —re·ci·proc·i·ty (res-ə-PROS-i-tee) *n.*

re·cite (ri-SIT) *vt.* (-cit·ed, -cit·ing) repeat aloud, *esp.* to audience —re·cit'al (-əl) *n.* musical performance, usu. by one person; act of reciting; narration of facts *etc.*; story; public entertainment of recitations *etc.* —rec·i·ta'tion *n.* recital, usu. from memory, of poetry or prose; recountal —rec·i·ta·tive (res-i-tə-TEEV) *n.* musical declamation

reck·less (REK-lis) *adj.* heedless, incautious

reck·on (REK-ən) *v.* count; include; consider; *inf.* think, deem; make calculations

re·claim (ri-KLAYM) *vt.* make fit for cultivation; bring back; reform; demand the return of —rec·la·ma'tion *n.*

re·cline (ri-KLIN) *vi.* (-clined, -clin·ing) sit, lie back or on one's side

re·cluse (REK-loos) *n.* hermit —*adj.* (ri-KLOOS) living in seclusion, shut off from the world —re·clu'sive *adj.*

rec·og·nize (REK-əg-niz) *vt.* (-nized, -niz·ing) know again; treat as valid; notice, show appreciation of —rec·og·ni'tion *n.* —rec·og·niz'a·ble *adj.* —re·cog·ni·zance (ri-KOG-nə-zəns) *n.* avowal; bond by which person undertakes before court to observe some condition; *obs.* recognition

re·coil (ri-KOIL) *vi.* draw back in horror *etc.*; go wrong so as to hurt the perpetrator; rebound (*esp.* of gun when fired) —*n.* (REE-koil) backward spring; retreat; recoiling

rec·ol·lect (rek-ə-LEKT) *vt.* call back to mind, remember

rec·om·mend (rek-ə-MEND) *vt.* advise, counsel; praise, commend; make acceptable —rec·om·men·da'tion *n.*

rec·om·pense (REK-əm-pens) *vt.* (-pensed, -pens·ing) reward; compensate, make up for —*n.* compensation; reward; requital

rec·on·cile (REK-ən-sil) *vt.* (-ciled, -cil·ing) bring back into friendship; adjust, settle, harmonize —rec·on·cil'a·ble *adj.* —rec·on·cil·i·a'tion *n.*

rec·on·dite (REK-ən-dit) *adj.* obscure, abstruse, little known

re·con·di·tion (ree-kən-DISH-ən) *vt.* restore to good condition, working order

re·con·noi·ter (ree-kə-NOI-tər) *vt.* make preliminary survey of;

survey position of enemy —vi.
make reconnaissance —re·con·
nais·sance (ri-KON-ɔ-sɔns) n. examination or survey for military
or engineering purposes; scouting

re·con·sti·tute (ree-KON-sti-toot)
vt. (-tut·ed, -tut·ing) restore
(food) to former state esp. by
addition of water to a concentrate

re·cord (REK-ɔrd) n. being recorded; document or other thing
that records; disk with indenta-
tions that phonograph transforms
into sound; best recorded
achievement; known facts about
person's past —v. (ri-KORD) preserve (sound, TV programs etc.)
on plastic disk, magnetic tape
etc. for reproduction on playback
device —vt. put in writing; register —re·cord′er n. one who, that
which records; type of flute —re·
cord′ing n. process of making
records from sound; something
recorded, eg radio or TV program —record player instrument
for reproducing sound on disks
—off the record not for publication

re·count (ri-KOWNT) vt. tell in
detail

re·coup (ri-KOOP) vt. recompense, compensate; recover
what has been expended or lost

re·course (REE-kors) n. (resort-
ing to) source of help; Law right
of action or appeal

re·cov·er (ri-KUV-ɔr) v. regain,
get back —vi. get back health
—re·cov′er·y n. (pl. -er·ies)

rec·re·ant (REK-ree-ɔnt) adj.
cowardly, disloyal n. recreant
person; renegade

rec·re·a·tion (rek-ree-AY-shɔn)
n. agreeable or refreshing occupation, relaxation, amusement

re·crim·i·nate (ri-KRIM-ɔ-nayt)

vi. (-nat·ed, -nat·ing) make
countercharge or mutual accusation —re·crim·i·na′tion n. mutual
abuse and blame

re·cru·desce (ree-kroo-DES) vi.
(-desced, -desc·ing) break out
again —re·cru·des′cent adj.

re·cruit (ri-KROOT) n. newly-
enlisted soldier; one newly joining society etc. —vt. enlist fresh
soldiers etc.

rec·tan·gle (REK-tang-gɔl) n. oblong four-sided figure with four
right angles —rec·tang′u·lar adj.
shaped thus

rec·ti·fy vt. (-fied, -fy·ing) put
right, correct, remedy, purify
—rec·ti·fi·ca′tion n. act of setting
right; Electricity conversion of
alternating current into direct
current —rec′ti·fi·er (-fi-ɔr) n.
person or thing that rectifies

rec·ti·lin·e·ar (rek-tl-IN-ee-ɔr)
adj. in straight line; characterized by straight lines

rec·ti·tude (REK-ti-tood) n. moral uprightness; honesty of purpose

rec·to (REK-toh) n. (pl. -tos)
right-hand page of book, front of
leaf

rec·tor (REK-tɔr) n. member of
clergy with care of parish; head
of certain institutions, chiefly
academic —rec′to·ry n. rector's
house

rec·tum (REK-tɔm) n. final section of large intestine —rec′tal
(-tl) adj.

re·cum·bent (ri-KUM-bɔnt) adj.
lying down —re·cum′ben·cy n.

re·cu·per·ate (ri-KOO-pɔr-ayt) v.
(-at·ed, -at·ing) restore, be restored from illness, losses etc.;
convalesce —re·cu·per·a′tion n.

re·cur (ri-KUR) vi. (-curred,
-cur·ring) happen again; return
again and again; go or come
back in mind —re·cur′rence

(-ons) *n.* repetition —**re·cur′rent** (-ont) *adj.*

**re·cy·cle** (ree-SĪ-kəl) *vt.* (-cled, -cling) reprocess a manufactured substance for use again; reuse

**red** *adj.* of color varying from crimson to orange and seen in blood, rubies, glowing fire *etc.* —*n.* the color; communist —**red′-den** *v.* make red; become red; flush —**red′dish** *adj.* —**red-blood·ed** (-blud-id) *adj.* vigorous; virile —**red′coat** *n.* in American Revolution, a British soldier —**red flag** danger signal —**red-hand′ed** *adj.* (caught) in the act —**red herring** topic introduced to divert attention from main issue —**red-hot** red with heat; creating excitement —**red tape** excessive adherence to official rules —**red′wood** (-wuud) *n.* giant coniferous tree of California —**in the red** operating at loss; in debt —**see red** *inf.* be very angry

**re·deem** (ri-DEEM) *vt.* buy back; set free; free from sin; make up for —**re·demp′tion** (-DEM-shon) *n.* —**re·deem′a·ble** *adj.* —**The Redeem·er** Jesus Christ

**red·o·lent** (RED-l-ont) *adj.* smelling strongly, fragrant; reminiscent (of) —**red′o·lence** *n.*

**re·dou·ble** (ree-DUB-əl) *v.* (-bled, -bling) increase, multiply, intensify; double a second time

**re·doubt** (ri-DOWT) *n.* detached outwork in fortifications

**re·doubt·a·ble** (ri-DOWT-ə-bəl) *adj.* dreaded, formidable

**re·dound** (ri-DOWND) *vt.* contribute (to); recoil

**re·dress** (ri-DRES) *vt.* set right; make amends for —*n.* (REE-dres) compensation, amends

**re·duce** (ri-DOOS) *vt.* (-duced, -duc·ing) bring down, lower; lessen, weaken; bring by force or necessity to some state or action; slim; simplify; dilute; *Chem.* separate substance from others with which it is combined —**re·duc′-i·ble** *adj.* —**re·duc′tion** (-DUK-shon) *n.* —**reducing agent** substance used to deoxidize or lessen density of another substance

**re·dun·dant** (ri-DUN-dont) *adj.* superfluous —**re·dun′dan·cy** *n.*

**reed** *n.* various marsh or water plants; tall straight stem of one; *Mus.* vibrating cane or metal strip of certain wind instruments —**reed′y** *adj.* (reed·i·er, reed·i·est) full of reeds; like reed instrument, harsh and thin in tone

**reef** *n.* ridge of rock or coral near surface of sea; vein of ore; part of sail that can be rolled up to reduce area —*vt.* take in a reef of —**reef′er** *n.* sailor's close-fitting jacket; *sl.* marijuana cigarette

**reek** *n.* strong (unpleasant) smell —*vi.* emit fumes; smell

**reel** *n.* spool on which film is wound; *Motion Pictures* portion of film; winding apparatus; bobbin; thread wound on this; lively dance; music for it; act of staggering —*vt.* wind on reel; draw (in) by means of reel —*vi.* stagger, sway, rock —**reel off** recite, write fluently, quickly

**re·fec·to·ry** (ri-FEK-tə-ree) *n.* (*pl.* -ries) dining room in monastery, college *etc.* —**re·fec′tion** *n.* a meal

**re·fer** (ri-FUR) *v.* (-ferred, -fer·ring) —*vi.* relate (to), allude —*vt.* send to for information; trace, ascribe to; submit for decision —**re·fer′ral** *n.* act, instance of referring —**ref·er·ee′** *n.* arbitrator; person willing to whom scientific paper *etc.* is sent for judgment of its quality *etc.*; umpire —*v.* (-eed, -ee·ing) act as referee —**ref′er·ence** (-ins) *n.* act of referring; citation or direction in book; appeal to judgment of another; testimonial; one to whom inquiries as to character *etc.* may be made —**ref·er·en'·dum** *n.* (*pl.* -**da** *pr.* -**do**) submitting of question to electorate

**re·fine** (ri-FĪN) *vt.* (-**fined**, -**fin·ing**) purify —**re·fine'ment** *n.* subtlety; improvement, elaboration; fineness of feeling, taste or manners —**re·fin'er·y** *n.* (*pl.* -**er·ies**) place for refining sugar, oil *etc.*

**re·fla·tion** (ri-FLAY-shən) *n.* (steps taken to produce) increase in economic activity of country *etc.*

**re·flect** (ri-FLEKT) *vt.* throw back, *esp.* rays of light; cast (discredit *etc.*) upon —*vi.* meditate —**re·flec'tion** (-FLEK-shən) *n.* act of reflecting; return of rays of heat, light, or waves of sound, from surface; image of object given back by mirror *etc.*; conscious thought; meditation; expression of thought —**re·flec'tive** *adj.* meditative, quiet, contemplative; throwing back images —**re·flec'tor** *n.* polished surface for reflecting light *etc.*

**re·flex** (REE-fleks) *n.* reflex action; reflected image; reflected light, color *etc.* —*adj.* (of muscular action) involuntary; reflected; bent back —**re·flex·ive** (ri-FLEK-siv) *adj. Grammar* describes verb denoting agent's action on self —**reflex action** involuntary response to (nerve) stimulation

**re·form** (ri-FORM) *v.* improve; abandon evil practices; reconstruct —*n.* improvement —**ref·or·ma·tion** (ref-ər-MAY-shən) *n.* —**re·form'a·to·ry** *n.* (*pl.* -**ries**) institution for reforming juvenile offenders

**re·fract** (ri-FRAKT) *vi.* change course of light *etc.* passing from

one medium to another —**re·frac'tion** *n.*

**re·frac·to·ry** (ri-FRAK-tə-ree) *adj.* unmanageable; difficult to treat or work; *Med.* resistant to treatment; resistant to heat

**re·frain¹** (ri-FRAYN) *vi.* abstain (from)

**re·frain²** *n.* phrase or verse repeated regularly *esp.* in song or poem; chorus

**re·fran·gi·ble** (ri-FRAN-jə-bəl) *adj.* that can be refracted

**re·fresh** (ri-FRESH) *vt.* give freshness to; revive; renew; brighten; provide with refreshment —**re·fresh'er** *n.* that which refreshes —**re·fresh'ment** *n.* that which refreshes, *esp.* food, drink; restorative

**re·frig·er·ate** (ri-FRIJ-ə-rayt) *vt.* (-**at·ed**, -**at·ing**) freeze; cool —**re·frig'er·ant** *n.* refrigerating substance —*adj.* —**re·frig'er·a·tor** *n.* apparatus in which foods, drinks are kept cool

**ref·uge** (REF-yooj) *n.* shelter, protection, retreat, sanctuary —**ref·u·gee** (ref-yuu-JEE) *n.* one who seeks refuge, *esp.* in foreign country

**re·ful·gent** (ri-FUL-jənt) *adj.* shining, radiant —**re·ful'gence** *n.* —**re·ful'gen·cy** *n.* splendor

**re·fund** (ri-FUND) *vt.* pay back —*n.* (REE-fund)

**re·fur·bish** (ree-FUR-bish) *vt.* furbish, furnish or brighten anew

**re·fuse¹** (ri-FYOOZ) *v.* (-**fused**, -**fus·ing**) decline, deny, reject —**re·fus'al** *n.* denial of anything demanded or offered; option

**ref·use²** (REF-yoos) *n.* rubbish, useless matter

**re·fute** (ri-FYOOT) *vt.* (-**fut·ed**, -**fut·ing**) disprove —**re·fut'a·ble** *adj.* —**ref·u·ta·tion** (ref-yuu-TAY-shən) *n.*

**re·gal** (REE-gəl) *adj.* of, like a

king —re·ga·li·a (ri-GAY-lee-ə) n. pl. insignia of royalty, as used at coronation etc.; emblems of high office, an order etc. —re·gal·i·ty (ri-GAL-i-tee) n. (pl. -ties)

re·gale (ri-GAYL) vt. (-galed, -gal·ing) give pleasure to; feast

re·gard (ri-GAHRD) vt. look at; consider; relate to; heed —n. look; attention; particular respect; esteem —pl. expression of good will —re·gard'ful adj. heedful, careful —re·gard'less adj. heedless —adv. in spite of everything

re·gat·ta (ri-GAT-ə) n. meeting for yacht or boat races

re·gen·er·ate (ri-JEN-ə-rayt) v. (-at·ed, -at·ing) cause spiritual rebirth; reform morally; reproduce, re-create; reorganize —adj. (-ə-rit) born anew —re·gen·er·a'tion n. —re·gen'er·a·tive adj.

re·gent (REE-jənt) n. ruler of kingdom during absence, minority etc., of its monarch —adj. ruling —re'gen·cy n. status, (period of) office of regent

reg·gae (REG-ay) n. style of popular West Indian music with strong beat

reg·i·cide (REJ-ə-sīd) n. one who kills a king; this crime

re·gime (rə-ZHEEM) n. system of government, administration

reg·i·men (REJ-ə-mən) n. prescribed system of diet etc.; rule

reg·i·ment (REJ-ə-mənt) n. organized body of troops as unit of army —vt. (REJ-ə-ment) discipline, organize rigidly or too strictly —reg·i·men'tal adj. of regiment

re·gion (REE-jən) n. area, district; stretch of country; part of the body; sphere, realm; administrative division of a country —re'gion·al adj.

reg·is·ter (REJ-ə-stər) n. list; catalogue; roll; device for registering; written record; range of voice or instrument —v. show, be shown on meter, face etc. —vt. enter in register; record; show; set down in writing; Printing, Photography cause to correspond precisely —reg'is·trar (-trahr) n. keeper of a register esp. in college or university —reg·is·tra'tion n. —reg'is·try n. (pl. -tries) registering; place where registers are kept, esp. of births, marriages deaths

re·gorge (ri-GORJ) v. (-gorged, -gorg·ing) vomit up

re·gress (ri-GRES) vi. return, revert to former place, condition etc. —n. —re·gres'sion (-shən) n. act of returning; retrogression —re·gres'sive adj. falling back

re·gret (ri-GRET) vt. (-gret·ted, -gret·ting) feel sorry, distressed for loss of or on account of —n. sorrow, distress for thing done or left undone or lost —re·gret'ful adj. —re·gret'ta·ble adj.

reg·u·lar (REG-yə-lər) adj. normal; habitual; done, occurring, according to rule; periodical; straight; level; living under rule; belonging to standing army —n. regular soldier; regular customer —reg·u·lar'i·ty n. —reg'u·lar·ize vt. (-ized, -iz·ing)

reg·u·late (REG-yə-layt) vt. (-lat·ed, -lat·ing) adjust; arrange; direct; govern; put under rule —reg·u·la'tion n. —reg'u·la·tor n. contrivance to produce uniformity of motion, as flywheel, governor etc.

re·gur·gi·tate (ri-GUR-ji-tayt) v. vomit; bring back (swallowed food) into mouth

re·ha·bil·i·tate (ree-hə-BIL-i-tayt) vt. (-tat·ed, -tat·ing) help (person) to readjust to society after a period of illness, imprisonment *etc.*; restore to reputation or former position; make fit again; reinstate

**re·hash** (ree-HASH) *vt.* rework, reuse —*n.* (REE-hash) old materials presented in new form

**re·hearse** (ri-HURS) *vt.* (-hearsed, -hears·ing) practice (play *etc.*); repeat aloud; say over again; train, drill —**re·hears'al** *n.*

**reign** (rayn) *n.* period of sovereign's rule —*vi.* be ruler; be supreme

**re·im·burse** (ree-im-BURS) *vt.* (-bursed, -burs·ing) refund; pay back —**re·im·burse'ment** *n.*

**rein** (rayn) *n.* narrow strap attached to bit to guide horse; instrument for governing —*vt.* check, manage with reins; control —**give free rein** to remove restraints

**re·in·car·na·tion** (ree-in-kahr-NAY-shon) *n.* rebirth of soul in successive bodies; one of series of such transmigrations —**re·in·car'nate** (-KAHR-nayt) *vt.* (-nat·ed, -nat·ing)

**rein·deer** (RAYN-deer) *n.* deer of cold regions, eg Lapland

**re·in·force** (ree-in-FORS) *vt.* (-forced, -forc·ing) strengthen with new support, material, force; strengthen with additional troops, ships *etc.* —**re·in·force'ment** *n.* —**reinforced concrete** concrete strengthened internally by steel bars

**re·in·state** (ree-in-STAYT) *vt.* (-stat·ed, -stat·ing) replace, restore, reestablish

**re·it·er·ate** (ree-IT-ʒ-rayt) *vt.* (-at·ed, -at·ing) repeat again and again —**re·it·er·a'tion** *n.* repetition —**re·it'er·a·tive** (-ʒr-ʒ-tiv) *adj.*

**re·ject** (ri-JEKT) *vt.* refuse to accept; put aside; discard; renounce —*n.* (REE-jekt) person or thing

rejected as not up to standard —**re·jec'tion** *n.* refusal

**re·joice** (ri-JOIS) *v.* (-joiced, -joic·ing) make or be joyful, merry; gladden; exult

**re·join** (ree-JOIN) *vt.* reply; join again —**re·join·der** (ri-JOIN-dʒr) *n.* answer, retort

**re·ju·ve·nate** (ri-JOO-vʒ-nayt) *vt.* (-nat·ed, -nat·ing) restore to youth —**re·ju·ve·na'tion** *n.* —**re·ju·ve·nes·cence** (ri-joo-vʒ-NES-ʒns) *n.* process of growing young again

**re·lapse** (ri-LAPS) *vi.* (-lapsed, -laps·ing) fall back into evil, illness *etc.* —*n.* (REE-laps)

**re·late** (ri-LAYT) *v.* (-lat·ed, -lat·ing) —*vt.* narrate, recount; establish relation between; have reference or relation to —*vi.* (with to) form sympathetic relationship

**re·la·tion** (ri-LAY-shon) *n.* relative quality or condition; connection by blood or marriage; connection between things; act of relating; narrative —**re·la'tion·ship** *n.* —**rel·a·tive** (REL-ʒ-tiv) *adj.* dependent on relation to something else, not absolute; having reference or relation (to) —*n.* one connected by blood or marriage; relative word or thing —**rel·a·tiv'i·ty** *n.* state of being relative; subject of two theories of Albert Einstein, dealing with relationships of space, time and motion, and acceleration and gravity

**re·lax** (ri-LAKS) *vt.* make loose or slack —*vi.* become loosened or slack; ease up from effort or attention; become more friendly, less strict —**re·lax·a'tion** (ree-) *n.* relaxing recreation; alleviation; abatement

**re·lay** (REE-lay) *n.* fresh set of people or animals relieving others; *Electricity* device for making or breaking local circuit —*vt.* pass on, as message (-layed, -laying) —**relay race** race between teams of which each runner races part of distance

**re·lease** (ri-LEES) *vt.* (-leased, -leas·ing) give up, surrender, set free; permit public showing of (movie *etc.*) —*n.* setting free; releasing; written discharge; permission to show publicly; film, record *etc.* newly issued

**rel·e·gate** (REL-i-gayt) *vt.* (-gat·ed, -gat·ing) banish, consign; demote —**rel·e·ga'tion** *n.*

**re·lent** (ri-LENT) *vi.* give up harsh intention, become less severe —**re·lent'less** (-lis) *adj.* pitiless; merciless

**rel·e·vant** (REL-ə-vənt) *adj.* having to do with the matter in hand, to the point —**rel'e·vance** *n.*

**reliable, reliance** *see* RELY

**rel·ic** (REL-ik) *n.* thing remaining, *esp.* as memorial of saint; memento —*pl.* remains, traces

**re·lief** (ri-LEEF) *n.* alleviation, end of pain, distress *etc.*; money, food given to victims of disaster, poverty *etc.*; release from duty; one who relieves another; freeing of besieged city *etc.*; projection of carved design from surface; distinctness, prominence —**re·lieve** (ri-LEEV) *vt.* (-lieved, -liev·ing) bring or give relief to —**relief map** map showing elevations and depressions of country in relief

**re·li·gion** (ri-LIJ-ən) *n.* system of belief, in worship of a supernatural power or god —**re·li'gious** *adj.* pert. to religion; pious; conscientious —**re·li'gious·ly** *adv.* in religious manner; scrupulously; conscientiously

**re·lin·quish** (ri-LING-kwish) *vt.* give up, abandon

**rel·i·quar·y** (REL-i-kwer-ee) *n.* (*pl.* -quar·ies) case or shrine for holy relics

**rel'ish** *v.* enjoy, like —*n.* liking, gusto; appetizing taste; taste or flavor

**re·luc·tant** (ri-LUK-tənt) *adj.* unwilling, loath, disinclined —**re·luc'tance** *n.*

**re·ly** (ri-LI) *vi.* (-lied, -ly·ing) depend (on); trust —**re·li·a·bil'i·ty** *n.* —**re·li'a·ble** *adj.* trustworthy, dependable —**re·li'ance** (ri-LI-əns) *n.* trust; confidence; dependence —**re·li'ant** (-ənt) *adj.* confident; trustful

**re·main** (ri-MAYN) *vi.* stay, be left behind; continue; abide; last —**re·mains** *n. pl.* relics, *esp.* of ancient buildings; dead body —**re·main'der** *n.* rest, what is left after subtraction —*vt.* offer (end of consignment of goods, material *etc.*) at reduced prices

**re·mand** (ri-MAND) *vt.* send back, *esp.* into custody

**re·mark** (ri-MAHRK) *vi.* make casual comment (on) —*vt.* comment, observe; say; take notice of —*n.* observation, comment —**re·mark'a·ble** *adj.* noteworthy, unusual —**re·mark'a·bly** *adv.* exceedingly; unusually

**rem·e·dy** (REM-i-dee) *n.* (*pl.* -dies) means of curing, counteracting or relieving disease, trouble *etc.* —*vt.* (-died, -dy·ing) put right —**re·me'di·a·ble** *adj.* —**re·me'di·al** *adj.* designed, intended to correct specific disability, handicap *etc.* —**re·me'di·a'tion** *n.*

**re·mem·ber** (ri-MEM-bər) *vt.* retain, recall to memory —*vi.* have in mind —**re·mem'brance** (-brəns) *n.* memory; token; souvenir; reminiscence

**re·mind** (ri-MIND) *vt.* cause to remember; put in mind (of) —**mind'er** *n.*

**rem·i·nisce** (rem-ɔ-NIS) *vi.* (-nisced, -nisc·ing) talk, write of past times, experiences *etc.* —**rem·i·nis'cence** *n.* remembering; thing recollected —*pl.* memoirs —**rem·i·nis'cent** *adj.* reminding or suggestive of

**re·miss** (ri-MIS) *adj.* negligent, careless

**re·mit** (ri-MIT) *v.* (-mit·ted, -mit·ting) send money for goods, services *etc.*, *esp.* by mail; refrain from exacting; give up; restore, return; slacken; forgive (sin *etc.*) —*n. Law* transfer of court record to another court —**re·mis'sion** *n.* abatement; reduction in length of prison term; pardon, forgiveness —**re·mit'tance** *n.* sending of money; money sent

**rem·nant** (REM-nɔnt) *n.* fragment or small piece remaining; oddment

**re·mon·strate** (ri-MON-strayt) *vi.* (-strat·ed, -strat·ing) protest, reason with, argue —**re·mon'strance** (-strɔns) *n.*

**re·morse** (ri-MORS) *n.* regret and repentance —**re·morse'ful** (-fɔl) *adj.* —**re·morse'less** (-lis) *adj.* pitiless

**re·mote** (ri-MOHT) *adj.* (-mot·er, -mot·est) far away, distant; aloof; slight —**re·mote'ly** *adv.* —remote control control of apparatus from a distance by electrical device

**re·move** (ri-MOOV) *v.* (-moved, -mov·ing) —*vt.* take away or off; transfer; withdraw —*vi.* go away, change residence —*n.* degree of difference —**re·mov·a·ble** *adj.* —**re·mov'al** *n.*

**re·mu·ner·ate** (ri-MYOO-nɔ-rayt) *vt.* reward, pay —**re·mu·ner·a'tion** *n.* —**re·mu'ner·a·tive** *adj.*

**ren·ais·sance** (ren-ɔ-SAHNS) *n.* revival, rebirth, *esp.* (R-) revival of learning in 14th to 16th centuries (*also* **re·nas'cence** *pr.* ri-NAS-ɔns)

**re·nal** (REEN-l) *adj.* of the kidneys

**re·nas·cent** (ri-NAS-ɔnt) *adj.* springing up again into being

**rend** *v.* (rent, rend·ing) tear, wrench apart; burst, break, split

**ren·der** (REN-dɔr) *vt.* submit, present; give in return, deliver up; cause to become; portray, represent; melt down; cover with plaster

**ren·dez·vous** (RAHN-de-voo) *n.* (*pl.* same form *pr.* -vooz) meeting place; appointment; haunt; assignation —*vi.* (-voused *pr.* -vood, -vous·ing *pr.* -voo·ing) meet, come together

**ren·di·tion** (ren-DISH-ɔn) *n.* performance; translation

**ren·e·gade** (REN-i-gayd) *n.* deserter; outlaw; rebel —*adj.*

**re·nege** (ri-NIG) *vi.* (-neged, -neg·ing) (*usu. with* on) go back on (promise *etc.*); in cards, break rule

**re·new** (ri-NOO) *vt.* begin again; reaffirm; make valid again; make new; revive; restore to former state; replenish —*vi.* be made new; grow again —**re·new·a·bil'i·ty** *n.* quality of being renewable —**re·new'a·ble** *adj.* —**re·new'al** *n.* revival, restoration; regeneration

**ren·net** (REN-it) *n.* lining membrane of calf's fourth stomach; preparation from this membrane for curdling milk

**re·nounce** (ri-NOWNS) *vt.* (-nounced, -nounc·ing) give up, cast off, disown; abjure; resign, as title or claim —**re·nun·ci·a'tion** *n.*

**ren·o·vate** (REN-ɔ-vayt) *vt.* restore, repair, renew, do up —**ren·o·va'tion** *n.*

**re·nown** (ri-NOWN) *n.* fame

**rent¹** *n.* payment for use of land,

buildings, machines *etc.* —*vt.* hold by lease; hire; let —**rent·al** (RENT-əl) *n.* sum payable as rent

**rent²** *n.* tear; fissure —*pt./pp. of* REND

**renunciation** *see* RENOUNCE

**rep** *n.* fabric with corded surface for upholstery *etc.*

**rep²** *adj./n.* short for REPERTORY (COMPANY)

**rep³** *n.* short for REPRESENTATIVE

**re·paid** (ri-PAYD) *pt./pp. of* REPAY

**re·pair¹** (ri-PAIR) *vt.* make whole, sound again; mend; patch; restore —*n.* —**re·pair'a·ble** *adj.* —**rep·a·ra·tion** (rep-ə-RAY-shən) *n.* repairing; amends, compensation

**repair²** *vi.* resort (to), go

**rep·ar·tee** (rep-ər-TEE) *n.* witty retort; interchange of reports

**re·past** (ri-PAST) *n.* a meal

**re·pa·tri·ate** (ri-PAY-tree-ayt) *vt.* (-at·ed, -at·ing) send (someone) back to own country

**re·pay** (ri-PAY) *vt.* (-paid, -paying) pay back, refund; make return for —**re·pay'ment** *n.*

**re·peal** (ri-PEEL) *vt.* revoke, annul, cancel —*n.* act of repealing

**re·peat** (ri-PEET) *vt.* say, do again; reproduce; recur —*vi.* recur; of food, be tasted repeatedly for some time after being eaten —*n.* act, instance of repeating, *esp.* TV show broadcast again —**re·peat'ed·ly** *adv.* again and again; frequently —**re·peat'er** *n.* firearm that can be discharged many times without reloading; watch that strikes hours —**rep· e·ti·tion** (rep-i-TISH-ən) *n.* act of repeating; thing repeated; piece learned by heart and repeated —**rep·e·ti'tious** *adj.* repeated unnecessarily —**re·pet'i·tive** *adj.* repeated

**re·pel** (ri-PEL) *vt.* (-pelled, -pel·ling) drive back, ward off, refuse; be repulsive to —**re·pel'lent** (-ənt) *adj.* distasteful; resisting water *etc.* —*n.* that which repels, *esp.* chemical to repel insects

**re·pent** (ri-PENT) *vi.* wish one had not done something; feel regret for deed or omission —*vt.* feel regret for —**re·pent'ance** (-əns) *n.* contrition —**re·pent'ant** (-ənt) *adj.*

**re·per·cus·sion** (ree-pər-KUSHən) *n.* indirect effect, oft. unpleasant; recoil; echo

**rep·er·to·ry** (REP-ər-tor-ee) *n.* (*pl.* -ries) repertoire, collection; store —**rep'er·toire** (-twahr) *n.* stock of plays, songs *etc.* that performer or company can give —**repertory** (theater, company, group) (theater *etc.*) with permanent company producing succession of plays

**repetition, repetitious, repetitive** *see* REPEAT

**re·pine** (ri-PĪN) *vi.* (-pined, -pining) fret, complain

**re·place** (ri-PLAYS) *vt.* (-placed, -plac·ing) substitute for; put back

**re·play** (REE-play) *n.* immediate reshowing on TV of incident in sport, *esp.* in slow motion (*also* **instant replay**); replaying of a match —*vt.* (ree-PLAY)

**re·plen·ish** (ri-PLEN-ish) *vt.* fill up again —**re·plen'ish·ment** *n.*

**re·plete** (ri-PLEET) *adj.* filled, gorged

**rep·li·ca** (REP-li-kə) *n.* exact copy; facsimile, duplicate —**rep·li·cate** (REP-li-kayt) *vt.* (-cat·ed, -cat·ing) make, be a copy of —**rep·li·ca'tion** *n.* —**rep'li·ca·ble** *adj.*

**re·ply** (ri-PLĪ) *v.* (-plied, -ply·ing) answer —*n.* (*pl.* -lies)

**re·port** (ri-PORT) *n.* account,

statement; written statement of child's progress at school; rumor; repute; bang —vt. announce, relate; make, give account of; take down in writing; complain about —vi. make report; act as reporter; present oneself (to) —re·port'er n. one who reports, esp. for newspaper

re·pose (ri-POHZ) n. peace; composure; sleep —v. (-posed, -pos-ing) —vi. rest; lay to rest; place; rely, lean (on) —re·pos'i·tor·y (-POZ-i-tor-ee) n. (pl. -tor·ies) place where valuables are deposited for safekeeping; store

rep·re·hend (rep-ri-HEND) vt. find fault with —rep·re·hen'si·ble adj. deserving censure; unworthy —rep·re·hen'sion n. censure

rep·re·sent (rep-ri-ZENT) vt. stand for; deputize for; act, play; symbolize; make out to be; call up by description or portrait —rep·re·sen·ta'tion n. —rep·re·sent'a·tive n. one chosen to stand for group; (traveling) salesman; (R-) member of US House of Representatives, congressman —adj. typical

re·press (ri-PRES) vt. keep down or under, quell, check —re·pres'-sion (-PRESH-ən) n. restraint —re·pres'sive adj.

re·prieve (ri-PREEV) vt. (-prieved, -priev·ing) suspend execution of (condemned person); give temporary relief (to) —n. postponement or cancellation of punishment; respite; last-minute intervention

rep·ri·mand (REP-rə-mand) n. sharp rebuke —vt. rebuke sharply

re·pris·al (ri-PRĪ-zəl) n. retaliation

re·proach (ri-PROHCH) vt. blame, rebuke —n. scolding, upbraiding;

expression of this; thing bringing discredit —re·proach'ful (-fəl) adj.

rep·ro·bate (REP-rə-bayt) adj. depraved; rejected by God —n. depraved or disreputable person —vt. (-bat·ed, -bat·ing) disapprove of, reject

re·pro·duce (ree-prə-DOOS) v. (-duced, -duc·ing) —vt. produce copy of; bring new individuals into existence; re-create, produce anew —vi. propagate; generate —re·pro·duc'i·ble adj. —re·pro·duc'tion n. process of reproducing; that which is reproduced; facsimile, as of painting etc. —re·pro·duc'tive adj.

re·prove (ri-PROOV) vt. (-proved, -prov·ing) censure, rebuke —re·proof' n.

rep·tile (REP-til) n. cold-blooded, air breathing vertebrate with horny scales or plates, as snake, tortoise etc. —rep·til'i·an adj.

re·pub·lic (ri-PUB-lik) n. country without monarch in which supremacy of people or their elected representatives is formally acknowledged —re·pub'li·can adj./n.

re·pu·di·ate (ri-PYOO-dee-ayt) vt. (-at·ed, -at·ing) reject authority or validity of; cast off, disown —re·pu·di·a'tion n.

re·pug·nant (ri-PUG-nənt) adj. offensive; distasteful; contrary —re·pug'nance n. dislike, aversion; incompatibility

re·pulse (ri-PULS) vt. (-pulsed, -puls·ing) drive back; rebuff; repel —n. driving back, rejection, rebuff —re·pul'sion (-shən) n. distaste, aversion; Physics force separating two objects —re·pul'-sive adj. loathsome, disgusting

re·pute (ri-PYOOT) v. (-put·ed, -put·ing) reckon, consider —n. reputation, credit —rep'u·ta·ble *adj.* of good repute; respectable —**rep·u·ta·tion** *n.* estimation in which person is held; character; good name

**re·quest** (ri-KWEST) *n.* asking; thing asked for —*vt.* ask

**Req·ui·em** (REK-wee-əm) *n.* Mass for the dead; (also r-) music for this

**re·quire** (ri-KWIR) *vt.* (-quired, -quir·ing) want, need; demand —**re·quire'ment** *n.* essential condition; specific need; want

**req·ui·site** (REK-wə-zit) *adj.* necessary; essential —*n.*

**req·ui·si·tion** (rek-wə-ZISH-ən) *n.* formal demand, *eg* for materials or supplies —*vt.* demand (supplies); press into service

**re·quite** (ri-KWIT) *vt.* (-quit·ed, -quit·ing) repay

**re·scind** (ri-SIND) *vt.* cancel, annul —**re·scis·sion** (-SIZH-ən) *n.*

**res·cue** (RES-kyoo) *vt.* (-cued, -cu·ing) save, deliver, extricate —*n.* —**res'cu·er** *n.*

**re·search** (ri-SURCH) *n.* investigation, *esp.* scientific study to discover facts —*v.* carry out investigations on, into

**re·sem·ble** (ri-ZEM-bəl) *vt.* (-bled, -bling) be like; look like —**re·sem'blance** *n.*

**re·sent** (ri-ZENT) *vt.* show, feel indignation at; retain bitterness about —**re·sent'ful** (-fəl) *adj.* —**re·sent'ment** (-mənt) *n.*

**re·serve** (ri-ZURV) *vt.* (-served, -serv·ing) hold back, set aside, keep for future use —*n.* (*also pl.*) something, *esp.* money, troops *etc.* kept for emergencies; area of land reserved for particular purpose or for use by particular group of people *etc.* (*also* **re·ser·va'tion**) reticence, concealment of feelings or friendliness —**res·ervation** *n.* reserving; thing reserved; doubt; exception or limitation —**reserved** *adj.* not showing feelings, lacking cordiality —**re·serv'ist** *n.* one serving in reserve

**res·er·voir** (REZ-ər-vwahr) *n.* enclosed area for storage of water, *esp.* for community supplies; receptacle for liquid, gas *etc.*; place where anything is kept or stored

**re·side** (ri-ZID) *vi.* (-sid·ed, -sid·ing) dwell permanently —**res·i·dence** (REZ-i-dəns) *n.* home; house —**res'i·den·cy** *n.* dwelling; position or period of medical resident —**res'i·dent** (-dənt) *adj./n.* —**res·i·den'tial** *adj.* (of part of town) consisting mainly of residences; of, connected with residence; providing living accommodation —**resident** *n.* physician in residence at hospital and serving on staff to obtain advanced training

**res·i·due** (REZ-i-doo) *n.* what is left, remainder —**re·sid'u·al** (ri-ZIJ-oo-əl) *adj.* —**residuals** *n.* additional payments to performers for reruns of film, TV programs *etc.* in which they appear

**re·sign** (ri-ZIN) *vt.* give up —*vi.* give up office, employment *etc.*; reconcile (oneself) to —**res·ig·na'tion** (-ig-NAY-shən) *n.* resigning; being resigned, submission —**re·signed'** (-ZIND) *adj.* content to endure

**re·sil·ient** (ri-ZIL-yənt) *adj.* capable of returning to normal after stretching *etc.*, elastic; (of person) recovering quickly from shock *etc.* —**re·sil'ience**, **-ien·cy** *n.*

**res·in** (REZ-in) *n.* sticky substance formed in and oozing from plants, *esp.* firs and pines —**res'in·ous** (-nəs) *adj.* of, like resin

**re·sist** (ri-ZIST) *v.* withstand, oppose —**re·sist'ance** (-əns) *n.* act of resisting; opposition; hindrance; *Electricity* opposition offered by circuit to passage of current through it —re·sist'ant (-ənt) *adj.* —re·sist'i·ble *adj.* —re·sis·tiv'i·ty *n.* measure of electrical resistance —re·sist'or *n.* component of electrical circuit producing resistance

res·o·lute (REZ-ə-loot) *adj.* determined —res·o·lu'tion *n.* resolving; firmness; purpose or thing resolved upon; decision or vote of assembly

re·solve (ri-ZOLV) *vt.* (-solved, -solv·ing) make up one's mind; decide with effort of will; form by resolution of vote; separate component parts of; make clear —*n.* resolution; fixed purpose

res·o·nance (REZ-ə-nəns) *n.* echoing, *esp.* in deep tone; sound produced by body vibrating in sympathy with neighboring source of sound —res'o·nant (-nənt) *adj.* —res'o·nate *vi./vt.* (-nat·ed, -nat·ing)

re·sort (ri-ZORT) *vi.* have recourse; frequent —*n.* place of recreation *eg* beach; recourse; frequented place; haunt

re·sound (ri-ZOWND) *vi.* echo, ring, go on sounding —re·sound'ing *adj.* echoing; thorough

re·source (ri-ZORS) *n.* capability, ingenuity; that to which one resorts for support; expedient —*pl.* source of economic wealth; supply that can be drawn on; means of support, funds —re·source'ful (-fəl) *adj.*

re·spect (ri-SPEKT) *n.* deference, esteem; point or aspect; reference, relation —*vt.* treat with esteem; show consideration for —re·spect·a·bil'i·ty *n.* —re·spect'a·ble *adj.* worthy of respect, decent; fairly good —re·spect'ful *adj.* —re·spect'ing *prep.*

concerning —re·spect'ive *adj.* relating separately to each of those in question; several, separate

res·pi·ra·tion *n.* (res-pə-RAY-shən) breathing —res'pi·ra·tor *n.* apparatus worn over mouth and breathed as protection against dust, poison gas *etc.* or to provide artificial respiration —re·spi·ra·to·ry (-rə-tor-ee) *adj.*

res·pite (RES-pit) *n.* pause; interval; suspension of labor; delay; reprieve

re·splend·ent (ri-SPLEN-dənt) *adj.* brilliant, splendid; shining —re·splend'en·cy (-ən-see) *n.*

re·spond (ri-SPOND) *vi.* answer; act in answer to stimulus; react —re·spond'ent *adj.* replying —*n.* one who answers; defendant —re·sponse' *n.* answer —re·spon'sive *adj.* readily reacting to some influence

re·spon·si·ble (ri-SPON-sə-bəl) *adj.* liable to answer for; accountable; dependable; involving responsibility; of good credit or position —re·spon·si·bil'i·ty *n.* state of being answerable; duty; charge; obligation

rest¹ *n.* repose; freedom from exertion *etc.*; that on which anything rests or leans; pause, *esp.* in music; support —*vi.* take rest; be supported —*vt.* give rest to; place on support —rest'ful (-fəl) *adj.* —rest'less (-lis) *adj.* offering no rest; uneasy, impatient —rest home residential establishment providing care for aged, convalescent *etc.*

rest² *n.* remainder; others —*vi.* remain; continue to be

res·tau·rant (RES-tər-ənt) *n.* commercial establishment serving food —res·tau·ra·teur' (-ə-TUR) *n.* keeper of one

res·ti·tu·tion (res-ti-TOO-shən) *n.*

giving back or making up; reparation, compensation

**res·tive** (RES-tiv) *adj.* restless; resisting control, impatient

**re·store** (ri-STOR) *vt.* (-stored, -stor·ing) build up again, repair, renew; reestablish; give back —**res·to·ra'tion** *n.* —**re·stor'a·tive** *adj.* restoring —*n.* medicine to strengthen *etc.* —**re·stor'er** *n.*

**re·strain** (ri-STRAYN) *vt.* check, hold back; prevent; confine —**re·straint'** *n.* restraining, control, *esp.* self-control

**re·strict** (ri-STRIKT) *vt.* limit, bound —**re·stric'tion** *n.* limitation; restraint; rule —**re·stric'tive** *adj.* —**restricted** neighborhood, club *etc.* one denying residence, membership to persons of certain races, ethnic groups *etc.*

**re·sult** (ri-ZULT) *vi.* follow as consequence; happen; end —*n.* effect, outcome —**re·sul'tant** (-ZULTnt) *adj.* arising as result

**re·sume** (ri-ZOOM) *vt.* (-sumed, -sum·ing) begin again —**ré·su·mé** (REZ-uu-may) *n.* summary, abstract; brief statement of one's qualifications for employment, public office *etc.* —**re·sump'tion** (ri-ZUM-shən) *n.* resuming; fresh start

**re·sur·gence** (ri-SUR-jəns) *n.* rising again —**re·sur'gent** *adj.*

**res·ur·rect** (rez-ə-REKT) *vt.* restore to life, resuscitate; use once more (something discarded *etc.*) —**res·ur·rec'tion** *n.* rising again (*esp.* from dead); revival

**re·sus·ci·tate** (ri-SUS-i-tayt) *vt.* (-tat·ed, -tat·ing) revive to life, consciousness

**re·tail** (REE-tayl) *n.* sale in small quantities —*adv.* at retail —*v.* sell, be sold, retail; (ri-TAYL) recount

**re·tain** (ri-TAYN) *vt.* keep; engage services of —**re·tain'er** *n.* fee to retain professional adviser, *esp.* lawyer —**re·ten'tion** (-shən) *n.* —**re·ten'tive** *adj.* capable of retaining, remembering

**re·tal·i·ate** (ri-TAL-ee-ayt) *v.* (-at·ed, at·ing) repay in kind; revenge —**re·tal·i·a'tion** *n.* —**re·tal'i·a·to·ry** *adj.*

**re·tard** (ri-TAHRD) *vt.* make slow or late; keep back; impede development of —**re·tard'ed** *adj.* underdeveloped, *esp.* mentally —**re·tar·da'tion** *n.*

**retch** (rech) *vi.* try to vomit

**ret·i·cent** (RET-ə-sənt) *adj.* reserved in speech; uncommunicative —**ret'i·cence** *n.*

**ret·i·na** (RET-n-ə) *n.* (*pl.* -nas) light-sensitive membrane at back of eye —**ret'i·nal** *adj.* —**ret·i·ni'tis** (-NI-tis) *n.* inflammation of retina

**ret·i·nue** (RET-n-yoo) *n.* band of followers or attendants

**re·tire** (ri-TIR) *v.* (-tired, -tir·ing) —*vi.* give up office or work; go away; withdraw; go to bed —*vt.* cause to retire —**re·tired'** *adj.* that has retired from office *etc.* —**re·tire'ment** (-mənt) *n.* —**re·tir'ing** *adj.* unobtrusive, shy

**re·tort** (ri-TORT) *vt.* reply; repay in kind, retaliate; hurl back (charge *etc.*) —*vi.* reply with countercharge —*n.* vigorous reply or repartee; vessel with bent neck used for distilling

**re·touch** (ree-TUCH) *vt.* touch up, improve by new touches, *esp.* of paint *etc.*

**re·trace** (ri-TRAYS) *vt.* (-traced, -trac·ing) go back over (a route *etc.*) again

**re·tract** (ri-TRAKT) *v.* draw back, recant —**re·tract'a·ble** *adj.* —**re·trac'tion** *n.* drawing or taking back, *esp.* of statement *etc.* —**re·trac'tor** *n.* muscle; surgical instrument

**re·tread** (ree-TRED) vt. restore tread to worn rubber tire —n. (REE-tred) retreaded tire; sl. person returned to work after dismissal; person training for new type of work; inf. reworked old idea etc.

**re·treat** (ri-TREET) vi. move back from any position; retire —n. act of, or military signal for, retiring, withdrawal; place to which anyone retires esp. for meditation; refuge; sunset call on bugle

**re·trench** (ri-TRENCH) vt. reduce expenditure, esp. by dismissing staff; cut down

**ret·ri·bu·tion** (re-trə-BYOO-shən) n. recompense, esp. for evil deeds; vengeance

**re·trieve** (ri-TREEV) vt. (-trieved, -triev·ing) fetch back again; restore; rescue from ruin; recover, esp. information from computer; regain —**re·triev'al** n. —**re·triev'er** n. dog trained to retrieve game

**ret·ro·ac·tive** (re-troh-AK-tiv) adj. applying or referring to the past

**ret·ro·grade** (RE-trə-grayd) adj. going backward, reverting; reactionary —**ret·ro·gres'sion** (-GRE-shən) n. —**ret·ro·gres'sive** adj.

**ret·ro·spect** (RE-trə-spekt) n. looking back, survey of past —**ret·ro·spec'tion** (-SPEK-shən) n. —**ret·ro·spec'tive** adj.

**re·trous·sé** (ri-troo-SAY) adj. of nose, turned upward

**re·turn** (ri-TURN) vi. go, come back —vt. give, send back; report officially; elect —n. returning, being returned; profit; official report esp. tax return

**re·un·ion** (ree-YOON-yən) n. gathering of people who have been apart

**Rev.** Revelations

**rev** n. inf. revolution (of engine) —v. (revved, rev·ving) (oft. with up) increase speed of revolution (of engine)

**re·val·ue** (ree-VAL-yoo) v. (-ued, -u·ing) adjust exchange value of currency upward

**re·vamp** (ree-VAMP) vt. renovate, restore

**re·veal** (ri-VEEL) vt. make known; show —**re·ve·la'tion** n.

**rev·eil·le** (REV-ə-lee) n. morning bugle call etc. to waken soldiers

**rev·el** (REV-əl) vi. (-eled, -el·ing) take pleasure (in); make merry —n. (usu. pl.) merrymaking —**rev'el·ry** n. festivity

**re·venge** (ri-VENJ) n. retaliation for wrong done; act that satisfies this; desire for this —v. (-venged, -veng·ing) —vt. avenge; make retaliation for —vt. refl. avenge oneself —**re·venge'ful** (-fəl) adj. vindictive; resentful

**rev·e·nue** (REV-ən-yoo) n. income, esp. of nation, as taxes etc.

**re·ver·ber·ate** (ri-VUR-bə-rayt) v. (-at·ed, -at·ing) echo, resound, throw back (sound etc.)

**re·vere** (ri-VEER) vt. (-vered, -ver·ing) hold in great regard or religious respect —**rev'er·ence** (-əns) n. revering; awe mingled with respect and esteem; veneration —**rev'er·end** adj. (esp. as prefix to clergyman's name) worthy of reverence —**rev'er·ent** (-ənt) adj. showing reverence —**rev·er·en'tial** adj. marked by reverence

**rev·er·ie** (REV-ə-ree) n. daydream, absent-minded state

**re·verse** (ri-VURS) v. (-versed, -vers·ing) of vehicle) (cause to) move backward —vt. turn upside down or other way round; change completely —n. opposite, contrary; side opposite, obverse; defeat; reverse gear —adj. opposite, contrary —re·ver'sal (-səl) n. —re·vers'i·ble adj. —reverse gear mechanism enabling vehicle to move backward

**re·vert** (ri-VURT) vi. return to former state; come back to subject; refer to a second time; turn backward —re·ver'sion (-VUR-zhən) n. (of property) rightful passing to owner or designated heir etc.

**re·vet·ment** (ri-VET-mənt) n. facing of stone, sandbags etc. for wall

**re·view** (ri-VYOO) vt. examine; look back on; reconsider; hold, make, write review of —n. general survey; critical notice of book etc.; periodical with critical articles; inspection of troops; revue —re·view'er n. writer of reviews

**re·vile** (ri-VIL) vt. (-viled, -vil·ing) be viciously scornful of, abuse

**re·vise** (ri-VIZ) vt. (-vised, -vis·ing) look over and correct; change, alter —re·vi'sion (-zhən) n. reexamination for purpose of correcting; act of revising; revised copy —re·vi'sion·ism n. departure from generally accepted theory, interpretation —re·vi'sion·ist adj./n.

**re·vive** (ri-VIV) v. (-vived, -viv·ing) bring, come back to life, vigor, use etc. —re·viv'al (-vəl) n. reviving, esp. of religious fervor —re·viv'al·ist n. organizer of religious revival

**re·voke** (ri-VOHK) vt. (-voked, -vok·ing) take back, withdraw; cancel —rev'o·ca·ble (-ə-kə-bəl) adj. —rev·o·ca'tion n. repeal

**re·volt** (ri-VOHLT) v. rebellion —vi. rise in rebellion; feel disgust —vt. affect with disgust —re·volt'ing adj. disgusting, horrible

**re·volve** (ri-VOLV) v. (-volved, -volv·ing) —vi. turn around, rotate; be centered on —vt. rotate —rev·o·lu'tion n. violent overthrow of government; great change; complete rotation, turning or spinning around —rev·o·lu'tion·ar·y adj./n. —rev·o·lu'tion·ize vt. (-ized, -iz·ing) change considerably; bring about revolution in

**re·volv·er** (ri-VOL-vər) n. repeating pistol with revolving cylinder

**re·vue, re·view** (ri-VYOO) n. theatrical entertainment with topical sketches and songs

**re·vul·sion** (ri-VUL-shən) n. sudden violent change of feeling; marked repugnance or abhorrence

**re·ward** (ri-WORD) vt. pay, make return for service, conduct etc. —n. —re·ward'ing adj. giving personal satisfaction, worthwhile

**Rh** Chem. rhodium

**rhap·so·dy** (RAP-sə-dee) n. (pl. -dies) enthusiastic or high-flown (musical) composition or utterance —rhap·sod'ic adj. —rhap'so·dize (-sə-diz) v. (-dized, -diz·ing)

**rhe·o·stat** (REE-ə-stat) n. instrument for regulating the value of the resistance in an electric circuit

**rhe·sus** (REE-səs) n. small, long-tailed monkey of S Asia —rhesus factor (also Rh factor) feature distinguishing different types of human blood

**rhet·o·ric** (RET-ər-ik) n. art of effective speaking or writing; artificial or exaggerated language —rhe·tor·i·cal (ri-TOR-i-kəl) adj. (of question) not requiring an answer —rhet·o·ri'cian (-RISH-ən) n.

**rheu·ma·tism** (ROO-mə-tiz-əm) n. painful inflammation of joints or muscles —rheu·mat·ic (ruu-MAT-ik) *adj./n.* —**rheu·ma·toid** (ROO-mə-toid) *adj.* of, like rheumatism

**Rh factor** *see* RHESUS

**rhi·no·cer·os** (rī-NOS-ər-əs) *n.* (*pl.* -os·es) large thick-skinned animal with one or two horns on nose

**rho·di·um** (ROH-dee-əm) *n.* hard metal like platinum

**rhom·bus** (ROM-bəs) *n.* (*pl.* -bus·es, -bi *pr.* -bī) equilateral but not right-angled parallelogram, diamond-shaped figure

**rhu·barb** (ROO-bahrb) *n.* garden plant of which the fleshy stalks are cooked and used as fruit; laxative from root of allied Chinese plant; *sl.* argument, fight

**rhyme** (rīm) *n.* identity of sounds at ends of lines of verse, or in words; word or syllable identical in sound to another; verse marked by rhyme —*vt.* (rhymed, rhym·ing) make rhymes

**rhythm** (RITH-əm) *n.* measured beat or flow, *esp.* of words, music *etc.* —**rhyth·mic** *adj.* —**rhyth'mi·cal·ly** *adv.*

**rib**[1] *n.* one of curved bones springing from spine and forming framework of upper part of body; cut of meat including rib(s); curved timber of framework of boat; raised series of rows in knitting *etc.* —*vt.* (ribbed, rib·bing) furnish, mark with ribs; knit to form a rib pattern —**rib'bing** *n.*

**rib**[2] *vt. inf.* (ribbed, rib·bing) tease, ridicule —**rib'bing** *n.*

**rib·ald** (RIB-əld) *adj.* irreverent, scurrilous; indecent —*n.* ribald person —**rib'al·dry** *n.* vulgar, indecent talk

**rib·bon** (RIB-ən) *n.* narrow band of fabric used for trimming, tying *etc.*; long strip or line of anything —**ribbon development** building of

houses *etc.* along main road leading out of town *etc.*

**ri·bo·fla·vin** (RĪ-boh-flay-vin) *n.* form of vitamin B

**rice** (rīs) *n.* cereal plant; its seeds as food —**rice paper** fine (edible) Chinese paper

**rich** *adj.* (-er, -est) wealthy; fertile; abounding; valuable; (of food) containing much fat or sugar; mellow; amusing —**the** wealthy classes —**rich·es** (RICH-iz) *n. pl.* wealth —**rich'ly** *adv.*

**rick·ets** (RIK-its) *n.* disease of children marked by softening of bones, bow legs *etc.*, caused by vitamin D deficiency —**rick'et·y** *adj.* (-et·i·er, -et·i·est) shaky, insecure, unstable; suffering from rickets

**rick·shaw** (RIK-shaw) *n.* light two-wheeled man-drawn Asian vehicle

**ric·o·chet** (rik-ə-SHAY) *vi.* (-cheted *pr.* -SHAYD, -chet·ing *pr.* -SHAY-ing) (of bullet) rebound or be deflected by solid surface or water —*n.* bullet or shot to which this happens

**rid** *vt.* (rid *or* rid·ded, rid·ding) clear, relieve of; free; deliver —**rid·dance** (RID-ns) *n.* clearance; act of ridding; deliverance; relief

**rid·den** (RID-n) *pp.* of RIDE —*adj.* (*in combination*) afflicted, affected, as disease-ridden

**rid·dle**[1] (RID-l) *n.* question made puzzling to test one's ingenuity; enigma; puzzling thing, person —*vi.* (-dled, -dling) speak in, make riddles

**rid·dle**[2] *vt.* (-dled, -dling) pierce with many holes —**riddled with** full of, *esp.* holes

**ride** (rīd) *v.* (rode, rid·den, rid·ing) sit on and control or propel (horse, bicycle *etc.*); be carried on or across —*vi.* go on horseback or in vehicle; lie at anchor —vt. travel over —n. journey on horse etc., or in any vehicle —rid'er n. one who rides; supplementary clause; addition to a document

**ridge** (rij) n. long narrow hill; long, narrow elevation on surface; line of meeting of two sloping surfaces —vt. (ridged, ridg·ing) form into ridges

**ri·dic·u·lous** (ri-DIK-yə-ləs) adj. deserving to be laughed at, absurd, foolish —rid·i·cule (RID-i-kyool) n. treatment of person or thing as ridiculous —vt. (-culed, -cul·ing) laugh at, deride

**rife** (rīf) adj. prevalent, common

**rif·fle** (RIF-əl) v. (-fled, -fling) flick through (pages etc.) quickly

**riff'raff** n. rabble, disreputable people

**ri·fle** (RĪ-fəl) vt. (-fled, -fling) search and rob; ransack; make spiral grooves in (gun barrel etc.) —n. firearm with long barrel —rifling n. arrangement of grooves in gun barrel; pillaging

**rift** n. crack, split, cleft

**rig** vt. (rigged, rig·ging) provide (ship) with spars, ropes etc.; equip; set up, esp. as makeshift; arrange in dishonest way —n. way ship's masts and sails are arranged; apparatus for drilling for oil and gas; tractor-trailer truck; style of dress —rigging n. ship's spars and ropes, lifting tackle

**right** (rīt) adj. just; in accordance with truth and duty; true; correct; proper; of side that faces east when front is turned to north; Politics conservative or reactionary (also with wing); straight; upright; of outer or more finished side of fabric —vt. bring back to vertical position; do justice to —vi. come back to vertical posi-

tion —n. claim, title etc. allowed or due; what is right, just or due; conservative political party; punch, blow with right hand —adv. straight; properly; very; on or to right side —right'ful (-fəl) adj. —right'ly adv. —right angle angle of 90 degrees —right of way Law right to pass over someone's land; path used; right to driver to proceed

**right·eous** (RĪ-chəs) adj. just, upright; godly; virtuous; good; honest

**rig·id** (RIJ-id) adj. inflexible; harsh, stiff —ri·gid'i·ty n.

**rig·ma·role** (RIG-mə-rohl) n. meaningless string of words; long, complicated procedure

**rig·or¹** (RIG-ər) n. sudden coldness attended by shivering —rigor mor'tis stiffening of body after death

**rigor²** n. harshness, severity, strictness; hardship —rig'or·ous adj. stern, harsh, severe

**rile** (rīl) vt. inf. (riled, ril·ing) anger, annoy

**rill** n. small stream

**rim** n. edge, border, margin; outer ring of wheel —vt. (rimmed, rim·ming) furnish with rim; coat or encrust; Basketball, Golf of ball, go around basket, hole, and not drop in —rimmed adj. bordered, edged —rim'less adj.

**rime** (rīm) n. hoarfrost —rim'y adj. (rim·i·er, rim·i·est)

**rind** (rīnd) n. outer coating of fruits etc.

**ring¹** n. circle of gold etc., esp. for finger; any circular band, coil, rim etc.; circle of persons; enclosed area, esp. roped-in square for boxing —vt. (ringed, ring·ing) put ring round; mark (bird etc.) with ring —ring'er n. one who rings bells; sl. student, athlete, racehorse etc. participating in examination, sporting event *etc.* under false pretenses or fraudulently in place of another —**dead ringer** *sl.* person, thing apparently identical to another —**ring'-lead·er** (-leed-ər) *n.* instigator of mutiny, riot *etc.* —**ring'let** (-lit) *n.* curly lock of hair —**ring'worm** (-wurm) *n.* fungal skin disease in circular patches

**ring** *vi.* (**rang, rung, ring·ing**) give out clear resonant sound, as bell; resound; cause (bell) to sound; telephone *etc.* —*n.* a ringing; telephone call

**rink** (ringk) *n.* sheet of ice for skating or hockey; floor for roller skating

**rinse** (rins) *vt.* (**rinsed, rins·ing**) remove soap (from washed clothes, hair *etc.*) by applying clean water; wash lightly —*n.* a rinsing; liquid to tint hair

**ri·ot** (Rī-ət) *n.* tumult, disorder; loud revelry; disorderly, unrestrained disturbance; profusion —*vi.* make, engage in riot —**ri'ot·ous** *adj.* unruly, rebellious, wanton

**R.I.P.** requiescat in pace (*Lat.,* rest in peace)

**rip**[1] *vt.* (**ripped, rip·ping**) cut, tear away, slash, rend —*n.* rent, tear —**rip'cord** *n.* cord pulled to open parachute —**rip'saw** *n.* saw with coarse teeth (used for cutting wood along grain) —**rip off** *sl.* steal, cheat, overcharge —**rip'off** *n. sl.* act of stealing, overcharging *etc.*

**rip**[2] *n.* strong current, *esp.* one moving away from the shore

**ri·par·i·an** (ri-PAIR-ee-ən) *adj.* of, on banks of river

**ripe** (rīp) *adj.* (**rip·er, rip·est**) ready to be reaped, eaten *etc.;* matured; (of judgment *etc.*) sound —**rip'en** *v.* grow ripe; mature

**ri·poste** (ri-POHST) *n.* verbal retort; counterstroke; *Fencing* quick lunge after parry

**rip·ple** (RIP-əl) *n.* slight wave, ruffling of surface; anything like this; sound like ripples of water *v.* (**-pled, -pling**) —*vi.* flow, form into little waves; (of sounds) rise and fall gently —*vt.* form ripples on

**rise** (rīz) *vi.* (**rose, ris·en, ris·ing**) get up; move upward; appear above horizon; reach higher level; increase in value or price; rebel; adjourn; have its source —*n.* rising; upslope; increase, *esp.* of prices —**ris'er** *n.* one who rises, esp. from bed; vertical part of stair step —**rising** *n.* revolt —*adj.* increasing in rank, maturity

**ris·i·ble** (RIS-ə-bəl) *adj.* inclined to laugh; laughable —**ris·i·bil'i·ty** *n.* (*pl.* **-ties**)

**risk** *n.* chance of disaster or loss —*vt.* venture; put in jeopardy; take chance of —**risk'y** *adj.* (**risk·i·er, risk·i·est**) dangerous; hazardous

**ri·sot·to** (ri-SAW-toh) *n.* dish of rice cooked in stock with various other ingredients

**ris·qué** (ri-SKAY) *adj.* suggestive of indecency

**rite** (rīt) *n.* formal practice or custom, *esp.* religious —**rit·u·al** (RICH-oo-əl) *n.* prescribed order or book of rites; regular, stereotyped action or behavior —*adj.* concerning rites —**rit'u·al·ism** *n.* practice of ritual

**ri·val** (Rī-vəl) *n.* one that competes with another for favor, success *etc.* —*vt.* (**-valed, -val·ing**) vie with —*adj.* in position of rival —**ri'val·ry** *n.* keen competition

**riv·er** (RIV-ər) *n.* large natural stream of water; copious flow

**riv·et** (RIV-it) *n.* bolt for fastening

metal plates, the end being put through holes and then beaten flat —vt. (-et·ed, -et·ing) fasten with rivets; cause to be fixed or held firmly, esp. (fig.) in surprise, horror etc. —riv'et·er n.

riv·u·let (RIV-yə-lit) n. small stream

**Rn** Chem. radon

**roach** (rohch) n. cockroach; sl. butt of marijuana cigarette

**road** (rohd) n. track, way prepared for passengers, vehicles etc.; direction, way; street —road'block n. barricade across road to stop traffic for inspection etc. —road hog selfish, aggressive driver —road'run·ner n. large cuckoo of W US, Mexico, C Amer. able to run quickly —road'side n./adj. —road'ster n. obs. touring car —road'work (-wurk) n. repairs to road; running, jogging along country roads as exercise for boxers —road'wor·thy (-wur-thee) adj. (of vehicle) mechanically sound

**roam** (rohm) v. wander about, rove —roam'er n.

**roan** (rohn) adj. (of horses) having coat in which main color is thickly interspersed with another, esp. bay, sorrel or chestnut mixed with white or gray —n. roan horse

**roar** (ror) v. make or utter loud deep hoarse sound as of lion, thunder, voice in anger etc. —n. such a sound —roar'ing adj. brisk and profitable —adv. noisily

**roast** (rohst) v. bake, cook in closed oven; cook by exposure to open fire; make, be very hot —n. piece of meat for roasting; inf. roasting —adj. roasted —roast'ing n. severe criticism, scolding; session of good-natured scolding by way of tribute to honored person

**rob** vt. (robbed, rob·bing) plunder, steal from; pillage, defraud —rob'ber n. —rob'ber·y n. (pl. -ber·ies)

**robe** (rohb) n. long outer garment, often denoting rank or office —v. (robed, rob·ing) —vt. dress —vi. put on robes, vestments

**rob'in** n. large thrush with red breast —robin's-egg blue pale green to light blue

**ro·bot** (ROH-bot) n. automated machine, esp. performing functions in human manner; person of machine-like efficiency —ro·bot·ics (roh-BOT-iks) n. with sing. v. science of designing and using robots

**ro·bust** (roh-BUST) adj. sturdy, strong —ro·bust'ness (-nis) n.

**roc** (rok) n. monstrous bird of Arabian mythology

**rock**[1] (rok) n. stone; large rugged mass of stone; sl. diamond, gem —rock'er·y n. (pl. -er·ies) mound or grotto of stones or rocks for plants in a garden —rock'y adj. (rock·i·er, rock·i·est) having many rocks; rugged, presenting difficulty —rock bottom lowest possible level —between a rock and a hard place between equally unattractive alternatives

**rock**[2] v. (cause to) sway to and fro —n. style of pop music derived from rock-'n'-roll —rock'er n. curved piece of wood etc. on which thing may rock; rocking chair —rock-'n'-roll n. popular dance rhythm —rock the boat inf. disrupt smooth routine of company etc. —off one's rocker sl. insane

**rock·et** (ROK-it) n. self-propelling device powered by burning of explosive contents (used as firework, for display, signaling, line carrying, weapon etc.); vehicle propelled by rocket engine, as weapon or carrying spacecraft —vi. move fast, esp. upward, as rocket —rock′et·ry n.

ro·co·co (rə-KOH-koh) adj. of furniture, architecture etc. having much conventional decoration in style of early 18th cent. work in France; tastelessly florid

rod n. slender straight bar; stick; cane; old measure (5½ yards)

rode pt. of RIDE

ro·dent (ROHD-ənt) n. gnawing animal, eg rat

ro·de·o (ROH-dee-oh) n. display of skills, competition, with bareback riding, cattle handling techniques etc.

roe (roh) n. mass of eggs in fish

roent·gen (RENT-gən) n. measuring unit of radiation dose

rogue (rohg) n. rascal, knave, scoundrel; mischief-loving person or child; wild beast of savage temper, living apart from herd —ro′guish adj.

rois·ter (ROI-stər) vi. be noisy, boisterous, bragging —roist′er·er n. reveler

role, rôle (rohl) n. actor's part; specific task or function

roll (rohl) v. move by turning over and over —vt. wind around; smooth out with roller —vi. move, sweep along; undulate; of ship, swing from side to side; of aircraft, turn about a line from nose to tail in flight —n. act of lying down and turning over and over or from side to side; piece of paper etc. rolled up; any object thus shaped, eg jelly roll; list, catalogue; bread baked into small oval or round; continuous sound, as of drums, thunder etc. —roll′er n. cylinder of wood, stone, metal etc. used for pressing, crushing, smoothing, supporting thing to be moved, winding thing on etc.; long wave of sea —roll call act, time of calling over list of names, as in schools or army —roller bearings bearings of hardened steel rollers —roller coaster small gravity railroad in amusement park with steep ascents and descents for frightening riders; any experience with similar ups and downs —roller skate skate with wheels instead of runner —roller towel loop of towel on roller —rolling pin cylindrical roller for pastry or dough —rolling stock locomotives, freight cars etc. of railroad —roll top n. in desk, flexible lid sliding in grooves; such a desk —roll up appear, turn up; increase, accumulate

rol·lick·ing (ROL-i-king) adj. boisterously jovial and merry

ro·ly-po·ly (ROH-lee-poh-lee) —adj. round, plump —n. round, plump person or thing

Rom. Romans

Ro·man (ROH-mən) adj. of Rome or Roman Catholic Church —Roman Catholic member of Roman Catholic Church —Roman Catholic Church the Christian church that acknowledges supremacy of the Pope —Roman numerals letters I, V, X, L, C, D, M used to represent numbers in manner of Romans —roman type plain upright letters, ordinary style of printing

roman à clef (roh-mah-na-KLAY) (pl. romans à clef, same pr.) French novel that disguises real events and people

ro·mance (roh-MANS) n. love affair, esp. intense and happy one; mysterious or exciting quality; tale of chivalry; tale with scenes remote from ordinary life; literature like this; picturesque falsehood —v. (-manced, -manc·ing)

—*vi.* exaggerate, fantasize —*vt. inf.* woo, court —**Romance language** any of vernacular languages of certain countries, developed from Latin, as French, Spanish *etc.* —**ro·man'tic** *adj.* characterized by romance; of or dealing with love; of literature *etc.*, preferring passion and imagination to proportion and finish —*n.* —**ro·man'ti·cism** (-ti-sizm) *n.* —**ro·man'ti·cize** *vi.* (-cized, -ciz·ing)

**Ro·man·esque** (rohm-ən-NESK) *adj./n.* (in) style of round-arched vaulted architecture of period between Classical and Gothic

**romp** *vi.* run, play wildly, joyfully —*n.* spell of romping; easy victory —**romp'ers** (-ərz) *n. pl.* child's loose one-piece garment —**romp home** win easily

**ron·deau** (RON-doh) *n.* (*pl.* -deaux *pr.* -dohz) short poem with opening words used as refrain —**ron·del'** *n.* extended rondeau —**ron·de·let** (ron-dl-ET) *n.* short rondeau

**ron·do** (RON-doh) *n.* (*pl.* -dos) piece of music with leading theme to which return is continually made

**roof** *n.* (*pl.* roofs) outside upper covering of building; top, covering part of anything —*vt.* put roof on, over

**rook'**[1] (ruuk) *n.* bird of crow family —*vt.* swindle, cheat —**rook'er·y** *n.* (*pl.* -er·ies) colony of rooks

**rook'**[2] *n.* piece at chess (*also* castle)

**rook·ie** (RUUK-ee) *n.* recruit, *esp.* in army; *Sports* professional athlete playing his first season

**room** *n.* space; space enough; division of house; scope, opportunity —*pl.* lodgings —**room'y**

*adj.* (room·i·er, room·i·est) spacious

**roost** *n.* perch for poultry —*vi.* perch —**roost'er** *n.* male of domestic fowl; cock

**root'**[1] *n.* part of plant that grows down into earth and conveys nourishment to plant; plant with edible root, *eg* carrot; vital part; (*also* roots) source, origin, original cause of anything; *Anatomy* embedded portion of tooth, nail, hair *etc.*; primitive word from which other words are derived; factor of a quantity that, when multiplied by itself the number of times indicated, gives the quantity —*v.* (cause to) take root; pull by roots; dig, burrow

**root'**[2] *vi.* cheer; applaud; encourage —**root'er** *n.*

**rope** (rohp) *n.* thick cord —*vt.* (roped, rop·ing) secure, mark off with rope —**rope** in *inf.* entice, lure by deception

**ro·sa·ry** (ROH-zə-ree) *n.* (*pl.* -ries) series of prayers; string of beads for counting these prayers as they are recited; rose garden, bed of roses

**rose'**[1] (rohz) *n.* shrub, climbing plant *usu.* with prickly stems and fragrant flowers; the flower; perforated flat nozzle for hose, watering can *etc.*; pink color —*adj.* of this color —**ro·se·ate** (ROH-zee-it) *adj.* rose-colored, rosy —**ro·sette** (roh-ZET) *n.* rose-shaped bunch of ribbon; rose-shaped architectural ornament —**ros'y** *adj.* (ros·i·er, ros·i·est) flushed; hopeful, promising —**rose-colored** *adj.* having color of rose; unwarrantably optimistic —**rose window** circular window with series of mullions branching from center —**rose of Sharon** (SHAR-ən) low, spreading small tree or shrub with white, purplish or red flowers

**rose**[2] *pt. of* RISE

**ro·sé** (roh-ZAY) *n.* pink wine

**rose·mar·y** (ROHZ-mair-ee) *n.* evergreen fragrant flowering shrub; its leaves and flowers used as seasoning

**Ro·si·cru·cian** (roh-zi-KROO-shən) *n.* member of secret order devoted to occult law —*adj.* —**Ro·si·cru·cian·ism** *n.*

**ros·in** (ROZ-in) *n.* resin *esp.* used for rubbing on bows of violins *etc.*

**ros·ter** (ROS-tər) *n.* list or plan showing turns of duty

**ros·trum** (ROS-trəm) *n.* (*pl.* -*tra pr.* -trə, -**trums**) platform, stage, pulpit; beak or bill of a bird

**rot** *v.* (rot·ted, rot·ting) decompose naturally; corrupt —*n.* decay, putrefaction; any disease producing decomposition of tissue; nonsense —**rot'ten** *adj.* decomposed, putrid; corrupt

**ro·ta·ry** (ROH-tə-ree) *adj.* (of movement) circular; operated by rotary movement —**ro·tate** (ROH-tayt) *v.* (-tat·ed, -tat·ing) (cause to) move around center or on pivot —**ro·ta'tion** *n.* rotating; regular succession —**Rotary Club** one of international association of businessmen's clubs —**Ro·tar'i·an** *n.* member of such

**rote** (roht) *n.* habitual, mechanical repetition —**by rote** by memory

**ro·tis·ser·ie** (roh-TIS-ə-ree) *n.* (electrically driven) rotating spit for cooking meat

**ro·tor** (ROH-tər) *n.* rotating portion of a dynamo motor or turbine

**rotten** *see* ROT

**ro·tund** (roh-TUND) *adj.* round; plump; sonorous —**ro·tun'di·ty** *n.*

**rouble** *see* RUBLE

**rou·é** (roo-AY) *n.* dissolute or dissipated man; rake

**rouge** (roozh) *n.* red powder, cream used to color cheeks —*v.* (rouged, roug·ing) color with rouge

**rough** (ruf) *adj.* (-er, -est) not smooth, of irregular surface; violent, stormy, boisterous; rude; uncivil; lacking refinement; approximate; in preliminary form —*vt.* make rough; plan out approximately; (*with* it) live without usual comforts *etc.* —*n.* rough condition or area; sketch —**diamond in the rough** excellent, valuable but unsophisticated person —**rough'en** (-n) *vt.* —**rough'age** (RUF-ij) *n.* unassimilated portion of food promoting proper intestinal action —**rough'house** (-hows) *n./v.* (-housed, -hous·ing) fight, row

**rou·lette** (roo-LET) *n.* game of chance played with revolving dishlike wheel and ball

**round** (rownd) *adj.* (-er, -est) spherical, cylindrical, circular, curved; full, complete; roughly correct; large, considerable; plump; unqualified, positive —*adv.* with circular or circuitous course —*n.* thing round in shape; recurrent duties; stage in competition; customary course, as of postman; game (of golf); one of several periods in boxing match *etc.*; cartridge for firearm; rung; movement in circle —*prep.* about; on all sides of —*v.* make, become round —*vt.* move around —**round'ers** *n. with sing.* English ball game resembling baseball —**round'ly** *adv.* plainly; thoroughly —**round·a·bout'** *adj.* not straightforward —**round robin** sports tournament in which all contestants play one another

—**round up** drive (cattle) together; collect and arrest criminals

**roun·de·lay** (ROWN-dl-ay) n. simple song with refrain

**rouse** (rowz) v. (**roused, rousing**) —vt. wake up, stir up, excite to action; cause to rise —vi. waken —**roust·a·bout** (ROWST-ə-bowt) n. laborer working in circus, oil rig etc.

**rout** (rowt) n. overwhelming defeat, disorderly retreat; noisy rabble —vt. scatter and put to flight

**route** (root) n. road, chosen way —**go the route** inf. see through to the end; Baseball pitch complete game

**rou·tine** (roo-TEEN) n. regularity of procedure, unvarying round; regular course —adj. ordinary, regular

**roux** (roo) n. fat and flour cooked together as thickener for sauces

**rove** (rohv) v. (**roved, rov·ing**) wander, roam —**rov'er** n. one who roves; pirate

**row**[1] (roh) n. number of things in a straight line; rank; file; line

**row**[2] v. propel boat by oars —n. spell of rowing —**row'boat** n.

**row**[3] (rhymes with cow) n. dispute; disturbance —vi. quarrel noisily

**row·dy** (ROW-dee) adj. (**-di·er, -di·est**) disorderly, noisy and rough —n. person like this

**roy·al** (ROI-əl) adj. of, worthy of, befitting, patronized by, king or queen; splendid —**roy'al·ist** n. supporter of monarchy —**roy'al·ty** n. royal dignity or power; royal persons; payment to owner of land for right to work minerals, or to inventor for use of invention; payment to author depending on sales

**Ru** Chem. ruthenium

**rub** v. (**rubbed, rub·bing**) —vt. apply pressure to with circular or backward and forward movement; clean, polish, dry, thus; pass hand over; abrade, chafe; remove by friction —vi. come into contact accompanied by friction; become frayed or worn by friction —n. rubbing; impediment

**rub·ber**[1] (RUB-ər) n. coagulated sap of rough, elastic consistency, of certain tropical trees; piece of rubber etc. used for erasing; thing for rubbing; person who rubs; sl. condom —adj. of rubber —**rub'ber·ize** vt. (**-ized, -iz·ing**) coat, impregnate, treat with rubber —**rub'ber·y** adj. —**rub'ber·neck** v. gawk at —**rubber stamp** device for imprinting dates etc.; automatic authorization

**rubber**[2] n. series of odd number of games or contests at various games eg bridge; two out of three games won —**rubber match** deciding contest between tied opponents

**rub·bish** (RUB-ish) n. refuse, waste material, garbage; anything worthless; trash, nonsense —**rub'bish·y** adj. valueless

**rub·ble** (RUB-əl) n. fragments of stone etc.; builders' rubbish

**ru·bel·la** (roo-BEL-ə) n. mild contagious viral disease, German measles

**ru·bi·cund** (ROO-bi-kund) adj. ruddy

**ru·ble, rou·ble** (ROO-bəl) n. Russian monetary unit

**ru·bric** (ROO-brik) n. title, heading; direction in liturgy; instruction

**ru·by** (ROO-bee) n. (**-bies**) precious red gem; its color —adj. of this color

**ruck·sack** (RUK-sak) n. pack carried on back, knapsack

**ruck·us** (RUK-əs) n. uproar, disturbance

**ruc·tion** (RUK-shən) n. noisy disturbance

**rud·der** (RUD-ər) n. flat piece hinged to boat's stern or rear of aircraft to steer by

**rud·dy** (RUD-ee) adj. (-di·er, -di·est) of fresh and healthy red color; rosy; florid

**rude** (rood) adj. impolite; coarse; vulgar; primitive; roughly made; uneducated; sudden, violent —**rude'ly** adv. —**rude'ness** n.

**ru·di·ments** (ROO-də-mənts) n. pl. elements, first principles —**ru·di·men'ta·ry** adj.

**rue**[1] (roo) v. (rued, ru·ing) grieve for; regret; deplore; repent —n. sorrow; repentance —**rue'ful** (-fəl) adj. sorry; regretful; dejected; deplorable

**rue**[2] n. plant with evergreen bitter leaves

**ruff** n. starched and frilled collar; natural collar of feathers, fur etc. on some birds and animals; type of shore bird —**ruf'fle** vt. (-fled, -fling) rumple, disorder; annoy, put out; frill, pleat —n. frilled trimming

**ruff**[2] n./v. Cards trump

**ruf·fi·an** (RUF-ee-ən) n. violent, lawless person

**rug** n. small, oft. shaggy or thickpiled floor mat; thick woolen wrap, coverlet; sl. toupee, hairpiece

**rug·by** (RUG-bee) n. form of football with two teams of 15 players

**rug·ged** (RUG-id) adj. rough; broken; unpolished; harsh, austere

**ru·in** (ROO-in) n. decay, destruction; downfall; fallen or broken state; loss of wealth, position etc. —pl. ruined buildings etc. —vt. reduce to ruins; bring to decay or destruction; spoil; impoverish —**ru·in·a'tion** n. —**ru'in·ous** adj.

causing or characterized by ruin or destruction

**rule** (rool) n. principle; precept; authority; government; what is usual; control; measuring stick —vt. (ruled, rul·ing) govern; decide; mark with straight lines; draw (line) —**rul'er** n. one who governs; stick for measuring or ruling lines

**rum** n. liquor distilled from sugar cane

**rum·ba** (RUM-bə) n. (pl. -bas) rhythmic dance, orig. Cuban; music for it

**rum·ble** (RUM-bəl) vi. (-bled, -bling) make noise as of distant thunder, heavy vehicle etc.; sl. engage in gang street fight —n. noise like thunder etc.; gang street fight

**ru·mi·nate** (ROO-mə-nayt) vi. (-nat·ed, -nat·ing) chew cud; ponder over; meditate —**ru'mi·nant** (-nənt) adj./n. cud-chewing (animal) —**ru·mi·na'tion** (-NAY-shən) n. quiet meditation and reflection —**ru'mi·na·tive** (-mə-nə-tiv) adj.

**rum·mage** (RUM-ij) v. (-maged, -mag·ing) search thoroughly —n. —**rummage sale** sale of miscellaneous, usu. secondhand, items

**rum·my** (RUM-ee) n. card game; sl. (pl. -mies) drunkard

**ru·mor** (ROO-mər) n. hearsay, common talk, unproved statement —vt. put out as, by way of, rumor

**rump** n. tail end; buttocks

**rum·ple** (RUM-pəl) v./n. (-pled, -pling) crease, wrinkle

**rum·pus** (RUM-pəs) n. (pl. -us·es) disturbance; noise and confusion

**run** v. (ran, run, run·ning) —vi. move with more rapid gait than walking; go quickly; flow; flee; compete in race, contest, election; revolve; continue; function;

travel according to schedule; fuse; melt; spread over; have certain meaning —*vt.* cross by running; expose oneself (to risk *etc.*); cause to run; (of newspaper) print, publish; transport and dispose of (smuggled goods); manage; operate —*n.* act, spell of running; rush; tendency; course; period; sequence; heavy demand; enclosure for domestic poultry, animals; ride in car; series of unraveled stitches, ladder; score of one at baseball; steep snow-covered course for skiing —**run'ner** *n.* racer; messenger; curved piece of wood on which sleigh slides; any similar appliance; slender stem of plant running along ground forming new roots at intervals; strip of cloth, carpet —**running** *adj.* continuous; consecutive; flowing; discharging; effortless; entered for race; used for running —*n.* act of moving or flowing quickly; management —**run'ny** *adj.* (**-ni·er, -ni·est**) tending to flow or exude moisture —**run'down** *n.* summary —**run-down** *adj.* exhausted —run down stop working; reduce; exhaust; denigrate —**run'way** *n.* level stretch where aircraft take off and land —in the running having fair chance in competition

**rung**[1] *n.* crossbar or spoke, *esp.* in ladder

**rung**[2] *pp. of* RING[2]

**runt** *n.* small animal, below usual size of species; *offens.* undersized person

**ru·pee** (roo-PEE) *n.* monetary unit of India and Pakistan

**rup·ture** (RUP-chər) *n.* breaking, breach; hernia —*v.* (**-tured, tur·ing**) break; burst, sever

**ru·ral** (RUUR-əl) *adj.* of the country; rustic

**ruse** (rooz) *n.* stratagem, trick

**rush**[1] *vt.* impel, carry along violently and rapidly; take by sudden assault —*vi.* cause to hurry; move violently or rapidly —*n.* rushing, charge; hurry; eager demand for; heavy current (of air, water *etc.*) —*adj.* done with speed; characterized by speed —**rush hour** period at beginning and end of day when many people are traveling to and from work

**rush**[2] *n.* marsh plant with slender pithy stem; the stems as material for baskets

**rusk** *n.* kind of sweet raised bread *esp.* used for feeding babies

**rus·set** (RUS-it) *adj.* reddish-brown —*n.* the color; apple with skin of this color

**rust** *n.* reddish-brown coating formed on iron by oxidation; disease of plants —*v.* contract, affect with rust —**rust'y** *adj.* (**rust·i·er, rust·i·est**) coated with rust, of rust color; out of practice —**rust'proof** *adj.*

**rus·tic** (RUS-tik) *adj.* of, or as of, country people; rural; of rough manufacture; made of untrimmed tree limbs —*n.* country person, peasant —**rus'ti·cate** *v.* (**-cat·ed, -cat·ing**) send into, house in, country —*vi.* live a country life

**rus·tle**[1] (RUS-əl) *vi.* (**-tled, -tling**) make sound as of blown dead leaves *etc.* —*n.* this sound

**rus·tle**[2] *vt.* (**-tled, -tling**) steal (cattle) —**rus'tler** *n.* cattle thief

**rut**[1] *n.* furrow made by wheel; settled habit or way of living; groove —**rut'ty** *adj.* (**-ti·er, -ti·est**)

**rut**[2] *n.* periodic sexual excitement among animals —*vi.* (**rut·ted, rut·ting**) be under influence of this

**ruth·less** (ROOTH-lis) adj. pitiless, merciless

**rye** (rī) n. grain used for forage and bread; plant bearing it; whiskey made from rye

# S

**S** Chem. sulfur

**Sab·bath** (SAB-əth) n. Saturday, devoted to worship and rest from work in Judaism and certain Christian churches; Sunday, observed by Christians as day of worship and rest —**sab·bat·i·cal** (sə-BAT-i-kəl) adj./n. (denoting) leave granted to university staff etc. for study

**sa·ber** (SAY-bər) n. curved cavalry sword; fencing sword having two cutting edges and blunt point

**sa·ble** (SAY-bəl) n. small weasellike animal of cold regions; its fur; black —adj. black

**sab·o·tage** (SAB-ə-tahzh) n. intentional damage done to roads, machines etc.; escape secretly in war —v. (-taged, -tag·ing) —**sab·o·teur** (sab-ə-TUR) n.

**sac** (sak) n. pouchlike structure in an animal or vegetable body

**sac·cha·rin** (SAK-ər-in) n. artificial sweetener —**sac·cha·rine** (-in) adj. lit./fig. excessively sweet

**sac·er·do·tal** (sas-ər-DOHT-l) adj. of priests

**sa·chet** (sa-SHAY) n. small envelope or bag, esp. one holding scented powder

**sack** (sak) n. large bag, orig. of coarse material; sl. dismissal; sl. bed —vt. pillage (captured town); sl. fire (person) from a job —**sack'ing** n. material for sacks —**sack·cloth** (SAK-

klawth) n. coarse fabric used for sacks and worn as sign of mourning

**sac·ra·ment** (SAK-rə-mənt) n. one of certain ceremonies of Christian church esp. Eucharist —**sac·ra·men'tal** adj.

**sa·cred** (SAY-krid) adj. dedicated, regarded as holy; set apart, reserved; inviolable; connected with, intended for religious purpose

**sac·ri·fice** (SAK-rə-fis) n. giving something up for sake of something else; act of giving up; thing so given up; making of offering to a god; thing offered —vt. (-ficed, -fic·ing) offer as sacrifice; give up; sell at very cheap price —**sac·ri·fi'cial** (-FISH-l) adj.

**sac·ri·lege** (SAK-rə-lij) n. misuse, desecration of something sacred —**sac·ri·le'gious** (-LEEJ-əs) adj. profane; desecrating

**sac·ris·ty** (SAK-ri-stee) n. (pl. -ties) room where sacred vessels etc. are kept

**sac·ro·sanct** (SAK-roh-sangkt) adj. preserved by religious fear against desecration or violence; inviolable

**sac·rum** (SAK-rəm) n. (pl. sac·ra pr. SAK-rə) five vertebrae forming compound bone at base of spinal column

**sad** adj. (sad·der, sad·dest) sorrowful; unsatisfactory, deplorable —**sad·den** (SAD-n) vt. make sad

**sad·dle** (SAD-l) n. rider's seat to fasten on horse, bicycle etc.; anything resembling a saddle; cut of mutton, venison etc. for roasting; ridge of hill —vt. (-dled, -dling) put saddle on; lay burden, responsibility on —adj. resembling a saddle, as in **sad·dle·back**

**sa·dism** (SAY-diz-əm) n. form of (sexual) perversion marked by

love of inflicting pain —**sa′dist** n.
—**sa·dis·tic** (sə-DIS-tik) adj.

**sa·fa·ri** (sə-FAH-ree) n. (party
making) overland (hunting) journey, esp. in Africa —**safari park**
park where lions etc. may be
viewed by public from automobiles

**safe** (sayf) adj. (**saf·er**, **saf·est**)
secure, protected; uninjured, out
of danger; not involving risk;
trustworthy; sure, reliable; cautious —n. strong lockable container; structure for storing meat
etc. —**safe′ly** adv. —**safe′ty** n.
—**safe-conduct** (KON-dukt) n. a
permit to pass somewhere
—**safe′guard** (-gahrd) n. protection —vt. protect —**safety glass**
glass resistant to fragmenting
when broken

**saf·fron** (SAF-rən) n. crocus; orange colored flavoring obtained
from it; the color —adj. orange

**sag** vi. (**sagged**, **sagging**) sink in
middle; hang sideways; curve
downward under pressure; give
way; tire; (of clothes) hang loosely —n. droop

**sa·ga** (SAH-gə) n. legend of Norse
heroes; any long (heroic) story

**sa·ga·cious** (sə-GAY-shəs) adj.
wise —**sa·ga′cious·ly** adv. —**sa·
gac′i·ty** (-GAS-i-tee) n.

**sage**[1] (sayj) n. very wise person
—adj. (**sag·er**, **sag·est**) wise

**sage**[2] n. aromatic herb

**said** (sed) pt./pp. of SAY

**sail** (sayl) n. piece of fabric
stretched to catch wind for propelling ship etc.; act of sailing;
journey upon the water; ships
collectively; arm of windmill
—vi. travel by water; move
smoothly; begin voyage —vt.
navigate —**sail′or** n. seaman; one
who sails —**sail′board** (-bord) n.
craft used for windsurfing like

surfboard with mast and single
sail

**saint** (saynt) n. (title of) person
formally recognized (esp. by R.C.
Church) after death, as having
gained by holy deeds a special
place in heaven; exceptionally
good person —**saint′ed** (-id) adj.
canonized; sacred —**saint′li·ness**
(-nis) n. holiness —**saint′ly** adj.

**sake**[1] (sayk) n. cause, account;
end, purpose —**for the sake of** in
behalf of; to please or benefit

**sa·ke**[2] (SAH-kee) n. Japanese alcoholic drink made of fermented
rice

**sa·laam** (sə-LAHM) n. bow of salu-
tation, mark of respect in East
—vt. salute

**salable** adj. see SALE

**sa·la·cious** (sə-LAY-shəs) adj. excessively concerned with sex,
lewd

**sal·ad** (SAL-əd) n. mixed vegetables, or fruit, used as food without
cooking, oft. combined with fish,
meat etc. —adj. —**salad days** period of youthful inexperience
—**salad dressing** oil, vinegar,
herbs etc. mixed together as
sauce for salad

**sal·a·man·der** (SAL-ə-man-dər)
n. variety of lizard; mythical
lizardlike fire spirit; portable
space heater

**sa·la·mi** (sə-LAH-mee) n. variety
of highly-spiced sausage

**sal·a·ry** (SAL-ə-ree) n. (pl. -**ries**)
fixed regular payment to persons
employed usu. in nonmanual
work —**sal′a·ried** adj.

**sale** (sayl) n. selling; selling of
goods at unusually low prices;
auction —**sal′a·ble** adj. capable
of being sold —**sales′per·son** n.
one who sells goods etc. in store;
one traveling to sell goods, esp.
as representative of firm
—**sales′man·ship** n. art of selling

or presenting goods in most effective way

**sa·li·ent** (SAY-lee-ənt) *adj.* prominent, noticeable; jutting out —*n.* salient angle, *esp.* in fortification or line of battle —**sa'li·ent·ly** *adv.*

**sa·line** (SAY-leen) *adj.* containing, consisting of a chemical salt, *esp.* common salt; salty —**sa·lin·i·ty** (sə-LIN-i-tee) *n.*

**sa·li·va** (sə-LI-və) *n.* liquid that forms in mouth, spittle —**sal·i·vary** (SAL-ə-ver-ee) *adj.* —**sal'i·vate** *v.* (-vat·ed, -vat·ing)

**sal·low** (SAL-oh) *adj.* of unhealthy pale or yellowish color

**sal·ly** (SAL-ee) *n.* (*pl.* -lies) rushing out, *esp.* by troops; outburst; witty remark —*vi.* (-lied, -ly·ing) rush; set out

**salm·on** (SAM-ən) *n.* large silvery fish with orange-pink flesh valued as food; color of its flesh —*adj.* of this color

**sal·mo·nel·la** (sal-mə-NEL-ə) *n.* (*pl.* -lae *pr.* -nee) bacteria causing disease (*esp.* food poisoning)

**sa·lon** (sə-LON) *n.* (reception room for) guests in fashionable household; commercial premises of hairdressers, beauticians *etc.*

**sa·loon** (sə-LOON) *n.* principal cabin or sitting room in passenger ship; bar; public room for specified use, *eg* billiards

**salt** (sawlt) *n.* white powdery or granular crystalline substance consisting mainly of sodium chloride, used to season or preserve food; chemical compound of acid and metal; wit —*vt.* season, sprinkle with, spread, preserve with salt —**salt'less** (-less) *adj.* —**salt'y** *adj.* (salt·i·er, salt·i·est) of, like salt —**old salt** sailor —**salt'cel·lar** (-sel-ər) *n.* salt shaker —**salt lick** deposit, block of salt licked by game, cattle *etc.* —**salt pan** *n.* depression encrusted with

salt after partial draining away of water —**salt·pe·ter** (sawlt-PEE-tər) *n.* potassium nitrate used in gunpowder —**with a pinch, grain, of salt** allowing for exaggeration —**worth one's salt** efficient

**sa·lu·bri·ous** (sə-LOO-bree-əs) *adj.* favorable to health, beneficial

**Sa·lu·ki** (sə-LOO-kee) *n.* tall hound with silky coat

**sal·u·tary** (SAL-yə-ter-ee) *adj.* wholesome, resulting in good

**sa·lute** (sə-LOOT) *v.* (-lut·ed, -lut·ing) —*vt.* greet with words or sign; acknowledge with praise —*vi.* perform military salute —*n.* word, sign by which one greets another; motion of arm as mark of respect to superior *etc.* in military usage; firing of guns as military greeting of honor —**sal·u·ta'tion** (-yə-TAY-shən) *n.*

**sal·vage** (SAL-vij) *n.* act of saving ship or other property from danger of loss; property so saved —*vt.* (-vaged, -vag·ing)

**sal·va·tion** (sal-VAY-shən) *n.* fact or state of being saved, *esp.* of soul

**salve** (sav) *n.* healing ointment —*vt.* (salved, salv·ing) anoint with such, soothe

**sal·ver** (SAL-vər) *n.* (silver) tray for presentation of food, letters *etc.*

**sal·vo** (SAL-voh) *n.* (*pl.* -vos, -voes) simultaneous discharge of guns *etc.*

**Sam.** Samuel

**Sa·mar·i·tan** (sə-MAR-i-tn) *n.* native of ancient Samaria; (s-) benevolent person

**sam·ba** (SAM-bə) *n.* dance of S Amer. origin; music for it

**same** (saym) *adj.* identical, not different, unchanged; uniform; just mentioned previously

—**same′ness** (-nis) *n.* similarity; monotony

**sam·o·var** (SAM-ɔ-vahr) *n.* Russian tea urn

**Sam·o·yed** (sam-ɔ-YED) *n.* dog with thick white coat and tightly curled tail

**sam′pan** *n.* small oriental boat

**sam·ple** (SAM-pɔl) *n.* specimen —*vt.* (-pled, -pling) take, give sample of; try; test; select —**sam′pler** *n.* beginner's exercise in embroidery —**sampling** *n.* the taking of samples; sample

**sam·u·rai** (SAM-uu-rī) *n.* (*pl. same form*) member of ancient Japanese warrior caste

**san·a·to·ri·um** (san-ɔ-TOR-ee-ɔm) *n.* (*pl.* -ri·ums, -ri·a *pr.* -ree-ɔ) hospital, *esp.* for chronically ill; health resort

**sanc·ti·fy** (SANGK-tɔ-fī) *vt.* (-fied, -fying) set apart as holy; free from sin —**sanc·ti·fi·ca·tion** *n.* —**sanc′ti·ty** *n.* (*pl.* -ti·ties) saintliness; sacredness; inviolability —**sanc′tu·ar·y** (-choo-er-ee) *n.* (*pl.* -ar·ies) holy place; part of church nearest altar; place of special holiness in synagogue; place where fugitive was safe from arrest or violence; place protected by law where animals *etc.* can live without interference —**sanc′tum** (SANGK-tɔm) *n.* sacred place or shrine; person's private room —**sanctum sanc·to·rum** (sangk-TOR-ɔm) *n.* holy of holies in Temple in Jerusalem; sanctum

**sanc·ti·mo·ni·ous** (sangk-tɔ-MOH-nee-ɔs) *adj.* making a show of piety, holiness —**sanc·ti·mo′ni·ous·ness** *n.*

**sanc·tion** (SANGK-shɔn) *n.* permission, authorization; penalty for breaking law —*pl.* boycott or other coercive measure *esp.* by one country against another re-garded as having violated a law, right *etc.* —*vt.* allow, authorize, permit

**sand** *n.* substance consisting of small grains of rock or mineral, *esp.* on beach or in desert —*pl.* stretches or banks of this, usually forming seashore —*vt.* polish, smooth with sandpaper; cover, mix with sand —**sand′er** *n.* (power) tool for smoothing surfaces —**sand′y** *adj.* (sand·i·er, sand·i·est) like sand; sand-colored; consisting of, covered with sand —**sand′bag** *n.* bag filled with sand or soil, used as protection against gunfire, floodwater *etc.* and as weapon —*vt.* (-bagged, -bagging) beat, hit with sandbag; *inf.* in football, tackle passer as if from ambush —**sand′blast** *n.* jet of sand blown from a nozzle under pressure for cleaning, grinding *etc.* —*vt.* —**sand′pa·per** *n.* paper with sand stuck on it for scraping or polishing wood *etc.* —**sand′pit, sand′box** *n.* quantity of sand for children to play in —**sand′stone** *n.* rock composed of sand

**san·dal** (SAN-dl) *n.* shoe consisting of sole attached by straps

**sand′wich** *n.* two slices of bread with meat or other food between; anything resembling this —*vt.* insert between two other things

**sane** (sayn) *adj.* (san·er, san·est) of sound mind; sensible, rational —**san·i·ty** (SAN-i-tee) *n.*

**sang** *pt. of* SING

**sang-froid** (sahn-FRWAH) *n.* Fr. composure; indifference; self-possession

**san·guine** (SANG-gwin) *adj.* cheerful, confident; ruddy in complexion —**san·gui·nar·y** (SANG-gwɔ-ner-ee) *adj.* accompanied by bloodshed; bloodthirsty

—**san'guine·ly** adv. hopefully, confidently

**san·i·tar·y** (SAN-i-ter-ee) adj. helping protection of health against dirt etc. —**san·i·ta'tion** n. measures, apparatus for preservation of public health

**sank** pt. of SINK

**San'skrit** n. ancient language of India

**sap**[1] n. moisture that circulates in plants; energy —v. (sapped, sapping) drain off sap —**sap'ling** n. young tree

**sap**[2] v. (sapped, sapping) undermine; destroy insidiously; weaken —n. trench dug in order to approach or undermine an enemy position —**sap'per** (-pər) n. soldier doing this

**sap**[3] n. sl. foolish, gullible person

**sa·pi·ent** (SAY-pee-ənt) adj. (usu. ironical) wise; discerning; shrewd; knowing —**sa'pi·ence** n.

**Sap'phic** (SAF-ik) adj. of Sappho, a Grecian poet; denoting a kind of verse —n. Sapphic verse —**sap'phism** (SAF-iz-əm) n. lesbianism

**sap·phire** (SAF-īr) n. (usu. blue) precious stone; deep blue —adj.

**sar·a·band** (SAR-ə-band) n. slow, stately Spanish dance; music for it

**sar·casm** (SAHR-kaz-əm) n. bitter or wounding ironic remark; such remarks; taunt; sneer; irony; use of such expressions —**sar·cas'tic** (-KAS-tik) adj. —**sar·cas'ti·cal·ly** adv.

**sar·coph·a·gous** (sahr-KOF-ə-gəs) adj. carnivorous

**sar·coph·a·gus** (sahr-KOF-ə-gəs) n. (pl. -gi pr. -jī) stone coffin

**sar·dine** (sahr-DEEN) n. small fish of herring family, usu. preserved in oil

**sar·don·ic** (sahr-DON-ik) adj.

characterized by irony, mockery or derision

**sar·don·yx** (sahr-DON-iks) n. gemstone, variety of chalcedony

**sar·gas·sum** (sahr-GAS-əm), **sar·gas·so** (-GAS-oh) n. gulfweed, type of floating seaweed

**sa·ri** (SAHR-ee) n. (pl. -ris) Hindu woman's robe

**sa·rong** (sə-RAWNG) n. skirtlike garment worn in Asian and Pacific countries

**sar·sa·pa·ril·la** (sas-pə-RIL-ə) n. (flavor of) drink like root beer orig. made from root of plant

**sar·to·ri·al** (sahr-TOR-ee-əl) adj. of tailor, tailoring, or men's clothes

**sash**[1] n. decorative belt, ribbon, wound around the body

**sash**[2] n. window frame opened by moving up and down in grooves

**sat** pt./pp. of SIT

**Sa·tan** (SAYT-n) n. the devil —**sa·tan'ic** (sə-TAN-ik), **sa·tan'i·cal** adj. devilish, fiendish

**satch·el** (SACH-əl) n. small bag, oft. with shoulder strap

**sate** (sayt) vt. (sat·ed, sat·ing) satisfy a desire or appetite fully or excessively

**sat·el·lite** (SAT-l-īt) n. celestial body or manmade projectile orbiting planet; person, country etc. dependent on another

**sa·ti·ate** (SAY-shee-ayt) vt. (-at·ed, -at·ing) satisfy to the full; surfeit —**sa·ti·a'tion** n. —**sa·ti·e·ty** (sə-TĪ-i-tee) n. feeling of having had too much

**sat·in** (SAT-n) n. fabric (of silk, nylon etc.) with glossy surface on one side —**sat'in·y** adj. of, like satin

**sat·ire** (SAT-īr) n. composition in which vice, folly or foolish person is held up to ridicule; use of ridicule or sarcasm to expose vice and folly —sa·tir·i·cal (sə-TIR-i-kəl) *adj.* of nature of satire; sarcastic; bitter —sat'i·rist *n.* —sat'i·rize *vt.* (-rized, -riz·ing) make object of satire; censure thus

sat·is·fy (SAT-is-fi) *vt.* (-fied, -fy·ing) content, meet wishes of; pay; fulfill, supply adequately; convince —sat·is·fac'tion *n.* —sat·is·fac'to·ry *adj.*

sa·trap (SAY-trap) *n.* provincial governor in ancient Persia; subordinate ruler, oft. despotic

sat·u·rate (SACH-ə-rayt) *vt.* (-rat·ed, -rat·ing) soak thoroughly; cause to absorb maximum amount; *Chem.* cause substance to combine to its full capacity with another; shell or bomb heavily —sat·u·ra'tion *n.* act, result of saturating

Sat·urn (SAT-ərn) *n.* Roman god; one of planets —sat·ur·nine (SAT-ər-nin) *adj.* gloomy; sluggish in temperament, dull, morose —Sat·ur·na'li·a (-NAY-lee-ə) *n.* (*pl.* -li·as) ancient festival of Saturn; (*also* s-) noisy revelry, orgy

sa·tyr (SAY-tər) *n.* woodland deity, part man, part goat; lustful man

sauce (saws) *n.* liquid added to food to enhance flavor; *inf.* impudence; *sl.* whiskey —*vt.* (sauced, sauc·ing) add sauce to; *inf.* be cheeky, impudent to —sau'ci·ly *adv.* —sau'cy *adj.* (-ci·er, -ci·est) impudent —sauce'pan *n.* cooking pot with long handle

sau·cer (SAW-sər) *n.* curved plate put under cup; shallow depression

sau·er·bra·ten (SOW-ər-braht-n) *n.* German pot roast marinated in vinegar *etc.*

sau·er·kraut (SOW-ər-krowt) *n.*

German dish of finely shredded and pickled cabbage

sau·na (SAW-nə) *n.* steam bath, *orig.* Finnish

saun·ter (SAWN-tər) *vi.* walk in leisurely manner, stroll —*n.* leisurely walk or stroll

sau·ri·an (SOR-ee-ən) *n.* one of the order of reptiles including the alligator, lizard *etc.*

sau·sage (SAW-sij) *n.* chopped seasoned meat enclosed in thin tube of animal intestine or synthetic material —sausage meat meat prepared for this

sau·té (soh-TAY) *adj.* cooked or browned in pan with little butter, oil *etc.* —*vt.* (-téed, -té·ing) cook in this way

Sau·ternes (soh-TURN) *n.* sweet white Fr. wine —sau·terne *n.* California or other wine resembling this

sav·age (SAV-ij) *adj.* wild; ferocious; brutal; uncivilized, primitive —*n.* member of savage tribe, barbarian —*vt.* (-aged, -ag·ing) attack ferociously —sav'age·ry *n.*

sa·van·na(h) (sə-VAN-ə) *n.* extensive open grassy plain

sa·vant (sa-VAHNT) *n.* person of learning

save (sayv) *v.* (saved, sav·ing) —*vt.* rescue, preserve; protect; secure; keep for future, lay by; prevent need of; spare —*vi.* lay by money —*prep.* except —*conj.* but —saving *adj.* frugal; thrifty; delivering from sin; excepting; compensating —*prep.* except —*n.* economy —*pl.* money, earnings put by for future use

sav·ior (SAYV-yər) *n.* person who rescues another; (S-) Christ

sa·voir-faire (sav-wahr-FAIR) *n.* Fr. ability to do, say, the right thing in any situation

sa·vor (SAY-vər) *n.* characteristic

taste; flavor; odor; distinctive quality —vi. have particular smell or taste; have suggestion (of) —vt. give flavor to; have flavor of; enjoy, appreciate —**sa'vor·y** adj. attractive to taste or smell; not sweet

**sa·vor·y** (SAY-və-ree) n. (pl. -vor·ies) aromatic herb used in cooking

**sav·vy** (SAV-ee) vt. inf. (-vied, -vy·ing) understand —n. wits, intelligence

**saw**[1] n. tool for cutting wood etc. by tearing it with toothed edge —v. (sawed, sawed or sawn, saw·ing) cut with saw; make movements of sawing —**saw'dust** n. fine wood fragments made in sawing —**saw'mill** n. mill where timber is sawed by machine into planks etc.

**saw**[2] pt. of SEE

**saw**[3] n. wise saying, proverb

**sax·i·frage** (SAK-sə-frij) n. alpine or rock plant

**Sax·on** (SAK-sən) n. member of West Germanic people who settled widely in Europe in the early Middle Ages —adj.

**sax·o·phone** (SAK-sə-fohn) n. keyed wind instrument

**say** vt. (said pr. sed, say·ing; says pr. sez 3rd pers. sing. pres. ind.) speak; pronounce; state; express; take as example or as near enough; form and deliver opinion —n. what one has to say; chance of saying it; share in decision —**saying** n. maxim, proverb

**Sb** Chem. antimony

**scab** (skab) n. crust formed over wound; skin disease; disease of plants; strikebreaker —**scab'by** (-bi·er, -bi·est) adj.

**scab·bard** (SKAB-ərd) n. sheath for sword or dagger

**scab·rous** (SKAYB-rəs) adj. having rough surface; thorny; indecent; risky

**scaf·fold** (SKAF-əld) n. temporary platform for workmen; gallows —**scaf'fold·ing** n. (material for building) scaffold

**sca·lar** (SKAY-lər) n. variable quantity, eg time, having magnitude but no direction —adj.

**scald** (skawld) vt. burn with hot liquid or steam; clean, sterilize with boiling water; heat (liquid) almost to boiling point —n. injury by scalding

**scale**[1] (skayl) n. one of the thin, overlapping plates covering fishes and reptiles; thin flake; incrustation that forms in boilers etc. —v. (scaled, scal·ing) —vt. remove scales from —vi. come off in scales —**scal'y** adj. (scal·i·er, scal·i·est) resembling or covered in scales —**scale insect** plant pest covered by waxy secretion

**scale**[2] (chiefly in pl.) weighing instrument —vt. (scaled, scal·ing) weigh in scales; have weight of

**scale**[3] n. graduated table or sequence of marks at regular intervals used as reference or for fixing standards, as in making measurements; in music etc.; ratio of size between a thing and a model or map of it; (relative) degree, extent —vt. (scaled, scal·ing) climb —**scale up** or **down** increase or decrease proportionately

**sca·lene** (skay-LEEN) adj. (of triangle) with three unequal sides

**scal·lop** (SKOL-əp) n. edible shellfish; edging in small curves like edge of scallop shell —vt. shape like scallop shell; cook in scallop shell or dish like one

**scalp** (skalp) n. skin and hair of top of head —vt. cut off scalp of

**scal·pel** (SKAL-pəl) n. small surgical knife

**scamp** (skamp) n. mischievous person or child —v. do or make hastily or carelessly

**scamp·er** (SKAM-pər) vi. run about; run hastily from place to place —n.

**scam·pi** (SKAM-pee) n. (pl. same form) large shrimp; dish of these sautéed in oil or butter and garlic

**scan** (skan) v. (scanned, scanning) look at carefully, scrutinize; measure or read (verse) by metrical feet; examine, search by systematically varying the direction of a radar or sonar beam; glance over quickly; (of verse) conform to metrical rules —n. scanning —**scan'ner** n. device, esp. electronic, that scans —**scan'sion** (-shən) n.

**scan·dal** (SKAN-dl) n. action, event generally considered disgraceful; malicious gossip —**scan'dal·ize** (-ized, -iz·ing) n. shock —**scan'dal·ous** (-dl-əs) adj. outrageous, disgraceful

**scant** (skant) adj. (-er, -est) barely sufficient or not sufficient —**scant'i·ly** adv. —**scant'y** (scant·i·er, scant·i·est) adj. —**scant·ies** (SKAN-teez) n. very brief underpants esp. for women

**scape·goat** (SKAYP-goht) n. person bearing blame due to others —**scape'grace** (-grays) n. rascal; unscrupulous person

**scap·u·la** (SKAP-yə-lə) n. (pl. -las) shoulder blade —**scap'u·lar** (-lər) adj. of scapula n. loose sleeveless monastic garment

**scar** (skar) n. mark left by healed wound, burn or sore; change resulting from emotional distress —v. (scarred, scar·ring) mark, heal with scar

**scar·ab** (SKA-rəb) n. sacred beetle of ancient Egypt; gem cut in shape of this

**scarce** (skairs) adj. hard to find; existing or available in insufficient quantity; uncommon —**scarce'ly** adv. only just; not quite; definitely or probably not —**scar'ci·ty** (-si-tee) n.

**scare** (skair) vt. (scared, scaring) frighten —n. fright, sudden panic —**scar'y** adj. (scar·i·er, scar·i·est) —**scare'crow** (-kroh) n. thing set up to frighten birds from crops; badly dressed or miserable looking person —**scare·mon·ger** (-mung-gər) n. one who spreads alarming rumors

**scarf¹** (skarf) n. (pl. scarfs or scarves) long narrow strip, large piece of material to put around neck, head etc.

**scarf²** n. (pl. scarfs) part cut away from each of two pieces of timber to join them edge to edge longitudinally; joint so made —vt. cut or join in this way

**scar·i·fy** (SKA-rə-fi) vt. (-fied, -fy·ing) scratch, cut slightly all over; lacerate; stir surface soil of; criticize mercilessly

**scar·let** (SKAHR-lit) n. a brilliant red color; cloth or clothing of this color —adj. of this color; immoral, esp. unchaste —**scarlet fever** infectious fever with scarlet rash

**scarp** (skahrp) n. steep slope; inside slope of ditch in fortifications

**scathe** (skayth) (usu. now as pp./adj. scathed and un·scathed) n. injury, harm, damage —vt. (scathed, scath·ing) injure, damage —**scath'ing** adj. harshly critical; cutting; damaging

**scat·ter** (SKAT-ər) v. throw in various directions; put here and there; sprinkle —vi. disperse —n. —**scat'ter·brain** (-brayn) n. silly, careless person

**scav·enge** (SKAV-inj) v. (-enged, -eng·ing) search for (anything usable) usu. among discarded material —**scav'en·ger** n. person who scavenges; animal, bird that feeds on refuse

**scene** (seen) n. place of action of novel, play etc.; place of any action; subdivision of play; view; episode; display of strong emotion —**scen'er·y** n. (pl. -er·ies) natural features of area; constructions of wood, canvas etc. used on stage to represent a place where action is happening —**sce'nic** adj. picturesque; of or on the stage —**sce·nar·i·o** (si-NAIR-ee-oh) n. (pl. -i·os) summary of plot (of play etc.) or plan

**scent** (sent) n. distinctive smell, esp. pleasant one; trail, clue; perfume —vt. detect or track (by smell); suspect, sense; fill with fragrance

**scep·ter** (SEP-tər) n. ornamental staff as symbol of royal power; royal dignity

**sched·ule** (SKEJ-uul) n. plan of procedure for a project; list; timetable —vt. (-uled, -ul·ing) enter in schedule; plan to occur at certain time —**on schedule** on time

**sche·ma** (SKEE-mə) n. (pl. -ma·ta pr. -mə·tə, -mas) overall plan or diagram —**sche·mat'ic** adj. presented as plan or diagram —**sche'ma·tize** (-tīz) v. (-tized, -tiz·ing)

**scheme** (skeem) n. plan, design; project; outline —v. (schemed, schem·ing) devise, plan, esp. in underhand manner —**schem'er** n.

**scher·zo** (SKERT-soh) n. Mus. light playful composition

**schism** (SIZ-əm) n. (group resulting from) division in political party, church etc. —**schis·mat'ic** n./adj.

**schist** (shist) n. crystalline rock that splits into layers

**schiz·o·phre·ni·a** (skit-sə-FREE-nee-ə) n. mental disorder involving deterioration of, confusion about personality —**schiz·o·phren'ic** (-FREN-ik) adj./n. —**schiz'oid** (-soid) adj. relating to schizophrenia

**schmaltz** (shmahlts) n. excessive sentimentality —**schmaltz'y** adj. (schmaltz·i·er, schmaltz·i·est)

**schnapps** (shnops) n. spirit distilled from potatoes; any strong spirit

**schnit·zel** (SHNIT-səl) n. thin slice of meat, esp. veal, as WIENER SCHNITZEL

**scholar** n. see SCHOOL¹

**school¹** (skool) n. institution for teaching children or for giving instruction in any subject; buildings of such institution; group of thinkers, writers, artists etc. with principles or methods in common —vt. educate; bring under control, train —**school'man** n. medieval philosopher —**schol'ar** (SKOL-ər) n. learned person; one taught in school; one quick to learn —**schol'ar·ly** adj. learned, erudite —**schol'ar·ship** n. learning; prize, grant to student for payment of school or college fees —**scho·las'tic** (skə-LAS-tik) adj. of schools or scholars, or education; pedantic

**school²** n. large number (of fish, whales etc.)

**schoon·er** (SKOO-nər) n. fore-and-aft rigged vessel with two or more masts; tall glass

**schot·tische** (SHOT-ish) n. kind of dance; music for this

**sci·at·i·ca** (sī-AT-i-kə) n. neuralgia of hip and thigh; pain in sciatic nerve —**sci·at'ic** *adj.* of the hip; of sciatica

**sci·ence** (SI-əns) *n.* systematic study and knowledge of natural or physical phenomena; any branch of study concerned with observed material facts —**sci·en·tif'ic** *adj.* of the principles of science; systematic —**sci·en·tif'i·cal·ly** *adv.* —**sci'en·tist** *n.* one versed in natural sciences —**science fiction** stories set in the future making imaginative use of scientific knowledge

**scim·i·tar** (SIM-i-tər) *n.* oriental curved sword

**scin·til·late** (SIN-tl-ayt) *vi.* (-lated, -lat·ing) sparkle; be animated, witty, clever —**scin·til·la'tion** *n.*

**sci·on** (SI-ən) *n.* descendant, heir; slip for grafting

**scis·sors** (SIZ-ərs) *n. with sing. or pl. v.* (*esp.* pair of scissors) cutting instrument of two blades pivoted together —*n./adj.* (with) scissorlike action of limbs in swimming, athletics *etc.*, eg scissors kick

**scle·ro·sis** (skli-ROH-sis) *n.* (*pl.* -ses *pr.* -seez) a hardening of bodily organs, tissues *etc.* —**scle·rot'ic** (-ROT-ik) *adj.*

**scoff** (skof) *vt.* express derision for —*n.* derision; mocking words —**scoff'er** *n.*

**scold** (skohld) *v.* find fault; reprimand, be angry with —*n.* someone who does this —**scold'ing** *n.*

**sconce** (skons) *n.* bracket candlestick on wall

**scone** (skohn) *n.* small plain biscuit baked on griddle or in oven

**scoop** (skoop) *n.* small shovellike tool for ladling, hollowing out *etc.*; *inf.* exclusive news item; *inf.* information —*vt.* ladle out; hollow out, rake in with scoop; make

sudden profit; beat (rival newspaper *etc.*)

**scoot** (skoot) *vi. inf.* move off quickly —**scoot'er** *n.* child's vehicle propelled by pushing on ground with one foot; light motorcycle *also* motor scooter

**scope** (skohp) *n.* range of activity or application; room, opportunity

**scorch** (skorch) *v.* burn, be burned, on surface; parch; shrivel; wither —*n.* slight burn —**scorch'er** *n. inf.* very hot day

**score** (skor) *n.* points gained in game, competition; group of 20; a lot (*esp. pl.*); musical notation; mark or notch, *esp.* to keep tally; reason, account; grievance —*v.* (scored, scor·ing) —*vt.* gain points in game; mark; cross out; arrange music (for) —*vi.* keep tally of points; succeed

**scorn** (skorn) *n.* contempt, derision —*vt.* despise —**scorn'ful** (-fəl) *adj.* derisive —**scorn'ful·ly** *adv.*

**scor·pi·on** (SKOR-pee-ən) *n.* small lobster-shaped animal with sting at end of jointed tail

**Scot** (skot) *n.* native of Scotland —**Scot'tish** *adj.* (*also* **Scotch, Scots**)—**Scotch** *n.* Scotch whisky —**Scots'man** (-mən) *n.*

**scotch** (skoch) *vt.* put an end to; wound

**scot-free** (skot-free) *adj.* without harm or loss

**scoun·drel** (SKOWN-drəl) *n.* villain, blackguard —**scoun'drel·ly** *adj.*

**scour**[1] (skowr) *vt.* clean, polish by rubbing; clear or flush out

**scour**[2] *v.* move rapidly along or over (territory) in search of something

**scourge** (skurj) *n.* whip; lash; severe affliction; pest; calamity —*vt.* (scourged, scourg·ing) flog; punish severely

**scout** (skowt) *n.* one sent out to reconnoiter; (S-) member of Boy Scouts, Girl Scouts organizations to develop character and responsibility —*vi.* go out, act as scout; reconnoiter —**scout'mas·ter** *n.* leader of troop of Boy Scouts

**scow** (skow) *n.* unpowered barge

**scowl** (skowl) *vi.* frown gloomily or sullenly —*n.* angry or gloomy expression

**scrab·ble** (SKRAB-əl) *v.* (-bled, -bling) scrape at with hands, claws in disorderly manner —*n.* (S-) R word game

**scrag** (skrag) *n.* lean person or animal; lean end of a neck of mutton —**scrag'gy** *adj.* (-gi·er, -gi·est) thin, bony

**scrag·gly** (SKRAG-lee) *adj.* (-gli·er, -gli·est) untidy

**scram**[1] (skram) *v.* *inf.* (scrammed, scram·ming) (*oft. imp.*) go away hastily, get out

**scram**[2] *n.* emergency shutdown of nuclear reactor —*v.* (scrammed, scram·ming)

**scram·ble** (SKRAM-bəl) *v.* (-bled, -bling) —*vi.* move along or up by crawling, climbing *etc.*; struggle with others (for); (of aircraft, aircrew) take off hurriedly —*vt.* mix up; cook (eggs) beaten up with milk; render (speech) unintelligible by electronic device —*n.* scrambling; rough climb; disorderly proceeding; emergency takeoff of military aircraft

**scrap** (skrap) *n.* small piece or fragment; leftover material; *inf.* fight —*v.* (scrapped, scrap·ping) break up, discard as useless; fight —**scrap'py** *adj.* (-pi·er, -pi·est) unequal in quality; badly finished —**scrap'book** (-buuk) *n.* book in which newspaper clippings *etc.* are kept

**scrape** (skrayp) *vt.* (scraped, scrap·ing) rub with something sharp; clean, smooth thus; grate; scratch; rub with harsh noise —*n.* act, sound of scraping; awkward situation, *esp.* as result of escapade —**scrap'er** *n.* instrument for scraping; contrivance on which mud *etc.* is scraped from shoes

**scratch** (skrach) *vt.* score, make narrow surface wound with claws, nails, or anything pointed; make marks on with pointed instruments; scrape (skin) with nails to relieve itching; remove, withdraw from list, race *etc.* —*vi.* use claws or nails, *esp.* to relieve itching —*n.* wound, mark or sound made by scratching; line or starting point —*adj.* got together at short notice; impromptu; *Golf* without any allowance —**scratch'y** *adj.* (scratch·i·er, scratch·i·est) —**scratch hit** *Baseball* weak hit barely enabling batter to reach first base

**scrawl** (skrawl) *vt.* write, draw untidily —*n.* thing scrawled; careless writing

**scrawn·y** (SKRAW-nee) *adj.* (scrawn·i·er, scrawn·i·est) thin, bony

**scream** (skreem) *vi.* utter piercing cry, *esp.* of fear, pain *etc.*; be very obvious —*vt.* utter in a scream —*n.* shrill, piercing cry; *inf.* very funny person or thing

**scree** (skree) *n.* loose shifting stones; slope covered with these

**screech** (skreech) *vi./n.* scream

**screed** (skreed) *n.* long (tedious) letter, passage or speech; thin layer of cement; in masonry, board used to make level

**screen** (skreen) *n.* device to shelter from heat, light, draft, observation *etc.*; anything used for such purpose; mesh over doors, windows to keep out insects; white or silvered surface on which photographic images are projected; windscreen; wooden or stone partition in church —*vt.* shelter, hide; protect from detection; show (film); scrutinize; examine (group of people) for presence of disease, weapons *etc.*; examine for political motives; *Electricity* protect from stray electric or magnetic fields —**the screen** motion pictures generally

**screw** (skroo) *n.* (nail-like device or cylinder with) spiral thread cut to engage similar thread or to bore into material (wood *etc.*) to pin or fasten; anything resembling a screw in shape, esp. in spiral form; propeller; twist —*vt.* fasten with screw; twist around; extort —**screw'y** *adj. sl.* (**screw-i-er, screw-i-est**) crazy, eccentric —**screw'driv-er** *n.* tool for turning screws; drink of vodka and orange juice —**screw up** *sl.* bungle, distort

**scrib-ble** (SKRIB-əl) *v.* (**-bled, -bling**) write, draw carelessly; make meaningless marks with pen or pencil —*n.* something scribbled

**scribe** (skrīb) *n.* writer; copyist —*v.* (**scribed, scrib-ing**) scratch a line with pointed instrument

**scrim-mage** (SKRIM-ij) *n.* scuffle; *Football* a play —*v.* (**-maged, -mag-ing**) engage in scrimmage

**scrimp** (skrimp) *vt.* make too small or short; treat meanly —**scrimp'y** *adj.* (**scrimp-i-er, scrimp-i-est**)

**scrip** (skrip) *n.* written certificate *esp.* of holding fractional share of stock; paper certificates issued in place of money

**script** (skript) *n.* (system or style of) handwriting; written characters; written text of film, play, radio or television program —*vt.* write a script

**scrip-ture** (SKRIP-chər) *n.* sacred writings; (**S-**) the Bible —**scrip'tur-al** *adj.*

**scrof-u-la** (SKROF-yə-lə) *n.* tuberculosis of lymphatic glands, *esp.* of neck —**scrof'u-lous** (-ləs) *adj.*

**scroll** (skrohl) *n.* roll of parchment or paper; list; ornament shaped thus

**scro-tum** (SKROH-təm) *n.* (*pl.* **-tums**) pouch of skin containing testicles

**scrounge** (skrownj) *v.* (**scrounged, scroung-ing**) get without cost, by begging —**scroung'er** *n.*

**scrub**[1] (skrub) *vt.* (**scrubbed, scrub-bing**) clean with hard brush and water; scour; *sl.* cancel, get rid of —*n.* scrubbing —**scrubbing brush**

**scrub**[2] *n.* stunted trees; brushwood —**scrub'by** *adj.* (**-bi-er, -bi-est**) covered with scrub; stunted; shabby

**scruff** (skruf) *n.* nape (of neck)

**scrum** (skrum) *n.* *Rugby* restarting of play in which opposing packs of forwards push against each other to gain possession of the ball

**scru-ple** (SKROO-pəl) *n.* doubt or hesitation about what is morally right; weight of 20 grains —*vi.* (**-pled, -pling**) hesitate —**scru'pu-lous** (-pyə-ləs) *adj.* extremely conscientious; thorough, attentive to small points

**scru-ti-ny** (SKROOT-n-ee) *n.* (*pl.* **-nies**) close examination; critical investigation; searching look —**scru'ti-nize** *vt.* (**-nized, -niz-ing**) examine closely

**scu-ba** (SKOO-bə) *n./adj.* (relating to) *s*elf-*c*ontained *u*nderwater *b*reathing *a*pparatus

**scud** (skud) *vi.* (**scud-ded, scud-ding**) run fast; run before wind

**scuff** (skuf) *vi.* drag, scrape with

feet in walking —vt. scrape with feet; scratch (something) by scraping —n. act, sound of scuffing —pl. thong sandals —**scuffed** adj. (of shoes) scraped or slightly grazed

**scuf·fle** (SKUF-əl) vi. (-fled, -fling) fight in disorderly manner; shuffle —n.

**scull** (skul) n. oar used in stern of boat; short oar used in pairs —v. propel, move by means of scull(s)

**scul·ler·y** (SKUL-ə-ree) n. (pl. -ler·ies) place for washing dishes etc. —**scul·lion** (SKUL-yən) n. despicable person; kitchen servant doing menial work

**sculp·ture** (SKULP-chər) n. art of forming figures in relief or solid; product of this art —vt. (-tured, -tur·ing) represent by sculpture —**sculpt** v. —**sculp·tur·al** adj. with qualities proper to sculpture —**sculp·tor** n. (**sculp·tress** (-tris) fem.)

**scum** (skum) n. froth or other floating matter on liquid; waste part of anything; vile person(s) or thing(s) —**scum·my** adj. (-mi·er, -mi·est)

**scup·per** (SKUP-ər) n. hole in ship's side level with deck to carry off water

**scurf** (skurf) n. flaky matter on scalp, dandruff —**scurf·y** adj. (scurf·i·er, scurf·i·est)

**scur·ril·ous** (SKUR-ə-ləs) adj. coarse, indecently abusive —**scur·ril·i·ty** (skə-RIL-i-tee) n. pl. (-ties)

**scur·ry** (SKUR-ee) vi. (-ried, -ry·ing) run hastily —n. (pl. -ries) bustling haste; flurry

**scut·tle²** (SKUT-l) n. fireside container for coal

**scuttle²** vt. (-tled, -tling) rush away; run hurriedly —n.

**scuttle³** vt. (-tled, -tling) make

hole in ship to sink it; abandon, cause to be abandoned

**scur·vy** (SKUR-vee) n. disease caused by lack of vitamin C —adj. (-vi·er, -vi·est) afflicted with the disease; mean, contemptible

**scut·work** (SKUT-wurk) n. inf. menial work

**scythe** (sīth) n. manual implement with long curved blade for cutting grass, grain —vt. (scythed, scyth·ing) cut with scythe

**Se** Chem. selenium

**sea** (see) n. mass of salt water covering greater part of Earth; broad tract of this; waves; swell; large quantity; vast expanse —**sea'board** (-bord) n. coast —**sea'far·ing** (-fair·ing) adj. occupied in sea voyages —**sea horse** fish with bony plated body and horselike head —**sea lion** kind of large seal —**sea'man** (-mən) n. sailor —**sea'sick·ness** n. nausea caused by motion of ship —**sea'- sick** adj. —**sea urchin** marine animal, echinus —**sea'weed** n. plant growing in sea —**sea'- wor·thy** (-wurth·ee) adj. (-thi·er, -thi·est) in fit condition to put to sea

**seal¹** (seel) n. piece of metal or stone engraved with device for impression on wax etc.; impression thus made (on letters etc.); device, material preventing passage of water, air, oil etc. (also **seal'er**) —vt. affix seal to ratify, authorize; mark with stamp as evidence of some quality; keep close or secret; settle; make watertight, airtight etc.

**seal²** n. amphibious furred carnivorous mammal with flippers as limbs —vi. hunt seals —**seal'er** n. person or ship engaged in sealing —**seal′skin** *n.* skin, fur of seals

**seam** (seem) *n.* line of junction of two edges, *eg* of two pieces of cloth, or two planks; thin layer, stratum —*vt.* mark with furrows or wrinkles —**seam′less** (-lis) *adj.* —**seam′y** *adj.* (**seam·i·er, seam·i·est**) sordid; marked with seams —**seam′stress** (-stris) *n.* sewing woman

**sé·ance** (SAY-ahns) *n.* meeting of spiritualists

**sear** (seer) *vt.* scorch, brand with hot iron; deaden

**search** (surch) *v.* look over or through to find something; probe into, examine —*n.* act of searching; quest —**search′ing** *adj.* keen; thorough; severe —**search′light** *n.* powerful electric light with concentrated beam

**sea·son** (SEE-zən) *n.* one of four divisions of year associated with type of weather and stage of agriculture; period during which thing happens, grows, is active *etc.*; proper time —*vt.* flavor with salt, herbs *etc.*; make reliable or ready for use; make experienced —**sea′son·a·ble** *adj.* appropriate for the season; opportune; fit —**sea′son·al** (-əl) *adj.* depending on, varying with seasons —**sea′son·ing** *n.* flavoring —**in season** (of an animal) in heat —**season ticket** one for series of events within a certain time

**seat** (seet) *n.* thing for sitting on; buttocks; base; right to sit (*eg* in legislature *etc.*); place where something is located, centered; locality of disease, trouble *etc.*; country house —*vt.* make to sit; provide sitting accommodation for; install firmly

**se·ba·ceous** (si-BAY-shəs) *adj.* of, pert. to fat; secreting fat, oil

**se·cant** (SEE-kant) *n.* Math. (se-cant of an angle) reciprocal of its cosine; line that intersects a curve

**se·cede** (si-SEED) *vi.* (**-ced·ed, -ced·ing**) withdraw formally from federation, union *etc.* —**se·ces′sion** (-SESH-ən) *n.*

**se·clude** (si-KLOOD) *vt.* (**-clud·ed, -clud·ing**) guard from, remove from sight, view, contact with others —**secluded** *adj.* remote; private —**se·clu′sion** (-KLOO-zhən) *n.*

**sec·ond** (SEK-ənd) *adj.* next after first; alternate, additional; of lower quality —*n.* person or thing coming second; attendant; sixtieth part of minute; SI unit of time; moment; (*esp. pl.*) inferior goods —*vt.* support; support (motion in meeting) so that discussion may be in order —**sec·ond-hand′** *adj.* bought after use by another; not original —**second sight** faculty of seeing events before they occur

**sec·ond·ar·y** (SEK-ən-der-ee) *adj.* subsidiary, of less importance; developed from, or dependent on, something else; *Education* after primary stage —**sec′ond·ar·i·ly** *adv.*

**se·cret** (SEE-krit) *adj.* kept, meant to be kept from knowledge of others; hidden; private —*n.* thing kept secret —**se′cre·cy** (-krə-see) *n.* (*pl.* **-cies**) keeping or being kept secret —**se′cre·tive** *adj.* given to having secrets; uncommunicative; reticent —**se′cre·tive·ness** (-tiv-nis) *n.*

**sec·re·tar·y** (SEK-ri-ter-ee) *n.* (*pl.* **-tar·ies**) one employed by individual or organization to deal with papers and correspondence, keep records, prepare business *etc.*; member of presidential cabinet —**sec·re·tar′i·al** (-TAIR-ee-əl) *adj.* —**sec·re·tar′i·at** (-ət) *n.* body of secretaries; building occupied by secretarial staff

**se·crete** (si-KREET) *vt.* (-cret·ed, -cret·ing) hide; conceal; (of gland *etc.*) collect and supply particular substance in body —**se·cre'tion** *n.*

**sect** (sekt) *n.* group of people (within religious body *etc.*) with common interest; faction —**sec·tar'i·an** (-TAIR-ee-ən) *adj.* of a sect; narrow-minded

**sec·tion** (SEK-shən) *n.* part cut off; division; portion; distinct part of city, country, people *etc.*; cutting; drawing of anything as if cut through —**sec'tion·al** *adj.*

**sec·tor** (SEK-tər) *n.* part or subdivision; part of circle enclosed by two radii and the arc they cut off

**sec·u·lar** (SEK-yə-lər) *adj.* worldly; lay, not religious; not monastic; lasting for, or occurring once in, an age; centuries old —**sec'u·lar·ism** *n.* —**sec'u·lar·ist** *n.* one who believes that religion should have no place in civil affairs —**sec·u·lar·i·za'tion** *n.* —**sec'u·lar·ize** *vt.* (-ized, -iz·ing) transfer from religious to lay possession or use

**se·cure** (si-KYOOR) *adj.* safe; free from fear, anxiety; firmly fixed; certain, sure, confident —*vt.* (-cured, -cur·ing) gain possession of; make safe; free (creditor) from risk of loss; make firm —**se·cu'ri·ty** *n.* (*pl.* -ties) state of safety; protection; that which secures; assurance; anything given as bond, caution or pledge; one who becomes surety for another

**se·dan** (si-DAN) *n.* enclosed automobile body with two or four doors —**sedan chair** *Hist.* closed chair for one person, carried on poles by bearers

**se·date**[1] (si-DAYT) *adj.* calm, collected, serious

**sedate**[2] *vt.* (-dat·ed, -dat·ing) make calm by sedative —**se·da'tion** *n.* —**sed'a·tive** *adj.* having soothing or calming effect —*n.* sedative drug

**sed·en·ta·ry** (SED-n-ter-ee) *adj.* done sitting down; sitting much

**Se·der** (SAY-dər) *n.* ritual for the first or first two nights of Passover

**sed·i·ment** (SED-ə-mənt) *n.* matter that settles to the bottom of liquid; dregs, lees —**sed·i·men'ta·ry** *adj.*

**se·di·tion** (si-DISH-ən) *n.* speech or action threatening authority of a state —**se·di'tious** (-shəs) *adj.*

**se·duce** (si-DOOS) *vt.* (-duced, -duc·ing) persuade to commit some (wrong) deed, *esp.* sexual intercourse; tempt; attract —**se·duc'er** *n.* (**se·duc'tress** *fem.*) —**se·duc'tion** (-DUK-shən) *n.* —**se·duc'tive** *adj.* alluring; winning

**sed·u·lous** (SEJ-ə-ləs) *adj.* diligent; industrious; persevering, persistent —**se·du·li·ty** (si-DOO-li-tee) *n.*

**see**[1] *v.* (saw, seen, see·ing) perceive with eyes or mentally; observe; watch; find out; reflect; come to know; interview; make sure; accompany; perceive; consider; understand —**seeing** *conj.* since; in view of the fact that

**see**[2] *n.* diocese, office, or jurisdiction of bishop

**seed** *n.* reproductive germs of plants; one grain of this; such grains saved or used for sowing; origin; sperm; offspring —*vt.* sow with seed; arrange draw for tennis or other tournament, so that best players do not meet in early rounds —*vi.* produce seed

—**seed·ling** n. young plant raised from seed —**seed·y** adj. (**seed·i·er, seed·i·est**) shabby; gone to seed; unwell, ill

**seek** v. (sought pr. sawt, **seek·ing**) make search or inquiry for; search

**seem** vi. appear (to be or to do); look; appear to one's judgment —**seem·ing** adj. apparent but not real —**seem·ing·ly** adv.

**seem·ly** (SEEM-lee) adj. (**-li·er, -li·est**) becoming and proper —**seem·li·ness** (-nis) n.

**seen** pp. of SEE

**seep** vi. trickle through slowly, as water, ooze

**seer** n. prophet

**seer·suck·er** (SEER-suk-ər) n. light cotton fabric with slightly crinkled surface

**see·saw** n. game in which children sit at opposite ends of plank supported in middle and swing up and down; plank used for this —vi. move up and down

**seethe** (seeth) vi. (**seethed, seeth·ing**) boil, foam; be very agitated; be in constant movement (as large crowd etc.)

**seg·ment** (SEG-mənt) n. piece cut off; section —v. (SEG-ment) to divide into segments —**seg·men·ta'tion** n.

**seg·re·gate** (SEG-ri-gayt) vt. (**-gat·ed, -gat·ing**) set apart from rest; dissociate; separate; isolate —**seg·re·ga'tion** n.

**se·gue** (SAY-gway) vi. (**-gued, -gue·ing**) proceed from one section or piece of music to another without break; make a transition smoothly eg from one topic of conversation to another —n.

**seis·mic** (SĪZ-mik) adj. pert. to earthquakes —**seis'mo·graph** (-mə-graf) n. instrument to record earthquakes —**seis·mo·log'i·cal** adj. pert. to seismology —**seis·mol'o·gist** (-MOL-ə-jist) n. one versed in seismology —**seis·mol'o·gy** n. science concerned with study of earthquakes

**seize** (seez) v. (**seized, seiz·ing**) —vt. grasp; lay hold of; capture —vi. in machine, of bearing or piston, to stick tightly through overheating —**seiz·ure** (SEE-zhər) n. act of taking, esp. by legal writ, as goods; sudden onset of disease

**sel·dom** (SEL-dəm) adv. not often, rarely

**se·lect** (si-LEKT) vt. pick out, choose —adj. choice, picked; exclusive —**se·lec'tion** n. —**se·lec'tive** adj. —**se·lec·tiv'i·ty** n.

**se·le·ni·um** (si-LEE-nee-əm) n. nonmetallic element with photoelectric properties

**sel·e·nog·ra·phy** (sel-ə-NOG-rə-fee) n. study of surface of moon

**self** pron. (pl. **selves**), used reflexively or to express emphasis —adj. (of color etc.) same throughout, uniform —n. one's own person or individuality —**self'ish** adj. concerned unduly over personal profit or pleasure; lacking consideration for others; greedy —**self'ish·ly** adv. —**self'less** (-lis) adj. having no regard for self; unselfish

**self-** (comb. form) of oneself or itself, as in the words below

| | | |
|---|---|---|
| self-ad·dressed' | self-con·trol' | self-in·dul'gent |
| self-as·sured' | self-de·fense' | self-in'ter·est |
| self-cen'tered | self-de·ni'al | self-pit'y |
| self-con'fi·dent | self-em·ployed' | self-re·li'ant |
| self-con·tained' | self-ev'i·dent | self-sac'ri·fice |

**self-con·scious** (-KON-shəs) adj. unduly aware of oneself; conscious of one's acts or states

**self-de·ter·mi·na·tion** (-di-tur-mə-NAY-shən) n. the right of person or nation to decide for itself

**self-made** (-mayd) adj. having achieved wealth, status etc. by one's own efforts

**self-pos·sessed** (-pə-ZEST) adj. calm, composed —**self-pos·ses·sion** (-pə-ZESH-ən) n.

**self-re·spect′** (-ri-SPEKT) n. proper sense of one's own dignity and integrity

**self-right′eous** (-RI-chəs) adj. smugly sure of one's own virtue

**self-same** (-saym) adj. very same

**self-seek′ing** adj./n. (having) preoccupation with one's own interests

**self-serv′ice** (-SUR-vis) adj./n. (of) the serving of oneself in a store or restaurant

**self-suf·fi′cient** (-sə-FISH-ənt) adj. sufficient in itself; relying on one's own powers

**self-will′** n. obstinacy; willfullness —**self-willed′** adj. headstrong

**sell** v. (sold, sell·ing) hand over for a price; stock, have for sale; make someone accept; find purchasers; inf. betray, cheat —n. inf. hoax —**sell′er** n. —**sell′out** n. disposing of completely by selling; betrayal

**selt·zer** (SELT-sər) (**water**) n. effervescent (mineral) water

**sel·vage** (SEL-vij) n. finished, unfraying edge of cloth

**se·man·tic** (si-MAN-tik) adj. relating to meaning of words or symbols —**se·man′tics** n. with sing. v. study of linguistic meaning

**sem·a·phore** (SEM-ə-for) n. post with movable arms for signaling; system of signaling by human or mechanical arms

**sem·blance** (SEM-blans) n. (false) appearance; image, likeness

**se·men** (SEE-mən) n. fluid carrying sperm of male animals; sperm

**se·mes·ter** (si-MES-tər) n. (half-year) session of academic year in many universities, colleges

**sem·i** (SEM-I) n. inf. semitrailer

**semi-** (comb. form) half, partly, as in semicircle

**sem·i·breve** (SEM-ee-breev) n. musical note half the length of a breve

**sem·i·cir·cle** (SEM-i-sur-kəl) n. half of circle —**sem·i·cir′cu·lar** (-SUR-kyə-lər) adj.

**sem·i·co·lon** (SEM-i-koh-lən) n. punctuation mark (;)

**sem·i·de·tached** (sem-ee-di-TACHT) adj./n. (of) house joined to another on one side only

**sem·i·fi·nal** (sem-ee-FIN-l) n. match, round etc. before final

**sem·i·nal** (SEM-ə-nl) adj. capable of developing; influential, important; rudimentary; of semen or seed

**sem·i·nar** (SEM-ə-nahr) n. meeting of group of (students) for discussion

**sem·i·nar·y** (SEM-ə-ner-ee) n. (pl. -nar·ies) college for priests —**sem·i·nar′i·an** n. student at seminary

**sem·i·pre·cious** (sem-ee-PRESH-əs) adj. (of gemstones) having less value than precious stones

**sem·i·skilled** (sem-ee-SKILD) adj. partly skilled, trained but not for specialized work

self-sat′is·fied · · · · · · · · · · self-sup·port′ing

**Sem·ite** (SEM- īt) n. member of ancient and modern peoples including Jews and Arabs; Jew —**Se·mit·ic** (sə-MIT-ik) adj. denoting a Semite; Jewish

**sem·i·tone** (SEM-ee-tohn) n. musical half tone

**sem·i·trail·er** (SEM-i-tray-lər) n. trailer used for hauling freight, having wheels at back but supported by towing vehicle in front

**sem·o·li·na** (sem-ə-LEE-nə) n. milled product of durum wheat, used for pasta etc.

**sen·ate** (SEN-it) n. upper legislative body of country; upper council of university etc.—**sen·a·tor** (-ə-tər) n. —**sen·a·to·ri·al** (-TOR-ee-əl) adj.

**send** vt. (sent, send·ing) cause to go or be conveyed; dispatch; transmit (by radio)

**se·nile** (SEE-nīl) adj. showing weakness of old age —**se·nil·i·ty** (si-NIL-i-tee) n.

**sen·ior** (SEEN-yər) adj. superior in rank or standing; older —n. superior; elder person —**sen·ior·i·ty** (-YOR-i-tee) n.

**se·ñor** (sayn-YOR) n. Sp. title of respect, like Mr. —**se·ño·ra** n. Mrs. —**se·ño·ri·ta** (-REE-tə) n. Miss

**sen·sa·tion** (sen-SAY-shən) n. operation of sense, feeling, awareness; excited feeling, state of excitement; exciting event; strong impression; commotion —**sen·sa·tion·al** adj. producing great excitement; melodramatic; of perception by senses —**sen·sa·tion·al·ism** n. use of sensational language etc. to arouse intense emotional excitement; doctrine that sensations are basis of all knowledge

**sense** (sens) n. any of bodily faculties of perception or feeling; sensitiveness of any or all of these faculties; ability to perceive, mental alertness; consciousness; meaning; coherence, intelligible meaning; sound practical judgment —vt. (sensed, sens·ing) perceive; understand —**sense·less** (-lis) adj.

**sen·si·ble** (SEN-sə-bəl) adj. reasonable, wise; perceptible by senses; aware, mindful; considerable, appreciable —**sen·si·bil'·i·ty** n. ability to feel esp. emotional or moral feelings —**sen'·si·bly** adv.

**sen·si·tive** (SEN-si-tiv) adj. open to, acutely affected by, external impressions; easily affected or altered; easily upset by criticism; responsive to slight changes —**sen·si·tiv'·i·ty** n. —**sen'·si·tize** (tīz) vt. (-tized, -tiz·ing) make sensitive, esp. make (photographic film etc.) sensitive to light

**sen·sor** (SEN-sər) n. device that responds to stimulus

**sen·so·ry** (SEN-sə-ree) adj. relating to organs, operation, of senses

**sen·su·al** (SEN-shoo-əl) adj. of senses only and not of mind; given to pursuit of pleasures of sense; self-indulgent; licentious —**sen'su·al·ist** n.

**sen·su·ous** (SEN-shoo-əs) adj. stimulating, or apprehended by, senses esp. in aesthetic manner

**sent** pt./pp. of SEND

**sen·tence** (SEN-tns) n. combination of words that is complete as expressing a thought; judgment passed on criminal by court or judge —vt. (-tenced, -tenc·ing) pass sentence on, condemn —**sen·ten'tial** (-TEN-shəl) adj. of sentence —**sen·ten'tious** (-shəs) adj. full of axioms and maxims; pithy; pompously moralizing —**sen·ten'tious·ness** n.

**sen·tient** (SEN-shənt) adj. capable of feeling; feeling; thinking —sen'tience n.

sen·ti·ment (SEN-tə-mənt) n. tendency to be moved by feeling rather than reason; verbal expression of feeling; mental feeling, emotion; opinion —sen·ti·men'tal adj. given to indulgence in sentiment and in its expression; weak; sloppy —sen·ti·men'tal·i·ty n.

sen·ti·nel (SEN-tn-l) n. sentry

sen·try (SEN-tree) n. (pl. -tries) soldier on watch

se·pal (SEE-pəl) n. leaf or division of the calyx of a flower

sep·a·rate (SEP-ə-rayt) v. (-rat·ed, -rat·ing) —vt. part; divide; sever; put apart; occupy place between —vi. withdraw, become parted from —adj. (SEP-ər-it) disconnected, apart, distinct, individual —sep'a·ra·ble adj. —sep·a·ra'tion (-RAY-shən) n. disconnection; Law living apart of married people without divorce —sep'a·ra·tor n. that which separates; apparatus for separating cream from milk

se·pi·a (SEE-pee-ə) n. reddish-brown pigment made from a fluid secreted by the cuttlefish —adj. of this color

sep'sis n. presence of pus-forming bacteria in body

sep·ten·ni·al (sep-TEN-ee-əl) adj. lasting, occurring every seven years

sep·tet' n. music for seven instruments or voices; group of seven performers

sep·tic (SEP-tik) adj. of, caused by, sepsis; (of wound) infected —sep·ti·ce'mi·a (-SEE-mee-ə) n. blood poisoning

sep·tu·a·ge·nar·i·an (sep-choo-ə-jə-NAIR-ee-ən) adj. aged between seventy and eighty —n.

sep·ul·cher (SEP-əl-kər) n. tomb;

burial vault —se·pul·chral (sə-PUL-krəl) adj. of burial, or the grave; mournful; gloomy —sep'ul·ture (-əl-chər) n. burial

se·quel (SEE-kwəl) n. consequence; continuation, eg of story

se·quence (SEE-kwəns) n. arrangement of things in successive order; section, episode of motion picture —se·quen'tial (si-KWEN-shəl) adj.

se·ques·ter (si-KWES-tər) vt. separate; seclude; put aside —se·ques'trate (-KWES-trayt) vt. (-trat·ed, -trat·ing) confiscate; divert or appropriate income of property to satisfy claims against its owner —se·ques·tra'tion (-TRAY-shən) n.

se·quin (SEE-kwin) n. small ornamental metal disk or spangle on dresses etc.; orig. Venetian gold coin

se·quoi·a (si-KWOI-ə) n. giant Californian coniferous tree

se·ragl·io (si-RAL-yoh) n. (pl. -ragl·ios) harem, palace, of Turkish sultan

ser·aph (SER-əf) n. (pl. -a·phim pr. -ə·fim) member of highest order of angels

ser·e·nade (ser-ə-NAYD) n. sentimental piece of music or song of type addressed to woman by lover esp. at evening —v. (-nad·ed, -nad·ing) sing serenade (to someone)

ser·en·dip·i·ty (ser-ən-DIP-i-tee) n. faculty of making fortunate discoveries by accident

se·rene (sə-REEN) adj. calm, tranquil; unclouded; quiet, placid —se·ren'i·ty (-REN-i-tee) n.

serf (surf) n. one of class of medieval laborers bound to, and transferred with, land —serf'dom (-dəm) n.

serge (surj) n. strong hard-wearing twilled worsted fabric

**ser·geant** (SAHR-jənt) n. noncommissioned officer in Army, Marine Corps, police department —**sergeant major** noncommissioned Army officer serving as chief administrative assistant; noncommissioned officer ranking above first sergeant in Marine Corps —**sergeant at arms** legislative, organizational officer assigned to keep order etc.

**se·ries** (SEER-eez) n. (pl. same form) sequence; succession; set (eg of radio, TV programs with same characters, setting, but different stories) —**se·ri·al** (SEER-ee-əl) n. story or play produced in successive episodes or installments; periodical publication —adj. —**se·ri·al·ize** v. (-ized, -iz·ing) publish, present as serial —**serial killer** murderer who commits series of murders in same pattern oft. in same locality

**ser·if** n. small line finishing off stroke of letter

**se·ri·ous** (SEER-ee-əs) adj. thoughtful, solemn; earnest, sincere; of importance; giving cause for concern

**ser·mon** (SUR-mən) n. discourse of religious instruction or exhortation spoken or read from pulpit; any similar discourse —**ser'·mon·ize** vi. (-ized, -iz·ing) talk like preacher; compose sermons

**ser·pent** (SUR-pənt) n., snake —**ser'·pen·tine** (-teen) adj. like, shaped like, serpent

**ser·rate** (SER-ayt), **ser·rat·ed** (SER-ay-tid) adj. having notched, sawlike edge —**ser·ra'tion** n.

**se·rum** (SEER-əm) n. (pl. -rums) watery animal fluid, esp. thin part of blood as used for inoculation or vaccination

**serve** (surv) v. (served, serv·ing) (mainly tr.) work for, under, another; attend (to customers) in store etc.; provide; help to (food etc.); present (food etc.) in particular way; provide with regular supply of; be member of military unit; pay homage to; spend time doing; be useful, suitable enough; Tennis etc. put (ball) into play —n. Tennis etc. act of serving ball —**ser'vant** (-vənt) n. personal or domestic attendant —**serv·ice** (SUR-vis) n. the act of serving, helping, assisting; system organized to provide for needs of public; maintenance of vehicle; use; readiness, availability for use; set of dishes etc.; form, session, of public worship —pl. armed forces —vt. (-iced, -ic·ing) overhaul —**serv'ice·a·ble** adj. in working order, usable; durable —**service road** narrow road giving access to houses, stores etc. —**service station** place supplying fuel, oil, maintenance for motor vehicles

**ser·vile** (SUR-vil) adj. slavish, without independence; cringing; fawning; menial —**ser·vil'i·ty** n.

**ser·vi·tude** (SUR-vi-tood) n. bondage, slavery

**ser·vo·mech·an·ism** (SER-voh-mek-ə-niz-əm) n. electronic device for converting small mechanical, hydraulic or other type of force into larger, esp. in steering mechanisms

**ses·a·me** (SES-ə-mee) n. plant with seeds used as herbs and for making oil

**ses·sion** (SESH-ən) n. meeting of court etc.; assembly; continuous series of such meetings; any period devoted to an activity; school or university term eg summer session

**set** v. (set, set·ting) (mainly tr.) put or place in specified position or condition; cause to sit; fix, point, put up; make ready; become firm or fixed; establish; prescribe, allot; put to music; of hair, arrange while wet, so that it dries in position; of sun, go down; have direction —*adj.* fixed, established; deliberate; formal, arranged beforehand; unvarying —*n.* act or state of being set; bearing, posture; *Radio, TV* complete apparatus for reception or transmission; *Theater, Motion Pictures etc.* organized settings and equipment to form ensemble of scene; number of things, persons associated as being similar, complementary or used together; *Math.* group of numbers, objects *etc.* with at least one common property —**set'back** *n.* anything that hinders or impedes —**set'up** *n.* position; organization —**set·up** establish; *inf.* treat, as to drinks; *inf.* frame, entrap; *inf.* lure into embarrassing, dangerous, situation —**set shot** *Basketball* shot at basket taken from standing position and relatively distant from basket

**set·tee'** *n.* couch

**set·ter** (SET-ər) *n.* various breeds of gun dog

**set·ting** (SET-ing) *n.* background; surroundings; scenery and other stage accessories; act of fixing; decorative metalwork holding precious stone *etc.* in position; tableware and cutlery for (single place at) table; descending below horizon of sun; music for song

**set·tle** (SET-l) *v.* (-tled, -tling) —*vt.* arrange, put in order; establish, make firm or secure or quiet; decide upon; end (dispute *etc.*); pay; bestow (property) by legal deed —*vi.* come to rest; subside; become clear; take up residence; subside, sink to bottom; come to agreement —**set'**-

**tle·ment** (-mənt) *n.* act of settling; place newly inhabited; money bestowed legally; subsidence (of building) —**set·tler** (SET-lər) *n.* colonist

**sev·en** (SEV-ən) *adj./n.* cardinal number, next after six —**sev'·enth** *adj.* the ordinal number —**sev'en·teen'** (-teen') *adj./n.* ten and seven —**sev'en·ty** *adj./n.* (*pl.* -ties) ten times seven

**sev·er** (SEV-ər) *v.* separate, divide; cut off —**sev·er·ance** (-əns) *n.* —**severance pay** compensation paid by a firm to an employee for loss of employment

**sev·er·al** (SEV-ər-əl) *adj.* some, a few; separate; individual; various; different —*pron.* indefinite small number —**sev'er·al·ly** *adv.* apart from others; singly

**se·vere** (sə-VEER) *adj.* (-ver·er, -ver·est) strict; rigorous; hard to do; harsh; austere; extreme —**se·ver'i·ty** (-VER-i-tee) *n.*

**sew** (soh) *v.* (sewed, sewn or sewed, sew·ing) join with needle and thread; make by sewing

**sew·age** (SOO-ij) *n.* refuse, waste matter, excrement conveyed in sewer —**sew'er** (SOO-ər) *n.* underground drain to remove waste water and refuse —**sew'er·age** *n.* arrangement of sewers; sewage

**sex** (seks) *n.* state of being male or female; males or females collectively; sexual intercourse —*adj.* concerning sex —*vt.* ascertain sex of —**sex'ism** *n.* discrimination on basis of sex —**sex'ist** *n./adj.* —**sex·u·al** (SEK-shoo-əl) *adj.* —**sex'y** *adj.* (sex·i·er, sex·i·est) —**sexual intercourse** act of procreation in which male's penis is inserted into female's vagina

**sex·a·ge·nar·i·an** (sek-sə-jə-NAIR-ee-ən) *adj./n.* (person) sixty to seventy years old

**sex·tant** (SEK-stənt) *n.* navigator's instrument for measuring elevations of heavenly body *etc.*

**sex·tet** (seks-TET) *n.* (composition for) six singers or players; group of six *Also* **ses·tet'**, **sex·tette'**

**sex·ton** (SEK-stən) *n.* official who takes care of church building and its contents and sometimes assists in burial of dead; official who takes care of synagogue and sometimes assists cantor in conducting services

**shab·by** (SHAB-ee) *adj.* (-bi·er, -bi·est) faded, worn, ragged; poorly dressed; mean, dishonorable; stingy —**shab'bi·ly** *adv.* —**shab'bi·ness** (-nis) *n.*

**shack** (shak) *n.* rough hut —**shack up** (**with**) *sl.* live (with) *esp.* as husband and wife without being legally married

**shack·le** (SHAK-əl) *n.* metal ring or fastening for prisoner's wrist or ankle; anything that confines —*vt.* (-led, -ling) fasten with shackles; hamper

**shade** (shayd) *n.* partial darkness; shelter, place sheltered from light, heat *etc.*; darker part of anything; depth of color; tinge; ghost; screen; anything used to screen; window blind —*pl.* *sl.* sunglasses —*vt.* (shad·ed, shad·ing) screen from light, darken; represent shades in drawing —**shad'y** *adj.* (shad·i·er, shad·i·est) shielded from sun; dim; dubious; dishonest; dishonorable

**shad·ow** (SHAD-oh) *n.* dark figure projected by anything that intercepts rays of light; patch of shade; slight trace; indistinct image; gloom; inseparable companion —*vt.* cast shadow over; follow and watch closely —**shad'ow·y** *adj.*

**shaft** *n.* straight rod, stem, handle; arrow; ray, beam (of light); revolving rod for transmitting power; one of the bars between which horse is harnessed; entrance boring of mine

**shag**[1] *n.* matted wool or hair; long-napped cloth; coarse shredded tobacco —**shag'gy** *adj.* (-gi·er, -gi·est) covered with rough hair or wool; tousled; unkempt

**shag**[2] *vt.* (shagged, shag·ging) chase after; *Baseball* in practice, chase and catch fly balls

**shah** *n.* formerly, ruler of Iran

**shake** (shayk) *v.* (shook *pt.* shuuk, shak·en) (cause to) move with quick vibrations; tremble; grasp the hand (of another) in greeting; upset; wave, brandish —*n.* act of shaking; vibration; jolt; *inf.* short period of time, jiffy —**shak'i·ly** *adv.* —**shak'y** *adj.* (shak·i·er, shak·i·est) unsteady, insecure

**shale** (shayl) *n.* flaky, sedimentary rock

**shall** (shal) *v. aux.* (should *pt. pr.* shuud) makes compound tenses or moods to express obligation, command, condition or intention

**shal·lot** (SHAL-ət) *n.* kind of small onion

**shal·low** (SHAL-oh) *adj.* (-er, -est) not deep; having little depth of water; superficial; not sincere —*n.* shallow place

**sham** *adj./n.* imitation, counterfeit —*v.* (shammed, sham·ming) pretend, feign

**sham·ble** (SHAM-bəl) *vi.* (-bled, -bling) walk in shuffling, awkward way

**sham·bles** (SHAM-bəlz) *n.* with *sing.* or *pl. v.* messy, disorderly thing or place

**shame** (shaym) *n.* emotion caused by consciousness of guilt or dishonor in one's conduct or state; cause of disgrace; ignominy; pity, hard luck —vt. (shamed, sham·ing) cause to feel shame; disgrace; force by shame (into) —shame'ful (-fəl) adj. disgraceful —shame·less (-lis) adj. with no sense of shame; indecent —shame'faced (-fuysd) adj. ashamed

**sham·poo** n. various preparations of liquid soap for washing hair, carpets etc.; this process —vt. (-pooed, -poo·ing) use shampoo to wash

**sham·rock** (SHAM-rok) n. cloverlike plant with three leaves on each stem, esp. as Irish emblem

**shang·hai** (SHANG-hī) v. (-haied, -hai·ing) force, trick someone to do something

**shank** n. lower leg; shinbone; stem of thing —shank of the evening best or main part of the evening

**shan'tung** n. soft, natural Chinese silk

**shan·ty**[1] (SHAN-tee) n. (pl. -ties) temporary wooden building; crude dwelling

**shanty**[2] see CHANTEY

**shape** (shayp) n. external form or appearance, esp. of a woman; mold, pattern; condition, esp. of physical fitness —v. (shaped, shap·ing) —vt. form, mold, fashion, make —vi. develop —shape'less (-lis) adj. —shape'ly adj. (-li·er, -li·est) well-proportioned

**shard** (shahrd) n. broken fragment, esp. of earthenware

**share**[1] (shair) n. portion; quota; lot; unit of ownership in corporation —v. (shared, shar·ing) give, take a share; join with others in doing, using, something —share'-hold·er n.

**share**[2] n. blade of plow

**shark** (shahrk) n. large some-times predatory sea fish; person who cheats others; inf. person of great ability in cards etc.

**sharp** (shahrp) adj. (-er, -est) having keen cutting edge or fine point; keen; not gradual or gentle; brisk; clever; harsh; dealing cleverly but unfairly; shrill; strongly marked, esp. in outline —adv. promptly —n. Mus. note half a tone above natural pitch; (also sharp'er) cheat, swindler —sharp'en vt. make sharp —sharp'shoot·er n. marksman

**shat·ter** (SHAT-ər) v. break in pieces; ruin (plans etc.); disturb (person) greatly

**shave** (shayv) v. (shaved, shaved or shav·en, shav·ing) cut close, esp. hair of face or head; pare away; graze; reduce —n. shaving —shav'ings n. pl. parings —close shave narrow escape

**shawl** n. piece of fabric to cover woman's shoulders or head

**she** (shee) pron. 3rd person singular feminine pronoun

**sheaf** (sheef) n. (pl. sheaves) bundle, esp. corn; loose leaves of paper

**shear** (sheer) vt. (sheared, sheared or shorn, shear·ing) clip hair, wool from; cut through; trim (eg hedge); fracture —shears n. pl. large pair of scissors; mechanical shearing, cutting instrument

**sheath** (sheeth) n. (pl. sheaths pr. sheethz) close-fitting cover, esp. for knife or sword; scabbard; condom —sheathe (sheeth) vt. (sheathed, sheath·ing) put into sheath

**she·bang** (shə-BANG) n. inf. situation, matter, esp. whole shebang

**shed**[1] n. roofed shelter used for storage or as workshop

**shed**[2] vt. (shed, shed·ding) (cause

to) pour forth (*eg* tears, blood); cast off

**sheen** *n.* gloss

**sheep** *n.* ruminant animal bred for wool and meat —**sheep′ish** *adj.* embarrassed, shy —**sheep-dip** *n.* solution in which sheep are immersed to kill vermin and germs in fleece —**sheep′dog** *n.* dog of various breeds *orig.* for herding sheep —**sheep′skin** *n.* skin of sheep (with fleece) used for clothing, rug or without fleece for parchment; *inf.* diploma

**sheer**[1] *adj.* (**-er, -est**) perpendicular; of material, very fine, transparent; absolute, unmitigated

**sheer**[2] *vi.* deviate from course; swerve; turn aside

**sheet**[1] *n.* large piece of cotton *etc.* to cover bed; broad piece of any thin material; large expanse —*vt.* cover with sheet

**sheet**[2] *n.* rope fastened in corner of sail —**sheet anchor** large anchor for emergency

**sheik** (shayk) *n.* Arab chief

**shek-el** (SHEK-əl) *n.* Israeli paper money or coin; —*pl.* (**shekels**) money, cash

**shelf** *n.* (*pl.* **shelves**) board fixed horizontally (on wall *etc.*) for holding things; ledge

**shell** *n.* hard outer case (*esp.* of egg, nut *etc.*); husk; explosive projectile; outer part of structure left when interior is removed; racing shell —*vt.* take shell from; take out of shell; fire at with shells —**racing shell** long light racing boat for rowing by crew of one or more —**shell′fish** *n.* mollusk; crustacean —**shell shock** battle fatigue, nervous disorder caused by bursting of shells or bombs —**shell out** *inf.* pay up

**shel-lac** (shə-LAK) *n.* varnish

—*vt.* (**-lacked, -lack·ing**) coat with shellac

**shel·ter** (SHEL-tər) *n.* place, structure giving protection; protection; refuge; haven —*vt.* give protection to; screen —*vi.* take shelter

**shelve** (shelv) *v.* (**shelved, shelving**) —*vt.* put on a shelf; put off; cease to employ; defer indefinitely —*vi.* slope gradually

**she-nan·i·gan** (shə-NAN-i-gən) *n.* *inf. usu. pl.* frolicking; playing tricks *etc.*

**shep-herd** (SHEP-ərd) *n.* person who tends sheep (**shep′herd·ess** (-is) *fem.*) —*vt.* guide, watch over

**sher-bet** (SHUR-bit) *n.* frozen fruit-flavored dessert like ices but with gelatin *etc.* added

**sher′iff** *n.* law enforcement officer

**Sher·pa** (SHUR-pə) *n.* (*pl.* **-pas, -pa**) member of a Tibetan people

**sher·ry** (SHER-ee) *n.* (*pl.* **-ries**) fortified wine

**shib-bo·leth** (SHIB-ə-lith) *n.* custom, word *etc.* distinguishing people of particular class or group; test word, pet phrase of sect or party

**shield** (sheeld) *n.* piece of armor carried on arm; any protection used to stop blows, missiles *etc.*; any protective device; sports trophy —*vt.* cover, protect

**shift** *v.* (cause to) move, change position —*n.* relay of workers; time of their working; evasion; expedient; removal; woman's underskirt or dress —**shift′i·ness** (-nis) *n.* —**shift′less** (-lis) *adj.* lacking in resource or character —**shift′y** *adj.* (**shift·i·er, shift·i·est**) evasive, of dubious character

**shil·le·lagh** (shə-LAY-lə) *n.* (in Ireland) cudgel

**shil′ling** *n.* former Brit. coin, now

5 pence; monetary unit in various countries

**shil·ly-shal·ly** (SHIL-ee-shal-ee) *vi.* (-lied, -ly·ing) waver —*n.* wavering, indecision

**shim·mer** (SHIM-ər) *vi.* shine with quivering light —*n.* such light; glimmer

**shin** *n.* front of lower leg —*v.* (shinned, shin·ning) climb with arms and legs —**shin'bone** (-bohn) *n.* tibia

**shin'dig** *n. inf.* elaborate party, dance *etc.*

**shine** (shīn) *v.* (shone, shin·ing) give out, reflect light; perform very well, excel; cause to shine by polishing —*n.* brightness, luster; polishing —**shin'y** (shin·i·er, shin·i·est) *adj.*

**shin·gle**[1] (SHIN-gəl) *n.* wooden roof and wall tile —*vt.* (-gled, -gling) cover with shingles

**shingle**[2] *n.* mass of pebbles

**shin·gles** (SHIN-gəlz) *n.* disease causing inflammation along a nerve

**Shin·to** (SHIN-toh) *n.* native Japanese religion —**Shin'to·ism** *n.*

**ship** *n.* large seagoing vessel —*v.* (shipped, ship·ping) put on or send (*esp.* by ship); embark; take employment on ship —**ship'ment** (-mənt) *n.* act of shipping; goods shipped —**ship'ping** *n.* freight transport business; ships collectively —**ship'shape** (-shayp) *adj.* orderly, trim —**ship'wreck** (-rek) *n.* destruction of a ship through storm, collision *etc.* —*vt.* cause to undergo shipwreck —**ship'yard** *n.* place for building and repair of ships —**ship out** leave by ship; *inf.* quit, resign, be fired

**shirk** (shurk) *vt.* evade, try to avoid (duty *etc.*)

**shirr** (shur) *vt.* gather (fabric) into parallel rows —*n.* also **shirr'ing**

**shirt** (shurt) *n.* garment for upper part of body

**shiv** *n. sl.* knife

**shiv·er**[1] (SHIV-ər) *vi.* tremble, usu. with cold or fear; shudder; vibrate —*n.* act, state, of shivering

**shiv·er**[2] *v.* splinter, break in pieces —*n.* splinter

**shoal** (shohl) *n.* stretch of shallow water; sandbank or bar —*v.* make, become, shallow

**shock**[1] (shok) *vt.* horrify, scandalize —*n.* violent or damaging blow; emotional disturbance; state of weakness, illness, caused by physical or mental shock; paralytic stroke; collision; effect on sensory nerves of electric discharge —**shock'er** *n.* person or thing that shocks or distresses —**shock absorber** device (*esp.* in automobiles) to absorb shocks

**shock**[2] *n.* group of corn sheaves placed together

**shock**[3] *n.* mass of hair —*adj.* shaggy —**shock'head·ed** (-hed-id) *adj.*

**shod·dy** (SHOD-ee) *adj.* (-di·er, -di·est) worthless, trashy, second-rate, of poor material

**shoe** (shoo) *n.* (*pl.* shoes) covering for foot, not enclosing ankle; metal rim or curved bar put on horse's hoof; various protective plates or undercoverings —*vt.* (shod *or* shoed, shod *or* shoed, shoe·ing) protect, furnish with shoe or shoes —**shoe'string** *adj./n.* very small (amount of money *etc.*)

**shone** *pt./pp. of* SHINE

**shoo** *interj.* go away! —*vt.* (shooed, shoo·ing) drive away

**shook** (shuuk) *pt. of* SHAKE

**shoot** *v.* (shot, shoot·ing) hit, wound, kill with missile fired from weapon; discharge weapon; send, slide, push rapidly; photograph, film; hunt; sprout —*n.*

young branch, sprout; shooting competition; hunting expedition

**shop** *n.* store, place for retail sale of goods and services; workshop, factory —*vi.* (shopped, shop-ping) visit stores to buy or examine —**shop′lift·er** *n.* one who steals from store —**shop stew′ard** (STOO-ərd) labor union representative of workers in factory *etc.* —**talk shop** talk of one's business *etc.* at unsuitable moments

**shore**¹ (shor) *n.* edge of sea or lake

**shore**² *vt.* (shored, shor·ing) prop (up)

**shorn** *pp. of* SHEAR

**short** *adj.* (-er, -est) not long; not tall; brief, hasty; not reaching quantity or standard required; wanting, lacking; abrupt, rude; *Stock Exchange* not in possession of stock shares when selling them —*adv.* suddenly, abruptly; without reaching end —*n.* short film —*pl.* short trousers —**short′-age** (-ij) *n.* deficiency —**short′en** *v.* —**short′ly** *adv.* soon; briefly —**short′bread** (-bred) *n.* butter cookie —**short′cake** (-kayk) cake made of butter, flour and sugar; dessert of biscuit dough with fruit topping —**short circuit** *Electricity* connection, often accidental, of low resistance between two parts of circuit —**short′com·ing** (-kum-ing) *n.* failing; defect —**short′hand** *n.* method of rapid writing by signs or contractions —**short′-hand·ed** *adj.* lacking the usual or necessary number of workers, helpers —**short list** selected list of candidates (*esp.* for job) from which final selection will be made —**short shrift** summary treatment —**short ton** ton (2000 lbs.) —**short wave** radio

wave of frequency greater than 1600 kHz

**short·en·ing** (SHORT-ning) *n.* fat used to make cake *etc.* rich and crumbly; *pr.p. of* SHORTEN

**shot** *n.* act of shooting; missile; lead in small pellets; marksman, shooter; try, attempt; photograph; short film sequence; dose; hypodermic injection —*adj.* woven so that color is different, according to angle of light —*pt./pp. of* SHOOT

**should** (shuud) (*used to express condition*); *pt. of* SHALL

**shoul·der** (SHOHL-dər) *n.* part of body to which arm or foreleg is attached; anything resembling shoulder; side of road —*vt.* undertake; bear (burden); accept (responsibility); put on one's shoulder —*vi.* make way by pushing —**shoulder blade** (blayd) shoulder bone

**shout** (showt) *n.* loud cry —*v.* utter (cry *etc.*) with loud voice

**shove** (shuv) *vt.* (shoved, shov-ing) push —*n.* push —**shove off** *inf.* go away

**shovel** (SHUV-əl) *n.* instrument for scooping, lifting earth *etc.* —*vt.* (-eled, -el·ing) lift, move (as) with shovel

**show** (shoh) *v.* (showed, shown, show-ing) expose to view; point out; display; exhibit; explain; prove; guide; accord (favor *etc.*); appear; be noticeable —*n.* display, exhibition; spectacle; theatrical or other entertainment; indication; competitive event; ostentation; semblance; pretense —**show′i·ly** *adv.* —**show′y** *adj.* (show·i·er, show·i·est) gaudy; ostentatious—**show′down** *n.* confrontation; final test —**show jump·ing** horse-riding competition to demonstrate skill in jumping obstacles —**show′man** (-mən) (*pl.* **-men**) *n.* organizer of theatrical events, circuses *etc.*; one skilled at presenting anything in effective way —**show off** exhibit to invite admiration; behave in this way —**show-off** *n.* —**show up** reveal; expose; embarrass; arrive

**show·er** (SHOW-ər) *n.* short fall of rain; anything coming down like rain; kind of bath in which person stands while being sprayed with water; party to present gifts to a person, as a prospective bride —*vt.* bestow liberally —*vi.* take bath in shower —**show′er·y** *adj.*

**shrank** *pt. of* SHRINK

**shrap·nel** (SHRAP-nəl) *n.* shell filled with pellets that scatter on bursting; shell splinters

**shred** *n.* fragment, torn strip; small amount —*vt.* (**shred** *or* **shred·ded, shred·ding**) cut, tear to shreds

**shrew** (shroo) *n.* animal like mouse; bad-tempered woman; scold —**shrew′ish** *adj.* nagging

**shrewd** (shrood) *adj.* (**-er, -est**) astute, intelligent; crafty —**shrewd′ness** (-nis) *n.*

**shriek** (shreek) *n.* shrill cry; piercing scream —*v.* screech

**shrike** (shrīk) *n.* bird of prey

**shrill** *adj.* piercing, sharp in tone —*v.* utter in such tone —**shril′ly** *adv.*

**shrimp** *n.* (*pl.* **shrimp, shrimps**) small edible crustacean; *inf.* (*pl.* **shrimps**) undersized person —*vi.* go catching shrimps

**shrine** (shrīn) *n.* place (building, tomb, alcove) of worship, usu. associated with saint

**shrink** (shreenk) *v.* (**shrank** *or* **shrunk, shrunk** *or* **shrunk·en, shrink·ing**) become smaller; retire, flinch, recoil; make smaller

—*n. sl.* psychiatrist, psychotherapist —**shrink′age** (-ij) *n.*

**shrive** (shrīv) *vt.* (**shrove** *or* **shrived, shriv·en** *or* **shrived, shriv·ing**) give absolution to —**shrift** *n. obs.* confession; absolution

**shriv·el** (SHRIV-əl) *vi.* (**-eled, -el·ing**) shrink and wither

**shroud** (shrowd) *n.* sheet, wrapping, for corpse; anything that covers, envelops like shroud —*pl.* set of ropes to masthead —*vt.* put shroud on; screen, veil; wrap up

**Shrove Tuesday** (shrohv) day before Ash Wednesday

**shrub** *n.* bushy plant; drink of fruit juices *etc.* oft. with alcohol —**shrub′ber·y** (-ər-ee) *n.* (*pl.* **-ber·ies**) planting of shrubs; shrubs collectively

**shrug** *v.* (**shrugged, shrug·ging**) raise shoulders, as sign of indifference, ignorance *etc.*; move (shoulders) thus; (*with* **off**) dismiss as unimportant —*n.* shrugging

**shrunk(en)** *pp. of* SHRINK

**shuck** (shuk) *n.* shell, husk, pod —*vt.* remove husks *etc.* from —**shucks** *interj. inf.* used as mild expression of regret

**shud·der** (SHUD-ər) *vi.* shake, tremble involuntarily, *esp.* with horror —*n.* shuddering, tremor

**shuf·fle** (SHUF-əl) *v.* (**-fled, -fling**) —*vi.* move feet without lifting them; dance like this; act evasively —*vt.* mix (cards); (*with* **off**) evade, pass to another —*n.* shuffling; rearrangement

**shun** *vt.* (**shunned, shun·ning**) avoid; keep away from

**shunt** *vt.* push aside; divert; move (train) from one line to another

**shut** *v.* (**shut, shut·ting**) close; bar; forbid entrance to —**shut′ter** (-ər) *n.* movable window screen, usu. hinged to frame; device in camera admitting light as required to film or plate —**shut down** close or stop factory, machine etc.

**shut·tle** (SHUT-l) n. instrument that threads weft between threads of warp in weaving; similar appliance in sewing machine; plane, bus etc. traveling to and fro over short distance —v. (-tled, -tling) (cause to) move back and forth —**shut'tle·cock** n. small, light cone with cork stub and fan of feathers used as a ball in badminton

**shy¹** (shī) adj. (**shy·er** or **shi·er**, **shy·est** or **shi·est**) awkward in company; timid, bashful; reluctant; scarce, lacking (esp. in card games, not having enough money for bet etc.) —vi. (**shied, shy·ing**) start back in fear; show sudden reluctance —n. (pl. **shies**) start of fear by horse —**shy'ly** adv. —**shy'ness** (-nis) n.

**shy²** vt./n. (**shied, shy·ing**) throw

**shy·ster** (SHI-stər) n. inf. dishonest, deceitful person, esp. unprofessional lawyer

**SI** Fr. Système International (d'Unités), international system of measurement based on units of ten

**Si** Chem. silicon

**Si·a·mese cat** (SI-ə-MEEZ) breed of cat with blue eyes

**Siamese twins** twins born joined to each other by some part of body

**sib·i·lant** (SIB-ə-lənt) adj. hissing —n. speech sound with hissing effect

**sib'ling** n. person's brother or sister —adj.

**sib·yl** (SIB-əl) n. woman endowed with spirit of prophecy —**sib'yl·line** (-een) adj. occult

**sic** (sik) Lat. thus: oft. used to call attention to a quoted mistake

**sick** (sik) adj. (**-er, -est**) inclined to vomit, vomiting; not well or healthy, physically or mentally; macabre, sadistic, morbid; bored, tired; disgusted —**sick'en** (-ən) v. make, become, sick; disgust; nauseate —**sick'ly** adv. unhealthy, weakly; inducing nausea —**sick'ness** (-nis) n. —**sick bay** place set aside for treating sick people, esp. aboard ships

**sick·le** (SIK-əl) n. reaping hook

**side** (sīd) n. one of the surfaces of object, esp. upright inner or outer surface; either surface of thing having only two; part of body that is to right or left; region nearer or farther than, or right or left of, dividing line etc.; region; aspect or part; one of two parties or sets of opponents; sect, faction; line of descent traced through one parent —adj. at, in, the side; subordinate, incidental —vi. (**sid·ed, sid·ing**) take up cause of (usu. with with) —**sid'ing** n. short line of rails on which trains or wagons are shunted from main line —**side'board** (-bord) n. piece of furniture for holding dishes etc. in dining room —**side'burns** (-burnz) n. pl. man's side whiskers —**side'car** n. small car attached to side of motorcycle; cocktail made with brandy, orange liqueur and lemon juice —**side'kick** n. inf. assistant —**side'light** (-līt) n. esp. either of two lights on vessel for use at night; item of incidental information —**side'line** n. Sports boundary of playing area; subsidiary interest or activity —**side'long** (-lawng) adj. lateral, not directly forward —adv. obliquely —**side'man** (pl. -men) n. instrumentalist in band —**side'track** v. deviate from main topic —n. —**side'walk** n. footpath beside road —**side′ways** (-wayz) *adv.* to or from the side; laterally

**si·de·re·al** (sī-DEER-ee-əl) *adj.* relating to, fixed by, stars

**si·dle** (SĪD-l) *vi.* (-dled, -dling) move in furtive or stealthy manner; move sideways

**SIDS** sudden infant death syndrome, unexplained death of baby while asleep

**siege** (seej) *n.* besieging of town or fortified place

**si·en·na** (see-EN-ə) *n.* (pigment of) brownish-yellow color

**si·er·ra** (see-ER-ə) *n.* range of mountains with jagged peaks

**si·es·ta** (see-ES-tə) *n.* rest, sleep in afternoon

**sieve** (siv) *n.* device with network or perforated bottom for sifting —*v.* (sieved, siev·ing) sift; strain

**sift** *vt.* separate (*eg* with sieve) coarser portion from finer; examine closely —**sift′er** *n.*

**sigh** (sī) *v./n.* (utter) long audible breath —**sigh** for yearn for, grieve for

**sight** (sīt) *n.* faculty of seeing; seeing; thing seen; view; glimpse; device for guiding eye; spectacle; *inf.* pitiful or ridiculous or unusual object; *inf.* large number, great deal —*vt.* catch sight of; adjust sights of gun *etc.* —**sight** for sore eyes *inf.* person or thing one is glad to see —**sight′less** (-lis) *adj.* —**sight-read** (-reed) *v.* (-read *pr.* -red, -read·ing *pr.* -reed·ing) play, sing music without previous preparation —**sight′see** *v.* visit (place) to look at interesting sights

**sign** (sīn) *n.* mark, gesture *etc.* to convey some meaning; (board, placard, bearing) notice, warning *etc.*; symbol; omen; evidence —*vt.* put one's signature to; ratify —*vi.* make sign or gesture; affix signature; use symbols of sign

language —**sign language** gestures used for communicating with deaf people

**sig·nal** (SIG-nəl) *n.* sign to convey order or information, *esp.* on railroads; that which in first place imparts any action; *Radio etc.* sequence of electrical impulses transmitted or received —*adj.* remarkable, striking —*v.* (-naled, -nal·ing) make signals to; give orders *etc.* by signals —**sig′nal·ize** *vt.* (-ized, -iz·ing) make notable

**sig·na·to·ry** (SIG-nə-tor-ee) *n.* (pl. -ries) one of those who sign agreements, treaties

**sig·na·ture** (SIG-nə-chər) *n.* person's name written by self; act of writing it —**signature tune** theme song

**sig·net** (SIG-nit) *n.* small seal

**sig·nif·i·cant** (sig-NIF-i-kənt) *adj.* revealing; designed to make something known; important —**sig·nif′i·cance** (-kəns) *n.* import, weight; meaning —**sig·ni·fi·ca′tion** *n.* meaning

**sig·ni·fy** (SIG-nə-fī) *v.* (-fied, -fy·ing) mean; indicate; denote; imply; be of importance

**si·gnor** (SEEN-yor) *n.* Italian title of respect, like Mr. —**si·gno·ra** (sin-YOR-ə) *n.* Mrs. —**si·gno·ri′na** (seen-yə-REEN-ə) *n.* Miss

**Sikh** (seek) *n.* believer in monotheistic Indian religion

**si·lage** (SĪ-lij) *n.* fodder crop harvested while green and stored in state of partial fermentation

**si·lence** (SĪ-ləns) *n.* absence of noise; refraining from speech —*vt.* (-lenced, -lenc·ing) make silent; put a stop to —**si′lenc·er** *n.* device to reduce noise of firearm —**si′lent** *adj.*

**sil·hou·ette** (sil-oo-ET) *n.* outline of object seen against light; profile portrait in black —*vt.*

(-et·ted, -et·ting) show in or as if in silhouette

**sil·i·ca** (SIL-i-kə) n. naturally occurring dioxide of silicon —**si·li·ceous** (sə-LEE-shəs) adj. —**si·li·co·sis** (si-li-KOH-sis) n. lung disease caused by inhaling silica dust over a long period

**sil·i·con** (SIL-i-kən) n. brittle metalloid element found in sand, clay, stone, widely used in chemistry, industry —**sil'i·cone** (-kohn) n. large class of synthetic substances, related to silicon and used in chemistry, industry, medicine

**silk** n. fiber made by larvae (silk'worms) of certain moth; thread, fabric made from this —**silk'en** adj. made of, like silk; soft; smooth; dressed in silk —**silk'i·ness** (-nis) n.

**sill** n. ledge beneath window; bottom part of door or window frame

**sil·ly** (SIL-ee) adj. (-li·er, -li·est) foolish; trivial; feebleminded —**sil'li·ness** (-nis) n.

**si·lo** (SI-loh) n. (pl. -los) pit, tower for storing fodder or grain; underground missile launching site

**silt** n. mud deposited by water —v. fill, be choked with silt —**sil·ta'tion** n.

**sil·ver** (SIL-vər) n. white precious metal; things made of it; silver coins; cutlery —adj. made of silver; resembling silver or its color; having pale luster, as moon; soft, melodious, as sound; bright —vt. coat with silver —**sil'ver·y** adj. —**silver birch** tree having silvery white peeling bark —**silver wedding** 25th wedding anniversary

**sim·i·an** (SIM-ee-ən) adj. of, like apes

**sim·i·lar** (SIM-ə-lər) adj. resembling, like —**sim·i·lar'i·ty** n. likeness; close resemblance

**sim·i·le** (SIM-ə-lee) n. comparison of one thing with another, using "as" or "like," esp. in poetry

**si·mil·i·tude** (si-MIL-i-tood) n. outward appearance, likeness; guise

**sim·mer** (SIM-ər) v. keep or be just bubbling or just below boiling point; to be in state of suppressed anger or laughter

**sim·per** (SIM-pər) vi. smile, utter in silly or affected way —n.

**sim·ple** (SIM-pəl) adj. (-pler, -plest) not complicated; plain; not combined or complex; ordinary, mere; guileless; stupid —**sim'ple·ton** (-tən) n. foolish person —**sim·plic'i·ty** (-PLIS-ə-tee) n. (pl. -ties) simpleness, clearness, artlessness —**sim·pli·fi·ca'tion** n. —**sim'pli·fy** vt. (-fied, -fy·ing) make simple, plain or easy —**sim·plis'tic** adj. extremely simple, naive —**sim'ply** adv. —**simple fraction** one in which both the numerator and the denominator are whole numbers

**sim·u·late** (SIM-yə-layt) vt. (-lat·ed, -lat·ing) make pretense of; reproduce, copy, esp. conditions of particular situation —**sim·u·la'tion** n. —**sim'u·la·tor** n.

**si·mul·ta·ne·ous** (sī-məl-TAY-nee-əs) adj. occurring at the same time —**si·mul·ta·ne'i·ty** (-tə-NEE-i-tee) n. —**simultane·ous·ly** adv.

**sin** n. transgression of divine or moral law, esp. committed consciously; offense against principle or standard —vi. (sinned, sin·ning) commit sin —**sin'ful** (-fəl) adj. of nature of sin; guilty of sin —**sin'ful·ly** adv.

**since** (sins) prep. during or throughout period of time after

—*conj.* from time when; because —*adv.* from that time

**sin·cere** (sin-SEER) *adj.* not hypocritical, actually moved by or feeling apparent emotions; true, genuine; unaffected —**sin·cere′ly** *adv.* —**sin·cer′i·ty** (-SER-i-tee) *n.*

**sine** (sīn) *n.* mathematical function, *esp.* ratio of length of hypotenuse to opposite side in right triangle

**si·ne·cure** (SĪ-ni-kyuur) *n.* office with pay but minimal duties

**si·ne di·e** (SĪ-nee DĪ-ee) *Lat.* with no date, indefinitely postponed

**si·ne qua non** (SĪ-nee kway non) *Lat.* essential condition or requirement

**sin·ew** (SIN-yoo) *n.* tough, fibrous cord joining muscle to bone —*pl.* muscles, strength —**sin′ew·y** *adj.* stringy; muscular

**sing** *v.* (**sang, sung, sing·ing**) utter musical sounds; hum, whistle, ring; utter (words) with musical modulation; celebrate in song or poetry —**sing′song** (-sawng) *adj.* monotonously regular in tone, rhythm

**singe** (sinj) *vt.* (**singed, singe·ing**) burn surface of —*n.* act or effect of singeing

**sin·gle** (SING-gəl) *adj.* one only; alone, separate; unmarried; for one; formed of only one part, fold *etc.*; wholehearted, straightforward —*n.* single thing; phonograph record with one short item on each side; *Baseball* one-base hit —*vt.* (**-gled, -gling**) pick (out); make single —**sin′gly** *adv.* —**sin·gle file** persons, things arranged in one line —**single-hand·ed** *adj.* without assistance —**singles** bar bar or club that is social meeting place esp. for single people

**sin·gu·lar** (SING-gyə-lər) *adj.* remarkable; unusual; unique; denoting one person or thing —**sin-**

**gu·lar·i·ty** *n.* (*pl.* **-ties**) something unusual —**sin·gu·lar·ly** (-lər-lee) *adv.* particularly; peculiarly

**sin·is·ter** (SIN-ə-stər) *adj.* threatening; evil-looking; wicked; unlucky; *Heraldry* on bearer's left-hand side —**sin′is·trous** (-trəs) *adj.* ill-omened

**sink** (singk) *v.* (**sank** *or* **sunk, sunk** *or* **sunk·en, sink·ing**) become submerged (in water); drop, give way; decline in value, health *etc.*; penetrate (into); cause to sink; make by digging out; invest —*n.* receptacle with pipe for carrying away waste water; cesspool; place of corruption, vice —**sink′er** *n.* weight for fishing line —**sink′hole** (-hohl) *n.* low land where drainage collects; cavity formed in rock by water —**sinking fund** money set aside at intervals for payment of particular liability at fixed date

**Sinn Fein** (shin fayn) Irish republican political movement

**Sino-** (*comb. form*) Chinese, of China

**sin·u·ous** (SIN-yoo-əs) *adj.* curving, devious, lithe —**sin·u·os′i·ty** (-OS-i-tee) *n.* (*pl.* **-ties**)

**si·nus** (SĪ-nəs) *n.* (*pl.* **-nus·es**) cavity, *esp.* air passages in bones of skull —**si·nus·i′tis** (-SĪ-tis) *n.* inflammation of sinus

**sip** *v.* (**sipped, sip·ping**) drink in very small portions —*n.*

**si·phon** (SĪ-fən) *n.* device, *esp.* bent tube, that uses atmospheric or gaseous pressure to draw liquid from container —*v.* draw off thus; draw off in small amounts

**sir** (sur) *n.* polite term of address for a man; (**S-**) title of knight or baronet

**sire** (sīr) *n.* male parent, *esp.* of horse or domestic animal; term of address to king —*v.* (**sired, sir·ing**) beget

**si·ren** (SĪ-rən) *n.* device making loud wailing noise, *esp.* giving warning of danger; legendary sea nymph who lured sailors to destruction; alluring woman

**sir·loin** (SUR-loin) *n.* prime cut of loin of beef

**si·sal** (SĪ-səl) *n.* (fiber of) plant used in making ropes

**sis·sy** (SIS-ee) *adj./n.* (*pl.* -sies) weak, cowardly (person); effeminate boy or man

**sis·ter** (SIS-tər) *n.* daughter of same parents; woman fellow member *esp.* of religious body —*adj.* closely related, similar —**sis'ter·hood** (-huud) *n.* relation of sister; order, band of women —**sis'ter·ly** *adj.* —**sister-in-law** *n.* sister of husband or wife; brother's wife

**sit** *v.* (*mainly intr.*) (sat, sit·ting) adopt posture or rest on buttocks, thighs; perch; incubate; pose for portrait; occupy official position; hold session; remain; take examination; keep watch over baby *etc.* —**sit in** in protest by refusing to move from place —**sit-in** *n.* such a protest

**si·tar** (si-TAHR) *n.* stringed musical instrument, *esp.* of India —**si·tar'ist** *n.*

**site** (sīt) *n.* place, location; space for, with, a building

**sit·u·ate** (SICH-oo-ayt) *v.* (-at·ed, -at·ing) place, locate —**sit·u·a'tion** *n.* place, position; state of affairs; employment, post

**six** (siks) *adj./n.* cardinal number one more than five —**sixth** *adj.* ordinal number —*n.* sixth part —**six'teen'** *n./adj.* six and ten —**six'ty** *n./adj.* (*pl.* -ties) six times ten

**size**[1] (sīz) *n.* bigness, dimensions; one of series of standard measurements of clothes *etc.*; *inf.* state of affairs —*vt.* (sized, siz·ing) arrange according to size —**siz'a·ble**, **size'a·ble** *adj.* quite large —**size up** *inf.* assess (person, situation *etc.*)

**size**[2] *n.* gluelike sealer, filler —*vt.* (sized, siz·ing) coat, treat with size

**siz·zle** (SIZ-l) *v./n.* (-zled, -zling) (make) hissing, spluttering sound as of frying —**siz'zler** (-lər) *n. inf.* hot day

**skate**[1] (skayt) *n.* steel blade attached to boot, for gliding over ice —*vi.* (skat·ed, skat·ing) glide as on skates —**skat'er** *n.* —**skate'board** *n.* small board mounted on roller-skate wheels

**skate**[2] *n.* large marine ray

**ske·dad·dle** (ski-DAD-l) *vi. inf.* (-dled, -dling) flee; run away hurriedly

**skeet** *n.* shooting sport with clay target propelled from trap to simulate flying bird

**skein** (skayn) *n.* quantity of yarn, wool *etc.* in loose knot; flight of wildfowl

**skel·e·ton** (SKEL-i-tn) *n.* bones of animal; bones separated from flesh and preserved in their natural position; very thin person; outline, draft, framework; nucleus —*adj.* reduced to a minimum; drawn in outline; not in detail —**skel'e·tal** (-təl) *adj.* —**skeleton key** filed down so as to open many different locks

**skep·tic** (SKEP-tik) *n.* one who maintains doubt or disbelief; agnostic; unbeliever —**skep'ti·cal** (-kəl) *adj.* —**skep'ti·cism** (-siz-əm) *n.*

**sketch** (skech) *n.* rough drawing; brief account; essay; short humorous play —*v.* make sketch (of) —**sketch'y** *adj.* (sketch·i·er, sketch·i·est) omitting detail; incomplete; inadequate

**skew** (skyoo) *vi.* move obliquely —*adj.* slanting; crooked

**skew·er** (SKYOO-ər) *n.* pin to fasten (meat) together —*v.* pierce or fasten (as though) with skewer

**ski** (skee) *n.* (*pl.* skis) long runner fastened to boot for sliding over snow or water —*v.* (skied, ski·ing) slide on skis; go skiing

**skid** *v.* (skid·ded, skid·ding) slide (sideways), *esp.* vehicle out of control with wheels not rotating —*n.* instance of this; device to facilitate sliding, *eg* in moving heavy objects —skid'dy (-ee) *adj.* (-di·er, -di·est)

**skiff** *n.* small boat

**skill** *n.* practical ability, cleverness, dexterity —skilled *adj.* having, requiring knowledge, united with readiness and dexterity —skill'ful (-fəl) *adj.* expert, masterly; adroit

**skil·let** (SKIL-it) *n.* small frying pan

**skim** *v.* (skimmed, skim·ming) remove floating matter from surface of liquid; glide over lightly and rapidly; read thus; move thus —skim *or* skimmed milk milk from which cream has been removed

**skimp** *vt.* give short measure; do thing imperfectly —skimp'y *adj.* (skimp·i·er, skimp·i·est) meager; scanty

**skin** *n.* outer covering of vertebrate body, lower animal or fruit; animal skin used as material or container; film on surface of cooling liquid *etc.*; complexion —*vt.* (skinned, skin·ning) remove skin of —skin'ny *adj.* (-ni·er, -ni·est) thin —skin-deep *adj.* superficial; slight —skin diving underwater swimming using breathing apparatus —skin'flint *n.* miser, niggard —skin graft

transplant of piece of healthy skin to wound to form new skin —skin-tight (-tīt) *adj.* fitting close to skin

**skip**[1] *v.* (skipped, skip·ping) leap lightly; jump a rope as it is swung under one; pass over, omit —*n.* act of skipping

**skip**[2] *n.* large bucket, container for transporting people, materials in mines *etc.*

**skip·per** (SKIP-ər) *n.* captain of ship, plane or team —*vt.* captain

**skirl** (skurl) *n.* sound of bagpipes

**skir·mish** (SKUR-mish) *n.* fight between small parties, small battle —*vi.* fight briefly or irregularly

**skirt** (skurt) *n.* woman's garment hanging from waist; lower part of woman's dress, coat *etc.*; outlying part; *sl.* offens. woman —*v.* border; go around —skirt'ing *n.* material for women's skirts

**skit** *n.* short satirical piece, *esp.* theatrical sketch

**skit·tish** *adj.* frisky, frivolous

**skit·tles** (SKIT-əlz) *n. with sing. v.* ninepins

**skoal** (skohl) *interj.* (as a toast) to your health

**skul·dug·ger·y** (skul-DUG-ə-ree) *n.* (*pl.* -ger·ies) trickery

**skulk** *vi.* sneak out of the way; lurk —skulk'er *n.*

**skull** *n.* bony case that encloses brain —skull'cap *n.* close-fitting cap

**skunk** *n.* small N Amer. animal that emits evil-smelling fluid; *inf.* mean person

**sky** (skī) *n.* (*pl.* skies) apparently dome-shaped expanse extending upward from the horizon; outer space; heavenly regions —*vt. inf.* (skied, sky·ing) hit, throw (ball) high —sky'div·ing *n.* parachute jumping with delayed opening of parachute —sky'light (-līt) *n.*

window in roof or ceiling —**sky'-scrap·er** (-skrayp-ər) *n.* very tall building

**slab** *n.* thick, broad piece

**slack** (slak) *adj.* loose; sluggish; careless, negligent; not busy —*n.* loose part, as of rope —*vi.* be idle or lazy —**slack'en** *v.* become looser; become slower, abate

**slacks** (slaks) *n. pl.* informal trousers worn by men or women

**slag** *n.* refuse of smelted metal

**slain** *pp.* of SLAY

**slake** (slayk) *vt.* (slaked, slak·ing) satisfy (thirst, desire *etc.*); combine (lime) with water to produce calcium hydroxide

**sla·lom** (SLAH-ləm) *n./v.* race over winding course in skiing, automobile racing *etc.*

**slam** *v.* (slammed, slam·ming) shut noisily; bang; hit; dash down; *inf.* criticize harshly —*n.* (noise of) this action —**grand slam** *Cards* winning of all tricks; *Sports* winning of selected group of major tournaments in one year

**slan·der** (SLAN-dər) *n.* false or malicious statement about person —*v.* utter such statement —**slan'der·ous** *adj.*

**slang** *n.* words *etc.* or meanings of these used very informally for novelty or vividness or for the sake of unconventionality

**slant** *v.* slope; put at angle; write, present (news *etc.*) with bias —*n.* slope; point of view; idea —*adj.* sloping, oblique —**slant'wise** (-wiz) *adv.*

**slap** *n.* blow with open hand or flat instrument —*vt.* (slapped, slap·ping) strike thus; put on, down carelessly or messily —**slap'dash** *adj.* careless and abrupt —**slap'stick** *n.* broad boisterous comedy

**slash** *vt.* gash; lash; cut, slit; criti-

cize unmercifully —*n.* gash; cutting stroke

**slat** *n.* narrow strip of wood or metal as in window blinds *etc.*

**slate** (slayt) *n.* kind of stone that splits easily in flat sheets; piece of this for covering roof or, formerly, for writing on —*vt.* (slat·ed, slat·ing) cover with slates

**slath·er** (SLATH-ər) *n. inf.* generous amount —*vt. inf.* (-ered, -er·ing) spread, apply thickly

**slat·tern** (SLAT-ərn) *n.* slut —**slat'tern·ly** *adj.* slovenly, untidy

**slaugh·ter** (SLAW-tər) *n.* killing —*vt.* kill —**slaugh'ter·ous** *adj.* —**slaugh'ter·house** (-hows) *n.* place for butchering animals for food

**slave** (slayv) *n.* captive, person without freedom or personal rights; one dominated by another or by a habit *etc.* —*vi.* (slaved, slav·ing) work like slave —**slav'er** *n.* person, ship engaged in slave traffic —**slav'er·y** *n.* —**slav'ish** *adj.* servile

**slav·er** (SLAV-ər) *vi.* dribble saliva from mouth; fawn —*n.* saliva running from mouth

**slay** *vt.* (slew, slain, slay·ing) kill; *inf.* impress, *esp.* by being very funny —**slay'er** *n.* killer

**slea·zy** (SLEE-zee) *adj.* (-zi·er, -zi·est) sordid —**sleaze** (sleez) *n. sl.* sordidness; contemptible person

**sled** *n.* carriage on runners for sliding on snow; toboggan —*v.* (sled·ded, sled·ding)

**sledge** (slej) *n.* sledgehammer; sled

**sledge·ham·mer** (SLEJ-ham-ər) *n.* heavy hammer with long handle

**sleek** *adj.* (-er, -est) glossy, smooth, shiny

**sleep** *n.* unconscious state regularly occurring in humans and animals; slumber; repose; *inf.* dried particles *oft.* found in corners of eyes after sleeping —*v.* (**slept, sleep·ing**) take rest in sleep, slumber; accommodate for sleeping —**sleep′er** *n.* one who sleeps; railroad sleeping car; *inf.* person, firm etc. that succeeds unexpectedly —**sleep′i·ly** *adv.* —**sleep′i·ness** (-nis) *n.* —**sleep′less** (-lis) *adj.* —**sleep′y** *adj.* (**sleep·i·er, sleep·i·est**) —**sleeping sickness** *Afr.* disease spread by tsetse fly

**sleet** *n.* rain and snow or hail falling together

**sleeve** (sleev) *n.* part of garment that covers arm; case surrounding shaft; phonograph record cover —*vt.* (**sleeved, sleev·ing**) furnish with sleeves —**sleeved** *adj.* —**sleeve′less** (-lis) *adj.* —**have up one's sleeve** have something prepared secretly for emergency or as trick

**sleigh** (slay) *n.* sled

**sleight** (slit) *n.* dexterity; trickery; deviousness —**sleight-of-hand** (manual dexterity in) conjuring, juggling; legerdemain

**slen·der** (SLEN-dər) *adj.* slim, slight; feeble

**slept** *pt./pp. of* SLEEP

**sleuth** (slooth) *n.* detective; bloodhound —*vt.* track

**slew**¹ (sloo) *pt. of* SLAY

**slew**² *v.* swing around

**slew**³ *n. inf.* large number or quantity

**slice** (slis) *n.* thin flat piece cut off; share; spatula; slice of pizza —*vt.* (**sliced, slic·ing**) cut into slices; cut cleanly; hit with bat, club etc. at angle

**slick** (slik) *adj.* smooth; smooth-tongued; flattering; superficially attractive; sly —*vt.* make glossy, smooth —*n.* slippery area; patch of oil on water

**slide** (slid) *v.* (**slid, slid** *or* **slidden, slid·ing**) slip smoothly along; glide, as over ice; pass imperceptibly; deteriorate morally —*n.* sliding; surface, track for sliding; sliding part of mechanism; piece of glass holding object to be viewed under microscope; photographic transparency —**slide rule** mathematical instrument of two parts, one of which slides upon the other, for rapid calculations —**sliding scale** schedule for automatically varying one thing (*eg* wages) according to fluctuations of another (*eg* cost of living)

**slight** (slit) *adj.* small, trifling; not substantial, fragile; slim, slender —*vt.* disregard; neglect —*n.* indifference; act of discourtesy

**slim** *adj.* (**slim·mer, slim·mest**) thin; slight —*v.* (**slimmed, slim·ming**) reduce person's weight by diet and exercise —**slim′ness** *n.* —**slim′line** *adj.* appearing slim; pert. to slimness

**slime** (slim) *n.* greasy, thick, liquid mud or similar substance —**slim′y** *adj.* (**slim·i·er, slim·i·est**) like slime; fawning

**sling** *n.* strap, loop with string attached at each end for hurling stone; bandage for supporting wounded limb; rope, belt etc. for hoisting, carrying weights —*vt.* (**slung, sling·ing**) throw; hoist, swing by rope

**slink** *vi.* (**slunk, slink·ing**) move stealthily, sneak —**slink′y** *adj.* (**slink·i·er, slink·i·est**) sinuously graceful; (of clothes etc.) figure-hugging

**slip**¹ *v.* (**slipped, slip·ping**) (cause to) move smoothly, easily, quietly; pass out of (mind etc.); (of motor vehicle clutch) engage partially, fail —*v.* lose balance by sliding; fall from person's grasp; make mistake (*usu.* with up); decline in health, morals —vt. put on or take off easily, quickly; let go (anchor etc.); dislocate (bone) —n. act or occasion of slipping; mistake; petticoat; small piece of paper; plant cutting; launching slope on which ships are built; covering for pillow; small child —**slip′shod** adj. slovenly, careless —**slip′stream** n. Aviation stream of air driven astern by engine

**slip²** n. clay mixed with water to creamy consistency, used for decorating ceramic ware

**slip·per** (SLIP-ər) n. light shoe for indoor use —**slip′pered** adj.

**slip·per·y** (SLIP-ə-ree) adj. so smooth as to cause slipping or to be difficult to hold or catch; changeable; unreliable; crafty; wily

**slit** vt. (slit, slit·ting) make long straight cut in; cut in strips —n.

**slith·er** (SLITH-ər) vi. slide unsteadily (down slope etc.)

**sliv·er** (SLIV-ər) n. thin small piece torn off something; splinter

**slob** n. slovenly, coarse person

**slob·ber** (SLOB-ər) v. slaver; be weakly and excessively demonstrative —n. running saliva; maudlin speech

**sloe** (sloh) n. blue-black, sour fruit of blackthorn —**sloe-eyed** adj. dark-eyed; slanty-eyed —**sloe gin** (jin) liqueur of sloes steeped in gin

**slog** v. (slogged, slog·ging) hit vigorously, esp. in boxing; work or study with dogged determination; move, work with difficulty —n.

**slo·gan** (SLOH-gən) n. distinctive phrase (in advertising etc.)

**sloop** n. small one-masted vessel; Hist. small warship

**slop** v. (slopped, slop·ping) spill; splash —n. spilled liquid; watery

food; dirty liquid —pl. liquid refuse —**slop′py** adj. (-pi·er, -pi·est) careless, untidy; sentimental; wet, muddy

**slope** (slohp) n. v. (sloped, slop·ing) —vt. place slanting —vi. lie in, follow an inclined course; go furtively —n. slant; upward, downward inclination

**slosh** n. watery mud etc. —v. splash —**sloshed** adj. sl. drunk

**slot** n. narrow hole or depression; slit for coins —v. (slot·ted, slot·ting) put in slot; sort; place in series, organization —**slot machine** automatic machine worked by insertion of coin

**sloth** (slawth) n. sluggish S Amer. animal; sluggishness —**sloth′ful** (-fəl) adj. lazy, idle

**slouch** (slowch) vi. walk, sit etc. in lazy or ungainly, drooping manner —n. —adj. (of hat) with wide, flexible brim

**slough¹** (slow rhymes with cow) n. bog

**slough²** (sluf) n. skin shed by snake —v. shed (skin); drop off

**slov·en** (SLUV-ən) n. dirty, untidy person —**slov′en·ly** adj. (-li·er, -li·est) untidy; careless; disorderly —adv.

**slow** (sloh) adj. (-er, -est) lasting a long time; moving at low speed; behind the true time; dull —v. slacken speed (of) —**slow motion** motion picture showing movement greatly slowed down —**slow′poke** (-pohk) n. person slow in moving, acting, deciding etc.

**sludge** (sluj) n. slush, ooze; sewage

**slug¹** n. land snail with no shell; bullet —**slug′gard** (-ərd) n. lazy, idle person —**slug′gish** adj. slow; lazy, inert; not functioning well —**slug′gish·ness** n.

**slug²** v. (slugged, slug·ging) hit,

slog —n. inf. heavy blow; shot of whiskey —slug'ger n. hard-hitting boxer, baseball batter

sluice (sloos) n. gate, door to control flow of water —vt. (sluiced, sluic·ing) pour water over, through

slum n. squalid street or neighborhood —vi. (slummed, slumming) visit slums —slum'lord n. landlord who owns buildings in slums and neglects them

slum·ber (SLUM-bər) vi./n. sleep —slum'ber·er n.

slump v. fall heavily; relax ungracefully; decline suddenly in value, volume or esteem —n. sudden decline; (of prices etc.) sharp fall; depression

slung pt./pp. of SLING

slunk pt./pp. of SLINK

slur vt. (slurred, slur·ring) pass over lightly; run together (words, musical notes); disparage —n. slight, stigma; Mus. curved line above or below notes to be slurred

slurp v. eat, drink noisily

slur·ry (SLUR-ee) n. (pl. -ries) muddy liquid mixture as cement, mud etc.

slush n. watery, muddy substance; excessive sentimentality —slush'y adj. (slush·i·er, slush·i·est) —slush fund fund for financing bribery, corruption

slut n. dirty (immoral) woman —slut'tish adj.

sly (slī) adj. (sly·er or sli·er, sly·est or sli·est) cunning, wily, knowing; secret, deceitful —sly'ly, sli'ly adv. —sly'ness (-nis) n.

smack[1] (smak) n. taste, flavor; sl. heroin —vi. taste (of); suggest

smack[2] vt. slap; open and close (lips) with loud sound —n. smacking slap; crack; such sound; loud kiss —adv. inf.

squarely; directly —smack'dab' adv. inf. smack

smack[3] n. small sailing vessel, usu. for fishing

small (smawl) adj. (-er, -est) little, unimportant; petty; short; weak; mean —n. small slender part esp. of the back —small hours hours just after midnight —small-mind·ed (-mind-id) adj. having narrow views; petty —small'pox n. contagious disease —small talk light, polite conversation

smarm·y (SMAHR-mee) adj. (smarm·i·er, smarm·i·est) unpleasantly suave; fawning

smart (smahrt) adj. (-er, -est) astute; brisk; clever, witty; impertinent; trim, well dressed; fashionable; causing stinging pain —v. feel, cause pain —n. sharp pain —smart'en vt. —smart'ly adv. —smart'ness (-nis) n. —smart al'eck conceited person, know-it-all —smart ass sl. offens. smart aleck

smash vt. break violently; strike hard; ruin; destroy —vi. break; dash violently against —n. heavy blow; collision (of vehicles etc.); total financial failure; inf. popular success —smashed adj. sl. very drunk or affected by drugs —smash'er n. attractive person, thing

smat·ter·ing (SMAT-ər-ing) n. slight superficial knowledge

smear (smeer) vt. rub with grease etc.; smudge, spread with dirt, grease etc. —n. mark made thus; sample of secretion for medical examination; slander

smell v. (smelled or smelt, smell'-ing) perceive by nose; suspect; give out odor; use nose —n. faculty of perceiving odors by nose; anything detected by sense of smell —smell'y adj. (smell·i·er,

**smell·i·est**) with strong (unpleasant) smell

**smelt**[1] vt. extract metal from ore —**smelt′er** n.

**smelt**[2] n. fish of salmon family

**smid·gen** (SMIJ-ən) n. very small amount

**smile** (smīl) n. curving or parting of lips in pleased or amused expression —v. (**smiled, smil·ing**) wear, assume a smile; approve, favor

**smirch** (smurch) vt. dirty, sully; disgrace, discredit —n. stain; disgrace

**smirk** (smurk) n. smile expressing scorn, smugness —v.

**smite** (smīt) vt. (**smote, smit′ten** or **smit, smit′ing**) strike; attack; afflict; affect, esp. with love or fear

**smith** n. worker in iron, gold etc. —**smith′y** n. (pl. **smith·ies**) blacksmith's workshop; blacksmith

**smith·er·eens** (SMITH-ər-eenz) n. pl. small bits

**smock** (smok) n. loose outer garment —vt. gather by sewing in honeycomb pattern —**smock′ing** n.

**smog** n. mixture of smoke and fog

**smoke** (smohk) n. cloudy mass of suspended particles that rises from fire or anything burning; spell of tobacco smoking —v. (**smoked, smok·ing**) —vi. give off smoke; inhale and expel tobacco smoke —vt. use (tobacco) by smoking; expose to smoke (esp. in curing fish etc.) —**smok′er** n. one who smokes; informal party

**smol·der** (SMOHL-dər) vi. burn slowly without flame; (of feelings) exist in suppressed state

**smooch** v./n. inf. kiss, cuddle

**smooth** (smooth) adj. (-er, -est) not rough, even of surface or texture; sinuous; flowing; calm,

soft, soothing; suave, plausible; free from jolts —vt. make smooth; quiet —**smooth′ly** adv.

**smor·gas·bord** (SMOR-gəs-bord) n. buffet meal of assorted dishes

**smote** pt. of SMITE

**smoth·er** (SMUTH-ər) v. suffocate; envelop; suppress —vi. be suffocated

**smudge** (smuj) v. (**smudged, smudg·ing**) make smear, stain, dirty mark (on) —n.

**smug** adj. (**smug·ger, smug·gest**) self-satisfied, complacent —**smug′ly** adv.

**smug·gle** (SMUG-əl) vt. (-**gled, -gling**) import, export without paying customs duties; conceal, take secretly —**smug′gler** n.

**smut** n. piece of soot, particle of dirt; lewd or obscene talk etc.; disease of grain —vt. (**smut·ted, smut·ting**) blacken, smudge —**smut′ty** adj. (-**ti·er, -ti·est**) soiled with smut, soot; obscene, lewd

**Sn** Chem. tin

**snack** (snak) n. light portion of food eaten hastily between meals —vi. eat thus —**snack bar** lunchroom at which light meals are served

**snag** n. difficulty; sharp protuberance; hole, loop in fabric caused by sharp object; obstacle (eg tree branch etc. in river bed) —vt. (**snagged, snag′ging**) catch, damage on snag

**snail** (snayl) n. slow-moving mollusk with shell; slow, sluggish person —**snail′like** adj.

**snake** (snayk) n. long scaly limbless reptile, serpent —v. (**snaked, snak·ing**) move like snake —**snak′y** adj. (**snak·i·er, snak·i·est**) of, like snakes —**snake in the grass** hidden enemy

**snap** v. (**snapped, snap·ping**) break suddenly; make cracking sound; bite (at) suddenly; speak suddenly, angrily —*n.* act of snapping; fastener; snapshot; *inf.* easy task; brief period, *esp.* of cold weather —*adj.* sudden, unplanned, arranged quickly —snap'py *adj.* (-pi·er, -pi·est) irritable; *inf.* quick; *inf.* well-dressed, fashionable —snap'drag·on *n.* plant with flowers that can be opened like a mouth —snap'shot *n.* informal photograph

**snare** (snair) *n.* (noose used as) trap —*vt.* (snared, snar·ing) catch with one

**snarl** (snahrl) *n.* growl of angry dog; tangle, knot —*vi.* utter snarl; grumble

**snatch** (snach) *v.* make quick grab or bite (at); seize, catch —*n.* grab; fragment; short spell

**sneak** (sneek) *vi.* (sneaked, sneak·ing) slink; move about furtively; act in mean, underhand manner —*n.* mean, treacherous person —sneak'ing *adj.* secret but persistent —sneak pre'view unannounced showing of movie before general release

**sneak·ers** (SNEEK-ərz) *n. pl.* flexible, informal sports shoes

**sneer** *n.* scornful, contemptuous expression or remark —*v.*

**sneeze** (sneez) *vi.* (sneezed, sneez·ing) emit breath through nose with sudden involuntary spasm and noise —*n.*

**snick·er** (SNIK-ər) *n./v.* sly, disrespectful laugh, *esp.* partly stifled —*v.*

**snide** (snid) *adj.* (snid·er, snid·est) malicious, supercilious

**sniff** *vi.* inhale through nose with sharp hiss; (*with* at) express disapproval *etc.* by sniffing —*vt.* take up through nose, smell —*n.* —snif'fle *vi.* (-fled, -fling) sniff noisily through nose, *esp.* when

suffering from a cold in the head; snuffle

**snig·ger** (SNIG-ər) *n.* snicker

**snip** *vt.* (snipped, snip·ping) cut, cut bits off —*n.* act, sound of snipping; bit cut off; *inf.* small, insignificant, impertinent person —snip·pet (SNIP-it) *n.* shred, fragment, clipping —snips *n. pl.* tool for cutting

**snipe** (snip) *n.* wading bird —*v.* (sniped, snip·ing) shoot at enemy from cover; (*with* at) criticize, attack (person) slyly —snip'er *n.*

**snit** *n.* irritated state of mind

**snitch** (snich) *vt. inf.* steal —*vi.* inform —*n.* informer

**sniv·el** (SNIV-əl) *vi.* (-eled, -el·ing) sniffle to show distress; whine

**snob** *n.* one who pretentiously judges others by social rank *etc.* —snob'ber·y *n.* —snob'bish *adj.* of or like a snob

**snook·er** (SNUUK-ər) *n.* game like pool played with 21 balls —*vt.* leave (opponent) in unfavorable position; place (someone) in difficult situation; *sl.* cheat

**snoop** *v.* pry, meddle; peer into —*n.* one who acts thus; snooping

**snoot·y** (SNOOT-ee) *adj. inf.* (snoot·i·er, snoot·i·est) haughty

**snooze** (snooz) *vi.* (snoozed, snooz·ing) take short sleep —*n.* nap

**snore** (snor) *vi.* (snored, snor·ing) breathe noisily when asleep —*n.*

**snor·kel** (SNOR-kəl) *n.* tube for breathing underwater —*vi.* swim, fish using this

**snort** *vi.* make (contemptuous) noise by driving breath through nostrils; *sl.* inhale drug —*n.* noise of snorting; *sl.* shot of liquor; *sl.* amount of drug inhaled

**snot** *n. vulg.* mucus from nose —snot·ty (-tee) *adj. inf.* (-ti·er, -ti·est) arrogant

**snout** (snowt) *n.* animal's nose

**snow** (snoh) *n.* frozen vapor that falls in flakes; *sl.* cocaine —*v.* fall, sprinkle as snow; let fall, throw down like snow; cover with snow; *sl.* overwhelm; *sl.* deceive —**snow′y** *adj.* (**snow·i·er, snow·i·est**) of, like snow; covered with snow; very white —**snow′ball** *n.* snow pressed into hard ball for throwing —*v.* increase rapidly; play, fight with snowballs —**snow blind·ness** temporary blindness due to brightness of snow —**snow′drift** *n.* bank of deep snow —**snow fence** fence for erecting in winter beside exposed road —**snow job** *sl.* attempt to deceive by flattery or exaggeration —**snow line** elevation above which snow does not melt —**snow′shoes** (-shooz) *n. pl.* shoes like rackets for traveling on snow —**snow under** cover and block with snow; *fig.* overwhelm

**snub** *vt.* (**snubbed, snub·bing**) insult (*esp.* by ignoring) intentionally —*n.* —*adj.* short and blunt —**snub-nosed** *adj.*

**snuff**[1] *n.* powdered tobacco for inhaling through nose —**up to snuff** *inf.* up to a standard

**snuff**[2] *v.* extinguish (*esp.* candle *etc.*)

**snuf·fle** (SNUF-əl) *vi.* (-**fled,** -**fling**) breathe noisily, with difficulty

**snug** *adj.* (-**ger,** -**gest**) warm, comfortable —**snug′gle** *v.* (-**gled,** -**gling**) lie close to for warmth or affection —**snug′ly** *adv.*

**so**[1] (soh) *adv.* to such an extent; in such a manner; very; the case being such; accordingly —*conj.* therefore; in order that; with the result that —*interj.* well! —**so-called** *adj.* called by but doubtful-

ly deserving that name —**so long** *inf.* goodbye

**so**[2] *see* SOL

**soak** (sohk) *v.* steep; absorb; drench; lie in liquid; *sl.* overcharge (customer) —*n.* soaking; *sl.* habitual drunkard

**soap** (sohp) *n.* compound of alkali and oil used in washing —*vt.* apply soap to —**soap′y** *adj.* (**soap·i·er, soap·i·est**) —**soap opera** radio or TV serial of domestic life

**soar** (sor) *vi.* fly high; increase, rise (in price *etc.*)

**sob** *vi.* (**sobbed, sob·bing**) catch breath, *esp.* in weeping —*n.* sobbing —**sob story** tale of personal distress told to arouse sympathy

**so·ber** (SOH-bər) *adj.* (-**ber·er,** -**ber·est**) not drunk; temperate; subdued; dull, plain; solemn —*v.* make, become sober —**so·bri·e·ty** (sə-BRĪ-i-tee) *n.* state of being sober

**so·bri·quet** (SOH-brə-kay) *n.* nickname; assumed name

**soc·cer** (SOK-ər) *n.* ball game played with feet and spherical ball

**so·cia·ble** (SOH-shə-bəl) *adj.* friendly; convivial —**so·cia·bil′i·ty** *n.*

**social** (SOH-shəl) *adj.* living in communities; relating to society; sociable —*n.* informal gathering —**so′cial·ite** *n.* member of fashionable society —**so′cial·ize** *v.* (-**ized,** -**iz·ing**) —**so′cial·ly** *adv.* —**social security** government-sponsored provision for the disabled, unemployed, aged *etc.* —**social work** work to improve welfare of others

**so·cial·ism** (SOH-shə-liz-əm) *n.* political system that advocates public ownership of means of production, distribution and exchange —**so′cial·ist** *n./adj.*

**so·ci·e·ty** (sə-SĪ-i-tee) n. (pl. -ties) living associated with others; those so living; companionship; company; association; club; fashionable people collectively

**so·ci·ol·o·gy** (soh-see-OL-ə-jee) n. study of societies

**sock**[1] (sok) n. cloth covering for foot

**sock**[2] vt. hit —n. blow

**sock·et** (SOK-it) n. hole or recess for something to fit into

**So·crat·ic** (sə-KRAT-ik) adj. of, like Greek philosopher Socrates

**sod** n. lump of earth with grass

**so·da** (SOH-də) n. compound of sodium; soda water —soda water water charged with carbon dioxide

**sod·den** (SOD-n) adj. soaked; drunk; heavy and lumpy

**so·di·um** (SOH-dee-əm) n. metallic alkaline element —sodium bicarbonate white crystalline soluble compound (also bicarbonate of soda)

**sod·om·y** (SOD-ə-mee) n. anal or oral intercourse —sod'om·ite n.

**so·fa** (SOH-fə) n. upholstered couch with back and arms, for two or more people

**soft** (sawft) adj. (-er, -est) yielding easily to pressure, not hard; mild; easy; subdued; quiet, gentle; (too) lenient; oversentimental; foolish, stupid; (of water) containing few mineral salts; (of drugs) not liable to cause addiction —soft'en (SAWF-ən) v. make, become soft or softer; mollify; lighten; mitigate; make less loud —soft'ly adv. gently, quietly —soft drink one that is nonalcoholic —soft goods nondurable goods eg curtains, rugs —soft soap inf. flattery —soft'ware n. computer programs, tapes etc. —soft'wood (-wuud) n. wood of coniferous tree

**sog·gy** (SOG-ee) adj. (-gi·er, -gi·est) soaked with liquid; damp and heavy

**soil**[1] n. earth, ground; country, territory

**soil**[2] v. make, become dirty; tarnish, defile —n. dirt; sewage; stain

**soi·ree** (swah-RAY) n. private evening party esp. with music

**so·journ** (SOH-jurn) vi. stay for a time —n. short stay —so'journ·er n.

**sol, so** n. fifth sol-fa note

**sol·ace** (SOL-is) n./vt. (-aced, -ac·ing) comfort in distress

**so·lar** (SOH-lər) adj. of the sun —solar plex'us network of nerves at pit of stomach

**so·lar·i·um** (sə-LAIR-ee-əm) n. (pl. -i·ums) room built mainly of glass to give exposure to sun

**sold** pt./pp. of SELL

**sol·der** (SOD-ər) n. easily-melted alloy used for joining metal —vt. join with it —soldering iron

**sol·dier** (SOHL-jər) n. one serving in army —vi. serve in army; inf. loaf; (with on) persist doggedly —sol'dier·ly adj.

**sole**[1] (sohl) adj. one and only, unique; solitary —sole'ly adv. alone; only; entirely

**sole**[2] n. underside of foot; underpart of shoe etc. —vt. (soled, sol·ing) furnish with sole

**sole**[3] n. small edible flatfish

**sol·e·cism** (SOL-ə-siz-əm) n. breach of grammar or etiquette

**sol·emn** (SOL-əm) adj. serious; formal; impressive —sol'emn·ly adv. —so·lem·ni·ty (sə-LEM-ni-tee) n. —sol·em·nize (SOL-əm-nīz) vt. (-nized, niz·ing) celebrate, perform; make solemn

**so·le·noid** (SOH-lə-noid) n. coil of wire as part of electrical apparatus

**sol-fa** (sohl-FAH) n. Mus. system

of syllables sol, fa *etc.* sung in scale

**so·lic·it** (sə-LIS-it) *vt.* request; accost; urge; entice —**so·lic·i·ta'tion** *n.* —**so·lic'i·tor** *n.* one who solicits —**so·lic'i·tous** *adj.* anxious; eager; earnest —**so·lic'i·tude** *n.*

**sol'id** *adj.* not hollow; compact; composed of one substance; firm; massive; reliable, sound —*n.* body of three dimensions; substance not liquid or gas —**sol·i·dar'i·ty** *n.* unity of interests; united condition —**so·lid'i·fy** *v.* (-fied, -fy·ing) make, become solid or firm; harden —**so·lid'i·ty** *n.*

**so·lil·o·quy** (sə-LIL-ə-kwee) *n.* (*pl.* -quies) (*esp.* in drama) thoughts spoken by person while alone —**so·lil'o·quize** *vi.* (-quized, -quiz·ing)

**sol·ip·sism** (SOL-ip-siz-əm) *n.* doctrine that self is the only thing known to exist —**sol'ip·sist** *n.*

**sol·i·tar·y** (SOL-i-ter-ee) *adj.* alone, single —*n.* hermit —**sol·i·taire** *n.* game for one person played with cards or with pegs set in board; single precious stone set by itself —**sol'i·tude** *n.* state of being alone; loneliness

**so·lo** (SOH-loh) *n.* (*pl.* -los) music for one performer —*adj.* not concerted; unaccompanied; alone; piloting airplane alone —**so'lo·ist** *n.*

**sol·stice** (SOL-stis) *n.* either shortest (winter) or longest (summer) day of year

**solve** (solv) *vt.* (solved, solv·ing) work out, explain; find answer to —**sol·u·bil'i·ty** (sol·yə-BIL-i-tee) *n.* —**sol'u·ble** *adj.* capable of being dissolved in liquid; able to be solved or explained —**so·lu'tion** (sə-LOO-shən) *n.* answer to problem; dissolving; liquid with something dissolved in it —**solv'a·ble** *adj.* —**sol'ven·cy** (-vən-see) *n.* —**sol'vent** *adj.* able to meet financial obligations —*n.* liquid with power of dissolving

**som·ber** (SOM-bər) *adj.* dark, gloomy

**som·bre·ro** (som-BRAIR-oh) *n.* (*pl.* -bre·ros) wide-brimmed hat worn in Mexico, Spain *etc.*

**some** (sum) *adj.* denoting an indefinite number, amount or extent; one or other; amount of; certain; approximately —*pron.* portion, quantity —**some'bod·y** *n.* some person; important person unknown —**some'how** *adv.* by some means —**some'thing** *n.* thing not clearly defined; indefinite amount, quantity or degree —**some'time** *adv.* formerly; at some (past or future) time —*adj.* former —**some'times** *adv.* occasionally; now and then —**some'what** (-hwot) *adv.* to some extent, rather —**some'where** (-hwair) *adv.*

**som·er·sault** (SUM-ər-sawlt) *n.* tumbling head over heels

**som·nam·bu·list** (som-NAM-byə-list) *n.* sleepwalker —**som·nam'bu·lism** *n.*

**som·no·lent** (SOM-nə-lənt) *adj.* drowsy; causing sleep —**som'no·lence** *n.*

**son** (sun) *n.* male child —**son-in-law** *n.* daughter's husband

**so·nar** (SOH-nahr) *n.* device like echo sounder

**so·na·ta** (sə-NAH-tə) *n.* piece of music in several movements —**son·a·ti·na** (son-ə-TEE-nə) *n.* short sonata

**son et lumière** (saw-nay-luu-MYAIR) *Fr.* entertainment staged at night at famous place, building, giving dramatic history of it with lighting and sound effects

**song** (sawng) *n.* singing; poem

*etc.* for singing —**song'ster** *n.* singer; songbird (**song'stress** *fem.* -stris)

**sonic** (SON-ik) *adj.* pert. to sound waves —**sonic boom** explosive sound caused by aircraft traveling at supersonic speed

**son·net** (SON-it) *n.* fourteen-line poem with definite rhyme scheme —**son·net·eer** (son-i-TEER) *n.* writer of this

**so·no·rous** (sə-NOR-əs) *adj.* giving out (deep) sound, resonant —**so·nor'i·ty** *n.*

**soon** *adv.* in a short time; before long; early, quickly

**soot** (suut) *n.* black powdery substance formed by burning of coal *etc.* —**soot'y** *adj.* (**soot·i·er, soot·i·est**) of, like soot

**sooth** *n.* truth —**sooth'say·er** *n.* one who foretells future; diviner

**soothe** (sooth) *vt.* (**soothed, sooth·ing**) make calm, tranquil; relieve (pain *etc.*)

**sop** *n.* piece of bread *etc.* soaked in liquid; concession, bribe —*vt.* (**sopped, sop·ping**) steep in water *etc.*; soak (up) —**sop·ping** *adj.* completely soaked

**soph·ist** (SOF-ist) *n.* fallacious reasoner, quibbler —**soph'ism** (-izm) *n.* specious argument —**soph'ist·ry** *n.*

**so·phis·ti·cate** (sə-FIS-ti-kayt) *vt.* (**-cat·ed, -cat·ing**) make artificial, spoil, falsify, corrupt —*n.* (-kit) sophisticated person —**so·phis·ti·ca·tion** *n.* —**so·phis'ti·cat·ed** *adj.* having refined or cultured tastes, habits; worldly wise; superficially clever; complex —**so·phis·ti·ca'tion** *n.*

**soph·o·more** (SOF-ə-mor) *n.* student in second year at high school or college —**soph·o·mor'ic** intellectually pretentious

**sop·o·rif·ic** (sop-ə-RIF-ik) *adj.* causing sleep (*esp.* by drugs)

**so·pra·no** (sə-PRAN-oh) *n.* (*pl.* -pran·os) highest voice in women and boys; singer with this voice; musical part for it

**sor·bet** (sor-BAY) *n.* sherbet

**sor·cer·er** (SOR-sər-ər) *n.* magician (**sor·cer·ess** *fem.* -ris) —**sor'cer·y** *n.* (*pl.* -ies) witchcraft, magic

**sor'did** *adj.* mean, squalid; ignoble, base —**sor'did·ly** *adv.* —**sor'did·ness** (-nis) *n.*

**sore** (sor) *adj.* (**sor·er, sor·est**) painful; causing annoyance; severe; distressed; annoyed —*adv. obs.* grievously, intensely —*n.* sore place, ulcer, boil *etc.* —**sore'ly** *adv.* grievously; greatly

**sor·ghum** (SOR-gəm) *n.* kind of grass cultivated for grain

**sor·rel** (SOR-əl) *n.* plant; reddish-brown color; horse of this color —*adj.* of this color

**sor·row** (SOR-oh) *n.* pain of mind, grief, sadness —*vi.* grieve —**sor'row·ful** (-fəl) *adj.*

**sor·ry** (SOR-ee) *adj.* (-ri·er, -ri·est) feeling pity or regret; distressed; miserable, wretched; mean, poor —**sor'ri·ly** *adv.*

**sort** *n.* kind or class —*vt.* classify —**sort'er** *n.*

**sor·tie** (SOR-tee) *n.* sally by besieged forces

**SOS** *n.* international code signal of distress; call for help

**so-so** (SOH-soh) *adj.* mediocre —*adv.* tolerably

**sot** *n.* habitual drunkard

**sot·to vo·ce** (SOT-oh VOH-chee) *It.* in an undertone

**souf·flé** (soo-FLAY) *n.* dish of eggs beaten to froth, flavored and baked; dessert like this of various ingredients

**sough** (sow *rhymes with* cow) *n.* low murmuring sound as of wind in trees

**sought** (sawt) *pt./pp. of* SEEK

**soul** (sohl) *n.* spiritual and immortal part of human being; example, pattern; person; (*also* soul music) type of African-American music combining urban blues with jazz, pop *etc.* —**soul′ful** (-fəl) *adj.* full of emotion or sentiment —**soul′less** (-lis) *adj.* mechanical; lacking sensitivity or nobility; heartless, cruel

**sound**[1] (sownd) *n.* what is heard; noise —*vi.* make a sound; seem; give impression of —*vt.* cause to sound; utter —**sound barrier** hypothetical barrier to flight at speed of sound waves —**sound track** recorded sound accompaniment of motion picture *etc.*

**sound**[2] *adj.* (-er, -est) in good condition; solid; of good judgment; legal; solvent; thorough; effective; watertight; deep —**sound′ly** *adv.* thoroughly

**sound**[3] *vt.* find depth of, as water; ascertain views of; probe —**sound′ings** *n. pl.* measurements taken by sounding

**sound**[4] *n.* channel; strait

**soup** (soop) *n.* liquid food made by boiling or simmering meat, vegetables *etc.* —**soup′y** *adj.* (soup-i-er, soup-i-est) like soup; murky; sentimental

**sour** (sowr) *adj.* acid; gone bad; rancid; peevish; disagreeable —*v.* make, become sour —**sour′ness** (-nis) *n.* —**sour′puss** (-puus) *n. inf.* sullen, sour-faced person

**source** (sors) *n.* origin, starting point; spring

**souse** (sows *rhymes with* louse) *v.* (soused, sous·ing) plunge, drench; pickle —*n.* sousing; brine for pickling; *sl.* drunkard —**soused** *adj. sl.* drunk

**south** (sowth) *n.* cardinal point opposite north; region, part of country *etc.* lying to that side —*adj./adv.* (that is) toward south —**south′ward** (-wərd) *adj./adv.*

—**south′wards** (-wərdz) *adv.* —**south·er·ly** (SUTH-ər-lee) *adj.* toward south —*n.* (pl. -lies) wind from the south —**south·ern** (SUTH-ərn) *adj.* in south

**south-west·er** (sowth-WES-tər) *n.* wind, storm from the southwest

**sou·ve·nir** (soo-və-NEER) *n.* keepsake, memento

**sou′west·er** (sow-WES-tər) *n.* waterproof hat; southwester

**sov·er·eign** (SOV-rin) *n.* king, queen; former British gold coin worth 20 shillings —*adj.* supreme; efficacious —**sov′er·eign·ty** *n.* (pl. -ties) supreme power and right to exercise it; dominion; independent state

**so·vi·et** (SOH-vee-et) *n.* elected council at various levels of government in USSR; (S-) official or citizen of USSR —*adj.* of, pert. to USSR, its people, government

**sow**[1] (soh) *v.* (sowed, sown *or* sowed, sow·ing) *v.* scatter, plant seed —*vt.* scatter, deposit (seed); spread abroad

**sow**[2] (*rhymes with* cow) *n.* female adult pig

**soy·bean** (SOI-been) *n.* edible bean used as livestock feed, meat substitute *etc.*

**soy sauce** (SOI saws) sauce made by fermenting soybeans in brine

**spa** (spah) *n.* medicinal spring; place, resort with one

**space** (spays) *n.* extent; room; period; empty place; area; expanse; region beyond Earth's atmosphere —*vt.* (spaced, spac·ing) place at intervals —**spa′cious** (-shəs) *adj.* roomy, extensive —**space′craft, space′ship** *n.* vehicle for travel beyond Earth's atmosphere —**space shuttle** vehicle for repeated space flights —**space′suit** *n.* sealed, pressurized suit worn by astronaut

**spade**[1] (spayd) n. tool for digging —**spade work** arduous preparatory work

**spade**[2] n. leaf-shaped black symbol on playing card

**spa·ghet·ti** (spə-GET-ee) n. pasta in form of long strings

**spake** (spayk) obs. pt. of SPEAK

**span** n. space from thumb to little finger as measure; extent, space; stretch of arch etc.; abbrev. of **wing'span**, distance from wing tip to wing tip —vt. (**spanned, span·ning**) stretch over; measure with hand

**span·gle** (SPANG-gəl) n. small shiny metallic ornament —vt. (-**gled, -gling**) decorate with spangles

**span·iel** (SPAN-yəl) n. breed of dog with long ears and silky hair

**spank** (spangk) vt. slap with flat of hand etc. esp. on buttocks —n. —**spank'ing** n. series of spanks —adj. quick, lively; large, fine

**span·ner** (SPAN-ər) n. type of wrench for gripping nut or bolt head

**spar**[1] (spahr) n. pole, beam, esp. as part of ship's rigging

**spar**[2] vi. (**sparred, spar·ring**) box; dispute, esp. in fun —n. sparring

**spar**[3] n. any of kinds of crystalline mineral

**spare** (spair) vt. (**spared, spar·ing**) leave unhurt; show mercy; abstain from using; do without; give away —adj. additional; in reserve; thin; lean; scanty —n. spare part (for machine) —**spar·ing** adj. economical, careful

**spark** (spahrk) n. small glowing or burning particle; flash of light produced by electrical discharge; vivacity, humor; trace; in internal-combustion engines, electric spark (in spark plug) that ignites explosive mixture in cylinder —v. emit sparks; kindle, excite; obs. woo

**spar·kle** (SPAHR-kəl) vi. (-**kled, -kling**) glitter; effervesce; scintillate —n. small spark; glitter; flash; luster —**sparkling** adj. flashing; glittering; brilliant; lively; (of wines) effervescent

**spar·row** (SPA-roh) n. small finch

**sparse** (spahrs) (**spars·er, spars·est**) adj. thinly scattered

**Spar·tan** (SPAHR-tn) adj. hardy; austere; frugal; undaunted

**spasm** (SPAZ-əm) n. sudden convulsive (muscular) contraction; sudden burst of activity etc. —**spas·mod·ic** (spaz-MOD-ik) adj. occurring in spasms

**spas·tic** (SPAS-tik) adj. affected by spasms, suffering cerebral palsy —n.

**spat**[1] pt. of SPIT[1]

**spat**[2] n. short gaiter

**spat**[3] n. slight quarrel —vi. (**spat·ted, spat·ting**) quarrel

**spate** (spayt) n. rush, outpouring; flood

**spa·tial** (SPAY-shəl) adj. of, in space

**spat·ter** (SPAT-ər) vt. splash, cast drops over —vi. be scattered in drops —n. slight splash; sprinkling

**spat·u·la** (SPACH-ə-lə) n. utensil with broad, flat blade for various purposes

**spav·in** n. injury to, growth on horse's leg —**spav'ined** adj. lame, decrepit

**spawn** n. eggs of fish, frog etc. —vi. (of fish or frog) cast eggs; produce in great numbers

**spay** vt. remove ovaries from (animal)

**speak** (speek) v. (**spoke, spo·ken, speak·ing**) utter words; converse; deliver discourse; utter; pronounce; express; communicate in —**speak'er** n. one who speaks;

one who specializes in speech-making; (*oft.* **S-**) official chairman of US House of Representatives, other legislative bodies; loudspeaker

**spear** (speer) *n.* long pointed weapon; slender shoot, as of asparagus —*vt.* transfix, pierce, wound with spear —**spear'head** (-hed) *n.* leading force in attack, campaign —*vt.*

**spear·mint** (SPEER-mint) *n.* type of mint

**spec** (spek) *n.* (*esp.* on spec) speculation or gamble; specification

**spe·cial** (SPESH-əl) *adj.* beyond the usual; particular, individual; distinct; limited —**spe'cial·ist** *n.* one who devotes self to special subject or branch of subject —**spe'cial·ty** *n.* (*pl.* **-ties**) special product, skill, characteristic *etc.* —**spe'cial·ize** *v.* (**-ized, -iz·ing**) —*vi.* be specialist; be adapted to special function or environment —*vt.* make special

**spe·cie** (SPEE-shee) *n.* coined, as distinct from paper, money

**spe·cies** (SPEE-sheez) *n.* (*pl.* same form) sort, kind, *esp.* animals *etc.*; class; subdivision

**spe·cif·ic** (spə-SIF-ik) *adj.* definite; exact in detail; characteristic of a thing or kind —**spe·cif'i·cal·ly** *adv.* —**spec'i·fy** *vt.* (**-fied, -fy·ing**) state definitely or in detail —**spec·i·fi·ca'tion** (-KAY-shən) *n.* detailed description of something to be made, done —**specific gravity** ratio of density of substance to that of water

**spec·i·men** (SPES-ə-mən) *n.* part typifying whole; individual example

**spe·cious** (SPEE-shəs) *adj.* deceptively plausible, but false —**spe'cious·ly** *adv.* —**spe'cious·ness** (-nis) *n.*

**speck** (spek) *n.* small spot, particle —*vt.* spot —**speck·le** (SPEK-l) *n./vt.* (**-led, -ling**) speck

**spec·ta·cle** (SPEK-tə-kəl) *n.* show; thing exhibited; ridiculous sight —*pl.* eyeglasses —**spec·tac'u·lar** *adj.* impressive; showy; grand; magnificent —*n.* lavishly produced performance —**spec·ta·tor** (SPEK-tay-tər) *n.* one who looks on

**spec·ter** (SPEK-tər) *n.* ghost; image of something unpleasant —**spec'tral** (-trəl) *adj.* ghostly

**spec·trum** (SPEK-trəm) *n.* (*pl.* **-tra** *pr.* **-trə**) band of colors into which beam of light can be decomposed *eg* by prism; range (of *eg* opinions, occupations) —**spec'tro·scope** (-trə-skohp) *n.* instrument for producing, examining physical spectra

**spec·u·late** (SPEK-yə-layt) *vi.* (**-lat·ed, -lat·ing**) guess, conjecture; engage in (risky) commercial transactions —**spec·u·la'tion** *n.* —**spec'u·la·tive** (-lə-tiv) *adj.* given to, characterized by speculation —**spec'u·la·tor** *n.*

**spec·u·lum** (SPEK-yə-ləm) *n.* (*pl.* **-lums**) mirror; reflector of polished metal, *esp.* in reflecting telescopes

**speech** *n.* act, faculty of speaking; words, language; conversation; discourse; (formal) talk given before audience —**speech'i·fy** *vi.* (**-fied, -fy·ing**) make speech, *esp.* long and tedious one —**speech'less** (-lis) *adj.* mute; at a loss for words

**speed** *n.* swiftness; rate of progress; degree of sensitivity of photographic film; *sl.* amphetamine —*v.* (**sped** *or* **speed·ed, speed·ing**) move quickly; drive vehicle at high speed; further; expedite —**speed'ing** *n.* driving (vehicle) at high speed, *esp.* over legal limit —**speed′i·ly** adv. —**speed′y** adj. (**speed·i·er, speed·i·est**) quick; rapid; nimble; prompt —**speed′boat** n. light fast motorboat —**speed·om′e·ter** (-OM-ə-tər) n. instrument to show speed of vehicle —**speed′way** n. track for automobile or motorcycle racing

**spe·le·ol·o·gy** (spee-lee-OL-ə-jee) n. study, exploring of caves —**spe·le·ol′o·gist** n.

**spell**[1] vt. (**spelled** or **spelt**, **spell·ing**) give letters of in order; read letter by letter; indicate, result in —**spelling** n. **spell out** make explicit

**spell**[2] n. magic formula; enchantment —**spell′bound** (-bownd) adj. enchanted; entranced

**spell**[3] n. (short) period of time, work

**spend** vt. (**spent, spend·ing**) pay out; pass (time) on activity etc.; use up completely —**spend′thrift** n. wasteful person

**sperm** (spurm) n. male reproductive cell; semen —**sper·mat′ic** adj. of sperm —**sperm′i·cide** (-sīd) n. drug etc. that kills sperm

**sper·ma·cet·i** (spur-mə-SET-ee) n. white, waxy substance obtained from oil from head of sperm whale —**sperm whale** large, toothed whale

**spew** (spyoo) v. vomit; gush

**sphag·num** (SFAG-nəm) n. moss that grows in bogs

**sphere** (sfeer) n. ball, globe; range; field of action; status; position; province —**spher·i·cal** (SFER-i-kəl) adj.

**sphinc·ter** (SFINGK-tər) n. ring of muscle surrounding opening of hollow bodily organ

**sphinx** (sfingks) n. (pl. **-es**) figure in Egypt with lion's body and human head; (S-) the great statue of this near the pyramids of Giza;

(s-) monster, half woman, half lion; enigmatic person

**spice** (spīs) n. aromatic or pungent vegetable substance; spices collectively; anything that adds flavor, relish, piquancy, interest etc. —vt. (**spiced, spic·ing**) season with spices, flavor —**spic′y** (**spic·i·er, spic·i·est**) adj. flavored with spices; slightly indecent, risqué

**spick-and-span** (SPIK-ən-SPAN) adj. spotlessly clean; neat, smart, new-looking

**spi·der** (SPĪ-dər) n. small eight-legged creature that spins web to catch prey —**spi′der·y** adj.

**spiel** (speel) n. inf. glib (sales) talk —vi. deliver spiel, recite —**spiel′er** n.

**spig·ot** (SPIG-ət) n. peg or plug; faucet

**spike** (spīk) n. sharp point; sharp pointed object; long flower cluster with flowers attached directly to the stalk —vt. (**spiked, spik·ing**) pierce, fasten with spike; render ineffective; add alcohol to (drink)

**spill** v. (**spilled** or **spilt, spill·ing**) (cause to) pour from, flow over, fall out, esp. unintentionally; upset; be lost or wasted —n. spillway; spillage —**spill′age** (-ij) n. amount spilled —**spill′way** n. passageway through which excess water spills

**spin** v. (**spun, spin·ning**) (cause to) revolve rapidly; whirl; twist into thread; prolong; tell (a story); fish with lure —n. spinning; (of aircraft) descent in dive with continued rotation; rapid run or ride; Politics interpretation (of event, speech etc.) to gain partisan advantage —**spinning** n. act, process of drawing out and twisting into threads, as wool, cotton, flax etc. —**spinning wheel** household machine with large wheel turned by treadle for spinning wool *etc.* into thread —spin-dry *vt.* (-dried, -dry-ing) spin clothes in (washing) machine to remove excess water

spin-ach (SPIN-ich) *n.* garden vegetable

spin-dle (SPIN-dl) *n.* rod, axis for spinning —spin'dly *adj.* (-dli-er, -dli-est) long and slender; attenuated

spin'drift *n.* spray blown along surface of sea

spine (spīn) *n.* backbone; thin spike, *esp.* on fish *etc.*; ridge; back of book —spi'nal (-əl) *adj.* —spine'less (-lis) *adj.* lacking spine; cowardly

spin-et (SPIN-it) *n.* small piano; small harpsichord

spin-na-ker (SPIN-ə-kər) *n.* large yacht sail

spin-ster (SPIN-stər) *n.* unmarried woman

spi-ral (SPĪ-rəl) *n.* continuous curve drawn at ever increasing distance from fixed point; anything resembling this; *Football* kick or pass turning on longer axis —*v.* (-raled, -ral-ing) of *eg* football or inflation, (cause to) take spiral course —*adj.*

spire (spīr) *n.* pointed part of steeple; pointed stem of plant

spir'it *n.* life principle animating body; disposition; liveliness; courage; frame of mind; essential character or meaning; soul; ghost; liquid got by distillation, alcohol —*pl.* emotional state; strong alcoholic drink *eg* whiskey —*vt.* carry away mysteriously —spir'it-ed (-id) *adj.* lively —spir'it-less (-lis) *adj.* listless, apathetic —spir-it-u-al (-choo-əl) *adj.* given to, interested in things of the spirit —*n.* religious song, hymn —spir'it-u-al-ism *n.* belief

that spirits of the dead communicate with the living —spir'it-u-al-ist *n.* —spir'it-u-ous *adj.* alcoholic —spirit level glass tube containing bubble in liquid, used to check horizontal, vertical surfaces

spirt *n. see* SPURT

spit¹ *v.* (spit *or* spat, spit-ting) eject saliva; eject from mouth —*n.* spitting, saliva —spit-tle (SPIT-l) *n.* saliva —spit'ball *n.* illegal pitch of baseball moistened with saliva by pitcher; ball of chewed paper used as missile —spit-toon' *n.* vessel to spit into —spit'fire *n.* person, *esp.* woman or girl, with fiery temper

spit² *n.* sharp rod to put through meat for roasting; sandy point projecting into the sea —*vt.* (spit-ted, spit-ting) thrust through

spite (spīt) *n.* malice —*vt.* (spit-ed, spit-ing) thwart spitefully —spite'ful (-fəl) *adj.* —in spite of *prep.* regardless of; notwithstanding

splash *v.* scatter liquid about or on, over something; print, display prominently —*n.* sound of this; patch, *esp.* of color; (effect of) extravagant display; small amount

splat *n.* wet, slapping sound

splat-ter (SPLAT-ər) *v./n.* spatter

splay *adj.* spread out; slanting; turned outward —*vt.* spread out; twist outward —*n.* slanted surface —splay'foot-ed (-fuut-id) *adj.* flat and broad (of foot)

spleen *n.* organ in the abdomen; anger; irritable or morose temper —sple-net-ic (splə-NET-ik) *adj.*

splen'did *adj.* magnificent, brilliant, excellent —splen'did-ly *adv.* —splen'dor (-dər) *n.*

splice (splīs) *vt.* (spliced, splicing) join by interweaving strands; join (wood) by overlapping; *inf.* join in marriage —*n.* spliced joint

**spline** (splīn) *n.* narrow groove, ridge, strip, *esp.* joining wood *etc.*

**splint** *n.* rigid support for broken limb *etc.*

**splin·ter** (SPLIN-tər) *n.* thin fragment —*vi.* break into fragments, shiver —**splinter group** group that separates from main party, organization, *oft.* after disagreement

**split** *v.* (**split, split·ting**) break asunder; separate; divide; *sl.* depart —*n.* crack, fissure; dessert of fruit, *usu.* banana, and ice cream

**splotch** (sploch) *n./v.* splash, daub —**splotch'y** (**splotch·i·er, splotch·i·est**)

**splurge** (splurj) *v.* (**splurged, splurg·ing**) spend money extravagantly —*n.*

**splut·ter** (SPLUT-ər) *v.* make hissing, spitting sounds; utter incoherently with spitting sounds —*n.*

**spoil** *v.* (**spoiled** *or* **spoilt, spoil·ing**) damage, injure; damage manners or behavior of (*esp.* child) by indulgence; pillage; go bad —*n.* booty; waste material, *esp.* in mining (*also* **spoil'age** pr. ij) —**spoil'er** *n.* slowing device on aircraft wing *etc.* —**spoiling for** eager for

**spoke**[1] (spohk) *pt.,* **spo·ken** *pp.* of SPEAK —**spokes'per·son, -wo·man, -man** *n.* one deputed to speak for others

**spoke**[2] *n.* radial bar of a wheel

**spo·li·a·tion** (spoh-lee-AY-shən) *n.* act of spoiling; robbery; destruction —**spo'li·ate** (-ayt) *v.* (**-at·ed, -at·ing**) despoil, plunder, pillage

**spon·dee** *n.* metrical foot consisting of two long syllables

**sponge** (spunj) *n.* marine animal;

its skeleton, or a synthetic substance like it, used to absorb liquids; type of light cake *v.* (**sponged, spong·ing**) —*vt.* wipe with sponge —*vi.* live meanly at expense of another; cadge —**spong'er** *n. sl.* one who cadges, or lives at expense of others —**spon'gy** *adj.* (**-gi·er, -gi·est**) spongelike; wet and soft

**spon·sor** (SPON-sər) *n.* one promoting, advertising something; one who agrees to give money to a charity on completion of specified activity by another; one taking responsibility (*esp.* for welfare of child at baptism, *as* godparent); guarantor —*vt.* act as sponsor —**spon'sor·ship** *n.*

**spon·ta·ne·ous** (spon-TAY-nee-əs) *adj.* voluntary; natural; not forced; produced without external force —**spon·ta·ne'i·ty** (-tə-NEE-i·tee) *n.*

**spoof** *n.* mild satirical mockery; trick, hoax —*v.*

**spook** *n.* ghost —*vt.* haunt —**spook'y** *adj.* (**spook·i·er, spook·i·est**)

**spool** *n.* reel, bobbin

**spoon** *n.* implement with shallow bowl at end of handle for carrying food to mouth *etc.* —*vt.* lift with spoon —**spoon'ful** (-fəl) *n.* (*pl.* **-fuls** -fəlz) —**spoon'fed** *adj.* fed (as if) with spoon; pampered

**spoon·er·ism** (SPOO-nə-riz-əm) *n.* amusing transposition of initial consonants, *eg* half-warmed fish *for* half-formed wish

**spoor** (spuur) *n.* trail of wild animals —*v.* follow spoor

**spo·rad·ic** (spə-RAD-ik) *adj.* intermittent; scattered; single —**spo·rad'i·cal·ly** *adv.*

**spore** (spor) *n.* minute reproductive organism of some plants and protozoans

**sport** *n.* game, activity for pleasure, competition, exercise; enjoyment; mockery; cheerful person, good loser —*vi.* wear (*esp.* ostentatiously) —*vi.* frolic; play (sport) —**sport'ing** *adj.* of sport; behaving with fairness, generosity —**sport'ive** *adj.* playful —**sports car** fast (open) car —**sports jacket** man's casual jacket —**sports'man** (-mən) *n.* (*pl.* -men) one who engages in sport; good loser —**sports'man·ship** *n.*

**spot** *n.* small mark, stain; blemish; pimple; place; (difficult) situation —*vt.* (**spot·ted**, **spot'ting**) mark with spots; detect; observe; blemish —**spot'less** (-lis) *adj.* unblemished; pure —**spot'less·ly** *adv.* —**spot'ty** *adj.* (-ti·er, -ti·est) with spots; uneven —**spot check** random examination —**spot'light** *n.* powerful light illuminating small area; center of attention

**spouse** (spows) *n.* husband or wife —**spous·al** (SPOWZ-əl) *n./adj.* (of) marriage

**spout** (spowt) *v.* pour out; *inf.* speechify —*n.* projecting tube or lip for pouring liquids; copious discharge

**sprain** *n./vt.* wrench or twist (of muscle *etc.*)

**sprang** *pt. of* SPRING

**sprat** *n.* small sea fish

**sprawl** *vi.* lie or sit about awkwardly; spread in rambling, unplanned way —*n.* sprawling

**spray**[1] *n.* (device for producing) fine drops of liquid —*vt.* sprinkle with shower of fine drops

**spray**[2] *n.* branch, twig with buds, flowers *etc.*; floral ornament, brooch *etc.* like this

**spread** (spred) *v.* (**spread**, **spread'ing**) extend; stretch out; open out; scatter; distribute; unfold; cover —*n.* extent; increase; ample meal; food that can be

spread on bread *etc.* —**spread'-ea·gle** *adj.* with arms and legs outstretched

**spree** *n.* session of overindulgence; romp

**sprig** *n.* small twig; ornamental design like this; small headless nail

**spright·ly** (SPRĪT-lee) *adj.* (-li·er, -li·est) lively, brisk —**spright'li·ness** (-nis) *n.*

**spring** *v.* (**sprang**, **sprung**, **spring·ing**) leap; shoot up or forth; come into being; appear; grow; become bent or split; produce unexpectedly; set off (trap) —*n.* leap; recoil; piece of coiled or bent metal with much resilience; flow of water from earth; first season of year —**spring'y** *adj.* (**spring·i·er**, **spring·i·est**) elastic —**spring'-board** (-bord) *n.* flexible board for diving; anything that supplies impetus for action

**sprin·kle** (SPRING-kəl) *vt.* (-kled, -kling) scatter small drops on, strew —**sprin'kler** *n.* —**sprinkling** *n.* small amount or number

**sprint** *vt.* run short distance at great speed —*n.* such run, race —**sprint'er** *n.* one who sprints

**sprit** *n.* small spar set diagonally across a fore-and-aft sail in order to extend it

**sprite** (sprit) *n.* fairy, elf

**sprock·et** (SPROK-it) *n.* projection on wheel or capstan for engaging chain; wheel with these

**sprout** (sprowt) *vi.* put forth shoots, spring up —*n.* shoot —**Brus'sels** (-səlz) **sprout** kind of miniature cabbage

**spruce**[1] (sproos) *n.* variety of fir

**spruce**[2] *adj.* (**spruc·er**, **spruc·est**) neat in dress —*v.* (**spruced**, **spruc·ing**) (*with* up) make (oneself) spruce

**sprung** *pp. of* SPRING

**spry** (spri) *adj.* (**spry·er** *or* **spri-**

**er, spry·est** or **spri·est**) nimble, vigorous

**spud** n. inf. potato

**spume** (spyoom) n./v. (**spumed, spum·ing**) foam, froth

**spun** pt./pp. of SPIN

**spunk** n. courage, spirit

**spur** n. pricking instrument attached to horseman's heel; incitement; stimulus; projection on rooster's leg; projecting mountain range; branch (road etc.) —vt. (**spurred, spur·ring**) equip with spurs; urge on

**spu·ri·ous** (SPYUUR-ee-əs) adj. not genuine

**spurn** vt. reject with scorn, thrust aside

**spurt** v. send, come out in jet; rush suddenly —n. jet; short sudden effort, esp. in race

**sput·nik** (SPUUT-nik) n. one of series of Russian satellites

**sput·ter** (SPUT-ər) v. splutter

**spu·tum** (SPYOO-təm) n. (pl. **-ta** pr. -tə) spittle

**spy** (spī) n. (pl. **spies**) one who watches (esp. in rival countries, companies etc.) and reports secretly —v. (**spied, spy·ing**) act as spy; catch sight of —**spy·glass** n. small telescope

**squab·ble** (SKWOB-əl) vi. (**-bled, -bling**) engage in petty, noisy quarrel, bicker —n.

**squad** (skwod) n. small party, esp. of soldiers or police —**squad car** police patrol automobile (also **patrol car**) —**squad·ron** (-rən) n. division of cavalry regiment, fleet or air force

**squal·id** (SKWOL-id) adj. mean and dirty —**squal'or** (-ər) n.

**squall** (skwawl) n. harsh cry; sudden gust of wind; short storm —vi. yell

**squan·der** (SKWON-dər) vt. spend wastefully, dissipate

**square** (skwair) n. equilateral rectangle; area of this shape; in town, open space (of this shape); product of a number multiplied by itself; instrument for drawing right angles; sl. person behind the times —adj. square in form; honest; straight; even; level; equal; denoting a measure of area; inf. straightforward, honest; sl. ignorant of current trends in dress, music etc., conservative —v. (**squared, squar·ing**) —vt. make square; find square of; pay —vi. fit, suit —**square'ly** adv. —**square meter** etc. area equal to that of square with sides one meter etc. long —**square off** get ready to dispute or fight —**square root** number that, multiplied by itself, gives number of which it is factor

**squash** (skwosh) vt. crush flat; pulp; suppress; humiliate (person) —n. act of squashing; game played with rackets and soft balls in walled court (also **squash racquets**); plant bearing gourds used as a vegetable

**squat** (skwot) vi. (**squat·ted** or **squat, squat·ting**) sit on heels; act as squatter —adj. (**squat·ter, squat·test**) short and thick —**squatter** n. one who settles on land or occupies house without permission

**squaw** (skwaw) n. offens. Amer. Indian woman; sl. wife

**squawk** (skwawk) n. short harsh cry, esp. of bird —v. utter this

**squeak** (skweek) v./n. (make) short shrill sound

**squeal** (skweel) n. long piercing squeak —vi. make one; sl. turn informer, supply information (about another) —**squeal'er** n.

**squeam·ish** (SKWEEM-ish) adj. easily nauseated; easily shocked; overscrupulous

**squee·gee** (SKWEE-jee) n. tool

with rubber blade for clearing water (from glass *etc.*), spreading wet paper *etc.* —*vt.* (-**geed**, -**gee**·**ing**) press, smooth with a squeegee

**squeeze** (skweez) *vt.* (**squeezed**, **squeez**·**ing**) press; wring; force; hug; subject to extortion —*n.* act of squeezing; period of hardship, difficulty caused by financial weakness

**squelch** (skwelch) *vt.* squash; silence with crushing rebuke *etc.* —*vi.* make, walk with wet sucking sound, as in walking through mud —*n.*

**squib** (skwib) *n.* small (faulty) firework; short piece of writing; short news story

**squid** (skwid) *n.* type of cuttlefish

**squig·gle** (SKWIG-əl) *n.* wavy, wriggling mark —*vt.* (-**gled**, -**gling**) wriggle; draw squiggle

**squint** (skwint) *vi.* look with eyes partially closed; have the eyes turned in different directions; glance sideways; look askance —*n.* partially closed eyes; crossed eyes; *inf.* a glance

**squire** (skwir) *n.* country gentleman

**squirm** (skwurm) *vi.* wriggle; be embarrassed —*n.*

**squir·rel** (SKWUR-əl) *n.* small graceful bushy-tailed tree animal —*vt.* (-**reled**, -**rel**·**ing**) store or hide (possession) for future use

**squirt** (skwurt) *v.* (of liquid) force, be forced through narrow opening —*n.* jet; *inf.* short or insignificant person; *inf.* (impudent) youngster

**squish** (skwish) *v.*/*n.* (make) soft splashing sound

**Sr** *Chem.* strontium

**stab** *v.* (**stabbed**, **stab**·**bing**) pierce, strike (at) with pointed weapon —*n.* blow, wound so inflicted; sudden sensation, *eg* of fear; attempt

**sta·bil·ize** (STAY-bə-līz) *vt.* (-**ized**, -**iz**·**ing**) make steady, restore to equilibrium, *esp.* of money values, prices and wages —**sta·bi·li·za'tion** *n.* —**sta'bil·iz·er** *n.* device to maintain equilibrium of ship, aircraft *etc.*

**sta·ble** (STAY-bəl) *n.* building for horses; racehorses of particular owner, establishment; such establishment —*vt.* (-**bled**, -**bling**) put into, lodge in, a stable

**stable²** *adj.* (-**bler**, -**blest**) firmly fixed; steadfast, resolute —**sta·bil·i·ty** (stə-BIL-ə-tee) *n.* steadiness; ability to resist change of any kind —**sta'bly** *adv.*

**stac·ca·to** (stə-KAH-toh) *adj.*/*adv.* *Mus.* with notes sharply separated; abrupt

**stack** (stak) *n.* ordered pile, heap; chimney —*vt.* pile in stack; control aircraft waiting to land so that they fly safely at different altitudes

**sta·di·um** (STAY-dee-əm) *n.* (*pl.* -**di·ums**) open-air or covered arena for athletics *etc.*

**staff** *n.* (*pl.* **staffs**) body of officers or workers; personnel; pole; (*pl.* **staffs** or **staves**) five lines on which music is written —*vt.* employ personnel; supply with personnel

**stag** *n.* adult male deer —*adj.* for men only, as in **stag party**

**stage** (stayj) *n.* period, division of development; raised floor or platform; (platform of) theater; scene of action; stopping place of stagecoach *etc.* on road, distance between two of them; separate unit of space rocket, which may usu. be jettisoned —*vt.* (**staged**, **stag**·**ing**) put (play) on stage; arrange, bring about —**stag'y** *adj.* (**stag**·**i·er**, **stag**·**i·est**) theatrical

—by easy stages unhurriedly; gradually —**stage whisper** loud whisper intended to be heard by audience

**stag·ger** (STAG-ər) vi. walk unsteadily —vt. astound; arrange in overlapping or alternating positions, times; distribute over a period —n. act of staggering —**stag'gers** n. with sing. v. form of vertigo; disease of horses —**stag'ger·ing** adj. astounding

**stag·nate** (STAG-nayt) vi. (-nat·ed, -nat·ing) cease to flow or develop —**stag·na'tion** n. —**stag'nant** (-nənt) adj. sluggish; not flowing; foul, impure

**staid** (stayd) adj. of sober and quiet character, sedate —**staid'ly** adv. —**staid'ness** (-nis) n.

**stain** (stayn) v. spot, mark; apply liquid coloring to (wood etc.); bring disgrace upon —n. —**stain'less** adj. —**stainless steel** rustless steel alloy

**stairs** (stairz) n. pl. set of steps, esp. as part of house —**stair'case**, **-way** n. structure enclosing stairs; stairs —**stair'well** n. vertical opening enclosing staircase

**stake** (stayk) n. sharpened stick or post; money wagered or contended for —vt. (staked, stak·ing) secure, mark out with stakes; wager, risk

**sta·lac·tite** (stə-LAK-tīt) n. lime deposit like icicle on roof of cave

**sta·lag·mite** (stə-LAG-mīt) n. lime deposit like pillar on floor of cave

**stale** (stayl) adj. (stal·er, stal·est) old, lacking freshness; hackneyed; lacking energy, interest through monotony —**stale'mate** n. Chess draw through one player being unable to move; deadlock, impasse

**stalk**[1] (stawk) n. plant's stem; anything like this

**stalk**[2] v. follow, approach stealthily; walk in stiff and stately manner —n. stalking —**stalking-horse** n. pretext

**stall** (stawl) n. compartment in stable etc.; booth for display and sale of goods; seat in choir or chancel of church; slowdown —v. put in stall; stick fast; (motor engine) unintentionally stop; (aircraft) lose flying speed; delay; hinder

**stal·lion** (STAL-yən) n. uncastrated male horse, esp. for breeding

**stal·wart** (STAWL-wərt) adj. strong, brave; staunch —n. stalwart person

**sta·men** (STAY-mən) n. male organ of a flowering plant

**stam·i·na** (STAM-ə-nə) n. power of endurance, vitality

**stam·mer** (STAM-ər) v. speak, say with repetition of syllables, stutter —n. habit of so speaking —**stam'mer·er** n.

**stamp** vi. put down foot with force —vt. impress mark on; affix postage stamp; fix in memory; reveal, characterize —n. stamping with foot; imprinted mark; appliance for marking; piece of gummed paper printed with device as evidence of postage etc.; character

**stam·pede** (stam-PEED) n. sudden frightened rush, esp. of herd of cattle, crowd —v. (-ped·ed, -ped·ing) cause, take part in stampede

**stance** (stans) n. manner, position of standing; attitude; point of view

**stanch** (stawnch) vt. stop flow (of blood) from

**stan·chion** (STAN-shən) n. upright bar, support —vt. make secure with stanchion

**stand** v. (stood pr. stuud, stand·ing) have, take, set in upright position; remain; be situated; remain firm or stationary; cease to move; endure; adhere to principles; offer oneself as a candidate; be symbol etc. of; provide free treat to —n. holding firm; position; halt; something on which thing can be placed; structure from which spectators watch sport etc.; stop made by traveling entertainer etc. eg one-night **stand —standing** n. reputation, status; duration —adj. erect; permanent, lasting; stagnant; performed from standing position (as standing jump) —**stand'by** (-bī) n. (pl. -bys pr. -bīz) someone, something that can be relied on —**stand in** act as substitute (for) —**stand-in** n. substitute —**stand over** watch closely; postpone

**stand·ard** (STAN-dərd) n. accepted example of something against which others are judged; degree, quality; flag; weight or measure to which others must conform; post —adj. usual, regular; average; of recognized authority, competence; accepted as correct —**stand'ard·ize** vt. (-ized, -iz·ing) regulate by a standard

**stand·off** (STAND-awf) n. (objectionable) aloofness; Sports a tie —adj. (objectionably) aloof; reserved

**stand'point** n. point of view, opinion; mental attitude

**stank** pt. of STINK

**stan·nous** (STAN-əs) adj. of, containing tin

**stan·za** (STAN-zə) n. (pl. -zas) group of lines of verse

**sta·ple** (STAY-pəl) n. U-shaped piece of metal with pointed ends to drive into wood for use as ring; paper fastener; main product; fiber; pile of wool etc. —adj. principal; regularly produced or made for market —vt. (-pled,

-pling) fasten with staple; sort, classify (wool etc.) according to length of fiber —**sta'pler** n. small device for fastening papers together

**star** (stahr) n. celestial body, seen as twinkling point of light; asterisk (*); celebrated player, actor; medal, jewel etc. of apparent shape of star —v. (starred, star·ring) adorn with stars; mark (with asterisk); feature as star performer; play leading role in film etc. —adj. leading, most important, famous —**star'ry** adj. (-ri·er, -ri·est) covered with stars —**star'dom** (-dəm) pr. —**star'fish** n. small star-shaped sea creature —**Star Wars** U.S. proposed system of artificial satellites armed with lasers, etc. to destroy enemy missiles in space (also SDI)

**star·board** (STAHR-bərd) n. righthand side of ship, looking forward —adj. of, on this side

**starch** n. substance forming the main food element in bread, potatoes etc., and used mixed with water, for stiffening laundered fabrics; inf. boldness; vigor; energy —vt. stiffen thus —**starch'y** adj. (starch·i·er, starch·i·est) containing starch; stiff; formal; prim

**stare** (stair) vi. (stared, star·ing) look fixedly at; gaze with eyes wide open; be obvious or visible to —n. staring, fixed gaze —**stare down** abash by staring at; defeat by staring

**stark** (stahrk) adj. (-er, -est) blunt, bare; desolate; absolute —adv. completely

**start** (stahrt) vt. begin; set going —vi. begin, esp. journey; make sudden movement —n. beginning; abrupt movement; advantage of a lead in a race —**start'er** n. electric motor starting car engine; competitor in, supervisor of, start of race

**star·tle** (STAHR-tl) *vt.* (-**tled**, -**tling**) give a fright to

**starve** (stahrv) *v.* (**starved**, **starv-ing**) (cause to) suffer or die from hunger —**star·va'tion** (-VAY-shən) *n.*

**stash** *vt.* put away, store, hide —*n.* anything stashed; place for this; *sl.* supply of illicit drugs

**state** (stayt) *n.* condition; place, situation; politically organized people *eg* any of the fifty states of the USA; government; rank; pomp —*vt.* (**stat·ed, stat·ing**) express in words —**stated** *adj.* fixed; regular; settled —**state'ly** *adj.* (-**li·er, -li·est**) dignified, lofty —**state'ment** (-mənt) *n.* expression in words; account —**state'-room** (-ruum) *n.* private cabin on ship —**states'man** (-mən) *n.* (*pl.* -**men**) respected political leader —**states'man·ship** *n.* statesman's art

**stat·ic** (STAT-ik) *adj.* motionless, inactive; pert. to bodies at rest, or in equilibrium —*n.* electrical interference in radio reception —**stat'i·cal·ly** *adv.*

**sta·tion** (STAY-shən) *n.* place where thing stops or is placed; stopping place for railroad trains, buses; local office for police force, fire department *etc.*; place equipped for radio or television transmission; post; status; position in life —*vt.* put in position —**sta'tion·ar·y** (-er-ee) *adj.* not moving, fixed; not changing

**sta·tion·er** (STAY-shən-ər) *n.* dealer in writing materials *etc.* —**sta'tion·er·y** *n.*

**sta·tis·tics** (stə-TIS-tiks) *n.* (*with pl. v.*) numerical facts collected systematically and arranged; (*with sing. v.*) the study of them —**sta·tis'ti·cal** (-kəl) *adj.* —**stat-**

**is·ti·cian** (stat-i-STISH-ən) *n.* one who compiles and studies statistics

**stat·ue** (STACH-oo) *n.* solid carved or cast image of person, animal *etc.* —**stat'u·ar·y** (-er-ee) *n.* statues collectively —**stat·u-esque'** (-esk) *adj.* like statue; dignified

**stat·ure** (STACH-ər) *n.* bodily height; greatness

**sta·tus** (STAY-təs) *n.* position, rank; prestige; relation to others —**status quo** (kwoh) existing state of affairs

**stat·ute** (STACH-oot) *n.* written law —**stat'u·to·ry** (-ə-tor-ee) *adj.* enacted, defined or authorized by statute

**staunch** (stawnch) *adj.* (-**er, -est**) trustworthy, loyal

**stave** (stayv) *n.* one of the pieces forming barrel; verse, stanza; *Mus.* staff —*vt.* (**staved** *or* **stove, stav·ing**) break hole in; ward (off)

**stay**[1] *v.* (**stayed, stay·ing**) remain; sojourn; pause; wait; endure; stop; hinder; postpone —*n.* remaining, sojourning; check; restraint; deterrent; postponement

**stay**[2] *n.* support, prop, rope supporting mast *etc.* —*pl.* formerly, laced corsets

**stead** (sted) *n.* place —**in stead** in place (of) —**in good stead** of service

**stead·y** (STED-ee) *adj.* (**stead·i-er, stead·i·est**) firm; regular; temperate; industrious; reliable —*vt.* (**stead·ied, stead·y·ing**) make steady —**stead'i·ly** *adv.* —**stead'i·ness** (-nis) *n.* —**stead'-fast** (-fəst) *adj.* firm, fixed, unyielding —**stead'fast·ly** *adv.*

**steak** (stayk) *n.* slice of meat, *esp.* beef; slice of fish

**steal** (steel) *v.* (**stole, sto·len,**

steal·ing) rob; move silently; take without right or leave

**stealth** (stelth) *n.* secret or underhanded procedure, behavior —**stealth'i·ly** *adv.* —**stealth'y** *adj.* (stealth·i·er, stealth·i·est)

**steam** (steem) *n.* vapor of boiling water; *inf.* power, energy —*vi.* give off steam; rise in vapor; move by steam power —*vt.* cook or treat with steam —**steam'er** *n.* steam-propelled ship; vessel for cooking or treating with steam —**steam engine** engine worked or propelled by steam —**steam'-roll·er** *n.* large roller, *orig.* moved by steam, for leveling road surfaces *etc.*; any great power used to crush opposition —*vt.* crush

**steed** *n. Poet.* horse

**steel** *n.* hard and malleable metal made by mixing carbon in iron; tool, weapon of steel —*vt.* harden —**steel'y** *adj.* (steel·i·er, steel·i·est)

**steep**[1] *adj.* (-er, -est) rising, sloping abruptly; precipitous; (of prices) very high or exorbitant; unreasonable —**steep'en** *v.* —**steep'ly** *adv.* —**steep'ness** *n.*

**steep**[2] *v.* soak, saturate —*n.* act or process of steeping; the liquid used

**stee·ple** (STEE-pəl) *n.* church tower with spire —**stee'ple-chase** *n.* horse race with ditches and fences to jump; foot race with hurdles *etc.* to jump —**stee'ple·jack** *n.* one who builds, repairs chimneys, steeples *etc.*

**steer**[1] *vt.* guide, direct course of vessel, motor vehicle *etc.* —*vi.* direct one's course —**steer'age** (-ij) *n.* formerly, cheapest accommodation on ship —**steer'ing gear, wheel** *etc.* mechanism for steering

**steer**[2] *n.* castrated bull

**stein** (stīn) *n.* (usu.) earthenware beer mug

**ste·le** (STEE-lee) *n.* ancient carved stone pillar or slab

**stel·lar** (STEL-ər) *adj.* of stars

**stem**[1] *n.* stalk, trunk; long slender part, as in tobacco pipe; part of word to which inflections are added; foremost part of ship

**stem**[2] *vt.* (stemmed, stem·ming) check, stop, dam up

**stench** *n.* evil smell

**sten·cil** (STEN-səl) *n.* thin sheet pierced with pattern which is brushed over with paint or ink, leaving pattern on surface under it; the pattern; the plate; pattern made —*vt.* (-ciled, -cil·ing)

**ste·nog·ra·phy** (stə-NOG-rə-fee) *n.* shorthand writing —**sten·og'ra·pher** *n.* —**sten·o·graph'ic** *adj.*

**sten·to·ri·an** (sten-TOR-ee-ən) *adj.* (of voice) very loud

**step** *v.* (stepped, step·ping) move and set down foot; proceed (in this way); measure in paces —*n.* act of stepping; sound made by stepping; mark made by foot; manner of walking; series of foot movements forming part of dance; gait; pace; measure, act, stage in proceeding; board, rung *etc.* to put foot on; degree in scale; mast socket; promotion —*pl.* portable ladder with hinged prop attached, stepladder —**step'lad·der** *n.* four-legged ladder having broad flat steps

**step·child** (STEP-chīld) *n.* (*pl.* -chil·dren *pr.* -CHIL-drən) child of husband or wife by former marriage; person, organization, idea *etc.* treated improperly —**step'broth·er** *n.* —**step'fa·ther** *n.* —**step'moth·er** *n.* —**step'sis·ter** *n.*

**steppe** (step) *n.* extensive treeless plain in European and Asiatic Russia

**stere** (steer) *n.* cubic meter

**ster·e·o·phon·ic** (ster-ee-ɔ-FON-ik) *adj.* (of sound) giving effect of coming from many directions —**ste′re·o** *adj./n.* (of, for) stereophonic record player *etc.*

**ster·e·o·scop·ic** (ster-ee-ɔ-SKOP-ik) *adj.* having three-dimensional effect

**ster·e·o·type** (STER-ee-ɔ-tīp) *n.* metal plate for printing cast from type; something (monotonously) familiar, conventional, predictable —*vt.* (-typed, -typing) make stereotype of

**ster·ile** (STER-ǝl) *adj.* unable to produce fruit, crops, young *etc.*; free from (harmful) germs —**ste·ril·i·ty** (stɔ-RIL-ɔ-tee) *n.* —**ster·i·li·za′tion** *n.* process or act of making sterile —**ster′i·lize** *vt.* (-lized, -liz·ing) render sterile

**ster·ling** (STUR-ling) *adj.* genuine, true; of solid worth, dependable; in British money —*n.* British money

**stern**[1] (sturn) *adj.* severe, strict —**stern′ly** *adv.* —**stern′ness** (-nis) *n.*

**stern**[2] *n.* rear part of ship

**ster·num** (STUR-nɔm) *n.* the breast bone

**ster·to·rous** (STUR-tɔr-ɔs) *adj.* with sound of heavy breathing, hoarse snoring

**stet** *Lat.* let it stand (proofreader's direction to cancel alteration previously made)

**steth·o·scope** (STETH-ɔ-skohp) *n.* instrument for listening to action of heart, lungs *etc.*

**Stet·son** (STET-sɔn) *n.* R type of broad-brimmed felt hat *esp.* cowboy hat

**ste·ve·dore** (STEE-vi-dor) *n.* one who loads or unloads ships

**stew** (stoo) *n.* food cooked slowly in closed vessel; state of excitement, agitation or worry —*v.*

cook by stewing; worry —**stew in one's own juice** suffer consequences of one's own actions

**stew·ard** (STOO-ɔrd) *n.* one who manages another's property; official managing race meeting, assembly *etc.*; attendant on ship's or aircraft's passengers (**stew′ard·ess** (-is) *fem.*)

**stick** (stik) *n.* long, thin piece of wood; anything shaped like a stick; *inf.* uninteresting person —*v.* (stuck, stick·ing) —*vt.* pierce, stab; place, fasten, as by pins, glue; protrude; bewilder; *inf.* impose disagreeable responsibility on (someone) —*vi.* adhere; come to stop, jam; remain; be fastened; protrude —**stick′er** *n.* *esp.* adhesive label, bumper sticker —**stick′y** *adj.* (stick·i·er, stick·i·est) covered with, like adhesive substance; (of weather) warm, humid; *inf.* difficult, unpleasant —**stick shift** automobile transmission with manually operated shift lever

**stick·ler** (STIK-lɔr) *n.* person who insists on something

**stiff** *adj.* (-er, -est) not easily bent or moved; rigid; awkward; difficult; thick, not fluid; formal; stubborn; unnatural; strong or fresh, as breeze; *inf.* excessive —*n.* *sl.* corpse; *sl.* a drunk —*vt.* *sl.* fail to tip (waiter *etc.*) —**stiff′en** (-in) *v.* —**stiff′ly** *adv.* —**stiff-necked** (-nekt) *adj.* obstinate, stubborn; haughty

**sti·fle** (STĪF-ɔl) *vt.* (-fled, -fling) smother, suppress

**stig·ma** (STIG-mɔ) *n.* (*pl.* -mas, -ma·ta *pr.* -MAH-tɔ) distinguishing mark *esp.* of disgrace —**stig′ma·tize** *vt.* (-tized, -tiz·ing) mark with stigma

**sti·let·to** (sti-LET-oh) *n.* (*pl.* -tos, -toes) small dagger; small boring tool —*adj.* thin, pointed like a stiletto

**still**[1] *adj.* (-er, -est) motionless, noiseless, at rest —*vt.* quiet —*adv.* to this time; yet; even —*n.* photograph *esp.* of motion picture scene —**still'born** *adj.* born dead —**still life** (*pl.* **lifes**) a painting of inanimate objects

**still**[2] *n.* apparatus for distilling

**stilt** *n.* pole with footrests for walking raised from ground; long post supporting building *etc.* —**stilt'ed** (-id) *adj.* stiff in manner, pompous

**stim·u·lus** (STIM-yə-ləs) *n.* (*pl.* -li *pr.* -lī) something that rouses to activity; incentive —**stim'u·lant** (-lənt) *n.* drug *etc.* acting as a stimulus —**stim'u·late** *vt.* (-lated, -lat·ing) rouse up, spur —**stim'u·lat·ing** *adj.* acting as stimulus —**stim·u·la'tion** *n.* —**stim'u·la·tive** (-lə-tiv) *adj.*

**sting** *v.* (**stung**, **sting·ing**) thrust sting into; cause sharp pain to; *sl.* cheat, take advantage of, *esp.* by overcharging; feel sharp pain —*n.* (wound, pain, caused by) sharp pointed organ, often poisonous, of certain insects and animals; *sl.* illegal operation conducted by police *etc.* to collect evidence against criminals

**stin·gy** (STIN-jee) *adj.* (-gi·er, -gi·est) mean; avaricious; niggardly —**stin'gi·ness** (-nis) *n.*

**stink** *vi.* (**stank** or **stunk**, **stunk**, **stink·ing**) give out strongly offensive smell; *inf.* be markedly inferior —*n.* such smell, stench; *inf.* fuss, bother; scandal

**stint** *vt.* be frugal, miserly to (someone) or with (something) —*n.* allotted amount of work or time; limitation, restriction

**sti·pend** (STĪ-pend) *n.* payment, *esp.* scholarship or fellowship allowance given to student —**sti-**

**pen'di·ar·y** (-dee-er-ee) *adj.* receiving stipend

**stip·ple** (STIP-əl) *vt.* (-pled, -pling) engrave, paint in dots —*n.* this process

**stip·u·late** (STIP-yə-layt) *vi.* (-lated, -lat·ing) specify in making a bargain —**stip·u·la'tion** *n.* proviso; condition

**stir** (stur) *v.* (**stirred**, **stir·ring**) (begin to) move; rouse; cause trouble; set, keep in motion; excite —*n.* commotion, disturbance

**stir·rup** (STUR-əp) *n.* metal loop hung from strap for supporting foot of rider on horse

**stitch** (stich) *n.* movement of needle in sewing *etc.*; its result in the work; sharp pain in side; least fragment (of clothing) —*v.* sew

**stock** (stok) *n.* goods, material stored, *esp.* for sale or later use; reserve, fund; shares in, or capital of, company *etc.*; standing, reputation; farm animals (livestock); plant, stem from which cuttings are taken; handle of gun, tool *etc.*; liquid broth produced by boiling meat *etc.*; flowering plant; lineage —*pl. Hist.* frame to secure feet, hands (of offender); frame to support ship during construction —*adj.* kept in stock; standard, hackneyed —*vt.* keep, store; supply with livestock, fish *etc.* —**stock'y** *adj.* (**stock·i·er, stock·i·est**) thickset —**stock'brok·er** (-brohk-ər) *n.* agent for buying, selling stocks and bonds —**stock car** ordinary automobile strengthened and modified for a form of racing in which automobiles often collide —**stock ex·change** institution for buying and selling shares —**stock'pile** *v.* acquire and store large quantity of (something) —**stock-still** *adj.* motionless —**stock'tak·ing** *n.* examination, counting and valuing of goods in a store *etc.* —**put stock** in believe, trust

**stock·ade** (sto-KAYD) *n.* enclosure of stakes, barrier

**stock·ing** (STOK-ing) *n.* close-fitting covering for leg and foot

**stodg·y** (STOJ-ee) *adj.* (stodg·i·er, stodg·i·est) heavy, dull

**sto·gie** (STOH-gee) *n.* (*pl.* -gies) cheap cigar

**sto·ic** (STOH-ik) *adj.* capable of much self-control, great endurance without complaint —*n.* stoical person —**sto'i·cal** (-kəl) *adj.*

**stoke** (stohk) *v.* (stoked, stok·ing) feed, tend fire or furnace —**stok'er** *n.*

**stole**[1] (stohl) *pt.* —**sto'len** (-ən) *pp.* of STEAL

**stole**[2] *n.* long scarf or shawl

**stol·id** *adj.* hard to excite; heavy, slow, apathetic

**stom·ach** (STUM-ək) *n.* sac forming chief digestive organ in any animal; appetite; desire, inclination —*vt.* put up with

**stomp** *vi.* put down foot with force

**stone** (stohn) *n.* (piece of) rock; gem; hard seed of fruit; hard deposit formed in kidneys, bladder; British unit of weight, 14 lbs. —*vt.* (stoned, ston·ing) throw stones at; free (fruit) from stones —**stoned** *adj. sl.* stupefied by alcohol or drugs —**ston'i·ly** *adv.* —**ston'y** *adj.* (ston·i·er, ston·i·est) of, like stone; hard; cold —**stone-broke** (-brohk) *adj.* with no money left —**stone-dead** *adj.* completely dead —**stone-deaf** *adj.* completely deaf —**stone'wall** *v.* stall; evade; filibuster —**stone'ware** (-wair) *n.* heavy common pottery

**stood** (stuud) *pt./pp.* of STAND

**stooge** (stooj) *n. Theater etc.* performer always the butt of

another's jokes; anyone taken advantage of by another

**stool** *n.* backless chair; excrement

**stoop**[1] *vi.* lean forward or down, bend; swoop; abase, degrade oneself —*n.* stooping carriage of the body

**stoop**[2] *n.* steps or small porch in front of house

**stop** *v.* (stopped, stop·ping) check, bring to halt; prevent; interrupt; suspend; desist from; fill up an opening; cease, come to a halt; stay —*n.* stopping or becoming stopped; any device for altering or regulating pitch; set of pipes in organ having tones of a distinct quality —**stop'page** (-ij) *n.* —**stop'per** (-ər) *n.* plug for closing bottle *etc.* —**stop'gap** *n.* temporary substitute —**stop'off, stop'o·ver** *n.* short break in journey —**stop'watch** *n.* one that can be stopped for exact timing *eg* of race —**pull out all the stops** use all available means

**store** (stor) *vt.* (stored, stor·ing) stock, furnish, keep —*n.* retail store; abundance; stock; place for keeping goods; warehouse —*pl.* stocks of goods, provisions —**stor'age** *n.* —**in store** in readiness; imminent

**stork** *n.* large wading bird

**storm** *n.* violent weather with wind, rain, hail, sand, snow *etc.*; assault on fortress; violent outbreak, discharge —*vt.* assault; take by storm —*vi.* rage —**storm'y** *adj.* (storm·i·er, storm·i·est) like storm; (emotionally) violent

**sto·ry**[1] (STOR-ee) *n.* (*pl.* -ries) (book, piece of prose *etc.*) telling about events, happenings; lie

**sto·ry**[2] *n.* (*pl.* -ries) horizontal division of a building

**stoup** (stoop) n. small basin for holy water

**stout** (stowt) adj. (-er, -est) fat; sturdy, resolute —n. kind of beer —**stout'ly** adv. —**stout'ness** (-nis) n.

**stove**[1] (stohv) n. apparatus for cooking, heating etc.

**stove**[2] pt./pp. of STAVE

**stow** (stoh) vt. pack away —**stow'age** (-ij) n. —**stow'a·way** n. one who hides in ship to obtain free passage

**strad·dle** (STRAD-l) v. (-dled, -dling) bestride —vi. spread legs wide —n.

**strafe** (strayf) vt. (strafed, strafing) attack (esp. with bullets, rockets) from air

**strag·gle** (STRAG-əl) vi. (-gled, -gling) stray, get dispersed, linger —**strag'gler** n.

**straight** (strayt) adj. (-er, -est) without bend; honest; level; in order; (of whiskey) undiluted; neat; expressionless; (of drama, actor etc.) serious; sl. heterosexual —n. straight condition or part —adv. direct —**straight'en** (-in) v. —**straight'a·way** adv. immediately —**straight·for'ward** (-word) adj. open, frank; simple; honest

**strain**[1] (strayn) vt. stretch tightly; stretch to full or to excess; filter —vi. make great effort —n. stretching force; violent effort; injury from being strained; burst of music or poetry; great demand; (condition caused by) overwork, worry etc.; tone of speaking or writing —**strain'er** (-ər) n. filter, sieve

**strain**[2] n. breed or race; type (esp. in biology); trace, streak

**strait** (strayt) n. channel of water connecting two larger areas of water —pl. position of difficulty or distress —adj. narrow; strict —**strait'en** (-in) vt. make strait,

narrow; press with poverty —**strait'jack·et** n. jacket to confine arms of violent person —**strait-laced** (-laysd) adj. austere, strict; puritanical

**strand**[1] v. run aground; leave, be left in difficulties or helpless

**strand**[2] n. one single string or wire of rope etc.

**strange** (straynj) adj. (strang·er, strang·est) odd; queer; unaccustomed; foreign; uncommon; wonderful; singular —**stran'ger** n. unknown person; foreigner; one unaccustomed (to) —**strange'ness** (-nis) n.

**stran·gle** (STRANG-gəl) vt. (-gled, -gling) kill by squeezing windpipe; suppress —**stran·gu·la'tion** (-yə-LAY-shən) n. strangling

**strap** n. strip, esp. of leather —vt. (strapped, strap·ping) fasten, beat with strap —**strap'ping** adj. tall and powerful —**strap'hang·er** n. in bus, subway car, one who has to stand, steadying self with strap provided for this purpose

**strat·a·gem** (STRAT-ə-jəm) n. plan, trick —**strat'e·gy** n. (pl. -gies) art of war; overall plan —**strat'e·gist** n. —**stra·te·gic** (strə-TEE-jik) adj.

**strat·o·sphere** (STRAT-ə-sfeer) n. upper part of the atmosphere from approx. 11 km to 50 km above Earth's surface

**stra·tum** (STRAY-təm) n. (pl. stra·ta pr. -tə) layer, esp. of rock; class in society —**strat'i·fy** v. (-fied, -fy·ing) form, deposit in layers —**strat·i·fi·ca'tion** n.

**straw** n. stalks of grain; single stalk; long, narrow tube used to suck up liquid —**straw'ber·ry** n. creeping plant producing a red, juicy fruit; the fruit

**stray** vi. wander; digress; get lost —adj. strayed; occasional, scattered —n. stray animal

**streak** (streek) *n.* long line or band; element, trace —*vt.* mark with streaks —*vi.* move fast; run naked in public —**streak'y** *adj.* (**streak·i·er, streak·i·est**) having streaks; striped

**stream** (streem) *n.* flowing body of water or other liquid; steady flow —*vi.* flow; run with liquid; float, wave in the air —*vt.* discharge, send in stream —**stream'er** (-ər) *n.* (paper) ribbon, narrow flag

**stream·lined** (STREEM-līnd) *adj.* (of train, plane *etc.*) built so as to offer least resistance to air

**street** *n.* road in town *etc.* usu. lined with houses —**street'car** *n.* vehicle (*esp.* electrically driven and for public transport) running usu. on rails laid on roadway —**street'walk·er** *n.* prostitute —**street'wise, -smart** *adj. inf.* adept at surviving in urban, oft. criminal, environment

**strength** (strength) *n.* capacity of being strong; power; capacity for exertion or endurance; vehemence; force; full or necessary number of people —**strength'en** *v.* make stronger, reinforce —**on the strength of** relying on, because of

**stren·u·ous** (STREN-yoo-əs) *adj.* energetic; earnest

**strep·to·coc·cus** (strep-tə-KOK-əs) *n.* (*pl.* **-coc·ci** *pr.* **-KOK-sī**) genus of bacteria

**strep·to·my·cin** (strep-tə-MĪ-sin) *n.* antibiotic drug

**stress** *n.* emphasis; strain; impelling force; effort; tension —*vt.* emphasize; accent; put mechanical stress on

**stretch** (strech) *vt.* extend; exert to utmost; tighten, pull out; reach out —*vi.* reach; have elasticity —*n.* stretching, being stretched, expanse; spell —**stretch'er** *n.*

person, thing that stretches; appliance on which disabled person is carried; bar linking legs of chair

**strew** (stroo) *vt.* (**strewed, strewn** or **strewed, strew·ing**) scatter over surface, spread

**stri·ate** (STRĪ-ayt) *vt.* (**-at·ed, -at·ing**) mark with streaks; score —**stri·a'tion** *n.* —**striated** *adj.* streaked, furrowed, grooved

**strick·en** (STRIK-ən) *adj.* seriously affected by disease, grief, famine; afflicted; *pp.* of STRIKE

**strict** (strikt) *adj.* (**-er, -est**) stern, not lax or indulgent; defined; without exception

**stric·ture** (STRIK-chər) *n.* critical remark; constriction

**stride** (strīd) *vi.* (**strode, stridden, strid·ing**) walk with long steps —*n.* single step; its length; regular pace —**hit one's stride** reach the level at which one consistently functions best

**stri·dent** (STRĪD-nt) *adj.* harsh in tone; loud; urgent

**strife** (strīf) *n.* conflict; quarreling

**strike** (strīk) *v.* (**struck, struck** or **strick·en, strik·ing**) hit (against); ignite; (of snake) bite; arrive at, come upon; of plants (cause to) take root; attack; hook (fish); sound (time) as bell in clock *etc.*; *Baseball* swing and miss a pitch *etc.* —*vt.* affect; enter mind of; discover (gold, oil *etc.*); dismantle, remove; make (coin) —*vi.* cease work as protest or to make demands —*n.* act of striking —**strik'er** *n.* —**striking** *adj.* noteworthy, impressive —**strike it rich** meet unexpected financial success —**strike off** remove —**strike out** fail in a venture; *Baseball* make three strikes

**string** *n.* (length of) thin cord or other material; strand, row; series; fiber in plants —*pl.* conditions —*vt.* (strung, string·ing) provide with, thread on string; form in line, series —**stringed** *adj.* (of musical instruments) furnished with strings —**string'y** *adj.* (string·i·er, string·i·est) like string; fibrous

**strin·gent** (STRIN-jənt) *adj.* strict, rigid, binding —**strin'gen·cy** *n.* severity

**strip** *v.* (stripped, strip·ping) lay bare, take covering off; dismantle; deprive (of); undress —*n.* long, narrow piece —**strip'per** *n.* striptease artiste —**strip'tease** (-teez) *n.* nightclub or theater act in which stripper undresses in time to music

**stripe** (strīp) *n.* narrow mark, band; chevron as symbol of military rank; style, kind

**strip'ling** *n.* a youth

**strive** (strīv) *vi.* (strove or strived, striv·en or strived, striv·ing) try hard, struggle, contend

**strobe** (strōb) *n.* apparatus that produces high-intensity flashing light

**strode** (strōd) *pt. of* STRIDE

**stroke** (strōk) *n.* blow; sudden action, occurrence; apoplexy; mark of pen, pencil, brush *etc.*; chime of clock; completed movement in series; act, manner of striking (ball *etc.*); style, method of swimming; rower sitting nearest stern setting the rate; act of stroking —*vt.* (stroked, strok·ing) set time in rowing; pass hand lightly over

**stroll** (strōl) *vi.* walk in leisurely or idle manner —*n.*

**strong** (strawng) *adj.* (-er, -est) powerful, robust, healthy; difficult to break; noticeable; intense; emphatic; not diluted; having a certain number —**strong'hold** (-hōld) *n.* fortress

**stron·ti·um** (STRON-shee-əm) *n.* silvery-white chemical element —**strontium 90** radioactive isotope of strontium present in fallout of nuclear explosions

**strop** *n.* leather for sharpening razors —*vt.* (stropped, strop·ping) sharpen on one

**strove** (strōv) *pt. of* STRIVE

**struck** *pt./pp. of* STRIKE

**struc·ture** (STRUK-chər) *n.* (arrangement of parts in) construction, building *etc.*; form; organization —*vt.* (-tured, -tur·ing) give structure to —**struc'tur·al** (-chər-əl) *adj.*

**strug·gle** (STRUG-əl) *vi.* (-gled, -gling) contend; fight; proceed, work, move with difficulty and effort —*n.*

**strum** *v.* (strummed, strum·ming) strike notes of guitar *etc.*

**strum·pet** (STRUM-pit) *n.* promiscuous woman; prostitute

**strung** *pt./pp. of* STRING

**strut** *vi.* (strut·ted, strut·ting) walk affectedly or pompously —*n.* brace; rigid support, usu. set obliquely; strutting gait

**strych·nine** (STRIK-nin) *n.* poison obtained from nux vomica seeds

**stub** *n.* remnant of anything, eg pencil, cigarette *etc.*; retained portion of check *etc.* —*vt.* (stubbed, stub·bing) strike (eg toes) against fixed object; extinguish by pressing against surface —**stub'by** *adj.* (-bi·er, -bi·est) short, broad

**stub·ble** (STUB·əl) *n.* stumps of cut grain *etc.* after cutting; short growth of beard

**stub·born** (STUB·ərn) *adj.* unyielding, obstinate —**stub'born·ness** (-nis) *n.*

**stuc·co** (STUK-oh) *n.* (*pl.* -coes, -cos) plaster —*vt.* (-coed, -co·ing) apply stucco to (wall)

**stuck** *pt./pp. of* STICK

**stud**[1] *n.* nail with large head; type of button; vertical wall support —*vt.* (**stud′ded, stud′ding**) set with studs —**stud′ding** *n.*

**stud**[2] *n.* stallion, set of horses, kept for breeding; *sl.* man known for sexual prowess —**stud′book** (-buuk) *n.* book giving pedigree of noted or thoroughbred animals, *esp.* horses —**stud farm** establishment where horses are kept for breeding

**stu·di·o** (STOO-dee-oh) *n.* (*pl.* -di·os) workroom of artist, photographer *etc.*; building, room where motion pictures, TV or radio shows are made, broadcast; apartment of one main room

**stud·y** (STUD-ee) *v.* (**stud·ied, stud·y·ing**) be engaged in learning; make study of; try constantly to do; consider; scrutinize —*n.* (*pl.* **stud·ies**) effort to acquire knowledge; subject of this; room to study in; book, report *etc.* produced as result of study; sketch —**stu·dent** (STOOD-nt) *n.* one who studies, *esp.* at college *etc.* —**studied** *adj.* carefully designed, premeditated —**stu·di·ous** (STOO-dee-əs) *adj.* fond of study; thoughtful; painstaking; deliberate —**stu′di·ous·ly** *adv.*

**stuff** *v.* pack, cram, fill (completely); eat large amount; fill with seasoned mixture; fill (animal's skin) with material to preserve lifelike form —*n.* material, fabric; any substance —**stuff′ing** *n.* material for stuffing, *esp.* seasoned mixture for inserting in poultry *etc.* before cooking —**stuff′y** *adj.* (**stuff·i·er, stuff·i·est**) lacking fresh air; dull, conventional —**stuffed shirt** pompous person

**stul·ti·fy** (STUL-tə-fī) *vt.* (-**fied, -fy·ing**) make ineffectual —**stul·ti·fi·ca′tion** *n.*

**stum·ble** (STUM-bəl) *vi.* (-**bled, -bling**) trip and nearly fall; falter —*n.* —**stumbling block** obstacle

**stump** *n.* remnant of tree, tooth *etc.*, when main part has been cut away; part of leg or arm remaining after amputation —*vt.* confuse, puzzle —*vi.* walk heavily, noisily —**stump′y** *adj.* (**stump·i·er, stump·i·est**) short and thickset

**stun** *vt.* (**stunned, stun·ning**) knock senseless; amaze

**stung** *pt./pp.* of STING

**stunk** *pp.* of STINK

**stunt**[1] *vt.* check growth of, dwarf —**stunt′ed** *adj.* underdeveloped; undersized

**stunt**[2] *n.* feat of dexterity or daring; anything spectacular, unusual done to gain publicity

**stu·pe·fy** (STOO-pə-fī) *vt.* (-**fied, -fy·ing**) make insensitive, lethargic; astound —**stu·pe·fac′tion** *n.*

**stu·pen·dous** (stoo-PEN-dəs) *adj.* astonishing, amazing; huge

**stu·pid** (STOO-pid) *adj.* (-**er, -est**) slow-witted; silly; in a stupor —**stu·pid′i·ty** *n.* (*pl.* -ties)

**stu·por** (STOO-pər) *n.* dazed state; insensibility —**stu′por·ous** *adj.*

**stur·dy** (STUR-dee) *adj.* (-**di·er, -di·est**) robust, strongly built; vigorous —**stur′di·ly** *adv.*

**stur·geon** (STUR-jən) *n.* fish yielding caviar

**stut·ter** (STUT-ər) *v.* speak with difficulty; stammer —*n.*

**sty**[1] (stī) *n.* (*pl.* **sties**) place to keep pigs in; hovel, dirty place

**sty**[2] *n.* (*pl.* **sties**) inflammation on edge of eyelid

**Styg·i·an** (STIJ-ee-ən) *adj.* of river Styx in Hades; gloomy; infernal

**style** (stīl) *n.* manner of writing, doing *etc.*; designation; sort; elegance, refinement; superior manner, quality; design —*vt.* (**styled, styl·ing**) shape, design;

adapt; designate —**styl'ish** adj. fashionable —**styl'ist** n. one cultivating style in literary or other execution; designer; hairdresser —**styl·is'tic** adj. (**-ized, -iz·ing**) give conventional stylistic form to

**sty·lus** (STĪ-ləs) n. (pl. **-lus·es**) writing instrument; (in record player) tiny point running in groove of record

**sty·mie** (STĪ-mee) vt. (**-mied, -my·ing**) hinder, thwart

**styp·tic** (STIP-tik) adj./n. (designating) a substance that stops bleeding

**suave** (swahv) adj. (**suav·er, suav·est**) smoothly polite, affable, bland —**suav'i·ty** n.

**sub** short for submarine, submarine sandwich; substitute —vi. inf. (**subbed, sub·bing**) serve as substitute

**sub-** (prefix) under, less than, in lower position, forming subdivision etc., as in **subaquatic** adj., **subheading** n., **subnormal** adj., **subsoil** n. Such words are not given here where the meaning can easily be inferred from the simple word

**sub·com·mit·tee** (SUB-kə-mit-ee) n. section of committee functioning separately from main body

**sub·con·scious** (sub-KON-shəs) adj. acting, existing without one's awareness —n. Psychology that part of the human mind unknown, or only partly known to possessor

**sub·cu·ta·ne·ous** (sub-kyoo-TAY-nee-əs) adj. under the skin

**sub·di·vide** (sub-di-VĪD) vt. (**-vid·ed, -vid·ing**) divide again —**sub'di·vi·sion** (-vizh-ən) n.

**sub·due** (səb-DOO) v. (**-dued, -du·ing**) overcome —**subdued'**

adj. cowed, quiet; (of light) not bright or intense

**subject** (SUB-jikt) n. theme, topic; that about which something is predicated; conscious self; one under power of another —adj. owing allegiance; subordinate; dependent; liable (to) —vt. (səb-JEKT) cause to undergo; make liable; subdue —**sub·jec'tion** (-JEK-shən) n. act of bringing, or state of being, under control —**sub·jec'tive** adj. based on personal feelings, not impartial; of the self; existing in the mind; displaying artist's individuality —**sub·jec·tiv'i·ty** n.

**sub ju·di·ce** (sub JOO-di-see) Lat. under judicial consideration

**sub·ju·gate** (SUB-jə-gayt) vt. (**-gat·ed, -gat·ing**) force to submit; conquer —**sub·ju·ga'tion** n.

**sub·junc·tive** (səb-JUNGK-tiv) n. mood used mainly in subordinate clauses expressing wish, possibility —adj. in, of, that mood

**sub·let'** vt. (**-let, -let·ting**) (of tenant) let to another all or part of what tenant has rented

**sub·li·mate** (SUB-lə-mayt) vt. Psychology (**-mat·ed, -mat·ing**) direct energy (esp. sexual) into activities considered more socially acceptable; refine —n. Chem. (-mit) material obtained when substance is sublimed —**sub·li·ma'tion** n. Psychology unconscious diversion of sexual impulses towards new aim and activities; Chem. process in which a solid changes directly into a vapor

**sub·lime** (sə-BLĪM) adj. elevated; eminent; majestic; inspiring awe; exalted —v. Chem. (**-limed, -lim·ing**) change or cause to change from solid to vapor —**sub·lime'ly** adv.

**sub·lim·i·nal** (sub-LIM-ə-nl) adj.

resulting from processes of which the individual is not aware

**sub·ma·rine** (sub-mə-REEN) *n.* ship that can travel below surface of sea and remain submerged for long periods —*adj.* below surface of sea **submarine sandwich** overstuffed sandwich of meats, cheese *etc.* in long loaf of Italian bread

**sub·merge** (sob-MURJ) *v.* (-merged, -merg·ing) place, go under water —**sub·mer'sion** (-MUR-zhon) *n.*

**sub·mit** (sob-MIT) *v.* (-mit·ted, -mit·ting) surrender; put forward for consideration; give in, comply, defer —**sub·mis'sion** (-MISH-ən) *n.* —**sub·mis'sive** *adj.* meek, obedient

**sub·or·di·nate** (sə-BOR-dn-it) *adj.* of lower rank or less importance —*n.* inferior; one under order of another —*vt.* (-dn-ayt) (-nat·ed, -nat·ing) make, treat as subordinate —**sub·or·di·na'tion** (-NAY-shən) *n.*

**sub·orn** (sə-BORN) *vt.* bribe to do evil —**sub·or·na·tion** (sub-or-NAY-shən) *n.*

**sub·poe·na** (sə-PEE-nə) *n.* writ requiring attendance at court of law —*vt.* (-naed, -na·ing) summon by such order

**sub·scribe** (sob-SKRĪB) *vt.* (-scribed, -scrib·ing) pay, promise to pay (contribution); write one's name at end of document —**sub·scrip'tion** *n.* subscribing; money paid

**sub·se·quent** (SUB-si-kwənt) *adj.* later, following or coming after in time

**sub·ser·vi·ent** (sob-SUR-vee-ənt) *adj.* submissive, servile —**sub·ser'vi·ence** *n.*

**sub·side** (sob-SĪD) *vi.* (-sid·ed, -sid·ing) abate, come to an end; sink; settle; collapse —**sub·sid'ence** *n.*

**sub·sid·i·ar·y** (sob-SID-ee-er-ee) *adj.* secondary; auxiliary —*n.* (*pl.* -ar·ies)

**sub·si·dize** (SUB-si-dīz) *vt.* (-dized, -diz·ing) help financially; pay grant to —**sub'si·dy** (-dee) *n.* money granted (*pl.* -dies)

**sub·sist** (sob-SIST) *vi.* exist, sustain life —**sub·sist'ence** (-əns) *n.* the means by which one supports life; livelihood

**sub·son·ic** (sub-SON-ik) *adj.* concerning speeds less than that of sound

**sub·stance** (SUB-stəns) *n.* matter; particular kind of matter; chief part, essence; wealth —**sub·stan·tial** (sob-STAN-shəl) *adj.* considerable; of real value; solid, big, important; really existing —**sub·stan'ti·ate** (-shee-ayt) *vt.* (-at·ed, -at·ing) bring evidence for, confirm, prove —**sub·stan·ti·a'tion** *n.* —**sub'stan·tive** (-stən-tiv) *adj.* having independent existence; real, fixed —*n.* noun

**sub·sti·tute** (SUB-sti-toot) *v.* (-tut·ed, -tut·ing) put, serve in exchange (for) —*n.* thing, person put in place of another; deputy —**sub·sti·tu'tion** *n.*

**sub·sume** (sob-SOOM) *vt.* (-sumed, -sum·ing) incorporate (idea, case *etc.*) under comprehensive heading, classification

**sub·tend** (sob-TEND) *vt.* be opposite to and delimit

**sub·ter·fuge** (SUB-tər-fyooj) *n.* trick, lying excuse used to evade something

**sub·ter·ra·ne·an** (sub-tə-RAY-nee-ən) *adj.* underground; in concealment

**sub·ti·tle** (SUB-tīt-l) *n.* secondary title of book; written translation of film dialogue, superimposed on film

**sub·tle** (SUT-l) adj. (-tler, -tlest) not immediately obvious; ingenious, acute; crafty; intricate; delicate; making fine distinctions —**sub'tle·ty** (-tee) n. (pl. -ties)

**sub·tract** (sob-TRAKT) vt. take away, deduct —**sub·trac'tion** (-TRAK-shon) n.

**sub·trop·i·cal** (sub-TROP-i-kol) adj. of regions bordering on the tropics

**sub·urb** n. residential area on outskirts of city —**sub·ur·ban** (so-BUR-bon) adj. —**sub·ur'bi·a** (-bee-o) n. suburbs of a city

**sub·ven·tion** (sob-VEN-shon) n. subsidy

**sub·vert** (sob-VURT) vt. overthrow; corrupt —**sub·ver'sion** (-zhon) n. —**sub·ver'sive** (-siv) adj.

**sub'way** n. underground passage; underground railroad

**suc·ceed** (sok-SEED) vi. accomplish purpose; turn out satisfactorily; follow —vt. follow, take place of —**suc·cess'** n. favorable accomplishment, attainment, issue or outcome; successful person or thing —**suc·cess'ful** (-fol) adj. —**suc·ces'sion** (-SESH-on) n. following; series; succeeding —**suc·ces'sive** (-siv) adj. following in order; consecutive —**suc·ces'sor** (-or) n.

**suc·cinct** (sok-SINGKT) adj. terse, concise —**suc·cinct'ly** adv. —**suc·cinct'ness** (-nis) n.

**suc·cor** (SUK-or) n. help in distress

**suc·cu·bus** (SUK-yo-bos) n. (pl. -bi pr. -bī) female demon fabled to have sexual intercourse with sleeping men

**suc·cu·lent** (SUK-yo-lont) adj. juicy, full of juice; (of plant) having thick, fleshy leaves —n. such plant —**suc'cu·lence** (-lins) n.

**suc·cumb** (so-KUM) vi. yield, give way; die

**such** adj. of the kind or degree mentioned; so great, so much; so made etc.; of the same kind —**such'like** adj. such —pron. other such things

**suck** (suk) vt. draw into mouth; hold (dissolve) in mouth; draw in —n. sucking —**suck'er** n. person, thing that sucks; organ, appliance that adheres by suction; shoot coming from root or base of stem of plant; inf. person easily deceived or taken in

**suck·le** (SUK-ol) v. (-led, -ling) feed from the breast —**suck'ling** n. unweaned infant

**suc·tion** (SUK-shon) n. drawing or sucking of air or fluid; force produced by difference in pressure

**sud·den** (SUD-n) adj. done, occurring unexpectedly; abrupt, hurried —**sud'den·ness** (-don-is) n.

**su·dor·if·ic** (soo-do-RIF-ik) adj. causing perspiration —n. medicine that produces sweat

**suds** (sudz) n. pl. froth of soap and water, lather; sl. beer

**sue** (soo) v. (sued, su·ing) —vt. prosecute; seek justice from —vi. make application or entreaty; beseech

**suede** (swayd) n. leather with soft, velvety finish

**su·et** (SOO-it) n. hard animal fat from sheep, cow etc.

**suf·fer** (SUF-or) v. undergo, endure, experience (pain etc.); allow —**suf'fer·a·ble** adj. —**suf'fer·ance** (-ons) n. toleration

**suf·fice** (so-FĪS) v. (-ficed, fic·ing) be adequate, satisfactory (for) —**suf·fi·cien·cy** (so-FISH-on-see) n. adequate amount —**suf·fi'cient** adj. enough, adequate

**suf·fix** (SUF-iks) n. letter or word

added to end of word —*vt.* add, annex to the end

**suf·fo·cate** (SUF-ə-kayt) *v.* (-cat·ed, -cat·ing) kill, be killed by deprivation of oxygen; smother

**suf·frage** (SUF-rij) *n.* vote or right of voting —**suf'fra·gist** *n.* one claiming a right of voting (suf·fra·gette' *fem.*)

**suf·fuse** (sə-FYOOZ) *vt.* (-fused, -fus·ing) well up and spread over —**suf·fu'sion** (-FYOO-zhən) *n.*

**sug·ar** (SHUUG-ər) *n.* sweet crystalline vegetable substance —*vt.* sweeten, make pleasant (with sugar) —**sug'ar·y** *adj.* —**sugar cane** plant from whose juice sugar is obtained —**sugar daddy** *inf.* wealthy (elderly) man who pays for (*esp.* sexual) favors of younger woman

**sug·gest** (səg-JEST) *vt.* propose; call up the idea of —**sug·gest'i·ble** *adj.* easily influenced —**sug·ges'tion** (-chən) *n.* hint; proposal; insinuation of impression, belief *etc.*, into mind —**sug·gest'ive** *adj.* containing, open to suggestion, *esp.* of something indecent

**su·i·cide** (SOO-ə-sīd) *n.* (act of) one who takes own life —**su·i·cid'al** (-əl) *adj.*

**suit** (soot) *n.* set of clothing; garment worn for particular event, purpose; one of four sets in pack of cards; action at law —*v.* make, be fit or appropriate for; be acceptable to (someone) —**suit'a·ble** *adj.* fitting, proper, convenient; becoming —**suit'a·bly** *adv.* —**suit'case** (-kays) *n.* flat rectangular traveling case

**suite** (sweet) *n.* matched set *esp.* furniture; set of rooms

**suit·or** (SOOT-ər) *n.* wooer; one who sues; petitioner

**sul·fate** (SUL-fayt) *n.* salt formed by sulfuric acid in combination with any base

**sul·fon·a·mides** (sul-FON-ə-mīdz) *n.* group of drugs used as internal germicides in treatment of many bacterial diseases

**sul·fur** (SUL-fər) *n.* pale yellow nonmetallic element —**sul·fur'ic** (sul-FYUUR-ik) *adj.*

**sulk** *vi.* be silent, resentful, *esp.* to draw attention to oneself —*n.* this mood —**sulk'y** *adj.* (sulk·i·er, sulk·i·est)

**sul·len** (SUL-ən) *adj.* unwilling to talk or be sociable, morose; dismal; dull

**sul·ly** (SUL-ee) *vt.* (-lied, -ly·ing) stain, tarnish, disgrace

**sul·tan** (SUL-tn) *n.* ruler of Muslim country —**sul·tan'a** *n.* sultan's wife or concubine; kind of raisin

**sul·try** (SUL-tree) *adj.* (-tri·er, -tri·est) (of weather) hot, humid; (of person) looking sensual

**sum** *n.* amount, total; problem in arithmetic —*v.* (summed, sum·ming) add up; make summary of main parts

**sum·ma·ry** (SUM-ə-ree) *n.* (*pl.* -ries) abridgment or statement of chief points of longer document, speech *etc.*; abstract —*adj.* done quickly —**sum·mar·i·ly** (sə-MAIR-ə-lee) *adv.* speedily; abruptly —**sum'ma·rize** (-ə-rīz) *vt.* (-rized, -riz·ing) make summary of; present briefly and concisely

**sum·mer** (SUM-ər) *n.* second, warmest season —*vi.* pass the summer —**sum'mer·y** *adj.*

**sum'mit** *n.* top, peak —**summit conference** meeting of heads of governments —**sum'mit·ry** (-mi-tree) *n.* practice, art of holding summit conferences

**sum·mon** (SUM-ən) *vt.* demand attendance of; call on; bid witness appear in court; gather up (energies *etc.*) —**sum′mons** *n.* call; authoritative demand

**sump** *n.* place or receptacle (*esp.* as oil reservoir in engine) where fluid collects

**sump·tu·ous** (SUMP-choo-əs) *adj.* lavish, magnificent; costly —**sump′tu·ous·ness** (-nis) *n.* —**sump′tu·ar·y** (-er-ee) *adj.* pert. to or regulating expenditure

**sun** *n.* luminous body around which Earth and other planets revolve; its rays —*v.* (sunned, sun·ning) expose (self) to sun's rays —**sun′ny** *adj.* (-ni·er, -ni·est) like the sun; warm; cheerful —**sun′bath·ing** (-bay*th*-ing) *n.* exposure of whole or part of body to sun's rays —**sun′beam** (-beem) *n.* ray of sun —**sun′burn** *n.* inflammation of skin due to excessive exposure to sun —**sun′down** *n.* sunset —**sun′spot** *n.* dark patch appearing temporarily on sun's surface —**sun′stroke** (-strohk) *n.* illness caused by prolonged exposure to intensely hot sun —**sun′tan** *n.* coloring of skin by exposure to sun

**sun·dae** (SUN-day) *n.* ice cream topped with fruit *etc.*

**Sun·day** *n.* first day of the week; Christian Sabbath —**Sunday school** school for religious instruction of children

**sun·der** (SUN-dər) *vt.* separate, sever

**sun·dry** (SUN-dree) *adj.* several, various —**sun′dries** *n. pl.* odd items not mentioned in detail

**sung** *pp. of* SING

**sunk, sunk′en** (-in) *pp. of* SINK

**sup** *v.* (supped, sup·ping) take by sips; take supper —*n.* mouthful of liquid

**su·per** (SOO-pər) *adj.* very good —*n.* short for superintendent

**super-** (*prefix*) above, greater, exceeding(ly), as in **superhuman**

*adj.*, **superman** *n.*, **supertanker** *n.* Such compounds are not given here where the meaning can be inferred easily from the simple word

**su·per·a·ble** (SOO-pər-ə-bəl) *adj.* capable of being overcome; surmountable

**su·per·an·nu·ate** (soo-pər-AN-yoo-ayt) *vt.* (-at·ed, -at·ing) pension off; discharge or dismiss as too old

**su·perb** (suu-PURB) *adj.* splendid, grand, impressive

**su·per·charge** (SOO-pər-chahrj) *vt.* (-charged, -charg·ing) charge, fill to excess —**su′per·charg·er** *n.* (internal-combustion engine) device to ensure complete filling of cylinder with explosive mixture when running at high speed

**su·per·cil·i·ous** (soo-pər-SIL-ee-əs) *adj.* displaying arrogant pride, scorn, indifference —**su·per·cil′i·ous·ness** (-nis) *n.*

**su·per·fi·cial** (soo-pər-FISH-əl) *adj.* of or on surface; not careful or thorough; without depth, shallow

**su·per·flu·ous** (suu-PUR-floo-əs) *adj.* extra, unnecessary; excessive; left over —**su·per·flu′i·ty** (-FLOO-i-tee) *n.* (*pl.* -ties) superabundance; unnecessary amount

**su·per·in·tend** (soo-pər-in-TEND) *v.* have charge of; overlook; supervise —**su·per·in·ten′dent** (-dint) *n. esp.* person in charge of building maintenance

**su·pe·ri·or** (sə-PEER-ee-ər) *adj.* greater in quality or quantity; upper, higher in position, rank or quality; showing consciousness of being so —**su·pe·ri·or′i·ty** *n.* quality of being higher, greater, or more excellent

**su·per·la·tive** (sə-PUR-lə-tiv) *adj.* of, in highest degree or quality; surpassing; *Grammar* denoting form of adjective, adverb meaning "most" —n. Grammar superlative degree of adjective or adverb

**su·per·mar·ket** (SOO-pər-mahr-kit) n. large self-service store selling chiefly food and household goods

**su·per·nal** (suu-PUR-nl) adj. celestial

**su·per·nat·u·ral** (soo-pər-NACH-ər-əl) adj. being beyond the powers or laws of nature; miraculous —n. being, place etc. of miraculous powers

**su·per·nu·mer·a·ry** (soo-pər-NOO-mə-rer-ee) adj. in excess of normal number, extra —n. (pl. -ar·ies) extra person or thing

**su·per·script** (SOO-pər-skript) n./adj. (character) printed, written above the line

**su·per·sede** (soo-pər-SEED) vt. (-sed·ed, -sed·ing) take the place of; set aside, discard, supplant

**su·per·son·ic** (soo-pər-SON-ik) adj. denoting speed greater than that of sound

**su·per·sti·tion** (soo-pər-STISH-ən) n. religion, opinion or practice based on belief in luck or magic —su·per·sti'tious (-STI-shəs) adj.

**su·per·vene** (soo-pər-VEEN) vi. (-vened, -ven·ing) happen, as an interruption or change —su·per·ven'tion (-shən) n.

**su·per·vise** (SOO-pər-viz) vt. (-vised, -vis·ing) oversee; direct; inspect and control; superintend —su·per·vi'sion (-VIZH-ən) n. —su'per·vis·or n.

**su·pine** (soo-PIN) adj. lying on back with face upward; indolent —n. (SOO-pin) Latin verbal noun

**sup·per** (SUP-ər) n. (light) evening meal

**sup·plant** (sə-PLANT) vt. take the place of, esp. unfairly; oust

**sup·ple** (SUP-əl) adj. (-pler, -plest) pliable; flexible; compliant —sup·ply (SUP-lee) adv.

**sup·ple·ment** (SUP-lə-mənt) n. thing added to fill up, supply deficiency, esp. extra part added to book etc.; additional number of periodical, usu. on special subject; separate, often illustrated section published periodically with newspaper —vt. add to; supply deficiency —sup·ple·men'ta·ry (-tə-ree) adj. additional

**sup·pli·ant** (SUP-lee-ənt) adj. petitioning —n. petitioner

**sup·pli·cate** (SUP-li-kayt) v. (-cat·ed, -cat·ing) beg humbly, entreat —sup'pli·cant (-li-kənt) n. —sup·pli·ca'tion (-KAY-shən) n. —sup'pli·ca·to·ry (-kə-tor-ee) adj.

**sup·ply** (sə-PLI) vt. (-plied, -ply·ing) furnish; make available; provide —n. (pl. -plies) supplying, substitute; stock, store

**sup·port** (sə-PORT) vt. hold up; sustain; assist —n. supporting, being supported; means of support —sup·port'a·ble adj. —sup·port'er n. adherent —sup·port'ing adj. (of motion picture etc. role) less important —sup·port'ive adj.

**sup·pose** (sə-POHZ) vt. (-posed, pos·ing) assume as theory; take for granted; accept as likely; (in passive) be expected, obliged; ought —sup·posed' adj. —sup·pos·ed·ly (sə-POH-zid-lee) adv. —sup·po·si'tion (-ZISH-ən) n. assumption; belief without proof; conjecture —sup·po·si'tious (sə-pə-ZISH-əs) adj. sham; spurious; counterfeit

**sup·pos·i·to·ry** (sə-POZ-i-tor-ee) n. (pl. -ries) medication (in capsule) for insertion in orifice of body

**sup·press** (sə-PRES) vt. put

down, restrain; crush, stifle; keep or withdraw from publication —sup·pres'sion (-PRESH-ən) n.

sup·pu·rate (SUP-yə-rayt) vi. (-rat·ed, -rat·ing) fester, form pus —sup·pu·ra'tion (-shən) n.

supra- (prefix) above, over, as in supranational adj. involving more than one nation Such words are not given here where the meaning can easily be inferred from the simple word

su·preme (sə-PREEM) adj. highest in authority or rank; utmost —su·prem·a·cy (-PREM-ə-see) n. position of being supreme

sur·cease (sur-SEES) vi. (-ceased, -ceas·ing) cease, desist —n. cessation

sur·charge (SUR-chahrj) n. additional charge —vt. (sur-CHAHRJ) (-charged, -charg·ing) make an additional charge

sure (shuur) adj. certain; trustworthy; without doubt —adv. inf. certainly —sure'ly adv. —sure·ty (SHUUR-i-tee) n. (pl. -ties) one who takes responsibility for another's obligations; security against failure etc.; certainty

surf n. waves breaking on shore —v. swim in, ride surf —surf'ing n. this sport —surf'er n. one who (often) goes surfing —surf'board n. board used in surfing

sur·face (SUR-fis) n. outside face of body; exterior; plane; top, visible side; superficial appearance, outward impression —adj. involving the surface only; going no deeper than surface —v. (-faced, -fac·ing) (cause to) come to surface; put a surface on

sur·feit (SUR-fit) n. excess; disgust caused by excess —v. feed to excess; provide anything in excess

surge (surj) n. wave; sudden increase; Electricity sudden rush

of current in circuit —vi. (surged, surg·ing) move in large waves; swell, billow; rise precipitately

sur·geon (SUR-jən) n. physician who performs operations —sur'ger·y n. medical treatment by operation —sur'gi·cal (-kəl) adj.

sur·ly (SUR-lee) adj. (-li·er, -li·est) gloomily morose; ill-natured; cross and rude —sur'li·ness (-nis) n.

sur·mise (sər-MIZ) v./n. (-mised, -mis·ing) guess, conjecture

sur·mount (sər-MOWNT) vt. get over, overcome —sur·mount'a·ble adj.

sur·name (SUR-naym) n. family name

sur·pass (sər-PAS) vt. go beyond; excel; outstrip —sur·pass'a·ble adj. —sur·pass'ing adj. excellent; exceeding others

sur·plice (SUR-plis) n. loose white vestment worn by clergy and choir members

sur'plus n. what remains over in excess

sur·prise (sər-PRIZ) vt. (-prised, -pris·ing) cause surprise to; astonish; take, come upon unexpectedly; startle (someone) into action thus —n. what takes unawares; something unexpected; emotion aroused by being taken unawares

sur·re·al·ism (sə-REE-ə-liz-əm) n. movement in art and literature emphasizing expression of the unconscious —sur·re'al adj. —sur·re'al·ist n./adj.

sur·ren·der (sə-REN-dər) vt. hand over, give up —vi. yield; cease resistance; capitulate —n. act of surrendering

sur·rep·ti·tious (sur-əp-TISH-əs) adj. done secretly or stealthily; furtive

sur·ro·gate (SUR-ə-gayt) n. deputy, *esp.* of bishop; substitute; judicial officer supervising probate of wills —**surrogate mother** woman who bears child on behalf of childless woman

**sur·round** (sə-ROWND) *vt.* be, come all around, encompass, encircle; hem in —*n.* border, edging —**sur·round'ings** *n. pl.* conditions, scenery *etc.* around a person, place, environment

**sur·tax** (SUR-taks) *n.* additional tax

**sur·veil·lance** (sər-VAY-ləns) *n.* close watch, supervision —**surveil'lant** *adj./n.*

**sur·vey** (sər-VAY) *vt.* view, scrutinize; inspect, examine; measure, map (land) —*n.* (SUR-vay) (*pl.* -veys) a surveying; inspection; report incorporating results of survey —**sur·vey'or** (-ər) *n.*

**sur·vive** (sər-VIV) *v.* (-vived, -viv·ing) —*vt.* outlive; come through alive —*vi.* continue to live or exist —**sur·viv'al** (-əl) *n.* continuation of existence of persons, things *etc.* —**sur·viv'or** (-ər) *n.* one left alive when others have died; one who continues to function despite setbacks

**sus·cep·ti·ble** (sə-SEP-tə-bəl) *adj.* yielding readily (to); capable (of); impressionable —**sus·cep·ti·bil'i·ty** *n.*

**sus·pect** (sə-SPEKT) *vt.* doubt innocence of; have impression of existence or presence of; be inclined to believe that; mistrust —*adj.* (SUS-pekt) of suspected character —*n.* (SUS-pekt) suspected person

**sus·pend** (sə-SPEND) *vt.* hang up; cause to cease for a time; debar from an office or privilege; keep inoperative; sustain in fluid —**sus·pend'ers** *n. pl.* straps for supporting trousers *etc.*

**sus·pense** (sə-SPENS) *n.* state of

uncertainty, *esp.* while awaiting news, an event *etc.*; anxiety, worry —**sus·pen'sion** (-shən) *n.* state of being suspended; springs on axle or body of vehicle —**suspen'so·ry** (-sə-ree) *adj.*

**sus·pi·cion** (sə-SPISH-ən) *n.* suspecting, being suspected; slight trace —**sus·pi'cious** *adj.*

**sus·tain** (sə-STAYN) *vt.* keep, hold up; endure; keep alive; confirm —**sus·tain'a·ble** *adj.* —**sus'te·nance** (-nəns) *n.* food

**su·ture** (SOO-chər) *n.* act of sewing; sewing up of a wound; material used for this; a joining of the bones of the skull —*vt.* (-tured, -tur·ing) join by suture

**su·ze·rain** (SOO-zə-rin) *n.* sovereign with rights over autonomous state; feudal lord —**su'ze·rain·ty** (-tee) *n.*

**svelte** (svelt) *adj.* (svelt·er, svelt·est) lightly built, slender; sophisticated

**swab** (swob) *n.* mop; pad of surgical cotton *etc.* for cleaning, taking specimen *etc.*; *sl.* sailor, low or unmannerly fellow —*vt.* (swabbed, swab'bing) clean with swab

**swad·dle** (SWOD-l) *vt.* (-dled, -dling) swathe —**swaddling clothes** *Hist.* long strips of cloth for wrapping infant

**swag** *n. sl.* stolen property

**swag·ger** (SWAG-ər) *vi.* strut; boast —*n.* strutting gait; boastful, overconfident manner

**swain** *n.* rustic lover

**swal·low**[1] (SWOL-oh) *v.* cause, allow to pass down gullet; engulf; suppress, keep back; believe gullibly —*n.*, act of swallowing

**swal·low**[2] *n.* migratory bird with forked tail and skimming manner of flight

**swam** *pt. of* SWIM

**swamp** (swomp) *n.* bog —*vt.* entangle in swamp; overwhelm; flood —**swamp'y** adj. (**swamp·i·er, swamp·i·est**)

**swan** (swon) n. large, web-footed water bird with graceful curved neck —**swan song** fabled song of a swan before death; last act etc. before death

**swank** (swangk) vi. swagger; show off —n. smartness; style —**swank'y** adj. (**swank·i·er, swank·i·est**) smart; showy

**swap** (swop) n./v. (**swapped, swap·ping**) exchange; barter

**swarm** (sworm) n. large cluster of insects; vast crowd —vi. (of bees) be on the move in swarm; gather in large numbers

**swarth·y** (SWOR-*thee*) adj. (**swarth·i·er, swarth·i·est**) of dark complexion

**swash·buck·ler** (SWOSH-buk-lor) n. swaggering daredevil person —**swash'buck·ling** adj.

**swas·ti·ka** (SWOS-ti-kə) n. form of cross with arms bent at right angles, used as emblem by Nazis

**swat** (swot) vt. (**swat·ted, swat·ting**) hit smartly; kill, esp. insects

**swath** (swoth) n. line of grass or grain cut and thrown together by scythe or mower; whole sweep of scythe or mower

**swathe** (swo*th*) vt. (**swathed, swath·ing**) cover with wraps or bandages

**sway** v. swing unsteadily; (cause to) vacillate in opinion etc.; influence opinion etc. —n. control; power; swaying motion

**swear** (swair) v. (**swore, sworn, swear·ing**) —vt. promise on oath; cause to take an oath —vi. declare; use profanity

**sweat** (swet) n. moisture oozing from, forming on skin, esp. in humans —v. (**sweat** or **sweat·ed, sweat·ing**) (cause to) exude sweat; toil; employ at wrongfully

low wages; worry; wait anxiously —**sweat'y** adj. (**sweat·i·er, sweat·i·est**) —**sweat·shirt** (-shurt) n. long-sleeved cotton pullover

**sweat·er** (SWET-ər) n. knitted pullover or cardigan with or without sleeves

**sweep** v. (**swept, sweep·ing**) —vi. effect cleaning with broom; pass quickly or magnificently; extend in continuous curve —vt. clean with broom; carry impetuously —n. act of cleaning with broom; sweeping motion; wide curve; range; long oar; one who cleans chimneys —**sweep'ing** adj. wide-ranging; without limitations, reservations —**sweep'stakes** n. with sing. or pl. v. gamble in which winner takes stakes contributed by all; type of lottery; risky venture promising great return

**sweet** adj. (-**er**, -**est**) tasting like sugar; agreeable; kind, charming; fresh, fragrant; in good condition; tuneful; gentle, dear, beloved —n. small piece of sweet food; something pleasant —pl. ...**cake** etc. containing much sugar —**sweet'en** (-in) v. **sweet'en·er** (-ən-ər) n. —**sweet'bread** (-bred) n. animal's pancreas used as food —**sweet'heart** n. lover —**sweetheart contract** collusive contract between labor union and company benefiting latter —**sweet'meat** n. sweetened delicacy eg small cake, candy —**sweet potato** trailing plant; its edible, sweetish, starchy tubers —**sweet talk** inf. flattery —**sweet-talk** v. inf. coax, flatter

**swell** v. (**swelled, swol·len** pr. SWOHL-ən or **swelled, swel·ling**) expand —vi. be greatly filled with pride, emotion —n. act of swelling or being swollen; wave of sea; mechanism in organ to vary volume of sound; *inf.* person of high social standing —*adj. inf.* stylish, socially prominent; fine

**swel·ter** (SWEL-tər) *vi.* be oppressed with heat

**swept** *pt./pp.* of SWEEP

**swerve** (swurv) *vi.* (swerved, swerv·ing) swing around, change direction during motion; turn aside (from duty *etc.*) —*n.* swerving

**swift** *adj.* (-er, -est) rapid, quick, ready —*n.* bird like a swallow

**swig** *n. inf.* large swallow of drink —*v. inf.* (swigged, swig·ging) drink thus

**swill** *v.* drink greedily; feed (pigs) with swill —*n.* liquid or wet pig food; greedy drinking; kitchen refuse; drivel

**swim** *v.* (swam, swum, swim·ming) —*vi.* support and move oneself in water; float; be flooded; have feeling of dizziness —*vt.* cross by swimming; compete in by swimming —*n.* spell of swimming —**swim'ming·ly** *adv.* successfully, effortlessly

**swin·dle** (SWIN-dl) *n./v.* (-dled, -dling) cheat —**swind'ler** (-lər) *n.* —**swind'ling** *n.*

**swine** (swin) *n.* (*pl.* same form) pig; contemptible person —**swin'ish** *adj.*

**swing** *v.* (swung, swing·ing) (cause) to move to and fro; (cause) to pivot, turn; hang; arrange, play music with (jazz) rhythm —*vi.* be hanged; hit out (at) —*n.* act, instance of swinging; seat hung to swing on; fluctuation (*esp. eg* in voting pattern) —**swing'er** *n. sl.* person regarded as modern and lively or sexually promiscuous

**swipe** (swīp) *v.* (swiped, swip·ing) strike with wide, sweeping or glancing blow; *inf.* steal

**swirl** (swurl) *v.* (cause to) move with eddying motion —*n.* such motion

**swish** *v.* (cause to) move with audible hissing sound —*n.* the sound; *sl.* effeminate homosexual male —*adj. sl.* effeminate

**switch** (swich) *n.* mechanism to complete or interrupt electric circuit *etc.*; abrupt change; flexible stick or twig; tufted end of animal's tail; type of women's hairpiece —*vi.* shift, change; swing —*vt.* affect (current *etc.*) with switch; change abruptly; strike with switch —**switch'back** *n.* road, railway with steep rises and descents —**switch'board** (-bord) *n.* installation for establishing or varying connections in telephone and electric circuits

**swiv·el** (SWIV-əl) *n.* mechanism of two parts that can revolve the one on the other —*v.* (-eled, -el·ing) turn (on swivel)

**swollen** (SWOH-lən) *pp.* of SWELL

**swoon** *vi./n.* faint

**swoop** *vi.* dive, as hawk —*n.* act of swooping; sudden attack

**sword** (sord) *n.* weapon with long blade for cutting or thrusting

**swore** *pt.* —**sworn** *pp.* of SWEAR

**swum** *pp.* of SWIM

**swung** *pt./pp.* of SWING

**syb·a·rite** (SIB-ə-rīt) *n.* person who loves luxury —**syb·a·rit'ic** (-RIT-ik) *adj.*

**syc·o·phant** (SIK-ə-fənt) *n.* one using flattery to gain favors —**syc·o·phan'tic** (-FAN-tik) *adj.* —**syc'o·phan·cy** (-fən-see) *n.*

**syl·la·ble** (SIL-ə-bəl) *n.* division of word as unit for pronunciation —**syl·lab'ic** *adj.* —**syl·lab'i·fy** (-fied, -fy·ing)

**syl·la·bus** (SIL-ə-bəs) *n.* (*pl.* -bi *or* -bī) outline of a course of study; list of subjects studied in course

**syl·lo·gism** (SIL-ə-jiz-əm) *n.* form

of logical reasoning consisting of two premises and conclusion —syl·lo·gis'tic *adj.*

sylph (silf) *n.* slender, graceful woman; sprite

syl·van (SIL-vən) *adj.* of forests, trees

sym- *see* SYN-, used before labial consonants

sym·bi·o·sis (sim-bee-OH-sis) *n.* (*pl.* -ses *pr.* -seez) living together of two organisms of different kinds, *esp.* to their mutual benefit —sym·bi·ot·ic (-OT-ik) *adj.*

sym·bol (SIM-bəl) *n.* sign; thing representing or typifying something —sym·bol'ic *adj.* —sym·bol'i·cal·ly *adv.* —sym'bol·ism *n.* use, of representation by symbols; movement in art holding that work of art should express idea in symbolic form —sym'bol·ist *n./adj.* —sym'bol·ize *vt.* (-ized, iz·ing)

sym·me·try (SIM-ə-tree) *n.* (*pl.* -tries) proportion between parts; balance of arrangement between two sides; order —sym·met'ri·cal *adj.* having due proportion in its parts; harmonious; regular

sym·pa·thy (SIM-pə-thee) *n.* (*pl.* -thies) feeling for another in pain *etc.*; compassion, pity; sharing of emotion, interest, desire *etc.*; fellow feeling —sym·pa·thet'ic *adj.* —sym'pa·thize (-thīz) *vi.* (-thized, -thiz·ing)

sym·pho·ny (SIM-fə-nee) *n.* (*pl.* -nies) composition for full orchestra; harmony of sounds —sym·phon'ic (-FON-ik) *adj.* —sym·pho'ni·ous (-FOH-nee-əs) *adj.* harmonious

sym·po·si·um (sim-POH-zee-əm) *n.* (*pl.* -si·a *pr.* -zee-ə) conference, meeting; discussion, writings on a given topic

symp·tom (SIMP-təm) *n.* change in body indicating its state of health or disease; sign, token —symp·to·mat'ic *adj.*

syn- (*prefix*) with, together, alike

syn·a·gogue (SIN-ə-gog) *n.* (place of worship of) Jewish congregation

syn·chro·nize (SING-krə-nīz) *v.* (-nized, -niz·ing) —*vt.* make agree in time —*vi.* happen at same time —syn·chro·ni·za'tion *n.* —syn'chro·nous (-nis) *adj.* simultaneous

syn·co·pate (SIN-kə-payt) *vt.* (-pat·ed, -pat·ing) accentuate weak beat in bar of music —syn·co·pa'tion *n.*

syn·di·cate (SIN-di-kit) *n.* body of people, delegates associated for some enterprise —*v.* (-kayt) (-cat·ed, -cat·ing) form syndicate —*vt.* publish in many newspapers at the same time

syn·drome (SIN-drohm) *n.* combination of several symptoms in disease; symptom, set of symptoms or characteristics

syn·ec·do·che (si-NEK-də-kee) *n.* figure of speech by which whole of thing is put for part or part for whole, *eg* sail for ship

syn·od (SIN-əd) *n.* church council; convention

syn·o·nym (SIN-ə-nim) *n.* word with (nearly) same meaning as another —syn·on·y·mous (si-NON-ə-məs) *adj.*

syn·op·sis (si-NOP-sis) *n.* (*pl.* -ses *pr.* -seez) summary, outline —syn·op'tic *adj.* of, like synopsis; having same viewpoint

syn·tax (SIN-taks) *n.* part of grammar treating of arrangement of words in sentence —syn·tac'tic *adj.*

syn·the·sis (SIN-thə-sis) *n.* (*pl.* -ses *pr.* -seez) putting together, combination —syn'the·size *v.* (-sized, -siz·ing) make artificially —syn'the·siz·er (-sīz-ər) *n.* electronic keyboard instrument capable of reproducing a wide range of musical sounds —**syn·thet·ic** adj. artificial; of synthesis

**syph·i·lis** (SIF-ə-lis) n. contagious venereal disease —**syph·i·lit'ic** adj.

**sy·ringe** (sə-RINJ) n. instrument for drawing in liquid by piston and forcing it out in fine stream or spray; squirt —vt. -**ringed,** -**ring·ing** spray, cleanse with syringe

**syr·up** (SIR-əp) n. thick solution obtained in process of refining sugar, molasses etc.; any liquid like this, esp. in consistency —**syr'up·y** adj.

**sys·tem** (SIS-təm) n. complex whole, organization; method; classification —**sys·tem·at'ic** adj. methodical —**sys·tem·a·tize** (-tiz) vt. (-**tized,** -**tiz·ing**) reduce to system; arrange methodically —**sys·tem'ic** adj. affecting entire body or organism

**sys·to·le** (SIS-tə-lee) n. contraction of heart and arteries for expelling blood and carrying on circulation —**sys·tol'ic** (sis-TOL-ik) adj. contracting; of systole

# T

**T** Chem. tritium —**to a T** precisely, to a nicety

**tab** n. tag, label, short strap —**keep tabs on** inf. keep watchful eye on

**tab·er·na·cle** (TAB-ər-nak-əl) n. portable shrine of Israelites; receptacle containing reserved Eucharist; place of worship

**ta·ble** (TAY-bəl) n. piece of furniture consisting of flat board supported by legs; food; set of facts, figures arranged in lines or columns —vt. (-**bled,** -**bling**) lay on table; lay aside (motion etc.) for possible but unlikely consideration in future —**ta'ble·land** n. plateau, high flat area —**ta'ble·spoon** n. spoon used for serving food etc. —**under the table** secretly; as bribe; drunk

**tab·leau** (ta-BLOH) n. (pl. -**leaux,** -**leaus,** pr. -BLOHZ) group of persons, silent and motionless, arranged to represent some scene; dramatic scene

**ta·ble d'hôte** (TAH-bəl DOHT) Fr. (pl. **ta·bles d'hôte** same pr.) meal, with limited choice of dishes, at a fixed price

**tab·let** (TAB-lit) n. pill of compressed powdered medicinal substance; writing pad; slab of stone, wood etc., esp. used formerly for writing on

**tab'loid** n. (illustrated) popular small-sized newspaper usu. with terse, sensational headlines

**ta·boo** (tə-BOO) adj. forbidden or disapproved of —n. (pl. -**boos**) prohibition resulting from social conventions etc.; thing prohibited —vt. (-**booed,** -**boo·ing**) place under taboo

**tab·u·lar** (TAB-yə-lər) adj. shaped, arranged like a table —**tab·u·late** (-layt) vt. (-**lat·ed,** -**lat·ing**) arrange (figures, facts etc.) in tables

**tacho-** (comb. form) speed

**ta·chom·e·ter** (ta-KOM-i-tər) n. device for measuring speed, esp. of revolving shaft (eg in automobile) and hence revolutions per minute

**tac·it** (TAS-it) adj. implied but not spoken; silent —**tac'it·ly** adv. —**tac'i·turn** adj. talking little; habitually silent

**tack**[1] (tak) n. small nail; long loose stitch; Naut. course of ship obliquely to windward; course, direction —vt. nail with tacks; stitch lightly; append, attach; sail to windward

**tack²** n. riding harness for horses

**tack·le** (TAK-əl) n. equipment, apparatus, esp. for fishing; lifting appliances with ropes; *Football* lineman between guard and end —vt. (-led, -ling) take in hand; grip, grapple with; undertake to cope with, master etc.; *Football* seize, bring down (ball-carrier)

**tack·y** (TAK-ee) adj. (tack·i·er, tack·i·est) sticky; not quite dry; dowdy, shabby —**tack′i·ness** (-nis) n.

**tact** (takt) n. skill in dealing with people or situations; delicate perception of the feelings of others —**tact′ful** (-fəl) adj. —**tact′less** (-lis) adj.

**tac·tics** (TAK-tiks) n. pl. art of handling troops, ships in battle; adroit management of a situation; plans for this —**tac·ti·cal** (TAK-ti-kəl) adj. —**tac·ti′cian** (-TISH-ən) n.

**tac·tile** (TAK-til) adj. of, relating to the sense of touch

**tad′pole** (TAD-pohl) n. immature frog, in its first state before gills and tail are absorbed

**taf·fe·ta** (TAF-i-tə) n. smooth, stiff fabric of silk, nylon etc.

**taf·fy** (TAF-ee) n. (pl. -fies) candy of molasses and sugar

**tag¹** n. label identifying or showing price of (something); ragged, hanging end; pointed end of shoelace etc.; trite saying or quotation; any appendage —vt. (tagged, tag·ging) append, add (on); trail (along) behind

**tag²** n. children's game where one being chased becomes the chaser upon being touched —vt. (tagged, tag·ging) touch —**tag wrestling** wrestling match for

teams of two, where one partner may replace the other upon being touched on hand

**tail** (tayl) n. flexible prolongation of animal's spine; lower or inferior part of anything; appendage; rear part of aircraft; inf. person employed to follow another —pl. reverse side of coin; tail coat —vt. remove tail of; inf. follow closely, trail —**tail′ings** n. pl. waste left over from some (eg industrial) process —**tail′less** (-lis) adj. —**tail′board** (-bord) n. removable or hinged rear board on truck etc. —**tails** n. pl. man's full-dress coat —**tail end** last part —**tail′light** n. light carried at rear of vehicle —**tail′spin** n. spinning dive of aircraft; sudden (eg emotional, financial) collapse —**tail′wind** n. wind coming from behind —**tail off** diminish gradually, dwindle —**turn tail** run away

**tai·lor** (TAY-lər) n. maker of outer clothing, esp. for men —**tailor-made** adj. made by tailor; well-fitting; appropriate

**taint** (taynt) v. affect or be affected by pollution, corruption etc. —n. defect, flaw; infection, contamination

**take** (tayk) v. (took pr. tuuk, tak·en, tak·ing) —vt. grasp, get hold of; get; receive, assume; adopt; accept; understand; consider; carry, conduct; use; capture; consume; subtract; require —vi. be effective; please; go —n. esp. *Motion Pictures* (recording of) scene, sequence photographed without interruption; inf. earnings, receipts —**tak′ing** adj. charming —**take′off** n. instant at which aircraft becomes airborne; commencement of flight —**take after** resemble in face or character —**take down** write down; dismantle; humiliate

—take in understand; make (garment *etc.*) smaller; deceive —take in vain blaspheme; be facetious —take off (of aircraft) leave ground; *inf.* go away; *inf.* mimic —take to become fond of

tal·cum pow'der (TAL-kəm) powder, *usu.* scented, to absorb body moisture, deodorize *etc.*

tale (tayl) *n.* story, narrative, report; fictitious story

tal·ent (TAL-ənt) *n.* natural ability or power; ancient weight or money —tal'ent·ed (-id) *adj.* gifted

tal·is·man (TAL-is-mən) *n.* (*pl.* -mans) object supposed to have magic power; amulet —tal·is·man'ic (-MAN-ik) *adj.*

talk (tawk) *vi.* express, exchange ideas *etc.* in words —*vt.* express in speech, utter; discuss —*n.* speech, lecture; conversation; rumor —talk'a·tive (-tiv) *adj.* fond of talking —talking-to *n.* (*pl.* -tos) reproof —talk show TV or radio program in which guests are interviewed informally

tall (tawl) *adj.* high; of great stature; incredible, untrue, as tall story

tal·low (TAL-oh) *n.* melted and clarified animal fat —*vt.* smear with this

tal·ly (TAL-ee) *vi.* (-lied, -ly·ing) correspond one with the other; keep record —*n.* (*pl.* -lies) record, account, total number

Tal·mud (TAHL-muud) *n.* body of Jewish law —Tal·mud'ic (-MUUD-ik) *adj.*

tal·on (TAL-ən) *n.* claw

tam·bou·rine (tam-bə-REEN) *n.* flat half-drum with jingling disks of metal attached

tame (taym) *adj.* (tam·er, tam·est) not wild, domesticated; subdued; uninteresting —*vt.*

make tame —tame'ly *adv.* in a tame manner; without resisting

tamp *vt.* pack, force down by repeated blows

tam·per (TAM-pər) *vi.* interfere (with) improperly; meddle

tam'pon *n.* plug of lint, cotton *etc.* inserted in wound, body cavity, to stop flow of blood, absorb secretions *etc.*

tan *adj./n.* (adj. tan·ner, tan·nest) (of) brown color of skin after long exposure to rays of sun *etc.* —*v.* (tanned, tan·ning) (cause to) go brown; (of animal hide) convert to leather by chemical treatment —tan'ner *n.* —tan'ner·y *n.* place where hides are tanned —tan'nic *adj.* —tan'nin *n.* vegetable substance used as tanning agent —tan'bark *n.* bark of certain trees, yielding tannin

tang *n.* strong pungent taste or smell; trace, hint; spike, barb —tang'y *adj.* (tang·i·er, tang·i·est)

tan·gent (TAN-jənt) *n.* line that touches a curve without cutting; divergent course —*adj.* touching, meeting without cutting —tan·gen'tial (-JEN-shəl) *adj.* —tan·gen'tial·ly *adv.*

tan·ge·rine (tan-jə-REEN) *n.* citrus tree; its fruit, a variety of orange

tan·gi·ble (TAN-jə-bəl) *adj.* that can be touched; definite; palpable; concrete

tan·gle (TANG-gəl) *n.* confused mass or situation —*vt.* (-gled, -gling) twist together in muddle; contend (with)

tan·go (TANG-goh) *n.* (*pl.* -gos) dance of S Amer. origin

tank *n.* storage vessel for liquids or gas; armored motor vehicle moving on tracks; cistern; reservoir —tank'er *n.* ship, truck *etc.* for carrying liquid in bulk

**tan·kard** (TANG-kərd) n. large drinking cup of metal or glass; its contents, esp. beer

**tannin** see TAN

**tan·ta·lize** (TAN-tə-līz) vt. (-**lized**, -**liz·ing**) torment by appearing to offer something desired; tease

**tan·ta·mount** (TAN-tə-mownt) adj. equivalent in value or signification; equal, amounting (to)

**tan·trum** (TAN-trəm) n. childish outburst of temper

**tap**[1] v. (**tapped**, **tap·ping**) strike lightly but with some noise —n. slight blow, rap

**tap**[2] n. valve with handle to regulate or stop flow of fluid in pipe etc.; stopper, plug permitting liquid to be drawn from cask etc.; steel tool for forming internal screw threads —vt. (**tapped**, **tap·ping**) put tap in; draw off with or as with tap; make secret connection to telephone wire to overhear conversation on it; make connection for supply of electricity at intermediate point in supply line; form internal threads in

**tape** (tayp) n. narrow long strip of fabric, paper etc.; magnetic recording of music, data etc. —vt. (**taped**, **tap·ing**) record (speech, music etc.) —**tape deck**, **tape player** device for playing magnetic tape recordings —**tape measure** tape of fabric, metal marked off in centimeters, inches etc. —**tape recorder** apparatus for recording sound on magnetized tape and playing it back —**tape′worm** (-wurm) n. long flat worm parasitic in animals and people

**ta·per** (TAY-pər) vi. become gradually thinner toward one end —n. thin candle; long wick covered with wax; a narrowing

**tap·es·try** (TAP-ə-stree) n. (pl. -**tries**) fabric decorated with designs in colors woven by needles —**tap′es·tried** adj.

**tap·i·o·ca** (tap-ee-OH-kə) n. bead-like starch made from cassava root, used esp. in puddings, as thickener etc.

**ta·pir** (TAY-pər) n. Amer. animal with elongated snout, allied to pig

**tap′root** n. large single root growing straight down

**tar**[1] (tahr) n. thick black liquid distilled from coal etc. —vt. (**tarred**, **tar·ring**) coat, treat (as though) with tar —**tarred with same brush** (made to appear) guilty of same misdeeds

**tar**[2] n. inf. sailor

**tar·an·tel·la** (ta-rən-TEL-ə) n. lively Italian dance; music for it

**ta·ran·tu·la** (tə-RAN-chuu-lə) n. (pl. -**las**) any of various large (poisonous) hairy spiders

**tar·dy** (TAHR-dee) adj. (-**di·er**, -**di·est**) slow, late —**tar′di·ly** adv.

**tare** (tair) n. weight of wrapping, container for goods; unladen weight of vehicle

**tar·get** (TAHR-git) n. mark to aim at in shooting; thing aimed at; object of criticism

**tar·iff** (TA-rif) n. tax levied on imports etc.; list of charges; bill

**tarn** (tahrn) n. small mountain lake

**tar·nish** (TAHR-nish) v. (cause to) become stained, lose shine or become dimmed or sullied —n. discoloration, blemish

**ta·ro** (TAHR-oh) n. (pl. -**ros**) plant of Pacific islands now cultivated widely; its edible tuber

**tar·ot** (TA-roh) n. one of special pack of cards now used mainly in fortunetelling

**tar·pau·lin** (tahr-PAW-lin) n. (sheet of) heavy hard-wearing waterproof fabric

**tar·ry** vi. (-ried, -ry·ing) linger, delay; stay behind

**tart**[1] n. small pie filled with fruit, jam etc.; sl. promiscuous woman; prostitute

**tart**[2] adj. (-er, -est) sour; sharp; bitter

**tar·tan** (TAHR-tn) n. woolen cloth woven in pattern of colored checks, esp. in colors, patterns associated with Scottish clans; such pattern

**tar·tar**[1] (TAHR-tər) n. crust deposited on teeth; deposit formed during fermentation of wine

**tartar**[2] n. ill-tempered person, difficult to deal with; (T-) member of group of peoples including Mongols and Turks

**task** n. piece of work (esp. unpleasant or difficult) set or undertaken —vt. assign task to; exact —**task force** naval or military unit dispatched to carry out specific undertaking; any similar group in government, industry —**task'mas·ter** n. (stern) overseer —**take to task** reprove

**tas·sel** (TAS-əl) n. ornament of fringed knot of threads etc.; tuft —**tas'seled** adj.

**taste** (tayst) n. sense by which flavor, quality of substance is detected by the tongue; this act or sensation; (brief) experience of something; small amount; preference, liking; power of discerning, judging; discretion, delicacy —v. (tast·ed, tast·ing) observe or distinguish the taste of a substance; take small amount into mouth; experience —vi. have specific flavor —**taste'ful** (-fəl) adj. in good style; with, showing good taste —**taste'less** (-lis) adj. —**tast'y** adj. (tast·i·er, tast·i·est) pleasantly or highly flavored —**taste bud** small organ of taste on tongue

**tat** v. (tat·ted, tat·ting) make by tatting —**tatting** n. type of handmade lace

**tat·ter** (TAT-ər) v. make or become ragged, worn to shreds —n. ragged piece

**tat·tle** vi./n. (v. -tled, -tling) gossip, chatter

**tat·too**[1] (ta-TOO) n. (pl. -toos) beat of drum and bugle call; military spectacle or pageant

**tattoo**[2] vt. (-tooed, -too·ing) mark skin in patterns etc. by pricking and filling punctures with indelible colored inks —n. (pl. -toos) mark so made

**tat·ty** (TAT-ee) adj. (-ti·er, -ti·est) shabby, worn out

**taught** (tawt) pt./pp. of TEACH

**taunt** (tawnt) vt. provoke, deride with insulting words etc. —n. instance of this; words used for this

**taut** (tawt) adj. (-er, -est) drawn tight; under strain

**tau·tol·o·gy** (taw-TOL-ə-gee) n. (pl. -gies) needless repetition of same thing in other words in same sentence —**tau·to·log'i·cal** (-tə-LOJ-ə-kəl) adj.

**tav·ern** (TAV-ərn) n. bar; inn

**taw·dry** (TAW-dree) adj. (-dri·er, -dri·est) showy, but cheap and without taste, flashy —**taw'dri·ness** (-nis) n.

**taw·ny** (TAW-nee) adj./n. adj. (-ni·er, -ni·est) (of) light (yellowish) brown

**tax** (taks) n. compulsory payments by wage earners, companies etc. imposed by government to raise revenue; heavy demand on something —vt. impose tax on; strain; accuse, blame —**tax'a·ble** adj. —**tax·a'tion** n. levying of taxes —**tax'pay·er** n. —**tax return** statement supplied to authorities of personal income and tax due

**tax·i** (TAK-see) n. (pl. **tax·is**) motor vehicle (also **tax'i·cab**) for hire with driver —vi. (**tax·ied, tax·i·ing** or **tax·y·ing**) (of aircraft) run along ground under its own power; ride in taxi

**tax·i·der·my** (TAK-si-dur-mee) n. art of stuffing, mounting animal skins to give them lifelike appearance —**tax'i·der·mist** n.

**tax·on·o·my** (tak-SON-ə-mee) n. science, practice of classification, esp. of biological organisms

**Tb** Chem. terbium

**T-bone steak** loin steak with T-shaped bone

**Tc** Chem. technetium

**te** see TI

**Te** Chem. tellurium

**tea** (tee) n. dried leaves of plant cultivated esp. in (sub)tropical Asia; infusion of it as beverage; various herbal beverages; tea, cakes etc. as light afternoon meal; sl. marijuana —**tea bag** small porous bag of paper containing tea leaves —**tea'spoon** n. small spoon for stirring tea etc.

**teach** (teech) v. (**taught** pr. tawt, **teach·ing**) instruct; educate; train; impart knowledge of; act as teacher —**teach'er** n.

**teak** (teek) n. East Indian tree; very hard wood obtained from it

**teal** (teel) n. type of small duck; greenish-blue color

**team** (teem) n. set of animals, players of game etc. in activity —vi. (usu. with **up**) (cause to) make a team —**team'ster** n. driver of truck or team of draft animals —**team spirit** subordination of individual desire for good of team —**team'work** n. cooperative work by team acting as unit

**tear¹** (teer) n. drop of fluid appearing in and falling from eye —**tear'ful** (-fəl) adj. inclined to weep; involving tears —**tear gas** irritant gas causing abnormal watering of eyes, and temporary blindness —**tear-jerk·er** (TEER-jur-kər) n. inf. excessively sentimental story, moving picture etc.

**tear²** (tair) v. (**tore, torn, tear·ing**) pull apart, rend; become torn; rush —n. hole, cut or split

**tease** (teez) vt. (**teased, teas·ing**) tantalize, torment, irritate, bait; pull apart fibers of —n. one who teases

**teat** (teet) n. nipple of female breast; rubber nipple of baby's feeding bottle

**tech·ni·cal** (TEK-ni-kəl) adj. of, specializing in industrial, practical or mechanical arts and applied sciences; skilled in practical and mechanical arts; belonging to particular art or science; according to letter of the law —**tech·ni·cal'i·ty** n. point of procedure; state of being technical —**tech·ni'cian** (-NISH-ən) n. one skilled in technique of an art —**tech·nique** (tek-NEEK) n. method of performance in an art; skill required for mastery of subject —**technical college** higher educational institution specializing in mechanical and industrial arts and applied science etc. —**technical knockout** Boxing termination of bout by referee who judges that one boxer is not fit to continue

**tech·noc·ra·cy** (tek-NOK-rə-see) n. government by technical experts; example of this —**tech'no·crat** (-nə-krat) n.

**tech·nol·o·gy** (tek-NOL-ə-gee) n. (pl. **-gies**) application of practical, mechanical sciences to industry, commerce; technical methods, skills, knowledge —**tech·no·log'i·cal** adj.

**tec·ton·ic** (tek-TON-ik) adj. of

construction or building; *Geology* pert. to (forces or condition of) structure of Earth's crust —**tec·ton′ics** *n.* (*with sing. v.*) art, science of building

**te·di·ous** (TEE-dee-əs) *adj.* causing fatigue or boredom, monotonous —**te′di·um** (-əm) *n.* monotony

**tee** *n. Golf* slightly raised ground from which first stroke of hole is made; small peg supporting ball for this stroke —**tee off** make first stroke of hole in golf; *sl.* scold; *sl.* irritate

**teem** *vi.* abound with; swarm; be prolific; pour, rain heavily

**teens** (teenz) *n. pl.* years of life from 13 to 19 —**teen′age** *adj.* —**teen′ag·er** *n.* person in teens

**teepee** *n. see* TEPEE

**tee·ter** (TEE-tər) *vi.* seesaw or make similar movements; vacillate

**teeth** *pl.* of TOOTH

**teethe** (teeth) *vi.* (**teethed, teeth·ing**) (of baby) grow first teeth —**teething** ring ring on which baby can bite

**tee·to·tal** (tee-TOHT-l) *adj.* pledged to abstain from alcohol —**tee·to′tal·er** *n.*

**tele-** (*comb. form*) at a distance, and from far off

**tel·e·cast** (TEL-i-kast) *v./n.* (-**cast** *or* -**cast·ed**, -**cast·ing**) (broadcast) TV program

**tel·e·com·mu·ni·ca·tions** (tel-i-kə-myoo-ni-KAY-shənz) *n.* (*with sing. v.*) science and technology of communications by telephony, radio, TV *etc.*

**tel·e·gram** (TEL-i-gram) *n.* message sent by telegraph

**tel·e·graph** (TEL-i-graf) *n.* electrical apparatus for transmitting messages to a distance; any signaling device for transmitting messages —*v.* communicate by telegraph —**tel·e·graph′ic** *adj.* —**te·leg′ra·pher** *n.* one who works telegraph —**te·leg′ra·phy** *n.* science of telegraph; use of telegraph

**tel·e·ol·o·gy** (tel-ee-OL-ə-jee) *n.* doctrine of final causes; belief that things happen because of the purpose or design that will be fulfilled by them

**tel·e·mar·ket·ing** (tel-ə-MAHR-ki-ting) *n.* selling or advertising by telephone, television

**te·lep·a·thy** (tə-LEP-ə-thee) *n.* action of one mind on another at a distance —**tel·e·path′ic** (-ə-PATH-ik) *adj.*

**tel·e·phone** (tel-ə-FOHN) *n.* apparatus for communicating sound to hearer at a distance —*v.* (-**phoned, -phon·ing**) communicate, speak by telephone —**tel·e·phon′ic** (-FON-ik) *adj.* —**te·leph·o·ny** (tə-LEF-ə-nee) *n.*

**tel·e·pho·to** (TEL-ə-foh-toh) *adj.* (of lens) producing magnified image of distant object

**Tel·e·Promp·Ter** (TEL-ə-promp-tər) *n.* R off-camera device to enable TV performer to refer to magnified script out of sight of the cameras

**tel·e·scope** (TEL-ə-skohp) *n.* optical instrument for magnifying images of distant objects —*v.* (-**scoped, -scop·ing**) slide or drive together, *esp.* parts designed to fit one inside the other; make smaller, shorter —**tel·e·scop′ic** (-SKOP-ik) *adj.*

**tel·e·text** (TEL-i-tekst) *n.* electronic system that shows information, news, graphics on subscribers' TV screens

**tel·e·vi·sion** (TEL-ə-vizh-ən) *n.* system of producing on screen images of distant objects, events *etc.* by electromagnetic radiation; device for receiving this transmission and converting it to optical images; programs *etc.* viewed on TV set —**tel′e·vise** (-vīz) *vt.* (-vised, -vis·ing) transmit by TV; make, produce as TV program

**tell** *v.* (told, tel·ling) —*vt.* let know; order, direct; narrate, make known; discern; distinguish; count —*vi.* give account; be of weight, importance; reveal secrets —**tel′ler** *n.* narrator; bank cashier —**tell′ing** *adj.* effective, striking —**tell′tale** *n.* sneak; automatic indicator —*adj.* revealing

**tel·lu′ri·um** (te-LUUR-ee-əm) *n.* nonmetallic bluish-white element —**tel·lu′ric** *adj.*

**tem·blor** (TEM-blər) *n.* earthquake

**te·mer·i·ty** (tə-MER-i-tee) *n.* boldness, audacity

**temp** *n.* *inf.* one employed on temporary basis

**tem·per** (TEM-pər) *n.* frame of mind; anger, oft. noisy; mental constitution; degree of hardness of steel *etc.* —*vt.* restrain, qualify, moderate; harden; bring to proper condition

**tem·per·a** (TEM-pər-ə) *n.* emulsion used as painting medium; painting made with this

**tem·per·a·ment** (TEM-pər-ə-mənt) *n.* natural disposition; emotional mood; mental constitution —**tem·per·a·men′tal** *adj.* given to extremes of temperament, moody; of, occasioned by temperament

**tem·per·ate** (TEM-pər-it) *adj.* not extreme; showing, practicing moderation —**tem′per·ance** (-əns) *n.* moderation; abstinence, *esp.* from alcohol

**tem·per·a·ture** (TEM-pər-ə-chər) *n.* degree of heat or coldness; *inf.* (abnormally) high body temperature

**tem·pest** (TEM-pist) *n.* violent storm —**tem·pes·tu·ous** (tem-PES-choo-əs) *adj.* turbulent; violent, stormy

**tem·plate** (TEM-plit) *n.* mold, pattern to help shape something accurately

**tem·ple**[1] (TEM-pəl) *n.* building for worship; shrine

**temple**[2] *n.* flat part on either side of forehead

**tem·po** (TEM-poh) *n.* (*pl.* -pos) rate, rhythm, *esp.* in music

**tem·po·ral** (TEM-pə-rəl) *adj.* of time; of this life or world, secular

**tem·po·rar·y** (TEM-pə-rer-ee) *adj.* lasting, used only for a time —*n.* (*pl.* -ies) person employed on temporary basis —**tem·po·rar′i·ly** *adv.*

**tem·po·rize** (TEM-pə-rīz) *vi.* (-ized, -iz·ing) use evasive action; hedge; gain time by negotiation *etc.*; conform to circumstances —**tem′po·riz·er** *n.*

**tempt** *vt.* try to persuade, entice, *esp.* to something wrong or unwise; dispose, cause to be inclined to —**temp·ta′tion** (-TAY-shən) *n.* act of tempting; thing that tempts —**tempt′er** *n.* (-ress *fem.*) —**tempt′ing** *adj.* attractive, inviting

**ten** *n./adj.* cardinal number next after nine —**tenth** *adj./n.* ordinal number

**ten·a·ble** (TEN-ə-bəl) *adj.* able to be held, defended, maintained

**te·na·cious** (tə-NAY-shəs) *adj.* holding fast; retentive; stubborn —**te·nac′i·ty** (-NAS-i-tee) *n.*

**ten·ant** (TEN-ənt) *n.* one who holds lands, house *etc.* on rent or lease —**ten′an·cy** *n.* (*pl.* -cies)

**tend**[1] *vi.* be inclined; be conducive; make in direction of —**ten′den·cy** (-dən-see) *n.* (*pl.* -cies) inclination, bent —**ten·den′tious**

(-DEN-shəs) adj. having, showing tendency or bias; controversial

**tend²** vt. take care of, watch over —**tend′er** n. small boat carried by yacht or ship; carriage for fuel and water attached to steam locomotive; one who tends, eg **bartender**

**ten·der¹** (TEN-dər) adj. not tough or hard; easily injured; gentle, loving, affectionate; delicate, soft —**ten′der·ness** (-nis) n. —**ten′der·ize** vt. (-ized, -iz·ing) soften (meat) by pounding or by treating (it) with substance made for this purpose —**ten′der·foot** (-fuut) n. (pl. -feet or -foots) newcomer, esp. to ranch etc.

**tender²** vt. offer —vi. make offer or estimate —n. offer; offer or estimate for contract to undertake specific work; what may legally be offered in payment

**ten·don** (TEN-dən) n. sinew attaching muscle to bone etc. —**ten·di·ni′tis** (-NĪ-tis) n. inflammation of tendon

**ten′dril** n. slender curling stem by which climbing plant clings to anything; curl, as of hair

**ten·e·ment** (TEN-ə-mənt) n. rundown apartment house, esp. in slum

**ten·et** (TEN-it) n. doctrine, belief

**ten′nis** n. game in which ball is struck with racket by players on opposite sides of net, lawn tennis —**tennis elbow** strained muscle as a result of playing tennis

**ten·on** (TEN-ən) n. tongue put on end of piece of wood etc., to fit into a mortise

**ten·or** (TEN-ər) n. male voice between alto and bass; music for, singer with this; general course, meaning

**tense¹** (tens) n. modification of verb to show time of action

**tense²** adj. (tens·er, tens·est)

stretched tight; strained; taut; emotionally strained —v. (tensed, tens·ing) make, become tense —**ten′sile** (-səl) adj. of, relating to tension; capable of being stretched —**ten′sion** (-shən) n. stretching; strain when stretched; emotional strain or excitement; hostility, suspense; Electricity voltage

**tent** n. portable shelter of canvas etc.

**ten·ta·cle** (TEN-tə-kəl) n. elongated, flexible organ of some animals (eg octopus) used for grasping, feeding etc.

**ten·ta·tive** (TEN-tə-tiv) adj. done as a trial; experimental, cautious

**ten·ter·hooks** (TEN-tər-huuks) n. pl. —on tenterhooks in anxious suspense

**ten·u·ous** (TEN-yoo-əs) adj. flimsy, uncertain; thin, fine, slender

**ten·ure** (TEN-yər) n. (length of time of) possession, holding of office, position etc.

**te·pee, tee·pee** (both TEE-pee) n. N Amer. Indian cone-shaped tent of animal skins

**tep′id** adj. moderately warm, lukewarm; half-hearted

**te·qui·la** (tə-KEE-lə) n. Mexican alcoholic liquor

**ter·bi·um** (TUR-bee-əm) n. rare metallic element

**ter·cen·ten·a·ry** (tur-sen-TEN-ə-ree) adj./n. (pl. -nar·ies) (of) three-hundredth anniversary

**term** (turm) n. word, expression; limited period of time; period during which courts sit, schools are open etc.; limit, end —pl. conditions; mutual relationship —vt. name, designate

**ter·mi·nal** (TUR-mə-nl) adj. at, forming an end; pert. to, forming a terminus; (of disease) ending in death —n. terminal part or structure; extremity; point where current enters, leaves electrical device (*eg* battery); device permitting operation of computer at some distance from it

**ter·mi·nate** (TUR-mə-nayt) v. (-nat·ed, -nat·ing) bring, come to an end —**ter·mi·na′tion** (-shən) n.

**ter·mi·nol·o·gy** (tur-mə-NOL-ə-jee) n. (pl. -gies) set of technical terms or vocabulary; study of terms

**ter·mi·nus** (TUR-mə-nəs) n. (pl. -ni pr. -nī) finishing point; farthest limit; railroad station, bus station *etc.* at end of long-distance line

**ter·mite** (TUR-mīt) n. insect, some species of which feed on and damage wood (*also called* white ant)

**ter·race** (TER-əs) n. raised level place; level cut out of hill; row, street of houses built as one block —vt. (-raced, -rac·ing) form into, furnish with terrace

**ter·ra cot·ta** (TER-ə KOT-ə) hard unglazed pottery; its color, a brownish-red

**ter·ra fir·ma** (FUR-mə) *Lat.* firm ground; dry land

**ter·rain** (tə-RAYN) n. area of ground, *esp.* with reference to its physical character

**ter·ra·pin** (TER-ə-pin) n. type of aquatic tortoise

**ter·rar·i·um** (tə-RAIR-ee-əm) n. (pl. -i·ums) enclosed container in which small plants, animals are kept

**ter·raz·zo** (tə-RAZ-oh) n. floor, wall finish of chips of stone set in mortar and polished

**ter·res·tri·al** (tə-RES-tree-əl) adj. of the earth; of, living on land

**ter·ri·ble** (TER-ə-bəl) adj. serious, dreadful, frightful; excessive; causing fear —**ter′ri·bly** adv.

**ter·ri·er** (TER-ee-ər) n. small dog

of various breeds, *orig.* for following quarry into burrow

**ter·rif·ic** (tə-RIF-ik) adj. very great; *inf.* good, excellent; terrible, awe-inspiring

**ter·ri·fy** (TER-ə-fī) vt. (-fied, -fy·ing) fill with fear, dread

**ter·ri·to·ry** (TER-i-tor-ee) n. (pl. -ries) region; geographical area under control of a political unit, *esp.* a sovereign state; area of knowledge —**ter·ri·to′ri·al** adj.

**ter·ror** (TER-ər) n. great fear; *inf.* troublesome person or thing —**ter′ror·ism** n. use of violence, intimidation to achieve ends; state of terror —**ter′ror·ist** n./adj. —**ter′ror·ize** vt. (-ized, -iz·ing) force, oppress by fear, violence

**terse** (turs) adj. (ters·er, ters·est) expressed in few words, concise; abrupt

**ter·ti·ary** (TUR-shee-ər-ee) adj. third in degree, order *etc.* —n. (T-) geological period before Quaternary

**tes·sel·late** (TES-ə-layt) vt. (-lat·ed, -lat·ing) make, pave, inlay with mosaic of small tiles; (of identical shapes) fit together exactly —**tes′ser·a** (-ər-ə) n. (pl. -ae pr. -ee) stone used in mosaic

**test** vt. try, put to the proof; carry out test(s) on —n. (critical) examination; means of trial —**test′ing** adj. difficult —**test case** lawsuit viewed as means of establishing precedent —**test tube** narrow cylindrical glass vessel used in scientific experiments —**test-tube baby** baby conceived in artificial womb

**tes·ta·ment** (TES-tə-mənt) n. *Law;* declaration; (T-) one of the two main divisions of the Bible —**tes·ta·men′ta·ry** adj.

**tes·tate** (TES-tayt) adj. having left a valid will —**tes′ta·cy** n. (-tə-see) state of being testate —**tes′****ta**·**tor** (-tay-tər) n. maker of will (**tes**·**ta**·**trix** pr. te-STAY-triks fem.)

**tes**·**ti**·**cle** (TES-ti-kəl) n. either of two male reproductive glands

**tes**·**ti**·**fy** (TES-ti-fī) v. (-fied, -fying) declare; bear witness (to)

**tes**·**ti**·**mo**·**ny** (TES-tə-moh-nee) n. (pl. -nies) affirmation; evidence —**tes**·**ti**·**mo**′**ni**·**al** (-əl) n. certificate of character, ability etc.; gift, reception etc. by organization or person expressing regard for recipient —adj.

**tes**·**tis** n. (pl. -tes pr. -teez) testicle

**tes′**·**ty** adj. (-ti·er, -ti·est) irritable, short-tempered —**tes′**·**ti**·**ly** adv.

**tet**·**a**·**nus** (TET-ə-nəs) n. acute infectious disease producing muscular spasms, contractions (also called lockjaw)

**tête**-à-**tête** (TAYT-ə-TAYT) Fr. (pl. **tête**-à-**têtes** pr. -tayts) private conversation

**teth**·**er** (TETH-ər) n. rope or chain for fastening (grazing) animal —vt. tie up with rope —**be at the end of one′s tether** have reached limit of one′s endurance

**Teu**·**ton**·**ic** (too-TON-ik) adj. German; of ancient Teutons

**text** (tekst) n. (actual words of) book, passage etc.; passage of Scriptures etc., esp. as subject of discourse —**tex′tu**·**al** (-choo-əl) adj. of, in a text—**text′book** n. book of instruction on particular subject

**tex**·**tile** (TEKS-tīl) n. any fabric or cloth, esp. woven —adj. of (the making of) fabrics

**tex**·**ture** (TEKS-chər) n. character, structure; consistency

**Th** Chem. thorium

**tha**·**lid**·**o**·**mide** (thə-LID-ə-mīd) n. drug formerly used as sedative, but found to cause abnormalities in developing fetus

**thal**·**li**·**um** (THAL-ee-əm) n. highly toxic metallic element —**thal′lic** adj.

**than** (than) conj. introduces second part of comparison

**thank** (thangk) vt. express gratitude to; say thanks; hold responsible —**thanks** n. pl. words of gratitude —**thank′ful** (-fəl) adj. grateful, appreciative —**thank′****less** (-lis) adj. having, bringing no thanks; unprofitable —**Thanksgiv′ing Day** public holiday in US, Canada

**that** (that) adj. demonstrates or particularizes (pl. those) —demonstrative pron. particular thing meant (pl. those) —adv. as —relative pron. which, who —conj. introduces noun or adverbial clauses

**thatch** (thach) n. reeds, straw etc. used as roofing material —vt. to roof (a house) with reeds, straw etc. —**thatch′er** n.

**thaw** v. melt; (cause to) unfreeze; defrost; become warmer, or more genial —n. a melting of frost etc.)

**the** (thə, thee) is the definite article

**the**·**a**·**ter** (THEE-ə-tər) n. place where plays etc. are performed; drama, dramatic works generally; large room with (tiered) seats, used for lectures etc.; surgical operating room —**the**·**at′ri**·**cal** adj. of, for the theater; exaggerated, affected

**thee** (thee) pron. obs. objective and dative of THOU

**theft** n. stealing

**their** (thair) adj./pron. of THEM; possessive of THEY —**theirs** poss. pron. belonging to them

**the**·**ism** (THEE-iz-əm) n. belief in

creation of universe by one god —**the'ist** *n.*

**them** (them) *pron.* objective case of THEY; those persons or things —**them·selves'** (them-) *pron.* emphatic and reflexive form of THEY

**theme** (theem) *n.* main idea or topic of conversation, book *etc.*; subject of composition; recurring melody in music —**the·mat·ic** (thə-MAT-ik) *adj.* —**theme park** leisure area designed around one subject —**theme song** one associated with particular program, person *etc.*

**then** (then) *adv.* at that time; next; that being so

**thence** (thens) *adv. obs.* from that place, point of reasoning *etc.*

**the·oc·ra·cy** (thee-OK-rə-see) *n.* (*pl.* -**cies**) government by a deity or a priesthood —**the·o·crat'ic** (-ə-KRAT-ik) *adj.*

**the·od·o·lite** (thee-OD-l-īt) *n.* surveying instrument for measuring angles

**the·ol·o·gy** (thee-OL-ə-jee) *n.* (*pl.* -**gies**) systematic study of religion(s) and religious belief(s) —**the·o·lo·gian** (thee-ə-LOH-jən) *n.*

**the·o·rem** (THEE-ər-əm) *n.* proposition that can be demonstrated by argument

**the·o·ry** (THEE-ə-ree) *n.* (*pl.* -**ries**) supposition to account for something; system of rules and principles; rules and reasoning *etc.* as distinguished from practice —**the·o·ret'i·cal** *adj.* based on theory; speculative, as opposed to practical —**the'o·rize** *vi.* (-rīzed, -rīz·ing) form theories, speculate

**the·os·o·phy** (thee-OS-ə-fee) *n.* any of various religious, philosophical systems claiming pos-

sibility of intuitive insight into divine nature

**ther·a·py** (THER-ə-pee) *n.* (*pl.* -**pies**) healing treatment: *usu.* in compounds as RADIOTHERAPY —**ther·a·peu'tic** (-PYOO-tik) *adj.* of healing; serving to improve or maintain health —**ther·a·peu'tics** *n. with sing.* v. art of healing —**ther'a·pist** *n. esp.* psychotherapist

**there** (thair) *adv.* in that place; to that point —**there·by'** *adv.* by that means —**there'fore** *adv.* in consequence, that being so —**there·up·on** *conj.* at that point, immediately afterward

**therm** (thurm) *n.* unit of measurement of heat —**ther'mal** (-əl) *adj.* of, pert. to heat; hot, warm (*esp.* of a spring *etc.*)

**therm·i·on** (THURM-ī-ən) *n.* ion emitted by incandescent body —**therm·i·on·ic** (thur·mee-ON-ik) *adj.* pert. to thermion

**thermo-** (*comb. form*) related to, caused by or producing heat

**ther·mo·dy·nam·ics** (thur-moh-dī-NAM-iks) *n.* (with *sing.* v.) the science that deals with the interrelationship and interconversion of different forms of energy

**ther·mom·e·ter** (thə-MOM-ə-tər) *n.* instrument to measure temperature —**ther·mo·met·ric** (thur-mə-MET-rik) *adj.*

**ther·mo·nu·cle·ar** (thur-moh-NOO-klee-ər) *adj.* involving nuclear fusion

**ther·mo·plas·tic** (thur-mə-PLAS-tik) *n.* plastic that retains its properties after being melted and solidified —*adj.*

**ther·mos** (THUR-məs) *n.* double-walled flask with vacuum between walls, for keeping contents of inner flask at temperature at which they were inserted

**ther·mo·stat** (THUR-mə-stat) *n.*

apparatus for automatically regulating temperature —**ther·mo·stat′ic** adj.

**the·sau·rus** (thi-SOR-əs) n. book containing lists of synonyms and antonyms; dictionary of selected words, topics

**these** (theez) pl. of THIS

**the·sis** (THEE-sis) n. (pl. -ses pr. -seez) written work submitted for degree, diploma; theory maintained in argument

**thes·pi·an** (THES-pee-ən) adj. theatrical —n. actor, actress

**they** (thay) pron. the third person plural pronoun

**thick** (thik) adj. (-er, -est) having great thickness, not thin; dense, crowded; viscous; (of voice) throaty; inf. stupid, insensitive; inf. friendly —n. busiest, most intense part —**thick·en** (THIK-ən) v. make, become thick; become more involved, complicated —**thick′ly** adv. —**thick′ness** (-nis) n. dimensions of anything measured through it, at right angles to length and breadth; state of being thick; layer —**thick·et** (THIK-it) n. thick growth of small trees —**thick′set** adj. sturdy and solid of body; set closely together

**thief** (theef) n. one who steals (pl. **thieves**) —**thieve** (theev) v. (**thieved, thiev·ing**) steal —**thiev′ish** adj.

**thigh** (thī) n. upper part of leg

**thim·ble** (THIM-bəl) n. cap protecting end of finger when sewing

**thin** adj. (thin·ner, thin·nest) of little thickness; slim; lean; of little density; sparse; fine; loose, not close-packed; inf. unlikely —v. (**thinned, thin·ning**) make, become thin —**thin′ness** (-nis) n.

**thine** (thīn) pron./adj. obs. belonging to thee

**thing** n. material object; any possible object of thought

**think** (thingk) v. (**thought** pr. **thawt, think·ing**) —vi. have one's mind at work; reflect, meditate; reason; deliberate; imagine; hold opinion —vt. conceive, consider in the mind; believe; esteem —**think′a·ble** adj. able to be conceived, considered, possible, feasible —**think′ing** adj. reflecting —**think tank** group of experts studying specific problems

**third** (thurd) adj. ordinal number corresponding to three —n. third part —**third degree** see DEGREE —**third party** Law, Insurance etc. person involved by chance or only incidentally in legal proceedings etc. —**Third World** developing countries of Africa, Asia, Latin Amer.

**thirst** (thurst) n. desire to drink; feeling caused by lack of drink; craving; yearning —v. feel lack of drink —**thirst′y** adj. (**thirst·i·er, thirst·i·est**)

**thir·teen** (thur-TEEN) adj./n. three plus ten —**thir′ty** n./adj. (pl. -ties) three times ten

**this** (this) demonstrative adj./pron. denotes thing, person near, or just mentioned (pl. **these** pr. theez)

**this·tle** (THIS-əl) n. prickly plant with dense flower heads

**thong** (thawng) n. narrow strip of leather, strap

**thor·ax** (THOR-aks) n. part of body between neck and belly —**tho·rac·ic** (thaw-RAS-ik) adj.

**tho·ri·um** (THOR-ee-əm) n. radioactive metallic element

**thorn** n. prickle on plant; spine; bush noted for its thorns; anything that causes trouble or annoyance —**thorn′y** adj. (**thorn·i·er, thorn·i·est**)

**thor·ough** (THUR-oh) adj. careful, methodical; complete, entire —**thor'ough·ly** *adv.* —**thor'ough-bred** *adj.* of pure breed —*n.* pure-bred animal, *esp.* horse —**thor'ough·fare** (-fair) *n.* road or passage open at both ends; right of way

**those** (thohz) *pron., pl.* of THAT; denoting, as a correlative of THESE, the former, as distinguished from the latter

**thou** (thow) *pron. obs.* the second person singular pronoun (*pl.* ye, you)

**though** (thoh) *conj.* in spite of the fact that, even if —*adv.* nevertheless

**thought** (thawt) *n.* process of thinking; what one thinks; product of thinking; meditation —*pt./pp.* of THINK —**thought'ful** (-fəl) *adj.* considerate; showing careful thought; engaged in meditation; attentive —**thought'-less** (-lis) *adj.* inconsiderate, careless, heedless

**thou·sand** (THOW-zənd) *n./adj.* cardinal number, ten hundred

**thrall** (thrawl) *n.* slavery; slave, bondsman —**thrall'dom** (-dəm) *n.* bondage

**thrash** *vt.* beat, whip soundly; defeat soundly; thresh —*vi.* move, plunge (*esp.* arms, legs) in wild manner —**thrash out** argue about from every angle; solve by exhaustive discussion

**thread** (thred) *n.* fine cord; yarn; ridge cut spirally on screw; theme, meaning —*vt.* put thread into; fit film, magnetic tape *etc.* into machine; put on thread; pick (one's way *etc.*) —**thread'bare** (-bair) *adj.* worn, with nap rubbed off; meager; shabby

**threat** (thret) *n.* declaration of intention to harm, injure *etc.*; person or thing regarded as dangerous —**threat·en** (THRET-n) *vt.* utter threats against; menace

**three** *n./adj.* cardinal number, one more than two —**three-ply** (-plī) *adj.* having three layers (as wood) or strands (as wool) —**three'some** (-səm) *n.* group of three —**three-di·men'sion·al**, 3-D *adj.* having three dimensions; simulating the effect of depth

**thresh** *v.* beat, rub (wheat *etc.*) to separate grain from husks and straw; thrash

**thresh·old** (THRESH-ohld) *n.* bar of stone or wood forming bottom of doorway; entrance; starting point; point at which a stimulus is perceived, or produces a response

**threw** (throo) *pt.* of THROW

**thrice** (thrīs) *adv.* three times

**thrift** *n.* saving, economy; genus of plant, sea pink —**thrift'y** *adj.* (**thrift·i·er, thrift·i·est**) economical, frugal, sparing

**thrill** *n.* sudden sensation of excitement and pleasure —*v.* (cause to) feel a thrill; vibrate, tremble —**thrill'er** *n.* book, motion picture *etc.* with story of mystery, suspense —**thrill'ing** *adj.* exciting

**thrive** (thrīv) *vi.* (thrived or throve *pr.* throhv, thrived or thriv·en, thriv·ing) grow well; flourish, prosper

**throat** (throht) *n.* front of neck; either or both of passages through it —**throat'y** *adj.* (**throat·i·er, throat·i·est**) (of voice) hoarse

**throb** *vi.* (throbbed, throb·bing) beat, quiver strongly, pulsate —*n.* pulsation, beat; vibration

**throes** (throhz) *n. pl.* condition of violent pangs, pain *etc.* —**in the throes of** in the process of

**throm·bo·sis** (throm-BOH-sis) *n.*

formation of clot of coagulated blood in blood vessel or heart

**throne** (throhn) *n.* ceremonial seat, powers and duties of king or queen —*vt.* (throned, thron·ing) place on throne, declare king *etc.*

**throng** (thrawng) *n./v.* crowd

**throt·tle** (THROT-l) *n.* device controlling amount of fuel entering engine and thereby its speed —*vt.* (-tled, -tling) strangle; suppress; restrict (flow of liquid *etc.*)

**through** (throo) *prep.* from end to end, from side to side of; between the sides of; in consequence of; by means or fault of —*adv.* from end to end; to the end —*adj.* completed; finished; continuous; (of transport, traffic) not stopping —**through·out'** (-OWT) *adv./prep.* in every part (of) —**through'put** (-puut) *n.* quantity of material processed, *esp.* by computer —**through train, bus** *etc.* train *etc.* that travels whole (unbroken) length of long journey —**carry through** accomplish

**throve** (throhv) *pt. of* THRIVE

**throw** (throh) *vt.* (threw *pr.* throo, thrown, throw·ing) fling, cast; move, put abruptly, carelessly; give, hold (party *etc.*); cause to fall; shape on potter's wheel; move (switch, lever *etc.*) *inf.* baffle, disconcert —*n.* act or distance of throwing —**throw'·back** *n.* one who, that which reverts to character of an ancestor; this process

**thrush**[1] *n.* songbird

**thrush**[2] *n.* fungal disease of mouth, *esp.* in infants; foot disease of horses

**thrust** *v.* (thrust, thrust·ing) push, drive; stab; push one's way —*n.* lunge, stab with pointed weapon *etc.*; cutting remark; propulsive force or power

**thud** *n.* dull heavy sound —*vi.* (thud·ded, thud·ding) make thud

**thug** *n.* brutal, violent person

**thumb** (thum) *n.* first, shortest, thickest finger of hand —*vt.* handle, dirty with thumb; make hitchhiker's signal to get ride; flick through (pages of book *etc.*)

**thump** *n.* dull heavy blow; sound of one —*vt.* strike heavily

**thun·der** (THUN-dǝr) *n.* loud noise accompanying lightning —*vi.* rumble with thunder; make noise like thunder —*vt.* utter loudly —**thun'der·ous** (-ǝs) *adj.* —**thun'der·bolt** (-bohlt), **-clap** *n.* lightning flash followed by peal of thunder; anything totally unexpected and unpleasant —**thun'der·struck** *adj.* amazed

**thus** (thus) *adv.* in this way; therefore

**thwack** (thwak) *vt./n.* whack

**thwart** (thwort) *vt.* foil, frustrate, baffle —*adv. obs.* across —*n.* seat across a boat

**thy** (thi) *adj. obs.* belonging to thee —**thy·self'** *pron.* emphasized form of THOU

**thyme** (tim) *n.* aromatic herb

**thy·mus** (THI-mǝs) *n.* small ductless gland in upper part of chest

**thy·roid** (THI-roid) **gland** endocrine gland controlling body growth, situated (in people) at base of neck

**ti, te** (*pr.* tee) seventh sol-fa note

**Ti** *Chem.* titanium

**ti·ar·a** (tee-AR-ǝ) *n.* woman's jeweled head ornament, coronet

**tib·i·a** (TIB-ee-ǝ) *n.* (*pl.* **-i·as**) thicker inner bone of lower leg

**tic** (tik) *n.* spasmodic twitch in muscles, *esp.* of face

**tick**[1] (tik) *n.* slight tapping sound, as of watch movement; small mark (✓) —*vt.* mark with tick —*vi.* make the sound —**tick·er tape** continuous paper ribbon

—**tick off** mark off; reprimand; make angry —**tick over** (of engine) idle; continue to function smoothly

**tick**[2] *n.* small insect-like parasite living on and sucking blood of warm-blooded animals

**tick**[3] *n.* mattress case —**tick'ing** *n.* strong material for mattress covers

**tick·et** (TIK-it) *n.* card, paper entitling holder to admission, travel *etc.*; list of candidates for election —*vt.* attach label to; issue tickets to

**tick·le** (TIK-əl) *v.* (**-led, -ling**) —*vt.* touch, stroke, poke (person, part of body *etc.*) to produce laughter *etc.*; please, amuse —*vi.* be irritated, itch —*n.* act, instance of this —**tick'lish** *adj.* sensitive to tickling; requiring care or tact

**tid'bit** *n.* tasty morsel of food; pleasing scrap (of scandal *etc.*)

**tide** (tīd) *n.* rise and fall of sea happening twice each lunar day; stream; season, time —**tid'al** (-əl) *adj.* of, like tide —**tidal wave** great wave, *esp.* produced by earthquake —**tide** over help someone for a while, *esp.* by loan *etc.*

**ti·dings** (TĪ-dingz) *n. pl.* news

**ti·dy** (TĪ-dee) *adj.* (**-di·er, -di·est**) orderly, neat; of fair size —*vt.* (**-died, -dy·ing**) put in order

**tie** (tī) *v.* (**tied, ty·ing**) equal (score of) —*vt.* fasten, bind, secure, restrict —*n.* that with which anything is bound; restriction, restraint; long, narrow piece of material worn knotted around neck; bond; connecting link; drawn game, contest; match, game in eliminating competition —**tie'-dye·ing** *n.* way of dyeing cloth in patterns by tying sections tightly so they will not absorb dye

**tier** (teer) *n.* row, rank, layer

**tiff** *n.* petty quarrel

**ti·ger** (TĪ-gər) *n.* large carnivorous feline animal

**tight** (tīt) *adj.* (**-er, -est**) taut, tense; closely fitting; secure, firm; not allowing passage of water *etc.*; cramped; *inf.* mean, stingy; *sl.* drunk —**tights** *n. pl.* one-piece clinging garment covering body from waist to feet —**tight'en** (-ən) *v.* —**tight'rope** *n.* rope stretched taut above the ground, on which acrobats perform

**tile** (tīl) *n.* flat piece of ceramic, plastic *etc.* material used for roofs, walls, floors, fireplaces *etc.* —*vt.* (**tiled, til·ing**) cover with tiles

**till**[1] *prep.* up to the time of —*conj.* to the time that

**till**[2] *vt.* cultivate —**till'er** *n.*

**till**[3] *n.* drawer for money in store; cash register

**til·ler** (TIL·ər) *n.* lever to move rudder of boat

**tilt** *v.* incline, slope, slant; tip up —*vi.* take part in medieval combat with lances; thrust, aim (at) —*n.* slope, incline; *Hist.* combat for mounted men with lances, joust

**tim·ber** (TIM-bər) *n.* wood for building *etc.*; trees suitable for the sawmill —**tim'bered** *adj.* made of wood; covered with trees —**timber line** geographical limit beyond which trees will not grow

**tim·bre** (TAM-bər) *n.* quality of musical sound, or sound of human voice

**time** (tīm) *n.* existence as a succession of states; hour; duration; period; point in duration; opportunity; occasion; leisure; tempo —*vt.* (**timed, tim·ing**) choose time for; note time taken by

—**time'ly** adj. at opportune or appropriate time —**tim'er** (-ər) n. person, device for recording or indicating time —**time bomb** bomb designed to explode at arranged time; situation resembling this —**time-honored** (-onərd) adj. respectable because old —**time-lag** n. period of time between cause and effect —**time'piece** (-pees) n. watch, clock —**time-sharing** n. system of part ownership of vacation property for specified period each year, also **time share**; Computers system enabling users at different terminals to communicate with computer apparently at same time —**time'ta·ble** n. plan showing hours of work, times of arrival and departure etc. —**Greenwich** (GREN-ich) **Mean Time** world standard time, time as settled by passage of sun over the meridian at Greenwich, England

**tim'id** adj. easily frightened; lacking self-confidence —**ti·mid'i·ty** n. —**tim'or·ous** (-ər-əs) adj. timid; indicating fear

**tim·pa·ni** (TIM-pə-nee) n. pl. set of kettledrums —**tim'pa·nist** n.

**tin** n. malleable metal —vt. (tinned, tin·ning) coat with tin —**tin'ny** adj. (-ni·er, -ni·est) (of sound) thin, metallic; cheap, shoddy

**tinc·ture** (TINGK-chər) n. solution of medicinal substance in alcohol; color, stain —vt. (-tured, -tur·ing) color, tint

**tin·der** (TIN-dər) n. dry easily-burning material used to start fire

**tine** (tīn) n. tooth, spike of fork, antler etc.

**tinge** (tinj) n. slight trace, flavor —vt. (tinged, tinge·ing) color, flavor slightly

**tin·gle** (TING-gəl) vi. (-gled,

-gling) feel thrill or pricking sensation —n.

**tin'ker** (TING-kər) n. formerly, traveling mender of pots and pans —vi. fiddle, meddle (eg with machinery) oft. inexpertly

**tin·kle** (TING-kəl) v. (-kled, -kling) (cause to) give out series of light sounds like small bell —n. this sound or action

**tin·sel** (TIN-səl) n. glittering metallic substance for decoration; anything sham and showy

**tint** n. color; shade of color; tinge —vt. dye, give tint to

**ti·ny** (TĪ-nee) adj. (-ni·er, -ni·est) very small, minute

**tip¹** n. slender or pointed end of anything; piece of metal, leather etc. protecting an extremity —vt. (tipped, tip·ping) put a tip on

**tip²** n. small present of money given for service rendered; helpful piece of information; warning, hint —vt. (tipped, tip·ping) give tip to —**tip'ster** (-stər) n. one who sells tips about races etc.

**tip³** v. (tipped, tip·ping) —vt. tilt, upset; touch lightly —vi. topple over

**tip·ple** (TIP-əl) v. (-pled, -pling) drink (liquor) habitually, esp. in small quantities —n. drink of liquor —**tip'pler** (-lər) n.

**tip·sy** adj. (-si·er, -si·est) drunk, partly drunk

**tip·toe** vi. (-toed, -to·ing) walk on ball of foot and toes; walk softly

**ti·rade** (TĪ-rayd) n. long speech, generally vigorous and hostile, denunciation

**tire¹** (tīr) v. (tired, tir·ing) —vt. reduce energy of, esp. by exertion; bore; irritate —vi. become tired, wearied, bored —**tire'some** (-səm) adj. wearisome, irritating, tedious

**tire²** n. (inflated) rubber or synthetic rubber ring over rim of road vehicle

**tis·sue** (TISH-oo) *n.* substance of animal body, plant *etc.*; fine, soft paper, *esp.* used as handkerchief *etc.*; fine woven fabric; interconnection *eg* of lies

**tit**[1] *n.* varieties of small birds, usu. in combination, *eg* **tufted tit-mouse**

**tit**[2] *n. vulg. sl.* female breast

**ti·tan·ic** (tī-TAN-ik) *adj.* huge, epic

**ti·ta·ni·um** (tī-TAY-nee-əm) *n.* rare metal of great strength and rust-resisting qualities

**tit for tat** blow for blow, retaliation

**tithe** (tīth) *n.* tenth part *esp. Hist.* of agricultural produce paid for the upkeep of the clergy or paid as tax —*v.* (**tithed, tith·ing**) —*vt.* exact tithes from —*vi.* give, pay tithe

**ti·tian** (TISH-ən) *adj.* (of hair) reddish-gold, auburn

**tit·il·late** (TIT-l-ayt) *vt.* (**-lat·ed, -lat·ing**) tickle, stimulate agreeably

**ti·tle** (TĪT-l) *n.* name of book; heading; name; appellation denoting rank; legal right or document proving it; *Sports* championship —**title deed** legal document as proof of ownership

**tit·ter** (TIT-ər) *vi.* laugh in suppressed way —*n.* such laugh

**tit·tle** (TIT-l) *n.* whit, detail

**tit·tle-tat·tle** (TIT-l-tat-l) *n./vi.* (**-tled, -tling**) gossip

**tit·u·lar** (TICH-ə-lər) *adj.* pert. to title; nominal; held by virtue of a title

**tiz·zy** (TIZ-ee) *n. sl.* (*pl.* **-zies**) state of confusion, anxiety

**to** *prep.* toward, in the direction of; as far as; used to introduce a comparison, ratio, indirect object, infinitive *etc.* —*adv.* to the

required or normal state or position

**toad** (tohd) *n.* animal like frog —**toad′y** *n.* (*pl.* **toad·ies**) obsequious flatterer, sycophant —*vi.* (**toad·ied, toad·y·ing**) do this —**toad′stool** *n.* fungus like mushroom, but usu. poisonous

**toast** (tohst) *n.* slice of bread crisped and browned on both sides by heat; tribute, proposal of health, success *etc.* made by company of people and marked by drinking together; one toasted —*vt.* crisp and brown (as bread); drink toast to; dry or warm at fire —**toast′er** *n.* electrical device for toasting bread

**to·bac·co** (tə-BAK-oh) *n.* (*pl.* **-cos, -coes**) plant with leaves used for smoking; the prepared leaves

**to·bog·gan** (tə-BOG-ən) *n.* sled for sliding down slope of snow —*vi.* slide on one

**toc·ca·ta** (tə-KAH-tə) *n.* rapid piece of music for keyboard instrument

**toc·sin** (TOK-sin) *n.* alarm signal, bell

**to·day** (tə-DAY) *n.* this day —*adv.* on this day; nowadays

**tod·dle** (TOD-l) *vi.* (**-dled, -dling**) walk with unsteady short steps —*n.* toddling —**tod′dler** (-lər) *n.* child beginning to walk

**tod·dy** (TOD-ee) *n.* (*pl.* **-dies**) sweetened mixture of alcoholic liquor, hot water *etc.*

**to-do** (tə-DOO) *n. inf.* (*pl.* **-dos**) fuss, commotion

**toe** (toh) *n.* digit of foot; anything resembling toe in shape or position —*vt.* (**toed, toe·ing**) reach, touch with toe —**toe the line** conform

**tof·fee** (TAW-fee) *n.* brittle candy made of sugar and butter *etc.*

**to·ga** (TOH-gə) *n.* (*pl.* **-gas**) loose

outer garment worn by ancient Romans

**to·geth·er** (tə-GETH-ər) adv. in company, simultaneously —adj. sl. (well) organized

**tog·gle** (TOG-əl) n. small wooden, metal peg fixed crosswise on cord, wire etc. and used for fastening as button; any similar device

**togs** (togz) n. pl. clothes

**toil** n. heavy work or task —vi. labor —toil'worn adj. weary with toil; hard and lined

**toi·let** (TOI-lit) n. lavatory; ceramic toilet bowl; process of washing, dressing; articles for this

**to·ken** (TOH-kən) n. sign or object used as evidence; symbol; disk used as money —adj. nominal, slight

**told** (tohld) pt./pp. of TELL.

**tol·er·ate** (TOL-ər-ayt) vt. (-at·ed, -at·ing) put up with; permit —tol'er·a·ble adj. bearable; fair, moderate —tol'er·ance (-əns) n. (degree of) ability to endure stress, pain, radiation etc. —tol'er·ant (-ənt) adj. disinclined to interfere with others' ways or opinions; forbearing; broad-minded

**toll¹** (tohl) vt. make (bell) ring slowly at regular intervals; announce death thus —vi. ring thus —n. tolling sound

**toll²** n. tax, esp. for the use of bridge or road; loss, damage incurred through accident, disaster etc.

**tom** n. male of some animals, esp. cat

**tom·a·hawk** (TOM-ə-hawk) n. formerly, fighting ax of N Amer. Indians —vt. strike, kill with one

**to·ma·to** (tə-MAY-toh) n. (pl. -toes) plant with red fruit; the fruit, used in salads etc.

**tomb** (toom) n. grave; monument over one —tomb'stone n. gravestone

**tom·boy** (TOM-boi) n. girl who acts, dresses in boyish way

**tome** (tohm) n. large book or volume

**tom·fool·er·y** (tom-FOO-lə-ree) n. (pl. -er·ies) nonsense, silly behavior

**to·mog·ra·phy** (tə-MOG-rə-fee) n. x-ray method of displaying selected plane(s) within human body eg through CAT or CT scan computerized axial tomography

**to·mor·row** (tə-MOR-oh) adv./n. (on) the day after today

**tom-tom** n. drum associated with N Amer. Indians or with Asia

**ton** (tun) n. measure of weight, 2000 lbs. (907 kg) (also called short ton); measure of weight, 2240 lbs. (1016 kg) (also called long ton) —ton'nage (TUN-ij) n. carrying capacity; charge per ton; ships collectively

**tone** (tohn) n. quality of musical sound; quality of voice, color etc.; general character, style; healthy condition —vt. (toned, ton·ing) give tone to; blend, harmonize (with) —ton'er (-ər) n. substance that modifies color or composition —ton'al (-əl) adj. —to·nal'i·ty n. (pl. -ties) —tone poem orchestral work based on story, legend etc.

**tongs** (tongz) n. pl. large pincers, esp. for handling coal, sugar

**tongue** (tung) n. muscular organ inside mouth, used for speech, taste etc.; various things shaped like this; language, speech, voice

**ton·ic** (TON-ik) n. medicine to improve bodily tone or condition; Mus. keynote; first note of scale —adj. invigorating, restorative; of tone —tonic (water) mineral water oft. containing quinine

**to·night** (tə-NĪT) *n.* this night; the coming night —*adv.* on this night

**ton·sil** (TON-səl) *n.* gland in throat —**ton·sil·li·tis** (-LĪ-tis) *n.* inflammation of tonsils —**ton·sil·lec·to·my** (-sə-LEK-tə-mee) *n.* (*pl.* -mies) surgical removal of tonsil(s)

**ton·sure** (TON-shər) *n.* shaving of part of head as religious or monastic practice; part shaved —*vt.* (-sured, -sur·ing) shave thus

**ton·tine** (ton-TEEN) *n.* fund, subscribers to which receive annuities increasing as number of subscribers decreases

**too** *adv.* also, in addition; in excess, overmuch

**took** (tuuk) *pt. of* TAKE

**tool** *n.* implement or appliance for mechanical operations; servile helper; means to an end —*vt.* work on with tool, *esp.* chisel stone; indent design on leather book cover *etc.* —**tool′ing** *n.* decorative work; setting up *etc.* of tools, *esp.* for machine operation

**tooth** *n.* (*pl.* **teeth**) bonelike projection in gums of upper and lower jaws of vertebrates; various pointed things like this; prong, cog

**top¹** *n.* highest part, summit; highest meat; first in merit; garment for upper part of body; lid, stopper of bottle *etc.* —*vt.* (**topped**, **top′ping**) cut off, pass, reach, surpass top; provide top for —**top′less** (-lis) *adj.* (of costume, woman) with no covering for breasts —**top′most** (-mohst) *adj.* supreme; highest —**top′-dress** *vt.* spread soil, fertilizer *etc.* on surface of land —**top dressing** *n.* —**top hat** man's hat with tall cylindrical crown —**top-heavy** *adj.* unbalanced; with top too heavy for base —**top′notch** *adj.* excellent, first-class —**top-secret** *adj.* needing highest level of secrecy, security —**top′soil** *n.* surface layer of soil; more fertile soil spread on lawns *etc.*

**top²** *n.* toy that spins on tapering point or ball bearing

**to·paz** (TOH-paz) *n.* precious stone of various colors

**to·pee** (toh-PEE) *n.* lightweight hat made of pith

**to·pi·ar·y** (TOH-pee-er-ee) *adj.* (of shrubs) shaped by cutting or pruning, made ornamental by trimming or training —*n.*

**top·ic** (TOP-ik) *n.* subject of discourse, conversation *etc.* —**top′i·cal** (-ik-əl) *adj.* up-to-date, having news value; of topic

**to·pog·ra·phy** (tə-POG-rə-fee) *n.* (*pl.* -phies) (description of) surface features of a place —**to·pog′ra·pher** *n.*

**top·ple** (TOP-əl) *v.* (-pled, -ling) (cause to) fall over, collapse

**top·sy·tur·vy** (TOP-see-TUR-vee) *adj./adv.* upside down, in confusion

**tor** *n.* high, rocky hill

**To·rah** (TOH-rə) *n.* parchment for which is written the Pentateuch

**torch** *n.* portable hand light containing electric battery and bulb; burning brand *etc.*; any apparatus burning with hot flame, *esp.* for welding —**torch′bear·er** (-bair-ər) *n.*

**tore** *pr.* —**torn** *pp. of* TEAR²

**tor·e·a·dor** (TOR-ee-ə-dor) *n.* bullfighter

**tor·ment** *v.* torture in body or mind; afflict; tease —*n.* (TOR-ment) suffering, torture, agony of body or mind

**tor·na·do** (tor-NAY-doh) *n.* (*pl.* -does) whirlwind; violent storm

**tor·pe·do** (tor-PEE-doh) *n.* (*pl.* -does) cylindrical self-propelled underwater missile with explosive warhead, fired *esp.* from submarine —*vt.* (-doed, -do·ing) strike, sink with, as with, torpedo

**tor'pid** *adj.* sluggish, apathetic —**tor·por** (TOR-pər) *n.* torpid state

**torque** (tork) *n.* collar, similar ornament of twisted gold or other metal; *Mechanics* rotating or twisting force

**tor·rent** (TOR-ənt) *n.* a rushing stream; downpour —**tor·ren·tial** (tə-REN-shəl) *adj.* resembling a torrent; overwhelming

**tor·rid** (TOR-id) *adj.* parched, dried with heat; highly emotional —**Torrid Zone** land between tropics

**tor·sion** (TOR-shən) *n.* twist, twisting

**tor'so** (TOR-soh) *n.* (*pl.* -sos) (statue of) body without head or limbs; trunk

**tort** *n.* *Law* private or civil wrong

**tor·til·la** (tor-TEE-yə) *n.* (*pl.* -til·las) thin Mexican pancake

**tor·toise** (TOR-təs) *n.* four-footed reptile covered with shell of horny plates —**tor'toise·shell** *n.* mottled brown shell of hawksbill turtle used commercially —*adj.*

**tor·tu·ous** (TOR-choo-əs) *adj.* winding, twisting; involved, not straightforward

**tor·ture** (TOR-chər) *n.* infliction of severe pain —*vt.* (-tured, -tur·ing) subject to torture —**tor'·tur·er** *n.* torture chamber

**toss** (taws) *vt.* throw up, about —*vi.* be thrown, fling oneself about —*n.* act of tossing

**tot¹** *n.* very small child;

**tot²** *v.* (tot·ted, tot·ting) (*with* up) add up; amount to

**to·tal** (TOHT-l) *n.* whole amount; sum, aggregate —*adj.* complete, entire, full, absolute —*v.* (-taled, -tal·ing) amount to; add up —**to·tal'i·ty** *n.* (*pl.* -ties) —**to·tal·i·za·tor** (TOHT-l-ə-zay-tər) *n.* machine

to operate system of betting at racetrack in which money is paid out to winners in proportion to their bets

**to·tal·i·tar·i·an** (toh-tal-i-TAIR-ee-ən) *adj.* of dictatorial, one-party government

**tote¹** (toht) *n.* short for TOTALIZATOR

**tote²** *vt.* (tot·ed, tot·ing) haul, carry

**to·tem** (TOH-təm) *n.* tribal badge or emblem —**totem pole** post carved, painted with totems, *esp.* by Amer. Indians

**tot·ter** (TOT-ər) *vi.* walk unsteadily; begin to fall

**touch** (tuch) *n.* sense by which qualities of object *etc.* are perceived by touching; characteristic manner or ability; touching; slight blow, stroke, contact, amount *etc.* —*vt.* come into contact with; put hand on; reach; affect emotions of; deal with, handle; eat, drink; *sl.* (try to) borrow from —*vi.* be in contact; (*with* on) refer to —**touch'ing** *adj.* emotionally moving —*prep.* concerning —**touch'y** *adj.* (**touch·i·er, touch·i·est**) easily offended, sensitive —**touch'down** *n.* *Football* crossing of goal line with football; act of, moment of, landing of aircraft —**touch'stone** *n.* criterion —**touch and go** precarious (situation)

**tou·ché** (too-SHAY) *interj.* acknowledgment that blow (*orig.* in fencing), remark *etc.* has been successful

**tough** (tuf) *adj.* (-er, -est) strong, resilient, not brittle; sturdy; able to bear hardship, strain; difficult; needing effort to chew; rough; uncivilized; violent; unlucky, unfair —*n.* rough, violent person —**tough'en** (-ən) *v.* —**tough'ness** (-nis) *n.*

**tou·pee** (too-PAY) *n.* man's hairpiece, wig

**tour** (toor) *n.* traveling around; journey to one place after another; excursion —*v.* make tour (of) —**tour′ism** *n.* tourist travel; this as an industry —**tour′ist** *n.* one who travels for pleasure

**tour de force** (toor də FORS) Fr. brilliant stroke, achievement

**tour·ma·line** (TUUR-mə-lin) *n.* crystalline mineral used for optical instruments and as gem

**tour·na·ment** (TUUR-nə-mənt) *n.* competition, contest usu. with several stages to decide overall winner —**tour·ney** (TUUR-nee) *n.* (*pl.* **-neys**) tournament

**tour·ni·quet** (TUR-ni-kit) *n.* bandage, surgical instrument to constrict artery and stop bleeding

**tou·sle** (TOW-zəl) *vt.* (**-sled,** **-sling**) tangle, ruffle; treat roughly

**tout** (towt) *vi.* solicit trade (usu. in undesirable fashion); obtain and sell information about racehorses *etc.* —*n.* one who touts

**tow**[1] (toh) *vt.* drag along behind, *esp.* at end of rope —*n.* towing or being towed; vessel, vehicle in tow —**tow′path** *n.* path beside canal, river, orig. for towing

**tow**[2] *n.* fiber of hemp, flax —**towhead·ed** (-hed-id) *adj.* with pale-colored, or rumpled hair

**to·ward** (tord) *prep.* in direction of; with regard to; as contribution to (*also* **towards**)

**tow·el** (TOW-əl) *n.* cloth for wiping off moisture after washing —**tow′el·ing** *n.* material used for making towels

**tow·er** (TOW-ər) *n.* tall strong structure often forming part of church or other large building; fortress —*vi.* stand very high; loom (over)

**town** *n.* collection of dwellings *etc.* larger than village and smaller than city —**town′ship** *n.* small town —**towns′peo·ple** *n.*

**tox·ic** (TOK-sik) *adj.* poisonous; due to poison —**tox·e·mi·a** (tok-SEEM-ee-ə) *n.* blood poisoning —**tox·ic′i·ty** (-IS-i-tee) *n.* strength of a poison —**tox·i·col·o·gy** (tok-si-KOL-ə-jee) *n.* study of poisons —**tox′in** *n.* poison of bacterial origin

**toy** (toi) *n.* something designed to be played with; (miniature) replica —*adj.* very small —*vi.* act idly, trifle

**trace**[1] (trays) *n.* track left by anything; indication; minute quantity —*vt.* (**traced,** **trac·ing**) follow course, track of; find out; make plan of; draw or copy exactly, *esp.* using tracing paper —**trace element** chemical element occurring in very small quantity in soil *etc.* —**tracer bul·let,** shell *etc.* one that leaves visible trail so that aim can be checked —**tracing paper** transparent paper placed over drawing, map *etc.* to enable exact copy to be taken

**trace**[2] *n.* chain, strap by which horse pulls vehicle —**kick over the traces** become defiant, independent

**tra·che·a** (TRAY-kee-ə) *n.* (*pl.* **-che-as**) windpipe —**tra′che·al** (-əl) *adj.* —**tra·che·ot′o·my** (-OT-ə-mee) *n.* (*pl.* **-mies**) surgical incision into trachea

**tra·cho·ma** (trə-KOH-mə) *n.* contagious viral disease of eye

**track** (trak) *n.* mark, line of marks, left by passage of anything; path; rough road; course; railroad line; distance between two road wheels on one axle; circular jointed metal band driven by wheels as on tank, bulldozer *etc.*; course for running or racing; separate section on phonograph record; class, division of schoolchildren grouped together because of similar ability —*vt.* follow trail or path of; find thus —**track record** past accomplishments of person, company *etc.*

**tract**[1] (trakt) *n.* wide expanse, area; *Anat.* system of organs *etc.* with particular function

**tract**[2] *n.* treatise or pamphlet, *esp.* religious one —**trac'tate** (-tayt) *n.* short tract

**trac·ta·ble** (TRAK-tə-bəl) *adj.* easy to manage, docile, amenable

**trac·tion** (TRAK-shən) *n.* action of drawing, pulling —**traction engine** locomotive running on surfaces other than tracks

**trac·tor** (TRAK-tər) *n.* motor vehicle for hauling, pulling *etc.*

**trade** (trayd) *n.* commerce, business; buying and selling; any profitable pursuit; those engaged in trade —*v.* (trad·ed, trad·ing) engage in trade; buy and sell; barter —**trade-in** *n.* used article given in part payment for new —**trade'mark**, **-name** *n.* distinctive mark (secured by legal registration) on maker's goods —**trades'man** (-mən) *n.* (*pl.* -men) person engaged in trade; skilled worker —**trade union** society of workers for protection of their interests —**trade wind** wind blowing constantly toward equator in certain parts of globe

**tra·di·tion** (trə-DISH-ən) *n.* unwritten body of beliefs, facts *etc.* handed down from generation to generation; custom, practice of long standing; process of handing down

**tra·duce** (trə-DOOS) *vt.* (-duced, -duc·ing) slander

**traf·fic** (TRAF-ik) *n.* vehicles

passing to and fro in street, town *etc.*; (illicit) trade —*vi.* (-ficked, -fick·ing) trade, *esp.* in illicit goods, *eg* drugs —**traf'fick·er** *n.* trader —**traffic lights** set of colored lights at road junctions *etc.* to control flow of traffic

**trag·e·dy** (TRAJ-i-dee) *n.* (*pl.* -dies) sad or calamitous event; dramatic, literary work dealing with serious, sad topic and with ending marked by (inevitable) disaster —**tra·ge·di·an** (trə-JEE-dee-ən) *n.* actor in, writer of tragedies —**trag'ic** *adj.* of, in manner of tragedy; disastrous; appalling —**trag'i·cal·ly** *adv.*

**trail** (trayl) *vt.* drag behind one —*vi.* be drawn behind; hang, grow loosely —*n.* trace or trace; thing that trails; rough ill-defined track in wild country —**trail'er** *n.* vehicle towed by another vehicle; trailing plant; *Motion Pictures* advertisement of forthcoming film

**train** (trayn) *vt.* educate, instruct, exercise; cause to grow in particular way; aim (gun *etc.*) —*vi.* follow course of training, *esp.* to achieve physical fitness for athletics —*n.* line of railroad vehicles joined to locomotive; succession, *esp.* of thoughts, events *etc.*; procession of animals, vehicles *etc.* traveling together; trailing part of dress; body of attendants —**train·ee'** *n.* one training to be skilled worker, *esp.* in industry

**traipse** (trayps) *vi. inf.* (traipsed, traips·ing) walk wearily

**trait** (trayt) *n.* characteristic feature

**trai·tor** (TRAY-tər) *n.* one who betrays or is guilty of treason —**trai'tor·ous** (-əs) *adj.* disloyal; guilty of treachery

**tra·jec·to·ry** (trə-JEK-tə-ree) *n.*

(*pl.* -ries) line of flight, (curved) path of projectile

**tram·mel** (TRAM-əl) *n.* anything that restrains or holds captive; type of compasses —*vt.* (-meled, -mel·ing) restrain; hinder

**tramp** *vi.* travel on foot, *esp.* as vagabond or for pleasure; walk heavily —*n.* homeless person who travels about on foot; walk; tramping; vessel that takes cargo wherever shippers desire

**tram·ple** (TRAM-pəl) *vt.* (-pled, -pling) tread on and crush under foot

**tram·po·line** (tram-pə-LEEN) *n.* tough canvas sheet stretched horizontally with elastic cords *etc.* to frame, for gymnastic, acrobatic use

**trance** (trans) *n.* unconscious or dazed state; state of ecstasy or total absorption

**tran·quil** (TRANG-kwil) *adj.* calm, quiet; serene —**tran·quil'i·ty** *n.* —**tran'quil·ize** *vt.* (-ized, -iz·ing) make calm —**tran'quil·iz·er** (-er) *n.* drug that induces calm, tranquil state

**trans-** (*prefix*) across, through, beyond

**trans·act** (tran-SAKT) *vt.* carry through; negotiate; conduct (affair *etc.*) —**trans·ac'tion** *n.* performing of any business; that which is performed; single sale or purchase —*pl.* proceedings; reports of a society

**trans·ceiv·er** (tran-SEE-vər) *n.* combined radio transmitter and receiver

**trans·cend** (tran-SEND) *vt.* rise above; exceed, surpass —**trans·cend'ent** *adj.* —**tran·scen·den'tal** *adj.* surpassing experience; supernatural; abstruse —**tran·scendental meditation** process seeking to induce detachment

from problems *etc.* by system of meditation

**tran·scribe** (tran-SKRĪB) *vt.* (-scribed, -scrib·ing) copy out; record for later broadcast; arrange (music) for different instrument —**tran'script** *n.* copy

**tran'sept** *n.* transverse part of cruciform church; either of its arms

**trans·fer** (trans-FUR) *vt.* (-ferred, -fer·ring) move, send from one person, place *etc.* to another —*n.* (TRANS-fur) removal of person or thing from one place to another; design that can be transferred from one surface to another by pressure, heat *etc.* —**trans·fer'a·ble** *adj.* —**trans·fer'ence** *n.* transfer

**trans·fig·ure** (trans-FIG-yər) *vt.* (-ured, -ur·ing) alter appearance of

**trans·fix** (trans-FIKS) *vt.* astound, stun; pierce

**trans·form'** *vt.* change shape, character of —**trans·for·ma'tion** *n.* —**trans·form'er** *n.* Electricity apparatus for changing voltage of alternating current

**trans·fuse** (trans-FYOOZ) *vt.* (-fused, -fus·ing) convey from one vessel to another, *esp.* blood from healthy person to one injured or ill —**trans·fu'sion** (-FYOO-zhən) *n.*

**trans·gress** (trans-GRES) *vt.* break (law); sin —**trans·gres'sion** (-GRESH-ən) *n.* —**trans·gres'sor** *n.*

**tran·sient** (TRAN-shənt) *adj.* fleeting, not permanent —**tran'sience** *n.*

**tran·sis·tor** (tran-ZIS-tər) *n.* Electronics small semiconducting device used to amplify electric currents; *inf.* portable radio using transistors

**tran'sit** *n./v.* (-sit·ed, -sit·ing) (make) passage, crossing —**tran-**

**si'tion** (-ZISH-ən) *n.* change from one state to another —**tran·si'tion·al** *adj.* —**tran'si·tive** *adj.* (of verb) requiring direct object —**tran'si·to·ry** *adj.* not lasting long, transient

**trans·late** (trans-LAYT) *vt.* (-lat·ed, -lat·ing) turn from one language into another; interpret —**trans·la'tion** *n.* —**trans·la'tor** *n.*

**trans·lit·er·ate** (trans-LIT-ər-ayt) *vt.* (-at·ed, -at·ing) write in the letters of another alphabet —**trans·lit·er·a'tion** *n.*

**trans·lu·cent** (trans-LOO-sənt) *adj.* letting light pass through, semitransparent —**trans·lu'cence** *n.*

**trans·mi·grate** (trans-MĪ-grayt) *vi.* (-grat·ed, -grat·ing) (of soul) pass into another body —**trans·mi·gra'tion** *n.*

**trans·mit** (trans-MIT) *vt.* (-mit·ted, -mit·ting) send, cause to pass to another place, person *etc.*; communicate; send out (signals) by means of radio waves; broadcast (radio, television program) —**trans·mis'sion** *n.* transference; gear by which power is communicated from engine to road wheels —**trans·mit'tal** *n.* transmission

**trans·mog·ri·fy** (trans-MOG-rə-fī) *vt. inf.* (-fied, -fy·ing) change completely *esp.* into bizarre form

**trans·mute** (trans-MYOOT) *vt.* (-mut·ed, -mut·ing) change in form, properties, or nature —**trans·mu·ta'tion** *n.*

**tran·som** (TRAN-səm) *n.* window above door; crosspiece separating the door and window

**trans·par·ent** (trans-PA-rənt) *adj.* letting light pass without distortion; that can be seen through distinctly; obvious —**trans·par'en·cy** *n.* (*pl.* -cies) quality of being transparent;

photographic slide; picture made visible by light behind it

**tran·spire** (tran-SPĪR) *vi.* (-spired, -spir·ing) become known; *inf.* happen; (of plants) give off water vapor through leaves —**tran·spi·ra'tion** *n.*

**trans·plant** (trans-PLANT) *vt.* move and plant again in another place; transfer organ surgically from one body to another —*n.* (TRANS-plant) surgical transplanting of organ; anything transplanted —**trans·plan·ta'tion** *n.*

**trans·port** (trans-PORT) *vt.* convey from one place to another; enrapture —*n.* (TRANS-port) means of conveyance; ships, aircraft *etc.* used in transporting supplies, troops *etc.*; a ship *etc.* so used

**trans·pose** (trans-POHZ) *vt.* (-posed, -pos·ing) change order of; interchange; put music into different key —**trans·po·si'tion** (-pə-ZISH-ən) *n.*

**tran·sub·stan·ti·a·tion** *n.* (tran-səb-stan-shee-AY-shən) doctrine that substance of bread and wine changes into substance of Christ's body when consecrated in Eucharist

**trans·verse** (trans-VURS) *adj.* lying across; at right angles

**trans·ves·tite** (trans-VES-tīt) *n.* person seeking sexual pleasure by wearing clothes normally worn by opposite sex

**trap** *n.* snare, device for catching game *etc.*; anything planned to deceive, betray *etc.*; arrangement of pipes to prevent escape of gas; movable opening, *esp.* through ceiling *etc.*; *sl.* mouth —*vt.* (trapped, trap·ping) catch, ensnare —**trap'per** *n.* one who traps animals for their fur

—**trap'door** n. door in floor or roof

**tra·peze** (tra-PEEZ) n. horizontal bar suspended from two ropes for use in gymnastics, acrobatic exhibitions *etc.* —**trapeze artist** one who performs on trapeze

**trap·e·zoid** (TRAP-ə-zoid) n. quadrilateral with two parallel sides

**trap·pings** (TRAP-ingz) n. pl. equipment, ornaments

**trash** n. rubbish; nonsense —**trash'y** adj. (trash·i·er, trash·i·est) worthless, cheap

**trau·ma** (TROW-mə) n. nervous shock; injury —**trau·mat'ic** adj. of, causing, caused by trauma

**tra·vail** (trə-VAYL) vi./n. labor, toil

**trav·el** (TRAV-əl) v. (-eled, -el·ing) go, move from one place to another —n. act of traveling, *esp.* as tourist; *Machinery* distance component is allowed to move —pl. (account of) traveling —**trav'el·er** n. —**trav·e·logue** (TRAV-ə-log) n. film *etc.* about travels

**tra·verse** (trə-VURS) vt. (-ersed, -ers·ing) cross, go through or over; (of gun) move laterally —n. (TRA-vurs) anything set across; partition; *Mountaineering* face, steep slope to be crossed from side to side —adj. being, lying across

**trav·es·ty** (TRAV-ə-stee) n.(pl. -ties) farcical, grotesque imitation; mockery —vt. (-tied, -ty·ing) make, be a travesty of

**trawl** n. net dragged at deep levels behind special boat, to catch fish, shrimp *etc.* —vi. fish with one —**trawl'er** n. trawling vessel

**tray** n. flat board, usu. with rim, for carrying things; any similar utensil

**treach·er·y** (TRECH-ə-ree) n. (pl. -er·ies) deceit, betrayal —**treach'er·ous** (-əs) adj. disloyal; unreliable, dangerous

**trea·cle** (TREE-kəl) n. cloying sentimentally; *Brit.* molasses

**tread** (tred) v. (trod, trod·den or trod, tread·ing) set foot on; trample; oppress; walk —n. treading; fashion of walking; upper surface of step; part of motor vehicle tire in contact with ground —**tread'mill** n. dreary routine *etc.*

**trea·dle** (TRED-l) n. lever worked by foot to turn wheel

**trea·son** (TREE-zən) n. violation by citizen of allegiance to country or ruler; treachery; disloyalty —**trea'son·a·ble** adj. constituting treason —**trea'son·ous** adj.

**treas·ure** (TREZH-ər) n. riches; stored wealth or valuables —vt. (-ured, -ur·ing) prize, cherish; store up —**treas'ur·er** n. official in charge of funds —**treas'ur·y** n. (pl. -ur·ies) place for treasure; government department in charge of finance —**treasure-trove** (-trohv) n. treasure found hidden (with no evidence of ownership)

**treat** n. (treet) pleasure, entertainment given —vt. deal with, act toward; give medical treatment to; (with of) discourse on; entertain, *esp.* with food or drink —vi. negotiate —**treat'ment** (-mənt) n. method of counteracting a disease; act or mode of treating; manner of handling an artistic medium

**trea·tise** (TREE-tis) n. book discussing a subject, formal essay

**trea·ty** (TREE-tee) n. (pl. -ties) signed contract between nations *etc.*

**tre·ble** (TREB-l) adj. threefold, triple; *Mus.* high-pitched —n. soprano voice; part of music for it;

singer with such voice —v. (-bled, -bling) increase threefold —tre′bly (-blee) adv.

**tree** n. large perennial plant with woody trunk; beam; anything (eg genealogical chart) resembling tree, or tree's structure —v. (treed, tree·ing) force, drive up tree; plant with trees

**tre·foil** (TREE-foil) n. plant with three-lobed leaf, clover; carved ornament like this

**trek** vi./n. (trekked, trek·king) (make) long difficult journey

**trel·lis** (TREL-is) n. lattice or grating of light bars fixed crosswise —vt. screen, supply with one

**trem·ble** (TREM-bəl) vi. (-bled, -bling) quiver, shake; feel fear, anxiety —n. involuntary shaking; quiver; tremor

**tre·men·dous** (tri-MEN-dəs) adj. vast, immense; exciting, unusual, excellent

**trem·o·lo** (TREM-ɔ-loh) n. (pl. -los) quivering or vibrating effect in singing or playing

**trem·or** (TREM-ɔr) n. quiver; shaking; minor earthquake

**trem·u·lous** (TREM-yə-ləs) adj. quivering slightly; fearful, agitated

**trench** n. long narrow ditch, esp. as shelter in war —vt. cut grooves or ditches in —trench coat double-breasted waterproof overcoat

**trench·ant** (TRENCH-ənt) —adj. cutting, incisive, biting

**trench·er·man** (TRENCH-ər-mən) n. (pl. -men) heavy eater

**trend** n. direction, tendency, inclination, drift —trend′y adj./n. (trend·i·er, trend·i·est) consciously fashionable (person) —trend′i·ness (-nis) n.

**tre·pan** (tri-PAN) n. instrument for cutting circular pieces, esp.

from skull —vt. (-panned, -panning)

**trep·i·da·tion** (trep-i-DAY-shən) n. fear, anxiety

**tres·pass** (TRES-pəs) vi. intrude (on) property etc. of another; transgress, sin —n. wrongful entering on another's land; wrongdoing

**tress** n. long lock of hair

**tres·tle** (TRES-l) n. board fixed on pairs of spreading legs and used as support; structural member of bridge

**tri-** (comb. form) three

**tri·ad** (TRI-ad) n. group of three; Chem. element, radical with valence of three

**tri·al** (TRI-əl) n. act of trying, testing; experimental examination; Law conduct of case before judge, jury; thing, person that strains endurance or patience

**tri·an·gle** (TRI-ang-gəl) n. figure with three angles; percussion musical instrument —tri·an′gu·lar (-lər) adj.

**tribe** (trib) n. subdivision of race of people —trib′al (-əl) adj.

**trib·u·la·tion** (trib-yə-LAY-shən) n. misery, trouble, affliction, distress; cause of this

**tri·bu·nal** (tri-BYOON-l) n. law court; body appointed to inquire into and decide specific matter; place, seat of judgment

**trib·u·tar·y** (TRIB-yə-ter-ee) n. (pl. -tar·ies) stream flowing into another —adj. auxiliary; contributory; paying tribute

**trib·ute** (TRIB-yoot) n. sign of honor or recognition; tax paid by one country to another as sign of subjugation

**trice** (tris) n. moment —in a trice instantly

**tri·chi·na** (tri-KĪ-nə) n. (pl. -nae pr. -nee) minute parasitic worm

—**trich·i·no·sis** n. (tri-kə-NOH-sis) disease caused by this

**trick** (trik) n. deception; prank; mannerism; illusion; feat of skill or cunning; knack; cards played in one round; spell of duty; *sl.* prostitute's customer, sexual act —vt. cheat; hoax; deceive —**trick'ster** n. —**trick'y** adj. (**trick·i·er**, **trick·i·est**) difficult, needing careful handling; crafty

**trick·le** (TRIK-l) v. (-led, -ling) (cause to) run, flow, move in thin stream or drops

**tri·col·or** (TRI-kul-ər) adj. three colored —n. tricolor flag, eg of France

**tri·cy·cle** (TRI-si-kəl) n. child's three-wheeled bike

**tri·dent** (TRID-nt) n. three-pronged fork or spear

**tri·en·ni·al** (trī-EN-ee-əl) adj. happening every, or lasting, three years

**tri·fle** (TRI-fəl) n. insignificant thing or matter; small amount —vi. (-fled, -fling) toy (with); act, speak idly —**tri'fler** (-flər) n.

**trig·ger** (TRIG-ər) n. catch that releases spring esp. to fire gun —vt. (*oft.* with off) start, set in action *etc.* —**trigger-happy** adj. tending to irresponsible, ill-considered behavior, *esp.* in use of firearms

**trig·o·nom·et·ry** (trig-ə-NOM-i-tree) n. branch of mathematics dealing with relations of sides and angles of triangles —**trig·o·no·met'ric** (-nə-MET-rik) adj.

**tri·lat·er·al** (trī-LAT-ər-əl) adj. having three sides

**trill** vi. sing with quavering voice; sing lightly; warble —n. such singing or sound

**tril·lion** (TRIL-yən) n. number 1 followed by 12 zeroes

**tril·o·gy** (TRIL-ə-jee) n. (pl. -gies)

series of three related (literary) works

**trim** adj. (**trim·mer**, **trim·mest**) neat, smart; slender; in good order —vt. (**trimmed**, **trim·ming**) shorten slightly by cutting; prune; decorate; adjust; put in good order; adjust balance of (ship, aircraft) —n. decoration; order, state of being trim; haircut that neatens existing style; upholstery, accessories in automobile; edging material, as inside woodwork around doors, windows *etc.* —**trimming** n. (*oft.* pl.) decoration, addition; *inf.* a defeat; pl. garnish to main dish

**tri·ma·ran** (TRI-mə-ran) n. three-hulled vessel

**trin·i·ty** (TRIN-i-tee) n. the state of being threefold; (T-) the three persons of the Godhead —**trin·i·tar'i·an** (-TAIR-ee-ən) n./adj.

**trin·ket** (TRING-kit) n. small ornament, trifle

**tri·o** (TREE-oh) n. (pl. tri·os) group of three; music for three parts

**tri·ode** (TRI-ohd) n. *Electronics* three-electrode vacuum tube

**trip** n. (short) journey for pleasure; stumble; switch; *sl.* hallucinatory experience caused by drug —v. (**tripped**, **trip·ping**) (cause to) stumble; (cause to) make false step, mistake —vi. run lightly; skip; dance; *sl.* take hallucinatory drugs —vt. operate (switch)

**tri·par·tite** (trī-PAHR-tīt) adj. having, divided into three parts

**tripe** (trīp) n. stomach of cow *etc.* prepared for food; *sl.* nonsense

**tri·ple** (TRIP-əl) adj. threefold —v. (-pled, -pling) treble; hit triple —n. *Baseball* three-base hit —**trip·let** (TRIP-lit) n. three of a kind; one of three offspring born at one birth —**trip'lex** adj. threefold; (of apartment) having three floors —**trip'ly** (-lee) *adv.*

**trip·li·cate** (TRIP-li-kit) *adj.* threefold —*n.* state of being triplicate; one of set of three copies —*vt.* (-kayt) (-cat·ed, -cat·ing) make threefold

**tri·pod** (TRI-pod) *n.* stool, stand *etc.* with three feet

**trip·tych** (TRIP-tik) *n.* carving, set of pictures (*esp.* altarpiece) on three panels hinged side by side

**trite** (trīt) *adj.* hackneyed, banal

**trit·i·um** (TRIT-ee-əm) *n.* radioactive isotope of hydrogen

**tri·umph** (TRI-əmf) *n.* great success; victory; exultation —*vi.* achieve great success or victory; prevail; exult —**tri·um'phal** (-UMF-əl) *adj.* —**tri·um'phant** (-fənt) *adj.* victorious

**tri·um·vi·rate** (trī-UM-vər-it) *n.* joint rule by three persons

**triv·et** (TRIV-it) *n.* metal bracket or stand for pot or kettle

**triv·i·a** (TRIV-ee-ə) *n. pl.* petty, unimportant things, details —**triv'i·al** *adj.* of little consequence; commonplace —**triv·i·al'i·ty** *n.* (*pl.* -ties)

**tro·chee** (TROH-kee) *n.* in verse, foot of two syllables, first long and second short —**tro·cha'ic** (-KAY-ik) *adj.*

**trod** *pt.*, **trod'den** *pr.* TROD-ən, **trod** *pp.* of TREAD

**trog·lo·dyte** (TROG-lə-dīt) *n.* cave dweller

**Tro·jan** (TROH-jən) *adj./n.* (inhabitant) of ancient Troy; steadfast or persevering (person)

**troll**[1] (trohl) *vt.* fish for by dragging baited hook or lure through water

**troll**[2] *n.* supernatural being in Scandinavian mythology and folklore

**trol·ley** (TROL-ee) *n.* (*pl.* -leys)

small wheeled table for food and drink; wheeled cart for moving goods *etc.*; streetcar

**trol·lop** (TROL-əp) *n.* promiscuous or slovenly woman

**trom·bone** (trom-BOHN) *n.* deep-toned brass wind instrument with sliding tube —**trom·bon'ist** *n.*

**troop** *n.* group or crowd of persons or animals; unit of cavalry —*pl.* soldiers —*vi.* move in a troop, flock —**troop'er** *n.* cavalry soldier; state police officer

**trope** (trohp) *n.* figure of speech

**tro·phy** (TROH-fee) *n.* (*pl.* -phies) prize, award, as shield, cup; memorial of victory, hunt *etc.*

**trop·ic** (TROP-ik) *n.* either of two lines of latitude at 23½° N (tropic of Cancer) or 23½° S (tropic of Capricorn) —*pl.* area of Earth's surface between these lines —**trop'i·cal** (-kəl) *adj.* pert. to, within tropics; (of climate) very hot

**trot** *vi.* (trot·ted, trot·ting) (of horse) move at medium pace, lifting feet in diagonal pairs; (of person) run easily with short strides —*n.* trotting, jog —**trot'·ter** *n.* horse trained to trot in race; foot of certain animals, *esp.* pig

**troth** (trawth) *n.* fidelity, truth

**trou·ba·dour** (TROO-bə-dor) *n.* one of school of early poets and singers

**trou·ble** (TRUB-əl) *n.* state or cause of mental distress, pain, inconvenience *etc.*; care, effort —*v.* (-bled, -bling) —*vt.* be trouble to —*vi.* be inconvenienced, concerned (about); be agitated; take pains, exert oneself —**trou'ble·some** (-səm) *adj.*

**trough** (trawf) *n.* long open vessel, *esp.* for animals' food or water; hollow between two waves; *Meteorology* area of low pressure

**trounce** (trowns) *vt.* (**trounced, trounc·ing**) beat thoroughly, thrash

**troupe** (troop) *n.* company of performers —**troup'er** *n.*

**trou·sers** (TROW-zərz) *n. pl.* two-legged outer garment with legs reaching to the ankles

**trous·seau** (TROO-soh) *n.* (*pl.* -**seaux** *pr.* -sohz) bride's outfit of clothing

**trout** (trowt) *n.* freshwater sport and food fish

**trow·el** (TROW-əl) *n.* small tool like spade for spreading mortar, lifting plants *etc.* —*vt.* (-**eled, -el·ing**) work with or as if with trowel

**troy weight** (troi) system of weights used for gold, silver and gems

**tru·ant** (TROO-ənt) *n.* one absent without leave, *esp.* child so absenting self from school —*adj.* —**tru'an·cy** (-ən-see) *n.* (*pl.* -**cies**)

**truce** (troos) *n.* temporary cessation of fighting; respite, lull

**truck**[1] (truk) *n.* wheeled (motor) vehicle for moving goods

**truck**[2] *n.* barter; dealing, *esp.* in **have no truck with**; payment of workmen in goods

**truck·le** (TRUK-əl) *vi.* (-**led, -ling**) yield weakly (to)

**truc·u·lent** (TRUK-yə-lənt) *adj.* aggressive, defiant —**truc·u·lence** (-ləns) *n.*

**trudge** (truj) *vi.* (**trudged, trudg·ing**) walk laboriously —*n.* laborious or wearisome walk

**true** (troo) *adj.* (**tru·er, tru·est**) in accordance with facts; faithful; exact, correct; genuine —**tru·ism** (TROO-iz-əm) *n.* self-evident truth —**tru'ly** *adv.* exactly; really; sincerely —**truth** (trooth) *n.* state of being true; something that is true

—**truth'ful** (-fəl) *adj.* accustomed to speak the truth; accurate, exact

**truf·fle** (TRUF-əl) *n.* edible fungus growing underground; candy resembling this

**truism** (TROO-iz-əm) *n.* see TRUE

**trump** *n.* card of suit temporarily ranking above others —*vt.* take trick with a trump —**trump up** concoct, fabricate

**trump·er·y** (TRUM-pə-ree) *adj.* showy but worthless —*n.* (*pl.* -**er·ies**) worthless finery; trash; worthless stuff

**trum·pet** (TRUM-pit) *n.* metal wind instrument like horn —*vi.* blow trumpet; make sound like one, as elephant —*vt.* proclaim, make widely known

**trun·cate** (TRUNG-kayt) *vt.* (-**cat·ed, -cat·ing**) cut short

**trun·cheon** (TRUN-chən) *n.* police officer's club; staff of office or authority; baton

**trun·dle** (TRUN-dəl) *vt.* (-**dled, -dling**) roll, as a thing on little wheels —**trundle bed**

**trunk** *n.* main stem of tree; person's body without or excluding head and limbs; box for clothes *etc.*; elephant's proboscis —*pl.* man's bathing suit —**trunk line** main line of railroad, telephone *etc.*

**truss** *vt.* fasten up, tie up —*n.* support; medical device of belt *etc.* to hold hernia in place; pack, bundle; cluster of flowers at end of single stalk

**trust** *n.* confidence; firm belief; reliance; combination of producers to remove competition and keep up prices; care, responsibility; property held for another —*vt.* rely on; believe in; expect, hope; consign for care —**trust·ee'** *n.* one legally holding property on another's behalf; trusty

—trust·ee′ship *n.* —trust′ful (-fəl) *adj.* inclined to trust; credulous —trust′wor·thy (-wur-*thee*) *adj.* reliable; dependable; honest; safe —trust′y *adj.* (trust·i·er, trust·i·est) faithful; reliable —*n.* (*pl.* trust·ies) trustworthy convict with special privileges

**truth** (trooth) *see* TRUE

**try** (trī) *v.* (tried, try·ing) —*vi.* attempt, endeavor —*vt.* attempt; test; make demands upon; investigate (case); examine (person) in court of law; purify or refine (as metals) —*n.* (*pl.* tries) attempt, effort —**tried** *adj.* proved; afflicted —**try′ing** *adj.* upsetting, annoying; difficult

**tryst** (trist) *n.* appointment to meet; place appointed

**tsar** (zahr) *see* CZAR

**tset·se** (TSET-see) *n.* Afr. blood-sucking fly whose bite transmits various diseases to man and animals

**T-shirt** (TEE-shurt) *n.* informal (short-sleeved) undershirt, sweater *usu.* of cotton

**T square** *n.* T-shaped ruler for drawing parallel lines, right angles *etc.*

**tub** (tub) *n.* open wooden vessel like bottom half of barrel; small round container; bath; *inf.* short, fat person; old, slow ship *etc.*

**tu·ba** (TOO-bə) *n.* (*pl.* -bas) valved brass wind instrument of low pitch

**tube** (toob) *n.* long, narrow, hollow cylinder; flexible cylinder with cap to hold liquids, pastes —**tu′bu·lar** (-byə-lər) *adj.* like tube

**tu·ber** (TOO-bər) *n.* fleshy underground stem of some plants, *eg* potato —**tu′ber·ous** (-əs) *adj.*

**tu·ber·cle** (TOO-bər-kəl) *n.* any small rounded nodule on skin *etc.*; small lesion of tissue, *esp.*

produced by tuberculosis —**tu·ber·cu·lar** *adj.* (tuu-BUR-kyə-lər) —**tu·ber′cu·lin** *n.* extraction from bacillus used to test for and treat tuberculosis —**tu·ber·cu·lo′sis** *n.* communicable disease, *esp.* of lungs

**tuck** (tuk) *vt.* push, fold into small space; gather, stitch in folds; draw, roll together —*n.* stitched fold —**tuck′er** *n.* strip of linen or lace formerly worn across bosom by women —*vt. inf.* weary; tire

**tu·fa** (TOO-fə) *n.* porous rock formed as deposit from springs *etc.*

**tuf·fet** (TUF-it) *n. obs.* small mound or seat

**tuft** *n.* bunch of feathers, threads *etc.*

**tug** (tug) *vt.* (tugged, tug·ging) pull hard or violently; haul; jerk forward —*n.* violent pull; ship used to tow other vessels —**tug of war** contest in which two teams pull against one another on a rope; hard-fought contest for supremacy

**tu·i·tion** (too-ISH-ən) *n.* teaching, instruction; fee for instruction

**tu·lip** (TOO-lip) *n.* plant with bright cup-shaped flowers

**tulle** (tool) *n.* kind of fine thin silk or lace

**tum·ble** (TUM-bəl) *v.* (-bled, -bling) (cause to) fall or roll, twist *etc.* (*esp.* in play); rumple, disturb —*n.* fall; somersault —**tum′bler** *n.* stemless drinking glass; acrobat; spring catch in lock —**tum′ble-down** *adj.* dilapidated —**tumble to** *inf.* realize, understand

**tu·me·fy** (TOO-mə-fī) *v.* (-fied, -fy·ing) (cause to) swell —**tu·mes·cence** (too-MES-əns) *n.* —**tu·mes′cent** (-ənt) *adj.* (becoming) swollen

**tu·mor** (TOO-mər) *n.* abnormal growth in or on body

**tu·mult** (TOO-məlt) *n.* violent uproar, commotion —**tu·mult'u·ous** (-MUL-choo-əs) *adj.*

**tu·na** (TOO-nə) *n.* large marine food and game fish

**tun·dra** (TUN-drə) *n.* vast treeless zone between ice cap and timber line of N America and Eurasia

**tune** (toon) *n.* melody; quality of being in pitch; adjustment of musical instrument; concord; frame of mind —*vt.* (tuned, tun·ing) put in tune; adjust machine to obtain most efficient running; adjust radio circuit —**tune'ful** (-fəl) *adj.* —**tun'er** (-ər) *n.* —**tune** in adjust (radio, TV) to receive (a station, program)

**tung·sten** (TUNG-stən) *n.* grayish-white metal, used in lamp filaments, some steels *etc.*

**tu·nic** (TOO-nik) *n.* close-fitting jacket forming part of uniform; loose hip-length or knee-length garment

**tun·nel** (TUN-l) *n.* underground passage, *esp.* as track for railroad line; burrow of a mole *etc.* —*v.* (-neled,-nel·ing) make tunnel (through)

**tur·ban** (TUR-bən) *n.* in certain countries, man's headdress, made by coiling length of cloth around head or a cap; woman's hat like this

**tur'bid** *adj.* muddy, not clear; disturbed —**tur·bid'i·ty** *n.*

**tur·bine** (TUR-bin) *n.* rotary engine driven by steam, gas, water or air playing on blades

**turbo-** (*comb. form*) of, relating to, or driven by a turbine

**tur·bu·lent** (TUR-byə-lənt) *adj.* in commotion; swirling; riotous —**tur'bu·lence** (-ləns) *n. esp.* instability of atmosphere causing gusty air currents *etc.*

**tu·reen** (tuu-REEN) *n.* serving dish for soup

**turf** *n.* (*pl.* turfs) short grass with earth bound to it by matted roots; grass, *esp.* as lawn; *sl.* claimed territory of gang —*vt.* lay with turf

**tur·gid** (TUR-jid) *adj.* swollen, inflated; bombastic —**tur·gid'i·ty** *n.*

**tur·key** (TUR-kee) *n.* large bird reared for food; *sl.* loser, naive person; *Theater sl.* a flop

**Turk·ish** (TUR-kish) *adj.* of, pert. to Turkey, the Turks —**Turkish bath** steam bath —**Turkish delight** gelatin candy flavored and coated with powdered sugar

**tur'moil** *n.* confusion and bustle, commotion

**turn** *v.* move around, rotate; change, reverse, alter position or direction (of); (*oft.* with into) change in nature, character *etc.* —*vt.* make, shape on lathe —*n.* act of turning; inclination *etc.*; period, spell; turning; short walk; (part of) rotation; performance —**turn'ing** *n.* road, path leading off main route —**turn'coat** (-koht) *n.* one who forsakes own party or principles —**turn'out** *n.* number of people appearing for some purpose, occasion; way in which person is dressed, equipped —**turn'o·ver** *n.* total sales made by business over certain period; rate at which employees leave and are replaced; small pastry; *Football, Basketball* loss of ball to opponents through mistake —**turn'pike** *n. Hist.* (gate across) road where toll was paid; highway —**turn'stile** *n.* revolving gate for controlling admission of people —**turn'ta·ble** *n.* revolving platform —**turn down** refuse —**turn up** appear; be found; increase (flow, volume)

**tur·nip** n. plant with globular root used as food

**tur·pen·tine** (TUR-pən-tīn) n. resin obtained from certain trees; oil made from this —**turps** n. *short for* turpentine

**tur·pi·tude** (TUR-pi-tood) n. depravity

**tur·quoise** (TUR-kwoiz) n. bluish-green precious stone; this color

**tur·ret** (TUR-it) n. small tower; revolving armored tower for guns on warship, tank *etc.*

**tur·tle** (TUR-tl) n. ( *esp.* sea) tortoise

**tusk** n. long pointed side tooth of certain animals, *eg* elephant, wild boar

**tus·sle** (TUS-əl) n./v. (-**sled**, -**sling**) fight, wrestle, struggle

**tu·te·lage** (TOOT-l-ij) n. act, office of tutor or guardian —**tu'te·lar·y** (-ler-ee) adj.

**tu·tor** (TOO-tər) n. one teaching individuals or small groups —v. teach thus —**tu·to'ri·al** (-TOR-ee-əl) n. period of instruction with tutor

**tu·tu** (TOO-too) n. (pl. -**tus**) short, stiff skirt worn by ballerinas

**tux·e·do** (tuk-SEE-doh) n. (pl. -**dos**) dinner jacket

**TV** television —**TV dinner** frozen meal in tray for heating before serving —**TV game** game played on TV screen using special attachment

**twad·dle** (TWOD-l) n. silly talk

**twain** (twayn) n. two in **twain** asunder

**twang** n. vibrating metallic sound; nasal speech —v. (cause to) make such sounds

**tweak** (tweek) vt. pinch and twist or pull —n.

**tweed** n. rough-surfaced cloth used for clothing —pl. suit of tweed

**tweet** n./vi. chirp —**tweet'er** n.

small loudspeaker reproducing high-frequency sounds

**tweez·ers** (TWEE-zərz) n. pl. small forceps or tongs

**twelve** (twelv) n./adj. cardinal number two more than ten —**twelfth** adj. the ordinal number —n.

**twen·ty** (TWEN-tee) n./adj. (pl. -**ties**) cardinal number, twice ten —**twen'ti·eth** (-tee-ith) adj. the ordinal number —n.

**twerp** (twurp) n. sl. silly person

**twice** (twīs) adv. two times

**twid·dle** (TWID-l) v. (-**dled**, -**dling**) fiddle; twist

**twig** n. small branch, shoot

**twi·light** (TWI-līt) n. soft light after sunset

**twill** n. fabric woven so as to have surface of parallel ridges

**twin** n. one of pair, *esp.* of two children born together —adj. being a twin —v. (**twinned, twinning**) pair, be paired

**twine** (twīn) v. (**twined, twin·ing**) twist, coil around —n. string, cord

**twinge** (twinj) n. momentary sharp, shooting pain; qualm

**twin·kle** (TWING-kəl) vi. (-**kled**, -**kling**) shine with dancing or quivering light, sparkle —n. twinkling; flash; gleam of amusement in eyes —**twinkling** n. very brief time

**twirl** (twurl) vt. turn or twist round quickly; whirl; twiddle

**twist** v. make, become spiral, by turning with one end fast; distort, change; wind —n. thing twisted —**twist'er** n. person or thing that twists; inf. tornado, whirlwind —**twist'y** adj. (**twist·i·er, twist·i·est**)

**twit** n. inf. foolish person —vt. (**twit·ted, twit·ting**) taunt

**twitch** (twich) v. give momentary sharp pull or jerk (to) —n.

such pull or jerk; spasmodic jerk, spasm

**twit·ter** (TWIT-ər) vi. giggle; talk idly; (of birds) utter succession of tremulous sounds —n. such succession of notes

**two** (too) n./adj. cardinal number, one more than one —two'·fold adj./adv. —two-faced adj. double-dealing, deceitful; with two faces —two-stroke (-strohk) adj. (of internal-combustion engine) making one explosion to every two strokes of piston

**ty·coon** (tī-KOON) n. powerful, influential businessperson

**tyke** (tīk) n. small, cheeky child; small (mongrel) dog

**tympani** see TIMPANI

**type** (tīp) n. class; sort; model; pattern; characteristic build; specimen; block bearing letter used for printing; such pieces collectively —vt. (typed, typ·ing) print with typewriter; typify; classify —type'script n. typewritten document or copy —type'writ·er n. keyed writing machine —typ'ist n. one who operates typewriter —typo n. inf. (pl. ty·pos) error in typing, printing

**ty·phoid** (TĪ-foid) n. acute infectious disease, affecting esp. intestines —adj. —ty·phus (TĪ-fəs) n. infectious disease

**ty·phoon** (tī-FOON) n. violent tropical storm or cyclone

**typ·i·cal** (TIP-i-kəl) adj. true to type; characteristic —typ'i·cal·ly adv.

**typ·i·fy** (TIP-i-fī) vt. (-fied, -fy·ing) serve as type or model of

**ty·pog·ra·phy** (tī-POG-rə-fee) n. art of printing; style of printing —ty·po·graph'i·cal adj. —ty·pog'ra·pher (-POG-rə-fər) n.

**ty·rant** (TĪ-rənt) n. oppressive or cruel ruler; one who forces own will on others cruelly and arbi-

trarily —ty·ran·ni·cal (ti-RAN-i-kəl) adj. despotic; ruthless —tyr·an·nize (TIR-ə-nīz) v. (-nized, -niz·ing) exert ruthless or tyrannical authority (over) —tyr'an·nous (-ə-nəs) adj. —tyr'an·ny (-ee) n. despotism

**ty·ro** (tī-roh) n. (pl. -ros) novice, beginner

# U

**U** Chem. uranium

**u·biq·ui·tous** (yoo-BIK-wi-təs) adj. everywhere at once; omnipresent —u·biq'ui·ty n.

**ud·der** (UD-ər) n. milk-secreting organ of cow etc.

**ug·ly** (UG-lee) adj. (-li·er, -li·est) unpleasing, repulsive to the sight, hideous; ill-omened; threatening —ug'li·ness (-nis) n.

**u·kase** (yoo-KAYS) n. an arbitrary command

**u·ku·le·le** (yoo-kə-LAY-lee) n. small four-stringed guitar, esp. of Hawaii

**ul·cer** (UL-sər) n. open sore on skin, mucous membrane that is slow to heal —ul'cer·ate v. (-at·ed, -at·ing) make, form ulcer(s) —ul·cer·a'tion n.

**ul·lage** (UL-ij) n. quantity by which a container falls short of being full

**ul·na** (UL-nə) n. (pl. -nae pr. -nee) longer of two bones of forearm

**ul·te·ri·or** (ul-TEER-ee-ər) adj. lying beneath, beyond what is revealed or evident (eg motives); situated beyond

**ul·ti·mate** (UL-tə-mit) adj. last; highest; most significant; fundamental —ul·ti·ma'tum (-MAY-təm) n. (pl. -tums, -ta pr. -tə) final proposition; final terms offered

**ul·tra-** (*prefix*) beyond, excessively, as in *ultramodern adj.*

**ul'tra·high frequency** (UL-trǝ-hī) (band of) radio waves of very short wavelength

**ul·tra·ma·rine** (ul-trǝ-mǝ-REEN) *n.* blue pigment

**ul·tra·son·ic** (ul-trǝ-SON-ik) *adj.* of sound waves beyond the range of human ear

**ul·tra·vi·o·let** (ul-trǝ-VI-ǝ-lit) *adj.* of electromagnetic radiation (*eg* of sun *etc.*) beyond limit of visibility at violet end of spectrum

**um·bel** (UM-bǝl) *n.* umbrella-like flower cluster with stalks springing from central point —**um·bel'lif·er·ous** (-LIF-ǝr-ǝs) *adj.* bearing umbel(s)

**um·ber** (UM-bǝr) *n.* dark brown pigment

**um·bil·i·cal** (um-BIL-i-kǝl) *adj.* of

(region of) navel —**umbilical cord** cordlike structure connecting fetus with placenta of mother; cord joining astronaut to spacecraft *etc.*

**um·brage** (UM-brij) *n.* offense, resentment

**um·brel·la** (um-BREL-ǝ) *n.* folding circular cover of nylon *etc.* on stick, carried in hand to protect against rain, heat of sun; anything shaped or functioning like an umbrella

**um·pire** (UM-pīr) *n.* person chosen to decide question, or to decide disputes and enforce rules in a game —*v.* (-pired, -pir·ing) act as umpire (in)

**un-** (*prefix*) indicating not, contrary to, opposite of, reversal of an action, removal from, release or deprivation The list below contains some of the more common compounds

| | | |
|---|---|---|
| un·ac·cept'a·ble | un·de·mand'ing | un·fa·mil'iar |
| un·ac·com'pa·nied | un·de·served' | un·fa'vor·a·ble |
| un·ac·cus'tomed | un·de·sir'a·ble | un·feel'ing |
| un·af·fect'ed | un·de·terred' | un·feigned' |
| un·ap·proach'a·ble | un·dif·fer·en'ti·at·ed | un·fin'ished |
| un·at·tached' | un·di·min'ished | un·fit' |
| un·at·trac'tive | un·dis·ci·plined' | un·fold' |
| auth'or·ized | un·dis·cov'ered | un·for·get'ta·ble |
| un·bear'a·ble | un·dis·turbed' | un·for'tu·nate |
| un·be·liev'a·ble | un·drink'a·ble | un·found'ed |
| un·bi'ased | un·earned' | un·gov'ern·a·ble |
| un·break'a·ble | un·eat'a·ble | un·gra'cious |
| un·cer'tain | un·ec·o·nom'ic | un·gram·mat'i·cal |
| un·char·ac·ter·is'tic | un·ed·u·cat·ed | un·guard'ed |
| un·char'i·ta·ble | un·e·mo'tion·al | un·hap'py |
| un·com'fort·a·ble | un·end'ing | un·harmed' |
| un·com·mit'ted | une'qualed | un·health'y |
| un·com'mon·ly | un·e·quiv'o·cal | un·heat'ed |
| un·con·di'tion·al | un·eth'i·cal | un·help'ful |
| un·con·sti·tu'tion·al | un·e·vent'ful | un·hur'ried |
| un·con·ven'tion·al | un·ex·pect'ed | un·hurt' |
| un·co·or'di·nat·ed | un·ex·plained' | un·hy·gi·e'nic |
| un·crit'i·cal | un·fail'ing | |
| un·de·cid'ed | un·fair' | |

**un·ac·count·a·ble** (un-ə-KOWNT-ə-bəl) *adj.* that cannot be explained

**u·nan·i·mous** (yoo-NAN-ə-məs) *adj.* in complete agreement; agreed by all —**u·na·nim·i·ty** (yoo-nə-NIM-ə-tee) *n.*

**un·as·sum·ing** (un-ə-SOO-ming) *adj.* not pretentious, modest

**un·a·vail·ing** (un-ə-VAY-ling) *adj.* useless, futile

**un·a·ware** (un-ə-WAIR) *adj.* not aware, uninformed —**un·a·wares'** (-WAIRZ) *adv.* without previous warning; unexpectedly

**un·bos·om** (un-BUUZ-əm) *vt.* tell or reveal (one's secrets *etc.*)

**un·can·ny** (un-KAN-ee) *adj.* weird, mysterious; extraordinary

**un·cle** (UNG-kəl) *n.* brother of father or mother; husband of aunt

**un·com·pli·men·ta·ry** (un-kom-plə-MEN-tə-ree) *adj.* not complimentary; insulting, derogatory

**un·con·scion·a·ble** (un-KON-shə-nə-bəl) *adj.* unscrupulous, unprincipled; excessive

**un·con·scious** (un-KON-shəs) *adj.* insensible; not aware; not knowing; of thoughts, memories *etc.* of which one is not normally aware —*n.* these thoughts —**un·con'scious·ness** (-nis) *n.*

**un·couth** (un-KOOTH) *adj.* clumsy, boorish; without ease or polish

**unc·tion** (UNGK-shən) *n.* anoint-

un·i·den'ti·fied
un·i·mag'i·na·tive
un·im·paired'
un·im·por'tant
un·im·pressed'
un·in·hab'it·ed
un·in·hib'it·ed
un·in·spired'
un·in·sured'
un·in·tel'li·gi·ble
un·in·ten'tion·al
un·in'ter·est·ing
un·in·ter·rupt'ed
un·in·vit'ed
un·jus'ti·fied
un·la'beled
un·law'ful
un·lim'it·ed
un·lined'
un·locked'
un·luck'y
un·man'age·a·ble
un·mar'ried
un·men'tion·a·ble
un·mer'it·ed
un·mis·tak·a·ble
un·moved'
un·mu'si·cal

un·named'
un·nat'u·ral
un·nec'es·sar·y
un·no'ticed
un·ob·serv'ant
un·ob·tain'a·ble
un·ob·tru'sive
un·of·fi'cial
un·o'pened
un·op·posed'
un·or'tho·dox
un·paid'
un·par'don·a·ble
un·pleas'ant
un·pop'u·lar
un·prec'e·dent·ed
un·pre·pared'
un·ques'tion·a·bly
un·re·al·is'tic
un·rea'son·a·ble
un·re·lent'ing
un·rep·re·sent'a·tive
un·re·quit'ed
un·re·solved'
un·re·strained'
un·ri'valed
un·roll'
un·ruf'fled

un·safe'
un·sal'a·ble
un·sat·is·fac'to·ry
un·sched'uled
un·self·con'scious
un·shak'a·ble
un·so·lic'it·ed
un·spec'i·fied
un·spo'ken
un·suc·cess'ful
un·suit'a·ble
un·sweet'ened
un·sym·pa·thet'ic
un·sys·tem·at'ic
un·trained'
un·trust'wor·thy
un·typ'i·cal
un·us'a·ble
un·u'su·al
un·ut'ter·a·ble
un·want'ed
un·war'rant·ed
un·whole'some
un·will'ing
un·wind'
un·wise'
un·wrap'

ing; excessive politeness; soothing words or thoughts —**unc′tu·ous** (-choo-əs) *adj.* slippery, greasy; oily in manner; gushing

**un·der** (UN-dər) *prep.* below, beneath; bound by, included in; less than; subjected to; known by; in the time of —*adv.* in lower place or condition —*adj.* lower

**under-** (*as prefix*) beneath, below, lower, as in underground

**un·der·car·riage** (UN-dər-ka-rij) *n.* landing gear of vehicle *esp.* aircraft

**un·der·charge** (un-dər-CHAHRJ) *vt.* (-charged, -charg·ing) charge less than proper amount —*n.* (UN-dər-chahrj) too low a charge

**un·der·coat** (UN-dər-koht) *n.* coat of paint applied before top coat

**un·der·go** (un-dər-GOH) *vt.* (-went, -gone, -go·ing) experience, endure, sustain

**un·der·grad·u·ate** (un-dər-GRAJ-oo-it) *n.* student at college who has not received degree

**un·der·ground** (UN-dər-grownd) *adj.* under the ground; secret —*adv.* secretly —*n.* secret but organized resistance to government in power; subway

**un·der·hand** (UN-dər-hand) *adj.* secret, sly; *Sports* (of softball pitch *etc.*) with hand swung below shoulder level

**un·der·lie** (un-dər-LI) *vt.* (-lay, -lain, -ly·ing) be situated under, lie beneath

**un·der·line** (UN-dər-lin) *vt.* (-lined, -lin·ing) put line under; emphasize

**un·der·ling** (UN-dər-ling) *n.* subordinate

**un·der·mine** (un-dər-MIN) *vt.* (-mined, -min·ing) wear away base, support of; weaken insidiously

**un·der·neath** (un-dər-NEETH)

*adv.* below —*prep.* under —*adj.* lower —*n.* bottom; lowest part

**un·der·pass** (UN-dər-pas) *n.* section of road passing under another road, railroad line *etc.*

**un·der·stand** (un-dər-STAND) *v.* (-stood *pr.* -STUUD, -stand·ing) know and comprehend; realize —*vt.* infer; take for granted —**un·der·stand′a·ble** *adj.* —**un·der·stand′ing** *n.* intelligence; opinion; agreement —*adj.* sympathetic

**un·der·stud·y** (UN-dər-stud-ee) *n.* (*pl.* -stud·ies) one prepared to take over theatrical part from performer if necessary —*vt.* (-stud·ied, -stud·y·ing) work as understudy to (performer)

**un·der·take** (un-dər-TAYK) *vt.* (-took *pr.* -TUUK, -tak·en, -tak·ing) make oneself responsible for; enter upon; promise —**un′der·tak·er** *n.* one who arranges funerals —**un′der·tak·ing** *n.* that which is undertaken; project; guarantee

**un·der·tone** (UN-dər-tohn) *n.* quiet, dropped tone of voice; underlying tone or suggestion

**un·der·tow** (UN-dər-toh) *n.* backwash of wave; current beneath surface moving in different direction from surface current

**un·der·wear** (UN-dər-WAIR) *n.* garments worn next to skin (*also* **un′der·clothes** *pr.* -klohz)

**un·der·world** (UN-dər-wurld) *n.* criminals and their associates; *Myth.* abode of the dead

**un·der·write** (UN-dər-RIT) *vt.* (-wrote, -writ·ten, -writ·ing) agree to pay; accept liability in insurance policy —**un′der·writ·er** *n.* agent for insurance or stock issue

**un·do** (un-DOO) *vt.* (-did, -done, -do·ing) untie, unfasten; reverse; cause downfall of —**un·do′ing** *n.*

—**un·done** *adj.* (un-DUN) ruined; not performed

**un·du·late** (UN-jə-layt) *v.* (-lat-ed, -lat·ing) move up and down like waves —**un·du·la·tion** *n.*

**un·earth** (un-URTH) *vt.* dig up; discover

**un·eas·y** (un-EE-zee) *adj.* (-eas·i·er, -eas·i·est) anxious; uncomfortable —**un·eas·i·ness** (-nis) *n.*

**un·em·ployed** (un-im-PLOID) *adj.* having no paid employment, out of work —**un·em·ploy·ment** (-mənt) *n.*

**un·err·ing** (un-ER-ing) *adj.* not missing the mark; consistently accurate

**un·gain·ly** (un-GAYN-lee) *adj.* (-li·er, -li·est) awkward, clumsy —**un·gain·li·ness** (-nis) *n.*

**un·guent** (UNG-gwənt) *n.* ointment

**uni-** (*comb. form*) one, as in *unicorn, uniform* etc. Such words are not given here where the meanings can easily be inferred from the simple word

**u·ni·corn** (YOO-ni-korn) *n.* mythical horselike animal with single long horn

**u·ni·form** (YOO-ni-form) *n.* identifying clothes worn by members of same group *eg* soldiers, nurses *etc.* —*adj.* not changing, unvarying; regular, consistent; conforming to same standard or rule —**u·ni·form·i·ty** *n.* sameness —**u'ni·form·ly** *adv.*

**u·ni·fy** (YOO-ni-fī) *v.* (-fied, -fy·ing) make or become one —**u·ni·fi·ca·tion** (-KAY-shən) *n.*

**u·ni·lat·er·al** (yoo-nə-LAT-ər-əl) *adj.* one-sided; (of contract) binding one party only

**un·ion** (YOON-yən) *n.* joining into one; state of being joined; result of being joined; federation, combination of states *etc.*; labor union, trade union —**un'ion·ize** *v.*

(-ized, -iz·ing) organize (workers) into labor union

**u·nique** (yoo-NEEK) *adj.* being only one of its kind; unparalleled

**u·ni·son** (YOO-ni-sən) *n. Mus.* singing *etc.* of same note as others; agreement, harmony, concord

**u·nit** (YOO-nit) *n.* single thing or person; standard quantity; group of people or things with one purpose

**u·nite** (yoo-NĪT) *v.* (u·nit·ed, u·nit·ing) —*vt.* join into one, connect; associate; cause to adhere —*vi.* become one; combine —**u'ni·ty** (-nə-tee) *n.* state of being one; harmony; agreement, uniformity; combination of separate parts into connected whole; *Mathematics* the number one

**u·ni·verse** (YOO-nə-vurs) *n.* all existing things considered as constituting systematic whole; the world —**u·ni·ver·sal** (-səl) *adj.* relating to all things or all people; applying to all members of a community —**u·ni·ver·sal'i·ty** (-SAL-ə-tee) *n.*

**u·ni·ver·si·ty** (yoo-nə-VUR-si-tee) *n.* (*pl.* -ties) educational institution for research, study, examination and award of degrees in various branches of learning

**un·kempt** (un-KEMPT) *adj.* of rough or uncared-for appearance

**un·less** *conj.* if not, except

**un·rav·el** (un-RAV-əl) *vt.* (-eled, -el·ing) undo, untangle

**un·re·mit·ting** (un-ri-MIT-ing) *adj.* never slackening or stopping

**un·ru·ly** (un-ROO-lee) *adj.* (-li·er, -li·est) badly behaved, ungovernable, disorderly

**un·sa·vor·y** (un-SAY-və-ree) *adj.* distasteful, disagreeable

**un·sight·ly** (un-SĪT-lee) *adj.* ugly

**un·ten·a·ble** (un-TEN-ə-bəl) *adj.*

(of theories *etc.*) incapable of being maintained, defended

un·think·a·ble (un-THING-kə-bəl) *adj.* out of the question; inconceivable; unreasonable

un·til′ *conj.* to the time that; (with a negative) before —*prep.* up to the time of

un·to (UN-too) *prep.* to

un·touched (un-TUCHT) *adj.* not touched; not harmed —un·touch′a·ble *adj.* not able to be touched —*n. esp.* formerly, noncaste Hindu, forbidden to be touched by one of caste

un·to·ward (un-TORD) *adj.* awkward, inconvenient

un·tram·meled (un-TRAM-əld) *adj.* not confined, not constrained

un·wield·y (un-WEEL-dee) *adj.* (-wield·i·er, -wield·i·est) awkward, big, heavy to handle; clumsy

un·wit·ting *adj.* not knowing; not intentional

up *prep.* from lower to higher position; along —*adv.* in or to higher position, source, activity *etc.*; indicating completion —up′ward (-ward) *adj./adv.* —up′wards (-wardz) *adv.* —up against confronted with

up- (*comb. form*) up, upper, upwards as in uproot, upgrade *etc.* Such words are not given here where the meaning can easily be found from the simple word

up·braid (up-BRAYD) *vt.* scold, reproach

up′bring·ing *n.* rearing and education of children

up·date (up-DAYT) *vt.* (-dat·ed, -dat·ing) bring up to date

up·front (up-frunt) *adj. inf.* open, frank —*adj./adv. inf.* (of money) paid out at beginning of business arrangement

up·grade (up-GRAYD) *vt.* (-grad-

ed, -grad·ing) promote to higher position; improve

up·heav·al (up-HEE-vəl) *n.* sudden or violent disturbance

up·hold (up-HOHLD) *vt.* (-held, -hold·ing) maintain, support *etc.*

up·hol·ster (up-HOHL-stər) *vt.* fit springs, padding and coverings on chairs *etc.* —up·hol′ster·er *n.* one who does this work —up·hol′ster·y *n.*

up′keep *n.* act, process or cost of keeping something in good repair

up·lift *vt.* raise aloft —*n.* (UP-lift) a lifting up; mental, social or emotional improvement

up·on (ə-PON) *prep.* on

up·per (UP-ər) *adj.* higher, situated above —*comp. of* UP —*n.* upper part of boot or shoe —up′per·cut *n.* short-arm upward blow —up′per·most (-mohst) *adj. sup. of* UP

up′pish, up·pi·ty (UP-i-tee) *adj. inf.* self-assertive; arrogant; affectedly superior

up·right (UP-rīt) *adj.* erect; honest, just —*adv.* vertically —*n.* thing standing upright, *eg* post in framework

up·ris·ing (UP-rī-zing) *n.* rebellion, revolt

up·roar (UP-ror) *n.* tumult, disturbance —up·roar′i·ous (-ee-əs) *adj.* rowdy

up·set′ *vt.* (-set, -set·ting) overturn; distress; disrupt; make ill —*n.* (UP-set) unexpected defeat; confusion; trouble; overturning

up′shot *n.* outcome, end

up·stage (up-stayj) *adj.* of back of stage —*vt.* (-staged, -stag·ing) draw attention away from another to oneself

up·start (UP-stahrt) *n.* one suddenly raised to wealth, power *etc.*

up·tight (up-tīt) *adj. sl.* displaying

tense nervousness, irritability; repressed

**u·ra·ni·um** (yuu-RAY-nee-əm) *n.* white radioactive metallic element, used as chief source of nuclear energy

**U·ra·nus** (YUUR-ə-nəs) *n.* Greek god, personification of sky; seventh planet from the sun

**ur·ban** (UR-bən) *adj.* relating to town or city —**ur·ban·ize** *vt.* (**-ized, -iz·ing**) change countryside to residential or industrial area

**ur·bane** (ur-BAIN) *adj.* elegant, sophisticated —**ur·ban·i·ty** (-BAN-i-tee) *n.*

**ur·chin** *n.* mischievous, unkempt child

**u·re·a** (yuu-REE-ə) *n.* substance occurring in urine

**u·re·thra** (yuu-REE-thrə) *n.* canal conveying urine from bladder out of body

**urge** (urj) *vt.* (**urged, urg·ing**) exhort earnestly; entreat; drive on —*n.* strong desire —**ur'gen·cy** (-jən-see) *n.* (**pl. -cies**) —**ur'gent** (-jənt) *adj.* pressing; needing attention at once —**ur'gent·ly** *adv.*

**u·rine** (YUUR-in) *n.* fluid excreted by kidneys to bladder and passed as waste from body —**u'ric** *adj.* —**u·ri·nal** (YUUR-ə-nl) *n.* (place with) sanitary fitting used by men for urination —**ur·i·nar·y** *adj.* —**u'ri·nate** *vi.* (**-nat·ed, -nat·ing**) discharge urine

**urn** *n.* vessel like vase, *esp.* for ashes of the dead; large container with tap for making and dispensing tea, coffee *etc.*

**ur·sine** (UR-sin) *adj.* of, like a bear

**us** *pron. pl.* the objective case of the pronoun WE

**use** (yooz) *vt.* (**used, us·ing**) employ, avail oneself of; exercise; exploit; consume —*n.* (yoos) employment, application to a purpose; need to employ; serviceableness; profit; habit —**us·a·ble** (YOO-zə-bəl) *adj.* fit for use —**us·age** (YOOS-ij) *n.* act of using; custom; customary way of using —**used** (yoozd) *adj.* secondhand, not new —**use·ful** (YOOS-fəl) *adj.* of use; helpful; serviceable —**use'ful·ness** (-nis) *n.* —**use'·less·ness** (-lis-nis) *n.* —**used** to (yoost) *adj.* accustomed to —*vt.* did so formerly —**us·er** (YOO-zər) friendly (of computer *etc.*) easily understood and operated

**ush·er** (USH-ər) *n.* doorkeeper, one showing people to seats *etc.* —*vt.* introduce; announce; inaugurate

**u·su·al** (YOO-zhoo-əl) *adj.* habitual, ordinary —**u'su·al·ly** *adv.* as a rule; generally, commonly

**u·surp** (yoo-SURP) *vt.* seize wrongfully —**u·sur·pa·tion** (-sər-PAY-shən) *n.* violent or unlawful seizing of power —**u·surp'er** *n.*

**u·su·ry** (YOO-zhə-ree) *n.* lending of money at excessive interest; such interest —**u'su·rer** *n.* money lender —**u·su'ri·ous** (-ZHUUR-ee-əs) *adj.*

**u·ten·sil** (yoo-TEN-səl) *n.* vessel, implement, *esp.* in domestic use

**u·ter·us** (YOO-tər-əs) *n.* (**pl. -us·es**) womb —**u·ter·ine** (-tər-in) *adj.*

**u·til·i·ty** (yoo-TIL-i-tee) *n.* (**pl. -ties**) usefulness; benefit; useful thing; a public service *eg* electric-light system —*adj.* made for practical purposes —**u·til·i·tar'i·an** (-TAIR-ee-ən) *adj.* useful rather than beautiful —**u·til·i·tar'i·an·ism** *n.* doctrine that morality of actions is to be tested by their utility, *esp.* that the greatest good of the greatest number should be the sole end of public action —u·ti·li·za'tion (-ZAY-shən) n. —u'ti·lize vt. (-lized, -liz·ing) make use of

ut·most (UT-mohst) adj. to the highest degree; extreme, furthest —n. greatest possible amount

u·to·pi·a (yoo-TOH-pee-ə) n. imaginary state with perfect political and social conditions, or constitution —u·to'pi·an (-pee-ən) adj. ideally perfect but impracticable

ut·ter¹ (UT-ər) vt. express, emit audibly, say; put in circulation (forged bills, counterfeit coin) —ut'ter·ance (-əns) n. act of speaking; expression in words; spoken words

utter² adj. complete, total, absolute —ut'ter·ly adv

ut·ter·most (UT-ər-mohst) adj. farthest out; utmost —n. highest degree

u·vu·la (YOO-vyə-lə) n. (pl. -las, -lae pr. -lee) pendent fleshy part of soft palate —u'vu·lar (-lər) adj.

ux·o·ri·ous (uk-SOR-ee-əs) adj. excessively fond of one's wife

# V

V Chem. vanadium

va·cant (VAY-kənt) adj. without thought, empty; unoccupied —va'can·cy (-kən-see) n. (pl. -cies) state of being unoccupied; unfilled position, accommodation etc.

va·cate (VAY-kayt) vt. (-cat·ed, -cat·ing) quit, leave empty —va·ca'tion (-KAY-shən) n. act of vacating; holidays; time when schools and courts etc. are closed

vac·ci·nate (VAK-sə-nayt) vt. (-nat·ed, -nat·ing) inoculate with vaccine as protection against a specific disease —vac·ci·na'tion n. —vac·cine (vak-SEEN) n. any substance used for inoculation against disease

vac·il·late (VAS-ə-layt) vi. (-lat·ed, -lat·ing) fluctuate in opinion; waver; move to and fro —vac·il·la'tion n. indecision; wavering; unsteadiness

vac·u·um (VAK-yoom) n. (pl. -u·ums) place, region containing no matter and from which all or most air, gas has been removed —v. clean with vacuum cleaner —va·cu·i·ty (va-KYOO-i-tee) n. —vac·u·ous (VA-kyoo-əs) adj. vacant; expressionless; unintelligent —vacuum cleaner apparatus for removing dust by suction

vag·a·bond (VAG-ə-bond) n. person with no fixed home; wandering beggar or thief —adj. like a vagabond

va·gar·y (və-GAIR-ee) n. (pl. -gar·ies) something unusual, erratic; whim

va·gi·na (və-JĪ-nə) n. (pl. -nas) passage from womb to exterior —vag·i·nal (VAJ-ə-nl) adj.

va·grant (VAY-grənt) n. vagabond, tramp —adj. wandering, esp. without purpose —va'gran·cy n. (pl. -cies)

vague (vayg) adj. (vaguer pr. -gər, vaguest pr. -gəst) indefinite or uncertain; indistinct; not clearly expressed; absent-minded

vain (vayn) adj. (-er, -est) conceited; worthless, useless; unavailing; foolish —vain'ly adv

vain·glo·ry (VAYN-glor-ee) n. boastfulness, vanity —vain·glo'ri·ous adj

val·ance (VAL-əns) n. short curtain around base of bed etc.

vale (vayl) n. Poet. valley

val·e·dic·tion (val-i-DIK-shən) n. farewell —val·e·dic·to'ri·an (-TOR-ee-ən) n. —val·e·dic'to·ry

(-DIK-tə-ree) n. farewell address —adj.

**va·lence** (VAY-ləns), **va·len·cy** (-lən-see) n. Chem. combining power of element or atom

**val·en·tine** (VAL-ən-tin) n. (one receiving) card, gift, expressing affection, on Saint Valentine's Day, Feb. 14th

**val·et** (va-LAY) n. gentleman's personal servant

**val·e·tu·di·nar·y** (val-i-TOOD-ner-ee) adj. sickly; infirm —**val·e·tu·di·nar'i·an** (-NAIR-ee-ən) n. person obliged or disposed to live the life of an invalid

**Val·hal·la** (val-HAL-ə) n. Norse Myth. place of immortality for heroes slain in battle

**val·iant** (VAL-yənt) adj. brave, courageous

**val'id** adj. sound; capable of being justified; of binding force in law —**va·lid·i·ty** (və-LID-i-tee) n. soundness; power to convince; legal force —**val'i·date** vt. (-dat·ed, -dat·ing) make valid

**va·lise** (və-LEES) n. traveling bag

**Val·kyr·ie** (val-KEER-ee) n. one of the Norse war goddesses who chose the slain and guided them to Valhalla

**val·ley** (VAL-ee) n. (pl. -leys) low area between hills; river basin

**val·or** (VAL-ər) n. bravery —**val'or·ous** (-əs) adj.

**val·ue** (VAL-yoo) n. worth; utility; equivalent; importance —pl. principles, standards —vt. (-ued, u·ing) estimate value of; hold in respect; prize —**val'u·a·ble** (-ə-bəl) adj. precious; worthy; capable of being valued —n. usu. pl. valuable thing —**val·u·a'tion** (-AY-shən) n. estimated worth —**val'ue·less** (-lis) adj. worthless —**value added tax** on difference between cost of basic ma-

terials and cost of article made from them

**valve** (valv) n. device to control passage of fluid etc. through pipe; Anat. part of body allowing one-way passage of fluids; any of separable parts of shell of mollusk; Mus. device on brass instrument for lengthening tube

**va·moose** (va-MOOS) v. sl. (-moosed, -moos·ing) depart quickly

**vamp¹** n. woman who deliberately allures men —v. exploit (man) as vamp

**vamp²** n. something patched up; front part of shoe upper —vt. patch up, rework; Jazz improvise

**vam·pire** (VAM-pir) n. (in folklore) corpse that rises from dead to drink blood of the living —**vampire bat** one that sucks blood of animals

**van¹** n. large covered truck, esp. for furniture; smaller such vehicle for camping etc.

**van²** n. short for VANGUARD

**va·na·di·um** (və-NAY-dee-əm) n. metallic element used in manufacture of hard steel

**van·dal** (VAN-dl) n. one who wantonly and deliberately damages or destroys —**van'dal·ism** n. —**van'dal·ize** vt. (-ized, -iz·ing)

**vane** (vayn) n. weather vane; blade of propeller; fin on bomb etc.; sight on quadrant

**van·guard** (VAN-gahrd) n. leading, foremost group, position etc.

**va·nil·la** (və-NIL-ə) n. tropical climbing orchid; its seed(pod); essence of this for flavoring

**van·ish** vi. disappear; fade away

**van·i·ty** (VAN-i-tee) n. (pl. -ties) excessive pride or conceit; ostentation

**van·quish** (VANG-kwish) vt. subdue in battle; conquer, overcome

**vap′id** *adj.* flat, dull, insipid —**va-pid·i·ty** (və-PID-i-tee) *n.*

**va·por** (VAY-pər) *n.* gaseous form of a substance more familiar as liquid or solid; steam; mist; invisible moisture in air —**va′por·ize** (-pə-rīz) *v.* (-ized, -iz·ing) convert into, pass off in, vapor

**var′i·a·ble** *see* VARY

**var·i·cose** (VAR-i-kohs) *adj.* of vein, swollen, twisted

**var·i·e·gate** (VA-ree-i-gayt) *vt.* (-gat·ed, -gat·ing) diversify by patches of different colors —**var′i·e·gat·ed** *adj.* streaked, spotted, dappled

**va·ri·e·ty** (və-RĪ-i-tee) *n.* (*pl.* -ties) state of being varied or various; diversity; varied assortment; sort or kind

**var·i·o·rum** (va-ree-OR-əm) *adj./n.* (edition) with notes by various commentators

**var·i·ous** (VA-ree-əs) *adj.* manifold, diverse, of several kinds

**var·nish** (VAHR-nish) *n.* resinous solution put on a surface to make it hard and shiny —*vt.* apply varnish to

**var·y** (VAIR-ee) *v.* (var·ied, var·y·ing) (cause to) change, diversify, differ, deviate —**var·i·a·bil′i·ty** *n.* —**var′i·a·ble** *adj.* changeable; unsteady or fickle —*n.* something subject to variation —**var′i·ance** (-əns) *n.* state of discord, discrepancy —**var′i·ant** (-ənt) *adj.* different —*n.* difference in form; alternative form or reading —**var·i·a′tion** (-AY-shən) *n.* alteration; extent to which thing varies; modification —**var′ied** *adj.* diverse; modified; variegated

**vas** *n.* (*pl.* va·sa *pr.* VA·sə) vessel, tube carrying bodily fluid

**vas·cu·lar** (VAS-kyə-lər) *adj.* of, with vessels for conveying sap, blood *etc.*

**vase** (vayz) *n.* vessel, jar as ornament or for holding flowers

**vas·ec·to·my** (va-SEK-tə-mee) *n.* (*pl.* -mies) contraceptive measure of surgical removal of part of vas bearing sperm from testicle

**vas·sal** (VAS-əl) *n.* holder of land by feudal tenure; dependent

**vast** *adj.* (-er, -est) very large —**vast′ly** (-lee) *adv.* —**vast′ness** (-nis) *n.*

**vat** *n.* large tub, tank

**Vat·i·can** (VAT-i-kən) *n.* Pope's palace; papal authority

**vaude·ville** (VAWD-vil) *n.* theatrical entertainment with songs, juggling acts, dance *etc.*

**vault**[1] (vawlt) *n.* arched roof; arched apartment; cellar; burial chamber; place for storing valuables —*vt.* build with arched roof

**vault**[2] *v.* spring, jump over with the hands resting on something —*n.* such jump —**vaulting horse** padded apparatus for support of hands in gymnastics

**veal** (veel) *n.* calf flesh as food

**vec·tor** (VEK-tər) *n.* quantity (*eg* force) having both magnitude and direction; disease-carrying organism, *esp.* insect; compass direction, course

**veer** *vi.* change direction; change one's mind

**veg·e·ta·ble** (VEJ-tə-bəl) *n.* plant, *esp.* edible one; *inf.* person who has lost use of mental and physical faculties; dull person —*adj.* of, from, concerned with plants

**veg·e·tar·i·an** (vej-i-TAIR-ee-ən) *n.* one who does not eat meat —*adj.* —**veg·e·tar′i·an·ism** *n.*

**veg·e·tate** (VEJ-i-tayt) *vi.* (-tat·ed, -tat·ing) (of plants) grow, develop; (of person) live dull, unproductive life —**veg-**

**e·ta'tion** n. plants collectively; plants growing in a place; process of plant growth —**veg'e·ta·tive** (-tay-tiv) adj.

**ve·he·ment** (VEE-ə-mənt) adj. marked by intensity of feeling; vigorous; forcible —**ve'he·mence** (-məns) n.

**ve·hi·cle** (VEE-i-kəl) n. means of conveying; means of expression; medium —**ve·hic'u·lar** (-HIK-yə-lər) adj.

**veil** (vayl) n. light material to cover face or head; mask, cover —vt. cover with, as with, veil —**veiled** adj. disguised —**take the veil** become a nun

**vein** (vayn) n. tube in body taking blood to heart; rib of leaf or insect's wing; fissure in rock filled with ore; streak; distinctive trait, strain etc.; mood —vt. mark with streaks —**ve·nous** (VEE-nəs) adj. of veins

**veld, veldt** (both pr. velt) n. elevated grassland in S Afr.

**vel·lum** (VEL-əm) n. parchment of calf skin used for manuscripts or bindings; paper imitating this

**ve·loc·i·ty** (və-LOS-i-tee) n. (pl. -ties) rate of motion in given direction, esp. of inanimate things; speed

**ve·lour** (və-LUUR) n. fabric with velvety finish

**ve·lum** (VEE-ləm) n. Zool. (pl. -la pr. -lə) membranous covering or organ; soft palate

**vel·vet** (VEL-vit) n. silk or cotton fabric with thick, short pile —**vel·vet·een'** n. cotton fabric resembling velvet —**vel'vet·y** adj. of, like velvet; soft and smooth

**ve·nal** (VEEN-l) adj. guilty of taking, prepared to take, bribes; corrupt —**ve·nal'i·ty** n.

**vend** vt. sell —**ven·dor** (VEN-dər) n. —**vending machine** one that automatically dispenses goods when money is inserted

**ven·det·ta** (ven-DET-ə) n. bitter, prolonged feud

**ve·neer** (və-NEER) n. thin layer of fine wood; superficial appearance —vt. cover with veneer

**ven·er·a·ble** (VEN-ər-ə-bəl) adj. worthy of reverence —**ven·er·ate** (VEN-ə-rayt) vt. (-at·ed, -at·ing) look up to, respect, revere —**ven·er·a'tion** n.

**ve·ne·re·al** (və-NEER-ee-əl) adj. (of disease) transmitted by sexual intercourse; infected with venereal disease; of, relating to genitals or sexual intercourse

**ven·er·y** (VEN-ə-ree) n. obs. pursuit of sexual gratification

**ve·ne·tian** (və-NEE-shən) n. blind window blind made of thin horizontal slats arranged to turn so as to admit or exclude light

**ven·geance** (VEN-jəns) n. revenge; retribution for wrong done —**venge'ful** (-fəl) adj.

**ve·ni·al** (VEE-nee-əl) adj. pardonable

**ven·i·son** (VEN-ə-sən) n. flesh of deer as food

**ven·om** (VEN-əm) n. poison; spite —**ven'om·ous** (-əs) adj. poisonous

**venous** (VEE-nəs) see VEIN

**vent**[1] n. small hole or outlet —vt. give outlet to; utter; pour forth

**vent**[2] n. vertical slit in garment esp. at back of jacket

**ven·ti·late** (VEN-tl-ayt) vt. (-lat·ed, -lat·ing) supply with fresh air; bring into discussion —**ven'ti·la·tor** n.

**ven·tral** (VEN-trəl) adj. abdominal

**ven·tri·cle** (VEN-tri-kəl) n. cavity, hollow in body, esp. in heart or brain —**ven·tric'u·lar** (-TRIK-yə-lər) adj.

**ven·tril·o·quist** (ven-TRIL-ə-kwist) n. one who can so speak that the sounds seem to come from some other person or place —ven·tril'o·quism n.

ven·ture (VEN-chər) v. (-tured, -tur·ing) vt. expose to hazard; risk —vi. dare; have courage to do something or go somewhere —n. risky undertaking; speculative commercial undertaking —ven'ture·some (-səm) adj.

ven·ue (VEN-yoo) n. Law district in which case is tried; meeting place; location

Ve·nus (VEE-nəs) n. Roman goddess of love; planet between Earth and Mercury —Venus's flytrap insect-eating plant

ve·ra·cious (və-RAY-shəs) adj. truthful; true —ve·rac'i·ty (-RAS-i-tee) n.

ve·ran·da(h) (və-RAN-də) n. open or partly enclosed porch on outside of house

verb (vurb) n. part of speech used to express action or being —ver·bal (VUR-bəl) adj. of, by, or relating to words (spoken rather than written); of, like a verb —ver·bal·ize v. (-ized, -iz·ing) put into words, speak —ver'bal·ly adv. —ver·ba·tim (vər-BAY-tim) adv./adj. word for word, literal

ver·bi·age (VUR-bee-ij) n. excess of words —ver·bose (vər-BOHS) adj. wordy, long-winded —ver·bos'i·ty (-BOS-i-tee) n.

ver·dant (VUR-dnt) adj. green and fresh —ver·dure (-jər) n. greenery; freshness

ver·dict (VUR-dikt) n. decision of a jury; opinion reached after examination of facts

ver·di·gris (VUR-di-grees) n. green film on copper

verdure (VUR-jər) see VERDANT

verge (vurj) n. edge; brink —vi. (verged, verg·ing) come close to; be on the border of

ver·i·fy (VER-i-fi) vt. (-fied, -fy-ing) prove, confirm truth of; test accuracy of —ver'i·fi·a·ble adj.

ver·i·si·mil·i·tude n. (ver-ə-si-MIL-i-tood) appearance of truth; likelihood

ver·i·ta·ble (VER-i-tə-bəl) adj. actual, true, genuine —ver'i·ta·bly adv.

ver·i·ty (VER-i-tee) n. (pl. -ties) truth; reality; true assertion

ver·mi·cide (VUR-mə-sid) n. substance to destroy worms —ver'mi·form adj. shaped like a worm (eg vermiform appendix)

ver·mil·ion (vər-MIL-yən) adj./n. (of) bright red color or pigment

ver·min (VUR-min) n. pl. injurious animals, parasites etc.

ver·mouth (vər-MOOTH) n. wine flavored with aromatic herbs etc.

ver·nac·u·lar (vər-NAK-yə-lər) n. commonly spoken language or dialect of particular country or place —adj. of vernacular; native

ver·nal (VUR-nl) adj. of spring

ver·ni·er (VUR-nee-ər) n. sliding scale for obtaining fractional parts of subdivision of graduated scale

ver·sa·tile (VUR-sə-tl) adj. capable of or adapted to many different uses, skills etc.; liable to change —ver·sa·til'i·ty n.

verse (vurs) n. stanza or short subdivision of poem or the Bible; poetry; line of poetry —ver·si·fy (VUR-sə-fi) v. (-fied, -fy·ing) turn into verse —ver·si·fi·ca'tion n. —versed in skilled

ver·sion (VUR-zhən) n. description from certain point of view; translation; adaptation

ver·so (VUR-soh) n. back of sheet of printed paper, left-hand page

ver·sus (VUR-səs) prep. against

ver·te·bra (VUR-tə-brə) n. (pl. -brae pr. -bree) single section of backbone —ver'te·bral (-brəl) adj. of the spine —ver'te·brate

(-brit) n. animal with backbone —adj.

**ver·tex** (VUR-teks) n. (pl. -ti·ces pr. -tə-seez) summit

**ver·ti·cal** (VUR-ti-kəl) adj. at right angles to the horizon; upright; overhead

**ver·ti·go** (VUR-ti-goh) n. (pl. -goes) giddiness —ver·tig·i·nous (vər-TIJ-ə-nəs) adj. dizzy

**verve** (vurv) n. enthusiasm; spirit; energy, vigor

**ver·y** (VER-ee) adj. exact, ideal; same; complete; actual —adv. extremely; to great extent

**ves·i·cle** (VES-i-kəl) n. small blister, bubble, or cavity —ve·sic·u·lar (və-SIK-yə-lər adj.)

**ves·pers** (VES-pərz) n. pl. evening church service; evensong

**ves·sel** (VES-əl) n. any object used as a container, esp. for liquids; ship, large boat; tubular structure conveying liquids (eg blood) in body

**vest** n. sleeveless garment worn under jacket or coat —vt. place; bestow; confer; clothe —vest'·ment (-mənt) n. robe or official garment —vested interest strong personal interest in particular state of affairs

**ves·tal** (VES-tl) adj. pure, chaste

**ves·ti·bule** (VES-tə-byool) n. entrance hall, lobby

**ves·tige** (VES-tij) n. small trace, amount —ves·tig'i·al (-TIJ-ee-əl) adj.

**ves·try** (VES-tree) n. (pl. -tries) room in church for keeping vestments, holding meetings etc.

**vet** n. short for VETERAN, VETERINARIAN —vt. (vet·ted, vet·ting) examine; check

**vet·er·an** (VET-ər-ən) n. one who has served a long time, esp. in fighting services —adj. longserving

ee·ən) —n. one qualified to treat animal ailments —vet'er·i·nar·y (-ner-ee) adj. of, concerning the health of animals —n. veterinarian

**ve·to** (VEE-toh) n. (pl. -toes) power of rejecting piece of legislation, or preventing it from coming into effect; any prohibition —vt. (-toed, -to·ing) enforce veto against; forbid with authority

**vex** (veks) vt. annoy; distress —vex·a'tion n. cause of irritation; state of distress —vex·a'tious adj. —vexed adj. cross; annoyed; much discussed

**Vi** Chem. virginium

**vi·a** (VĪ-ə) adv. by way of

**vi·a·ble** (VĪ-ə-bəl) adj. practicable; able to live and grow independently —vi·a·bil'i·ty n.

**vi·a·duct** (VĪ-ə-dukt) n. bridge over valley for a road or railroad

**vi·al** (VĪ-əl) n. small bottle for medicine etc.

**vi·ands** (VĪ-əndz) n. pl. food esp. delicacies

**vi·bra·harp** (VĪ-brə-hahrp) n. musical instrument like xylophone, but with electronic resonators, that produces a gentle vibrato (also vi'bra·phone)

**vi·brate** (VĪ-brayt) v. (-brat·ed, -brat·ing) (cause to) move to and fro rapidly and continuously; give off (light or sound) by vibration —vi. oscillate; quiver —vi'brant (-brənt) adj. throbbing; vibrating; appearing vigorous, lively —vi·bra'tion n. a vibrating —pl. inf. instinctive feelings about a place, person etc. —vi·bra·to (vi-BRAH-toh) n. (pl. -os) vibrating effect in music

**vic·ar** (VIK-ər) n. member of clergy in charge of parish —vic'ar·age (-ij) n. vicar's house —vi·car·i·al (vi-KAIR-ee-əl) adj. of vicar

**vi·car·i·ous** (vī-KAIR-ee-əs) adj.

obtained, enjoyed or undergone through sympathetic experience of another's experiences; suffered, done *etc.* as substitute for another

**vice** (vīs) *n.* evil or immoral habit or practice; criminal immorality *esp.* prostitution; fault, imperfection

**vice-** (*comb. form*) in place of, second to, as in *vice-chairman, viceroy etc.* These are not given here where meaning can be inferred from simple word

**vice-roy** (VĪS-roi) *n.* ruler acting for king in province or dependency (**vice-reine** *pr.* -rayn *n. fem.*)

**vi-ce ver-sa** (VĪ-sə VUR-sə) *Lat.* conversely, the other way round

**vi-cin-i-ty** (vi-SIN-i-tee) *n.* (*pl.* -ties) neighborhood

**vi-cious** (VISH-əs) *adj.* wicked, cruel; ferocious, dangerous; leading to vice

**vi-cis-si-tude** (vi-SIS-i-tood) *n.* change of fortune —*pl.* ups and downs of fortune

**vic-tim** (VIK-tim) *n.* person or thing killed, injured *etc.* as result of another's deed, or accident, circumstances *etc.*; person cheated; sacrifice —**vic-tim-i-za'-tion** (-ZAY-shən) *n.* —**vic'ti-mize** *vt.* (-mized, -miz-ing) punish unfairly; make victim of

**vic-tor** (VIK-tər) *n.* conqueror; winner —**vic-to-ri-ous** (vik-TOR-ee-əs) *adj.* winning; triumphant —**vic'to-ry** (-tə-ree) *n.* (*pl.* -ries) winning of battle *etc.*

**vict-ual** (VIT-l) *n.* (*usu. in pl.*) food —*v.* (-ualed, -ual-ing) supply with or obtain food

**vi-cu-na** (vī-KOO-nə) *n.* S Amer. animal like llama; fine, light cloth made from its wool

**vi-de** (VĪ-dee) *Lat.* see —**vide in-**fra (IN-frə) see below —**vide supra** (SOO-prə) see above

**vi-de-li-cet** (vi-DEL-ə-sit) *Lat.* namely

**vid-e-o** (VID-ee-oh) *adj.* relating to or used in transmission or production of TV image —*n.* apparatus for recording TV programs; film *etc.* on videocassette for viewing on this apparatus —**vid'e-o-cas-sette** cassette containing videotape —**video-cassette recorder** tape recorder for vision and sound signals, used for recording and playing back TV programs and films on cassette —**video game** any of various games played on video screen using electronic control —**vid'e-o-porn** *n. inf.* film, *usu.* made for video, that is explicitly pornographic —**video-tape** magnetic tape on which to record TV program —**videotape recorder** tape recorder for signals for TV broadcast —**vid'e-o-tex** *n.* means of providing written or graphical representation of computerized information on TV screen for information retrieval, shopping at home *etc.*

**vie** (vī) *vi.* (vied, vy-ing) (*with* with *or* for) contend, compete against or for someone, something

**view** (vyoo) *n.* survey by eyes or mind; range of vision; picture; scene; opinion; purpose —*vt.* look at; survey; consider —**view'er** *n.* one who views; one who watches TV; optical device to assist viewing of photographic slides —**view'find-er** *n.* device on camera enabling user to see what will be included in photograph —**view'point** *n.* way of regarding a subject; position commanding view of landscape

**view·da·ta** (VYOO-day-tə) *n.* videotex service in which consumer is linked to a computer by telephone or television cable

**vig·il** (VIJ-əl) *n.* a keeping awake, watch; eve of church festival —**vig'i·lance** (-ləns) *n.* —**vig'i·lant** (-lənt) *adj.* watchful, alert

**vig·i·lan·te** (vij-ə-LAN-tee) *n.* one (*esp.* as member of group) who unofficially takes on duty of enforcing law

**vi·gnette** (vin-YET) *n.* short literary essay, sketch; photograph or portrait with the background shaded off

**vig·or** (VIG-ər) *n.* force, strength; energy, activity —**vig'or·ous** (-əs) *adj.* strong; energetic; flourishing

**Vi·king** (VI-king) *n.* medieval Scandinavian seafarer, raider, settler

**vile** (vil) *adj.* (vil·er, vil·est) very wicked, shameful; disgusting; despicable —**vil·i·fy** (VIL-ə-fi) *vt.* (-fied, -fy·ing) speak ill of; slander —**vil·i·fi·ca·tion** (-fi-KAY-shən) *n.*

**vil·la** (VIL-ə) *n.* large, luxurious, country house

**vil·lage** (VIL-ij) *n.* small group of houses in country area

**vil·lain** (VIL-ən) *n.* wicked person; *inf.* mischievous person —**vil'lain·ous** (-əs) *adj.* wicked; vile —**vil'lain·y** *n.* (*pl.* -lain·ies)

**vim** *n.* force, energy

**vin·ai·grette** (vin-ə-GRET) *n.* small bottle of smelling salts; type of salad dressing —*adj.* (of food) served with vinaigrette

**vin·di·cate** (VIN-di-kayt) *vt.* (-cat·ed, -cat·ing) clear of charges; justify; establish the truth or merit of —**vin·di·ca'tion** *n.*

**vin·dic·tive** (vin-DIK-tiv) *adj.* revengeful; inspired by resentment

**vine** (vin) *n.* climbing plant bearing grapes —**vine'yard** (VIN-yərd) *n.* plantation of vines —**vin'tage** (-tij) *n.* gathering of the grapes; the yield; wine of particular year; time of origin —*adj.* best and most typical —**vint'ner** (-nər) *n.* dealer in wine

**vin·e·gar** (VIN-i-gər) *n.* acid liquid obtained from wine and other alcoholic liquors —**vin'e·gar·y** *adj.* like vinegar; sour; bad-tempered

**vi·nyl** (VIn-l) *n.* plastic material with variety of domestic and industrial uses

**vi·ol** (VI-əl) *n.* early stringed instrument preceding violin —**vi·o·la**[1] (vee-OH-lə) *n.* large violin with lower range —**vi·o·la**[2] (vI-OH-lə) *n.* single-colored variety of pansy

**vi·o·late** (VI-ə-layt) *vt.* (-lat·ed, -lat·ing) break (law, agreement *etc.*), infringe; rape; outrage, desecrate —**vi'o·la·ble** (-lə-bəl) *adj.* —**vi·o·la'tion** (-LAY-shən) *n.*

**vi·o·lent** (VI-ə-lənt) *adj.* marked by, due to, extreme force, passion or fierceness; of great force; intense —**vi·o·lence** (-lins) *n.*

**vi·o·let** (VI-ə-lit) *n.* plant with small bluish-purple or white flowers; the flower; bluish-purple color —*adj.* of this color

**vi·o·lin** (vI-ə-LIN) *n.* small four-stringed musical instrument —**vi·o·lin'ist** *n.* —**vi·o·lon·cel·lo** (vee-ə-lən-CHEL-oh) *n.* *see* CELLO

**vi·per** (VI-pər) *n.* venomous snake

**vi·ra·go** (vi-RAH-goh) *n.* (*pl.* -goes, -gos) abusive woman

**vir·gin** (VUR-jin) *n.* one who has not had sexual intercourse —*adj.* without experience of sexual intercourse; unsullied; fresh; (of land) untilled —**vir·gin·al** (VUR-jə-nl) *adj.* of, like virgin —*n.* type of spinet —**vir·gin'i·ty** *n.*

**vir·ile** (VIR-əl) *adj.* (of male) capable of copulation or procreation; strong, forceful —**vi·ril′i·ty** (-RIL·i·tee) n.

**vi·rol·o·gy** (vī-ROL-ə-jee) see VIRUS

**vir·tu·al** (VUR-choo-əl) adj. so in effect, though not in appearance or name —**vir′tu·al·ly** adv. practically, almost

**vir·tue** (VUR-choo) n. moral goodness; good quality; merit; inherent power —**vir′tu·ous** (-əs) adj. morally good; chaste

**vir·tu·o·so** (vur-choo-OH-soh) n. (pl. -sos, -si pr. -see) one with special skill, esp. in a fine art —**vir·tu·os′i·ty** n. great technical skill, esp. in a fine art as music

**vir·u·lent** (VIR-yə-lənt) adj. very infectious, poisonous etc.; malicious

**vi·rus** (VĪ-rəs) n. various submicroscopic organisms, some causing disease —**vi·rol′o·gy** n. study of viruses

**vi·sa** (VEEZ-ə) n. (pl. -sas) endorsement on passport permitting the bearer to travel into country of issuing government —**visa** vt. (-saed, -sa·ing) approve visa for (someone)

**vis·age** (VIZ-ij) n. face

**vis-a-vis** (vee-zə-VEE) Fr. in relation to, regarding; opposite to

**vis·cer·a** (VIS-ər-ə) n. pl. large internal organs of body, esp. of abdomen —**visc′er·al** (-əl) adj.

**vis·cid** (VIS-id) adj. sticky, of a consistency like molasses —**vis·cid′i·ty** n.

**vis·cous** (VIS-kəs) adj. thick and sticky —**vis·cos′i·ty** n. (pl. -ties)

**vise** (vis) n. appliance with screw jaw for holding things while working on them

**vis·i·ble** (VIZ-ə-bəl) adj. that can be seen —**vis·i·bil′i·ty** n. degree of clarity of atmosphere, esp. for navigation —**vis′i·bly** adv.

**vi·sion** (VIZH-ən) n. sight; insight;

dream; phantom; imagination —**vi′sion·ar·y** (-er-ee) adj. marked by vision; impractical —n. (pl. -ar·ies) mystic; impractical person

**vis·it** (VIZ-it) v. go, come and see, stay temporarily with (someone) —n. stay; call at person's home etc.; official call —**vis·it·a′tion** (-ə-TAY-shən) n. formal visit or inspection; affliction or plague —**vis′i·tor** n.

**vi·sor** (VĪ-zər) n. front part of helmet made to move up and down before the face; eyeshade, esp. on car; peak on cap

**vis·ta** (VIS-tə) n. view, esp. distant view

**vis·u·al** (VIZH-oo-əl) adj. of sight; visible —**vis′u·al·ize** vt. (-ized, -iz·ing) form mental image of —**vis·u·al·i·za′tion** n.

**vi·tal** (VĪT-l) adj. necessary to, affecting life; lively, animated; essential; highly important —**vi′tals** n. pl. vital organs of body —**vi·tal′i·ty** n. life, vigor —**vi′tal·ize** (-ə-līz) vt. (-ized, -iz·ing) give life to; lend vigor to —**vi′tal·ly** adv.

**vi·ta·min** (VĪ-tə-min) n. any of group of substances occurring in foodstuffs and essential to health

**vi·ti·ate** (VISH-ee-ayt) vt. (-at·ed, -at·ing) spoil; deprive of efficacy; invalidate —**vi·ti·a′tion** n.

**vit·re·ous** (VI-tree-əs) adj. of glass; glassy —**vit′ri·fy** (VI-trə-fī) v. (-fied, -fy·ing) convert into glass, or glassy substance —**vit·ri·fi·ca′tion** n.

**vit·ri·ol** (VI-tree-əl) n. sulfuric acid; caustic speech —**vit·ri·ol′ic** adj.

**vi·tu·per·ate** (vī-TOO-pə-rayt) vt. (-at·ed, -at·ing) abuse in words, revile —**vi·tu′per·a·tive** adj.

**vi·va·cious** (vi-VAY-shəs) adj.

lively, gay, sprightly —**vi·vac'i·ty** (-VAS-i-tee) n.

**vi·va vo·ce** (VĪ-və VOH-see) Lat. by word of mouth —n. in European universities, oral examination

**viv'id** adj. bright, intense; clear; lively, animated; graphic —**viv'id·ly** adv.

**viv·i·fy** (VIV-ə-fī) vt. (-fied, -fy-ing) animate, inspire

**vi·vip·a·rous** (vī-VIP-ər-əs) adj. bringing forth young alive

**viv·i·sec·tion** (viv-ə-SEK-shən) n. dissection of, or operating on, living animals —**viv·i·sec'tion·ist** n.

**vix·en** (VIK-sən) n. female fox; spiteful woman —**vix'en·ish** adj.

**viz.** short for VIDELICET, namely

**vi·zier** (vi-ZEER) n. (formerly) high official in some Muslim countries

**vo·cab·u·lar·y** (voh-KAB-yə-lair-ee) n. (pl. -lar·ies) list of words, usu. in alphabetical order; stock of words used in particular language etc.

**vo·cal** (VOH-kəl) adj. of, with, or giving out voice; outspoken, articulate —n. piece of popular music that is sung —**vo'cal·ist** n. singer —**vo'cal·ize** vt. (-ized, -iz·ing) utter with voice

**vo·ca·tion** (voh-KAY-shən) n. (urge, inclination, predisposition to) particular career, profession etc. —**vo·ca'tion·al** (-əl) adj.

**voc·a·tive** (VOK-ə-tiv) n. in some languages, case of nouns used in addressing a person

**vo·cif·er·ate** (voh-SIF-ə-rayt) v. (-at·ed, -at·ing) exclaim, cry out —**vo·cif'er·ous** (-əs) adj. shouting, noisy

**vod·ka** (VOD-kə) n. Russian spirit distilled from grain, potatoes etc.

**vogue** (vohg) n. fashion, style; popularity

**voice** (vois) n. sound given out by person in speaking, singing etc.; quality of the sound; expressed opinion; (right to) share in discussion; verbal forms proper to relation of subject and action —vt. (voiced, voic·ing) give utterance to, express —**voice'less** (-lis) adj.

**void** adj. empty; destitute; not legally binding —n. empty space —vt. make ineffectual or invalid; empty out

**vol·a·tile** (VOL-ə-tl) adj. evaporating quickly; lively; fickle, changeable —**vol·a·til'i·ty** n. —**vol'a·ti·lize** (-lized, -liz·ing) v. (cause to) evaporate

**vol·ca·no** (vol-KAY-noh) n. (pl. -noes, -nos) hole in Earth's crust through which lava, ashes, smoke etc. are discharged; mountain so formed —**vol·can'ic** adj. —**vol·can·ol'o·gy** (-kə-NOL-ə-jee) n. study of volcanoes and volcanic phenomena, vulcanology

**vole** (vohl) n. small rodent

**vo·li·tion** (voh-LISH-ən) n. act, power of willing; exercise of the will

**vol·ley** (VOL-ee) n. (pl. -leys) simultaneous discharge of weapons or missiles; rush of oaths, questions etc.; Tennis flight, return of moving ball before it touches ground —v. (-leyed, -ley·ing) discharge; utter; fly, strike etc. in volley —**vol'ley·ball** n. team game where large ball is hit by hand over high net

**volt** (vohlt) n. unit of electric potential —**volt'age** (-ij) n. electric potential difference expressed in volts —**volt'me·ter** n.

**volte-face** (vohlt-FAHS) Fr. n. (same form in pl.) complete reversal of opinion or direction

**vol·u·ble** (VOL-yə-bəl) adj. talking

easily, readily and at length
—**vol·u·bly** *adv.* —**vol·u·bil'i·ty** *n.*

**vol·ume** (VOL-yəm) *n.* space occupied; bulk, mass; amount; power, fullness of voice or sound; control on radio *etc.* for adjusting this; book; part of book bound in one cover —**vol·u·met'ric** *adj.* pert. to measurement by volume —**vo·lu·mi·nous** (və-LOO-mə-nəs) *adj.* bulky, copious

**vol·un·ta·ry** (VOL-ən-ter-ee) *adj.* having, done by free will; done without payment; supported by freewill contributions; spontaneous —*n.* (*pl.* **-ta·ries**) organ solo in church service —**vol·un·tar'i·ly** *adv.* —**vol·un·teer'** *n.* one who offers service, joins force *etc.* of own free will —*v.* offer oneself or one's services

**vo·lup·tu·ous** (və-LUP-choo-əs) *adj.* of, contributing to pleasures of the senses —**vol·up'tu·a·ry** (-er-ee) *n.* (*pl.* **-ar·ies**) one given to luxury and sensual pleasures

**vo·lute** (və-LOOT) *n.* spiral or twisting turn, form or object

**vom·it** *v.* eject (contents of stomach) through mouth —*n.* matter vomited

**voo·doo** *n.* (*pl.* **-doos**) practice of black magic, *esp.* in W Indies, witchcraft —*vt.* (**-dooed, -doo·ing**) affect by voodoo

**vo·ra·cious** (vaw-RAY-shəs) *adj.* greedy, ravenous —**vo·rac'i·ty** (-RAS-i-tee) *n.*

**vor·tex** (VOR-teks) *n.* (*pl.* **-ti·ces** *pr.* -tə-seez) whirlpool; whirling motion

**vo·ta·ry** (VOH-tə-ree) *n.* (*pl.* **-ta·ries**) one vowed to service or pursuit —**vo'tive** (-tiv) *adj.* given, consecrated by vow

**vote** (voht) *n.* formal expression of choice; individual pronouncement; right to give it, in question or election; result of voting; that which is given or allowed by vote —*v.* (**vot·ed, vot·ing**) express, declare opinion, choice, preference *etc.* by vote; authorize, enact *etc.* by vote

**vouch** (vowch) *vi.* (*usu.* *with for*) guarantee, make oneself responsible for —**vouch'er** *n.* document proving correctness of item in accounts, or to establish facts; ticket as substitute for cash —**vouch·safe'** (-SAYF) *vt.* (**-safed, -saf·ing**) agree, condescend to grant or do something

**vow** *n.* solemn promise, *esp.* religious one —*vt.* promise, threaten by vow

**vow·el** (VOW-əl) *n.* any speech sound pronounced without stoppage or friction of the breath; letter standing for such sound, as *a, e, i, o, u*

**voy·age** (VOI-ij) *n.* journey, *esp.* long one, by sea or air —*vi.* (**-aged, -ag·ing**) make voyage —**voy'ag·er** *n.*

**vo·yeur** (vwah-YUR) *n.* one obtaining sexual pleasure by watching sexual activities of others

**vul·can·ize** (VUL-kə-nīz) *vt.* (**-ized, -iz·ing**) treat (rubber) with sulfur at high temperature to increase its durability —**vul'can·ite** *n.* rubber so hardened —**vul·can·i·za'tion** (-nə-ZAY-) *n.* —**vul·can·ol'o·gy** *see* VOLCANOLOGY

**vul·gar** (VUL-gər) *adj.* offending against good taste; coarse; common —**vul·gar'i·an** (-GAIR-ee-ən) *n.* vulgar (rich) person —**vul'gar·ism** *n.* coarse, obscene word, phrase —**vul·gar'i·ty** *n.* (*pl.* **-ties**) —**vul·gar·i·za'tion** (-gə-ri-ZAY-shən) *n.* —**vul'gar·ize** *vt.* (**-ized, -iz·ing**) make vulgar or too common

**Vul·gate** (VUL-gayt) *n.* fourth-century Latin version of the Bible

**vul·ner·a·ble** (VUL-nər-ə-bəl) *adj.* capable of being physically or emotionally wounded or hurt; exposed, open to attack, persuasion *etc.*

**vul·pine** (VUL-pin) *adj.* of foxes; foxy

**vul·ture** (VUL-chər) *n.* large bird that feeds on carrion —**vul'turous** (-əs) *adj.* of vulture; rapacious

**vul·va** (VUL-və) *n.* (*pl.* -vas) external genitals of human female

**vy·ing** (VĪ-ing) *pr. p. of* VIE

# W

**W** *Chem.* tungsten

**wad** (wod) *n.* small pad of fibrous material; thick roll of paper money; sum of money —*vt.* (**wad·ded, wad·ding**) line, pad, stuff *etc.* with wad —**wadding** *n.* stuffing

**wad·dle** (WOD-l) *vi.* (-dled, -dling) walk like duck —*n.* this gait

**wade** (wayd) *vi.* (**wad·ed, wad·ing**) walk through something that hampers movement, *esp.* water; proceed with difficulty —**wad'er** *n.* person or bird that wades —*pl.* angler's high waterproof boots

**wa·di** (WO-dee) *n.* (*pl.* -dis) in the East, watercourse that is dry except in wet season

**wa·fer** (WAY-fər) *n.* thin, crisp biscuit; thin slice of anything; thin disk of unleavened bread used in the Eucharist

**waf·fle¹** (WOF-əl) *n.* kind of batter cake with gridlike design

**waf·fle²** *vi. inf.* (-fled, -fling) speak, write in vague wordy

manner —*n. inf.* vague speech *etc.*; nonsense

**waft** (wahft) *vt.* convey smoothly through air or water —*n.* breath of wind; odor, whiff

**wag** *v.* (**wagged, wag·ging**) (cause to) move rapidly from side to side —*n.* instance of wagging; humorous, witty person —**wag'gish** *adj.*

**wage** (wayj) *n.* payment for work done (*oft. in pl.*) —*vt.* (**waged, wag·ing**) carry on

**wa·ger** (WAY-jər) *n./vt.* bet

**wag·on** (WAG-ən) *n.* four-wheeled vehicle for heavy loads —**off the wagon** *sl.* drinking alcoholic beverages again —**on the wagon** *sl.* abstaining from alcoholic beverages

**waif** (wayf) *n.* homeless person, *esp.* child

**wail** (wayl) *v.* cry out, lament —*n.* mournful cry

**wain·scot** (WAYN-skət) *n.* wooden lining of walls of room —*vt.* (-scot·ed, -scot·ing) line thus

**waist** (wayst) *n.* part of body between hips and ribs; various narrow central parts —**waistcoat** (WES-kət) *n.* Brit. vest —**waist'line** *n.* line, size of waist (of person, garment)

**wait** (wayt) *v.* stay in one place, remain inactive in expectation (of something); be prepared (for something); delay —*vi.* serve in restaurant *etc.* —*n.* act or period of waiting —**wait'er** *n.* attendant serving diners at hotel, restaurant *etc.* (**wait·ress** (WAY-tris) *fem.*); one who waits

**waive** (wayv) *vt.* (**waived, waiving**) forgo; not to insist on —**waiv'er** *n.* (written statement of) this act

**wake¹** (wayk) *v.* (**waked** *or* **woke, waked** *or* **wok·en, wak·ing**) rouse from sleep; stir up —*n.*

vigil; watch beside corpse —**wak·en** (WAY-kən) v. wake —**wake·ful** (-fəl) adj.

**wake**[2] n. track or path left by anything that has passed, as track of turbulent water behind ship

**walk** (wawk) v. (cause, assist to) move, travel on foot at ordinary pace —vt. cross, pass through by walking; escort, conduct by walking —n. act, instance of walking; path or other place or route for walking; manner of walking; occupation, career —**walk'er** n. one who walks; framework of metal for support while walking —**walk·ie-talk·ie** (WAW·kee-TAW·kee) n. portable radio set containing both transmission and receiver units —**walking stick** stick, cane carried while walking —**Walk·man** (WAWK·man) n. R small portable cassette player, radio etc. equipped with headphones —**walk'out** n. strike; act of leaving as a protest —**walk'o·ver** n. unopposed or easy victory

**wall** (wawl) n. structure of brick, stone etc. serving as fence, side of building etc.; surface of one; anything resembling this —vt. enclose with wall; block up with wall —**wall'flow·er** n. garden flower, often growing on walls; at dance, person who remains seated for lack of partner —**wall'pa·per** n. paper, usu. patterned, to cover interior walls

**wal·la·by** (WOL-ə-bee) n. (pl. -bies) Aust. marsupial similar to and smaller than kangaroo

**wal·let** (WOL-it) n. small folding case, esp. for paper money, documents etc.

**wall-eyed** (WAWL-īd) adj. having eyes turned outward in squint; having eyes with pale irises

**wal·lop** (WOL-əp) vt. inf. beat soundly; strike hard —n. stroke or blow —**wal'lop·er** n. inf. one who wallops —**wal'lop·ing** n. inf. thrashing —adj./adv. inf. very, great(ly)

**wal·low** (WOL-oh) vi. roll (in liquid or mud); revel (in) —n.

**wal·nut** (WAWL-nut) n. large nut with crinkled shell splitting easily into two halves; the tree; its wood

**wal·rus** (WAWL-rəs) n. large sea mammal with long tusks

**waltz** (wawlts) n. ballroom dance; music for it —v.

**wam·pum** (WOM-pəm) n. beads made of shells, formerly used by N Amer. Indians as money and for ornament

**wan** (won) adj. (wan·ner, wan·nest) pale, sickly complexioned, pallid

**wand** (wond) n. stick, usu. straight and slender, esp. as carried by magician etc.

**wan·der** (WON-dər) v. roam, ramble —vi. go astray, deviate —n. —**wan'der·er** n. —**wan'der·lust** n. irrepressible urge to wander or travel

**wane** (wayn) vi./n. (waned, wan·ing) decline; (of moon) decrease in apparent size

**wan·gle** (WANG-gəl) vt. inf. (-gled, -gling) manipulate, manage in skillful way

**want** (wont) v. desire; lack —n. desire; need; deficiency —**want'ed** (-id) adj. being sought, esp. by the police —**want'ing** adj. lacking; below standard

**wan·ton** (WON-tən) adj. dissolute; without motive, thoughtless; unrestrained —n. wanton person

**war** (wor) n. fighting between nations; state of hostility; conflict, contest —vi. (warred, war·ring) make war —**war'like** adj. of, for war; fond of war —**war·ri·or** (WOR-ee-ər) n. fighter —**war cry** cry used by attacking troops in war; distinctive word, phrase used by political party etc. —**war'fare** (-fair) n. hostilities —**war'head** (-hed) n. part of missile etc. containing explosives —**war·mon·ger** (WOR-mung-gər) n. one fostering, encouraging war —**war'ship** n. vessel armed, armored for naval warfare

**war·ble** (WOR-bəl) vi. (-bled, -bling) sing with trills —**war·bler** (-blər) n. person or bird that warbles; any of various kinds of small songbirds

**ward** (word) n. division of city, hospital etc.; minor under care of guardian; guardianship; curved bar in lock, groove in key that prevents incorrectly cut key opening lock —**ward'room** n. officers' mess on warship —**ward** off avert, repel

**war·den** (WOR-dn) n. person, officer in charge of prison

**ward·robe** (WOR-drohb) n. piece of furniture for hanging clothes in; person's supply of clothes; costumes of theatrical company

**ware** (wair) n. goods; articles collectively —pl. goods for sale; commodities; merchandise —**ware'house** n. storehouse for goods prior to distribution and sale —vt. store for future shipment or use

**war·lock** (WOR-lok) n. wizard, sorcerer

**warm** (worm) adj. moderately hot; serving to maintain heat; affectionate; ardent; earnest; hearty; (of color) having yellow or red for a basis —v. make, become warm —**warm'ly** adv. —**warmth** n. mild heat; cordiality; vehemence, anger

**warn** (worn) vt. put on guard; caution, admonish; give advance information to; notify authoritatively —**warn'ing** n. hint of harm etc.; admonition; advance notice of

**warp** (worp) v. (cause to) twist (out of shape); pervert or be perverted —n. state, condition of being warped; lengthwise threads on loom

**war·rant** (WOR-ənt) n. authority; document giving authority —vt. guarantee; authorize, justify —**war·ran·tee'** n. person given warranty —**war'ran·tor** (-tər) n. person, company giving warranty —**war'ran·ty** (-tee) n. (pl. -ties) guarantee of quality of goods; security —**warrant officer** officer in certain armed services holding rank between commissioned and noncommissioned officer

**war·ren** (WOR-ən) n. (burrows inhabited by) colony of rabbits

**warrior** (WOR-ee-ər) n. see WAR

**wart** (wort) n. small hard growth on skin —**wart hog** kind of Afr. wild pig

**war·y** (WAIR-ee) adj. (war·i·er, war·i·est) watchful, cautious, alert —**war'i·ly** adv.

**was** (wuz, woz) pt. first and third person sing. of BE

**wash** (wosh) v. clean (oneself, clothes etc.) esp. with water, soap etc. —vi. be washable; inf. be able to be proved true —vt. move, be moved by water; flow, sweep over, against —n. act of washing; clothes washed at one time; sweep of water, esp. set up by moving ship; thin coat of color —**wash'a·ble** adj. capable of being washed without damage etc. —**wash'er** n. one who, that which, washes; ring put under a nut —**wash'ing** n. clothes to be washed —**wash'y** adj. (wash·i·er, wash·i·est) dilute; watery; insipid

—**wash'out** n. rainout; *inf.* complete failure

**wasp** (wosp) n. striped stinging insect resembling bee —**wasp'ish** adj. irritable, snappish —**wasp waist** very small waist

**waste** (wayst) v. (**wast·ed, wast·ing**) —vt. expend uselessly, use extravagantly; fail to take advantage of; lay desolate —vi. dwindle; pine away —n. act of wasting; what is wasted; desert —adj. worthless, useless; desert; wasted —**wast'age** (WAY-stij) n. loss by use or decay; losses as result of wastefulness —**waste'ful** (-fəl) adj. extravagant —**waste'fulness** (-nis) n. —**waste** product discarded material in manufacturing process; excreted urine, feces —**wast·rel** (WAY-strəl) n. wasteful person, spendthrift

**watch** (woch) vt. observe closely; guard —vi. wait expectantly (for); be on watch —n. portable timepiece for wrist, pocket *etc.*; state of being on the lookout; guard; spell of duty —**watch'ful** (-fəl) adj. —**watch'mak·er** n. one skilled in making and repairing watches —**watch'man** (-mən) n. (pl. **-men**) person guarding building *etc.*, *esp.* at night —**watch'word** (-wurd) n. password; rallying cry

**wa·ter** (WAW-tər) n. transparent, colorless, odorless, tasteless liquid, substance of rain, river *etc.*; body of water; river; lake; sea; tear; urine —vt. put water on or into; irrigate or provide with water —vi. salivate; (of eyes) fill with tears; take in or obtain water —**wa'ter·y** adj. —**water buffalo** oxlike Asian animal —**water closet** (KLOZ-it) toilet —**wa'ter·col·or** n. pigment mixed with water; painting in this —**wa'ter·course** n. stream

—**wa'ter·cress** n. plant growing in clear ponds and streams —**wa'ter·fall** n. perpendicular descent of waters of river, stream —**wa'ter·logged** adj. saturated, filled with water —**wa'ter·mark** n. faint translucent design stamped on substance of sheet of paper —**wa'ter·proof** adj. not letting water through —v. make waterproof —**wa'ter·shed** n. area drained by a river; important division between conditions, phases —**water-ski·ing** n. sport of riding over water on ski towed by speedboat —**water sports** various sports, as swimming, windsurfing, that take place in or on water —**water·tight** (-tīt) adj. so fitted as to prevent water entering or escaping; with no loopholes or weak points

**watt** (wot) n. unit of electric power —**watt'age** (-ij) n. electric power expressed in watts

**wat·tle** (WOT-l) n. fleshy pendent lobe on head or neck of certain birds, *eg* turkey

**wave** (wayv) v. (**waved, wav·ing**) move to and fro, as hand in greeting or farewell; signal by waving; give, take shape of waves (as hair *etc.*) —n. ridge and trough on water *etc.*; act, gesture of waving; vibration, as in radio waves, of electric and magnetic forces alternating in direction; prolonged spell of something; upsurge; wavelike shapes in the hair *etc.* —**wav'y** (-ee) adj. (**wav·i·er, wav·i·est**) —**wave'length** n. distance between same points of two successive sound waves

**wav·er** (WAY-vər) vi. hesitate, be irresolute; be, become unsteady

**wax**[1] (waks) n. yellow, soft, pliable material made by bees; this or similar substance used for sealing, making candles *etc.*; waxy secretion of ear —*vt.* (waxed, wax·ing) put wax on —wax′y (-ee) *adj.* (wax·i·er, wax·i·est) like wax —wax′wing *n.* small songbird —wax′work (-wurk) *n.* lifelike figure, *esp.* of famous person, reproduced in wax

**wax²** *vi.* (waxed, wax·ing) grow, increase

**way** *n.* manner; method; means; track; direction; path; passage; course; route; progress; state or condition —way′far·er (-fair·ər) *n.* traveler, *esp.* on foot —way′lay *vt.* (-laid, -lay·ing) lie in wait for and accost, attack —way′side *n.* side or edge of a road —*adj.* —way′ward (-wərd) *adj.* capricious, perverse, willful —way′ward·ness (-nis) *n.*

**we** (wee) *pron.* first person nominative plural

**weak** (week) *adj.* (-er, -est) lacking strength; feeble; fragile; defenseless; easily influenced; faint —weak·en (WEE-kən) *v.* —weak′ling *n.* feeble creature —weak′ly *adj.* weak; sickly —*adv.*

**wealth** (welth) *n.* riches; abundance —wealth′y *adj.* (wealth·i·er, wealth·i·est)

**wean** (ween) *vt.* accustom to food other than mother's milk; win over, coax away from

**weap·on** (WEP·ən) *n.* implement to fight with; anything used to get the better of an opponent —wea′pon·ry (-ree) *n.*

**wear** (wair) *v.* (wore, worn, wear·ing) —*vt.* have on the body; show; produce (hole *etc.*) by rubbing *etc.*; harass or weaken —*vi.* last; become impaired by use; (of time) pass slowly —*n.* act of wearing; things to wear; damage

caused by use; ability to resist effects of constant use

**wea·ry** (WEER·ee) *adj.* (-ri·er, -ri·est) tired, exhausted, jaded; tiring; tedious —*v.* (-ried, -ry·ing) make, become weary —wea′ri·ness (-ree·nis) *n.* —wea′ri·some (-ree·səm) *adj.* causing weariness

**wea·sel** (WEE·zəl) *n.* small carnivorous mammal with long body and short legs

**weath·er** (WETH·ər) *n.* day-to-day meteorological conditions, *esp.* temperature, cloudiness *etc.* of a place —*adj.* toward the wind —*vt.* affect by weather; endure; resist; come safely through; sail to windward of —weath′er·vane (-vain) *n.* rotating vane to show which way wind blows

**weave** (weev) *v.* (wove *or* weaved, wo·ven *or* wove, weav·ing) —*vt.* form into texture or fabric by interlacing, *esp.* on loom; fashion, construct —*vi.* become woven; make one's way, *esp.* with side to side motion —weav′er (-ər) *n.*

**web** *n.* woven fabric; net spun by spider; membrane between toes of waterfowl, frogs *etc.* —web′bing *n.* strong fabric woven in strips

**web·er** (WEB·ər) *n.* SI unit of magnetic flux

**wed** *vt.* (wed·ded, wed·ding) marry; unite closely —wedding *n.* act of marrying, nuptial ceremony —wed′lock *n.* marriage

**wedge** (wej) *n.* piece of wood, metal *etc.*, thick at one end, tapering to a thin edge —*vt.* (wedged, wedg·ing) fasten, split with wedge; stick by compression or crowding

**weed** *n.* plant growing where undesired; *inf.* tobacco; *sl.* marijuana; thin, sickly person, animal —*vt.* clear of weeds —weed′y _adj._ (weed·i·er, weed·i·est) full of weeds; thin, weakly —**weed out** remove, eliminate what is unwanted

**weeds** (weedz) _n. pl. obs._ (widow's) mourning clothes

**week** _n._ period of seven days, _esp._ one beginning on Sunday and ending on Saturday; hours, days of work in seven-day period —**week'ly** _adj./adv._ happening, done, published _etc._ once a week —_n._ —**week'day** _n._ any day of week except Sunday and _usu._ Saturday —**week'end** _n._ (at least) Saturday and Sunday, _esp._ considered as rest period

**weep** _v._ (wept, weep·ing) shed tears (for); grieve —**weep'y** _adj._ (weep·i·er, weep·i·est) —**weeping willow** willow with drooping branches

**wee·vil** (WEE-vəl) _n._ small beetle harmful to cotton _etc._

**weft** _n._ cross threads in weaving, woof

**weigh** (way) _vt._ find weight of; consider; raise (anchor) —_vi._ have weight; be burdensome —**weight** _n._ measure of the heaviness of an object; quality of heaviness; heavy mass; object of known mass for weighing; unit of measurement of weight; importance, influence —_vt._ add weight to —**weight'y** _adj._ (weight·i·er, weight·i·est) heavy; onerous; important; momentous

**weir** (weer) _n._ river, stream dam; fence or net in stream _etc._ for catching fish

**weird** (weerd) _adj._ (-er, -est) unearthly, uncanny; strange, bizarre

**wel·come** (WEL-kəm) _adj._ received gladly; freely permitted —_n./interj._ kindly greeting —_vt._ (-comed, -com·ing) greet with pleasure; receive gladly

**weld** _vt._ unite metal by softening with heat; unite closely —_n._ welded joint —**weld'er** _n._ person who welds; machine used in welding —**weld'ment** (-mənt) _n._ welded assembly

**wel·fare** (WEL-fair) _n._ well-being —**welfare state** system in which the government takes responsibility for the social, economic _etc._ security of its citizens

**well**[1] _adv._ in good manner or degree; suitably; intimately; fully; favorably, kindly; to a considerable degree —_adj._ (bet·ter, best) in good health; suitable —_interj._ exclamation of surprise, interrogation _etc._ —**well-being** _n._ state of being well, happy, or prosperous —**well-disposed** _adj._ inclined to be friendly, kindly (toward) —**well-mannered** _adj._ having good manners —**well-off** _adj._ fairly rich —**well-read** (-red) _adj._ having read much —**well-spoken** _adj._ speaking fluently, graciously, aptly

**well**[2] _n._ hole sunk into the earth to reach water, gas, oil _etc._; spring; any shaft like a well —_vi._ spring, gush

**Welsh** _adj._ of Wales —_n._ language, people of Wales —**Welsh rabbit, rarebit** dish of melted cheese, beer, spices on toast

**welsh** _vi. inf._ fail to pay debt or fulfill obligation (_also_ **welch**) —**welsh'er** (-ər), **welch·er** (WELCH-ər) _n._

**welt** _n._ raised, strengthened seam; weal —_vt._ provide with welt; thrash

**wel·ter** (WEL-tər) _vi._ roll or tumble —_n._ turmoil, disorder

**wel·ter·weight** (WEL-tər-wayt) _n._ Boxing weight between light and middle; boxer of this weight

**wen** _n._ cyst, _esp._ on scalp

**wench** n. obs. now oft. facetious young woman

**wend** v. go, travel

**went** pt. of GO

**wept** pt./pp. of WEEP

**were** (wur) past indicative, plural and subjunctive sing. and pl. of BE

**were·wolf** (WAIR-wuulf) n. (pl. -wolves) (in folklore) human being turned into wolf

**west** n. part of sky where sun sets; part of country etc. lying to this side; occident —adj. that is toward or in this region —adv. to the west —**west'er·ly** (-ɔr-lee) adj. —**west'ward** (-wɔrd) adj./adv. —**west'ward(s)** adv. toward the west —**west'ern** (-ɔrn) adj. of, in the west —n. film, story etc. about cowboys or frontiersmen in western US —**go west** inf. die

**wet** adj. (wet·ter, wet·test) having water or other liquid on a surface or being soaked in it; rainy; not yet dry (paint, ink etc.) —vt. (wet or wet·ted, wet·ting) make wet —n. moisture, rain —**wet blanket** one depressing spirits of others —**wet'land** (-lɔnd) n. area of swamp or marsh —**wet nurse** woman suckling another's child —**wet suit** close-fitting rubber suit worn by divers etc.

**whack** (hwak) vt. strike with sharp resounding blow —n. such blow; sl. share; inf. attempt —**whack'ing** adj. inf. big, enormous

**whale** (hwayl) n. large fish-shaped sea mammal —**whal'er** n. person, ship employed in hunting whales —**whale'bone** n. horny elastic substance from projections of upper jaw of certain whales —**whal'ing** n. —**a whale of a** inf. very large, fine, example of something

**wharf** (hworf) n. platform at harbor, on river etc. for loading and unloading ships

**what** (hwut, hwot) pron. which thing; that which; request for statement to be repeated —adj. which; as much as; how great, surprising etc. —interj. exclamation of surprise, anger etc. —**what·ev'er** pron. anything which; of what kind it may be —**what'not** n. small stand with shelves; something, anything of same kind

**wheat** (hweet) n. cereal plant with thick four-sided seed spikes of which bread is chiefly made —**wheat'en** (-ɔn) adj. —**wheat germ** (-jurm) embryo of wheat kernel

**whee·dle** (HWEED-l) v. (-dled, -dling) coax, cajole

**wheel** (hweel) n. circular frame or disk (with spokes) revolving on axle; anything like a wheel in shape or function; steering wheel —v. (cause to) turn as if on axis; (cause to) move on or as if on wheels; (cause to) change course, esp. in opposite direction —**wheel'bar·row** (-ba-roh) n. barrow with one wheel —**wheel'base** (-bays) n. distance between front and rear hubs of vehicle —**wheel'chair** n. chair mounted on large wheels, used by people who cannot walk

**wheeze** (hweez) vi. (wheezed, wheez·ing) breathe with difficulty and whistling noise —n. this sound; story etc. told too often —**wheez'y** (-ee) adj. (wheez·i·er, wheez·i·est)

**whelp** (hwelp) n. (oft. jocular, disparaging) pup, cub —v. produce whelps

**when** (hwen) adv. at what time

—*conj.* at the time that; although; since —*pron.* at which (time) —when·ev'er *adv./conj.* at whatever time

**whence** (hwens) *adv./conj.* from what place or source; how

**where** (hwair) *adv./conj.* at what place; at or to the place in which —where'a·bouts *adv./conj.* in what, which place —n. present position —where·as' *conj.* considering that; while, on the contrary —where·by' (-BĪ) *conj.* by which —where'fore *adv. obs.* why —*conj.* consequently —where·up·on' *conj.* at which point —wher·ev'er *adv.* at whatever place —where'with·al (-with-awl) *n.* necessary funds, resources *etc.*

**whet** (hwet) *vt.* (whet·ted, whet·ting) sharpen; stimulate —whet'stone *n.* stone for sharpening tools

**wheth·er** (HWETH-ər) *conj.* introduces the first of two alternatives, of which the second may be expressed or implied

**whey** (hway) *n.* watery part of milk left after separation of curd in cheese making

**which** (hwich) *adj.* used in requests for a selection from alternatives —*pron.* which person or thing; the thing "who" —which·ev'er *pron.*

**whiff** (hwif) *n.* brief smell or suggestion of; puff of air —*v.* smell

**while** (hwīl) *conj.* in the time that; in spite of the fact that, although; whereas —*vt.* (whiled, whil·ing) pass (time, usu. idly) —*n.* period of time

**whim** (hwim) *n.* sudden, passing fancy —whim'si·cal (-zi-kəl) *adj.* fanciful; full of whims —whim·si·cal'i·ty (-zi-KAL-i-tee) *n.* (*pl.* -ties)

—whim'sy (-zee) *n.* (*pl.* -sies) whim; caprice

**whim·per** (HWIM-pər) *vi.* cry or whine softly; complain in this way —*n.* such cry or complaint

**whine** (hwīn) *n.* high-pitched plaintive cry; peevish complaint —*vi.* (whined, whin·ing) utter this

**whin·ny** (HWIN-ee) *vi.* (-nied, -ny·ing) neigh softly —*n.*

**whip** (hwip) *v.* (whipped, whip·ping) —*vt.* strike with whip; thrash; beat (cream, eggs) to a froth; lash; pull, remove, quickly; —*vi.* dart —*n.* lash attached to handle for urging or punishing; one who enforces attendance, voting *etc.* of political party; elastic quality permitting bending in mast, fishing rod *etc.*; whipped dessert —whip'lash *n.* injury to neck as result of sudden jerking of unsupported head —whipping boy scapegoat

**whip·pet** (HWIP-it) *n.* racing dog like small greyhound

**whir** (hwur) *v.* (whirred, whir·ring) (cause to) fly, spin *etc.* with buzzing or whizzing sound; bustle —*n.* this sound

**whirl** (hwurl) *v.* swing rapidly around; move rapidly in a circular course; drive at high speed —*n.* whirling movement; confusion, bustle, giddiness —whirl'pool *n.* circular current, eddy —whirl'wind *n.* wind whirling around while moving forward —*adj.*

**whisk** (hwisk) *v.* brush, sweep, beat lightly; move, remove, quickly; beat to a froth —*n.* light brush; eggbeating implement

**whisk·er** (HWIS-kər) *n.* any of the long stiff hairs at side of mouth of cat or other animal; any of hairs on a man's face —by a whisker only just

**whis·key** (HWIS-kee) n. (pl. -keys) alcoholic liquor distilled from fermented cereals —**whis'·ky** n. (pl. -kies) Scotch or Canadian whiskey

**whis·per** (HWIS-pər) v. speak in soft, hushed tones, without vibration of vocal cords; rustle —n. such speech; trace or suspicion; rustle

**whist** (hwist) n. card game

**whis·tle** (HWIS-əl) v. (-tled, -tling) —vi. produce shrill sound by forcing breath through rounded, nearly closed lips; make such a sound —vt. utter, summon etc. by whistle —n. such sound; any similar sound; instrument to make it —**whis'·tler** (HWIS-lər) n. —**whistle-blower** n. person who informs on or puts stop to something

**whit** (hwit) n. jot, particle (usu. in not a whit)

**white** (hwit) adj. (whit·er, whit·est) of the color of snow; pale; light in color; having a light-colored skin —n. color of snow; white pigment; white part; clear fluid round yolk of egg; Caucasian person —**whi'·ten** (-ən) v. —**white ant** termite —**white-collar** adj. denoting nonmanual salaried workers —**white elephant** useless, unwanted, or possession —**white flag** white banner or cloth used as signal of surrender or truce —**white hope** one (formerly, a white person) expected to bring honor or glory to his group, team etc. —**white lie** minor, unimportant lie —**white paper** government report on matter recently investigated —**white slave** woman, child forced or enticed away for purposes of prostitution —**white'·wash** (-wosh) n. substance for whitening walls etc. —vt. apply

this; cover up, gloss over, suppress

**whith·er** (HWITH-ər) adv. to what place; to which

**whit·tle** (HWIT-l) vt. (-tled, -tling) cut, carve with knife; pare away —**whittle down** reduce gradually, wear (away)

**whiz** (hwiz) n. loud hissing sound; inf. person skillful at something —v. (whizzed, whiz·zing) move with such sound, or make it; inf. move quickly

**who** (hoo) pron. relative and interrogative pronoun, always referring to persons —**who·dun'it** n. inf. detective story —**who·ev'er** pron. who, any one or every one that

**whole** (hohl) adj. complete; containing all elements or parts; entire; not defective or imperfect; healthy —n. complete thing or system —**whol'·ly** adv. —**whole·heart'ed** (-HART-id) adj. sincere; enthusiastic —**whole'·sale** (-sayl) n. sale of goods in large quantities to retailers —adj. dealing by wholesale; extensive —vt. (-saled, -sal·ing) —**whole'sal·er** n. —**whole'·some** (-səm) adj. producing good effect, physically or morally —**whole·wheat** adj. of, pert. to flour that contains the complete wheat kernel —**on the whole** taking everything into consideration; in general

**whom** (hoom) pron. objective case of WHO

**whoop** (hwuup) n. shout or cry expressing excitement etc.

**whoop·ee** (HWUUP-ee) n. inf. gay, riotous time —**make whoopee** participate in wild noisy party; go on spree

**whoop·ing cough** (HUUP-ing) infectious disease of mucous membrane lining air passages, marked by convulsive coughing with loud whoop or indrawing of breath

**whop·per** (HWOP-ər) n. inf. anything unusually large; monstrous lie —whop'ping n.

**whore** (hor) n. prostitute

**whorl** (hwurl) n. ring of leaves or petals; turn of spiral; anything forming part of circular pattern, eg lines of human fingerprint

**whose** (hooz) pron. possessive case of WHO and WHICH used as adjective

**why** (hwī) adv. for what cause or reason

**wick** (wik) n. strip of thread feeding flame of lamp or candle with oil, grease etc.

**wick·ed** (WIK-id) adj. evil, sinful; very bad; mischievous —wick'ed·ness (-nis) n.

**wick·er** (WIK-ər) n. woven cane etc. basketwork (also wick·er·work)

**wick·et** (WIK-it) n. small window, gate; Croquet wire arch

**wide** (wid) adj. (wid·er, wid·est) having a great extent from side to side, broad; having considerable distance between; spacious; liberal; vast; far from the mark; opened fully —adv. to the full extent; far from the intended target —wi·den (WID-n) v. —width n. breadth —wide'-spread (-spred) adj. extending over a wide area

**wid·ow** (WID-oh) n. woman whose husband is dead and who has not married again —vt. make a widow of —wid'ow·er n. man whose wife is dead and who has not married again —wid'ow·hood (-huud) n.

**wield** (weeld) vt. hold and use; brandish; manage

**wife** (wif) n. (pl. wives) a man's partner in marriage, married woman —wife'ly adj.

**wig** n. artificial hair for the head —wigged adj.

**wig·gle** (WIG-əl) v. (-gled, -gling) (cause to) move jerkily from side to side —n.

**wig·wam** (WIG-wom) n. N Amer. Indian's hut or tent

**wild** (wild) adj. (-er, -est) not tamed or domesticated; not cultivated; savage; stormy; uncontrolled; random; excited; rash; frantic; (of party etc.) rowdy, unrestrained —wild'ly adv. —wild'ness (-nis) n. —wild'cat n. any of various undomesticated feline animals; wild, savage person —adj. unsound, irresponsible; sudden, unofficial, unauthorized —wildcat strike strike called without sanction of labor union —wild-goose chase futile pursuit —wild'life n. wild animals and plants collectively

**wil·der·ness** (WIL-dər-nis) n. desert, waste place; state of desolation or confusion

**wild-fire** (WILD-fir) n. raging, uncontrollable fire; anything spreading, moving fast

**wile** (wil) n. trick —wil'y adj. (wil·i·er, wil·i·est) crafty, sly

**will** v. aux. forms moods and tenses indicating intention or conditional result (would pt. & pr. wuud) —vi. have a wish —vt. wish; intend; leave as legacy —n. faculty of deciding what one will do; purpose; volition; determination; wish; directions written for disposal of property after death —will'ing adj. ready; given cheerfully —will'ing·ly adv. —will'ing·ness (-nis) n. —will'pow·er n. ability to control oneself, one's actions, impulses

**will·ful** (WIL-fəl) adj. obstinate,

self-willed; intentional —**will'ful·ness** (-nis) n.

**will-o'-the-wisp** (WIL-ə-thə-WISP) n. brief pale flame or phosphorescence sometimes seen over marshes; elusive person or hope

**wil·low** (WIL-oh) n. tree (eg weeping willow) with long thin flexible branches; its wood —**wil'low·y** adj. lithe, slender, supple

**wil·ly-nil·ly** (WIL-ee-NIL-ee) adv./adj. (occurring) whether desired or not

**wilt** v. (cause to) become limp, drooping or lose strength etc.

**wimp** n. inf. feeble, ineffective person

**wim·ple** (WIM-pəl) n. garment worn by nun, around face

**win** v. (won, win·ning) —vi. be successful, victorious —vt. get by labor or effort; reach; lure; be successful in; gain the support, consent etc. of —n. victory, esp. in games —**winning** adj. charming —**winnings** n. pl. sum won in game, betting etc.

**wince** (wins) vi. (winced, winc·ing) flinch, draw back, as from pain etc. —n. this act

**winch** n. machine for hoisting or hauling using cable wound around drum —vt. move (something) by using a winch

**wind¹** n. air in motion; breath; flatulence; idle talk; hint or suggestion; scent borne by air —vt. (wind·ed, wind·ing) render short of breath, esp. by blow etc.; get the scent of —**wind'ward** (-wərd) n. side against which wind is blowing —**wind'y** adj. (**wind·i·er, wind·i·est**) exposed to wind; flatulent; talking too much —**wind'fall** n. unexpected good luck; fallen fruit —**wind instru·ment** musical instrument played

by blowing or air pressure —**wind'mill** n. wind-driven apparatus with fanlike sails for raising water, crushing grain etc. —**wind'pipe** n. passage from throat to lungs —**wind'shield** (-sheeld) n. protective sheet of glass etc. in front of driver or pilot —**wind'sock** n. cone of material flown on mast at airfield to indicate wind direction —**wind'surf·ing** n. sport of sailing standing up on sailboard holding special boom to control sail

**wind²** (wīnd) v. (wound pr. wownd, wind·ing) —vi. twine; meander —vt. twist around, coil; wrap; make ready for working by tightening spring —n. act of winding; single turn of something wound; a turn, curve

**wind·lass** (WIND-ləs) n. winch, esp. simple one worked by a crank

**win·dow** (WIN-doh) n. hole in wall (with glass) to admit light, air etc.; anything similar in appearance or function; area for display of goods behind glass of store front —**window dressing** arrangement of goods in a shop window; deceptive display

**wine** (wīn) n. fermented juice of grape etc. —**wine'press** n. apparatus for extracting juice from grape

**wing** n. feathered limb a bird uses in flying; one of organs of flight of insect or some animals; main lifting surface of aircraft; lateral extension; side portion of building projecting from main central portion; one of sides of a stage; flank corps of army on either side; administrative, tactical unit of air force; faction esp. of political party —pl. insignia worn by qualified aircraft pilot; sides of stage —vi. fly; move, go very fast —*vt.* disable, wound slightly

**wink** (wingk) *v.* close and open (an eye) rapidly, *esp.* to indicate friendliness or as signal; twinkle —*n.* act of winking

**win·now** (WIN-oh) *vt.* blow free of chaff; sift, examine

**win·some** (WIN-səm) *adj.* charming, winning —**win'some·ly** *adv.*

**win·ter** (WIN-tər) *n.* the coldest season —*vi.* pass, spend the winter —**win'try** *adj.* (-tri·er, -tri·est) of, like winter; cold

**wipe** (wīp) *vt.* (wiped, wip·ing) rub so as to clean —*n.* wiping —**wi'per** *n.* one that wipes; automatic wiping apparatus (*esp.* windshield wiper) —**wipe out** erase; annihilate; *inf.* kill; *sl.* beat decisively —**wiped-out** *adj. sl.* exhausted; intoxicated —**wipe'out** *n. inf.* murder; decisive defeat

**wire** (wīr) *n.* metal drawn into thin, flexible strand; something made of wire, *eg* fence; telegram —*vt.* (wired, wir·ing) provide, fasten with wire; send by telegraph —**wiring** *n.* system of wires —**wir'y** *adj.* (wir·i·er, wir·i·est) like wire; lean and tough —**wire-haired** *adj.* (of various breeds of dog) with short stiff hair

**wire·less** (WIR-lis) *n.* old-fashioned term for radio, radio set —*adj.*

**wise**[1] (wīz) *adj.* (wis·er, wis·est) having intelligence and knowledge; sensible —**wis·dom** (WIZ-dəm) *n.* (accumulated) knowledge, learning; erudition —**wise'ly** *adv.* —**wise'a·cre** (WIZ-ay-kər) *n.* one who wishes to seem wise —**wisdom tooth** third molar usually cut about 20th year

**wise**[2] *n. obs.* manner

**wise·crack** (WIZ-krak) *n. inf.* flippant (would-be) clever remark

**wish** *vi.* have a desire —*vt.* desire

—*n.* desire; thing desired —**wish'ful** (-fəl) *adj.* desirous; too optimistic —**wish'bone** *n.* V-shaped bone above breastbone of fowl

**wisp** *n.* light, delicate streak, as of smoke; twisted handful, usu. of straw *etc.*; stray lock of hair —**wisp'y** *adj.* (wisp·i·er, wisp·i·est)

**wist·ful** (WIST-fəl) *adj.* longing, yearning; sadly pensive —**wist'ful·ly** *adv.*

**wit** *n.* ingenuity in connecting amusingly incongruous ideas; person gifted with this power; sense; intellect; understanding; ingenuity; humor —**wit'ti·cism** (-ti·sizm) *n.* witty remark —**wit'ti·ly** *adv.* —**wit'ting·ly** *adv.* on purpose; knowingly —**wit'less** (-lis) *adj.* foolish —**wit'ty** *adj.* (-ti·er, -ti·est)

**witch** (wich) *n.* person, usu. female, believed to practice, practicing, or professing to practice (black) magic, sorcery; ugly, wicked woman; fascinating woman —**witch'craft** *n.* —**witch doctor** in certain societies, person appearing to cure or cause injury, disease by magic

**with** (with) *prep.* in company or possession of; against; in relation to; through; by means of —**with·al** (with-AWL) *adv.* also, likewise —**with·in'** *prep./adv.* in, inside —**with·out'** *prep.* lacking; *obs.* outside

**with·draw** (with-DRAW) *v.* (-drew, -drawn, -draw·ing) draw back or out —**with·draw'al** *n.* —**with·drawn'** *adj.* reserved, unsociable

**with·er** (WITH-ər) *v.* (cause to) wilt, dry up, decline —**with'er·ing** *adj.* (of glance *etc.*) scornful

**with·ers** (WITH-ərz) *n. pl.* ridge

between a horse's shoulder blades

**with·hold** (with-HOHLD) *vt.* (-held, -hold·ing) restrain; keep back; refrain from giving

**with·stand'** *vt.* (-stood *pr.* -stuud, -stand·ing) oppose, resist, *esp.* successfully

**wit·ness** (WIT-nis) *n.* one who sees something; testimony; one who gives testimony —*vi.* see testimony —*vt.* see; attest; and sign as having seen

**wiz·ard** (WIZ-ərd) *n.* sorcerer, magician; conjurer —**wiz'ard·ry** *n.*

**wiz·ened** (WIZ-ənd) *adj.* shriveled, wrinkled

**wob·ble** (WOB-əl) *vi.* (-bled, -bling) move unsteadily; sway —*n.* an unsteady movement —**wob'bly** *adj.* (-bli·er, -bli·est)

**woe** (woh) *n.* grief —**woe·be·gone** (WOH-bi-gawn) *adj.* looking sorrowful —**woe'ful** (-fəl) *adj.* sorrowful; pitiful; wretched —**woe'ful·ly** *adv.*

**wolf** (wuulf) *n.* (*pl.* wolves) wild predatory doglike animal of northern countries; *inf.* man who habitually tries to seduce women —*vt.* eat ravenously —**wolf whis·tle** whistle by man expressing admiration for a woman —**cry wolf** raise false alarm

**wolf·ram** (WUUL-frəm) *n.* tungsten

**wol·ver·ine** (wuul-və-REEN) *n.* carnivorous mammal inhabiting northern regions

**wom·an** (WUUM-ən) *n.* (*pl.* wom·en *pr.* WIM-in) adult human female; women collectively —**wom'an·hood** (-huud) *n.* —**wom'an·ish** *adj.* effeminate —**wom'an·ize** *vi.* (-ized, -iz·ing) (of man) indulge in many casual affairs with women —**wom'an·kind** (-kīnd) *n.* —**wom'an·ly** *adj.*

of, proper to woman —**women's liberation** movement for removal of attitudes, practices that preserve social, economic *etc.* inequalities between women and men (*also* women's lib)

**womb** (woom) *n.* female organ of conception and gestation, uterus

**won** (wun) *pt./pp. of* WIN

**won·der** (WUN-dər) *n.* emotion excited by amazing or unusual thing; marvel, miracle —*vi.* be curious about; feel amazement —**won'der·ful** (-fəl) *adj.* remarkable; very fine —**won'der·ment** (-mənt) *n.* surprise —**won'drous** (-drəs) *adj.* inspiring wonder; strange

**wont** (wawnt) *n.* custom —*adj.* accustomed —**wont'ed** (-id) *adj.* habitual, established

**woo** *vt.* court, seek to marry —**woo'er** (-ər) *n.* suitor

**wood** (wuud) *n.* substance of trees, timber; firewood; tract of land with growing trees —**wood'ed** (-id) *adj.* having (many) trees —**wood'en** (-n) *adj.* made of wood; obstinate; without expression —**wood'y** *adj.* —**wood'chuck** *n.* Amer. burrowing rodent —**wood'cut** *n.* engraving on wood; impression from this —**wood'land** (-lənd) *n.* woods, forest —**wood'peck·er** *n.* bird that searches tree trunks for insects —**wood'wind** *adj./n.* (of) wind instruments of orchestra, *orig.* made of wood

**woof** (wuuf) *n.* Brit. the threads that cross the warp in weaving

**woof·er** (WUUF-ər) *n.* loudspeaker for reproducing low-frequency sounds

**wool** (wuul) *n.* soft hair of sheep, goat *etc.*; yarn spun from this —**wool'en** (-n) *adj.* —**wool'ly** *adj.* (-li·er, -li·est) of wool; vague, muddled —*n.* knitted woolen garment, *esp. pl.* **wool·ies** (-eez) warm undergarment —**wool'-gath·er·ing** n. daydreaming

**word** (wurd) n. unit of speech or writing regarded by users of a language as the smallest separate meaningful unit; term; message; brief remark; information; promise; command —vt. express in words, *esp.* in particular way —**word'ing** n. choice and arrangement of words —**word'y** adj. (**word·i·er, word·i·est**) using more words than necessary, verbose —**word processor** keyboard, microprocessor and monitor for electronic organization and storage of written text

**wore** pt., **worn** pp. of WEAR

**work** (wurk) n. labor; employment; occupation; task; toil; something made or accomplished; production of art or science; book; needlework —pl. factory; total of person's deeds, writings *etc.*; *inf.* everything, full or extreme treatment; mechanism of clock *etc.* —**gum up the works** *sl.* spoil something through blunder or stupidity —vt. cause to operate; make, shape —vi. apply effort; labor; operate; be engaged in trade, profession *etc.*; turn out successfully; ferment —**work'-a·ble** adj. —**work·a·hol·ic** (wurk-ə-HAW-lik) n. person addicted to work —**work'ing class** social class consisting of wage earners, *esp.* manual —**working-class** adj. —**work·man** (WURK-mən) n. (pl. -men) manual worker; male worker —**work'man·ship** n. skill of workman; way thing is finished; style —**work'shop** n. place where things are made; discussion group, seminar

**world** (wurld) n. the universe; Earth; sphere of existence; mankind, people generally; society

—**world'ly** adj. earthly; mundane; absorbed in the pursuit of material gain, advantage; carnal

**worm** (wurm) n. small limbless creeping snakelike creature; anything resembling worm in shape or movement; gear wheel with teeth forming part of screw threads; *inf.* weak, despised person —pl. (disorder caused by) infestation of worms, *esp.* in intestines —vi. crawl —vt. work (oneself) in insidiously; extract (secret) craftily; rid of worms —**worm'-eaten** adj. full of holes gnawed by worms; old, antiquated —**worm'y** adj. (**worm·i·er, worm·i·est**)

**worm·wood** (WURM-wuud) n. bitter herb; bitterness

**worn** pp. of WEAR

**wor·ry** (WUR-ee) v. (-ried, -ry·ing) —vi. be (unduly) concerned —vt. trouble, pester, harass; (of dog) seize, shake with teeth —n. (pl. -ries) (cause of) anxiety, concern —**wor'ri·er** n.

**worse** (wurs) adj./adv. comp. of BAD or BADLY —n. —**worst** adj./adv. sup. of BAD or BADLY —n. —**wors'en** (-in) v. make, grow worse; impair; deteriorate

**wor·ship** (WUR-ship) vt. (-shiped, -ship·ing) show religious devotion to; adore; love and admire —n. act of worshiping —**wor'ship·er** n.

**wor·sted** (WUUS-tid) n. woolen yarn —adj. made of woolen yarn; spun from wool

**worth** (wurth) adj. having or deserving to have value specified; meriting —n. excellence; merit, value; virtue; usefulness; price; quantity to be had for a given sum —**wor·thy** (WUR-thee) adj. (-thi·er, -thi·est) virtuous; meriting —n. one of eminent worth; celebrity —**wor'thi·ness** (-thee-nis) *n.* —**worth·less** (WURTH-lis) *adj.* useless —**worth·while** (wurth-hwīl) *adj.* worth the time, effort *etc.* involved

**would** (wuud) *v. aux.* expressing wish, intention, probability; *pt. of* WILL —**would-be** (WUUD-bee) *adj.* wishing, pretending to be

**wound**[1] (woond) *n.* injury, hurt from cut, stab *etc.* —*vt.* inflict wound on, injure; pain

**wound**[2] (wownd *rhymes with* sound) *pt./pp. of* WIND[2]

**wove** (wohv) *pt.*, **wo'ven** *pp. of* WEAVE

**wow** *interj.* of astonishment —*n. inf.* object of astonishment, admiration *etc.*; variation, distortion in pitch in record player *etc.*

**wraith** (rayth) *n.* apparition of a person seen shortly before or after death; specter

**wran·gle** (RANG-gǝl) *vi.* (-gled, -gling) quarrel (noisily); dispute; herd cattle —*n.* noisy quarrel; dispute —**wran'gler** (-glǝr) *n.* cowboy; disputant

**wrap** (rap) *v.* (wrapped, wrap·ping) cover, *esp.* by putting something around; put around —**wrap'per** *n.* loose garment; covering —**wrapping** *n.* material used to wrap

**wrath** (rath) *n.* anger —**wrath'ful** (-fǝl) *adj.* —**wrath'ful·ly** *adv.*

**wreak** (reek) *vt.* inflict (vengeance); cause

**wreath** (reeth) *n.* something twisted into ring form, *esp.* band of flowers *etc.* as memorial or tribute on grave *etc.* —**wreathe** (reeth) *vt.* (wreathed, wreath·ing) form into wreath; surround; wind around

**wreck** (rek) *n.* destruction of ship; wrecked ship; ruin; something ruined —*vt.* cause the wreck of —**wreck'age** (-ij) *n.* —**wreck'er** *n.* person or thing

that destroys, ruins; vehicle for towing disabled, wrecked *etc.* automobiles, a tow truck

**wren** (ren) *n.* kind of small song-bird

**wrench** (rench) *vt.* twist; distort; seize forcibly; sprain —*n.* violent twist; tool for twisting or turning; tool for gripping nut or bolt head; sudden pain caused *esp.* by parting

**wrest** (rest) *vt.* take by force; twist violently

**wres·tle** (RES-ǝl) *vi.* (-tled, -tling) fight (*esp.* as sport) by grappling and trying to throw down; strive (with); struggle —*n.* —**wrest'ler** (-lǝr) *n.*

**wretch** (rech) *n.* despicable person; miserable creature —**wretch'ed** (-id) *adj.* (-ed·er, -ed·est) miserable, unhappy; worthless —**wretch'ed·ly** *adv.* —**wretch'ed·ness** (-nis) *n.*

**wrig·gle** (RIG-ǝl) *v.* (-gled, -gling) move with twisting action, as worm; squirm —*n.* this action

**wring** (ring) *vt.* (wrung, wring·ing) twist; extort; pain; squeeze out

**wrin·kle** (RING-kǝl) *n.* slight ridge or furrow on surface; crease in the skin; fold; pucker; *inf.* (useful) trick, hint —*v.* (-kled, -kling) make, become wrinkled, pucker

**wrist** (rist) *n.* joint between hand and arm —**wrist'let** (-lit) *n.* band worn on wrist

**writ** (rit) *n.* written command from law court or other authority

**write** (rīt) *v.* (wrote, writ·ten, writ·ing) —*vi.* mark paper *etc.* with the symbols that are used to represent words or sounds; compose; send a letter —*vt.* set down in words; compose; communicate in writing —**writ'er** *n.* one who writes; author —**write-off** *n.* cancellation from accounts as loss; *inf.* person or thing considered hopeless —**write-up** *n.* written (published) account of something

**writhe** (rīth) *v.* (writhed, writhing) twist, squirm in or as in pain *etc.* —*vi.* be acutely embarrassed *etc.*

**wrong** (rawng) *adj.* not right or good; not suitable; wicked; incorrect; mistaken; not functioning properly —*n.* that which is wrong; harm; evil —*vt.* do wrong to; think badly of without justification —**wrong'do·er** (-doo-ər) *n.* one who acts immorally or illegally —**wrong'ful** (-fəl) *adj.* —**wrong'ful·ly** *adv.*

**wrote** (rōht) *pt.* of WRITE

**wrought** (rawt) *adj.* (of metals) shaped by hammering or beating —**wrought** iron pure form of iron used *esp.* in decorative railings *etc.*

**wrung** *pt./pp.* of WRING

**wry** (rī) *adj.* (wri·er, wri·est) turned to one side, contorted, askew; sardonic, dryly humorous

# X

**X** Christ; Christian; cross; Roman numeral, 10; mark indicating something wrong, a choice, a kiss, signature *etc.* —*n.* unknown, mysterious person, factor

**Xe** *Chem.* xenon

**xe·nog·a·my** (zə-NOG-ə-mee) *n.* pollination from another plant; cross-fertilization

**xe·non** (ZEE-non) *n.* colorless, odorless gas occurring in very small quantities in air

**xen·o·pho·bi·a** (zen-ə-FOH-bee-ə) *n.* dislike, hatred, fear, of strangers or aliens —**xen·o·pho'bic** *adj.*

**xe·rog·ra·phy** (zi-ROG-rə-fee) *n.* photocopying process

**Xmas** (KRIS-məs, *oft. facetiously* EKS-məs) *n.* short for CHRISTMAS

**x-rays** (EKS-rayz) *n. pl.* radiation of very short wavelengths, capable of penetrating solid bodies, and printing on photographic plate shadow picture of objects not permeable by rays —**x-ray** *v.* photograph by x-rays

**xy·lo·carp** (Zl-lə-kahrp) *n.* hard, woody fruit —**xy·lo·carp'ous** *adj.* having fruit that becomes hard or woody

**xy·lo·graph** (Zl-lə-graf) *n.* wood engraving; impression from wood block

**xy·loid** (Zl-loid) *adj.* pert. to wood; woody, ligneous

**xy·lo·phone** (Zl-lə-fohn) *n.* musical instrument of wooden bars that sound when struck

# Y

**yacht** (yot) *n.* vessel propelled by sail or power, used for racing, pleasure *etc.* —**yachts·man** (YOTS-mən) *n.* (*pl.* -men)

**ya·hoo** (YAH-hoo) *n.* (*pl.* -hoos) crude, coarse person

**Yah·weh** (YAH-we) *n.* Jehovah, God

**yak** *n.* shaggy-haired, long-horned ox of Central Asia

**yam** *n.* large edible tuber, sweet potato

**yank** (yangk) *v.* jerk, tug; pull quickly —*n.* quick tug

**Yank** (yangk), **Yank'ee** *adj./n. inf.* American

**yap** *vi.* (yapped, yap·ping) bark (as small dog); *sl.* talk shrilly, idly —*n.* a bark; *sl.* the mouth

**yard**[1] (yahrd) *n.* unit of length, 3

feet (36 inches, .9144 meter); spar slung across ship's mast to extend sails —**yard'stick** n. 36-inch ruler; formula or standard of measurement or comparison —**yard'age** (-ij) n. measurement of distance in yards; length in yards

**yard²** n. piece of enclosed ground adjoining building and used for some specific purpose, as garden, storage, holding livestock etc. —**yard'age** n. use of yard; charge made for this

**yar·mul·ke** (YAHR-məl-kə) n. skullcap worn by Jewish men and boys, esp. in synagogue

**yarn** (yahrn) n. spun thread; tale —vi. inf. tell a tale, also spin a yarn

**yash·mak** (yahsh-MAHK) n. face veil worn by Muslim women

**yaw** vi. of aircraft etc., turn about vertical axis; deviate temporarily from course

**yawl** n. two-masted sailing vessel

**yawn** vi. open mouth wide, esp. in sleepiness; gape —n. a yawning

**yaws** (yawz) n. with sing. v. contagious tropical skin disease

**ye** (yee) pron. obs. you

**yea** (yay) interj. yes —n. affirmative vote

**year** (yeer) n. time taken by one revolution of Earth around sun, about 365 days; twelve months —**year'ling** n. animal one year old —**year'ly** adv. every year, once a year —adj. happening etc. once a year

**yearn** (yurn) vi. feel longing, desire; be filled with pity, tenderness —**yearn'ing** n.

**yeast** (yeest) n. substance used as fermenting, leavening agent, esp. in brewing and in baking bread —**yeast'y** adj. (yeast·i·er, yeast·i·est) of, like yeast; frothy,

fermenting; (of time) characterized by excitement, change etc.

**yell** v. cry out in loud shrill tone; speak in this way —n. loud shrill cry; a cheer, shout

**yel·low** (YEL-oh) adj. (-er, -est) of the color of lemons, gold etc.; inf. cowardly —n. this color —**yel'low·bel·ly** n. sl. (pl. -lies) coward —**yellow fever** acute infectious disease of (sub)tropical climates —**yellow jacket** type of wasp; sl. yellow capsule of phenobarbital

**yelp** vi./n. (produce) quick, shrill cry

**yen¹** n. Japanese monetary unit

**yen²** n. inf. longing, craving

**yeo·man** (YOH-mən) n. (pl. -men) petty officer in U.S. Navy having mainly clerical duties; Brit. Hist. farmer cultivating own land —adj. performed in valiant, thorough manner

**yes** interj. affirms or consents, gives an affirmative answer —n. (pl. yes·ses) affirmative reply —**yes-man** n. (pl. -men) weak person willing to agree to anything

**yes·ter·day** (YES-tər-day) n. day before today; recent time —adv./adj.

**yet** adv. now, still, besides, hitherto; nevertheless —conj. but, at the same time, nevertheless

**yet·i** (YET-ee) n. see ABOMINABLE SNOWMAN

**yew** (yoo) n. evergreen tree with dark leaves; its wood

**Yid·dish** (YID-ish) adj./n. (of, in) language used by many Jews in or from Europe, orig. a form of German written in Hebrew letters, with words from Hebrew and many other languages

**yield** (yeeld) vt. give or return as food; produce; provide; concede; give up, surrender —vi. produce;

submit; comply; surrender, give way —n. amount produced, return, profit, result

**yo·del** (YOHD-l) vi. (-deled, -del·ing) warble in falsetto tone —n. falsetto warbling as practiced by Swiss mountaineers

**yo·ga** (YOH-gə) n. Hindu philosophical system aiming at spiritual, mental and physical wellbeing by means of certain physical and mental exercises —yo'gi (-gee) n. (pl. -gis) one who practices yoga

**yo·gurt** (YOH-gərt) n. thick, custard-like preparation of curdled milk

**yoke** (yohk) n. wooden bar put across the necks of two animals to hold them together and to which plow etc. can be attached; various objects like a yoke in shape or use; fitted part of garment, esp. around neck, shoulders; bond or tie; domination —vt. (yoked, yok·ing) put a yoke on, couple, unite

**yo·kel** (YOH-kəl) n. disparaging term for (old-fashioned) country dweller

**yolk** (yohk) n. yellow central part of egg; oily secretion of skin of sheep

**yon** adj. obs. or dial. that or those over there —yon·der (YON-dər) adj. yon —adv. over there, in that direction

**yore** (yor) n. Poet. the distant past

**York·shire pudding** (YORK-shər) baked batter eaten with roast beef

**you** (yoo) pron. referring to person(s) addressed, or to unspecified person(s)

**young** (yung) adj. (-er, -est) not far advanced in growth, life or existence; not yet old; immature; junior; recently formed; vigorous

—n. offspring —young'ster (-stər) n. child

**your** (yuur) adj. belonging to you —yours pron. —your·self' pron. (pl. -selves)

**youth** (yooth) n. state or time of being young; state before adult age; young man; young people —youth'ful (-fəl) adj.

**yowl** v./n. (produce) mournful cry

**yo-yo** (YOH-yoh) n. (pl. -yos) toy consisting of a spool attached to a string, by which it can be spun out and reeled in while attached to the finger

**yuc·ca** (YUK-ə) n. tropical plant with stiff lancelike leaves

**Yule** (yool) n. the Christmas festival or season

**yup·pie** (YUP-ee) n. young urban professional —adj.

# Z

**za·ba·glio·ne** (zah-bəl-YOH-nee) n. Italian custardlike dessert of whipped and heated egg yolks, sugar and Marsala wine

**za·ny** (ZAY-nee) adj. (-ni·er, -ni·est) comical, funny in unusual way —n. (pl. -nies) eccentric person; silly person

**zap** vt. inf. (zapped, zap·ping) attack, kill or destroy; Computers clear from screen, erase —vt. change (TV channels) rapidly by remote control; skip over or delete sound of (commercials)

**zeal** (zeel) n. fervor; keenness, enthusiasm —zeal·ot (ZEL-ət) n. fanatic; enthusiast —zeal·ous (-əs) adj. ardent; enthusiastic; earnest —zeal'ous·ly adv.

**ze·bra** (ZEE-brə) n. (pl. -bras) striped Afr. animal like a horse

**ze·bu** (ZEE-byoo) *n.* humped Indian ox or cow

**Zen** *n.* Japanese school teaching contemplation, meditation

**ze·nith** (ZEE-nith) *n.* point of the heavens directly above an observer; summit; peak; climax — point opposite nadir

**zeph·yr** (ZEF-ər) *n.* soft, gentle breeze

**zep·pe·lin** (ZEP-ə-lin) *n.* large, cylindrical, rigid airship

**ze·ro** (ZEER-oh) *n.* (*pl.* -ros, -roes) nothing; figure 0; point on graduated instrument from which positive and negative quantities are reckoned; the lowest point —*vt.* (-roed, -ro·ing) reduce to zero; adjust (instrument *etc.*) to zero

**zest** *n.* enjoyment; excitement; interest, flavor; peel of orange or lemon —**zest′ful** (-fəl) *adj.*

**zig·zag** *n.* line or course characterized by sharp turns in alternating directions —*vi.* (-zagged, -zag·ging) move along in zigzag course

**zinc** (zingk) *n.* bluish-white metallic element with wide variety of uses, *esp.* in alloys as brass *etc.*

**zin·ni·a** (ZIN-ee-ə) *n.* plant with daisylike, brightly colored flowers

**Zi·on** (ZĪ-ən) *n.* hill on which Jerusalem stands; Judaism; Christian Church; heaven —**Zi′on·ism** *n.* movement to found, support Jewish homeland in what now is state of Israel —**Zi′on·ist** *n./adj.*

**zip** *n.* short whizzing sound; energy, vigor —*vt.* (zipped, zip·ping) move with zip

**zip code** (kohd) *n.* system of numbers used to aid sorting of mail (*also* ZIP code)

**zip·per** (ZIP-ər) *n.* device for fastening with two rows of flexible metal or plastic teeth, interlocked and opened by a sliding clip — fasten with zipper

**zir·con** (ZUR-kon) *n.* mineral used as gemstone and in industry

**zith·er** (ZITH-ər) *n.* flat stringed instrument

**Zn** *Chem.* zinc

**zo·di·ac** (ZOH-dee-ak) *n.* imaginary belt of the heavens along which the sun, moon, and chief planets appear to move, divided crosswise into twelve equal areas, called signs of the zodiac, each named after a constellation —**zo·di·a·cal** (zoh-DĪ-ə-kəl) *adj.*

**zom·bie** (ZOM-bee) *n.* person appearing lifeless, apathetic *etc.*; corpse supposedly brought to life by supernatural spirit

**zone** (zohn) *n.* region with particular characteristics or use; any of the five belts into which tropics and arctic and antarctic circles divide Earth

**zoo** *n.* place where wild animals are kept, studied, bred and exhibited (*in full* zoological garden)

**zo·og·ra·phy** (zoh-OG-rə-fee) *n.* descriptive zoology —**zo·og′ra·pher**, **zo·og′ra·phist** *n.* —**zo·o·graph′i·cal** *adj.*

**zo·ol·o·gy** (zoh-OL-ə-jee) *n.* scientific study of animals; characteristics of particular animals or of fauna of particular area —**zo·o·log′i·cal** *adj.* —**zo·ol′o·gist** *n.*

**zoom** *v.* (cause to) make loud buzzing, humming sound; (cause to) go fast or rise, increase sharply —*vi.* (of camera) use lens of adjustable focal length to make subject appear to move closer or farther away —**zoom lens** lens used in this way

**zo·o·phyte** (ZOH-ə-fīt) *n.* plantlike animal, *as* sponge —**zo·o·phyt′ic** (-FIT-ik) *adj.*

**zuc·chi·ni** (zoo-KEEN-ee) *n.* (*pl.*

-ni, -nis) green-skinned summer squash

**Zu·lu** (ZOO-loo) *n.* member, language of S Afr. Bantu tribes

**zy·gote** (ZĪ-goht) *n.* fertilized egg cell

**zy·mot·ic** (zī-MOT-ik) *adj.* of, or caused by fermentation; of, caused by infection

# PUNCTUATION MARKS AND OTHER SYMBOLS

| | |
|---|---|
| **,** | comma. |
| **;** | semicolon. |
| **:** | colon. |
| **.** | period. |
| **—** | dash. |
| **!** | exclamation mark. |
| **?** | interrogation or doubt. |
| **-** | hyphen; as in *follow-up*. |
| **'** | apostrophe; as in *Peter's dog*. |
| **( )** | parentheses. |
| **[ ]** | brackets. |
| **}** | brace, to enclose two or more lines. |
| **´** | acute accent; as in *blasé*. |
| **` ^** | grave accent } as in circumflex } *tête-à-tête*. |
| **~** | tilde, used over *n* in certain Spanish words to denote the sound of *ny*; as in *señor*. |
| **ç** | cedilla, to denote that *c* is pronounced soft; as in *façade*. |
| **" "** | quotation marks. |
| **' '** | quotation marks, when used within a quotation; as in *"He said, 'I will go at once' and jumped into a cab."* |
| **¯** | macron, to mark length of sound; as in *cōbra*. |
| **˘** | breve, marking a short sound; as in *līnen*. |
| **··** | dieresis; as in *daïs*. |
| **··** | in German, used to denote modification of the vowel sound; as in *Köln* (Cologne). |
| **^** | caret, marking a word or letter to be inserted in the line. |

| | |
|---|---|
| **. . .**, **—**, or **- - - -** | ellipsis to indicate a break in a narrative, an omission, or part of a quoted sentence that is deliberately omitted. |
| **⁂** or **⁂** | asterism, used to call attention to a particular passage. |
| **. . . .** or **- - - -** | leaders, to direct the eye to a certain point. |
| **¶** | paragraph. |
| **\*** | asterisk; (1) a reference mark; (2) used in philology to denote forms assumed to have existed though not recorded. |
| **†** | dagger, obelisk; (1) a reference mark; (2) obsolete or dead. |
| **‡** | double dagger, a reference mark. |
| **²** | superior figure, used as a reference mark. |
| **ª** | superior letter. |
| **§** | section mark. |
| **‖** | parallel mark. |
| **☛** | index, hand, fist. |
| **#** | number; space. |
| **„** | ditto. |
| **&** | ampersand, and. |
| **&c** | et cetera. |
| **@** | at. |
| **%** | per cent, per hundred. |
| **©** | copyright. |
| **®** | registered; registered trademark. |
| **♂** | male. |
| **♀** | female. |

613

# PUNCTUATION AND THE USE OF CAPITAL LETTERS

**apostrophe** The sign ('), used to indicate possession. In the singular - 's is used (eg, *day's end*); in the plural the apostrophe is added to the end of the word (eg, *the neighbors' dog*). Plurals that do not end in -s also take - 's (eg, *sheep's eyes*). Except for a few traditional exceptions (like *Jesus', Keats'*) proper names ending in -s take - 's at the end (eg, *Thomas's, the Jones's*).

**parentheses** These serve to isolate part of a sentence that could be omitted and still leave an intelligible statement. Punctuation of the rest of the sentence should run as if the parenthetical portion were not there, eg *That house over there (with the blue door) is ours.* Square brackets are used where the writer inserts his own information into a quotation, eg, *I was raised in Columbus [Georgia].*

**capital letters** These are used at the beginning of a sentence or quoted speech, and for proper names and titles of people and organizations, eg *Mr. Robertson, Dr. Smith, South America, House of Representatives.* They are not used when speaking of a general topic like *the pay of miners, the manufacture of cosmetics.* If an initial *the* is included in a title it has a capital, eg *We went to see The Tempest.*

**colons and semicolons** The function of these marks is to provide more of a break than a comma, and less than a period. The colon is used to make an abrupt break between two related statements, eg *Take it or leave it: the choice is yours.* It is also used to introduce a list, quotation, or summary. Semicolons can be used instead of conjunctions to link two sentences or parts of them, eg *Two of the lights were working; two were out.*

**commas** 1. These make divisions in sentences, eg, *She stormed out, slamming the door behind her.*
2. Commas are used to divide units in a series of nouns, adjectives, or phrases, eg *The cupboard was full of pots, pans, and crockery.* In such a series the last comma (before "and" or "or") is optional. It is not customary to place a comma between the last of a series of adjectives and the noun, eg, *It was a long, hot, humid day.*
3. Commas also serve to mark off a word or phrase in a sentence that can stand grammatically complete on its own, as can dashes and parentheses. Commas give the lightest degree of separation, dashes produce a jerky effect, and parentheses cut off part of a sentence most firmly, eg, *He hurried home, taking a short cut, but still arrived too late. It's a long time — over two years — since last we met. They both went to Athens (unaware of each other's plans) and stayed in the same hotel.*
4. When two clauses are linked by a conjunction a comma is used if the subject changes eg, *She was dark, but her brother was fair.*
5. When addressing a person,

614

commas are used before and after the person's name or title, eg *Well, Mrs. Smith, how are you today?*

**exclamation marks** These should only be used after genuine exclamations and not after ordinary statements.

**periods (full stops)** Normally, these appear only at the end of a complete sentence containing a main verb, except in reported speech and where a passage takes the form of an argument, eg, *You may think you can get away with it. Not a chance.* Periods are also used after abbreviations and initial letters standing for the whole word (as in *fig., a.m., R.C.*) but they are often omitted after abbreviations of much-used titles like *CIA, USA, UCLA.* As usage is currently in a state of flux, the above should be taken only as a guide to common practice.

**hyphens** Compound words, like *open-hearted* or *smart ass*, or words with a prefix, like *unpick*, may or may not contain a hyphen. It is generally used when the compound is new and dropped as it becomes familiar. When a compound adjective comes before a noun, it should be hyphenated to stress that the constituent parts are not to be used independently, eg *He bit into a half-rotten apple.*

**quotation marks (quotes, inverted commas)** 1. These are used for direct quotation, not for indirect speech. It is usual to have a comma before and after a quotation if the sentence is resumed, eg, *He said, "Follow me", and set off down the street.*
2. Single quotation marks can be used to indicate a title or quotation within a speech, eg, *"I loved 'War and Peace'," she said, "but it took so long to read."*

**question marks** These are used at the end of direct questions, but not after reported ones.

# PLURALS OF NOUNS

Plurals are formed by adding -s except in the following cases.

1. When a word ends in -ch, -s, -sh, -ss, -x, the plural is formed by adding -es (eg, *benches, gases, dishes, crosses, taxes*).

2. When a word ends in -y preceded by a consonant, the plural form is -ies (eg, *parties, bodies, policies*). When a word ends in -y preceded by a vowel, the plural is formed by adding -s (eg, *trays, joys, keys*).

3. When a word ends in -o, the more common plural ending is -oes (eg, *cargoes, potatoes, heroes*). In many less familiar words or when the final -o is preceded by a vowel, the plural ending is -os (eg, *avocados, armadillos, studios, cameos*).

4. When a word ends in -f, the plural is formed either by adding -s (eg, *beliefs, cuffs, whiffs*) or by changing the -f to -v and adding -es (eg, *wives, thieves, loaves*). Some words may take both forms (eg, *scarf, hoof, wharf*).

5. When a word ends in -ex or -ix, the more formal plural ending is -ices. In more general contexts

-es is used (eg, *appendices, appendixes; indices, indexes*).

6. When a word from Latin ends in -is the plural form is -es (eg, *crises, analyses*).

With compound words (like *mother-in-law*) it is usually the more important part that is pluralized (eg, *brigadier generals, mothers-in-law*).

In certain cases the plural form of a word is the same as the singular (eg, *deer, sheep, grouse*) and in some words both forms end in -s (eg, *measles, corps*).

There are two main types of plurals that take either singular or plural verbs:

a. words like *media* and *data*. These are in common use as singular nouns although, strictly, this is incorrect.

b. words ending in -ics. Generally, these are treated as plural when the word relates to an individual person or thing (eg, *your statistics are out-of-date; the hall's acoustics are good*) and as singular when the word is regarded more strictly as a science (eg, *statistics is an important subject*).

# PRESIDENTS OF THE UNITED STATES OF AMERICA

| | |
|---|---|
| 1. George Washington (F) | 1789-97 |
| 2. John Adams (F) | 1797-1801 |
| 3. Thomas Jefferson (D-R) | 1801-09 |
| 4. James Madison (D-R) | 1809-17 |
| 5. James Monroe (D-R) | 1817-25 |
| 6. John Quincy Adams (D-R) | 1825-29 |
| 7. Andrew Jackson (D) | 1829-37 |
| 8. Martin Van Buren (D) | 1837-41 |
| 9. William Henry Harrison (W) | 1841 |
| 10. John Tyler (W) | 1841-45 |
| 11. James K. Polk (D) | 1845-49 |
| 12. Zachary Taylor (W) | 1849-50 |
| 13. Millard Fillmore (W) | 1850-53 |
| 14. Franklin Pierce (D) | 1853-57 |
| 15. James Buchanan (D) | 1857-61 |
| 16. Abraham Lincoln (R) | 1861-65 |
| 17. Andrew Johnson (R) | 1865-69 |
| 18. Ulysses S. Grant (R) | 1869-77 |
| 19. Rutherford B. Hayes (R) | 1877-81 |
| 20. James A. Garfield (R) | 1881 |
| 21. Chester A. Arthur (R) | 1881-85 |
| 22. Grover Cleveland (D) | 1885-89 |
| 23. Benjamin Harrison (R) | 1889-93 |
| 24. Grover Cleveland (D) | 1893-97 |
| 25. William McKinley (R) | 1897-1901 |
| 26. Theodore Roosevelt (R) | 1901-09 |
| 27. William Howard Taft (R) | 1909-13 |
| 28. Woodrow Wilson (D) | 1913-21 |
| 29. Warren G. Harding (R) | 1921-23 |
| 30. Calvin Coolidge (R) | 1923-29 |
| 31. Herbert C. Hoover (R) | 1929-33 |
| 32. Franklin D. Roosevelt (D) | 1933-45 |
| 33. Harry S. Truman (D) | 1945-53 |
| 34. Dwight D. Eisenhower (R) | 1953-61 |
| 35. John F. Kennedy (D) | 1961-63 |
| 36. Lyndon B. Johnson (D) | 1963-69 |
| 37. Richard M. Nixon (R) | 1969-74 |
| 38. Gerald R. Ford (R) | 1974-77 |
| 39. James E. Carter, Jr. (D) | 1977-81 |
| 40. Ronald W. Reagan (R) | 1981-89 |
| 41. George H. W. Bush (R) | 1989- |

(D) Democratic; (D-R) Democratic Republican; (F) Federalist;
(R) Republican; (W) Whig.

# STATES OF THE U.S.A.

| | Zip Code | Capital | Area (sq. mi.) | Estimated population (1990) |
|---|---|---|---|---|
| Alabama | AL | Montgomery | 51 705 | 4 181 000 |
| Alaska | AK | Juneau | 591 004 | 576 000 |
| Arizona | AZ | Phoenix | 114 000 | 3 752 000 |
| Arkansas | AR | Little Rock | 53 187 | 2 427 000 |
| California | CA | Sacramento | 158 706 | 29 126 000 |
| Colorado | CO | Denver | 104 091 | 3 434 000 |
| Connecticut | CT | Hartford | 5 018 | 3 279 000 |
| Delaware | DE | Dover | 2 045 | 666 000 |
| Florida | FL | Tallahassee | 55 664 | 12 818 000 |
| Georgia | GA | Atlanta | 58 910 | 6 663 000 |
| Hawaii | HI | Honolulu | 6 471 | 1 141 000 |
| Idaho | ID | Boise | 83 564 | 1 017 000 |
| Illinois | IL | Springfield | 56 345 | 11 612 000 |
| Indiana | IN | Indianapolis | 36 185 | 5 550 000 |
| Iowa | IO | Des Moines | 56 275 | 2 758 000 |
| Kansas | KS | Topeka | 82 277 | 2 492 000 |
| Kentucky | KY | Frankfort | 40 410 | 3 745 000 |
| Louisiana | LA | Baton Rouge | 47 752 | 4 513 000 |
| Maine | ME | Augusta | 33 265 | 1 212 000 |
| Maryland | MD | Annapolis | 10 460 | 4 729 000 |
| Massachusetts | MA | Boston | 8 284 | 5 880 000 |
| Michigan | MI | Lansing | 58 527 | 9 293 000 |
| Minnesota | MN | St. Paul | 84 402 | 4 324 000 |
| Mississippi | MS | Jackson | 47 689 | 2 699 000 |
| Missouri | MO | Jefferson City | 69 697 | 5 192 000 |
| Montana | MT | Helena | 147 046 | 805 000 |
| Nebraska | NE | Lincoln | 77 355 | 1 588 000 |
| Nevada | NV | Carson City | 110 561 | 1 076 000 |
| New Hampshire | NH | Concord | 9 279 | 1 142 000 |
| New Jersey | NJ | Trenton | 7 787 | 7 899 000 |
| New Mexico | NM | Santa Fe | 121 593 | 1 632 000 |
| New York | NY | Albany | 49 108 | 17 773 000 |
| North Carolina | NC | Raleigh | 52 669 | 6 690 000 |
| North Dakota | ND | Bismarck | 70 702 | 660 000 |
| Ohio | OH | Columbus | 41 330 | 10 791 000 |
| Oklahoma | OK | Oklahoma City | 69 956 | 3 285 000 |
| Oregon | OR | Salem | 97 073 | 2 766 000 |
| Pennsylvania | PA | Harrisburg | 45 308 | 11 827 000 |
| Rhode Island | RI | Providence | 1 212 | 1 002 000 |
| South Carolina | SC | Columbia | 31 113 | 3 549 000 |
| South Dakota | SD | Pierre | 77 116 | 708 000 |

## STATES OF THE U.S.A.

| | Zip Code | Capital | Area (sq. mi.) | Estimated population (1990) |
|---|---|---|---|---|
| Tennessee | TN | Nashville | 42 144 | 4 972 000 |
| Texas | TX | Austin | 266 807 | 17 712 000 |
| Utah | UT | Salt Lake City | 84 899 | 1 776 000 |
| Vermont | VT | Montpelier | 9 614 | 562 000 |
| Virginia | VA | Richmond | 40 767 | 6 157 000 |
| Washington | WA | Olympia | 68 139 | 4 657 000 |
| West Virginia | WV | Charleston | 24 232 | 1 856 000 |
| Wisconsin | WI | Madison | 56 153 | 4 808 000 |
| Wyoming | WY | Cheyenne | 97 809 | 502 000 |
| | | | | |
| District of Columbia | DC | — | 69 | 614 000 |

# ESTIMATED POPULATION OF SELECTED U.S. CITIES

| City | Population | City | Population |
|---|---|---|---|
| Akron, OH | 222 060 | Jersey City, NJ | 219 480 |
| Albany, NY | 101 727 | Kansas City, MO | 441 170 |
| Albuquerque, NM | 366 750 | Las Vegas, NV | 192 000 |
| Amarillo, TX | 166 000 | Lincoln, NE | 183 050 |
| Anaheim, CA | 240 730 | Little Rock, AR | 181 030 |
| Anchorage, AK | 235 000 | Long Beach, CA | 396 280 |
| Atlanta, GA | 421 910 | Los Angeles, CA | 3 259 300 |
| Austin, TX | 467 000 | Louisville, KY | 286 000 |
| Baltimore, MD | 752 800 | Macon, GA | 118 420 |
| Baton Rouge, LA | 241 130 | Memphis, TN | 653 000 |
| Birmingham, AL | 277 510 | Miami, FL | 374 000 |
| Bismarck, ND | 44 485 | Milwaukee, WI | 605 090 |
| Boise, ID | 108 000 | Minneapolis, MN | 356 840 |
| Boston, MA | 573 600 | Mobile, AL | 203 260 |
| Buffalo, NY | 324 820 | Montgomery, AL | 194 290 |
| Cambridge, MA | 95 322 | Montpelier, VT | 8 241 |
| Charleston, SC | 68 900 | Nashville, TN | 473 670 |
| Charleston, WV | 59 371 | Newark, NJ | 316 300 |
| Charlotte, NC | 352 000 | New Haven, CT | 123 000 |
| Cheyenne, WY | 47 283 | New Orleans, LA | 554 500 |
| Chicago, IL | 3 009 530 | New York, NY | 8 529 000 |
| Cincinnati, OH | 370 000 | Norfolk, VA | 274 800 |
| Cleveland, OH | 535 830 | Oakland, CA | 356 960 |
| Colorado Springs, CO | 273 000 | Oklahoma City, OK | 446 000 |
| Columbus, OH | 566 030 | Omaha, NE | 349 000 |
| Corpus Christi, TX | 263 900 | Paterson, NJ | 139 160 |
| Dallas, TX | 1 003 520 | Peoria, IL | 110 290 |
| Dayton, OH | 179 000 | Philadelphia, PA | 1 642 900 |
| Denver, CO | 505 000 | Phoenix, AZ | 894 000 |
| Des Moines, IO | 192 000 | Pierre, SD | 11 973 |
| Detroit, MI | 1 086 220 | Pittsburgh, PA | 387 490 |
| Duluth, MN | 92 811 | Portland, ME | 61 572 |
| El Paso, TX | 492 000 | Portland, OR | 387 870 |
| Fort Lauderdale, FL | 149 000 | Providence, RI | 157 200 |
| Fort Worth, TX | 430 000 | Raleigh, NC | 180 430 |
| Gary, IN | 136 790 | Richmond, VA | 217 700 |
| Grand Rapids, MI | 187 000 | Rochester, NY | 235 970 |
| Hartford, CT | 138 000 | Sacramento, CA | 323 550 |
| Helena, MT | 24 289 | St. Louis, MO | 426 000 |
| Honolulu, HI | 372 330 | St. Paul, MN | 263 680 |
| Houston, TX | 1 728 910 | Salt Lake City, UT | 158 400 |
| Indianapolis, IN | 719 820 | San Antonio, TX | 914 350 |
| Jackson, MS | 208 440 | San Bernardino, CA | 138 610 |
| Jacksonville, FL | 609 614 | San Diego, CA | 1 015 190 |

## ESTIMATED POPULATION OF SELECTED U.S. CITIES

| | | | |
|---|---|---|---|
| San Francisco, CA | 749 000 | Syracuse, NY | 160 750 |
| San Jose, CA | 712 080 | Tallahassee, FL | 119 000 |
| Santa Ana, CA | 237 000 | Tampa, FL | 278 000 |
| Santa Fe, NM | 55 000 | Toledo, OH | 340 680 |
| Savannah, GA | 146 800 | Topeka, KS | 118 580 |
| Seattle, WA | 486 200 | Trenton, NJ | 92 124 |
| Shreveport, LA | 220 380 | Tucson, AZ | 359 000 |
| Sioux Falls, SD | 81 071 | Tulsa, OK | 374 000 |
| Spokane, WA | 172 890 | Washington, DC | 626 000 |
| Springfield, IL | 100 290 | Wichita, KS | 289 000 |
| Springfield, MA | 149 410 | Yonkers, NY | 186 080 |

# TIME ZONES OF THE U.S.

**EASTERN STANDARD TIME (12 noon)**

*Applies in:*
Connecticut, Delaware, Florida, Georgia, Indiana, Maine, Maryland, Massachusetts, Michigan, New Jersey, New Hampshire, New York, North Carolina, Ohio, Pennsylvania, Rhode Island, South Carolina, Vermont, Virginia, Washington DC, West Virginia, eastern Kentucky, eastern Tennessee.

**CENTRAL STANDARD TIME (11 a.m.)**

*Applies in:*
Alabama, Arkansas, Illinois, Iowa, Kansas, Louisiana, Minnesota, Mississippi, Missouri, Oklahoma, Texas, western Kentucky, western Tennessee, eastern Nebraska, eastern North Dakota, eastern South Dakota.

**MOUNTAIN STANDARD TIME (10 a.m.)**

*Applies in;*
Arizona, Colorado, Idaho, Montana, New Mexico, Utah, Wyoming, western Nebraska, western North Dakota, western South Dakota.

**PACIFIC STANDARD TIME (9 a.m.)**

*Applies in:*
California, Nevada, Oregon, Washington (State).

**ALASKA STANDARD TIME (8 a.m.)**

*Applies in:*
Alaska

**HAWAII-ALEUTIAN STANDARD TIME (7 a.m.)**

*Applies in:*
Hawaii, Aleutian Islands

## POPULATIONS
### (estimated in thousands) of selected urban areas

| | | | |
|---|---:|---|---:|
| Tokyo, Japan | 25 434 | Philadelphia, U.S.A. | 4 025 |
| Mexico City, Mexico | 16 901 | Barcelona, Spain | 3 842 |
| São Paulo, Brazil | 14 911 | San Francisco — Oakland, | |
| New York, U.S.A. | 14 598 | U.S.A. | 3 790 |
| Seoul, S. Korea | 13 665 | Sydney, Australia | 3 396 |
| Osaka-Kobe-Kyoto, | | Athens, Greece | 3 252 |
| Japan | 13 562 | Detroit, U.S.A. | 3 133 |
| Buenos Aires, | | Miami — Fort Lauderdale, | |
| Argentina | 10 750 | U.S.A. | 3 123 |
| Calcutta, India | 10 462 | Wuhan, China | 3 048 |
| Bombay, India | 10 033 | Berlin, Germany | 3 033 |
| Rio de Janeiro, Brazil | 10 116 | Toronto, Canada | 2 972 |
| Moscow, U.S.S.R. | 9 873 | Rome, Italy | 2 944 |
| Los Angeles, U.S.A. | 9 638 | Naples, Italy | 2 862 |
| London, England | 9 442 | Melbourne, Australia | 2 852 |
| Paris, France | 8 638 | Cleveland, U.S.A. | 2 834 |
| Cairo, Egypt | 8 595 | Montreal, Canada | 2 827 |
| Manila, Philippines | 8 485 | Singapore | 2 556 |
| Jakarta, Indonesia | 8 122 | Kiev, U.S.S.R. | 2 489 |
| Essen — Dortmund — | | Dallas — Fort Worth, | |
| Duisburg, Germany | 7 604 | U.S.A. | 2 486 |
| Tehran, Iran | 7 354 | Boston, U.S.A. | 2 470 |
| Delhi — New Delhi, | | Washington DC, U.S.A. | 2 456 |
| India | 6 993 | St. Louis, U.S.A. | 2 358 |
| Shanghai, China | 6 698 | Budapest, Hungary | 2 297 |
| Chicago, U.S.A. | 6 511 | Pittsburgh, U.S.A. | 2 264 |
| Karachi, Pakistan | 6 351 | Bucharest, Romania | 2 095 |
| Beijing, China | 5 608 | Havana, Cuba | 1 951 |
| Lima, Peru | 5 447 | Hamburg, Germany | 1 824 |
| Hong Kong | 5 415 | Warsaw, Poland | 1 621 |
| Istanbul, Turkey | 5 389 | Lisbon, Portugal | 1 611 |
| Bangkok, Thailand | 4 998 | Vienna, Austria | 1 562 |
| Madras, India | 4 983 | Johannesburg, S. Africa | 1 441 |
| Santiago, Chile | 4 700 | Stockholm, Sweden | 1 389 |
| Milan, Italy | 4 635 | Munich, Germany | 1 287 |
| Tianjin, China | 4 622 | Cape Town, S. Africa | 1 108 |
| Leningrad, U.S.S.R. | 4 569 | Turin, Italy | 1 104 |
| Madrid, Spain | 4 137 | Lagos, Nigeria | 1 061 |
| Shenyang (Mukden), China | 4 086 | Rotterdam, Netherlands | 1 025 |

# COUNTRIES, RELATED NOUNS, ADJECTIVES, AND CURRENCIES

| Country | Noun/Adjective | Currency Unit |
|---|---|---|
| Afghanistan | Afghan | afghani |
| Albania | Albanian | lek |
| Algeria | Algerian | dinar |
| Andorra | Andorran | franc/peseta |
| Angola | Angolan | kwanza |
| Argentina | Argentine or Argentinian | austral |
| Australia | Australian | dollar |
| Austria | Austrian | schilling |
| Bahamas | Bahamian | dollar |
| Bahrain | Bahraini | dinar |
| Bangladesh | Bangladeshi | taka |
| Barbados | Barbadian | dollar |
| Belgium | Belgian | franc |
| Benin | Beninese | franc |
| Bermuda | Bermudan | dollar |
| Bhutan | Bhutanese | ngultrum |
| Bolivia | Bolivian | boliviano |
| Botswana | | pula |
| Brazil | Brazilian | cruzado |
| Brunei | | dollar |
| Bulgaria | Bulgarian | lev |
| Burkina-Faso | | franc |
| Burma | Burmese | kyat |
| Burundi | Burundian | franc |
| Cambodia | Cambodian | riel |
| Cameroon | Cameroonian | franc |
| Canada | Canadian | dollar |
| Cape Verde | Cape Verdean | escudo |
| Central African Republic | | franc |
| Chad | Chadian | franc |
| Chile | Chilean | peso |
| China | Chinese | yuan |
| China (Taiwan) | Chinese | dollar |
| Colombia | Colombian | peso |
| Congo | Congolese | franc |
| Costa Rica | Costa Rican | colon |
| Cuba | Cuban | peso |
| Cyprus | Cypriot | pound |
| Czechoslovakia | Czech, Czechoslovak or Czechoslovakian | koruna |

# COUNTRIES, RELATED NOUNS, ADJECTIVES & CURRENCIES

| Country | Noun/Adjective | Currency Unit |
|---------|----------------|---------------|
| Denmark | Dane; Danish | krone |
| Djibouti | | franc |
| Dominica | Dominican | dollar |
| Dominican Republic | Dominican | peso |
| Ecuador | Ecuadorean | sucre |
| Egypt | Egyptian | pound |
| El Salvador | Salvadorean | colon |
| Equatorial Guinea | | ekpwele |
| Ethiopia | Ethiopian | birr |
| Fiji | Fijian | dollar |
| Finland | Finn; Finnish | markka |
| France | Frenchman, -woman; French | franc |
| Gabon | Gabonese | franc |
| Gambia | Gambian | dalasi |
| Germany, Federal Republic of | German | deutschmark |
| Ghana | Ghanaian | cedi |
| Greece | Greek | drachma |
| Grenada | Grenadian | dollar |
| Guatemala | Guatemalan | quetzal |
| Guinea | Guinean | franc |
| Guinea-Bissau | | peso |
| Guyana | Guyanese | dollar |
| Haiti | Haitian | gourde |
| Honduras | Honduran | lempira |
| Hungary | Hungarian | forint |
| Iceland | Icelander; Icelandic | krona |
| India | Indian | rupee |
| Indonesia | Indonesian | rupiah |
| Iran | Iranian | rial |
| Iraq | Iraqi | dinar |
| Ireland, Republic of | Irishman, -woman; Irish | punt |
| Israel | Israeli | shekel |
| Italy | Italian | lira |
| Ivory Coast | | franc |
| Jamaica | Jamaican | dollar |
| Japan | Japanese | yen |
| Jordan | Jordanian | dinar |
| Kenya | Kenyan | shilling |
| Korea, North | North Korean | won |
| Korea, South | South Korean | won |

# COUNTRIES, RELATED NOUNS, ADJECTIVES, & CURRENCIES

| Country | Noun/Adjective | Currency Unit |
|---|---|---|
| Kuwait | Kuwaiti | dinar |
| Laos | Laotian | kip |
| Lebanon | Lebanese | pound |
| Lesotho | | loti |
| Liberia | Liberian | dollar |
| Libya | Libyan | dinar |
| Liechtenstein | | franc |
| Luxembourg | | franc |
| Madagascar | Madagascan | franc |
| Malawi | Malawian | kwacha |
| Malaysia | Malaysian | ringgit |
| Maldives | Maldivian | rufiyaa |
| Mali | Malian | franc |
| Malta | Maltese | pound |
| Mauritania | Mauritanian | ouguiya |
| Mauritius | Mauritian | rupee |
| Mexico | Mexican | peso |
| Monaco | Monegasque | franc |
| Mongolian People's Republic | Mongolian | tugrik |
| Morocco | Moroccan | dirham |
| Mozambique | Mozambican | escudo |
| Nauru | Nauruan | dollar |
| Nepal | Nepalese | rupee |
| Netherlands | Dutchman, -woman, Netherlander; Dutch | guilder |
| New Zealand | New Zealander | dollar |
| Nicaragua | Nicaraguan | cordoba |
| Niger | | franc |
| Nigeria | Nigerian | naira |
| Norway | Norwegian | krone |
| Oman | Omani | rial |
| Pakistan | Pakistani | rupee |
| Panama | Panamanian | balboa |
| Papua New Guinea | Papuan | kina |
| Paraguay | Paraguayan | guarani |
| Peru | Peruvian | inti |
| Philippines | Filipino or Philippine | peso |
| Poland | Pole; Polish | zloty |
| Portugal | Portuguese | escudo |
| Qatar | Qatari | riyal |
| Romania | Romanian | leu |

# COUNTRIES, RELATED NOUNS, ADJECTIVES & CURRENCIES

| Country | Noun/Adjective | Currency Unit |
|---|---|---|
| Rwanda | Rwandan | franc |
| San Marino | San Marinese or Sammarinese | lira |
| Saudi Arabia | Saudi Arabian | riyal |
| Senegal | Senegalese | franc |
| Seychelles | | rupee |
| Sierra Leone | Sierra Leonean | leone |
| Singapore | Singaporean | dollar |
| Somalia | Somalian | shilling |
| South Africa | South African | rand |
| Spain | Spaniard; Spanish | peseta |
| Sri Lanka | Sri Lankan | rupee |
| Sudan | Sudanese | pound |
| Surinam | Surinamese | guilder |
| Swaziland | Swazi | |
| Sweden | Swede; Swedish | krona |
| Switzerland | Swiss | franc |
| Syria | Syrian | pound |
| Tanzania | Tanzanian | shilling |
| Thailand | Thai | baht |
| Togo | Togolese | franc |
| Tonga | Tongan | pa'anga |
| Trinidad and Tobago | Trinidadian, Tobagan | dollar |
| Tunisia | Tunisian | dinar |
| Turkey | Turk; Turkish | lira |
| Uganda | Ugandan | shilling |
| U.S.S.R. | Russian or Soviet | ruble |
| United Arab Emirates | | dirham |
| United Kingdom | Briton; British | pound |
| USA | American | dollar |
| Uruguay | Uruguayan | peso |
| Vatican City | | lira |
| Venezuela | Venezuelan | bolivar |
| Vietnam | Vietnamese | dong |
| Western Samoa | Samoan | tala |
| Yemen | Yemeni | riyal, dinar |
| Yugoslavia | Yugoslav or Yugoslavian | dinar |
| Zaire | Zairean | zaire |
| Zambia | Zambian | kwacha |
| Zimbabwe | Zimbabwean | dollar |

## SIGNS OF THE ZODIAC

| | | |
|---|---|---|
| ♈ | Aries, the Ram | 21 March—19 April |
| ♉ | Taurus, the Bull | 20 April—20 May |
| ♊ Ⅱ | Gemini, the Twins | 21 May—21 June |
| ♋ | Cancer, the Crab | 22 June—22 July |
| ♌ | Leo, the Lion | 23 July—22 August |
| ♍ | Virgo, the Virgin | 23 August—22 September |
| ♎ | Libra, the Balance | 23 September—21 October |
| ♏ | Scorpio, the Scorpion | 22 October—21 November |
| ♐ | Sagittarius, the Archer | 22 November—21 December |
| ♑ ♒ | Capricorn, the Goat | 22 December—19 January |
| ♒ | Aquarius, the Water Bearer | 20 January—18 February |
| ♓ | Pisces, the Fish | 19 February—20 March |

## ROMAN NUMERALS

| | | | | | | |
|---|---|---|---|---|---|---|
| I | = | 1 | | XX | = | 20 |
| II | = | 2 | | XXX | = | 30 |
| III | = | 3 | | XL | = | 40 |
| IV or IIII | = | 4 | | L | = | 50 |
| V | = | 5 | | LX | = | 60 |
| VI | = | 6 | | LXX | = | 70 |
| VII | = | 7 | | LXXX | = | 80 |
| VIII | = | 8 | | XC | = | 90 |
| IX | = | 9 | | C | = | 100 |
| X | = | 10 | | CC | = | 200 |
| XI | = | 11 | | CCC | = | 300 |
| XII | = | 12 | | CCCC or CD | = | 400 |
| XIII | = | 13 | | D | = | 500 |
| XIV | = | 14 | | DC | = | 600 |
| XV | = | 15 | | DCC | = | 700 |
| XVI | = | 16 | | DCCC | = | 800 |
| XVII | = | 17 | | CM | = | 900 |
| XVIII | = | 18 | | M | = | 1000 |
| XIX | = | 19 | | MM | = | 2000 |

# CHEMICAL SYMBOLS

Each element is placed in alphabetical order of its symbol and is followed by its atomic number.

| | | |
|---|---|---|
| **Ac** actinium, 89 | **H** hydrogen, 1 | **Pt** platinum, 78 |
| **Ag** silver, 47 | **Ha** hahnium, 105 | **Pu** plutonium, 94 |
| **Al** aluminum, 13 | **He** helium, 2 | **Ra** radium, 88 |
| **Am** americium, 95 | **Hf** hafnium, 72 | **Rb** rubidium, 37 |
| **Ar** argon, 18 | **Hg** mercury, 80 | **Re** rhenium, 75 |
| **As** arsenic, 33 | **Ho** holmium, 67 | **Rf** rutherfordium, |
| **At** astatine, 85 | **I** iodine, 53 | 104 |
| **Au** gold, 79 | **In** indium, 49 | **Rh** rhodium, 45 |
| **B** boron, 5 | **Ir** iridium, 77 | **Rn** radon, 86 |
| **Ba** barium, 56 | **K** potassium, 19 | **Ru** ruthenium, 44 |
| **Be** beryllium, 4 | **Kr** krypton, 36 | **S** sulfur, 16 |
| **Bi** bismuth, 83 | **La** lanthanum, 57 | **Sb** antimony, 51 |
| **Bk** berkelium, 97 | **Li** lithium, 3 | **Sc** scandium, 21 |
| **Br** bromine, 35 | **Lr** lawrencium, 103 | **Se** selenium, 34 |
| **C** carbon, 6 | **Lu** lutetium, 71 | **Si** silicon, 14 |
| **Ca** calcium, 20 | **Md** mendelevium, 101 | **Sm** samarium, 62 |
| **Cd** cadmium, 48 | **Mg** magnesium, 12 | **Sn** tin, 50 |
| **Ce** cerium, 58 | **Mn** manganese, 25 | **Sr** strontium, 38 |
| **Cf** californium, 98 | **Mo** molybdenum, 42 | **Ta** tantalum, 73 |
| **Cl** chlorine, 17 | **N** nitrogen, 7 | **Tb** terbium, 65 |
| **Cm** curium, 96 | **Na** sodium, 11 | **Tc** technetium, 43 |
| **Co** cobalt, 27 | **Nb** niobium, 41 | **Te** tellurium, 52 |
| **Cr** chromium, 24 | **Nd** neodymium, 60 | **Th** thorium, 90 |
| **Cs** cesium, 55 | **Ne** neon, 10 | **Ti** titanium, 22 |
| **Cu** copper, 29 | **Ni** nickel, 28 | **Tl** thallium, 81 |
| **Dy** dysprosium, 66 | **No** nobelium, 102 | **Tm** thulium, 69 |
| **Er** erbium, 68 | **Np** neptunium, 93 | **U** uranium, 92 |
| **Es** einsteinium, 99 | **O** oxygen, 8 | **V** vanadium, 23 |
| **Eu** europium, 63 | **Os** osmium, 76 | **W** tungsten, 74 |
| **F** fluorine, 9 | **P** phosphorus, 15 | **Xe** xenon, 54 |
| **Fe** iron, 26 | **Pa** protactinium, 91 | **Y** yttrium, 39 |
| **Fm** fermium, 100 | **Pb** lead, 82 | **Yb** ytterbium, 70 |
| **Fr** francium, 87 | **Pd** palladium, 45 | **Zn** zinc, 30 |
| **Ga** gallium, 31 | **Pm** promethium, 61 | **Zr** zirconium, 40 |
| **Gd** gadolinium, 64 | **Po** polonium, 84 | |
| **Ge** germanium, 32 | **Pr** praseodymium, 59 | |

# PLANETS IN THE SOLAR SYSTEM

| Planet | Equatorial diameter (miles) | Mean distance from sun (millions of miles) | Period of rotation (length of 'day') | Period of revolution or Sidereal period (length of 'year') | Number of known moons |
|---|---|---|---|---|---|
| Mercury | 3,000 | 36 | 58.6 days | 87.97 days | 0 |
| Venus | 7,700 | 67.2 | 243 days | 224.70 days | 0 |
| Earth | 7,926 | 93 | 23.9 hrs | 365.26 days | 1 |
| Mars | 4,200 | 141.5 | 24.6 hrs | 686.98 days | 2 |
| Jupiter | 88,700 | 484 | 9.8 hrs | 11.86 years | 16 |
| Saturn | 75,000 | 887.2 | 10.2 hrs | 29.46 years | 22 |
| Uranus | 29,300 | 1,783 | 10.7 hrs | 84.01 years | 15 |
| Neptune | 27,700 | 2,793 | 16 hrs | 164.79 years | 8 |
| Pluto | 1,863 | 3,663 | 6.3 days | 247.70 years | 1 |

# COLLINS BILINGUAL GEM DICTIONARIES

A wealth of language information in a handy pocket-size volume, with all the well-known features of Collins bilingual dictionaries:

- more entries than any other comparable dictionary
- thousands of current phrases and constructions
- meanings and usage clearly indicated

Titles available:

| | |
|---|---|
| **COLLINS GEM FRENCH DICTIONARY** | ISBN 0-00-458539-9 |
| **COLLINS GEM GERMAN DICTIONARY** | ISBN 0-00-458926-2 |
| **COLLINS GEM GREEK DICTIONARY** | ISBN 0-00-458548-8 |
| **COLLINS GEM ITALIAN DICTIONARY** | ISBN 0-00-458546-1 |
| **COLLINS GEM LATIN DICTIONARY** | ISBN 0-00-458644-1 |
| **COLLINS GEM PORTUGUESE DICTIONARY** | ISBN 0-00-458666-2 |
| **COLLINS GEM RUSSIAN DICTIONARY** | ISBN 0-00-458665-4 |
| **COLLINS GEM SPANISH DICTIONARY** | ISBN 0-00-458544-5 |

---

## ALSO AVAILABLE IN THE GEM SERIES

**COLLINS GEM THESAURUS**

- Over 120,000 synonyms and 9,250 entries
- The ideal companion to the Collins Gem Webster's Dictionary